Roget's Thesaurus

of English Words and Phrases

Roget's Thesaurus

of English Words and Phrases

By Peter Mark Roget, M.D., F.R.S.
Enlarged by John Lewis Roget, M.A.
Classic American Edition originally revised
and enlarged by
Samuel Romilly Roget, M.A.

CHAIN SALES MARKETING, INC.
NEW YORK, N.Y. 10016

This edition is published by Chain Sales Marketing, Inc.,
New York, NY 10016 by arrangement with Gramercy Books,
distributed by Outlet Book Company, Inc., a Random House
Company.

Printed and bound in the United States of America

Library of Congress Cataloging-in-Publication Data

8 7 6 5 4 3 2 1

FOREWORD

FOR over three generations, *Roget's Thesaurus* has served the needs of writers, speakers, students, and translators. Peter Mark Roget first compiled and organized his guide to English words and phrases in 1805; the work was published in 1852 and was immediately recognized as a valuable tool for anyone concerned with the proper and creative use of the English language. Three generations of Rogets have worked on the thesaurus, preserving Peter Mark Roget's original concept, organization, and format.

Roget recognized that writing and speaking difficulties are not necessarily the result of a poor vocabulary or ill-formed ideas. He grasped what many writers, orators, and translators had long had to contend with: the necessity of finding the exactly appropriate word or phrase from a group of synonyms. In every language, words are subject to a variety of shadings and implications. A living, growing language contains words that have specific meanings—meanings either embedded in the root of a word or that have developed in the course of history and usage. Words that at first seem synonymous and therefore completely interchangeable, prove otherwise in certain contexts. The word first chosen on impulse may interrupt the mood of a piece of writing or a speech and may jar the reader or the listener by its lack of specificity, or, more seriously, may imply a completely different intent than that which the author had in mind.

The translator is especially concerned with the problems of mood and intent, for even the most formal scholarly works depend on the idiomatic expressions of a language. The richness of poetry and fiction sometimes depends totally on an exact and idiomatic turn of phrase. These expressions are inaccessible to literal translation; a translator must find a matching idiom to retain the author's original sense.

A standard dictionary provides little assistance in these situations. Dictionaries serve only to define words, giving little indication of their use within a language. More importantly, dictionaries are not designed to allow the playing with words that is so important to creating individual nuance.

With the thesaurus, a whole new approach to creative expression is possible, because the thesaurus stresses the importance of the *idea* first. It functions almost as a reverse dictionary: as a dictionary goes from word to idea, a thesaurus starts with a concept and leads to specific words. In this way, the thesaurus becomes both thought-expressing and thought-provoking. A writer or speaker who has a general idea in mind must find the word or phrase that will convey his meaning most clearly and succinctly. The thesaurus, with its exhaustive compilation of synonyms, permits on-the-spot, rapid comparisons of similar words. In addition, while glancing over the list of words, one may decide to modify or strengthen his initial concept. The thesaurus user may come upon an expression or word that had not occurred to him before. And, finally, the selection of a word may start off new trains of thoughts and ideas.

FOREWORD

THE DESIGN OF THE THESAURUS

The format of *Roget's Thesaurus* is well adapted to the needs of the user. It is organized by general categories that reflect the most common patterns of words and their usage in the English language. The six general categories are:

1) Abstract relations
2) Space
3) Matter
4) Intellect
5) Volition
6) Affections

Of course, many words fit under more than one of these categories, and they will be found in each relevant one. For example, *work*, because of its multiple meanings, has a place in "abstract relations," "space," "intellect," "volition" and "affections." An introductory synopsis of the general categories describes in detail the subcategories within each general category, making it easy for the thesaurus user to pinpoint and clarify in his own mind the precise meaning he is looking for.

The format of the thesaurus embodies the principle that form must follow function. And the function of the thesaurus is to facilitate the precise expression of ideas; it encourages the exploration of shades of meaning, of comparing directly one word with another that is almost synonymous. In addition, each subcategory is printed beside the subcategory that most nearly reflects its antithesis. For example, *superiority* and *inferiority* appear in parallel columns, as do *safety* and *danger*, *vanity* and *modesty*, and so on.

The thesaurus functions in another way also. The index at the back of the book is arranged by individual words. Within the entry, each word is further broken down into its various meanings, with references to the subcategory in the text proper. When the thought is clear, but the word is missing, the index functions as a quick, easy guide. The index is so specific that a word may have as many as twenty different references. *Rude*, for example, is broken down into ten possible contexts, reflecting the variety of meanings it may assume—"violent," "shapeless," "inelegant," "uncivil," and so on.

The arrangement of words and phrases within each subcategory remains constant throughout the book, and is again designed for easy use. The keyword of each subcategory is printed in bold-faced type. It is followed by a list of synonymous nouns, then verbs, adjectives, adverbs, etc. Under each part of speech, the most closely related synonyms are grouped together in paragraphs. Finally, there is a list of phrases and idiomatic expressions, for often a phrase is the only way to get at the true thought. Slang expressions (indicated as such) that have become a part of the language are also given. Foreign words that have been naturalized are included, as are those foreign words that have no literal translation in English and serve a distinctive role in the English language.

Because further refinements may be necessary, all entries are internally cross-referenced. For example, under *disobedience*, one finds references to *disorder*, *resistance*, *defy*.

THE THESAURUS AS AN INDISPENSABLE TOOL

The aim of *Roget's Thesaurus* is twofold. It is a quick reference of synonyms for someone looking for a fresh word or a word with a slightly different meaning than the word in the writer's mind. These thesaurus users will depend heavily on the index, where they will find references to the literal, figurative, and derivative senses of any word. Others might depend more on the general categories. These are the users who immerse themselves in the rich lists of words and phrases, thereby getting a total feeling of the concept under consideration and all its ramifications.

The purpose of the thesaurus is not to regulate word usage in the English language. Rather, it expands anyone's appreciation of English, supplying a rich vocabulary and suggesting new forms of expression, possibly even new ideas.

ELLEN LEVENTHAL

PLAN OF CLASSIFICATION

TABULAR SYNOPSIS OF CATEGORIES

Class I. ABSTRACT RELATIONS

I. EXISTENCE

1°. ABSTRACT	1. Existence.	2. Inexistence.
2°. CONCRETE	3. Substantiality.	4. Unsubstantiality.
3°. FORMAL	*Internal.*	*External.*
	5. Intrinsicality.	6. Extrinsicality.
4°. MODAL	*Absolute.*	*Relative.*
	7. State.	8. Circumstance.

II. RELATION

	9. Relation.	10. Irrelation.
	11. Consanguinity.	
1°. ABSOLUTE	12. Correlation.	
	13. Identity.	14. Contrariety.
	15. Difference.	
2°. CONTINUOUS	16. Uniformity.	16a. Non-uniformity.
	17. Similarity.	18. Dissimilarity.
3°. PARTIAL	19. Imitation.	20. Non-imitation.
	20a. Variation.	
	21. Copy.	22. Prototype.
4°. GENERAL	23. Agreement.	24. Disagreement.

III. QUANTITY

	Absolute.	*Relative.*
1°. SIMPLE	25. Quantity.	26. Degree.
	27. Equality.	28. Inequality.
	29. Mean.	
	30. Compensation.	
	By Comparison with a Standard.	
2°. COMPARATIVE	31. Greatness.	32. Smallness.
	By Comparison with a similar Object.	
	33. Superiority.	34. Inferiority.
	Changes in Quantity.	
	35. Increase.	36. Decrease.

VI. TIME

1°. ABSOLUTE ....
106. Time.	107. Neverness.
Definite.	*Indefinite.*
108. Period.	109. Course.
108a. Contingent Duration.	
110. Diuturnity.	111. Transientness.
112. Perpetuity.	113. Instantaneity.
114. Chronometry.	115. Anachronism.

2°. REL-ATIVE

1. *to Succession*
116. Priority.	117. Posteriority.
118. Present time.	119. Different time.
120. Synchronism.	

2. *to a Period*
121. Futurity.	122. Preterition.
123. Newness.	124. Oldness.
125. Morning.	126. Evening.
127. Youth.	128. Age.
129. Infant.	130. Veteran.
131. Adolescence.	

3. *to an Effect or purpose*
132. Earliness.	133. Lateness.
134. Occasion.	135. Intempestivity.

3°. RECURRENT ....
136. Frequency.	137. Infrequency.
138. Periodicity.	139. Irregularity.

VII. CHANGE

1°. SIMPLE ....
140. Change.	141. Permanence.
142. Cessation.	143. Continuance.
144. Conversion.	
	145. Reversion.
146. Revolution.	

2°. COMPLEX ....
147. Substitution.	148. Interchange.
149. Changeableness.	150. Stability.
Present.	*Future.*
151. Eventuality.	152. Destiny.

VIII. CAUSATION

1°. CONSTANCY OF SE-QUENCE ....
153. { *Constant Ante-cedent.* Cause.	154. { *Constant Sequent.* Effect.

2°. CONNECTION BE-TWEEN CAUSE AND EFFECT.........
155. { *Assignment of Cause.* Attribution.	156. { *Absence of As-signment.* Chance.
157. Power.	158. Impotence.
Degrees of Power.	
159. Strength.	160. Weakness.
161. Production.	162. Destruction.
163. Reproduction.	

3°. POWER IN OPERA-TION ....
164. Producer.	165. Destroyer.
166. Paternity.	167. Posterity.
168. Productiveness.	169. Unproductiveness.
170. Agency.	
171. Energy.	172. Inertness.
173. Violence.	174. Moderation.

Class IV. INTELLECT

Division (I.). Formation of Ideas

SYNOPSIS OF CATEGORIES

Class V. VOLITION

Division (I.). Individual Volition

I. Volition in General..

1°. Acts....

600. Will.	601. Necessity.
602. Willingness.	603. Unwillingness.
604. Resolution.	605. Irresolution.
604a. Perseverance. ⎫ 606. Obstinacy. ⎭	607. Tergiversation.
	608. Caprice.
609. Choice.	609a. Absence of Choice. 610. Rejection.
611. Predetermination.	612. Impulse.
613. Habit.	614. Desuetude.

2°. Causes

615. Motive.	615a. Absence of Motive. 616. Dissuasion.
617. Plea.	

3°. Objects

618. Good.	619. Evil.

II. Prospective Volition....

1°. Conceptional

620. Intention.	621. Chance.
622. Pursuit.	623. Avoidance.
	624. Relinquishment.
625. Business.	
626. Plan.	
627. Method.	
628. Mid-Course.	629. Circuit.
630. Requirement.	

2°. Subservience to Ends

1. Actual Subservience.

631. Instrumentality.	
632. Means.	
633. Instrument.	
634. Substitute.	
635. Materials.	
636. Store.	
637. Provision.	638. Waste.
639. Sufficiency.	
641. Redundance.	640. Insufficiency.

2. Degree of Subservience.

642. Importance.	643. Unimportance.
644. Utility.	645. Inutility.
646. Expedience.	647. Inexpedience.
648. Goodness.	649. Badness.
650. Perfection.	651. Imperfection.
652. Cleanness.	653. Uncleanness.
654. Health.	655. Disease.
656. Salubrity.	657. Insalubrity.

SYNOPSIS OF CATEGORIES

CLASS VI. AFFECTIONS

SYNOPSIS OF CATEGORIES

ABBREVIATIONS, &c.

Adj.	*adj.*	Adjectives, Participles, and Words having the power of Adjectives.
Adv.	*adv.*	Adverbs and Adverbial Expressions.
Int.	*int.*	Interjections.
Phr.	*phr.*	Phrases.
V.	*v.*	Verbs.

The numbers are those of the headings, or Categories.

Words in italics within parentheses are not intended to explain the meanings of the words which precede them, but to indicate the nature of allied groups of words under the numbers which follow them.

Roget's Thesaurus
of English Words and Phrases

CLASS I

Words Expressing
ABSTRACT RELATIONS

Section I. EXISTENCE

1°. Being, in the Abstract

1. Existence.—N. existence, being, entity, *ens, esse*, subsistence, quiddity.

reality, realness, actuality; positiveness &c. *adj.*; fact, matter of fact, sober reality; truth &c. 494; actual existence.

presence &c. (*existence in space*) 186; coexistence &c. 120.

stubborn fact; not a -dream &c. 515; no joke.

substance, essence, prime constituent, hypostatis.

[Science of existence], ontology.

V. exist, be; have -being &c. *n.*; subsist, live, breathe, stand, obtain, be the case; occur &c. (*event*) 151; have place, rank, prevail; find oneself, pass the time, vegetate.

consist in, lie in, reside in, inhere in.

come into -existence &c. *n.*; arise &c. (*begin*) 66; come forth &c. (*appear*) 446.

become &c. (*be converted*) 144; bring into existence &c. 161; coexist, preexist, endure &c. 141.

Adj. existing &c *v.*; existent, subsistent, under the sun; in -existence &c. *n.*; extant; afloat, on foot, current, prevalent, rife, in force, -vogue; undestroyed.

real, actual, positive, absolute; true &c. 494; substan-tial, -tive; self-existing, -ent.

2. Inexistence.—N. inexistence; nonexistence, -subsistence; nonentity, *nil*;

negativeness &c. *adj.*; nullity; nihil-ity, -ism; *tabula rasa*, blank; abeyance; absence &c. 187; no such thing &c. 4; nothingness, oblivion, *non esse*.

annihilation; extinction &c. (*destruction*) 162.

V. not -exist &c. 1; have no -existence &c. 1; be null and void; cease to -exist &c. 1; pass away, perish; be –, become-extinct &c. *adj.*; die out; disappear &c. 449; melt away, dissolve, leave not a rack behind, leave no trace; go, be no more; die &c. 360.

annihilate, render null, nullify; abrogate &c. 756; destroy &c. 162; take away; remove &c. (*displace*) 185.

Adj. inexistent, non-existent &c. 1; negative, blank, null and void; missing, omitted; absent &c. 187; visionary &c. 515.

unreal, potential, virtual; baseless, *in nubibus*; unsubstantial &c. 4; vain.

un-born, -created, -begotten, -conceived, -produced, -made.

perished, annihilated &c. *v.*; extinct, exhausted, gone, lost, departed; defunct &c. (*dead*) 360; *spurlos versenkt*.

fabulous, ideal &c. (*imaginary*) 515; supposititious &c. 514.

Adv. negatively, virtually, &c. *adj.* well-founded, -grounded; un-ideal, -imagined; not -potential &c. 2.

Adv. actually &c. *adj.*; in -fact, – point of fact, – reality; indeed; *de –, ipso-facto.*

1

2°. BEING, IN THE CONCRETE

3. Substantiality.—N. substantiality, *hypostasis*; person, thing, object, article; something, a being, an existence; creature, body, substance, flesh and blood, stuff, *substratum*; matter &c. 316; physical nature.

[Totality of existences], world &c. 318; *plenum*.

Adj. substan-tive, -tial, concrete; hypostatic; personal, bodily; tangible &c. (*material*) 316; real, corporeal, evident.

Adv. substantially &c. *adj.*; bodily, essentially.

4. Unsubstantiality.—N. un-, insubstantiality; nothingness, nihility.

nothing, naught, *nil*, nullity, zero, cipher, no one, nobody; never –, ne'er -a one; no such thing, none in the world; nothing -whatever, – at all, – on earth; not a -particle &c. (*smallness*) 32; all -talk, – moonshine, – stuff and nonsense, matter of no import.

thing of naught, man of straw, John Doe and Richard Roe; *nominis umbra*, nonentity, figurehead, lay figure; flash in the pan, *vox et præterea nihil*.

shadow; phantasm, phantom &c. (*fallacy of vision*) 443; dream &c. (*imagination*) 515; *ignis fatuus* &c. (luminary) 423; 'such stuff as dreams are made of'; air, thin air; bubble &c. 353; 'baseless fabric of a vision'; mockery.

hollowness, blank; vacuity, void &c. (*absence*) 187.

inanity, fool's paradise, fatuity, stupidity, emptiness of mind.

V. vanish, evaporate, fade, sink, fly –, die –, melt- away, dissolve, disappear &c. 449, become extinct, become invisible.

Adj. unsubstantial; fleeting; base-, ground-less; ungrounded; without –, having no- foundation.

visionary &c. (*imaginary*) 515; im-material &c. 317; spectral &c. 980; dreamy; shadowy; ethereal, airy, imponderable, tenuous, vague.

vacant, vacuous; empty &c. 187; eviscerated; blank, hollow; nominal; null; inane.

Phr. there's nothing in it.

3°. FORMAL EXISTENCE

Internal conditions

5. Intrinsicality.—N. intrinsicality, inbeing, inherence, inhesion, immanence; subjectiveness; *ego*; essence; essentialness &c. *adj.*; essential part, essential stuff, substance, quintessence, incarnation, quiddity, gist, pith, core, kernel, marrow, sap, life-blood, backbone, heart, soul, life, flower; important part &c. (*importance*) 642.

principle, nature, constitution, character, ethos, type, quality, crasis, *diathesis*.

habit; temper, -ament; spirit, humour, grain, disposition, streak, tendency &c. 176.

endowment, capacity; capability &c. (*power*) 157; moods, declensions, features, aspects; peculiarities &c. (*specialty*) 79; idiosyncrasy; idiocrasy; diagnostics.

V. be –, run- in the blood; be born so; be -intrinsic &c. *adj.*

Adj. derived from within, subjective; idiocratic, idiosyncratic, intrin-sic, -sical; fundamental, cardinal, normal; inherent, essential, natural; in-nate, -born, -bred, -dwelling, -grained, -wrought; radical, incarnate, thorough-bred, hereditary, inherited, immanent; congen-ital, -ite; connate, running in the blood; coeval with birth, genetic, ingenerate, -genite; indigenous; in the -grain &c. *n.*; bred in the bone, instinctive; inward, internal &c. 221; to the manner born; virtual.

characteristic &c. (*special*) 79, (*indicative*) 550; invariable, incurable, ineradicable, fixed, settled, constant, unchanging.

Adv. intrinsically &c. *adj.*; at bottom, in the main, in effect, essentially, practically, virtually, substantially, *au fond*; fairly.

External conditions

6. Extrinsicality.—N. extrinsicality, objectiveness, *non ego*; extraneousness &c. 57; accident; letter of the law.

Adj. derived from without; objective; extrin-sic, -sical; extraneous &c. (*foreign*) 57; modal, adventitious, additional, supervenient, fortuitous; a-, ad-scititious; incidental, casual, accidental, unessential, non-essential, accessory.

implanted, ingrafted, instilled, inculcated.

outward &c. (*external*) 220.

Adv. extrinsically &c. *adj.*

4°. MODAL EXISTENCE

Absolute

7. State.—N. state, condition, category, estate, lot, case, trim, mood, pickle, plight &c. 704; temper; aspect &c. (*appearance*) 448.

constitution, habitude, *diathesis*; frame, fabric &c. 329; stamp, set, fit, mould.

mode, modality, schesis; fettle; form &c. (*shape*) 240.

tone, tenor, turn; trim, guise, fashion, light, complexion, style, character.

V. be in -, possess -, enjoy -, labour under- a -state &c. *n.*; be on a footing, do, fare; come to pass.

Adj. conditional, modal, formal; structural, organic.

Adv. conditionally &c. *adj.*; as -the matter stands, - things are; such being the case &c. 8.

Relative

8. Circumstance.—N. circumstance, situation, phase, position, posture, attitude, place, point; terms; *régime*; footing, standing, status.

occasion, juncture, conjuncture; contingency &c. (*event*) 151.

predicament; emergen-ce, -cy; exigency, crisis, pinch, pass, push; turning point; crossroads.

bearings, how the land lies.

Adj. circumstantial; given, conditional, provisional; critical; modal; contingent, incidental; adventitious &c. (*extrinsic*) 6.

Adv. in the circumstances &c. *n.*, under the conditions &c. 7; thus, in such wise.

accordingly; that -, such- being the case; that being so, since, seeing that.

as matters stand; as -things, - times-go.

conditionally, provided, if, in case; if -so, - so be, - it be so; if it so -happen, - turn out; in the event of; in such a -contingency, - case, - event; provisionally, unless, without.

according to -circumstances, - the occasion; as it may -happen, - turn out, - be; as the -case may be, - wind blows; *pro re natâ*.

Section II. RELATION

1°. Absolute Relation

9. Relation.—N. relation, bearing, reference, connection, apposition, interconnection, concern, cognation; applicability, appositeness; correlation &c. 12; analogy; similarity &c. 17; affinity, intimacy, friendship; homology, alliance, homogeneity, association, rapport; approximation &c. (*nearness*) 197; filiation &c. (*consanguinity*) 11; interest; relevancy &c. 23; relationship, relative position; relativity; interrelation &c. 12.

comparison &c. 464; ratio, proportion.

link, tie, bond, bond of union.

V. be-related &c. *adj.*; have a relation &c. *n.*; relate -, refer- to; bear upon, regard, concern, touch, affect, have to do with; pertain -, belong -, appertain- to; have respect to; answer to; interest.

bring -into relation with, - to bear upon; connect, associate, draw a parallel; link &c. 43.

Adj. relative; correlative &c. 12; cognate; relating to &c. *v.*; relative to, in relation with, referable *or* referrible to; belonging to &c. *v.*; appurtenant to, in common with.

related, connected; implicated, associated, affiliated, akin, allied to; collateral, cognate, congenial, kindred, affinitive, *en rapport*, in touch with.

approxima-tive, -ting; approaching; proportion-al, -ate, -able; allusive, comparable.

in the same -category &c. 75; like &c. 17; relevant &c. (*apt*) 23.

Adv. relatively &c. *adj.*; pertinently &c. 23.

thereof; as -to, - for, - respects, - regards; about; concerning &c. *v.*; anent; relating -, as relates- to; with

-relation, - reference, -respect, - regard-to; in respect of; while speaking -, *à propos-* of; in connection with; by the -way, - by; whereas; for -, in -as much as; in point of, as far as; on the -part, - score- of; *quoad hoc; pro re natâ*; under the -head &c. (*class*) 75- of; in the matter of, *in re*.

Phr. 'thereby hangs a tale.'

10. [Want, or absence of relation.] **Irrelation.—N.** irrelation, dissociation; inapplicability; inconnection; multifariousness; disconnection &c. (*disjunction*) 44; inconsequence, independence; incommensurability; irreconcilableness &c. (*disagreement*) 24; heterogeneity; unconformity &c. 83; irrelevancy, impertinence, *nihil ad rem*; intrusion &c. 24.

V. have no -relation &c. 9 to, - bearing upon, - concern &c. 9 with, - business with; not -concern &c. 9; have -nothing to do with, - no business there; intrude, &c. 24.

bring -, drag -, haul -, lug- in head and shoulders.

Adj. irrelative, irrespective, unrelated, irrelated; arbitrary; independent, unallied; un-, dis-connected; adrift, isolated, insular; extraneous, strange, alien, foreign, outlandish, exotic.

not comparable, incommensurable, heterogeneous; unconformable &c. 83.

irrelevant; rambling &c. 279; inapplicable; not -pertinent, - to the purpose; impertinent, inapposite, beside the mark, *à propos de bottes*; away from -, foreign to -, beside- the -purpose, - question, - transaction, - point; misplaced &c. (*intrusive*) 24.

remote, far fetched, out of the way,

forced, neither here nor there, quite another thing; detached, segregated, segregate.

multifarious; discordant &c. 24.

incidental, parenthetical, *obiter dictum*, episodic.

Adv. parenthetically &c. *adj.*; by the -way, – by; *en passant*, incidentally; irrespectively &c. *adj.*; without reference, – regard- to; in the abstract &c. 87; *a se.*

11. [Relations of kindred.] **Consanguinity.—N.** consanguinity, relationship, kindred, blood; parentage &c. (*paternity*) 166; filiation, affiliation; lineage, agnation, connection, cognation, alliance; family -connection, – tie; ties of blood; blood relationship; nepotism.

kins-man, -folk; people; kith and kin; rela-tion, -tive; connection; sib; next of kin; uncle, aunt, nephew, niece; cousin, -german; first –, second- cousin; cousin -once, – twice &c.- removed; near –, distant- relation; brother, sister, one's own flesh and blood.

family, patriarch, matriarch; fraternity; brother-, sister-, cousin-hood.

race, stock, generation; sept &c. 166; stirps, side; strain; breed, clan, tribe.

V. be -related &c. *adj.* – to; claim -relationship &c. *n.*- with.

Adj. related, akin, consanguineous, matrilinear, patrilineal, of the blood, family, allied, collateral; cog-, ag-, connate; kindred; affiliated, affine; fraternal, avuncular.

intimately –, nearly –, closely –, remotely –, distantly- related, – allied; german.

12. [Double or reciprocal relation.] **Correlation.—N.** reciprocalness &c. *adj.*; recipro-city, -cality, -cation; mutuality, correlation, correspondence, interdependence; interchange &c. 148; exchange, barter; interrelation, interconnection; alternation, see-saw.

V. reciprocate, alternate; interchange &c. 148; exchange; counterchange; interact, correspond, mutualize, give and take.

Adj. reciprocal, mutual, commutual, correlative; alternate; interchangeable; international; correspondent, complementary, analogous.

Adv. *mutatis mutandis; vice versâ;* each other; by turns &c. 148; reciprocally &c. *adj.*; to and fro &c. 314.

13. Identity.—N. identity, sameness, oneness, ditto, homogeneity; unity, coincidence, coalescence; convertibility; equality &c. 27; selfness, self, oneself; identification.

monotony, tautology &c. (*repetition*) 104.

synonym.

fac-simile &c. (*copy*) 21; *alter ego* &c. (*similar*) 17; *ipsissima verba* &c. (*exactness*) 494; same; self–, very –, one and the- same; very –, actual- thing; no other.

V. be -identical &c. *adj.*; match, coincide, coalesce.

treat as –, render- -the same, –identical; identify; recognize the identity of.

Adj. identical; self, ilk; the -same &c. *n.*; self same; synonymous; one and the same.

coincid-, coalesc-ent, -ing; indistinguishable; one; equivalent &c. (*equal*) 27; much -the same, – of a muchness; unaltered.

Adv. identically &c. *adj.*; on all fours; *ibid-, -em.*

14. [Non-coincidence.] **Contrariety.—N.** contrariety, contrast, foil, antithesis, oppositeness; counterpole; contradiction; antagonism &c. (*opposition*) 708; counteraction &c. 179.

inversion &c. 218; the -opposite, – reverse, – inverse, – converse, – antipodes, – other extreme &c. 237.

antonym.

V. be -contrary &c. *adj.*; contrast with, oppose; differ *toto cœlo.*

invert, reverse, turn the tables &c. 218.

contra-dict, -vene; antagonize &c. 708.

Adj. contrar-y, -ious, -iant; opposite, counter, dead against; ad-, con-, reverse; opposed, antithetical, contrasted, antipodean, antagonistic, opposing; conflicting, inconsistent, contradictory, at cross purposes; negative; hostile &c. 708.

differing *toto cœlo*; diametrically opposite; as opposite as -black and white, – light and darkness, – fire and water, – the poles, as different as chalk from cheese; 'Hyperion to a satyr'; quite the -contrary, – reverse; no such thing, just the other way, *tout au contraire*.

Adv. contrarily &c. *adj.; contra*, contrariwise, *per contra*, on the contrary, nay rather; topsy-turvey; *vice versâ*; on the other hand &c. (*in compensation*) 30.

15. Difference.—N. difference, unlikeness; heterogeneity; vari-ance, -ation, -ety; diversity, dissimilarity &c. 18; disagreement &c. 24; disparity &c. (*inequality*) 28; distinction, contradistinction; distinctness; discrepancy, divergence, contrast &c. 18; nonconformity, incompatibility, antithesis.

discord &c. 713.

modification, moods and tenses.

nice –, fine –, delicate –, subtle- distinction; shade of difference, *nuance*; discrimination &c. 465; *differentia*.

different thing, something else, variant, apple off another tree, horse of another colour, another pair of shoes; this that or the other.

V. be -different &c. *adj.*; differ, vary, ablude, mismatch, contrast; diverge –, depart–, deviate-from; divaricate; differ -*toto cœlo*, – *longo intervallo*.

disagree &c. 713.

vary, modify &c. (*change*) 140.

discriminate &c. 465.

Adj. differing &c. *v.*; different, diverse, divided, heterogeneous; distinguishable; varied, modified; divergent, incongruous, diversified, various; discrepant, dissentient, differential; divers, all manner of; variform &c. 81; discordant &c. 713.

other, another, not the same; unequal &c. 28; unmatched; widely apart.

distinctive, characteristic; discriminative; distinguishing.

Adv. differently &c. *adj.*

Phr. *il y a fagots et fagots; tot nomines tot sententiœ*; one man's meat is another man's poison.

2°. CONTINUOUS RELATION

16. Uniformity.—N. uniformity; homogene-ity, -ousness; continuity, stability, consistency; connatural-ity, -ness; homology; accordance; conformity &c. 82; agreement &c. 23.

regularity, constancy, even tenor, routine; monotony, evenness, sameness, dead level; steadiness, equability, unity.

V. b -uniform &c. *adj.*; accord with &c. 23; run through.

become -uniform &c. *adj.*; conform to &c. 82.

render uniform &c. *adj.*; assimilate, level, smooth, dress.

Adj. uniform; homo-geneous, -logous; of a piece, consistent, steady; connatural; monotonous, changeless, dreary, even, invariable, equable, level, regular, stereotyped, unchanged, unvarying; methodical &c. 60; habitual &c. 613.

Adv. uniformly &c. *adj.*; uniformly with &c. (*conformably*) 82; in harmony with &c. (*agreeing*) 23; in a -rut, – groove.

always, ever &c. 112; invariably, without exception, never otherwise; by clock-work; endlessly &c. 112.

Phr. *ab uno disce omnes.*

16a. [Absence of want of uniformity.] **Non-uniformity.—N.** diversity, irregularity, unevenness; multiformity &c. 81; unconformity &c. 83; roughness &c. 256; heterogeneity, heteromorphism.

Adj. diversified, varied, irregular, uneven, rough &c. 256; multifarious; multiform &c. 81; of various kinds; all -manner, – sorts, – kinds- of.

Adv. in all manner of ways, here there and everywhere.

3°. PARTIAL RELATION

17. Similarity.—N. similarity, resemblance, likeness, similitude, semblance; affinity, approximation, parallelism; parity; agreement &c. 23; ana-logy, -logicalness; correspondence, equality &c.

connatural-ness, -ity; brotherhood, family likeness.

alliteration, rhyme, pun.

repetition &c. 104; sameness &c. (*identity*) 13; uniformity &c. 16.

analogue; the like; match, *pendant*, fellow, companion, pair, mate, twin, double, counterpart, brother, sister; one's second self, *alter ego*, chip of the old block, *par nobile fratrum*, *Arcades ambo*, birds of a feather, *et hoc genus omne*.

parallel; simile; type &c. (*metaphor*) 521; image &c. (*representation*) 554; photograph; close-, striking -, speaking -, faithful &c. *adj.* - likeness, - resemblance.

V. be -similar &c. *adj.*; look like, resemble, bear resemblance, favour; savour -, smack- of; approximate; parallel, match, rhyme with; take after; imitate &c. 19; run in pairs.

render -similar &c. *adj.*; assimilate, approximate, bring near; connaturalize, make alike; rhyme, pun.

Adj. similar; resembling &c. *v.*; like, alike; twin.

analog-ous, -ical; parallel, of a piece; such as, so.

connatural, congeneric, allied to; corresponding, cognate; akin to &c. (*consanguineous*) 11.

approximate, much the same, near, close, something like, such like; a show of; mock, *pseudo*, simulating, representing.

exact &c. (*true*) 494; lifelike, faithful, realistic; true to -nature, - the life; the -very image - picture- of; for all the world like, *comme deux gouttes d'eau*; as like as -two peas, - it can stare; *instar omnium*, cast in the same mould, ridiculously like.

Adv. as if, so to speak; as -, as if- it were; *quasi*, just as, *veluti in speculum*.

18. Dissimilarity.—N. dissimil-arity, -itude; unlikeness, diversity, disparity, dissemblance; divergence, inequality, difference &c. 15; novelty; variation, variety, originality, disguise.

V. be -unlike &c. *adj.*; vary &c. (*differ*) 15; bear no resemblance to, differ *toto cœlo*.

render -unlike &c. *adj.*; vary &c. (*diversify*) 140.

Adj. dissimilar, unlike, disparate; of a different kind &c. (*class*) 75; unmatched, unique; new, novel; unprecedented &c. 83; original.

nothing of the kind; no such -, quite another- thing; far from it, other than, cast in a different mould, *tertium quid*, as like a dock as a daisy, 'very like a whale'; as different as -chalk from cheese, - Macedon and Monmouth; *lucus a non lucendo*.

diversified &c. 16*a*.

Adv. otherwise, *alias*.

19. Imitation.—N. imitation; copying &c. *v.*; transcription; repetition, mimeograph, mimeotype, duplication, reduplication; quotation; reproduction.

mockery, mimicry, mime, simulation, personation; representation &c. 554; semblance, simulacrum; pretence; copy &c. 21; assimilation.

paraphrase, parody &c. 21.

plagiarism; forgery &c. (*falsehood*) 544.

imitator, echo, cuckoo, parrot, ape, monkey, mocking-bird, mimic, impersonator; copyist.

V. imitate, copy, mirror, reflect, reproduce, repeat, borrow; do like, echo, re-echo, catch; transcribe; match, parallel.

mock, take off, mimic, ape, simulate, personate, impersonate; forge; act &c. (*drama*) 599; represent &c. 554;

counterfeit, duplicate; portray, parody, travesty, caricature, burlesque.

follow -, tread- in the- -steps, - footsteps, - wake- of; pattern after, take pattern by; follow -suit, - the example of; walk in the shoes of, take a leaf out of another's book, strike in with; take -, model -after; emulate.

Adj. imitated &c. *v.*; mock, mimic; counterfeit, false, pseudo; modelled after, moulded on, paraphrastic; literal; imitative, apish; second-hand; imitable; sham &c. 545.

Adv. literally, to the letter, strictly, precisely, *verbatim, literatim, sic, totidem verbis,* word for word, *mot à mot.*

Phr. like master like man.

20. Non-Imitation.—N. no imitation, genuineness, originality; creativeness.

Adj. unimitated, uncopied; unmatched, unparalleled; inimitable &c. 33; *unique,* original, primordial, primary, pristine, underived, first-hand, archetypal, prototypal.

20a. Variation.—N. variation; alteration &c. (*change*) 140.

modification, moods and tenses; modulation

divergency &c. 291; deviation &c. 279; aberration; innovation.

V. vary &c. (*change*) 140; deviate &c. 279; diverge &c. 291.

Adj. varied &c. *v.*; modified; dissimilar &c. 18; diversified &c. 16*a.*

21. [Result of imitation.] Copy.—N. copy, fac-simile, counterpart, *effigies*, effigy, symbol, image, form, likeness, similitude, semblance, resemblance, cast, electrotype, stereotype, tracing, ectype; imitation &c. 19; model, representation, adumbration, study; counterfeit presentment, portrait &c. (*representment*) 554.

duplicate; transcript, -ion; reflex, -ion; shadow, echo; chip of the old block; reprint, reproduction, casting, engraving, replica; transfer; second edition &c. (*repetition*) 104; *réchauffé*; apograph, fair copy, revise.

parody, caricature, cartoon, burlesque, travesty, paraphrase.

servile -copy, - imitation; counterfeit &c. (*deception*) 545; *pasticcio.*

Adj. faithful; lifelike &c. (*similar*) 17.

22. [Thing copied.] Prototype.—N. prototype, original, model, pattern, founding, precedent, standard, scantling, type, arche-, anti-type; protoplast, copy-book, module, exemplar, example, ensample, specimen; paradigm; guide; templet; lay-figure.

text, copy, manuscript, MS., design; fugleman, keynote.

die, mould; matrix, engraving, last, plasm; pro-, proto-plasm; mint; seal, punch, *intaglio*, negative, stamp.

V. be -, set- an example; set a copy; standardize.

4°. GENERAL RELATION

23. Agreement.—N. agreement; accord, -cordance; unison, harmony, syntony; concord &c. 714; concordance, concert, understanding, convention, *entente -cordiale, consortium*, consensus of opinion, pact, mutual understanding, unanimity.

conformity &c. 82; conformance; uniformity &c. 16; consonance, consentaneousness, consistency; congruity, -ence; keeping; congeniality; correspondence, concinnity, parallelism, apposition, union.

fitness, aptness &c. *adj.*; relevancy; pertinen-ce, -cy; sortance; case in point; aptitude, coaptation, propriety, applicability, admissibility, commensurability, compatibility, suitability; cognation &c. (*relation*) 9.

adaptation, adjustment, arrangement, graduation, accommodation; reconciliation -ement; assimilation; attunement.

consent &c. (*assent*) 448; concurrence &c. 178; co-operation &c. 709.

right man in the right place, very thing; quite -, just- the thing.

V. be -accordant &c. *adj.*; agree, accord, harmonize; correspond, tally, respond; meet, suit, fit, befit, do, adapt itself to; fall in -, chime in -, square -, quadrate -, consort -, comport- with; dovetail, assimilate; fit like a glove; fit to a -tittle, - T; match &c. 17; become one.

consent &c. (*assent*) 488.

render -accordant &c. *adj.*; fit, suit, adapt, accommodate; graduate; adjust &c. (*render equal*) 27; dress, regulate, readjust; accord, harmonize, reconcile; fadge, dovetail, square.

Adj. agreeing, suiting &c. *v.*; in accord, accordant, concordant, consonant, congruous, consentaneous, correspondent, corresponding, homologous, congenial; becoming; harmonious, reconcilable, conformable; in -accordance, - harmony, - keeping, - unison, &c. *n.*- with; at one with, of one mind, of a piece; consistent, compatible, proportionate, answerable; commensurate; on all fours.

apt, apposite, pertinent, pat; to the -point, - purpose; happy, felicitous, germane, *ad rem*, in point, bearing upon, applicable, relevant, admissible.

fit, adapted, *in loco*, *à propos*, appropriate, seasonable, sortable, suitable, idoneous, deft; meet &c. (*expedient*) 646.

at home, in one's proper element.

Adv. *à propos of*; pertinently &c. *adj.*; *pro rata*.

Phr. *rem acu tetigisti*, the cap fits.

24. Disagreement.—N. disagreement; dis-cord, -cordance; disunion, dissonance, dissidence, discrepancy; unconformity &c. 83; incongru-ity, -ence; discongruity, *mésalliance, oxymoron*; jarring &c. *v.*; clash, collision,

dissension &c. 713; conflict &c. (*opposition*) 708; controversy &c. 720; falling out, wrangle, argument.

disparity, mismatch, misfit, disproportion; disproportionateness &c. *adj.*; variance, divergence, repugnance.

unfitness &c. *adj.*; inaptitude, impropriety; inapplicability &c. *adj.*; inconsistency, inconcinnity; irrelevancy &c. (*irrelation*) 10.

misjoin-ing, -der; syncretism, intrusion, interference; *concordia discors*.

fish out of water.

V. disagree; clash, quarrel, jar &c. (*discord*) 713; interfere, intrude, come amiss; not concern &c. 10; mismatch; *hymano capiti cervicem jungere equinam*.

Adj. disagreeing &c. *v.*; discordant, discrepant; at -variance, - war; hostile, antagonistic, repugnant, factious, contradictory, dissentious, incompatible, irreconcilable, inconsistent with; unconformable, exceptional &c. 83; intrusive, incongruous; disproportionate, -ed; unharmonious; unconsonant; divergent, repugnant to.

inapt, unapt, inappropriate, inept, infelicitous, improper; unsuit-ed, -able; inapplicable; un-fit, -fitting, -befitting; unbecoming; ill-timed, ill-adapted, unseasonable, *mal à propos*, inadmissible; inapposite &c. (*irrelevant*) 10.

uncongenial; ill-assorted, -sorted, -matched; mis-matched, -mated, -joined, -placed; unaccommodating, irreducible, uncommensurable, unsympathetic.

out of -character, - keeping, - proportion, - joint, - tune, - place, - season, - its element; at -odds, - variance with.

Adv. in -defiance, - contempt, - spite- of; discordantly &c. *adj.*; *à tort et à travers.*

SECTION III. QUANTITY

1°. SIMPLE QUANTITY

25. [Absolute quantity.] **Quantity.—**
N. quantity, magnitude; size &c. (*dimensions*) 192; amplitude, mass, amount, *quantum*, measure, measurement, substance, strength.

[Science of quantity.] Mathematics, Mathesis.

[Definite or finite quantity] arm-, hand-, mouth-, spoon-, thimble-, capful; stock, batch, lot, dose, ration, quotum, quota, pittance, driblet, part, portion &c. 51.

Adj. quantitative, some, any, more or less.

Adv. to the tune of.

26. [Relative quantity.] **Degree.—N.**
degree, grade, extent, measure, proportion, amount, ratio, stint, standard, height, pitch; reach, amplitude, range, scope, size, calibre; gradation, shade; tenor, compass; sphere, station, rank, standing; rate, way, sort.

point, mark, step, stage &c. (*term*) 71; intensity, strength &c. (*greatness*) 31.

V. compare, graduate, calibrate, measure.

Adj. comparative; gradual, shading off, gradational; within the bounds &c. (*limit*), 233.

Adv. by degrees, gradually, inasmuch, *pro tanto*; how-ever, -soever; step by step, bit by bit, little by little, inch by inch, drop by drop, gradatim; by -inches, - slow degrees, - little and little; in some -degree, - measure; to some extent; just a bit.

2°. COMPARATIVE QUANTITY

27. [Sameness of quantity or degree.]
Equality.—N. equality, parity, co-

extension, symmetry, balance, poise; evenness, monotony, level.

equivalence; equi-pollence, -poise, -librium, -ponderance; par, quits; not a pin to choose; distinction without a difference, six of one and half a dozen of the other; identity &c. 13; similarity &c. 17; isotropism; coequality.

equalization, equation; equilibration, co-ordination, adjustment, readjustment.

drawn -game, -battle, draw, stalemate; neck and neck race; tie, dead heat.

match, peer, compeer, equal, mate, fellow, brother; equivalent.

V. be -equal &c. *adj.*; equal, match, reach, keep pace with, run abreast; come -, amount -, come up- to; be -, lie- on a level with; balance; cope with; come to the same thing; level off.

render -equal &c. *adj.*; equalize, level, dress, balance, equate, handicap, give points, trim, adjust, poise; fit, accommodate; adapt &c. (*render accordant*) 23; strike a balance; establish -, restore- equality, - equilibrium; readjust; stretch on the bed of Procrustes.

Adj. equal, even, level, monotonous, coequal, symmetrical, coordinate; on a -par, - level, - footing- with; up to the mark; equiparent.

equivalent, tantamount; quits; homologous; synonymous &c. 522; resolvable into, convertible, much at one, as broad as long, neither more nor less; much the same -, the same thing -, as good- as; all -one, - the same; equi-pollent, -ponderant, -ponderous, -balanced; equalized &c. *v.*; drawn; half and half; isochronous; isoperimetrical.

Adv. equally &c. *adj.; pari passu, ad eundem, cœteris paribus; in equilibrio;* to all intents and purposes.

Phr. it -comes, -adds up, – amounts-to the same thing.

28. [Difference of quantity or degree.] **Inequality.—N.** inequality; dis-, im-parity; odds; difference &c. 15; ill-balanced; unevenness; inclination of the balance, partiality; shortcoming; casting – make- weight; superiority &c. 33; inferiority &c. 34.

V. be -unequal &c. *adj.*; countervail; have –, give- the advantage; turn the scale; kick the beam; topple, -over; over-match &c. 33; not come up to &c. 34.

Adj. unequal, uneven, disparate, partial; un-, over-balanced; top-heavy, lop-sided.

Adv. *haud passibus æquis.*

29. Mean.—N. mean, medium, inter-medium, average, run of the mill, normal, balance; mediocrity, generality, rule, ordinary -run, -ruck; golden mean &c. (*mid-course*) 628; middle &c. 68; compromise &c. 774; neutrality; middle point, middle course.

V. split the difference; take the -average &c. *n.*; reduce to a -mean &c. *n.*; strike a balance, pair off.

Adj. mean, intermediate; medial; middle &c. 68; average, normal, standard; neutral; middling, moderate.

médiocre, middle-class; *bourgeois*, commonplace &c. (*unimportant*) 643.

Adv. on an average, in the long run; taking -one with another, – all things together, – it for all in all; *communibus annis*, in round numbers.

30. Compensation.—N. compensation, equation; commutation; indemnification; compromise &c. 774; neutralization, nullification; counteraction &c. 179; reaction; measure for measure; retaliation &c. 718; equalization &c. 27; redemption, recoupment, recompense.

set-off, offset; make- casting-weight; counterpoise, equipoise, ballast; indemnity, reparation &c. 790; equivalent, *quid pro quo*; bribe, hushmoney, tribute &c. 784; amends &c. (*atonement*) 952; counterclaim, counterbalance, equiponderance, countervail, cross demand.

V. make -amends, – compensation; com-pensate, -pense; indemnify; counter-act, -vail, -poise; equiponderate; balance; out-, over-, counter-balance; set off, offset, cancel; hedge, square, give and take; make up -for, – lee way; cover, fill up, neutralize, nullify; equalize &c. 27; make good; redeem &c. (*atone*) 952; recoup, pay &c. 973.

Adj. compensat-ing, -ory; amendatory, reparative, countervailing &c. *v.*; in the opposite scale; equivalent &c. (*equal*) 27.

Adv. in -return, – consideration; but, however, yet, still, notwithstanding; neverthe-, nath-less; although, though; al-, how-beit; in spite of, despite; maugre; at -all events, – any rate; be that as it may, for all that, even so, on the other hand, at the same time, *quoad minus, quand même*, however that may be; after all, – is said and done; taking one thing with another &c. (*average*) 29.

31. Greatness.—N. greatness &c. *adj.*; magnitude; size &c. (*dimensions*) 192; multitude &c. (*number*) 102; immensity, enormity; infinity &c. 105; might, strength, intensity, fulness; importance &c. 642; fame &c. 873.

great quantity, quantity, deal, power, sight, pot, volume, world; mass, heap &c. (*assemblage*) 72; stock &c. (*store*) 636; peck, bushel, load, cargo; cart –, wagon –, car –, truck –, ship- load; flood, spring tide; abundance &c. (*sufficiency*) 639.

principal –, chief –, main –, greater –, major –, best –, essential- part; bulk, mass &c. (*whole*) 50.

V. be -great &c. *adj.*; run high, soar, loom up, tower, bulk large, transcend; rise –, carry- to a great height; know no bounds; scale, overtop, ascend.

enlarge &c. (*increase*) 35, (*expand*) 194.

Adj. great; greater &c. 33; large, considerable, fair, above par; big, massive, huge &c. (*large in size*) 192; ample; abundant &c. (*enough*) 639;

Herculean &c. 159; full, intense, strong, sound, passing, heavy, plenary, deep, high; signal, at its height, in the zenith.

world-wide, wide-spread, extensive; wholesale; many &c. 102.

goodly, noble, precious, mighty; sad, grave, serious; far gone, arrant, downright; utter, -most; crass, gross, arch, profound, intense, consummate; rank, unmitigated, red-hot, desperate; glaring, flagrant, stark staring; thoroughpaced, -going; roaring, thumping, thundering, strapping, whacking; extraordinary; important &c. 642; unsurpassed &c. (*supreme*) 33; complete &c. 52.

vast, immense, enormous, extreme; inordinate, excessive, extravagant, exorbitant; outrageous, preposterous, unconscionable, swinging, monstrous, over-grown; towering, stupendous, prodigious, astonishing, incredible; terrific, frightful; marvellous &c. (*wonder*) 870; grand.

unlimited &c. (*infinite*) 105; unapproachable, unutterable, indescribable, ineffable, unspeakable, inexpressible, beyond expression, fabulous.

un-diminished, -abated, -reduced, -restricted.

absolute, positive, stark, decided, unequivocal, essential, perfect, finished.

remarkable, of mark, marked, pointed, veriest; noticeable, uncommon, noteworthy, eminent &c. 873.

Adv. [in a positive degree] truly &c. (*truth*) 494; decidedly, unequivocally, purely, absolutely, seriously, essentially, fundamentally, radically, downright, in all conscience; for the most part, in the main.

[in a complete degree] entirely &c. (*completely*) 52; abundantly, &c. (*sufficiently*) 639; widely, far and wide.

[in a great or high degree] greatly &c. *adj.*; much, muckle, well, indeed, very, very much, a deal, no end of, most not a little; pretty, – well; enough, in a great measure, passing richly; to a -large, – great, – gigantic- extent; on a large scale; so; never –, ever- so; ever so much; by wholesale; mightily, mighty,

powerfully; with a witness, *ultra*, in the extreme, extremely, exceedingly, intensely, exquisitely, acutely, indefinitely, immeasurably; beyond -compare, – comparison, – measure, – all bounds; incalculably, infinitely.

[in a supreme degree] pre-eminently, superlatively &c. (*superiority*) 33.

[in a too great degree] immoderately, unduly, monstrously, grossly, preposterously, inordinately, exorbitantly, excessively, enormously, out of all proportion, with a vengeance.

[in a marked degree] particularly, remarkably, singularly, curiously, uncommonly, unusually, peculiarly, notably, signally, strikingly, pointedly, mainly, chiefly; famously, egregiously, prominently, glaringly, emphatically, strangely, wonderfully, amazingly, surprisingly, astonishingly, incredibly, marvellously, awfully, stupendously.

[in an exceptional degree] peculiarly &c. (*unconformity*) 83.

[in a violent degree] furiously &c. (*violence*) 173; severely, desperately, tremendously, extravagantly, confoundedly, deucedly, devilishly, with a vengeance; *à* –, *à toute- outrance*.

[in a painful degree] painfully, sadly, grossly, sorely, bitterly, piteously, grievously, miserably, cruelly, woefully, lamentably, shockingly, frightfully, dreadfully, fearfully, terribly, horribly, distressingly, balefully.

32. Smallness.—N. smallness &c. *adj.*; littleness &c. (*small size*) 193; tenuity; paucity; fewness &c. (*small number*) 103; meanness, insignificance &c. (*unimportance*) 643; mediocrity, moderation.

small quantity, *modicum, minimum*; vanishing point; material point, electron, atom, particle, molecule, corpuscle, point, dab, fleck, speck, dot, mote, jot, iota, ace; *minutiæ*, details; look, thought, idea, *soupçon*, whit, tittle, shade, shadow; spark, *scintilla*, gleam; touch, cast; grain, scruple, granule, globule, minim, sup, sip, sop, spice, drop, droplet, sprinkling, dash, smack, tinge, tincture; inch, patch, scantling, dole; scrap, shred, tag, splinter, rag, tatter, cantlet, flitter, gobbet, mite, bit, morsel, crumb, seed, fritter, shive; snip, -pet; snick, snack, snatch, slip, scrag; chip, -ping; shiver, sliver, driblet, clipping, paring, shaving, hair.

nutshell; thimble-, spoon-, hand-, cap-, mouth-ful; fragment; fraction &c. (*part*) 51; drop in the ocean, drop in the bucket.

animalcule &c. 193.

trifle &c. (*unimportant thing*) 643; mere -, next to- nothing; hardly anything; just enough to swear by; the shadow of a shade.

finiteness, finite quantity.

V. be -shall &c. *adj.*; lie in a nutshell.

diminish &c. (*decrease*) 36, (*contract*) 195.

Adj. small, little, tiny, weeny; diminutive &c. (*small in size*) 193; minute; minikin, fine, inconsiderable, dribbling, paltry &c. (*unimportant*) 643; faint &c. (*weak*) 160; slender, light, slight, scanty, scant, limited; meagre &c. (*insufficient*) 640; sparing; few &c. 103; low, so-so, middling, tolerable, no great shakes; below -, under- -par, - the mark; at a low ebb; halfway; moderate, modest; tender, subtle; petty, shallow, skin-deep.

inappreciable, evanescent, infinitesimal, homœopathic, very small, atomic, molecular, ultra-, -microscopic.

petty, shallow &c. 499.

mere, simple, sheer, stark, bare; near run.

Adv. [in a small degree] to a small extent, on a small scale; a -little, - wee, - tiny bit; slightly &c. *adj.*; imperceptibly; miserably, wretchedly; insufficiently &c. 640; imperfectly; faintly &c. 160; passably, pretty well, well enough.

[in a certain or limited degree] partially, in part; in -, to a certain degree; to a certain extent; comparatively; some, rather; in some -degree, -measure; some-thing, -what; simply, only, purely, merely; at -, at the- -least, - most; ever

so little, as little as may be, *tant soit peu*, in ever so small a degree; thus far, *pro tanto*, within bounds, in a manner, after a fashion.

almost, nearly, well nigh, short of, not quite, all but; near -, close- upon; *peu s'en faut*, near the mark; within an -ace, - inch- of; on the brink of; scarcely, hardly, barely, only just, no more than.

[in an uncertain degree] about, thereabouts, somewhere about, nearly, say; be the same -more, - little more- or less.

[in no degree] no- ways, - wise; not -at all, - in the least, - a bit, - a bit of it, - a whit, - a jot, - a shadow; in no -wise, - respect; by no -means, - manner of means; on no account, at no hand.

QUANTITY BY COMPARISON WITH A SIMILAR OBJECT

33. Superiority.—**N.** supremacy, superiority, majority; greatness &c. 31; advantage, odds, pull; preponderance, -ation; predominance, vantage ground, coign of vantage, prevalence, partiality; personal superiority; sovereignty &c. 737; nobility &c. (*rank*) 875; Triton among the minnows, *primus inter pares*, *nulli secundus*, superman; captain &c. 475.

supremacy, pre-eminence; primacy, lead, *maximum*; record; climax, crest, top; culmination &c. (*summit*) 210; transcendence; *ne plus ultra*; lion's share, Benjamin's mess; excess; bisque, surplus &c. (*remainder*) 40, (*redundance*) 641.

V. be -superior &c. *adj.*; exceed, excel, transcend; out-do, -balance, -weigh, -rival, -Herod, outrank, pass, surpass, surmount, get ahead of; over-top, -ride, -pass, -balance, -weigh, -match; top, o'er-top, cap, beat, win out, cut out; beat hollow; outstrip &c. 303; eclipse, throw into the shade, take the shine out of, put one's nose out of joint; have the -upper hand, - whip hand of, - advantage; turn the scale, play first fiddle &c. (*importance*) 642; preponderate, predominate, prevail; precede, take precedence, come first; come to a head, culminate; beat &c. all others, bear the palm; break the record, take the cake.

become -, render- -larger, &c. (*increase*) 35, (*expand*) 194.

Adj. superior, greater, major, higher; exceeding &c. *v.*; great &c. 31; distinguished, *ultra*; vaulting; more than a match for.

supreme, greatest, maximal, maximum, utmost, paramount, preeminent, foremost, crowning; first-rate &c. (*important*) 642, (*excellent*) 648; unrivalled; peer-, match-less; none such, second to none, *sans pareil*; unparagoned, -paralleled, -equalled, -approached, -surpassed; superlative, inimitable, *facile princeps*, incomparable, sovereign, without parallel, *nulli secundus, ne plus ultra*; beyond -compare, - comparison; culminating &c. (*topmost*) 210; transcend-ent, -ental; *plus royaliste que le Roi.*

increased &c. (*added to*) 35; enlarged &c. (*expanded*) 194.

Adv. beyond, more, over; over -, above- the mark; above par; upwards -, in advance- of; over and above; at the top of the scale, on the crest, at its height.

[in a superior or supreme degree] eminently, egregiously, preeminently, surpassing, prominently, superlatively, supremely, above all, of all things, the most, to crown all, *par excellence*, principally, especially, particularly, peculiarly, *a fortiori*, even, yea, still more.

Phr. 'we shall not look upon his like again.'

34. Inferiority.—N. inferiority, minority, subordinancy; shortcoming, deficiency; handicap; *minimum*; smallness &c. 32; imperfection, shabbiness.

[personal inferiority] commonalty &c. 876; subordinate, substitute, sub.

V. be -inferior &c. *adj.*; fall -, come-short of; not -pass, - come up to; want.

become -, render- smaller &c. (*decrease*) 36, (*contract*) 195; hide its diminished head, retire into the shade,

yield the palm, play second fiddle, take a back seat; bow.

Adj. inferior, smaller; small &c. 32; minor, less, lesser, deficient, minus, lower, subordinate, secondary; second-rate &c. (*imperfect*) 651; sub, subaltern; thrown into the shade; weighed in the balance and found wanting; not fit to hold a candle to.

least, smallest &c. (*see* little, small &c. 193); lowest.

diminished &c. (*decreased*) 36; reduced &c. (*contracted*) 195; unimportant &c. 643.

Adv. less; under -, below- -the mark, - par; at -the bottom of the scale, - a low ebb, - a disadvantage; short of, under.

CHANGES IN QUANTITY

35. Increase—N. increase, augmentation, addition, enlargement, extension; dilatation &c. (*expansion*) 194; multiplication; increment, accretion; accession &c. 37; production &c. 161; development, growth; aggrandizement, aggravation, intensification; rise; ascent &c. 305; anabasis; ex-aggeration, -acerbation; spread &c. (*dispersion*) 73; flood-, spring-, -tide; gain, produce, profit &c. 618; booty, plunder &c. 793.

V. increase, augment, add to, enlarge; dilate &c. (*expand*) 194; grow, wax, mount, swell, get ahead, gain strength; advance; run -, shoot- up; rise; ascend &c. 305; sprout &c. 194.

aggrandize; raise, exalt; deepen, heighten; lengthen; thicken; strengthen; intensify, enhance, inflate, magnify, double, redouble; multiply; aggravate, exaggerate; ex-asperate, -acerbate; add fuel to the flame, *oleum addere camino*, superadd &c. (*add*) 37; spread &c. (*disperse*) 73.

Adj. increased &c. *v.*; on the increase, undiminished; additional &c. (*added*) 37; increasing &c. *v.*; growing, crescent, intensive, cumulative.

Adv. *crescendo*, increasingly.

Phr. *vires acquirit eundo.*

36. Non-Increase, Decrease.—N.
decrease, diminution; lessening &c. *v.*;
subtraction &c. 38; reduction, abatement, declension; shrinkage &c. (*contraction*) 195; coarctation; abridgment
&c. (*shortening*) 201; extenuation.

subsidence, catabasis, wane, ebb-,
neap-tide, decline; descent &c. 306;
decrement, reflux, depreciation; erosion, wear and tear, deterioration &c.
659; anticlimax; mitigation &c. (*moderation*) 174.

V. decrease, diminish, lessen; abridge
&c. (*shorten*) 201; shrink &c. (*contract*)
195; drop -, fall -, tail- off; fall away,
waste, wear, erode; wane, ebb, decline;
descend &c. 306; subside; deliquesce,
melt -, die -away; retire into the shade,
hide its diminished head, fall to a low
ebb, run low, languish, decay, crumble,
consume away.

bate, abate, dequantitate; discount;
depreciate; extenuate, lower, weaken,
attenuate, fritter away; mitigate &c.
(*moderate*) 174; belittle, minimize;
dwarf, throw into the shade; keep down,
reduce &c. 195; shorten &c. 201; subtract &c. 38.

Adj. unincreased &c. (*see* increase
&c. 35); decreased &c. *v.*; decreasing
&c. *v.*; on the -wane &c. *n.*; deliquescent.

Adv. *diminuendo, decrescendo*, decreasingly.

3°. Conjunctive Quantity

37. Addition.—N. addition, annex-
ation, adjection; junction &c. 43; superposition, -addition, -junction, -fetation;
accession, reinforcement; increase &c.
35; increment, supplement; accompaniment &c. 88; interposition &c. 228; insertion &c. 300; summation &c. 85; adjunct &c. 39.

V. add, annex, adject, affix, attach,
superadd, subjoin, superpose; clap -,
saddle- on; tack to, postfix, append, tag;

ingraft; saddle with; sprinkle; introduce
&c. (*interpose*) 228; insert &c. 300.

become added, accrue; ad-, supervene; add up &c. 85.

reinforce, strengthen, swell the ranks
of; augment &c. 35.

Adj. added &c. *v.*; additional; supplement, -al, -ary; suppletory, subjunc-
tive; adjec-, adsci-, asci-titious; additive, extra, spare, further, fresh, more,
new, ulterior, other, auxiliary, supernumerary, accessory.

Adv. in addition, more, plus, extra;
and, also, likewise, too, furthermore,
further, item; and -also, - eke; else, besides, to boot, *et cætera*; &c.; and so -
on, - forth; into the bargain, *cum multis
aliis*, over and above, moreover.

with, withal; including, inclusive, as
well as, not to mention, let alone; together -, along -, coupled -, in con-
junction- with; conjointly; jointly &c.
43.

38. Non-Addition. Subduction.—N.
sub-traction, -duction; deduction, retrenchment; removal; ab-, sub-lation;
abstraction &c. (*taking*) 789; garbling
&c. *v.*; mutilation, detruncation; ampu-
tation, severance; abs-, ex-, re-cision;
curtailment &c. 201; minuend, subtrahend; decrease &c. 36; abrasion.

V. sub-tract, -duct; rebate, de-duct,
-duce; bate, retrench; remove, withdraw;
take -from, - away; detract.

garble, mutilate, amputate, sever, detruncate; cut -off, - away, - out; expurgate; abscind, excise; pare, thin, prune;
decimate; abrade, scrape, file; geld, castrate, emasculate, unman, spay, caponize; eliminate.

diminish &c. 36; curtail &c. (*short-
en*) 201; deprive of &c. (*take*) 789;
weaken.

Adj. subtracted &c. *v.*; subtractive.
tailless, acáudal.

Adv. in -deduction &c. *n.*; less; short
of; minus, without, except, excepting,
with the exception of, barring, bar, save,
exclusive of, save and except, with a reservation.

39. [Thing added.] **Adjunct.—N.** adjunct; addit-ion, -ament; *additum*, affix, appendage, annex; augment, -ation; increment, reinforcement, supernumerary, accessory, item; garnish, sauce; accompaniment &c. 88; adjective, *addendum*, accession, complement, supplement; continuation; extension, subscript, tag, appendix, postscript, interlineation, interpolation, insertion.

rider, codicil, off-shoot, episode, side issue, corollary; piece; flap, lapel, label, tab, strip, fold, lappet, apron, skirt, embroidery, trappings, *cortège*; tail, suffix &c. (*sequel*) 65; wing.

Adj. additional &c. 37.

Adv. in addition &c. 37.

40. [Thing remaining.] **Remainder.—N.** remainder, residue; remains, *remanet*, remnant, rest, relic, relict; leavings, heel-tap, odds and ends, cheese-parings, candle ends, orts; *residuum*; dottle, dregs &c. (*dirt*) 653; refuse &c. (*useless*) 645; stubble, result, educt; fag-end, stub; ruins, wreck, skeleton, stump; *alluvium*.

surplus, overplus, excess; balance, complement, superfluity &c. (*redundance*) 641; surviv-al, -ance; afterglow.

V. remain; be -left &c. *adj.*; exceed, survive; leave.

Adj. remaining, left; left -behind, -over; residu-al, -ary; over, odd; unconsumed, sedimentary; surviving; net; exceeding, over and above; out-lying, -standing; cast off &c. 782; superfluous &c. (*redundant*) 641.

40a. [Thing deducted.] **Decrement.—N.** decrement, discount, rebate, defect, loss, deduction, eduction, tare; drawback; waste, wastage; reprise.

41. [Forming a whole without coherence.] **Mixture.—N.** mix-, admix-, commix-ture, -tion, mingling; commixion, immixture, interfusion, intermixture, alloyage, matrimony; junction &c. 43; combination &c. 48; entanglement, interlacing; miscegenation, interbreeding.

impregnation; in-, dif-, suf-, transfusion; infiltration; seasoning, sprinkling, interlarding; interpolation &c. 228; adulteration, sophistication.

[Thing mixed] tinge, tincture, touch, dash, smack, sprinkling, spice, seasoning, infusion, *soupçon*.

[Compound resulting from mixture] alloy, brass, bronze, pewter &c.; amalgam, *magma*, blend, half-and-half, *mélange, tertium, quid*, miscellany, *ambigu*, medley, mess, hash, hotchpotch, hodgepodge, *pasticcio*, patchwork, odds and ends, all sorts; jumble &c. (*disorder*) 59; salad, sauce, mash, *omnium gatherum*, gallimaufry, ragout, *olla podrida, olio*, salmagundi, *pot-pourri*, Noah's ark; texture, mingled yarn; mosaic &c. (*variegation*) 440.

half-blood, -caste, -breed, Eurasian; mulatto; terc-, quart-, quint-eron &c.; quad-, octo-roon; *griffo, zambo*; cross, hybrid, mongrel &c. 83.

V. mix; join &c. 43; combine &c. 48; com-, im-, inter-mix; mix up with, mingle; com-, inter-, be-mingle; shuffle &c. (*derange*) 61; pound together; hash -, stir- up; knead, brew; impregnate with; interlard &c. (*interpolate*) 228; intertwine, -weave &c. 219; associate with, miscegenate, interbreed.

be mixed &c.; get among, be entangled with.

instil, imbue; in-, suf-, trans-fuse; infiltrate, dash, tinge, tincture, season, sprinkle, besprinkle, attemper, medicate, blend, cross; alloy, amalgamate, compound, adulterate, sophisticate, infect.

Adj. mixed &c. *v.*; implex, composite, half-and-half, linsey-wolsey, hybrid, mongrel, heterogeneous; motley &c. (*variegated*) 440; miscellaneous, promiscuous, indiscriminate; miscible.

Adv. among, amongst, amid, amidst, with; in the midst of, in the crowd.

42. [Freedom from mixture.] **Simpleness.—N.** simpleness &c. *adj.*; purity, homogeneity.

elimination; sifting &c. *v.*; purification &c. (*cleanness*) 652.

V. render -simple &c. *adj.*; simplify.

sift, winnow, bolt, eliminate; narrow down; get rid of, exclude &c. 55; clear; purify &c. (*clean*) 652; disentangle &c. (*disjoin*) 44.

Adj. simple, uniform, of a piece, homogeneous, single, pure, clear, sheer, neat; Attic.

un-mixed, -mingled, -blended, -combined, -compounded; elementary, undecomposed; un-adulterated, -sophisticated, -alloyed, -tinged, -fortified; pure and simple.

free –, exempt- from; exclusive.

Adv. simply &c. *adj.*; only.

43. Junction.—N. junction; joining &c. *v.*; joinder, union; con-nection, -junction, -jugation, compendency, annex-ion, -ation, -ment; coalition; astriction, attachment, compagination, vincture, ligation, alligation; accouplement; marriage &c. (*wedlock*) 903; infibulation, inosculation, symphysis, anastomosis, confluence, communication, concatenation; concurrence, meeting, reunion; assemblage &c. 72.

copulation, coition, intercourse.

joint, joining, juncture, chiasma, pivot, hinge, articulation, commissure, seam, suture, gusset, stitch, splice; link &c. 45; mitre, mortise.

closeness, tightness &c. *adj.*; coherence &c. 46; combination &c. 48.

V. join, unite; con-join, -nect; associate; put –, lay –, clap –, hang –, lump –, hold –, piece –, tack –, fix –, bind up- together; embody; re-embody; roll into one.

attach, fix, affix, saddle on, fasten, bind, secure, clinch, twist, make -fast &c. *adj.*; tie, pinion, string, strap, sew, lace, stitch, tack, paste, knit, button, buckle, hitch, lash, truss, bandage, braid, splice, swathe, gird, tether, moor, picket, harness, chain; fetter &c. (*restrain*) 751; lock, latch, belay, brace, hook, grapple, leash, couple, accouple,

link, yoke, bracket; marry &c. (*wed*) 903; bridge over, span.

pin, nail, bolt, hasp, clasp, clamp, screw, rivet; impact, solder, braze, cement, set; weld –, fuse- together; wedge, rabbet, mortise, mitre, jam, dovetail, enchase; graft, ingraft, inosculate; en-, in-twine; inter-link, -lace, -twine, -twist, -weave; entangle; twine round, belay; tighten; trice –, screw-up.

be -joined &c.; hang –, hold- together; cohere &c. 46.

Adj. joined &c. *v.*; joint; con-joint, -junct; corporate, compact; hand in hand.

firm, fast, close, tight, taut, taught, tense, secure, set, intervolved; inseparable, -dissoluble, -secable, -severable.

Adv. jointly &c. *adj.*; in conjunction with &c. (*in addition to*) 37; fast, firmly &c. *adj.*; intimately.

44. Disjunction.—N. dis-junction, -connection, -unity, -union, -association, -engagement, -sociation; discontinuity &c. 70; inconnection; abstraction, -edness; isolation; insul-arity, -ation; oasis; separateness &c. *adj.*; severalty; *disjecta membra*; dispersion &c. 73; apportionment &c. 786.

separation; parting &c. *v.*; detachment, segregation; divorce, sejunction, seposition, diduction, diremption, discerption; elision; *cæsura*, division, sub-division, break, fracture, rupture; compartition; dis-memberment, -integration, -location; luxation; sever-, dis-severance; scission; re-, ab-scission; circumcision; lacer-, dilacer-ation; dis-, abruption; avulsion, divulsion; section, resection, cleavage; fission; separability; separatism.

fissure, breach, rent, split, rift, crack, slit, slot, incision.

dissection, anatomy; decomposition &c. 49; cutting instrument &c. (*sharpness*) 253; saw.

V. be -disjoined &c.; come –, fall-off, – to pieces; peel off; get loose.

dis-join, -connect, -engage, -unite, -sociate, -pair; divorce, part, dispart, detach, uncouple, separate, cut off, rescind, segregate; set -, keep- apart; insulate, isolate; throw out of gear; cut adrift; loose; un-loose, -do, -bind, -tie, -hitch, -chain, -lock &c. (*fix*) 43, -pack, -ravel; disentangle; set free &c. (*liberate*) 750.

sunder, divide, subdivide, sectionalize, sever, dissever, abscind; cut; segment; in-cide, -cise; circumcise; saw, snip, nib, nip, cleave, rive, rend, slit, split, splinter, chip, crack, snap, break, tear, burst; rend &c. -asunder, - in twain; wrench, rupture, shatter, shiver, cranch, crunch, craunch, chop; rip up; hack, hew, slash; whittle; haggle, hackle, discind, lacerate, scamble, mangle, gash, hash, slice.

cut up, carve, quarter, dissect, anatomize; take -, pull -, pick -, tear- to pieces; tear to tatters, - piecemeal; divellicate; skin &c. 226; dis-integrate, -member, -branch, -band; disperse &c. 73; dis-locate, -joint; break up; mince; comminute &c. (*pulverize*) 330; distribute, apportion &c. 786.

part, - company; separate, leave; alienate, estrange.

Adj. disjoined &c. *v.*; discontinuous &c. 70; bipartite, multipartite, abstract; digitate; disjunctive; isolated &c. *v.*; insular, separate, disparate, discrete, apart, asunder, far between, loose, free; unattached, -annexed, -associated, -connected; distinct; adrift; straggling; rift, reft, cleft, split.

[capable of being divided] scissile, partible, divisible, separable, severable, detachable.

Adv. separately &c. *adj.*; one by one, severally, apart; adrift, asunder, in twain; in the abstract, abstractedly.

45. [Connecting medium.] Vinculum.—N. vinculum, link, *nexus*; connec-tive, -tion; junction &c. 43; bond of union, copula, intermedium, hyphen; bracket; bridge, stepping-stone, isthmus.

bond, tendon, tendril; fibre; cord, -age; riband, ribbon, rope, guy, cable,

line, halser, hawser, painter, moorings, wire, chain; string &c. (*filament*) 205.

fastening, tie; liga-ment, -ture; strap; bowline, halliard, tackle, lanyard, rigging, shrouds; standing -, running- rigging; traces, harness; yoke; band, -age; brace, roller, fillet; inkle; with, withe, withy; thong, braid; girder, tie-beam; girt, cinch, girth, girdle, cestus, garter, braces, suspenders, halter, noose, lasso, lariat, surcingle, knot, hitch, running knot, frog.

pin, corking pin, nail, brad, tack, skewer, staple, cleat, clamp; cramp, screw, button, buckle, clasp, hasp, hinge, hank, catch, latch, bolt, ring, latchet, pawl, tag: tooth; stud; hook, - and eye; morse, lock, holdfast, padlock, rivet; anchor, grappling-iron, drawbar, coupler, drawhead, coupling, treenail, trennel, stake, pale, pile, post, bollard.

cement, glue, gum, paste, size, wafer, solder, lute, putty, bird-lime, mortar, stucco, plaster, grout.

shackle, rein &c. (*means of restraint*) 752; suspender &c. 214; prop &c. (*support*) 215.

V. bridge over, span; connect &c. 43; hang &c. 214.

46. Coherence.—N. co-, ad-herence; -hesion, -hesiveness; concretion, accretion; con-, ag-glutination, -glomeration; aggregation; consolidation, set, cementation; sticking, soldering &c. *v.*; connection.

tenacity, toughness; stickiness &c. 352; insepara-bility, -bleness; bur, remora.

conglomerate, concrete &c. (*density*) 321.

V. cohere, adhere, stick, cling, cleave, hold, take hold of, hold fast, close with, embrace, clasp, hug; grow -, hang-together; twine round &c. (*join*) 43.

stick like -a leech, - wax; stick close; cling like -ivy, - a bur; adhere like -a remora, - Dejanira's shirt.

glue; ag-, con-glutinate; cement, lute, paste, gum; solder, weld; cake, coagulate, consolidate &c. (*solidify*) 321; agglomerate.

Adj. co-, ad-hesive, -hering &c. *v.*; tenacious, tough; sticky &c. 352.

united, unseparated, sessile, inseparable, inextricable, infrangible; compact &c. (*dense*) 321.

47. [Want of adhesion, non-adhesion, immiscibility.] **Incoherence.**—**N.** non-adhesion; immiscibility; incoherence; looseness &c. *adj.*; laxity; relaxation; loosening &c. *v.*; freedom; disjunction &c. 44; rope of sand.

V. make -loose &c. *adj.*; loosen, slacken, relax; un-glue &c. 46; detach &c. (*disjoin*) 44.

Adj. non-adhesive, immiscible; incoherent, detached, loose, slack, baggy, lax, relaxed, flapping, streaming; dishevelled; segregated, like grains of sand; un-consolidated &c. 321, -combined &c. 48; non-cohesive.

48. Combination.—**N.** combination; mixture &c. 41; alloy; junction &c. 43; union, unification, synthesis, incorporation, amalgamation, embodiment, coalescence, crasis, fusion, blend, blending, absorption, centralization, federation.

compound, amalgam, composition, *tertium quid*; resultant, impregnation.

V. combine, unite, incorporate, alloy, intertwine &c. 41; amalgamate, embody, absorb, re-embody, blend, merge, fuse, melt into one, consolidate, coalesce, centralize, impregnate; put -, lump- together; federate, associate; fraternize; cement a union, marry, wed, couple, pair, ally.

Adj. combined &c. *v.*; conjunctive, conjugate, conjoint, allied, confederate; impregnated with, ingrained, inoculated.

49. Decomposition.—**N.** decomposition, analysis, diæresis, dissection, resolution, catalysis, electrolysis, hydrolysis, photolysis, dissolution; dispersion &c. 73; disjunction &c. 44; disintegration, decay, rot, putrefaction, putrescence, caries, necrosis, corruption &c. (*uncleanness*) 653.

V. decom-pose, -pound; analyze, dis-

embody, dissolve; resolve -, separate-into its elements; electrolyze; dissect, decentralize, break up; disintegrate; disperse &c. 73; unravel &c. (*unroll*) 313; crumble into dust; decay &c. *n.*; deteriorate &c. 659.

Adj. decomposed &c. *v.*; catalytic, analytical.

4°. Concrete Quantity

50. Whole. [Principal part.]—**n.** whole, totality, integrity; totalness &c. *adj.*; entirety, *ensemble*, collectiveness; unity &c. 87; completeness &c. 52; in-divisibility, indiscerptibility; integration, embodiment; integer, integral.

all, the whole, total, aggregate, one and all, gross amount, sum, sum-total, *tout ensemble*, length and breadth of, Alpha and Omega, 'be all and end all,' lock, stock and barrel.

bulk, mass, lump, tissue, staple, body, torso, *compages*; trunk, bole, hull, hulk, skeleton; greater -, major -, best -, principal -, main- part; essential part &c. (*importance*) 642; lion's share, Benjamin's mess; the long and the short; nearly -, almost- all.

V. form -, constitute- a whole; integrate, embody, amass; aggregate &c. (*assemble*) 72; amount to, come to.

Adj. whole, total, integral, entire; complete &c. 52; one, individual.

un-broken, -cut, -divided, -severed, -clipped, -cropped, -shorn; seamless; un-diminished; un-demolished, -dissolved, -destroyed, -bruised.

in-divisible, -dissoluble, -dissolvable, -discerptible.

wholesale, sweeping, comprehensive.

Adv. wholly, altogether; totally &c. (*completely*) 52; entirely, all, all in all, considering all things, in a body, collectively, all put together; in the -aggregate, - lump, - mass, - gross, - main, - long run; *en masse*, on the whole, as a whole, bodily, *en block, in extenso*, throughout, every inch; substantially.

51. Part.—N. part, portion; dose; item, particular; aught, any; division, ward; subdivision, section; chapter, verse; article, clause, count, paragraph, passage; phrase; number, volume, book, fascicule; sector, segment; fraction, fragment; cantle, -t; frustum; detachment, parcel, unit, class &c. 75.

piece, lump, bit; cut, -ting; chip, chunk, collop, slice, scale, shard; lamina &c. 204; moiety; small part; morsel, scrap, crumb; particle &c. (*smallness*) 32; instalment, dividend; share &c. (*allotment*) 786.

débris, odds and ends, oddments, *detritus*; *excerpta*; member, limb, lobe, lobule, arm, wing, scion, branch, bough, joint, link, offshoot, ramification, twig, stipule, tendril, bush, spray, sprig; runner; leaf, -let; stump; constituent, ingredient, component part &c. 56.

compartment; department &c. (*class*) 75; county &c. (*region*) 181.

V. part, divide, break &c. (*disjoin*) 44; partition &c. (*apportion*) 786.

Adj. fractional, fragmentary; sectional, aliquot; divided &c. *v.*; in compartments, multifid, incomplete, partial, divided &c. 44.

Adv. partly, in part, partially; piecemeal, part by part; by -instalments, - snatches, - inches, - driblets; bit by bit, inch by inch, foot by foot, drop by drop; in -detail, - lots.

52. Completeness.—N. completeness &c. *adj.*; completion &c. 729; integration; integrality.

entirety; universality; totality; perfection &c. 650; solid-ity, -arity; unity; all; *ne plus ultra*, ideal, limit.

complement, supplement, make-weight; filling up &c. *v.*

impletion; satur-ation, -ity; high water; high -, flood -, spring- tide; fill, load, bumper, bellyful; brimmer; sufficiency &c. 639.

V. be -complete &c. *adj.*; come to a head.

render -complete &c. *adj.*; complete &c. (*accomplish*) 729; fill, charge, load,

replenish; make-up, - good; piece -, eke- out; supply deficiencies; fill -up, - in, - to the brim, - the measure of; saturate &c. 869.

go the whole -hog, - length, go all lengths.

Adj. complete, entire; whole &c. 50; perfect &c. 650; full, good, absolute, thorough, plenary; solid, undivided; with all its parts.

exhaustive, radical, sweeping, thorough-going; dead.

regular, consummate, unmitigated, sheer, unqualified, unconditional, free; abundant &c. (*sufficient*) 639.

brimming; brim-, top-ful; chock -, choke- full; as full as -an egg is of meat, - a vetch, - a tick; saturated, crammed; replete &c. (*redundant*) 641; fraught, laden, full-laden, -fraught, -charged; heavy laden.

completing &c. *v.*; supplement-al, -ary; ascititious.

Adv. completely &c. *adj.*; altogether, outright, wholly, totally, in *toto*, quite; over head and ears; effectually, for good and all, nicely, fully, through thick and thin, head and shoulders; neck and -heel, - crop; all out; in -all respects, - every respect; at all points, out and out, to all intents and purposes; *toto cœlo*; utterly, clean, - as a whistle; to the -full, - utmost, - backbone; hollow, stark; heart and soul, root and branch; down to the ground.

to the top of one's bent, as far as possible, *à outrance*.

throughout; from -first to last, - beginning to end, - end to end, - one end to the other, - Dan to Beersheba, - head to foot, - head to heels, - top to toe, - top to bottom; *de fond en comble; à fond, a capite ad calcem, ab ovo usque ad mala*, fore and aft; every -whit, - inch; *cap-à-pie*, to the end of the chapter; up to the -brim, - ears, - eyes; as . . . as can be.

on all accounts; *sous tous les rapports*; with a -vengeance, - witness.

53. Incompleteness.—N. incompleteness &c. *adj.*; deficiency, short -measure, – weight; shortcoming &c. 304; insufficiency &c. 640; imperfection &c. 651; immaturity &c. (*nonpreparation*) 674; half measures.

[part wanting] defect, deficit, shortage, ullage, defalcation, omission, *caret*; interval &c. 198; break &c. (*discontinuity*) 70; non-completion &c. 730; missing link.

V. be -incomplete &c. *adj.*; fall short of &c. 304; lack &c. (*be insufficient*) 640; neglect &c. 460.

Adj. incomplete; imperfect &c. 651; unfinished; uncompleted &c. (*see* complete &c. 729); defective, deficient, wanting; failing; in -default, – arrear; short, – of; hollow, meagre, lame, half-and-half, perfunctory, sketchy; crude &c. (*unprepared*) 674.

mutilated, garbled, mangled, docked, lopped, truncated; bobtailed, cropped, bobbed, shingled.

in -progress, – hand; going on, proceeding.

Adv. incompletely &c. *adj.*; by halves.

Phr. *cætera desunt; caret.*

54. Composition.—N. composition, constitution, crasis, synthesis; makeup; combination &c. 48; inclusion, admission, comprehension, reception; embodiment, formation, conformation, production.

compilation &c. 72; (*musical*) composition &c. 415; painting &c. 556; writing &c. 590; typography &c. 591.

V. be -composed, – made, – formed, – made up- of; consist of, be resolved into.

include &c. (*in a class*) 76; subsume; synthesize; contain, hold, comprehend, take in, admit, embrace, embody; involve; implicate, drag into.

compose, constitute, form, make; make –, fill –, build- up; weave, construct, fabricate; compile; write, draw; set up (*printing*); enter into the composition of &c. (*be a component*) 56.

Adj. containing, constituting &c. *v.*

55. Exclusion.—N. exclusion, non-admission, omission, exception, rejection, repudiation; exile &c. (*seclusion*) 893; preclusion, lock out, ostracism, prohibition; disbarment, expulsion, ban.

separation, segregation, seposition, elimination, coffer-dam.

V. be excluded from &c.

exclude, bar, ban; leave –, shut –, thrust –, bar- out; reject, repudiate, spurn, blackball; ostracize, boycott; lay –, put –, set -apart, – aside; relegate, segregate; throw overboard; strike -off, – out; neglect &c. 460; banish &c. (*seclude*) 893; separate &c. (*disjoin*) 44.

pass over, omit; garble; eliminate, weed, winnow.

Adj. excluding &c. *v.*; exclusive.

excluded &c. *v.*; unrecounted, not included in; inadmissible; preventive, interdictive.

Adv. exclusive of, barring; except; with the exception of; save, bating.

56. Component.—N. component; component –, integral –, integrant- part; element, constituent, ingredient, leaven; part and parcel; contents; appurtenance; feature; member &c. (*part*) 51; personnel.

V. enter into, – the composition of; be a -component &c. *n.*; be –, form-part of; merge –, be merged- in; be implicated in; share in &c. (*participate*) 778; belong –, appertain- to.

form, make, constitute, compose.

Adj. forming &c. *v.*; inclusive; inherent &c. 5.

57. Extraneousness.—N. extraneousness &c. *adj.*; extrinsicality &c. 6; exteriority &c. 220; alienism.

foreign -body, – substance, – element; alien, stranger, intruder, interloper, foreigner, tramontane, *novus homo*, new comer, immi-, emi-grant; creole, Afrikander; outsider, outlander, tenderfoot.

Adj. extraneous, foreign, alien, ulterior; exterior, external, outside, outlandish; oversea; tra-, ultra-montane.

excluded &c. 55; inadmissible; exceptional.

Adv. in foreign -parts, – lands; abroad, beyond seas, overseas.

SECTION IV. ORDER

1°. ORDER IN GENERAL

58. Order.—**N.** order, regularity &c.
80; uniformity, symmetry, *lucidus ordo*;
harmony, music of the spheres.

gradation, progression; series &c.
(*continuity*) 69.

subordination; course, even tenor,
routine; method, disposition, arrangement, array, system, economy, discipline; orderliness &c. *adj.*

rank, place, &c. (*term*) 71.

V. be -, become- in order &c. *adj.*;
form, fall in, draw up; arrange -, range
-, place- itself; adjust; fall into -, take-
-one's place, - rank; rally round; arrange &c. 60.

Adj. orderly, regular; in -order, -
trim, - apple-pie order, according to
Cocker, - its proper place, neat, neat as
a pin, tidy, *en règle*, well regulated, correct, methodical, uniform, symmetrical,
ship-shape, business-like, systematic;
habitual; unconfused &c. (*see* confuse
&c. 61) arranged &c. 60.

Adv. in order; methodically &c. *adj.*;
in -turn, - its turn; step by step; by regular -steps, - gradations, - stages, - intervals; *seriatim*, systematically, by
clockwork, *gradatim*; at stated periods
&c. (*periodically*) 138.

59. [Absence, or want of Order, &c.]
Disorder.—**N.** disorder; derangement
&c. 61; irregularity; anomaly &c. (*unconformity*) 83; anar-chy, -chism; want
of method; dishevelment, untidiness &c.
adj.; disunion; discord &c. 24.

confusion; confusedness &c. *adj.*;
disarray, jumble, mix-up, huddle, litter,
lumber; *cahotage*; farrago; mess, muss,
mash, muddle, hash; hotchpotch; *imbroglio*, chaos, *omnium gatherum*, medley; mere -mixture &c. 41; fortuitous

concourse of atoms, *disjecta membra,
rudis indigestaque moles.*

complexity; complexness &c. *adj.*;
com-, im-plication; intri-cacy, -cation;
perplexity; network, maze, labyrinth;
wilderness, jungle; involution, ravel-
ling, entanglement; coil &c. (*convolution*) 248; sleave, tangled skein, knot,
Gordian knot, kink, web; wheels within
wheels.

turmoil; ferment, &c. (*agitation*) 315;
to do, trouble, pudder, pother, row, disturbance, convulsion, tumult, pandemonium, uproar, riot, rumpus, stour,
scramble, *fracas*, embroilment, *mêlée*;
spill and pelt, rough and tumble; whirlwind &c. 349; bear garden, Babel, Saturnalia, Donnybrook Fair, confusion
worse confounded, most admired disorder, *concordia discors*; Bedlam -, hell-
broke loose; bull in a china shop; all the
fat in the fire, *diable à quatre*, Devil to
pay; pretty kettle of fish; pretty piece of
-work, - business.

slattern, slut, sloven, draggle-tail.

V. be -disorderly &c. *adj.*; ferment,
play at cross purposes.

put out of order; derange &c. 61; ravel &c. 219; ruffle, rumple; bungle,
botch.

Adj. disorderly, orderless; out of
-order, - place, - gear, - whack; irregular, desultory; anomalous &c. (*unconformable*) 83; acephalous, disorganized,
straggling; un-, im-methodical; unsymmetric; unsystematic; untidy, slovenly,
bedraggled, messy; dislocated; out of
sorts; promiscuous, indiscriminate; cha-
otic, anarchical, lawless; unarranged
&c. 60; confused, tumultuous, turbulent, tempestuous; deranged &c. 61;

topsy turvy &c. (*inverted*) 218; shapeless &c. 241; disjointed, out of joint.

com-plex, -plexed; intricate, complicated, perplexed, involved, ravelled, entangled, knotted, tangled, inextricable; irreducible.

troublous; riotous &c. (*violent*) 173.

Adv. irregularly &c. *adj.* by fits and -snatches, – starts; pell-mell; higgledy-piggledy; helter-skelter; harum-scarum; in a ferment; at -sixes and sevens, – cross purposes; upside down &c. 218.

Phr. the cart before the horse, chaos is come again.

60. [Reduction to Order.] Arrangement.—N. arrangement; plan &c. 626; preparation &c. 673; dispos-al, -ition; col-, al-location; distribution; sorting &c. *v.*; assortment, allotment; grouping; apportionment, *taxis*, taxonomy, *syn-taxis*, graduation, organization, grading; re-organization, rationalization.

analysis, classification, division, digestion; systematism.

[Result of arrangement] order, orderliness, form, array; digest, synopsis &c. (*compendium*) 596; *syntagma*, table, atlas; register &c. (*record*) 551; score &c. 415; cosmos, organism, architecture.

[Instrument for sorting] sieve &c. 260; file, card index.

V. reduce to –, bring into- order; introduce order into; rally.

arrange, dispose, place, form; put –, set –, place- in order; straighten up, tidy up; set out, collocate, allocate, pack, marshal, range, size, rank, array, group, parcel out, allot, space, distribute, deal; cast –, assign- the parts; dispose of, assign places to; assort, sort; sift, riddle; put –, set- -to rights, – into shape, – in trim, – in array.

class, -ify; divide; file, string together, thread; register &c. (*record*) 551; list, catalogue, tabulate, index, alphabeticize, graduate, digest, grade, codify; orchestrate, score.

methodize, regulate, systematize, standardize, co-ordinate, organize, settle, fix.

unravel, disentangle, ravel, card; disembroil.

Adj. arranged &c. *v.*; embattled, in battle array; cut and dried; methodical, orderly, regular, systematic, tabular.

61. [Subversion of Order; bringing into disorder.] Derangement.—N. derangement &c. *v.*; disorder &c. 59; evection, discomposure, disturbance; dis-, de-organization; involvement; dislocation; perturbation, interruption; shuffling &c. *v.*; inversion &c. 218; corrugation &c. (*fold*) 258; insanity &c. 503.

V. derange; dis-, mis-arrange; dis-, mis-place; mislay, discompose, disorder, de-, dis-organize; embroil, unsettle, disturb, confuse, trouble, perturb, jumble, tumble; huddle, shuffle, muddle, toss, hustle, fumble, riot; bring –, put –, throw- into -disorder &c. 59; break the ranks, disconcert, convulse; break in upon.

unhinge, dislocate, put out of joint, throw out of gear.

turn topsy-turvy &c. (*invert*) 218; bedevil; complicate, involve, perplex, confound; im-, em-brangle; tangle, entangle, ravel, tousle, dishevel, ruffle, rumple &c. (*fold*) 258; dement.

litter, scatter; mix &c. 41.

Adj. deranged &c. *v.*; syncre-tic, -tistic.

2°. CONSECUTIVE ORDER

62. Precedence.—N. precedence; coming before &c. *v.*; the lead, *le pas*; superiority &c. 33; importance &c. 642; anteced-ence, -ency; anteriority &c. (*front*) 234; precursor &c. 64; priority &c. 116; precession &c. 280; anteposition, preference.

V. precede; come -before, – first; forerun, head, lead, take the lead; lead the -way, – dance; introduce, usher in; have the *pas*; set the fashion &c.

(*influence*) 175; lead off, kick off, open the ball; take –, have- precedence; outrank; have the start &c. (*get before*) 280.

place before; prefix; premise, prelude, preface.

Adj. preceding &c. *v.*; pre-, antecedent; anterior; prior &c. 116; before; former, foregoing; before-, abovementioned; aforesaid, said; precurs-ory, -ive; prevenient, preliminary, prefatory, introductory; prelus-ive, -ory; proemial, preparatory.

Adv. before; in advance &c. (*precession*) 280.

Phr. *seniores priores.*

63. Sequence.—N. sequence, coming after; going after &c. (*following*) 281; consecution, succession; posteriority &c. 117.

continuation; prolongation, order of succession; successiveness; Elijah's mantle.

secondariness; subordinancy &c. (*inferiority*) 34.

V. succeed; come -after, – on, – next; follow, ensue, step into the shoes of; alternate.

place after, suffix, append.

Adj. succeeding &c. *v.*; sequent; sub-, con-sequent; sequacious, proximate, next; consecutive &c. (*continuity*) 69; alternate, amœbæan.

latter; posterior &c. 117.

Adv. after, subsequently; behind &c. (*rear*) 235.

64. Precursor.—N. precursor, antecedent, precedent, predecessor; forerunner, van-courier, *avant-coureur*, pioneer, prodrome, *prodromos*, outrider; leader, bell-wether; herald, harbinger; dawn.

prelude, preamble, preface, prologue, foreword, *avant-propos*, *protasis*, prolusion, proem, *prolepsis*, *prolegomena*, prefix, introduction; lead, heading, frontispiece, groundwork; preparation &c. 673; overture, voluntary, *exordium*, symphony, *ritornello*; premises.

prefiguration &c. 511; omen &c. 512.

Adj. precursory; prelu-sive, -sory,

-dious; proemial, introductory, prefatory, prodromous, inaugural, preliminary; precedent &c. (*prior*) 116.

65. Sequel.—N. sequel, suffix, successor; tail, *queue*, train, wake, trail, rear; retinue, suite; appendix, postscript, subscript; epilogue; conclusion, peroration; codicil; continuation, *sequela*; appendage &c. 39; tail -, heelpiece; tag, more last words; *colophon*.

follower, after-glow, -growth, -crop, -taste, -math.

after-part, -piece, -course, -thought, -game; *arrière pensée*, second thoughts.

66. Beginning.—N. beginning, commencement, opening, outset, incipience, inception, inchoation; introduction &c. (*precursor*) 64; *alpha*; initial; foundation; inauguration, *début*, *le premier pas*, embarcation, rising of the curtain; zero hour; exordium, curtain raiser; maiden speech; prelude; outbreak, onset, brunt; initiative, move, first move; gambit, narrow –, thin- end of the wedge; fresh start, new departure; forefront.

origin &c. (*cause*) 153; source, rise; bud, germ &c. 153; egg, rudiment; genesis, birth, nativity, cradle, infancy, incunabula; start, starting-point &c. 293; dawn &c. (*morning*) 125.

title-page; head, -ing, caption; van &c. (*front*) 234.

en-trance, -try; inlet, orifice, mouth, chops, lips, porch, portal, portico, *propylon*, door; gate, -way; postern, wicket, threshold, vestibule; skirts, border &c. (*edge*) 231; tee.

first -stage, – blush, – glance, – impression, – sight.

rudiments, elements, outlines, *principia*, grammar, *protasis*; alphabet, ABC.

V. begin, commence, inchoate, rise, arise, originate, institute, conceive, initiate, open, dawn, set in, take its rise, enter upon, start; enter; set out &c. (*depart*) 293; embark in.

usher in; lead -off, – the way; take the -lead, – initiative; inaugurate, head;

stand -at the head, – first, – for; lay the foundations &c. (*prepare*) 673; found &c. (*cause*) 153; set -up, – on foot, – agoing, – abroach, – the ball in motion; apply the match to a train; launch, broach; open -up, – the door to; set -about, – to work; make a -beginning, – start; handsel; take the first step, lay the first stone, cut the first turf; break -ground, – the ice, – cover; pass –, cross- the Rubicon; open -fire, – the ball; ventilate, air; undertake &c. 676.

come into -existence, – the world; make one's *début*, take birth; burst forth, break out; spring –, crop- up.

begin -at the beginning, – *ab ovo*, – again, – *de novo*; start afresh, make a fresh start, shuffle the cards, resume, recommence.

Adj. beginning &c. *v.*; initi-al, -atory, -ative; inceptive, introductory, incipient; proemial, inaugural; incho-ate, -ative; embryonic, rudimental; primogenial; primeval &c. (*old*) 124; rudimentary, aboriginal; natal, nascent.

first, foremost, front, leading, head; maiden.

begun &c. *v.*; just -begun &c. *v.*

Adv. at –, in- the beginning &c. *n.*; first, in the first place, *imprimis*, first and foremost; *in limine*; in -the bud, – embryo, – its infancy; from -the beginning, – its birth; *ab -initio*, – *ovo*, – *incunabilis*, primarily, originally.

67. End.—N. end, close, termination; desinence, conclusion, *finis*, *finale*, period, term, *terminus*, last, *omega*; extreme, -tremity; gable –, butt –, fagend; tip, nib, point; tail &c. (*rear*) 235; verge &c. (*edge*) 231; tag, epilogue, peroration; *bonne bouche*; bitter end, tail end; terminal; *apodosis*; appendix.

consummation, *dénouement*; finish &c. (*completion*) 729; fate; doom, -sday; crack of doom, day of Judgment, fall of the curtain, wind-up; goal, destination; limit, stoppage, end all, determination; expiration, expiry; death &c. 360; end of all things; finality; eschatology.

break up, *commencement de la fin*, last stage, turning point; *coup de grâce*, death-blow; knock-out.

V. end, close, finish, terminate, conclude, be all over; expire; die &c. 360; come –, draw- to a -close &c. *n.*; have run its course; run out, pass away.

bring to an -end &c. *n.*; put an end to, make an end of; determine; get through; achieve &c. (*complete*) 729; stop &c. (*make to cease*) 142; shut up shop.

Adj. ending &c. *v.*; final, terminal, definitive, conclusive; crowning &c. (*completing*) 729; last, ultimate; hindermost; rear &c. 235; caudal.

contermin-ate, -ous, -able.

ended &c. *v.*; at an end; settled, decided, over, played out, set at rest.

penultimate; last but -one, – two, &c.

unbegun, uncommenced; fresh.

Adv. finally &c. *adj.*; in fine; at the last; once for all.

68. Middle.—N. middle, midst, mediety; mean &c. 29; medium, middle term; centre &c. 222, mid-course &c. 628; *mezzo termine*; *juste milieu* &c. 628; half-way house, nave, navel, omphalos; nucle-us, -olus.

equidistance, bisection, half-distance; equator, diaphragm, midriff; interjacence &c. 228.

Adj. middle, medial, mesial, mean, mid; middle-, mid-most; middling; mediate; intermediate &c. (*interjacent*) 228; equidistant; central &c. 222; mediterranean, equatorial.

Adv. in the middle; in the thick; mid-, half-way; midships, *in medias res*.

69. [Uninterrupted sequence.] Continuity.—N. continuity; consecu-tion, -tiveness &c. *adj.*; succession, round, suite, progression, series, train, chain; cat-, concat-enation; catena; scale; gradation, course, constant flow, perpetuity.

procession, column; retinue, *cortège*, cavalcade, rank and file, line of battle, array.

pedigree, genealogy, lineage, race &c. 166.

rank, file, line, row, range, tier, string, thread, team; suit; colonnade.

V. follow in –, form- a series &c. *n.*; fall in.

arrange in a -series &c. *n.*; string together, catenate, file, thread, graduate, tabulate.

Adj. continu-ous, -ed; consecutive; progressive, gradual; serial, successive; immediate, unbroken, entire; linear; in a -line, – row &c. *n.*; uninter-rupted, -mitting; unremitting; perennial, evergreen; constant.

Adv. continuously &c. *adj.*; *seriatim*; in a -line &c. *n.*; in -succession, – turn; running, gradually, step by step, *gradatim*, at a stretch; in -file, – column, – single file, – Indian file.

70. [Interrupted sequence.] Discontinuity.—N. discontinuity; disjunction &c. 44; anacoluthon; interruption, break, fracture, flaw, fault, split, crack, cut; gap &c. (*interval*) 198; solution of continuity, *cæsura*; broken thread; parenthesis, episode; rhapsody, patchwork; intermission; alternation &c. (*periodicity*) 138; dropping fire.

V. be -discontinuous &c. *adj.*; alternate, intermit.

discontinue, pause, interrupt; intervene; break, – in upon; interpose &c. 228; break –, snap- the thread; disconnect &c. (*disjoin*) 44.

Adj. discontinuous, unsuccessive, broken, interrupted, *décousu*; dis-, unconnected, discrete, disjunctive; fitful &c. (*irregular*) 139; spasmodic, desultory, intermit-ting &c. *v.*, -tent; alternate; recurrent &c. (*periodic*) 138; few and far between.

Adv. at intervals; by -snatches, – jerks, – skips, – catches, – fits and starts; skippingly, *per saltum*; *longo intervallo*.

71. Term.—N. term, rank, station, stage, step; degree &c. 26; scale, remove, grade, link, peg, round –, rung- of the ladder, *status*, position, place,

point, mark, *pas*, period, pitch; stand, -ing; footing, range.

V. hold –, occupy –, fall into- a place &c. *n.*

3°. COLLECTIVE ORDER

72. Assemblage.—N. assemblage; col-lection, -location, -ligation; compilation, levy, gathering, ingathering, mobilization, meet, foregathering, muster, *attroupement*; con-course, -flux, -gregation, -tesseration, -vergence &c. 290; meeting, *levée*, *réunion*, drawing room, at home; conversazione &c. (*social gathering*) 892; assembly, congress, eisteddfod; conven-tion, -ticle; gemote; conclave, &c. (*council*) 696; posse, *posse comitatûs*; Noah's ark.

miscellany, *collectanea*, symposium; museum, menagerie, &c. (*store*) 636.

crowd, throng, multitude; flood, rush, deluge; rout, rabble, mob, press, crush, *cohue*, jam, horde, body, tribe; crew, gang, knot, squad, band, party; swarm, shoal, school, covey, flock, herd, drove, kennel; array, bevy, galaxy; *corps*, company, troop, *troupe*; army, force, regiment, &c. (*combatants*) 726; host &c. (*multitude*) 102; populousness.

clan, brotherhood, association &c. (*party*) 712.

volley, shower, storm, cloud.

group, cluster, Pleiades, clump, pencil; set, batch, lot, pack; budget, *dossier*, assortment, bunch; parcel; pack-et, -age; bundle, *fasciculus*, fascine, bale; ser-on, -oon; faggot, wisp, truss, tuft; shock, rick, fardel, stack, sheaf, swath, gavel, haycock, stook.

accumulation &c. (*store*) 636; congeries, heap, lump, pile, *rouleau*, tissue, mass, pyramid; drift; snow-ball, -drift; acervation, cumulation; amassment, glom-, agglom-eration; conglobation; conglomeration, -ate; coacervation, coagmentation, aggregation, concentration, congestion, *omnium gatherum*, *spicilegium*, black hole of Calcutta; quantity &c. (*greatness*) 31.

collector, gatherer; whip, -per in.

V. [be or come together] assemble, collect, muster; meet, unite, join, rejoin; cluster, flock, swarm, surge, stream, herd, crowd, throng, associate; con-gregate, -glomerate, -centrate; centre round, *rendezvous*, resort; come -, flock -, get -, pig- together; forgather; huddle; reassemble.

[get or bring together] assemble, muster, mobilize; bring -, get -, put -, draw -, scrape -, lump- together; col-lect, -locate, -ligate; get -, whip- in; gather; hold a meeting; con-vene, -voke, -vocate; rake up, dredge; heap, mass, pile; pack, put up, truss, cram; acervate; ag-glomerate, -gregate; compile; group, aggroup, concentrate, unite; collect -, bring- into a focus; amass, accumulate &c. (*store*) 636; collect in a drag-net; heap Ossa upon Pelion.

Adj. assembled &c. *v.*; closely packed, dense, serried, crowded to suffocation, teeming, swarming, populous; as thick as hops; all of a heap, fasciculated; cumulative.

Phr. the plot thickens.

73. Non-assemblage. Dispersion.—N. dispersion; disjunction &c. 44; divergence &c. 291; scattering &c. *v.*; dissemination, broadcasting, diffusion, dissipation, distribution; apportionment &c. 786; spread, respersion, circumfusion, interspersion, spargefaction.

waifs and estrays, flotsam and jetsam, *disjecta membra*.

V. disperse, scatter, sow, disseminate, radiate, diffuse, shed, spread, ted, bestrew, overspread, dispense, disband, disembody, demobilize, dismember, distribute; apportion &c. 786; blow off, let out, dispel, cast forth, draught off; strew, straw, strow; spirtle, cast, sprinkle, shatter; issue, deal out, retail, utter; re-, inter-sperse; set abroach, circumfuse.

turn -, cast- adrift; scatter to the winds; sow broadcast.

spread like wildfire, disperse themselves.

Adj. unassembled &c. (*see* assemble &c. 72); dispersed &c. *v.*; sparse, dispread, broadcast, sporadic, widespread; farflung; epidemic &c. (*general*) 78; adrift, stray; dishevelled, streaming.

Adv. *sparsim*, here and there, *passim.*

74. [Place of meeting.] **Focus.—N.** focus; point of- convergence &c. 290; corradiation; centre &c. 222; gathering-place, resort; haunt; retreat; *venue, rendezvous*; rallying point, head-quarters, home, club; *dépôt* &c. (*store*) 636; tryst, trysting-place; place of -meeting, - resort, - assignation; *point de -, lieu de-réunion*; issue.

V. bring to- a point, - a focus, - an issue; focus.

4°. DISTRIBUTIVE ORDER

75. Class.—N. class, category, *categorema*, head, order, section; division, subdivision; department, province, domain, sphere.

kind, sort, genus, species, variety, branch, family, race, tribe, caste, sept, clan, breed; *clique, coterie*; type, kit, sect, set; assortment, feather, kidney; suit; range; gender, sex, kin.

manner, description, denomination, persuasion, connection, designation, character, stamp; predicament; conviction &c. 484.

similarity &c. 17.

76. Inclusion. [Comprehension under, or reference to a class.]—**N.** inclusion, admission, incorporation, comprehension, reception.

composition &c. (*inclusion in a compound*) 54.

V. be -included in &c.; come -, fall -, range- under; belong -, pertain- to; range with; merge in.

include, compromise, comprehend, contain, admit, embrace, receive;

enclose &c. (*circumscribe*) 229; incorporate, cover, embody, encircle.

reckon –, enumerate –, number- among; refer to; place –, arrange- under, – with; take into account.

Adj. includ-ed, -ing &c. *v.*; inclusive; comprehensive, all-embracing; congener, -erous: of the same -class &c. 75.

Phr. *et hoc genus omne*, &c.; *et ca etera*.

77. Exclusion.*—N. exclusion &c. 55.

78. Generality.—N. general-ity, -ization; universality; catholic-ity, -ism; miscel-lany, -laneousness; dragnet.

every-one, -body; all hands, all the world and his wife; any body, N or M, all sorts; *tout le monde*.

prevalence, run.

V. be -general &c. *adj.*; prevail, obtain, be going about, stalk abroad.

render -general &c. *adj.*; generalize; spread, broadcast.

Adj. general, usual, current, generic, collective; broad, comprehensive, sweeping; encyclopedical, panoramic, widespread &c. (*dispersed*) 73.

universal; catho-lic, -lical; common, world-wide; œ-, e-cumenical; transcendental; prevalent, prevailing, rife, epidemic, besetting; all over, covered with.

every, all; indeterminate, indefinite, unspecified, impersonal.

customary &c. (*habitual*) 613.

Adv. what-ever, -soever; to a man, one and all, without exception.

generally &c. *adj.*; always, for better for worse; in general, generally speaking; speaking generally; for the most part; in the long run &c. (*on an average*) 29.

79. Specialty.—N. speciality, *spécialité*; individ-uality, -uity; particularity,

* The same set of words is used to express *Exclusion from a class* and *Exclusion from a compound.* Reference is therefore made to the former at 55. This identity does not occur with regard to *Inclusion,* which therefore constitutes a separate category.

peculiarity; idiocrasy &c. (*tendency*) 176; personality, characteristic, mannerism, idiosyncrasy, attribute specificness &c. *adj.*; singularity &c. (*unconformity*) 83; reading, version, lection; state; *trait*; distinctive feature; technicality; *differentia*.

particulars, details, minutiæ, items, counts.

I, self, I myself, *ego*; my-, him-, her-, it-self.

V. specify, particularize, individualize, realize, specialize, designate, differentiate, determine, define, denote, indicate, itemize, detail.

descend to particulars, enter into detail, come to the point.

Adj. special, particular, individual, specific, proper, personal, intimate, original, private, respective, definite, concrete, determinate, especial, certain, esoteric, endemic, partial, party, peculiar, marked, appropriate, several, characteristic, diagnostic, exact, exclusive; singular &c. (*exceptional*) 83; idiomatic; typical, representative, distinctive.

this, that; yon, -der.

Adv. specially &c. *adj.*; in particular, *in propriâ personâ*; *ad hominem*; for my part.

each, apiece, one by one; severally, respectively, each to each; *seriatim*, in detail, bit by bit; *pro hac vice*, – *re natâ*.

namely, that is to say, *videlicet*, viz.; to wit.

5°. ORDER AS REGARDS CATEGORIES

80. Rule.—N. regularity, uniformity &c. 16; clock-work precision; punctuality &c. (*exactness*) 494; routine &c. (*custom*) 613; formula; system; rut; canon, convention, maxim; rule &c. (*form, regulation*) 697; key-note, standard, model; precedent &c. (*prototype*) 22; conformity &c. 82.

nature, principle; law; order of things; normal –, natural –, ordinary –, model-

-state, - condition; standing -dish, - order; normality; Procrustean law; law of the Medes and Persians; hard and fast rule.

Adj. regular, uniform, symmetrical, constant, steady; according to rule &c. (*conformable*) 82; customary &c. 613; orderly &c. 58.

81. Multiformity.—N. multi-, omniformity; variety, diversity; multifariousness &c. *adj.*

Adj. multi-form, -fold, -farious, -generous; multiplex, variform, manifold, many-sided, multiplicate; omniform, -genous, -farious; polymorphic; protean; heterogeneous, motley, mosaic; epicene, indiscriminate, desultory, irregular, diversified, different, divers; all manner of; of -every description, - all sorts and kinds; *et hoc genus omne*; and what not? *de omnibus rebus et quibusdam aliis.*

82. Conformity.—N. conform-ity, -ance; observance.

naturalization; conventionality &c. (*custom*) 613; agreement &c. 23.

example, instance, specimen, sample, quotation; exemplification, illustration, case in point; object lesson.

conventionalist, formalist, Philistine.

pattern &c. (*prototype*) 22.

V. conform to, - rule; accommodate -, adapt- oneself to; rub off corners.

be -regular &c. *adj.*; move in a groove; follow -, observe -, go by -, bend to -, obey- -rules, - precedents; comply -, tally -, chime in -, fall in-with; be -guided, - regulated- by; fall into a -custom, - usage; follow the -fashion, - multitude; pass muster, do as others do, *hurler avec les loups*; do at Rome as the Romans do; go -, swim-with the -stream, - current, - tide; tread the beaten track &c. (*habit*) 613; rubber-stamp; keep one in countenance.

exemplify, illustrate, cite, quote, put a case; produce an- instance &c. *n.*

Adj. conformable to rule, adaptable, compliant, consistent, agreeable; regular &c. 80; according to -regulation, - rule, - Cocker; *en règle, selon les règles*, well regulated, orderly; symmetric &c. 242.

conventional, commonplace &c. (*customary*) 613; of -daily, - every day- occurrence; in the natural order of things; ordinary, common, - or garden, prosaic, habitual, usual.

in the order of the day; naturalized.

typical, normal, formal; canonical, orthodox, sound, strict, rigid, positive, uncompromising, Procrustean; point device.

secundum artem, ship-shape, technical.

exemplary, illustrative, in point.

Adv. conformably &c. *adj.*; by rule; agreeably to; in -conformity, - accordance, - keeping- with; according to; consistently with; as usual, *ad instar, instar omnium; more -solito, - majorum.*

for the sake of conformity; of -, as a matter of- course; *pro formâ*, for form's sake, by the card; according to plan.

invariably &c. (*uniformly*) 16.

for -example, - instance; *exempli gratiâ; e.g.; inter alia.*

Phr. *cela va sans dire; ex pede Herculem, noscitur a sociis.*

83. Unconformity.—N. nonconformity &c. 82; un-, dis-conformity; unconventionality, informality, abnormity, anomaly; anomalousness &c. *adj.*; exception, peculiarity, &c. 79; infraction -, breach -, violation -, infringement- of -law, - custom, - usage; eccentricity, *bizarrerie*, oddity, *je ne sais quoi*, monstrosity, rarity; freak of Nature.

individuality, idiosyncrasy, singularity, originality, mannerism.

aberration; irregularity; variety; singularity; exemption; salvo &c. (*qualification*) 469.

nonconformist; nondescript, character, original, nonsuch, monster, prodigy, wonder, miracle, curiosity, missing link, flying fish, black swan, *lusus naturæ, rara avis*, queer fish; mongrel; half-caste, -blood, -breed; *métis*, cross breed, hybrid, mule, mulatto, sacatra, marabou; *tertium quid*, hermaphrodite, gynander, androgyn.

phœnix, chimera, hydra, sphinx, minotaur; griff-in, -on; centaur; hippogriff, -centaur; sagittary; kraken, cockatrice, wyvern, roc, liver, dragon, seaserpent; mermaid; unicorn; Cyclops, 'men whose heads do grow beneath their shoulders'; Teratology.

fish out of water; neither -one thing nor another, -fish flesh nor fowl nor good red herring; one in a -way, – thousand; out-cast, -law; Ishmael, pariah; oasis.

V. be -unconformable &c. *adj.*; leave the beaten -track, – path; infringe –, break –, violate- a law, – habit, – usage, – custom; drive a coach and six through; stretch a point; have no business there; baffle –, beggar- all description.

Adj. unconformable, exceptional; abnorm-al, -ous; anomal-ous, -istic; out of -order, – place, – keeping, – tune, – one's element; irregular, arbitrary; lawless, informal, aberrant, stray, wandering, wanton; peculiar, exclusive, unnatural, eccentric, crotchety, egregious; out of the -beaten track, – common, – common run, – pale of; misplaced; funny.

un-usual, -accustomed, -customary, -wonted, -common; rare, singular, *unique*, curious, odd, extraordinary, strange, monstrous; wonderful &c. 870; unexpected, unaccountable; *outré*, out of the way, remarkable, noteworthy; queer, quaint, nondescript, none such, *sui generis*; original, unconventional, Bohemian, unfashionable; un-described, -precedented, -paralleled, -exampled, -heard of, -familiar; fantastic, newfangled, grotesque, *bizarre*; outlandish, exotic, *tombé des nues*, preternatural; denaturalized.

heterogeneous, heteroclite, amorphous, mongrel, amphibious, epicene, half-blood, hybrid; androgyn-ous, -al; unsymmetric &c. 243.

qualified &c. 469.

Adv. unconformably &c. *adj.*; except, unless, save, barring, beside, without, save and except, let alone.

however, yet, but.

Int. what -on earth! – in the world!

Phr. never was -seen, – heard, – known- the like.

Section V. NUMBER

1°. Number in the Abstract

84. Number.—N. number, symbol, numeral, figure, cipher, digit, integer; counter; round number; formula; function; series.

sum, total, aggregate, difference, complement, subtrahend; product; multipli-cand, -er, -cator; coefficient, multiple; dividend, divisor, factor, quotient, sub-multiple, fraction; mixed number; numerator, denominator; decimal, circulating decimal, repetend; common measure, aliquot part; reciprocal; prime number; totitive, totient.

permutation, combination, variation; election.

ratio, proportion; progression; arithmetical –, geometrical –, harmonical-progression; percentage.

figurate –, pyramidal –, polygonal-numbers.

power, root, exponent, index, logarithm, antilogarithm; modulus.

differential, integral, fluxion, fluent.

Adj. numeral, complementary, divisible, aliquot, reciprocal, prime, fractional, decimal, figurate, incommensurable.

proportional, exponential, logarithmic, logometric, differential, fluxional, integral.

positive, negative; rational, irrational; surd, radical, real, imaginary, impossible.

85. Numeration.—N. numeration; numbering &c. *v.*; pagination; tale, tally, recension, enumeration, summation, reckoning, computation, supputation; calcu-lation, -lus; algorithm, rhabdology, dactylonomy; measurement &c. 466; statistics.

arithmetic, analysis, algebra, fluxions; differential -, integral -, infinitesimal- calculus; calculus of differences.

[Statistics] dead reckoning, muster, poll, census, capitation, roll-call, recapitulation; account &c. (*list*) 86.

[Operations] notation, addition, subtraction, multiplication, division, proportion, rule of three, practice, equations, extraction of roots, reduction, involution, evolution, approximation, interpolation, differentiation, integration.

[Instruments] abacus, swan-pan, logometer, sliding -, slide- rule, tallies, Napier's bones, calculating -, adding-machine, difference engine; cash register.

arithmetician, calculator, abacist; mathematician, actuary, statistician, surveyor, geodesist.

V. number, count, tell; call -, run-over, take an account of, enumerate, call the roll, muster, poll, recite, recapitulate; sum; sum -, cast- up; tell off, score, cipher, compute, calculate, set a price, reckon, - up, estimate; suppute, add, subtract, multiply, divide, extract roots.

check, prove, demonstrate, balance, audit, overhaul, take stock; affix numbers to, page, foliate, paginate.

amount -, come- to.

Adj. numer-al, -ical; arithmetical, analytic, algebraic, statistical, numerable, computable, calculable; commensurable, -ate; incommensur-able, -ate.

86. List.—N. list, catalogue, enumer-ation, inventory, schedule; register &c. (*record*) 551; account; bill, - of costs; syllabus; terrier, tally, file; almanac, calendar, index, table, atlas, contents, card index; rota, ticket; book, ledger; synopsis, *catalogue raisonné; tableau*; scroll, manifest, invoice, bill of lading; prospectus, *programme*; bill of fare, *menu, carte*; score, census, statistics, returns; Red -, Blue -, Domesday-book; *cadastre*; directory, gazetteer, dictionary, glossary, lexicon, thesaurus, gradus.

roll; check -, chequer -, bead- roll, - of honour; muster -roll, - book; roster, panel; cartulary, diptych.

V. list, enrol, schedule, register &c. *n.*; indent, post, docket; matriculate.

Adj. cadastral, listed &c. *v.*

2°. DETERMINATE NUMBER

87. Unity.—N. unity; oneness &c. *adj.*; individuality; solitude &c. (*seclusion*) 893; isolation &c. (*disjunction*) 44; unification &c. 48.

one, unit, ace; item; individual; solo, none else, no other, naught beside.

V. be -one, - alone &c. *adj.*; dine with Duke Humphrey.

isolate &c. (*disjoin*) 44.

render one; unite &c. (*join*) 43, (*combine*) 48.

Adj. one, sole, single, solitary, only-begotten; individual, apart, alone; kithless.

un-accompanied, -attended; *solus*, single-handed; singular, odd, unique, unrepeated, azygous, first and last; isolated &c. (*disjoined*) 44; insular; unitary.

lone; lone-ly, -some; desolate, dreary. in-secable, -severable, -discerptible; compact, irresolvable.

Adv. singly &c. *adj.*; alone, by itself, *per se*, only, apart, in the singular number, in the abstract; one -by one, - at a time; simply; one and a half, *sesqui-*.

Phr. *natura il fece, e poi roppe la stampa.*

88. Accompaniment.—N. accompaniment; appurtenance, adjunct &c. 39; context.

coexistence, concomitance, company, association, companionship; part-, co-part-nership; coefficiency.

concomitant, accessory, coefficient; companion, attendant, fellow, associate, consort, spouse, colleague, *fidus Achates*; part-, co-part-ner; satellite, hanger on, shadow; escort, *entourage*, suite, *cortège*; convoy, follower &c. 65; attribute.

V. accompany, coexist, attend, convoy, chaperon; hang –, wait- on; go hand in hand with; synchronize &c. 120; bear –, keep- company; row in the same boat; bring in its train, associate –, couple- with.

Adj. accompanying &c. *v.*; concomitant, fellow, twin, joint; associated –, coupled- with; accessory, attendant, *obbligato*.

Adv. with, withal; together –, along –, in company- with; hand in hand, side by side; cheek by -jowl, – jole; arm in arm; there–, here-with; and &c. (*addition*) 37.

together, in a body, collectively.

89. Duality.—N. dual-ity, -ism; duplicity; bi-plicity, -formity; span, polarity.

two, deuce, couple, couplet, doublet, brace, pair, cheeks, twins, Castor and Pollux, *gemini,* Siamese twins; fellows; yoke, conjugation, dyad, distich.

V. [unite in pairs] pair, couple, bracket, yoke; conduplicate, mate.

Adj. two, twain; dual, -istic; binary, binomial; twin, biparous; dyadic; conduplicate; duplex &c. 90; *tête-à-tête*; paired; dihedral.

coupled &c. *v.*; conjugate.

both, – the one and the other.

90. Duplication.—N. duplication; doubling &c. *v.*; gemi-, ingemi-nation;

reduplication; iteration &c. (*repetition*) 104; renewal.

V. double; re-double, -duplicate; geminate; repeat &c. 104; renew &c. 660; duplicate, copy &c. 21.

Adj. double; doubled &c. *v.*; bicameral, bicapital, bi-fold, -form, -lateral, -farious, -facial; two-fold, -sided, -headed, -edged &c.; duplex; double-faced; twin, duplicate, ingeminate; second; dual &c. 29.

Adv. twice, once more; over again &c. (*repeatedly*) 104; as much again, twofold.

secondly, in the second place, again.

91. [Division into two parts.] Bisection.—N. bi-section, -partition; di-, subdi-chotomy; halving &c. *v.*; dimidiation; *hendiadis*.

bifurcation, forking, branching, furcation, ramification, divarication; fork, prong; fold.

half, moiety.

V. bisect, halve, divide, split, cut in two, cleave, dimidiate, dichotomize, divaricate.

go halves, divide with.

separate, fork, bifurcate; branch -off, – out; ramify.

Adj. bisected &c. *v.*; cloven, cleft; bipartite, biconjugate, bicuspid, bifid; bifur-cous, -cate, -cated; semi-, demi-, hemi-.

92. Triality.—N. triality, trinity,* triplicity.

three, triad, triplet, trey, trio, ternion, trinomial, leash; tierce; triennium; trefoil, triangle, trident, tripod, triumvirate, *troika.*

third power, cube.

Adj. three; tri-form, -nal, -nomial; tertiary; triune.

93. Triplication.—N. tripli-cation, -city; trebleness, trine, trilogy.

V. treble, triple, triplicate, cube.

Adj. treble, triple; tern, -ary; triplex,

---

* *Trinity* is hardly ever used except in a theological sense; *see* Deity 976.

triplicate, threefold, trilogistic; third; trinal; trihedral.

Adv. three -times, – fold; thrice, in the third place, thirdly; trebly &c. *adj.*

94. [Division into three parts.] **Trisection.—N.** tri-section, -partition, -chotomy; third, – part.

V. trisect, divide into three parts, trifurcate.

Adj. trifid; trisected &c. *v.*; tripartite, -chotomous, -sulcate.

95. Quaternity.—N. quaternity, four, tetrad, quartet, quaternion, square, quadrature, quarter, quadruplet; quadrilateral, quadrangle, quatrefoil; *quadriga.*

V. reduce to a square, square.

Adj. four; quat-ernary, -ernal; quadratic; quartile, quartic, tetractic, tetrad, tetrahedral; quadrennial; quadrivalent.

96. Quadruplication.—N. quadruplication.

V. multiply by four, quadruplicate, biquadrate.

Adj. fourfold; quad-ruple, -ruplicate, -rible; quadruplex; fourth.

Adv. four times; in the fourth place, fourthly.

97. [Division into four parts.] **Quadrisection.—N.** quadri-section, -partition; quartering &c. *v.*; fourth; quart, -er, -ern; farthing (*i.e.* fourthing); quarto.

V. quarter, divide into four parts, quadrisect.

Adj. quartered &c. *v.*; quadri-fid, -partite.

98. Five, &c.—N. five, cinque, quint, quincunx, quintuplet, quintet, pentagon, pentameter, Pentateuch; six, half-a-dozen, sextet, hexagon, hexameter; seven, Heptarchy; eight, octet, octagon, octave; nine, three times three; ten, decade; eleven; twelve, dozen; thirteen; long –, baker's- dozen.

twenty, score; twenty-four, four and twenty, two dozen; twenty-five, five and twenty, quarter of a hundred; forty, two score; fifty, half a hundred; sixty, three score, sexagenarian; seventy, three score and ten, septuagenarian; eighty, four score, octogenarian; ninety, four score and ten, nonagenarian.

hundred, centenary, hecatomb, century; hundredweight, cwt.; one hundred and forty-four, gross; bicentenary, tercentenary &c.

thousand, chiliad; myriad, millennium, ten thousand; lac, lakh, one hundred thousand, plum; million; thousand million, *milliard.*

billion, trillion &c.

V. centuriate.

Adj. five, quinary, quintuple; fifth; senary, sextuple; sixth; seventh; octuple; eighth; ninefold, ninth; tenfold, decimal, denary, decuple, tenth; eleventh; duo-denary, -denal; twelfth; in one's 'teens, thirteenth.

vices-, viges-imal; twentieth; twenty-fourth &c. *n.*

cent-uple, -uplicate, -ennial, -enary, -urial; secular, hundredth; thousandth; millenary &c.

99. Quinquesection, &c.—N. division by -five &c. 98; quinquesection &c.; fifth &c.; decimation.

V. decimate, quinquesect.

Adj. quinque-fid, -partite; quinquarticular; octifid; decimal, tenth, tithe, teind; duodecimal, twelfth; sexagesimal, -genary; hundredth, centesimal; millesimal &c.

3°. INDETERMINATE NUMBER

100. [More than one.] **Plurality.—N.** plurality; a -number, – certain number; one or two, two or three &c.; a few, several; multitude &c. 102.

Adj. plural, more than one, upwards of, some, certain; not -alone &c. 87.

Adv. *et cætera*, &c., etc.

Phr. *non deficit alter.*

100a. [Less than one.] **Fraction.—N.** fraction, fractional part, fragment; part &c. 51.

Adj. fractional, fragmentary, partial.

101. Zero.—N. zero, nothing, naught, nought, duck's egg, goose egg; cipher, none, nobody; not a soul; *âme qui vive*; absence &c. 187; unsubstantiality &c. 4.

Adj. not -one, - any.

102. Multitude.—N. multitude; numerousness &c. *adj.*; numer-osity, -ality; multiplicity; profusion &c. (*plenty*) 639; legion, host; great -, large -, round -, enormous- number; a quantity, numbers, array, sight, army, sea, galaxy; scores, peck, bushel, school, shoal, swarm, draft, bevy, cloud, flock, herd, drove, flight, covey, hive, brood, litter, farrow, fry, nest; mob, crowd &c. (*assemblage*) 72; lots, loads, heaps; all the world and his wife.

[Increase of number] greater number, majority; multiplication, multiple.

V. be -numerous &c. *adj.*; swarm -, teem -, crawl -, creep -with; crowd, swarm, come thick upon; outnumber, multiply; people; swarm like -locusts, - bees.

Adj. many, several, sundry, divers, various, not a few; a -hundred, - thousand, - myriad, - million, - thousand and one; some -ten or a dozen, - forty or fifty &c.; half a -dozen, - hundred &c.; very -, full -, ever so- many; numer-ous, -ose; profuse, in profusion; manifold, multiplied, multitudinous, multiferous, multiple, multinomial, teeming, crawling, populous, peopled, crowded, thick, studded; galore.

thick coming, many more, more than one can tell, a world of; no end -of, - to; *cum multis aliis*; thick as -hops, - hail; plenty as blackberries; numerous as the -stars in the firmament, - sands on the sea-shore, - hairs on the head; and -what not, - heaven knows what; endless &c. (*infinite*) 105.

Phr. their name is 'Legion.'

103. Fewness.—N. fewness &c. *adj.*; paucity, small number; small quantity &c. 32; scarcity, sparsity; rarity; infre-quency &c. 137; handful; maniple; minority, exiguity.

[Diminution of number] reduction; weeding &c. *v.*; elimination, sarculation, decimation.

V. be -few &c. *adj.*

render -few &c. *adj.*; reduce, diminish the number, weed, eliminate, thin, decimate.

Adj. few; scarce; scant, -y; thin, rare, thinly scattered, few and far between; exiguous; infrequent &c. 137; *rari nantes*; hardly -, scarcely- any; to be counted on one's fingers; reduced &c. *v.*; unrepeated.

Adv. here and there.

104. Repetition.—N. repetition, iteration, reiteration, duplication, ding-dong, alliteration; *epistrophe*; harping, recurrence, succession, run; batto-, tauto-logy; monotony, tautophony; rhythm &c. 138; pleonasm, redundancy, diffuseness.

chimes, repetend, echo, *ritornello*, burden of a song, *refrain*; rehearsal; encore; *réchauffé*, *rifacimento*, recapitulation.

cuckoo &c. (*imitation*) 19; reverberation &c. 408; drumming &c. (*roll*) 407; renewal &c. (*restoration*) 660.

twice-told tale; old -story, - song, chestnut; second -, new- edition; reprint, new impression; return game, return match, reappearance, reproduction; periodicity &c. 138.

V. repeat, iterate, reiterate, reproduce, parrot, echo, re-echo, drum, harp upon, battologize, hammer, redouble.

recur, revert, return, reappear; renew &c. (*restore*) 660.

rehearse; do -, say- over again; ring the changes on; harp on the same string; din -, drum- in the ear; conjugate in all its moods, tenses and inflexions, begin again, go over the same ground, go the same round, never hear the last of; resume, return to; recapitulate, reword.

Adj. repeated &c. *v.*; repetition-al, -ary; recur-rent, -ring; ever recurring, thick coming; frequent, incessant, redundant, pleonastic, tautological.

monotonous, harping, iterative; mocking, chiming; retold; aforesaid, -named; above-mentioned, said; habitual &c. 613; another.

Adv. repeatedly, often, again, afresh, anew, over again, once more; ditto, *encore, de novo, bis, da capo.*

again and again; over and over, – again; many times over; time- and again, – after time; year after year; day by day &c.; many –, several –, a number of-times; many –, full many- a time; times out of number, year in and year out, morning, noon and night; frequently &c. 136.

Phr. *ecce iterum Crispinus, toujours perdrix,* cut and come again; 'tomorrow and tomorrow.'

105. Infinity.—N. infini-ty, -tude, -teness &c. *adj.*; perpetuity &c. 112.

V. be -infinite &c. *adj.*; know –, have- no -limits, – bounds; go on for ever.

Adj. infinite; immense; number-, count-, sum-, measure-less; in-numer-, immeasur-, incalcul-, illimit-, intermin-, unfathom-, unapproach-able; exhaustless, inexhaustible, indefinite; without -number, – measure, – limit, – end; incomprehensible; limit-, end-, bound-, termless; un-told, -numbered, -measured, -bounded, -limited; illimited; perpetual &c. 112.

Adv. infinitely &c. *adj.*; *ad infinitum.*

Section VI. TIME

1°. Absolute Time

106. Time.—N. time, duration; period, term, stage, space, span, spell, season; the whole -time, – period; course &c. 109.

intermediate time, while, *interim,* interval, bit, pendency; inter-vention, -mission, -mittence, -regnum, -lude; respite.

era, epoch, æon, cycle; time of life, age, year, date; decade &c. (*period*) 108; moment, &c. (*instant*) 113; reign &c. 737.

glass –, ravages –, whirligig –, noise-less foot- of time; scythe.

V. continue, last, endure, go on, hold out, remain, stay, persist, abide, run; intervene; elapse &c. 109.

take –, take up –, fill –, occupy- time.

pass –, pass away –, spend –, while away –, consume –, talk against –, kill-time; tide over; use –, employ- time; tarry &c. 110; seize an opportunity &c. 134; waste time &c. (*be inactive*) 683.

Adj. continuing &c. *v.*; on foot; permanent &c. (*durable*) 110.

Adv. while, whilst, during, pending; during the -time, – interval; in the course of; for the time being, day by day; in the time of, when; mean-time, -while; in the -meantime, – *interim; ad interim, pendente lite; de die in diem;* from -day to day, – hour to hour &c.; hourly, always; for a -time, – season; till, until, up to, yet; the whole –, all the- time; all along; throughout &c. (*completely*) 52; for good &c. (*diuturnity*) 110.

here-, there-, where-upon; then; *anno, – Domini;* A.D.; *ante Christum;* A.C.; before Christ; B.C.; *anno urbis conditæ;* A.U.C.; *anno regni;* A.R.; once upon a time, one fine morning.

Phr. time -runs, – runs against; *tempus fugit.*

107. Neverness.*—N. 'neverness';

* A term introduced by Bishop Wilkins.

absence of time, no time; *dies non*; Tib's eve; Greek Kalends.

Adv. never; at no -time, – period; on no occasion, never in all one's born days, nevermore, *sine die*.

108. [Definite duration, or portion of time.] **Period.—N.** period; second, minute, hour, day, week, sennight, octave, month, moon, quarter, semester, year, *lustrum, quinquennium*, decade, *decennium*, indiction, lifetime, generation, epoch, era, cycle.

century, age, *millennium; annus magnus*.

Adj. horary; hourly, annual &c. (*periodical*) 138.

108a. Contingent Duration.—Adv. during -pleasure, – good behaviour; *quamdiu se bene gesserit.*

109. [Indefinite duration.] **Course.— N.** course –, progress –, process –, succession –, lapse –, flow –, flux –, effluxion, stream –, tract –, current –, sweep –, tide –, march –, step –, flight- of time; duration &c. 106.

[Indefinite time] aorist.

V. elapse, lapse, flow, run, proceed, advance, pass; roll –, wear –, press –, drag- on; flit, fly, slip, slide, glide, crawl; run -its course.

out; expire; go –, pass- by; be -past &c. 122.

Adj. elapsing &c. *v.*; aoristic; progressive, transient &c. 111.

Adv. in due -time, – season; in -course, – process, – the fulness- of time; in time.

Phr. *labitur et labetur; truditur dies die; fugaces labuntur anni;* 'tomorrow and tomorrow and tomorrow creeps in this petty pace from day to day.'

110. [Long duration.] **Diuturnity. —N.** diuturnity; a -long –, length of- time; an age, a century, an eternity; æons; slowness &c. 275; perpetuity &c. 112; blue moon.

dura-bleness, -bility; persistence, lastingness &c. *adj.*; continuance, assiduity, endurance, standing; permanence

&c. (*stability*) 150; survi-val, -vance; longevity &c. (*age*) 128; distance of time.

protraction –, prolongation –, extension- of time; delay &c. (*lateness*) 133.

V. last, endure, stand, remain, abide, continue, brave a thousand years.

tarry &c. (*be late*) 133; drag -on, – its slow length along, – a lengthening chain; protract, prolong; spin –, eke –, draw –, lengthen- out; temporize; gain –, make –, talk against- time.

out-last, -live; survive; live to fight again.

Adj. durable; perdurable; lasting &c. *v.*; of long -duration, – standing; permanent, chronic, long-standing; intransi-ent, -tive; intransmutable, persistent; life-, live-long; longeval, long-lived, macrobiotic, diuturnal, sempervirent, evergreen, perennial; unin-, ter-, unremitting; perpetual &c. 112.

lingering, protracted, prolonged, spun out &c. *v.*; long-pending, -winded; slow &c. 275.

Adv. long; for -a long time, – an age, – ages, – ever so long, – many a long day; long ago &c. (*in a past time*) 122; *longo intervallo.*

all the -day long, – year round; the livelong day, as the day is long, morning, noon and night; hour after hour, day after day, &c.; for good; permanently &c. *adj.*

111. [Short duration.] **Transient-ness.—N.** transientness &c. *adj.*; evanescence, impermanence, fugacity, transitoriness, volatility, caducity, mortality, span; flash in the pan, nine days' wonder, bubble, May-fly; spurt, temporary arrangement, interregnum.

velocity &c. 274; suddenness &c. 113; changeableness &c. 149.

V. be -transient &c. *adj.*; flit, pass away, fly, gallop, vanish, fade, fleet, melt away, evaporate; pass away like a -cloud, – summer cloud, – shadow, – dream.

Adj. transi-ent, -tory, -tive; passing, evanescent, fleeting; flying &c. *v.*;

fug-acious, -itive; shifting, slippery; spasmodic.

tempor-al, -ary; provis-ional, -ory; cursory, short-lived, ephemeral, deciduous; perishable, mortal, precarious; impermanent.

brief, quick, brisk; cometary, meteoric, extemporaneous, summary; pressed for time &c. (*haste*) 684; sudden, momentary &c. (*instantaneous*) 113.

Adv. temporarily &c. *adj.*; *pro tempore*; for -the moment, – a time; awhile, *en passant*, *in transitu*; in a short time; soon &c. (*early*) 132; briefly &c. *adj.*; at short notice; on the -point, – eve -of; *in articulo*; between cup and lip.

Phr. one's days are numbered; the time is up; here to-day and gone tomorrow; *non semper erit œstas*; *eheu! fugaces labuntur anni*; *sic transit gloria mundi.*

112. [Endless duration.] **Perpetuity.—N.** perpetuity, eternity, timelessness; everness,* aye, sempiternity, immortality, athanasia; everlastingness &c. *adj.*; perpetuation; infinite duration.

V. last –, endure –, go on- for ever; have no end.

eternize, eternify, perpetuate, immortalize.

Adj. perpetual, eternal, eterne; everlasting, -living, -flowing; continual, constant, sempiternal; co-eternal; endless, unending; ceaseless, incessant, uninterrupted, indesinent, unceasing; interminable, having no end; unfading, evergreen, amaranthine; never-ending, -dying, -fading; deathless, immortal, undying, imperishable.

Adv. perpetually &c. *adj.*; always, ever, evermore, aye; for -ever, – aye, – evermore, – ever and a day, – ever and ever; in all ages, from age to age; without end; world –, time- without end; *in sæcula sæculorum*; to the -end of time, – crack of doom, – 'last syllable of re-

corded time'; till doomsday; constantly &c. (*very frequently*) 136.

Phr. *esto perpetuum*; *labitur et labetur in omne volubilis ævum.*

113. [Point of time.] **Instantaneity.**
—N. instantane-ity, -ousness; sudden-, abrupt-ness.

moment, instant, second, minute; twinkling, trice, flash, breath, crack, jiffy, *coup*, burst, flash of lightning, stroke of time.

epoch, time; time of -day, – night; hour, minute; very -minute &c., – time, – hour; present –, right –, true –, exact –, correct- time.

V. be -instantaneous &c. *adj.*; twinkle, flash.

Adj. instantaneous, momentary, extempore, sudden, instant, abrupt; subitaneous, hasty; quick as -thought,* – lightning, – a flash; rapid as electricity.

Adv. instantaneously &c. *adj.*; in –, in less than- no time; *presto, subito, instanter*, suddenly, at a stroke, like- a shot, – greased lightning; in a trice, in a moment &c. *n.*; eftsoons, in the twinkling of -an eye, – a bed post; at one jump, in the same breath, *per saltum, uno saltu*; at –, all at- once; in one's tracks; plump, slap; 'at one fell swoop'; at the same -instant &c. *n.*; immediately &c. (*early*) 132; *extempore*, on the -spot, – spur of the moment, – dot; just then; slap- dash &c. (*haste*) 684; before you could -turn round, – say -knife, – Jack Robinson.

Phr. touch and go; no sooner said than done.

114. [Estimation, measurement, and record of time.] **Chronometry.—N.** chrono-, horo-metry, -logy; date, epoch; style, era.

almanac, calendar, ephemeris; register, -try; chronicle, annals, journal, diary, chronogram.

[Instruments for the measurement of time] clock, watch; chrono-meter, -scope, -graph; repeater, alarum;

---

* Bishop Wilkins.   * See note on 264.

time-keeper, -piece; dial, sun-dial, *gnomon*, *pendule*, horologe, pendulum, hourglass, water clock, clepsydra.

mean -, Greenwich -, solar -, sidereal -, local -, summer- time; daylight saving.

chrono-grapher, -loger, -logist; annalist.

V. fix -, mark- the time; date, register, chronicle; measure -, beat -, mark-time; bear date.

Adj. chrono-logical, -metrical, -grammatical; isochronal.

Adv. o'clock; *a.m.*, *p.m.*

115. [False estimate of time.] Anachronism.—N. ana-, meta-, para-, prochronism; *prolepsis*, misdate; anticipation, antichronism.

disregard -, neglect -, oblivion- of time.

intempestivity &c. 135.

V. mis-, ante-, post-, over-date; anticipate; take no note of time.

Adj. misdated &c. *v.*; undated; overdue; out of date; anachronous &c. *n.*

2°. RELATIVE TIME

1. *Time with reference to Succession*

116. Priority.—N. priority, antecedence, anteriority, pre-existence, precedence &c. 62; precession &c. 280; precursor &c. 64; the past &c. 122; premises.

V. precede, come before; forerun; antecede, go before &c. (*lead*) 280; preexist; dawn; premise, presage &c. 511.

be -beforehand &c. (*be early*) 132; steal a march upon, anticipate, forestall; have -, gain- the start.

Adj. prior, previous; preced-ing, -ent; anterior, antecedent; pre-existing, -existent; foresighted; former, foregoing; afore -, before-, above-mentioned; aforesaid, said; introductory &c. (*precursory*) 64; pre-war.

Adv. before, prior to; earlier; previ-

ously &c. *adj.*; afore, ere, theretofore, erewhile; ere -, before- -then, - now; erewhile, already, yet, beforehand; aforetime, on the eve of, in anticipation.

117. Posteriority.—N. posteriority; succession, sequence; following &c. 281; subsequence, supervention; futurity &c. 121; successor; sequel &c. 65; remainder, reversion.

V. follow &c. 281 -, come -, go-after; ensue, result; succeed, supervene; step into the shoes of.

Adj. subsequent, posterior, following, after, later, succeeding, postliminious, postnate; successive &c. 63; postdiluvi-al, -an; *puisné*; posthumous; post-war, future &c. 121.

Adv. subsequently, after, afterwards, since, later; at a -subsequent, - later-period; next, in the sequel, close upon thereafter, thereupon, upon which, eftsoons; from that -time, - moment; after a -while, - time; in process of time.

postcenal, postcibal, postprandial, after-dinner.

118. The Present Time.—N. the present -time, - day, - moment, - juncture, - occasion; the times, existing time, time being; twentieth century; nonce, crisis, epoch, day, hour.

age, time of life.

Adj. present, actual, instant, current, latest, existing, that is.

Adv. at this -time, - moment &c. 113; at the -present time &c. *n.*; now, at present.

at this time of day, to-day, now-a-days; already; even -, but -, just-now; on the present occasion; for the -time being, - nonce; *pro hâc vice*; on the -nail, - spot; on the spur of the -moment, - occasion.

until now; to -this, - the present day.

119. [Time different from the present.] Different Time.—N. different -, other- time.

[Indefinite time] aorist.

Adj. aoristic.

Adv. at that -, at which- time,

– moment, – instant; then, on that occasion, upon.

when; when-ever, -soever; upon which, on which occasion; at -another, – a different, – some other, – any- time; at various times; some –, one-of these days, – fine morning, – day; sooner or later; some time or other; once upon a time, once.

120. Synchronism.—N. synchronism; coexistence, coincidence; simultaneousness &c. *adj.*; concurrence, concomitance, unity of time, interim.

[Having equal times] isochronism, syntony.

contemporary, coetanian.

V. coexist, concur, accompany, go hand in hand, keep pace with; synchronize, isochronize.

Adj. synchron-ous, -al, -ical, -istical; simultaneous, coexisting, coincident, concomitant, concurrent; coev-al, -ous; contempora-ry, -neous; coetaneous; coterminous, coeternal; isochronous.

Adv. at the same time; simultaneously &c. *adj.*; together, in concert, during the same time; in the same breath; *pari passu*; in the interim.

at the -very moment &c. 113; just as, as soon as; meanwhile &c. (*while*) 106.

121. [Prospective time.] **Futurity.** —**N.** futur-ity, -ition; future, hereafter, time to come; approaching –, coming –, after- -time, – age, – days, – hours, – years, –ages, – life; morrow, to-morrow, by and by; millennium, doomsday, day of judgment, crack of doom, remote future.

approach of time, advent, time drawing on, womb of time; destiny &c. 152; eventuality.

heritage, heirs, posterity, descendants.

prospect &c. (*expectation*) 507; foresight &c. 510.

V. look forwards; anticipate &c. (*expect*) 507, (*foresee*) 510; forestall &c. (*be early*) 132.

come –, draw- on; draw near; ap-

proach, await, threaten; impend &c. (*be destined*) 152.

Adj. future, to come; coming &c. (*impending*) 152; next, near; near –, close- at hand; eventual, ulterior; expectant, prospective, in prospect &c. (*expectation*) 507.

Adv. prospectively, hereafter, on the knees of the gods, in future; to-morrow, the day after to-morrow; in -course, – process, – the fulness- of time; eventually, ultimately, sooner or later; *proximo*; *paulo post futurum*; in after time; one of these days; after a -time, – while.

from this time; hence-forth, -forwards; thence; thence-forth, -forward; whereupon, upon which.

soon &c. (*early*) 132; on the -eve, – point, – brink- of; about to; close upon.

122. [Retrospective time.] **Preterition.—N.** preterition; priority &c. 116; the past, past time; days –, times- -of yore, – of old, – past, – gone by; bygone days, good old days; old –, ancient –, former -times; fore time; yesterdays; the olden –, good old-time; auld lang syne; eld.

antiquity, antiqueness, *status quo*; time immemorial; distance of time; remote -age, – time; ancient history; remote past; rust of antiquity; ancientness.

pale-ontology, -ography, -ology; palætiology,* archæology; archaism, antiquarianism, mediævalism, pre-Raphaelitism; retrospection, looking back, memory &c. 505.

laudator temporis acti; mediævalist, pre-Raphaelite; antiqu-ary, -arian; archæologist &c.; Oldbuck, Dryasdust.

ancestry &c. (*paternity*) 166.

V. be -past &c. *adj.*; have -expired &c. *adj.*, – run its course, – had its day; pass; pass –, go- -by, – away, – off; lapse, blow over.

look –, trace –, cast the eyes- back; exhume.

Adj. past, gone, gone by, over, passed

* Whewell.

away, bygone, foregone; elapsed, lapsed, preterlapsed, expired, no more, run out, blown over, that has been, whilom, extinct, never to return, exploded, forgotten, irrecoverable; obsolete &c. (*old*) 124; extinct as the dodo.

former, pristine, *quondam*, *ci-devant*, late; ancestral.

foregoing; last, latter; recent, overnight; past, preterite, preter-perfect, -pluperfect, past perfect.

looking back &c. *v.*; retro-spective, -active; archæological &c. *n.*

Adv. formerly; of -old, – yore; erst, whilom, erewhile, time was, ago, over; in -the olden time &c. *n.*; anciently, long -ago, – since; a long -while, – time- ago; years –, ages- ago; some time -ago, – since, – back.

yesterday, the day before yesterday; last -year, – season, – month &c.; *ultimo*; lately &c. (*newly*) 123.

retrospectively; ere –, before –, till-now; hitherto, heretofore; no longer; once, – upon a time; from time immemorial; in the memory of man; time out of mind; already, yet, up to this time; *ex post facto*.

Phr. time was; the time -has, – hath-been.

2. Time with reference to a particular Period

123. Newness.—N. newness &c. *adj.*; neologism, neoterism; novelty, recency; immaturity; youth &c. 127; gloss of novelty.

innovation; renovation &c. (*restoration*) 660.

modernist, neologist, neoteric.

modernism, modernity; mushroom; latest fashion, *dernier cri*.

upstart, *parvenu*, *nouveau riche*.

V. renew &c. (*restore*) 660; modernize.

Adj. new, novel, recent, fresh, green; young &c. 127; evergreen; raw, immature; virgin; un-tried, -handseled, -used, -trodden, -beaten; fledgling.

late, modern, neoteric; new-born,

-fashioned, -fangled, -fledged; of yesterday; just out, brand –, span-new, up to date, topical; vernal, renovated; innovatory.

fresh as -a rose, – a daisy, – paint; spick and span.

Adv. newly &c. *adj.*; afresh, anew, lately, just now, only yesterday, the other day; latterly, of late.

not long –, a short time- ago.

124. Oldness.—N. oldness &c. *adj.*; age, antiquity; cobwebs of antiquity.

maturity, ripeness; decline, decay; senility &c. 128.

seniority, eldership, primogeniture.

archaism &c. (*the past*) 122; thing –, relic- of the past; megatherium.

tradition, prescription, custom, folklore, immemorial usage, common law.

V. be -old &c. *adj.*; have -had, – seen- its day; become -old &c. *adj.*; age, fade.

Adj. old, olden, ancient, antique; of long standing, time-honoured, venerable; eld-er, -est; first-born.

prime; prim-itive, -eval, -igenous; primordi-al, -nate; aboriginal &c. (*beginning*) 66; diluvian, antediluvian; prehistoric; patriarchal, preadamite; palæocrystic; fossil, paleozoic, preglacial, ante-mundane; archaic, classic, mediæval, pre-Raphaelite, ancestral, black-letter.

immemorial, traditional, prescriptive, customary, whereof the memory of man runneth not to the contrary; inveterate, rooted.

antiquated, of other times, rococo, of the old school, after-age, obsolete; fusty, moth-eaten; out of -date, – fashion; stale, old-fashioned, behind the -age, – times; exploded; gone out, – by; *passé*, outworn, run out; disused; senile &c. 128; time-worn; crumbling &c. (*deteriorated*) 659; second-hand.

old as -the hills, – Methuselah, – Adam, – history.

Adv. since the -world was made, – year one, – days of Methuselah.

125. Morning. [Noon.]**—N.** morning,

morn, matins, forenoon, *a.m.*, prime, dawn, daybreak, daylight, sun-up, peep -, break- of day; aurora, Eos; first blush -, prime- of the morning; twilight, crepuscule, sunrise, cockcrow.

spring; vernal equinox.

noon; mid-, noon-day; noontide, meridian, prime.

summer, midsummer; summer solstice.

Adj. matin, matutinal; vernal, æstival.

Adv. at -sunrise &c. *n.*; with the lark, when the morning dawns.

126. Evening. [Midnight.]—**N.** evening, eve; decline -, fall -, close- of day; eventide, evensong, vespers; candlelight, nightfall, curfew, dusk, twilight, blind man's holiday; eleventh hour; sunset, -down; going down of the sun, cockshut, dewy eve, gloaming, bed-time.

afternoon, *post meridiem, p.m.*

autumn; fall, - of the leaf; autumnal equinox, Indian summer, harvest-time.

midnight; dead -, witching time- of night; winter, - solstice.

Adj. vespertine, autumnal, nocturnal, wintry, brumal, hiemal.

127. Youth.—**N.** youth; juven- -ility, -escence; juniority; infancy; baby-, child-, boy-, girl-, youth-hood; *incunabula*; minority, immaturity, nonage, teens, tender age, bloom.

cradle, nursery, leading-strings, pupilage, puberty, *pucelage*.

prime -, flower -, spring-tide -, seedtime-, golden season- of life; heyday of youth, school days; rising generation, younger generation.

Adj. young, youthful, juvenile, green, callow, budding, sappy, *puisné*, beardless, unfledged, unripe, under age, in one's teens; *in statu pupillari*; younger, junior.

128. Age.—**N.** age; oldness &c. *adj.*; old -, advanced- age; sen-ility, -essence; years, anility, grey hairs, climacteric, grand climacteric, declining years, decrepitude, hoary age, caducity, super-

annuation; second childhood, -ishness; dotage; vale of years, decline of life, 'sear and yellow leaf'; three-score years and ten; green old age, ripe old age; longevity; time of life.

seniority, eldership; elders &c. (*veteran*) 130; firstling; *doyen*, dean, father; primogeniture; nostology.

V. be -aged &c. *adj.*; grow -, get- old &c. *adj.*; age; decline, wane.

Adj. aged; old &c. 124; elderly, senile; matronly, anile; in years; ripe, mellow, run to seed, declining, waning, past one's prime; grey, -headed; hoar, -y; venerable, time-worn, antiquated, *passé*, effete, doddering, decrepit, superannuated; advanced in -life, - years; stricken in years; wrinkled, marked with the crow's foot; having one foot in the grave; doting &c. (*imbecile*) 499.

old-, eld-er, -est; senior; first-born.

turned of, years old; of a certain age, no chicken, old as Methuselah; gerontic; ancestral; patriarchal &c. (*ancient*) 124.

129. Infant.—**N.** infant, babe, baby; nurse-, suck-, year-, wean-ling; *papoose, bambino*.

child, bairn, little- one, - tot, - mite, chick, brat, chit, kid, urchin; bant-, bratling; elf.

youth, boy, lad, slip, sprig, stripling, youngster, cub, unlicked cub, younker, callant, whipster, whipper-snapper, schoolboy, hobbledehoy, hopeful, cadet, minor, master.

scion; sap-, seed-ling; tendril, olivebranch, nestling, chicken, duckling; larva, caterpillar, chrysalis, cocoon; tadpole, whelp, cub, pullet, fry, callow; codlin, -g; *fœtus*, calf, colt, pup, foal, kitten; lamb, -kin.

girl; lass, -ie; wench, miss, damsel, *demoiselle*, damozel; maid, -en; virgin; nymph; colleen; minx, baggage, schoolgirl; tomboy, flapper, hoyden.

Adj. infant-ine, ile; puerile; boy-, girl-, child-, baby-, kitten-ish; baby; new-born, unfledged, new-fledged, callow.

in -the cradle, – swaddling clothes, – long clothes, – arms, – leading strings; at the breast; in one's teens; young &c. 127.

130. Veteran.—N. veteran, old man, seer, patriarch, greybeard, dugout, grand-father, -sire; grandam, beldam; gaffer, gammer; hag, crone; pantaloon; sexage-, octoge-, nonage-, cente-narian; old stager; dotard &c. 501.

preadamite, Methuselah, Nestor, Rip van Winkle, old Parr; elders; forefathers &c. (*paternity*) 166.

131. Adolescence.—N. adolescence, pubescence, majority; adultness &c. *adj.*; manhood, virility, maturity; flower of age; prime –, meridian- of life.

man &c. 373; woman &c. 374; adult, no chicken.

V. come -of age, – to man's estate, – to years of discretion; attain majority, assume the *toga virilis*; have -cut one's eye-teeth, – sown one's wild oats, settle down.

Adj. adolescent, pubescent, of age; of -full, – ripe- age; out of one's teens, grown up, mature, full- blown, – grown, in one's prime, in full bloom, manly, virile, adult; womanly, matronly; marriageable, nubile.

3. Time with reference to an Effect or Purpose

132. Earliness.—N. earliness &c. *adj.*; morning &c. 125

punctuality; promptitude &c. (*activity*) 682; haste &c. (*velocity*) 274; suddenness &c. (*instantaneity*) 113.

prematurity, precocity, precipitation, anticipation; prevenience, a stitch in time.

V. be -early &c. *adj.*, – beforehand &c. *adv.*; keep time, take time by the forelock, anticipate, forestall; have –, gain- the start; steal a march upon; gain time, draw on futurity; bespeak, secure, engage, pre-engage.

accelerate; expedite &c. (*quicken*) 274; make haste &c. (*hurry*) 684.

Adj. early, prime, timely, in time, punctual, forward; prompt &c. (*active*) 682; summary.

premature, precipitate, precocious; prevenient, anticipatory; rathe.

sudden &c. (*instantaneous*) 113; unexpected &c. 508; impending, imminent; near, – at hand; immediate.

Adv. early, soon, anon, betimes, rathe; eft, -soons; ere –, before- long; punctually &c. *adj.*; to the minute; in time; in -good, – military, – pudding, – due- time; time enough.

beforehand; prematurely &c. *adj.*; precipitately &c. (*hastily*) 684; too soon; before -its, – one's- time; in anticipation; unexpectedly &c. 508.

suddenly &c. (*instantaneously*) 113; before one can say 'Jack Robinson,' at short notice, extempore; on the spur of the -moment, – occasion; at once; on the -spot, – instant; at sight; off –, out of- hand; *à vue d'œil*; straight, -way, -forth; forthwith, incontinently, summarily, instanter, immediately, briefly, shortly, quickly, speedily, apace, before the ink is dry, almost immediately, presently, at the first opportunity, in no long time, by and by, in a while, directly.

Phr. touch and go, no sooner said than done.

133. Lateness.—N. lateness &c. *adj.*; tardiness &c. (*slowness*) 275.

de-lay, -lation; cunctation, procrastination; detention; deferring &c. *v.*; filibuster, postponement, adjournment, prorogation, retardation, respite, reprieve, stay; protraction, prolongation, moratorium; contango; demurrage; remand; Fabian policy, *médecine expectante*, chancery suit; leeway; high time.

V. be -late &c. *adj.*; tarry, wait, stay, bide, take time; dawdle &c. (*be inactive*) 683; linger, loiter, saunter, lag behind; bide –, take- one's time; hang -about, – around, – back, – in the balance; gain time; hang fire; stand –, lie-over.

put off, defer, delay, lay over, suspend; shift -, stave- off; waive, retard, remand, postpone, adjourn; procrastinate; dally; prolong, protract; spin -, draw -, lengthen- out; prorogue; keep back; tide over; push -, drive- to the last; let the matter stand over; reserve &c. (*store*) 636; temporize; consult one's pillow, sleep upon it.

shelve, table, lay on the table.

lose an opportunity &c. 135; be kept waiting, dance attendance; kick -, cool- one's heels; *faire antichambre*; wait impatiently; await &c. (*expect*) 507; sit up, - at night.

Adj. late, tardy, slow, behindhand, belated, postliminious, posthumous, backward, unpunctual; dilatory &c. (*slow*), overdue 275; delayed &c. *v.*; in abeyance.

Adv. late; late-, back-ward; late in the day; at -sunset, - the eleventh hour, - length, - last, - long; ultimately; after -, behind- time; too late; too late for &c. 135.

slowly, leisurely, deliberately, at one's leisure; *ex post facto*; *sine die*.

Phr. *nonum prematur in annum.*

134. Occasion.—N. occasion, opportunity, opening, room, scope, field; suitable -, proper- -time, - season; high time; opportuneness &c. *adj.*; tempestivity.

crisis, turn, juncture, emergency, conjuncture; turning point, given time.

nick of time; golden -, well-timed -, fine -, favourable- opportunity; clear stage, fair field; *mollia tempora*; *fata Morgana*; spare time &c. (*leisure*) 685.

V. seize &c. (*take*) 789 -, use &c. 677 -, give &c. 784- an -opportunity, - occasion; improve the occasion.

suit the occasion &c. (*be expedient*) 646.

strike the iron while it is hot, *battre le fer sur l'enclume*, make hay while the sun shines, take time by the forelock, *prendre la balle au bond*.

Adj. opportune, timely, well-timed, timeous, timeful, seasonable.

providential, lucky, fortunate, happy, favourable, propitious, auspicious, critical; suitable &c. 23; *obiter dicta*.

Adv. opportunely &c. *adj.*; in -proper, - due- -time, - course, - season; for the nonce; in the -nick, - fulness- of time; all in good time; just in time, at the eleventh hour, now or never.

by the -way, - by; *en passant*, *à propos*; *pro -re natâ*, - *hac vice*; *par parenthèse*, parenthetically, by way of parenthesis; while -speaking of, - on this subject; *ex tempore*; on the spur of the -moment, - occasion; on the spot &c. (*early*) 132.

Phr. *carpe diem*; *occasionem cognosce*; one's hour is come, the time is up; that reminds me.

135. Intempestivity.—N. intempestivity; unseasonableness; unsuitable -, improper-time; unreasonableness &c. *adj.*; evil hour; *contretemps*; intrusion; anachronism &c. 115.

V. be -ill timed &c. *adj.*; mistime, intrude, come amiss, break in upon; have other fish to fry; be -busy, - engaged, - tied up, - occupied.

lose -, throw away -, waste -, neglect &c. 460- an opportunity; allow -, suffer- the -opportunity, - occasion- to -pass, - slip, - go by, - escape, - lapse; waste time &c. (*be inactive*) 683; let slip through the fingers, lock the stable door when the steed is stolen.

Adj. ill-, mis-timed; untimely, intrusive, unseasonable; out of -date, - season; inopportune, timeless, untoward, *mal à propos*, unlucky, inauspicious, unpropitious, unfortunate, unfavourable; unsuited &c. 24; inexpedient &c. 647.

unpunctual &c (*late*) 133; too late for; premature &c. (*early*) 132; too soon for; wise after the event.

Adv. inopportunely &c. *adj.*; as ill luck would have it, in an evil hour, the time having gone by, a day after the fair.

Phr. after meat mustard, after death the doctor.

3°. RECURRENT TIME

136. Frequency.—N. frequency, oftness; repetition, &c. 104.

V. recur &c. 104; do nothing but; keep, - on.

Adj. frequent, many times, not rare, thickcoming, incessant, perpetual, continual, constant, recurrent, repeated &c. 104; habitual &c. 613; hourly, &c. 138.

Adv. often, often to be met with, oft; oft-, often-times; frequently; repeatedly &c. 104; unseldom, not unfrequently; in -quick, - rapid- succession; many a time and oft; daily, hourly &c.; every -day, - hour, - moment &c.

perpetually, continually, constantly, incessantly, without ceasing, at all times, daily and hourly, night and day, day and night, day after day, morning noon and night, ever and anon.

most often; commonly &c. (*habitually*) 613.

sometimes, occasionally, at times, now and then, from time to time, there being times when, *toties quoties*, often enough, again and again &c. 104.

137. Infrequency.—N. infrequency, infrequence, rareness, rarity; fewness &c. 103; seldomness, uncommonness.

V. be -rare &c. *adj.*

Adj. un-, in-frequent; uncommon, sporadic, rare, - as a blue diamond; few &c. 103; scarce; almost unheard of, unprecedented, which has not occurred within the memory of the oldest inhabitant, not within one's previous experience.

Adv. seldom, rarely, scarcely, hardly; not often, unfrequently, infrequently, unoften; scarcely -, hardly- ever; once in a blue moon.

once; once -for all, - in a way; *pro hac vice*; like angels' visits, few and far between.

138. Regularity of recurrence. **Periodicity.—N.** periodicity, intermittence;

beat; oscillation &c. 314; pulse, pulsation; rhythm; alter-nation, -nateness, -nativeness, -nity.

bout, round, revolution, rotation, turn.

anniversary, birthday, jubilee, centenary, bi-, ter-centenary.

[Regularity of return] rota, cycle, period, stated time, routine; days of the week; Sunday, Monday &c.; months of the year; January &c; feast, fast, saint's day &c.; Christmas, Easter, New Year's Day &c. 998; quarter-, Lady-, Midsummer-, Michaelmas-day; May Day, the King's Birthday; leap year; seasons.

punctuality, regularity, steadiness.

V. recur in regular -order, - succession; return, revolve, rotate; come -again, - in its turn; come round, - again; beat, pulsate; alternate; intermit.

Adj. periodic, -al; serial, recurrent, cyclic-, -al, rhythmic-, -al, even; recurring &c. *v.*; inter-, re-mittent; alternate, every other.

hourly; diurnal, daily; quotidian, tertian, weekly; hebdomad-al, -ary; bi-weekly, fortnightly; monthly, menstrual, catamenial; yearly, annual; biennial, triennial, &c.; bissextile; centennial, secular; paschal, lenten, &c.

regular, steady, punctual, constant, methodical, regular as clockwork.

Adv. periodically &c. *adj.*; at -regular intervals, - stated times; at -fixed, - established- periods; punctually &c. *adj.*; *de die in diem*; from day to day, day by day.

by turns; in -turn, - rotation; alternately, every other day, off and on, ride and tie, round and round.

139. Irregularity of recurrence.—**N.** irregularity, uncertainty, unpunctuality; fitfulness &c. *adj.*

Adj. irregular, uneven, uncertain, unpunctual, capricious, erratic, desultory, fitful, flickering; rambling, rhapsodical; spasmodic, unsystematic, unequal, variable, halting.

Adv. irregularly &c. *adj.*; by fits and starts &c. (*discontinuously*) 70.

SECTION VII. CHANGE

1°. SIMPLE CHANGE

140. [Difference at different times.]
Change.— N. change, alteration, mutation, permutation, variation, modification, modulation, inflexion, mood, qualification, innovation, *metastasis*, deviation, shift, turn; diversion; break.

transformation, transfiguration; metamorphosis; metabolism; transmutation; transubstantiation; metagenesis, transanimation, transmigration, metempsychosis; version; metathesis; transmogrification; catalysis; *avatar*; alterative.

conversion &c. (*gradual change*) 144; revolution &c. (*sudden or radical change*) 146; inversion &c. (*reversal*) 218; displacement &c. 185; transference &c. 270.

changeableness &c. 149; tergiversation &c. (*change of mind*) 607.

V. change, alter, vary, wax and wane; modulate, diversify, qualify, tamper with; turn, shift, veer, jibe, tack, chop, shuffle, swerve, dodge, warp, deviate, turn aside, evert, intervert; pass to, take a turn, turn the corner, resume.

work a change, modify, vamp, revamp, superinduce; trans-form, –mute, -ume, -figure &c. *n.*; metamorphose, ring the changes; convert, resolve; revolutionize; chop and change; patch, reshape.

innovate, introduce new blood, shuffle the cards, spin the wheel; give a -turn, - colour- to; influence, turn the scale; shift the scene, turn over a new leaf.

recast &c. 146; reverse &c. 218; disturb &c. 61; convert into &c. 144.

Adj. changed &c. *v.*; new-fangled; changeable &c. 149; transitional; modifiable; alterative.

Adv. *mutatis mutandis.*

Int. *quantum mutatus!*
Phr. 'a change came o'er the spirit of my dream'; *nous avons changé tout cela*; *tempora mutantur et nos mutamur in illis*; *non sum qualis eram.*

141. [Absence of change.] **Permanence.—N.** stability &c. 150; quiescence &c. 265; obstinacy &c. 606.

permanence, -cy, persistence, fixity, fixity of purpose, endurance, durability; standing, *status quo*; maintenance, preservation, conservation; conservatism; *laissez-faire*; law of the Medes and Persians; standing dish.

V. let -alone, - be; persist, remain, stay, tarry, rest; hold, - on; last, endure, bide, abide, aby, dwell, maintain, keep; stand, - still, - fast; subsist, live, outlive, survive; hold -, keep- one's -ground, - footing; hold good.

Adj. stable &c. 150; persisting &c. *v.*; permanent; established, fixed; durable; unchanged &c. (change &c. 140); unrenewed; intact, inviolate; persistent; monotonous, uncheckered; unfailing.

un-destroyed, -repealed, -suppressed; conservative, *qualis ab incepto*; prescriptive &c. (*old*) 124; stationary &c. 265.

Adv. *in statu quo*; for good, finally; at a stand, -still; *uti possidetis*; without a shadow of turning.

Phr. as you were!; *j'y suis j'y reste*; *esto perpetua*; *nolumus leges Angliæ mutari*; let sleeping dogs lie.

142. [Change from action to rest.] **Cessation.—N.** cessation, discontinuance, desistance, desinence.

inter-, re-mission; sus-pense, -pension; interruption, hitch; hartal; stop;

stopping &c. *v.*; closure, stoppage, halt; arrival &c. 292.

pause, rest, lull, respite, truce, armistice, drop; interregnum, abeyance.

closure &c. 261.

dead -stop, – stand, – lock; checkmate; comma, colon, semicolon, period, full stop; end &c. 67; death &c. 360; *cæsura*.

V. cease, discontinue, desist, stay; break –, leave- off; hold, stop, pull up, stall, stop short, check; stick, deadlock, hang fire; halt; pause, rest.

have done with, give over, surcease, shut up shop; give up &c. (*relinquish*) 624.

hold –, stay- one's hand; rest on one's oars, repose on one's laurels.

come to a -stand, – standstill, – dead lock, – full stop; arrive &c 292; go out, die away, peter out; wear -away, – off; pass away &c. (*be past*) 122; be at an end.

intromit, interrupt, suspend, interpel; inter-, re-mit; put -an end, – a stop, – a period- to; bring to a stand, -still; stop, cut out, cut short, arrest, avast; stem the -tide, – torrent; pull the check string; switch off.

Int. halt! hold! stop! enough! avast! have done! a truce to! soft! leave off! shut up! give over! chuck it!

143. Continuance in action.—**N.** continu-ance, -ation; run; extension, prolongation; maintenance, perpetuation; persistence &c. (*perseverance*) 604*a*; repetition &c. 104.

V. continue, persist; go –, jog –, keep –, carry –, run – hold- on; abide, keep, pursue, stick to; endure; take –, maintain- its course; keep up.

sustain, uphold, hold up, keep on foot; follow up, perpetuate, prolong; maintain; preserve &c. 604*a*; harp upon &c. (*repeat*) 104.

keep -going, – alive, – at it, – the pot boiling, – the ball rolling, – up the ball; plod-, plug- along; slog on; die in harness; hold on –, pursue- the even tenor of one's way.

let be; *stare super antiquas vias*; *quieta non movere*; let things take their course.

Adj. continuing &c. *v.*; uninterrupted, unintermitting, unremitting, unvarying, unshifting; unreserved, unstopped, unrevoked, unvaried; sustained; undying &c. (*perpetual*) 112; inconvertible.

follow-up.

Int. carry on! right away!

Phr. *vestigia nulla retrorsum*; *labitur et labetur*.

144. [Gradual change to something different.] **Conversion.**—**N.** conversion, reduction, transmutation, transformation, development, resolution, assimilation; assumption; naturalization.

chemistry, alchemy; progress, growth, lapse, flux.

passage; transit, -ion; transmigration, shifting &c. *v.*; conjugation; convertibility.

crucible, alembic, caldron, retort, test tube &c.

convert, neophyte, proselyte, pervert, renegade, deserter, apostate, turncoat.

V. be converted into; become, get, wax; come –, turn- -to, – into; turn out, lapse, shift; run –, fall –, pass –, slide –, glide –, grow –, ripen –, open –, resolve itself –, settle –, merge- into; melt, grow, come round to, mature, mellow; assume the -form, – shape, – state, – nature, – character- of; illapse; assume a new phase, undergo a change.

convert –, resolve- into; make, render; mould, form &c. 240; remodel, new model, refound, reform, reorganize; assimilate –, bring –, reduce- to; transform.

Adj. converted into &c. *v.*; convertible, resolvable into; transitional; naturalized.

Adv. gradually &c. (*slowly*) 275; *in transitu* &c. (*transference*) 270.

145. Reversion.—**N.** reversion, return; revulsion; reaction.

turning point, turn of the tide; *status quo ante bellum*; calm before a storm.

alternation &c. (*periodicity*) 138; inversion &c. 219; recoil &c. 277; regression &c. 283; restoration &c. 660; relapse &c. 661; vicinism, atavism, throwback.

V. revert, turn back, return; relapse &c. 661; recoil &c. 277; retreat &c. 283; restore &c. 660; undo, unmake; turn the -tide, - scale; escheat.

Adj. reverting &c. *v.*; revulsive, reactionary.

Adv. *à rebours*, wrong side out.

146. [Sudden or violent change.] **Revolution.—N.** revolution, *bouleversement*, subversion, break up; destruction &c. 162; sudden -, radical -, sweeping -, organic - change; clean sweep, *coup d'état*, overthrow, *débâcle*; counterrevolution, rebellion &c. 742.

transilience, jump, leap, plunge, jerk, start; explosion; spasm, convulsion, throe, revulsion; storm, earthquake, eruption, upheaval, cataclysm.

legerdemain &c. (*trick*) 545.

V. revolutionize; new model, remodel, recast; strike out something new, break with the past; change the face of, unsex; revert &c. 742.

Adj. unrecognizable.

Revolutionary, Bolshevik &c. 742.

147. [Change of one thing for another.] **Substitution.—N.** substitution, subrogation, commutation; supplanting &c. *v.*, supersession, metonymy &c. (*figure of speech*) 521.

[Thing substituted] substitute, *succedaneum*, make-shift, temporary expedient, shift, *pis aller*, stop-gap, jury-mast, *locum tenens*, warming-pan, dummy, goat, scape-goat; double; changeling; *quid pro quo*, alternative; remount; representative &c. (*deputy*) 759; palimpsest.

price, purchase-money, consideration, equivalent.

V. substitute, put in the place of, change for; make way for, give place to; supply -, take- the place of; supplant, supersede, replace, cut out, serve as a substitute; step into -, stand in- the shoes

of; make a shift -, put up- with; borrow of Peter to pay Paul; commute, redeem, compound for.

Adj. substituted &c. *v.*; vicarious, subdititious; substitutional.

Adv. instead; in -place, - lieu, - the stead, - the room- of; *faute de mieux*.

148. [Double or mutual change.] **Interchange.—N.** inter-, ex-change; com-, per-, inter-mutation; reciprocation, transposal, transposition, shuffling; reciprocity, castling [at chess]; hocuspocus.

interchange-ableness, -ability.

barter &c. 794; tit for tat &c. (*retaliation*) 718; cross fire, battledore and shuttlecock; *quid pro quo*.

V. inter-, ex-, counter-change; bandy, transpose, shuffle, change hands, swap, trade, permute, reciprocate, commute; give and take, return the compliment; play at -puss in the corner, - battledore and shuttlecock; retaliate &c. 718; barter &c. 794.

Adj. interchanged &c. *v.*; reciprocal, mutual, commutative, interchanged &c. *v.*; interchangeable, intercurrent.

Adv. in exchange, *vice versâ, mutatis mutandis*, backwards and forwards, by turns, turn and turn about, turn about; each -, every one- in his turn.

2°. COMPLEX CHANGE

149. Changeableness.—N. changeableness &c. *adj.*; mutability, inconstancy; versatility, mobility; instability, unstable equilibrium; vacillation &c. (*irresolution*) 605; fluctuation, vicissitude; alternation &c. (*oscillation*) 314.

restlessness &c. *adj.*; fidgets, disquiet; dis-, in-quietude; unrest; agitation &c. 315.

moon, Proteus, chameleon, kaleidoscope, quicksilver, shifting sands, weathercock, harlequin, Cynthia of the minute, April showers; wheel of Fortune; transientness &c. 111.

V. fluctuate, vary, waver, flounder,

flicker, flitter, flit, flutter, shift, shuffle, shake, totter, tremble, vacillate, wamble, turn and turn about, ring the changes; sway -, shift- to and fro; change and change about; oscillate &c. 314; vibrate -, oscillate- between two extremes; alternate; have as many phases as the moon.

Adj. change-able, -ful; changing &c. 140; mutable, variable, checkered, ever changing, kaleidoscopic, prote-an, -iform; versatile.

unstaid, inconstant; un-steady, -stable, -fixed, -settled; fluctuating &c. *v.*; restless; mercurial; agitated &c. 315; erratic, fickle; irresolute &c. 605; capricious &c. 608; touch-and-go; inconsonant, fitful, spasmodic; vibratory; vagrant, wayward, wavering; desultory; afloat; alternating; alterable, plastic, mobile; fleeting, transient &c. 111.

Adv. see-saw &c. (*oscillation*) 314; off and on.

150. Stability.—N. stability; immutability &c. *adj.*; unchangeableness &c. *adj.*; constancy; stable equilibrium, immobility, soundness, vitality, stabiliment, stabilization, stiffness, ankylosis, solidity, *aplomb*.

establishment, fixture; rock, pillar, tower, foundation, leopard's spots, Ethiopian's skin, law of the Medes and Persians.

stabilimeter, stabilisator.

permanence &c. 141; obstinacy &c. 606.

V. be -firm &c. *adj.*; stick fast; stand -, keep -, remain- firm; weather the storm.

settle, establish, stablish, ascertain, fix, set, stabilitate, stabilize; retain, stet, keep hold; make -good, - sure; fasten &c. (*join*) 43; set on its legs, float; perpetuate.

settle down; strike -, take- root; take up one's abode &c. 184; build one's house on a rock.

Adj. unchangeable, immutable; unalter-ed, -able; not to be changed, constant; permanent &c. 141; invariable,

undeviating; stable, durable; perennial &c. (*diuturnal*) 110.

fixed, steadfast, firm, fast, steady, balanced; confirmed, valid, fiducial, immovable, irremovable, riveted, rooted; settled, established &c. *v.*; vested; incontrovertible, stereotyped, indeclinable.

tethered, anchored, moored, at anchor, on a rock, firm as a rock; firmly -seated, - established &c. *v.*; deeprooted, ineradicable; inveterate; obstinate &c. 606.

transfixed, stuck fast, aground, high and dry, stranded.

indefeasible, irretrievable, intransmutable, incommutable, irresoluble, irrevocable, irreversible, reverseless, inextinguishable, irreducible; indissoluble, -vable; indestructible, undying, imperishable, indelible, indeciduous; insusceptible, - of change.

Int. *stet.*

Present Events

151. Eventuality.—N. eventuality, event, occurrence, incident, affair, transaction, proceeding, fact; matter of -, naked- fact; phenomenon; advent.

business, concern; circumstance, particular, casualty, happening, accident, adventure, passage, crisis, pass, emergency, contingency, consequence &c. 154.

the world, life, things, doings, affairs, matters; things -, affairs- in general; the times, state of affairs, order of the day; course -, tide -, stream -, current -, run -, march- of -things, - events; ups and downs of life; chapter of accidents &c. (*chance*) 156; situation &c. (*circumstances*) 8.

V. happen, occur; take -place, - effect; come, become of; come -off, - about, - round, - into existence, - forth, - to pass, - on: pass, present itself; fall; fall -, turn- out; run, be on foot, fall in; be-fall, -tide, -chance; prove, eventuate, draw on; turn -, crop -, spring -, castup; super-, sur-vene; issue, emanate, arrive, ensue, arise, start, hold, take its course; pass off &c. (*be past*) 122.

meet with; experience; fall to the lot of; be one's -chance, - fortune, - lot; find; encouter, undergo; pass -, go-through; endure &c. (*feel*) 821.

Adj. happening &c. *v.*; going on, doing, current; in the wind, afloat; on -foot, - the *tapis*; at issue, in question; incidental.

eventful, momentous, signal; stirring, bustling, full of incident.

Adv. eventually, ultimately, in -the event of, - case; in the course of things; in the -natural, - ordinary- course of things; as -things, - times- go; as the world -goes, -wags; as the -tree falls, - cat jumps; as it may -turn out, - happen.

Phr. the plot thickens.

Future Events

152. Destiny.—N. destiny &c. (*necessity*) 601; hereafter, future -, post-existence; future state, next world, world to come, after life; futurity &c. 121; everlasting -life, - death; prospect &c. (*expectation*) 507.

V. impend; hang -, lie -, hover- over; threaten, loom, await, come on, approach, stare one in the face; fore-, pre-ordain; predestine, doom, foredoom, foreshadow, have in store for.

Adj. impending &c. *v.*; destined; about to -be, - happen; coming, in store, to come, going to happen, instant, at hand, near; near -, close- at hand; over-hanging, hanging over one's head, imminent; brewing, preparing, forthcoming; in the wind, on the cards, in reserve; that -will, - is to- be; in prospect &c (*expected*) 507; looming in the -distance, - horizon, - future; unborn, in embryo; in the womb of -time; - futurity; on the knees of the gods; pregnant &c (*producing*) 161.

Adv. in -time, - the long run; all in good time; eventually &c. 151; whatever may happen &c. (*certainly*) 474; as -chance &c. 156- would have it.

SECTION VIII. CAUSATION

1°. CONSTANCY OF SEQUENCE IN EVENTS

153. [Constant antecedent.] Cause.—N. cause, origin, source, principle, element; occasioner, prime mover, engine, turbine, motor, *primum mobile*; *vera causa*; author &c. (*producer*) 164; main-spring, agent; dynamo, generator, battery (electric); leaven; groundwork, foundation &c. (*support*) 215.

spring, fountain, well, font; fountain -, spring- head; *fons et origo*, genesis; descent &c. (*paternity*) 166; remote cause; influence.

pivot, hinge, turning-point, lever; key; kernel, core; proximate cause, *causa causans*; last straw that breaks the camel's back.

ground; reason, - why; why and wherefore, rationale, occasion, derivation; final cause &c. (*intention*) 620; *le dessous des cartes*; undercurrents.

rudiment, egg, germ, embryo, fœtus bud, root, *radix*, radical, etymon, nucleus, seed, stem, stalk, stock, *stirps*, trunk, tap-root; latent organism.

nest, cradle, nursery, womb, *nidus*, birth-, breeding-place, hot-bed.

caus-ality, -ation; origination; production &c. 161.

V. be the -cause &c. *n.*- of; originate; give -origin, - rise, - occasion- to; cause, occasion, sow the seeds of, kindle, suscitate; bring -on, - to pass,

– about; produce; create &c. 161; set -up, – afloat, – on foot; found, broach, institute, lay the foundation of, inaugurate; lie at the root of.

procure, induce, draw down, open the door to, superinduce, evoke, entail, operate; elicit, provoke.

conduce to &c. (*tend to*) 176; contribute; promote; have a -hand in, – finger in- the pie; determine, decide, turn the scale, give the casting vote; have a common origin; derive its origin &c. (*effect*) 154.

Adj. caused &c. *v*.; causal, original; prim-ary, -itive, -ordial; aboriginal; radical; inceptive, embry-onic, -otic; *in -embryo, – ovo*; seminal, germinal; formative, productive &c. 168; at the bottom of; connate, having a common origin.

Adv. because &c. 155; behind the scenes.

154. [Constant sequent.] **Effect.—N.** effect, consequence, sequela; deriva-tive, -tion; result; result-ant, -ance; upshot, issue, *dénouement*; outcome; termination, end &c. 67; development, outgrowth, fruit, crop, harvest, product, bud, blossom, florescence, ear.

production, produce, product, finished product, work, handiwork, fabric, performance; creature, creation; offspring, -shoot; first-fruits, -lings; *prémices*.

V. be the -effect &c. *n*.- of; be -due, – owing- to; originate -in, – from; rise –, arise –, take its rise –, spring –, proceed –, emanate –, come –, grow –, bud –, sprout –, germinate –, issue –, flow –, result –, follow –, derive its origin –, accrue- from; come -to, – of, – out of; depend –, hang –, hinge –, turn- upon.

take the consequences, sow the wind and reap the whirlwind.

Adj. owing to; resulting from &c. *v*.; resultant; derivable from; due to; caused &c. by, 153; dependent upon; derived –, evolved- from; derivative; hereditary.

Adv. of course, it follows that, naturally, consequently; as a –, in- conse-

quence; through all, all along of, necessarily, eventually.

Phr. *cela va sans dire*, thereby hangs a tale.

155. [Assignment of cause.] **Attribution.—N.** attribution, theory, etiology, ascription, reference to, rationale; accounting for &c. *v*.; palætiology,* imputation, derivation from.

fil-, affil-iation; pedigree &c. (*paternity*) 166.

explanation &c. (*interpretation*) 522; reason why &c. (*cause*) 153.

V. attribute –, ascribe –, impute –, refer –, lay –, point –, trace –, bring home- to; put –, set- down- to; charge –, ground- on; invest with, assign as cause, charge with, blame, lay at the door of, father upon; saddle with; affiliate; account for, derive from, point out the -reason &c. 153; theorize; tell how it comes; put the saddle on the right horse.

Adj. attributed &c. *v*.; attributable &c. *v*.; refer-able, -rible; due to, derivable from; owing to &c. (*effect*) 154; putative.

Adv. hence, thence, therefore, for, since, on account of, because, owing to; on that account; from -this, – that- cause; thanks to, forasmuch as; whence, *propter hoc*.

why? wherefore? whence? how -comes, – is, – happens- it? how does it happen?

in -some, – some such- way; somehow, – or other.

Phr. that is why; *hinc illæ lachryma e*; *cherchez la femme*.

156. [Absence of assignable cause.] **Chance.†—N.** chance, indetermination, accident, fortune, hazard, hap, haphazard, chance-medley, random, luck,

---

* Whewell, 'History of the Inductive Sciences,' book xviii, vol. iii, p. 397 (3rd edit.).
† The word *Chance* has two distinct meanings: the first, the absence of assignable *cause*, as above; and the second, the absence of *design*—for the latter see 621.

raccroc, casualty, fortuity, contingence, coincidence, adventure, hit; fate &c. (*necessity*) 601; equal chance; lottery, raffle, tombola, sweepstake; toss up &c. 621; turn of the -table, - cards; hazard of the die, chapter of accidents; cast -, throw- of the dice; heads or tails, wheel of Fortune, whirligig of chance; *sortes, - Virgilianæ.*

probability, possibility, contingency, odds, long odds, run of luck; mainchance.

theory of -probabilities, - chances; book-making; assurance; speculation, gamble, gaming &c. 621.

V. chance, hap, turn up; fall to one's lot; be one's -fate &c. 601; stumble on, light -, blunder -, hit- upon; take one's chance &c. 621.

Adj. casual, fortuitous, accidental, haphazard, random, stray, adventitious, adventive, causeless, incidental, contingent, uncaused, undetermined, indeterminate; possible &c. 470; unintentional &c. 621.

Adv. by -chance, - accident; casually; perchance &c. (*possibly*) 470; for aught one knows; as -good, - bad, - ill-luck &c. *n.-* would have it; as it may -be, - chance, - turn up, - happen; as the case may be.

2°. CONNECTION BETWEEN CAUSE AND EFFECT

157. Power.—N. power; poten-cy, -tiality; puissance, might, force; energy &c. 171; dint; right -hand, - arm; ascendency, sway, control; pre-potency, -pollence; almightiness, omnipotence; authority &c. 737; strength &c. 159.

ability; ableness &c. *adj.*; competency; effi-ciency, -cacy; validity, cogency; enablement; vantage ground; influence &c. 175; horse power; dynamometer.

pressure; elasticity; gravity, electricity, magnetism, galvanism, voltaic electricity, voltaism, electro-magnetism, electrostatics, electrification, electric

current &c; attraction, repulsion; *vis - inertiæ, - mortua, - viva*; potential -, dynamic -, kinetic -, electrical -, chemical -, atomic- energy; friction, suction.

capability, capacity; *quid valeant humeri quid ferre recusent*; faculty, quality, attribute, endowment, virtue, gift, property, qualification, susceptibility.

V. be -powerful &c. *adj.*; gain -power &c. *n.*

belong -, pertain- to; lie -, be- in one's power; can.

give -, confer -, exercise- power &c. *n.*; empower, enable, invest; in-, en-due; endow, arm; strengthen &c. 159; compel &c. 744.

Adj. powerful, puissant; potent, -ial; capable, able; equal -, up- to; cogent, valid; effect-ive, -ual; efficient, efficacious, adequate, competent; multi-, pleni-, omni-, armi- potent; mighty, ascendent; almighty.

electric, electrical &c.

forcible &c. *adj.* (*energetic*) 171; influential &c. 175; productive &c. 168.

Adv. powerfully &c. *adj.*; by -virtue, - dint- of.

158. Impotence.—N. impotence; in-, dis-ability; disablement, impuissance, imbecility, caducity; incapa-city, -bility; inapt-, inept-itude; indocility; invalidity, inefficiency, incompetence, disqualification.

telum imbelle, brutum fulmen, blank cartridge, flash in the pan, *vox et præterea nihil,* dead letter, bit of waste paper, dummy; scrap of paper.

inefficacy &c. (*inutility*) 645; failure &c. 732.

helplessness &c. *adj.*; prostration, paralysis, palsy, ataxia, apoplexy, syncope, sideration, *deliquium,* collapse, exhaustion, softening of the brain, emasculation, inanition, senility &c. 128; castrato, eunuch.

cripple, old woman, muff, mollycoddle, milksop.

V. be -impotent &c. *adj.*; not have a leg to stand on.

*vouloir -rompre l'anguille au genou,
- prendre la lune avec les dents.*

collapse, faint, swoon, fall into a
swoon, drop; go by the board; end in
smoke &c. (*fail*) 732.

render -powerless &c. *adj.*; deprive of
power; decontrol; dis-able, -enable; disarm, incapacitate, disqualify, unfit, invalidate, undermine, deaden, cramp, tie
the hands; double up, prostrate, paralyze, muzzle, cripple, becripple, maim,
lame, hamstring, draw the teeth of;
throttle, strangle, *garrotte*; ratten, silence, sprain, clip the wings of, render
hors de combat, spike the guns; take the
wind out of one's sails, scotch the snake,
put a spoke in one's wheel; break the
-neck, - back; un-hinge, -fit; put out of
gear.

unman, unnerve, devitalize, attenuate, enervate; emasculate, spay, caponize, castrate, geld; effeminize.

shatter, exhaust; weaken &c. 160.

Adj. powerless, impotent, unable, incapable, incompetent; ineff-icient, -
ective; inept; un-fit, -fitted; un-, dis-
qualified; unendowed; in-, un-apt; crippled, decrepit, disabled &c. *v.*; armless.

harmless, unarmed, weaponless, defenceless, *sine ictu*, unfortified, indefensible, vincible, pregnable, untenable.

para-lytic, -lyzed; palsied, imbecile;
nerve-, sinew-, marrow-, pith-, lust-less;
emasculate, disjointed; out of -joint, -
gear; un- -nerved, -hinged; water-
logged, on one's beam ends, rudderless;
laid on one's back; done up, dead beat,
exhausted, shattered, demoralized;
gravelled &c. (*in difficulty*) 704; helpless, unfriended, fatherless; without a
leg to stand on, *hors de combat*, laid on
the shelf.

null and void, nugatory, inoperative,
good for nothing; dud; invertebrate; ineffectual &c. (*failing*) 732; inadequate
&c. 640; inefficacious &c. (*useless*) 645.

159. [Degree of power.] **Strength.—**
N. strength; power &c. 157; energy &c.
171; vigour, force; main -, physical -,

brute- force; spring, elasticity, tone,
tension, tonicity.

stoutness &c. *adj.*; lustihood, stamina, nerve, muscle, sinew, thews and sinews, *physique*; pith, -iness; virility, vi-
tality.

athlet-ics, -icism; gymnastics, feats of
strength.

adamant, steel, iron, oak, heart of
oak; iron grip; grit, bone.

athlete, gymnast, tumbler, acrobat;
Atlas, Hercules, Antæus, Samson, Cyclops, Goliath, Titan; tower of strength;
giant refreshed.

strengthening &c. *v.*; invigoration,
refreshment, refocillation.

[Science of forces] dynamics, statics.

V. be -strong &c. *adj.*, - stronger;
overmatch.

render -strong &c. *adj.*; give -strength
&c. *n.*; strengthen, invigorate, brace,
nerve, fortify, buttress, sustain, harden,
case-harden, steel; gird; screw -, wind
-, set- up; gird -, brace- up one's loins;
recruit, set on one's legs; vivify; refresh
&c. 689; refect; reinforce &c. (*restore*)
660.

Adj. strong, mighty, vigorous, forcible, hard, adamantine, stout, robust,
sturdy, hardy, powerful, potent, puissant, valid.

resistless, irresistible, invincible,
proof against, impregnable, unconquerable, indomitable, inextinguishable, unquenchable; incontestable; more than a
match for; over-powering, -whelming;
all-powerful; sovereign.

able-bodied; athletic, gymnastic;
Herculean, Cyclopean, Atlantean; muscular, husky, brawny, wiry, well-knit,
broad-shouldered, sinewy, strapping,
stalwart, gigantic.

man-ly, -like, -ful; masculine, male,
virile, in the prime of manhood.

un-weakened, -allayed, -withered,
-shaken, -worn, -exhausted; in full -force,
- swing; in the plenitude of power.

stubborn, thick-ribbed, made of iron,
deep-rooted; strong as -a lion, - a horse,
- brandy; sound as a roach; in -fine,

- high- feather; in fine fettle; like a giant refreshed.

Adv. strongly &c. *adj.*; by -force &c. *n.*; by main force &c. (*by compulsion*) 744.

Phr. 'our withers are unwrung.'

160. Weakness.—N. weakness &c. *adj.*; debility, atony, relaxation, languor, enervation; impotence &c. 158; infirmity; effeminacy, feminality; fragility, flaccidity; inactivity &c. 683.

declension -, loss -, failure- of strength; delicacy, invalidation, decrepitude, asthenia, adynamy, cachexy, *cachexia*, anæmia, bloodlessness, sprain, strain.

reed, thread, rope of sand, broken reed, house -of cards, - built on sand.

soft-, weak-ling; infant &c. 129; youth &c. 127.

V. be -weak &c. *adj.*; drop, crumble, give way, totter, tremble, shake, halt, limp, fade, languish, decline, flag, fail, have one foot in the grave.

render -weak &c. *adj.*; weaken, enfeeble, debilitate, shake, deprive of strength, relax, enervate; un-brace, -nerve; cripple, unman, &c. (*render powerless*) 158; cramp, reduce, sprain, strain, blunt the edge of; dilute, impoverish; decimate; extenuate; reduce -in strength, - the strength of; invalidate; *mettre de l'eau dans son vin*.

Adj. weak, feeble, debile; impotent &c. 158; relaxed, unnerved &c. *v.*; sap-, strength-, power-less; weakly, unstrung, flaccid, adynamic, asthenic; nervous.

soft, effeminate, feminate, womanish.

frail, fragile, shattery, frangible, brittle &c. 328; flimsy, unsubstantial, gimcrack, gingerbread; rickety, cranky; creachy; dropping, tottering &c. *v.*; broken, lame, halt, game, withered, shattered, shaken, crazy, shaky, tumbledown; palsied &c. 158; decrepit; C3.

languid, poor, poorly, infirm; faint, -ish; sickly &c. (*disease*) 655; dull, slack, evanid, spent, short-winded, effete; weatherbeaten; decayed, rotten, worn,

seedy, languishing, wasted, washy, wishy-washy, laid low, pulled down, the worse for wear.

un-strengthened &c. 159, -supported, -aided, -assisted; aidless, defenceless &c. 158.

on its last legs; weak as a -child, - baby, - chicken, - cat, - rat; weak as -water, - water gruel, - gingerbread, - milk and water; colourless &c. 429.

Phr. *non sum qualis eram.*

3°. POWER IN OPERATION

161. Production.—N. production, creation, construction, formation, fabrication, manufacture; building, architecture, erection, edification; coinage; organization; *nisus formativus*; putting together &c. *v.*; establishment; workmanship, performance; achievement &c. (*completion*) 729; effect &c. 154.

flowering, fructification, fruition.

bringing forth &c. *v.*; parturition, birth, birth-throe, child-birth, delivery, confinement, *accouchement*, travail, labour, midwifery, obstetrics; geniture; gestation &c. (*maturation*) 673; evolution, development, growth; genesis, fertilization, breeding, conception, germination, generation, *epigenesis*, procreation, -generation, -pagation; fecundation, impregnation; spontaneous generation; *arche-genesis*, -*biosis*; *bio-, abio-, homo-, xeno-genesis.* *

authorship, publication; works, *œuvre, opus.*

edifice, building, structure, fabric, erection, pile, tower, flower, fruit.

V. produce, perform, operate, do, make, gar, form, construct, fabricate, frame, contrive, manufacture; weave, forge, coin, carve, chisel; build, raise, edify, rear, erect, put together; set -, run- up; establish, constitute, compose, organize, institute, get up; achieve, accomplish &c. (*complete*) 729.

* Huxley.

flower, sprout, blossom, burgeon, bear fruit, fructify, spawn, teem, ean, yean, farrow, drop, calf, pup, whelp, kitten, kindle; bear, lay, bring forth, give birth to, lie in, be brought to bed of, evolve, pullulate, usher into the world.

make productive &c. 168; create; beget, conceive, get, generate, fecundate, impregnate; pro-create, -generate, -pagate; engender; bring –, call- into -being, – existence; breed, hatch, develop, bring up.

induce, superinduce; suscitate; cause &c. 153; acquire &c. 775.

Adj. produc-ed, -ing &c. *v.*; productive of; prolific &c. 168; creative; formative; gen-etic, -ial, -ital; fertile, pregnant; *enceinte*, big –, fraught- with; with child, in the family way, teeming, parturient, in the straw, brought to bed of; puerper-al, -ous.

architectonic; constructive.

162. [Non-production.] **Destruction.—N.** destruction; waste, dissolution, breaking up; di-, dis-ruption; consumption; disorganization.

fall, downfall, ruin, perdition, crash, smash, havoc, *délabrement*, *débâcle*; break -down, – up; prostration; desolation, *bouleversement*, wreck, crack-up, crash, wrack, shipwreck, cataclysm; Caudine Forks, Sedan.

extinction, annihilation; destruction of life &c. 361; knock-out, knock-down blow; doom, crack of doom.

destroying &c. *v.*; demo-lition, -lishment; biblioclasm; overthrow, subversion, suppression; abolition &c. (*abrogation*) 756; sacrifice; ravage, devastation, *sabotage*, *razzia*; incendiarism; revolution &c. 146; extirpation &c. (*extraction*) 301; *commencement de la fin*, road to ruin; dilapidation &c. (*deterioration*) 659.

V. be -destroyed &c.; perish; fall, – to the ground; tumble, topple; go –, fall- to pieces; break up; crumble, – to dust; go to -the dogs, – the wall, – smash, – shivers, – wreck, – pot, – wrack and ruin; go -by the board, – all to smash,

– to pieces, – under; be all -over, – upwith; totter to its fall.

destroy; do –, make- away with; nullify; annul &c. 756; sacrifice, demolish; tear up; over-turn, -throw, -whelm; upset, subvert, put an end to; seal the doom of, do for, dish, undo; break -, cut- up; break –, cut –, pull –, mow –, blow –, beat- down; suppress, quash, put down; cut short, take off, blot out; dispel, dissipate, dissolve; consume.

smash, – to smithereens, quell, squash, squelch, crumple up, shatter, shiver; batter; tear –, crush –, cut –, shake –, pull –, pick- to pieces; nip; tear to -rags, – tatters; crush –, knock- to atoms; pulverize; ruin; strike out; throw –, knock- -down, – over; lay by the heels; fell, sink, swamp, scuttle, wreck, crash, shipwreck, engulf, submerge; lay in -ashes, – ruins; sweep away, erase, expunge, strike out, delete, efface, raze; level, – with the -ground, – dust.

deal destruction, lay waste, ravage, gut; disorganize; dismantle &c. (*render useless*) 645; devour, swallow up, desolate, devastate, sap, mine, blast, confound; exterminate, extinguish, quench, annihilate; snuff –, put –, stamp –, trample- out; lay –, trample- in the dust; prostrate; tread –, crush –, trample- under foot; lay the axe to the root of; make -short work, – a clean sweep, – mincemeat- of; cut up root and branch; fling –, scatter- to the winds; throw overboard; strike at the root of, sap the foundations of, spring a mine, blow up; ravage with fire and sword; cast to the dogs; eradicate &c. 301.

Adj. destroyed &c. *v.*; perishing &c. *v.*; trembling –, nodding –, tottering- to its fall; in course of -destruction &c. *n.*; extinct.

destructive, subversive, ruinous, incendiary, deletory; destroying &c. *v.*; suicidal; deadly &c. (*killing*) 361.

Adv. with -crushing effect, – a sledgehammer.

Phr. *delenda est Carthago.*

163. Reproduction.—N. reproduction,

renovation; restoration &c. 660; renewal; new edition, reprint &c. 21; revival, regeneration, palingenesia, reviv-
ification; apotheosis; resuscitation,
reanimation, resurrection, resurgence,
reappearance, atavism; Phœnix; reincarnation.
　generation &c. (*production*) 161;
multiplication.
　V. reproduce; restore &c. 660; revive, renovate, renew, regenerate, revivify, resuscitate, reanimate, refashion, stir
the embers, put into the crucible; multiply, repeat, resurge.
　crop up, spring up like mushrooms.
　Adj. reproduced &c. *v.*; renascent,
reappearing; reproductive; resurgent;
progenitive; Hydra-headed.

　164. Producer.—N. producer, creator, deviser, designer, originator, inventor, author, founder, generator, mover,
architect; grower, constructor, maker
&c. (*agent*) 690.

　165. Destroyer.—N. destroyer &c.
(destroy &c. 162); cankerworm &c.
(*bane*) 663; iconoclast; assassin &c.
(*killer*) 361; executioner &c. (*punish*)
975; Hun, Vandal, nihilist, anarchist.

　166. Paternity.—N. paternity; parentage; fatherhood; consanguinity &c.
11.
　parent, father, sire, dad, daddy, papa,
governor, *pater*, *paterfamilias*, *abba*;
genitor, progenitor, procreator, begetter; ancestor; grand-sire, -father; great-
grandfather.
　house, stem, trunk, tree, stock, *stirps*,
pedigree, lineage, line, family, tribe,
sept, race, clan; genealogy, descent, extraction, birth, ancestry; forefathers,
forbears, patriarchs.
　motherhood, maternity; mother, dam,
mamma, *materfamilias*; grand-mother;
matriarch.
　Adj. paternal, parental; maternal;
family, ancestral, linear, matrilinear,
patrilineal, patriarchal.

　167. Posterity.—N. posterity, progeny, breed, issue, offspring, brood, litter,
seed, farrow, spawn, spat; family, children, grandchildren, heirs; great-
grandchild.
　child, son, daughter; kid; infant &c.
129; bantling, scion; shoot, sprout, olive
branch, sprit, branch; off-shoot, -set;
ramification; descendant; heir, -ess; heir
-apparent, – presumptive; chip of the old
block; heredity; rising generation.
　straight descent, sonship, line, lineage, filiation, primogeniture.
　Adj. filial.

　168. Productiveness.—N. productiveness &c. *adj.*; fecundity, fertility,
luxuriance, uberty.
　pregnancy, pullulation, fructification,
multiplication, propagation, procreation; superfetation.
　milch cow, rabbit, hydra, warren,
seed-plot, land flowing with milk and
honey; second crop, after-crop, -growth,
-math; fertilization.
　V. make -productive &c. *adj.*; fructify; procreate, generate, fertilize, spermatize, impregnate; fecund-ate, -ify;
teem, pullulate, multiply; produce &c.
161; conceive.
　Adj. productive, prolific; teem-ing,
-ful; fertile, fruitful, frugiferous, fruit-
bearing; fructiferous; fecund, luxuriant;
pregnant, uberous.
　procre-ant, -ative; generative, life-
giving, spermatic; originative; multiparous; omnific; propagable.
　parturient &c. (*producing*) 161; profitable &c. (*useful*) 644.

　169. Unproductiveness.—N. unproductiveness &c. *adj.*; infertility, steril-e,
-ity; infecundity; impotence &c. 158;
unprofitableness &c. (*inutility*) 645.
　waste, desert, Sahara, wild, wilderness, howling wilderness.
　V. be -unproductive &c. *adj.*; hang
fire, flash in the pan, come to nothing.
　Adj. unproductive, inoperative, barren, addle, unfertile, unprolific, arid,
sterile, unfruitful, acarpous, infecund;
sine prole; fallow; teem-, issue-, fruit-
less; unprofitable &c. (*useless*) 645; null
and void, of no effect.

170. Agency.—N. agency, operation, force, working, strain, function, office, maintenance, exercise, work, swing, play; inter-working, -action, procuration, procurement.

causation &c. 153; instrumentality &c. 631; influence &c. 175; action &c. (*voluntary*) 680; *modus operandi* &c. 627.

quickening –, maintaining- power; home stroke.

V. be -in action &c. *adj.*; operate, work; act, – upon; perform, play, support, sustain, strain, maintain, take effect, quicken, strike.

come –, bring- into -operation, – play; have -play, – free play; bring to bear upon.

Adj. operative, efficient, efficacious, practical, effectual.

at work, on foot; acting &c. (*doing*) 680; in -operation, – force, – action, – play, – exercise; acted –, wrought- upon.

Adv. by the -agency &c. *n.*- of; through &c. (*instrumentality*) 631; by means of &c. 632.

171. Physical Energy.—N. energy, physical energy, force; keenness &c. *adj.*; intensity, vigour, strength, elasticity; go; pep, live wire, high pressure; backbone, mettle, fire, vim.

acri-mony, -tude, -dity; causticity, virulence, poignancy; harshness &c. *adj.*; severity, edge, point; pungency &c. 392.

cantharides; Spanish fly; seasoning &c. (*condiment*) 393, stimulant, excitant.

activity, agitation, effervescence; ferment, -ation; ebullition, splutter, perturbation, stir, bustle; voluntary energy &c. 682; quicksilver.

resolution &c. (*mental energy*) 604; exertion &c. (*effort*) 686; excitation &c. (*mental*) 824.

V. give -energy &c. *n.*; energize, stimulate, kindle, excite, activate, exert; sharpen, pep up, intensify; inflame &c. (*render violent*) 173; wind up &c. (*strengthen*) 159.

strike, – into, – hard, – home; make an impression.

Adj. strong, energetic, forcible, active; strenuous, forceful, mettlesome, enterprising, go ahead; intense, deepdyed, severe, keen, vivid, sharp, acute; incisive, trenchant, brisk, vigorous, live.

rousing, irritating; poignant; virulent, caustic, corrosive, mordant, harsh, stringent; double-edged, – shotted, – distilled; drastic, escharotic; racy &c. (*pungent*) 392; sarcastic &c. 932.

potent &c. (*powerful*) 157; radioactive.

Adv. strongly &c. *adj.*; *fortiter in re*; with telling effect.

Phr. the steam is up; *vires acquirit eundo.*

172. Physical Inertness.—N. inertness, dullness &c. *adj.*; inertia, *vis inertiæ*, inertion, inactivity, torpor, languor; dormancy, quiescence &c. 265; latency, inaction, passivity.

mental inertness; sloth &c. (*inactivity*) 683; inexcitability &c. 826; irresolution &c. 605; obstinacy &c. 606; permanence &c. 141.

V. be -inert &c. *adj.*; hang fire, smoulder.

Adj. inert, inactive, passive, pacific; torpid &c. 683; sluggish, stagnant, dull, heavy, flat, slack, tame, slow, blunt; lifeless, dead, uninfluential.

latent, dormant, smouldering, unexerted.

Adv. inactively &c. *adj.*; in -suspense, -abeyance.

173. Violence.—N. violence, inclemency, vehemence, might, impetuosity; boisterousness &c. *adj.*; effervescence, ebullition; turbulence, bluster; uproar, riot, row, rumpus, *le diable à quatre*, devil to pay, all the fat in the fire.

severity &c. 739; ferocity, rage, berserk, fury; exacerbation, exasperation, malignity; fit, paroxysm, orgasm; force, brute force; outrage; *coup de main*; strain, shock, shog; spasm, convulsion, throe; hysterics, passion &c. (*state of excitability*) 825.

out-break, -burst; burst, bounce, dissilience, discharge, volley, explosion, blow up, blast, detonation, rush, eruption, displosion, torrent.

turmoil &c. (*disorder*) 59; ferment &c. (*agitation*) 315; storm, tempest, rough weather; squall &c. (*wind*) 349; earthquake, volcano, thunderstorm.

fury, dragon, demon, tiger, beldame, Tisiphone, Megæra, Alecto, madcap, wild beast; fire-eater &c. (*blusterer*) 887.

V. be -violent &c. *adj.*; run high; ferment, effervesce; romp, rampage; run -wild, - riot; break the peace; rush, tear; rush head-long, -foremost; run amuck, raise a storm, make a riot; make -, kick up- a row, - a fuss; bluster, rage, roar, riot, storm; boil, - over; fume, foam, come in like a lion, wreak, bear down, ride roughshod, out-Herod Herod; spread like wildfire.

break -, fly -, burst- out; bounce, shock, strain; break-, pry, force-, prize-open.

render -violent &c. *adj.*; sharpen, stir up, quicken, excite, incite, urge, lash, stimulate; irritate, inflame, exacerbate, kindle, suscitate, foment; accelerate, aggravate, exasperate, convulse, infuriate, madden, lash into fury; fan -, add fuel to- the flame; *oleum addere camino.*

explode, go off, displode, fly, detonate, thunder, blow up, flash, flare, erupt, burst; let -off, - fly; discharge, detonize, fulminate.

Adj. violent, vehement, forcible; warm; acute, sharp; rough, rude, ungentle, bluff, boisterous, wild, vicious; brusque, abrupt, waspish; impetuous; rampant.

turbulent; disorderly; blustering, raging &c. *v.*; troublous, riotous; tumultuary, -ous; obstreperous, uproarious; extravagant, unmitigated; ravening, tameless; frenzied &c. (*insane*) 503; desperate &c. (*rash*) 863; infuriate, towering, furious, outrageous, frantic, hysteric, in hysterics.

fiery, flaming, scorching, hot, red-hot, ebullient.

savage, fierce, ferocious, fierce as a tiger.

excited &c. *v.*; un-quelled, -quenched, -extinguished, -repressed, -bridled, -ruly; headstrong; un-governable, -appeasable, -mitigable; un-, in-controllable; insup-, irre-pressible.

spasmodic, convulsive, explosive; detonating &c. *v.*; volcanic, meteoric; stormy &c. (*wind*) 349.

Adv. violently &c. *adj.*; amain; by -storm, - force, - main force; with might and main; tooth and nail, *vi et armis*, at the point of the -sword, - bayonet; at one fell swoop; with a high hand, through thick and thin; in desperation, with a vengeance; *à -*, *à toute-outrance*; head-long, -foremost, -first; like a bull at a gate.

174. Moderation.—N. moderation; lenity &c. 740; temperance, temperateness, gentleness &c. *adj.*; sobriety; quiet; mental calmness &c. (*inexcitability*) 826.

moderating &c. *v.*; relaxation, remission, mitigation &c. 834; tranquillization, alleviation, assuagement, appeasement, contemporation, pacification.

measure, *juste milieu*, golden mean &c. 29.

moderator; lullaby, sedative, lenitive, demulcent, rose-water, balm, soothing syrup, poppy, opiate, anodyne, milk, opium, laudanum, 'poppy or mandragora'; wet blanket; palliative, calmative.

V. be -moderate &c. *adj.*; keep within -bounds, - compass; sober -, settle- down; keep the peace, remit, relent; take in sail.

moderate, soften, mitigate, temper, accoy; at-, con-temper; mollify, lenify, dull, take off the edge, blunt, obtund, sheathe, subdue, chasten; sober -, tone -, smooth-down; censor, blue-pencil, weaken &c. 160; lessen &c. (*decrease*) 36, check; palliate.

tranquillize, assuage, appease, dulcify, swage, lull, soothe, compose, still, calm, cool, quiet, hush, quell, sober, pacify, tame, damp, lay, allay, rebate, slacken, smooth, alleviate, rock to sleep, deaden,

smother; throw -cold water on, – a wet
blanket over; slake; curb &c. (*restrain*)
751; tame &c. (*subjugate*) 749; smooth
over; pour oil on the -waves, – troubled
waters; pour balm into, *mettre de l'eau
dans son vin*.

go out like a lamb, 'roar you as gently
as any sucking dove.'

Adj. moderate; lenient &c. 740; gentle, mild; cool, sober, temperate, reasonable, measured; tempered &c. *v*.; calm,
unruffled, quiet, tranquil, still; slow,
smooth, untroubled; tame; peaceful, -
able; pacific, halcyon.

un-exciting, -irritating; soft, bland, oily,
demulcent, lenitive, anodyne; hypnotic
&c. 683; sedative; assuaging.

mild as mother's milk; milk and water;
gentle as a lamb.

Adv. moderately &c. *adj*.; gingerly; *piano*; under easy sail, at half speed; within
-bounds, – compass; in reason.

Phr. *est modus in rebus*.

4°. INDIRECT POWER

175. Influence.—N. influence; importance &c. 642; weight, pressure, preponderance, prevalence, sway, pull; predominance, -nancy; ascendency; control, dominance, reign; authority &c. 737; capability &c. (*power*) 157; interest; spell, magic, magnetism.

footing; purchase &c. (*support*) 215;
play, leverage, vantage ground.

tower of strength, host in himself; protection, patronage, auspices.

V. have -influence &c. *n*.; be
-influential &c. *adj*.; carry weight, actuate, sway, bias, weigh, tell; have a hold
upon, magnetize, bear upon, gain a
footing, work upon; take -root, – hold;
strike root in.

run through, pervade; prevail, dominate, predominate, subject; out-, overweigh; over-ride, -bear, – come; gain
head; rage; be -rife &c. *adj*.; spread like
wildfire; have -, get -, gain- -the upper
hand, – full play.

be -recognized, – listened to; make
one's voice heard, gain a hearing; play a
-part, – leading part- in; lead, control,
rule, master; get the mastery over; make
one's influence felt, cut ice with; take
the lead, pull the strings; turn -, throw
one's weight into- the scale; set the fashion, lead the dance.

Adj. influential; important &c. 642;
weighty; prevailing &c. *v*.; prevalent,
rife, rampant, dominant, regnant, predominant, in the ascendant, hegemoni-
cal; authoritative, recognized, telling,
with authority.

Adv. with telling effect.

175a. Absence of Influence.—N. impotence &c. 158; inertness &c. 172; irrelevancy &c. 10.

V. have no -influence &c. 175.

Adj. uninfluential; unconduc-ing, -ive,
-ting to; powerless &c. 158; irrelevant
&c. 10.

176. Tendency.—N. tendency; apt-
ness, -itude; proneness, proclivity, bent,
turn, tone, bias, set, warp, leaning to,
predisposition, inclination, conatus,
propensity, susceptibility; liability &c.
177; quality, nature, temperament; characteristic, idio-crasy, -syncrasy; cast,
vein, grain; humour, mood; drift &c.
(*direction*)   278;   con-duciveness,
-ducement; applicability &c. (*utility*) 644;
subservience &c. (*instrumentality*) 631.

V. tend, contribute, conduce, lead,
dispose, incline, verge, bend to, warp,
turn, trend, affect, carry, redound to, bid
fair to, gravitate towards; promote &c.
(*aid*) 707.

Adj. tending &c. *v*.; conducive,
working towards, in a fair way to, calculated to; liable &c. 177; subservient
&c. (*instrumental*) 631; useful &c. 644;
subsidiary &c. (*helping*) 707.

Adv. for, whither.

177. Liability.—N. lia-bility, -bleness;
possibility, contingency; suscepti-vity, -
bility.

V. be -liable &c. *adj*.; incur, lay oneself open to; run the -, stand a- chance;

lie under, expose oneself to, open a door to.

Adj. liable, subject; in danger &c. 665; open –, exposed –, obnoxious- to; answerable, responsible, accountable, amenable; unexempt from; apt to; dependent on; incident to.

contingent, incidental, possible, on the cards, within range of, at the mercy of.

5°. COMBINATIONS OF CAUSES

178. Concurrence.—N. concurrence, cooperation, coagency; coincidence, consilience; union; agreement &c. 23; consent &c. (*assent*) 488; alliance; concert &c. 709; partnership &c. 712; collaboration, conformity.

V. con-cur, -duce, -spire, -tribute; agree, unite, harmonize; hang –, pull-together &c. (*co-operate*) 709; help to &c. (*aid*) 707.

keep pace with, run parallel to; go –, go along –, go hand in hand- with.

Adj. concurring &c. *v.*; concurrent, conformable, joint, co-operative, concordant, coincident, concomitant, harmonious; in alliance with, banded to-gether, of one mind, at one with; parallel.

Adv. with one consent.

179. Counteraction.—N. counteraction, opposition; contrariety &c. 14; antagonism, polarity; clashing &c. *v.*; collision, interference, resistance, renitency, friction; reaction; retroaction; repercussion &c. (*recoil*) 277; counterblast; neutralization &c. (*compensation*) 30; *vis inertiæ*; check &c. (*hindrance*) 706.

voluntary -opposition &c. 708, – resistance &c. 719; repression &c. (*restraint*) 751.

V. counteract; run counter, clash, cross; interfere –, conflict- with; jostle; go –, run –, beat –, militate- against; stultify; antagonize, frustrate, oppose &c. 708; withstand &c. (*resist*) 719; hinder &c. 706; repress &c. (*restrain*) 751; react &c. (*recoil*) 277.

undo, neutralize, cancel; counterpoise &c. (*compensate*) 30; overpoise.

Adj. counteracting &c. *v.*; antagonistic, conflicting, retroactive, renitent, reactionary; contrary &c. 14.

Adv. although &c. 30; in spite of &c. 708; *malgré*; against.

CLASS II

Words Relating to SPACE

Section I. SPACE IN GENERAL

1°. Abstract Space

180. [Indefinite space.] **Space.—N.**
space, extension, extent, superficial extent, expanse, stretch; capacity, room, accommodation, scope, range, latitude, field, way, expansion, compass, sweep, play, swing, spread.

spare –, elbow –, house- room; stowage, roomage, margin; opening, sphere, arena; lee-, sea-, head-way.

open –, free- space; wide open spaces; void &c. (*absence*) 187; waste; wild-, wilder-ness, up-, bottom-, moor -land; *campagna*, *veldt*, prairie, steppe.

abyss &c. (*interval*) 198; unlimited space; infinity &c. 105; world, wide world; ubiquity &c. (*presence*) 186; length and breadth of the land.

proportions, acreage; acres, – roods and perches; square -inches, – yards &c.

Adj. spacious, roomy, extensive, expansive, capacious, ample; wide-spread, vast, world-wide, uncircumscribed; boundless &c. (*infinite*) 105; shore-, track-, path-less; large &c. 192.

Adv. extensively &c. *adj.*; wherever; everywhere; far and -near, – wide; right and left, all over, all the world over; throughout the -world, – length and breadth of the land; under the sun, in every quarter; in all -quarters, – lands; here, there and everywhere; from -pole to pole, – China to Peru, – Indus to the pole, – Dan to Beersheba, – end to end; on the face of the earth, in the wide world, from all points of the compass; to the -four winds, – uttermost parts of the earth.

180a. Inextension.—N. in-, nonextension; point; atom &c. (*smallness*) 32; pinprick; limitation &c. 229.

181. [Definite space.] **Region.—N.**
region, sphere, sphere of influence, corridor, ground, soil, area, realm, hemisphere, quarter, district, beat, orb, circuit, circle; pale &c. (*limit*) 233; com-, de-partment; domain, tract, territory, terrain, country, canton, county, shire, province, *arrondissement*, diocese, parish, township, borough, constituency, *commune*, ward, wapentake, hundred, riding, lathe, garth, soke, tithing, bailiwick; empire, kingdom, principality, duchy, grand –, arch-duchy, palatinate; republic, commonwealth, dominion, colony, state, island.

arena, precincts, *enceinte*, walk, march; patch, plot, enclosure, &c. 232; close, *enclave*, field, court; street &c. (*abode*) 189.

clime, climate, zone, meridian, latitude.

Adj. territorial, local, parochial, provincial, insular.

182. [Limited space.] **Place.—N.**
place, lieu, spot, point, dot; niche, nook, &c. (*corner*) 244; hole; pigeonhole &c. (*receptacle*) 191; compartment; premises, precinct, station, confine; area, court, yard, quadrangle, square, compound; abode &c. 189; locality &c. (*situation*) 183.

ins and outs; every hole and corner.

Adv. somewhere, in some place,

wherever it may be, here and there, in various places, *passim*.

2°. RELATIVE SPACE

183. Situation.—N. situation, position, locality, *locale*, *status*, latitude and longitude; footing, standing, standpoint, post; stage; aspect, attitude, posture, *pose*.

place, site, base, station, seat, *venue*, whereabouts, environment, neighbourhood; bearings &c. (*direction*) 278; spot &c. (*limited space*) 182.

top-, ge-, chor-ography; map &c. 554.
V. be -situated, - situate; lie; have its seat in.
Adj. situ-ate, -ated; local, topical, topographical &c. *n.*
Adv. in -*situ*, - *loco*; here and there, *passim*; here-, there-, whereabouts; in place, here, there.

in -, amidst- such and such--surroundings, - *environs*, - *entourage*.

184. Location.—N. loca-tion, -lization; lodgment; de-, re-position; stow-, package; collocation; packing, lading; establishment, settlement, installation; fixation; insertion &c. 300.

anchorage, roadstead, mooring, mooring mast, encampment, camp, bivouac.

plantation, colony, settlement, cantonment, encampment, reservation; colonization, domestication, situation; habitation &c. (*abode*) 189; cohabitation; 'a local habitation and a name'; indenization, naturalization.

V. place, situate, locate, localize, make a place for, put, lay, set, seat, station, lodge, quarter, post, install; storehouse, stow; establish, fix, pin, root; graft; plant &c. (*insert*) 300; shelve, pitch, camp, lay down, deposit, reposit; cradle; moor, tether, picket; pack, tuck in; embed; vest, invest in.

billet on, quarter upon, saddle with; load, lade, freight; pocket, put up, bag.

inhabit &c. (*be present*) 186; domes-ticate, colonize, populate, people; take -, strike- root; anchor; cast -, come to an- anchor; sit -, settle-down; settle; take up one's -abode, - quarters; plant -, establish -, locate- oneself; squat, perch, hive, *se nicher*, bivouac, burrow, get a footing; encamp, pitch one's tent; put up -at, - one's horses at; keep house.

indenizen, naturalize, adopt.

put back, replace &c. (*restore*) 660.
Adj. placed &c. *v.*; situate, posited, ensconced, embedded, embosomed, rooted; domesticated; vested in, unremoved.

moored &c. *v.*; at anchor.

185. Displacement.—N. displacement, elocation, transposition.

ejectment &c. 297; exile &c. (*banishment*) 893; removal &c. (*transference*) 270; unshipment.

misplacement, dislocation &c. 61; fish out of water.

V. dis-place, -plant, -lodge, -nest, -establish; misplace, unseat, disturb; exile &c. (*seclude*) 893; ablegate, set aside, remove; take -, cart- away; take -, draft- off; lade &c. 184, unship.

unload, empty &c. (*eject*) 297; transfer &c. 270; dispel.

vacate; depart &c. 293.
Adj. displaced &c. *v.*; un-placed, -housed, -harboured, -established, -settled; house-, home-less; out of -place, - a situation.

misplaced, out of its element.

3°. EXISTENCE IN SPACE

186. Presence.—N. presence; occupancy, -ation; attendance; whereness.

permeation, pervasion; diffusion &c. (*dispersion*) 73.

ubi-ety, -quity, -quitariness; omnipresence.

bystander &c. (*spectator*) 444.
V. exist in space, be -present &c. *adj.*; assist at; make one -of, - at; look on, attend, remain; find -, present-

oneself; show one's face; fall in the way of, occur in a place; lie, stand; occupy.

people; inhabit, dwell, reside, stay, sojourn, live, room, abide, bunk, lodge, nestle, roost, perch; take up one's abode &c. (*be located*) 184; tenant, occupy.

resort to, frequent, haunt; revisit.

fill, pervade, permeate; be -diffused, – disseminated- through; over-spread, -run; run through; meet one at every turn.

Adj. present; occupying, inhabiting &c. *v.*; moored &c. 184; residential, resi-ant, -dent, -dentiary; domiciled.

ubiquit-ous, -ary; omnipresent.

peopled, populous, full of people, inhabited.

Adv. here, there, where, everywhere, aboard, on board, at home, afield; on the spot; here, there and everywhere &c. (*space*) 180; in presence of, before; under the -eyes, – nose- of; in the face of; *in propriâ personâ*.

187. [Nullibiety.*] Absence.—N. absence; inexistence &c. 2; non-residence, absenteeism; non-attendance, *alibi*.

emptiness &c. *adj.*; void, *vacuum*; vac-uity, -ancy, *tabula rasa*; exemption; *hiatus* &c. (*interval*) 198; no man's land.

truant, absentee.

nobody; nobody -present, – on earth; no one; not a soul; *âme qui vive*.

V. be -absent &c. *adj.*; keep -away, – out of the way; play truant, absent oneself, stay away.

withdraw, make oneself scarce, vacate; go away, slip out, slip away, retreat &c. 293.

Adj. absent, not present, away, nonresident, gone, from home; missing; lost; wanted, wanting; omitted; nowhere to be found; inexistent &c. 2.

empty, void; blank, vac-ant, -uous; untenanted, -occupied, -inhabited; tenantless; desert, -ed; devoid; un-, uninhabitable.

exempt from, not having.

Adv. without, *minus*, nowhere; else-

where; neither here nor there; in default of; *sans*; behind one's back.

Phr. the bird has flown, *non est inventus*.

188. Inhabitant.—N. inhabitant; habitant, resident, -iary; dweller, indweller; occup-ier, -ant, farmer, planter; householder, lodger, boarder, paying guest; inmate, tenant, renter, incumbent, sojourner, *locum tenens*, commorant; settler, squatter, backwoodsman, colonist; islander; denizen, citizen; burgher, oppidan, cockney, cit, townsman, burgess; villager; cot-tager, -tier, -ter; compatriot.

native, indigene, aboriginal, aborigines, autochthones; Briton, Englishman, John Bull; new-comer &c. (*stranger*) 57.

garrison, crew; population; people &c. (*mankind*) 372; colony, settlement; household.

V. inhabit &c. (*be present*) 186; indenizen &c. (*locate oneself*) 184.

Adj. indigenous; enchorial; national, nat-ive, -al; autochthonous; British, English; colonial; domestic; domicil-iated, -ed; naturalized, vernacular, domesticated; domiciliary.

in the occupation of; garrisoned –, occupied- by.

189. [Place of habitation, or resort.] Abode.—N. abode, dwelling, lodging, -s; diggings, domicile, residence, address, habitation, where one's lot is cast, local habitation, berth, seat, lap, sojourn, housing, quarters, headquarters, resiance, tabernacle, throne, ark.

home, fatherland, mother country, country &c. 181; home-stead, -stall; fireside, chimney corner; hearth, – stone; household gods, *lares et penates*, roof, household, housing, *dulce domum*, paternal domicile; native -soil, – land, blighty.

nest, *nidus*, snuggery; arbour, bower &c. 191; lair, den, cave, hole, hidingplace, cell, *sanctum sanctorum*, aerie, eyry, rookery, hive; *habitat*, haunt, covert, resort, retreat, perch, roost; nidification.

---

* Bishop Wilkins.

bivouac, camp, encampment, cantonment, castrametation; barrack, casemate, casern.

tent &c. (*covering*) 223; building &c. (*construction*) 161; chamber &c. (*receptacle*) 191.

tenement, messuage, farm, farmhouse, grange, *hacienda*.

cot, cabin, log cabin, shack, hut, *châlet*, croft, shed, booth, stall, hovel, bothy, shanty, igloo, tepee, wigwam; pen &c. (*inclosure*) 232; barn, bawn; kennel, sty, dog-hole, cote, coop, hutch, byre; cow-house, -shed; stable, dovecote, shippen.

house, mansion, place, villa, cottage, box, lodge, hermitage, *rus in urbe*, folly, rotunda, tower, *château*, castle, pavilion, hotel, court, manor-house, capital messuage, hall, palace, alcazar; country seat; kiosk, bungalow; temple &c. 1000; home of rest, alms-, poor-, work-house, asylum; boarding-, lodging-house; flat, maisonette, duplex, penthouse, suite of rooms, apartments, rooms, room, building &c. 161; Mansion House, town hall, Capitol.

assembly-room, auditorium, coliseum, meeting-house, pump-room, spa, health resort, watering-place; club; theatre &c. 840; drill hall, gymnasium, church &c. 1000; Houses of Parliament &c. 696; school &c. 542; inn; hostel, -ry; hotel, tavern, caravansary, khan, hospice; public-, ale-, pot-, mug-house; gin-palace, gin mill; coffee-, eating-house; canteen, *restaurant*, *rôtisserie*, cafeteria, grill-room, *buffet*, *café*, *estaminet*, *posada*, *bodega*; bar; saloon, speakeasy, shebeen.

hamlet, village, thorp, dorp, ham, kraal; borough, burgh, town, county-seat, - town, city, capital, metropolis; suburb, quarter, parish &c. 181; ghetto; province, country.

street, place, terrace, parade, esplanade, promenade, pier, embankment, road, villas, row, walk, lane, alley, court, quadrangle, quad, wynd, close, yard, passage, rents, mansions, buildings, mews.

square, polygon, circus, crescent, mall, *piazza*, arcade, colonnade, peristyle, cloister; gardens, grove, residences; block of buildings, marketplace, *place*.

anchorage, roadstead, roads; dock, basin, wharf, quay, port, harbour; dry-, graving-, floating-dock.

garden, park, pleasure-ground, pleasance, demesne.

V. take up one's abode &c. (*locate oneself*) 184; inhabit &c. (*be present*) 186.

Adj. urban, oppidan, metropolitan; suburban; provincial, rural, rustic; countrified; regional, parochial, domestic; cosmopolitan; palatial.

190. [Things contained.] **Contents.—N.** contents; cargo, lading, freight, shipment, load, bale, burden; cart-, shipload; cup -, basket -, &c. (*receptacle*) 191- of; inside &c. 221; stuffing, ullage.

V. load, lade, ship, charge, fill, stuff.

191. Receptacle.—N. receptacle, container; inclosure &c. 232; recipient, receiver, reservatory.

compartment; cell, -ule; follicle; hole, corner, niche, recess, nook; crypt, stall, pigeon-hole, cove, oriel; cave &c. (*concavity*) 252.

capsule, vesicle, cyst, pod, calyx, *cancelli*, utricle, bladder, udder.

stomach, paunch, *venter*, abdomen, ventricle, crop, craw, ingluvies, maw, gizzard, bread-basket, belly, little Mary; mouth.

pocket, pouch, fob, sheath, scabbard, socket, bag, vanity bag, compact, sac, sack, saccule, despatch -, attaché-, tachy- case, wallet, scrip, card-, note-case, billfold, poke, knit, knap-, haver-, ruck-sack, sachel, satchel, reticule, budget, net; ditty-, -box, -bag, kitbag; portfolio; saddlebags, holster; quiver &c. (*magazine*) 636.

chest, box, coffer, caddy, case, casket, pyx, pix, *caisson*, desk, *bureau*, reliquary; shrine; trunk, portmanteau, band-box, *valise*, suitcase, hand-, traveling-, overnight-, Gladstone-, carpet-bag, brief case; boot, imperial; *vache*; cage, manger, rack.

vessel, vase, bushel, barrel; canister, jar; pottle, basket, punnet, pannier, buck-basket, hopper, maund, creel, cran, crate, cradle, bassinet, wisket, whisket, *jardinière*, *corbeille*, hamper, wastepaper basket, dosser, dorser, tray, hod, scuttle, utensil, spittoon, cuspidor.

[For liquids] cistern &c. (*store*) 636; vat, caldron, barrel, cask, puncheon, keg, rundlet, tun, butt, firkin, hogshead, kilderkin, carboy, amphora, ampulla, bottle, jar, leather bottle, decanter, ewer, cruse, carafe, crock, kit, canteen, flagon; demijohn; flask, -et; stoup, noggin, vial, phial, ampoulé, cruet, caster; gourd; urn, *épergne*, salver, *patella*, *tazza*, *patera*; pig-, big-gin; tea-, coffeepot, percolator, *samovar*; tyg, nipperkin, pocket-pistol; tub, bucket, pail, skeel, pot, tankard, jug, pitcher, toby, mug, pipkin; gal-, gall-ipot, pannikin; matrass, receiver, retort, alembic, bolthead, can, kettle; bowl, basin, jorum, punch-bowl, cup, goblet, chalice, tumbler, glass, wineglass, rummer, beaker, tass, horn, saucepan, skillet, posnet, tureen, terrine, *casserole*, sauce-, gravy-boat.

plate, platter, paten, dish, vegetable –, *entrée-* dish, trencher, calabash, porringer, potager, saucer, pan, crucible.

shovel, trowel, spoon; table-, dessert-, tea-, egg-, salt-spoon; spatula, ladle; dipper; baler; watch-glass, thimble.

closet, commode, cupboard, cellaret, *chiffonnière*, locker, bin, bunker, *buffet*, press, safe, sideboard, drawer, chest of drawers, till, *scrutoire*, *secrétaire*, *és-critoire*, davenport, book-case, cabinet, canterbury; corner cupboard, wardrobe.

chamber, apartment, room, cabin; office, court, hall, atrium; suite of rooms, flat, story; saloon, *salon*, parlour; presence-chamber; sitting-, drawing-, reception-, state-, living-, work-room; gallery, cabinet, closet, cubicle; pew, box; *boudoir*; *adytum*, *sanctum*; bed-room, dormitory, dressing-room; refectory, dining-room, *salle-à-manger*; nursery, school-room; library, study; *studio*; billiard-, bath-, smoking-room; den, canteen, mess, officers' mess; gun-, ward-, mess-room.

attic, loft, garret, cockloft, clerestory; cellar, vault, hold, cockpit; *entre-sol*; mezzanine floor; ground-floor, *rez-de-chaussée*; basement, kitchen, cookhouse, galley, pantry, scullery, offices; store-room &c. (*depository*) 636; lumber-room; dust-hole, -bin; dairy, laundry, coach-house; *garage*; *hangar*; out-, pent-house; lean-to.

portico, porch, piazza, verandah, lobby, court, hall, vestibule, corridor, passage; ante-room, -chamber; lounge; *foyer*, *loggia*.

conservatory, green-house, glass-house, vinery, bower, arbour, summer-house, alcove, grotto, hermitage, pergola.

lodging &c. (*abode*) 189; bed &c. (*support*) 215; carriage &c. (*vehicle*) 272.

Adj. capsular; saccu-lar, -lated; recipient; ventricular, cystic, vascular, vesicular, cellular, camerated, locular, multilocular, poly-gastric; marsupial; siliqu-ose, -ous.

SECTION II. DIMENSIONS

1°. GENERAL DIMENSIONS

192. Size.—N. size, magnitude, dimension, bulk, volume; largeness &c. *adj.*; greatness &c. (*of quantity*) 31; expanse &c. (*space*) 180; amplitude, mass; proportions.

capacity; ton-, tun-nage; calibre, scantling.

turgidity &c. (*expansion*) 194; corpulence, obesity; plumpness, &c. *adj.*; *embonpoint*, corporation, flesh and blood, lustihood.

hugeness &c. *adj.*; enormity, immensity, monstrosity.

giant, Brobdingnagian, Antæus, Goliath, Gog and Magog, Gargantua, monster, mammoth, Cyclops; whale, porpoise, behemoth, leviathan, elephant, hippopotamus; colossus; tun, lump, bulk, block, loaf, mass, clod, nugget, bushel, thumper, whopper, spanker, strapper; Triton among the minnows.

mountain, mound; heap &c. (*assemblage*) 72.

largest portion &c. 50; full-, life-size.

V. be- large &c. *adj.*; become -large &c. (*expand*) 194.

Adj. large, big; great &c (*in quantity*) 31; considerable, bulky, voluminous, ample, massive, massy; capacious, comprehensive; spacious &c. 180; mighty, towering, fine, magnificent.

corpulent, stout, fat, plump, squab, full, lusty, strapping, bouncing; portly, burly, well-fed, full-grown; stalwart, brawny, fleshy; goodly; in good -case, - condition; in condition; chopping, jolly; chub-, chubby-faced.

lubberly, hulky, unwieldy, lumpish, gaunt, spanking, whacking, whopping, thumping, thundering, hulking; overgrown; puffy &c. (*swollen*) 194.

huge, immense, enormous, mighty; vast, -y; amplitudinous, stupendous; monst-er, -rous; gigantic, elephantine; giant, -like; colossal, Cyclopean, Brobdingnagian, Gargantuan, Titanic; infinite &c. 105.

large as life; plump as a -dumpling, - partridge; fat as -a pig, - a quail, - butter, - brawn, - bacon.

193. Littleness.—N. littleness &c. *adj.*; smallness &c. (*of quantity*) 32; exiguity, inextension; parvi-tude, -ty; duodecimo; Elzevir edition, epitome, microcosm; rudiment; vanishing point; thinness &c. 203.

dwarf, pigmy, atomy, Liliputian, midget, chit, pigwidgeon, urchin, elf; doll, puppet; Tom Thumb, Hop-o'-my thumb, Humpty-dumpty; man-, mannikin; *homunculus*, dapperling, fingerling, dandiprat, cock-sparrow, scalawag.

animalcule, monad, mite, insect, emmet, fly, midge, gnat, shrimp, minnow, worm, maggot, entozoon; *bacillus*, microbe, micro-organism, *bacteria*; *infusoria*; microbe; grub; tit, tomtit, runt, mouse, small fry; millet-, mustard-seed; barley-corn; pebble, grain of sand; molehill, button, bubble.

point; atom &c. (*small quantity*) 32; fragment &c. (*small part*) 51; powder &c. 330; point of a pin, mathematical point; *minutiæ* &c. (*unimportance*) 643.

micro-graphy, -meter, -scope; vernier; scale.

V. be -little &c. *adj.*; lie in a nutshell; become small &c. (*decrease*) 36, (*contract*) 195.

Adj. little; small &c. (*in quantity*) 32; minute, diminutive, microscopic; inconsiderable &c. (*unimportant*) 643; exiguous, puny, tiny, wee, petty, minikin,

miniature, pigmy, elfin; under sized;
dwarf, -ed, -ish; spare, stunted, limited;
cramp, -ed; pollard, Liliputian, dapper,
pocket; port-ative, -able; duodecimo;
dumpy, squat; compact, handy; short
&c. 201.

impalpable, intangible, evanescent,
imperceptible, invisible, inappreciable,
infinitesimal, homœopathic; atomic,
corpuscular, molecular; rudiment-ary,
-al; embryonic.

weazen, scant, scraggy, scrubby; thin
&c. (*narrow*) 203; granular &c. (*powdery*) 330; shrunk &c. 195.

Adv. in a -small compass, – nutshell;
on a small scale.

194. Expansion.—N. expansion; increase &c. 35 -of size; enlargement, extension, augmentation; ampli-fication,
-ation; aggrandizement, spread, increment, growth, development, pullulation,
swell, dilation, dilatation, rarefaction;
turg-escence, -idness, -idity;.obesity &c.
(*size*) 192; dropsy, tumefaction, intumescence, swelling, tumour, *diastole*,
distension; puff-ing, -iness; inflation;
pandiculation.

dilatability, expansibility.

germination, growth, upgrowth; accretion &c. 35.

over-growth, -distension; hypertrophy, tympany.

bulb &c. (*convexity*) 250; plumper;
superiority of size.

V. become -larger &c. (large &c.
192); expand, widen, enlarge, extend,
grow, increase, incrassate, swell, gather; fill out; deploy, take open order, dilate, stretch, spread; mantle, wax; grow
–, spring- up; bud, bourgeon, shoot,
sprout, germinate, put forth, vegetate,
pullulate, open, burst forth, flower, blow
&c. 734; gain –, gather- flesh; outgrow;
spread like wildfire, overrun.

be larger than; surpass &c. (*be superior*) 33.

render -larger &c. (large &c. 192);
expand, spread, extend, aggrandize, distend, develop, amplify, spread out, wid-
en, magnify, rarefy, inflate, puff, puff

out, blow up, stuff, pad, cram; exaggerate; fatten.

Adj. expanded &c. *v.*; larger &c.
(large &c. 192); swollen; expansive;
wide-open, -spread; fan-shaped; flabelliform; overgrown, exaggerated, bloated, fat, turgid, tumid, hypertrophied,
dropsical; pot-, swag-bellied; œdematous, obese, puffy, pursy, blowzy, distended; patulous; bulbous &c. (*convex*)
250; full-blown, -grown, -formed; big
&c. 192.

195. Contraction.—N. contraction,
reduction, diminution; decrease &c. 36;
of size; defalcation, decrement; lessening, shrinkage; collapse, emaciation, attenuation, tabefaction, consumption,
marasmus, atrophy; systole, neck, hour-
glass.

condensation, compression, constraint, compactness; compendium &c.
596; squeezing &c. *v.*; strangulation;
corrugation; astringency, constringency;
astringents, sclerotics; contractility,
compressibility; coarctation.

inferiority in size.

V. become -small, – smaller; lessen,
decrease &c. 36; grow less, dwindle,
shrink, contract, narrow, shrivel, collapse, wither, lose flesh, wizen, fall
away, waste, wane, ebb; decay &c. (*deteriorate*) 659.

be smaller than, fall short of; not
come up to &c. (*be inferior*) 34.

render smaller, lessen, diminish, contract, draw in, narrow, coarctate; constrict, constringe; condense, compress,
boil down, deflate, exhaust, empty;
squeeze, corrugate, crush, crumple up,
warp, purse up, pack, stow; pinch,
tighten, strangle; cramp; dwarf, bedwarf; shorten &c. 201; circumscribe
&c. 229; restrain &c. 751; fold &c. 258.

pare, reduce, attenuate, rub down,
scrape, file, grind, chip, shave, shear.

Adj. contracting &c. *v.*; astringent;
shrunk, contracted &c. *v.*; strangulated,
tabid, wizened, stunted; tabescent; ma-
rasmic; waning &c. *v*; neap; compact.

unexpanded &c. (expand &c. 194);

inswept; contractile; compressible; smaller &c. (small &c. 193).

196. Distance.—N. distance; space &c. 180; remoteness, farness; far- cry to; longinquity, elongation; offing, background; removedness; parallax; reach, span, stride; drift.

out-post, -skirt; horizon, sky-line; aphelion; foreign parts, *ultima Thule*, *ne plus ultra*, antipodes; long range, giant's stride.

dispersion &c. 73.

V. be -distant &c. *adj.*; extend -, stretch -, reach -, spread -, go -, get -, stretch away- to; range, outrange, outreach.

remain at a distance; keep -, stand- -away, - off, - aloof, - clear of.

Adj. distant; far-off, - away; remote, telescopic, distal, wide of; stretching to &c. *v.*; yon, -der; ulterior; trans-marine, -pontine, -atlantic, -alpine; tramontane; ultra-montane, -mundane; hyper-borean, antipodean; inaccessible, out of the way; unapproach-ed, -able; incontiguous.

Adv. far -off, - away; afar, -off; off; away; a -long, - great, - good- way off; wide away, aloof; wide -, clear- of; out of -the way, - reach; abroad, yonder, farther, further, beyond; *outre mer*, over the border, far and wide, over the hills and far away; from pole to pole &c. (*over great space*) 180; to the -uttermost parts, - ends- of the earth; out of -hearing, - range, nobody knows where, *à perte de vue*, out of the sphere of, wide of the mark; a far cry to.

apart, asunder; wide -apart, - asunder; *longo intervallo*; at arm's length.

197. Nearness.—N. nearness &c. *adj.*; proximity, propinquity; vicinity, -age; neighbourhood, adjacency; contiguity &c. 199.

short -distance, - step, - cut; earshot, close quarters, stone's throw; bow -, gun -, pistol- shot; hair's breadth, span; close-up.

purlieus, neighbourhood, vicinage, *environs*, *alentours*, suburbs, confines, *banlieue*, borderland; whereabouts.

bystander; neighbour, broderer.

approach &c. 286; convergence &c. 290; perihelion.

V. be -near &c. *adj.*; adjoin, hang about, trench on; border -, verge upon; stand by, approximate, tread on the heels of, cling to, clasp, hug; cuddle, huddle; hang upon the skirts of, hover over; burn; abut.

bring -, draw- -near &c. 286; converge &c. 290; crowd &c. 72; place -side by side &c. *adv.*

Adj. near, nigh; close -, near- at hand; close, neighbouring, propinquent, bordering upon; adjacent, adjoining, limitrophe; proxim-ate, -al; at hand, handy; near the mark, near run; home, intimate.

Adv. near, nigh; hard -, fast- by; close -to, - upon, - up; at the point of; next door to; within -reach, - call, - hearing, - earshot, - range; within an ace of; but a step, not far from, at no great distance; on the -verge, - brink, - skirts- of; in the -environs &c. *n.*; at one's -door, - feet, - elbow, - finger's end, - side; on the tip of one's tongue; under one's nose; within a -stone's throw &c. *n.*; in -sight, - presence- of; at close quarters; cheek by -jole, - jowl; beside, alongside, side by side, *tête-à-tête*; in juxtaposition &c. (*touching*) 199; yard-arm to yard-arm; at the heels of; on the confines of, at the threshold, bordering upon, verging to; in the way.

about; here-, there-abouts; roughly, in round numbers; approxim- -ately; -atively; as good as, well nigh.

198. Interval.—N. interval, inter-space; separation &c. 44; break, gap, opening; hole &c. 260; chasm, *hiatus*, cæsura; inter-ruption, -regnum; inter-stice, *lacuna*, cleft, mesh, crevice, chink, rime, creek, cranny, crack, chap, slit, slot, fissure, scissure, rift, flaw, breach, fracture, rent, gash, cut, leak, dike, ha-ha.

gorge, defile, ravine, cañon, *crevasse*, abyss, abysm; gulf; inlet, frith, strait, gully, gulch, nullah; pass; notch; furrow

&c. 259; yawning gulf; *hiatus -maxime, – valde- deflendus*; parenthesis &c. (*interjacence*) 228; void &c. (*absence*) 187; incompleteness &c. 530.

V. gape &c. (*open*) 260.

Adj. with an interval, far between.

Adv. at intervals &c. (*discontinuously*) 70; *longo intervallo*.

199. Contiguity.—N. contiguity, contact, proximity, apposition, juxtaposition, touching &c. *v.*; abutment, osculation; meeting, appulse, appulsion, *rencontre*, rencounter, syzygy, coincidence, conjunction, coexistence; adhesion &c. 46.

border-land; frontier &c. (*limit*) 233; tangent.

V. be -contiguous &c. *adj.*; join, adjoin, abut on, march with, border; tick, graze, touch, meet, osculate, kiss, come in contact, coincide; coexist; adhere &c. 46.

Adj. contiguous; touching &c. *v.*; in -contact &c. *n.*; conterminous, end to end, osculatory; pertingent; tangential.

hand to hand; close to &c. (*near*) 197; with no -interval &c. 198.

2°. LINEAR DIMENSIONS

200. Length.—N. length, longitude, span, extent, mileage.

line, bar, rule, stripe, streak, spoke, radius.

lengthening &c. *v.*; pro-longation, -duction, -traction; ten-sion, -sure; extension.

[Measures of length] line, nail, inch, hand, palm, foot, cubit, yard, ell, fathom, rod, pole, perch, furlong, mile, league; chain, metre, kilo-, centi-, mill- &c. -metre.

pedometer, perambulator, odometer, odograph, speedometer, cyclometer, log, telemeter, range finder; scale &c. (*measurement*) 466.

V. be -long &c. *adj.*; stretch out, sprawl; extend -, reach -, stretch- to;

make a long arm, 'drag its slow length along.'

render -long &c. *adj.*; lengthen, extend, elongate; stretch; pro-long, -duce, -tract; let -, pay -, draw -, spin- out; drawl.

enfilade, look along, view in perspective.

Adj. long, -some; lengthy, lank, wiredrawn, outstretched; lengthened &c. *v.*; sesquipedalian &c. (*words*) 577; interminable, no end of.

line-ar, -al; longitudinal, oblong.

as long as -my arm, – to-day and tomorrow; unshortened &c. (shorten &c. 201).

Adv. lengthwise, at length, longitudinally, endlong, along; *tandem*; in a line &c. (*continuously*) 69; in perspective.

from -end to end, – stem to stern, – head to foot, – the crown of the head to the sole of the foot, – top to toe, – head to heels; fore and aft.

201. Shortness.—N. shortness &c. *adj.*; brevity; littleness &c. 193; a span.

shortening &c. *v.*; abbrevia-tion, -ture; abridgment, concision, retrenchment, curtailment, decurtation; reduction &c. (*contraction*) 195; epitome &c. (*compendium*) 596.

abridger, abstractor, epitomiser.

elision, ellipsis; conciseness &c. (*in style*) 572.

V. be -short &c. *adj.*; render -short &c. *adj.*; shorten, curtail, abridge, abbreviate, take in, reduce; compress &c. (*contract*) 195; epitomize &c. 596.

retrench, cut short, obtruncate; scrimp, cut, chop up, hack, hew; cut -, pare- down; clip, snip, dock, lop, prune; shear, shave, mow, reap, crop; snub; truncate, pollard, stunt, nip, nip in the bud, check the growth of; [in drawing] foreshorten.

Adj. short, brief, curt; compendious, compact; stubby, scrimp; shorn, stubbed; stumpy, thickset, podgy, stocky, pug; squab, -by; squat, dumpy; little &c. 193; curtailed of its fair

proportions; short by; oblate; concise
&c. 572; summary.
Adv. shortly &c. *adj.*; in short &c.
(*concisely*) 572.

202. Breadth. Thickness.—N.
breadth, width, latitude, amplitude; diameter, bore, calibre, radius; superficial
extent &c. (*space*) 180.
thickness, crassitude; corpulence &c.
(*size*) 192; dilatation &c. (*expansion*)
194.
V. be -broad &c. *adj.*; become –,
render- -broad &c. *adj.*; expand &c.
194; thicken, widen.
Adj. broad, wide, ample, extended;
discous; fan-like; out-spread, -stretched;
wide as a church-door.
thick, dumpy, squab, squat, thickset,
tubby; thick as a rope, stubby &c. 201.

203. Narrowness. Thinness.—N.
narrowness &c. *adj.*; closeness, exility;
exiguity &c. (*little*) 193.
line; hair's –, finger's -breadth; strip,
streak, vein.
thinness &c. *adj.*; tenuity; emaciation, macilency, *marcor*.
shaving, slip, &c. (*filament*) 205;
threadpaper, skeleton, shadow, scrag,
anatomy, spindle-shanks, barebones,
lantern jaws, mere skin and bone.
middle constriction, stricture, neck,
waist, isthmus, wasp, hour-glass; ridge,
ghaut, pass; ravine &c. 198.
narrowing, coarctation, angustation,
tapering; contraction &c. 195.
V. be -narrow &c. *adj.*; narrow, taper, contract &c. 195; render -narrow
&c. *adj.*
Adj. narrow, close; slender, thin,
fine; *svelte*; thread-like &c. (*filament*)
205; finespun, taper, slim, gracile,
slight, slight-made; scant, -y; spare,
delicate, incapacious; contracted &c.
195; unexpanded &c. (expand &c. 194);
slender as a thread, capillary.
emaciated, lean, meagre, gaunt, macilent; lank, -y; weedy, skinny, scrawny,
scraggy; starv-ed, -eling; attenuated,
shrivelled, wizened, pinched, peaky,
skeletal, spindling, spindle- -legged,

-shanked; extenuated, tabid, marcid,
bare-bone, raw-boned; herring-gutted;
worn to a shadow, lean as a rake; thin
as a -lath, – whipping post, – wafer;
hatchet-faced; lantern-jawed.

204. Layer.—N. layer, stratum,
course, bed, zone, *substratum*, floor,
flag, stage, story, tier, slab, escarpment,
table, tablet, panel, plaque; board,
plank; trencher, platter.
plate; lam-ina, -ella; sheet, flake, foil,
wafer, scale, coat, peel, pellicle, ply,
thickness, membrane, film, leaf, slice,
shive, cut, rasher, shaving, integument
&c. (*covering*) 223.
stratification, lamination, scaliness,
nest of boxes, coats of an onion.
V. slice, shave, pare, peel; plate, coat,
veneer; cover &c. 223.
Adj. lamell-ar, -ated, -iform; lami-
nated, -iferous; micaceous; shist-ose,
-ous; scaly, filmy, membranous, flaky,
squamous; folia-ted, -ceous; strati-fied,
-form; tabular, discoid, spathic.

205. Filament.—N. filament, line; fibre, fibril; funicle, vein, hair, capillament, *cilium*, tendril, gossamer; hair-
stroke; harl.
wire, string, thread, packthread, cotton, sewing-silk, twine, twist, whipcord, cord, rope, cable, yarn, hemp, oakum, jute, wool, worsted.
strip, shred, slip, spill, list, band, fillet, *fascia*, ribbon, riband, tape, roll,
lath, slat, strake, splinter, shiver, shaving.
beard &c. (*roughness*) 256; ramification; strand.
Adj. fil-amentous, -aceous, -iform;
fibr-ous, -illous; thread-like, wiry,
stringy, ropy; capill-ary, -iform; funicular, wire-drawn; anguilliform; flagelliform; hairy &c. (*rough*) 256; ligulate.

206. Height.—N. height, altitude, elevation, ceiling; eminence, pitch; loftiness &c. *adj.*; sublimity.
tallness &c. *adj.*; stature, procerity;
prominence &c. 250.

colossus &c. (*size*) 192; giant, grenadier, giraffe.

mount, -ain; hill, butte, monticle, fell, knap; cape; head-, fore-land; promontory; ridge, hog's back, dune; rising –, vantage- ground; down; moor, -land; Alp; up-, high-lands; heights &c. (*summit*) 210; knoll, hummock, hillock, barrow, mound, mole, *kopje*; steeps, bluff, cliff, craig, tor, peak, pike, clough; escarpment, edge, ledge, brae; dizzy height.

tower, pillar, column, pylon, obelisk, monument, steeple, spire, minaret, *campanile*, belfry, turret, roof, dome, cupola, pagoda, pyramid; sky scraper; Eiffel tower.

pole, pikestaff, maypole, flagstaff; mast, top -, topgallant- mast.

ceiling &c. (*covering*) 223.

high water; high -, flood -, spring-tide.

altimetry &c. (*angle*) 244; altimeter, height-finder, hypsometer, barograph.

V. be -high &c. *adj.*; tower, soar, command; hover; cap, culminate; overhang, hang over, impend, beetle; bestride, ride, mount; perch, surmount; cover &c. 233; overtop &c. (*be superior*) 33; stand on tiptoe.

become -high &c. *adj.*; grow, - higher, - taller; upgrow; rise &c. (*ascend*) 305.

render -high &c. *adj.*; heighten &c. (*elevate*) 307.

Adj. high, elevated, eminent, exalted, lofty, supernal; tall; gigantic &c. (*big*) 192; Patagonian; towering, beetling, soaring, hanging [gardens]; elevated &c. 307; upper; highest &c. (*topmost*) 210; monticolous, perching, hill-dwelling.

up-, moor-land; hilly, mountainous, alpine, sub-alpine, heaven-kissing; cloud-topt, -capt, -touching; aerial.

overhanging &c. *v.*; incumbent, overlying; super-incumbent, -natant, -imposed; prominent &c. 250.

tall as a -maypole, - poplar, - steeple; lanky &c. (*thin*) 203.

Adv. on high, high up, aloft, up, above, aloof, overhead; up -, abovestairs; in the clouds; on -tiptoe, - stilts, - the shoulders of; over head and ears; breast high.

over, upwards; from top to bottom &c. (*completely*) 52.

207. Lowness.—N. lowness &c. *adj.*; debasement, depression; prostration &c. (*horizontal*) 213; depression &c. (*concave*) 252.

molehill; lowlands; bottomlands; basement- ground-floor; *rez de chaussée* &c. 211; hold; feet, heels.

low water; low -, ebb -, neap -, spring- tide.

V. be -low &c. *adj.*; lie -low, - flat; underlie; crouch, slouch, wallow, grovel; lower &c. (*depress*) 308.

Adj. low, neap, debased; nether, -most; flat, level with the ground; lying low &c. *v.*; crouched, subjacent, squat, prostrate &c. (*horizontal*) 213.

Adv. under; be-, under-neath; below; down, -wards; adown, at the foot of; under-foot, -ground; down -, below- stairs; at a low ebb; below par.

208. Depth.—N. depth; deepness &c. *adj.*; profundity, depression &c. (*concavity*) 252.

hollow, pit, shaft, well, crater, abyss; gulf &c. 198; bowels of the earth, bottomless pit, hell.

soundings, depth of water, water, draught, submersion; plummet, sound, probe; sounding -rod, - line, - machine; lead; submarine, diving bell, bathysphere; diver.

V. be -deep &c. *adj.*; render -deep &c. *adj.*; deepen.

plunge &c. 310; sound, heave the lead, take soundings, dig &c. (*excavate*) 252.

Adj. deep, -seated; profound, sunk, buried; submerged &c. 310; subaqueous, -marine, -terranean, -terrene; underground.

bottom-, sound-, fathom-less; unfathomed, -able; abysmal; deep as a well, deep-sea.

knee-, ankle-deep.

Adv. beyond –, out of- one's depth; over head and ears, over one's head.

209. Shallowness.—N. shallowness &c. *adj.*; shoals; mere scratch.

Adj. shallow, superficial; skin –, ankle –, knee- deep; just enough to wet one's feet; shoal, -y

210. Summit.—N. summit, -y; top, vertex, apex, zenith, pinnacle, acme, acropolis, culmination, meridian, utmost height, *ne plus ultra*, height, pitch, maximum, climax, apogee; culminating –, crowning –, turning- point; turn of the tide, fountain head; water-shed, -parting; sky, pole.

tip, -top; crest, crow's nest, cap, truck, peak, nib; end &c. 67; crown, brow; head, nob, noddle, pate.

high places, heights.

top-, top-gallant mast, sky scraper; quarter –, hurricane- deck.

architrave, frieze, cornice, coping, coping-stone, zoophorus, capital, headpiece, capstone, epistyle, sconce, pediment, entablature; tympanum; ceiling &c. (*covering*) 223.

attic, loft, garret, house-top, upper story, roof.

V. culminate, cap, crown, top; overtop &c. (*be superior to*) 33.

Adj. highest &c. (high &c. 206); top; top-, upper-most; tip-top; culminating &c. *v.*; meridi-an, -onal; capital, head, polar, supreme, supernal, top-gallant.

Adv. a-top, at the top of – the tree, – the heap.

211. Base.—N. base, -ment; plinth, dado, wainscot, baseboard; foundation &c. (*support*) 215; substructure, *sub stratum*, sump, ground, earth, pavement, floor, paving, flag, carpet, ground-floor, deck; footing, groundwork, basis; hold, bilge, orlop deck.

bottom, nadir, foot, sole, toe, hoof, keel, kelson, root.

Adj. bottom; under-, nether-most; fundamental; founded –, based –, grounded –, built- on.

212. Verticality.—N. verticality;

erectness &c. *adj.*; perpendicularity; right angle, normal; azimuth circle.

wall, palisade, precipice, cliff, steep, bluff.

elevation, erection; square, plumbline, plummet.

V. be -vertical &c. *adj.*; stand -up, – on end, – erect, – upright; stick –, cockup.

render -vertical &c. *adj.*; set –, stick –, raise –, cock- up; erect, rear, raise, pitch, raise on its legs.

Adj. vertical, upright, erect, perpendicular, normal, plumb, straight, bolt upright; rampant; straight –, standing-up &c. *v.*; rectangular, orthogonal.

Adv. vertically &c. *adj.*; up, on end; up –, right- on end; *à plomb*, endwise; on one's legs; at right angles.

213. Horizontality.—N. horizontality; flatness; level, plane; stratum &c. 204; dead -level, – flat; level plane.

recumbency; lying down &c. *v.*; reclination, decumbence; de-, discumbency; proneness &c. *adj.*; accubation, supination, resupination, prostration; azimuth.

plain, floor, platform, bowling-green; cricket-ground; court; gridiron; baseball diamond; hockey rink; tennis-, croquetground, – lawn; billiard table; terrace, estrade, esplanade, *parterre*, table-land, *plateau*, ledge.

spirit-, level; T-square.

V. be -horizontal &c. *adj.*; lie, recline, couch; lie -down, – flat, – prostrate; sprawl, loll; sit down.

render -horizontal &c. *adj.*; lay, – down, – out; level, flatten, even, raze, equalize, smooth, align; prostrate, knock down, floor, fell, ground.

Adj. horizontal, level, even, plane; flat &c. 251; flat as a -billiard table, – bowling green; alluvial; calm, – as a mill-pond; smooth, – as glass.

re-, de-, pro-, ac-cumbent; lying &c. *v.*; prone, supine, couchant, jacent, prostrate.

Adv. horizontally &c. *adj.*; on -one's back, – all fours, – its beam ends.

214. Pendency.—N. pend-, dependency; suspension, hanging &c. *v.*

pendant, drop, tippet, tassel, lobe, tail, train, flap, lappet, skirt, pig-tail, queue, pendulum.

peg, knob, button, hook, nail, stud, ring, staple, tenterhook; davit; fastening &c. 45; spar, horse.

chande-, gase-, electro-lier.

V. be -pendent &c. *adj.*; hang, depend, swing, dangle, droop, sag; swag; daggle, flap, trail, flow.

suspend, hang, sling, hook up, hitch, fasten to, append.

Adj. pend-ent, -ulous; pensile; hanging &c. *v.*; dependent; suspended &c. *v.*; lowering, overhanging, beetling, decumbent; loose, flowing.

having a -peduncle &c. *n.*; pedunculate, tailed, caudate.

215. Support.—N. support, ground, foundation, base, basis; *terra firma*; bearing, fulcrum, *point d'appui*, caudex, purchase, footing, hold, -*locus standi*; landing, - stage, - place; stage, platform; block; rest, resting-place; groundwork, *substratum*, sustentation, subvention; floor &c. (*basement*) 211.

supporter; aid &c. 707; prop, stand, anvil, fulciment; hod, stay, shore, skid, rib, sprag, truss, bandage; sleeper; stirrup, stilts, shoe, sole, heel, splint, lap; bar, rod, boom, sprit, outrigger.

staff, stick, crutch, alpenstock, bourdon; *bâton*, maulstick, colstaff, cowlstaff, staddle; stalk, ped-icel, -icle, - uncle.

post, pillar, shaft, column, pilaster; pediment, pedestal; plinth, shank, leg, socle, zocle; buttress, jamb, mullion, abutment; pile, baluster, banister, stanchion, king post; balustrade.

frame, -work, body, *chassis*, *fuselage*; scaffold, skeleton, beam, rafter, girder, lintel, joist, cantilever, travis, trave, corner-stone, summer, transom; rung, round, step, sill.

columella, back-bone; key-stone; axle, -tree; axis; arch, ogive, mainstay.

trunnion, pivot, rowlock; peg &c.

(*pendency*) 214; tie-beam &c. (*fastening*) 45; thole pin.

board, ledge, shelf, hob, bracket, trevet, trivet, arbor, rack, hatrack; mantel, -piece, -shelf; slab, console; counter, dresser; flange, corbel; table, trestle, teapoy; shoulder; perch; horse; easel, desk; retable, predella.

seat, throne, dais; divan, musnud; chair, bench, form, stool, camp-stool, sofa, settee, davenport, stall, miserere, arm -, easy -, elbow -, rocking- chair; couch, day bed, *fauteuil*, woolsack, ottoman, settle, squab, bench, box, dicky; saddle, pannel, pillion; side -, pack-saddle; pommel.

bed, berth, pallet, tester, crib, cot, bassinet, hammock, shakedown, camp bed, bunk, truckle-bed, cradle, litter, stretcher, bedstead; four-poster, French bed; bedding, mattress, *paillasse*; pillow, bolster; mat, rug, cushion.

stool, footstool, hassock, faldstool, *prie-dieu*; tabouret; tripod.

Atlas, Persides, Atlantes, Caryatides, Hercules.

V. be -supported &c.; lie -, sit -, recline -, lean -, loll -, rest -, stand -, step -, repose -, abut -, beat -, be based &c.- on; have at one's back; be-stride, -straddle.

support, bear, carry, hold, sustain, shoulder; hold -, back -, bolster -, shore- up; up-hold, -bear; prop; under-prop, -pin, -set; bandage &c. 43; brace, truss; cradle, pillow.

give -, furnish -, afford -, supply -, lend- support; - foundations; bottom, found, base, ground, embed.

maintain, keep on foot; aid &c. 707.

Adj. support-ing, -ed, &c. *v.*; atlantean, columellar; sustentative, fundamental, basal.

Adv. astride on, astraddle; pick-a-back.

216. Parallelism.—N. parallelism; coextension, cocentricity, collimation.

V. be -, lie- parallel to; collimate.

Adj. parallel; coextensive, collateral, concentric, concurrent.

Adv. alongside, abreast &c. (*laterally*) 236.

217. Obliquity.—N. obliquity, inclination, skew, slope, slant; crookedness &c. *adj.*; slopeness; leaning &c. *v.*; bevel, bezel, ramp, tilt; bias, list, twist, swag, cant, lurch; distortion &c. 243; bend &c. (*curve*) 245; tower of Pisa.

acclivity, rise, ascent, grade, gradient, *glacis*, rising ground, hill, bank, declivity, downhill, dip, fall, devexity; gentle –, rapid- slope; easy -ascent, – descent; shelving beach; *talus*; *montagne Russe*; *facilis descensus Averni*.

steepness &c. *adj.*; cliff, precipice &c. (*vertical*) 212; escarpment, scarp.

[Measure of inclination] clinometer, theodolite, level, sextant, quadrant, protractor; angle, sine, cosine, tangent &c. hypothenuse.

diagonal; zigzag, chevron.

V. be -oblique &c. *adj.*; slope, slant, lean, incline, shelve, stoop, decline, descend, bend, heel, careen, sag, swag, seel, slouch, cant, sidle.

render -oblique &c. *adj.*; sway, bias; slope, slant; incline, bend, crook; cant, tilt; distort &c. 243.

Adj. oblique, inclined; sloping &c. *v.*; tilted &c. *v.*; recumbent, clinal, skew, askew, slant, aslant, bias, plagiedral, indirect, wry, awry, ajee, crooked; knock-kneed &c. (*distorted*) 243; bevel, out of the perpendicular.

uphill, rising, ascending, acclivous; downhill, falling, descending; declining, declivous, devex, anticlinal; steep, abrupt, precipitous, breakneck.

diagonal; trans-verse, -versal; athwart, antiparallel; curved &c. 245.

Adv. obliquely &c. *adj.*; on –, all on- one side; askew, askant, askance, aslope, asquint, edgewise, at an angle; side-long, -ways; slope-, slant-wise; by a side wind.

218. Inversion.—N. in-, e-, sub-, re-, retro-, intro-version; contraposition &c. 237; contrariety &c. 14; reversal; turn of the tide.

overturn; somer-sault, -set; summer-set; *culbute*; revulsion; *pirouette*.

transposition, transposal, anastrophy, *metastasis*, *hyperbaton*, *anastrophe*, *hysteron-proteron*, hypallage, *synchysis*, *tmesis*, parenthesis; *metathesis*; palindrome; Spoonerism.

pronation and supination.

V. be -inverted &c.; turn –, go –, wheel- -round, – about, – to the right about; turn –, go –, tilt –, topple-over; capsize, turn turtle.

in-, sub-, retro-, intro-vert; reverse; up-, over-turn, -set; turn -topsy turvy &c. *adj.*; *culbuter*; transpose, put the cart before the horse, turn the tables.

Adj. inverted &c. *v.*; wrong side -out, – up; inside out, upside down; bottom –, keel -upwards; supine, on one's head; topsy turvy, *sens dessus sens dessous*.

inverse; reverse &c. (*contrary*) 14; opposite &c. 237.

topheavy, unstable.

Adv. inversely &c. *adj.*; hirdie-girdie; heels over head, head over heels.

219. Crossing.—N. crossing &c. *v.*; inter-section, – lacement, – twinement, -digitation; decussation, transversion; convolution &c. 248.

reticulation, meshwork, network; in-osculation, anastomosis, intertexture, mortise.

net, *plexus*, web, mesh, twill, skein, sleeve, felt, lace; wicker; mat, -ting; plait, trellis, wattle, lattice, grating, *grille*, gridiron, tracery, fretwork, filigree, reticle; tissue, netting, mokes.

cross, crucifix, rood, crisscross, crux; chain, wreath, braid, cat's cradle, knot; entanglement &c. (*disorder*) 59.

[woven fabrics] cloth, linen, muslin, cambric, drill, homespun, tweed, broad-cloth &c.

V. cross, decussate; inter-sect, -lace, -twine, -twist, -weave, -digitate, -link.

twine, entwine, weave, inweave, twist, wreathe; anastomose, inosculate, dovetail, splice, link.

mat, plait, plat, braid, felt, twill;

tangle, entangle, ravel; net, knot; dishevel, raddle.

Adj. crossing &c. *v.*; crossed, matted
&c. *v.*; transverse.

cross, cruciform, crucial; reti-form,
-cular, -culated; areolar, cancellated,
mullioned, latticed, grated, barred,
streaked; textile, secant, plexal; interfretted.

Adv. across, thwart, athwart, trans-
versely, crosswise.

3°. Centrical Dimensions*

1. General

220. Exteriority.—N. exteriority;
outside, exterior; surface, superficies;
skin &c. (*covering*) 223; *superstratum*;
disk, disc; face, facet.

excentricity; circumjacence &c. 227.

V. be -exterior &c. *adj.*; lie around
&c. 227.

place -exteriorly, - outwardly, - outside; put -, turn- out.

Adj. exter-ior, -nal; extraneous, outer, -most; out-ward, -lying, -side, -door;
round about &c. 227; extramural.

superficial, skin-deep; frontal, discoid.

extraregarding; eccentric; outstanding; extrinsic &c. 6.

Adv. externally &c. *adj.*; out, without, over, outwards, *ab extra*, out of
doors; *extra muros*.

in the open air; *sub -Jove, - dio*; *à la
belle étoile, al fresco*.

221. Interiority.—N. interiority; inside, interior, endocrine; interspace,
subsoil, *substratum*.

contents &c. 190; substance, pith,
marrow; backbone &c. (*centre*) 222;
heart, bosom, breast, abdomen; vitals,
viscera, entrails, bowels, belly, intes-
tines, guts, chitterlings, womb, lap;
gland, cell; internal organs, *penetralia*,

recesses, innermost recesses; cave &c.
(*concavity*) 252.

inhabitant &c. 188.

V. be -inside &c. *adj.*, - within &c.
adv.

place -, keep- within; enclose &c.
(*circumscribe*) 229; intern; embed &c.
(*insert*) 300.

Adj. inter-ior, -nal; inner, inside, intimate, inward, intraregarding; in-, in-
ner-most; deep-seated; visceral, intestine, -tinal; inland; subcutaneous;
interstitial &c. (*interjacent*) 228; in-
wrought &c. (*intrinsic*) 5; enclosed
&c. *v.*

home, domestic, indoor, intramural,
vernacular; endemic.

Adv. internally &c. *adj.*; inwards,
within, in, inly; here-, there-, where-in;
ab intra, withinside; in -, within- doors;
at home, in the bosom of one's family.

222. Centrality.—N. centrality,
centricalness, centre; middle &c. 68;
focus &c. 74.

core, kernel; nucleus, nucleolus;
heart, pole, axis, pivot, fulcrum, bull's
eye; hub, nave, navel; *umbilicus*, spine,
backbone, marrow, pith; hot-bed; concentration &c. (*convergence*) 290; centralization; symmetry.

centre of -gravity, - pressure, - percussion, - oscillation, - buoyancy &c.
metacentre.

V. be -central &c. *adj.*; converge &c.
290.

render central, centralize, concentrate; bring to a focus.

Adj. centr-al, -ical; middle &c. 68;
axial, pivotal, focal, umbilical, concentric; middlemost, nuclear, centric, cen-
traidal; spinal, vertebral.

Adv. middle; midst; centrally &c.
adj.

223. Covering.—N. covering, cover;
canopy, tilt, awning, baldachin, tent,
marquee, *tente d'abri*, umbrella, parasol, sunshade; veil (*shade*) 424; shield
&c. (*defence*) 717; hall.

roof, dome, copola, mansard roof;
ceiling; thatch, tile; pan-, pen-tile;

* That is, Dimensions having reference to a centre.

tiling, shingles, slates, slating, leads; shed &c. (*abode*) 189.

top, lid, covercle, door, *operculum*, eyelid, blind, curtain.

bandage, plaster, lint, wrapping, dossil, finger stall.

coverlet, counterpane, sheet, quilt, comforter, eiderdown; tarpaulin, blanket, rug, drugget, linoleum, oilcloth; housing.

in-, tegument; skin, pellicle, fleece, fell, fur, ermine, miniver, sable, sealskin &c.; fabrikoid, leather, morocco, calf, pigskin, elk, kid, cowhide &c.; shagreen, hide; pelt, -ry; cuticle, *dermis*, scarf-skin, *epidermis*.

clothing &c. 225; mask &c. (*concealment*) 530.

peel, crust, bark, rind, *cortex*, husk, shell, coat.

capsule; ferrule; sheath, -ing; pod, cod; casing, case, theca; *elytron*; *involucrum*; wrapp-ing, -er, cellophane; envelope, vesicle; dermatology, conchology.

armour, -plate, armouring; veneer, facing; pavement; scale &c. (*layer*) 204; coating, paint, stain; varnish &c. (*resin*) 356*a*; anointing &c. *v.*; inunction; incrustation, superposition, obduction, ground, enamel, whitewash, plaster, stucco, rough cast, pebble dash, compo; rendering; cerement; ointment &c. (*grease*) 356.

V. cover; super-pose, -impose; overlay, -spread; wrap &c. 225; incase; face, case, veneer, pave, paper; tip, cap, bind, revet.

coat, paint, varnish, pay, incrust, stucco, cement, dab, plaster, tar; wash; be-, smear; be-, daub; anoint, do over; gild, plate, electroplate, japan, lacquer, lacker, enamel, whitewash; lay it on thick.

over-lie, -arch; conceal &c. 528.

Adj. covering &c. *v.*; cutaneous, dermal, cortical, cuticular, tegumentary, skinny, scaly, squamous; covered &c. *v.*; imbricated, loricated, armour-plated, iron-clad; under cover, hooded, cloaked, cowled.

224. Lining.—N. lining, inner coating; coating &c. (*covering*) 223; stalactite, -agmite.

filling, stuffing, wadding, padding, bushing.

wainscot, *parietes*, wall, brattice.

V. line, stuff, incrust, wad, pad, fill.

Adj. lined &c. *v.*

225. Investment.—N. investment; covering &c. 223; dress, clothing, raiment, drapery, costume, attire, guise, toilet, *toilette*, trim; habiliment; vesture, -ment; garment, garb, palliament, apparel, wardrobe, wearing apparel, clothes, things.

array; tailoring, millinery; best bib and tucker; finery &c. (*ornament*) 847; full dress &c. (*show*) 882; garniture; theatrical properties.

outfit, equipment, *trousseau*; uniform, khaki, regimentals; academicals, canonicals &c. 999; livery, gear, harness, turn out, accoutrement, caparison, suit, rigging, trappings, traps, slops, togs, toggery; masquerade.

dishabille, morning dress, lounge suit, tea-gown, *kimono*, *négligé*, dressing-gown, *peignoir*, wrapper, undress; shooting-coat; smoking-jacket, mufti; rags, tatters, old clothes; mourning, weeds; duds; slippers.

robe, tunic, dolman, *paletot*, habit, gown, coat, coatee, frock, blouse, *pelisse*, middy, sagum, *toga*, smock-frock; frock-, dress-, morning-, tail-coat; dress-suit, – clothes, swallow-tail coat, dinner-, Eton-jacket.

cloak, pall; mantle, mantlet, mantua, shawl, *pelisse*, veil, yashmak; cape, tippet, kirtle, plaid, muffler, comforter, Balaclava helmet, haik, huke, chlamys, mantilla, tabard, housing, horse-cloth, burnous, *roquelaure*; *houppelande*; sur-, top, over-, great-coat; *surtout*, spencer, cardigan, sweater, blazer; mackintosh, waterproof, slicker, raincoat, oilskin, trench coat, ulster, monkey-, pea-, pilot-jacket, redingote; wraprascal, poncho, cardinal, pelerine, talma.

jacket, jumper, vest, jerkin,

waistcoat, doublet, *camisole*, gabardine; stays, *corsage*, corset, corselet, bodice; stomacher; skirt, petticoat, slip, farthingale, kilt, jupe, crinoline, bustle, hobble skirt, *panier*, apron, pinafore; loin cloth.

trousers; breeches; trews, pantaloons, unmentionables, inexpressibles, overalls, pyjamas, smalls, small-clothes; tights, pants, shorts, drawers; knickerbockers, knickers, plus fours, bloomers, divided skirt; phil-, fill-ibeg.

head-dress, -gear; cap, *béret*, tam o' shanter, glengarry, topee, sombrero; hat; cocked –, high –, tall –, top –, silk –, opera –, crush -hat, *gibus*, beaver, castor, bonnet, tile, wideawake, billycock; bowler; soft felt –, straw –, leghorn -hat, panama; toque; wimple; night-, mob-, skull-cap, biretta; hood, cowl, coif; capote, calach; scull-cap; kerchief, snood; head, *coiffure*; crown &c. (*circle*) 247; *chignon*, pelt, wig, front, peruke, periwig; caftan, turban, fez, *tarboosh*, taj, shako, csako, busby; *képi*, forage cap, bearskin; helmet &c. 717; mask, domino.

body clothes; linen; shirt, sark, smock, shift, *chemise*, *lingerie*; nightgown, -shirt; bed-gown, *sac de nuit*; jersey, guernsey; under-clothing, -waistcoat.

neck-erchief, -cloth; tie, ruff, collar, cravat, stock, handkerchief, bandana, scarf; bib, tucker; dicky; boa; girdle &c. (*circle*) 247; cummerbund.

shoe, pump, brogue, boot, slipper, sandal, galoche, goloshes, arctics, rubber boots, overshoes, patten, clog, sabot; high-low; Blucher –, Wellington –, Hessian –, jack –, top- boot; Balmoral; legging, puttee, buskin, greave, galligaskin, moccasin, *gamache*, gambado, gaiter, spatter-dash, spat, antigropeles; stocking, hose, gaskins, trunk-hose, sock, hosiery.

glove, gauntlet, mitten, cuff, muffettee, wristband, sleeve.

swaddling cloth, baby-linen, *layette*; pocket-handkerchief.

shroud &c. 363.

clothier, tailor, milliner, *costumier*, sempstress, seamstress, snip; dress-, habit-, breeches-, shoe-maker; cordwainer, cobbler, Crispin, hosier, hatter; draper, linendraper, haberdasher, mercer.

V. invest; cover &c. 223; envelop, lap, involve; in-, en-wrap; wrap; fold –, wrap –, lap –, muffle- up; overlap; sheathe, swathe, swaddle, roll up in, shroud, circumvest.

vest, clothe, array, dress, dight, drape, robe, enrobe, attire, tire, garb, habilitate, apparel, accoutre, rig, fit out; bedizen, deck &c. (*ornament*) 847; perk; equip, harness, caparison; dress up.

wear; don; put –, huddle –, slip- on; mantle.

Adj. invested &c. *v.*; habited; dight, -ed; clad, *costumé*, shod, *chaussé*; en grande tenue &c. (*show*) 882.

sartorial.

226. Divestment.—N. divestment; taking off &c. *v.*

nudity; bareness &c. *adj.*; undress; dishabille &c. 225, altogether; nu-, denu-dation; decortication, depilation, excoriation, desquamation; moulting; exfoliation.

baldness, alopecia, acomia.

V. divest; uncover &c. (*cover* &c. 223); denude, bare, strip; undress, unclothe, disrobe &c. (dress, enrobe, &c. 225); uncoif; dismantle; uncase; put –, take –, cast- off; shed, doff; husk, peel, pare, decorticate, desquamate, excoriate, skin, scalp, flay, bark, expose, lay open; exfoliate, moult, mew; cast the skin.

Adj. divested &c. *v.*; bare, naked, nude; un-dressed, -draped, -clad, -clothed, -appareled; exposed; in dishabille; *décolleté*; bald, threadbare, ragged, callow, roofless.

in -a state of nature, – nature's garb, – buff, – native buff, – birthday suit; *in puris naturalibus*; with nothing on, stark naked; bald as a coot, bare as the back of one's hand; out at elbows; barefoot; bareback; leaf-, nap-, hairless, shaved,

clean shaven, tonsured, beardless, bald-
headed, acomous.

227. Circumjacence.—N. circumjacence, -ambience; environment, encom-
passment; atmosphere, medium; surroundings, *entourage*.

outpost; border &c. (*edge*) 231; girdle
&c. (*circumference*) 230; outskirts, *bou-
levards*, suburbs, purlieus, precincts,
faubourgs, environs, *banlieue*, neighbourhood, vicinity.

V. lie -around &c. *adv.*; surround,
beset, compass, encompass, environ,
inclose, enclose, encircle, circle, embrace, circumvent, lap, gird; begird,
girdle, engird; skirt, twine round; hem
in &c. (*circumscribe*) 229; besiege, invest, blockade.

Adj. circum-jacent, -ambient, -fluent;
ambient; surrounding &c. *v.*; circumferential, suburban.

Adv. around, about; without; on -
every side, - all sides; right and left, all
round, round about; in the neighbourhood.

228. Interjacence.—N. inter-jacence,
-currence, -venience, -location, -digitation,
-penetration; permeation.

inter-jection, -polation, -lineation,
-spersion, -calation; embolism.

inter-vention, -ference, -position; in-,
ob-trusion; insinuation; insertion &c.
300; dovetailing; infiltration; intromission.

intermedi-um, -ary; go-between,
agent, middleman, medium, bodkin, intruder, interloper; parenthesis, episode;
fly-leaf.

partition, *septum*, diaphragm, midriff;
party-wall, panel, vail, bulkhead, brattice, *cloison*; half-way house.

V. lie -, come -, get- between; intervene, slide in, interpenetrate, permeate.

put between, introduce, intromit, import; throw -, wedge -, edge -, jam -,
worm -, foist -, run -, plough -, work-
in; inter-pose, -ject, -calate, -polate,
-line, -leave, -sperse, -weave, -lard,
-digitate; let in, dovetail, splice, mortise,
insinuate, smuggle; infiltrate, ingrain.

interfere, put in an oar, thrust one's
nose in; intrude, obtrude; have a finger
in the pie; introduce the thin end of the
wedge; thrust in &c. (*insert*) 300.

Adj. inter-jacent, -current, -venient,
-vening &c. *v.*, -mediate, -mediary,
-calary, -stitial, -costal, -mural, -planetary,
-stellar; embolismal.

parenthetical, episodic; mediterranean; intrusive; embosomed; merged,
mean, middle, medium, median.

Adv. between, betwixt; 'twixt;
among, -st; amid, -st; 'mid, -st; in the
thick of; betwixt and between; sandwich-wise; parenthetically, *obiter dictum*.

229. Circumscription.—N. circumscription, limitation, inclosure; confinement &c. (*restraint*) 751; circumvallation, encincture; envelope &c. 232.

V. circumscribe, limit, bound, confine, enclose; surround &c. 227; compass about; imprison &c. (*restrain*) 751;
hedge -, wall -, rail- in; fence -, hedge-
round; embar; picket, corral.

enfold, bury, incase, pack up, enshrine, inclasp; wrap up &c. (*invest*)
225; embosom.

Adj. circumscribed &c. *v.*; begirt,
lapt; circumambient; buried -, im-
mersed- in; embosomed, in the bosom
of, imbedded, encysted, mewed up; imprisoned &c. 751; land-locked, in a ring
fence.

230. Outline.—N. outline, circumference; peri-meter, -phery; ambit, circuit, lines, *tournure*, *contour*, profile,
silhouette, lineaments; bounds, coast-
line.

zone, belt, girth, band, baldric, zodiac, girdle, tire, cingle, clasp, girt;
cordon &c. (*inclosure*) 232; circle &c.
247.

V. outline, delineate, *silhouette*, circumscribe &c. 229; profile, block out.

Adj. outlined &c. *v.*; circumferential,
perimetric, peripheral.

231. Edge.—N. edge, verge, brink,
brow, brim, margin, border, confines,

skirt, rim, felloe, felly, flange, side, mouth; jaws, chops, chaps, *fauces*; lip, muzzle.

threshold, door, porch; portal &c. (*opening*) 260; coast, shore, strand, beach, bank, wharf, quay, dock.

frame, fringe, flounce, frill, list, trimming, edging, skirting, hem, selvedge, welt; furbelow, valance, exergue.

Adj. border, marginal, skirting; labial, labiated, marginated.

232. Inclosure.—N. inclosure, enclosure, envelope; case &c. (*receptacle*) 191; wrapper; girdle &c. 230.

pen, fold, croft, sty; pen-, in-, sheepfold; paddock, pound, corral, kraal; yard, compound; net, seine net.

wall; hedge, -row; *espalier*; fence &c. (*defence*) 717; pale, paling, balustrade, rail, railing, gunwale; quickset hedge, park paling, circumvallation, *enceinte*, ring fence.

barrier, barricade; gate; -way; door, hatch, *cordon*; prison &c. 752.

dike, dyke, ditch, fosse, moat, trench.

V. inclose, circumscribe &c. 229.

233. Limit.—N. limit, boundary, bounds, confine, *enclave*, term, bourn, verge, kerb-stone, curbstone, but, pale; termin-ation, -us; stint, frontier, precinct, marches.

boundary line, landmark; line of -demarcation, – circumvallation; pillars of Hercules; Rubicon, turning-point; *ne plus ultra*; sluice, flood-gate.

V. limit, bound, confine, define, circumscribe, demarcate, delimit, encompass.

Adj. definite; contermin-ate, -able; terminable, limitable; terminal, frontier, border, bordering, boundary.

Adv. thus far, – and no further.

2. *Special*

234. Front.—N. front; fore, – part; foreground; forefront, face, disk, disc, frontage, *façade*, *proscenium*, facia, frontispiece; priority, anteriority; obverse [of a medal].

fore -, front- rank, first line; van, -guard; advanced guard; outpost, scout.

brow, forehead, visage, physiognomy, phiz, features, countenance, map, mug; rostrum, beak, bow, stem, prow, prore, jib, bowsprit; forecastle.

pioneer &c. (*precursor*) 64; metoposcopy.

V. be -, stand- in front &c. *adj.*; front, face, confront, breast, brave; bend forwards; come to the -front, – fore.

Adj. fore, forward, anterior, front, frontal.

Adv. before; in -front, – the van, – advance; ahead, right ahead; fore-, headmost; in the foreground; before one's -face, – eyes; face to face, *vis-à-vis*.

235. Rear.—N. rear, back, posteriority; rear -rank, – guard; background, *hinterland*.

occiput, nape, scruff, chine; heels; tail, rump, croup, buttock, posteriors, bottom, seat, backside, scut, breech, *dorsum*, loin; dorsal -, lumbar- region; hind quarters.

stern, poop, after-part, counter; postern, heel-, tail-piece, crupper.

wake; train &c. (*sequence*) 281.

reverse; other side of the shield.

V. be -behind &c. *adv.*; fall astern; bend backwards; bring up the rear; follow &c. 622; tail, shadow.

Adj. back, rear; hind, -er, -most, -ermost; post-ern, -erior; dorsal, after; caudal, lumbar; mizzen.

Adv. behind; in the -rear, – ruck, – back-ground; behind one's back; at the -heels, – tail, – back- of; back to back.

after, -most, aft, abaft, astern, sternmost, aback, rear-, hind-, back-ward.

236. Laterality.—N. laterality; side, flank, beam, quarter, lee; hand; cheek, jowl, jole, wing; profile; temple, *parietes*, loin, haunch, hip.

gable, -end; broadside; lee side.

points of the compass; East, Orient, Levant; West, occident; orientation.

V. be -on one side &c. *adv.*; flank, outflank; sidle; skirt, border.

Adj. lateral, sidelong; collateral;

parietal, flanking, skirting; flanked; sideling.

many-sided; multi-, bi-, tri-, quadrilateral.

East-ern, -ward, -erly; orient, -al, auroral, Levantine; West-ern, -ward, -erly; occidental, Hesperian; equatorial.

Adv. side-ways, -long, broadside on; on one side, abreast, abeam, alongside, beside, aside; by, – the side of it; side by side; cheek by jowl &c. (*near*) 197; to -windward, – leeward; laterally &c. *adj.*; right and left; on her beam ends.

237. Contraposition.—N. contraposition, opposition; polarity; inversion &c. 218; opposite side; antithesis; reverse, inverse; counterpart; antipodes; opposite poles, North and South.

V. be -opposite &c. *adj.*; subtend.

Adj. opposite; reverse, inverse; antipodal, subcontrary; fronting, facing, diametrically opposite.

Northern, Septentrional, Boreal, arctic; Southern, Austral, antarctic, polar.

Adv. over, – the way, – against; against; face to face, *vis-à-vis*; as poles asunder.

238. Dextrality.—N. dextrality; right, – hand; dexter, offside, starboard.

Adj. dextral, right-handed; ambidextral, dexterous, dextrorsal &c.

239. Sinistrality.—N. sinistrality; left, – hand; *sinister*, nearside, larboard, port.

Adj. sinistral, sinister, sinistrorsal &c., left-handed, sinistromanual, sinistrous.

Section III. FORM

1°. General Form

240. Form.—N. form, figure, shape; con-formation, -figuration; make, formation, frame, construction, design, cut, set, build, trim, cut of one's jib; stamp, type, cast, mould; fashion; contour &c. (*outline*) 230; structure &c. 329.

feature, lineament, outline, turn; phase &c. (*aspect*) 448; posture, attitude, *pose*.

[Science of form] morphology.

[Similarity of form] isomorphism.

forming &c. *v.*; form-, figur-, efformation; sculpture.

V. form, shape, figure, fashion, efform, carve, cut, chisel, hew, cast; rough-hew, -cast; sketch; block –, hammer- out; trim; lick –, put- into shape; model, knead, work up into, set, mould, sculpture; cast, stamp; built &c. (*construct*) 161.

Adj. formed &c. *v.*

[Receiving form] plastic, fictile, full-fashioned &c.

[Giving form] plasmic &c.

[Similar in form] isomorphous &c.

241. [Absence of form.] Amorphism.—N. amorphism, informity, uncouthness; unlicked cub, rough diamond; *rudis indigestaque moles*; disorder &c. 59; deformity &c. 243.

disfigure-, deface-ment, deformation; mutilation.

V. [Destroy form] deface, disfigure, deform, mutilate, truncate; derange &c. 61.

Adj. shapeless, amorphous, malformed, formless; un-formed, -hewn, -fashioned, -shapen; rough, rude, Gothic, barbarous, rugged, in the rough; misshapen &c. 243.

242. [Regularity of form.] Symmetry.—N. symmetry, shapeliness, finish;

beauty &c. 845; proportion, eurythmy, eurythmic, uniformity, parallelism; bi-, tri-, multi-lateral symmetry; centrality &c. 222.

arborescence, branching, ramification.

Adj. symmetrical, shapely, well set, finished; beautiful &c. 845; classic, chaste, severe.

regular, uniform, balanced; equal &c. 27; parallel, coextensive.

arbor-escent, -iform; dendr-iform, -oid; branching; ramous, ramose.

243. [Irregularity of form.] **Distortion.—N.** dis-, de-, con-tortion; knot, mop, warp, buckle, screw, twist; crookedness &c. (*obliquity*) 217; grimace; deformity; mal-, malcon-formation; monstrosity, misproportion, want of symmetry, *anamorphosis*; ugliness &c. 846; teratology.

V. distort, contort, twist, warp &c. *n.*; wrest, writhe, make faces, deform, misshape.

Adj. distorted &c. *v.*; out of shape, irregular, unsymmetric, awry, wry, askew, crooked, sinuous; anamorphous; not -true, - straight; on one side, crump, deformed; mis-shapen, -begotten; mis-, ill-proportioned; ill-made; grotesque, crooked as a ram's horn; hump-, hunch-, bunch-, crook-backed; bandy; bandy-, bow-legged; bow-, knock-kneed; splay-, club-footed; taliped; round-shouldered; snub-nosed; curtailed of one's fair proportions; scalene, stumpy &c. (*short*) 201; gaunt &c. (*thin*) 203; bloated &c. 194.

Adv. all manner of ways.

2°. SPECIAL FORM

244. Angularity.—N. angular-ity, -ness; aduncity; angle, cusp, bend; fold &c. 258; notch &c. 257; fork, bifurcation.

elbow, knee, knuckle, ankle, groin, crotch, crutch, crane, fluke, scythe, sickle, zigzag, kimbo.

corner, nook, recess, niche, oriel.

right angle &c. (*perpendicular*) 212; obliquity &c. 217; angle of 45°, mitre; acute -, obtuse -, salient -, re-entrant -, spherical -, solid -, dihedral- angle.

angular -measurement, - elevation, - distance, - velocity; trigon-, goniometry; altimetry; clin-, graph-, goniometer; theodolite; transit circle; sextant, quadrant; dichotomy.

triangle, trigon, wedge; rectangle, square, lozenge, diamond; rhomb, -us; quadr-angle, -ilateral; parallelogram; quadrature; poly-, penta-, hexa-, hepta-, ota-, deca-gon.

Platonic bodies; cube, rhomboid; tetra-, penta-, hexa-, octa-, dodeca-, icosahedron; prism, pyramid; parallelopiped.

V. bend, fork, bifurcate, crinkle, divaricate, branch, ramify.

Adj. angular, bent, crooked, aduncous, uncinated, aquiline, jagged, serrated; falc-iform, -ated; furcular, furcated, forked, bifurcate, crotched; zigzag; dovetailed; knock-kneed, crinkled, akimbo, kimbo, geniculated; oblique &c. 217.

fusiform, wedge-shaped, cuneiform; tri-angular, -gonal, -lateral; quadrangular, -ilateral; rectangular, square, foursquare, multilateral; polygonal &c. *n.*; cubical, rhomboidal, pyramidal.

245. Curvature.—N. curv-ature, -ity, -ation; incurv-ity, -ation; bend; flex-ure, -ion; conflexure; crook, hook, bought, bending; de-, inflexion; arcuation, devexity, turn; deviation, *détour*, sweep; curl, -ing; bough; recurv-ity, -ation; sinuosity &c. 248; aduncity.

curve, arc, arch, arcade, vault, dome, bow, crescent, *meniscus*, half-moon, lunule, horse-shoe, loop, crane-neck; para-, hyper-bola; catenary, festoon; conch-, cardi-oid; caustic, instep; tracery.

V. be -curved &c. *adj.*; sweep, swag, sag; deviate &c. 279; turn; re-enter.

render -curved &c. *adj.*; bend, curve, incurvate; de-, in-flect; crook; turn; round, arch, arcuate, arch over, loop the

loop, concamerate; bow, coil, curl, re-
curve, frizzle.

Adj. curved &c. *v.*; curvi-form,
-lineal, -linear; devex, devious; recurv-
ed, -ous; *retroussé*; crump; bowed &c.
v.; vaulted; hooked; falc-iform, -ated;
semicircular, crescentic; lun-iform,
-ular; semilunar, meniscal; conchoidal;
cord-iform, -ated; cardioid; heart-, bell-,
pear-, fig-shaped; reniform; lenti-form,
-cular; bow-legged &c. (*distorted*) 243;
oblique &c. 217; circular &c. 247.

246. Straightness.—N. straightness,
rectilinearity, directness; inflexibility
&c. (*stiffness*) 323; straight –, right –,
direct-, bee- line; short cut.

V. be -straight &c. *adj.*; have no turning; not -incline, – bend, – turn, – de-
viate- to either side; go straight; steer for
&c. (*direction*) 278.

render straight, straighten, rectify; set
–, put- straight; un-bend, -fold, -curl &c.
248, -ravel &c. 219, -wrap.

Adj. straight; rectiline-ar, -al; direct,
even, right, true, in a line; unbent &c.
v.; un-deviating, -turned, -distorted,
-swerving; straight as an arrow &c. (*direct*) 278; inflexible &c. 323.

**247. [Simple circularity.] Circulari-
ty.—N.** circularity, roundness; rotundity
&c. 249.

circle, circlet, ring, washer, areola,
hoop, roundlet, *annulus*, annulet, bracelet, armlet, armilla; ringlet, eye, loop,
wheel; cycle, orb, orbit, rundle, zone,
belt, *cordon*, band; sash, girdle, cestus,
cincture, baldric, fillet, *fascia*, wreath,
garland; crown, corona, coronet, chaplet, snood, necklace, collar; noose, lasso, lariat.

ellipse, oval, ovule; ellipsoid, cycloid; epi-cycloid, -cycle; semi-circle;
quadrant, sextant, sector.

V. make -round &c. *adj.*; round.

go round; encircle &c. 227; describe
-a circle &c. 311.

Adj. round, rounded, circular, annular, orbicular; oval, ovate; elliptic, -al;
ovoid, egg-shaped; pear-shaped &c.
245; cycloidal &c.*n.*; spherical &c. 249.

**248. [Complex circularity.] Convo-
lution.—N.** winding &c. *v.*; con-, in-,
circum-volution; wave, undulation, tor-
tuosity, anfractuosity; sinu-osity, -ation,
sinuousness; meandering, circuit, circumbendibus, twist, twirl, windings and
turnings, *ambages*; torsion; inosculation; reticulation &c. (*crossing*) 219.

coil, roll, curl, buckle, spire, spiral,
helix, corkscrew, worm, volute, whorl,
rundle; tendril; scollop, scallop, escal-
lop; kink.

serpent, snake, eel, maze, labyrinth.

V. be -convoluted &c. *adj.*; wind,
twine, turn and twist, twirl; wave, undulate, meander; inosculate; entwine,
intwine; twist, coil, roll; wrinkle, curl,
crisp, twill; frizz, -le; crimp, crape, indent, scollop, scallop; wring, intort;
contort; wreathe &c. (*cross*) 219.

Adj. convoluted; winding, twisted
&c. *v.*; tortile, tortive; wavy; und-ated,
-ulatory; circling, snaky, snake-like;
serpentine; serpent-, anguill-, verm-
iform; vermicular; mazy, tortuous, an-
fractuous, sinuous, flexuous, wavy, sigmoidal.

involved, intricate, complicated, perplexed; labyrinth-ic, -ian, -ine; circuitous; peristaltic; dædalian, curly.

wreathy, frizzly, *crêpé*, buckled; ravelled &c. (*in disorder*) 59.

spiral, coiled, helical, turbinated.

Adv. in and out, round and round.

249. Rotundity.—N. rotundity;
roundness &c. *adj.*; cylindricity; spher-
icity, -oidity; globosity.

cylin-der, -droid; barrel, drum; roll,
-er; *rouleau*, column, rolling-pin, rundle; chimney-pot, drain-pipe.

cone, conoid; pear-, egg-, bell-shape.

sphere, globe, ball, boulder, bowlder;
spher-, ellips-, ge-, glob-oid, oblong –,
oblate- spheroid; drop, spherule, globule, vesicle, bulb, bullet, pellet, *pelote*,
clew, pill, marble, pea, knob, pommel,
knot.

V. render -spherical &c. *adj.*; form
into a sphere, sphere, roll into a ball;
give -rotundity &c. *n.*; round.

Adj. rotund; round &c. (*circular*) 247; cylindr-ic, -ical, -oid; columnar, lumbriciform; conic, -al; spher-ical, -oidal; glob-ular, -ated, -ous, -ose; egg-, bell-, pear-shaped; ov-oid, -iform; gibbous; campan-iform, -ulate, -iliform; fungiform, bead-like, moniliform, pyriform, bulbous; *teres atque rotundus*; round as -an orange, – an apple, – a ball, – a billiard ball, – a cannon ball.

3°. SUPERFICIAL FORM

250. Convexity.—N. convexity, prominence, projection, swelling, gibbosity, bilge, bulge, protuberance, protrusion; excrescency, camber.

intumescence; tumour, tumor; tubercle, -osity; excrescence; hump, hunch, bunch, gnarl.

tooth, knob, elbow, process, *apophysis*, condyle, bulb, node, nodule, nodosity, tongue, *dorsum*, boss, embossment, bump, clump; sugar-loaf &c. (*sharpness*) 253; bow; mamelon.

pimple, wen, wheal, *papula*, postule, pock, proud flesh, growth, goitre, *sarcoma*, caruncle, corn, bunion, wart, furnuncle, polypus, adenoid, fungus, fungosity, *exostosis*, bleb, blister, blain; boil &c. (*disease*) 655; bubble, blob.

papilla, nipple, teat, pap, breast, dug, mammilla; proboscis, nose, neb, beak, snout, nozzle, snozzle; Adam's apple; belly, paunch, corporation; withers, back, shoulder, lip, flange.

peg, button, stud, ridge, rib, jutty, trunnion, snag.

cupola, dome, bee-hive; arch, balcony, eaves; pilaster.

relief, relievo, *cameo*; *basso-*, *mezzo-*, *alto-rilievo*; low-, bas-, high-relief.

hill &c. (*height*) 206; cape, promontory, mull; fore-, head-land; point of land, naze, ness, mole, jetty, hummock, ledge, spur.

V. be -prominent &c. *adj.*; project, bulge, protrude, bag, belly, pout, bouge, bunch; jut -, stand -, stick -, poke- out;

stick -, bristle -, start -, cock -, shoot-up; swell -, hang -, bend- over; beetle.

render -prominent &c. *adj.*; raise 307; emboss, chase.

Adj. convex, prominent, protuberant, underhung, undershot; projecting &c. *v.*; bossed, bossy, nodular, bunchy; clavate, -ated; hummocky, *moutonné*, mammiform; papul-ous, -ose; hemispheric, bulbous; bowed, arched; bold; bellied; tuber-ous, -culous; tumorous; cornute, knobby, odontoid; lenti-form, -cular; gibbous.

salient, in relief, raised, *repoussé*; bloated &c. (*expanded*) 194.

251. Flatness.—N. flatness &c. *adj.*; smoothness &c. 255.

plane; level &c. 213; plate, platter, table, tablet, slab.

V. render flat, flatten, squash; level &c. 213.

Adj. flat, plane, even, flush, scutiform, discoid; level &c. (*horizontal*) 213; smooth, flat as -a pancake, – a fluke, – a flounder, – a board, – my hand.

252. Concavity.—N. concavity, depression, dip; hollow, -ness; indentation, *intaglio*, cavity, antrum, dent, dint, dimple, follicle, pit, *sinus*, alveolus, *lacuna*; excavation, trench, sap, mine, tunnel, burrow; trough &c. (*furrow*) 259; honeycomb.

cup, basin, crater, punch-bowl; cell &c. (*receptacle*) 191; socket, faucet.

valley, vale, dale, dell, gap, dingle, combe, bottom, slade, strath, glade, grove, glen, cave, cavern, cove; grot, -to; alcove, *cul-de-sac*, blind alley; gully &c. 198; arch &c. (*curve*) 245; bay &c. (*of the sea*) 343.

excavator, sapper, miner.

V. be -concave &c. *adj.*; retire, cave in.

render -concave &c. *adj.*; depress, hollow; scoop, – out; gouge, dig, delve, excavate, dent, dint, mine, sap, undermine, burrow, tunnel, stave in.

Adj. depressed &c. *v.*; concave, hollow, stove in; dished; spoon-like;

retiring; retreating; cavernous; porous &c. (*with holes*) 260; cellular, spongy, spongious; honeycombed, alveolar; infundibul-ar, -iform; funnel-, bell-shaped; campaniform, capsular; vaulted, arched.

253. Sharpness.—N. sharpness &c. *adj.*; acuity, acumination; spinosity.

point, spike, spine, *spiculum*, tine; needle, pin; tack, nail; prick, -le; spur, rowel, barb; spit, cusp; horn, antler; snag; tag; thorn, bristle.

nib, tooth, incisor, tusk; spoke, cog, ratchet.

crag, crest, *arête*, cone, peak, sugar-loaf, pike, *aiguille*; spire, pyramid, steeple.

beard, *chevaux de frise*, porcupine, hedgehog, brier, bramble, thistle; comb, awn, bur.

wedge; knife-, cutting- edge; blade, edge-tool, cutlery, knife, penknife, whittle, razor; scalpel, bistoury, lancet; chisel; plough-share, coulter; hatchet, axe, pick-axe, mattock, pick, adze, bill; bill-hook, cleaver, cutter; skiver; scythe, sickle, scissors, shears; sword &c. (*arms*) 727; bodkin &c. (*perforator*) 262.

sharpener, hone, strop; grind-, whet-stone; steel, emery.

V. be -sharp &c. *adj.*; taper to a point; bristle with.

render -sharp &c. *adj.*; sharpen, point, aculeate, acuminate, whet, barb, spiculate, set, strop, grind.

cut &c. (*sunder*) 44.

Adj. sharp, keen; acute; aci-cular, -form; acu-leated, -minated; pointed; tapering; conical, pyramidal; mucron-ate, -ated; spindle-, needle-shaped; spiked, spiky, ensiform, peaked, salient, cusp-ed, -idate, -idated; corn-ute, -uted, -iculate; prickly; spiny, spinous; thorny, bristling, muricated, pectinated, studded, thistly, briery; craggy &c. (*rough*) 256; snaggy; digitated, two-edged, fusiform; denti-form, -culated; toothed; odontoid; star-like; stell-ated, -iform; arrow-headed; arrowy, barbed, spurred,

sagittal; spear-shaped, hastate; horned; conical.

cutting; sharp-, knife-edged; sharp -, keen- as a razor; sharp as a needle; sharpened &c. *v.*; set.

254. Bluntness.—N. bluntness &c. *adj.*

V. be -, render- blunt &c. *adj.*; obtund, dull; take off the -point, - edge; turn.

Adj. blunt, obtuse, dull, bluff.

255. Smoothness.—N. smoothness &c. *adj.*; polish, gloss; lubric-ity, -ation.

down, velvet, silk, satin; slide; bowling green &c. (*level*) 213; glass, ice; asphalt, pavement, flags.

roller, steam-roller; iron, flat-iron, tailor's goose; sand-, emery-paper; burnisher, turpentine and bees-wax.

V. smooth, -en; plane; file; mow, shave; level, roll; macadamize; polish, burnish, planish, levigate, calender, glaze; iron, hot-press, mangle; lubricate &c. (*oil*) 332.

Adj. smooth; polished &c. *v.*; even; level &c. 213; plane &c. (*flat*) 251; sleek, glossy; silken, silky; lanate, downy, velvety; glabrous, slippery, glassy, lubricous, oily, soft; unwrinkled; smooth as -glass, - ice, - velvet, - oil; slippery as an eel; woolly &c. (*feathery*) 256.

256. Roughness.—N. roughness &c. *adj.*; tooth, grain, texture, ripple; asperity, rugosity, salebrosity, corrugation, nodosity; arborescence &c. 242.

brush, hair, beard, shag, mane, whisker, mutton-chops, *moustache*, *mustachio*, imperial, Van Dyke, tress, lock, curl, ringlet, *fimbriæ*, *cilia*, *villi*; eyelashes, eye-brows, love-lock.

plum-age, -osity, plume, *panache*, crest; feather, tuft, tussock, fringe, toupee.

wool, velvet, plush, nap, pile, floss, fluff, fur, down; byssus, moss, bur.

V. be -rough &c. *adj.*; go against the grain.

render -rough &c. *adj.*; roughen,

rough cast, knurl; ruffle, crisp, crumple, crinkle, corrugate, engrail; set on edge, stroke -, rub- the wrong way, rumple.

Adj. rough, uneven; scabrous, knotted; nodular; rug-ged, -ose, -ous; asperous, crisp, salebrous, gnarled, unpolished, unsmooth, rough-hewn; knurled, cross-grained, crag-gy, -ged; crankling, scraggy, jagged, unkempt, prickly &c. (*sharp*) 253; arborescent &c 242; leafy, well-wooded; feathery; plum-ose, -igerous; tufted, fimbriated, hairy, bristly, ciliated, filamentous, hirsute; crinose, -ite; bushy, hispid, villous, pappous, bearded, pilous, shaggy, shagged; fringed, befringed; set-ous, -ose, -aceous; 'like quills upon the fretful porcupine'; rough as a -nutmeg grater, - bear.

downy, velvety, flocculent, woolly; lan-ate, -ated; lanugin-ous, -ose; tomentous.

Adv. against the grain, in the rough, on edge.

257. Notch.—N. notch, dent, nick, cut; indent, -ation; serration; dimple.

embrasure, battlement, machicolation; saw, tooth, crenelle, scallop, scollop, vandyke.

V. notch, nick, cut, pink, mill, score, dent, indent, jag, scarify, scotch, crimp, scollop, crenulate, vandyke.

Adj. notched &c. *v.*; crenate, -d; dentate, -d; denticulate, -d; toothed, palmated, serrated.

258. Fold.—N. fold, plicature, pleat, plait, ply, crease; tuck, gather; flexion, flexure, joint, elbow, doubling, duplicature, wrinkle, rimple, crinkle, crankle, crumple, rumple, rivel, ruck, ruffle, dog's ear, corrugation, frounce, flounce, lapel; pucker, crow's feet.

V. fold, double, plicate, pleat, plait, crease, wrinkle, crinkle, crankle, curl, smock, cockle up, crocker, rimple, rumple, frizzle, frounce, rivel, twill, corrugate, ruffle, crimple, crumple, pucker; turn -, double-down, - under; tuck, ruck, hem, gather.

Adj. folded &c. *v.*

259. Furrow.—N. furrow, groove, rut, *sulcus*, scratch, streak, *striae*, crack, score, incision, slit; chamfer, fluting.

channel, gutter, trench, ditch, dike, dyke, moat, fosse, trough, kennel; ravine &c. (*interval*) 198.

V. furrow &c. *n.*; flute, groove, carve, corrugate, plough; incise, chase, enchase, grave, engrave, etch, bite in, cross-hatch.

Adj. furrowed &c. *v.*; ribbed, striated, sulcated, fluted, canaliculated; bisulc-ous, -ate; trisulcate; corduroy.

260. Opening.—N. hole, foramen; puncture, blow-out, perforation; pin-, key-, loop-, port-, peep-, mouse-, pigeon-hole; eye, - of a needle; eyelet; slot.

opening; apert-ure, -ness; hiation, yawning, oscitancy, dehiscence, patefaction, pandiculation; gap, chasm &c. (*interval*) 198.

embrasure, window, casement, light; sky-, fan-light; lattice; bay-, bow-window; oriel; dormer, lantern.

out-, in-let; vent, vomitory; *embouchure*; orifice, mouth, sucker, muzzle, throat, gullet, placket, weasand, wizen, nozzle, *æsophagus*.

portal, porch, gate, ostiary, postern, wicket, trap-door, hatch, door; arcade; gate-, door-, hatch-, gang-way; lych-gate.

way, path &c. 627; thoroughfare; channel, passage, tube, pipe; water-pipe &c. 350; air-pipe &c. 351; vessel, tubule, canal, gut, fistula; adjutage, ajutage; chimney, smoke stack, flue, tap, funnel, gully, tunnel, main; mine, pit, adit, shaft; gallery.

alley, aisle, glade, lane, vista.

bore, calibre; pore; blind orifice.

por-ousness, -osity; sieve, cullender, colander; grater, shredder; cribble, riddle, screen; honeycomb.

apertion, perforation; piercing &c.

v.; terebration, empalement, pertusion, puncture, acupuncture, penetration.

opener, key, master-key, *passe-partout*.

V. open, ope, gape, dehisce, yawn, bilge; fly open.

perforate, pierce, empierce, tap, bore, drill; mine &c. (*scoop out*) 252; tunnel; trans-pierce, -fix; enfilade, impale, spike, spear, gore, spit, stab, pink, puncture, lance, trepan, trephine, stick, prick, riddle, punch; stave in.

cut a passage through; make -way, -room- for.

un-cover, -close, -rip; lay -, cut -, rip -, throw- open.

Adj. open; perforated &c. *v.*; perforate; wide open, agape, ajar; un-closed, -stopped; oscitant, gaping, yawning; patent.

tubular, cannular, fistulous; per-vious, -meable; foraminous; vesi-, vas-cular; porous, follicular, cribriform, honeycombed, infundibular, riddled; tubulous, -ated, piped.

opening &c. *v.*; aperient.

Int. *open sesame!*

261. Closure.—N. closure, occlusion, blockade; shutting up &c. *v.*; obstruction &c. (*hindrance*) 706; gag; embolism; contraction &c. 195; infarction; con-, ob-stipation; blind -alley, - corner; *cul-de-sac, cæcum*; imper-foration, -viousness &c. *adj.*, -meability; stopper &c. 263; *operculum*.

V. close, occlude, plug; block -, stop -, fill -, bung -, cork -, button -, stuff -, shut -, dam- up, obturate; blockade; obstruct &c. (*hinder*) 706; bar, bolt, stop, seal, plumb; choke, throttle; ram down, tamp, dam, cram; trap, clinch; put to -, shut- the door; batten down the hatches.

Adj. closed &c. *v.*; shut, operculated; unopened.

unpierced, imporous, cæcal; imperforate, -vious, -meable; impenetrable; un-, im-passable; invious; path-, wayless; untrodden.

unventilated; air-, water-tight; hermetically sealed; tight, snug.

262. Perforator.—N. perforator, piercer, borer, auger, gimlet, stylet, drill, wimble, awl, bradawl, scoop, terrier, corkscrew, dibble, trocar, trepan, trephine, probe, bodkin, needle, stiletto, broach, reamer, rimer, warder, lancet; punch, -eon; spikebit, gouge; spear &c. (*weapon*) 727.

263. Stopper.—N. stopper, stopple; plug, cork, bung, spike, spill, stop-cock, tap; rammer; ram, -rod; piston; stopgap; wadding, stuffing, padding, stopping, dossil, pledget, tompion, tourniquet, obturator; wad.

cover &c. 223; valve, slide valve; vent-peg, spigot.

janitor, door -, gate- keeper, porter, commissionaire, *concierge*, warder, beadle, Cerberus, usher, guard, sentry, sentinel; ostiary.

SECTION IV. MOTION

1°. MOTION IN GENERAL

264. [Successive change of place.*]
Motion.—N. motion, movement, move;
motivity, motility, going &c. *v.*; unrest.

stream, current, flow, flux, run,
course, stir; conduction, evolution; kinematics.

step, rate, pace, tread, stride, gait,
clip, port, footfall, cadence, carriage,
velocity, angular velocity; progress, locomotion; journey &c. 266; voyage &c.
267; transit &c. 270.

restlessness &c. (*changeableness*) 149;
mobility; movableness, motive power;
laws of motion; mobilization.

V. be -in motion &c. *adj.*; move, go,
hie, gang, budge, stir, pass, flit; hover
-round, - about; shift, slide, slither,
glide; roll, - on; flow, stream, run, drift,
sweep along; wander &c. (*deviate*) 279;
walk &c. 266; change -, shift- one's
-place, - quarters; dodge; keep -going,
- moving.

put -, set- in motion; move; impel
&c. 276; propel &c. 284; render movable, mobilize.

Adj. moving &c. *v.*; in motion; motile, transitional; motory, motive; shifting, movable, mobile, mercurial, unquiet; restless &c. (*changeable*) 149;
nomadic &c. 266; erratic &c. 279.

Adv. under way; on the -move, -
wing, - tramp, - march.

265. Quiescence.—N. rest; stillness
&c. *adj.*; quiescence; stag-nation,

* A thing cannot be said to *move* from one place
to another, unless it passes in succession through
every intermediate place; hence motion is only such
a change of place as is *successive*. 'Rapid, swift,
&c., as thought' are therefore incorrect expressions.

-nancy; fixity, immobility, catalepsy; indisturbance; quietism.

quiet, tranquillity, calm; repose &c.
687; peace; dead calm, anticyclone;
statue-like repose; silence &c. 403; not
a -breath of air, - mouse stirring; sleep
&c. (*inactivity*) 683.

pause, lull &c. (*cessation*) 142; stand,
- still; standing still &c. *v.*; lock; dead
-lock, - stop, - stand; full stop; fix; embargo.

resting-place; bivouac; home &c.
(*abode*) 189; pillow &c. (*support*) 215;
haven &c. (*refuge*) 666; goal &c.
(*arrival*) 292.

V. be -quiescent &c. *adj.*; stand -,
lie- still; keep quiet, repose, hold the
breath.

remain, stay; stand, lie to, ride at anchor, remain *in situ*, mark time, tarry;
bring -, heave -, lay- to; pull -, draw-
up; hold, halt; stop, - short; rest, pause,
anchor; cast -, come to an- anchor; rest
on one's oars; repose on one's laurels,
take breath; stop &c. (*discontinue*) 142.

stagnate, vegetate; *quieta non movere*; let -alone, - well alone; abide, rest
and be thankful; keep within doors, stay
at home, go to bed.

dwell &c. (*be present*) 186; settle &c.
(*be located*) 184; alight &c. (*arrive*) 292.

stick, - fast; stand, - like a post; not
stir a -peg, - step; be at a -stand &c. *n.*

quell, becalm, hush, stay, lull to sleep,
lay an embargo on; put the brake on.

Adj. quiescent, still; motion-, moveless; fixed; stationary; at -rest, - a stand,
- a stand-still, - anchor; stock-still; immotile, standing still &c. *v.*; sedentary,
untravelled, stay-at-home; becalmed,
stagnant, quiet; un-moved, -disturbed,
-ruffled; calm, restful; cataleptic;

immovable &c. (*stable*) 150; sleeping &c. (*inactive*) 683; silent &c. 403; still as -a statue, – a post, – a mouse, – death.

Adv. at a stand &c. *adj.*; *tout court*; at the halt.

Int. stop! stay! avast! halt! hold, – hard! whoa!

Phr. *requiescat in pace.*

266. [Locomotion by land.] **Journey.—N.** travel; travelling &c. *v.*; wayfaring, campaigning.

journey, excursion, expedition, tour, trip, grand tour, circuit, peregrination, discursion, ramble, pilgrimage, *trek*, course, ambulation, march, walk, hike, promenade, constitutional, stroll, saunter, tramp, jog-trot, turn, stalk, perambulation; noctambulation; somnambulism, sleep walking; outing, ride, drive, airing, jaunt.

equitation, horsemanship, riding, *manège*, ride and tie.

roving, vagrancy, pererration; marching and countermarching; nomadism; vagabond-ism, -age; gadding; flit, -ting; migration; e-, im-, de-, inter-migration.

plan, itinerary, guide; hand-, roadbook; Baedeker, Murray, Bradshaw, time table.

procession, parade, cavalcade, caravan, file, *cortège*, column.

[Organs and instruments of locomotion] vehicle &c. 272; locomotive &c. 271; legs, feet, pegs, pins, trotters.

traveller &c. 268.

V. travel, journey, course; tour; take –, go- a journey; take –, go out for- -a walk &c. *n.*; have a run; take the air.

flit, take wing; migrate, emigrate, *trek*; rove, prowl, roam, range, patrol, pace up and down, traverse; scour –, traverse- the country; peragrate; per-, circum-ambulate; nomadize, wander, ramble, stroll, saunter, hover, go one's rounds, straggle; gad, – about; expatiate.

walk, march, step, tread, pace, plod, wend; promenade; trudge, tramp; stalk, stride, straddle, strut, foot it, stump,

bundle, bowl along, toddle; paddle; tread –, follow –, pursue- a path.

take horse, ride, drive, trot, amble, canter, prance, fisk, frisk, *caracoler*; gallop &c. (*move quickly*) 274; motor, cycle, taxi; go by -car, – train, – tram, – bus, – plane.

peg –, jog –, wag –, shuffle- on; stir one's stumps; bend one's -steps, – course; make –, find –, wend –, pick –, thread –, plough- one's way; coast, slide, glide, skim, skate, ski; march in procession, file off, defile.

go –, repair –, resort –, hie –, betake oneself- to.

Adj. travelling &c. *v.*; ambulatory, itinerant, peripatetic, perambulatory, roving, rambling, gadding, discursive, vagrant, migratory, nomadic; circumforane-an, -ous; somnambular, nocti-, mundi- vagrant; locomotive, automotive, self-moving.

way-faring, -worn; travel-stained.

Adv. on -foot, – horseback, – Shanks's mare; by the Marrowbone stage; *in transitu* &c. 270; *en route* &c. 282.

Int. come along!

267. [Locomotion by water, or air.] **Navigation.—N.** navigation; aquatics; boating, cruising, yachting; ship &c. 273; oar, scull, sweep, punt pole, paddle, – wheel, screw, propeller, stern wheel, sail, canvas.

natation, swimming; fin, flipper, fish's tail.

aerial navigation, air service, airways, airmanship, aero-donetics, -dynamics, -mechanics, -station, -statics, -nautics; ballooning, balloonry; balloon &c. 273; flying, flight, aviation, volitation; wing, pinion, *aileron*.

voyage, sail, cruise, passage, circumnavigation, *periplus*; head-, stern-, lee-way.

mariner, aeronaut &c. 269.

V. sail; put to sea &c. (*depart*), 293; take ship, get under way; spread -sail, – canvas; gather way, have way on; make

–, carry- sail; plough the -waves, – deep, – main, – ocean; walk the waters.

navigate, warp, luff, scud, boom, kedge; drift, course, cruise, coast; hug the -shore, – land; circumnavigate.

ply the oar, row, paddle, pull, scull, punt, steam.

swim, float; buffet the waves, ride the storm, skim *effleurer*, dive, wade.

fly, aviate, be wafted, hover, soar, drift, glide, plane, sideslip, *volplane*, pique, dive, spin, roll, loop, flutter; take -wing, – a flight; wing one's -flight, – way.

Adj. sailing &c. *v.*; seafaring, nautical, maritime, naval; sea-going, coasting; afloat; navigable, aquatic, natatory.

volitant, volant, aerostatic, aerial, aeronautic; alar, alate, pennate.

Adv. under -way, – sail, – canvas, – steam; on the wing.

268. Traveller.—N. traveller, wayfarer, voyager, itinerant, passenger.

tourist, excursionist, globe-trotter; explorer, adventurer, mountaineer, Alpine Club; peregrinator, wanderer, rover, straggler, rambler; bird of passage; gad-about, -ling; vagrant, scatterling, landloper, waifs and estrays, wastrel, stray; loafer; tramp, -er, hobo, beachcomber, vagabond, nomad, Bohemian, gipsy, Arab, Wandering Jew, Hadji, pilgrim, palmer; peripatetic; somnambulist, sleep walker, noctambulist; emigrant, fugitive, refugee, *émigré*.

runner, courier, King's messenger; Mercury, Iris, Ariel, comet.

pedestrian, walker, foot-passenger; cyclist; wheelman.

rider, horseman, equestrian, cavalier, jockey, rough rider, trainer, breaker, huntsman.

driver, coachman, whip, Jehu, charioteer, postilion, post-boy, carter, wagoner, drayman, truckman; cab-man, -driver; *voiturier*, *vetturino*, *condottiere*; engine-driver; stoker, fireman, guard, brakeman, conductor; chauffeur, automobilist, motorist, motor –, truck –, taxi- driver.

269. Mariner.—N. sailor, mariner, navigator, argonaut; sea-man, -farer, -faring man; yachtsman; tar, jack tar, salt, gob, sea-dog, shellback, able seaman, A.B.; man-of-war's man, bluejacket, marine, jolly; midshipman, middy, reefer; captain, commander, master mariner, skipper, mate; ship-, boat-, ferry-, water-, lighter-, barge-, longshore- man, hoveller; bargee, gondolier; oar-, -sman; rower; boat-, cock-swain; coxswain; steersman, helmsman, pilot; crew; lascar.

aerial navigator, aeronaut, balloonist, Icarus, aviator, pilot, observer, flyer, airman.

270. Transference.—N. transfer, -ence; trans-, e-location; displacement; *meta-stasis*, *-thesis*; removal; re-, a-motion; relegation; de-, as-portation; extradition, conveyance, draft; carrying, carriage; convection, -duction, -tagion, infection; transfusion; transfer &c. (*of property*) 783.

transit, transition; passage, ferry, gestation; portage, porterage, carting, cartage; shovelling &c. *v.*; vect-ion, -ure, -itation; shipment, freight, wafture; transmission, -port, -portation, -umption, -plantation, -lation; shift-, dodg-ing; dispersion &c. 73; transposition &c. (*interchange*) 148; traction &c. 285.

[Thing transferred] drift, alluvium, detritus, *moraine*; gift, legacy, bequest, lease; freight, mails, cargo, luggage, baggage, goods.

V. trans-fer, -mit, -port, -place, -plant; convey, assign, carry, bear, fetch and carry; carry –, ferry- over; hand, pass, forward; shift; conduct, convoy, bring, fetch, reach.

send, delegate, consign, mail, post, relegate, turn over to, pass the buck, deliver; ship, embark; waft; switch, shunt; transpose &c. (*interchange*) 148; displace &c. 185; throw &c. 284; drag &c. 285.

shovel, lade, dip, ladle, bale, decant, draft off, transfuse.

Adj. transferred &c. *v.*; drifted; movable; port-able, -ative; conductive; contagious, infectious.

transferable, assignable, conveyable, devisable, negotiable, transmissible.

Adv. from -hand to hand, – pillar to post.

on –, by- the way; on the -road, – wing; as one goes; *in transitu*, *en route*, *chemin faisant*, *en passant*, in mid-progress.

271. Carrier.—N. carrier, porter, red cap, bearer, messenger, postman, tranter, conveyer; stevedore; coolie; conductor, locomotive, tractor, caterpillar tractor, motor.

beast of burden, cattle, horse, steed, nag, palfrey, Arab, blood horse, thorough-bred, galloway, charger, courser, racer, hunter, jument, pony, filly, colt, foal, barb, roan, jade, hack, *bidet*, pad, cob, tit, punch, roadster, goer; race-, pack-, draft-, cart-, dray-, post-horse, mount; Shetland pony, sheltie; garran; jennet, genet, bayard, mare, stallion, gelding; stud.

Pegasus, Bucephalus, Rozinante.

ass, donkey, jackass, mule, hinny; sumpter -horse, – mule; reindeer; camel, dromedary, mehari, llama, elephant; carrier pigeon.

carriage &c. (*vehicle*) 272; ship &c. 273.

Adj. equine, asinine.

272. Vehicle.—N. vehicle, conveyance, carriage, car, caravan, van, furniture van, pantechnicon; wagon, wain, dray, cart, lorry.

carriole; sledge, sled, sleigh, bobsleigh, toboggan, *luge*, truck, tram; limber, tumbrel, pontoon; barrow; wheel-, hand- -barrow, – cart, trolley; perambulator; Bath –, wheel –, sedan chair, jinriksha, rickshaw; ekka; chaise; palankeen, -quin; litter, horse-litter, brancard, crate, hurdle, stretcher, ambulance; velocipede, hobby-horse, coaster, scooter, go-cart; cycle; bi-, tri-, quadri-cycle; tandem, safety; skate, roller skate; ski, snow-shoe.

equipage, turn-out; coach, chariot, *quadriga*, chaise, phaëton, break, brake, nail-phaëton, wagonette, drag, curricle, tilbury, whisky, landau, *barouche*, victoria, brougham, clarence, calash, *calèche*, britzska, *araba*, kibitka; berlin; sulky, *désobligeant*, sociable, *vis-à-vis*, *dormeuse*; jaunting –, outside- car; *tarantass*; runabout; shay.

post-chaise; diligence, stage; stage –, mail –, hackney –, glass- coach; stagewagon; car, omnibus, bus, fly, *cabriolet*, cab, hansom, shofle, four-wheeler, growler, *droshki*, drosky.

dog-cart, trap, gig, whitechapel, buggy, four-in-hand, unicorn, random, tandem; shandredhan, *char-à-banc*.

automobile, motor-, auto-, touring-, racing-, cycle-, side-, steam-, electric-car; motor-, -omnibus, – bus, – cab, – cycle; limousine, landaulette, cabriolet, *coupé*, *voiturette*, runabout, electromobile, taxi, -cab.

train; passenger –, express –, freight –, subway –, special –, corridor –, parliamentary –, luggage –, goods- train, *train de luxe*; 1st-, 2nd-, 3rd- class--train, – carriage, – compartment; Pullman –, sleeping-, club-, observation-, dining-, restaurant-car; mail-, luggage-, brake-van, coach, car, carriage; rolling stock; horse-box, cattle-truck.

tramcar, trolley-omnibus, trackless trolley.

shovel, spoon, spatula, ladle, hod, hoe; spade, spaddle, loy; spud; pitchfork.

Adj. vehicular.

273. Ship.—N. ship, vessel, sail; craft, bottom.

navy, marine, fleet, flotilla, squadron; shipping.

man of war &c. (*combatant*) 726; transport, tender, store-ship; merchant ship, merchantman; packet, liner; whaler, slaver, collier, coaster, tanker, freighter, freight steamer, cargo boat, lighter; fishing-, pilot- boat; trawler, drifter; cable ship; hulk; yacht; floating palace, ocean greyhound.

ship, bark, barque, brig, snow, hermaphrodite brig; brigantine, barquentine; schooner; topsail –, fore and aft –, three masted- schooner; *chasse-marée*; sloop, cutter, corvette, clipper, foist, yawl, dandy, ketch, smack, lugger, barge, hoy, cat-, -boat, buss; sail-er, -ing vessel, wind jammer; steam-er, -boat, -ship; mail –, paddle –, screw –, sternwheel- steamer; tug; train-ferry; line of steamers &c.

boat, pinnace, launch, motor-boat, picket-boat; hydroplane; life-, long-, jolly-, bum-, fly-, cock-, ferry-, canalboat, dory, dugout, galliot; shallop, gig, funny, skiff, dingy, scow, cockleshell, wherry, coble, punt, cog, lerret; eight-, four-, pair- oar; randan; outrigger; float, raft, pontoon; prame, ice-yacht.

state barge, bucentaur.

catamaran, coracle, gondola, carvel, caravel; felucca, caique, canoe; trireme; galley, – foist; bilander, dogger, hooker, howker; argosy, carack; galliass, galleon; galliot, polacca, polacre, corsair, tartane, junk, lorcha, praam, proa, prahu, saick, sampan, xebec, dhow; dahabeah; nuggar, cayak, piroque; trireme.

submarine, submersible.

aircraft (*combatant*) &c. 726; flying machine, air mail, aero-, air-, mono-, bi-, tri-, hydro aero-plane, plane, cabin plane, transport plane, *avion*, flying boat, glider, *aviette*, helicopter; balloon, air-, fire-, gas-, Mongolfier-, pilot-, captive-, free-, kite-, dirigible- balloon, air-ship, *Zeppelin*, blimp; kite, parachute.

nacelle, car, gondola, aileron; hangar, airport, landing field, airdrome; catwalk, controls, rudder, tail.

Adj. marine, maritime, naval, nautical, seafaring, sea-, ocean-going, seaworthy.

aerial, aeronautical, air-worthy, flying &c. *n.*

Adv. afloat, aboard; on -board, – ship board, – board ship.

2°. DEGREES OF MOTION

274. Velocity.—N. velocity, speed, celerity; swiftness &c. *adj.*; rapidity, eagle speed; expedition &c. (*activity*) 682; pernicity; acceleration; haste &c. 684.

spurt, rush, dash, race, steeplechase; smart –, lively –, swift &c. *adj.* –, rattling –, spanking –, strapping- -rate, – pace; round pace; flying, flight.

gallop, canter, trot, round trot, run, scamper; hand –, full- gallop; swoop.

lightning, light, electricity, wind; cannon-ball, rocket, arrow, dart, quicksilver; telegraph, express train; torrent; swallow flight.

eagle, antelope, courser, race-horse, gazelle, greyhound, hare, doe, squirrel.

Mercury, Ariel, Camilla, Harlequin.

[Measurement of velocity] speedometer, log, -line, tachometer.

V. move quickly, trip, fisk; speed, hie, hasten, sprint, spurt, post, spank, scuttle; scud, -dle; scurry; scour, – the plain; scamper; run, – like mad; fly, race, run a race, cut away, cut and run, shoot, tear, whisk, whiz, sweep, skim, brush; cut –, bowl- along; rush &c. (*be violent*) 173; dash -on, – off, – forward; bolt, trot, gallop, bound, flit, spring, dart, boom; march in -quick, – doubletime; ride hard, get over the ground, scorch.

hurry &c. (*hasten*) 684; accelerate, put on; quicken; quicken –, mend- one's pace; clap spurs to one's horse; make -haste, – rapid strides, – forced marches, – the best of one's way; put one's best leg foremost, stir one's stumps, wing one's way, set off at a score; carry –, crowd- sail; go off like a shot, go ahead, gain ground; outstrip the wind, fly on the wings of the wind.

keep -up, – pace- with; outstrip &c. 303.

Adj. fast, speedy, swift, rapid, quick, fleet; nimble, agile, expeditious;

express; active &c. 682; flying, galloping &c. *v.*; light-, nimble-footed; winged, eagle-winged, mercurial, electric, telegraphic; light-legged, light of heel; swift as -an arrow &c. *n.*; quick as -lightning &c. *n.*, – thought.*

Adv. swiftly &c. *adj.*; with -speed &c. *n.*; apace; at -a great rate, – full speed, – railway speed; full -drive, – gallop; post-haste, in full sail, tantivy; trippingly; instantaneously &c. 113; like a shot.

under press of -sail, – canvas, – sail and steam; *velis et remis*, on eagle's wing, in double quick time; with -rapid, – giant- strides; *à pas de géant*; in seven league boots; whip and spur; *ventre à terre*; as fast as one's -legs, – heels- will carry one; as fast as one can lay feet to the ground, at the top of one's speed; by leaps and bounds; with haste &c. 684; in- high – gear, – speed.

Phr. *vires acquirit eundo*.

275. Slowness.—N. slowness &c. *adj.*; languor &c. (*inactivity*) 683; drawl; creeping &c. *v.*, lentor.

retardation; slackening &c. *v.*; delay &c. (*lateness*) 133; claudication.

jog-, dog-trot, walk; mincing steps; slow -march, – time.

slow -goer, – coach, – back; lingerer, loiterer, sluggard, tortoise, snail; dawdle &c. (*inactive*) 683.

V. move -slowly, &c. *adv.*; creep, crawl, lag, slug, walk, drawl, linger, loiter, saunter; plod, trudge, stump along, lumber; trail; drag; dawdle &c. (*be inactive*) 683; grovel, worm one's way, steal along; jog –, rub –, bundle- on; toddle, waddle, wabble, slug; traipse, slouch, shuffle, halt, hobble, limp, claudicate, shamble; flag, falter, totter, stagger; mince, step short; march in -slow time, – funeral procession; take one's time; hang fire &c. (*be late*) 133.

retard, relax; slacken, check, moderate, rein in, curb; reef; strike –, shorten –, take in- sail; put on the drag, apply

the brake; clip the wings; reduce the speed, decelerate; slacken -speed, – one's pace, lose ground; back -water, – pedal, put the engines astern, throttle down.

Adj. slow, slack; tardy; dilatory &c. (*inactive*) 683; gentle, easy; leisurely; deliberate, gradual; insensible, imperceptible; languid, sluggish, apathetic, phlegmatic, slow-paced, tardigrade, snail-like; creeping &c. *v.*

Adv. slowly &c. *adj.*; leisurely; *piano, adagio*; *largo, larghetto*; at half speed, under easy sail; at a -foot's, – snail's, – funeral- pace; slower than molasses in January; in slow time; with -mincing steps, – clipped wings; *haud passibus æquis*; in- low –, gear, – speed.

gradually &c. *adj.*; *gradatim*; by -degrees, – slow degrees, – inches, – little and little; step by step; inch by inch, bit by bit, little by little, *seriatim*; consecutively.

3°. Motion Conjoined with Force

276. Impulse.—N. impulse, impulsion, impetus; momentum; push, pulsion, thrust, shove, jog, jolt, brunt, booming, boost, throw; explosion &c. (*violence*) 173; propulsion &c. 284.

percussion, concussion, collision, occursion, clash, encounter, cannon, *carambole*, appulse, shock, crash, bump; impact; *élan*; charge &c. (*attack*) 716; beating &c. (*punishment*) 972.

blow, dint, stroke, knock, tap, rap, slap, smack, pat, dab; fillip; slam, bang; hit, whack, thwack, clout; cuff &c. 972; squash, dowse, whap, swap, punch, thump, swipe, jab, pelt, kick, punce, calcitration; *ruade*; arietation; cut, thrust, lunge, yerk.

hammer, sledge-hammer, mall, maul, mallet, flail; ram, -mer; battering-ram, monkey, pile-driver, punch, bat, tamper, tamping iron; cudgel &c. (*weapon*) 727; axe &c. (*sharp*) 253.

* See note on 264.

[Science of mechanical forces] mechanics, dynamics &c.

V. give an -impetus &c. *n*.; impel, push; start, give a start to, set going; drive, urge, boom; thrust, prod, foin; cant; elbow, shoulder, jostle, justle, hustle, hurtle, shove, jog, jolt, bean, encounter; run -, bump -, butt- against; knock -, run- one's head against; impinge.

strike, knock, hit, bash, tap, rap, bat, slap, flap, dab, pat, thump, beat, bang, slam, dash; punch, thwack, whack; hit -, strike- hard; swap, batter, dowse, baste; pelt, patter, skelter, buffet, belabour, tamp; fetch one a blow, swat; poke at, pink, lunge, yerk; kick, calcitrate; butt; strike at &c. (*attack*) 716; whip &c. (*punish*) 972; propel &c. 284.

come -, enter- into collision; collide; foul; fall -, run- foul of.

throw &c. (*propel*) 284.

Adj. impelling &c. *v*.; im-pulsive, -pellent; booming; dynamic, -al; impelled &c. *v*.

277. Recoil.—N. recoil; re-, retroaction; revulsion; rebound, *ricochet*; repercussion, -calcitration; kick, *contrecoup*; springing back &c. *v*.; elasticity &c. 325; reflexion, reflex, reflux; reverberation &c. (*resonance*) 408; rebuff, repulse; return.

ducks and drakes; boomerang; spring; reactionist, reactionary.

V. recoil, resile, react; spring -, fly -, bound- back; rebound, reverberate, repercuss, recalcitrate, echo, *ricochet*.

Adj. recoiling &c. *v*.; re-fluent, -percussive, -calcitrant, -actionary; retroactive.

Adv. on the -recoil &c. *n*.

4°. MOTION WITH REFERENCE TO DIRECTION

278. Direction.—N. direction, bearing, course, set, drift, tenor; tendency &c. 176; incidence; bending, trending &c. *v*.; dip, tack, aim, collimation; steer-ing, -age.

point of the compass, cardinal -, half -, quarter- points; North, East, South, West; N by E, ENE, NE by N, NE &c.; rhumb, azimuth, line of collimation.

line, path, road, range, quarter, line of march; a-, al-lignment; straight shot, bee-line.

V. tend -, bend -, point- towards; conduct -, go- to; point -to, - at; bend, trend, verge, incline, dip, determine.

steer -, make- -for, - towards; aim -, level- at; take aim; keep -, hold- a course; be bound for; bend one's steps towards; direct -, steer -, bend -, shape-one's course; align -, allign- one's march; go straight, - to the point; march -on, - on a point.

ascertain one's -direction &c. *n*.; *s'orienter*, see which way the wind blows; box the compass.

Adj. directed &c. *v*., - towards; pointing towards &c. *v*.; bound for; aligned -, alligned- with; direct, straight; undeviating, -swerving; straightforward; North, -ern, -erly, &c. *n*.

directable &c. *v*.

Adv. towards; on the -road, - high road- to; *versus*, to; hither, thither, whither; directly; straight, - forwards, - as an arrow; point blank; in a -direct, - straight- line -to, - for, - with; in a line with; full tilt at, as the crow flies.

before -, near -, close to -, against-the wind; windwards, in the wind's eye.

through, *via*, by way of; in all -directions, - manner of ways; *quaquaversum*, from the four winds.

279. Deviation.—N. deviation; swerving &c. *v*.; obliquation, warp, refraction; flection, flexion; sweep; deflection, -flexure; declination.

diversion, digression, departure from, aberration, drift, sheer; divergence &c. 291; zigzag; *détour* &c. (*circuit*) 629.

[Desultory motion] wandering &c. *v*.; vagrancy, evagation; by-paths and crooked ways.

[Motion sideways, oblique motion] sidling &c. *v.*; *échelon*, leeway; knight's move (at chess).

V. alter one's course, deviate, depart from, turn, trend; bend, curve &c. 245; swerve, heel, bear off.

intervert; deflect; divert, - from its course; put on a new scent, shift, shunt, switch, wear, draw aside, crook, warp, short circuit.

stray, straggle; sidle, edge; diverge &c. 291; tralineate, digress, divagate, wander; wind, twist, meander, meander around Robin Hood's barn; veer, tack, sheer; turn -aside, - a corner, - away from; wheel, steer clear of; ramble, rove, drift; go -astray, - adrift; yaw, dodge; step aside, ease off, make way for, shy.

fly off at a tangent; glance off; turn, wheel -, face- about; turn -, face- to the right about; wabble &c. (*oscillate*) 314; go out of one's way &c. (*perform a circuit*) 629; lose one's way.

Adj. deviating &c. *v.*; aberrant, errant; ex-, dis-cursive; devious, desultory, loose; rambling; stray, erratic, vagrant, undirected; circuitous, indirect, zigzag; crab-like.

Adv. astray from, round about, wide of the mark; to the right about; all manner of ways; circuitously &c. 629.

obliquely, sideling, like the move of the knight on a chessboard.

280. [Going before.] **Precession.—N.** precession, leading, heading; precedence &c. 62; priority &c. 116; the lead, *le pas*; van &c. (*front*) 234; precursor &c. 64.

V. go -before, - ahead, - in the van, - in advance; precede, forerun; usher in, introduce, herald, head, take the lead; lead, - the way, - the dance; get -, have-the start; steal a march; get -before, - ahead, - in front of; outstrip &c. 303; take precedence &c. (*first in order*) 62.

Adj. foremost, first, leading &c. *v.*

Adv. in advance, before, ahead, in the van; fore-, head-most; in front.

Phr. *seniores priores.*

281. [Going after.] **Sequence.—N.** sequence, run; coming after &c. (*order*) 63; (*time*) 117; following; pursuit &c. 622.

follower, attendant, satellite, shadow, dangler, train.

V. follow; pursue &c. 622; go -, fly-after.

attend, beset, dance attendance on, dog, be-dog; tread -in the steps of, - close upon; be -, go -, follow- in the -wake, - trail, - rear- of; trail, follow as a shadow, hang on the skirts of; tread -, follow- on the heels of, tag after.

lag, get behind.

Adj. following &c. *v.*

Adv. behind; in the -rear &c. 235, - train of, wake of; after &c. (*order*) 63, (*time*) 117.

282. [Motion forwards; progressive motion.] **Progression.—N.** progress, -ion, -iveness; advancing &c. *v.*; advance, -ment; ongoing; flood-tide, head-way; march &c. 266; rise; improvement &c. 658.

V. advance; proceed, progress; get -on, - along, - over the ground; gain ground; jog -, rub -, wag- on; go with the stream; keep -, hold on- one's course; go -, move -, come -, get -, pass -, push -, press- -on, - forward, - forwards, - ahead; press onwards, step forward; make -, work -, carve -, push -, force -, edge -, elbow- one's way; make -progress, - head, - way, - headway, - advances, - strides, - rapid strides &c. (*velocity*) 274; go -, shoot-ahead; distance; make up leeway.

Adj. advancing &c. *v.*; pro-gressive, -fluent; advanced.

Adv. forward, onward; forth, on ahead, under way, *en route* for, on -one's way, - the way, - the road, - the high road- to; in -progress, - mid progress; *in transitu* &c. 270.

Phr. *vestigia nulla retrorsum.*

283. [Motion backwards.] **Regression.—N.** regress, -ion; retro-cession, -gression, -gradation, -action; *reculade*; retreat, withdrawal, retirement, remigration; recession &c. (*motion from*) 287; recess; crab-like motion.

re-fluence, -flux; backwater, regurgitation, ebb, return; resilience; reflexion (*recoil*) 277; *volte-face*.

counter -motion, – movement, – march; veering, tergiversation, recidivation, backsliding, fall, relapse; deterioration &c. 659.

turning-point &c. (*reversion*) 145.

V. re-cede, -grade, -turn, -vert, -treat, -tire; retro-grade, -cede; back, – down, – out, crawl; withdraw; rebound &c. 277; go –, come –, turn –, hark –, draw –, fall –, get –, put –, run- back; lose ground; fall –, drop- astern; back water, put about; veer, – round; double, wheel, counter-march; ebb, regurgitate; jib, shrink, shy.

turn -tail, – round, – upon one's heel, – one's back upon; retrace one's steps, dance the back step; sound –, beat- a retreat; go home.

Adj. receding &c. *v.*; retro-grade, -gressive; re-gressive, -fluent, -flex, -cidivous, -silient; crab-like; reactionary &c. 277; counter-clockwise.

Adv. back, -wards; reflexively, to the right about; *à reculons, à rebours*.

Phr. *revenons à nos moutons*, as you were.

284. [Motion given to an object situated in front.] **Propulsion.—N.** propulsion, -jection; *vis a tergo*; push &c. (*impulse*) 276; e-, jaculation; ejection &c. 297; throw, fling, toss, shot, discharge, shy.

[Science of propulsion] gunnery, ballistics, archery.

missile, projectile, ball, *discus*, javelin, hammer, quoit, brickbat, shot, bullet; arrow, shaft, gun &c. (*arms*) 727.

shooter, shot; gunner, gun-layer; archer, toxophilite; bow-, rifle-, marksman; good –, crack- shot; sharpshooter &c. (*combatant*) 726.

V. propel, project, throw, fling, cast, pitch, chuck, toss, jerk, heave, shy, hurl; flirt, fillip.

dart, lance, tilt; e-, jaculate; fulminate, bolt, drive, sling, pitchfork.

send; send –, let –, fire- off; discharge, shoot; launch, send forth, let fly; dash.

put –, set- in motion; set agoing, start; give -a start, – an impulse- to; push, impel &c. 276; trundle &c. (*set in rotation*) 312; expel &c. 297.

carry one off one's legs; put to flight.

Adj. propelled &c. *v.*; propelling &c. *v.*; pro-pulsive, -jectile.

285. [Motion given to an object situated behind.] **Traction.—N.** traction; drawing &c. *v.*; draught, pull, haul; rake; 'a long pull, a strong pull and a pull all together'; towage, haulage.

V. draw, pull, haul, lug, rake, drag, draggle, tug, tow, trail, trawl, train; take in tow.

wrench, jerk, twitch.

Adj. drawing &c. *v.*; tractive, tractile; ductile.

286. [Motion towards.] **Approach.— N.** approach, approximation, appropinquation; access; appulse; afflux, -ion; advent &c. (*approach of time*) 121; pursuit &c. 622; convergence &c. 290.

V. approach, approximate; near; get –, go –, draw- near; come, – near, – to close quarters; move –, set in- towards; drift; make up to; gain upon; pursue &c. 622; tread on the heels of; bear up; make the land; hug the -shore, – land.

Adj. approaching &c. *v.*; approximative; convergent; affluent; impending, imminent &c. (*destined*) 152.

Adv. on the road.

Int. come hither! approach! here! come! come near!

287. [Motion from.] **Recession.—N.** recession, retirement, withdrawal, retreat; retrocession &c. 283; departure &c. 293; recoil &c. 277; flight &c. (*avoidance*) 623.

V. recede, go, move from, retire, ebb, withdraw, shrink; come –, move –, go –, get –, drift- away; depart &c. 293; retreat &c. 283; move –, stand –, sheer-

off; swerve from; fall back, stand aside;
run away &c. (*avoid*) 623.

remove, shunt, side track, switch off.

Adj. receding &c. *v.*

288. [Motion towards, actively.] **Attraction.**—**N.** attract-ion, -iveness; pull;
drawing to, pulling towards, adduction,
magnetism, gravity, attraction of gravitation; lure, bait, decoy.

lode-stone, -star; magnet, siderite,
magnetite.

V. attract; draw –, pull –, drag- towards; adduce.

lure, bait, decoy.

Adj. attracting &c. *v.*; attrahent, attractive, adducent, adductive.

289. [Motion from, actively.] **Repulsion.**—**N.** repulsion; driving from &c.
v.; repulse; abduction.

V. repel; push –, drive – &c. 276;
from; chase, dispel; retrude; abduce,
abduct; send away, repulse, dismiss.

keep at arm's length, turn one's back
upon, give the cold shoulder; send packing; send -off, – away- with a flea in
one's ear, – about one's business.

Adj. repelling &c. *v.*; repellant, repulsive; abducent, abductive.

290. [Motion nearer to.] **Convergence.**—**N.** con-vergence, -fluence,
-course, -flux, -gress, -currence,
-centration; appulse, meeting; corradiation.

assemblage &c. 72; resort &c. (*focus*) 74; asymptote.

V. converge, concur; come together,
unite, meet, fall in with; close -with, –
in upon; centre -round, – in; enter in;
pour in.

gather together, unite, concentrate,
bring into a focus.

Adj. converging &c. *v.*; con-vergent,
-fluent, -current; centripetal; asymptotical.

291. [Motion further off.] **Divergence.**—**N.** diverg-ence, -ency; divarication, ramification, radiation; separation &c. (*disjunction*) 44; dispersion &c.

73; deviation &c. 279; aberration, declination.

V. diverge, divaricate, radiate; ramify; branch –, glance –, file- off; fly off,
– at a tangent; spread, scatter, disperse
&c. 73; deviate &c. 279; part &c. (*separate*) 44; splay apart.

Adj. diverging &c. *v.*; divergent, radiant, centrifugal; aberrant.

292. [Terminal motion at.] **Arrival.**—
N. arrival, advent; landing; de-, disembarkation; reception, welcome, *vin
d'honneur.*

home, goal, bourn; landing-place,
-stage; resting –, stopping -place; destination, harbour, haven, port; terminal,
terminus, railway station, depot, airport; halt, halting -place, – ground; anchorage &c. (*refuge*) 666.

return, recursion, remigration; meeting; ren-, en-counter.

completion &c. 729.

V. arrive; get to, come to; come;
reach, attain; come up, – with, – to;
overtake; make, fetch; complete &c.
729; join, rejoin.

light, alight, dismount; land, go
ashore; debark, disembark; put -in, –
into; visit, cast anchor, pitch one's tent;
sit down &c. (*be located*) 184; get to
one's journey's end; make the land; be
in at the death; come –, get- -back, –
home; return; come in &c. (*ingress*) 294;
make one's appearance &c. (*appear*)
446; drop in; detrain; outspan.

come to hand; come -at, – across; hit;
come –, light –, pop –, bounce –, plump
–, burst –, pitch- upon; meet; en- rencounter; come in contact.

Adj. arriving &c. *v.*; homeward-
bound; terminal.

Adv. here, hither.

Int. welcome! hail! all hail! good-day,
– morrow; greetings! hullo! well!

293. [Initial motion from.] **Departure.**—**N.** departure, decession, decampment; embarkation; take-off; outset, start; removal; exit &c. (*egress*) 295;
exodus, Hejira, flight.

leave-taking, *congé*, valediction,

valedictory, adieu, farewell, good-bye, stirrup-cup.

starting -point, – post; point –, place- of -departure; – embarkation; port of embarkation.

V. depart; go, – away; take one's de- parture, set out; set –, march –, put –, start –, be –, move –, get –, whip –, pack –, go –, take oneself- off; start, is- sue, march out, debouch; go –, sally- forth; sally, set forward; be gone.

leave a place, quit, vacate, evacuate, abandon; go off the stage, make one's exit; retire, withdraw, remove; go -one's way, – along, – from home; take -flight, – wing; spring, fly, flit, wing one's flight; fly –, whip- away; take off, hop off; embark; go -on board, – aboard; set sail; put –, go- to sea; sail, take ship; hoist blue Peter; get under way, weigh anchor; strike tents, break camp, de- camp; walk one's chalks, make tracks, cut one's stick; cut and run; take leave; say –, bid- -good-bye &c. *n.*; disappear &c. 449; abscond &c. (*avoid*) 623; en- train, embus, emplane; saddle –, har- ness –, hitch- up; inspan.

Adj. departing &c. *v.*; valedictory; outward bound.

Adv. whence, hence, thence; with a foot in the stirrup; on the -wing, – move.

Int. begone! &c. (*ejection*) 297; to horse! all aboard! farewell! adieu! good- bye, – day! *au revoir! auf wiedersehen!* fare you well! so long! God -bless you, – speed! *bon voyage!*

294. [Motion into.] **Ingress.—N.** in- gress; entrance, entry; introgression; in- flux; intrusion, inroad, incursion, inva- sion, irruption; pene-, interpenetration; illapse, import, importation, infiltra- tion; immigration; admission &c. (*re- ception*) 296; insinuation &c. (*interjac- ence*) 228; insertion &c. 300.

inlet; way in; mouth, door &c. (*open- ing*) 260; path &c. (*way*) 627; conduit &c. 350; immigrant, visitor, incomer, newcomer, colonist.

V. have the *entrée*; enter; go –, come –, pour –, flow –, creep –, slip –, pop

–, break –, burst- -into, – in; set foot on; burst –, break- in upon; invade, in- trude, butt in, horn in, crash; insinuate itself; inter-, penetrate; infiltrate; find one's way –, wriggle –, worm oneself- into.

give entrance to &c. (*receive*) 296; in- sert &c. 300.

Adj. incoming, ingressive &c. *n.*; in- ward bound.

Adv. inward.

295. [Motion out of.] **Egress.—N.** egress, exit, issue; emer-sion, -gence; disemboguement; out-break, -burst; e-, pro-ruption; emanation; evacuation; ex- , trans-udation; extravasation, perspira- tion, sweating, leakage, percolation, distillation, oozing; gush &c. (*water in motion*) 348; outpour, -ing; effluence, ef- fusion; efflux, -ion; drain; dribbling &c. *v.*; defluxion; drainage; out-come, -put; discharge &c. (*excretion*) 299.

export; expatriation; e-, re-migration; *débouche;* exodus &c. (*departure*) 293; emigrant, migrant, *émigré,* colonist.

outlet, vent, spout, tap, sluice, flood- gate; pore; vomitory, out-gate, sally- port; way out; mouth, door &c. (*open- ing*) 260; path &c. (*way*) 627; conduit &c. 350; air-pipe &c. 351.

V. emerge, emanate, issue; go –, come –, move –, pass –, pour –, flow- out of; pass off, evacuate; migrate.

ex-, trans-ude; leak; run, – out, – through; per-, trans-colate; seep; strain, distil; perspire, sweat, drain, ooze; fil- ter, filtrate; dribble, gush, spout, flow out; well, – out; pour, trickle &c. (*wa- ter in motion*) 348; effuse, extravasate, disembogue, discharge itself, debouch; come –, break- forth; burst- out, – through; find vent, escape &c. 671.

Adj. effused &c. *v.*; outgoing, out- ward bound.

Adv. outward.

296. [Motion into, actively.] **Recep- tion.—N.** reception; admission, admit- tance, *entrée,* importation; initia- tion; intro-duction, -mission, -ception; immission, ingestion, imbibition, absorption, ingurgitation, inhalation; suction, sucking; eating, drinking &c. (*food*)298; insertion &c. 300; interjection &c. 228.

V. give -entrance to, – admittance to, – the *entrée*; intro-duce, -mit; usher, admit, receive, import, initiate, bring in, open the door to, throw open, ingest, absorb, imbibe, inhale, infiltrate; let –, take –, suck- in; re-admit, -sorb, -absorb; snuff up; swallow, ingurgitate; engulf, engorge; gulp; eat, drink &c. (*food*) 298.

Adj. admit-ting &c. *v.*, -ted &c. *v.*; admissible; absorbent; introductory, introceptive, intromittent, initiatory.

297. [Motion out of, actively.] **Ejection.—N.** ejection, emission, effusion, rejection, expulsion, eviction, extrusion, trajection; discharge.

egestion, evacuation, vomition, disgorgement, voidance, eruption, eruptiveness; ruc-, eruc-tation, blood-letting, venesection, phlebotomy, paracentesis; tapping, drainage; clear-ance, -age, voidance; vomiting, excretion &c. 299.

deportation; banishment &c. (*punishment*) 972; rogue's march; relegation, extradition; dislodgment.

V. give -exit, – vent- to; let –, give –, pour –, send- out; des-, dis-patch; exhale, excern, excrete, disembogue, secrete, secern; extravasate, shed, void, evacuate, egest, emit; open the -sluices, – floodgates; turn on the tap; extrude, detrude; effuse, spend, expend; pour forth; squirt, spirt, spill, slop; perspire &c. (*exude*) 295; breathe, blow &c. (*wind*) 349.

tap, draw off; bale –, lade- out; let blood, broach.

eject, reject; expel, discard; cut, send to Coventry, boycott, ostracize; *chasser*; banish &c. (*punish*) 972; throw &c. 284 -out, – up, – off, – away, – aside; push &c. 276 -out, – off, – away, – aside; shovel –, sweep- -out, – away; brush –, whisk –, turn –, send- -off, – away; discharge; send –, turn –, cast- adrift; turn –, bundle- out; throw overboard; give the

sack to; send -packing, – about one's business, – to the right about; strike off the roll &c. (*abrogate*) 756; turn out- neck and heels, – head and shoulders, – neck and crop; pack off; send away with a flea in the ear; send to Jericho; bow out, show the door to, dismiss, fire, sack.

turn out of -doors, – house and home; evict, oust; exorcise, un-house, -kennel; dislodge; un-, dis-people; depopulate; relegate, deport.

empty; drain, – to the dregs; sweep off; clear, – off, – out, – away; suck, draw off, extract; clean out, make a clean sweep of, clear decks, purge.

em-, dis-, disem-bowel; eviscerate, gut; unearth, root -out, – up; averruncate; weed –, get out; eliminate, get rid of, do away with, shake off; exenterate.

vomit, spew, puke, keck, retch; belch, – out, eruct, eructate; cast –, bring- up; disgorge; expectorate, salivate, clear the throat, hawk, spit, sputter, splutter, slobber, drool, drivel, slaver, slabber.

unpack, unlade, unload, unship; break bulk.

be let out; ooze &c. (*emerge*) 295.

Adj. emitt-ing, -ed &c. *v.*

begone! get you gone! get –, go- -away, – along, – along with you! go your way! away, – with! off with you! go, – about your business! be off! avaunt! aroynt! get out!

298. [Eating.] **Food.—N.** eating &c. *v.*; deglutition, gulp, epulation, mastication, manducation, rumination, gastronomy, gastrology; panto-, hippo-, ichthyo-phagy &c.; gluttony &c. 957; carnivorousness, vegetarianism.

mouth, jaws, mandible, mazard, chops.

drinking &c. *v.*; potation, draught, libation; carousal &c. (*amusement*) 840; drunkenness &c. 959.

food, *pabulum*; aliment, nourishment, nutriment; susten-ance, -tation; nurture, subsistence, provender, feed, fodder, provision, ration, keep, commons, board; commissariat &c.

(*provision*) 637; prey, forage, pasture, pasturage; fare, cheer; diet, -ary; regimen; belly timber, staff of life; bread, -and cheese; proteins, carbohydrates, vitamins.

comestibles, eatables, victuals, edibles, *ingesta*; grub, prog, tack, hard tack, meat; bread, -stuffs; cereals; viands, cates, delicacy, dainty, creature comforts, contents of the larder, fleshpots; festal board; ambrosia; good -cheer, – living.

hors-d'œuvre; soup, pottage, *potage*, broth, *bouillon*, *consommé*, *purée*, *borsch*, stock, skilly, gumbo; fish, – cakes, – pie; joint, *rôti*, *pièce de résistance*, *relevé*, hash, *réchauffé*, stew, *ragoût*, fricassee, mince, *salim*, *goulash*, *bouillabaisse*, remove, *entrée*, *croquette*, *rissole*, sausage, curry, bubble and squeak; haggis, collops, giblets; poultry, game &c.; biscuit, bun, scone, rusk, pancake, pie, pastry, pasty, patty, *patisserie*, tart, turnover, *vol-au-vent*, *soufflé*, dumpling, pudding, duff, *compote*, fritters, cake, napoleon, blancmange, custard, jelly, jam, sweets &c. 396; *entremet*; oatmeal, porridge, hasty pudding, gruel; eggs, omelet, cheese, matzoon, savoury; vegetable, salad, *mayonnaise*, fruit; sauce, condiment &c. 393; kickshaws.

table, *cuisine*, bill of fare, *menu*, *table d'hôte*, ordinary, *à la carte*; cover.

meal, repast, feed, spread; mess; dish, plate, course, side dish; regale; regale-, refresh-, entertain-ment; refection, collation, picnic, feast, banquet, junket; breakfast; lunch, -eon; *déjeuner*, bever, tiffin, tea, dinner, supper, snack, whet, bait, dessert; pot-luck, *table d'hôte*, *dèjeuner à la fourchette*; hearty –, square –, substantial –, full- -meal; blow out; light refreshment; pemmican.

mouthful, bolus, gobbet, tit-bit, morsel, sop, sippet.

drink, beverage, liquor, broth, soup; potion, dram, draught, drench, swill; nip, peg, sip, sup, gulp.

wine, champagne, spirits, *liqueur*, beer, porter, stout, ale, malt liquor, julep, Sir John Barleycorn, stingo, heavy wet, bitter, lager-beer, cider; grog, toddy, flip, purl, punch, negus, cup, bishop, posset, wassail; bitters, *apéritif*, high-ball, cocktail; whisky, rum, absinthe; gin &c. (*intoxicating liquor*) 959; coffee, chocolate, cocoa, tea, *maté*, the cup that cheers but not inebriates.

eating-house &c. 189.

V. eat, feed, fare, devour, swallow, take; gulp, bolt, snap; fall to; despatch, dispatch; discuss; take –, get –, gulp-down; lay –, tuck- in; lick, pick, peck; gormandize &c. 957; bite, champ, munch, cranch, craunch, crunch, chew, masticate, nibble, gnaw, mumble.

live on; feed –, batten –, fatten –, feast- upon; browse, graze, crop, regale; carouse &c. (*make merry*) 840; eat heartily, do justice to, play a good knife and fork, banquet.

break -bread, – one's fast; breakfast, lunch, dine, take tea, sup.

drink, – in, – up, – one's fill; quaff, sip, sup; suck, – up; lap; swig; swill, tipple &c. (*be drunken*) 959; empty one's glass, drain the cup; toss -off, – one's glass; wash down, crack a bottle, wet one's whistle.

cater, purvey &c. 637.

Adj. eatable, edible, esculent, comestible, alimentary; cereal, cibarious; dietetic; culinary; nutri-tive, -tious; succulent; drinkable, pot-able, -ulent; bibulous.

omn-, carn-, herb-, frug-, gran-, gramin-, phyt-ivorus; ichthyophagous.

prandial.

299. Excretion.—N. excretion, discharge, emanation; ejection &c. 297; exhalation, exudation, extrusion, secretion, effusion, extravasation, *ecchymosis*, evacuation, cacation, defecation, dysentery, dejection, *fæces*, excrement; perspiration, sweat; sub-, exud-ation; *diaphoresis*; sewage.

saliva, spittle, rheum; ptyalism, salivation, catarrh, distemper; diarrhœa; *ejecta*, *egesta*, *sputum*, *sputa*; *excreta*; lava; *exuviæ* &c. (*uncleanness*) 653.

hemorrhage, bleeding; catamenia, menses; outpouring &c. (*egress*) 295; leucorrhea.

V. excrete &c. (*eject*) 297; emanate &c. (*come out*) 295.

Adj. excretory, fæcal, secretory; ejective, eliminant.

300. [Forcible ingress.] **Insertion.—N.** insertion, implantation, intercalation, embolism, introduction; interpolation, insinuation &c. (*intervention*) 228; planting &c. *v.*; injection, inoculation, importation, infusion; forcible -ingress &c. 294; immersion; submersion, -gence; dip, plunge; bath &c. (*water*) 337; interment &c. 363.

V. insert; intro-duce, -mit; put -, run-into; import; inject; interject &c. 228; infuse, instil, inoculate, impregnate, imbue, imbrue.

graft, ingraft, bud, plant, implant; dovetail.

obtrude; thrust -, stick -, ram -, stuff -, tuck -, press -, drive -, pop -, whip -, drop -, put- in; impact; empierce &c. (*make a hole*) 260.

embed; immerse, immerge, merge; bathe, soak &c. (*water*) 337; dip, plunge &c. 310.

bury &c. (*inter*) 363.

insert &c.-itself; plunge *in medias res*.

Adj. inserted &c. *v.*

301. [Forcible egress.] **Extraction.—N.** extraction; extracting &c. *v.*; removal, elimination, extrication, eradication, evolution.

evulsion, avulsion; wrench; expression, squeezing; extirpation, extermination; ejection &c. 297; export &c. (*egress*) 295; distillation.

extractor, corkscrew, forceps, pliers.

V. extract, draw, pit; take -, draw -, pull -, tear -, pluck -, pick -, get- out; wring from, wrench; extort; root -, weed -, grub -, rake- up, - out; eradicate; pull -, pluck- up by the roots; averruncate; unroot; uproot, pull up, extirpate, dredge.

remove; educe, elicit; evolve, extri-

cate; eliminate &c. (*eject*) 297; eviscerate &c. 297.

express, squeeze -, press- out; distil.

Adj. extracted &c. *v.*

302. [Motion through.] **Passage.—N.** passage, transmission; permeation; pene-, interpene-tration; transudation, infiltration; *osmosis*, osmose, endos-, exos-mose; intercurrence; ingress &c. 294; egress &c. 295; path &c. 627; conduit &c. 350; opening &c. 260; journey &c. 266; voyage &c. 267.

V. pass, - through; perforate &c. (*hole*) 260; penetrate, permeate, thread, thrid, enfilade; go -through, - across; go -, pass- over; cut across; ford, cross; pass and repass, work; make -, thread -, worm -, force- one's way; make -, force- a passage; cut one's way through; find its -way, - vent; transmit, make way, clear the course; traverse, go over the ground.

Adj. passing &c. *v.*; intercurrent; osmotic &c. *n.*

Adv. *en passant* &c. (*transit*) 270.

303. [Motion beyond.] **Overstep.—N.** trans-cursion, -ilience, -gression; infraction, intrusion; trespass; encroach-, infringe-ment; extravagation, transcendence; redundance &c. 641; ingress &c. 294.

V. transgress, surpass, pass; go- beyond, - by; show in -, come to the-front; shoot ahead of; steal a march -, gain- upon.

over-step, -pass, -reach, -go, -ride, -leap, -jump, -skip, -lap, -shoot the mark; out-strip, -leap, -jump, -go, -step, -run, -ride, -rival, -do; beat, - hollow; distance; leave in the -lurch, - rear; go one better, throw into the shade; exceed, transcend, surmount; soar &c. (*rise*) 305.

encroach, intrude, trespass, infringe, invade, trench upon, intrench on; strain; stretch -, strain- a point; pass the Rubicon.

Adj. surpassing &c. *v.*

Adv. beyond the mark, ahead.

304. [Motion short of.] **Shortcoming.—N.** shortcoming, failure; delinquency; falling short &c. *v.*; de-fault, -falcation; leeway; labour in vain, no go.

incompleteness &c. 53; imperfection &c. 651; insufficiency &c. 640; noncompletion &c. 730; failure &c. 732.

V. come -, fall -, stop- -short, - short of; not reach; want; keep within - bounds, - the mark, - compass.

break down, stick in the mud, collapse, come to nothing; fall -through, - to the ground, - down; cave in, end in smoke, fizzle out, miss the mark, fail; lose ground; miss stays, slump.

Adj. unreached; deficient; short, - of; *minus*; out of depth; perfunctory &c. (*neglect*) 460.

Adv. within -the mark, - compass, - bounds; behindhand; *re infectâ*; to no purpose; far from it.

Phr. the bubble burst.

305. [Motion upwards.] **Ascent.—N.** ascent, ascension; rising &c. *v.*; rise, upgrowth; leap &c. 309; acclivity, hill &c. 217; stair, stairs, stair-case, -way, flight of -steps, - stairs; ladder, companion, - way; lift, elevator &c. 307.

rocket, lark; sky-rocket, -lark; Alpine Club.

V. ascend, rise, mount, arise, uprise; go -, get -, work one's way -, start -, spring -, shoot- up; zoom; aspire.

climb, clamber, ramp, scramble, swarm, *escalade*, surmount; scale, - the heights.

tower, soar, hover, spire, plane, swim, float, surge; leap &c. 309.

Adj. rising &c. *v.*; scandent, buoyant; super-natant, -fluitant; excelsior.

Adv. uphill.

306. [Motion downwards.] **Descent.—N.** descent, descension, declension, declination; fall; falling &c. *v.*; drop, cadence; subsidence, lapse; comedown, downfall, tumble, slip, tilt, trip, lurch, cropper, *culbute*; titubation, stumble; fate of Icarus; dive, nose-dive, *volplané*.

avalanche, *débâcle*, landslip, slide.

declivity, dip, hill; decline, drop.

V. descend; go -, drop -, comedown; fall, gravitate, drop, slip, slide, glissade, dive, plunge, settle; decline, slump, set, sink, droop, come down a peg.

dismount, alight, light, get down; swoop; stoop &c. 308; fall prostrate, precipitate oneself; let fall &c. 308.

tumble, trip, stumble, titubate, lurch, pitch, swag, topple; topple -, tumble-down, - over; tilt, sprawl, plump down, come a cropper.

Adj. descending &c. *v.*; descendent, declivitous; downcast; decur-rent, sive; labent, deciduous; nodding to its fall.

Adv. down, -hill, -wards.

307. **Elevation.—N.** elevation; raising &c. *v.*; erection, lift; sublevation, upheaval; sublimation, exaltation; prominence &c. (*convexity*) 250.

lever &c. 633; crane, derrick, windlass, capstan, winch, dredger, lift, elevator, escalator, dumb waiter.

V. heighten, elevate, raise, lift, erect; set -, stick -, perch -, perk -, tilt- up; rear, hoist, heave; up-lift, -raise, -rear, -bear, -cast, -hoist, -heave; buoy, weigh, mount, give a lift; exalt, sublimate; place -, set- on a pedestal.

take -, drag -, fish- up; dredge.

stand -, rise -, get -, jump- up; spring to one's feet; hold -oneself, - one's head-up; draw oneself up to his full height.

Adj. elevated &c. *v.*; standing up; stilted, attollent, rampant.

Adv. on -stilts, - the shoulders of, - one's legs, - one's hind legs.

308. **Depression.—N.** lowering &c. *v.*; depression; dip &c. (*concavity*) 252; abasement; detrusion; reduction.

over-throw, -set, -turn; upset; prostration, subversion, precipitation.

bow; courtesy, curtsy; genuflexion, *kowtow*, obeisance, *salaam*.

V. depress, lower; let -, take- -down, - down a peg; cast; let -drop, - fall; sink, debase, bring low, abase, slash, reduce, detrude, pitch, precipitate.

over-throw, -turn, -set; upset, subvert,

prostrate, level, fell; cast –, take –, throw –, fling –, dash –, pull –, cut –, knock –, hew- down; raze, – to the ground; humiliate, trample in the dust, pull about one's ears.

sit, – down; couch, squat, crouch, stoop, bend, bow, courtsey, curtsy; bob, duck, dip, genuflect, kneel; *kowtow, salaam*, make obeisance, prostrate oneself; bend, bow- the -head, – knee; incline the head; bow down; cower; recline &c. (*be horizontal*) 213.

Adj. depressed &c. *v.*; at a low ebb; prostrate &c. (*horizontal*) 213; detrusive.

309. Leap.—N. leap, jump, hop, spring, bound, vault, saltation.

dance, caper, gambol; curvet, caracole; *gam-bade, -bado*; capriole, demivolt; buck, – jump; hop, skip and jump.

kangaroo, jerboa, chamois, goat, frog, grasshopper, flea.

V. leap; jump -up, – over the moon; hop, spring, bound, vault, ramp, cut capers, gambol, trip, skip, dance, caper; curvet, *caracole*; foot it, bob, bounce, flounce, start, frisk &c. (*amusement*) 840; jump about &c. (*agitation*) 315; trip it on the light fantastic toe, dance oneself off one's legs.

Adj. leaping &c. *v.*; saltatory, frisky.

Adv. on the light fantastic toe.

310. Plunge.—N. plunge, dip, dive, header; ducking &c. *v.*; submergence, immersion, diver.

V. plunge, dip, souse, duck; dive, plump; take a -plunge, – header, make a plunge; bathe &c. (*water*) 337.

sub-merge, -merse; immerse, douse, sink, engulf, send to -the bottom, – Davy Jones' locker.

get out of one's depth; go -to the bottom, – down like a stone; founder, welter, wallow.

311. [Curvilinear motion.] **Circuition.—N.** circuition, circulation; turn, curvet; excursion; circum-vention, -navigation, -ambulation; north-west

passage; ambit, gyre, lap, circuit &c. 629.

turning &c. *v.*; wrench; evolution; coil, helix, spiral; corkscrew.

V. turn, bend, wheel; go –, put-about; heel; go –, turn -round, – to the right about; turn on one's heel; make –, describe- a -circle, – complete circle; encircle; go –, pass- through -180°, – 360°.

circum-navigate, -aviate, -ambulate, -vent; put a girdle round the earth, go the round, make the round of.

turn –, round- a corner; double a point.

wind, circulate, meander; whisk, twirl; twist &c. (*convolution*) 248; make a *détour* &c. (*circuit*) 629.

Adj. turning &c. *v.*; circuitous; circum-foraneous, -fluent; devious, roundabout, circum-ambient, -flex, -navigable.

Adv. round about.

312. [Motion in a continued circle.] **Rotation.—N.** rotation, revolution, gyration, circulation, roll; circum-rotation, -volution, -gyration; volutation, circination, turbination, *pirouette*, convolution.

verticity; whir, whirl, swirl, eddy, vortex, whirlpool, gurge; cyclone, tornado; surge; *vertigo*, dizzy round; Maelstrom, Charybdis; Ixion; wheel of Fortune.

wheel, screw, propeller, whirligig, rolling stone, windmill; top, teetotum, merry-go-round; roller; cog-, fly-wheel; spit; jack; caster.

axis, axle, spindle, spool, pivot, pin, hinge, pole, swivel, gimbals, arbor, bobbin, mandrel, shaft.

[Science of rotatory motion] trochilics, gyrostatics.

V. rotate; roll, – along; revolve, spin; turn, – round; circumvolve; circulate, gyre, gyrate, wheel, whirl, swirl, twirl, trundle, troll, bowl; slew round.

roll up, furl; wallow, welter; box the compass; spin like a -top, – teetotum.

Adj. rotating &c. *v.*; rota-tory, -ry;

circumrotatory, trochilic, vertiginous, gyratory; vortic-al, -ose.

Adv. head over heels, round and round, like a horse in a mill.

313. [Motion in a reverse circle.] **Evolution.—N.** evolution, unfolding, development; eversion &c. (*inversion*) 218.

V. evolve; un-fold, -roll, -wind, -coil, -twist, -furl, -twine, -ravel; disentangle; develop.

Adj. evolving &c. *v.*; evolved &c. *v.*

314. [Reciprocating motion, motion to and fro.] **Oscillation.—N.** oscillation; vibration, libration; motion of a pendulum; nutation; undulation; pulsation; pulse; throb; seismic disturbance.

alternation; coming and going &c. *v.*; ebb and flow, flux and reflux, ups and downs; wave, vibratiuncle, swing, beat, shake, wag, see-saw, dance, lurch, dodge; fluctuation; vacillation &c. (*irresolution*) 605.

seismometer, vibroscope, seismograph.

V. oscillate; vi-, li-brate; alternate; undulate, wave; sway, rock, swing; pulsate, beat; wag, -gle; nod, bob, courtesy, curtsy; tick; play; chatter, wamble, wabble; teeter, dangle, swag.

fluctuate, dance, curvet, reel, quake; quiver, quaver, shake, flicker; wriggle; roll, toss, pitch; flounder, stagger, totter, waddle; move -, bob- up and down &c. *adv.*; pass and repass, ebb and flow, come and go, shuttle; vacillate &c. 605.

brandish, shake, flourish.

Adj. oscillating &c. *v.*; oscill-, undul-, puls-, libr-atory; vibrat-ory, -ile; pendulous, shutterwise, seismic.

Adv. to and fro, up and down, backwards and forwards, see-saw, zig-zag, wibble-wabble, in and out, from side to side, like buckets in a well.

315. [Irregular motion.] **Agitation.—N.** agitation, stir, tremor, shake, ripple, jog, jolt, jar, jerk, shock, succussion, trepidation, quiver, quaver, dance; jac-tit-ation, -ance; shuffling &c. *v.*; twitter, flicker, flutter.

disquiet, perturbation, commotion, turmoil, turbulence; tumult, -uation; hubbub, rout, bustle, fuss, racket, *subsultus*, staggers, megrims, epilepsy, fits, twitching, vellication, St. Vitus' dance.

spasm, throe, throb, palpitation, convulsion, paroxysm; tetanus.

disturbance &c. (*disorder*) 59, restlessness &c. (*changeableness*) 149.

ferment, -ation; ebullition, effervescence, hurly burly, *cahotage*; tempest, storm, ground swell, heavy sea, whirlpool, vortex &c. 312; whirlwind &c. (*wind*) 349.

V. be -agitated &c.; shake; tremble, – like an aspen leaf; quiver, quaver, quake, shiver, twitter, twire, dither, dodder; twitch, writhe, toss, shuffle, tumble, stagger, bob, reel, sway; wag, -gle, wiggle; wriggle, – like an eel; squirm; dance, stumble, shamble, flounder, totter, flounce, flop, curvet, prance.

throb, pulsate, beat, palpitate, go pit-a-pat; flutter, flitter, flicker, bicker; bustle.

ferment, effervesce, foam; boil, – over; bubble, – up; simmer.

toss -, jump- about; jump like a parched pea; shake like an aspen leaf; shake to its -centre, – foundations; be the sport of the winds and waves; reel to and fro like a drunken man; move -, drive- from post to pillar and from pillar to post; keep between hawk and buzzard.

agitate, shake, convulse, toss, tumble, bandy, wield, brandish, flap, flourish, whisk, jerk, hitch, jolt; jog, -gle; jostle, buffet, hustle, disturb, stir, shake up, churn, jounce, wallop, whip, vellicate.

Adj. shaking &c. *v.*; agitated, tremulous; de-, sub-sultory; shambling; giddy-paced, saltatory, convulsive, jerky, unquiet, restless, all of a twitter.

Adv. by fits and starts; subsultorily &c. *adj.*; *per saltum*; hop, skip and jump; in -convulsions, – fits, pit-a-pat.

CLASS III

WORDS RELATING TO MATTER

SECTION I. MATTER IN GENERAL

316. Materiality.—N. material-ity, -ness; materialization; corpor-eity, -ality; substantiality, material existence, incarnation, flesh and blood, *plenum*; physical condition.

matter, body, substance, brute matter, stuff, element, principle, protoplasm, plasma, *parenchyma*, material, *substratum*, hyle, *corpus*, *pabulum*; frame.

object, article, thing, something; still life; stocks and stones; materials &c. 635.

[Science of matter] physics; somatology, -ics; natural –, experimental-philosophy; physical science, *philosophie positive*, materialism, hylism; materialist, physicist.

V. materialize, incorporate, incarnate, substantiate, embody.

Adj. material, bodily; corpor-eal, -al; physical; somat-ic, -oscopic; sensible, tangible, ponderable, palpable, substantial; fleshly, incarnate.

objective, impersonal, neuter, unspiritual, materialistic.

317. Immateriality.—N. immateriality, -ness; incorporeity, dematerialization, unsubstantiality, spirituality; inextension; astral plane.

personality; I, myself, me; *ego*, spirit &c. (*soul*) 450; astral body; immaterialism; spiritual-ism, -ist; subliminal –, subconscious- self.

V. disembody, spiritualize, dematerialize.

Adj. immateri-al, -ate; incorpor-eal, -al; asomatous, unextended; un-, disembodied; extramundane, supersensi-ble, unearthly; pneumatoscopic; spiritual &c. (*psychical*) 450; aery.

personal, subjective.

318. World.—N. world, creation, nature, universe; earth, globe, wide world; *cosmos*; terraqueous globe, sphere; macro-, mega-cosm; music of the spheres.

heavens, sky, welkin, empyrean; starry -heaven, – host; firmament; vault –, canopy- of heaven; celestial spaces.

heavenly bodies, stars, luminaries, nebulæ; galaxy, milky way, galactic circle, *via lactea*.

sun, orb of day, Apollo, Phœbus; photo-, chromo-sphere; solar system; planet, -oid, asteroid; comet; satellite; moon, orb of night, Diana, Luna; aerolite, meteor; falling –, shooting- star; meteorite.

constellation, zodiac, signs of the zodiac, Charles's wain, Great Bear, Southern Cross, Orion's belt, Cassiopeia's chair, Pleiades &c.

colures, equator, ecliptic, orbit.

[Science of heavenly bodies] astronomy; urano-graphy, -logy; cosmo-logy, -graphy, -gony; *eidouranion*, orrery; geography; geodesy &c. (*measurement*) 466; star-gazing, -gazer; astronomer; cosmogonist, geodesist, geographer; observatory.

Adj. cosmic, cosmical, mundane; terr-estrial, -estrious, -aqueous, -ene, -eous; telluric, earthly, geotic, geodetic, cosmogonal, under the sun; sub-lunary, -astral.

solar, heliacal; lunar; celestial,

heavenly, empyreal, sphery; starry, stellar; sider-eal, -al; astral; nebular.

Adv. in all creation, on the face of the globe, here below, under the sun.

319. Gravity.—N. gravi-ty, -tation; weight; heaviness &c. *adj.*; specific gravity; ponderosity, pressure, load; burden, -then; ballast, counterpoise; lump -, mass -, weight- of.

lead, millstone, mountain, Ossa on Pelion.

weighing, ponderation, trutination; weights; avoirdupois -, troy -, apothecaries'- weight; grain, scruple, drachm, ounce, pound, lb., load, stone, hundredweight, cwt., ton, quintal, carat, pennyweight, tod, gramme, kilogramme &c.

[Weighing instrument] balance, scales, steelyard, beam, weighbridge, spring balance, weighing machine.

[Science of gravity] statics.

V. be -heavy &c. *adj.*; gravitate, weigh, press, cumber, load.

[Measure the weight of] weigh, poise.

Adj. weighty; weighing &c. *v.*; heavy, - as lead; ponder-ous, -able; lump-ish, -y; cumber-, burden-some; cumbrous, unwieldy, massive.

in-, superin-cumbent.

320. Levity.—N. levity; lightness &c. *adj.*; imponderability, imponderables, buoyancy, volatility.

feather, dust, mote, down, thistle-down, flue, cobweb, gossamer, straw, cork, bubble; float, buoy; ether, air.

leaven, ferment, barm, yeast, enzyme.

V. be -light &c. *adj.*; float, swim, be buoyed up.

render -light &c. *adj.*; lighten, levitate; leaven.

Adj. light, subtile, subtle, airy; imponder-ous, -able; astatic, weightless, ethereal, sublimated; uncompressed, volatile; buoyant, floating &c. *v.*; barmy, frothy; portable.

light as -a feather, - thistle down, - air.

fermenting &c. *n.*

SECTION II. INORGANIC MATTER

1°. SOLID MATTER

321. Density.—N. density, solidity; solidness &c. *adj.*; impenetra-, impermeability; incompressibility; imporosity; cohesion &c. 46; constipation, consistence, spissitude.

specific gravity; hydro-, areo-meter.

condensation; solid-ation, -ification; consolidation; concretion, caseation, coagulation; petrifaction &c. (*hardening*) 323; crystallization, precipitation; deposit, precipitate, silt; inspissation; thickening &c. *v.*

indivisibility, indiscerptibility, indissolvableness.

solid body, mass, block, knot, lump; con-cretion, -crete, -glomerate; cake,

clot, stone, curd, coagulum, grume; bone, gristle, cartilage.

V. be -dense &c. *adj.*; become -, render- solid &c. *adj.*; solid-ify, -ate; concrete, set, take a set, consolidate, congeal, coagulate; curd, -le; fix, clot, cake, candy, precipitate, deposit, cohere, crystallize; petrify &c. (*harden*) 323.

condense, thicken, inspissate, incrassate; compress, squeeze, ram down, constipate.

Adj. dense, solid; solidified &c. *v.*; cohe-rent, -sive &c. 46; compact, close, serried, thickset; substantial, massive, lumpish; impenetrable, impermeable, imporous; incompressible; constipated; concrete &c. (*hard*) 323; knot-ted, -ty; gnarled; crystal-line, -lizable; thick, grumous, stuffy.

un-dissolved, -melted, -liquefied, -thawed.

in-divisible, -discerptible, -frangible, -dissolvable, -dissoluble, -soluble, -fusible.

322. Rarity.—N. rarity; tenuity; absence of -solidity &c. 321; subtility; sponginess, compressibility.

rarefaction, expansion, dilatation, inflation, subtilization.

ether &c. (*gas*) 334.

V. rarefy, expand, dilate, subtilize, attenuate, thin.

Adj. rare, subtile, thin, fine, tenuous, compressible, flimsy, slight; light &c. 320; cavernous, spongy &c. (*hollow*) 252.

rarefied &c. *v.*; unsubstantial; uncompact, -pressed.

323. Hardness.—N. hardness &c. *adj.*; rigidity, renitence, inflexibility, temper, callosity, durity.

induration, petrifaction; lapidification, -escence; vitri-, ossi-, cornification; crystallization.

stone, pebble, flint, marble, rock, fossil, crag, crystal, quartz, granite, adamant; bone, cartilage; heart of oak, block, board, deal board; iron, steel; cast -, wrought- iron; nail; brick, concrete; cement.

V. render -hard &c. *adj.*; harden, stiffen, indurate, petrify, temper, ossify, vitrify.

Adj. hard, rigid, stubborn, stiff, firm; starch, -ed; stark, unbending, unlimber, unyielding; inflexible, tense; indurate, -d; gritty, proof.

adamant-ine, -ean; concrete, stony, rocky, lithic, granitic, vitreous; crystalline; horny, corneous; bony; oss-eous, -ific; cartilaginous; hard as a -stone &c. *n.*; stiff as -buckram, - a poker.

324. Softness.—N. softness, pliableness &c. *adj.*; flexibility; pli-ancy, -ability; sequacity, malleability; flabbiness; duct-, tract-ility; extend-, extensibility; plasticity; inelasticity, flaccidity, laxity.

clay, wax, butter, dough, pudding; cushion, pillow, feather-bed, pad, down, padding, wadding.

mollification; softening &c. *v.*

V. render -soft &c. *adj.*; soften, mollify, mellow, relax, temper; mash, knead, squash, *massage*.

bend, yield, relent, relax, give.

Adj. soft, tender, supple; pli-ant, -able; flex-ible, -ile; lithe, -some; lissom, limber, plastic; ductile, tract-ile, -able; malleable, extensile, sequacious, inelastic, mollient.

yielding &c. *v.*; flabby, limp, flimsy.

flaccid, flocculent, downy; spongy, œdematous, medullary, doughy, argillaceous, mellow.

soft as -butter, - down, -silk; yielding as wax; tender as a chicken.

325. Elasticity.—N. elasticity, springiness, spring, resilience, renitency, buoyancy.

india-rubber, caoutchouc, guttapercha, whalebone, gum elastic.

V. be -elastic &c. *adj.*; spring back &c. (*recoil*) 277.

Adj. elastic, tensile, springy, ductile, resilient, renitent, buoyant.

326. Inelasticity.—N. want of-, absence of- elasticity &c. 325; inelasticity &c. (*softness*) 324.

Adj. inelastic &c. (*soft*) 324.

327. Tenacity.—N. tenacity, toughness, strength; cohesion &c. 46; sequacity; stubbornness &c. (*obstinacy*) 606; viscidity &c. 352.

leather; gristle, cartilage.

V. be -tenacious &c. *adj.*; resist fracture.

Adj. tenacious, tough, cohesive, adhesive, strong, resisting, sequacious, stringy, gristly, cartilaginous, leathery, coriaceous, tough as whit-leather; stubborn &c. (*obstinate*) 606.

328. Brittleness.—N. brittleness &c. *adj.*; frag-, friab-, frangib-, fiss-ility; frailty; house of -cards, – glass.

V. be -brittle &c. *adj.*; live in a glass house.

break, crack, snap, split, shiver, splinter, crumble, break short, burst, fly, give way; fall to pieces; crumble -to, – into- dust.

Adj. breakable, brittle, frangible, fragile, frail, friable, delicate, gimcrack, shivery, fissile; splitting &c. *v.*; lacerable, splintery, crisp, crimp, short, brittle as glass.

329. [Structure.] Texture.—N. structure, organization, anatomy, frame, mould, fabric, construction; framework, carcass, architecture; stratification, cleavage.

substance, stuff, *compages*, *parenchyma*; constitution, staple, organism.

[Science of structures] organ-, oste-, my-, splanchn-, neur-, angi-, adenology; angi-, aden-ography.

texture; inter-, con-texture; tissue, grain, web, surface; warp and -woof, – weft; tooth, nap &c. (*roughness*) 256; fineness –, coarseness- of grain.

[Science of textures] histology.

Adj. structural, organic; anatomic, -al.

text-ural, -ile; fine-, coarse-grained; fine, delicate, subtile, gossamery, filmy; coarse; home-spun; linsey-woolsey.

330. Pulverulence.—N. [State of powder.] pulverulence; sandiness &c. *adj.*; efflorescence; friability.

powder, dust, sand, shingle; sawdust; grit; attrition; meal, bran, flour, *farina*, spore, sporule; crumb, seed, grain; particle &c. (*smallness*) 32; thermion; limature, filings, *débris*, *detritus*, scobs, magistery, fine powder; *flocculi*.

smoke; cloud of -dust, – sand, –

smoke; puff –, volume -of smoke; sand –, dust- storm.

[Reduction to powder] pulverization, comminution, attenuation, granulation, disintegration, subaction, contusion, trituration, levigation, abrasion, detrition, multure; limation; filing &c. *v.*

[Instruments for pulverization] mill, millstone, grater, rasp, file, pestle and mortar, nutmeg grater, teeth, molar, grinder, chopper, grindstone, kern, quern, muller.

V. come to dust; be -disintegrated, – reduced to powder &c.

reduce –, grind- to powder; pulverize, comminute, granulate, triturate, levigate; scrape, file, abrade, rub down, grind, grate, rasp, pound, bray, bruise; con-tuse, -tund; beat, crush, cranch, craunch, crunch, muller, scranch, crumble, disintegrate; attenuate &c. 195.

Adj. powdery, pulverulent, granular, mealy, floury, farinaceous, branny, furfuraceous, flocculent, dusty, sandy, sabulous; aren-ose, -arious, -aceous; gritty; efflorescent, impalpable.

pulverizable; friable, crumbly, shivery; pulverized &c. *v.*; attrite; in pieces.

331. Friction.—N. friction, attrition; rubbing &c. *v.*; erasure; con-frication, -trition, affriction, abrasion, arrosion, limature, frication, rub; elbow-grease; rosin; *massage*.

V. rub, scratch, abrade, scrape, scrub, fray, rasp, graze, curry, scour, polish, rub out, erase, gnaw; file, grind &c. (*reduce to powder*) 330; *massage*.

set one's teeth on edge; rosin.

Adj. anatriptic, abrasive.

332. [Absence of friction. Prevention of friction.] Lubrication.—N. smoothness &c. 255; unctuousness &c. 355.

lubri-cation, -fication; anointment; oiling &c. *v.*

synovia; lubricant, graphite, glycerine, oil &c. 356; saliva; lather.

V. lubri-cate, -citate; oil, grease, lather, soap; wax.

Adj. lubricated &c. *v.*

2°. FLUID MATTER

1. *Fluids in General*

333. Fluidity.—N. fluidity, liquidity; liquidness &c. *adj.*; gaseity &c. 334; liquefaction &c. 334.

fluid, inelastic fluid; liquid, liquor; lymph, humour, juice, sap, serum, blood, serosity, gravy, rheum, ichor, sanies.

solu-bility, -bleness.

[Science of liquids] hydro-logy, -statics, -dynamics, hydraulics &c.

V. be -fluid &c. *adj.*; flow &c. (*water in motion*) 348; liquefy &c. 335.

Adj. liquid, fluid, serous, juicy, succulent, sappy; fluent &c. (*flowing*) 348. liquefied &c. 335; uncongealed; soluble, hydrostatic &c. *n.*

334. Gaseity.—N. gaseity, gaseousness; vapourousness &c. *adj.*; flatulence, -lency; volatility, aeration, gasification.

elastic fluid, gas, air, vapour, ether, steam, fume, reek, *effluvium, flatus*; cloud &c. 353.

[Science of elastic fluids] pneumat-ics, -ostatics; aero-statics, -dynamics &c.

gas-, gaso-meter.

V. gassify, aerate, aerify; emit vapour &c. 336.

Adj. gaseous, aeriform, ethereal, aerial, airy, vaporous, volatile, evaporable; flatulent; aerostatic &c. *n.*

335. Liquefaction.—N. liquefaction; liquescen-ce, -cy, deliquescence; melting &c. (*heat*) 384; colliqu-ation, -efaction; thaw; de-, liquation; lixiviation, dissolution.

solution, apozem, lixivium, infusion, decoction, flux.

solvent, diluent, menstruum, alkahest, *aqua fortis*.

V. render -liquid &c. 333; liquefy, run, deliquesce; melt &c. (*heat*) 384; solve; dissolve, resolve; liquate; hold in solution; leach, lixiviate.

Adj. lique-fied &c. *v.*, -scent, -fiable; deliquescent, soluble, colliquative; solvent.

336. Vaporization.—N. vapor-, volatilization; gasification; e-, vaporation; distillation, cohobation, sublimation, exhalation; volatility.

vaporizer, still, retort, spray, atomizer; fumigation, steaming.

V. render -gaseous &c. 334; vaporize, volatilize; distil, sublime; evaporate, exhale, smoke, transpire, emit vapour, fume, reek, steam, fumigate.

Adj. volatilized &c. *v.*; reeking &c. *v.*; volatile; evaporable, vaporizable.

2. *Specific Fluids*

337. Water.—N. water; serum, serosity; lymph; rheum; diluent.

dilution, maceration, lotion; washing &c. *v.*; im-, mersion; humectation, infiltration, spargefaction, affusion, irrigation, *douche*, balneation, bath.

deluge &c. (*water in motion*) 348; high water, flood-, spring-tide.

V. be -watery &c. *adj.*; reek.

add water, water, wet; moisten &c. 339; dilute, dip, immerse; merge; im-, sub-merge; plunge, souse, duck, drown; soak, steep, macerate, pickle, wash, sprinkle, sparge, lave, bathe, affuse, splash, swash, douse, slosh, drench; dabble, slop, slobber, irrigate, inundate, deluge; syringe, inject, gargle; infiltrate, percolate.

Adj. watery, aqueous, aquatic, lymphatic; balneal, diluent; drenching &c. *v.*; diluted &c. *v.*; weak; wet &c. (*moist*) 339.

Phr. the waters are out.

338. Air.—N. air &c. (*gas*) 334; common -, atmospheric- air; atmosphere, stratosphere, isothermal layer, troposphere, Heaviside layer.

open, - air; sky, welkin; blue, - sky; cloud &c. 353.

weather, climate, rise and fall of the barometer, isobar.

[Science of air] pneumatics,

aero-logy, -scopy, -graphy; meteorology, climatology; eudio-, baro-, aero-meter; aneroid, baro-graph, -scope; weather-gauge, -glass, -cock.

exposure to the -air, – weather; ventilation; aero-station, -nautics, -naut &c. 265 and 269.

V. air, ventilate; fan &c. (*wind*) 349.

Adj. containing air, flatulent, effervescent; windy &c. 349.

atmospheric, airy; aeri-al, -form; pneumatic; meteorological; weatherwise.

Adv. in the open air, out of doors, *à la belle étoile, al fresco; sub -Jove, -dio.*

339. Moisture.—N. moisture; moistness &c. *adj.*; hum-idity, -ectation; madefaction, dew; *serein*; marsh &c. 345; Hygromet-ry, -er.

V. moisten, wet; humect, -ate; sponge, damp, dampen, bedew; imbue, imbrue, infiltrate, saturate; seethe, sop; soak, drench &c. (*water*) 337.

be -moist &c. *adj.*; not have a dry thread; perspire &c. (*exude*) 295.

Adj. moist, damp; watery &c. 337; undried, humid, wet, dank, muggy, dewy; roric; roscid; juicy.

wringing wet; wet -through, – to the skin; saturated &c. *v.*

swashy, soggy, dabbled; reeking, seething, dripping, soaking, soft, sodden, sloppy, muddy; swampy &c. (*marshy*) 345; irriguous.

340. Dryness.—N. dryness &c. *adj.*; siccity, aridity, drought, ebb-, neap-tide, low water.

drying, ex-, de-siccation; evaporation; dehydration; arefaction, dephlegmation, drainage.

drier, desiccator.

V. be -dry &c. *adj.*; render -dry &c. *adj.*; dry; dry –, soak- up; sponge, swab, wipe; ex-, de-siccate, dehydrate, anhydrate; drain, parch.

be fine, hold up.

Adj. dry, anhydrous, arid, waterless; dried &c. *v.*; undamped; juice-, sap-less; sear; husky; rainless, without rain, fine;

dry as -a bone, – dust, – a stick, – a mummy, – a biscuit; desiccated; dehydrated; water-proof, -tight.

341. Ocean.—N. sea, ocean, main, deep, brine, salt water, waters, waves, billows, high seas, offing, great waters, watery waste, 'vasty deep,' briny ocean, herring pond, steamer track, the seven seas; wave, tide &c.(*water in motion*) 348.

hydrograph-y, -er, oceanography; Neptune, Thetis, Triton, Naiad, Nereid; sea-nymph, Siren, mer-maid, -man; trident, dolphin.

Adj. oceanic; mar-ine, -itime; pleagic, -ian; sea-going, -worthy; hydrographic.

Adv. at –, on- sea; afloat, on the high seas.

342. Land.—N. land, earth, ground, dry land, *terra firma*.

continent, mainland, peninsula, delta; tongue –, neck- of land; isthmus; oasis; promontory &c. (*projection*) 250; highland &c. (*height*) 206.

coast, shore, scar, strand, beach; bank, lea; seaboard, -side, -shore, -bank, -coast, -beach; rock-, iron-bound coast; loom of the land; derelict; innings; *alluvium*, alluvion.

soil, glebe, clay, loam, marl, cledge, chalk, gravel, mould, subsoil, clod, clot; rock, crag, cliff.

acres; real estate &c. (*property*) 780; landsman, land-lubber, farmer.

geography &c. 318; agriculture &c. 371.

V. land, come to land; set foot on -the soil, – dry land; come –, go- ashore.

Adj. earthy; continental, midland; littoral, riparian, ripuarian; alluvial; terrene &c. (*world*) 318; landed, predial, territorial.

Adv. ashore; on -shore, – land.

343. Gulf. Lake.—N. land covered with water, gulf, gulph, bay, inlet, bight, estuary, arm of the sea, fiord, armlet; frith, firth, ostiary, mouth; lagune, lagoon; indraught; cove, creek; natural harbour; roads; strait, narrows; Euripus; sound, belt, gut, kyles.

lake, loch, lough, mere, tarn, plash, broad, pond, pool, lin, puddle, well, artesian well, tank, sump; standing -, dead -, sheet of- water; fish -, mill-pond; race; ditch, dike, dyke, dam; reservoir &c. (*store*) 636.
Adj. lacustrine; land locked.

344. Plain.—N. plain, table land, mesa, face of the country; open -, champaign-country; basin, downs, waste, weary waste, desert, tundra, wild, steppe, pampas, savanna, prairie, champaign, heath, common, wold, veld; moor, -land, uplands, fell; bush; *plateau* &c. (*level*) 213; *campagna.*

meadow, mead, haugh, pasturage, park, field, lawn, green, plat, plot, grass-plat, greensward, sward, grass, turf, sod, heather; lea, ley, lay; grounds.
Adj. campestrian, champaign, alluvial.

345. Marsh.—N. marsh, swamp, morass, marish, moss, fen, bog, quagmire, slough, sump, wash; mud, squash, slush.
Adj. marsh, -y; swampy, boggy, plashy, poachy, quaggy, soft; muddy, sloppy, squashy, spongy; paludal; moorish, -y; fenny.

346. Island.—N. island, isle, islet, eyot, ait, holm, reef, atoll, breaker; archipelago; islander.
Adj. insular, sea-girt.

3. *Fluids in Motion*

347. [Fluid in motion.] **Stream.—N.** stream &c. (*of water*) 348, (*of air*) 349.
V. flow &c. 348; blow &c. 349.

348. [Water in motion.] **River.—N.** running water.

jet, spirt, squirt, spout, splash, swash, rush, gush, *jet d'eau;* sluice, chute.

water-spout, -fall; fall, cascade, force, foss; lin, -n; ghyll, Niagara; cata-ract, -dupe, -clysm; *débâcle,* inundation, deluge.

rain, -fall; *serein;* shower, scud; downpour, cloud burst; driving -, pouring -, drenching- rain; hyeto-logy, -graphy; rainy season, monsoon; predominance of Aquarius, reign of St. Swithin; mizzle, drizzle, *stillicidium,* plash; dropping &c. *v.*

stream, course, flux, flow, profluence; effluence &c. (*egress*) 295; defluxion; flowing &c. *v.*; current, tide, race.

spring; fount, -ain; rill, rivulet, gill, gullet, rillet; stream-, brook-let; runnel, sike, burn, beck, brook, stream, river; reach; tributary.

body of water, torrent, rapids, flush, flood, swash, spate; spring -, high -, full-tide; bore; eagre, *hygre;* fresh, -et; undertow, indraught, reflux, undercurrent, eddy, vortex, gurge, whirlpool, Maelström, regurgitation, overflow; confluence, corrivation.

wave, billow, surge, swell, ripple; roller, ground swell, surf, breaker, white horses; comber, beach-comber; rough -, heavy -, cross -, long -, short -, chopping -, choppy- sea, choppiness; tidal wave.

[Science of fluids in motion] Hydrodynamics; Hydraul-ics &c.; rain-gauge &c.

water-bearer, - carrier, Aquarius.

irrigation &c. (*water*) 337; pump; watering-pot, - cart; hydrant, standpipe, hose, sprinkler, drencher; fire-engine, squirt, syringe.

V. flow, run; meander; gush, pour, spout, roll, jet, well, issue; drop, drip, dribble, plash, squirt, spurt, spirtle, trill, trickle, distil, percolate; stream, over-flow, inundate, deluge, flow over, splash, swash; guggle, murmur, babble, bubble, purl, gurgle, sputter, regurgitate; ooze, flow out &c. (*egress*) 295.

rain, - hard, - in torrents, - cats and dogs, - pitchforks; come down in sheets; pour with rain, drizzle, mizzle, spit, sprinkle, set in.

flow -, fall -, open -, drain- into; discharge itself, disembogue.

[Cause a flow] pour; pour out &c.

(*discharge*) 297; shower down; irrigate, drench &c. (*wet*) 337; spill, splash.

[Stop a flow] stanch; dam, -up &c. (*close*) 261; obstruct &c. 706.

Adj. fluent; dif-, pro-, af-fluent; tidal; flowing &c. *v.*; meand-ering, -ry, -rous; fluvi-al, -atile; streamy, showery, rainy, drizzly, drizzling, pluvial, pluviose, stillicidous.

349. [Air in motion.] **Wind.—N.** wind, draught, *flatus*, *afflatus*, air; breath, - of air; puff, whiff, zephyr; blow, drift; *aura*; stream, current; under-current.

gust, blast, breeze, squall, gale, half a gale, storm, tempest, hurricane, whirlwind, tornado, samiel, cyclone, typhoon; simoon; harmattan, monsoon, trade wind, sirocco, *mistral*, *bise*, *föhn*, tramontane, levanter; capful of wind; fresh -, stiff- breeze; keen blast; blizzard.

windiness &c. *adj.*; ventosity; rough -, dirty -, ugly -, stress of- weather; dirty-, windy-, mackerel- sky; mare's tail; thick -, black -, white- squall.

anemography, aerodynamics; wind-gauge, anemometer, weather-cock, vane.

suf-, insuf-, per-, in-, af-flation; blowing, fanning &c. *v.*; ventilation.

sneezing &c. *v.*; sternutation; hiccup, -cough; catching of the breath; breathing &c.

Eolus, Eurus, Boreas, Zephyr, cave of Eolus.

air-pump, lungs, bellows, blow-pipe, fan, blower; pulmotor, ventilator, punkah, aspirator, exhauster, ejector.

V. blow, waft; blow -hard, - great guns, - a hurricane &c. *n.*; whistle, roar, howl, ring in the shrouds; stream, issue.

respire, breathe, in-, ex-hale, puff; whif, -fle; gasp, wheeze; snuff, -le; sniff, -le; sneeze, cough, belch.

fan, ventilate; in-, per-flate; blow -, pump- up.

Adj. blowing &c. *v.*; windy, airy, æolian, flatulent; breezy, gusty, squally;

stormy, tempestuous, blustering; boisterous &c. (*violent*) 173.

pulmon-ic, -ary.

350. [Channel for the passage of water.] **Conduit.—N.** conduit, channel, duct, watercourse, race; head -, tail-race; adit, aqueduct, canal, trough, flume, gutter, pantile; dike, canyon, ravine, gorge, hollow, main, gully, moat, ditch, drain, sewer, culvert, *cloaca*, sough, kennel, siphon, *piscina*; pipe &c. (*tube*) 260; funnel; tunnel &c. (*passage*) 627; water -, waste- pipe; emunctory, gully-hole, artery, aorta, vein, blood vessel; lymphatic; throat, alimentary canal, intestine; pore, spout, scupper; ad-, a-jutage; hose; gar-, gur-goyle; penstock, weir; flood-, water-gate; sluice, lock, valve; rose; waterworks.

Adj. vascular &c. (*with holes*) 260.

351. [Channel for the passage of air.] **Air-pipe.—N.** air-pipe, - shaft, - way, - passage, - tube; shaft, flue, chimney, funnel, vent, blow-hole, nostril, nozzle, throat, weasand, *trachea*; *bronch-us, -ia*; larynx, tonsils, wind-pipe, spiracle; venti-duct, -lator; louvre, Venetian blinds; blow-pipe &c. (*wind*) 349; pipe &c. (*tube*) 260.

3°. IMPERFECT FLUIDS

352. Semiliquidity.—N. semiliquidity; stickiness &c. *adj.*; visc-idity, -osity; gumm-, glutin-, muc-osity; spiss-, crassitude; lentor; adhesiveness &c. (*cohesion*) 46.

inspiss-, incrass-ation; thickening, coagulation.

jelly, aspic, mucilage, gelatin, isinglass; colloid, mucus, phlegm; pituite, lava; glair, starch, gluten, albumen, milk, cream, protein; syrup, treacle; gum, size, glue, paste; wax, bee's-wax; emulsoid, emulsion, soup; squash, mud, slush, slime, ooze; moisture &c. 339; marsh &c. 345.

V. inspiss-, incrass-ate; coagulate,

gelatinize, gelatinify, gel, jell, emulsify, thicken; mash, squash, churn, beat up.

Adj. semi-fluid, -liquid; half-melted, -frozen; milky, muddy &c. *n.*; lact-eal, -ean, -eous, -escent, -iferous; emulsive, curdled, thick, succulent, uliginous.

gelat-, album-, mucilag-, glut-inous; gelatine, mastic, amylaceous, ropy, clammy, clotted; vis-cid, -cous; sticky, tacky; slab, -by; lentous, pituitous; mucid, -culent, -cous.

353. [Mixture of air and water.] Bubble. [Cloud.]—N. bubble; foam, froth, head, fume, spume, lather, suds, spray, surf, yeast, barm, spindrift.

cloud, vapour, fog, mist, haze, steam; scud, rack, *nimbus*; *cumulus*, woolpack, *cirrus*, *stratus*; *cirro-*, *cumulo-stratus*; *cirro-cumulus*; mackerel sky, mare's tail, dirty sky.

[Science of clouds] nephelognosy, nephology.

effervescence, fermentation; bubbling &c. *v.*

nebula; cloudiness &c. (*opacity*) 426; nebulosity &c. (*dimness*) 422.

V. bubble, boil, foam, froth, spume, mantle, sparkle, guggle, gurgle; effervesce, ferment, fizzle; aerate; cloud, overcast, befog.

Adj. bubbling &c. *v.*; frothy, nappy, effervescent, sparkling, *mousseux*, up, fizzy, with a head on.

cloudy &c. *n.*; vaporous, nebulous, overcast; nubiferous, nephological; foggy, brumous.

354. Pulpiness.—N. pulpiness &c.

adj.; pulp, paste, dough, sponge, curd, pap, rob, jam, pudding, mush, fool, poultice, grume.

Adj. pulpy &c. *n.*; pultaceous, grumous.

V. pulp, pulpify, mash.

355. Unctuousness.—N. unctuousness &c. *adj.*; unctuosity, lubricity; ointment &c. (*oil*) 356; anointment; lubrication &c. 332.

V. oil &c. (*lubricate*) 332.

Adj. unctuous, oily, oleaginous, adipose, sebaceous; fat, -ty; greasy; waxy, butyraceous, soapy, saponaceous, pinguid, lardaceous; slippery.

356. Oil.—N. oil, fat, butter, cream, grease, tallow, suet, lard, dripping, margarine, oleomargarine, exunge, blubber; glycerine, stearine, elaine, oleagine; soap; soft soap, wax, cement; paraffin, spermaceti, adipocere; petroleum, mineral –, rock –, crystal- oil, kerosene, vegetable –, colza –, olive –, linseed –, cotton seed –, rape –, nut –, fusel- oil; animal –, neat's foot –, signal –, train-oil; ointment, unguent, liniment, salve, pomade, pomatum, brilliantine, spike –, nard.

356a. Resin.—N. resin, rosin, colophony; gum; lac, shellac, sealing-wax; amber, -gris; bitumen, pitch, tar, asphalt, -e, -um; varnish, copal, mastic, magilp, lacquer, japan.

V. varnish &c. (*overlay*) 223.

Adj. resinous, bituminous, pitchy, tarry.

SECTION III. ORGANIC MATTER

1°. VITALITY

1. *Vitality in General*

357. Organization.—N. organized -world, – nature; living –, animated- nature; living beings; organic remains, organism; fossils; animal and vegetable kingdom, *fauna* and *flora*, biota.

prot-oplasm, -ein; albumen; structure
&c. 329; organ-ization, -ism.

[Science of living beings] biology;
natural history,* organic -, bio-
chemistry, anatomy, physiology, embryology, morphology, evolution, Darwinism, Lamarkism, zoology &c. 368; botany &c. 369; naturalist, biologist &c.

Adj. organ-ic, -ized.

358. Inorganization.—N. mineral
-world, - kingdom; unorganized -, in-
organic -, brute -, inanimate- matter.

[Science of the mineral kingdom]
mineralogy; geo-logy, -gnosy, -scopy;
metall-urgy, -ography; lithology; oryc-
to-logy, -graphy.

V. turn to dust, pulverize.

Adj. in-organic, -animate; unorganized; azoic; mineral.

359. Life.—N. life; vi-tality, -ability;
animation; vital -spark, - flame, - force.

respiration, wind; breath -of life, - of
one's nostrils; life-blood; Archeus; existence &c. 1.

vivification, vitalization; revivifica-
tion &c. 163; Prometheus; life to come
&c. (*destiny*) 152.

[Science of life] physiology, etiology,
embryology, biology; animal economy.

nourishment, staff of life &c. (*food*)
298.

V. be -alive &c. *adj.*; live, breathe,
respire; subsist &c. (*exist*) 1; walk the
earth; strut and fret one's hour upon a
stage; be spared.

see the light, be born, come into the
world; fetch -, draw- -breath, - the
breath of life; quicken; revive; come to,
- life.

give birth to &c. (*produce*) 161; bring
to life, put into life, vitalize; vivi-fy,
-ficate; reanimate &c. (*restore*) 660; keep
-alive, - body and soul together, - the
wolf from the door; support life.

have nine lives like a cat.

---

* The term *Natural History* is also used as relating to all the objects in Nature whether organic
or inorganic, and including therefore *Mineralogy,
Geology, Meteorology,* &c.

Adj. living, alive; in -life, - the flesh,
- the land of the living; on this side of
the grave, above ground, breathing,
quick, animated, viable; lively &c. (*active*) 682; alive and kicking; tenacious of
life.

vital; vivi-fying, -fied &c. *v.*; Promethean.

Adv. *vivendi causâ.*

360. Death.—N. death, dying &c. *v.*;
de-cease, -mise; dissolution, departure,
obit, release, rest, *quietus*, fall; loss, bereavement.

end &c. 67 -, cessation &c. 142 -,
loss -, extinction -, ebb- of -life &c.
359.

death-warrant, -watch, -rattle, -bed;
stroke -, agonies -, shades -, valley of
the shadow -, jaws -, hand- of death;
last -breath, - gasp, - agonies; dying-
day, - breath, - agonies; swan song,
chant du cygne; *rigor mortis*; Stygian
shore; crossing the bar, the great adventure.

King -of terrors, - Death; Death, Angel of Death; mortality; doom &c. (*necessity*) 601.

euthanasia; happy release; break up
of the system; natural -death, - decay;
sudden -, violent- death; untimely end,
watery grave; suffocation, *asphyxia*;
heart failure; fatal disease &c. (*disease*)
655; death-blow &c. (*killing*) 361.

necrology, bills of mortality, obituary; death-song &c. (*lamentation*) 839.

V. die, expire, perish; meet one's
-death, - end; pass away, be taken; yield
-, resign- one's breath; resign one's
-being, - life; end one's -days, - life, -
earthly career; breathe one's last; cease
to -live, - breathe; depart this life; be
-no more &c. *adj.*; go -, drop -, pop
-off; lose -, lay down -, relinquish -,
surrender- one's life; drop -, sink- into
the grave; close one's eyes; fall -, drop-
dead, - down dead; break one's neck;
give -, yield- up the ghost; be all over
with one.

pay the debt to nature, shuffle off this
mortal coil, take one's last sleep; go the

way of all flesh; join the -greater number, - majority, - choir invisible, to life immortal awake; come -, turn- to dust; cross the Stygian ferry; go to -one's long account, - one's last home, - Davy Jones's locker, - the wall; receive one's death warrant, make one's will, die a natural death, go out like the snuff of a candle; come to an untimely end; catch one's death; go off the hooks, kick the bucket, peg out; go West; hop the twig, turn up one's toes; die a violent death &c. (*be killed*) 361; make the supreme sacrifice.

Adj. dead, lifeless; deceased, demised, departed, defunct; late, gone, no more; ex-, in-animate; out of the world, taken off, released; departed this life &c. *v.*; dead and gone; bereft of life, stone dead, dead as -a door nail, - a door post, - mutton, - a herring, - nits; launched into eternity, gathered to one's fathers, numbered with the dead, gone to a better land, behind the veil, beyond the grave, - mortal ken.

dying &c. *v.*; mori-bund, -ent, Acherontic; hippocratic; *in -articulo, - extremis*; in the -jaws, - agony- of death; going, - off; *aux abois*; on one's last legs, - death bed; at -the point of death, - death's door, - the last gasp; near one's end, given over, booked, fey; with one foot in -, tottering on the brink of- the grave.

still-born; mortuary; deadly &c. (*killing*) 361.

Adv. *post -obit, - mortem.*

Phr. life -ebbs, - fails, - hangs by a thread; one's -days are numbered, - hour is come, - race is run, - doom is sealed; Death -knocks at the door, - stares one in the face; the breath is out of the body; the grave closes over one; *sic itur ad astra*.

361. [Destruction of life; violent death.] **Killing.—N.** killing &c. *v.*; homicide, manslaughter, murder, assassination, trucidation, occision; lynching, effusion of blood; blood, -shed;

gore, slaughter, carnage, butchery; *battue*, gladiatorial combat.

massacre; *fusillade, noyade, pogrom*; thuggism; racketeering.

death blow, finishing stroke, *coup de grâce, quietus*; execution &c. (*capital punishment*) 972; judicial murder; martyrdom.

butcher, slayer, murderer, Cain, assassin, cut-throat, garrotter, *bravo*, thug, racketeer, gunman, mobster, gangster, Moloch, *matador, sabreur; guet-à-pens*; gallows, executioner &c. (*punishment*) 975; man-eater.

regicide, parricide, fratricide, infanticide, aborticide &c.

suicide, *felo de se, suttee, hara kiri*, Juggernaut; immolation, holocaust.

suffocation, strangulation, *garrotte*; hanging &c. *v.*

deadly weapon &c. (*arms*) 727; Aceldama; the potter's field, the field of blood.

fatal accident, violent death, casualty.

[Destruction of animals] slaughtering; phthiozoics;* sport, -ing; the chase, venery; hunting, coursing, shooting, fishing; pig-sticking; sports-, hunts-, fisher-man; hunter, Nimrod; slaughterer, knacker, slaughter-house, shambles, *abattoir*.

V. kill, put to death, slay, shed blood; murder, assassinate, butcher, slaughter; victimize, immolate; massacre; take away -, deprive of- life; make away with, put an end to; despatch, dispatch; burke settle, do, - to death, - for.

strangle, garrotte, hang, lynch, throttle, choke, stifle, suffocate, stop the breath, smother, asphyxiate, drown.

sabre; cut -down, - to pieces, - the throat; jugulate; stab, run through the body, bayonet; put to the -sword, - edge of the sword.

shoot, - dead; blow one's brains out; brain, knock on the head; stone, lapidate; give -, deal- a death blow; give a *-quietus, - coup de grâce*.

behead, bowstring &c. (*execute*) 972.

---

* Bentham, 'Chrestomathia.'

hunt, shoot &c. *n.*

cut off, nip in the bud, launch into eternity, send to one's last account, bump off, rub out, sign one's death warrant, strike the death knell of.

give no quarter, pour out blood like water; decimate; run amuck, wade knee-deep –, imbrue one's hands- in blood.

die a violent death, welter in one's blood; dash –, blow- out one's brains; commit suicide; kill –, -make away with –, put an end to- oneself.

Adj. killing &c. *v.*; murd-, slaughterous; sanguin-ary, -olent; blood-stained, -thirsty; homicidal, red-handed; bloody, -minded; ensanguined, gory, sanguineous.

mortal, fatal, lethal; dead-, death-ly; mort-, leth-iferous; unhealthy &c. 657; internecine; suicidal.

sporting; piscator-ial, -y.

Adv. in at the death.

362. Corpse.—N. corpse, corse, carcass, bones, skeleton, dry-bones; defunct, relics, *relinquiæ*, remains, mortal remains, dust, ashes, earth, clay; mummy; carrion; food for- worms, – fishes; tenement of clay, this mortal coil.

shade, ghost, *manes*, apparition &c. 980.

organic remains, fossils.

Adj. cadaverous, corpse-like; unburied &c. 363.

363. Interment.—N. interment, burial, inhumation, sepulture, entombment; in-, humation; obs-, ex-equies; funeral, wake, pyre, funeral pile; cremation.

funeral -rite, – solemnity; knell, passing bell, tolling; dirge &c. (*lamentation*) 839; cypress; *obit*, dead march, muffled drum; coroner, mortician, undertaker, mute, mourner, professional mourner, pall-bearer; elegy; funeral -oration, – sermon; epitaph.

grave clothes, shroud, winding-sheet, cere-cloth; cerement.

coffin, shell, sarcophagus, urn, pall, bier, hearse, catafalque, cinerary urn.

grave, pit, sepulchre, tomb, vault, crypt, catacomb, mausoleum, *Golgotha*,

house of death, narrow house, long home; cemetery, necropolis, boneyard; burial-place, -ground; grave-, churchyard; God's acre; mortuary, tope, cromlech, dolmen, menhir, barrow, tumulus, cairn; ossuary; bone-, charnel-, deadhouse; *Morgue*; lich-gate; crematorium.

sexton, grave-digger.

monument, memorial, cenotaph, shrine; grave-, head-, tomb-stone; *memento mori*; hatchment, stone, cross.

exhumation, disinterment; necropsy, autopsy, *post-mortem* examination.

V. inter, bury; lay in –, consign to- the -grave, – tomb; en-, in-tomb; inhume; lay out, prepare for burial, embalm, mummify; conduct a funeral, hold services; toll the knell; put to bed with a shovel.

exhume, disinter, unearth.

Adj. buried &c. *v.*; burial; fune-real, -brial; mortuary, sepulchral, cinerary; elegiac; necroscopic.

Adv. *in memoriam*; *post-obit, -mortem*; beneath –, under- the sod.

Phr. *hic jacet, ci-git, requiescat in pace.*

2. Special Vitality

364. Animality.—N. animal life; anima-tion, -lity, -lization; breath.

flesh, – and blood; corporeal nature; *physique*; strength &c. 159.

V. animalize, incorporate.

Adj. fleshly, incarnate, carnal, corporeal, human.

365. Vegetability.—N. vegetable life; vegeta-tion, -bility; herbage.

V. vegetate, germinate, sprout, shoot; cultivate.

Adj. vegetable &c. 367; rank, lush.

366. Animal.—N. animal, – kingdom; *fauna*; brute creation.

beast, brute, creature, created being; creeping –, living- thing; dumb -animal, – creature.

flocks and herds, live stock; domestic –, wild- animals; game, *feræ naturæ*;

beasts of the field, fowls of the air, denizens of the day.

vertebrate, bi-, quadru-ped, mammal, marsupial, bird, reptile, batrachian, amphibian, fish, crustacean, shell fish, articulate, mollusc, worm, insect, zoophyte; protozoon, animalcule &c. 193.

horse &c. (*beast of burden*) 271; cattle, kine, ox; bull, -ock; steer, stot; cow, milch-cow, calf, heifer, shorthorn; sheep; lamb, -kin; ewe -, pet- lamb; ewe, ram, tup; pig, swine, boar, hog, shoat, sow; tag, teg, wether.

dog, bitch, hound; pup, -py; whelp, cur, mutt, mongrel; house-, watch-, sheep-, shepherd's-, sporting-, fancy-, lap-, toy-, bull-, badger-dog; mastiff; blood-, grey-, stag-, deer-, fox-, otterhound; harrier, beagle, spaniel, pointer, setter, retriever; Newfoundland; water-dog, -spaniel; pug, poodle; dachshund; Pinscher; turnspit; terrier; fox -, Skye-terrier; Dandie Dinmont; colley.

cat; puss, -y; kitten; grimalkin; gib-, tom-cat; mouser; fox, Reynard, vixen, stag, deer, hart, buck, doe, roe, antelope.

bird; poultry, fowl, cock, hen, chicken, chanticleer, partlet, rooster, dunghill cock, barn-door fowl; feathered - tribes, - songster; singing -, dicky- bird; canary; finch; auk, dodo, moa, roc, phœnix.

snake, serpent, viper, adder; newt, eft; asp, vermin.

Adj. animal, zoological.

equine, bovine, vaccine, canine, feline; fishy; piscator-y, -ial; molluscous, vermicular.

367. Vegetable.—N. vegetable - kingdom; *flora*, vendure.

plant; tree, shrub, bush; creeper; vine; herb, -age; grass.

annual; per-, bi-, tri-ennial; exotic.

timber; primeval -, virgin- forest; wood, -lands; hurst, frith, holt, weald, park, chase, greenwood, brake, grove, copse, coppice, *bocage*, *tope*, clump of trees, thicket, spinet, spinney; under-, brush-wood; boscage, scrub; the oak and the ash and the bonny ivy tree.

bush, jungle, prairie; heath, -er; fern, bracken; furze, gorse, whin broom; grass, turf, grassland, greensward, green, lawn, meadow; pas-ture, -turage; turbary; sedge, rush, weed; fungus, mushroom, toadstool; lichen, moss, conferva, mould; seaweed &c.; growth, crop.

foliage, leafage, branch, bough, ramage; spray &c. 51; leaf, frond, flag, petal, shoot, tendril.

flower, blossom, bud, bloom, bine; flowering plant; tree, sapling, pollard; timber-, fruit-tree; palm-, gum-tree; pulse, legume.

Adj. veget-able, -ous; herb-aceous, -al; botanic; sylvan, silvan; arbor- ary, -eous, -escent, -ical; dendritic, dendriform; woody, grassy; ver-dant, -durous; floral, mossy; lign-ous, -eous; wooden, leguminous; end-, ex-ogenous.

368. [The science of animals.] **Zoology.—N.** zoo-logy, -nomy, -graphy, -tomy; anatomy; comparative anatomy; animal -, comparative- physiology; morphology.

anthrop-, ornith-, ichthy-, herpet-, ophi-, malac-, helminth-, entom-, oryct-, paleont-ology; ichthy- &c. -otomy; taxidermy.

zo- &c. -ologist.

Adj. zoological &c. *n.*

369. [The science of plants.] **Botany.—N.** botany; phyto-graphy, -logy, -tomy; vegetable physiology, herborization, dendr-, myc-, fung-, alg-ology; flora, pomona; botanist &c.; botanic garden &c. (*garden*) 371; *hortus siccus*, *herbarium*, herbal.

herb-ist, -arist, -alist, -orist, -arian &c.

V. botanize, herborize.

Adj. botanical &c. *n.*

370. [The economy or management of animals.] **Cicuration.—N.** taming &c. *v.*; cicuration, zoohygiantics;

domestication, -ity; *manège*; veterinary art; breeding, pisciculture, apiculture &c.

menagery, vivarium, zoological garden, zoo; bear-pit; aviary, apiary, hive; aquarium, fishery, fish hatchery; duck-, fish-pond; stud-farm; stock farm, dairy. [Destruction of animals] phthisozoics* &c. (*killing*) 361.

neat-, cow-, shep-herd, shepherdess; grazier, drover, cowboy, cowkeeper; trainer, breeder, groom, ostler &c. 746; veterinary surgeon, vet, horse doctor; farrier; keeper; game keeper.

cage &c. (*prison*) 752; hen-coop, bird-cage, cauf; sheep-fold &c (*inclosure*) 232.

V. tame, domesticate, acclimatize, breed, tend, break in, train, corral, round up; cage, bridle &c. (*restrain*) 751; ride &c. 266.

drive, yoke, harness, hitch; groom, curry-comb; milk; shear; hatch; incubate.

Adj. pastoral, bucolic; tame, domestic, domesticated, broken in, gentle, docile.

371. [The economy or management of plants.] **Agriculture.**—**N.** agriculture, cultivation, husbandry, farming; georgics, geoponics; tillage, tilth, agronomy, gardening, spade husbandry, vintage; hort-, arbor-, silv-, citr-, vit-, floriculture; intensive culture; landscape gardening; forestry, afforestation.

husbandman, horticulturist, citriculturist, gardener, florist; agricult-or, -urist; yeoman, farmer, cultivator, tiller of the soil, ploughman, sower, reaper; woodcutter, backwoodsman, forester; vine grower, vintager; Boer; Triptolemus.

field, meadow, garden; botanic -, winter -, ornamental -, flower -, kitchen -, truck -, market -, hop- garden; nursery; green-, hot-, glass-house; conservatory, cucumber frame, *cloche*, bed, border, seed-plot; grass-plat, lawn; park &c. (*pleasure ground*) 840; *parterre*,

shrubbery, plantation, avenue, *arboretum*, pinery, *pinetum*, orchard; vineyard, vinery; orangery; farm &c. (*abode*) 189.

V. cultivate; till, - the soil; farm, garden; sow, plant; reap, mow, cut; manure, dress the ground, dig, delve, dibble, hoe, plough, plow, harrow, rake, weed, lop and top, force, transplant, thin out, bed out, prune, graft.

Adj. agr-icultural, -arian, -estic.

arable; predial, rural, rustic, country, bucolic, Bœotian; horticultural.

372. Mankind.—**N.** man, -kind; human -race, - species, - nature; humanity, mortality, flesh, generation.

[Science of man] anthropo-logy, -graphy, -sophy; ethno-logy, -graphy; humanitarianism.

human being; person, -age; individual, creature, fellow creature, mortal, body, somebody, one; such a -, someone; soul, living soul; earthling; party, head, hand; *dramatis personæ*.

people, persons, folk, public, society, world; community, - at large; general public; nation, -ality; state, realm; common-weal, -wealth; republic, body politic; million &c. (*commonalty*) 876; population &c. (*inhabitant*) 188.

cosmopolite; lords of the creation; ourselves.

Adj. human, mortal, personal, individual, national, civic, public, cosmopolitan; anthropoid.

373. Man.—**N.** man, male, he; manhood &c. (*adolescence*) 131; gentleman, sir, master; yeoman, wight, swain, fellow, guy, blade, *beau*, chap, gaffer, good man; husband &c. (*married man*) 903; Mr., mister, *monsieur*, *sahib*, *Herr*, señor, *signor*; boy &c. (*youth*) 129; Adonis.

[Male animal] cock, drake, gander, dog, boar, stag, hart, buck, horse, entire horse, stallion; gib-, tom-cat; he-, Billy-goat; ram, tup; bull, -ock; capon, ox, gelding; steer, stot.

Adj. male, he, masculine; manly, virile; un-womanly, -feminine.

* Bentham.

374. Woman.—N. woman, she, female, petticoat, skirt, moll, broad.

feminality, femininity, muliebrity; womanhood &c. (*adolescence*) 131; feminism; gynecology, gyniatrics, gynics.

womankind; the -sex, – fair; fair –, softer- sex; weaker vessel; the distaff side.

dame, madam, *madame*, mistress, Mrs., lady, *mem-sahib*, *Frau*, *señora*, *signora*, *donna*, *belle*, matron, dowager, goody, gammer; good -woman, – wife; squaw; wife &c. (*marriage*) 903; matronage, -hood.

Venus, nymph, wench, *grisette*; little bit of fluff; girl &c. (*youth*) 129.

inamorata (love) &c. 897; courtesan &c. 962.

spinster, old maid, virgin, bachelor girl, new woman, amazon.

[Female animal] hen, slut, bitch, sow, doe, roe, mare; she-, Nanny-goat; ewe, cow; lioness, tigress; vixen.

gynecœum, harem, *seraglio*, *zenana*, *purdah*.

Adj. female, she; feminine, womanly, ladylike, matronly, maidenly; womanish, effeminate, unmanly, gynecic.

2°. SENSATION

(1.) *Sensation in General*

375. Physical Sensibility.—N. sensibility; sensitiveness &c. *adj.*; physical sensibility, feeling, perceptivity, anaphylaxis, susceptibility, æsthetics; moral sensibility &c. 822.

sensation, impression, effect; consciousness &c. (*knowledge*) 490.

external senses.

V. be -sensible &c. *adj.* -of; feel, perceive.

render, -sensible &c. *adj.*; excite, stir, sharpen, cultivate, tutor.

cause sensation, impress; excite –, produce- an impression.

Adj. sens-ible, -itive,-uous; æsthetic, perceptive, sentient; conscious &c.

(*aware*) 490; impressionable, responsive, alive to.

acute, sharp, keen, vivid, lively, impressive, thin-skinned.

Adv. to the quick.

376. Physical Insensibility.—N. insensibility, physical insensibility; obtuseness &c. *adj.*; palsy, paralysis, *ana esthesia*, *analgesia*, *narcosis*, *hypnosis*, twilight sleep, stupor, coma, trance, catalepsy; sleep &c. (*inactivity*) 683; moral insensibility &c. 823; numbness &c. 381.

anæsthetic agent, general –, local- anæsthetic, opium, ether, chloroform, cocaine, novocaine, chloral; nitrous oxide, laughing gas; refrigeration.

V. be -insensible &c. *adj.*; have a -thick skin, – rhinoceros hide.

render -insensible &c. *adj.*; blunt, pall, obtund, benumb, deaden, paralyze; anæsthetize, drug, dope; put under the influence of -chloroform &c. *n.*; hypnotize; stupefy, stun, narcotize.

Adj. insensible, unfeeling, senseless, comatose, dazed, impercipient, callous, thick-skinned, pachydermatous; hard, -ened; case-hardened; proof; obtuse, dull; anæsthetic; paralytic, palsied, numb, dead.

377. Physical Pleasure.—N. pleasure; physical -, sensual -, sensuous- pleasure; bodily enjoyment, animal gratification, sensuality; hedonism, luxuriousness &c. *adj.*; dissipation, round of pleasure; titillation, *gusto*, creature comforts, comfort, ease; pillow &c. (*support*) 215; luxury, lap of luxury; purple and fine linen; bed of -down, – roses; velvet, clover; cup of Circe &c. (*intemperance*) 954.

treat; diversion, divertisement, entertainment; refreshment, regale; feast; *délice*; dainty &c. 394; *bonne bouche*.

source of pleasure &c. 829; happiness &c. (*mental enjoyment*) 827.

V. feel -, experience -, receive- pleasure; enjoy, relish; luxuriate -, revel -, riot -, bask -, swim -, wallow-in; feast on; gloat -over, – on; smack the lips.

live -on the fat of the land, – in comfort &c. *adv.*; bask in the sunshine, *faire ses choux gras*.

give pleasure &c. 829.

Adj. enjoying &c. *v.*; luxurious, voluptuous, sensual, hedonistic, comfortable, cosy, snug, in comfort, at ease.

agreeable &c. 829; grateful, refreshing, comforting, cordial, genial; sensuous; palatable &c. 394; sweet &c. (*sugar*) 396; fragrant &c. 400; melodious &c. 413; lovely &c. (*beautiful*) 845.

Adv. in -comfort &c. *n.*; on -a bed of roses &c. *n.*; at one's ease.

378. Physical Pain.—N. pain; suffering, -ance; bodily – physical- -pain, – suffering; mental suffering &c. 828; dolour, ache, aching &c. *v.*; smart; shoot, -ing; twinge, twitch, gripe, head-, ear-, tooth-ache; *migraine*, neuralgia, neuritis, lumbago, gout, sciatica; hurt, cut; sore, -ness; discomfort, *malaise*; *tic douloureux*.

spasm, cramp; nightmare, *ephialtes*; crick, stitch, kink; thrill, convulsion, throe; throb &c. (*agitation*) 315; pang.

sharp -, piercing -, throbbing -, shooting -, gnawing -, burning- pain; anguish, agony.

torment, torture; rack; cruci-ation, -fixion; martyrdom; martyr, toad under a harrow, vivisection.

V. feel -, experience -, suffer -, undergo- pain &c. *n.*; suffer, ache, smart, bleed; tingle, shoot; twinge, twitch, lancinate; writhe, wince, make a wry face; sit on -thorns, – pins and needles.

give -, inflict- pain; pain, hurt, chafe, sting, bite, gnaw, gripe, stab, grind; pinch, tweak; grate, gall, fret, prick, pierce, wring, convulse; torment, torture; rack, agonize; crucify; ex-, cruci-ate; break on the wheel, put to the rack; flag &c. (*punish*) 972; grate on the ear &c. (*harsh sound*) 410.

Adj. in -pain &c. *n.*, – a state of pain; pained &c. *v.*

painful; aching &c. *v.*; biting, poignant; sore, raw, tender, with exposed nerve.

(2.) *Special Sensation*

1. Touch

379. [Sensation of pressure.] **Touch.—N.** touch; tact, -ion, -ility; feeling; palp-ation, -ability; manipulation; brush, tick, graze, contact &c. 199.

[Organ of touch] hand, finger, forefinger, thumb, paw, feeler, *antenna*.

V. touch, feel, handle, finger, thumb, paw, fumble, grope, grabble; twiddle, tweedle; pass -, run- the fingers over, massage, rub, knead; palpate, stroke, manipulate, wield; throw out a feeler.

Adj. tact-ual, -ile; tangible, palpable; lambent.

380. Sensations of Touch.—N. itching &c. *v.*; titillation, formication, *aura*.

V. itch, tingle, creep, thrill, sting; prick, -le; tickle, titillate.

Adj. itching &c. *v.*

381. [Insensibility to touch.] **Numbness.—N.** numbness &c. (*physical insensibility*) 376; pins and needles.

local anæsthetic, cocaine, novocaine &c.; morphia.

V. benumb &c. 376; freeze, dull, deaden.

Adj. numb; benumbed &c. *v.*; intangible, impalpable.

2. Heat

382. Heat.—N. heat, caloric; temperature, warmth, fervour, calidity; incal-, incand-, recal-, decal-escence; glow, flush, blush; fever, hectic.

phlogiston; fire, spark, scintillation, flash, flame, blaze; arc; bonfire; firework, pyrotechny; wild-fire; sheet of fire, lambent flame; devouring element; conflagration.

summer, dog-days, canicule; baking &c. 384 -, white -, tropical -, Afric -, Bengal -, summer -, blood- heat; heat wave, sirocco, simoon; broiling sun; isolation; warming &c. 384.

sun &c. (*luminary*) 423; fire worshipper &c. 991; furnace &c. 386.

geyser, hot spring, volcano.
[Science of heat] pyrology; thermology, -otics; thermometer &c. 389.

V. be -hot &c. *adj.*; glow, incandesce, flush, sweat, swelter, bask, smoke, reek, stew, simmer, seethe, boil, burn, singe, scorch, scald, grill, broil, blaze, flame; smoulder; parch, fume, pant.

heat &c. (*make hot*) 384; thaw, fuse, melt, give.

Adj. hot, heated, warm, mild, genial, tepid, lukewarm, unfrozen; therm-al, -ic; calorific; ferv-ent, -id; ardent; aglow.

sunny, torrid, tropical, estival, canicular; close, sultry, stifling, stuffy, suffocating, oppressive; reeking &c. *v.*; baking &c. 384.

red -, white -, smoking -, burning &c. *v.* -, piping- hot; like -a furnace, - an oven; hot as -fire, - pepper; hot enough to roast an ox.

fiery; incand-, incal-escent; candent, ebullient, glowing, smoking; on fire; blazing &c. *v.*; in -flames, - a blaze; alight, afire, ablaze; un-quenched, -extinguished; smouldering; in a -heat, - glow, - fever, - perspiration, - sweat; sudorific; swelter-ing, -ed; blood-hot, -warm; warm as -a toast, - wool; recalescent, thermogenic, pyrotechnic, feverish, febrile, inflamed.

volcanic, plutonic, igneous; isothermal, -mic, -al.

Phr. Not a breath of air.

383. Cold.—N. cold, -ness &c. *adj.*; frigidity, gelidity, algidity, inclemency, *fresco*.

winter; depth of -, hard- winter; Siberia, Nova Zembla; Ant-, arctic; North -, South- Pole.

ice; snow, - flake, - crystal, - drift; sleet; hail, -stone; rime, frost; hoar -, white -, hard -, sharp -, frost; icicle, thick-ribbed ice; fall of snow, snow storm, heavy fall, *avalanche*; ice-berg, -floe; floe, berg; *glacier*; *nevée, serac*.

[Sensation of cold] chilliness &c. *adj.*; chill; shivering &c. *v.*; goose-skin, -flesh; *rigor*, horripilation, chattering of teeth; frostbite, chilblain.

V. be -cold &c. *adj.*; shiver, starve, quake, shake, tremble, shudder, didder, quiver; perish with cold; chill &c. (*render cold*) 385.

Adj. cold, cool; chill, -y; gelid, frigid, algid; fresh, keen, bleak, raw, inclement, bitter, biting, niveous, cutting, nipping, piercing, pinching; clay-cold; starved &c. (*made cold*) 385; shivering &c. *v.*; aguish, *transi de froid*; frostbitten, -bound, -nipped.

cold as -a stone, - marble, - lead, - iron, - a frog, - charity, - Christmas; cool as -a cucumber, - custard.

icy, glacial, frosty, freezing, wintry, brumal, hibernal, boreal, arctic, antarctic, polar, Siberian, hyemal; hyperborean, -al; ice-bound; frozen out.

un-warmed, -thawed, -heated; isocheimal, -chimenal.

Adv. coldly, bitterly &c. *adj.*; *à pierre fendre*.

384. Calefaction.—N. increase of temperature; heating &c. *v.*; cale-, tepe-, torre-faction; melting, fusion; liquefaction &c. 335; burning &c. *v.*; kindling, combustion; in-, ac-cension; con-, cremation; scorification; cauter-y, -ization; ustulation, calcination; in-, cineration; cupellation; carbonization.

ignition, inflammation, adustion, flagration; de-, con-flagration; empyrosis, incendiarism; arson; *auto da fé*; suttee.

boiling &c. *v.*; coction, ebullition, estuation, elixation, decoction.

furnace &c. 386; blanket, flannel, fur, muffler, wrap; wadding &c. (*lining*) 224; clothing &c. 225.

match &c. (*fuel*) 388; incendiary, pyromaniac; *pétroleur, pétroleuse*; cauterant, caustic, lunar caustic, apozem, moxa.

sunstroke, *coup de soleil*; insolation, sunburn.

pottery, ceramics, crockery, porcelain, china; earthen-, stone-ware; pot, mug, *terra-cotta*, brick, clinker; cinder, ash, *scoriae*; embers, dress, slag, products of combustion, coke, carbon, charcoal.

inflamma-, combusti-bility.

[Transmission of heat] diathermancy, transcalency.

V. heat, warm, chafe, stive, foment; make -hot &c. 382; sun oneself, bask in the sun.

fire; set -fire to, - on fire; kindle, enkindle, light, ignite, strike a light; apply the -match, - torch- to; re-kindle, -lume; fan -, add fuel to- the flame; poke -, stir -, blow- the fire; make a bonfire of; burn at the stake.

melt, thaw, fuse; liquefy &c. 335.

burn, inflame, roast, toast, fry, grill, singe, parch, bake, torrefy, scorch; brand, cauterize, sear, burn in; corrode, char, carbonize, calcine, incinerate; smelt, cupel, scorify; reduce to ashes; burn to a cinder; commit -, consign- to the flames.

boil, digest, stew, cook, seethe, scald, parboil, simmer; do to rags.

take -, catch- fire; blaze &c. (*flame*) 382.

Adj. heated &c. *v.*; molten, sodden; *réchauffé*; heating &c. *v.*

inflammable, burnable, inflammatory, combustible; diatherm-al, -anous; burnt &c. *v.*; volcanic.

385. Refrigeration.—N. refrigeration, infrigidation, reduction of temperature; cooling &c *v.*; con-gelation, -glaciation; ice &c. 383; solidification &c. (*density*) 321; refrigerator &c. 387.

extincteur; fire, - engine, - extinguisher, - annihilator, - brigade, - man; sprinkler, hose, hydrant, standpipe.

incombusti-bility, -bleness &c. *adj.*

V. cool, fan, refrigerate, refresh, ice; congeal, freeze, glaciate; benumb, starve, pinch, chill, petrify, chill to the marrow, nip, cut, pierce, bite, make one's teeth chatter; damp, slack; quench; put -, stamp- out; extinguish.

go -, burn- out.

Adj. cooled &c. *v.*; frozen out; cooling &c. *v.*; frigorific.

incombustible; un-, unin-flammable; fire-proof.

386. Furnace.—N. furnace, blast furnace, fire-box, stove, incinerator, destructor, crematorium, crematory, kiln, oven, oast-house; hot-, bake-, washhouse; laundry; conservatory; hearth, focus; athanor, hypocaust, reverberatory; volcano; forge, fiery furnace; *tuyère*, brasier, salamander, heater, warmingpan, foot-warmer, hot-water bottle; radiator; boiler, geyser, caldron, seething caldron, pot; urn, kettle; chafing-dish; retort, crucible, alembic, still; saggar.

fire-place, -dog, -irons; hearth, ingle, grate, range, kitchener; kitchen range; oil-, gas-, electric, -cooker, -stove; fireless cooker; fire; galley; ca-, cam-boose; poker, tongs, shovel, hob, trivet; and-, grid-iron; frying-, stew-pan &c.

hot -, Turkish -, Russian -, vapour -, shower -, warm- bath; *calidarium, tepidarium, sudatorium*, sudatory; *hammam*.

387. Refrigerator.—N. refrigerator, -y; *frigidarium*; cold storage; refrigerating-plant, - machine; ice-house, -pail, -bag, -chest, -pack; cooler, damper; wine-cooler, freezing mixture.

388. Fuel.—N. fuel, firing, combustible, coal, wallsend, anthracite, bituminous coal, slack, culm, cannel coal, lignite, briquette, coke, carbon, charcoal; turf, peat, fire-wood, bobbing, faggot, log, yule log, ember, cinder &c. (*products of combustion*) 384; kindling wood, tinder, touch-wood; fumigator, sulphur, brimstone; incense; port-fire; fire-barrel, -ball, -brand.

fuel oil, gas, gasoline, electricity.

brand, torch, fuse; wick; spill, match, safety match, light, lucifer, congreve, vesuvian, vesta, fusee, locofoco; linstock; illuminant.

candle &c. (*luminary*) 423; oil &c. (*grease*), 356; petrol, gasoline, methylated -, spirit; gas, acetylene.

Adj. carbonaceous; combustible, inflammable.

V. stoke, fire, feed, add fuel to the flames.

389. Thermometer.—N. thermo-meter, -scope, -stat, -pile, differential thermometer; pyro-, calori-meter; radio micrometer &c.

3. Taste

390. Taste.—N. taste, flavour, gust, *gusto*, relish, savour; sapor, sapidity; twang, smack, smatch; after-taste, tang.

tasting; de-, gustation.

palate, tongue, tooth, stomach.

V. taste, savour, smatch, smack, fla-vour, twang; tickle the palate &c. (*sa-voury*) 394; smack the lips.

Adj. sapid, saporific; gusta-ble, -tory; strong; flavoured, spiced, savoury; pal-atable &c. 394.

391. Insipidity.—N. insipidity; taste-lessness &c. *adj.*

V. be -tasteless &c. *adj.*

Adj. void of -taste &c. 390; insipid; jejune; taste-, gust-, savour-less; ingus-tible, mawkish, milk and water, weak, stale, flat, vapid, *fade*, wishy-washy, mild; untasted.

392. Pungency.—N. pungency, pi-quancy, poignancy, *haut-goût*, strong taste, twang, race, tang.

sharpness &c. *adj.*; acrimony, acrid-ity; roughness &c. (*sour*) 397; unsa-vouriness &c. 395.

nitre, saltpetre; mustard, cayenne, caviare; seasoning &c. (*condiment*) 393; brine.

dram, cordial, nip, pick-me-up, brac-er, potion.

nicotine, tobacco, snuff, quid; segar; cigar, -ette, gasper, fag; cheroot; weed; fragrant -, Indian- weed; pipe, clay pipe, churchwarden, brier, meerschaum, hookah, hubble-bubble.

V. be -pungent &c. *adj.*; bite the tongue.

render -pungent &c. *adj.*; season, spice, salt, pepper, pickle, brine, devil, curry.

smoke, chew, take snuff.

Adj. pungent, strong; high-, full-flavoured; high-tasted, -seasoned; gamy; sharp, stinging, rough, *piquant*, racy; biting, mordant; spicy; seasoned &c. *v.*; hot, – as pepper; peppery, vellicating, escharotic, meracious; acrid, acrimoni-ous, bitter; rough &c. (*sour*) 397; un-savoury &c. 395.

salt, saline, brackish, briny; salt as -brine, – a herring, – Lot's wife.

393. Condiment.—N. condiment, flavouring, salt, mustard, pepper, cay-enne, curry, seasoning, sauce, spice, cinnamon, chillies, relish, *sauce pi-quante*, caviare, pot-herbs, onion, gar-lic, pickle, chutney, nutmeg &c.

V. season &c. (*render pungent*) 392.

394. Savouriness.—N. savouriness &c. *adj.*; relish, zest.

tit-bit, dainty, delicacy, ambrosia, nectar, *bonne bouche*; game, turtle, venison.

V. taste good, be -savoury &c. *adj.*; tickle the -palate, – appetite; flatter the palate.

render -palatable &c. *adj.*

relish, like, smack the lips.

Adj. savoury, well-tasted, to one's taste, tasty, good, palatable, nice, dain-ty, delectable; tooth-ful, -some; gustful, appetizing, lickerish, delicate, deli-cious, exquisite, rich, luscious, ambro-sial.

Adv. *per amusare la bocca.*

Phr. *cela se laisse manger.*

395. Unsavouriness.—N. unsavouri-ness &c. *adj.*; amaritude; acri-mony, -tude; roughness &c. (*sour*) 397; acerbity, austerity; gall and worm-wood, rue, quassia, aloes; sickener.

V. be -unpalatable &c. *adj.*; sicken, disgust, nauseate, pall, turn the stom-ach.

Adj. un-savoury, -palatable, -sweet; ill-flavoured, un-appetizing, -eatable, inedible; bitter, – as gall; acrid, acri-monious; rough.

offensive, repulsive, nasty; sickening

&c. *v.*; nauseous; loath-, ful-some; unpleasant &c. 830.

396. Sweetness.—N. sweetness, dulcitude, saccharinity.

sugar, cane-, beet-sugar; saccharine, glucose, syrup, treacle, molasses, honey, manna; confection, -ary; sweets, grocery, conserve, preserve, *confiture*, jam, marmalade, julep; sugar-candy, -plum; licorice, liquorice, plum, lollipop, *bon bon, jujube*, comfit, sweetmeat, caramel, toffee, butterscotch.

nectar; hydromel, mead, metheglin, honeysuckle, *liqueur*, sweet wine.

pastry, pie, tart, puff, pudding, cake.

dulc-ification, -oration.

V. be -sweet &c. *adj.*

render -sweet &c. *adj.*; sugar, saccharize, sweeten; edulcorate; dulc-orate, -ify; candy; mull.

Adj. sweet, sugary; sacchar-ine, -iferus; dulcet, honied, candied, luscious, nectarious, melliferous; sweetened &c. *v.*

sweet as -a nut, - sugar, - honey.

397. Sourness.—N. sourness &c. *adj.*.; acid, -ity; acetous fermentation; acerbity.

vinegar, verjuice, crab, alum.

V. be - , turn- -sour &c. *adj.*; set the teeth on edge.

render-sour &c. *adj.*; acid-ify, -ulate.

Adj. sour; acid, -ulous, -ulated; acerb; tart, crabbed; acet-ous, -ose; sour as vinegar, sourish, acescent, sub-acid; styptic, hard, rough; unripe, green.

4. Odour

398. Odour.—N. odour, smell, odorament, scent, effluvium; eman-, exhalation; fume, essence, trail, nidor, redolence.

sense of smell; scent; act of -smelling &c. *v.*

V. have an -odour &c. *n.*; smell, - of, - strong of; exhale; give out a -smell &c. *n.*; scent.

smell, scent; snuff, - up; sniff, nose, inhale.

Adj. odor-ous, -iferous; smelling, strong-scented; redolent, graveolent, nidorous, pungent.

[Relating to the sense of smell] olfactory, quick-scented.

399. Inodorousness.—N. inodorousness; absence -, want- of smell.

V. be -inodorous &c. *adj.*; not smell. deodorize.

Adj. inodor-ous, -ate; scentless; without -, wanting- smell &c. 398.

deodoriz-ed, -ing.

400. Fragrance.—N. fragrance, aroma, redolence, perfume, *bouquet*; sweet smell, aromatic perfume.

perfumery; incense; musk, frankincense; pastil, -le; myrrh, perfumes of Arabia, chypre; otto, ottar, attar; bergamot, balm, civet, *pot-pourri*, pulvil; nosegay, *boutonnière*; scent, -bag; *sachet*, scent-bottle, smelling bottle, *vinaigrette*; toilet water, *eau de Cologne*; thurible, censer, thurification.

perfumer; incense bearer.

V. be -fragrant &c. *adj.*; have a -perfume &c. *n.*; smell sweet, scent, perfume, thurify, embalm.

Adj. fragrant, aromatic, redolent, spicy, balmy, scented; sweet-smelling, -scented; perfum-ed, -atory; thuriferous; fragrant as a rose, muscadine, ambrosial.

401. Fetor.—N. fetor, fetidness; bad &c. *adj.*; -smell, - odour; stench, stink; mephitis, foul -, mal- odour; *empyreuma*; mustiness &c. *adj.*; rancidity; foulness &c. (*uncleanness*) 653.

stoat, polecat, skunk; assafœtida; fungus, garlic; stink-pot, -bomb.

V. have a -bad smell &c. *n.*; smell; stink, - in the nostrils, - like a polecat; smell -strong &c. *adj.*, - offensively.

Adj. fetid; strong-smelling; high, bad, strong, fulsome, offensive, noisome, rank, rancid, reasty, tainted, musty, fusty, frouzy; olid, -ous; nidorous; smelling, stinking; putrid &c. 653; suffocating, mephitic; empyreumatic.

5. *Sound*

(i.) SOUND IN GENERAL

402. Sound.—N. sound, noise, strain; accent, twang, intonation, tone, tune; cadence; sonority, sonorousness &c. *adj.*; audibility; resonance &c. 408; voice &c. 580.

[Science of sound] acou-, acu-stics; catacoustics, cataphonics; phon-ics, -etics, -ology, -ography; dia-coustics, -phonics.

telephone, phonograph &c. 418.

V. produce sound; sound, make a noise; give out -, emit- sound; phonetize, phonate; resound &c. 408.

Adj. sounding; soniferous; sonorific; resonant, audible, acoustic, auditory, distinct; stertorous; phonic, sonant; phonetic.

403. Silence.—N. silence; stillness &c. (*quiet*) 265; peace, hush, lull, rest; muteness &c. 581; solemn -, awful -, dead -, deathlike- silence.

V. be -silent &c. *adj.*; hold one's tongue &c. (*not speak*) 585.

render -silent &c. *adj.*; silence, still, hush; stifle, muffle, gag, stop; muzzle, put to silence &c. (*render mute*) 581.

Adj. silent; still, -y; calm, quiet; noise-, sound-, speech-less; hushed &c. *v.*; mute &c. 581; aphonic.

soft, solemn, awful, deathlike, silent as the grave; inaudible &c. (*faint*) 405.

Adv. silently &c. *adj.; sub silentio*; in perfect silence.

Int. hush! 'sh! silence! soft! whist! tush! chut! tut! *pax!* mum's the word! hold your tongue! shut up! be silent! be quiet! stop that noise! hold your row! dry up! peace, be still!

Phr. one might hear a -feather, - pindrop.

404. Loudness.—N. loudness, power; loud noise, din; clang, -or; clatter, noise, bombilation, roar, uproar, racket, static, grinders, hubbub, *fracas, charivari*, trumpet blast, blare, flourish of trumpets, fanfare, *tintamarre*, peal, swell, blast, alarum, boom; resonance &c. 408.

vociferation; pandemonium, hullaballoo &c. 411; lungs; Stentor; megaphone; siren.

artillery, cannon, gunfire, shell-burst, bomb; thunder.

V. be -loud &c. *adj.*; peal, swell, clang, boom, thunder, fulminate, roar; resound &c. 408; speak up, shout &c. (*vociferate*) 411; bellow &c. (*cry as an animal*) 412; give tongue.

rend the -air, - skies; fill the air; din -, ring -, thunder- in the ear; pierce -, split -, rend- the -ears, - head; deafen, stun; *faire le diable à quatre*; make one's windows shake; awaken -, startle- the echoes; make the welkin ring.

Adj. loud, sonorous; high-, big-sounding; blatant; deep, full, powerful, noisy, clangorous, multisonous, *fortissimo*; thundering, deafening &c. *v.*; trumpet-tongued; ear-splitting, -rending, -deafening; piercing; obstreperous, rackety, uproarious; enough to wake the -dead, - seven sleepers.

shrill &c. 410; clamorous &c. (*vociferous*) 411; stentor-ian, -ophonic.

Adv. loudly &c. *adj.*; aloud; at the top of one's voice, lustily, in full cry.

Phr. the air rings with.

405. Faintness.—N. faintness &c. *adj.*; faint sound, whisper, breath; undertone, -breath; murmur, hum, rustle, buzz, purr, plash; sough, moan, sigh, susurration; tinkle; 'still small voice.'

hoarseness &c. *adj.*; raucity.

silencer, soft pedal, damper, mute, *sourdine*.

V. whisper, breathe, murmur, purl, hum, gurgle, ripple, babble, flow; tinkle; mutter &c. (*speak imperfectly*) 583.

steal on the ear; melt in -, float on- the air.

muffle, mute, deaden, damp, stifle.

Adj. inaudible; scarcely -, just-audible; low, dull; stifled, muffled; hoarse, husky; gentle, soft, faint; floating; purling, flowing &c. *v.*; whispered

&c. *v.*; liquid; soothing; dulcet &c. (*melodious*) 413.

Adv. in a whisper, with bated breath, *sotto voce*, between the teeth, aside; *pian-o, -issimo; à la sourdine; con sordine*; out of earshot, inaudibly &c. *adj.*

(ii.) Specific Sounds*

406. [Sudden and violent sounds.] **Snap.—N.** snap &c. *v.*; rapping &c. *v.*; de-, crepitation; smack, clap, report; thud; burst, explosion, discharge, detonation, blow-out, back-fire, firing, salvo, volley, pistol-shot.

squib, cracker, gun, rifle, pop-gun.

V. rap, snap, tap, knock; click; clash; crack, -le; crash; pop; slam, bang, clap, thump, plump; toot; back-fire, explode, burst on the ear.

Adj. rapping &c. *v.*

Int. crash! bang!

407. [Repeated and protracted sounds.] **Roll.—N.** roll &c. *v.*; drumming &c. *v.*; tattoo; ding-dong; tantara; rataplan; whirr; rat-a-tat; rub-a-dub; pit-a-pat; quaver, clutter, *charivari*, racket; cuckoo; repetition &c. 104; peal of bells, devil's tattoo; reverberation &c. 408.

drumfire, barrage.

machine gun.

V. roll, drum, rumble, rattle, clatter, rustle, roar, drone, patter, clack.

hum, trill, shake; chime, peal, toll; tick, beat.

drum -, din- in the ear.

Adj. rolling &c. *v.*; monotonous &c. (*repeated*), 104; like a bee in a bottle.

408. Resonance.—N. resonance; ring &c. *v.*; ringing &c. *v.*; tintinnabulation; reflection, reverberation, clangor.

low -, base -, bass -, flat -, grave -, deep -, pedal- note; bass; *basso, - profondo*; bari-, bary-tone; *contralto*.

V. re-sound, -verberate, -echo; ring, ding, sing, jingle, gingle, chink, clink;

---

* [The author's classification of sounds has been retained, though it does not entirely accord with the theories of modern science.—Ed.]

---

tink, -le; chime; gurgle &c. 405; plash, guggle, echo, ring in the ear.

Adj. resounding &c. *v.*; resonant, tinnient, tintinnabulary; deep-toned, -sounding, -mouthed; hollow, sepulchral; gruff &c. (*harsh*) 410.

408a. Non-resonance.—N. thud, thump, dead sound; non-resonance; muffled drums, cracked bell; silencer, damper; mute, *sourdine*.

V. sound dead; stop -, damp- the -sound, - reverberations; deaden, muffle.

Adj. non-resonant, dead, muted, muffled.

409. [Hissing sounds.] **Sibilation.— N.** sibilation; hiss &c. *v.*; sternutation; high note &c. 410.

goose, serpent, snake.

V. hiss, whiz, rustle; fizz, -le, sizzle, swish; wheeze, whistle, snuffle; squash; sneeze.

Adj. sibilant; hissing &c. *v.*; wheezy.

410. [Harsh sounds.] **Stridor.—N.** creak &c. *v.*; creaking &c. *v.*; discord &c. 414; stridor; harshness, roughness, sharpness &c. *adj.*; cacophony.

acute -, high- note; *soprano*, treble, tenor, *alto*, falsetto, *voce di testa*; shriek, cry &c. 411.

piccolo, fife, penny -whistle, - trumpet.

V. creak, grate, jar, burr, pipe, twang, jangle, clank, clink; scream &c. (*cry*) 411; yelp &c. (*animal sound*) 412; buzz &c. (*hiss*) 409.

set the teeth on edge, *écorcher les oreilles*; pierce -, split- the -ears, - head; offend -, grate upon -, jar upon- the ear.

Adj. creaking &c. *v.*; strident, stridulous, harsh, coarse, hoarse, horrisonous, raucous, metallic, rough, gruff, grum, sepulchral.

sharp, high, acute, shrill, high-pitched; trumpet-toned; piercing, ear-piercing; cracked; discordant &c. 414; cacophonous.

411. Cry.—N. cry &c. *v.*; voice &c. (*human*) 580; bark &c. (*animal*) 412.

vociferation, outcry, hullaballoo,

chorus, clamour, hue and cry, plaint; lungs; stentor.

V. cry, roar, shout, bawl, brawl, halloo, halloa, hail, hoop, whoop, yell, bellow, howl, scream, screech, screak, shriek, shrill, squeak, squeal, squall, whine, whinny, pule, pipe, yaup.

cheer, hurrah; hoot; grumble, moan, groan.

snore, snort; grunt &c. (*animal sounds*) 412.

vociferate; raise –, lift up- the voice; call –, sing –, cry- out; exclaim; rend the air; thunder –, shout- at the -top of one's voice, – pitch of one's breath; *s'égosiller*; strain the -throat, – voice, – lungs; give a -cry &c.

Adj. crying &c. *v.*; clam-ant, -orous; vociferous; stentorian &c. (*loud*) 404; open-mouthed.

412. [Animal sounds.] Ululation.—N. cry &c. *v.*; crying &c. *v.*; ululation, latration, belling; reboation; call, note; bark, howl, yelp; twittering, woodnote; insect cry, fritinancy, drone; screech; cuckoo.

V. cry, ululate, howl, roar, bellow, blare, rebellow, bark, yelp; bay, – the moon; yap, growl, yarr, yawl, snarl, howl; grunt, -le; snort, squeak; neigh, bray; mew, mewl; purr, caterwaul, pule; bleat, low, moo; troat, croak, crow, screech, caw, coo, gobble, quack, cackle, gaggle, guggle; chuck, -le; cluck; clack; cheep, chirp, chirrup, twitter, sing, cuckoo; pout, wail, hum, buzz; hiss, blatter; hoot.

Adj. crying &c. *v.*; blatant, latrant; re-, mugient; deep-, full-mouthed.

Adv. in full cry.

(iii.) Musical Sounds

413. Melody. Concord.—N. melody, rhythm, measure; rhyme &c. (*poetry*) 597.

pitch, *timbre*, intonation, tone, overtone.

scale, gamut; diapason; diatonic –, chromatic –, enharmonic- scale; key, clef, chords.

modulation, temperament, syncope, syncopation, preparation, suspension, resolution.

staff, stave, line, space, brace; bar, rest; *appogia-to, -tura; acciaccatura,* shake, *arpeggio.*

note, musical note, notes of a scale; sharp, flat, natural; high note &c. (*shrillness*) 410; low note &c. 408; interval; semitone; second, third, fourth &c.; diatessaron.

breve, semibreve, minim, crotchet, quaver; semi-, demisemi-quaver; sustained note, drone, burden.

tonic; key-, leading-, fundamentalnote; supertonic, mediant, dominant; sub-mediant, -dominant, organ-, pedalpoint; octave, tetrachord; major –, minor- -mode, – scale, – key; Doric mode, passage, phrase.

concord, harmony; unison, -ance; chime, homophony; euphon-y, -ism; tonality; consonance; concent; part.

orchestration, harmonization, – phrasing.

[Science of harmony] harmon-y, -ics; thorough-, fundamental-bass; counterpoint; faburden.

piece of music &c. 415; composer, harmonist, contrapuntist.

V. be -harmonious &c. *adj.*; harmonize, chime, symphonize, transpose; put in tune, tune, accord, string; score, arrange, orchestrate.

Adj. hormoni-ous, -cal; in -concord &c. *n.*, – tune, – concert; unisonant, concentual, symphonizing, isotonic, homophonous, assonant, consonant.

measured, rhythmical, diatonic, chromatic, enharmonic.

melodious, musical; tuneful, tunable; sweet, dulcet, canorous; mell-ow, -ifluous; soft; clear, – as a bell; silvery; euphon-ious, -ic, -ical; symphonious; enchanting &c. (*pleasure-giving*) 829; fine-, full-, silver-toned.

Adv. harmoniously &c. *adj.*

414. Discord.—N. discord, -ance; dissonance, cacophony, caterwauling; harshness &c. 410; consecutive fifths.

[Confused sounds] Babel, pandemonium; Dutch –, cat's- concert; marrowbones and cleavers.

V. be -discordant &c. *adj.*; jar &c. (*sound harshly*) 410.

Adj. discordant; dis-, ab-sonant; out of tune, tuneless; un-musical, -tunable; un-, im-melodious; un-, in-harmonious; sing-song; cacophonous; jarring, harsh &c. 410.

415. Music.—N. music, classical –, modern –, descriptive- music; concert, recital; strain, tune, air, *motif*; melody &c. 413; *aria, arietta*; piece of music, *sonata; rond-o, -eau; pastorale, cavatina*, roulade, *fantasia, toccata, concerto*, overture, symphony, symphonic poem, tone poem, prelude, voluntary, *intermezzo*, variations, *cadenza*; cadence; fugue, canon, seranade, *nocturne, notturno*, rhapsody, romance, *aubade*, dithyramb; opera, operetta; oratorio; composition, movement; stave.

instrumental music; full-, orchestral-score; minstrelsy, tweedledum and tweedledee, band, orchestra &c. 416; concerted piece, *potpourri*, medley, *capriccio*, incidental music; improvisation; peal.

vocal music, vocalism; chaunt, chant; psalm, -ody; hymn; song &c. (*poem*) 597; canticle, canzonet, *cantata, bravura, coloratura*; lay, ballad, ditty, carol, barcarolle, pastoral, recitative, *recitativo, solfeggio*, tonic sol-fa.

Lydian measures; slow -music, -movement; *adagio* &c. *adv.*; minuet; siren strains, soft music, lullaby; *berceuse*, cradle song, dump; dirge &c. (*lament*) 839; pibroch; martial music, march, funeral-, dead- march; dance music; waltz &c. (*dance*) 840; rag-time, syncopation, jazz.

solo, duet, *duo, trio*; quartet; quintet, sextet, septet; part song, descant, glee, madrigal, catch, round, chorus, *chorale*; antiphon, -y; accompaniment, second –, alto –, tenor –, bass- part; score, thorough bass; counterpoint.

composer &c. 413; musician &c. 416.

V. compose, perform &c. 416; attune.

Adj. musical; instrumental, orchestral, vocal, choral, lyric, operatic; harmonious &c. 413.

Adv. *adagio; largo, larghetto, andante, -tino; alla capella; maestoso, moderato; allegr-o, -etto; spiritoso, vivace, veloce; prest-o, -issimo; pian-o, -issimo, fort-e, -issimo, sforzando; con brio; capriccioso; scherz-o, -ando; legato, sostenuto, staccato, crescendo, diminuendo, rallentando, affettuoso, arioso; parlante, cantabile; obbligato; pizzicato, tremolo, vibrato.*

416. Musician. [Performance of Music.]**—N.** musician, *artiste, virtuoso*, performer, player, minstrel; bard &c. (*poet*) 597; instrumental-, organ-, accompan-, pian-, violin-, flaut-, harp-ist; harper, fiddler, fifer, trumpeter, piper, drummer; catgut scraper.

band, orchestra, waits.

vocal-, melod-ist; singer, warbler; songst-, chaunt-er, -ress; *diva, cantatrice*, coloratura, soprano, mezzo-soprano, alto, contralto, tenor, baritone, bass, *basso, -profondo*.

choir, quire, chorister; chorus, – singer; choral society, festival, *eisteddfod*.

nightingale, philomel, thrush; siren; Orpheus, Apollo, the Muses, Erato, Euterpe, Terpsichore; tuneful -nine, –quire.

composer &c. 413.

performance, virtuosity, execution, touch, expression, solmization.

V. play, pipe, strike –, tune- up, sweep the chords, tickle –, paw- the ivories, vamp, tweedle, fiddle; strike the lyre, beat the drum; blow –, sound –, wind- the horn; grind the organ; touch the -guitar &c. (*insruments*) 417; thrum, strum, twang, drum, beat –, keep- time, conduct.

execute, perform; accompany; sing –, play- a second; compose, write music, set to music, arrange, harmonize, orchestrate.

sing, chaunt, chant, hum, warble, carol, chirp, chirrup, lilt, purl, quaver, trill, shake, twitter, whistle; sol-fa; intone.

have -an ear for music, – a musical ear, – a correct ear, – absolute pitch.
Adj. playing &c. *v.*; musical, lyric.
Adv. *adagio, andante* &c. (*music*) 415.

417. Musical Instruments.—N. musical instruments; band; string-, brass-, drum and fife-, military-, bugle-, German-, dance-, jazz-band; orchestra, string quartet; orchestrion, orchestrelle.

[Stringed instruments] mono-, polychord; harp, lyre, lute, archlute, thearbo; mandol-a, -in, -ine; guitar; *ukulele*; psaltery, zither; bandore, cither, -n; gittern, rebeck, *bandurria*, banjo, zither banjo, *balalaika, samisen*; plectrum.

viol, -in, Cremona, Stradivarius; fiddle, kit; *vielle, viola, – d'amore, – di gamba*; tenor, *violoncello*, cello; bass, bass-, base-viol; double-bass, *contrabasso, violone*, hurdy-gurdy; strings, catgut; bow, fiddlestick.

piano, -forte; grand –, concert grand –, baby –, upright –, cottage-piano; pianino, pianette; harpsi-, clavi-, clari-, mani-chord; *clavier*, spinet, virginals; dulcimer, *cymbalo*; Eolian harp; piano-organ, -player, electric piano, player-piano, pianola.

[Wind instruments] organ, church –, pipe –, American- organ; harmoni-um, -phon; accordion, seraphina, concertina; melodeon; barrel-organ; humming top.

flute, fife, piccolo, flageolet, penny-whistle, reed instrument; clari-net, -onet; bass clarionet; saxophone; basset horn, *corno di bassetto*; musette, shawm, oboe, hautboy, *cor Anglais, corno Inglese*, bassoon, double bassoon, *contrafagotto*; bag-, union-pipes; ocarina, Pandean pipes; calliope; sirene, pipe, pitch-pipe; sourdet; whistle, cat-call.

horn, bugle, key bugle, cornet, *cornet-à-pistons*, cornopean, clarion, trumpet, trombone, ophicleide, serpent; English-, French-, bugle-, sax-, flugel-, alt-, helicon-, post-horn; sackbut, euphonium, bombardon, tuba, bass tuba.

[Vibrating surfaces] cymbal, bell, gong, peal of bells, *carillon*; tambour, -ine; drum, tom-tom, tab-or, -ret, -ourine, -orin; *sistrum; grand caisse*, bass-, big-, side-, kettle-drum; *tympani*; war drums; tymbal, timbrel, castanet, bones; musical-glasses, -stones; harmonica, sounding-board, rattle; gramophone, phonograph.

[Vibrating bars] reed, tuning-fork, triangle, Jew's harp, musical box, harmonicon, xylophone, marimba, *celeste*.

sord-ine, pet; *sourd-ine, -et*; mute.

(iv.) PERCEPTION OF SOUND

418. [Sense of sound.] Hearing.—N. hearing &c. *v.*; audition, auscultation; eavesdropping; audibility; acoustics &c. 402.

acute –, nice –, delicate –, quick –, sharp –, correct –, musical -ear; ear for music.

ear, auricle, lug, acoustic organs, auditory apparatus, ear-drum, tympanum; ear-, speaking-trumpet, megaphone; telephone, radiophone, stethoscope, phonograph, gramophone, microphone.

hearer, auditor, listener, eavesdropper; audi-tory, -ence.

V. hear, overhear; hark, -en; list, -en; give –, lend –, bend- an ear; give attention; catch a sound, prick up one's ears; give -a hearing, – audience- to.

hang upon the lips of, be all ears, listen with both ears, monitor.

become audible; meet –, fall upon –, catch –, reach- the ear; be heard; ring in the ear &c. (*resound*) 408.

Adj. hearing &c. *v.*; auditory, auricular, aural, auditive, acoustic.

Adv. *arrectis auribus*.

Int. hark, – ye! hear! list, -en! *Oyez!* attention! lend me your ears!

419. Deafness.—N. deafness, hardness of hearing, surdity; inaudibility.
V. be -deaf &c. *adj.*; have no ear;

shut –, stop –, close- one's ears; turn a deaf ear to.

render deaf, stun, deafen.

Adj. deaf, earless, surd; hard –, dull- of hearing; deaf-mute, stunned, deafened; stone deaf; dead as -a post, – an adder, – a beetle, – a trunk-maker.

inaudible &c. 405; out of hearing.

6. Light

(i.) LIGHT IN GENERAL

420. Light.—N. light, ray, beam, stream, gleam, streak, pencil; sun-, moon-beam; dawn, aurora.

day; sunshine; light of -day, – heaven; sun &c. (*luminary*) 432, day-, broad day-, noontide- light; noon-tide, -day; glare.

glow &c. *v.*; afterglow, sunset; glimmering &c. *v.*; glint; play –, flood- of light; phosphorescence, lambent flame.

flush, halo, glory, nimbus, aureole, *aureola*.

spark, *scintilla; facula*; sparkling &c. *v.*; emication, scintillation, flash, blaze, coruscation, fulguration; flame &c. (*fire*) 382; lightning, *ignis fatuus*, &c. (*luminary*) 423, radio-activity.

lustre, sheen, shimmer, reflection; gloss, tinsel, spangle, brightness, brilliancy, splendour; ef-, re-fulgence; fulgor, -gidity; dazzlement, resplendence, transplendency; luminousness &c. *adj.*; luminosity; lucidity; renitency; radiance, -ation; irradiation, illumination, phosphorescence, luminescence.

radiation, radiant heat, infra-red rays, visible radiation, ultra-violet –, actinic- rays, actinism; X –, Roentgen-rays; phot-, heli-ography; optical instruments &c. 445.

[Science of light] optics; photo-logy, -metry; di-, cat-optrics.

[Distribution of light] *chiaroscuro, clair-obscur*, clear obscure, breadth, light and shade, black and white, tonality, half-tone, mezzotint.

reflection, refraction, dispersion, double refraction, polarization, diffraction, interference.

illuminant &c. 423.

V. shine, glow, glitter, phosphoresce; glis-ter, -ten; twinkle, gleam; flare, – up; glare, beam, shimmer, glimmer, flicker, sparkle, scintillate, coruscate, flash, fulgurate, blaze; be -bright &c. *adj.*; reflect light, daze, dazzle, bedazzle, radiate, shoot out beams.

clear up, brighten.

lighten, enlighten; light, – up; irradiate, shine upon; give –, hang out- a light; cast –, throw –, shed- -lustre, – light- upon; illum-e, -ine, -inate; relume, strike a light; kindle &c. (*set fire to*) 384.

Adj. shining &c. *v.*; lumin-ous, -iferous; luc-id, -ent, -ulent, -ific, -iferous; illuminating, light, -some; bright, vivid, splendent, nitid, lustrous, shiny, brilliant, beamy, scintillant, radiant, lambent; sheen, -y; glossy, burnished, glassy, sunny, orient, meridian; noon-day, -tide; cloudless, clear; unclouded, -obscured.

garish; re-, tran-splendent; re-, effulgent; ful-gid, -gent; relucent, splendid, blazing, in a blaze, ablaze, rutilant, meteoric, phosphorescent; aglow.

bright as silver; light –, bright- as -day, – noonday, – the sun at noonday.

optical, actinic; photo-genic, -graphic; heliographic, radioactive.

421. Darkness.—N. darkness &c. *adj.*; blackness &c. (*dark colour*) 431; obscurity, gloom, murk; dusk &c. (*dimness*) 422; tenebrosity, umbrageousness.

Cimmerian –, Stygian –, Egyptian- darkness; night; midnight; dead of –, witching time of- night; blind man's holiday; darkness -visible, – that can be felt; palpable, obscure; Erebus.

shade, shadow, umbra, penumbra; sciagraphy; *silhouette*; radiograph, skiagraph.

obscuration; ad-, ob-umbration; obtenebration, offuscation, caligation; extinction; eclipse, total eclipse; gathering of the clouds.

shading; distribution of shade; *chiaroscuro* &c. (*light*) 420.

noctivagation, noctograph, noctuary. obscurantist.

V. be -dark &c. *adj.*

darken, obscure, shade; dim; tone down, lower; over-cast, -shadow; cloud, eclipse; ob-, of-fuscate; ob-, adumbrate, cast into the shade; be-cloud, -dim, -darken; cast -, throw -, spread- a -shade, - shadow, - gloom.

extinguish; put -, blow -, snuff- out; doubt.

Adj. dark, -some, -ling; obscure, tenebrous, tenebrious, sombrous, pitch dark, pitchy; caliginous; black &c. (*in colour*) 431.

sunless, lightless &c. (*see* sun, light, &c. 423); sombre, dusky; unilluminated &c. (*see* illuminate &c. 420); nocturnal; dingy, lurid, gloomy; murk-y, -some; shady, umbrageous; overcast &c. (*dim*) 422; cloudy &c. (*opaque*) 426; darkened &c. *v.*

dark as -pitch, - a pit, - Erebus.

benighted; noctivag-ant, -ous.

Adv. in the -dark, - shade; at night.

422. Dimness.—N. dimness &c. *adj.*; darkness &c. 421; paleness &c. (*light colour*) 429.

half-light, *demi-jour*; partial -shadow, - eclipse; shadow of a shade; glimmer, -ing; nebulosity; cloud &c. 353; eclipse.

aurora, dusk, twilight, gloaming, blind man's holiday, shades of evening, crepuscule, cockshut time; break of day, daybreak, dawn.

moon-light, -beam, -shine; star-, owl's-, candle-, rush-, fire-light; farthing candle.

V. be -, grow- -dim &c. *adj.*; flicker, twinkle, glimmer, loom, lower; fade; darken; pale, - its ineffectual fire.

render -dim &c. *adj.*; dim, bedim, obscure.

Adj. dim, dull, lack-lustre, dingy, darkish, shorn of its beams; dark 421.

faint, shadowed forth; glassy; bleary; cloudy; misty &c. (*opaque*) 426; muggy, fuliginous; nebul-ous, -ar; obnubi-

lated, overcast, crepuscular, twilight, muddy, lurid, leaden, dun, dirty; looming &c. *v.*

pale &c. (*colourless*) 429; confused &c. (*invisible*) 447.

423. [Source of light &c.] **Luminary.—N.** luminary; light &c. 420; flame &c. (*fire*) 382.

spark, *scintilla*; phosphorescence.

sun, orb of day, day star, Phœbus, Apollo, Helios, Phaethon, Hyperion, Ra, Aurora; star, orb, meteor; falling -, shooting- star; blazing -, dog- star; Sirius, canicula, Aldebaran; morning star, Lucifer, Phosphor, evening star; Hesperus, Venus, planet, moon &c. 318; constellation, galaxy; northern light, *aurora -borealis*, *- australis*, zodiacal light; mock sun, parhelion.

lightning; fork -, sheet -, summer-lightning, St. Elmo's fire; phosphorus; *ignis fatuus*; Jack o' -, Friar's- lantern; Will o' the wisp, fire-drake, *Fata Morgana*.

glow-worm. fire-fly.

radium, luminous paint.

[Artificial light] gas; gas -, lime -, electric -, head -, search -, spot -, flash -, flood -, foot-light; lamp, oil -, gas -, arc -, incandescent- lamp; flare; lantern, -horn; dark lantern, bull's eye, projector; candle, *bougie*, tallow -, wax-candle; dip, farthing dip; taper, rush-light; oil &c. (*grease*) 356; wick, burner; Argand, moderator, duplex; torch, *flambeau*, link, brand; cresset; gase-, chande-, electro-lier; candelabrum, *girandole*, sconce, lustre, candle-stick.

firework, fizgig; pyrotechnics; Roman candle, Véry light, star shell, parachute light; rocket, lighthouse &c. (*signal*) 550.

V. illuminate &c. (*light*) 420.

Adj. self-luminous, incandescent; phosphor-ic, -escent; luminescent, fluorescent, radiant &c. (*light*) 420.

424. Shade.—N. shade; awning &c. (*cover*) 223; parasol, sunshade, umbrella; screen, curtain, shutter, blind, gauze, veil, mantle, mask; cloud, mist, gathering of clouds; smoke screen; smoked glasses, coloured spectacles; blinkers, blinders.

umbrage, glade; shadow &c. 421.

V. draw a curtain; put up –, close- a shutter; veil &c. *v.*; cast a shadow &c. (*darken*) 421; screen, obstruct the view.

Adj. shady, umbrageous, bowery.

425. Transparency.—N. transparence, -cy; translucen-ce, -cy; diapha-neity; luc-, pelluc-, limp-idity.

transparent medium, glass, crystal, mica; lymph, water.

V. be -transparent &c. *adj.*; transmit light.

Adj. transparent, pellucid, lucid, diaphanous; trans-, tra-lucent; limpid, clear, serene, crystalline, clear as crystal, vitreous, transpicuous, glassy, hyaline.

426. Opacity.—N. opacity; opaqueness &c. *adj.*

film; cloud &c. 353.

V. be -opaque &c. *adj.*; obstruct the passage of light; ob-, of-fuscate.

Adj. opaque, impervious to light.

dim &c. 422; turbid, thick, muddy, opacous, obfuscated, fuliginous, cloudy, hazy, foggy, vaporous, nubiferous, muggy.

smoky, fumid, murky, dirty.

427. Semitransparency.—N. semi-transparency, opalescence, milkiness, pearliness; gauze, muslin; film; mist &c. (*cloud*) 353; frosted glass.

Adj. semi-transparent, -pellucid, -diaphanous, -opacous, -opaque; opalescent, -ine; pearly, milky, frosted, mat; misty.

(ii.) Specific Light

428. Colour.—N. colour, hue, tint, tinge, dye, complexion, shade, tincture, cast, livery, coloration, chromatism, glow, flush; tone, key.

pure –, positive –, primary –, primitive –, complementary- colour; three primaries; spectrum, chromatic disper-

sion; broken –, secondary –, tertiary-colour.

local colour, colouring, keeping, tone, value, aerial perspective.

[Science of colour] chromatics, spectrum analysis; prism, spectroscope.

pigment, colouring matter, paint, dye, wash, distemper, strain; medium; mordant; oil-paint &c. (*painting*) 556.

V. colour, dye, tinge, stain, tint, tinct, tone, paint, wash, ingrain, grain, illuminate, emblazon, imbue; paint &c. (*fine art*) 556; daub.

Adj. coloured &c. *v.*; colorific, tingent, tinctorial; chromatic, prismatic; full-, high-, deep-coloured; doubly-dyed; polychromatic.

bright, vivid, intense, deep; fresh, unfaded; rich, gorgeous; highly coloured; gay; variegated &c. 440.

gaudy, florid; garish; showy, flaunting, flashy; raw, crude; glaring, flaring; discordant, inharmonious.

mellow, harmonious, pearly, sweet, delicate, tender, refined.

429. [Absence of colour.] Achromatism.—N. achromatism; de-, discoloration; pall-or, -idity; paleness &c. *adj.*; etiolation; neutral tint, monochrome, black-and-white.

V. lose -colour &c. 428; fade, fly, go; become -colourless &c. *adj.*; turn pale, pale, whiten.

deprive of colour, decolorize, bleach, tarnish, achromatize, blanch, etiolate, wash out, tone down.

Adj. uncoloured &c. (*see* colour &c. 428); colourless, achromatic, hueless, pale, pallid; pale-, tallow-faced; faint, dull, cold, muddy, leaden, dun, wan, sallow, dead, dingy, ashy, ashen, ghastly, cadaverous, glassy, lack-lustre; discoloured &c. *v.*

light-coloured, fair, *blond*; white &c. 430.

pale as -death, – ashes, – a witch, – a ghost, – a corpse.

430. Whiteness.—N. whiteness &c. *adj.*; argent.

albification, albescence, albinism, etiolation.

snow, paper, chalk, milk, lily, ivory,
silver, alabaster; white lead, chinese -,
flake -, ivory -, zinc- white, white-wash,
-ning, whiting.

V. be -white &c. *adj.*

render -white &c. *adj.*; whiten-bleach,
blanch, etiolate, whitewash, silver, frost.

Adj. white; milky, milk-, snow-white;
snowy, niveous, candid, chalky; hoar,
-y; frosted, silvery; argent, -ine; canescent.

whitish, creamy, pearly, ivory, fair,
blond, ash-blond, platinum blond;
blanched &c. *v.*; high in tone, light.

white as -a sheet, - driven show, - a
lily, - silver; like -ivory &c. *n.*

431. Blackness.—N. blackness &c.
adj.; darkness &c. (*want of light*) 421;
swarthness, lividity, dark colour, tone,
colour; *chiaroscuro* &c. 420.

nigrification, infuscation, denigra-
tion.

jet, ink, ebony, coal, pitch, soot,
smudge, charcoal, sloe, raven, crow;
negro, Ethiopian, black.

[Pigments] lamp -, ivory -, blue-
black; writing -, printing -, printer's -,
Indian- ink.

V. be -black &c. *adj.*

render -black &c. *adj.*; blacken, infuscate, denigrate; blot, -ch; smutch;
smirch; darken &c. 421.

Adj. black, sable, swarthy, sombre,
dark, inky, ebon, atramentous, jetty;
coal-, jet-black; fuliginous, pitchy,
sooty, swart, dusky, dingy, murky; low-
toned, low in tone; of the deepest dye.

black as -jet &c. *n.*, - my hat, - a
shoe, - a tinker's pot, - November, -
thunder, - midnight; nocturnal &c.
(*dark*) 421; nigrescent; gray &c. 432;
obscure &c. 421.

Adv. in mourning.

432. Gray.—N. gray &c. *adj.*; neutral tint, silver, pepper and salt, *chiaroscuro, grisaille*, grayness.

[Pigments] Payne's gray; black &c.
431.

Adj. gray, grey; steel -, iron- gray,
dun, drab, dingy, leaden, livid, sombre,
sad, pearly; silver, -y, -ed; ash-en, -y;
ciner-eous, -itious; grizzl-y, -ed; dove-,
slate-, stone-, mouse-, ash-coloured;
mole; cool.

433. Brown.—N. brown &c. *adj.*

[Pigments] bistre, ochre, sepia, Vandyke brown.

Adj. brown, adust, bay, dapple, auburn, chestnut, nutbrown, cinnamon,
hazel, fawn, puce, *écru*, russet, tawny,
fuscous, chocolate, maroon, foxy, tan,
brunette, whitey-brown; snuff-, liver-
coloured; brown as -a berry, - mahogany; reddish brown; copper-, rust- coloured; henna, bronze, khaki; russet,
roan, sorrel.

sun-burnt; tanned &c. *v.*

V. render -brown &c. *adj.*; tan, embrown, bronze.

Primitive Colours*

434. Redness.—N. red, scarlet, ver-
milion, cardinal, Post Office, red, carmine, crimson, pink, lake, *cerise*, cherry red, maroon, carnation, *couleur de
rose, rose du Barry*; magenta, damask;
flesh -colour, - tint; colour; fresh -,
high- colour; warmth; gules.

ruby, garnet, carbuncle; rose; rust,
iron-mould.

[Dyes and pigments] cinnabar, cochineal; fuchsine; ruddle, madder, red-
lead; Indian -, light -, Venetian- red;
red ink, annotto.

redness &c. *adj.*; rub-escence, -
icundity, -ification; erubescence, blush.

V. be -, become- red &c. *adj.*;
blush, flush, colour up, mantle, redden.

render -red &c. *adj.*; redden, rouge;
rub-ify, -ricate; incarnadine; ruddle.

Adj. red &c. *n.*, -dish; rufous, ruddy,
florid, incarnadine, sanguine, bloody,

* The author's classification of colours has been
retained, though it does not entirely accord with
the theories of modern science: Complete lists of
shades or pigments are beyond the scope of this
work.

gory; ros-y, -eate; blowz-y, -ed; brunt; rubi-cund, -form; lurid, stammel, blood-red; russet, murrey, carroty, sorrel, la-teritious.

rose-, ruby-, cherry-, claret-, wine-, plum-, flame-, flesh-, peach-, salmon-, brick-, brickdust-coloured, reddish brown &c. 433.

blushing &c. *v.*; erubescent; reddened &c. *v.*

red as -fire, – blood, – scarlet, – a turkeycock, – a lobster; warm, hot; foxy.

Complementary Colours

435. Greenness.—N. green &c. *adj.*; blue and yellow; vert.

emerald, verd antique, verdigris, malachite, beryl, aquamarine, reseda.

[Pigments] *terre verte*, verditer, bice, chlorophyl.

greenness, verdure, verdancy; viridity, -escence.

Adj. green, verdant; glaucous, olive; porraceous; green as grass.

emerald –, pea –, grass –, apple –, sea –, olive –, bottle –, leaf- green.

greenish; vir-ent, -escent.

436. Yellowness.—N. yellow &c. *adj.*; or.

[Pigments] gamboge; cadmium –, chrome –, Indian –, lemon- yellow; orpiment, yellow ochre, Claude tint, aureolin.

crocus, saffron, topaz, gold.

jaundice; London fog; yellowness &c. *adj.*

Adj. yellow, aureate, gold, golden, gilt, gilded, flavous, citrine, fallow; fulvous, -id; sallow, luteous, fawny, creamy, sandy; xanth-ic, -ous; jaundiced.

gold-, citron-, saffron-, lemon-, sulphur-, amber-, straw-, primrose-, cream-coloured; flaxen, yellowish, buff.

yellow as a -quince, – guinea, – crow's foot.

437. Purple.—N. purple &c. *adj.*; blue and red, bishop's purple; aniline dyes, gridelin, amethyst; purpure.

livid-ness, -ity.

V. empurple.

Adj. purple, violet, plum-coloured, lavender, lilac, puce, *mauve*; livid.

438. Blueness.—N. blue &c. *adj.*; garter-blue; watchet.

[Pigments] ultramarine, smalt, cobalt, cyanogen; Prussian –, syenite-blue; bice, indigo, woad.

lapis lazuli, sapphire, turquoise.

blue-, bluish-ness; bloom.

Adj. blue, azure, cerulean; sky-blue, -coloured, -dyed; navy-blue, aquamarine, electric blue, royal blue, cyanic; bluish; atmospheric, retiring; cold.

439. Orange.—N. orange, red and yellow; gold; or; flame &c. colour, *adj.*

[Pigments] ochre, Mars orange, cadmium.

V. gild, warm.

Adj. orange; ochreous; orange-, gold-, flame-, copper-, brass-, apricot-coloured; warm, hot, glowing.

440. Variegation.—N. variegation; di-, tri-chroism; iridescence, irisation, play of colours, polychrome, maculation, spottiness, striæ.

spectrum, rainbow, iris, tulip, peacock, chameleon, butterfly, tortoise-shell; mackerel, – sky; zebra, leopard, mother-of-pearl, nacre, opal, marble, batik.

check, plaid, tartan, patchwork; mar-, par-quetry; mosaic, *tesseræ*, tessellation, chess-board, checkers, chequers; harlequin; Joseph's coat; tricolour; patches, bands, stripes, spots &c. of colour.

V. be -variegated &c. *adj.*; variegate, stripe, streak, checker, chequer; be-, speckle, fleck; be-, sprinkle; stipple, maculate, dot, bespot; tattoo, inlay, tessellate, damascene; embroider, braid, quilt.

Adj. variegated &c. *v.*; many-coloured, -hued; divers-, parti-coloured; di-, poly-chromatic; bi-, tri-, versi-colour; of all -the colours of the rainbow, – manner of colours; kaleidoscopic.

iridescent; opal-ine, -escent; prismat-ic, nacreous, pearly, shot, *gorge de pi-geon, chatoyant*, irisated.

pied, piebald, skewbald; motley; mottled, marbled; pepper and salt, paned, dappled, clouded, cymophan-ous.

mosaic, tessellated, chequered, plaid; tortoiseshell &c. *n.*

spott-ed, -y; punctated, powdered; speckled &c. *v.*; freckled, flea-bitten, studded; fleck-ed, -ered; striated, barred, veined; brind-ed, -led; tabby; watered; grizzled; listed; embroidered &c. *v.*; dædal.

(iii.) PERCEPTIONS OF LIGHT

441. Vision.—N. vision, sight, op-tics, eye-sight. ·

view, look, espial, glance, ken, *coup d'œil*; glimpse, peep, glint; gaze, stare, leer; perlustration, contemplation; con-spect-ion, -uity; regard, survey; in-, in-tro-spection; *reconnaissance*, specula-tion, watch, espionage, *espionnage*, autopsy; ocular -inspection, - demon-stration; sight-seeing.

macrography, micrography.

point of view; view-, stand-point; ga-zebo, loop-hole, *belvedere*, watch-tower.

field of view; theatre, amphitheatre, arena. vista, horizon; commanding -, bird's eye -, panoramic- view; peri-scope.

visual organ, organ of vision; eye; na-ked -, unassisted- eye; eye-ball, retina, pupil, iris, cornea, white; optics, orbs; saucer -, goggle -, gooseberry-eyes.

short sight &c. 443; clear -, sharp -, quick -, eagle -, piercing -, penetrat-ing- -sight, - glance, - eye; perspicaci-ty, discernment; catopsis.

eagle, hawk; cat, lynx; Argus.

evil eye; basilisk, cockatrice.

spectacles, telescope &c. 445.

V. see, behold, discern, perceive, have in sight, descry, sight, make out, discover, distinguish, recognize, spy, espy, ken; get -, have -, catch- a -sight, - glimpse- of; command a view of; wit-ness, contemplate, speculate; cast -, set- the eyes on ; be a -spectator &c. 444- of; look on &c. (*be present*) 186; see sights &c. (*curiosity*) 455; see at a glance &c. (*intelligence*) 498.

look, view, eye; lift up the eyes, open one's eye; look -at, - on, - upon, - over, - about one, - round; survey, scan, in-spect; run the eye -over, - through; re-connoitre, glance -round, - on, - over; turn -, bend- one's looks upon; direct the eyes to, turn the eyes on, cast a glance, make eyes at.

observe &c. (*attend to*) 457; watch &c. (*care*) 459; see with one's own eyes; watch for &c. (*expect*) 507; peek, peep, peer, pry, take a peep; play at bo-peep.

look -full in the face, - hard at, - in-tently; strain one's eyes; fix -, rivet- the eyes upon; stare, gaze; pore over, gloat -over, - on; leer, ogle, glare; goggle; cock the eye, squint, gloat, look askance; give the glad eye.

Adj. seeing &c. *v.*; visual, ocular, -al; ophthalmic.

far-, clear-sighted &c. *n.*; eagel-, hawk-, lynx-, keen-, Argus-eyed.

visible &c. 446.

Adv. visibly &c. 446; in sight of, with one's eyes open.

at -sight, - first sight, - a glance, - the first blush; *primâ facie*.

Int. look! &c. (*attention*) 457.

Phr. the scales falling from one's eyes.

442. Blindness.—N. blindness, an-opsia, cecity, excecation, *amaurosis*, cataract, ablepsy, prestriction; dim-sightedness &c. 443.

V. be -blind &c. *adj.*; not see; lose sight of; have the eyes bandaged; grope in the dark.

not look; close -, shut -, turn away -, avert- the eyes; look another way; wink &c. (*limited vision*) 443; shut the eyes -, be blind- to; wink -, blink- at.

render -blind &c. *adj.*; blind, -fold; hoodwink, dazzle; put one's eyes out; throw dust into one's eyes; *jeter de la poudre aux yeux*; screen from sight &c. (*hide*) 528.

Adj. blind; eye-, sight-, vision-less; dark; stone-, sand-, stark-blind; undiscerning; dim-sighted &c. 443.

blind as -a bat, - a buzzard, - a beetle, - a mole, - an owl; wall-eyed.

blinded &c. *v.*

Adv. blind-ly, -fold; darkly.

443. [Imperfect vision.] **Dim-sightedness.** [Fallacies of vision.]—**N.** dim -, dull -, half -, short -, near -, long -, double -, astigmatic -, failing-sight; dim &c. -sightedness; snow blindness; purblindness, lippitude; my-, presby-opia; confusion of vision; astigmatism, nystagmus; colour-blindness, dichromism, chromato-pseudo-blepsis, Daltonism; nyctalopy; *strabismus*, strabism, squint, cast in the eye, swivel eye, goggle eyes; obliquity of vision.

winking &c. *v.*; nictitation; blinkard, albino.

dizziness, swimming, scotomy; cataract; ophthalmia.

[Limitation of vision] eye shade, blinker, blinder; screen &c. (*hider*) 530.

[Fallacies of vision] *deceptio visûs*; refraction, distortion, illusion, false light, *anamorphosis*, virtual image, *spectrum*, *mirage*, looming, phasma; phant-asm, -asma, -om; vision; spectre, apparition, ghost; *ignis fatuus* &c. (*luminary*) 423; spectre of the Brocken; magic mirror; magic lantern &c. (*show*) 448; mirror, lens &c. (*instrument*) 445.

V. be -dim-sighted &c. *n.*; see double; have a -mote in the eye, - mist before the eyes, - film over the eyes; see through a -prism, - glass darkly; wink, blink, nictitate; squint; look ask-ant, -ance; screw up the eyes, glare, glower.

dazzle, glare, blur, swim, loom.

Adj. dim-sighted &c. *n.*; my-, presby-opic; astigmatic; moon-, mope-, blear-, goggle-, gooseberry-, one-eyed; blind of one eye, monoculous; half-, pur-, colour-blind; dichromatic.

blind as a bat &c. (*blind*) 442; winking &c. *v.*

444. Spectator.—**N.** spectator, beholder, observer, inspector, viewer, looker-on, onlooker, witness, eye-witness, bystander, passer by; sight-seer.

spy, scout; sentinel &c. (*warning*) 668.

V. witness, behold &c. (*see*) 441; look on &c. (*be present*) 186.

445. Optical Instruments.—**N.** optical instruments; lens, meniscus, magnifier, reading -, burning- glass; micro-, mega-, teino-scope; spectacles, glasses, barnacles, goggles, giglamps, eyeglass, *pince-nez*, monocle; periscopic lens; telescope, glass, lorgnette, binocular; spy-, opera-, field-glass, periscope, range finder.

mirror, reflector, speculum; looking-, pier-, cheval-, hand-glass.

prism; camera, *camera-lucida*, *-obscura*; projector, stereopticon, magic lantern &c. (*show*) 448; chro-, thaumatrope; stereo-, pseudo-, poly-, kaleido-scope.

photo-, opto-, erio-, actino-, luci-, radio-, spectro-meter; polari-, polemo-, spectro-scope, diffraction grating.

optics, optician, optometry, optometrist; microscop-y, -ist; photometry, photography; photographer.

446. Visibility.—**N.** visibility, perceptibility; conspicuousness, distinctness &c. *adj.*; conspicuity; appearance &c. 448; exposure; manifestation &c. 525; ocular -proof, - evidence, - demonstration; field of view &c. (*vision*) 441.

V. be -, become- -visible &c. *adj.*; appear, emerge, open to the view; meet -, catch- the eye; present -, show -, manifest -, produce -, discover -, reveal -, expose -, betray-itself; stand -forth, - out; show; arise; peep -, peer -, crop- out; start -, spring -, show -, turn -, crop- up; glimmer, glitter, glow, loom; glare; burst forth, scintillate; burst upon the -view, - sight; heave in sight; come -in sight, - into view, - out, - forth, - forward; see the light of day; break through the clouds; make its appearance, show its face, materialize, appear to one's eyes, come upon the stage, enter; float before the eyes, speak for itself &c. (*manifest*) 525; attract the attention &c. 457; reappear; live in a glass house.

expose to view &c. 525.

Adj. visible, perceptible, perceivable, discernible, apparent; in -view, - full view, - sight; exposed to view, *en évidence*; unclouded.

obvious &c. (*manifest*) 525; plain, clear, distinct, definite; well- defined, -marked; in focus; recognizable, palpable, autoptical; glaring, staring, conspicuous; stereoscopic; in -bold, - strong, - high- relief.

periscopic, panoramic.

before -, under- one's eyes; before one, *à vue d'œil*, in one's eye, *oculis subjecta fidelibus*.

Adv. visibly &c. *adj.*; in sight of; before one's eyes &c. *adj.; veluti in speculum.*

447. Invisibility.—N. invisibility,
non-appearance, imperceptibility; indistinctness &c. *adj.*; mystery, delitescence.

concealment &c. 528; latency &c. 526.

V. be -invisible &c. *adj.*; be hidden &c. (*hide*) 528; lurk &c. (*lie hidden*) 526; escape notice.

render -invisible &c. *adj.*; conceal &c. 528; put out of sight.

not see &c. (*be blind*) 442; lose sight of.

Adj. invisible, imperceptible; un-, indiscernible; un-, non-apparent; out of -, not in- sight; *à perte de vue*; behind the -scenes, - curtain; view-, sight-less; in-, un-conspicuous; unseen &c. (*see* &c. 441); covert &c. (*latent*) 526; eclipsed, under an eclipse.

dim &c. (*faint*) 422; mysterious, dark, obscure, confused; indistin-ct, -guishable; shadowy, indefinite, undefined; ill-defined, -marked; blurred, fuzzy, out of focus; misty &c. (*opaque*)

426; veiled &c. (*concealed*) 528; delitescent.

448. Appearance.—N. appearance,
phenomenon, sight, spectacle, show, premonstration, scene, species, view, *coup d'œil*; look-out, out-look, prospect, vista, perspective, bird's-eye view, scenery, landscape, picture, *tableau*; display, exposure, *mise en scène*; scenery, *décor*; rising of the curtain.

phant-asm, -om &c. (*fallacy of vision*) 443.

pageant, *spectacle*; peep-, raree-, gallanty-show; *ombres chinoises*; projector, optical -, magic- lantern, phantasmagoria, dissolving views; cinema, -tograph; bio-scope, -graph; moving pictures, movies, film, screen &c.; pan-, di-, cosm-, ge-orama; *coup -, jeu- de théâtre*; pageantry &c. (*ostentation*) 882; insignia &c. (*indication*) 550.

aspect, phase, *phasis*, seeming; shape &c. (*form*) 240; guise, look, complexion, colour, image, mien, air, cast, carriage, port, demeanour; presence, expression, first blush, face of the thing; point of view, light.

lineament, feature, trait, lines; outline, -side; contour, *silhouette*, face, countenance, physiognomy, visage, phiz, mug, cast of countenance, profile, *tournure*, cut of one's jib, metoposcopy; outside &c. 220.

V. appear; be -, become- visible &c. 446; seem, look, show; present -, wear -, carry -, have -, bear -, exhibit -, take -, take on -, assume- the -appearance, - semblance; look like; cut a figure, figure; present to the view; show &c. (*make manifest*) 525.

Adj. apparent, seeming, ostensible; on view.

Adv. apparently; to all -seeming, - appearance; ostensibly, seemingly, as it seems, on the face of it, *primâ facie*; at the first blush, at first sight; in the eyes of; to the eye.

449. Disappearance.—N. disappearance, evanescence, eclipse, occultation.

departure &c. 293; exit, vanishing point; dissolving views.

V. disappear, vanish, dissolve, fade, melt away, pass, go, avaunt; be -gone &c. *adj.*; leave -no trace, – 'not a rack behind'; go off the stage &c. (*depart*) 293; suffer –, undergo- an eclipse; be lost to –, retire from- -sight, – view.

lose sight of.
efface &c. 552.

Adj. disappearing &c. *v.*; evanescent; missing, lost; lost to -sight, – view; gone; *spurlos versenkt*.

Int. vanish! disappear! avaunt! &c. (*ejection*) 297.

CLASS IV

WORDS RELATING TO THE
INTELLECTUAL FACULTIES

DIVISION (I.) FORMATION OF IDEAS

Section I.
OPERATIONS OF INTELLECT
IN GENERAL

450. Intellect.—N. intellect, mind, understanding, reason, thinking principle; rationality; cogitative -, cognitive -, intellectual- faculties; faculties, senses, consciousness, observation, percipience, apperception, mentality, intelligence, intellection, intuition, association of ideas, instinct, flair, conception, judgment, wits, parts, capacity, intellectuality, reasoning power, brains, genius; wit &c. 498; ability &c. (*skill*) 698; wisdom &c. 498.

soul, spirit, ghost, inner man, heart, breast, bosom, *penetralia mentis, divina particula auræ,* heart's core; ego, psyche, pneuma, subconsciousness, subconscious, subliminal self; dual personality.

organ -, seat- of thought; *sensorium,* sensory, brain, gray matter; head, -piece; pate, noddle, skull, scull, *pericranium, cerebrum, cranium,* brain-pan, -box; sconce, upper story.

[Science of mind] metaphysics; psychics, psycho-logy, -metry, -genesis, -analysis, -physics, psychi-atry, -cal research, thought reading &c. 992; ideology; mental -, moral- philosophy; philosophy of the mind; pneumat-, phrenology; no -, cranio-logy, -scopy.

ideal-ity, -ism; transcendental-, spiritual-ism; immateriality &c. 317.

metaphysician, psychologist &c.

V. note, notice, mark; take -notice, -

cognizance- of; be -aware, - conscious-of; realize; appreciate; ruminate &c. (*think*) 451; fancy &c. (*imagine*) 515; conceive, reason, understand.

Adj. [Relating to intellect] intellectual, mental, rational, subjective, metaphysical, nooscopic, spiritual; ghostly; psych-ical, -ological; cerebral.

immaterial &c. 317; endowed with reason.

Adv. *in petto.*

450a. Absence or want **of Intellect.—N.** absence -, want- of -intellect &c. 450; imbecility &c. 499; brutality; brute -instinct, - force.

Adj. unendowed with reason.

451. Thought.—N. thought; exercitation -, exercise- of the intellect; reflection, cogitation, consideration, meditation, study, lucubration, speculation, deliberation, pondering; head-, brain-work; cerebration; mentation, deep reflection; close study, application &c. (*attention*) 457.

abstract thought, abstraction, contemplation, musing; brown study &c. (*inattention*) 458; reverie, Platonism; depth of thought, workings of the mind, thoughts, inmost thoughts; self-counsel, -communing, -consultation.

association -, succession -, flow -, train -, current- of -thought, - ideas.

after -, mature- thought; reconsideration,

second thoughts; retrospection &c. (*memory*) 505; excogitation; examination &c. (*inquiry*) 461; invention &c. (*imagination*) 515.

thoughtfulness &c. *adj.*

V. think, reflect, reason, cogitate, excogitate, consider, deliberate; bestow - thought, - consideration- upon; speculate, contemplate, meditate, ponder, muse, dream, ruminate; brood -, con- over; animadvert, study; bend -, apply- the mind &c. (*attend*) 457; digest, discuss, hammer at, weigh, perpend; realize, appreciate; fancy &c. (*imagine*) 515; trow.

take into consideration; take counsel &c. (*be advised*) 695; commune with -, bethink- oneself; collect one's thoughts; revolve -, turn over -, run over- in the mind; chew the cud -, sleep- upon; take counsel of -, advise with- one's pillow.

rack -, ransack -, crack -, beat -, cudgel- one's brains; set one's -brain, - wits- to work.

harbour -, entertain -, cherish -, nurture- an -idea &c. 453; take into one's head; bear in mind; reconsider.

occur; present -, suggest- itself; come -, get- into one's head; strike one, flit across the view, come uppermost, run in one's head; enter -, pass in -, cross -, flash on -, flash across -, float in -, fasten itself on -, be uppermost in -, occupy- the mind; have in one's mind.

make an impression; sink -, penetrate- into the mind; engross the thoughts.

Adj. thinking &c. *v.*; thoughtful, pensive, meditative, reflective, cogitative, museful, wistful, contemplative, speculative, deliberative, studious, sedate, introspective, Platonic, philosophical.

lost -, engrossed -, rapt -, absorbed- in thought &c. (*inattentive*) 458; deep musing &c. (*intent*) 457.

in the mind, under consideration, in contemplation.

Adv. all things considered; taking everything into account.

Phr. the mind being on the stretch;

the -mind, - head- -turning, - running- upon.

452. [Absence or want of thought.] **Incogitancy.—N.** incogitancy, vacancy, inunderstanding; inanity, fatuity &c. 499; thoughtlessness &c. (*inattention*) 458.

V. not -think &c. 451; not think of; dismiss from the -mind, - thoughts &c. 451.

indulge in reverie &c. (*be inattentive*) 458.

put away thought; unbend -, relax -, divert- the mind.

Adj. vacant, unintellectual, unideal, unoccupied, unthinking, inconsiderate, thoughtless; absent &c. (*inattentive*) 458; diverted; irrational &c. 499; narrow-minded &c. 481.

un-thought of, -dreamt of, -considered; off one's mind; incogitable, not to be thought of, inconceivable.

453. [Object of thought.] **Idea.—N.** idea, notion, conception, thought, apprehension, impression, perception, image, sentiment, reflection, observation, consideration; abstract idea, principle; archetype.

view &c. (*opinion*) 484; theory &c. 514; conceit, fancy; phantasy &c. (*imagination*) 515.

point of view &c. (*aspect*) 448; field of view.

454. [Subject of thought.] **Topic.—N.** subject of -, material for- thought; food for the mind, mental *pabulum*.

subject, -matter; matter, theme, topic, what it is about, *thesis*, text, business, affair, matter in hand, argument; motion, resolution; head, chapter; case, point; proposition, theorem; field of inquiry; moot point, problem, &c. (*question*) 461.

V. float -, pass- in the mind &c. 451.

Adj. thought of; uppermost in the mind; *in petto*.

Adv. under -discussion, - consideration, - advisement; in -question, - the mind; on -foot, – the carpet, – the *tapis*; before the house, relative to &c. 9.

Section II. PRECURSORY CONDITIONS AND OPERATIONS

455. [The desire of knowledge.] **Curiosity.—N.** interest, thirst for knowledge; curi-osity, -ousness; inquiring mind; inquisitiveness.

sight-seer, quidnunc, newsmonger, Paul Pry, peeping Tom, eavesdropper; gossip &c. (*news*) 532; questioner, *enfant terrible.*

V. be -curious &c. *adj.*; take an interest in, stare, gape; prick up the ears, see sights, lionize; pry, speer; dig up.

Adj. curious, inquisitive, burning with curiosity, overcurious, nosey; inquiring &c. 461; prying; inquisitorial; agape &c. (*expectant*) 507; attentive &c. 457.

Phr. what's the matter? what next?

456. [Absence of curiosity.] **Incuriosity.—N.** incuriosity; incuriousness &c. *adj.*; *insouciance* &c. 866; indifference, apathy.

V. be -incurious &c. *adj.*; have no -curiosity &c. 455; take no interest in &c. 823; mind one's own business.

Adj. incurious, uninquisitive, uninterested, indifferent, bored; impassive &c. 823.

457. Attention.—N. attention; mindfulness &c. *adj.*; intent-ness, -iveness; thought &c. 451; adverten-ce, -cy; observ-ance, -ation; consideration, reflection, perpension; heed; particularity; notice, regard &c. *v.*; circumspection &c. (*care*) 459; study, scrutiny, once-over; in-, intro-spection; revision, -al.

active -, diligent -, exclusive -, minute -, close -, intense -, deep -, profound -, abstract -, laboured -, deliberate- -thought, – attention, – application, – study.

minuteness, attention to detail &c. 459.

absorption of mind &c. (*abstraction*) 458.

indication, calling attention to &c. *v.*

V. be -attentive &c. *adj.*; attend, advert to, observe, look, see, view, remark, notice, regard, take notice, mark; give –, pay- -attention, – heed-to; listen in, incline –, lend- an ear to; trouble one's head about; give a thought –, animadvert- to; occupy oneself with; contemplate &c. (*think of*) 451; look -at, – to, – after, – into, – over; see to; turn –, bend –, apply –, direct –, give- the -mind, – eye, – attention- to; have -an eye to, – in one's eye; bear in mind; take into -account, – consideration; keep in -sight, – view; have regard to, heed, mind, take cognizance of, be engaged in, entertain, recognize; make –, take-note of; note.

examine cursorily; glance -at, – upon, – over; cast –, pass- the eyes over; run over, turn over the leaves, dip into, perstringe; skim &c. (*neglect*) 460; take a cursory view of.

examine, – closely, – intently; scan, scrutinize, consider; give –, bend- one's mind to; overhaul, revise, pore over; inspect, review, pass under review; take stock of; fix –, rivet –, focus –, devote-the -eye, – mind, – thoughts, – attention- on *or* to; hear –, think- out; mind one's business.

revert –, hark back- to; watch &c. (*expect*) 507, (*take care of*) 459; hearken –, listen- to; prick up the ears; have –, keep- the eyes open; come to the point.

meet with attention; fall under one's -notice, – observation; be -under consideration &c. (*topic*) 454.

catch –, strike- the eye; attract notice; catch –, awaken –, wake –, invite –, solicit –, attract –, claim –, excite –, engage –, occupy –, strike –, arrest –, fix –, engross –, absorb –, rivet- the-attention, – mind, – thoughts; be -present to, – uppermost in- the mind.

bring under one's notice; point -out, – to, – at, – the finger at; lay the finger on, indigitate, indicate; direct –, call- attention to; show; put a -mark &c. (*sign*) 550- upon; call soldiers to 'attention'; bring forward &c. (*make manifest*) 525.

Adj. attentive, mindful, heedful, observant, regardful; alive -, awake- to, alert; observing &c. *v.*; taken up -, occupied- with; engaged -, engrossed -, interested -, wrapped- in; absorbed, rapt; breathless; pre-occupied &c. (*inattentive*) 458; watchful &c. (*careful*) 459; intent on, open-eyed, breathless, undistracted, upon the stretch; on the watch &c. (*expectant*) 507 steadfast.

Int. see! look, - here, - out, - alive, - you, - to it! mark! lo! behold! soho! hark, - ye! mind! halloo! observe! lo and behold! attention! *nota bene*; N.B.; *, †; I'd have you to know; notice! take notice! O yes! *Oyez!*

Phr. this is -, these are- to give notice.

458. Inattention.—N. in-attention, -consideration; inconsiderateness &c. *adj.*; oversight; inadverten-ce, -cy; non-observance, disregard.

supineness &c. (*inactivity*) 683; *étourderie*; want of thought; heedlessness &c. (*neglect*) 460; insouciance &c. (*indifference*) 866.

abstraction; absence -, absorption- of mind; preoccupation, distraction, reverie, brown study, deep musing, fit of abstraction, woolgathering.

V. be -inattentive &c. *adj.*; overlook, disregard; pass by &c. (*neglect*) 460; not -observe &c. 457; think little of.

close -, shut- one's eyes to; wink at; pay no attention to; dismiss -, discard -, discharge- from one's -thoughts, - mind; drop the subject, think no more of; set -, turn -, put- aside; turn -away from, - one's attention from, - a deaf ear to, - one's back upon.

abstract oneself, dream, indulge in reverie.

escape -notice, - attention; come in at one ear and go out at the other; forget &c. (*have no remembrance*) 506.

call off -, draw off -, call away -, divert -, distract- the -attention, - thoughts, - mind; put out of one's head; dis-concert, -compose; put out, confuse, perplex, bewilder, moider, fluster, muddle, dazzle; throw a sop to Cerberus.

Adj. inattentive; un-observant, -mindful, -heeding, -discerning; inadvertent; mind-, regard-, respect-less; listless &c. (*indifferent*) 866; blind, deaf; flighty, hand over head; cur-, percur-sory; giddy-, scatter-, hare-brained; unreflecting, *écervelé*, inconsiderate, off-hand, thoughtless, dizzy, muzzy, brainsick; giddy, - as a goose; wild, harum-scarum, rantipole, high-flying; heed-, care-less &c. (*neglectful*) 460.

absent, absent-minded, abstracted, *distrait*; lost; lost -, wrapped- in thought, woolgathering; rapt, in the clouds, bemused; dreaming -, musing- on other things; pre-occupied; engrossed &c. (*attentive*) 457; in a -reverie &c. *n.*; off one's guard &c. (*inexpectant*) 508; napping; dreamy.

disconcerted, put out &c. *v.*; rattled.

Adv. inattentively, inadvertently &c. *adj.*; *per incuriam, sub silentio.*

Int. stand -at ease, - easy!

Phr. the attention wanders; one's wits gone a -woolgathering, - bird's nesting; it never entered into one's head; the mind running on other things; one's thoughts being elsewhere; had it been a bear it would have bitten you.

459. Care. [Vigilance.]—N. care, solicitude, heed; heedfulness &c. *adj.*; scruple &c. (*conscientiousness*) 939.

watchfulness &c. *adj.*; vigilance, *surveillance*, eyes of Argus, watch, vigil, look out, watch and ward, *l'œil du maître*.

alertness &c. (*activity*) 682; attention &c. 457; prudence &c., circumspection &c. (*caution*) 864; forethought &c. 510; precaution &c. (*preparation*) 673; tidiness &c. (*order*) 58, (*cleanliness*) 652; accuracy &c. (*exactness*) 494; minuteness, attention to detail; meticulousness, nicety, circumstantiality.

V. be -careful &c. *adj.*; reck; take care &c. (*be cautious*) 864; pay attention to &c. 457; take care of; look -, see- -to, - after; keep -an eye, - a sharp eye- upon; keep -watch, - watch and ward; mount guard, set watch, watch; keep in -sight, - view; chaperon, play gooseberry; mind, - one's business.

look -sharp, - about one; look with one's own eyes; keep a -good, - sharp-look-out; have all one's -wits, - eyes-about one; watch for &c. (*expect*) 507; stand to; keep one's eyes -, have the eyes -, sleep with one eye- open.

take precautions &c. 673; protect &c. (*render safe*) 664.

do one's best &c. 682; mind one's Ps and Qs, speak by the card, pick one's steps.

Adj. care-, regard-, heed-ful; taking care &c. *v.*; particular; prudent &c. (*cautious*) 864; considerate; thoughtful &c. (*deliberative*) 451; provident &c. (*prepared*) 673; alert &c. (*active*) 682; sure-footed.

guarded, on one's guard; on the -*qui vive*, - alert, - watch, - look-out; awake, broad awake, vigilant; watch-, wake-, wist-ful; Argus-, lynx- eyed; wide awake &c. (*intelligent*) 498; on the watch for &c. (*expectant*) 507.

tidy &c. (*orderly*) 58, (*clean*) 652; accurate &c. (*exact*) 494; scrupulous &c. (*conscientious*) 939; *cavendo tutus* &c. (*safe*) 664.

Adv. carefully &c. *adj.*; with care, gingerly.

Phr. *quis custodiet ipsos custodes?*

460. Neglect.—N. neglect; carelessness &c. *adj.*; trifling &c. *v.*; negligence; omission, laches, default; remissness, slackness, procrastination; supineness &c. (*inactivity*) 683; inattention &c. 458; *nonchalance* &c. (*insensibility*) 823; imprudence, recklessness &c. 863; slovenliness &c. (*disorder*) 59, (*dirt*) 653; improvidence &c. 674; non-completion &c. 730; inexactness &c. (*error*) 495.

paraleipsis [in rhetoric].

trifler, slacker, waster, waiter on Providence; Micawber.

V. be -negligent &c. *adj.*; take no care of &c. (*take care of &c.* 459); neglect; let -slip, - go; lay -, set -, cast -, put- aside; keep -, leave- out of sight; lose sight of.

overlook, disregard; pass -over, - by; let pass; blink; wink -, connive- at; gloss over; take no -note, - notice, - thought, - account- of; pay no regard to; *laisser aller*; allow to lie on the table.

scamp; trifle, fribble; do by halves; skimp; cut; slight &c. (*despise*) 930; play -, trifle- with; slur; skim, - the surface; *effleurer*; take a cursory view of &c. 457.

slur -, slip -, skip -, jump- over; pretermit, miss, skip, jump, omit, give the go-by to, push aside, throw into the background, shelve, sink; ignore, shut one's eyes to, refuse to hear, turn a deaf ear to; leave out of one's calculation; not -attend to &c. 457, - mind; not trouble -oneself, - one's head -with, –about; forget &c. 506; be caught napping &c. (*not expect*) 508; leave a loose thread; let the grass grow under one's feet.

render -neglectful &c. *adj.*; put -, throw- off one's guard.

Adj. neglecting &c. *v.*; unmindful, negligent, neglectful; heedless, careless, thoughtless; perfunctory, remiss, slack.

inconsiderate; un-, in-circumspect; off one's guard; un-wary, -watchful, - guarded; offhand.

supine &c. (*inactive*) 683; inattentive &c. 458; *insouciant* &c. (*indifferent*) 823; imprudent, reckless &c. 863; slovenly &c. (*disorderly*) 59, (*dirty*) 653; inexact &c. (*erroneous*) 495; improvident &c. 674.

neglected &c. *v.*; un-heeded, -cared for, -perceived, -seen, -observed, -noticed, -noted, -marked, -attended to, -thought of, -regarded, -remarked, -missed; shunted, shelved.

un-examined, -studied, -searched, -scanned, -weighed, -sifted, -explored.

abandoned; buried in a napkin, hid under a bushel.

Adv. negligently &c. *adj.*; hand over head, anyhow; in an unguarded moment &c. (*unexpectedly*) 508; *per incuriam.*

Int. never mind, no matter, let it pass; it will be all the same a hundred years hence.

461. Inquiry. [Subject of Inquiry. Question.]—**N.** inquiry; request &c. 765; search, research, quest; pursuit &c. 622.

examination, review, scrutiny, investigation, indagation; per-quisition, -scrutation, -vestigation; inqu-est, -isition; exploration; *exploitation*, ventilation.

sifting; calculation, analysis, dissection, resolution, induction; Baconian method.

strict -, close -, searching -, exhaustive- inquiry; narrow -, strict-search; study &c. (*consideration*) 451.

scire facias, ad referendum; trial.

questioning &c. *v.*; interroga-tion, -tory; third degree; interpellation; challenge, examination, cross-examination, catechism; feeler, Socratic method, zetetic philosophy; leading question; discussion &c. (*reasoning*) 476; questionnaire, questionary.

reconnoitering, *reconnaissance*; prying &c. *v.*; espionage, *espionnage*; domiciliary visit, peep behind the curtain; lantern of Diogenes.

question, query, problem, *desideratum*, point to be solved, porism; subject -, field- of -inquiry, - controversy; point -, matter- in dispute; moot-point; issue, question at issue; bone of contention &c. (*discord*) 713; plain -, fair -, open-question; enigma &c. (*secret*) 533; knotty point &c. (*difficulty*) 704; *quodlibet*; threshold of an inquiry.

inquirer, investigator, experimenter, inquisitor, inspector, querist, examiner, catechist; scrut-ator, -ineer; analyst; quidnunc &c. (*curiosity*) 455.

V. make -inquiry &c. *n.*; inquire, seek, search, frisk, speer, look -for, -

about for, - out for; scan, reconnoitre, explore, sound, rummage, ransack, pry, peer, look round; look -, go- -over, -through; spy, over-haul.

scratch the head, slap the forehead.

look -, peer -, pry- into every hole and corner; look behind the scenes; trace up; hunt -, fish -, dig -, ferret- out; unearth; leave no stone unturned.

seek a -clue, - clew; hunt, track, trail, shadow, mouse, dodge, trace; follow the -trail, - scent; pursue &c. 622; beat up one's quarters; fish for; feel for &c. (*experiment*) 463.

investigate; take up -, institute -, pursue -, follow up -, conduct -, carry on -, prosecute- -an inquiry &c. *n.*; look -at, - into; pre-examine; discuss, canvass, agitate.

examine, study, consider, calculate; dip -, dive -, delve -, go deep- into; make sure of, probe, sound, fathom; probe to the -bottom, - quick; scrutinize, analyze, anatomize, dissect, parse, resolve, sift, winnow; view -, try- in all its phases; thresh out.

bring in question, subject to examination; put to the proof &c. (*experiment*) 463; audit, tax, pass in review; take into consideration &c. (*think over*) 451; take counsel &c. 695.

ask, question, demand; put -, pop -, propose -, propound -, moot -, start -, raise -, stir -, suggest -, put forth -, ventilate -, grapple with -, go into- a question.

put to the question, interrogate, catechize, pump, grill; cross-question, -examine; dodge; require an answer; pick -, suck- the brains of; feel the pulse.

be -in question &c. *adj.*; undergo examination.

Adj. inquiry &c. *v.*; inquisitive &c. (*curious*) 455; requisit-ive, -ory; catechetical, inquisitorial, analytic; in -search, - quest- of; on the look-out for, interrogative, zetetic; all-searching.

un-determined, -tried, -decided; in -question, - dispute, - issue, - course of inquiry; under -discussion, - consideration, - investigation &c. *n.*, *sub judice*, moot, proposed; doubtful &c. (*uncertain*) 475.

Adv. what? why? wherefore? whence? whither? where? *quære?* how -comes, – happens, – is- it? what is the reason? what's -the matter, – up, – in the wind? what on earth? when? who?

462. Answer.—N. answer, response, reply, replication, *riposte*, rejoinder, surrejoinder, rebutter, surrebutter, counter-evidence &c. 468, counter-charge, defence, plea; retort, repartee, contradiction &c. 536; rescript, -ion, antiphon, -y; acknowledgment; pass word; echo.

discovery &c. 480*a*; solution &c. (*explanation*) 522; rationale &c. (*cause*) 153; clue &c. (*indication*) 550.

Œdipus; oracle &c. 513; return &c. (*record*) 551.

V. answer, respond, reply, rebut, retort, rejoin; give –, return for- answer; acknowledge, echo.

explain &c. (*interpret*) 522; solve &c. (*unriddle*) 522; discover &c. 480*a*; fathom, hunt out &c. (*inquire*) 461; satisfy, set at rest, determine.

Adj. answering &c. *v.*; respon-sive, -dent; oracular; antiphonal; conclusive.

Adv. because &c. (*cause*) 153; on the -scent, – right scent.

Int. *eureka!*

463. Experiment.—N. experiment; essay &c. (*attempt*) 675; research &c. (*investigation*) 461; trial, tentative method, *tâtonnement*.

verification, probation, *experimentum crucis*, proof, criterion, diagnostic, test, tryout, crucial test, acid test.

crucible, reagent, check, touchstone, pix; assay ordeal; ring.

empiricism, rule of thumb.

feeler; pilot –, messenger- balloon, *ballon d'essai*; pilot engine; scout; straw to show the wind.

speculation, random shot, leap in the dark.

analy-zer, -st; adventurer, explorer, sourdough, prospector; experiment-er, -ist, -alist; assayer.

V. experiment; essay &c. (*endeavour*) 675; try, assay, sample; make -an experiment, – trial of; give a trial to; put upon –, subject to- trial; experiment upon; rehearse; put –, bring –, submit-to the -test, – proof; prove, verify, test, touch, practise upon, try one's strength.

grope; feel –, grope- -for, – one's way; fumble; *tâttonner, aller à tâtons*; put –, throw- out a feeler; send up a pilot balloon; see how the -land lies, – wind blows; consult the barometer; feel the pulse; fish –, bob- for; cast –, beat-about for; angle, trawl, cast one's net, beat the bushes.

venture, try one's fortune &c. (*adventure*) 675; explore &c. (*inquire*) 461.

Adj. experimental; probat-ive, -ory, -ionary; analytic, docimastic; tentative; empirical; speculative, tentative.

under probation, on one's trial, on trial, on approval.

464. Comparison.—N. comparison, collation, contrast; identification.

sim-ile, -ilitude; allegory &c. (*metaphor*) 521.

V. compare -to, – with; collate, confront; place side by side &c. (*near*) 197; set –, pit- against one another; contrast, balance.

identify, draw a parallel, parallel.

compare notes; institute a comparison; *parva componere magnis*.

Adj. comparative, relative; metaphorical &c. 521.

compared with &c. *v.*; comparable.

Adv. relatively &c. (*relation*) 9; as compared with &c. *v.*

465. Discrimination.—N. discrimination, distinction, differentiation, diagnosis, diorism; nice perception; perception –, appreciation- of difference; acuteness; estimation &c. 466; nicety, refinement; taste &c. 850; *critique*, judgement, tact; insight, discernment &c. (*intelligence*) 498; *nuances*.

V. discriminate, distinguish, differentiate –, severalize; separate; draw the line, sift; separate –, winnow- the chaff from the wheat; split hairs.

estimate &c. (*measure*) 466; know -which is which, – one's stuff, – one's way about, – what is what, – 'a hawk from a handsaw.'

take into -account, – consideration; give –, allow- due weight to; weigh carefully.

Adj. discriminating &c. *v.*; dioristic, discriminative, critical, distinctive; nice.

Phr. *il y a fagots et fagots; rem acu tetigisti.*

465a. Indiscrimination.—N. indiscrimination; promiscuity; indistinctness, -ion; uncertainty &c. (*doubt*) 475; obtuseness.

V. not -indiscriminate &c. 465; overlook &c. (*neglect*) 460- a distinction; con-found, -fuse, jumble; swallow whole.

Adj. indiscriminate, undiscriminating, promiscuous; undistinguish-ed, -able, -ing; unmeasured.

466. Measurement.—N. measurement, admeasurement, mensuration, survey, valuation, appriasement, assessment, assize; estim-ate, -ation; dead reckoning; reckoning &c. (*numeration*) 85; gauging &c. *v.*

metrology, weights and measures, compound arithmetic.

measure, yard measure, standard, rule, foot-rule, chain, tape, staff, compass, callipers; dividers; gage, gauge, planimeter; meter, line, rod, check.

volt, kilowatt, ampere, candle power; horse power; axle load; foot pound.

flood –, high water- mark; Plimsoll mark; index &c. 550.

scale; gradu-ation, -ated scale; nonius; vernier &c. (*minuteness*) 193; pedo (*length*)- 200, sounding line &c. (*depth*) 208, thermo (*heat* &c. 389)-, baro (*air* &c. 338)-, dynamo (*power*)- 276, anemo (*wind* 349)-, gonio (*angle* 244)- meter; landmark &c. (*limit*) 233; balance &c. (*weight*) 310; optical instruments &c. 445.

co-ordinates, ordinate and abscissa, polar co-ordinates, latitude and longi-

tude, declination and right ascension, altitude and azimuth.

geo-, stereo-, hypso-metry; metage; surveying, land- surveying; geo-desy, -detics, -desia; ortho-, alti-metry; *cadastre.*

astrolabe, armillary sphere.

land -surveyor; geometer, topographer, cartographer, hydrographer.

V. measure, meter, mete; value, assess, rate, appriase, estimate, form an estimate, set a value on; appreciate; standardize.

span, pace, step; apply the -compass &c. *n.*; gauge, plumb, probe, calliper, sound, fathom &c. 208; heave the -log, -lead; weigh &c. 319; survey.

take an average &c. 29; graduate.

Adj. measuring &c. *v.*; metric, -al; measurable; geodetical, cadastral, topographical.

Section III. MATERIALS FOR REASONING

467. Evidence [on one side.]**—N.** evidence; facts, premises *data, præcognita,* grounds.

indication &c. 550; criterion &c. (*test*) 463.

testi-mony, -fication; attestation; deposition &c. (*affirmation*) 535; examination.

admission &c. (*assent*) 488; authority, warrant, credential, diploma, voucher, certificate, docket; record &c. 551; document, muniments; *pièce justificative;* deed, warranty &c. (*security*) 771; signature, seal &c. (*identification*) 550; exhibit, citation, reference.

witness, indicator; eye-, ear-witness; deponent; sponsor.

oral –, documentary –, hearsay –, external –, extrinsic –, internal –, intrinsic –, circumstantial –, cumulative –, *ex parte* –, presumptive –, collateral –, constructive- evidence; proof &c. (*demonstration*) 478; evidence in chief; finger prints, dactylogram.

secondary evidence; confirmation, corroboration, adminicle, support; ratification &c. (*assent*) 488; authentication, verification; compurgation, wager of law, comprobation.

citation, reference.

V. be -evidence &c. *n.*; evince, show, betoken, tell of; indicate &c. (*denote*) 550; imply, involve, argue, bespeak, breathe.

have -, carry- weight; tell, speak volumes; speak for itself &c. (*manifest*) 525.

rest -, depend- upon; repose on.

bear -witness &c. *n.*; give -evidence &c. *n.*; testify, depose, witness, vouch for; sign, seal, undersign, set one's hand and seal, sign and seal, deliver as one's act and deed, certify, attest; acknowledge &c. (*assent*) 488.

make absolute, confirm, ratify, corroborate, endorse, countersign, support, bear out, vindicate, uphold, warrant.

adduce, attest, cite, quote; refer -, appeal- to; call, - to witness; bring -forward, - into court; allege, plead; produce -, confront- witnesses; collect -, bring together -, rake up- evidence.

have -, make out- a case; establish, circumstantiate, authenticate, substantiate, verify, make good, quote chapter and verse; bring -home to, - to book.

Adj. showing &c. *v.*; evidential, indica-tive, -tory; deducible &c. 478; grounded -, founded -, based- on; first hand, authentic, verifiable; corroborative, confirmatory; significant, conclusive.

Adv. by inference; according to, witness, *a fortiori*; still -more, - less; *raison de plus*; in corroboration &c. *n.* of; *valeat quantum*; under -seal, - one's hand and seal.

468. [Evidence on the other side, on the other hand.] **Counter-evidence.—N.** counter-evidence; evidence on the other -side, - hand; disproof; refutation &c. 479; negation &c. 536; conflicting evidence.

plea &c. 617; vindication &c. 937;

counter-protest; *tu quoque* argument; other side -, reverse- of the shield.

V. countervail, oppose; run counter; rebut &c. (*refute*) 479; subvert &c. (*destroy*) 162; check, weaken; contravene; contradict &c. (*deny*) 536; tell another story, turn the -tables, - scale; alter the case; cut both ways; prove a negative.

audire alteram partem.

Adj. countervailing &c. *v.*; contradictory, in rebuttal.

un-attested, -authenticated, -supported by evidence; supposititious, trumped up.

Adv. *per contra*, conversely, on the other hand.

469. Qualification.—N. qualification, limitation, modification, colouring.

allowance, grains of allowance, consideration, extenuating circumstances.

condition, proviso, exception; exemption; salvo, saving clause; discount &c. 813.

V. qualify, limit, modify, affect, temper, leaven, give a colour to, introduce new conditions.

allow -, make allowance- for; admit exceptions, take into account.

take exception, object.

Adj. qualifying &c. *v.*; conditional; extenuatory; exceptional &c. (*unconformable*) 83.

hypothetical &c. (*supposed*) 514; contingent &c. (*uncertain*) 475.

Adv. provided, - always; if, unless, but, yet; according as; conditionally, admitting, supposing; on the supposition of &c. (*theoretically*) 514; with the understanding, even, although, though, for all that, after all, at all events.

with grains of allowance, *cum grano salis*; *exceptis excipiendis*; wind and weather permitting; if possible &c. 470.

subject to; with this -proviso &c. *n.*

Degrees of Evidence

470. Possibility.—N. possibility, potentiality; what -may be, - is possible &c. *adj.*; compatibility &c. (*agreement*) 23.

practicability, feasibility; practicableness &c. *adj.*

contingency, chance &c. 156.

V. be -possible &c. *adj.*; stand a chance, have a leg to stand on; admit of, bear.

render -possible &c. *adj.*; put in the way of.

Adj. possible; on the -cards, - dice; *in posse*, within the bounds of possibility, conceivable, credible, imaginable; compatible &c. 23.

practicable, feasible, workable, performable, achievable; within -reach, - measurable distance; accessible, superable, surmountable; at-, ob-tainable; contingent &c. (*doubtful*) 475.

Adv. possibly, by possibility; perhaps, -chance, -adventure; may be, haply, mayhap.

if possible, wind and weather permitting, God willing, *Deo volente*, D.V.

471. Impossibility.—N. impossibility &c. *adj.*; what -cannot, - can never- be; sour grapes; infeasibility, impracticability, hopelessness &c. 859.

V. be -impossible &c. *adj.*; have no chance whatever.

attempt impossibilities; square the circle; discover the -philosopher's stone, - elixir of life, - secret of perpetual motion; skin a flint; make -a silk purse out of a sow's ear, - bricks without straw; have nothing to go upon; weave a rope of sand, build castles in the air, *prendre la lune avec les dents*, extract sunbeams from cucumbers, set the Thames on fire, milke a he-goat into a sieve, catch a weasel asleep, *rompre l'anguille au genou*, be in two places at once.

Adj. impossible; not -possible &c. 470; absurd, contrary to reason; unlikely, at variance with facts; unreasonable &c. 477; incredible &c. 485; beyond the bounds of -reason, - possibility; from which reason recoils; visionary; inconceivable &c. (*improbable*) 473; prodigious &c. (*wonderful*) 870; un-, inimaginable, unthinkable, not a Chinaman's chance.

impracticable, unachievable; un-, infeasible; insuperable; un-, insurmountable; unat-, unob-tainable; out of -reach, - the question; not to be -had, - thought of; beyond control; desperate &c. (*hopeless*) 859; incompatible &c. 24; inaccessible, uncomeatable, impassable, impervious, innavigable, inextricable.

out of -, beyond- one's -power, - depth, - reach, - grasp; too much for; *ultra crepidam*.

Phr. the grapes are sour; *non possumus; non nostrum tantas componere lites*.

472. Probability.—N. probability, likelihood; likeliness &c. *adj.*

vraisemblance, verisimilitude, plausibility; colour, semblance, show of; presumption; presumptive -, circumstantial- evidence; credibility.

reasonable -, fair -, good -, favourable-chance, - prospect; prospect, well-grounded hope; chance &c. 156.

V. be -probable &c. *adj.*; give -, lend- colour to; point to; imply &c. (*evidence*) 467; bid fair &c. (*promise*) 511; stand fair for; stand -, run- a good chance.

presume, infer, suppose, take for granted.

think likely, dare say, flatter oneself; expect &c. 507; count upon &c. (*believe*) 484.

Adj. probable, likely, hopeful, to be expected, in a fair way.

plausible, specious, ostensible, colourable, *ben trovato*, well-founded, reasonable, credible, easy of belief, presumable, presumptive, apparent.

Adv. probably &c. *adj.*; belike; in all -probability, - likelihood; very -, most-likely; as likely as not; like enough; ten &c. to one; apparently, seemingly, according to every reasonable expectation; *primâ facie*; to all appearance &c. (*to the eye*) 448.

Phr. the -chances, - odds- are; appearances -, chances- are in favour of; there is reason to -believe, - think, -

expect; I dare say; all Lombard Street to a China orange.

473. Improbability.—N. improbability, unlikelihood; unfavourable -, bad -, little -, small -, poor -, scarcely any -, no -, not a ghost of a- chance; bare possibility; long odds; incredibility &c. 485.

V. be -improbable &c. *adj.*; have a -small chance &c. *n.*

Adj. improbable, unlikely, contrary to all reasonable expectation, implausible.

rare &c. (*infrequent*) 137; unheard of, inconceivable; un-, in-imaginable; incredible &c. 485; more than doubtful.

Int. not likely! no fear!

Phr. the chances are against.

474. Certainty.—N. certainty; necessity &c. 601; certitude, certainness, surety, assurance, sureness; dead -, moral-certainty; infallibleness &c. *adj.*; infallibility, reliability.

gospel, scripture, church, pope, court of final appeal; *res judicata, ultimatum.*

positiveness; dogmat-ism, -ist, -izer; *doctrinaire*, know-all, bigot, -ry; opinionist, Sir Oracle; *ipse dixit*; zealot.

fact; positive -, matter of- fact; *fait accompli.*

V. be -certain &c. *adj.*; stand to reason.

render -certain &c. *adj.*; in-, en-, assure; clinch, make sure; determine, decide, set at rest, 'make assurance double sure'; know &c. (*believe*) 484; dismiss all doubt.

dogmatize, lay down the law.

Adj. certain, sure; assured &c. *v.*; solid, well-founded.

unqualified, absolute, positive, determinate, definite, clear, unequivocal, categorical, unmistakable, decisive, decided, ascertained.

inevitable, unavoidable, ineluctable, avoidless.

unerring, infallible; unchangeable &c. 150; to be depended on, trustworthy, reliable, bound.

un-impeachable, -deniable, -questionable; in-disputable, -contestable, -controvertible,

-defeasible, -dubitable; irrefutable &c. (*proven*) 478; conclusive, without power of appeal, final.

indubious; without -, beyond a -, without a shade or shadow of- -doubt - question; past dispute; beyond all -question, - dispute; un-doubted, -contested, -questioned, -disputed; question-, doubt-less.

bigoted, fanatical, dogmatic, opinion-at-ed, -ive, *doctrinaire.*

authoritative, authentic, official.

sure as -fate, - death and taxes, - a gun.

evident, self-evident, axiomatic; clear, - as day, - as the sun at noonday; obvious.

Adv. certainly &c. *adj.*; for certain, certes, sure, no doubt, doubtless, and no mistake, *flagrante delicto*, sure enough, to be sure, of course, as a matter of course, *à coup sur*, to a certainty, undoubtedly; in truth &c. (*truly*) 494; at -any rate, - all events; without fail; *coûte que coûte*; whatever may happen, if the worst come to the worst; come -, happen- what -may, - will; sink or swim; rain or shine.

Phr. *cela va sans dire*; there is -no question, - not a shadow of doubt; the die is cast &c. (*necessity*) 601.

475. Uncertainty.—N. uncertainty, incertitude, doubt; doubtfulness &c. *adj.*; dubi-ety, -tation, -tancy, -ousness.

hesitation, suspense; perplexity, embarrassment, dilemma, quandary, Morton's fork, bewilderment; timidity &c. (*fear*) 860; indecision, vacillation &c. 605; *diaporesis*, indetermination.

vagueness &c. *adj.*; haze, fog; obscurity &c. (*darkness*) 421; ambiguity &c. (*double meaning*) 520; contingency, double contingency, possibility upon a possibility; conjecture; open question &c. (*question*) 461; *onus probandi*; blind bargain, pig in a poke, leap in the dark, something or other; needle in a bottle of hay; roving commission.

fallibility, unreliability, untrustworthiness, precariousness.

V. be -uncertain &c. *adj.*; wonder whether.

lose the -clue, – clew, – scent; miss one's way.

not know -what to make of &c. (*unintelligibility*) 519, – which way to turn, – whether one stands on one's head or one's heels; float in a sea of doubt, hesitate, flounder; lose -oneself, – one's head, – one's way, wander aimlessly; muddle one's brains.

render -uncertain &c. *adj.*; put out, pose, puzzle, perplex, embarrass; confuse, -found; bewilder, mystify, bother, moider, nonplus, addle the wits, throw off the scent; *ambiguas in vulgus spargere voces*; keep in suspense.

doubt &c. (*disbelieve*) 485; hang –, tremble- in the balance; depend.

Adj. uncertain; casual; random &c. (*aimless*) 621; changeable &c. 149.

doubtful, dubious; indecisive; unsettled, -decided, -determined; in suspense, open to discussion; controvertible; in question &c. (*inquiry*) 461; insecure, unstable.

vague; in-determinate, -definite; ambiguous, equivocal; undefin-ed, -able; confused &c. (*indistinct*) 447; mystic, mysterious, veiled, obscure, cryptic, oracular.

perplexing &c. *v.*; enigmatic, para-doxical, apocryphal, problematical, hypothetical; experimental &c. 463.

fallible, questionable, precarious, slippery, ticklish, debatable, disputable; un-reliable, -trustworthy.

contingent, – on, dependent on; subject to; dependent on circumstances; occasional; provisional.

unauth-entic, -enticated, -oritative; un-ascertained, -confirmed; undemonstrated; un-told, -counted.

in a -state of uncertainty, – cloud, – maze; ignorant &c. 491; on the horns of a dilemma; afraid to say; out of one's reckoning, astray, adrift; at -sea, – fault, – a loss, – one's wit's end, – a *nonplus*; puzzled &c. *v.*; lost, abroad, *désorienté*; dis-tracted, -traught.

Adv. *pendente lite; sub spe rati.*

Phr. Heaven knows; who can tell? who shall decide when doctors disagree?

Section IV. REASONING PROCESSES

476. Reasoning.—N. reasoning; ratio-cination, -nalism; dialectics, induction, generalization.

discussion, comment; ventilation; inquiry &c. 461.

argumentation, controversy, debate; polemics, wrangling; contention &c. 720; logomachy; dis-putation, -ceptation; paper war.

art of reasoning, logic.

process –, train –, chain- of reasoning; de-, in-duction; synthesis, analysis.

argument; case, plea, *plaidoyer*, opening; *lemma*, proposition, terms, premises, postulate, *data*, starting point, principle; inference &c. (*judgment*) 480.

pro-, syllogism; enthymeme, sorites, dilemma, *perilepsis, a priori* reasoning, *reductio ad absurdum*, horns of a dilemma, *argumentum ad hominem*, comprehensive argument.

reasoner, logician, dialectician; disputant; controver-sialist, -tist; wrangler, arguer, debater, polemic, casuist, rationalist; scientist.

logical sequence; good case; correct –, just –, sound –, valid –, cogent –, logical –, forcible –, persuasive –, persuasory –, consectary –, conclusive &c. 478 –, subtle- reasoning; force of argument; strong -point, – argument.

arguments, reasons, pros and cons.

V. reason, argue, discuss, debate, dispute, wrangle; bandy -words, – arguments; chop logic; hold –, carry on-an argument; controvert &c. (*deny*) 536; canvass; comment –, moralize- upon; consider &c. (*examine*) 461.

open a -discussion, – case; join –, be at- issue; moot; come to the point; stir

–, agitate –, ventilate –, torture- a question; try conclusions; take up a -side, – case.

contend, take one's stand upon, insist, lay stress on; infer &c. 480.

follow from &c. (*demonstration*) 478.

Adj. rational; reasoning &c. *v.*; rationalistic; argumentative, controversial, dialectic, polemical; discurs-ory, -ive; disputatious.

debatable, controvertible.

logical; in-, de-ductive; synthetic, analytic; relevant &c. 23.

Adv. for, because, hence, whence, seeing that, since, sith, then, thence, so; for -that, – this, – which- reason; for-, inasmuch as; whereas *ex concesso*, considering, in consideration of; there-, where-fore; consequently, *ergo*, thus, accordingly; *a fortiori*.

in -conclusion, – fine; finally, after all, *au bout du compte*, on the whole, taking one thing with another.

rationally &c. *adj.*

477. [The absence of reasoning.] **Intuition.** [False or vicious reasoning; show of reason.] **Sophistry.—N.** intuition, instinct, association; presentiment; rule of thumb.

sophistry, paralogy, perversion, casuistry, jesuitry, equivocation, evasion, mental reservation; chicane, -ry; quiddit, quiddity; mystification; special pleading; speciousness &c. *adj.*; nonsense &c. 497; word-, tongue-fence.

false –, vicious- reasoning; *petitio principii, ignoratio elenchi; post hoc ergo propter hoc; non sequitur, ignotum per ignotius.*

misjudgment &c. 481; false teaching &c. 538.

sophism, solecism, paralogism; quibble, quirk, *elenchus*, elench, fallacy, *quodlibet*, subterfuge, subtlety, quillet; inconsistency, antilogy; 'a mockery, a delusion and a snare'; claptrap, mere words; 'lame and impotent conclusion.'

meshes –, cobwebs- of sophistry; flaw in an argument; weak point, bad case.

over-refinement; hair-splitting &c. *v.*

sophist, casuist, paralogist.

V. judge -intuitively, – by intuition; hazard a proposition, talk at random.

reason -ill, – falsely &c. *adj.*; paralogize; misjudge &c. 481.

pervert, quibble; equivocate, mystify, evade, elude; gloss over, varnish; mis-teach &c. 538; mislead &c. (*error*) 495; cavil, refine, subtilize, split hairs; misrepresent &c. (*lie*) 544.

beg the question, reason in a circle, cut blocks with a razor, beat about the bush, play fast and loose, blow hot and cold, prove that black is white and white black, travel out of the record, *parler à tort et à travers*, put oneself out of court, not have a leg to stand on.

Adj. intuitive, instinctive, impulsive; independent of –, anterior to- reason; gratuitous, hazarded; unconnected.

unreasonable, illogical, false, unsound, invalid; unwarranted, not following; inconsequent, -ial; inconsistent, incongruous; abson-ous, -ant; unscientific; untenable, inconclusive, incorrect; fallacious, -ible; groundless, unproved.

deceptive, sophistical, sophisticated, casuistical, jesuitical; illus-ive, -ory; specious, hollow, plausible, *ad captandum*, evasive; irrelevant &c. 10.

weak, feeble, poor, flimsy, loose, vague, irrational; nonsensical &c. (*absurd*) 497; foolish &c. (*imbecile*) 499; frivolous, pettifogging, quibbling; finespun, over-refined.

at the end of one's tether, *au bout de son latin.*

Adv. intuitively &c. *adj.*; by intuition; illogically &c. *adj.*

Phr. *non constat*; that goes for nothing.

478. Demonstration.—N. demonstration, proof; conclusiveness &c. *adj.*; *apodixis*, probation, comprobation.

logic of facts &c. (*evidence*) 467; *experimentum crucis* &c. (*test*) 463; argument &c. 476; irrefragability.

V. demonstrate, prove, establish, make good; show; evince &c. (*be evidence of*) 467; verify &c. 467; settle the question, reduce to demonstration, set the question at rest.

make out, – a case; prove one's point, have the best of the argument; draw a conclusion &c. (*judge*) 480.

follow, – of course; stand to reason; hold -good, – water.

Adj. demonstra-ting &c. *v.*, -tive, -ble; probative, unanswerable, conclusive; apodictic, -al; irre-sistible, -futable, -fragable, undeniable.

categorical, decisive, crucial.

demonstrated &c. *v.*; proven; unconfuted, -answered, -refuted; evident &c. 474.

deducible, consequential, consectary, inferential, following.

Adv. of course, in consequence, consequently, as a matter of course.

Phr. *probatum est*; there is nothing more to be said, Q.E.D., it must follow.

479. Confutation.—N. con-, refutation; answer, complete answer; disproof, conviction, redargution, invalidation; expos-ure, -ition; clincher; retort; *reductio ad absurdum*; knock down -, *tu quoque*- argument.

V. con-, re-fute; parry, negative, disprove, redargue, expose, show the fallacy of, rebut, defeat; demolish &c. (*destroy*) 162; over-throw, -turn; scatter to the winds, explode, invalidate; silence; put -, reduce- to silence; clinch -an argument, – a question; give one a set down, stop the mouth, shut up; have, – on the hip; get the better of; confound, convince.

not leave a leg to stand on, cut the ground from under one's feet.

be confuted &c.; fail; expose -, show- one's weak point.

Adj. confut-ing, -ed &c. *v.*; capable of refutation; re-, con-futable.

condemned -on one's own showing, – out of one's own mouth.

Phr. the argument falls to the ground, *cadit quæstio*, it does not hold water, *'suo sibi gladio hunc jugulo.'*

Section V. RESULTS OF REASONING

480. Judgment. [Conclusion.]**—N.** result, conclusion, upshot; deduction, inference, ergotism, illation; corollary, porism; moral.

estimation, valuation, appreciation, judication; di-, ad-judication; arbitrament, -ement, -ation; assessment, ponderation.

award, estimate; review, criticism, *critique*, notice, report.

decision, determination, judgment, finding, verdict, sentence, decree, – nisi, – absolute, – interlocutory; dictum; *res judicata*.

plébiscite, referendum, voice, casting vote; vote &c. (*choice*) 609; opinion &c. (*belief*) 484; good judgment &c. (*wisdom*) 498.

judge, jurist, umpire; arbi-ter, -trator; assessor, referee; censor, reviewer, critic; *connoisseur*; commentator &c. 524; inspector, inspecting officer.

V. judge, conclude; come to -, draw -, arrive at- a conclusion; ascertain, determine, make up one's mind.

deduce, derive, gather, collect, draw an inference, make a deduction, weet, ween.

form an estimate, estimate, size up, appreciate, value, count, assess, rate, rank, account; regard, consider, think of; look upon &c. (*believe*) 484.

settle; pass -, give- an opinion; decide, try, pronounce, rule; pass -judgment, – sentence; sentence, doom; find; give -, deliver- judgment; ad-judge, -icate; arbitrate, award, report; bring in a verdict; make absolute, set a question at rest; confirm &c. (*assent*) 488.

comment, criticize; review, pass under review &c. (*examine*) 457; investigate &c. (*inquire*) 461.

hold the scales, sit in judgment; try -, hear- a cause.

Adj. judging &c. *v.*; judicious &c.

(*wise*) 498; determinate, conclusive, censorious, critical &c. 932.

Adv. on the whole, all things considered.

480a. [Result of search or inquiry.] **Discovery.—N.** discovery, invention, detection, disenchantment, disclosure, find, ascertainment, revelation.

trover &c. 775.

V. discover, find, determine, evolve; fix upon; find -, trace -, make -, hunt -, fish -, worm -, ferret -, root- out; fathom; bring -, draw- out; educe, elicit, bring to light, invent; dig -, grub -, fish- up; unearth, disinter.

solve, resolve; un-riddle, -ravel, -lock; pick -, open- the lock; find a -clue, - clew- to; interpret &c. 522; disclose &c. 529.

trace, get at; hit it, have it; lay one's -finger, - hands- upon; spot; get -, arrive- at the -truth &c. 494; put the saddle on the right horse, hit the right nail on the head.

be near the truth, burn; smoke, scent, sniff, smell a rat.

open the eyes to; see -through, - daylight, - in its true colours, - the cloven foot; detect; catch, - tripping.

pitch -, fall -, light -, hit -, stumble -, pop- upon; come across; meet -, fall in- with.

recognize, realize, verify, make certain of, identify.

Int. *eureka!*

481. Misjudgment.—N. misjudgment, obliquity of -, warped- judgment; mis-calculation, -computation, -conception &c. (*error*) 495; hasty conclusion.

prejud-gment, -ication, -ice; foregone conclusion; pre-notion, -vention, -conception, -dilection, -possession, -apprehension, -sumption, -sentiment; fixed -, preconceived- idea; *idée fixe*; *mentis gratissimus error*; fool's paradise.

esprit de corps, party spirit, race -, class- prejudice, partisanship, clannishness, *prestige*.

bias, warp, twist; hobby, fad, whim, craze, quirk, crotchet, partiality, infatuation, blind side, mote in the eye.

one-sided -, partial -, narrow -, confined -, superficial- -views, - ideas, - conceptions, - notions; narrow mind; bigotry &c. (*obstinacy*) 606; *odium theologicum*; pedantry; hypercriticism. *doctrinaire* &c. (*positive*) 474.

V. mis-judge, -estimate, -think, -conjecture, -conceive &c. (*error*) 495; fly in the face of facts; mis-calculate, -reckon, -compute.

overestimate &c. 482; underestimate &c. 483.

pre-, fore-judge; pre-suppose, -sume, -judicate; dogmatize; have a -bias &c. *n.*; have only one idea; *jurare in verba magistri*, run away with the notion; jump -, rush- to a conclusion; look only at one side of the shield; view -with jaundiced eye, - through distorting spectacles; not see beyond one's nose; *dare pondus fumo*; get the wrong sow by the ear &c. (*blunder*) 699.

give a -bias, - twist; bias, warp, twist; pre-judice, -possess.

Adj. misjudging &c. *v.*; ill-judging, wrong-headed; prejudiced, prejudicial, &c. *v.*; jaundiced; short-sighted, purblind; partial, one-sided, superficial.

narrow-minded; confined, insular, provincial, parochial, illiberal, intolerant, narrow, besotted, infatuated, fanatical, cracked, warped, *entêté*, positive, dogmatic, dictatorial; conceited; opin-, opini-ative; opinion-ed, -ate, -ative, -ated; self-opinioned, wedded to an opinion, *opiniâtre*; bigoted &c. (*obstinate*) 606; crotchety, fussy, impracticable; un-reason-able, -ing; stupid &c. 499; credulous &c. 486.

misjudged &c. *v.*

Adv. *ex parte.*

Phr. nothing like leather; the wish the father to the thought.

482. Overestimation.—N. overestimation &c. *v.*; exaggeration &c. 549; vanity &c. 880; optim-, pessim-ism, -ist; megalomania.

much -cry and little wool, – ado about
nothing; storm in a teacup; fine talking,
rodomontade, gush, hot air, gas, bombast.

egotism &c. 880; boasting &c. 884.

V. over-estimate, -rate, -value, -prize,
-weigh, -reckon, -strain, -praise; estimate too highly, attach too much importance to, make mountains of molehills,
catch at straws; strain, magnify; exaggerate &c. 549; set too high a value
upon; think –, make- -much, – too
much- of; outreckon.

extol, – to the skies; make the -most,
– best, – worst- of, eulogize, panegyrize, gush, puff, boost; make two bites
of a cherry.

have too high an opinion of oneself
&c. (*vanity*) 880.

Adj. overestimated &c. *v.*; oversen-
sitive &c. (*sensibility*) 822; inflated,
puffed up, exaggerated &c. 549.

Phr. all his geese are swans; *parturiunt montes.*

483. Underestimation.—N. underestimation; depreciation &c. (*detraction*) 934; pessim-ism, -ist; undervalu-
ing &c. *v.*; modesty &c. 881.

V. under-rate, -estimate, -value,
-reckon; depreciate; disparage &c. (*detract*) 934; not do justice to; mis-, disprize; ridicule &c. 856; slight &c. (*despise*) 930; neglect &c. 460; slur over,
under-state.

make -light, – little, – nothing, – no
account- of; minimize, belittle, run
down, think nothing of; set -no store by,
– at naught; shake off as dewdrops from
the lion's mane.

Adj. depreciat-ing, -ed, -ive, -ory,
&c. *v.*; un-appreciated, -valued, -prized;
pejorative.

484. Belief.—N. belief; credence;
credit; assurance; faith, trust, troth,
confidence, presumption, sanguine expectation &c. (*hope*) 858; dependence
on, reliance on.

persuasion, conviction, convince-
ment, plerophory, self-conviction; certainty &c. 474; opinion, mind, view;

conception, thinking; impression &c.
(*idea*) 453; surmise &c. 514; conclusion
&c. (*judgment*) 480.

tenet, dogma, principle, way of thinking; popular belief &c. (*assent*) 488.

firm –, implicit –, settled –, fixed –,
rooted –, deep-rooted –, staunch –, unshaken –, steadfast –, inveterate –, calm
–, sober –, dispassionate –, impartial –,
well-founded- -belief, – opinion &c.;
uberrima fides.

system of opinions, school, doctrine,
articles, canons; declaration –, profes-
sion- of faith; tenets, *credenda*, creed;
thirty-nine articles &c. (*orthodoxy*)
983*a*; catechism; assent &c. 488; *propaganda* &c. (*teaching*) 537.

credibility &c. (*probability*) 472.

V. believe, credit; give -faith, – credit, – credence- to; see, realize; assume,
receive; set down –, take- for; have –,
take- it; consider, esteem, presume.

count –, depend –, calculate –, pin
one's faith –, reckon –, lean –, build –,
rely –, rest- upon; lay one's account for;
make sure of.

make oneself easy -about, – on that
score; take on -trust, – credit; take for
-granted, –gospel; allow –, attach- some
weight to.

know, – for certain; have –, make- no
doubt; doubt not; be – rest- -assured &c.
adj.; persuade –, assure –, satisfy- oneself; make up one's mind.

give one credit for; confide –, believe
–, put one's trust- in; place –, repose-
implicit confidence in; take -one's word
for, – at one's word; place reliance on,
rely upon, swear by, regard to.

think, hold; take, – it; opine, be of
opinion, conceive, trow, ween, fancy,
apprehend; have –, hold –, possess –,
entertain –, adopt –, imbibe –, embrace
–, get hold of –, hazard –, foster –, nurture –, cherish- -a belief, – an opinion
&c. *n.*

view –, consider –, take –, hold –,
conceive –, regard –, esteem –, deem –,
look upon –, account –, set down- as;
surmise &c. 514.

get –, take- it into one's head; come

round to an opinion; swallow &c. (*credulity*) 486.

cause to -be believed &c. *v.*; satisfy, persuade, have the ear of, gain the confidence of, assure; con-vince, -vict, -vert; put across, sell; wean, bring round; bring –, put –, win- over; indoctrinate &c. (*teach*) 537; cram down the throat; produce –, carry- conviction; bring –, drive- home to.

go down, find credence, pass current; be -received &c. *v.*, – current &c. *adj.*; possess –, take hold of –, take possession of- the mind.

Adj. believing &c. *v.*; certain, sure, assured, positive, cocksure, satisfied, confident, unhesitating, convinced, secure.

under the impression; impressed –, imbued –, penetrated- with.

confiding, trustful, suspectless; un-susp-ecting, -icious; void of suspicion; credulous &c. 486; wedded to.

believed &c. *v.*; accredited, putative; unsuspected.

worthy of –, deserving of –, commanding-belief, – confidence; credible, reliable, trusted, trustworthy, to be depended on, undoubted; satisfactory; probable &c. 472; fiduci-al, -ary; persuasive, impressive.

relating to belief, doctrinal.

Adv. in the -opinion, – eyes- of; *me judice*; me-seems, -thinks; to the best of one's belief; I -dare say, – doubt not, – have no doubt, – am sure; in my opinion; sure enough &c. (*certainty*) 474; depend –, rely- upon it; be –, rest- assured; I'll warrant you &c. (*affirmation*) 535.

485. Unbelief. Doubt.—N. un-, dis-, mis-belief; discredit, miscreance; infidelity &c. (*irreligion*) 989; dissent &c. 489; change of -opinion &c. 484; retraction &c. 607.

doubt &c. (*uncertainty*) 475; skepticism, misgiving, demur; dis-, mis-trust; misdoubt, suspicion, jealousy, scruple, qualm; *onus probandi*.

incredib-ility, -leness; incredulity; unbeliever &c. 487.

V. dis-believe, -credit; not -believe &c. 484; misbelieve; refuse to admit &c. (*dissent*) 489; refuse to believe &c. (*incredulity*) 487.

doubt; be -doubtful &c. (*uncertain*) 475; doubt the truth of; be -skeptical as to &c. *adj.*; diffide; dis-, mis-trust; suspect, smoke, scent, smell a rat; have –, harbour –, entertain- -doubts, – suspicions; have one's doubts.

demur, stick at, pause, hesitate, scruple, waver, stop and consider.

hang in -suspense, – doubt.

throw doubt upon, raise a question; bring –, call- in question; question, challenge, query; dispute; deny &c. 536; cavil; cause –, raise –, start –, suggest –, awake- a -doubt, – suspicion; ergotize.

startle, stagger; shake –, stagger- one's faith, – belief.

Adj. unbelieving; incredulous –, skeptical- as to; distrustful –, shy –, suspicious- of; doubting &c. *v.*

doubtful &c. (*uncertain*) 475; disputable; unworthy –, undeserving- of -belief &c. 484; questionable; sus-pect, -picious (en to -suspicion, – doubt; staggering, hard to believe, incredible, not to be believed, inconceivable.

fallible &c. (*uncertain*) 475; unde-monstrable; controvertible &c. (*untrue*) 495.

Adv. *cum grano salis.*

Phr. *fronti nulla fides; nimium ne crede colori; 'timeo Danaos et dona ferentes'; credat Judæus Apella;* let those believe who may.

486. Credulity.—N. credul-ity, -ousness &c. *adj.*; gull-, cull-ibility; gross credulity, infatuation; self-delusion, -deception; blind reasoning; superstition; one's blind side; bigotry &c. (*obstinacy*) 606; hyper-orthodoxy &c. 984; misjudgment &c. 481.

credulous person &c. (*dupe*) 547.

V. be -credulous &c. *adj.*; *jurare in verba magistri*; follow implicitly;

swallow, - whole, gulp down; take on trust; take for -granted, - gospel; run away with -a notion, - an idea; jump -, rush-to a conclusion; think the moon is made of green cheese; take -, grasp- the shadow for the substance; catch at straws.

impose upon &c. (*deceive*) 545.

Adj. credulous, gullible; easily -deceived &c. 545; simple, green, soft, childish, silly, stupid; over-credulous, -confident; infatuated, superstitious; confiding &c. (*believing*) 484.

Phr. the wish the father to the thought; *credo quia impossibile*.

487. Incredulity.—N. incredul-ous-ness, -ity; skepticism, pyrrhonism; want of faith &c. (*irreligion*) 989.

suspiciousness &c. *adj.*; scrupulosi-ty; suspicion &c. (*unbelief*) 485; dissent &c. 489.

unbeliever, skeptic, aporetic; atheist, agnostic, infidel, disbeliever, misbeliev-er, pyrrhonist &c. 989; heretic &c. (*heterodox*) 984.

V. be -incredulous &c. *adj.*; distrust &c. (*disbelieve*) 485; refuse to believe; shut one's -eyes, - ears- to; turn a deaf ear to; hold aloof; ignore; *nullis jurare in verba magistri*.

Adj. incredulous, skeptical, unbeliev-ing, inconvincible; hard -, shy- of be-lief; suspicious, scrupulous, distrustful, heterodox &c. 984.

488. Assent.—N. assent, -ment; ac-quiescence, admission; nod; accon-cord, -cordance; agreement &c. 23; affirm-ance, -ation; recognition, acknowledg-ment, avowal; confession, - of faith.

unanimity, common consent, *consen-sus*, acclamation, chorus, *vox populi*; popular -, current-belief, - opinion; public opinion; concurrence &c. (*of causes*) 178; co-operation &c. (*volun-tary*) 709.

ratification, confirmation, corrobora-tion, approval, acceptance, *visa*; in-dorsement &c. (*record*) 551.

consent &c. (*compliance*) 762.

affirmant, consenter, covenantor, sub-scriber, endorser, upholder.

V. assent; give -, yield -, nod- as-sent; acquiesce; agree &c. 23; receive, accept, accede, accord, concur, lend oneself to, consent, coincide, recipro-cate, go with; be -at one with &c. *adj.*; go along -, chime in -, strike in -, close-with; echo, enter into one's views, agree in opinion; vote -, give one's voice- for; recognize; subscribe -, conform -, defer- to; say -yes, - ditto, - amen, - aye-to.

acknowledge, own, admit, allow, avow, confess; concede &c. (*yield*) 762; come round to; abide by; permit &c. 760.

come to -, arrive at- -an understand-ing, - terms, - an agreement.

con-, af-firm; ratify, approve, en-dorse, countersign; visa; corroborate &c. 467.

go -, swim- with the stream, float with the current; be in the fashion, join in the chorus; be in every mouth.

Adj. assenting &c. *v.*; of one -accord, - mind; of the same mind, at one with, agreed, acquiescent, content; willing &c. 602.

un-contradicted, -challenged, -questioned, -controverted.

carried -, agreed- -*nem. con.* &c. *adv.*; unanimous; agreed on all hands, carried by acclamation.

affirmative &c. 535.

Adv. yes, yea, ay, aye, true; good; well; very -well, - true; well and good; granted; *placet*; even -, just- so; to be sure, surely, 'thou hast said'; truly, ex-actly, precisely, that's just it, indeed, certainly, certes, *ex concesso*; of course, unquestionably, assuredly, no doubt, doubtless, undoubtedly.

be it so; so -be it, - let it be, so mote it be; amen; with all my heart; willingly &c. 602.

affirmatively, in the affirmative.

with one -consent, - voice, - accord; unanimously, *unâ voce*, by common consent, in chorus, to a man, *nem. con.*; *nemine -contradicente*, - *dissentiente*; without a dissentient voice; as one man, one and all, on all hands.

489. Dissent.—N. dissent; discordance &c. (*disagreement*) 24; difference –, diversity- of opinion.

non-conformity &c. (*heterodoxy*) 984; protestantism, recusancy, schism; disaffection; secession &c. 624; recantation &c. 607.

dissension &c. (*discord*) 713; discontent &c. 832; cavilling.

protest; contradiction &c. (*denial*) 536; non-compliance &c. (*rejection*) 764; disapprobation &c. 932; hartal.

dissent-ient, -er; non-juror, -content; recusant, sectary, schismatic, protestant, non-conformist, separatist, non-cooperator, conscientious objector, passive resister.

V. dissent, demur; call in question &c. (*doubt*) 485; differ in opinion, disagree; say –no &c. 536; refuse -assent, – to admit; cavil, protest, raise one's voice against, make bold to differ; repudiate; contradict &c. (*deny*) 536; agree to differ.

have no notion of, differ *toto cœlo*; revolt -at, – from the idea.

shake the head, shrug the shoulders; look -askance, – askant.

secede; recant &c. 607.

Adj. dissenting &c. *v.*; negative &c. 536; diss-ident, -entient; unconsenting &c. (*refusing*) 764; non-content, -juring; protestant, recusant; uncon-vinced, -verted.

unavowed, unacknowledged; out of the question.

discontented &c. 832; unwilling &c. 603; extorted.

sectarian, denominational, schismatic, heterodox, intolerant.

Adv. no &c. 536; at -variance, – issue- with; under protest; *non placet*.

Int. God forbid! not for the world; not on your life; I beg to differ; I'll be hanged if; never tell me; your humble servant, pardon me; tell that to the marines.

Phr. many men many minds; *quot homines tot sententiæ*; *tant s'en faut*; *il s'en faut bien*.

490. Knowledge.—N. knowledge; cogn-izance, -ition, -oscence; acquaintance, experience, ken, privity, insight, familiarity; com-, ap-prehension; recognition; appreciation &c. (*judgment*) 480; intuition; consci-ence, -ousness; perception, precognition; acroamatics.

light, enlightenment; glimpse, inkling; side light; glimmer, -ing; dawn; scent, suspicion; impression &c. (*idea*) 453; discovery &c. 480a.

system –, body- of knowledge; science, philosophy, pansophy; theory, Etiology; circle of the sciences; pandect, doctrine, body of doctrine; cy-, encyclopædia; school &c. (*system of opinions*) 484.

tree of knowledge; republic of letters &c. (*language*) 560.

erudition, learning, lore, scholarship, reading, letters; literature; book learning, bookishness; biblio-mania, -latry; information, general information; store of -knowledge &c.; education &c. (*teaching*) 537; culture, attainments; acqui-rements, -sitions; accomplishments, proficiency; practical knowledge &c. (*skill*) 698; higher education, liberal education; dilettantism; rudiments &c. (*beginning*) 66.

deep –, profound –, solid –, accurate –, acroatic –, acroamatic –, vast –, extensive –, encyclopædical- -knowledge, – learning; omniscience, pantology.

march of intellect; progress -, advance- of -science, – learning; schoolmaster abroad.

V. know, ken, scan, wot; wot -, be aware &c. *adj.*- of; ween, weet, trow, have, possess.

conceive; ap-, com-prehend; take, realize, understand, appreciate; fathom, make out; recognize, discern, perceive, see, get a sight of, experience.

know full well; have –, possess- some knowledge of; be -*au courant* &c. *adj.*; have -in one's head, – at one's fingers' ends; know by -heart, – rote; be master of; *connaître le dessous des cartes*, know what's what &c. 698.

see one's way; learn, discover &c. 480*a*.

come to one's knowledge &c. (*information*) 527.

Adj. knowing &c. *v.*; cognitive, acroamatic.

aware -, cognizant -, conscious- of; acquainted -, made acquainted- with; privy -, no stranger- to; *au -fait*, - *courant*; in the secret; up -, alive- to; sensible of; behind the -scenes, - curtain; let into; apprized -, informed- of; undeceived.

proficient -, versed -, read -, forward -, strong -, at home- in; conversant -, familiar- with.

erudite, instructed, learned, lettered, educated; high-brow; well-conned, -informed, -read, -grounded, -educated; enlightened, shrewd, insightful, *savant*, blue, bookish, scholastic, solid, profound, deep-read, book-learned; accomplished &c. (*skilful*) 698; omniscient; self-taught, -educated.

known &c. *v.*; ascertained, well-known, recognized, received, notorious, noted; proverbial; familiar, - as household words, to every schoolboy; hackneyed, trite, commonplace.

knowable, cogn-oscible, -izable.

Adv. to -, to the best of- one's knowledge.

Phr. one's eyes being opened &c. (*disclosure*) 529.

491. Ignorance.—N. ignorance, nescience, *tabula rasa*, crass ignorance, *ignorance crasse*; unacquaintance; unconsciousness &c. *adj.*; dark-, blindness; incomprehension, inexperience, simplicity.

unknown quantities, *x, y, z*.

sealed book, *terra incognita*, virgin soil, unexplored ground; dark ages.

[Imperfect knowledge] smattering, superficiality, half-learning, sciolism, glimmering; bewilderment &c. (*uncertainty*) 475; incapacity.

[Affectation of knowledge] pedantry; charlatan-ry, -ism.

V. be -ignorant &c. *adj.*; not -know

&c. 490; know -not, - not what, - nothing of; have no -idea, - notion, - conception; not have the remotest idea; not know chalk from cheese.

ignore, be blind to; keep in ignorance &c. (*conceal*) 528.

see through a glass darkly; have a -film over the eyes, - glimmering &c. *n.*; wonder whether; not know what to make of &c. (*unintelligibility*) 519; not pretend -, not take upon oneself- to say.

Adj. ignorant, nescient; un-knowing, -aware, -acquainted, -apprized, -witting, -weeting, -conscious; wit-, weetless; a stranger to; unconversant.

un-informed, -cultivated, -versed, -instructed, -taught, -initiated, -tutored, -schooled, -guided, -enlightened; Philistine; behind the age.

shallow, superficial, green, rude, empty, half-learned, illiterate; un-read, -informed, -educated, -learned, -lettered, -bookish; empty-headed; lowbrow; pedantic.

in the dark; be-nighted, -lated; blinded; -fold; hoodwinked; misinformed; *au bout de son latin*, at the end of his tether; at fault; at sea &c. (*uncertain*) 475; caught tripping.

un-known, -apprehended, -explained, -ascertained, -investigated, -explored, -heard of, -perceived; concealed &c. 528; novel.

Adv. ignorantly &c. *adj.*; unawares; for -anything, - aught- one knows; not that one knows.

Int. God -, Heaven -, the Lord -, nobody- knows.

Phr. a little learning is a dangerous thing.

492. Scholar—N. scholar, *connoisseur*, *savant*, pundit, schoolman, professor, graduate, wrangler, moonshee; academ-ician, -ist; fellow, don, post graduate, advanced student; master -, bachelor- of arts; doctor, licentiate, gownsman; philo-sopher, -math; scientist, clerk; soph, -ist, -ister; linguist, classicist; glosso-, etymo-, philologist; philologer; lexico-, glosso-grapher;

scholiast, commentator, annotator, grammarian; *littérateur, literati, dilettanti, illuminati*; Mezzofanti, admirable Crichton, Mæcenas.

book-worm, *helluo librorum*, bibliophile, -maniac; blue-stocking, *bas-bleu*; big-wig, learned Theban.

learned -, literary- man; *homo multarum literarum*; man of -learning, - letters, - education; high-brow, intelligentsia.

antiquar-ian, -y; archæologist; sage &c. (*wise man*) 500.

pedant, *doctrinaire*; pedagogue, Dr. Pangloss; pantologist.

teacher &c. 540; schoolboy &c. (*learner*) 541.

Adj. learned &c. 490; brought up at the feet of Gamaliel.

493. Ignoramus.—N. ignoramus, illiterate, moron, dunce, numskull; wooden spoon; no scholar.

sciolist, smatterer, dabbler, half-scholar; *charlatan*; wiseacre.

novice, griffin; greenhorn &c. (*dupe*) 547; tyro &c. (*learner*) 541.

lubber &c. (*bungler*) 701; fool &c. 501; pedant &c. 492.

Adj. bookless, shallow, simple, dense, dumb, thick, dull, ignorant &c. 491.

494. [Object of knowledge.] **Truth.— N.** fact, reality &c. (*existence*) 1; plain matter of fact; nature &c. (*principle*) 5; truth, verity; gospel; orthodoxy &c. 983*a*; authenticity; veracity &c. 543.

accuracy, exactitude; exact-, preciseness &c. *adj.*; precision, delicacy; rigour, mathematical precision, punctuality; clockwork precision &c. (*regularity*) 80.

orthology; *ipsissima verba*; letter of the law, realism.

plain -, honest -, sober -, naked -, unalloyed -, unqualified -, stern -, exact -, intrinsic -, truth; *nuda veritas*; the very thing; not an -illusion &c. 495; real Simon Pure; unvarnished tale; the truth, the whole truth and nothing but the truth; just the thing.

V. be -true &c. *adj.*, - the case; stand the test; have the true ring; hold -good, - true, - water; conform to rule.

render -, prove- -true &c. *adj.*; substantiate &c. (*evidence*) 467.

get at the truth &c. (*discover*) 480*a*.

Adj. real, actual &c. (*existing*) 1; veritable, true; certain &c. 474; substantially -, categorically- true &c.; true -to the letter, - to life, - to scale, - the facts, - as gospel; unimpeachable; veracious &c. 543; unre-, uncon-futed; un-ideal, -imagined; realistic.

exact, accurate, definite, precise, well defined, just, right, correct, strict, severe; close &c. (*similar*) 17; literal; rigid, rigorous; scrupulous &c. (*conscientious*) 939; religiously exact, punctual, mathematical, scientific; faithful, constant, unerring; curious, particular, punctilious, meticulous, nice, delicate, fine.

genuine, authentic, legitimate, pukka; orthodox &c. 983*a*; official, *ex officio*.

pure, natural, sound, sterling; unsophisticated, -adulterated, -varnished, -coloured; in its true colours.

well-grounded, -founded; solid, substantial, tangible, valid; undis-torted, -guised; un-affected, -exaggerated, -romantic, -flattering.

Adv. truly &c. *adj.*; verily, indeed, in reality; as a matter of fact; beyond -doubt, - question; with truth &c. (*veracity*) 543; certainly &c. (*certain*) 474; actually &c. (*existence*) 1; in effect &c. (*intrinsically*) 5.

exactly &c. *adj.*; *ad amussim*; *verbatim*, - *et literatim*; word for word, literally, *literatim, totidem verbis, sic*, to the letter, chapter and verse, *ipsissimis verbis*; *ad unguem*; to an inch; to a -nicety, - hair, - tittle, - turn, - T; *au pied de la lettre*; neither more nor less; in -every respect, - all respects; *sous tous les rapports*; at -any rate, - all events; strictly speaking.

Phr. the -truth, - fact- is; *rem acu tetigisti.*

495. Error.—N. error, fallacy;

misconception, -apprehension, -under-standing; inexactness &c. *adj.*; laxity; misconstruction &c. (*misinterpretation*) 523; miscomputation &c. (*misjudgment*) 481; *non-sequitur* &c. 477; misstatement, -report; anachronism; malapropism.

mistake; miss, fault, blunder, boner, bloomer, howler, *quid pro quo*, cross purposes, oversight, misprint, *erratum*, *corrigendum*, slip, blot, flaw, loose thread; trip, stumble &c. (*failure*) 732; botchery &c. (*want of skill*) 699; slip of the -tongue, - pen; *lapsus -linguæ*, -*calami*, clerical error; bull &c. (*absurdity*) 497.

il-, de-lusion; false -impression, - idea; bubble; self-deceit, -deception; warped notion; mists of error; superstition, exploded notion.

heresy &c. (*heterodoxy*) 984; hallucination &c. (*insanity*) 503; false light &c. (*fallacy of vision*) 443; dream &c. (*fancy*) 515; fable &c. (*untruth*) 546; bias &c. (*misjudgment*) 481; misleading &c. *v.*

V. be -erroneous &c. *adj.*

cause error; mis-lead, -guide; lead -astray, - into error; beguile, misinform &c. (*misteach*) 538; delude; give a false -impression, - idea; falsify, garble, misstate; deceive &c. 545; lie &c. 544.

err; be -in error &c. *adj.*, - mistaken &c. *v.*; be deceived &c. (*duped*) 547; mistake, receive a false impression, deceive oneself; fall into -, lie under -, labour under- - an error &c. *n.*; be in the wrong, blunder; mis-apprehend, -conceive, -understand, -reckon, -count, -calculate &c. (*misjudge*) 481.

play -, be- at cross purposes &c. (*misinterpret*) 523.

trip, stumble; lose oneself &c. (*uncertainty*) 475; go astray; fail &c. 732; take the wrong sow by the ear &c. (*mismanage*) 699; put the saddle on the wrong horse; reckon without one's host; take the shadow for the substance &c. (*credulity*) 486; dream &c. (*imagine*) 515.

Adj. erroneous, untrue, false, devoid of truth, fallacious, faulty, apocryphal, unreal, ungrounded, groundless; unsubstantial &c. 4; heretical &c. (*heterodox*) 984; unsound; illogical &c. 477; wrong.

in-, un-exact; in-accurate, -correct; indefinite &c. (*uncertain*) 475.

illus-ive, -ory; delusive; mock; ideal &c. (*imaginary*) 515; spurious &c. 545; deceitful &c. 544; perverted.

controvertible, unsustain-able, -ed; unauthenticated, untrustworthy.

exploded, refuted, discarded.

in -, under an- error &c. *n.*; mistaken &c. *v.*; tripping &c. *v.*; out, - in one's reckoning; aberrant; beside -, wide of the- -mark, - truth; astray &c. (*at fault*) 475; on -a false, - the wrong- scent; in the wrong box; at cross purposes, all in the wrong, all abroad, at sea.

Adv. more or less.

496. Maxim.—N. maxim, aphorism; apo-, apoph-thegm; *dictum*, saying, gnome, adage, saw, proverb, epigram; sentence, *mot*, motto, word, by-word, precept, moral, phylactery, *protasis*, brocard.

axiom, postulate, theorem, *scholium*, truism.

reflection &c. (*idea*) 453; conclusion &c. (*judgment*) 480; golden rule &c. (*precept*) 697; principle, *principia*; profession of faith &c. (*belief*) 484; formula.

wise -, sage-, received -, admitted -, recognized- maxim &c.; true -, common -, hackneyed -, trite -, commonplace- saying &c.

Adj. aphoristic, proverbial, phylacteric; axiomatic, gnomic.

Adv. as -the saying is, - they say.

497. Absurdity.—N. absurd-ity, -ness &c. *adj.*; imbecility &c. 499; alogy, nonsense, paradox, inconsistency; stultiloqu-y, -ence, futility.

blunder, muddle, bull; Irish-, Hibernic-ism; slip-slop; anticlimax, bathos; sophism &c. 477.

farce, burlesque, *galimatias*, *amphigouri*, rhapsody; farrago &c. (*disorder*) 59; extravagance, romance; sciomachy.

joke, catch, sell, pun, verbal quibble, macaronic.

jargon, fustian, twaddle &c. (*no meaning*) 517; exaggeration &c. 549; moonshine, stuff; mare's nest.

vagary, tomfoolery, mummery, monkey trick, practical joke, *boutade*, *escapade*.

V. play the fool &c. 499; stultify, blunder, muddle; joke; talk nonsense, *parler à tort et à travers*; *battre la campagne*; be -absurd &c. *adj.*

Adj. absurd, nonsensical, preposterous, egregious, senseless, farcical, inconsistent, ridiculous, extravagant, quibbling, futile; macaronic, punning, paradoxical.

foolish &c. 499; sophistical &c. 477; unmeaning &c. 517; without rhyme or reason; fantastic.

Int. fiddle-de-dee! pish! pish and tush! pho! stuff and nonsense! rubbish! rot! bosh! in the name of the Prophet—figs!

Phr. *credat Judæus Apella*; tell it to the marines.

Faculties

498. Intelligence. Wisdom.—N. intelligence, capacity, comprehension, understanding; intellect &c. 450; nous, parts, sagacity, mother wit, wit, *esprit*, gumption, quick parts, grasp of intellect; acuteness &c. *adj.*; acumen, subtlety, penetration; perspica-cy, -city; discernment, long-headedness, due sense of, good judgment; discrimination &c. 465; craftiness, cunning &c. 702; refinement &c. (*taste*) 850.

head, brains, gray matter, headpiece, upper story, long head; eagle -eye, - glance; eye of a -lynx, - hawk.

wisdom, sapience, sense; good -, common -, plain -, horse- sense; clear thinking; rationality, reason; reasonableness &c. *adj.*; judgment; solidity, depth, profundity, calibre; enlarged views; reach -, compass- of thought; enlargement of mind.

genius, inspiration, *geist*, fire of ge-

nius, heaven-born genius, soul; talent &c. (*aptitude*) 698.

[Wisdom in action] prudence &c. 864; vigilance &c. 459; tact &c. 698; foresight &c. 510; sobriety, self-possession, *aplomb*, ballast, mental -poise, - balance.

a bright thought, inspiration, brainwave, not a bad idea.

V. be -intelligent &c. *adj.*; have all one's wits about one; understand &c. (*intelligible*) 518; catch -, take in- an idea; take a -joke, - hint.

see -through, - at a glance, - with half an eye, - far into, - through a millstone; penetrate; discern &c. (*descry*) 441; foresee &c. 510.

discriminate &c. 465; know what's what &c. 698; listen to reason.

Adj. [Applied to persons] intelligent, quick of apprehension, keen, acute, alive, brainy, awake, bright, quick, sharp; quick-, keen-, clear-, sharpeyed, -sighted, -witted; wide awake; canny, shrewd, astute; clear-headed; far-sighted &c. 510; discerning, perspicacious, penetrating, piercing; argute; nimble-, needle-witted; sharp as a needle; alive to &c. (*cognizant*) 490; clever &c. (*apt*) 698; arch &c. (*cunning*) 702; *pas si bête*; acute &c. 682.

wise, sage, sapient, sagacious, reasonable, rational, sound, in one's right mind, sensible, *abnormis sapiens*, judicious, strong-minded.

un-prejudiced, -biassed, -bigoted, -prepossessed; un-dazzled, -perplexed; of unwarped judgment, impartial, equitable, fair, broad-minded.

cool; cool-, long-, hard-, strongheaded; long-sighted, calculating, thoughtful, reflecting; solid, deep, profound.

oracular; heaven-directed, -born.

prudent &c. (*cautious*) 864; sober, staid, solid; considerate, politic, wise in one's generation; watchful &c. 459; provident &c. (*prepared*) 673; in advance of one's age; wise as -a serpent, - Solomon, - Solon.

[Applied to actions] wise, sensible,

reasonable, judicious; well-judged, -advised; prudent, politic; expedient &c. 646.

499. Imbecility. Folly.—N. want of -intelligence &c. 498, - intellect &c. 450; shallow-, silli-, foolish-ness &c. *adj.*; imbecility, incapacity, vacancy of mind, poverty of intellect, clouded perception, poor head, apartments to let; stup-, stol-idity; hebetude, dull understanding, meanest capacity; shortsightedness; incompetence &c. (*unskilfulness*) 699.

one's weak side; bias &c. 481; infatuation &c. (*insanity*) 503.

simplicity, puerility, babyhood; dotage, anility, second childishness, senile dementia, fatuity; idio-cy, -tism; drivelling.

folly, frivolity, desipience, irrationality, trifling, ineptitude, nugacity, inconsistency, lip-wisdom, conceit; sophistry &c. 477; giddiness &c. (*inattention*) 458; eccentricity &c. 503; extravagance &c. (*absurdity*) 497; rashness &c. 863. act of folly &c. 699.

V. be -imbecile &c. *adj.*; have no -brains, - sense &c. 498.

trifle, drivel, *radoter*, dote; ramble &c. (*madness*) 503; play the -fool, -monkey, - goat, take leave of one's senses; not see an inch beyond one's nose; stultify oneself &c. 699; talk nonsense &c. 497.

Adj. [Applied to persons] unintelligent, -intellectual, -reasoning; mind-, wit-, reason-, brain-less; having no -head &c. 498; not -bright &c. 498; inapprehensible.

weak-, addle-, puzzle-, blunder-, muddle-, muddy-, pig-, beetle-, maggoty-, gross-headed; beef-, fat- -witted, -headed.

weak-, feeble-minded; dull-, shallow-, rattle-, lack-brained; half-, nit-, short-, dull-, blunt-witted; shallow-, clod-, addle-pated; dim-, short-sighted; thick-skulled; weak in the upper story.

shallow, *borné*, weak, wanting, soft, nutty, sappy, spoony; dull, - as a beetle;

stupid, heavy, insulse, obtuse, blunt, stolid, doltish, asinine; inapt &c. 699; prosaic &c. 843.

child-ish, -like; infant-ine, -ile; baby-, bab-ish; puerile, anile; simple &c. (*credulous*) 486.

fatuous, idiotic, imbecile, moronic, drivelling; blatant, babbling; vacant; sottish; bewildered &c. 475.

blockish, unteachable; Bœot-ian, ic; bovine; un-gifted, -discerning, -enlightened, -wise, -philosophical; apish.

foolish, silly, senseless, irrational, insensate, nonsensical, inept; maudlin.

narrow-minded &c. 481; bigoted &c. (*obstinate*) 606; giddy &c. (*thoughtless*) 458; rash &c. 863; eccentric &c. (*crazed*) 503.

[Applied to actions] foolish, unwise, indiscreet, injudicious, improper, unreasonable, without reason, ridiculous, silly, stupid, asinine; ill-imagined, -advised, -judged, -devised; inconsistent, irrational, unphilosophical; extravagant &c. (*nonsensical*) 497; sleeveless, idle; useless &c. 645; inexpedient &c. 647; frivolous &c. (*trivial*) 643; absurd &c. 497.

Phr. *Davis sum non Œdipus.*

500. Sage.—N. sage, wise man; pundit; master -mind, - spirit of the age; longhead, thinker, philosopher.

authority, oracle, mentor, luminary, shining light, *esprit fort*, *magnus Apollo*, Solon, Solomon, Nestor, Magi, 'second Daniel.'

man of learning &c. 492; expert &c. 700; wizard &c. 994.

[Ironically] wiseacre, bigwig.

Adj. wise, learned; authoritative, oracular; erudite &c. 490; venerable, reverenced, revered, *emeritus*.

501. Fool.—N. fool, idiot, tomfool, wiseacre, simpleton, Simple Simon, nitwit, witling, dizzard, donkey, ass; ninny, -hammer; moron, dolt, booby, Tom Noddy, looby, hoddy-doddy, noddy, nonny, noodle, nizy, owl; goose, -cap; *imbécile*; gaby, *radoteur*, nincompoop, *badaud*, zany; trifler, babbler; pretty fellow; natural, *niais*.

child, baby, infant, innocent, milksop, sop.

oaf, lout, loon, lown, dullard, doodle, calf, colt, buzzard, block, put, stick, stock, numps, tony.

bull-, dunder-, addle-, block-, dull-, logger-, jolt-, jolter-, beetle-, gross-, thick-, giddy-head; num-, thick-skull; lack-, shallow-brain; half-, lack-wit; dunder-pate; fat-head, poor stick.

sawney, gowk; clod, -hopper; clod-, clot-poll, -pate; bull-calf; men of Bœotia, wise men of Gotham.

un sot à triple étage, sot; jobbernowl, changeling, mooncalf, *gobemouche*.

dotard, driveller; old -fogey, - woman; crone, grandmother.

greenhorn &c. (*dupe*) 547; dunce &c. (*ignoramus*) 493; lubber &c. (*bungler*) 701; madman &c. 504.

one who -will not set the Thames on fire, - did not invent gunpowder; *qui n'a pas inventé la poudre*; no conjuror.

502. Sanity.—N. sanity; soundness &c. *adj.*; rationality, normality, sobriety, lucidity, lucid interval; senses, sober senses, sound mind, *mens sana*.

V. be -sane &c. *adj.*; retain one's senses, - reason.

become -sane &c *adj.*; come to one's senses, sober down.

render -sane &c. *adj.*; bring to one's senses, sober.

Adj. sane, rational, reasonable, *compos mentis*, of sound mind; sound, -minded.

self-possessed; sober, -minded.

in one's -sober senses, - right mind; in possession of one's faculties.

Adv. sanely &c. *adj.*

503. Insanity.—N. disordered -reason, - intellect; diseased -, unsound -, abnormal- mind; derangement, unsoundness.

insanity, lunacy; madness &c. *adj.*; mania, *rabies*, *furor*, mental alienation; paranoia, aberration; *amentia*, dementation, -tia, -cy; *dementia præcox*; mo-

rosis, idiocy, phrenitis, frenzy, raving, incoherence, wandering, delirium, calenture of the brain, delusion, hallucination; lycanthropy, brain storm, *delirium tremens*, D.T.'s

vertigo, dizziness, swimming; sunstroke, *coup de soleil*, siriasis.

fanaticism, infatuation, craze; oddity, eccentricity, twist, monomania; klepto-, dipso-mania; hypochondriasis &c. (*low spirits*) 837; *melancholia*, hysteria.

screw -, tile -, slate- loose; bee in one's bonnet, rats in the upper story.

dotage &c. (*imbecility*) 499.

V. be -, become- -insane &c. *adj.*; lose one's senses, - reason, -faculties, - wits; go -, run- mad, run amuck; rave, dote, ramble, wander; drivel &c. (*be imbecile*) 499; have a -screw loose &c. *n.*, - devil; *avoir le diable au corps*; lose one's head &c. (*be uncertain*) 475.

derange, render -, drive- -mad &c. *adj.*; madden, dementate, addle the wits, derange the head, infatuate, befool; turn -the brain, - one's head.

Adj. insane, mad, lunatic; crazy, crazed, *aliéné*, *non compos mentis*; not right, cracked, touched; bereft of reason; unhinged, deranged, unsettled in one's mind; insensate, reasonless, beside oneself, demented, daft; phren-, fren-zied, -etic; possessed, - with a devil, far gone, maddened, moonstruck; shatterpated; barmy; mad-, scatter-, shatter-, crack-brained; off one's head; bug-house, *loco*.

maniacal; manic, manic-depressive; delirious, light-headed, incoherent, rambling, doting, wandering; frantic, raving, stark staring mad, amok, amuck.

corybantic, dithyrambic; rabid, giddy, vertiginous, dizzy, wild, haggard, mazed; flighty; distr-acted, -aught; bewildered &c. (*uncertain*) 475.

mad as a -March hare, - hatter; of -unsound mind &c. *n.*; touched -, wrong -, not right- in one's head, - mind, - wits, - upper story; out of one's -mind, - senses - wits; not in one's right mind.

fanatical, infatuated, odd, eccentric; hypp-ed, -ish.

imbecile, silly &c. 499.

Adv. like one possessed.

Phr. the mind having lost its balance; the reason under a cloud; *tête -exaltée, -montée.*

504. Madman.—N. madman, lunatic, maniac, bedlamite, candidate for Bedlam, raver, madcap; energumen; paranoiac; auto-, mono-, pyro-, megalo-, dipso-, klepto-maniac; hypochondriac &c. (*low spirits*) 837.

dreamer &c. 515; rhapsodist, seer, high-flier, enthusiast, crank, eccentric, nut, fanatic, *fanatico*; *exalté*; knight errant, Don Quixote.

idiot &c. 501.

Section VI. EXTENSION OF THOUGHT

1°. *To the Past*

505. Memory.—N. memory, remembrance; reten-tion, -tiveness; tenacity; *veteris vestigia flammœ*; tablets of the memory; readiness.

reminiscence, recognition, recurrence, recollection, rememoration; retrospect, -ion; after-thought.

suggestion &c. (*information*) 527; prompting &c. *v.*; hint, reminder, token of remembrance, *memento, souvenir*, keepsake, relic, *memorandum*; remembrancer, flapper; memorial &c. (*record*) 551; commemoration &c. (*celebration*) 883.

things to be remembered, *memorabilia.*

art of -, artificial- memory; *memoria technica*; mnemo-nics, -technics; phrenotypics; Mnemosyne; memorandum-, note-, engagement-, prompt-book.

retentive -, tenacious -, green -, trustworthy -, capacious -, faithful -, correct -, exact -, ready -, prompt-memory.

V. remember, mind; retain the -memory, - remembrance- of; keep in view.

have -, hold -, bear -, carry -, keep -, retain-in *or* in the -thoughts, - mind, - memory, - remembrance; be in -, live in -, remain in -, dwell in -, haunt -, impress- one's memory, - thoughts, - mind.

sink in the mind; run in the head; not be able to get it out of one's head; be deeply impressed with; rankle &c. (*revenge*) 919.

recur to the mind; flash -on the mind, - across the memory.

recognize, recollect, bethink oneself, recall, call up, conjure up, retrace; look -, trace- -back, - backwards; think -, look back- upon; review; call -, recall -, bring- to mind; remembrance; carry one's thoughts back; rake up the past.

suggest &c. (*inform*) 527; prompt; put -, keepin mind; remind; fan the embers; call -, summon -, rip- up; renew; *infandum renovare dolorem*; task -, tax -, jog -, flap -, refresh -, rub up -, awaken-the memory; pull by the sleeve; bring back to the memory, put in remembrance, memorialize.

get -, have -, lean -, know -, say -, repeat- by -heart - rote; drive -, get- into one's head; say one's lesson; repeat, - as a parrot; have at one's fingers' ends.

commit to memory; memorize; con, - over; fix -, rivet -, imprint -, impress -, stamp -, grave -, engrave -, store -, treasure up -, bottle up -, embalm -, enshrine- in the memory; load -, store -, stuff -, burden- the memory with.

redeem from oblivion; keep the memory -alive, - green; *tangere ulcus*; keep up the memory of; commemorate &c. (*celebrate*) 883.

make a note of &c. (*record*) 551.

Adj. remember-ing, -ed &c. *v.*; mindful, reminiscential; retaned in the memory &c. *v.*; pent up in one's memory; fresh; green, - in remembrance, still vivid; unforgotten, present to the mind; within one's -memory &c. *n.*; indelible; not to be forgotten, unforgettable, enduring; uppermost in one's thoughts; memorable &c. (*important*) 642.

Adv. by -heart, – rote; without book, *memoriter*.

in memory of; *in memoriam*; suggestive.

Phr. *manet altâ mente repostum; forsan et hæc olim meminisse juvabit.*

506. Oblivion.—N. oblivion; forgetfulness &c. *adj.*; obliteration &c. 552, of –, insensibility &c. 823 to- the past.

short –, treacherous –, loose –, slippery –, failing- memory; decay –, failure –, lapse- of memory; memory like a sieve; waters of -Lethe, – oblivion, *amnesia*.

pardon, acquittal, amnesty, oblivion; absolution.

V. forget; be -forgetful &c. *adj.*; fall –, sink- into oblivion; have -a short memory &c. *n.*, – no head.

forget one's own name, have on the tip of one's tongue, come in at one ear and go out at the other.

slip –, escape –, fade from –, die away from- the memory; lose, – sight of.

unlearn; efface &c. 552 –, discharge- from the memory; consign to -oblivion, – the tomb of the Capulets; think no more of &c. (*turn the attention from*) 458; cast behind one's back, wean one's thoughts from; let bygones be bygones &c. (*forgive*) 918.

Adj. forgotten &c. *v.*; unremembered, past recollection, bygone, out of mind; buried –, sunk- in oblivion; clean forgotten; gone out of one's -head, – recollection.

forgetful, oblivious, mindless, heedless, Lethean; insensible &c. 823- to the past.

Phr. *non mi ricordo*; the memory -failing, – deserting one, – being at (*or* in) fault.

2°. *To the Future*

507. Expectation.—N. expect-ation, -ance, -ancy; anticipation, reckoning, calculation; contingency; foresight &c. 510.

contemplation, prospection, look out; prospect, perspective, horizon, vista; destiny &c. 152.

suspense, waiting, abeyance: curiosity &c. 455; anxious –, ardent –, eager –, breathless –, sanguine- expectation; torment of Tantalus.

presumption, hope &c. 858; trust &c. (*belief*) 484; prognostication, auspices &c. (*prediction*) 511.

V. expect; look -for, – out for, – forward to; hope for, anticipate; have in -prospect, – contemplation; keep in view; contemplate, promise oneself; not -wonder &c. 870 -at, – if.

wait –, tarry –, lie in wait –, watch –, bargain- for; keep a -good, – sharp- look-out for; await; stand at 'attention,' abide, bide one's –, mark- time, watch.

foresee &c. 510; prepare for &c. 673; forestall &c. (*be early*) 132; count upon &c. (*believe in*) 484; think likely &c. (*probability*) 472; make one's mouth water.

lead one to expect &c. (*predict*) 511; have in store for &c. (*destiny*) 152.

prick up one's ears, hold one's breath.

Adj. expectant; expecting &c. *v.*; in -expectation &c. *n.*; on the watch &c. (*vigilant*) 459; open -eyed, -mouthed; agape, gaping, all agog; on -tenterhooks, – tiptoe, – the tiptoe of expectation; *aux aguets*; ready; curious &c. 455; looking forward to; prepared for; on the rack.

expected &c. *v.*; long expected, foreseen; in prospect &c. *n.*; prospective; in -one's eye, – view, – the horizon; impending &c. (*destiny*) 152.

Adv. expectantly; in the event of; on the watch &c. *adj.*; with -breathless expectation &c. *n.*, – bated breath, – eyes, – ears strained; *arrectis auribus*; on edge.

Phr. we shall see, *nous verrons*.

508. Inexpectation.—N. in-, non-expectation; false expectation &c. (*disappointment*) 509; miscalculation &c. 481; unforeseen contingency, the unforeseen, the unexpected.

surprise, sudden burst, thunderclap,

blow, shock; bolt out of the blue; eye-opener; wonder &c. 870.

V. not -expect &c. 507; be taken by surprise; start; miscalculate &c. 481; not bargain for; come –, fall- upon.

be -unexpected &c. *adj.*; come -unawares &c. *adv.*; turn up, pop, drop from the clouds; come –, burst –, flash –, bounce –, steal –, creep- upon one; come –, burst- like a thunderclap, -bolt; take –, catch- -by surprise, – unawares, – napping.

pounce –, spring a mine- upon.

surprise, startle, take aback, electrify, stun, stagger, take away one's breath, throw off one's guard; astonish &c. (*strike with wonder*) 870.

Adj. non-expectant; surprised &c. *v.*; un-warned, -aware; off one's guard; inattentive &c. 458.

un-expected, -anticipated, -prepared for, -looked for, -foreseen, -hoped for; dropped from the clouds; beyond –, contrary to –, against- expectation; out of one's reckoning; unheard of &c. (*exceptional*) 83; startling; sudden &c. (*instantaneous*) 113.

Adv. abruptly, unexpectedly, plump, pop, *à l'improviste*, unawares; without -notice, – warning, – saying 'by your leave'; like a -thief in the night, – thunderbolt; in an unguarded moment; suddenly &c. (*instantaneously*) 113.

Int. heyday! &c. (*wonder*) 870.

Phr. little did one -think, – expect; nobody would ever -suppose, – think, – expect; who would have thought?

509. [Failure of expectation.] Disappointment.—N. disappointment, disillusionment; blighted hope, balk; blow; slip 'twixt cup and lip; non-fulfilment of one's hopes; sad –, bitter- disappointment; trick of fortune; afterclap; false –, vain- expectation; miscalculation &c. 481; fool's paradise; much cry and little wool.

V. be disappointed; look -blank, – blue; look –, stand- -aghast &c. (*wonder*) 870; find to one's cost; laugh on the wrong side of one's mouth; find one a false prophet.

disappoint; crush –, dash –, balk –, disappoint –, blight –, falsify –, defeat –, not realize- one's -hope, – expectation; balk, jilt, bilk; play one -false, – a trick; dash the cup from the lips; tantalize; dumb-found, -founder; disillusion, -ize; dissatisfy, disgruntle.

Adj. disappointed &c. *v.*; disconcerted, aghast; out of one's reckoning; disgruntled.

Phr. the mountain brought forth a mouse; *nascitur ridiculus mus*; *parturiunt montes*; *diis aliter visum*, the bubble burst; one's countenance falling.

510. Foresight.—N. foresight, prospicience, prevision, longsightedness; anticipation; providence &c. (*preparation*) 673.

fore-thought, -cast; pre-deliberation, -surmise; foregone conclusion &c. (*prejudgment*) 481; prudence &c. (*caution*) 864.

foreknowledge; *prognosis;* precognition, -science, -notion, -sentiment; second sight; sagacity &c. (*intelligence*) 498.

prospect &c. (*expectation*) 507; foretaste; prospectus &c. (*plan*) 626.

V. foresee; look -forwards to, – ahead, – beyond; scent from afar; feel in one's bones; look –, pry –, peep- into the future.

see one's way; see how the -land lies, – wind blows, – cat jumps.

anticipate; expect &c. 507; be beforehand &c. (*early*) 132; predict &c. 511; fore-know, -judge, -cast; surmise; have an eye to the -future, – main chance; *respicere finem*; keep a sharp look-out &c. (*vigilance*) 459; forewarn &c. 668.

Adj. foreseeing &c. *v.*; prescient; anticipatory; far-seeing, -sighted; sagacious &c. (*intelligent*) 498; weather-wise; provident &c. (*prepared*) 673; prospective &c. 507.

Adv. against the time when.

511. Prediction.—N. prediction, announcement; program, programme &c.

(*plan*) 626; premonition &c. (*warning*) 668; *prognosis*, prophecy, vaticination, Mantology, prognostication, premonstration, augur-y, -ation; a-, ha-riolation; fore-, a-boding; bode-, abode-ment; omin-ation, -ousness, auspices, forecast; sign, presage, prognostic; omen &c. 512; horoscope, nativity; sooth, -saying; fortune-telling; divination; crystal gazing, necromancy &c. 992; prophet &c. 512.

[Divination by the stars] astrology, horoscopy, astromancy, judicial astrology.*

* The following terms, expressive of different forms of divination, have been collected from various sources, and are here given as a curious illustration of bygone superstitions:

Divination *by oracles*, Theomancy; *by the Bible*, Bibliomancy; *by ghosts*, Psychomancy; *by spirits seen in a magic lens*, Cristallomantia; *by shadows or manes*, Sciomancy; *by appearances in the air*, Aeromancy, Chaomancy; *by the stars at birth*, Genethliacs; *by meteors*, Meteoromancy; *by winds*, Austromancy; *by sacrificial appearances*, Aruspicy (*or* Haruspicy), Hieromancy, Hieroscopy; *by the entrails of animals sacrificed*, Hieromancy; *by the entrails of a human sacrifice*, Anthropomancy; *by the entrails of fishes*, Ichthyomancy; *by sacrificial fire*, Pyromancy; *by red-hot iron*, Sideromancy; *by smoke from the altar*, Capnomancy; *by mice*, Myomancy; *by birds*, Orniscopy, Ornithomancy; *by a cock picking up grains*, Alectryomancy (*or* Alectoromancy); *by fishes*, Ophiomancy; *by herbs*, Botanomancy; *by water*, Hydromancy; *by fountains*, Pegomancy; *by a wand*, Rhabdomancy; *by dough of cakes*, Crithomancy; *by meal*, Aleuromancy, Alphitomancy; *by salt*, Halomancy; *by dice*, Cleromancy; *by arrows*, Belomancy; *by a balanced hatchet*, Axinomancy; *by a balanced sieve*, Coscinomancy; *by a suspended ring*, Dactyliomancy; *by dots made at random on paper*, Geomancy; *by precious stones*, Lithomancy; *by pebbles*, Pessomancy; *by pebbles drawn from a heap*, Psephomancy; *by mirrors*, Catoptromancy; *by writings in ashes*, Tephramancy; *by dreams*, Oneiromancy; *by the hand*, Palmistry, Chiromancy; *by nails reflecting the sun's rays*, Onychomancy; *by finger rings*, Dactylomancy; *by numbers*, Arithmancy; *by drawing lots*, Sortilege; *by passages in books*, Stichomancy; *by the letters forming the name of the person*, Onomancy, Nomancy; *by the features*, Anthroposcopy; *by the mode of laughing*, Geloscopy; *by ventriloquism*, Gastromancy; *by walking in a circle*, Gyromancy; *by dropping melted wax into water*, Ceromancy; *by currents*, Bletonism.

[Place of prediction] *adytum.*
prefigur-ation, -ement; prototype, type.

V. predict, prognosticate, prophesy, vaticinate, divine, foretell, soothsay, augurate, tell fortunes; cast a -horoscope, – nativity; advise; forewarn &c. 668.

presage, augur, bode; a-, fore-bode, -cast; fore-, be-token; pre-figure, -show; portend; fore-show, -shadow, shadow forth, typify, ominate, signify, point to, precurse.

usher in, herald, premise, announce; lower.

hold out-, raise –, excite- -expectation, – hope; bid fair, promise, lead one to expect; be the -precursor &c. 64.

Adj. predicting &c. *v.*; predictive, prophetic, fatidical, vaticinal, oracular, Sibylline, haruspical, weatherwise.

ominous, presageful, portentous; augur-ous, -al, -ial; auspici-al; -ous; prescious, monitory, extispicious, premonitory, precusory, significant of, pregnant with, big with the fate of.

Phr. 'coming events cast their shadows before.'

512. Omen.—N. omen, portent, presage, prognostic, augury, auspice; sign &c. (*indication*) 550; herald, forerunner, harbinger &c. (*precursor*) 64.

bird of ill omen; signs of the times; gathering clouds; warning &c. 668.

prefigurement &c. 511.

513. Oracle.—N. oracle; prophet, -ess; seer, soothsayer, augur, fortune-teller, palmist, medium, clairvoyant, crystal gazer, witch, geomancer, *aruspex*; a-, ha-ruspice; Sibyl; Python, -ess; Pythia; Pythian –, Delphian- oracle; Monitor, Sphinx, Tiresias, Cassandra, Sibylline leaves; Zadkiel, Old Moore; sorcerer &c. 994; interpreter &c. 524.

Section VII. CREATIVE THOUGHT

514. Supposition.—N. supposition, assumption, postulation, condition, pre-supposition, hy-pothesis, postulate, *postulatum*, theory, *data*; pro-, position; *thesis*, theorem; proposal &c. (*plan*) 626.

bare -, vague -, loose- -supposition, - suggestion; conceit; conjecture; guess, - work; rough guess, shot; conjecturality; surmise, suspicion, inkling, suggestion, suggestiveness, association of ideas, hint; presumption &c. (*belief*) 484; divination, speculation.

theorist, speculator, doctrinarian, hypothesist.

V. suppose, conjecture, surmise, suspect, guess, divine; theorize; pre-sume, -surmise, -suppose; assume, fancy, wis, take it; give a guess, speculate, believe, dare say, take it into one's head, take for granted.

put forth; pro-pound, -pose; moot; hypothesize; start, put a case, submit, move, make a motion; hazard -, throw out -, put forward- a -suggestion, - conjecture.

allude to, suggest, hint, put it into one's head.

suggest itself &c. (*thought*) 451; run in the head &c. (*memory*) 505; marvel -, wonder- -if, -whether.

Adj. supposing &c. *v.*; given, mooted, postulatory; assumed &c. *v.* supposit-ive, -itious; gratuitous, speculative, conjectural, hypothetical, suppositional, theoretical, academic, supposable, presumptive, putative.

suggestive, allusive, stimulating.

Adv. if, - so be; an; on the -supposition &c. *n.*; *ex hypothesi*; in -case, - the event of; *quasi*, as if, provided; perhaps &c. (*by possibility*) 470; for aught one knows.

515. Imagination.—N. imagination; originality; invention; fancy; inspiration; *verve*; empathy.

warm -, heated -, excited -, sanguine -, ardent -, fiery -, boiling -, wild -, bold -, daring -, playful -, lively -, fertile- -imagination, - fancy.

'mind's eye'; 'such stuff as dreams are made of.'

ideal-ity, -ism; romanticism, utopianism, castle-building; dreaming; frenzy; ecs-, ex-tasy; calenture &c. (*delirium*) 503; reverie, brown study, trance; somnambulism.

conception, *vorstellung*, excogitation, 'a fine frenzy,' poetic frenzy, divine afflatus; cloud-, dream-land; flight -, fumes- of fancy; 'thick-coming fancies'; creation -, coinage- of the brain; imagery, word painting.

conceit, maggot, figment, myth, dream, vision, shadow, chimera; phantasm, -tasy; fantasy, fancy; whim, -sey; vagary, rhapsody, romance, *extravaganza*; air-drawn dagger, bugbear, nightmare; flying Dutchman, great sea-serpent, man in the moon, castle in the air, *château en Espagne*; Utopia, Atlantis, happy valley, millennium, fairy land; land of Prester John, kingdom of Micomicon; work of fiction &c. (*novel*) 594; poetry &c. 597; drama &c. 599; Arabian nights; *le pot au lait*; dream of Alnaschar &c. (*hope*) 858; day -, golden- dream.

illusion &c. (*error*) 495; phantom &c. (*fallacy of vision*) 443; *Fata Morgana* &c. (*ignis fatuus*) 423; vapour &c. (*cloud*) 353; stretch of the imagination &c. (*exaggeration*) 549.

idealist, romanticist, visionary; mopus; romancer, dreamer; somnambulist; rhapsodist &c. (*fanatic*) 504.

V. imagine, fancy, conceive; ideal-, real-ize; dream, - of; 'give to airy nothing a local habitation and a name.'

create, originate, devise, invent, coin, fabricate; improvise, strike out something new.

set one's wits to work; strain -, crack- one's invention; rack -, ransack -, cudgel- one's brains; excogitate.

give -play, – the reins, – a loose- to
the -imagination, – fancy; empathize;
indulge in reverie.

conjure up a vision; fancy –, represent –, picture –, figure- to oneself; envisage.

float in the mind; suggest itself &c.
(*thought*) 451.

Adj. imagined &c. *v.*; *ben trovato*;
air-drawn, -built.

imagin-ing &c. *v.*, -ative; original, inventive, creative, fertile, productive; ingenious.

romantic, high-flown, flighty, extravagant, fanatic, enthusiastic, Utopian,
Quixotic; preposterous, rhapsodical.

ideal, unreal; in the clouds, *in nubibus*; unsubstantial &c. 4; illusory &c.(
fallacious) 495; fictitious, theoretical,
hypothetical.

fabulous, legendary; myth-ic, -ological;
chimerical; imagin-, vision-ary; notional; fan-cy, -ciful, -tastic, -tastical;
whimsical; fairy, -like.

dreamy, entranced, vaporous.

DIVISION (II.) COMMUNICATION OF IDEAS

Section I.
NATURE OF IDEAS
COMMUNICATED

516. [Idea to be conveyed.] **Meaning.**
[Thing signified.]—**N.** meaning; signif-
ic-ation, -ance; sense, expression; im-,
pur-port; drift, tenor, implication, con-
notation, essence, force, spirit bearing,
colouring; scope.

matter; subject, -matter; argument,
text, sum and substance; gist &c. 5.

general –, broad –, substantial –, colloquial –, literal –, plain –, simple –,
accepted –, natural –, unstrained –, true
&c. (*exact*) 494–, honest &c. 543–, *primâ facie* &c. (*manifest*) 525-meaning.

literality; literal interpretation; after
acceptation; allusion &c. (*latency*) 526;
suggestion &c. (*information*) 527; synonym; figure of speech &c. 521; acceptation &c. (*interpretation*) 522.

V. mean, signify, express, connote,
denote; im-, pur-port; convey, imply,
breathe, indicate, bespeak, bear a sense;
tell –, speak- of; touch on; point –, al-
lude- to; drive at; involve &c. (*latency*)
526; declare &c. (*affirm*) 535.

understand by &c. (*interpret*) 522.

Adj. meaning &c. *v.*; expressive, sug-

gestive, meaningful, allusive; significant; -ative, -atory; pithy; full of –, pregnant with- meaning.

declaratory &c. 535; intelligible &c.
518; literal, metaphrastic; synonymous;
tantamount &c. (*equivalent*) 27; implied
&c. (*latent*) 526; explicit &c. 525; literal &c. 562.

Adv. to that effect; that is to say &c.
(*being interpreted*) 522.

literally; evidently, from the context.

517. [Absence of meaning.] **Unmeaningness.—N.** unmeaningness &c. *adj.*;
scrabble, scribble, scrawl, daub, (*painting*), strumming (*music*).

empty sound, dead letter, *vox et præterea nihil*; 'a tale told by an idiot, full
of sound and fury, signifying nothing';
'sounding brass and a tinkling cymbal.'

nonsense, jargon, gibberish, jabber,
mere words, hocus-pocus, fustian, rant,
bombast, balderdash, palaver, patter,
flummery, *verbiage*, babble, *bavardage*,
baragouin, platitude, *niaiserie*; inanity;
rigmarole, rodomontade; truism; *nugæ
canoræ*; twaddle, twattle, fudge, trash;

stuff, – and nonsense; bosh, rubbish, rot, drivel, moonshine, wish-wash, fiddle-faddle, flapdoodle; absurdity &c. 497; vagueness &c. (*unintelligibility*) 519.

V. mean nothing; be-unmeaning &c. *adj.*; twaddle, quibble, rant, gabble, scrabble &c. *n.*

Adj. unmeaning; meaning-, senseless; nonsensical; void of -sense &c. 516.

in-, un-expressive; vacant, fatuous; not significant; insignificant.

trashy, washy, inane, vague, trumpery, trivial, fiddle-faddle, twaddling, quibbling.

unmeant, not expressed; tacit &c. (*latent*) 526.

inexpressible, undefinable, incommunicable.

Int. rubbish! &c. 497.

518. Intelligibility.—N. intelligibility, clearness, clarity, explicitness &c. *adj.*; lucidity, perspicuity; legibility, plain speaking &c. (*manifestation*) 525; precision &c. 494; a word to the wise.

V. be -intelligible &c. *adj.*; speak -for itself, – volumes; tell its own tale, lie on the surface.

render -intelligible &c. *adj.*; popularize, simplify, clear up; elucidate &c. (*explain*) 522.

understand, comprehend; take, – in; catch, grasp, recognize, follow, collect, master, make out; see -with half an eye, – daylight, – one's way; enter into the ideas of; come to an understanding.

Adj. intelligible; clear, – as -day, – crystal, – noonday; lucid; per-, transpicuous; luminous, transparent; comprehensible.

easily understood, easy to understand, for the million, intelligible to the meanest capacity, popularized.

plain, distinct, explicit, clear-cut; positive; definite &c. (*precise*) 494.

graphic, vivid, telling; expressive &c. (*meaning*) 516; illustrative &c. (*explanatory*) 522.

un-ambiguous, -equivocal, -mistakable

&c. (*manifest*) 525, -confused; legible, recognizable; obvious &c. 525.

Adv. in plain -terms, – words, – English.

Phr. he that runs may read &c. (*manifest*) 525.

519. Unintelligibility.—N. unintelligibility, incomprehensibility, imperspicuity; inconceivableness, vagueness &c. *adj.*; obscurity; ambiguity &c. 520; doubtful meaning; uncertainty &c. 475; perplexity &c. (*confusion*) 59; spinosity; *obscurum per obscurius*; mystification &c. (*concealment*) 528; latency &c. 526; transcendentalism.

paradox; enigma, riddle &c. (*secret*) 533; *dignus vindice nodus*; sealed book; steganography, freemasonry.

pons asinorum, asses' bridge; double -, high- Dutch, Greek, Hebrew; jargon &c. (*unmeaning*) 517.

obscurantist.

V. be -unintelligible &c. *adj.*; require -explanation &c. 522; have a doubtful meaning, pass comprehension.

render -unintelligible &c. *adj.*; conceal &c. 528; darken &c. 421; confuse &c. (*derange*) 61; perplex &c. (*bewilder*) 475.

not -understand &c. 518; lose, – the clue; miss; not know what to make of, be able to make nothing of, give it up; not be able to -account for, – make either head or tail of; be at sea &c. (*uncertain*) 475; wonder &c. 870; see through a glass darkly &c. (*ignorance*) 491.

not understand one another; play at cross purposes &c. (*misinterpret*) 523.

Adj. un-intelligible, -accountable, -decipherable, -discoverable, -knowable, -fathomable; in-cognizable, -explicable, -scrutable; inap-, incom-prehensible; insol-vable, -uble; impenetrable.

illegible, indecipherable, as Greek to one, unexplained, paradoxical; enigmatic, -al; puzzling, baffling.

obscure, dark, muddy, clear as mud, seen through a mist, dim, nebulous, shrouded in mystery; undiscernible &c.

(*invisible*) 447; misty &c. (*opaque*) 426; hidden &c. 528; latent &c. 526.

indefinite &c. (*indistinct*) 447; perplexed &c. (*confused*) 59; undetermined, vague, loose, ambiguous; mysterious; mystic, -al; transcendental; occult, recondite, esoteric, abstruse, crabbed.

incon-ceivable, -ceptible; searchless; above -, beyond -, past-comprehension; beyond one's depth; unconceived.

inexpressible, undefinable, incommunicable, unutterable, ineffable, unpronounceable.

520. [Having a double sense.] **Equivocalness.—N.** equivocalness &c. *adj.*; double -meaning &c. 516; ambiguity, *double entendre*, pun, paragram, *calembour*, quibble, *équivoque*, anagram; conundrum &c. (*riddle*) 533; word-play &c. (*wit*) 842; homonym, -y; amphiboly, -logy; ambiloquy.

Sphinx, Delphic oracle.

equivocation &c. (*duplicity*) 544; white lie, mental reservation &c. (*concealment*) 528.

V. be -equivocal &c. *adj.*; have two -meanings &c. 516; equivocate &c. (*palter*) 544.

Adj. equivocal, ambiguous, amphibolous, homonymous; double-tongued &c. (*lying*) 544.

521. Metaphor.—N. figure of speech; *façon de parler*, way of speaking, colloquialism.

phrase &c. 566; figure, trope, metaphor, tralatition, metonymy, enallage, *catachresis, synecdoche, autonomasia*; irony, satire, figurativeness &c. *adj.*; image, -ry; *metalepsis*, type, anagoge, simile, personification, *prosopopæia*, allegory, apologue, parable, fable; allusion, adumbration; application; euphemism; euphuism.

V. employ -metaphor &c. *n.*; personify, allegorize, adumbrate, shadow forth, apply, allude -, refer- to.

Adj. metaphorical &c. *n.*; figurative, catachrestical, typical, tralatitious, par-

abolic, allegorical, allusive, anagogical; ironical; colloquial.

Adv. so to -speak, - say, - express oneself; as it were.

Phr. *mutato nomine de te fabula narratur.*

522. Interpretation.—N. interpretation, definition; explan-, explic-ation; solution, answer; rationale; plain -, simple -, strict- interpretation; meaning &c. 516.

translation; rend-ering, -ition; reddition; literal -, free- translation; key, crib; secret; clew &c. (*indication*) 550; Rosetta stone.

exegesis; ex-pounding, -position; Hermeneutics; comment, -ary; inference &c. (*deduction*) 480; illustration, exemplification; gloss, annotation, *scholium*, note; e-, di-lucidation, enucleation; *éclaircissement, mot de l'énigme*.

symptomat-, semei-ology; metoposcopy, physiognomy; diagnosis, prognosis; paleography &c. (*philology*) 560.

accept-ion, -ation, -ance; light, reading, lection, construction, version.

equivalent, - meaning &c. 516; synonym; para-, meta-phrase; convertible terms, apposition; dictionary &c. 562; polyglot.

V. interpret, explain, define, construe, translate, render; do -, turn- into; transfuse the sense of.

find out &c. 480*a*- -the meaning &c. 516- of; read; spell -, figure -, makeout; decipher, decode, unravel, disentangle, puzzle out; find the key of, enucleate, resolve, solve; read between the lines.

account for; find -, tell- the cause &c. 153- of; throw -, shed- -light, - new light, - a fresh light- upon; clear up, elucidate.

illustrate, exemplify; unfold, expound, comment upon, annotate; popularize &c. (*render intelligible*) 518.

take -, understand -, receive -, accept- in a particular sense; understand by, put a construction on, be given to understand.

Adj. explanatory, expository; explicative, -tory; exegetical; hermeneutic, interpretive, illustrative, elucidative, annotative, scholiastic.

polyglot; literal; para-, meta-phrastic; cosignificative, synonymous; equivalent &c. 27.

Adv. in -explanation &c. *n.*; that is to say, *id est*, *videlicet*, to wit, namely, in other words.

literally, strictly speaking; in -plain, – plainer- -terms, – words, – English; more simply.

523. Misinterpretation.—N. misinterpretation, -apprehension, -understanding, -acceptation, -construction, -application; *catachresis*; cross -reading, – purposes; mistake &c. 495.

misrepresentation, perversion, exaggeration &c. 549; false -colouring, – construction; abuse of terms; parody, travesty; falsification &c. (*lying*) 544.

V. mis-interpret, -apprehend, -understand, -conceive, -judge, -doubt, -spell, -translate, -construe, -apply; mistake &c. 495.

misrepresent, pervert; garble &c. (*falsify*) 544; distort, detort; travesty, play upon words; stretch –, strain –, wrest- the -sense, – meaning; explain away; put a -bad, – false- construction on; give a false colouring, look through -rose coloured –, – dark – spectacles.

be –, play- at cross purposes.

Adj. misinterpreted &c. *v.*; untranslat-ed, -able.

Adv. at cross purposes.

524. Interpreter.—N. interpreter, translator, ex-positor, -pounder, -ponent, -plainer; demonstrator.

scholiast, commentator, annotator; meta-, para-phrast.

spokesman, speaker, mouthpiece, prolocutor; diplomat &c. 758.

guide, courier, dragoman, *valet de place*, *cicerone*, showman; oneirocritic; Œdipus; oracle &c. 513.

Section II. MODES OF COMMUNICATION

525. Manifestation.—N. manifestation; unfolding; plainness &c. *adj.*; plain speaking; expression; showing &c. *v.*; exposition, demonstration, *séance*; exhibition, production; display, showing off &c. 882, premonstration. [Thing shown] exhibit, show.

indication &c. (*calling attention to*) 457; publicity &c. 531; disclosure &c. 529; openness &c. (*honesty*) 543; (*artlessness*) 703; *épanchement*, prominence.

V. make –, render- -manifest &c. *adj.*; bring -forth, – forward, – to the front, – into view; give notice; express; represent, set forth, exhibit; show, – up; expose; produce; hold up –, expose- to view; set –, place –, lay- before -one, – one's eyes; tell to one's face; trot out, put through one's paces, unfold, show off, show forth, unveil, bring to light, display, demonstrate, unroll; lay open; draw –, bring- out; bring out in strong relief; call –, bringinto notice; hold up the mirror; wear one's heart upon his sleeve; show one's -face, – colours; manifest oneself; speak out; make no -mystery, – secret- of; unfurl the flag; proclaim &c. (*publish*) 531.

indicate &c. (*direct attention to*) 457; disclose &c. 529; elicit &c. 480*a*; interpret &c. 522.

be -manifest &c. *adj.*; appear &c. (*be visible*) 446; transpire &c. (*be disclosed*) 529; speak for itself, stand to reason; stare one in the face; loom large, appear on the horizon, rear its head; give -token, – sign, – indication of; tell its own tale &c. (*intelligible*) 518; go without saying.

Adj. manifest, apparent; salient, striking, demonstrative, prominent, in the foreground, notable, pronounced.

flagrant; notorious &c. (*public*) 531; arrant; stark staring; unshaded, glaring.

defin-ed, -ite; distinct, conspicuous &c. (*visible*) 446; obvious, evident, incontestable, unmistakable, not to be mistaken, plain, clear, palpable, self-evident, autoptical; intelligible &c. 518; clear as -day, – daylight, – noonday; plain as -a pikestaff, – the sun at noonday, – the nose on one's face, – the way to the parish church.

ostensible; open, – as day; overt, patent, express, explicit; naked, bare, literal, downright, undisguised, exoteric.

unreserved; frank, plain spoken &c. (*artless*) 703; barefaced, brazen, bold, shameless, daring, flaunting, loud.

manifested &c. *v.*; disclosed &c. 529; expressible, capable of being shown, producible; in-, un-concealable.

Adv. manifestly, openly &c. *adj.*; before one's eyes, under one's nose, to one's face, face to face, above board, *cartes sur table*, on the stage, in plain sight, in open court, in the open, – streets; at the cross roads; in market overt; in the face of -day, – heaven; in -broad –, open- daylight; without reserve; at first blush, *primâ facie*, on the face of; in set terms.

Phr. *cela saute aux yeux*; he that runs may read; you can see it with half an eye; it needs no ghost to tell us; the meaning lies on the surface; *cela va sans dire*; *res ipsa loquitur*.

526. Latency.—N. latency, inexpression; hidden -, occult- meaning; occultness, occultism, mysticism, mystery, cabala, symbolism, anagoge; silence &c. (*taciturnity*) 585; concealment &c. 528; more than meets the -eye, – ear; Delphic oracle; *le dessous des cartes*, undercurrent.

allusion, insinuation, implication; innuendo &c. 527; adumbration; 'something rotten in the state of Denmark.'

snake in the grass &c. (*pitfall*) 667; secret &c. 533.

darkness, invisibility, imperceptibility.

latent influence, power behind the throne; friend at court, wire puller.

V. be -latent &c. *adj.*; lurk, smoulder, underlie, make no sign; escape -observation, – detection, – recognition; lie hid &c. 528.

laugh in one's sleeve; keep back &c. (*conceal*) 528.

involve, imply, implicate, connote, import, understand, allude to, infer, leaave an inference; symbolize; whisper &c. (*conceal*) 528.

Adj. latent; lurking &c. *v.*; secret &c. 528; occult, symbolic, mystic; implied &c. *v.*; dormant.

un-apparent, -known, -seen &c. 441; in the background; invisible &c. 447; indiscoverable, dark; impenetrable &c. (*unintelligible*) 519; un-spied, -suspected.

un -said, -written, -published, -breathed, -talked of, -told &c. 527, -sung, -exposed, -proclaimed, -disclosed &c. 529, -pronounced, -mentioned, -expressed; not expressed, tacit.

un-developed, -solved, -explained, -traced, -discovered &c. 480*a*, -tracked, -explored, -invented.

indirect, crooked, inferential; by -inference, – implication; implicit; constructive; allusive, covert, muffled; steganographic; under-stood, -hand, -ground; concealed &c. 528; delitescent.

Adv. by a side wind; *sub silentio*; in the background; behind -the scenes, – one's back, – the veil; below the surface; on the tip of one's tongue; secretly &c. 528; between the lines; by a mutual understanding.

Phr. 'thereby hangs a tale.' 'that is another story.'

527. Information.—N. information, enlightenment, acquaintance, knowledge &c. 490; publicity &c. 531.

communication, intimation; not-ice, -ification; e-, an-nunciation; announcement; representation, round robin, presentment.

case, estimate, specification, report, advice, monition; news &c. 532; return &c. (*record*) 551; account &c.

(*description*) 594; statement &c. (*affirmation*) 535.

mention; acquainting &c., *v.*; instruction &c. (*teaching*) 537; outpouring; intercommunication, communicativeness.

informant, authority, teller, announcer, annunciator, harbinger, herald, intelligencer, commentator, columnist, reporter, exponent, mouthpiece; informer, keek, eavesdropper, delator, detective, sleuth; *mouchard*, spy, stool pigeon, newsmonger; messenger &c. 534; *amicus curiœ*.

valet de place, *cicerone*, pilot, guide; guide-, hand-book; *vade mecum*; manual; map, plan, chart, gazetteer; itinerary &c. (*journey*) 266.

hint, suggestion, wrinkle, innuendo, inkling, whisper, passing word, word in the ear, subaudition, cue, by-play; gesture &c. (*indication*) 550; gentle – broad- hint; *verbum sapienti*; word to the wise; insinuation &c. (*latency*) 526.

V. tell; inform, – of; acquaint, – with; impart, – to; make acquainted with, bring to the ears of, apprise, advise, enlighten, awaken.

let fall, mention, express, intimate, represent, communicate, make known; publish &c. 531; notify, signify, specify, convey the knowledge of.

let one –, have one to- know; serve notice, give one to understand; give notice; set –, lay –, put- before; point out, put into one's head; put one in possession of; instruct &c. (*teach*) 537; direct the attention to &c. 457.

an-nounce, -nunciate; report, – progress; bring –, send –, leave –, write- word; tele-graph, -phone; ring –, call- up; wire; retail, render an account; give an account &c. (*describe*) 594; state &c. (*affirm*) 535.

disclose &c. 529; show cause; explain &c. (*interpret*) 522.

hint; give an inkling of; give –, drop –, throw out- a hint; insinuate; allude –, make allusion- to; glance at; tip off, tip the wink &c. (*indicate*) 550; suggest, prompt, give the cue, breathe; whisper, – in the ear.

give a bit of one's mind; tell one plainly, – once for all; speak volumes.

un-deceive, -beguile; set right, correct, open the eyes of, disabuse.

be -informed of &c.; know &c. 490; learn &c. 539; get scent of, gather from; awaken –, open one's eyes- to; become -alive, – awake- to; keep posted; hear, overhear, understand.

come to one's -ears, – knowledge; reach one's ears.

Adj. informed &c. *v.*; *communiqué*; reported &c. *v.*; published &c. 531; advisory.

expressive &c. 516; explicit &c. (*open*) 525, (*clear*) 518; plain-spoken &c. (*artless*) 703.

declara-, nuncupa-, exposi-tory; declarative, enunciative, communicat-ive, -ory; oral.

Adv. from information received; according to -rumour, – report; in the air; from what one can gather.

Phr. a little bird told me.

528. Concealment.—N. concealment; hiding &c. *v.*; occultation, mystification.

seal of secrecy; screen &c. 530; disguise &c. 530; masquerade; masked battery; hiding place &c. 530; cipher, code, crypt-, stegan-ography; invisible –, sympathetic- ink; palimpsest; freemasonry.

stealth, -iness; obreption; slyness &c. (*cunning*) 702.

latit-ancy, -ation; seclusion &c. 893; privacy, secrecy, secretness; *incognita*.

reticence; reserve; mental –, reservation, aside; *arrière pensée*, suppression, evasion, white lie, misprision; silence &c. (*taciturnity*) 585; suppression of truth &c. 544; underhand dealing; close-, secretive-ness &c. *adj.*, mystery.

latency &c. 526; snake in the grass; secret &c. 533.

V. conceal, hide, secrete, stow away, put out of sight; lock –, seal –, bottle- up.

cover, screen, cloak, veil, shroud; screen from -sight, – observation; draw the veil; draw –, close- the curtain; curtain, shade, eclipse, throw a veil over; be-cloud, -fog, -mask; mask, disguise; ensconce, muffle, smother; whisper.

keep -from, – back, – to oneself; keep -snug, – close, – secret, – dark; bury; sink, suppress; keep -from, – out of--view, – sight; keep in –, throw into- the -shade, – background; cover up one's tracks; stifle, hush up, withhold, reserve; fence with a question; ignore &c. 460.

code, codify, use a cipher.

keep -a secret, – one's own counsel; hold one's tongue &c. (*silence*) 585; make no sign, not let it go further; not breathe a -word, – syllable- about; not let the right hand know what the left is doing; hide one's light under a bushel, bury one's talent in a napkin.

keep –, leave- in -the dark, – ignorance; blind, – the eyes; blindfold, hoodwink, mystify; puzzle &c. (*render uncertain*) 475; bamboozle &c. (*deceive*) 545.

be -concealed &c. *v.*; suffer an eclipse; retire from sight, couch; hide oneself; lie -hid, – in ambush, – low, – *perdu*, – snug, – close; seclude oneself &c. 893; lurk, sneak, skulk, slink, pussy-foot, prowl; steal -into, – out of, – by, – along; play at -bopeep, – hide and seek; hide in holes and corners.

Adj. concealed &c. *v.*; hidden; veiled, secret, recondite, mystic, cabalistic, occult, dark; cryptic, -al; private, privy, *in petto*, auricular, clandestine, close, inviolate.

behind a -screen &c. 530; under -cover, – an eclipse; in -ambush, – hiding, – disguise; in a -cloud, – fog, – mist, – haze, – dark corner; in the -shade, – dark; clouded, wrapt in clouds; invisible &c. 447; buried, underground, *perdu*; incommunicado; secluded &c. 893.

un-disclosed &c. 529, -told &c. 527; covert &c. (*latent*) 526; mysterious &c. (*unintelligible*) 519.

irrevealable, inviolable; confidential; esoteric; not to be spoken of.

obreptitious, furtive, stealthy, feline; skulking &c. *v.*; surreptitious, underhand, hole and corner; sly &c. (*cunning*) 702; secretive, evasive, noncommittal, reserved, reticent, uncommunicative, buttoned up; close, – as wax; taciturn &c. 585.

Adv. secretly &c. *adj.*; in -secret, – private, – one's sleeve, – holes and corners; in the dark &c. *adj.*

januis clausis, with closed doors, *à huis clos*; hugger-mugger, *à la dérobée*; under the -cloak of, – rose, – table; *sub rosâ, en tapinois*, in the background, aside, on the sly, with bated breath, *sotto voce*, in a whisper, without beat of drum, *à la sourdine*.

in –, strict- confidence; confidentially &c. *adj.*; between -ourselves, – you and me; *entre nous, inter nos*, under the seal of secrecy; in -code, – cipher.

underhand, by stealth, like a thief in the night; stealthily &c. *adj.*; behind -the scenes, – the curtain, – one's back, – a screen &c. 530; *incognito; in camerâ*.

Phr. it -must, – will- go no further; 'tell it not in Gath,' nobody the wiser.

529. Disclosure.—N. disclosure; retection; unveiling &c. *v.*; deterration, revealment, revelation; divulgence, expos-ition, -ure; *exposé*; whole truth; telltale &c. (*news*) 532.

acknowledgment, avowal; confession, -al; shrift.

bursting of a bubble; *dénouement*.

V. dis-close, -cover, -mask; draw –, draw aside –, lift –, raise –, lift up –, remove –, tear- the -veil, – curtain; unmask, -veil, -fold, -cover, -seal, -kennel; take off –, break- the seal; lay -open, – bare; expose; open, – up; bare, bright to light; evidence; make - clear, – evident, – manifest; evince.

divulge, reveal, break; let into the secret; reveal the secrets of the prison-house; tell &c. (*inform*) 527; breathe, utter, blab, peach; let -out, – fall, – drop, – the cat out of the bag; betray; tell tales, – out of school; come out with;

give -vent, - utterance- to; open the lips, blurt out, vent, whisper about; speak out &c. (*make manifest*) 525; make public &c. 531; unriddle &c. (*find out*) 480*a*; split, blow the gaff; break the news.

acknowledge, allow, concede, grant, admit, own, confess, avow, throw off all disguise, turn inside out, make a clean breast; show one's -hand, - cards; unburden -, disburden- one's mind, - conscience, - heart; open -, lay bare -, tell a piece of- one's mind; unbosom oneself, own to the soft impeachment; say -, speak- the truth; turn -King's - Queen's, -State's- evidence.

raise -, drop -, lift -, remove -, throw off- the mask; expose; debunk; lay open; un-deceive, -beguile; disabuse, set right, correct, open the eyes of; *désillusionner*.

be -disclosed &c.; transpire, come to light; come in sight &c. (*be visible*) 446; become known, escape the lips; come -, ooze -, creep -, leak -, peep -, crop-out; show its -face, - colours; discover &c. itself; break through the clouds, flash on the mind.

Adj. disclosed &c. *v.*

Int. out with it!

Phr. the murder is out; a light breaks in upon one; the scales fall from one's eyes; the eyes are opened.

530. Ambush. [Means of concealment.]—**N.** hiding-place; secret -place, - drawer; recess, hole, funk hole, holes and corners; closet, crypt, *adytum*, abditory, *oubliette*, safe, - deposit.

am-bush, -buscade; stalking horse; lurking-hole, -place; secret path, back-stairs; retreat &c. (*refuge*) 666.

screen, cover, shade, blinker; veil, curtain, blind, *purdah*, cloak, cloud.

mask, vizor, visor, disguise, masquerade dress, domino; *camouflage*.

pitfall &c. (*source of danger*) 667; trap &c. (*snare*) 545.

V. ambush, ambuscade, lie in ambush &c. (*hide oneself*) 528; lie in wait for; set a trap for &c. (*deceive*) 545.

Adv. *aux aguets*.

531. Publication.—N. publication;

public -announcement &c. 527; promulgation, propagation, proclamation, pronouncement, encyclical, *pronunciamento*; circulation, indiction, edition, imprint, impression, printing; hue and cry.

publicity, notoriety, currency, flagrancy, cry, *bruit*; *vox populi*; report &c. (*news*) 532.

the Press, fourth estate, public press, newspaper, periodical, journal, gazette; house organ, trade publication, tabloid; daily, weekly, monthly, quarterly, annual, magazine, monograph, book; review; news sheet, special edition, supplement, feature, rotogravure, comic strips; leaflet, pamphlet; telegraphy; publisher &c. *v.*

circular, - letter; manifesto, advertisement, puff, placard, bill, *affiche*, broadside, poster; notice &c. 527; programme.

V. publish; make -public, - known &c. (*information*) 527; speak -, talk- of; broach, utter; put forward; circulate, propagate, promulgate; spread -, abroad; rumour, diffuse, disseminate, evulgate; put -, give -, send- forth; emit, edit, get out; issue; cover, report; bring -, lay -, drag- before the public; give -out, - to the world; put -, bandy -, hawk -, buzz -, whisper -, bruit -, blaze- about; drag into the -open day, - limelight; voice.

proclaim, herald, blazon; blaze -, noise- abroad; sound a trumpet; trumpet -, thunder- forth; give tongue; announce with -beat of drum, - flourish of trumpets; proclaim -from the housetops, - at Charing Cross, at the cross roads; declare, declaim.

advertise, placard; post, - up; *afficher*, publish in the Gazette, send round the crier.

raise a -cry, - hue and cry, - report; set news afloat.

telegraph, cable, wireless, broadcast.

be -published &c.; be -, become-public &c. *adj.*; come out; go -, fly -, buzz -, blow- about; get -about, - abroad, - afloat, - wind; find vent; see the light; go forth, take air, acquire currency, pass current; go -the rounds, – the round of the newspapers, – through the length and breadth of the land; *virum volitare per ora*; pass from mouth to mouth; spread; run –, spread- like wildfire.

Adj. published &c. *v.*; current &c. (*news*) 532; in circulation, public; notorious; flagrant, arrant; open &c. 525; trumpet-tongued; encyclical, promulgatory; exoteric.

Adv. publicly &c. *adj.*; in open court, with open doors; in the limelight.

Int. *Oyez!* O yes! notice!

Phr. notice is hereby given; this is –, these are- to give notice.

532. News.—N. news; information &c. 527; piece –, budget- of -news, – information; report, story, yarn, copy, filler, intelligence, tidings; stop press news.

word, advice, *aviso*, message; dis-, des-patch; radio, telegram, cable, wireless telegram, radio-gram, marconigram, communication, errand, embassy; *bulletin*.

rumour, hearsay, *on dit*, flying rumour, news stirring, cry, buzz, *bruit*, fame; talk, *ouï-dire*, scandal, eavesdropping; town –, tale- talk; tittle-tattle; *canard*, topic of the day, idea afloat.

fresh –, stirring –, old –, stale- news; glad tidings; old –, stale- story.

narrator &c. (*describe*) 594; news-, scandal-monger; tale-bearer; tell-tale, gossip, tattler, busy-body, chatterer; informer.

V. transpire &c. (*be disclosed*) 529; rumour &c. (*publish*) 531.

Adj. many-tongued; rumoured; publicly -, currently- rumoured, - reported; rife, current, floating, afloat, going about, in circulation, in everyone's mouth, all over the town.

Adv. as the story -goes, - runs; as they say, it is said.

533. Secret.—N. secret; dead -, profound- secret; *arcanum*, mystery; latency &c. 526; Asian mystery; sealed

books, secrets of the prison-house; *le dessous des cartes*.

enigma, riddle, puzzle, nut to crack, conundrum, charade, rebus, logogriph; mono-, ana-gram; acrostic, cross-word puzzle; Sphinx; *crux criticorum*.

maze, labyrinth, Hyrcynian wood.

problem &c. (*question*) 461; paradox &c. (*difficulty*) 704; unintelligibility &c. 519; *terra incognita* &c. (*ignorance*) 491.

Adj. secret &c. (*concealed*) 528.

534. Messenger.—N. messenger, envoy, emissary, legate; nuncio, internuncio; intermediary; ambassador &c. (*diplomatist*) 758.

marshal, flag-bearer, herald, crier, trumpeter, bellman, pursuivant, *parlementaire*, *apparitor*.

courier, runner, dawk, *estafette*; Hermes, Mercury, Iris, Ariel.

postman, letter carrier, telegraph boy, messenger boy, district messenger; despatch rider, commissionaire; errand-boy.

mail; post, -office; letter-bag; mail -boat, - train, - coach, - van, aerial mail; tele-graph, -phone; cable, wire; carrier-pigeon; wireless tele-graph, -phone; radiotele-graph, -phone.

journalist, newspaperman, reporter; gentleman -, representative- of the press; sob sister; penny-a-liner; special -, war -, own- correspondent; spy, scout, informer &c. 527.

535. Affirmation.—N. affirm-ance, -ation; statement, allegation, assertion, predication, declaration, word, averment.

asseveration, adjuration, swearing, oath, affidavit; deposition &c. (*record*) 551; avouchment, assurance; protest, -ation; profession; acknowledgment &c. (*assent*) 488; pledge.

vote, voice, suffrage, ballot.

remark, observation; position &c. (*proposition*) 514; saying, *dictum*, sentence, *ipse dixit*.

emphasis, positiveness, peremptoriness; dogmatism &c. (*certainty*) 474; dogmatist &c. 887.

V. assert; make -an assertion &c. *n.*;

have one's say; say, affirm, predicate, declare, state, represent; protest, profess.

put -forth, – forward; advance, allege, propose, propound, enunciate, enounce, broach, set forth, hold out, maintain, contend, pronounce, pretend.

depose, depone, aver, avow, avouch, asseverate, swear; make –, take one's-oath; make –, swear –, put in- an affidavit; take one's Bible oath, kiss the book, vow, *vitam impendere vero*; swear till -one is black in the face, – all's blue; be sworn, call Heaven to witness; vouch, warrant, certify, assure, swear by bell, book and candle.

swear by &c. (*believe*) 484; insist –, take one's stand- upon; emphasize, lay stress on; assert -roundly, – positively; lay down, – the law; raise one's voice, dogmatize, have the last word; rap out; repeat; re-assert, -affirm.

announce &c. (*information*) 527; acknowledge &c. (*assent*) 488; attest &c. (*evidence*) 467; adjure &c. (*put to one's oath*) 768.

Adj. asserting &c. *v.*; declaratory, predicatory, pronunciative, affirmative, *soi-disant*; positive; certain &c. 474; express, explicit &c. (*patent*) 525; absolute, emphatic, flat, broad, round, pointed, marked, distinct, decided, confident, assertive, insistent, trenchant, dogmatic, definitive, formal, solemn, categorical, peremptory; unretracted; predicable, affirmable.

Adv. affirmatively &c. *adj.*; in the affirmative.

with emphasis, *ex cathedrâ*, without fear of contradiction.

I must say, indeed, i' faith, let me tell you, why, give me leave to say, marry, you may be sure, I'd have you to know; upon my -word, – honour; by my troth, egad, I assure you; by -jingo, – Jove, – George, – &c.; troth, seriously, sadly; in -, in sober- -sadness, – truth, – earnest; of a truth, truly, pardi, perdy; in all conscience, upon oath; be assured &c. (*belief*) 484; yes &c. (*assent*) 488; I'll -warrant, – warrant you, – engage,

– answer for it, – be bound, – venture to say, – take my oath; in fact, as a matter of fact, forsooth, joking apart; so help me God; not to mince the matter.

Phr. quoth he; *dixi*.

536. Negation.—N. ne-, abne-gation; denial; dis-avowal, -claimer; abjuration; contra-diction, -vention; recusation, protest; rebuttal; recusancy &c. (*dissent*) 489; flat –, emphatic- -contradiction, – denial; *démenti*.

qualification &c. 469; repudiation &c. 610; retractation &c. 607; confutation &c. 479; refusal &c. 764; prohibition &c. 761.

V. deny; contra-dict, -vene; controvert, give denial to, gainsay, negative, shake the head.

dis-own, -affirm, -claim, -avow; recant &c. 607; revoke &c. (*abrogate*) 756.

dispute, impugn, traverse, rebut, join issue upon; bring –, call- in question &c. (*doubt*) 485.

deny -flatly, – peremptorily, – emphatically, – absolutely, – wholly, – entirely; give the lie to, belie.

repudiate &c. 610; set aside, ignore &c. 460; rebut &c. (*confute*) 479; qualify &c. 469; refuse &c. 764.

Adj. denying &c. *v.*; denied &c. *v.*; contradictory; nega-tive, -ory; revocatory; recusant &c. (*dissenting*) 489; at issue upon.

Adv. no, nay, not, nowise; not a -bit, – whit, – jot; not -at all, – in the least, – so; no such thing; nothing of the -kind, – sort; quite the contrary, *tout au contraire*, far from it, *tant s'en faut*; on no account, in no respect; by -no, – no manner of- means; negatively.

Phr. there never was a greater mistake; I know better; *non hæc in fœdera*.

537. Teaching.—N. teaching &c. *v.*; instruction; edification; education; pedagogy; tuition; tutor-, tutel-age; direction, guidance.

qualification, preparation; train-, school-ing &c. *v.*; discipline; exer-cise, -citation; drill, practice.

persuasion, proselytism, propagandism, *propaganda*; in-doctrination, -culcation, -oculation.

explanation &c. (*interpretation*) 522; lesson, lecture, sermon, homily; apologue, parable; discourse, prelection, preachment, disquisition.

exercise, task; *curriculum*; course, – of study; grammar, three R's, initiation, A. B. C. &c. (*beginning*) 66.

elementary –, primary –, secondary –, grammar school –, high school –, college –, university –, technical –, liberal –, classical –, religious –, denominational –, moral –, secular- education; technical –, vocational- training; university extension lectures; propædeutics, moral tuition; evening classes, correspondence course.

physical education, gymnastics, calisthenics, eurythmics; *sloyd*.

V. teach, instruct, edify, school, tutor; cram, prime, coach; enlighten &c. (*inform*) 527.

in-culcate, -doctrinate, -oculate, -fuse, -stil, -fix, -graft, -filtrate; imbue, -pregnate, -plant; graft, sow the seeds of, disseminate, propagandize.

give an idea of; put -up to, – in the way of; set right.

sharpen the wits, enlarge the mind; give new ideas, open the eyes, bring forward, 'teach the young idea how to shoot'; improve &c. 658.

expound &c. (*interpret*) 522; lecture; prelect; read –, give- a -lesson, – lecture, – sermon, – discourse; hold forth, preach; sermon-, moral-ize; point a moral.

train, discipline; bring up, – to; educate, form, ground, prepare, qualify, drill, exercise, practice, habituate, familiarize with, nurture, dry-nurse; breed, rear, take in hand; break, – in; tame; pre-instruct; initiate, inure &c. (*habituate*) 613.

put to nurse, send to school.

direct, guide; direct attention to &c. (*attention*) 457; impress upon the -mind, – memory; beat into, – the head; convince &c. (*belief*) 484.

Adj. teaching &c. *v.*; taught &c. *v.*; educational; scholastic, academic, doctrinal; disciplinal; instructive, didactic, hortative, pedagogic, tutorial.

Phr. the schoolmaster abroad.

538. Misteaching.—N. mis-teaching, -information, -intelligence, -guidance, -direction, -persuasion, -instruction, -leading &c. *v.*; perversion, false teaching; sophistry &c. 477; college of Laputa; the blind leading the blind.

V. mis-inform, -teach, -direct, -guide, -instruct, -correct; pervert; put on a false –, throw off the- scent; deceive &c. 545; mislead &c. (*error*) 495; misrepresent; lie &c. 544; *ambiguas in vulgum spargere voces*, preach to the wise, teach one's grandmother to suck eggs.

render unintelligible &c. 519; bewilder &c. (*uncertainty*) 475; mystify &c. (*conceal*) 528; unteach.

Adj. misteaching &c. *v.*; unedifying.

Phr. *piscem natare doces.*

539. Learning.—N. learning; acquisition of -knowledge &c. 490, – skill &c. 698; acquirement, attainment; edification, scholarship, erudition; lore; information; self-instruction; study, reading, perusal; inquiry &c. 461.

ap-, prenticeship; pupil-age, -arity; tutelage, novitiate, matriculation.

docility &c. (*willingess*) 602; aptitude &c. 698.

V. learn; acquire –, gain –, receive –, take in –, drink in –, imbibe –, pick up –, gather –, get –, obtain –, collect –, glean- -knowledge, – information, – learning.

acquaint oneself with, master; make oneself -master of, – acquainted with; grind, cram; get –, coach- up; learn by -heart, – rote.

read, spell, peruse; con –, pore –, thumb- over; wade through; dip into; run the eye -over, – through; turn over the leaves.

study; be -studious &c. *adj.*; consume the midnight oil, mind one's book.

go to -school, – college, – the university; serve -an (*or* one's) apprenticeship,

- one's time; learn one's trade; be
-informed &c. 527; be -taught &c. 537.

Adj. studious; schol-astic, -arly;
teachable; docile &c. (*willing*) 602; apt
&c. 698, industrious &c. 682; learned,
erudite.

Adv. at one's books; *in statu pupillari*
&c. (*learner*) 541.

540. Teacher.—N. teacher, trainer,
instructor, institutor, master, tutor, don,
director, Corypheus, dry nurse, coach,
grinder, crammer; governor, bear-
leader; governess, duenna; disciplinarian.

professor, lecturer, reader, prelector,
prolocutor, preacher; Boanerges; pastor
&c. (*clergy*) 996; schoolmaster, dominie, usher, pedagogue, abecedarian;
schoolmistress, dame, monitor, proctor,
pupil-teacher.

expositor &c. 524; preceptor, guide;
mentor &c. (*adviser*) 695; pioneer,
apostle, missionary, propagandist,
moonshee; example &c. (*model for imitation*) 22.

professorship &c. (*school*) 542.
tutelage &c. (*teaching*) 537.

Adj. professorial, tutorial &c. 537.

541. Learner.—N. learner, scholar,
student, *alumnus*, *élève*, pupil; ap-,
prentice; articled clerk; school-boy,
-girl, beginner, tyro, abecedarian, alphabetarian.

recruit, novice, neophyte, tenderfoot,
inceptor, *débutant*, catechumen, probationer; undergraduate; freshman, frosh;
sophomore, junior, senior; junior -, se-
nior-, soph; sophister, questionist, fel-
low-, commoner, pensioner, exhibition-
er, sizar, scholar, fellow, advanced -,
post graduate -, research- student.

class, form, grade, standard, remove;
pupilage &c. (*learning*) 539.

disciple, follower, apostle, proselyte;
fellow student, school-mate, -fellow,
class mate, condisciple.

Adj. in statu pupillari, in leading
strings, sophomoric.

542. School.—N. school, academy,

university, *alma mater*, college, semi-
nary, Lyceum; instit-ute, -ution, *conservatoire*; *palæstra*, *gymnasium*.

day -, boarding -, public -, preparatory -, elementary -, primary -, infant
-, dame's -, grammar -, middle class -,
Board -, County -, Council -, parochial -, denominational -, Sunday -,
National -, British and Foreign -, collegiate -, secondary -, continuation -,
night -, correspondence -, secretarial -,
military -, law -, medical -, business
-, technical- school; technical -, train-
ing- college; Polytechnic; training ship;
Kindergarten, nursery, *crèche*, reformatory.

pulpit, desk, reading desk, ambo,
class-, lecture-room, theatre, amphitheatre, forum, stage, rostrum, platform,
hustings, tribune.

school -, horn -, text- book; grammar, primer, abecedary, rudiments,
manual, *vade mecum*, Lindley Murray,
Cocker.

professor-, lecture-, reader-ship;
chair; schoolmaster &c. 540.

School Board, Council of Education;
propaganda.

Adj. scholastic, academic, collegiate;
educational.

Adv. ex cathedrâ.

543. Veracity.—N. veracity; truthful-
ness, frankness &c. *adj.*; truth, sooth,
sincerity, candour, honesty, fidelity;
plain dealing, *bona fides*; love of truth;
probity &c. 939; ingenuousness &c.
(*artlessness*) 703.

the truth the whole truth and nothing
but the truth; honest -, sober-truth &c.
(*fact*) 494; unvarnished tale; light of
truth.

V. speak -, tell- the truth; speak by
the card; paint in its -, show oneself in
one's-true colours; make a clean breast
&c. (*disclose*) 529; speak one's mind
&c. (*be blunt*) 703; not -lie &c. 544, -
deceive &c. 545.

Adj. truthful, true; ver-acious,
-edical; scrupulous &c. (*honourable*)
939; sincere, candid, frank, open,

straight-forward, unreserved; open-, true-, simple- hearted; honest, trustworthy; undissembling &c. (dissemble &c. 544); guileless, pure; unperjured, true blue, as good as one's word; unaffected, unfeigned, *bonâ fide*; outspoken, ingenuous &c. (*artless*) 703; undisguised &c. (*real*) 494.

Adv. truly &c. (*really*) 494; on oath, in plain words &c. 703; in -, with -, of a -, in good -, very- truth; as the -dial to the sun, - needle to the pole; honour bright; troth; in good -sooth, - earnest; unfeignedly, with no nonsense, in sooth, sooth to say, *bonâ fide*, *in foro conscientiae*; without equivocation; *cartes sur table*, from the bottom of one's heart; by my troth &c. (*affirmation*) 535.

544. Falsehood.—N. false-hood, -ness; fals-ity, -ification; misrepresentation; deception &c. 545; untruth &c. 546; guile; bad faith; lying &c. *v.*; misrepresentation; mendacity, perjury, false swearing; forgery, invention, fabrication; subreption; covin.

perversion -, suppression- of truth; *suppressio veri*; perversion, distortion, false colouring; exaggeration &c. 549; prevarication, equivocation, shuffling, fencing, evasion, fraud; *suggestio falsi* &c. (*lie*) 546; mystification &c. (*concealment*) 528; simulation &c. (*imitation*) 19; dis-simulation, -sembling; deceit.

sham; pretence, pretending, malingering.

lip- homage, - service; mouth honour; hollowness; mere -show, - outside, eye-wash, window dressing; duplicity, double dealing, insincerity, hypocrisy, cant, humbug, casuistry; jesuit-ism, -ry; pharisaism; Machiavelism, 'organized hypocrisy'; crocodile tears, mealy-mouthedness, quackery; charlatan-ism, -ry; gammon; bun-kum, -come; flam, bam, flim-flam, cajolery, flattery; Judas kiss; perfidy &c. (*bad faith*) 940; *il volto sciolto i pensieri stretti*.

unfairness &c. (*dishonesty*) 940; art-

fulness &c. (*cunning*) 702; misstatement &c. (*error*) 495.

V. be -false &c. *adj.*; - a liar &c. 548; speak -falsely &c. *adv.*; tell -a lie &c. 546; lie, fib; lie like a trooper; swear falsely, forswear, perjure oneself, bear false witness.

mis-state, -quote, -cite, -report, -represent; belie, falsify, pervert, distort; put a false construction upon &c. (*misinterpret*) 523.

prevaricate, equivocate, quibble; palter, - to the understanding; *répondre en Normand*; trim, shuffle, fence, mince the truth, beat about the bush, blow hot and cold, play fast and loose.

garble, gloss over, disguise, give a colour to; give -, put- a -gloss, - false colouring- upon; colour, varnish, cook, dress up, embroider: varnish right and puzzle wrong, exaggerate &c. 549.

invent, fabricate; trump -, get- up; forge, hatch, concoct; romance &c. (*imagine*) 515; cry 'wolf!'

dis-semble, -simulate; feign, assume, put on, pretend, make believe; play -false, - a double game; coquet; act -, play- a part; affect &c. 855; simulate, pass off for; counterfeit, fake, sham, make a show of; malinger; swing the lead; say the grapes are sour.

cant, play the hypocrite, sham Abraham, *faire pattes de velours*, put on the mask, clean the outside of the platter, lie like a conjuror; hang out -, hold out -, sail under- false colours; 'commend the poisoned chalice to the lips'; *ambiguas in vulgus spargere voces*; deceive &c. 545.

Adj. false, deceitful, mendacious, un-veracious, fraudulent, untruthful, dishonest; faith-, truth-, troth-less; un-fair, -candid; evasive; un-, dis-ingenuous; hollow, insincere, *Parthis mendacior*; forsworn; canting.

canting; hypocrit-, jesuit-, pharisaical; tartuffish; Machiavelian; double-tongued, -faced, -handed, -minded, -hearted, -dealing; two-faced, bare-faced; Janus-faced; smooth-faced, -spoken,

-tongued; plausible; mealy-mouthed; affected &c. 855.

collus-ive, -ory; artful &c. (*cunning*) 702; perfidious &c. 940, spurious &c. (*deceptive*) 545; untrue &c. 546; falsified &c. *v.*; covinous.

Adv. falsely &c. *adj.*; *à la Tartufe*, with a double tongue; out of whole cloth; slily &c. (*cunning*) 702.

545. Deception.—N. deception; falseness &c. 544; untruth &c. 546; impos-ition, -ture; fraud, deceit, guile; fraudulen-ce, -cy; covin; knavery &c. (*cunning*) 702; misrepresentation &c. (*falsehood*) 544.

delusion, gullery, bluff, spoof, *blague*; juggl-ing, -ery; sleight of hand, legerdemain; presti-giation, -digitation; magic &c. 992; conjur-ing, -ation; hocus pocus, jockeyship; trickery, coggery, hanky-panky, chicanery, pettifogging, sharp practice; *supercherie*, cozenage, circumvention, ingannation, collusion; treachery &c. 940; practical joke.

trick, cheat, wile, ruse, blind, feint, plant, bubble, fetch, catch, chicane, juggle, reach, hocus, bite; thimble-rig, card-sharping, artful dodge, machination, swindle, hoax; tricks upon travellers; confidence trick; stratagem &c. (*artifice*) 702; theft &c. 791.

snare, trap, pitfall, decoy, gin; spinge, -gle; noose, hook; bait, decoy-duck, tub to the whale, baited trap, *guet-à-pens*; cobweb, net, meshes, toils, mouse-trap, bird-lime; ambush &c. 530; trap-door, sliding panel, false bottom; spring-net, -gun; mask, -ed battery; mine; booby trap.

Cornish hug; wolf in sheep's clothing &c. (*deceiver*) 548; disguise, -ment; false colours, masquerade, mummery, borrowed plumes; *pattes de velours*.

mockery &c. (*imitation*) 19; copy &c. 21; counterfeit, sham, brum-magem, make-believe, forgery, fraud, fake; lie &c. 546; 'a mockery, a delusion, and a snare,' hollow mockery.

whited -, painted- sepulchre; tinsel,

paste, false jewellery, scagliola, ormolu, German silver, Britannia metal, paint; jerry building; man of straw.

illusion &c. (*error*) 495; *ignis fatuus* &c. 423; *mirage* &c. 443.

V. deceive, take in; defraud, cheat, jockey, do, cozen, diddle, nab, gyp, chouse, double cross, play one false, bilk, cully, jilt, bite, pluck, swindle, victimize; abuse; mystify; blind one's eyes; blindfold, hoodwink, spoof, bluff; throw dust into the eyes, 'keep the word of promise to the ear and break it to the hope,' 'draw a herring across the trail.'

impose -, practise -, play -, put -, palm -, foist- upon; snatch a verdict.

circumvent, overreach; out-reach, -wit, -manœuvre; steal a march upon, give the go-by to, leave in the lurch.

set -, lay- a -trap, - snare- for; bait the hook, forelay, spread the toils, lime; decoy, waylay, lure, beguile, delude, inveigle; tra-, tre-pan; kidnap; let-, hook-in; trick; en-, in-trap, -snare, entoil, be-net; nick, springe; catch, - in a trap; sniggle, entangle, illaqueate, hocus, practise on one's credulity, dupe, gull, hoax, fool, befool, bamboozle; hum, -bug; gammon, stuff up, dope, sell; play a -trick, - practical joke- upon one; balk, trip up, throw a tub to a whale; fool to the top of one's bent, send on -a wild goose chase, - a fool's errand; make -game, - a fool, - an April fool, - an ass- of; trifle with, cajole, flatter; come over &c. (*influence*) 615; gild the pill, make things pleasant, divert, put a good face upon; dissemble &c. 544.

cog, - the dice, play with marked cards; live by one's wits, play at hide and seek; obtain money under false pretences &c. (*steal*) 791; conjure, juggle, practise chicanery; gerrymander.

play -, palm -, foist -, fob- off.

lie &c. 544; misinform &c. 538; mislead &c. (*error*) 495; betray &c. 940; be -deceived &c. 547.

Adj. deceived &c. *v.*; deceiving &c. *v.*; cunning &c. 702; prestigi-ous, -atory; decept-ive, -ious; deceitful, covinous; delus-ive, -ory; illus-ive, -ory;

elusive, insidious, *ad captandum vulgus.*

untrue &c. 546; mock, sham, make-believe, counterfeit, faked, pseudo, spurious, so-called, pretended, feigned, trumped up, bogus, scamped, fraudulent, tricky, factitious, artificial, bastard; surreptitious, illegitimate, contraband, adulterated, sophisticated; unsound, rotten at the core; colourable; disguised; meretricious; tinsel, pinchbeck, plated; catch-penny; Brummagem; simulated &c. 544.

Adv. under -false colours, – the garb of, – cover of; over the left.

Phr. *fronti nulla fides.*

546. Untruth.—N. untruth, falsehood, lie, story, thing that is not, fib, bounce, crammer, taradiddle, whopper.

forgery, fabrication, invention; misstatement, -representation; perversion, falsification, gloss, *suggestio falsi*; exaggeration &c. 549.

fiction; fable, nursery tale; romance &c. (*imagination*) 515; untrue –, false –, trumped up- -story, – statement; thing devised by the enemy; *canard*; shave, sell, hum, yarn, traveller's tale, Canterbury tale, cock and bull story, fairy tale, clap-trap.

myth, moonshine, bosh, all my eye, -and Betty Martin, mare's nest, farce.

irony; half truth, white lie, pious fraud; mental reservation &c. (*concealment*) 528.

pretence, pretext; false -plea &c. 617; subterfuge, evasion, shift, shuffle, make-believe; sham &c. (*deception*) 545.

profession, empty words; Judas kiss &c. (*hypocrisy*) 544; disguise &c. (*mask*) 530.

V. have a false meaning; not ring true.

pretend, sham, feign, counterfeit, make believe.

Adj. untrue, false, trumped up; void of –, without- foundation; far from the truth, false as dicer's oaths; unfounded, *ben trovato*, invented, fabulous, fabricated, forged; fict-, fact-, supposit-, surrept-itious; e-, il-lusory; ironical; satir-ical; evasive; *soi-disant* &c. (*misnamed*) 565.

Phr. *se non e vero e ben trovato.*

547. Dupe.—N. dupe, gull, gudgeon, *gobemouche*, cull, cully, victim, sucker, pigeon, April fool; laughing stock &c. 857; Cyclops, simple Simon, flat, mug, greenhorn; fool &c. 501; puppet, cat's paw.

V. be -deceived &c. 545, – the dupe of; fall into a trap; swallow –, nibble at- the bait; bite; catch a Tartar.

Adj. credulous &c. 486; mistaken &c. (*error*) 495.

548. Deceiver.—N. deceiver &c. (deceive &c. 545); dissembler, hypocrite; sophist, Pharisee, Jesuit, Mawworm, Pecksniff, Joseph Surface, Tartufe, Janus; serpent; snake in the grass, cockatrice, Judas, wolf in sheep's clothing; Molly Maguire; jilt; shuffler.

liar &c. (lie &c. 544); story-teller, perjurer, false-witness, *menteur à triple étage*, Scapin.

impostor, pretender, capper, decoy, fraud, *soi-disant*, humbug; adventurer; Cagliostro, Fernam Mendez Pinto; ass in lion's skin &c. (*bungler*) 701; actor &c. (*stage player*) 599.

quack, *charlatan*, mountebank, saltimbanco, *saltimbanque*, empiric, quacksalver, medicaster.

conjuror, juggler, magician, necromancer, trickster, prestidigitator, medium, jockey; crimp; decoy-duck, stool pigeon; rogue, knave, cheat; swindler &c. (*thief*) 792; jobber.

549. Exaggeration.—N. exaggeration; expansion &c. 194; hyperbole, stretch, strain, colouring; high colouring, caricature, *caricatura*; extravagance &c. (*nonsense*) 497; Baron Munchausen; men in buckram, yarn, fringe, embroidery, traveller's tale; Pelion upon Ossa.

storm in a teacup; much ado about nothing &c. (*over-estimation*) 482; puffery &c. (*boasting*) 884; rant &c. (*turgescence*) 577.

figure of speech, *façon de parler*; stretch of -fancy, – the imagination; flight of fancy &c. (*imagination*) 515.

false colouring &c. (*falsehood*) 544; aggravation &c. 835.

V. exaggerate, magnify, pile up, aggravate; amplify &c. (*expand*) 194; overestimate &c. 482; hyperbolize; overcharge, -state, -draw, -lay, -shoot the mark, -praise; make -much, – the most- of; strain, – a point; stretch, – a point; go great lengths; spin a long yarn; draw –, shoot with- a long-bow; deal in the marvellous.

out-Herod Herod, run riot, talk at random.

heighten, overcolour; colour- highly, – too highly; embroider, *broder*; flourish; colour &c. (*misrepresent*) 544; puff &c. (*boast*) 884.

Adj. exaggerated &c. *v.*; overwrought; bombastic &c. (*magniloquent*) 577; hyperbolical, on stilts; fabulous, extravagant, preposterous, egregious, *outré*, high-flying.

Adv. hyperbolically &c. *adj.*

Section III.
MEANS OF COMMUNICATING IDEAS

1.° *Natural Means*

550. Indication.—N. indication; symbol-ism, -ization; semeio-logy, -tics; sign of the times.

lineament, feature, *trait*, characteristic, trick, diagnostic; divining-rod; cloven hoof; footfall; means of recognition; earmark.

sign, symbol; ind-ex, -ice, -icator; point, -er; marker; exponent, note, token, symptom.

type, figure, emblem, cipher, device; representation &c. 554; epigraph, motto, posy.

gest-ure, -iculation; pantomime; wink, glance, leer; nod, shrug, beck; touch, nudge; grip; dactylo-logy, -nomy;

freemasonry, telegraphy, chirology, byplay, dumb-show; cue; hint &c. 527; clue, clew, key, scent, track &c. 551.

signal, -post; rocket, blue light; watch-fire, -tower; telegraph, semaphore, flag-staff; cresset; calumet; heliograph, signal-, flash-lamp.

mark, line, stroke, dash, score, stripe, streak, scratch, tick, dot, point, notch, nick, blaze; asterisk, red letter, Italics, heavy type, inverted commas, quotation marks, sublineation, underlining, jotting; print; impr-int, -ess, -ession; note, annotation, mark of exclamation.

[For identification] badge, criterion; counter-check, -mark, -sign, -foil; duplicate, tally; label, tab, ticket, stub, billet, letter, counter, *tessera*, card, bill, check; witness, voucher; stamp; *cachet*; trade -, Hall-mark; broad arrow; signature; address -, visiting- card; *carte de visite*; credentials &c. (*evidence*) 467; passport, identity book; attestation; hand, – writing, sign-manual; cipher; monogram, – mark, seal, sigil, signet; autograph, -y; paraph, brand; superscription; in-, endorsement; title, heading, rubric, docket; *mot -de passe*, – *du guet*; *passe-parole*; shibboleth; watch-, catch-, pass-word; open *sesame*.

insignia; banner, -et, -ol; bandrol; flag, colours, streamer, standard, eagle, labarum, oriflamb, *oriflamme*; figurehead; ensign; pen-non, -nant, -dant; burgee, blue Peter, jack, ancient, gonfalon, union-jack; tricolour, stars and stripes; bunting.

heraldry, crest; coat of -, arms; armorial bearings, hatchment; e-, scutcheon; shield, supporters; livery, uniform; cockade, *epaulette*, brassard, chevron; garland, chaplet, love-knot, fillet, favour.

[Of locality] beacon, cairn, post, staff, flagstaff, hand, pointer, vane, cock, weathercock; guide-, hand-, finger-, directing-, sign-post; pillars of Hercules, pharos, signal fire; land-, sea-mark; lighthouse, balize; pole-, load-, lodestar; cynosure, guide; address, direction, name; sign, -board.

[Of the future] warning &c. 668; omen &c. 512; prefigurement &c. 511. [Of the past] trace record &c. 551. [Of danger] warning &c. 668; alarm &c. 669. [Of authority] sceptre &c. 747. [Of triumph] trophy &c. 733. [Of quantity] gauge &c. 466. [Of distance] mile-stone, -post. [Of disgrace] brand, fool's cap, stigma, mark of Cain. [For detection] check, tell-tale; test &c. (*experiment*) 463.

notification &c. (*information*) 527; advertisement &c. (*publication*) 531.

word of command, call; bugle-, trumpet-call; reveille, taps; bell, alarum, cry; battle –, rallying- cry.

church, bell, angelus, sacring bell; muezzin.

exposition &c. (*explanation*) 522; proof &c. (*evidence*) 463; pattern &c. (*prototype*) 22.

V. indicate; be the -sign &c. *n.*- of; denote, betoken; argue, testify &c. (*evidence*) 467; bear the -impress &c. *n.*- of; con-note, -notate.

represent, stand for; typify &c. (*prefigure*) 511; symbolize.

put -an indication, – a mark, – &c. *n.*; note, mark, tick, blaze, stamp, ear-mark; set one's seal upon; label, ticket, docket; dot, spot, score, dash, trace, chalk; print, im-print, -press, surprint; engrave, stereotype, electrotype.

make a -sign &c. *n.*; signalize; give –, hang out- a signal; beck, -on; gesture; nod; wink, glance, leer, nudge, shrug, tip the wink; gesticulate; raise –, hold up- the -finger, – hand; saw the air, suit the action to the word.

wave –, unfurl –, hoist –, hang out- a banner &c. *n.*; wave -the hand, – a kerchief; give the cue &c. (*inform*) 527; show one's colours; give –, sound- an alarm; beat the drum, sound the trumpets, raise a cry.

sign, seal, attest &c. (*evidence*) 467; underline &c. (*give importance to*) 642; call attention to &c. (*attention*) 457; give notice &c. (*inform*) 527.

Adj. indicat-ing &c. *v.*, -ive, -ory; de-, con-notative; diacritical, represen-tative, typical, symbolic, pantomimic, pathognomonic, symptomatic, ominous, characteristic, demonstrative, diagnostic, exponential, emblematic, armorial; individual &c. (*special*) 79.

known –, recognizable- by; indicated &c. *v*; pointed, marked.

[Capable of being denoted] denotable; indelible.

Adv. in token of; symbolically. &c. *adj.*; in dumb show.

Phr. *ecce signum; ex ungue leonem, ex pede Herculem.*

551. Record.—N. trace, vestige, relic, remains; scar, *cicatrix*; foot-step, -mark, -print; track, mark, wake, trail, spoor, scent, *piste.*

monument, hatchment, escutcheon, slab, tablet, trophy, achievement; obelisk, pillar, column, monolith, cromlech, dolmen; memorial, *memento* &c. (*memory*) 505; testimonial, medal, ribbon, order; commemoration &c. (*celebration*) 883.

record, note, minute; *dossier*; register, -try; census, roll &c. (*list*) 86; cartulary, diptych, Domesday book; entry, memorandum, indorsement, inscription, copy, duplicate, docket; notch &c. (*mark*) 550; muniment, deed &c. (*security*) 771; document, deposition, *procès-verbal*; affidavit; certificate &c. (*evidence*) 467.

note-, memorandum-, pocket-, commonplace-book; portfolio; scoring-board, -sheet; bulletin board; card index, file; pigeon-holes, *excerpta, adversaria,* jottings, dottings.

gazette, -er; newspaper, magazine &c. 531; alman-ac, -ack; calendar, ephemeris, noctuary, diary, log, journal, account-, cash-, day-book, ledger.

archive, scroll, state-paper, Congressional Record, return, blue book; statistics &c. 86; *compte rendu;* Acts –, Transactions –, Proceedings- of; Hansard's Debates; chronicle, annals; legend; history, biography &c. 594.

registration; en-, in-rolment; tabulation; entry, booking; signature &c.

(*identification*) 550; recorder &c. 553; journalism.

drawing, photograph &c. 554; phonograph –, gramophone- record; music roll.

V. record; put –, place- upon record; go on record; chronicle, calendar, hand down to posterity; keep up the memory of &c. (*remember*) 505; commemorate &c. (*celebrate*) 883; report &c. (*inform*) 527; commit to –, reduce to- writing; put –, set down- -in writing, – in black and white; put –, jot –, take –, write –, note –, set- down; note, minute, put on paper; take –, make- a -note, – minute, – memorandum; make a return.

mark &c. (*indicate*) 550; sign &c. (*attest*) 467.

enter, book; post, – up; insert, make an entry of; mark –, tick-off; register, list, docket, enroll, inscroll; file &c. (*store*) 636.

Adv. on record.

552. [Suppression of sign.] Obliteration.—N. obliteration; erasure, rasure; effacement; cancel, -lation; cassation; circumduction; deletion, blot; *tabula rasa*.

V. efface, obliterate, erase, rase, expunge, cancel; blot –, take –, rub –, scratch –, strike –, wipe –, wash –, sponge- out; wipe –, rub- off; wipe away; deface, render illegible; draw the pen through, apply the sponge.

be -effaced &c.; leave no -trace &c. 449; 'leave not a rack behind.'

Adj. obliterated &c. *v.*; out of print; printless; leaving no trace; intestate; unrecorded, -registered, -written.

Int. *dele*; out with it!

553. Recorder.—N. recorder, notary, clerk; regis-trar, -trary, -ter; prothonotary; amanuensis, secretary, scribe, stenographer, remembrancer, book-keeper, *custos rotulorum*, Master of the Rolls.

annalist; histori-an, -ographer; chronicler, journalist, reporter, columnist; biographer &c. (*narrator*) 594; antiquary &c. (*antiquity*) 122; memorialist.

draughtsman &c. 559; engraver 558;

photographer, cinematographer, camera man.

Recording instrument, recorder, camera, phonograph, gramophone, dictaphone, telegraphone, telautograph, printing telegraph, tape machine, ticker, time recorder, cash register, turnstile, speedometer, voting machine, seismograph, photostat.

554. Representation.—N. represent-ation, -ment; imitation &c. 19; illustration, delineation, depictment, portrayal; imagery, portraiture, iconography; design, -ing; art, fine arts; painting &c. 556; sculpture &c. 557; engraving &c. 558; photography, radiography, skiagraphy.

person-ation, -ification; impersonation; drama &c. 599.

picture, drawing, sketch, draught, draft; tracing; copy &c. 21; photo-, helio-graph; daguerreo-, talbo-, calo-, helio-type; cabinet, *carte-de-visite*, snapshot; X-ray photograph; radio-gram, -graph, skia-graph, -gram.

image, likeness, icon, portrait; striking –, speaking- likeness; very image; effigy, fac-simile.

figure, – head; puppet, doll, *figurine*, aglet, manikin, lay-figure, model, *marionnette*, *fantoccini*, bust; waxwork, statue, -tte, automaton, Robot.

hieroglyphic, anaglyph; dia-, monogram, -graph.

map, plan, chart; ground plan, projection, elevation; ichno-, carto-graphy; atlas; outline, scheme; view &c. (*painting*) 556.

artist, draughtsman &c. 559.

V. represent, delineate; depict, -ure; portray; picture; take –, catch- a likeness &c. *n.*; hit off, photograph, daguerreotype; figure; shadow -forth, – out; adumbrate; body forth; describe &c. 594; trace, copy; mould.

dress up; illustrate, symbolize.

paint &c. 556; carve &c. 557; engrave &c. 558.

person-ate, -ify; impersonate; assume a character; pose as; act; play &c.

(*drama*) 599; mimic &c. (*imitate*) 19;
hold the mirror up to nature.

Adj. represent-ing &c. *v.*, -ative; illustrative; represented &c. *v.*; imitative,
figurative.

like &c. 17; graphic &c. (*descriptive*)
594.

555. Misrepresentation.—N. misrepresentation, distortion, exaggeration;
daubing &c. *v.*; bad likeness, daub, sign-
painting; scratch, caricature; *anamorphosis*.

V. misrepresent, distort, overdraw,
travesty, parody, burlesque, exaggerate,
caricature, daub.

Adj. misrepresented &c. *v.*

556. Painting.—N. painting; depict-
ing; drawing &c. *v.*; design; perspective, skiagraphy; *chiaroscuro* &c. (*light*)
420; composition; treatment, values, atmosphere, tone, technique.

historical -, portrait -, miniature -,
landscape -, marine -, flower -, scene-
painting; scenography.

school, style; the grand style, high,
art, *genre*, portraiture; ornamental art
&c. 847.

mono-, poly-chrome; *grisaille*.

pallet, palette; easel; brush, pencil,
stump; blacklead, charcoal, crayons,
chalk, pastel; paint &c. (*colouring matter*) 428; water-, body-, oil-colour; oils,
oil-paint; varnish &c. 356*a*; *gouache*,
tempera, distemper, fresco, water-glass;
enamel; encaustic painting; *graffito*,
gesso; mosaic; tapestry.

picture, painting, piece, *tableau*, canvas; oil &c.- painting; fresco, cartoon;
easel -, cabinet- picture; drawing,
draught, draft; pencil &c. -, watercol-
our- drawing; sketch, outline; study.

portrait &c. (*representation*) 554;
whole -, full -, half- length; kitcat,
head; miniature; shade, *silhouette*; profile.

landscape, sea-piece, -scape; view,
scene, prospect; interior; bird's-eye
view; pan-, di-orama; still life.

picture -, art- gallery; *studio, atelier*.

V. paint, design, limn, draw, sketch,

pencil, scratch, shade, stipple, hatch,
dash off, chalk out, square up; colour,
dead-colour, wash, varnish; draw in
-pencil &c. *n.*; paint in -oils &c. *n.*; stencil; depict &c. (*represent*) 554.

Adj. painted &c. *v.*; pictorial, graphic, picturesque, decorative; classical, romantic, pre-Raphaelite, modern, cubist,
futurist, vorticist.

pencil, oil &c. *n.*

Adv. in -pencil &c. *n.*

Phr. *fecit, delineavit.*

557. Sculpture.—N. sculpture, insculpture; carving &c. *v.*; statuary ceramics, plastic arts.

high -, low -, bas- relief; relievo;
basso-, alto-, mezzo-relievo; *intaglio* anaglyph; medal, -lion; *cameo*.

marble, bronze, *terra cotta*; ceramic
ware, pottery, porcelain, china, earthenware, faïence, enamel, *cloisonné*.

statue &c. (*image*) 554; cast &c.
(*copy*) 21; glyptotheca.

V. sculpture, carve, cut, chisel, model, mould; cast.

Adj. sculptured &c. *v.*; in relief, an-
aglyptic, ceroplastic, ceramic; parian;
marble &c. *n.*

558. Engraving.—N. engraving,
chalcography; line -, mezzotint -, stipple -, chalk- engraving; dry-point; bur;
etching, aquatinta; plate -, copper-plate
-, steel -, wood-, process-, photo-
engraving; xylo-, ligno-, glypto-, cero-,
litho-, chromolitho-, photolitho-, zinco-,
glypho- graphy, -graph.

impression, print, engraving, plate;
steel-, copper-plate; etching; mezzo-,
aqua-, litho-tint; cut, woodcut, block;
stereo-, grapho-, auto-, helio-type; half-
tone; *photogravure, rotogravure*.

graver, *burin*, etching-point, style;
plate, stone, wood-block, negative; die,
punch, stamp.

printing; plate -, copper-plate -, intaglio -, anastatic -, lithographic -, colour -, three colour- printing; type-
printing &c. 591.

illustr-, illumin-ation; *vignette*, initial
letter, *cul de lampe*, tail-piece.

V. engrave, grave, stipple, scrape, etch; bite, - in; lithograph &c. *n.*; print.
Adj. insculptured; engraved &c. *v.*
Phr. *sculpsit, imprimit.*

559. Artist.—N. artist; painter, limner, drawer, sketcher, delineator; cartoon-, caricatur-ist, designer, engraver; draughtsman; copyist; enamel-ler, -list.

historical -, landscape -, genre -, marine -, flower -, portrait -, miniature -, scene -, sign- painter; engraver; Apelles, sculptor, carver, chaser, modeller, lapidary, *figuriste*, statuary; Phidias, Praxiteles; Royal Academician.

photographer, retoucher.

2°. Conventional Means

1. Language generally

560. Language.—N. language; phraseology &c. 569; speech &c. 582; tongue, lingo, vernacular, slang; mother -, vulgar -, native- tongue; household words; King's *or* Queen's English; idiom; dialect &c. 563.

volapuk, esperanto, ido, occidental, Ro.

confusion of tongues, Babel, *pasigraphie*; pantomime &c. (*signs*) 550; *onomatopœia.*

phil-, gloss-, glott-ology; linguistics, chrestomathy; paleo-logy; -graphy; comparative grammar.

literature, letters, polite literature, *belles lettres*, muses, humanities, *literæ humaniores*, republic of letters, dead languages, classics; genius of a language; scholarship &c. (*knowledge*) 490.

linguist &c. (*scholar*) 492.
V. speak, say, express by words &c. 566.
Adj. lingu-al, -istic; dialectic; vernacular, current, colloquial, slangy; bilingual, polyglot; literary.

561. Letter.—N. letter; character; hieroglyphic &c. (*writing*) 590; type &c. (*printing*) 591; capitals; majus-, minuscule; alphabet, ABC, abecedary, Christcross-row.

consonant, vowel, diphthong; mute, surd; sonant, liquid, labial, dental, palatal, guttural.

syllable; mono-, dis-, poly-syllable; affix, prefix, suffix.

spelling, orthography; phon-ography, -etic spelling; ana-, meta-grammatism.

cipher, monogram, anagram; double -, acrostic.

V. spell.
Adj. literal; alphabetical, abecedarian; syllabic; uncial &c. (*writing*) 590; phonetic, voiced, mute &c. *n.*

562. Word.—N. word, term, vocable; name &c. 564; phrase &c. 566; root, etymon; derivative; part of speech &c.(*grammar*) 567.

dictionary, vocabulary, word book, lexicon, index, glossary, thesaurus, *gradus*, *delectus*, concordance.

etymology, lexicology, derivation; phonology, orthoepy; gloss-, termin-, orism-ology; paleology &c. (*philology*) 560; comparative philology.

lexicograph-er, -y; glossographer &c. (*scholar*) 492; etymologist; logolept.

verbosity, verbiage, loquacity &c. 584.

Adj. verbal, literal; titular, nominal. [Similarly derived] conjugate, paronymous; derivative.

Adv. verbally &c. *adj.*; *verbatim* &c. (*exactly*) 494.

563. Neology.—N. neolo-gy, -gism; new-fangled expression; barbarism; caconym; archaism, black letter, monkish Latin; corruption; missaying, antiphrasis.

paronomasia, play upon words; wordplay &c. (*wit*) 842; *double-entente* &c. (*ambiguity*) 520; palindrome, paragram, clinch; abuse of -language, - terms.

dialect, brogue, *patois*, provincialism, broken English, *lingua franca*; Brit-, Gall-, Scott-, Hibern-icism; American-ism; Gipsy lingo, Romany, pidgin English.

dog Latin, macaronics, gibberish, confusion of tongues, Babel; jargon.

colloquialism &c. (*figure of speech*)

521; by-word; technicality, lingo, slang, cant, *argot*, St. Giles's Greek, thieves' Latin, peddler's French, flash tongue, Billingsgate, Wall Street slang.

pseudonym &c. (*misnomer*) 565; Mr. So-and-so; what d'ye call 'em, what's his name; thingum-my, -bob; *je ne sais quoi.*

neologist, coiner of words.

V. coin words.

Adj. neologic, -al; rare; archaic; obsolete &c. (*old*) 124; colloquial, dialectic, slang, cant.

564. Nomenclature.—N. nomenclature; naming &c. *v.*; nuncupation, nomination, baptism; orismology; onomatopæia; antonomasia.

name; appella-tion, -tive; designation; title; head, -ing, caption; denomination; by-name, epithet.

style, proper name; præ-, ag-, cognomen; patronymic, surname; cognomination; compellation, description; empty -title, - name; handle to one's name; namesake, eponym.

synonym, antonym.

term, expression, noun; by-word; convertible terms &c. 522; technical term; cant &c. 563.

V. name, call, term, denominate, designate, style, entitle, intitule, clepe, dub, christen, baptize, nickname, characterize, specify, define, distinguish by the name of; label &c. (*mark*) 550.

be -called &c. *v.*; take -, bear -, go (*or* be known) by -, go (*or* pass) under -, rejoice in- the name of.

Adj. named &c. *v.*; hight, yclept, known as; what one may -well, - fairly, - properly, - fitly- call.

nuncupa-tory, -tive; cognominal, titular, nominal; orismological.

565. Misnomer.—N. misnomer; *lucus a non lucendo*; Mrs. Malaprop; what d'ye call 'em &c. (*neologism*) 563.

nickname, *sobriquet*, by-name, handle, moniker; assumed -name, - title; *alias; nom de -guerre, -plume, - théâtre*; pseudonym, pen name, stage name.

V. mis-name, -call, -term; nickname; assume -a name, - an alias.

Adj. misnamed &c. *v.*; pseudonymous; *soi-disant*; self-called, -styled, -christened; so-called.

nameless, anonymous; without a -, having no- name; innominate, unnamed.

Adv. in no sense.

566. Phrase.—N. phrase, expression, set phrase; sentence, paragraph; figure of speech &c. 521; idi-om, -otism; turn of expression.

paraphrase &c. (*synonym*) 522; periphrase &c. (*circumlocution*) 573; motto &c. (*proverb*) 496.

phraseology &c. 569.

V. express, phrase; word, - it; give -words, - expression- to; voice; arrange in -, clothe in -, put into -, express bywords; couch in terms; find words to express; speak by the card.

Adj. expressed &c. *v.*; idiomatic.

Adv. in -round, - set, - good, setterms; in set phrases.

567. Grammar.—N. grammar, accidence, syntax, *praxis*, analysis, paradigm, punctuation; parts of speech; inflexion, case, declension, conjugation; *jus et norma loquendi*; Lindley Murray &c. (*school-book*) 542; correct style; philology &c. (*language*) 560.

V. parse, analyze; decline, conjugate; punctuate.

Adj. grammatical; syntactic; inflexional.

568. Solecism.—N. solecism; bad -, false -, faulty- grammar; slip, error; slip of the -pen, - tongue; *lapsus calami-, - linguæ; faux pas*; slip-slop; bull.

V. use -bad, - faulty- grammar; solecize, commit a solecism; murder the -King's, - Queen's- English; break Priscian's head.

Adj. ungrammatical; in-correct, -accurate; faulty, improper, incongruous, abnormal.

569. Style.—N. style, diction, phraseology, wording; manner, strain;

composition; mode of expression, choice of words, literary power, ready pen, pen of a ready writer; command of language &c. (*eloquence*) 582; authorship; *la morgue littéraire*.

V. express by words &c. 566; write.

Various Qualities of Style

570. Perspicuity.—N. perspicuity &c. (*intelligibility*) 518; plain speaking &c. (*manifestation*) 525; defin-iteness, -ition; exactness &c. 494; perspicuousness, logical acuteness.

Adj. lucid &c. (*intelligible*) 518; explicit &c. (*manifest*) 525; exact &c. 494.

571. Obscurity.—N. obscurity &c. (*unintelligibility*) 519; involution; hard words; ambiguity &c. 520; vagueness &c. 475, inexactness &c. 495; what d'ye call 'em &c. (*neologism*) 563; cloudiness, confusion.

Adj. obscure &c. *n.*; crabbed, involved, confused.

572. Conciseness.—N. conciseness &c. *adj.*; brevity, 'the soul of wit,' laconism; Tacitus; ellipsis; syncope; abridgment &c. (*shortening*) 201; compression &c. 195; epitome &c. 596; monostitch; portmanteau word, telescope word, protogram.

V. be -concise &c. *adj.*; condense &c. 195; abridge &c. 201; abstract &c. 596; come to the point.

Adj. concise, brief, short, terse, close; to the point, exact; neat, compact, condensed, pointed; laconic, curt, pithy, trenchant, summary; pregnant; compendious &c. (*compendium*) 596; succinct; elliptical, epigrammatic, crisp, sententious.

Adv. concisely &c. *adj.*; briefly, summarily; in -brief, - short, - a word, - few words, - a nutshell; for shortness sake; to -come to the point, - make a long story short, - cut the matter short, - be brief; it comes to this, the long and the short of it is.

573. Diffuseness.—N. diffuseness &c. *adj.*; amplification &c. *v.*; dilating &c.

v.; verbosity, *verbiage*, wordiness, cloud of words, *copia verborum*; flow of words &c. (*loquacity*) 584.

poly-, tauto-, batto-, perisso-logy; pleonasm, exuberance, redundance; thrice-told tale; prolixity; circumlocution, *ambages*; periphra-se, -sis; roundabout phrases; episode; expletive; penny-a-lining; padding, drivel, twaddle, rigmarole; richness &c. 577.

V. be -diffuse &c. *adj.*; run out on, descant, expatiate, enlarge, dilate, amplify, expand, inflate, pad; launch -, branch- out; rant.

maunder, prose; harp upon &c. (*repeat*) 104; dwell on, insist upon.

digress, ramble, *battre la compagne*, beat about the bush, perorate, spin a long yarn, protract; spin -, swell -, draw- out, drivel.

Adj. dif-, pro-fuse; wordy, verbose, largiloquent, copious, exuberant, effusive, pleonastic, lengthy; long, -some, -winded, -spun, -drawn out; diffusive, spun out, protracted, prolix, prosing, maundering; circumlocutory, periphrastic, ambagious, roundabout; digressive; dis-, ex-cursive; rambling, episodic; flatulent, frothy.

Adv. diffusely &c. *adj.*; at large, *in extenso*; about it and about it.

574. Vigour.—N. vigour, power, force; boldness, raciness &c. *adj.*; spirit, point, antithesis, piquancy; *verve*, glow, fire, warmth, ardour, enthusiasm; 'thoughts that breathe and words that burn'; strong language; punch; gravity, sententiousness; elevation, loftiness, sublimity.

eloquence; command of -words, - language.

Adj. vigorous, nervous, powerful, forcible, trenchant, mordant, biting, incisive, impressive; sensational.

spirited, lively, glowing, sparkling, racy, bold, slashing; pungent, *piquant*, full of point, pointed, pithy, antithetical; sententious.

lofty, elevated, sublime, grand,

weighty, ponderous; eloquent; vehement, petulant, impassioned; poetic.

Adv. in -glowing, – good set, – no measured- terms.

575. Feebleness.—N. feebleness &c. *adj.*

Adj. feeble, bald, tame, meagre, insipid, nerveless, jejune, vapid, trashy, cold, frigid, poor, dull, dry, languid; pros-ing, -y, -aic; unvaried, monotonous, weak, frail, washy, wishy-washy, sloppy; sketchy, slight; careless, slovenly, loose, lax; slip-shod, -slop; inexact; dis-jointed, -connected; puerile, childish; flatulent; rambling &c. (*diffuse*) 573.

576. Plainness.—N. plainness &c. *adj.*; simplicity, severity; plain -terms, – English; Saxon English; household words.

V. speak plainly; call a spade 'a spade'; plunge *in medias res*; come to the point.

Adj. plain, simple; un-ornamented, -adorned, -varnished; home-ly, -spun; neat; severe, chaste, pure, Saxon; commonplace, matter of fact, natural, prosaic, sober, unimaginative.

dry, unvaried, monotonous &c. 575.

Adv. in plain -terms, – words, – English, – common parlance; point blank.

577. Ornament.—N. ornament; floridness &c. *adj.*; turg-idity, -escence; altiloquence &c. *adj.*; orotundity; declamation, teratology; well-rounded periods; elegance &c. 578.

inversion, antithesis, alliteration, *paronomasia*; figurativeness &c. (*metaphor*) 521.

flourish; flowers of -speech, – rhetoric; euph-uism, -emism.

big-, high-sounding words; macrology, *sesquipedalia verba*, sesquipedalianism; Alexandrine; inflation, pretension; rant, bombast, fustian, bunkum, balderdash, prose run mad; fine writing; Minerva press.

phrasemonger; euph-uist, -emist.

V. ornament, overlay with ornament, overcharge; smell of the lamp.

Adj. ornamented &c. *v.*; beautified &c. 847; ornate, florid, rich, flowery; euph-uistic, -emistic; sonorous; high-, big-sounding; inflated, swelling, tumid; turg-id, -escent; pedantic, pompous, stilted; high-flown, -flowing; sententious, rhetorical, declamatory; grandiose; grand-, magn-, alt-iloquent; sesquipedal, -ian; Johnsonian, mouthy; bombastic; fustian; frothy, flashy, flaming, flamboyant.

antithetical, alliterative; figurative &c. 521; artificial &c. (*inelegant*) 579.

Adv. *ore rotundo*; with rounded phrase.

578. Elegance.—N. elegance, purity, grace, ease, felicity, distinction, gracefulness, refinement, readiness &c. *adj.*; concinnity, euphony, numerosity, balance, rhythm, symmetry, proportion; restraint; good taste, propriety.

well rounded –, well turned –, flowing- periods; the right word in the right place; antithesis &c. 577.

purist, stylist.

V. point an antithesis, round a period.

Adj. elegant, polished, classical, Attic, correct, Ciceronian, artistic; chaste, pure, Saxon, academical.

graceful, easy, readable, fluent, flowing, tripping; unaffected, natural, unlaboured; mellifluous; euph-onious, -emistic; rhythmical, balanced, symmetrical.

felicitous, happy, neat; well –, neatly- -put, – expressed.

579. Inelegance.—N. inelegance; vulgarity, bad taste; stiffness &c. *adj.*; unlettered Muse; barbarism; slang &c. 563; solecism &c. 568; mannerism &c. (*affectation*) 855; euphuism; fustian &c. 577; cacophony; want of balance; words that -break the teeth, – dislocate the jaw.

V. be -inelegant &c. *adj.*

Adj. inelegant, graceless, ungraceful, unpolished; harsh, abrupt; dry, stiff, cramped, formal, *guindé*; forced, laboured, awkward; artificial, mannered, ponderous; turgid &c. 577; affected, euphuistic; barbarous, uncouth, grotesque, rude, crude, halting; vulgar, offensive to ears polite.

2. Spoken Language

580. Voice.—N. voice; vocality; organ, lungs, bellows; good -, fine -, powerful &c. (*loud*) 404 -, musical &c. 413- voice; intonation; tone &c. (*sound*) 402- of voice.

vocalization; cry &c. 411; strain, utterance, prolation; exclam-, ejacul-, vocifer-ation; enunci-, articul-ation; articulate sound, distinctness; clearness, - of articulation; stage whisper; delivery; attack.

accent, -uation; emphasis, stress; broad -, strong -, pure -, native -, foreign- accent; pronunciation.

[Word similarly pronounced] homonym.

orthoepy; euphony &c. (*melody*) 413.

gastri-, ventri-loquism; ventriloquist; polyphon-ism, -ist.

[Science of voice] phonology &c. (*sound*) 402.

V. sing, speak, utter, breathe, voice; give -utterance, - tongue; cry &c. (*shout*) 411; ejaculate, rap out; vocalize, prolate, articulate, enunciate, enounce, pronounce, accentuate, aspirate, deliver, mouth; emit, murmur, whisper, - in the ear, croon, yodel.

Adj. vocal, phonetic, oral; ejaculatory, articulate, distinct, stertorous; enunciative; accentuated, aspirated; euphonious &c. (*melodious*) 413.

581. Aphony.—N. aphony, *aphonia*; dumbness &c. *adj.*; obmutescence; absence -, want- of voice; dysphony; silence &c. (*taciturnity*) 585; raucity; harsh &c. 410 -, unmusical &c. 414- voice; *falsetto*, 'childish treble'; mute, dummy, deaf mute.

V. keep silence &c. 585; speak -low, - softly; whisper &c. (*faintness*) 405.

silence; render -mute, - silent &c.

403; muzzle, muffle, suppress, smother, gag, strike dumb, dumb-found, -founder; drown the voice, put to silence, stop one's mouth, cut one short.

stick in the throat.

Adj. aphon-ous, -ic, dumb, mute; deaf-mute, - and dumb; mum; tongue-tied; breath-, tongue-, voice-, speech-, word-less; mute as a -fish, - stockfish - mackerel; silent &c. (*taciturn*) 585; muzzled; in-articulate, -audible.

croaking, raucous, hoarse, husky, dry, hollow, sepulchral, hoarse as a raven.

Adv. with -bated breath, - the finger on the lips; *sotto voce*; in a -low tone, - cracked voice, - broken voice; in an aside.

Phr. *vox faucibus hæsit.*

582. Speech.—N. speech, faculty of speech; locution, talk, parlance, verbal intercourse, prolation, oral communication, word of mouth, *parole*, palaver, prattle; effusion.

oration, recitation, delivery, say, address, speech, lecture, harangue, sermon, *tirade*, screed, formal speech, salutatory, peroration; prelection; speechifying; soliloquy &c. 589; allocution &c. 586; interlocution &c. 588.

oratory; elo-cution, -quence; rhetoric, declamation; grandi-, multiloquence; burst of eloquence; facundity; talkativeness; flow -, command of -words, - language; *copia verborum*; power of speech, gift of the gab; *usus loquendi.*

speaker &c. *v.*; spokesman; pro-, inter-locutor; mouthpiece, Hermes; orator, -trix, -tress; Demosthenes, Cicero; rhetorician; stump -, platform-orator, tub-thumper; elocutionist; speech-maker, patterer, *improvisatore.*

V. speak, - of; say, utter, pronounce, deliver, give utterance to; utter -, pour-forth; breathe, let fall, come out with; rap -, blurt- out; have on one's lips; have at the -end, - tip- of one's tongue.

break silence; open one's -lips, - mouth; lift -, raise- one's voice; give -, wag the- tongue; talk, outspeak; put in a word or two.

hold forth; make –, deliver- -a speech
&c. *n.*; speechify, harangue, declaim,
stump, flourish, spout, rant, recite, lecture, preach, sermonize, discourse, be
on one's legs; have –, say- one's say; expatiate &c. (*speak at length*) 573; speak
one's mind.
    soliloquize &c. 589; tell &c. (*inform*)
527; speak to &c. 586; talk together &c.
588.
    be -eloquent &c. *adj.*; have -a tongue
in one's head, – the gift of the gab
&c. *n.*
    pass –, escape- one's lips; fall from
the -lips, – mouth.
    Adj. speaking &c., spoken &c. *v.*;
oral, lingual, phonetic, not written,
unwritten, outspoken; elo-quent,
-cutionary; orat-, rhetorical; declamatory; grandiloquent &c. 577; talkative &c.
584.
    Adv. orally &c. *adj.*; by word of
mouth, *vivâ voce*, from the lips of.
    Phr. quoth –, said- he &c.

    **583. [Imperfect Speech.] Stammer-
ing.—N.** inarticulateness; stammering
&c. *v.*; hesitation &c. *v.*; impediment in
one's speech; aphasia, titubancy, traulism; whisper &c. (*faint sound*) 405;
lisp, drawl, tardiloquence; nasal -tone,
– accent; twang; *falsetto* &c. (*want of
voice*) 581; broken -voice, – accents, –
sentences.
    brogue &c. 563; slip of the tongue,
lapsus linguæ.
    V. stammer, stutter, hesitate, falter,
hammer; balbu-tiate, -cinate; haw, hum
and haw, be unable to put two words together.
    mumble, mutter; maund, -er; whisper
&c. 405; mince, lisp; jabber, gabble,
gibber; sp-, spl-utter; muffle, mump;
drawl, mouth; croak; speak -thick, –
through the nose; snuffle, clip one's
words; murder the -language, – King's
(*or* Queen's) English; mis-pronounce,
-say.
    Adj. stammering &c. *v.*; inarticulate,
guttural, nasal; tremulous.
    Adv. *sotto voce* &c. (*faintly*) 405.

    584. Loquacity.—N. loquac-ity,
-iousness; talkativeness &c. *adj.*; garrulity; multiloquence, much speaking,
effusion, wordiness.
    jaw; gab, -ble; jabber, chatter; prate,
prattle, cackle, clack; twaddle, twattle,
rattle; *caquet, -terie*; blabber, *bavardage*, bibble-babble, gibblegabble; smali
talk &c. (*converse*) 588.
    fluency, flippancy, volubility, flowing
tongue; flow, – of words; *flux de
-bouche, – mots, – paroles; copia verborum, cacoëthes loquendi*; verbosity
&c. (*diffuseness*) 573; gift of the gab &c.
(*eloquence*) 582.
    talker; chatter-er, -box; babbler &c.
v.; rattle; ranter; sermonizer, proser,
driveller; wind bag; gossip &c. (*converse*) 588; magpie, jay, parrot, poll,
Babel; *moulin à paroles*.
    V. be -loquacious &c. *adj.*; talk glib-
ly, pour forth, patter; prate, palaver,
prose, chatter, prattle, clack, jabber,
jaw; rattle, – on; twaddle, twattle; babble, gabble; out-talk; talk oneself -out of
breath, – hoarse; maunder, gush, blatter; talk a donkey's hind leg off; expatiate &c. (*speak at length*) 573; gossip &c.
(*converse*) 588; din in the ears &c. (*repeat*) 104; talk -at random, – nonsense
&c. 497; be hoarse with talking.
    Adj. loquacious, talkative, conversa-
tional, garrulous, linguacious, multilo-
quous; chattering &c. *v.*; chatty &c. (*sociable*) 892; declamatory &c. 582; open-
mouthed.
    fluent, voluble, glib, flippant; long-
tongued, -winded &c. (*diffuse*) 573.
    Adv. trippingly on the tongue; glibly
&c. *adj.*
    Phr. the tongue running -fast, – loose,
– on wheels.

    585. Taciturnity.—N. silence, mute-
ness, obmutescence; taciturnity, pauciloquy, costiveness, curtness; reserve, reticence &c. (*concealment*) 528;
aposiopesis.
    man of few words.
    V. be -silent &c. *adj.*; keep silence;
hold one's -tongue, – peace, – jaw; not

speak &c. 582; say nothing; seal –, close
–, put a padlock on- the -lips, – mouth;
put a bridle on one's tongue; keep one's
tongue between one's teeth; make no
sign, not let a word escape one; keep a
secret &c. 528; not have a word to say;
lay –, place- the finger on the lips; render mute &c. 581.

stick in one's throat.

Adj. silent, mute, mum; silent as -a
post, – a stone, – the grave &c. (*still*)
403; dumb &c. 581.

taciturn, sparing of words; close, –
mouthed, – tongued; laconic, costive,
inconversable, curt; reserved; reticent
&c. (*concealing*) 528.

Int. tush! silence! mum! hush! *chut!*
hist! tut! &c. 403.

586. Allocution.—N. allocution, alloquy, address; speech &c. 582; apostrophe, interpellation, appeal, invocation, salutation; word in the ear.

[Feigned dialogue] dialogism.

platform &c. 542; audience &c. (*interview*) 588.

V. speak to, address, accost, make up
to, apostrophize, appeal to, invoke; hail,
salute; call to, halloo.

take -aside, – by the button, button-
hole; talk to in private.

lecture &c. (*make a speech*) 582.

Int. soho! halloo! hey! hist! hi!

587. Response &c., *see* Answer 462.

588. Interlocution.—N. interlocution; collocution, colloquy, converse,
conversation, confabulation, talk, discourse, verbal intercourse; communion,
oral communication, commerce; dia-,
duo-, tria-logue.

causerie, chat, chit-chat; small –, table –, teatable –, town –, village –, idle-
talk; tattle, gossip, tittle-tattle; babble,
-ment; *tripotage*, cackle, prittle-prattle;
on dit; talk of the -town, – village.

conference, parley, interview, audience, *pourparler*; *tête-à-tête*; reception,
conversazione; congress &c. (*council*)
696; pow-wow.

hall of audience, *durbar*, coliseum,
assembly hall, auditorium.

palaver, debate, logomachy, war of
words, controversy.

talker, gossip, tattler; Paul Pry; tabby; chatterer &c. (*loquacity*) 584; inter-
locutor &c. (*spokesman*) 582; conver-
sation-ist, -alist; dialogist.

'the feast of reason and the flow of
soul'; *mollia tempora fandi.*

V. talk together, converse, confabu-
late; hold –, carry on –, join in –, engage in- a conversation; put in a word;
shine in conversation; bandy words; parley; palaver; chat, gossip, tattle; prate
&c. (*loquacity*) 584.

discourse –, confer –, commune –,
commercewith; hold -converse, – conference, – intercourse; talk it over; be
closeted with; talk with one -in private,
– *tête-à-tête.*

Adj. conversing &c. *v.*; interlocutory;
convers-ational, -able; discursive, -coursive;
chatty &c. (*sociable*) 892; colloquial, *tête-
à-tête*, confabulatory.

589. Soliloquy.—N. soliloquy, monologue, apostrophe.

solilo-quist, -quizer, monologist.

V. soliloquize; say –, talk- to oneself;
say aside, think aloud, apostrophize.

Adj. soliloquizing &c. *v.*

Adv. aside.

3. *Written Language*

590. Writing.—N. writing &c. *v.*;
chiro-, stelo-, cero-graphy, graphology;
stylography; pen-craft, -script, -manship;
quill-driving; typewriting.

writing, manuscript, MS., *literæ
scriptæ*; these presents.

stroke –, dash- of the pen; *coup de
plume*; line; pen and ink.

letter &c. 561; uncial writing, cuneiform character, arrow-head, Ogham,
Runes, futhorc; hieroglyphic, hieratic,
demotic; script; contraction.

short-hand; steno-, brachy-, tachygraphy; secret writing, writing in

cipher; crypt-, stegan-ography; phono-, pasi-, poly-, logo-graphy.

copy; tran-, re-script; draft, rough -, fair- copy; handwriting; signature, sign-manual; auto-, mono-, holo-graph; hand, fist; mark.

calligraphy; good -, running -, flowing -, cursive -, legible -, copper-plate -, round -, bold- hand.

cacography, *griffonage, barbouillage*; bad -, cramped -, crabbed -, illegible-hand; scribble &c. *v.*; *pattes de mouche*; ill-formed letters; pot-hooks and hangers.

stationery; pen, quill, goose-quill, reed; stylographic-, fountain-pen; pencil, style, stylus; paper, foolscap, parchment, vellum, papyrus, pad, tablet, block, note book, slate, marble, pillar, table, black board.

ink-bottle, -pot, -stand, -well, -horn; typewriter.

transcription &c. (*copy*) 21; inscription &c. (*record*) 551; superscription &c. (*indication*) 550.

composition, authorship; *cacoethes scribendi.*

writer, scribe, amanuensis, scrivener, secretary, clerk, penman, copyist, transcriber, quill-driver; writer for the press &c. (*author*) 593.

shorthand writer, stenographer; typewriter, typist.

V. write, pen; copy, engross; write out, - fair; transcribe; scribble, scrawl, scrabble, scratch; interline; stain paper; write down &c. (*record*) 551; sign &c. (*attest*) 467; take down, - in shorthand; typewrite, type.

compose, indite, draw up, redact, draft, formulate; dictate; inscribe, throw on paper, dash off; concoct.

take -up the pen, - pen in hand; shed -, spill -, dip one's pen in- ink.

Adj. writing &c. *v.*; written &c. *v.*; in -writing, - black and white; under one's hand.

uncial, Runic, cuneiform, hieroglyphical &c. *n.*

Adv. *currente calamo*; pen in hand.

591. Printing.—N. printing; block -, type- printing, lino-, mono-type; plate printing &c. (*engraving*) 558; the press &c. (*publicaton*) 531; composition.

print, letterpress, text, matter, standing type; context, note, page, column; over-running; head-, foot-line, title.

typography; stereo-, electro-, apro-type; type, black letter, heavy type, font, fount; pi, pie; capitals &c. (*letters*) 561; diamond, pearl, nonpareil, minion, brevier, bourgeois, long primer, small pica, pica, english, great primer.

folio &c. (*book*) 593; copy, impression, pull, proof, galley -, author's -, page- proof, revise.

printer, compositor, reader; printer's devil.

V. print; compose; put -, go- to press; pass -, see- through the press; publish &c. 531; bring out; appear in -, rush into- print.

Adj. printed &c. *v.*; in type; typographical &c. *n.*

592. Correspondence.—N. correspondence, letter, epistle, note, *billet*, post-, letter-card, missive, circular, form letter; favour, *billet-doux*; des-, dispatch; *bulletin*, communication &c. 532; these presents; rescript, -ion; post &c. (*messenger*) 534; letter writer, correspondent.

V. correspond, - with; write -, send a letter- to; keep up a correspondence; drop a line to; despatch; communicate with; circularize.

Adj. epistolary.

593. Book.—N. book, -let; writing, work, volume, tome, opuscule; tract, -ate; *livret*; *brochure, libretto*, handbook, treatise, text-book, codex, manual, pamphlet, monograph, enchiridion, circular, publication; book of poems; novel; chap-book.

part, issue, number, *livraison*; album, portfolio; periodical, serial, magazine, *ephemeris*, annual, journal.

paper, bill, sheet, broadsheet, screed; leaf, -let; fly-leaf, page; quire, ream.

chapter, section, head, article,

paragraph, passage, clause, supplement, appendix; *feuilleton.*

folio, quarto, octavo; duo-, sexto-, octo-decimo.

en-, cyclopædia, dictionary, lexicon, thesaurus, concordance, anthology, bibliography; compilation, compendium, catalogue &c. 86; library, bibliotheca; the press &c. (*publication*) 531.

writer, author, *littérateur*, essayist, journalist, publicist; scribe, penman, war -, special -, correspondent; pen, scribbler, the scribbling race; ghost, hack, literary hack, Grub-street writer; writer for -, gentleman of -, representative of- the press; reporter, penny-a-liner; editor, sub-editor; playwright &c. 599; poet &c. 597.

bookseller, publisher; biblio-pole, -polist, -grapher; librarian; book -collector, - worm.

book -shop, - club, circulating -, lending -, public- library; publishing house.

knowledge of books, bibliography; book-learning &c. (*knowledge*) 490.

594. Description.—N. description, account, statement, report; *exposé* &c. (*disclosure*) 529; specification, particulars, scenario, plot; state -, summary- of facts; brief &c. (*abstract*) 596; return &c. (*record*) 551; *catalogue raisonné* &c. (*list*) 86; guide-book &c. (*information*) 527.

delineation &c. (*representation*) 554; sketch, vignette; monograph; minute -, detailed -, particular -, circumstantial -, graphic- account; narration, recital, rehearsal, relation.

histori-, chron-ography; historic Muse, Clio; history; bi-, autobiography; necrology, obituary.

narrative, history; memoir, memorials; annals &c. (*chronicle*) 551; tradition, legend, saga, epic, epos, story, tale, historiette; personal narrative, journal, letters, life, adventures, fortunes, experiences, confessions; anecdote, ana, *trait.*

work of fiction, short story, novelette,

novel, romance, penny dreadful, shilling shocker, Minerva press; fairy -, nursery- tale; fable, allegory, parable, apologue.

relator &c. *v.*; *raconteur*; historian &c. (*recorder*) 553; biographer, fabulist, novelist, story teller, romancer, teller of tales, spinner of yarns, anecdotist.

V. describe; set forth &c. (*state*) 535; draw a picture, picture; portray &c. (*represent*) 554; characterize, particularize; narrate, relate, recite, recount, sum up, run over, recapitulate, rehearse, fight one's battles over again.

unfold &c. (*disclose*) 529- a tale; tell; give -, render- an account of; report, make a report, draw up a statement.

detail; enter into -, descend to- particulars, - details.

Adj. descriptive, graphic, narrative, epic, suggestive, well-drawn; historic; auto-, biographical, realistic, expository, tradition-al, -ary; legendary; fabulous, mythical; anecdotic, storied; described &c. *v.*

595. Dissertation.—N. dissertation, treatise, essay; *thesis*, theme; tract, -ate, -ation, excursus; discourse, memoir, disquisition, lecture, sermon, homily, pandect.

commentary, review, *critique*, criticism, article; lead-er, -ing article, editorial; argument, running commentary.

investigation &c. (*inquiry*) 461; study &c. (*consideration*) 451; discussion &c. (*reasoning*) 476; exposition &c. (*explanation*) 522.

commentator, critic, essayist, pamphleteer; publicist, reviewer, leader writer, editor, annotator.

V. dissert; descant -, write -, touch- upon a subject; dissertate; treat of -, take up -, ventilate -, discuss -, deal with -, go into -, canvass -, handle -, do justice to- a subject; comment, criticize, interpret &c. 522.

Adj. dis-cursive, -coursive; disquisitional, disquisitionary; expository, critical.

596. Compendium.—N. compend, -ium; abstract, *précis*, epitome, *multum in parvo*, analysis, pandect, digest, sum and substance, brief, abridgment, summary, *aperçu*, draft, minute, note; synopsis, text-book, *conspectus*, outlines, syllabus, contents, heads, prospectus.

album; scrap –, note –, memorandum –, commonplace-book; extracts, *excerpta*, cuttings; fugitive -pieces, – writings; *spicilegium*, flowers, anthology, miscellany, *collectanea, analecta*; compilation.

recapitulation, *résumé*, review.

abbrevia-tion, -ture; contraction; shortening &c. 201; compression &c. 195.

V. abridge, abstract, epitomize, summarize; make –, prepare –, draw –, compile- an abstract &c. *n*.

recapitulate, review, skim, run over, sum up.

abbreviate &c. (*shorten*) 201; condense &c. (*compress*) 195; compile &c. (*collect*) 72; edit, blue pencil.

Adj. compendious, synoptic, analectic, analytical; abridged &c. *v.*

Adv. in -short, – epitome, – substance, – few words.

Phr. it lies in a nutshell.

597. Poetry.—N. poetry, poetics, poesy, Muse, Calliope, tuneful Nine, Parnassus, Helicon, Pierides, Pierian spring, afflatus, inspiration.

versification, rhyming, making verses; prosody, scansion, orthometry.

poem; epic, – poem; epopee, *epopœa*, ode, epode, idyl, lyric, eclogue, pastoral, bucolic, georgic, dithyramb, anacreontic, sonnet, roundelay, *rondel, rondoletto, rondeau, rondo,* triolet; madrigal, canzonet, *cento,* monody, elegy, palinode; rhapsody.

dramatic –, lyric- poetry; opera; posy, anthology.

song, ballad, lay; love –, drinking –, war –, folk –, sea- song; lullaby; music &c. 415; nursery rhymes.

[Bad poetry] doggerel, Hudibrastic verse, prose run mad; macaronics; macaronic –, leonine- verse; runes.

canto, stanza, distich, verse, line, couplet, triplet, quatrain, sestet; *strophe, antistrophe,* refrain, chorus, burden.

verse, rhyme, assonance, crambo, metre, measure, foot, numbers, strain, rhythm; accentuation &c. (*voice*) 580; iambus, dactyl, spondee, trochee, anapæst &c.; hex-, pent-ameter; Alexandrine; blank verse, alliteration.

elegiacs &c. *adj.*; elegiac &c. *adj.* -verse, – metre, – poetry.

poet, – laureate; laureate; minor poet, bard, lyrist, scald, troubadour, *trouvère*; minstrel; minne-, meister-singer; *improvisatore*; versifier, sonneteer; ballad monger; rhym-er, -ist, -ester; poetaster.

V. poetize, sing, versify, make verses, rhyme, scan.

Adj. poetic, -al; lyric, -al; tuneful; epic; dithyrambic &c. *n.*; metrical; a-, catalectic; elegiac, iambic, trochaic; spondaic, anapæstic; Ionic, Sapphic, Alcaic, Pindaric.

598. Prose.—N. prose, – writer, prosaism, -aist, -er.

V. prose, write prose.

write -prose, – in prose.

Adj. pros-y, -aic; unpoetical.

rhymeless, unrhymed, in prose, not in verse.

599. The Drama.—N. the -drama, – stage, – theatre, – play; theatricals, dramaturgy, histrionic art, buskin, sock, *cothurnus*, Melpomene and Thalia, Thespis.

play, drama, stage-play, piece, five-act play, tragedy, comedy, opera, comic opera, *vaudeville, comedietta, lever de rideau,* curtain raiser, interlude, afterpiece, exode, farce, *divertissement, extravaganza,* burletta, harlequinade, pantomime, mimodrama, burlesque, *opéra bouffe,* musical comedy, review, revue, intimate revue, variety, cabaret entertainment, *ballet, spectacle,* masque, *drame, comédie drame*; melo-drama, -drame; *comédie larmoyante,* emotional drama, sensation drama, tragi-, farcical-comedy; mono-drame, -logue; duo-logue; trilogy; charade, *proverbe*; mystery, miracle –, morality- play.

act, scene, *tableau*; in-, intro-duction; pro-, epi-logue, curtain; *libretto*, book, script.

performance, representation, show, *mise en scène*, stagery, *jeu de théâtre*, stage-craft; acting; gesture &c. 550; impersonation &c. 554; stage business, gag, patter, buffoonery.

theatre; play-, opera-house; house; music hall; *cabaret*; amphitheatre, circus, hippodrome; puppet-show, *fantoccini*; *marionnettes*, Punch and Judy.

cinema, -tograph-, picture –, theatre, the pictures, the movies, the talkies.

auditory, *auditorium*, front of the house, stalls, boxes, balcony, dress –, upper- -circle, – boxes, amphitheatre, pit, gallery; *foyer*; green-room; dressing rooms, *coulisses*.

flat; drop, – scene; wing, screen, side-scene; transformation scene, curtain, act-drop, safety –, fire- curtain; *proscenium*, forestage.

stage, revolving stage, scene, the boards; star –, grave –, trap, mezzanine floor; flies; gridiron, floats, battens, footlights; lime –, spot –, flood –, bunch-lights; scenery, set, *décor*, orchestra.

theatrical -costume, – properties, props.

part, *rôle*, character, cast, *dramatis personœ*; *répertoire*.

actor, player; stage –, strolling- player; old –, stager, performer; mime, -r; *artiste*; com-, trag-edian, straight man; *tragédienne*, Thespian, Roscius, star.

pantomimist, clown, harlequin, *buffo*,

buffoon, *farceur*, *grimacier*, pantaloon, columbine; *Pierrot*, *Pierrette*; punch, -inello; *pulcinell-o*, *-a*; mute, *figurante*, general utility; super, -numerary, extra.

mummer, guiser, guisard, gysart, masque.

mountebank, Jack Pudding; tumbler, posture-master, acrobat, equilibrist, juggler, contortionist; *danseuse*, *ballerina*, ballet -dancer, – girl, *coryphée*; *bayadère*, *geisha*; chorus -singer, – girl.

company; first tragedian, *prima donna*, lead, leading lady, protagonist; *jeune premier*; juvenile lead, *débutant*, *-e*; light –, genteel –, low-comedy, – comedian; *soubrette*, walking gentleman, *amoroso*, heavy, heavy father, *ingénue*, *jeune veuve*, *commère*, *compère*.

property man, *costumier*, machinist, stage hand, electrician, prompter, callboy; director, manager; stage –, acting –, business- manager; *entrepreneur*, *impresario*, producer, press agent.

dramatic -author, – writer; play-writer, -wright; dramatist, mimographer; dramatic critic.

V. act, play, perform; stage, produce, put on the stage; personate &c. 554; mimic &c. (*imitate*) 19; enact; play –, act –, go through –, perform- a part; rehearse, spout, gag, rant; 'strut and fret one's hour upon a stage'; tread the -stage, – boards; come out; star.

Adj. dramatic; theatric, -al; scenic, histrionic, anctorial, comic, tragic, buskined, farcical, tragi-comic, melodramatic, operatic; stagey spectacular; stagestruck.

Adv. on the -stage, – boards; before -the floats, – an audience; in the limelight, behind the footlights; behind the scenes.

CLASS V

WORDS RELATING
TO THE VOLUNTARY POWERS*

DIVISION (I.) INDIVIDUAL VOLITION

Section I. VOLITION
IN GENERAL

1°. *Acts of Volition*

600. Will.—N. will, volition, conation†, velleity; will and pleasure, freewill; freedom &c. 748; discretion; choice, inclination, intent, purpose, option &c. (*choice*) 609; voluntariness; spontane-ity, -ousness; originality.

pleasure, wish, desire, mind; frame of mind &c. (*inclination*) 602; intention &c. 620; predetermination &c. 611; self-control &c. determination &c. (*resolution*) 604; will-power.

V. will, list; see -, think- fit; determine &c. (*resolve*) 604; settle &c. (*choose*) 609; volunteer.

have a will of one's own; do what one chooses &c. (*freedom*) 748; have it all one's own way; have one's -will, - own way.

use -, exercise- one's discretion; take -upon oneself, - one's own course, - the law into one's own hands; do -of one's own accord, - upon one's own -responsibility, - authority; take the bit between one's teeth; take responsibility; originate &c. (*cause*) 153.

Adj. voluntary, volitive, volitional, wilful; free &c. 748; optional; discretion-al, -ary; volitient; dictatorial.

minded &c. (*willing*) 602; prepense &c. (*predetermined*) 611; intended &c.

620; autocratic; unbidden &c. (bid &c. 741); spontaneous; original &c. (*causal*) 153.

Adv. voluntarily &c. *adj.*; at -will, - pleasure; *à -volonté, - discrétion; al piacere; ad -libitum, - arbitrium*; as -one thinks proper, - it seems good to.

of one's own -accord, - free will; *proprio -, suo -, ex mero- motu*; out of one's own head; by choice &c. 609; purposely &c. (*intentionally*) 620; deliberately &c. 611.

Phr. *stet pro ratione voluntas; sic volo sic jubeo.*

601. Necessity.—N. involuntariness; instinct, blind -, natural- impulse; inborn -, innate- proclivity; the force of circumstances.

necessi-ty, -tation, necessarianism; obligation; compulsion &c. 744; subjection &c. 749; stern -, hard -, dire -, imperious -, inexorable -, iron -, adverse- -necessity, - fate; what must be.

desti-ny, -nation; fatality, fate; *kismet*, doom, foredoom, election, predestination; pre-, fore-ordination; lot, fortune; fatalism, determinism; inevitableness &c. *adj.*; spell &c. 993.

star, -s; planet, -s; astral influence; sky, Fates, Norns, *Parcæ*, Sisters three, Clotho, Lachesis, Atropos; book of fate; God's will, will of Heaven; wheel of

---

* Conative powers or faculties (Hamilton).
† Hamilton.

Fortune, Ides of March, Hobson's choice.

last -shift, – resort; *dernier ressort*; *pis aller* &c. (*substitute*) 147; necessaries &c. (*requirement*) 630.

necess-arian, -itarian; fatalist, determinist; automaton.

V. lie under a necessity; be -fated, – doomed, – destined &c., – in for, – under the necessity of; have no -choice, – alternative; be- obliged –, forced –, driven –, one's -fate &c. *n.*- to; be -pushed to the wall, – driven into a corner, – unable to help, – drawn irresistibly.

destine, doom, foredoom, devote; predestine, -ordain; cast a spell &c. 992; necessitate; compel &c. 744.

Adj. necessary; needful &c. (*requisite*) 630.

fated; destined &c. *v.*; fateful; elect; spell-bound.

compulsory &c. (*compel*) 744; uncontrollable, inevitable, unavoidable, irresistible, irrevocable, inexorable, binding; avoid-, resist-less; written in the book of fate.

involuntary, instinctive, automatic, blind, mechanical, un-conscious, -witting, -thinking; unintentional &c. (*undesigned*) 621; impulsive &c. 612.

Adv. necessarily &c. *adv.*; of -necessity, – course; *ex necessitate rei*; needs must; perforce &c. 744; *nolens volens*; will he nil he, willy nilly, *bon gré mal gré*, willing or unwilling, *coûte que coûte*, forcefully.

faute de mieux; by stress of; if need be.

Phr. it cannot be helped; there is no-help for, – helping- it; it -will, - must, – must needs- be, – be so, – have its way; the die is cast; *jacta est alea*; *che sarà sarà*; 'it is written'; one's- days are numbered, – fate is sealed; *Fata obstant*; *diis aliter visum*.

602. Willingness.—N. willingness, voluntariness &c. *adj.*; willing mind, heart.

disposition, inclination, leaning, ani-

mus; frame of mind, humour, mood, vein; bent &c. (*turn of mind*) 820; penchant &c. (*desire*) 865; aptitude &c. 698.

doc-ility, -ibleness, tractability; persuasi-bleness, -bility; pliability &c. (*softness*) 324.

geniality, cordiality; goodwill; alacrity, readiness, earnestness, forwardness, enthusiasm; zeal, eagerness &c. (*desire*) 865.

assent &c. 488; compliance &c. 762; pleasure &c. (*will*) 600.

labour of love, self-appointed task; volunteer, -ing, gratuitous service; unpaid worker, amateur.

V. be -willing &c. *adj.*; incline, lean to, mind, propend; had as lief; lend –, give –, turn- a willing ear; have -a, – half a, – a great- mind to; hold –, cling-to; desire &c. 865.

see –, think- -good, – fit, – proper; acquiescence &c. (*assent*) 488; comply with &c. 762.

swallow –, nibble at- the bait; gorge the hook; swallow hook, line and sinker; have –, make- no scruple of; make no bones of; jump –, catch- at; meet half way; volunteer, offer oneself &c. 763.

Adj. willing, minded, fain, disposed, inclined, favourable; favourably-minded, -inclined, -disposed; nothing loth; in the -vein, – mood, – humour, – mind.

ready, forward, enthusiastic, earnest, eager; bent upon &c. (*desirous*) 865; predisposed, propense.

docile; persua-dable, -sible; suasible; easily persuaded, facile, easy-going; amenable; tractable &c. (*pliant*) 324; genial, gracious, cordial, hearty; content &c. (*assenting*) 488.

voluntary, gratuitous, spontaneous; unasked &c. (ask &c. 765); unforced &c. (*free*) 748.

Adv. willingly &c. *adj.*; fain, freely, as lief, heart and soul; with -pleasure, – all one's heart, – open arms; with -good, – right good- will; *de bonne volonté*, *ex animo*; *con amore*, heart in hand, nothing loth, without reluctance, of one's own accord, graciously, with a good grace, without demur.

à la bonne heure; by all -means, – manner of means; to one's heart's content; yes &c. (*assent*) 488.

Int. sure, -ly! of course!

603. Unwillingness.—N. unwillingness &c. *adj.*; indispos-ition, -edness; disinclination, aversation, aversion; nolleity, nolition; renitence; reluctance; indifference &c. 866; backwardness &c. *adj.*; slowness &c. 275; want of -alacrity, – readiness; indocility &c. (*obstinacy*) 606.

scrupul-ousness, -osity; qualms of conscience, delicacy, demur, scruple, qualm, shrinking, recoil; hesitation &c. (*irresolution*) 605; fastidiousness &c. 868.

averseness &c. (*dislike*) 867; dissent &c. 489; refusal &c. 764.

slacker, scrimshanker, *embusqué*, unwilling worker, forced labor.

V. be -unwilling &c. *adj.*; nill; dislike &c. 867; grudge, begrudge; not be able to find it in one's heart to, not have the stomach to.

demur, stick at, scruple, stickle; hang fire, run rusty, slack, shirk, scamp, give up, fight shy of, not pull fair; recoil, shrink, swerve; hesitate &c. 605; avoid &c. 623.

oppose &c. 708; dissent &c. 489; refuse &c. 764.

Adj. unwilling; not in the vein, loth, shy of, disinclined, indisposed, averse, reluctant, not content; adverse &c. (*opposed*) 708; laggard, backward, remiss, slack, slow to; renitent; indifferent &c. 866; scrupulous; squeamish &c. (*fastidious*) 868; repugnant &c. (*dislike*) 867; rest-iff, -ive; demurring &c. *v.*; unconsenting &c. (*refusing*) 764; involuntary &c. 601; grudging, irreconcilable.

Adv. unwillingly &c. *adj.*; grudgingly, with a heavy heart; with -a bad, – an ill- grace; against –, sore against- -one's wishes, – one's will, – the grain; *invitâ Minervâ*; *à contre cœur*; *malgré soi*; in spite of -one's teeth, – oneself; *nolens*

volens &c. (*necessity*) 601; perforce &c. 744; under protest; no &c. 536; not for the world, far be it from me; not if I can help it; if I must I must.

604. Resolution.—N. determination, will; iron –, unconquerable- will; will of one's own, decision, resolution, backbone, grit; strength of -mind, – will; resolve &c. (*intent*) 620; *intransigeance*; firmness &c. (*stability*) 150; energy, manliness, vigour; game, pluck; resoluteness &c. (*courage*) 861; zeal &c. 682; *aplomb*; desperation; devot-ion, -edness.

mastery over self; self-control, -command, -mastery, -possession, -reliance, -government, -restraint, -conquest, -denial; moral -courage, – strength, – fibre; perseverance &c. 604*a*; tenacity; obstinacy &c. 606; bulldog; British lion.

V. have -determination &c. *n.*; know one's own mind; be -resolved &c. *adj.*; make up one's mind, will, resolve, determine; decide &c. (*judgment*) 480; form –, come to- a -determination, – resolution, – resolve; conclude, fix, seal, determine once for all, bring to a crisis, drive matters to an extremity; take a decisive step &c. (*choice*) 609; take upon oneself &c. (*undertake*) 676.

devote oneself –, give oneself up- to; throw away the scabbard, kick down the ladder, nail one's colours to the mast, set one's back against the wall, set one's teeth, put one's foot down, burn one's bridges, take one's stand; stand firm &c. (*stability*) 150; steel oneself; stand no nonsense, not listen to the voice of the charmer.

buckle to; put –, lay –, set- one's shoulder to the wheel; put one's heart into; run the gantlet, make a dash at, take the bull by the horns; beard the lion in his den; rush –, plunge- *in medias res*; go in for; insist upon, make a point of; set one's heart, – mind- upon.

stick at nothing; make short work of &c. (*activity*) 682; not stick at trifles; go -all lengths, – the whole hog; persist &c.

(*persevere*) 604*a*; go down with colours flying, die game; go through fire and water, ride in the whirlwind and direct the storm.

Adj. resolved &c. *v.*; determined; strong-willed, -minded; resolute &c. (*brave*) 861; self-possessed, plucky, tenacious; decided, definitive, peremptory; un-hesitating, -flinching, -shrinking; firm, cast iron, indomitable, game to the backbone; inexorable, relentless, not to be -shaken, – put down; *tenax propositi*; inflexible &c. (*hard*) 323; obstinate &c. 606; steady &c. (*persevering*) 604*a*; unbending, unyielding, irrevocable; firm as a rock; grim.

earnest, serious; set –, bent –, intent-upon.

steeled –, proof- against; *in utrumque paratus*.

Adv. resolutely &c. *adj.*; in –, in good- earnest; seriously, joking apart, earnestly, heart and soul; on one's metal; manfully, like a man, with a high hand; with a strong hand &c. (*exertion*) 686.

at any -rate, – risk, – hazard, – price, – cost, – sacrifice; at all -hazards, – risks, – events; cost what it may; *coûte que coûte*; *à tort et à travers*; once for all; neck or nothing; rain or shine; with colours nailed to the mast.

Phr. *spes sibi quisque.*

604a. Perseverance.—N. perseverance; continuance &c. (*inaction*) 143; permanence &c. (*absence of change*) 141; firmness &c. (*stability*) 150.

constancy, steadiness; singleness –, tenacity- of purpose; persistence, plodding, patience; sedulity &c. (*industry*) 682; pertina-cy, -city, -ciousness; iteration &c. 104.

bottom, game, pluck, stamina, backbone, grit; indefatiga-bility, bleness; bulldog courage.

V. persevere, persist; hold -on, – out; die in the last ditch, be in at the death; stick –, cling –, adhere- to; stick to one's text, keep on; keep to –, maintain- one's -course, – ground; bear –, keep –, hold-up; plod; stick to work &c. (*work*) 686; continue &c. 143; follow up; die -in harness, – at one's post.

Adj. persevering, constant; stead-y, -fast; un-deviating, -wavering, -faltering, -swerving, -flinching, -sleeping, -flagging, -drooping; steady as time; uninter-, unremitting; plodding; industrious &c. 682; strenuous &c. 686; pertinacious; persisting, -ent.

solid, sturdy, staunch, stanch, true to oneself; unchangeable &c. 150; unconquerable &c. (*strong*) 159; indomitable, game to the last, indefatigable, untiring, unwearied, never tiring.

Adv. through -evil report and good report, – thick and thin, – fire and water; *per fas et nefas*; without fail, sink or swim, at any price, *vogue la galère*; in sickness and in health.

Phr. never say die; *vestigia nulla retrorsum.*

605. Irresolution.—N. irresolution, infirmity of purpose, indecision; in-, undetermination, loss of will power; unsettlement; uncertainty &c. 475; demur, suspense; hesi-tating &c. *v.*, -tation, -tancy; vacillation; ambivalence; changeableness &c. 149; fluctuation; alternation &c. (*oscillation*) 314; caprice &c. 608; lukewarmness.

fickleness, levity, *légèreté*; pliancy &c. (*softness*) 324; weakness; timidity &c. 860; cowardice &c. 862; half measures.

waverer, ass between two bundles of hay; shuttlecock, butterfly; timeserver, opportunist, turn coat.

V. be -irresolute &c. *adj.*; hang –, keep- in suspense; leave '*ad referendum*'; think twice about, pause; dawdle &c. (*inactivity*) 683; remain neuter; dilly dally, hesitate, boggle, hover, wobble, shilly-shally, hum and haw, demur, not know one's own mind; debate, balance; dally –, coquet- with; will and will not, *chasser-balancer*; go half-way, compromise, make a compromise; be thrown off one's balance, stagger like a drunken man; be afraid &c. 860;

let 'I dare not' wait upon 'I would'; falter, waver.

vacillate &c. 149; change &c. 140; retract &c. 607; fluctuate; alternate &c. (*oscillate*) 314; keep off and on, play fast and loose; blow hot and cold &c. (*caprice*) 608.

shuffle, palter, blink; trim.

Adj. irresolute, infirm of purpose, double-minded, half-hearted; un-decided, -resolved, -determined; drifting; shilly-shally, fidgety, tremulous; wobbly; hesitating &c. *v.*; off one's balance; at a loss &c. (*uncertain*) 475.

vacillating &c. *v.*; unsteady &c. (*changeable*) 149; unsteadfast, fickle, unreliable, irresponsible, unstable, without ballast; capricious &c. 608; volatile, frothy; light, -some, -minded; giddy; fast and loose.

weak, feeble-minded, frail; timid &c. 860; cowardly &c. 862; facile; pliant &c. (*soft*) 324; unable to say 'no,' easy-going.

revocable, reversible.

Adv. irresolutely &c. *adj.*; irresolvedly; in faltering accents; off and on; from pillar to post; see-saw &c. 314.

Int. 'how happy could I be with either!'

606. Obstinacy.—N. obstinateness &c. *adj.*; obstinacy, tenacity; perseverance &c. 604*a*; immovability; old school; inflexibility &c. (*hardness*) 323; obdur-acy, -ation; dogged resolution; resolution &c. 604; ruling passion; blind side.

self-will, contumacy, perversity; pervica-cy, -city; indocility.

bigotry, intolerance, dogmatism; opinia-try, -tiveness; fixed idea &c.; intractability, incorrigibility; (*prejudgment*) 481; fanaticism, zealotry, infatuation, monomania, opinionativeness.

mule; opin-ionist, -ionatist, -iator, -ator; stickler, dogmatist, die-hard, bitter-ender; bigot; zealot, enthusiast, fanatic.

V. be -obstinate &c. *adj.*; stickle, take no denial, fly in the face of facts; opi-

nionate, be wedded to an opinion, hug a belief; have one's own way &c. (*will*) 600; persist &c. (*persevere*) 604*a*; have -, insist on having- the last word.

die -hard, - fighting, fight -against destiny, - to the last ditch; not yield an inch, stand out.

Adj. obstinate, tenacious, stubborn, obdurate, case-hardened; inflexible &c. (*hard*) 323; immovable, not to be moved; inert &c. 172; unchangeable &c. 150; inexorable &c. (*determined*) 604; mulish, obstinate as a mule, pig-headed.

dogged; sullen, sulky; un-moved, -influenced, -affected.

wilful, self-willed, perverse; res-ty, -tive, -tiff; pervicacious, wayward, refractory, unruly; head-y, -strong; *entêté*; contumacious; cross-grained.

arbitrary, dogmatic, opinionated, positive, bigoted; prejudiced &c. 481; prepossessed, infatuated; stiff-backed, -necked, -hearted; hard-mouthed, hidebound; unyielding; im-pervious, -practicable, -persuasible; unpersuadable; in-, un-tractable; incorrigible, deaf to advice, impervious to reason; crotchety &c. 608.

Adv. obstinately &c. *adj.*

Phr. *non possumus*; no surrender.

607. Tergiversation.—N. change of -mind, - intention, - purpose; afterthought.

tergiversation, recantation; palin- ode, -ody; renunciation; abjur-ation, -ement; defection &c. (*relinquishment*) 624; going over &c. *v.*; apostasy; retract-ion, -ation; withdrawal, disavowal &c. (*negation*) 536; revo-cation, -kement; reversal; repentance &c. 950; *redintegratio amoris*.

coquetry, flirtation; vacillation &c. 605; back-sliding, recidivation.

turn-coat, -tippet; rat, apostate, renegade, mugwump; con-, per-vert; proselyte, deserter; backslider, recidivist; black leg.

time-server, -pleaser; timist, Vicar of Bray, trimmer, ambidexter; weathercock &c. (*changeable*) 149; Janus.

V. change one's -mind, – intention, – purpose, – note; abjure, renounce; withdraw from &c. (*relinquish*) 624; wheel –, turn –, veer- round; turn a *pirouette*; go over –, pass –, change –, skip- from one side to another; go to the right about; box the compass, shift one's ground, go upon another tack; back down, crawl, crawfish.

apostatize, change sides, go over, rat; recant, retract; revoke; rescind &c. (*abrogate*) 756; recall, forswear, abjure, unsay; come -over, – round- to an opinion.

draw in one's horns, eat one's words; eat –, swallow- the leek; swerve, flinch, back out of, retrace one's steps, think better of it; come back –, return- to one's first love; turn over a new leaf &c. (*repent*) 950.

trim, shuffle, play fast and loose, blow hot and cold, coquet, flirt, hold with the hare but run with the hounds; straddle; *nager entre deux eaux*; wait to see how the -cat jumps, – wind blows.

Adj. changeful &c. 149; irresolute &c. 605; ductile, slippery as an eel, trimming, ambidextrous, timeserving; coquetting &c. *v.*

revocatory, reactionary.

Phr. 'a change came o'er the spirit of my dream.'

608. Caprice.—N. caprice, fancy, humour; whim, -sey, -wham; crotchet, *capriccio*, quirk, freak, maggot, fad, vagary, prank, fit, flimflam, *escapade, boutade*, wild-goose chase; capriciousness &c. *adj.*; kink.

V. be -capricious &c. *adj.*; have a maggot in the brain; take it into one's head, strain at a gnat and swallow a camel; blow hot and cold; play -fast and loose, – fantastic tricks.

Adj. capricious; erratic, eccentric, fitful, hysterical; full of -whims &c. *n.*; maggoty; inconsistent, fanciful, fantastic, whimsical, crotchety, particular, humoursome, freakish, skittish, wanton, wayward; contrary; captious; arbitrary; unrestrained, undisciplined; not amenable to reason; uncomfortable &c. 83; penny wise and pound foolish; fickle &c. (*irresolute*) 605; frivolous, sleeveless, giddy, volatile.

Adv. by fits and starts, without rhyme or reason, at one's own sweet will.

Phr. *nil fuit unquam sic impar sibi*; the deuce is in him.

609. Choice.—N. choice, option; discretion &c. (*volition*) 600; preoption; alternative; dilemma; *embarras de choix*; adoption, co-optation; novation; decision &c. (*judgment*) 480.

election, poll, ballot, vote, voice, suffrage, plumper, cumulative vote; *plebiscitum, plébiscite, vox populi; referendum*, electioneering; voting &c. *v.*; franchise; ballot box; slate, ticket.

selection, excerption, gleaning, eclecticism; *excerpta*, gleanings, cuttings, scissors and paste; pick &c. (*best*) 650.

preference, prelation; predilection &c. (*desire*) 865.

V. offer for one's choice, set before; hold out –, present –, ó ffer- the alternative; put to the vote.

use –, exercise –, one's- -discretion, – option; adopt, take up, embrace, espouse; choose, elect, co-opt; take –, make- one's choice; make choice of, fix upon.

vote, poll, hold up one's hand; divide.

settle; decide &c. (*adjudge*) 480; list &c. (*will*) 600; make up one's mind &c. (*resolve*) 604.

select; pick, – and choose; pick –, single- out, excerpt; cull, glean, winnow; sift –, separate –, winnow- the chaff from the wheat; pick up, pitch upon; pick one's way; indulge one's fancy.

set apart, reserve, mark out for; mark &c. 550.

prefer; have -rather, – as lief; fancy &c. (desire) 865; be persuaded &c. 615.

take a -decided, – decisive- step; commit oneself to a course; pass –, cross- the Rubicon; cast in one's lot with; take for better or for worse.

Adj. optional; co-optative; discretional &c. (*voluntary*) 600; on approval.

eclectic; choosing &c. *v.*; preferential; chosen &c. *v.*; choice &c. (*good*) 648.

Adv. optionally &c. *adj.*; at pleasure &c. (*will*) 600; either, – the one or the other; or; at the option of; whether or not; once for all; for one's money.

by -choice, – preference; in preference; rather, before.

609a. Absence of Choice.—N. no –, Hobson's- choice; first come, first served; necessity &c. 601; not a pin to choose &c. (*equality*) 27; any, the first that comes.

neutrality, indifference; indecision &c. (*irresolution*) 605.

V. be -neutral &c. *adj.*; have no choice; waive, not vote; abstain –, refrain- from voting; leave undecided; make a virtue of necessity.

Adj. neu-tral, -ter; indifferent; undecided &c. (*irresolute*) 605.

Adv. either &c. (*choice*) 609.

610. Rejection.—N. rejection, repudiation, exclusion; declination; refusal &c. 764.

V. reject; set –, lay- aside; give up; decline &c. (*refuse*) 764; exclude, except, eliminate; pluck, spin; cast.

repudiate, scout, set at naught; fling –, cast –, thrown –, toss- -to the winds, – to the dogs, – overboard, – away; send to the right about; disclaim &c. (*deny*) 536; discard &c. (*eject*) 297, (*have done with*) 678.

Adj. rejected &c. *v.*; reject-aneous, -itious; not -chosen &c. 609, – to be thought of; out of the question.

Adv. neither, – the one nor the other; no &c. 536.

Phr. *non hæc in fœdera.*

611. Predetermination.—N. premeditation, -deliberation, -determination, -destination; foreordination; foregone conclusion; *parti pris*; resolve, propendency; intention &c. 620; project &c. 626.

V. pre-determine, -destine, -meditate, -resolve, -concert; foreordain; resolve beforehand.

Adj. pre-pense, -meditated &c. *v.*, -designed; advised, studied, designed, calculated; aforethought; intended &c. 620; foregone.

well-laid, -devised, -weighed; maturely considered; cut and dried; cunning.

Adv. advisedly &c. *adj.*; with premeditation, deliberately, all things considered, with eyes open, in cold blood; intentionally &c. 620.

612. Impulse.—N. impulse, sudden thought; *impromptu*, improvisation; inspiration, hunch, flash, spurt.

improvisatore, improvisatrice, improviser, extemporizer; creature of impulse.

V. flash on the mind.

say what comes uppermost; improvise, extemporize; rise to the occasion; spurt.

Adj. extemporaneous, impulsive, indeliberate; improvis-ed, -ate, -atory; un-, unpre-meditated; *improvisé*; unprompted, -guided; natural, unguarded; spontaneous &c. (*voluntary*) 600; instinctive &c. 601.

Adv. extem-pore, -poraneously; offhand, *impromptu, à l'improviste*; improviso; on the spur of the -moment, – occasion.

613. Habit.—N. habit, -ude; assuetude, -faction; wont; run, way.

common –, general –, natural –, ordinary –, habitual- -course, – run, – state- of things; matter of course; beaten -path, – track, – ground.

prescription, custom, use, usage, immemorial usage, practice; tradition; prevalence, observance; conventionalism, -ity; mode, fashion, vogue; *etiquette* &c. (*gentility*) 852; order of the day, cry; conformity &c. 82.

habitué, addict.

one's old way, old school, consuetude, *veteris vestigia flammæ; laudator temporis acti.*

rule, standing order, precedent, routine; red-tape, -tapism; pipe-clay; rut, groove.

cacoëthes; bad –, confirmed –, inveterate –, intrinsic &c. 5- habit; addiction, trick.

training &c. (*education*) 537; seasoning, hardening, inurement; radication; second nature, acclimatization; knack &c. (*skill*) 698.

V. be -wont &c. *adj.*

fall into a custom &c. (*conform to*) 82; tread –, follow- the beaten -track, - path; *stare super antiquas vias*; move in a rut, run on in a groove, go round like a horse in a mill, go on in the old jogtrot way.

habituate, inure, harden, season, caseharden; accustom, familiarize; naturalize, acclimatize; keep one's hand in; train &c. (*educate*) 537.

get into the -way, - knack- of; learn &c. 539; cling –, adhere- to; repeat &c. 104; acquire –, contract –, fall into- a -habit, - trick; addict oneself –, take-to; accustom oneself to.

be -habitual &c. *adj.*; prevail; come into use, become a habit, take root; gain –, grow- upon one.

Adj. habitual; ac-, customary; prescriptive; accustomed &c. *v.*; traditional; of -daily, - every-day- occurrence; wonted, usual, general, ordinary, common, frequent, every-day, household, jog-trot; well-trodden, -known; familiar, vernacular, trite, commonplace, banal, bromidic, conventional, regular, set, stock, officinal, established, stereotyped; pre-vailing, -valent; current, received, acknowledged, recognized, accredited; of course, admitted, understood.

conformable &c. 82; according to - use, - custom –, routine; in -vogue, - fashion; fashionable &c. (*genteel*) 852.

wont; used –, given –, addicted –, attuned –, habituated &c. *v.*- to; in the habit of; *habitué*; at home in &c. (*skilful*) 698; seasoned; permeated –, imbued- with; devoted –, wedded- to; never free from.

hackneyed, fixed, rooted, deep-rooted, ingrafted, permanent, inveterate, besetting; naturalized; ingrained &c.(*intrinsic*) 5.

Adv. habitually &c. *adj.*; always &c. (*uniformly*) 16.

as -usual, - is one's wont, - things go, - the world goes, - the sparks fly upwards; *more -suo*, - *solito*.

as a rule, for the most part; generally &c. *adj.*; most often, - frequently.

Phr. *cela s'entend.*

614. Desuetude.—N. desuetude, disusage; disuse &c. 678; want of -habit, - practice; inusitation; newness to; new brooms.

infraction of usage &c. (*unconformity*) 83; non-prevalence; 'a custom more honoured in the breach than the observance.'

V. be -unaccustomed &c. *adj.*; leave off –, cast off –, break off –, wean oneself of –, violate –, break through –, infringe- a habit, - a custom, - a usage; break one's fetters; disuse &c. 678; wear off.

Adj. un-accustomed, -used, -wonted, -seasoned, -inured, -habituated, -trained; new; green &c. (*unskilled*) 699; fresh, original, unhackneyed.

unusual &c. (*unconformable*) 83; unconventional, non-observant; disused &c. 678.

Adv. just for once.

2°. *Causes of Volition*

615. Motive.—N. motive, springs of action.

reason, ground, call, principle; mainspring, *primum mobile*, key-stone; the why and the wherefore; *pro* and *con*, reason why; secret –, ulterior- motive, *arrière-pensée*; intention &c. 620.

inducement, consideration; attraction &c. 288; loadstone; magnet, -ism, -ic force; allect-ation, -ive; temptation, enticement, *agacerie*, allurement, witchery; bewitch-ment, -ery; charm; spell &c. 993; fascination, blandishment, cajolery; seduc-tion, -ement; honeyed words, voice of the tempter, son of the Sirens; forbidden fruit, golden apple.

persuasi-bility, -bleness; attractability; impress-, suscept-ibility; softness; persuas-, attract-iveness; tantalization.

influence, prompting, dictate, instance; impuls-e, -ion; incit-ement, -ation; press, instigation; provocation &c. (*excitation of feeling*) 824; inspiration; per-, suasion; encouragement, advocacy; exhortation, advice &c. 695; solicitation &c. (*request*) 765; lobbying.

incentive, stimulus, spur, fillip, whip, goad, rowel, provocative, whet, dram.

bribe, lure; decoy, – duck; bait, trail of a red herring; bribery and corruption; sop, – for Cerberus.

prompter, tempter; seduc-er, -tor; suggester, coaxer, wheedler; instigator, firebrand, incendiary; Siren, Circe; *agent provocateur*; lobbyist.

V. induce, move; draw, – on; bring in its train, give an -impulse &c. *n*.- to; inspire; put up to; prompt; call up; attract; beckon.

stimulate &c. (*excite*) 824; spirit up, inspirit; a-, rouse; ecphorize; animate, incite, provoke, instigate, set on, actuate; act –, work –, operate- upon; encourage; pat –, clap- on the -back, – shoulder.

influence, weigh with, bias, sway, incline, dispose, predispose, turn the scale, inoculate; lead, – by the nose; have –, exercise- influence- -with, – over, – upon; go –, come- round one; turn the head, magnetize.

persuade; prevail -with, – upon; overcome, carry; bring -round, – to one's senses; draw –, win –, gain –, come –, talk- over; procure, enlist, engage; invite, court.

tempt, seduce, overpersuade, entice, allure, captivate, fascinate, intrigue, bewitch, carry away, charm, conciliate, wheedle, coax, lure, suggest; inveigle; tantalize; cajole &c. (*deceive*) 545.

tamper with, bribe, suborn, grease the palm, bait with a silver hook, gild the pill, make things pleasant, put a sop into the pan, throw a sop to, bait the hook.

enforce, force; impel &c. (*push*) 276; propel &c. 284; whip, lash, goad, spur, prick, urge; egg –, hound –, hurry- on; drag &c. 285; exhort; advise &c. 695; call upon &c., press &c. (*request*) 765; advocate.

set -an example, – the fashion; keep in countenance; back up.

be -persuaded &c.; yield to temptation, come round; concede &c. (*consent*) 762; obey a call; follow -advice, – the bent, – the dictates of; act on principle.

Adj. impulsive, motive; suas-, persuas-, hortat-ive, -ory; protreptical; inviting, tempting &c. *v*.; seductive, attractive, irresistible; fascinating &c. (*pleasing*) 829; provocative &c. (*exciting*) 824.

induced &c. *v*.; disposed; persuadable &c. (*docile*) 602; spellbound; instinct –, smitten- with; inspired &c. *v*.-by.

Adv. because, therefore &c. (*cause*) 155; from -this, – that- motive; for -this, – that- reason; for; by reason –, for the sake –, on the score –, on account- of; out of, from, as, forasmuch as.

for all the world; on principle.

615a. Absence of Motive.—N. absence of motive; caprice &c. 608; chance &c. (*absence of design*) 621.

V. have no motive; scruple &c. (*be unwilling*) 603.

Adj. without rhyme or reason; aimless &c. (*chance*) 621.

Adv. capriciously; out of mere caprice.

616. Dissuasion.—N. dissuasion, dehortation, expostulation, remonstrance; deprecation &c. 766.

discouragement, damper, wet blanket; warning.

cohibition &c. (*restraint*) 751; curb &c. (*means of restraint*) 752; check &c. (*hindrance*) 706.

reluctance &c. (*unwillingness*) 603; contraindication.

V. dissuade, dehort, cry out against, remonstrate, expostulate, warn, contra-indicate.

disincline, indispose, shake, stagger; dispirit; dis-courage, -hearten, -enchant; deter; hold -, keep- back &c. (*restrain*) 751; render -averse &c. 603; repel; turn aside &c. (*deviation*) 279; wean from; act as a drag &c. (*hinder*) 706; throw cold water on, damp, cool, chill, blunt, calm, quiet, quench; deprecate &c. 766.

Adj. dissuading &c. *v.*; dissuasive; dehortatory, expostulatory; monit-ive, -ory.

dissuaded &c. *v.*; uninduced &c. (induce &c. 615); unpersuadable &c. (*obstinate*) 606; averse &c. (*unwilling*) 603; repugnant &c. (*dislike*) 867.

617. [Ostensible motive, ground, or reason assigned.] **Plea.—N.** plea, pretext; allegation, advocation; ostensible -motive, - ground, - reason; excuse &c. (*vindication*) 937; colour; gloss, guise.

loop-, starting-hole; how to creep out of, salvo, come off.

handle, peg to hang on, room, *locus standi*; stalking-horse, *cheval de bataille*, cue.

pretence &c. (*untruth*) 546; put off, subterfuge, dust thrown in the eyes; blind; moonshine; mere -, shallow- pretext; lame -excuse, - apology; tub to a whale; false plea, sour grapes; makeshift, shift, white lie; special pleading &c. (*sophistry*) 477; soft sawder &c. (*flattery*) 933.

V. plead, allege; shelter oneself under the plea of; excuse &c. (*vindicate*) 937; gloss over; lend a colour to; furnish a -handle &c. *n.*; make a -pretext, - handle- of; use as a plea &c. *n.*; take one's stand upon, make capital out of; pretend &c. (*lie*) 544.

Adj. ostensible &c. (*manifest*) 525; excusing; alleged, apologetic; pretended &c. 545.

Adv. ostensibly; under -colour, - the plea, - the pretence- of.

3°. Objects of Volition

618. Good.—N. good, benefit, advantage; improvement &c. 658; interest, service, behoof, behalf; weal; main chance, *summum bonum*, common weal; 'consummation devoutly to be wished'; gain, boot; profit, harvest.

boon &c. (*gift*) 784; good turn; blessing, benison; world of good; piece of good -luck, - fortune; nuts, prize, windfall, godsend, waif, treasure trove.

good fortune &c. (*prosperity*) 734; happiness &c. 827.

[Source of good] goodness &c. 648; utility &c. 644; remedy &c. 662; pleasure-giving &c. 829.

Adj. commendable &c. 931; useful &c. 644; good &c., beneficial &c. 648.

V. benefit, profit, advantage, serve, help, avail; do good to, gain, prosper, flourish.

Adv. well, aright, satisfactorily, favourably, not amiss; all for the best; to one's -advantage &c. *n.*; in one's -favour, - interest &c. *n.*

Phr. so far so good.

619. Evil.—N. evil, ill, harm, hurt, mischief, nuisance; machinations of the devil, Pandora's box, ills that flesh is heir to.

blow, buffet, stroke, scratch, bruise, wound, gash, mutilation; mortal -blow, - wound; *immedicabile vulnus*; damage, loss &c. (*deterioration*) 659.

disadvantage, prejudice, drawback.

disaster, accident, casualty; mishap &c. (*misfortune*) 735; bad job, devil to pay; calamity, bale, woe, catastrophe, tragedy; ruin &c. (*destruction*) 162; adversity &c. 735.

mental suffering &c. 828. [Evil spirit] demon &c. 980. [Cause of evil] bane &c. 663. [Production of evil] badness &c. 649; painfulness &c. 830; evil doer &c. 913.

outrage, wrong, injury, foul play; bad -, ill- turn; disserve; spoliation &c. 791; grievance, crying evil.

V. be in trouble &c. (*adversity*) 735; harm, injure, hurt, do disservice to.

Adj. disastrous, bad &c. 649; awry, out of joint; disadvantageous, injurious, harmful.

Adv. amiss, wrong, ill, to one's cost.

Section II. PROSPECTIVE VOLITION*

1°. *Conceptional Volition*

620. Intention.—N. intent, -ion, -ionality; purpose; *quo animo*; project &c. 626; undertaking &c. 676; predetermination &c. 611; design, ambition.

contemplation, mind, *animus*, view, purview, proposal; study; look out.

final cause; *raison d'être*; *cui bono*; object, aim, end; 'the be all and the end all'; drift &c. (*meaning*) 516; tendency &c. 176; destination, mark, point, butt, goal, target, bull's-eye, quintain; prey; quarry, game.

decision, determination, resolve; set -, settled- purpose; *ultimatum*; resolution &c. 604; wish &c. 865; *arrière-pensée*; motive &c. 615.

[Study of final causes] teleology.

V. intend, purpose, design, mean; have to; propose to oneself; harbour a design; have in -view, - contemplation, - one's eye, - *petto*; have an eye to.

bid -, labour- for; be -, aspire -, endeavour- after; be -, aim -, drive -, point -, level - at; take aim; set before oneself; study to.

take upon oneself &c. (*undertake*) 676; take into one's head; meditate, contemplate; think -, dream -, talk-of; premeditate &c. 611; compass, calculate; dest-ine, -inate; propose.

project &c. (*plan*) 626; have a mind to &c. (*be willing*) 602; desire &c. 865; pursue &c. 622.

Adj. intended &c. *v.*; intentional, advised, express, determinate; prepense

* That is, volition having reference to a future object.

&c. 611; bound for; intending &c. *v.*; minded, disposed, inclined; bent upon &c. (*earnest*) 604; at stake, on the -anvil, - *tapis*; in -view; - prospect, - the breast of; *in petto*; teleological.

Adv. intentionally &c. *adj.*; advisedly, wittingly, knowingly, designedly, purposely, on purpose, by design, studiously, pointedly; with -intent &c. *n.*; deliberately &c. (*with premeditation*) 611; with one's eyes open, in cold blood.

for; with -a view, - an eye- to; in order -to, - that; to the end -, with the intent- that; for the purpose -, with the view -, in contemplation -, on account- of.

in pursuance of, pursuant to; *quo animo*; to all intents and purposes.

621. [Absence of purpose in the succession of events.] **Chance.†—N.** chance &c. 156; lot, fate &c. (*necessity*) 601; luck; good luck &c. (*good*) 618; bad luck &c. 735; wheel of fortune; mascot; swastika.

speculation, venture, stake, flutter, flier, gamble, game of chance; mere -, random- shot; blind bargain, leap in the dark; pig in a poke &c. (*uncertainty*) 475; fluke, pot-luck.

drawing lots; sorti-legy, -tion; *sortes, - Virgilianæ*; *rouge et noir*, hazard, *roulette*, pitch and toss, chuck-farthing, cup-tossing, heads or tails, cross and pile, wager; bet, -ting; risk, stake, plunge; gambling; the turf.

stock exchange, bourse, board of trade, curb exchange.

gaming-, gambling-, betting-house; hell; betting ring; totalisator; dice, - box; dicer; gam-bler, -ester, plunger, stock operator, manipulator, punter; man of the turf; adventurer, speculator; bookmaker, layer, backer.

V. chance &c. (*hap*) 156; stand a chance &c. (*be possible*) 470.

toss up; cast -, draw- lots; leave -, trust- -to chance, - to the chapter of accidents; tempt fortune; chance it, take

† See note on 156.

one's chance; run -, incur -, encounter-
the -risk, - chance; stand the hazard of
the die.

speculate, try one's luck, set on a cast,
raffle, put into a lottery, buy a pig in a
poke, shuffle the cards.

risk, venture, hazard, stake; lay, - a
wager; make a bet, wager, bet, gamble,
game, play for; play at chuck-farthing.

Adj. fortuitous &c. 156; unintentional, -ded; accidental; not meant; undesigned, -purposed; unpremeditated
&c. 612; never thought of.

indiscriminate, promiscuous; undirected, random; aim-, drift-, design-,
purpose-, cause-less; without purpose.

possible &c. 470.

Adv. casually &c. 156; unintention-
ally &c. *adj.*; unwittingly.

en passant, by the way, incidentally;
as it may happen; at -random, - a venture, - haphazard; as luck would have
it, by -chance, - good fortune; un-, -
luckily.

622. [Purpose in action.] **Pursuit.—**
N. pursuit; pursuing &c. *v.*; prosecution; pursuance; enterprise &c. (*undertaking*) 676; business &c. 625; adventure &c. (*essay*) 675; quest &c. (*search*)
461; scramble, hue and cry, game; hobby.

chase, hunt, *battue*, race, steeplechase,
hunting, coursing; ven-ation, -ery; fox-
chase; sport, -ing; shooting, angling,
fishing, hawking.

pursuer; hunt-er, -sman; sportsman,
Nimrod, the field; hound &c. 366.

V. pursue, prosecute, follow; run -,
make -, be -, hunt -, prowl- after; shadow; carry on &c. (*do*) 680; engage in
&c. (*undertake*) 676; set about &c. (*begin*) 66; endeavour &c. 675; court &c.
(*request*) 765; seek &c. (*search*) 461;
aim at &c. (*intention*) 620; follow the
trail &c. (*trace*) 461; fish for &c. (*experiment*) 463; press on &c. (*haste*) 684;
run a race &c. (*velocity*) 274.

chase, give chase, course, dog, hunt,
hound, stalk; tread -, follow- on the
heels of &c. (*sequence*) 281.

rush upon; rush headlong &c. (*violence*) 173; ride -, run- full tilt at; make
a leap -, jump -, snatch- at; run down;
start game.

tread a path; take -, hold- a course;
shape -, direct -, bend- one's -steps, -
course; play a game; fight -, elbow-
one's way; follow up; take -to, - up; go
in for; ride one's hobby.

Adj. pursuing &c. *v.*; in quest of &c.
(*inquiry*) 461; in -pursuit, - full cry, -
hot pursuit; on the scent.

Adv. in pursuance of &c. (*intention*)
620; after.

Int. tally-ho! yoicks! so-ho!

623. [Absence of pursuit.] **Avoidance.—N.** abst-ention, -inence; forbearance; refraining &c. *v.*; inaction &c.
681; neutrality.

avoidance, evasion, elusion; seclusion
&c. 893.

avolation, flight; escape &c. 671; retreat &c. 287; recoil &c. 277; departure
&c. 293; rejection &c. 610.

shirker &c. *v.*; slacker; truant; fugitive, refugee; runa-way, -gate; renegade; deserter.

V. abstain, refrain, spare, not attempt; not do &c. 681; maintain the even
tenor of one's way.

eschew, keep from, let alone, have
nothing to do with; keep -, stand -,
hold- -aloof, - off; take no part in, have
no hand in.

avoid, shun; steer -, keep- clear of;
fight shy of; keep -one's, - at a respect-
ful- distance; keep -, get- out of the way;
evade, elude, turn away from; set one's
face against &c. (*oppose*) 708; deny
oneself.

shrink; hang -, hold -, draw- back;
recoil &c. 277; retire &c. (*recede*) 287;
flinch, blink, blench, shy, shirk, dodge,
parry, make way for, give place to.

beat a retreat; turn -tail, - one's back;
take to one's heels; run, -away, - for
one's life; cut and run; be off, - like a
shot; fly, flee; fly -, flee -, run away-
from; take -, take to- flight; desert,
elope; make -, scamper -, sneak -,

shuffle –, sheer- off; break –, burst –, tear oneself –, slip –, slink –, steal- -away, – away from; slip cable, part company, turn on one's heel; sneak out of, play truant, give one the go by, give leg bail, take French leave, slope, decamp, flit, bolt, abscond, levant, skedaddle, absquatulate, cut one's stick, walk one's chalks, show a light pair of heels, make oneself scarce; escape &c. 671; go away &c. (*depart*) 293; abandon &c. 624; reject &c. 610.

lead one a -dance, – a merry chase, – pretty dance; throw off the scent, play at hide and seek.

Adj. unsought, unattempted; avoiding &c. *v.*; neutral; shy of &c. (*unwilling*) 603; elusive, evasive, distant; fugitive, runaway; shy, wild.

Adj. lest, in order to avoid.

Int. forbear! keep –, hands- off! *sauve qui peut!* devil take the hindmost!

624. Relinquishment.—N. relinquish-, abandon-ment; desertion, defection, secession, withdrawal; cave of Adullam; *nolle prosequi.*

discontinuance &c. (*cessation*) 142; renunciation &c. (*recantation*) 607; abrogation &c. 756; resignation &c. (*retirement*) 757; desuetude &c. 614; cession &c. (*of property*) 782.

V. relinquish, give up, abandon, desert, forsake, leave in the lurch; depart – secede –, withdraw- from; back – out of, – down from, leave, go back on one's word, quit, take leave of, bid a long farewell; vacate &c. (*resign*) 757.

renounce &c. (*abjure*) 607; forego, have done with, drop; write off; disuse &c. 678; discard &c. 782; wash one's hands of; drop all idea of; *nolle-pros.*; lose interest in.

break –, leave- off; desist; stop &c. (*cease*) 142; hold –, stay- one's hand; quit one's hold; give over, shut up shop.

throw up the -game, – cards; give up the -point, – argument; pass to the order of the day, move the previous question, table the motion.

Adj. unpursued; relinquished &c. *v.*; relinquishing &c.*v.*

Int. avast &c. ! (*stop*) 142.

625. Business.—N. business, occupation, employment; pursuit &c. 622; what one is doing-, – about; affair, concern, matter, case, undertaking.

matter in hand, irons in the fire; thing to do, *agendum*, task, work, job, chore, errand, transaction, commission, mission, charge, care; duty &c. 926.

part, *rôle*, cue; province, function, look-out, department, capacity, sphere, orb, field, line; walk, – of life; beat, round, routine; race, career.

office, place, post, incumbency, living; situation, appointment, billet, berth, employ; service &c. (*servitude*) 749; engagement; undertaking &c. 676.

vocation, calling, profession, *métier*, cloth, faculty; industry, art; industrial arts; craft, mystery, handicraft; trade &c. (*commerce*) 794.

exercise; work &c. (*action*) 680; avocation; press of business &c. (*activity*) 682.

V. pass –, employ –, spend- one's time in; employ oneself -in, – upon; occupy –, concern- oneself with; make it one's -business &c. *n.*; undertake &c. 676; enter a profession; betake oneself to, turn one's hand to; have to do with &c. (*do*) 680.

drive a trade; carry on –, do –, transact- -business, – a trade &c. *n.*; keep a shop; ply one's task, – trade; labour in one's vocation; pursue the even tenor of one's way; attend to -business, – one's work.

officiate, serve, act; act –, play- one's part; do duty; serve –, discharge –, perform- the -office, – duties, – functions-of; hold –, fill- -an office, – a place, – a situation; hold a portfolio.

be -about, – doing, – engaged in, – employed in, – occupied with, – at work on; have one's hands in, have in hand; have on one's -hands, – shoulders; bear the burden; have one's hands full &c. (*activity*) 682.

be -in the hands of, - on the stocks, - on the anvil; pass through one's hands.

Adj. business-like; work-a-day; professional; official, functional; busy &c. (*actively employed*) 682; on -, in- -hand, - one's hands; afoot; on -foot, - the anvil; going on; acting.

Adv. in the course of business, all in a day's work; professionally &c. *adj.*

626. Plan.—N. plan, scheme, design, project; propos-al, -ition; suggestion; resolution, motion; precaution &c. (*provision*) 673; deep-laid &c. (*premeditated*) 611- plan &c.; racket.

system &c. (*order*) 58; organization &c. (*arrangement*) 60; germ &c. (*cause*) 153; Five Year Plan.

sketch, skeleton, outline, draught, draft, *ébauche, brouillon*; rough -cast, - draft, - draught, - copy; copy; proof, revise.

forecast, *programme*, prospectus, scenario; *carte du pays*; card; bill, protocol; order of the day, list of agenda, *memorandum*; bill of fare &c. (*food*) 298; base of operations; platform, plank.

rôle; policy &c. (*line of conduct*) 692.

contrivance, invention, expedient, receipt, nostrum, artifice, device, gadget; stratagem &c. (*cunning*) 702; trick &c. (*deception*) 545; alternative, loophole, shift &c. (*substitute*) 147; last shift &c. (*necessity*) 601.

measure, step; stroke, - of policy; master stroke; trump-, court-card; *cheval de bataille*, great gun; *coup, - d'état*; clever -, bold -, good- -move, - hit, - stroke; bright -thought, - idea, great idea.

intrigue, cabal, plot, frame-up, conspiracy, complot, machination; under-, counter-plot.

schem-ist, -atist; strategist, machinator, schemer; projector, author, builder, artist, promoter, designer &c. *v.*; conspirator; *intrigant* &c. (*cunning*) 702.

V. plan, scheme, design, frame, contrive, project, forecast, sketch; conceive, devise, invent &c. (*imagine*) 515; set one's wits to work &c. 515; spring a project; fall -, hit- upon; strike -, chalk -, cut -, lay -, map-out; lay down a plan; shape -, mark- out a course; predetermine &c. 611; concert, preconcert, preestablish; prepare &c. 673; hatch, - a plot; concoct; take -steps, - measures.

cast, recast, systematize, organize; arrange &c. 60; digest, mature.

plot; counter-plot, -mine; dig a mine; lay a train; intrigue &c. (*cunning*) 702.

Adj. planned &c. *v.*; strategic, -al; planning &c. *v.*; in course of preparation &c. 673; under consideration; on the -*tapis*, - carpet, - table.

627. Method. [Path.]—N. method, way, manner, wise, gait, form, mole, fashion, tone, guise; *modus operandi*; procedure &c. (*line of conduct*) 692.

path, road, route, course; line of -way, - road; trajectory, orbit, track, beat, tack.

steps; stair, -case; flight of stairs, ladder, stile.

bridge, viaduct, gauntry, pontoon, stepping stone, plank, gangway, catwalk, drawbridge; pass, ford, ferry, tunnel, subway, elevated; pipe &c. 260.

door; gateway &c. (*opening*) 260; channel, passage, avenue, means of access, approach, perron, adit, entrance; artery, lane, alley, aisle, lobby, corridor, cloister; back- door, -stairs; secret passage; covert-way.

road-, path-, stair-way; thoroughfare; highway, pike, turnpike, trail, parkway, *boulevard*; turnpike -, royal -, coachroad; broad -, King's -, Queen's- highway; beaten -track. - path; horse -, bridle- road, - track, - path; pathway; walk, *trottoir*, foot-path, pavement, flags, side-walk; by -, cross- -road, - path, - way; cut; short -cut &c. (*midcourse*) 628; *carrefour*; private -, occupation- road; highways and byways; rail-, tram-road, -way; funicular, ropeway, causeway; defile, cutting; canal &c. (*conduit*) 350; street &c. (*abode*) 189.

Adv. how; in what -way, - manner; by what mode; so, in this way, after this fashion, on these lines.

one way or another, anyhow; somehow or other &c. (*instrumentality*) 631; by way of; *viâ; in transitu* &c. 270; on the high road to.

Phr. *hæ tibi erunt artes.*

628. Mid-course.—N. middle-, mid-course; moderation, mean &c. 29; middle &c. 68; *juste milieu, mezzo termine,* golden mean, *aurea mediocritas.*

straight &c. (*direct*) 278 -course, – path; short –, cross- cut; short-circuit; great circle sailing.

neutrality; half –, half and half-measures; compromise.

V. keep in –, steer –, preserve- -a middle, – an even- course; go straight &c. (*direct*) 278.

go half way, compromise, make a compromise.

Adj. neutral, average, even, impartial, moderate, straight &c. (*direct*) 278.

629. Circuit.—N. circuit, roundabout way, digression, divagation, *détour,* circum-ambience, -ambulation, bendibus, *ambages,* loop; winding &c. (*circuition*) 311; zigzag &c. (*deviation*) 279.

V. perform –, make- a circuit; go - round about, – out of one's way; make a *détour;* meander &c. (*deviate*) 27; circumambulate.

lead a pretty dance; beat about, – the bush; make two bites of a cherry.

Adj. circuitous, indirect, roundabout; zig-zag &c. (*deviating*) 279; circum-ambient, -ambulatory.

Adv. by -a side wind, – an indirect course; in a roundabout way; from pillar to post.

630. Requirement.—N. requirement, need, wants, necessities; necessaries, – of life; stress, exigency, pinch, *sine quâ non,* matter of necessity; case of -need, – life or death.

needfulness, essentiality, necessity, indispensability, urgency, prerequisite.

requisition &c. (*request*) 765, (*exaction*) 741; run upon; demand –, call- for.

desideratum &c. (*desire*) 865; want &c. (*deficiency*) 640.

charge, claim, command, injunction, requisition, mandate, order, *ultimatum.*

V. require, need, want, have occasion for, entail; not be able to -do without, – dispense with; prerequire.

render necessary, necessitate, create a necessity for, call for, put in requisition; make a requisition &c. (*ask for*) 765, (*demand*) 741.

stand in need of; lack &c. 640; desiderate; desire &c. 865; be -necessary &c. *adj.*

Adj. required &c. *v.*; requisite, needful, necessary, imperative, essential, indispensable, prerequisite; called for; in -demand, – request.

urgent, exigent, pressing, instant, crying, absorbing.

in want of; destitute of &c. 640.

Adv. *ex necessitate rei* &c. (*necessarily*) 601; of –, out of stern- necessity; at a pinch.

Phr. there is no time to lose; it cannot be -spared, – dispensed with.

2° Subservience to Ends

1. *Actual Subservience*

631. Instrumentality.—N. instrumentality; aid &c. 707; subservien-ce, -cy; mediation, inter-vention, -mediacy, medium, inter-medium, -mediary, vehicle, hand; agency &c. 170.

minister, handmaid, servant, slave, maid, valet; midwife, *accoucheur,* obstetrician; go-between; cat's paw; stepping-stone.

key; master –, pass –, latch- key; 'open sesame'; passport, *passe partout,* safe-conduct; influence.

instrument &c. 633; expedient &c. (*plan*) 626; means &c. 632.

V. subserve, minister, tend, mediate, intervene; come –, go- between, interpose; pull the strings; be -instrumental &c. *adj.*; pander to.

Adj. instrumental; useful &c. 644; ministerial, subservient, mediatorial; inter-mediate, -vening; conducive.

Adv. through, by, *per;* where-, there-,

here-by; by the -agency &c. 170- of; by dint of; by –, in- virtue of; through the -medium &c. *n.*- of; along with; on the shoulders of; by means of &c. 632; by –, with- -the aid &c. (*assistance*) 707- of.

per fas et nefas, by fair means or foul; somehow, – or other; by hook or by crook.

632. Means.—N. means, resources, revenue, wherewithal, ways and means, income; capital &c. (*money*) 800; stock in trade &c. 636; provision &c. 637; a shot in the locker; appliances &c. (*machinery*) 633; means and appliances; conveniences; cards to play; expedients &c. (*measures*) 626; two strings to one's bow; sheet anchor &c. (*safety*) 666; aid &c. 707; medium &c. 631.

V. find –, have –, possess- means &c. *n.*; provide the wherewithal.

Adj. instrumental &c. 631; mechanical &c. 633.

Adv. by means of, with; by -what, – all, – any, – some- means; where-, here-, there-with; wherewithal.

how &c. (*in what manner*) 627; through &c. (*by the instrumentality of*) 631; with –, by- the aid &c. (*assistance*) 707- of; by the -agency &c. 170- of.

633. Instrument.—N. machinery, mechanism, engineering.

instrument, organ, tool, implement, utensil, contrivance, machine, motor, engine, lathe, gin, mill, pump.

gear; tack-le, -ling, trice, rigging, gear, apparatus, appliances; plant, *matériel*; harness, trappings, fittings, accoutrements; equip-ment, -age; appointments, furniture, upholstery; chattels; paraphernalia &c. (*belongings*) 780; *impedimenta*.

mechanical powers; lever, -age; mechanical advantage; crow, -bar; hand-spike, gavelock, jemmy, arm, limb, wing; oar, paddle; pulley, sheave; parbuckle; wheel and axle; wheel-, clock-work; wheels within wheels; pinion, gear wheel, spur –, bevel- gearing, chains, belting, crank, winch, capstan, wind-

lass, crane, derrick, hoist, life &c. 307; cam; pedal; wheel &c. (*rotation*) 312; inclined plane; wedge; screw; jack; spring, mainspring.

handle, hilt, haft, shaft, heft, shank, blade, trigger, tiller, helm, treadle, key; turnscrew, screwdriver, spanner, wrench.

hammer &c. (*impulse*) 276; edge tool &c. (*cut*) 253; borer &c. 262; vice, teeth &c. (*hold*) 781; nail, rope &c. (*join*) 45; peg &c. (*hang*) 214; support &c. 215; spoon &c. (*vehicle*) 272; arms &c. 727; oar &c. (*navigation*) 267.

Adj. instrumental &c. 631; mechanical, machinal, automatic, self-acting; brachial.

634. Substitute.—N. substitute &c. 147; deputy &c. 759; proxy, alternative, understudy.

635. Materials.—N. material, raw material, stuff, stock, staple; building materials, bricks and mortar; metal; stone; clay, brick; crockery &c. 384; compo, -sition; reinforced –, ferro-, concrete; cement; wood, ore, timber; gravel, cobbles, macadam, asphalt, tarmac.

materials; supplies, munition, fuel, grist, household stuff; *pabulum* &c. (*food*) 298; ammunition &c. (*arms*) 727; contingents; relay, reinforcement; baggage &c. (*personal property*) 780; means &c. 632.

Adj. raw &c. (*unprepared*) 674; wooden &c. *n.*

636. Store.—N. stock, fund, mine, vein, lode, quarry; spring; fount, -ain; well, -spring; milch-cow.

stock in trade, supply; heap &c. (*collection*) 72; treasure; reserve, *corps de réserve*, reserve fund, nest-egg, savings, *bonne bouche*.

crop, harvest, mow, vintage; yield, product, gleanings.

store, accumulation, hoard, rick, stack; lumber; relay &c. (*provision*) 637.

store-house, -room, -closet; depository, *dépôt*, *cache*, safe deposit, vault, pantechnicon, re-pository, -servatory, -pertory; *repertorium*; promptuary, warehouse, *entrepôt*, magazine, dump, buttery, larder, pantry, panary, lanary, still-room, spence; crib, garner, granary, silo, barn; bunker; thesaurus; bank &c. (*treasury*) 802; armoury; arsenal; dock; gallery, musuem, library, conservatory, hot-house; menag-ery, -erie, aquarium, zoological gardens.

reservoir, cistern, tank, sump, pond, mill-pond; gasometer.

budget, quiver, bandolier, portfolio; coffer &c. (*receptacle*) 191.

conservation; storing &c. *v.*; storage.

dictionary &c. 562; list &c. 86.

V. store; put -, lay -, set- by; stow away; set -, lay- apart; store -, hoard -, treasure -, lay -, heap -, put -, garner -, save- up; *cache*; accumulate, amass, hoard, fund, garner, save, bank.

conserve, reserve; keep -, hold- back; husband, - one's resources.

deposit; stow, stack, load, dump; harvest; heap, collect &c. 72; lay -in, - down, - by, store &c. *adj.*; keep, file [papers]; lay in &c. (*provide*) 637; preserve &c. 670; put by for a rainy day.

Adj. stored &c. *v.*; in -store, - reserve, - ordinary; spare, supernumerary.

637. Provision.—N. provision, supply; grist, - to the mill; subvention &c. (*aid*) 707; resources &c. (*means*) 632.

providing &c. *v.*; purveyance; reinforcement; commissary, commissariat.

rations; iron -, emergency- rations; provender &c. (*food*) 298; *viaticum*; ensilage.

caterer, purveyor, commissary, quartermaster, steward, housekeeper, manciple, feeder, batman, victualler, storekeeper, grocer, provision merchant, green-, grocer, *comprador*, *restaurateur*; sutler &c. (*merchant*) 797; innkeeper, publican, confectioner, baker, butcher, wine merchant, vintner.

V. provide; make -provision, - due provision for; lay in, - a stock, - a store.

sup-ply, -peditate; furnish; find, - one in; arm.

cater, victual, provision, purvey, forage; beat up for; stock, - with; make good, replenish; fill, - up; recruit, feed, ration.

have in -store, - reserve; keep, - by one, - on foot; have to fall back upon; store &c. 636; provide against a rainy day &c. (*economy*) 817.

638. Waste.—N. consumption, expenditure, exhaustion; dispersion &c. 73; ebb; leakage &c. (*exudation*) 295; loss &c. 776; wear and tear; waste; prodigality &c. 818; misuse &c. 679; wasting &c. *v.*; rubbish &c. (*useless*) 645.

mountain in labour.

V. spend, expend, use, consume, swallow up, exhaust, deplete; impoverish; spill, drain, empty; disperse &c. 73.

cast -, throw -, fling -, fritter- away; burn the candle at both ends, waste; squander &c. 818.

'waste its sweetness on the desert air'; cast -one's bread upon the waters, - pearls before swine; employ a steam engine to crack a nut, waste powder and shot, break a butterfly on a wheel; labour in vain &c. (*useless*) 645; cut a whetstone with a razor, pour water into a sieve; tilt at windmills.

leak &c. (*run out*) 295; run to waste; ebb; melt away, run dry, dry up.

Adj. wasted &c. *v.*; at a low ebb.

wasteful &c. (*prodigal*) 818; penny wise and pound foolish.

Phr. *magno conatu magnas nugas*; *le jeu n'en vaut pas la chandelle.*

639. Sufficiency.—N. sufficiency, adequacy, enough, withal, *quantum sufficit*, satisfaction, competence; no less.

mediocrity &c. (*average*) 29.

fill; fulness &c. (*completeness*) 52; plen-itude, -ty; abundance; copiousness &c. *adj.*; amplitude, galore, lots, profusion; full measure; 'good measure pressed down, shaken together and running over.'

luxuriance &c. (*fertility*) 168;

affluence &c. (*wealth*) 803; fat of the land; 'a land flowing with milk and honey'; cornucopia; horn of -plenty, - Amalthæa; mine &c. (*stock*) 636.

outpouring; flood &c. (*great quantity*) 31; tide &c. (*river*) 348; repletion &c. (*redundance*) 641; satiety &c. 869; rich man &c. 803.

V. be -sufficient &c. *adj.*; suffice, do, just do, satisfy, pass muster; have - enough &c. *n.*; eat -, drink -, have-one's fill; roll -, swim- in; wallow in &c. (*superabundance*) 641.

abound, exuberate, teem, flow, stream, rain, shower down; pour, - in; swarm; bristle with.

render -sufficient &c. *adj.*; replenish &c. (*fill*) 52.

Adj. sufficient, enough, adequate, up to the mark, commensurate, competent, satisfactory, valid, tangible.

measured; moderate &c. (*temperate*) 953.

full &c. (*complete*) 52; ample; plenty, -tiful, -teous; plenty as blackberries; copious, abundant; abounding &c. *v.*; replete, enough and to spare, flush; choke-full; well-stocked, -provided; liberal; unstint-ed, -ing; stintless; without stint; un-sparing, -measured; lavish &c. 641; wholesale.

rich; luxuriant &c. (*fertile*) 168; affluent &c. (*wealthy*) 803; wantless; big with &c. (*pregnant*) 161.

un-exhausted, -wasted; exhaustless, inexhaustible.

Adv. sufficiently, amply &c. *adj.*; full; in -abundance &c. *n.*; with no sparing hand; to one's heart's content, *ad libitum*, without stint.

Phr. cut and come again.

640. Insufficiency.—N. insufficiency; inadequa-cy, -teness; incompetence &c. (*impotence*) 158; deficiency &c. (*incompleteness*) 53; imperfection &c. 651; shortcoming &c. 304; paucity; stint; scantiness &c. (*smallness*) 32; none to spare; bare subsistence.

scarcity, dearth; want, need, lack,

poverty, exigency; inanition, starvation, famine, drought.

dole, pittance, mite; short -allowance, - commons; half-rations; banyan -, fast-day, Lent.

emptiness, poorness &c. *adj.*; depletion, vacancy, flaccidity; ebb-tide; low water; 'a beggarly account of empty boxes'; indigence &c. (*poverty*) 804; insolvency &c. (*non-payment*) 808; poor man &c. 804; bankrupt &c. 808.

V. be -insufficient &c. *adj.*; not -suffice &c. 639; come short of &c. 304; run dry.

want, lack, need, require; *caret*; be in want &c. (*poor*) 804; live from hand to mouth.

render- insufficient &c. *adj.*; drain of resources; impoverish &c. (*waste*) 638; stint &c. (*begrudge*) 819; put on short -commons, - allowance.

do -insufficiently &c. *adv.*; scotch the snake.

Adj. insufficient, inadequate; too -little &c. 32; not -enough &c. 639; unequal to; incompetent &c. (*impotent*) 158; 'weighed in the balance and found wanting'; perfunctory &c. (*neglect*) 460; deficient &c. (*incomplete*) 53; wanting &c. *v.*; imperfect &c. 651; ill-furnished, -provided, -stored, -off.

slack, at a low ebb; empty, vacant, bare; short -, out -, destitute -, devoid -, bereft &c. 789 -, denuded- of; dry, drained.

un -provided, -supplied, -furnished; un-replenished, -fed; un-stored, -treasured; empty-handed.

meagre, poor, thin, scrimp, sparing, spare, stinted, stunted; skimpy; starv-ed, -eling; half-starved, emaciated, famine-stricken, famished, underfed, undernourished; jejune.

scant &c. (*small*) 32; scarce; not to be had, - for love or money, - at any price; scurvy; stingy &c. 819; at the end of one's tether; without -resources &c. 632; in want &c. (*poor*) 804; in debt &c. 806.

Adv. insufficiently &c. *adj.*; in default -, for want- of; failing.

641. Redundance.—N. redundance; too -much, - many; superabundance, -fluity, -fluence; -saturation; nimiety, transcendency, exuberance, profuseness; profusion &c. (*plenty*) 639; repletion, enough in all conscience, *satis superque*, lion's share; more than -enough &c. 639; plethora, engorgement, congestion, load, surfeit, sickener; turgescence &c. (*expansion*) 194; over-dose, -measure, -supply, -flow; inundation &c. (*water*) 348; *avalanche*.

accumulation &c. (*store*) 636; heap &c. 72; drug, - in the market; glut; crowd; burden.

excess; sur-, over-plus, epact; margin; remainder &c. 40; duplicate; surplusage, expletive; work of -, supererogation; *bonus*, *bonanza*.

luxury; intemperance &c. 954; extravagance &c. (*prodigality*) 818; exorbitance, lavishment.

pleonasm &c. (*diffuseness*) 573; too many irons in the fire; embarrassment of riches; money to burn.

V. super-, over-abound; know no bounds, swarm; meet one at every turn; creep -, bristle- with; overflow; run -, flow -, well -, brim-over; run riot; over-run, -stock, -lay, -charge, -dose, -feed, -burden, -load, -do, -whelm, -shoot the mark &c. (*go beyond*) 303; surcharge, supersaturate, gorge, glut, load, drench, whelm, inundate, deluge, flood; drug, - the market.

choke, cloy, accloy, suffocate; pile up, lay it on, - with a trowel, lay on thick; impregnate with; lavish &c. (*squander*) 818.

send -, carry- coals to Newcastle, - owls to Athens; teach one's grandmother to suck eggs; *pisces natare docere*; kill the slain, 'gild refined gold,' 'paint the lily'; butter one's bread on both sides, put butter upon bacon, employ a steam-engine to crack a nut &c. (*waste*) 638.

exaggerate &c. 549; wallow in; roll in &c. (*plenty*) 639; remain on one's hands, hang heavy on hand, go a begging.

Adj. redundant; too -much, - many; exuberant, inordinate, superabundant, excessive, overmuch, replete, profuse, lavish; prodigal &c. 818; exorbitant; overweening; extravagant; overcharged &c. *v.*; supersaturated, drenched, overflowing; running -over, - to waste, - down.

crammed -, filled- to overflowing; gorged, stuffed, ready to burst; dropsical, turgid, plethoric, full-blooded; obese &c. 194; voluminous.

superfluous, unnecessary, needless, supervacaneous, uncalled for, to spare, in excess; over and above &c. (*remainder*) 40; *de trop*; adscititious &c. (*additional*) 37; supernumerary &c. (*reserve*) 636; on one's hands, spare, duplicate, supererogatory, expletive; *un peu fort*.

Adv. over, too, over and above; over -, too- much; too far; without -, beyond -, out of- measure; with . . . to spare; over head and ears; up to one's -eyes, - ears; *extra*; beyond the mark &c. (*transcursion*) 303; over one's head.

Phr. it never rains but it pours.

2. *Degree of Subservience*

642. Importance.—N. importance, consequence, moment, prominence, consideration, mark, materialness.

import, significance, concern; emphasis, interest.

greatness &c. 31; superiority &c. 33; notability &c. (*repute*) 873; weight &c. (*influence*) 175; value &c. (*goodness*) 648; usefulness &c. 644.

gravity, seriousness, solemnity; no -joke, - laughing matter; pressure, urgency, stress; matter of life and death.

memorabilia, notabilia, great doings; red-letter day.

great -thing, - point; main chance, 'the be all and end all,' cardinal point, outstanding feature; substance, gist &c. (*essence*) 5; sum and substance, *gravamen*, head and front; important -, principal -, prominent -, essential -part; half the battle; *sine quâ non*; breath of one's nostrils &c. (*life*) 359; cream, salt, core, kernel, heart, nucleus; key, -note, -stone;

corner stone; trump-card &c. (*device*) 626; salient points.

top-sawyer, first fiddle, *prima donna*, chief, big-wig; triton among the minnows.

V. be -important &c. *adj.*, – somebody, – something; import, signify, matter, be an object; carry weight &c. (*influence*) 175; make a figure &c. (*repute*) 873; be in the ascendant, come to the front, lead the way, take the lead, play first fiddle, throw all else into the shade; lie at the root of; deserve –, merit –, be worthy- -of notice, – regard, – consideration.

attach –, ascribe –, give- importance &c. *n.*- to; value, care for; set store -upon, – by; mark &c. 550; mark with a white stone, underline; write –, put –, print- in -italics, – capitals, – large letters, – large type, – letters of gold; accentuate, emphasize, lay stress on.

make -a fuss, – a stir, – a piece of work, – much ado- about; make -of, – much of.

Adj. important; of -importance &c. *n.*; momentous, material; to the point; not to be -overlooked, – despised, – sneezed at; egregious; weighty &c. (*influential*) 175; of note &c. (*repute*) 873; notable, prominent, salient, signal; memorable, remarkable; worthy of -remark, – notice; never to be forgotten; stirring, eventful.

grave, serious, earnest, noble, grand, solemn, impressive, commanding, imposing.

urgent, pressing, critical, instant.

paramount, essential, vital, all-absorbing, radical, cardinal, chief, main, prime, primary, principal, leading, capital, foremost, overruling; of vital &c. importance.

in the front rank, first-rate, A1; superior &c. 33; considerable &c. (*great*) 31; marked &c. *v.*; rare &c. 137.

significant, telling, trenchant, emphatic, pregnant; *tanti*.

Adv. materially &c. *adj.*; in the main; above all, *par excellence*, to crown all.

643. Unimportance.—N. unimportance, insignificance, nothingness, immateriality.

triviality, trivia, fribble, levity, frivolity; paltriness &c. *adj.*; poverty; smallness &c. 32; vanity &c. (*uselessness*) 645; matter of -indifference &c. 866; no object; side issue.

nothing, – to signify, – worth speaking of, – particular, – to boast of, – to speak of; small –, no great –, trifling &c. *adj.* -matter; mere -joke, – nothing; hardly –, scarcely- anything; nonentity, cipher, figurehead; no great shakes, *peu de chose*; child's play; small beer.

toy, plaything, popgun, paper pellet, gimcrack, gewgaw, bauble, trinket, *bagatelle*, kickshaw, knicknack, whimwham, trifle, 'trifles light as air.'

trumpery, trash, rubbish, stuff, *fatras*, frippery; 'leather or prunello'; chaff, drug, froth, bubble, smoke, cobweb; weed; refuse &c. (*inutility*) 645; scum &c. (*dirt*) 653.

joke, jest, snap of the fingers; fudge &c. (*unmeaning*) 517; fiddlestick, – end; pack of nonsense, mere farce.

straw, pin, fig, continental, button, rush; bulrush, feather, halfpenny, farthing, brass farthing, doit, peppercorn, jot, rap, pinch of snuff, old song.

minutiæ, details, minor details, small fry; dust in the balance, feather in the scale, drop in the ocean, flea-bite, molehill; fingle-fangle.

nine days' wonder, *ridiculus mus*; flash in the pan &c. (*impotence*) 158; much ado about nothing &c. (*overestimation*) 482; storm in a teacup.

V. be -unimportant &c. *adj.*; not -matter &c. 642; go for –, matter –, signify- -little, – nothing, – little or nothing; not matter a -straw &c. *n.*

make light of &c. (*underestimate*) 483; catch at straws &c. (*overestimate*) 482.

Adj. unimportant; of -little, – small, – no- -account, – importance &c. 642; immaterial; un-, non-essential; not vital; irrelevant, incidental, indifferent.

subordinate &c. (*inferior*) 34;

médiocre &c. (*average*) 29; passable, fair, respectable, tolerable, commonplace; uneventful, mere, common; ordinary &c. (*habitual*) 613; inconsiderable, so-so, insignificant, inappreciable, nugatory.

trifling. trivial; slight, slender, light, flimsy, frothy, idle; puerile &c. (*foolish*) 499; airy, shallow; weak &c. 160; powerless &c. 158; frivolous, petty, niggling; pid-, ped-dling; fribble, inane, ridiculous, farcical; fini-cal, -kin; fiddlefaddle, namby-pamby, wishy-washy, milk and water.

poor, paltry, pitiful; contemptible &c. (*contempt*) 930; sorry, mean, meagre, shabby, miserable, wretched, vile, scrubby, scrannel, weedy, niggardly, scurvy, putid, beggarly, worthless, twopenny-halfpenny, cheap, trashy, catchpenny, gimcrack, trumpery, one-horse; toy.

not worth -the pains, - while, - mentioning, - speaking of, - a thought, - a curse, - a straw, - rap &c. *n.*; beneath -, unworthy of- -notice, - regard, - consideration, - contempt; *de lanâ caprinâ*; vain &c. (*useless*) 645.

Adv. slightly &c. *adj.*; rather, somewhat, pretty well, fairly well, tolerably. for aught one cares.

Int. no matter! pish! tush! pshaw! pugh! pooh, -pooh! fudge! bosh! humbug! fiddle-stick, -end! fiddlededee! never mind! *n'importe*! what -signifies, - matter, - boots it, - of that, -'s the odds! a fig for! stuff! nonsense! stuff and nonsense!

Phr. *magno conatu magnas nugas*; *le jeu n'en vaut pas la chandelle*; it -matters not, - does not signify; it is of no -consequence, - importance.

644. Utility.—N. utility; usefulness &c. *adj.*; efficacy, efficiency, adequacy; service, use, stead, avail; help &c. (*aid*) 707; applicability &c. *adj.*; subservience &c. (*instrumentality*) 631; function &c. (*business*) 625; value; worth &c. (*goodness*) 648; money's worth; productiveness &c. 168; *cui bono* &c. (*intention*) 620; utilization &c. (*use*) 677; step in the right direction.

common weal, public good; utilitarianism &c. (*philanthropy*) 910.

V. be -useful &c. *adj.*; avail, serve; subserve &c. (*be instrumental to*) 631; conduce &c. (*tend*) 176; answer -, serve- -one's turn, - a purpose.

act a part &c. (*action*) 680; perform -, discharge- -a function &c. 625; do -, render- -a service, - good service, - yeoman's service; bestead, stand one in good stead; be the making of; help &c. 707.

bear fruit &c. (*produce*) 161; bring grist to the mill; profit, remunerate; benefit &c. (*do good*) 648.

find one's -account, - advantage- in; reap the benefit of &c. (*be better for*) 658.

render useful &c. (*use*) 677.

Adj. useful; of -use &c. *n.*; serviceable, usable, proficuous, good for; subservient &c. (*instrumental*) 631; conducive &c. (*tending*) 176; subsidiary &c. (*helping*) 707.

advantageous &c. (*beneficial*) 648; profitable, gainful, remunerative, worth one's salt; in-, valuable; prolific &c. (*productive*) 168.

adequate; ef-ficient, -ficacious; effective, -ual; practicable, expedient &c. 646.

applicable, available, ready, handy, at hand, tangible; commodious, adaptable; of all work.

Adv. usefully &c. *adj.*; *pro bono publico*.

645. Inutility.—N. inutility; uselessness &c. *adj.*; inefficacy, futility; inep-, inap-titude; unsubservience; inadequacy &c. (*insufficiency*) 640; inefficiency &c. (*incompetence*) 158; unskilfulness &c. 699; disservice; unfruitfulness &c. (*unproductiveness*) 169; labour -in vain, - lost, - of Sisyphus; lost -trouble, - labour; work of Penelope; sleeveless errand, wild goose chase, mere farce.

tautology &c. (*repetition*) 104; supererogation &c. (*redundance*) 641.

vanitas vanitatum, vanity, inanity, worthlessness, nugacity; triviality &c. (*unimportance*) 643.

caput mortuum, waste paper, dead letter; blunt tool.

litter, rubbish, lumber, odds and ends, cast-off clothes; button-top; shoddy; rags, orts, trash, refuse, sweepings, scourings, off-scourings, dross, slag, waste, rubble, dottle, drast, *débris*; stubble, leavings; broken meat; dregs &c. (*dirt*) 653; weeds, tares; rubbish heap, dust hole; *rudera*, deads.

fruges consumere natus &c. (*drone*) 683.

V. be -useless &c. *adj.*; go a begging &c. (*redundant*) 641; fail &c. 732.

seek –, strive- after impossibilities; use vain efforts, labour in vain, roll the stone of Sisyphus, beat the air, lash the waves, *battre l'eau avec un bâton, donner un coup d'épée dans l'eau*, fish in the air, milk the ram, drop a bucket into an empty well, sow the sand; bay the moon; preach –, speak- to the winds; whistle jigs to a milestone; kick against the pricks, *se battre contre des moulins*; lock the stable door when the steed is stolen &c. (*too late*) 135; hold a farthing candle to the sun; cast pearls before swine &c. (*waste*) 638; carry coals to Newcastle &c. (*redundance*) 641; wash a blackamoor white &c. (*impossible*) 471.

render, -useless &c. *adj.*; dis-mantle, -mast, -mount, -qualify, -able; unrig; cripple, lame &c. (*injure*) 659; spike guns, clip the wings; put out of gear.

Adj. useless, inutile, inefficacious, futile, unavailing, bootless; inoperative &c. 158; inadequate &c. (*insufficient*) 640; in-, un-sub-servient; inept, inefficient &c. (*impotent*) 158; of no -avail &c. (*use*) 644; ineffectual &c. (*failure*) 732; incompetent &c. (*unskilful*) 699; 'stale, flat and unprofitable'; superfluous &c. (*redundant*) 641; dispensable; thrown away &c. (*wasted*) 638; abortive &c. (*immature*) 674.

worth-, value-less; unsaleable; not worth a straw &c. (*trifling*) 643; dear at any price.

vain, empty, inane; gain-, profit-, fruit-less, un-serviceable, -profitable; ill-spent; unproductive &c. 169; *hors de combat*; barren, sterile, impotent, un-productive; effete, past work &c. (*impaired*) 659; obsolete &c. (*old*) 124; fit for the -dust-hole, – wastepaper bas-ket; good for nothing; of no earthly use; not worth -having, – powder and shot; leading to no end, uncalled for; un-necessary, -needed, superfluous.

Adv. uselessly &c. *adj.*; to -little, – no, – little or no- purpose.

Int. *cui bono?* what's the good!

646. [Specific subservience.] **Expedience.—N.** expedien-ce, -cy; desirableness, -bility &c. *adj.*; fitness &c. (*agreement*) 23; utility &c. 644; propriety; advantage; opportunism, pragmatism.

high time &c. (*occasion*) 134.

V. be -expedient &c. *adj.*; suit &c. (*agree*) 23; befit; suit –, befit- the -time, – season, – occasion.

conform &c. 82.

Adj. expedient; desir-, advis-, acceptable; convenient; worth while, meet; fit, -ting; due, proper, eligible, seemly, be-coming; befitting &c. *v.*; opportune &c. (*in season*) 134; *in loco*; suitable &c. (*accordant*) 23; applicable &c. (*useful*) 644; practical, effective, pragmatical; suitable, handy.

Adv. in the right place; conveniently &c. *adj.*; in the nick of time.

Phr. *operæ pretium est.*

647. Inexpedience.—N. inexpedien-ce, -cy; undesira-bleness, -bility &c. *adj.*; discommodity, impropriety; unfit-ness &c. (*disagreement*) 24; inutility &c. 645; inconvenience, inadvisability; dis-advantage.

V. be -inexpedient &c. *adj.*; come amiss &c. (*disagree*) 24; embarrass &c. (*hinder*) 706; put to inconvenience; pay too dear for one's whistle.

Adj. inexpedient, undesirable; un-, in-advisable; objectionable, troublesome, in-apt, -eligible, -admissible, -convenient; in-, dis-commodious; disadvantageous; inappropriate, unsuitable, unfit &c. (*inconsonant*) 24.

ill-contrived, -advised; unsatisfactory; unprofitable &c., unsubservient &c. (*useless*) 645; inopportune &c. (*unseasonable*) 135; out of -, in the wrong-place; improper, unseemly.

clumsy, awkward; cum-brous, -bersome; lumbering, unwieldly, hulky; unmanageable &c. (*impracticable*) 704; impedient &c. (*in the way*) 706.

unnecessary &c. (*redundant*) 641.

Phr. it will never do.

648. [Capability of producing good. Good qualities.] **Goodness.—N.** goodness &c. *adj.*; excellence, merit; virtue &c. 944; value, worth, price.

super-excellence, -eminence; superiority &c. 33; perfection &c. 650; *coup de maître*; master-piece, *chef d'œuvre*, prime, flower, cream, *élite*, pick, A1, none such, *nonpareil*, *crème de la crème*, flower of the flock, cock of the roost, salt of the earth; champion.

tid-bit; gem, - of the first water; *bijou*, precious stone, jewel, pearl, diamond, ruby, brilliant, treasure; good thing; *rara avis*, one in a thousand.

beneficence &c. 906; good man &c. 948.

V. be -beneficial &c. *adj.*; produce -, do- -good &c. 618; profit &c. (*be of use*) 644; benefit; confer a -benefit &c. 618.

be the making of, do a world of good, make a man of.

produce a good effect; do a good turn, confer an obligation; improve &c. 658.

do no harm, break no bones.

be -good &c. *adj.*; excel, transcend &c. (*be superior*) 33; bear away the bell.

stand the -proof, - test; pass -muster, - an examination.

challenge comparison, vie, emulate, rival.

Adj. harm-, hurt-less; unobnoxious; in-nocuous, -nocent, -offensive.

beneficial, valuable, of value; service-able &c. (*useful*) 644; advantageous, profitable, edifying; salutary &c. (*healthful*) 656.

favourable; propitious &c. (*hope-giving*) 858; fair.

good, - as gold; excellent; better; superior &c. 33; above par; nice, fine; genuine &c. (*true*) 494.

best, choice, select, picked, elect, eximious, *recherché*, rare, priceless; unpara-goned, -lleled &c. (*supreme*) 33; superlatively &c. 33- good; super-fine, -excellent; bonzer; of the first water; first-rate, -class; high-wrought; exquisite, very best, crack, prime, tip-top, gilt-edged, capital, cardinal; standard &c. (*perfect*) 650; inimitable.

admirable, estimable; praiseworthy &c. (*approve*) 931; pleasing &c. 829; *couleur de rose*, precious, of great price; costly &c. (*dear*) 814; worth -its weight in gold, -a king's ransom; matchless, peerless, invaluable, inestimable, precious as the apple of the eye.

tolerable &c. (*not very good*) 651;

up to the mark, un-exceptionable, -objectionable; satisfactory, tidy.

in -good, - fair- condition; fresh; unspoiled; sound &c. (*perfect*) 650.

Adv. beneficially &c. *adj.*; well &c. 618.

649. [Capability of producing evil. Bad qualities.] **Badness.—N.** hurtfulness &c. *adj.*; virulence.

evil doer &c. 913; bane &c. 663; plague-spot &c. (*insalubrity*) 657; evil star, ill wind; snake in the grass, skeleton in the closet; *amari aliquid*, thorn in the side; Jonah, jinx, hoodoo.

malignity; malevolence &c. 907; tender mercies [ironically].

ill-treatment, annoyance, molestation, abuse, oppression, persecution, outrage; misusage &c. 679; injury &c. (*damage*) 659.

badness &c. *adj.*; peccancy, abomination; painfulness &c. 830; pestilence &c. (*disease*) 655; guilt &c. 947; depravity &c. 945.

V. be -hurtful &c. *adj.*; cause -, produce -, inflict -, work -, do- evil &c. 619; damnify, endamage, hurt, harm, scathe; injure &c. (*damage*) 659; pain &c. 830.

wrong, aggrieve, oppress, persecute; trample -, tread -, bear hard -, put-upon; overburden; weigh -down, - heavy on; victimize; run down; molest &c. 830.

maltreat, abuse; ill-use, -treat; thwart, buffet, bruise, scratch, maul; smite &c. (*scourge*) 972; do -violence, - harm, - a mischief; stab, pierce, outrage.

do -, make- mischief; bring -, get-into trouble.

destroy &c. 162.

Adj. hurt-, harm-, scath-, bane-, baleful; injurious, deleterious, detrimental, noxious, pernicious, mischievous, full of mischief, mischief-making, malefic, malignant, nocuous, noisome; prejudicial; dis-serviceable, -advantageous; wide-wasting.

unlucky, sinister; obnoxious, untoward, disastrous.

oppressive, burdensome, onerous; malign &c. (*malevolent*) 907.

corrupting &c. (corrupt &c. 659); virulent, venomous, envenomed, corrosive; poisonous &c. (*morbific*) 657; deadly &c. (*killing*) 361; destructive &c. (*destroying*) 162; inauspicious &c. 859.

bad, ill, arrant, as bad as bad can be, dreadful; hor-rid, -rible; dire; rank, peccant, foul, fulsome; rotten, - at the core.

vile, base, villainous; mean &c. (*paltry*) 643; injured &c., deteriorated &c. 659; unsatisfactory, exception, -able, indifferent; below par &c. (*imperfect*) 651; ill-contrived, -conditioned; wretched, sad, grievous, deplorable, lamentable; piti-ful, -able, woeful &c. (*painful*) 830.

evil, wrong; depraved &c. 945; shocking; reprehensible &c. (*disapprove*) 932.

hateful, - as a toad; abominable, detestable, execrable, cursed, accursed, confounded; damn-ed, -able; infernal; diabolic &c. (*malevolent*) 907.

inadvisable &c. (*inexpedient*) 647;

unprofitable &c. (*useless*) 645; incompetent &c. (*unskilful*) 699; irremediable &c. (*hopeless*) 859.

Adv. badly &c. *adj.*; wrong, ill; to one's cost; where the shoe pinches.

Phr. bad is the best; the worst come to the worst.

650. Perfection.—N. perfection; perfectness &c. *adj.*; indefectibility; impecc-ancy, -ability.

pink, *beau idéal*, phœnix, paragon; pink -, acme- of perfection; *ne plus ultra*; summit &c. 210.

cygne noir; philosopher's stone; chrysolite, Koh-i-noor, black tulip.

model, standard, pattern, mirror, admirable Crichton; trump; very prince of.

master-piece, -stroke, super-excellence &c. (*goodness*) 648; transcendence &c. (*superiority*) 33.

V. be -perfect &c. *adj.*; transcend &c. (*be supreme*) 33.

bring to perfection, perfect, ripen, mature; consummate, complete &c. 729; put in trim &c. (*prepare*) 673; put the finishing touch to.

Adj. perfect, faultless, ideal; indefective, -ficient, -fectible; immaculate, spotless, impeccable; free from -imperfection &c. 651; un-blemished, -injured &c. 659; sound, - as a roach; in perfect condition; scathless, intact, harmless; seaworthy &c. (*safe*) 644; right as a trivet; *in seipso totus teres atque rotundus*; consummate &c. (*complete*) 52; finished &c. 729; complete in itself.

best &c. (*good*) 648; model, standard; inimitable, unparagoned, unparalleled &c. (*supreme*) 33; superhuman, divine; beyond all praise &c. (*approbation*) 931; *sans peur et sans reproche*.

Adv. to perfection, to the limit; perfectly &c. *adj.*; *ad unguem*; clean, - as a whistle.

651. Imperfection.—N. imperfection; imperfectness &c. *adj.*; deficiency; inadequacy &c. (*insufficiency*) 640; peccancy &c. (*badness*) 649; immaturity &c. 674.

fault, defect, weak point; screw loose; rift within the lute; fly in the ointment; flaw &c. (*break*) 70; gap &c. 198; twist &c. 243; taint, attainder; bar sinister, hole in one's coat; blemish &c. 848; weakness &c. 160; half-blood, touch of the tar brush; shortcoming &c. 304; drawback; seamy side.

mediocrity: no great -shakes, - catch; not much to boast of.

V. be -imperfect &c. *adj.*; have a -defect &c. *n.*; lie under a disadvantage; spring a leak.

not -, barely- pass muster; fall short &c. 304.

Adj. imperfect; not -perfect &c. 650; de-ficient, -fective; faulty, unsound, mutilated, tainted; out of -order, - tune; cracked, leaky; sprung; warped &c. (*distort*) 243; lame; injured &c. (*deteriorated*) 659; peccant &c. (*bad*) 649; frail &c. (*weak*) 160; inadequate &c. (*insufficient*) 640; crude &c. (*unprepared*) 674; incomplete &c. 53; found wanting; below par; short-handed; below -, under- its full -strength, - complement.

indifferent, middling, ordinary, mediocre; average &c. 29; so-so; *così-così,* milk and water; tolerable, fair, passable; pretty -well, - good; rather -, moderately- good; good -, well-enough; decent; not -bad, - amiss; inobjection-able, admissible, bearable, only better than nothing.

secondary, inferior; second-rate, -best, one-horse.

Adv. almost &c.; to a limited extent, rather &c. 32; pretty, moderately; only; considering, all things considered, enough.

Phr. *surgit amari aliquid.*

652. Cleanness.—N. cleanness &c. *adj.*; purity; cleaning &c. *v.*; purification, defecation &c. *v.*; purgation, lustration; de-, abs-tersion; epuration, mundation, ablution, lavation, colature; disinfection &c. *v.*; drain-, sewer-age.

lavatory, bath, -room; swimming pool, natatorium; public baths; hot -, cold -, Turkish -, Swedish -, Russian -, vapour- bath; *hammam,* laundry, washhouse; washerwoman, laundress, laundryman; scavenger, cleaner, sweeper, goodie; crossing sweeper, white wings, dustman, sweep.

brush; broom, besom, carpet-sweeper, vacuum-cleaner, mop, squilgee, rake, shovel, sieve, riddle, screen, filter; scraper, strigil.

napkin, *serviette,* cloth, table-, carving-cloth, table-linen, napery, maukin, handkerchief, towel, sudary; doyley, doily, duster, sponge, mop, swab.

cover, drugget, mat, doormat.

soap, wash, lotion, detergent, cathartic, purgative; purifier &c. *v.*; dentifrice, tooth-powder, -paste; mouth wash; disinfectant.

V. be -, render- clean &c. *adj.*

clean, -se; mundify, rinse, wring, flush, full, wipe, mop, sponge, scour, swab, scrub, holystone, brush up.

wash, shampoo, lave, launder, buck; abs-, de-terge; clear, purify; de-purate, -spumate, -fecate; purge, expurgate; Bowdlerize; elutriate, lixiviate, edulcorate, clarify, refine, rack; fil-ter, -trate; drain, strain.

disinfect, sterilize, pasteurize, fumigate, ventilate, deodorize; whitewash.

sift, winnow, screen, riddle, pick, weed, comb, rake, brush, sweep.

rout -, clear -, sweep &c.- out; make a clean sweep of.

Adj. clean, -ly; pure; immaculate; spot-, stain-, taint-less; without a stain, un-stained, -spotted, -soiled, -sullied, -tainted, -infected, -adulterated; aseptic; sweet, - as a nut.

neat, spruce, tidy, trim, gimp, clean as a new penny, like a cat in pattens; cleaned &c. *v.*; kempt.

Adv. neatly &c. *adj.*; clean as a whistle.

653. Uncleanness.—N. uncleanness &c. *adj.*; impurity; immundi-ty, -city; impurity &c. [of mind] 961.

defilement, contamination &c. *v.*;

defœdation; soil-ure, -iness; abomination; leaven; taint, -ure; fetor &c. 401.

decay; putre-scence, -faction; corruption; mould, must, mildew, dry-rot, *mucor*, rubigo, caries.

slovenry; slovenliness &c. *adj.*; squalor.

dowdy, drab, slut, malkin, slattern, sloven, slammerkin, scrub, draggletail, mudlark, dustman, sweep; beast.

dirt, filth, soil, slop; dust, cobweb, flue; smoke, soot, smudge, smut, grime, raff.

sordes, dregs, grounds, lees; sedi-, settle-ment; heel-tap; dross, -iness; mother, precipitate, *scoriæ*, ashes, cinders, recrement, slag; scum, froth.

hog-wash, swill, ditch-, dish-, bilge-water; rinsings, cheese-parings; sweepings &c. (*useless refuse*) 645; off-, out-scourings; off-scum; *caput mortuum, residuum*, sprue, feculence, clinker, draff; scurf, -iness; *exuviæ*, morphew; fur, -fur; dandruff; tartar.

riffraff; vermin, louse, cootie, flea, bug.

mud, mire, quagmire, *alluvium*, silt, sludge, slime, slush, slosh.

spawn, offal, garbage, carrion; *excreta* &c. 299; slough, peccant humour, pus, matter, suppuration, *lienteria*; *fæces*, excrement, ordure, dung; sew-, sewerage; muck, coprolite; guano, manure, compost.

dunghill, *coluvies*, mixen, midden, bog, laystall, sink, w.c., water-, earth-closet, latrine, privy, jakes, John's; cess, -pool; sump, sough, *cloaca*, drain, sewer, common sewer; Cloacina; dust-hole.

sty, pig-sty, lair, den, Augean stable, sink of corruption; slum, rookery.

V. be -, become- unclean &c. *adj.*; rot, putrefy, fester, rankle, reek; stink &c. 401; mould, -er; go -bad &c. *adj.*

render -unclean &c. *adj.*; dirt, -y; soil, smoke, tarnish, slaver, spot, smear, daub, blot, blur, smudge, smutch, smirch; d-, dr-abble, -aggle; spatter, slubber; be-smear &c., -mire, -slime, -grime, -foul; splash, stain, distain, maculate, sully, pollute, defile, debase, con-taminate, taint, leaven; corrupt &c. (*injure*) 659; cover with -dust &c. *n.*; drabble in the mud.

wallow in the mire; slob-, slab-ber.

Adj. unclean, dirty, filthy, grimy; soiled &c. *v.*; not to be handled with kid gloves; dusty, snuffy, smutty, sooty, smoky; thick, turbid, dreggy; slimy.

uncleanly, slovenly, untidy, sluttish, dowdy, slatternly, draggle-tailed; un-combed, -kempt, -scoured, -swept, -wiped, -washed, -strained, -purified; squalid.

nasty, coarse, foul, impure, offensive, abominable, beastly, reeky, reechy; fetid &c. 401.

mouldy, lentiginous, musty, mildewed, rusty, moth-eaten, mucid, rancid, bad, gone bad, touched, fusty, reasty, rotten, corrupt, tainted, high, fly-blown, maggoty; putr-id, -escent, -efied; purulent, carious, peccant, fec-al, -ulent; stercoraceous, excrementitious; scurfy, impetiginous, gory, bloody; rotting &c. *v.*; rotten as -a pear, - cheese.

crapulous &c. (*intemperate*) 954; gross &c. (*impure in mind*) 961.

654. Health.—N. health, sanity; soundness &c. *adj.*; vigour; good -, perfect -, excellent -, rude -, robust-health; bloom, *mens sana in corpore sano*; Hygeia; incorrupti-on, -bility; good state -, clean bill- of health, eupepsia.

V. be in health &c. *adj.*; bloom, flourish.

keep -body and soul together, - on one's legs; enjoy -good, - a good state of- health; have a clean bill of health.

return to health; recover &c. 660; get better &c. (*improve*) 658; take a -new, - fresh- lease of life; convalesce, be convalescent, recruit; restore to health; cure &c. (*restore*) 660.

Adj. health-y, -ful; in -health &c. *n.*; well, sound, strong, fit, hearty, hale, fresh, blooming, green, whole; florid, flush, hardy, stanch, staunch, brave, robust, vigorous, weather-proof; convalescent.

un-scathed, -injured, -maimed, -marred, -tainted; sound of wind and limb, safe and sound; without a scratch.

on one's legs; sound as a -roach, - bell; fresh as -a daisy, - a rose, - April; picture of health; bursting with health; fit as a fiddle; hearty as a buck; in -fine, - high- feather; in -good case, - full bloom; in fine fettle; pretty bobbish, tolerably well, as well as can be expected.

sanitary &c. (*health-giving*) 656; sanatory &c. (*remedial*) 662.

655. Disease.*—N. disease; illness, sickness &c. *adj.*; ailing &c. *v.*; 'the ills that flesh is heir to'; morb-idity, -osity; infirmity, ailment, indisposition; complaint, disorder, malady; distemper, -ature.

visitation, attack, seizure, stroke, fit, epilepsy, apoplexy, shock, shell-shock.

delicacy, loss of health, valetudinarianism, invalidism, cachexy; *cachexia*, atrophy, *marasmus*; indigestion, *dyspepsia*; decay &c. (*deterioration*) 659; malnutrition, decline, consumption, palsy, paralysis, prostration; occupational diseases.

taint, pollution, infection, contagion, septicity, septicæmia, blood poisoning, pyæmia, epi-, en-demic; murrain, plague, pestilence, virus, pox.

sore, ulcer, abscess, fester, boil; pimple &c. (*swelling*) 250; carbuncle, gathering, whitlow, imposthume, peccant humour, issue; rot, canker, cancer, *carcinoma*, *caries*, mortification, corruption, gangrene, *spachelus*, leprosy, eruption, rash, breaking out, venereal disease.

fever, calenture; inflammation.

fatal &c. (*hopeless*) 859; -disease &c.; dangerous illness, galloping consumption, churchyard cough; general breaking up, break up of the system.

[Disease of mind] neurasthenia; idiocy &c. 499; insanity &c. 503.

martyr to disease; cripple; 'the halt,

the lame and the blind'; valetudinar-y, -ian; invalid, patient, case; sick-room, -chamber, hospital &c. 662.

[Science of disease] path-, eti-, nosology, therapeutics, diagnosis, prognosis.

V. be -ill &c. *adj.*; ail, suffer, labour under, be affected with, complain of; droop, flag, languish, halt; sicken, peak, pine, waste away, fail, lose strength; gasp.

keep one's bed; feign sickness &c. (*falsehood*) 544, malinger.

lay -by, - up; take -, catch- -a disease &c. *n.*; - an infection; be stricken by; break out.

Adj. diseased; ailing &c. *v.*; ill, - of; taken ill, seized with; indisposed, unwell, sick, squeamish, poorly, seedy; affected -, afflicted- with illness; laid up, confined, bed-ridden, invalided, in hospital, on the sick list; out of -health, - sorts; valetudinary.

un-sound, -healthy; sickly, morbose, healthless, infirm, chlorotic, unbraced, drooping, flagging, lame, halt, crippled, halting.

morbid, tainted, vitiated, peccant, contaminated, poisoned, septic, tabid, mangy, leprous, cankered; rotten, - to, - at- the core; withered, palsied, paralytic, tuberculous; dyspeptic.

touched in the wind, broken-winded, spavined, gasping; *hors de combat* &c. (*useless*) 645.

weak-ly, -ened &c. (*weak*) 160; decrepit; decayed &c. (*deteriorated*) 659; incurable &c. (*hopeless*) 859; in declining health; cranky; in a bad way, in danger, prostrate; moribund &c. (*death*) 360.

morbific, epidemic &c. 657.

656. Salubrity.—N. salubrity, salubriousness; healthiness &c. *adj.*

fine -air, - climate; eudiometer.

[Preservation of health] *hygiène*; valetudinarian, -ism, preventorium, sanitarian; *sanitarium, sanitorium*, immunity.

---

* Extended lists of different diseases are beyond the scope of this work.

V. be -salubrious &c. *adj.*; agree with, be good for; assimilate &c. 23.

Adj. salu-brious, -tary, -tiferous, wholesome; health-y, -ful; sanitary, prophylactic, benign, bracing, tonic, invigorating, good for, nutritious, hyg-eian, -ienic.

in-noxious, -nocuous, -nocent; harmless, uninjurious, uninfectious; immune.

sanative &c. (*remedial*) 662; restorative &c. (*reinstate*) 660; useful &c. 644.

657. Insalubrity.—N. insalubrity; unhealthiness &c. *adj.*; non-naturals; plague spot; malaria &c. (*poison*) 663; death in the pot, contagion.

Adj. insalubrious; un-healthy, -wholesome; noxious, noisome, foul; morbi-fic, -ferous; mephitic, septic, azotic, deleterious; pesti-lent, -ferous, -lential; virulent, venomous, envenomed, poisonous, toxic, narcotic.

contagious, infectious, catching, taking, communicable, epidemic, zymotic; sporadic, endemic, pandemic, epizoötic.

innutritious, indigestible, ungenial; uncongenial &c. (*disagreeing*) 24.

deadly &c. (*killing*) 361.

658. Improvement.—N. improvement; a-, melioration; betterment; mend, amendment, emendation; mending &c. *v.*; advancement; advance &c. (*progress*) 282; ascent &c. 305; promotion, preferment; elevation &c. 307; increase &c. 35.

cultiv-, civiliz-ation; menticulture, culture, march of intellect; eugenics, euthenics, meliorism, telesis.

reform, -ation; revision, radical reform; second thoughts, correction, *limae labor*, refinement, elaboration; purification &c. 652; repair &c. (*restoration*) 660; recovery &c. 660.

revise; revised -, new- edition.

reformer, radical, progressive.

V. improve; be -, become -, get-better; mend, amend.

advance &c. (*progress*) 282; ascend &c. 305; increase &c. 35; fructify, rip-en, mature; pick up, come about, rally, take a favourable turn; turn -over a new leaf, – the corner; raise one's head, sow one's wild oats; recover &c. 660.

be -better &c. *adj.* - improved by; turn to -right, – good, – best- account; profit by, reap the benefit of; make -good use of, – capital out of; place to good account; take advantage of.

render better, improve, emend, make over, better; a-, meliorate; correct.

improve -, refine- upon; rectify; enrich, mellow, elaborate, fatten.

promote, cultivate, advance, forward, enhance; bring -forward, – on; foster &c. 707; invigorate &c. (*strengthen*) 159.

touch -, rub -, brush -, furbish -, bolster -, vamp -, brighten -, warm-up; polish, cook, make the most of, set off to advantage; prune; repair &c. (*restore*) 660; put in order &c. (*arrange*) 60.

review, revise, edit, redact; make -corrections, – improvements &c. *n.*; doctor &c. (*remedy*) 662; purify &c. 652.

relieve, refresh, revive, infuse new blood into, recruit, re-invigorate, renew, revivify, freshen, build -afresh, – anew; uplift, inspire.

re-form, -model, -organise; new model, civilize.

view in a new light, think better of, appeal from Philip drunk to Philip sober.

palliate, mitigate; lessen &c. 36- an evil.

Adj. improving &c. *v.*; progressive, improved &c. *v.*; better, – off, – for; all the better for; better advised.

reform-, emend-atory; reparatory &c. (*restorative*) 660; remedial &c. 662.

corrigible, improvable, curable, accultural.

Adv. on -consideration, – reconsideration, – second thoughts, – better advice; *ad melius inquirendum*; on the -mend, – up grade.

659. Deterioration.—N. deterioration, debasement; want, ebb; recession

&c. 287; retrogradation &c. 283; decrease &c. 36.

degenera-cy, -tion, -teness; degradation; deprav-ation, -ement; depravity &c. 945; demoralization, retrogression.

impairment, inquination, injury, damage, loss, detriment, delaceration, outrage, havoc, inroad, ravage, scath; perversion, prostitution, vitiation, discoloration, oxidation, pollution, defœdation, poisoning, venenation, leaven, contamination, canker, corruption, adulteration, alloy.

decl-ine, -ension, -ination; decadence, -cy; falling off &c. *v.*; caducity, decrepitude, senility.

decay, dilapidation, ravages of time, wear and tear; cor-, e-rosion; mouldi-, rotten-ness; moth and rust, dry-rot, blight, marasmus, atrophy, collapse; disorganization; *délabrement* &c. (*destruction*) 162.

wreck, mere wreck, honeycomb, *magni nominis umbra*.

V. be -, become- -worse, - deteriorated &c. *adj.*; have seen better days, deteriorate, degenerate, fall off; wane &c. (*decrease*) 36; ebb; retrograde &c. 283; decline, droop; go down &c. (*sink*) 306; go -downhill, - on from bad to worse, - farther and fare worse; jump out of the frying pan into the fire.

run to -seed, - waste; swale, sweal; lapse, be the worse for; break, - down; spring a leak, crack, start; shrivel &c. (*contract*) 195; fade, go off, wither, moulder, rot, rankle, decay, go bad; go to -, fall into- decay; 'fall into the sear and yellow leaf,' rust, crumble, shake; totter, - to its fall; perish &c. 162; die &c. 360.

[Render less good] deteriorate; weaken &c. 160; put back; taint, infect, contaminate, poison, empoison, envenom, canker, corrupt, exulcerate, pollute, vitiate, inquinate; de-, em-base; denaturalize, leaven; de-flower, -bauch, -file, -prave, -grade; stain &c. (*dirt*) 653; discolour; alloy, adulterate, sophisticate, tamper with, prejudice.

pervert, prostitute, demoralize, brutalize; render vicious &c. 945; compromise.

embitter, ex-, acerbate, aggravate.

injure, impair, labefy, damage, harm, hurt, shend, scathe, spoil, mar, despoil, dilapidate, waste; overrun; ravage; pillage &c. 791.

wound, stab, pierce, maim, lame, surbate, cripple, hough, hamstring, hit between wind and water, scotch, mangle, mutilate, disfigure, blemish, deface, warp.

blight, rot; cor-, e-rode, eat away; wear -away, - out; gnaw, - at the root of; sap, mine, undermine, shake, sap the foundations of, break up; dis-organize, -mantle, -mast; destroy &c. 162.

damnify &c. (*aggrieve*) 649; do one's worst; knock down; deal a blow to; play -havoc, - sad havoc, - the mischief, - the deuce, - the very devil- -with, - among; decimate.

Adj. unimproved &c. (improve &c. 658); deteriorated &c. *v.*; altered, - for the worse; injured &c. *v.*; sprung; withering, spoiling, &c. *v.*; on the -wane, - decline; tabid; degenerate; worse; the -, all the- worse for; out of -repair, - tune; imperfect &c. 651; the worse for wear; battered; weather-ed, -beaten; stale, *passé*, shaken, dilapidated, frayed, faded, wilted, shabby, second-hand, second-rate, threadbare; worn, - to- -a thread, - a shadow, - the stump, rags; reduced, - to a skeleton, skeletonized; far gone.

decayed &c. *v.*; moth-, worm-eaten; mildewed, rusty, mouldy, spotted, seedy, time-worn, moss-grown; discoloured; effete, wasted, crumbling, mouldering, rotten, cankered, blighted, tainted; depraved &c. (*vicious*) 945; decrep-id, -it; broken down; done, - for, - up; worn out, used up; fit for the -dust-hole, - wastepaper basket; past work &c. (*useless*) 645.

at a low ebb, in a bad way, on one's last legs, washed -up, - out; undermined, deciduous; nodding to its fall &c. (*destruction*) 162; tottering &c. (*dangerous*) 665; past cure &c. (*hope-*

less) 859; fatigued &c. 688; backward, retrograde &c. (*retrogressive*) 283; deleterious &c. 649; behind the times.

Adv. on the down grade; beyond hope.

Phr. out of the frying pan into the fire; *ægrescit medendo*.

660. Restoration.—N. restor-ation, -al; re-instatement, -placement, -habilitation, -establishment, -construction; reproduction &c. 163; re-novation, -newal; revival, -escence; refreshment &c. 689; resuscitation, -animation, -vivification, -viction; Phœnix; reorganization.

renaissance, renascence, rebirth, second youth, rejuvenation, rejuvenescence, new birth; regenera-tion, -cy, -teness; palingenesis, reconversion, resurgence, resurrection.

redress, retrieval, reclamation, recovery; convalescence; resumption, *résumption*.

recurrence &c. (*repetition*) 104; *réchauffé, rifacimento*.

cure, recure, sanation; healing &c. *v.*; reintegration; rectification, instauration.

repair, reparation, mending; recruiting &c. *v.*; cicatrization; disinfection; tinkering.

reaction; redemption &c. (*deliverance*) 672; restitution &c. 790; relief &c. 834.

mender, repairer, renewer; tinker, cobbler; doctor &c. 662; *vis medicatrix* &c. (*remedy*) 662.

curableness.

V. return to the original state; recover, rally, revive; come -to, – round, – to oneself; pull through, weather the storm, be oneself again; get -well, – round, – the better of, – over, – about; rise from -one's ashes; – the grave; resurge, resurrect; survive &c. (*outlive*) 110; resume, reappear; come to, – life again; live –, rise- again; relive.

heal, skin over, cicatrize; right itself.

restore, put back, place *in statu quo*; re-instate, -place, -seat, -habilitate, -establish, -estate, -install.

re-construct,   -build,   -organize,

-constitute; reconvert; re-new, -novate; recondition; regenerate; rejuvenate.

re-deem, -claim, -cover, -trieve; rescue &c. (*deliver*) 672.

redress, recure; cure, heal, remedy, doctor, physic, medicate; break of; bring round, set on one's legs.

re-suscitate, -vive, -animate, -vivify, -call to life; reproduce &c. 163; warm up; reinvigorate, refresh &c. 689.

reintegrate, make whole; recoup &c. 790; make -good, – all square, rectify; put –, set- -right, – to rights, – straight; set up, correct, put in order &c. (*arrange*) 60; refit, recruit; fill up, – the ranks, reinforce.

repair, mend; put in -repair, – thorough repair, – complete repair; retouch, botch, vamp, tinker, doctor, cobble; do –, patch –, plaster –, vamp- up; darn, fine-draw, heel-piece; stop a gap, stanch, staunch, caulk, calk, career, splice, bind up wounds.

Adj. restored &c. *v.*; *redivivus*, convalescent; in a fair way; none the worse; rejuvenated, renascent.

restoring &c. *v.*; restorative, recuperative; sana-, repara-tive, -tory; curative, remedial.

restor-, recover-, san-, remedi-, retriev-, cur-able.

Adv. *in statu quo*; as you were.

Phr. *revenons à nos moutons*.

661. Relapse.—N. relapse, lapse; falling back &c. *v.*; retrogradation &c. (*retrogression*) 283; deterioration &c. 659.

[Return to, or recurrence of a bad state] backsliding, recidivation, recrudescence.

V. relapse, lapse; fall –, slide–, sink-back; have a relapse; return; retrograde &c. 283; recidivate; fall off &c. 659-again.

662. Remedy.—N. remedy, help, redress; antidote, anti-toxin, anti-, counter-poison, prophylactic, antiseptic, germicide, bactericide, corrective, restorative, stimulant, pick-me-up, tonic; sedative &c. 174; palliative; febrifuge; alter-ant, -ative; specific; emetic, carminative; narcotic &c. *adj.*; Nepenthe, Mithridate.

cure; radical –, perfect –, certain-cure; sovereign remedy.

physic, medicine, patent medicine, Galenicals, simples, drug, potion, draught, dose, pill, bolus, lozenge, tablet, tabloid, capsule; electuary; tinct-us, -ure; medicament.

nostrum, receipt, recipe, prescription; catholicon, panacea, elixir, *elixir vitæ*, philosopher's stone; balm, balsam, cordial, theriac, ptisan.

salve, ointment, cerate, oil, lenitive, lotion, cosmetic; plaster; epithem, embrocation, liniment, cataplasm, sinapism, arquebusade, traumatic, vulnerary, pepastic, poultice, collyrium, depilatory.

compress, pledget; bandage &c. (*support*) 215.

treatment, medical treatment, regimen; diet-ary, -etics; *vis medicatrix, – naturæ; médecine expectante*; seton, blood-letting, bleeding, venesection, phlebotomy, cupping, leeches; operation, surgical operation; tonsillectomy, appendectomy; injection, electrolysis, massage.

pharma-cy, -cology, -ceutics; acology; materia medica, pharmacopœia, therapeutics, therapy, posology, pathology &c. 655; homœœ-, hetero-, all-, hydr-opathy; cold water –, open air-cure; dietetics; sur-, chirur-gery, osteopathy; healing art, leechcraft, practice of medicine; ortho-pædy, -praxy; dentistry, midwifery, obstetrics, gynæcology.

faith -cure, – healing, Christian science; psycho-therapy, -analysis, psychiatry.

hospital, infirmary, clinic; pest-, lazar-house; lazaretto, lazaret; lock hospital; *maison de santé; ambulance*; dispensary; *sanatorium, sanitarium*, spa, baths, pump-room, well; *hospice*; Red Cross; nursing home; asylum.

doctor, physician, surgeon; medical –, general- practitioner, consultant, spe-cialist; medical attendant; medical student, medico; chemist, apothecary, pharmacopolist, druggist; leech; Æsculapius, Hippocrates, Galen; *accoucheur*, gynæcologist, midwife, oculist, aurist, dentist; operator; osteopath, bonesetter; nurse, monthly nurse, sister; dresser; *masseur, masseuse*.

V. apply a -remedy &c. *n.*; doctor, dose, physic, nurse, minister to, attend, dress the wounds, plaster, bandage, poultice; heal, cure, work a cure, kill or cure, remedy, stay (disease), snatch from the jaws of death; prevent &c. 706; relieve &c. 834; palliate &c. 658; restore &c. 660; drench with physic; consult, operate, extract, deliver; bleed, cup, let blood, transfuse; electrolyse; psycho-analyse.

Adj. remedial; restorative &c. 660; corrective, palliative, healing; sana-tory, -tive; prophylactic; salutiferous &c. (*salutary*) 656; medic-al, -inal; therapeutic, surgical, chirurgical, orthopedic, epulotic, paregoric, tonic, corroborant, analeptic, balsamic, anodyne, hypnotic, neurotic, narcotic, sedative, lenitive, demulcent, emollient; depuratory; deter-sive, -gent; abstersive, disinfectant, febrifugal, alternative; traumatic, vulnerary.

dietetic, alimentary; nutrit-ious, -ive; peptic; alexi-pharmic, -teric; remedi-, cur-able.

663. Bane.—N. bane, curse, thorn in the -side, -flesh, bugbear, *bête noire*; evil &c. 619; hurtfulness &c. (*badness*) 649; painfulness &c. (*cause of pain*) 830; scrouge &c. (*punishment*) 975; *damnosa hereditas*; white elephant.

sting, fang, thorn, tang, bramble, briar, nettle.

poison, leaven, virus, venom; intoxicant; arsenic, Prussic acid, antimony, tartar emetic, strychnine, nicotine, cyanide of potassium, corrosive sublimate; curare; hyoscine &c.; poison-, mustard-, tear-gas; carbon di-, monoxide; ptomaine poisoning, botulism; miasm, mephitis, malaria, azote, sewer gas; pest, stench &c. 401.

rust, worm, moth, moth and rust, fungus, mildew; dry-rot; canker, -worm; cancer; torpedo; viper &c. (*evil-doer*) 913; demon &c. 980.

hemlock, hellebore, nightshade, *belladonna*, henbane, aconite; Upas tree.

drugs, dope, opium, morphia, morphine, cocaine, heroin, hashish, bhang.

[Science of poisons] Toxicology.

Adj. baneful &c. (*bad*) 649; poisonous &c. (*unwholesome*) 657.

3. Contingent Subservience

664. Safety.—N. safety, security, impregnability; invulnera-bility, -bleness &c. *adj.*; danger -past, - over; storm blown over; coast clear; escape &c. 671; means of escape, safety-valve; safeguard, palladium, sheet anchor, rock, tower of strength.

guardian-, war-, warden-ship; tutelage, custody, safe keeping; preservation &c. 670; protection, auspices.

safe-conduct, escort, convoy; guard, shield &c. (*defence*) 717; guardian angel, tutelary -god, - deity, - saint; *genius loci.*

protector, guardian; ward-en, -er; preserver, custodian, *duenna*, *chaperon*, third person.

watch-, ban-dog; Cerberus; watch-, patrol-, police-man, constable, peeler, bobby, copper, cop, bull, flat-foot, detective, armed guard; sentinel, sentry, scout &c. (*warning*) 668; garrison; guard-ship.

[Means of safety] refuge &c., anchor &c. 666; precaution &c. (*preparation*) 673; quarantine, *cordon sanitaire.*

[Sense of security] confidence &c. 858.

V. be -safe &c. *adj.*; keep one's head above water, tide over, save one's bacon; ride out -, weather- the storm; light upon one's feet; bear a charmed life; escape &c. 671; possess nine lives.

make -, render- -safe &c. *adj.*; protect, watch over; take care of &c. (*care*) 459; preserve &c. 670; cover, screen,

shelter, shroud, flank, ward; guard &c. (*defend*) 717; secure &c. (*restrain*) 751; intrench, fence round &c. (*circumscribe*) 229; house, nestle, ensconce; take charge of.

escort, convoy; garrison; watch, mount guard, patrol, scout, spy.

make assurance double sure &c. (*caution*) 864; take up a loose thread; take precautions &c. (*prepare for*) 673; take in a reef; double reef topsails.

seek safety; take -, find- shelter &c. 666; run into port.

Adj. safe, secure, sure; in -safety, - security; have an anchor to windward; on the safe side; under the -shield of, - shade of, - wing of, - shadow of one's wing; under -cover, - lock and key; out of -danger, - the meshes, - harm's way; in -harbour, - port; on sure ground, at anchor, high and dry, above water, on *terra firma*; unthreatened, -molested; protected &c. *v.*; *cavendo tutus*; panoplied &c. (*defended*) 717.

snug, sea-, air-worthy; weather-, water-, fire-, bomb-proof.

defensible, tenable, proof against, invulnerable; un-assailable, -attackable; im-pregnable, -perdible; founded on a rock; inexpugnable.

safe and sound &c. (*preserved*) 670; harmless; scathless &c. (*perfect*) 650; unhazarded; not -dangerous &c. 665.

protecting &c. *v.*; guardian, tutelary; preservative &c. 670; trustworthy &c. 939.

Adv. *ex abundanti cautelâ*; with impunity.

Phr. all's well; all clear; *salva res est*; *suave mari magno*; safety first.

665. Danger.—N. danger, peril, insecurity, jeopardy, risk, hazard, venture, precariousness, slipperiness; instability &c. 149; defencelessness &c. *adj.*

exposure &c. (*liability*) 177; vulnerability; vulnerable point, heel of Achilles; forlorn hope &c. (*hopelessness*) 859.

[Dangerous course] leap in the dark &c. (*rashness*) 863; road to ruin, *facilis descensus Averni*, hair-breadth escape.

cause for alarm; source of danger &c.
667. [Approach of danger] rock -,
breakers- ahead; storm brewing; clouds
-in the horizon, - gathering; warning
&c. 668; alarm &c. 669. [Sense of dan-
ger] apprehension &c. 860.

V. be -in danger &c. *adj.*; be exposed
to -, run into -, incur -, encounter-
-danger &c. *n.*; run a risk; lay oneself
open to &c. (*liability*) 177; lean on -,
trust to- a broken reed; feel the ground
sliding from under one, have to run for
it; have the -chances, - odds- against
one.

hang by a thread, totter; tremble on
the -verge, - brink; sleep -, stand -on a
volcano; sit on a barrel of gunpowder,
live in a glass house.

bring -, place -, put- in -danger &c.
n.; endanger, expose to danger, imperil;
jeopard, -ize, compromise; sail too near
the wind &c. (*rash*) 863; put one's head
in the lion's mouth.

adventure, risk, hazard, venture,
stake, set at hazard; run the gauntlet &c.
(*dare*) 861; engage in a forlorn hope.

threaten &c. 909; danger; run one
hard; lay a trap for &c. (*deceive*) 545.

Adj. in -danger &c. *n.*; endangered
&c. *v.*; fraught with danger; danger-,
hazard-, peril-, parl-, pericul-ous; unsafe, unprotected &c. (safe, protect &c.
664); insecure, untrustworthy, unreliable; built upon sand, on a sandy basis.

defence-, fence-, guard-, harbourless;
unshielded; vulnerable, expugnable, unsheltered, exposed; open to &c. (*liable*)
177.

aux abois, at bay; on -the wrong side
of the wall, - a lee shore, - the rocks.

at stake, in question; precarious, aleatory, critical, ticklish; slip-pery, -py;
hanging by a thread &c. *v.*; with a halter
round one's neck; between -the hammer
and the anvil, - Scylla and Charybdis, -
two fires; on the -edge, - brink, - verge
of a- -precipice, - volcano; in the lion's
den, on slippery ground, under fire; not
out of the wood.

un-warned, -admonished, -advised;

unprepared &c. 674; off one's guard &c.
(*inexpectant*) 508.

tottering; un-stable, -steady; shaky,
top-heavy, tumble-down, ramshackle,
crumbling, waterlogged; help-, guideless; in a bad way; reduced to -, at- the
last extremity; trembling in the balance;
nodding to its fall &c. (*destruction*) 162.

threatening &c. 909; ominous, ill-
omened; alarming &c. (*fear*) 860; explosive; poisonous &c. 657.

adventurous &c. (*rash*) 863, (*bold*)
861.

Int. stop! look out! beware! take care!

Phr. *incidit in Scyllam qui vult vitare
Charybdim; nam tua res agitur paries
dum proximus ardet.*

666. [Means of safety.] **Refuge.—N.**
refuge, sanctuary, retreat, fastness;
stronghold, keep, last resort; ward; prison &c. 752; asylum, ark, home, almshouse, refuge for the destitute; hiding-
place &c. (*ambush*) 530; *sanctum sanctorum* &c. (*privacy*) 893.

roadstead, anchorage; breakwater,
mole, port, haven; harbour, - of refuge;
sea-port; pier, jetty, embankment, quay.

covert, shelter, abri, screen, lee-wall,
wing, shield, umbrella; splash-, dash-
board, mudguard.

wall &c. (*inclosure*) 232; fort &c.
(*defence*) 717.

anchor, kedge; grap-nel, -pling iron;
sheet-, mushroom-anchor, main-stay;
support &c. 215; check &c. 706; ballast.

jury-mast; vent-peg; safety -valve, -
lamp; lightning conductor.

means of escape &c. (*escape*) 671;
life-boat, swimming belt, cork jacket;
life preserver, breeches buoy; parachute, plank, stepping-stone.

safeguard &c. (*protection*) 664.

V. seek -, take -, find -refuge &c. *n.*;
seek -, find- safety &c. 664; throw oneself into the arms of; claim sanctuary;
take to the -hills, - woods; make port,
reach shelter, bar -, bolt -, lock -the
door, - gate; let the portcullis down;
raise the drawbridge.

667. [Source of danger.] Pitfall.—N.
rocks, reefs, coral reef, sunken rocks, snags; sands, quicksands, Goodwin sands, sandy foundation; slippery ground; breakers, shoals, shallows, bank, shelf, flat, lee shore, iron-bound coast; rock -, breakers- ahead; derelict.

precipice; abyss, chasm, pit, crevasse; maelstrom, whirlpool, eddy, vortex, rapids, current, bore, tidal wave; storm, squall, hurricane, whirl-wind; volcano; ambush &c. 530; pitfall, trap-door; trap &c. (*snare*) 545.

sword of Damocles; wolf at the door, snake in the grass, viper in one's bosom, death in the pot; latency &c. 526.

ugly customer, dangerous person, *le chat qui dort*; firebrand, hornet's nest.

Phr. *latet anguis in herbâ; proximus ardet Ucalegon.*

668. Warning.—N. warning, caution, *caveat*; notice &c. (*information*) 527; premoni-tion, -shment; prediction &c. 511; contraindication; symptom; lesson, dehortation; admonition, monition; alarm &c. 669.

handwriting on the wall, *tekel upharsin*, yellow flag; fog-signal, -horn; siren; monitor, warning voice, Cassandra, signs of the times, Mother Carey's chickens, stormy petrel, bird of ill omen, gathering clouds, clouds in the horizon, cloud no bigger than a man's hand, death-watch.

watch-tower, beacon, signal-post; light-house &c. (*indication of locality*) 550.

sent-inel, -ry; watch, -man; watch and ward; watch-, ban-, house- dog; patrol, vedette, picket, bivouac, scout, spy, spial; advanced -, rear-guard, lookout, flagman.

cautiousness &c. 864.

V. warn, caution; fore-, pre-warn; ad-, pre-monish; give -notice, - warning; menace &c. (*threaten*) 909; put on one's guard; sound the alarm &c. 669; croak.

beware, ware; take -warning, - heed at one's peril; watch out for; keep watch and ward &c. (*care*) 459.

Adj. warning &c. *v.*; premonitory, monitory, cautionary; admonitory, -tive; ominous, threatening, lowering, minatory, symptomatic.

warned &c. *v.*; on one's guard &c. (*careful*) 459, (*cautious*) 864.

Adv. *in terrorem* &c. (*threat*) 909.

Int. beware! ware! take care! mind -, take care-what you are about; mind! look out!

Phr. *ne reveillez pas le chat qui dort; fœnum habet in cornu.*

669. [Indication of danger.] Alarm.—N. alarm; alarum, larum, alarm bell, tocsin, *alerte*, beat of drum, sound of trumpet, note of alarm, hue and cry, signal of distress, S.O.S.; blue-lights; war-cry, -whoop; warning &c. 668; fog-signal, -horn; siren; yellow flag; danger signal; red -light, - flag; fire -bell, - alarm; burglar alarm, police whistle, watchman's rattle.

false alarm, cry of wolf; bug-bear, -aboo.

V. give -, raise -, sound -, beat- the *or* an -alarm &c. *n.*; alarm; warn &c. 668; ring the tocsin; *battre la générale*; cry wolf.

Adj. alarming &c. *v.*

Int. *sauve qui peut! qui vive?* who goes there?

670. Preservation.—N. preservation; safe keeping; conservation &c. (*storage*) 636; maintenance, upkeep, support, sustentation, conservatism; *vis conservatrix*; salvation &c. (*deliverance*) 672; drying &c. *v.*

[Means of preservation] prophylaxis; preserv-er, -ative; canned goods; cold pack; hygi-astics, -antics; cover, drug-get; *cordon sanitaire*.

[Superstitious remedies] charm &c. 993.

V. preserve, maintain, keep, sustain, support; keep -up, - alive; not willingly let die; shore -, bank- up; nurse; save, rescue; be -, make- -safe &c. 664; take care of &c. (*care*) 459; guard &c. (*defend*) 717.

stare super antiquas vias; hold one's

own; hold -, stand- -one's ground &c. (*resist*) 719.

embalm, dry, cure, smoke, salt, pickle, season, kyanize, bottle, pot, tin, can; husband &c. (*store*) 636.

Adj. preserving &c. *v.*; conservative; prophylactic; preserva-tory, -tive; hygienic.

preserved &c. *v.*; un-impaired, -broken, -injured, -hurt, -singed, -marred; safe, - and sound; intact, with a whole skin, without a scratch.

Phr. *nolumus leges Angliæ mutari.*

671. Escape.—N. escape, scape; avolation, elopement, flight, get-away; evasion &c. (*avoidance*) 623; retreat; narrow -, hairbreadth- escape; close -, near- shave; come off, impunity.

[Means of escape] loophole &c. (*opening*) 260; path &c. 627; secret -door, - passage; refuge &c. 666; vent, - peg; safety-valve; draw-bridge, fire-escape.

reprieve &c. (*deliverance*) 672; liberation &c. 750.

refugee &c. (*fugitive*) 623.

V. escape, scape; make -, effect -, make good- one's escape, make a get-away; get -off, - clear off, - well out of; *échapper belle*, save one's bacon; weather the storm &c. (*safe*) 664; escape scot-free.

elude &c., make off &c. (*avoid*) 623; march off &c. (*go away*) 293; give one the slip; slip through the -hands, - fingers; slip the collar, wriggle out of; break -loose, - from prison; break -, slip -, get- away; find -vent, - a hole to creep out of.

Adj. escap-ing, -ed &c. *v.*; stolen away, fled.

Phr. the bird has flown.

672. Deliverance.—N. deliverance, extrication, rescue; repriev-e, -al; respite; ransom; liberation &c. 750; truce, armistice; redemption, salvation; riddance; gaol delivery; exemption, day of grace; redeem-ableness.

V. deliver, extricate, rescue, save, redeem, ransom, free, liberate, release, set

free, emancipate; bring -off, - through; *tirer d'affaire*, get the wheel out of the rut; snatch from the jaws of death, come to the rescue; rid; retrieve &c. (*restore*) 660; be -, get- rid of.

Adj. saved &c. *v.*; extric-, redeem-, rescu-able.

Phr. to the rescue!

3°. *Precursory Measures*

673. Preparation.—N. preparation; providing &c. *v.*; provi-sion, -dence; anticipation &c. (*foresight*) 510; precaution, -concertation, -disposition; forecast &c. (*plan*) 626; rehearsal, note of preparation.

[Putting in order] arrangement &c. 60; clearance; adjustment &c. 23; tuning; equipment, outfit, accoutrement, armament, array.

ripening &c. *v.*; maturation, evolution; elaboration, concoction, digestion; gestation, hatching, incubation, sitting.

groundwork, datum, first stone, cradle, stepping-stone; foundation, scaffold &c. (*support*) 215; scaffolding, *échafaudage*.

[Preparation -of men] training &c. (*education*) 537; inurement &c. (*habit*) 613; novitiate; [- of food] cook-ing, -ery; brewing, culinary art; [- of the soil] till-, plough-, sow-ing; semination, cultivation.

[State of being prepared] prepared-, readi-, ripe-, mellow-ness; maturity; *un impromptu fait à loisir.*

[Preparer] preparer, teacher, coach, trainer, pioneer; *avant-courrier, -coureur*; sappers and miners, paviour, navvy; packer, stevedore; warming-pan; precursor &c. 64.

V. prepare; get -, make- ready; make preparations, settle preliminaries, get up, sound the note of preparation; address oneself to.

set -, put- in order &c. (*arrange*) 60; forecast &c. (*plan*) 626; prepare -, plough -, dress- the ground; till -, cultivate- the soil; predispose, sow the seed, lay a train, dig a mine; lay -, fix- the

-foundations; – basis, -groundwork; dig the foundations, erect the scaffolding; lay the first stone &c. (*begin*) 66.

rough-hew; cut out work; block –, hammer- out; lick into shape &c. (*form*) 240.

elaborate, mature, ripen, mellow, season, bring to maturity; nurture &c. (*aid*) 707; hatch, cook, brew; temper; anneal, smelt; dry, cure &c. 670.

equip, arm, man; fit-out, -up; furnish, rig, dress, garnish, betrim, accoutre, array, fettle, fledge; dress –, furbish –, brush –, vamp- up; refurbish; sharpen one's tools, trim one's foils, set, prime, attune; whet the -knife, – sword; wind –, screw- up; adjust &c. (*fit*) 27; put in -trim, – train, – gear, – working order, – tune, – a groove for, – harness; pack, stow away, store.

train &c. (*teach*) 537; inure &c. (*habituate*) 613; breed, prepare &c.- for; rehearse; make provision for; take - steps, – measures, – precautions; provide, – against; beat up for recruits; open the door to &c. (*facilitate*) 705.

set one's house in order, make all snug; clear -decks, – for action; close one's ranks; shuffle the cards.

prepare oneself; serve an apprenticeship &c. (*learn*) 539; lay oneself out for, get into harness, gird up one's loins, buckle on one's armour, *reculer pour mieux sauter*, prime and load, shoulder arms, get the steam up, put the horses to.

guard –, make sure- against; forearm, make sure, prepare for the evil day, have a rod in pickle, provide against a rainy day, feather one's nest; lay in provisions &c. 637; make investments; keep on foot.

be -prepared, – ready &c. *adj.*; hold oneself in readiness, watch and pray, keep one's powder dry; lie in wait for &c. (*expect*) 507; anticipate &c. (*foresee*) 510; *principiis obstare; veniente occurrere morbo*.

Adj. preparing &c. *v.*; in -preparation, – course of preparation, – agitation, – embryo, – hand, – train; afoot, afloat; on -foot, – the stocks, – the anvil; under consideration &c. (*plan*) 626; brewing, hatching, forthcoming, brooding; in -store for, – reserve.

precautionary, provident; preparative, -tory; provisional, inchoate, under revision; preliminary &c. (*precedent*) 62.

prepared &c. *v.*; in readiness; ready, – to one's hand, – made, cut and dried; ready for use, reach me down; made to one's hand, handy, on the table, made to order; in gear; in working -order, – gear; snug; in practice.

ripe, mature, mellow; practised &c. (*skilled*) 698; laboured, elaborate, highly-wrought, smelling of the lamp, worked up.

in -full feather, – best bib and tucker; in –, at- harness; in – the saddle, – arms, – battle array, – war paint; up in arms; armed -at all points, – to the teeth, – *cap-à-pie*; sword in hand; booted and spurred.

in utrumque –, semper- paratus; on the alert &c. (*vigilant*) 459; at one's post.

Adv. in -preparation, – anticipation of; afoot, astir, abroad; abroach.

674. Non-Preparation.—N. non-, absence of –, want of- preparation; unpreparedness; inculture, inconcoction, improvidence.

immaturity, crudity; rawness &c. *adj.*; abortion; disqualification.

[Absence of art] nature, state of nature; virgin soil, unweeded garden; rough diamond, neglect &c. 460.

rough copy &c. (*plan*) 626; germ &c. 153; raw material &c. 635.

improvisation &c. (*impulse*) 612.

V. be -unprepared &c. *adj.*; want –, lack- preparation; lie fallow; *s'embarquer sans biscuits*; live from hand to mouth.

[Render unprepared] dismantle &c. (*render useless*) 645; undress &c. 226.

extemporize, improvise.

surprise, pay a surprise visit, take by surprise, drop in upon, take unawares; take pot-luck.

Adj. un-prepared &c. [prepare &c. 673]; without -preparation &c. 673; incomplete &c. 53; rudimental, embryonic, abortive; immature, unripe, raw, green, crude; coarse; rough, -cast, -hewn; in the rough; un-hewn, -formed, -fashioned, -wrought, -laboured,-blown, -cooked, -boiled, -concocted, -cut, -polished.

callow, un-hatched, -fledged, -nurtured, -licked, -taught, -educated, -cultivated, -trained, -tutored, -drilled, -exercised; precocious, premature; un-, in-digested; unmellowed, -seasoned, -leavened.

fallow; un-sown, -tilled; natural, in a state of nature; undressed; in dishabille, *en déshabille, en négligé*.

un-, dis-qualified; unfitted, ill-digested; un-begun, -ready, -arranged, -organized, -furnished, -provided, -equipped, -trimmed; out of -gear, – order; dismantled &c. *v.*

shiftless, improvident, unthrifty, thoughtless, unguarded; happy-go-lucky; caught napping &c. (*inexpectant*) 508; unpremeditated &c. 612.

Adv. extempore &c. 612.

675. Essay.—N. essay, trial, endeavour, aim, attempt; venture, adventure, speculation, *coup d'essai, début*; probation &c. (*experiment*) 463.

V. try, essay; experiment &c. 463; endeavour, strive; tempt, tackle, take on, attempt, make an attempt; venture, adventure, speculate, take one's chance, tempt fortune; try one's -fortune, – luck, – hand; use one's endeavour; feel –, grope –, pick- one's way.

try hard, push, make a bold push, use one's best endeavour; do one's best &c. (*exertion*) 686.

Adj. essaying &c. *v.*; experimental &c. 463; tentative, empirical, probationary.

Adv. experimentally &c. *adj.*; on trial, at a venture; by rule of thumb.

if one may be so bold.

676. Undertaking.—N. undertaking; compact &c. 769; engagement &c. (*promise*) 768; enter-, em-prise; venture &c. 675; pilgrimage; matter in hand &c. (*business*) 625; move; first move &c. (*beginning*) 66.

V. undertake; engage -, embark- in; launch –, plunge- into; volunteer; apprentice oneself to; engage &c. (*promise*) 768; contract &c. 769; take upon -oneself, – one's shoulders; devote oneself to &c. (*determination*) 604.

take -up, – in hand; tackle; set –, go-about; set –, fall- -to, – to work; launch forth; set up shop; put in -hand, – executive; set forward; break the neck of a business, be in for; put one's hand to; betake oneself to, turn one's hand to, go to do; begin &c. 66; broach, institute, &c. (*originate*) 153; put –, lay- one's -hand to the plough, – shoulder to the wheel.

have in hand &c. (*business*) 625; have many irons in the fire &c. (*activity*) 682.

Adj. undertaking &c. *v.*; on the anvil &c. 625; adventurous, venturesome.

Int. here goes!

677. Use.—N. use; employ, -ment; exer-cise, -citation; appli-cation, -ance; adhibition, disposal; consumption; agency &c. (*physical*) 170; usufruct; usefulness &c. 644; recourse, resort, avail, pragmatism.

[Conversion to use] utilization, service, wear.

[Way of using] usage.

V. use, make use of, employ, put to use; apply, put in -action, – operation, – practice; set -in motion; – to work.

ply, work, wield, handle, manipulate; play, – off; exert, exercise, practise, avail oneself of, profit by; resort -, have recourse -, recur -, take -, betake oneself- to; take -up with, – advantage of; lay one's hands on, try.

render useful &c. 644; mould; turn to -account, – use; convert to use, utilize, administer; work up; call -, bring- into play; put into requisition; call – draw-forth; press -, enlist- into the service; bring to bear upon, devote, dedicate, consecrate, apply, adhibit, dispose of; make a -handle, - cat's paw- of.

fall back upon, make a shift with; make the -most, - best- of.

use -, swallow- up; consume, absorb, expend; tax, task, wear, put to task.

Adj. in use; used &c. *v.*; well-worn, -trodden.

useful &c. 644; subservient &c. (*instrumental*) 631; utilitarian; pragmatical.

678. Disuse.—N. forbearance, abstinence; disuse; relinquishment &c. 782; desuetude &c. (*want of habit*) 614.

V. not use; do without, dispense with, let alone, not touch, forbear, abstain, spare, waive, neglect; keep back, reserve.

lay -up, - by, - on the shelf, - up in a napkin; shelve; set -, put -, lay- aside; disuse, leave off, have done with; supersede; discard &c. (*eject*) 297; dismiss, give warning.

throw aside &c. (*relinquish*) 782; make away with &c. (*destroy*) 162; cast -, heave -, throw- overboard; cast to the -dogs, - winds; dismantle &c. (*render useless*) 645.

lie -, remain- unemployed &c. *adj.*

Adj. not used &c. *v.*; un-employed, -applied, -disposed of, -spent, -exercised, -touched, -trodden, -essayed, -gathered, -culled; uncalled for, not required.

disused &c. *v.*; done with; run down, used up, cast off.

679. Misuse.—N. mis-use, -usage, -employment, -application, -appropriation.

abuse, profanation, prostitution, desecration; waste &c. 638.

V. mis-use, -employ, -apply, -appropriate.

desecrate, abuse, profane, prostitute; waste &c. 638; over-task, -tax, -work; squander &c. 818.

cut a whetstone with a razor, employ a steam-engine to crack a nut; catch at a straw.

Adj. misused &c. *v.*

Section III. VOLUNTARY ACTION

1°. *Simple Voluntary Action*

680. Action.—N. action, performance; doing &c. *v.*; perpetration; exercise, -citation; movement, operation, evolution, work; labour &c. (*exertion*) 686; *praxis*, execution; procedure &c. (*conduct*) 692; handicraft; business &c. 625; agency &c. (*power at work*) 170.

deed, act, overt act, stitch, touch, gest; transaction, job, doings, dealings, proceeding, measure, step, manœuvre, bout, passage, move, stroke, blow; *coup, - de main, - d'état*; *tour de force* &c. (*display*) 882; feat, exploit, stunt; achievement &c. (*completion*) 729; handiwork, workmanship, craftsmanship; manufacture; stroke of policy &c. (*plan*) 626.

actor &c. (*doer*) 690.

V. do, perform, execute; achieve &c. (*complete*) 729; transact, enact; commit, perpetrate, inflict; exercise, prosecute, carry on, work, practise, play.

employ oneself, ply one's task; officiate, have in hand &c. (*business*) 625; labour &c. 686; be at work; pursue a course; shape one's course &c. (*conduct*) 692.

act, operate; take -action, - steps; strike a blow, lift a finger, stretch forth one's hand; take in hand &c. (*undertake*) 676; put oneself in motion; put in practice; carry into execution &c. (*complete*) 729; act upon.

be -an actor &c. 690; take -, act -, play -, perform- a part in; participate in; have a -hand in, - finger in the pie; have to do with; be a -party to, - participator in; bear -, lend- a hand; pull an oar, run in a race; mix oneself up with &c.(*meddle*) 682.

be in action; come into operation &c. (*power at work*) 170.

Adj. doing &c. *v.*; acting; in action; in harness; on duty; at work; in operation &c. 170; up to one's ears in work, in the midst of things.

Adv. in the -act, – midst of, – thick of; red-handed, *in flagrante delicto*; while one's hand is in.

681. Inaction.—N. inaction, passiveness, abstinence from action; non-interference; Fabian –, conservative-policy; neglect &c. 460; stagnation, vegetation; loafing.

inactivity &c. 683; rest &c. (*repose*) 687; quiescence &c., 265; want of –, in-occupation; unemployment; idle hours, time hanging on one's hands, *dolce far niente*; sinecure.

V. not -do, – act, – attempt; be -inactive &c. 683; abstain from doing, do nothing, hold, spare; not -stir, – move, – lift- a -finger, – foot, – peg; fold one's -arms, – hands; leave –, let- alone; let -be, – pass, – things take their course, – it have its way, – well alone; *quieta non movere*; *stare super antiquas vias*; rest and be thankful, live and let live; lie –, rest- upon one's oars; *laisser -aller*, – *faire*; stand aloof; refrain &c. (*avoid*) 623; keep oneself from doing; remit –, relax- one's efforts; desist &c. (*relinquish*) 624; stop &c. (*cease*) 142; pause &c. (*be quiet*) 265.

wait, lie in wait, bide one's time, take time, tide it over.

cool –, kick- one's heels; loaf, while away the -time, – tedious hours; pass –, fill up –, beguile- the time; talk against time; waste time &c. (*inactive*) 683.

lie -by, – on the shelf, – in ordinary, – idle, – to, – fallow; keep quiet, slug; have nothing to do, whistle for want of thought; twiddle one's thumbs.

undo, do away with; take -down, – to pieces; destroy &c. 162.

Adj. not doing &c. *v.*; not done &c. *v.*; undone; passive; un-occupied, – employed; out of -employ, – work, – a job; fallow; *désœuvré*.

Adv. *re infectâ*, at a stand, *les bras croisés*, with folded arms; with the hands -in the pockets, – behind one's back; *pour passer le temps*.

Int. so let it be! stop! &c. 142; hands off!

Phr. nothing doing; *cunctando restituit rem*.

682. Activity.—N. activity; briskness, liveliness &c. *adj.*; animation, life, vivacity, spirit, verve, dash, energy, go.

nimbleness, agility; smartness, quickness &c. *adj.*; velocity &c. 274; alacrity, promptitude; des-, dis-patch; expedition; haste &c. 684; punctuality &c. (*early*) 132.

eagerness, zeal, ardour, *perfervidum ingenium*, *empressement*, earnestness, intentness; *abandon*; vigour &c. (*physical energy*) 171; devotion &c. (*resolution*) 604; exertion &c. 686.

industry, assiduity; assiduousness &c. *adj.*; sedulity; laboriousness; drudgery &c. (*labour*) 686; painstaking, diligence; perseverance &c. 604*a*; indefatigation; habits of business.

vigilance &c. 459; wakefulness; sleep-, rest-lessness; *pervigilium*, *insomnia*; racketing.

movement, bustle, hustle, stir, fuss, ado, bother, pottering; fidget, -iness; flurry &c. (*haste*) 684.

officiousness; dabbling, meddling; inter-ference, -position, -meddling, butting in, intrusiveness; tampering with, intrigue.

press of business, no sinecure, plenty to do, many irons in the fire, great doings, busy hum of men, battle of life, thick of -things,– the action; the madding crowd.

housewife, busy bee; new brooms; sharp fellow, blade; hustler, devotee, enthusiast, fan, zealot, fanatic; meddler, intermeddler, intriguer, busybody, kibitzer, pickthank.

V. be -active &c. *adj.*; busy oneself in; stir, -about, – one's stumps; bestir –, rouse- onself; speed, hasten, peg away, lay about one, bustle, fuss; raise –, kick up- a dust; push; make a -push, – fuss, – stir; go ahead, push forward; flight –, elbow- one's way; make progress &c. 282; toil &c. (*labour*) 686; drudge, plod, persist &c. (*persevere*) 604*a*; keep -up the ball, - the pot boiling.

look sharp; have all one's eyes about one &c. (*vigilance*) 459; rise, arouse oneself, get up early, hustle, push; be about, keep moving, steal a march, kill two birds with one stone; seize the opportunity &c. 134; lose no time, not lose a moment, make the most of one's time, not suffer the grass to grow under one's feet, improve the shining hour, make short work of; dash off; make haste &c. 684; do one's best, take pains &c. (*exert oneself*) 686; do -, work- wonders.

have -many irons in the fire, - one's hands full, - much on one's hands; have other -things to do, - fish to fry; be busy; not have a moment -to spare, - that one can call one's own.

have one's fling, run the round of; go all lengths, stick at nothing, run riot.

outdo; over-do, -act, -lay, -shoot the mark; make a toil of a pleasure.

have a hand in &c. (*act in*) 680; take an active part, put in one's oar, have a finger in the pie, mix oneself up with, trouble one's head about, intrigue; agitate.

tamper with, meddle, moil; intermeddle, -fere, -pose; obtrude; poke -, thrust- one's nose in, butt in.

Adj. active; brisk, - as a lark, - as a bee; lively, animated, vivacious; alive, - and kicking; frisky, spirited, stirring.

nimble, - as a squirrel; agile; light-, nimble-footed; featly, tripping.

quick, prompt, yare, instant, ready, alert, spry, sharp, smart, slick, go-ahead; fast &c. (*swift*) 274; quick as a lamplighter, expeditious; awake, broad awake; wide awake &c. (*intelligent*) 498.

forward, eager, ardent, strenuous, zealous, enterprising, pushing, in earnest; resolute &c. 604.

industrious, assiduous, diligent, sedulous, notable, painstaking; intent &c. (*attention*) 457; indefatigable &c. (*persevering*) 604*a*; unwearied; unsleeping, sleepless, never tired; plodding, hardworking &c. 686; business-like, workaday.

bustling; restless, - as a hyæna; fussy, fidgety, pottering; busy, - as a hen with one chicken.

working, labouring, at work, on duty, in harness; up in arms; on one's legs, at call; up and -doing, - stirring.

busy, occupied; hard at -work, - it; up to one's ears in, full of business, busy as a bee.

meddling &c. *v.*; meddlesome, pushing, officious, overofficious, *intrigant*.

astir, stirring; a-going, -foot; on foot; in full swing; eventful; on the alert &c. (*vigilant*) 459.

Adv. actively &c. *adj.*; with -life and spirit, - might and main &c. 686, - haste &c. 684, - wings; full tilt, *in mediis rebus*.

Int. be -, look- -alive, - sharp! move -, push- on! keep moving! go ahead! stir your stumps! *age quod agis!*

Phr. *carpe diem* &c. (*opportunity*) 134; *nulla dies sine lineâ*; *nec mora nec requies*; no sooner said than done &c. (*early*) 132; catch a weasel asleep.

683. Inactivity.—N. inactivity; inaction &c. 681; inertness &c. 172; obstinacy &c. 606.

lull &c. (*cessation*) 142; quiescence &c. 265; rust, -iness.

idle-, remiss-ness &c. *adj.*; sloth, indolence, indiligence; otiosity, dawdling &c. *v.*

dullness &c. *adj.*; langour; segni-ty, -tude; lentor; sluggishness &c. (*slowness*) 275; procrastination &c. (*delay*) 133; torp-or, -idity, -escence; stupor &c. (*insensibility*) 823; somnolence; drowsiness &c. *adj.*; nodding &c. *v.*; oscitation, -ancy; pandiculation, hypnotism, lethargy; heaviness, heavy eye-lids, sand in the eyes.

sleep, slumber; sound -, heavy -, balmy- sleep; Morpheus, dreamland; coma, trance, catalepsy, hypnosis, *ecstasis*, dream, hibernation, nap, doze, snooze, *siesta*, wink of sleep, forty winks, snore; Hypnology.

dull work; pottering; relaxation &c. (*loosening*) 47; Castle of Indolence.

[Cause of inactivity] lullaby, *berceuse*; anæsthetic, sedative &c. 174; torpedo.

idler, drone, droil, dawdle, mopus; do-little, *fainéant*, dummy, sleeping partner; afternoon farmer; truant &c. (*runaway*) 623; lounger, *lazzarone*, floater, loafer, tramp, beggar, cadger; lub-ber, -bard; slow-coach &c. (*slow*) 275; opium -, lotus- eater; slug; lag-, slug-gard, lie-abed; slumberer, dormouse, marmot; waiter on Providence, *fruges consumere natus.*

V. be -inactive &c. *adj.*; do nothing &c. 681; more slowly &c. 275; let the grass grow under one's feet; take one's time, dawdle, poke, drawl, droil, lag, hang back, slouch; loll, -op; lounge, loaf, loiter; go to sleep over; sleep at one's post, *ne battre que d'une aile.*

take -it easy, - things as they come; lead an easy life, vegetate, swim with the stream, eat the bread of idleness; loll in the lap of -luxury, - indolence; waste -, consume -, kill -, lose- time; burn daylight, waste the precious hours.

idle -, trifle -, fritter -, fool- away time; spend -, take- time in; ped-, piddle; potter, putter, dabble, faddle, fribble, fiddle-faddle; dally, dilly-dally.

sleep, slumber, be asleep; hibernate; oversleep; sleep like a -top, - log, - dormouse; sleep -soundly, - heavily; doze, drowze, snooze, nap; take a -nap &c. *n.*; dream; snore; settle -, go -, go off- to sleep; drop off; fall -, drop- asleep; close -, seal up- -the -eyes, - eyelids; weigh down the eyelids; get sleepy, nod, yawn; go to bed, turn in.

languish, expend itself, flag, hang fire; relax.

render -idle &c. *adj.*; sluggardize; mitigate &c. 174.

Adj. inactive; motionless &c. 265; unoccupied &c. (*doing nothing*) 681.

indolent, lazy, slothful, idle, otiose, lusk, remiss, slack, inert, torpid, sluggish, languid, supine, heavy, dull, leaden, lumpish; exanimate, soulless; listless; dron-y, -ish; lazy as Ludlam's dog. dilatory, laggard; lagging &c. *v.*; slow

&c. 275; rusty, flagging; lackadaisical, maudlin, fiddle-faddle; pottering &c. *v.*; shilly-shally &c. (*irresolute*) 605.

sleeping &c. *v.*; asleep; fast -, dead -, sound- asleep; in a sound sleep; sound as a top, dormant, comatose; in the -arms, - lap- of Morpheus.

sleep-y, -ful; dozy, drowsy, somnolent, torpescent; lethargic, -al; heavy, - with sleep; napping; somni-fic, -ferous; sopor-ous, -ific, -iferous; hypnotic; balmy, dreamy; un-, una-wakened.

sedative &c. 174.

Adv. inactively &c. *adj.*; at leisure &c. 685.

Phr. the eyes begin to draw straws.

684. Haste.—N. haste, urgency; des-, dis-patch; acceleration, spurt, spirt, forced march, rush, dash; velocity &c. 274; precipit-ancy, -ation, -ousness &c. *adj.*; impetuosity; *brusquerie*; hurry, scurry, scuttle, drive, scramble, push, hustle, bustle, fuss, fidget, flurry, flutter, splutter.

V. haste, hasten; make -haste, - a dash &c. *n.*; hurry -, dash -, whip -, push -, press- on, - forward; hurry, skurry, scuttle along, bundle on, dart to and fro, bustle, flutter, scramble; plunge, - headlong; run, race, speed; dash off; rush &c. (*violence*) 173.

bestir oneself &c. (*be active*) 682; lose -no time, - not a moment, - not an instant; make short work of; make the best of one's -time, - way.

be -precipitate &c. *adj.*; jump at; be in -haste, - a hurry &c. *n.*; have -no time, - not a moment- -to lose, - to spare; work -under pressure, - against time.

quicken &c. 274; accelerate, expedite, put on, precipitate, urge, whip, spur, flog, goad.

Adj. hasty, hurried, *brusque*; scrambling, cursory, precipitate, headlong, furious, boisterous, impetuous, hotheaded; feverish, fussy; pushing.

in -haste, - a hurry &c. *n.*; in -hot, - all- haste; breathless, pressed for time, hard pressed, urgent.

Adv. with -haste, – all haste, – breathless speed; in haste &c. *adj.*; apace &c. (*swiftly*) 274; amain, all at once &c. (*instantaneously*) 113; at short notice &c., immediately &c. (*early*) 132; posthaste; by -express, – telegraph, – wire, – wireless, – air mail.

hastily, precipitately &c. *adj.*; helter-skelter, hurry-skurry, holus-bolus; slap-dash, -bang; full-tilt, -drive; heels over head, head and shoulders, headlong, *à corps perdu*.

by -fits and starts, – spurts; hop, skip and jump.

Phr. *sauve qui peut*, devil take the hindmost, no time to be lost; no sooner said than done &c. (*early*) 132; a word and a blow.

Int. hurry up! look alive! get a move on! buck up! double march! rush! urgent!

685. Leisure.—N. leisure; spare -time, – hours, – moments; vacant hour; time, – to spare, – on one's hands; holiday &c. (*rest*) 687; *otium cum dignitate*, ease.

V. have -leisure &c. *n.*; take one's -time, – leisure, – ease; repose &c. 687; move slowly &c. 275; while away the time &c. (*inaction*) 681; be -master of one's time, – an idle man; *desipere in loco*.

Adj. leisurely; slow &c. 275; deliberate, quiet, calm, undisturbed; at -leisure, – one's ease, – a loose end.

Phr. time hanging heavy on one's hands.

686. Exertion.—N. exertion, effort, strain, tug, pull, stress, force, pressure, throw, stretch, struggle, spell, spurt, spirt; stroke -, stitch- of work.

'a strong pull, a long pull and a pull all together'; dead lift; heft; gymnastics, sports; exer-cise, -citation; wear and tear; ado; toil and trouble; uphill -, hard -, warm- work; harvest time.

labour, work, toil, travail, manual labour, sweat of one's brow, swink, operoseness, drudgery, slavery, fagging, hammering; *limæ labor*.

trouble, pains, duty; resolution &c. 604; energy &c. (*physical*) 171.

V. exert oneself; exert -, tax- one's energies; use exertion.

labour, work, toil, moil, sweat, fag, drudge, slave, drag a lengthened chain, wade through, strive, strain; make -, stretch- a long arm; pull, tug, ply; ply -, tug at- the oar; do the work; take the labouring oar.

bestir oneself (*be active*) 682; take trouble, trouble oneself.

work hard; rough it; put forth -one's strength, – a strong arm; fall to work, bend the bow; buckle to, set one's shoulder to the wheel &c. (*resolution*) 604; work like a -Briton, – horse, – carthorse, – galley-slave, – coalheaver; labour -, work- day and night; redouble one's efforts; do double duty; work double -hours, – tides; sit up, burn the -midnight oil, – candle at both ends; stick to &c. (*persevere*) 604a; work -, fight-one's way; lay about one, hammer at.

take pains; do one's -best, – level best, – utmost; do -the best one can, – all one can, – all in one's power, – as much as in one lies, – what lies in one's power; use one's -best, – utmost- endeavour; try one's -best, – utmost; play one's best card; put one's -best, – right- leg foremost; have one's whole soul in one's work, put all one's strength into, strain every nerve; spare no -efforts, – pains; go all lengths; go through fire and water &c. (*resolution*) 604; move heaven and earth, leave no stone unturned.

Adj. labouring &c. *v.*

laborious, operose, elaborate; strained; toil-, trouble-, burden-, wearisome; uphill; herculean, gymnastic, athletic, palestric.

hardworking, painstaking, strenuous, energetic.

hard at work, on the stretch.

Adv. laboriously &c. *adj.*; lustily; with -might and main, – all one's might, – a strong hand, – sledge-hammer, – much ado; to the best of one's abilities, *totis viribus*, *vi et armis*, *manibus pedibusque*, tooth and nail, *unguibus et* *rostro,* hammer and tongs, heart and soul; through thick and thin &c. (*perseverance*) 604a.

by the sweat of one's brow, *suo Marte.*

687. Repose.—N. repose, rest, silken repose; sleep &c. 683.

relaxation, breathing time; halt, pause &c. (*cessation*) 142; respite.

day of rest, *dies non,* Sabbath, Lord's day, holiday, red-letter day, vacation, recess.

V. respose; rest, - and be thankful; take -rest, - one's ease.

relax, unbend, slacken; take breath &c. (*refresh*) 689; rest upon one's oars; pause &c. (*cease*) 142; stay one's hand.

lie down; recline, - on a bed of down, - on an easy chair; go to -rest, - bed, - sleep &c. 683.

take a holiday, shut up shop; lie fallow &c. (*inaction*) 681.

Adj. reposing &c. *v.;* unstrained.

Adv. at rest.

688. Fatigue.—N. fatigue; weariness &c. 841; yawning, drowsiness &c. 683; lassitude, tiredness, fatigation, exhaustion; sweat.

anhelation, shortness of breath, panting; faintness; collapse, prostration, swoon, fainting, *deliquium,* syncope, lipothymy.

V. be -fatigued &c. *adj.;* yawn &c. (*get sleepy*) 683; droop, sink, flag; lose -breath, - wind; gasp, pant, puff, blow, drop, swoon, faint, succumb.

fatigue, tire, weary, bore, irk, fag, jade, harass, exhaust, knock up, wear out, prostrate.

tax, task, strain; over-task, -work, -burden, -tax, -strain.

Adj. fatigued &c. *v.;* weary &c. 841; drowsy &c. 683; drooping &c. *v.;* haggard; toil-, way-worn; footsore, surbated, weatherbeaten; faint; done -, used -, knocked- up; exhausted, prostrate, spent; over-tired, -spent, -fatigued; forspent; unre-freshed, -stored.

worn, - out; battered, shattered, pulled down, seedy, altered.

breath-, wind-less; short of -, out of -breath, - wind; blown, puffing and blowing; short-breathed; anhelous; broken-, short-winded.

ready to drop, more dead than alive, dog -tired, - weary, walked off one's legs, tired to death, on one's last legs, played out, *hors de combat.*

fatiguing &c. *v.;* tire-, irk-, wearisome; weary; trying.

689. Refreshment.—N. bracing &c. *v.;* recovery of -strength &c. 159; restoration, revival &c. 660; repair, refection, refocillation, refreshment, regalement, bait; relief &c. 834.

V. brace &c. (*strengthen*) 159; reinvigorate; air, freshen up, refresh, recruit; repair &c. (*restore*) 660; fan, refocillate.

breathe, respire; draw -, take -, gather -, take a long -, regain -, recover-breath; get better, raise one's head; recover -, regain -, renew- one's strength &c. 159; perk up.

come to oneself &c. (*revive*) 660; feel like a giant refreshed.

Adj. refreshing &c. *v.;* recuperative &c. 660.

refreshed &c. *v.;* un-tired, -wearied.

690. Agent.—N. doer, actor, agent, performer, perpetrator, operator; executor, -trix; practitioner, worker, stager.

bee, ant, working bee, labouring oar, shaft horse, servant -, maid- of all work, general servant, factotum.

workman, artisan; crafts-, handicrafts-man; mechanic, operative; working -, labouring- man; hewers of wood and drawers of water, labourer, navvy; hand, man, day labourer, journeyman, hack; mere -tool &c. 633; porter, docker, stevedore, beast of burden, drudge, fag.

maker, artificer, artist, wright, manufacturer, architect, contractor, builder, mason, bricklayer, smith, forger, Vulcan; black-, tin-smith; carpenter; ganger, platelayer.

machinist, mechanician, engineer, electrician, plumber, gasfitter &c.

semp-, sem-, seam-stress; needle-, char-, work-woman; tailor, cord-wainer.

minister &c. (*instrument*) 631; servant &c. 746; representative &c. (*commissioner*) 758, (*deputy*) 759.

co-worker, fellow-worker, party to, participator in, co-operator, colleague, associate, collaborator, *particeps criminis, dramatis personæ; personnel.*

Phr. *'quorum pars magna fui.'*

691. Workshop.—N. work-shop, -house; laboratory; manufactory, mill, factory, armoury, arsenal, mint, forge, loom; cabinet, *studio, bureau, atelier*; hive, - of industry; nursery; hot-house; -bed; kitchen, kitchenette; dock, -yard; slip, yard, wharf; found-ry, -ery; furnace; vineyard, orchard, farm, kitchen garden.

melting pot, crucible, alembic, caldron, mortar, *matrix.*

2°. Complex Voluntary Action

692. Conduct.—N. dealing, transaction &c. (*action*) 680; business &c. 625.

tactics, game, policy, polity; general-, statesman-, seaman-ship; strate-gy, -gics; plan &c. 626.

husbandry; house-keeping, -wifery; stewardship; *ménage*; regimen, *régime*; econom-y, -ics; political economy; management; government &c. (*direction*) 693.

execution, manipulation, treatment, campaign, career, life, course, walk, race.

conduct; behaviour; de-, comportment; carriage, *maintien*, demeanour, guise, bearing, manner, mien, air, observance.

course -, line- of -conduct, - action, - proceeding; *rôle*; process, ways, practice, procedure, *modus operandi*; method &c., path &c. 627.

V. transact, execute; des-, dis-patch; proceed with, discharge; carry -on, - through, - out, - into effect; work out; go -, get- through; enact; put into practice; officiate &c. 625.

behave -, comport -, demean -, carry -, bear -, conduct -, acquit- oneself.

run a race, lead a life, play a game; take -, adopt- a course; steer -, shape- one's course; play one's- -part, - cards; shift for oneself; paddle one's own canoe.

conduct; manage &c. (*direct*) 693.

deal -, have to do- with; treat, handle a case; take -steps, - measures.

Adj. conducting &c. *v.*; strategical, business-like, practical, economic, executive.

693. Direction.—N. direction; manage-ment, -ry; government, gubernation, conduct, legislation, regulation, guidance; steer-, pilot-age; reins, - of government; helm, rudder, controls, joy stick, needle, compass, binnacle; guiding -, load -, lode -, pole- star; cynosure.

super-vision, -intendence; *surveillance*, oversight; eye of the master; control, charge, auspices; board of control &c. (*council*) 696; command &c. (*authority*) 737.

premier-, senator-ship; director &c. 694; chair, seat, portfolio.

statesmanship; state-, king-craft.

minis-try, -tration; administration; steward-, proctor-ship; agency.

V. direct, manage, govern, conduct; order, prescribe, cut out work for; head, lead; lead -, show- the way; take the lead, lead on; regulate, guide, steer, pilot; take -, be at- the helm; have -, handle -, hold -, take- the reins, handle the ribbons; drive, tool; tackle.

super-intend, -vise; overlook, control, keep in order, look after, see to, oversee, legislate for; administer, ministrate; patronize; have the -care, - charge- of; have -, take- the direction; pull the -strings, - wires; rule &c. (*command*) 737; have -, hold- -office, - the portfolio; preside, - at the board; take -, occupy -, be in- the chair; pull the stroke oar.

Adj. directing &c. *v.*; executive, supervisory, hegemonic.

Adv. at the -helm, – head of, in charge of; under the auspices of.

694. Director.—N. director, manager, governor, rector, comptroller; superintendent, -visor; intendant; over-seer, -looker; foreman, boss, straw boss; supercargo, husband, inspector, visitor, ranger, surveyor, ædile, moderator, monitor, taskmaster; master &c. 745; leader, ringleader, demagogue, corypheus, conductor, fugleman, precentor, bellwether, agitator.

guiding star &c. (*guidance*) 693; adviser &c. 695; guide &c. (*information*) 527; pilot; helmsman; steers-man, -mate; man at the wheel; wire-puller.

driver, whip, Jehu, charioteer; coach-, car-, cab-man, jarvey; postilion, *vetturino*, muleteer, teamster; whipper in; engineer, engine driver, motorman, *chauffeur*.

head, – man; principal, president, speaker; chair, -man; captain &c. (*master*) 745; superior; dean; mayor &c. (*civil authority*) 745; vice-president, prime minister, premier, vizier, grand vizier; dictator.

officer, functionary, minister, official, red-tapist, bureaucrat; man –, Jack- in office; office-bearer; person in authority &c. 745.

statesman, strategist, legislator, lawgiver, politician, administrator, statist, statemonger; Minos, Draco; arbiter &c. (*judge*) 967; king maker, power behind the throne.

board &c. (*council*) 696.

secretary, – of state; Reis Effendi; vicar &c. (*deputy*) 759; steward, factor; agent &c. 758; bailiff, middleman; ganger, clerk of works, landreeve; factotum, major-domo, seneschal, housekeep̀er, shepherd, *croupier*; proctor, procurator, curator, librarian.

Adv. *ex officio.*

695. Advice.—N. advice, counsel, adhortation; word to the wise; suggestion, submonition, recommendation, advocacy, consultation.

exhortation &c. (*persuasion*) 615; ex-

postulation &c. (*dissuasion*) 616; admonition &c. (*warning*) 668; guidance &c. (*direction*) 693.

instruction, charge, injunction.

adviser, prompter; counsel, -lor; monitor, mentor, Nestor, *magnus Apollo*, senator; teacher &c. 540.

guide, manual, chart &c. (*information*) 527.

physician, leech, archiater; arbiter &c. (*judge*) 967.

refer-ence, -ment; consultation, conference, parley, *pourparler* &c. 696.

V. advise, counsel; give -advice, – counsel, – a piece of advice; suggest, prompt, submonish, recommend, prescribe, advocate; exhort &c. (*persuade*) 615.

enjoin, enforce, charge, instruct, call; call upon &c. (*request*) 765; dictate.

expostulate &c. (*dissuade*) 616; admonish &c. (*warn*) 668.

advise with; lay heads –, consult- together; compare notes; hold a council, deliberate, be closeted with.

confer, consult, refer to, call in; take –, follow- advice; follow implicitly; be advised by, have at one's elbow, take one's cue from.

Adj. recommendatory; hortative &c. (*persuasive*) 615; dehortatory &c. (*dissuasive*) 616; admonitory &c. (*warning*) 668; consultative.

Int. go to!

696. Council.—N. council, committee, subcommittee, *comitia*, court, chamber, cabinet, board, bench, staff; consultation.

senate, *senatus*, parliament, house, – of Lords, – Peers, – Commons, legislature, legislative assembly, federal council, chamber of deputies, directory, *reichsrath, rigsdag, cortes*, storthing, witenagemote, *junta*, divan, *musnud, sanhedrim*, Amphictyonic council; *duma, zemstvo, soviet, cheka, ogpu; Dail Eireann*; caput, consistory, chapter, syndicate; court of appeal &c. (*tribunal*) 966; board of -control, - works; vestry; county –, borough –, district –, parish –, town- council, local board.

cabinet –, privy- council, royal commission; cockpit, convocation, synod, congress, congregation, convention, diet, states-general, aulic council.

League of Nations, assembly, *caucus*, conclave, *clique*, conventicle; meeting, sitting, *séance*, conference, session, hearing, palaver, *pourparler, durbar*, pow-wow, house; *quorum*.

senator; member, – of parliament; councillor, M.P., representative of the people.

Adj. senatorial, curule, parliamentary.

697. Precept.—N. precept, direction, instruction, charge; prescript, -ion; *recipe*, receipt; golden rule; maxim &c. 496.

commandment, rule, ruling, canon, law, code, *corpus juris, lex scripta*, common –, unwritten –, canon-law; the Ten Commandments; act, statute, convention, rubric, stage direction, regulation; form, -ula, -ulary; technicality; nice point.

order &c. (*command*) 741.

698. Skill.—N. skill, skilfulness, address; dexter-ity, -ousness; adroitness, expertness &c. *adj.*; proficiency, competence, craft, callidity, facility, knack, trick, sleight; master-y, -ship; excellence, panurgy; ambidext-erity, -rousness; sleight of hand &c. (*deception*) 545.

sea-, air-, marks-, horse-manship; tight-, rope-dancing.

accomplish-, acquire-, attain-ment; art, science; techn-icality, -ology, -ique; practical –, technical- knowledge; technocracy; finish, technic.

knowledge of the world, world wisdom, *savoir-faire*; tact; mother wit &c. (*sagacity*) 498; discretion &c. (*caution*) 864; *finesse*; craftiness &c. (*cunning*) 702; management &c. (*conduct*) 692; *ars celare artem*; self-help.

cleverness, talent, ability, ingenuity, capacity, parts, talents, faculty, endow-

ment, *forte*, turn, gift, genius, flair, feeling; intelligence &c. 498; sharpness, readiness &c. (*activity*) 682; invention &c. 515; apt-ness, -itude- turn –, capacity –, genius- for; felicity, capability, *curiosa felicitas*, qualification, habilitation.

proficient &c. 700.

masterpiece, *coup de maître, chef-d'œuvre, tour de force*; good stroke &c. (*plan*) 626.

V. be -skilful &c. *adj.*; excel in, be master of; have -a turn for &c. *n.*

know -what's what, – a hawk from a handsaw, – what one is about, – on which side one's bread is buttered, – what's o'clock, – a thing or two; have cut one's -eye, – wisdom- teeth.

see -one's way, – where the wind lies, – which way the wind blows; have -all one's wits about one, – one's hand in; *savoir vivre; scire quid valeant humeri quid ferre recusent*.

look after the main chance; cut one's coat according to one's cloth; live by one's wits; exercise one's discretion, feather the oar, sail near the wind; stoop to conquer &c. (*cunning*) 702; play one's -cards well, – best card; hit the right nail on the head, put the saddle on the right horse.

take advantage of, make the most of; profit by &c. (*use*) 677; make a hit &c. (*succeed*) 731; make a virtue of necessity; make hay while the sun shines &c. (*occasion*) 134.

Adj. skilful, dexterous, adroit, expert, apt, slick, handy, quick, deft, ready, resourceful, gain; smart &c. (*active*) 682; proficient, good at, up to, at home in, master of, a good hand at, *au fait*, thoroughbred, masterly, crack, accomplished; conversant &c. (*knowing*) 490.

experienced, practised, skilled; up –, well up- in; in -practice, – proper cue; competent, efficient, qualified, capable, fitted, fit for, up to the mark, trained, initiated, prepared, primed, finished.

clever, able, ingenious, felicitous, gifted, talented, endowed, cute, inventive &c. 515; shrewd, sharp &c. (*intelligent*) 498; cunning &c. 702; alive to, up to snuff, not to be caught with chaff; discreet.

neat-handed, fine-fingered, ambidextrous, sure-footed; cut out -, fitted- for.

technical, artistic, scientific, dædalian, shipshape; workman-, business-, statesman-like.

Adv. skillfully &c. *adj.*; well &c. 618; artistically; with -skill, - consummate skill; *secundum artem, suo Marte*; to the best of one's abilities &c. (*exertion*) 686; like a machine.

699. Unskilfulness.—N. unskilfulness &c. *adj.*; want of -skill &c. 698; incompeten-ce, -cy; in-ability, -felicity, -dexterity, -experience; clumsiness; disqualification, unproficiency; quackery.

folly, stupidity &c. 499; indiscretion &c. (*rashness*) 863; thoughtlessness &c. (*inattention*) 458, (*neglect*) 460.

mis-management, -conduct; impolicy; maladministration; mis-rule, -government, -application, -direction, -feasance.

absence of rule, rule of thumb; bungling &c. *v.*; failure &c. 732; screw loose; too many cooks.

blunder &c. (*mistake*) 495; *étourderie, gaucherie*, act of folly, *balourdise*; botch, -ery; bad job, sad work.

sprat sent out to catch a whale, much ado about nothing, wildgoose chase.

bungler &c. 701; fool &c. 501.

layman, amateur.

V. be -unskilful &c. *adj.*; not see an inch beyond one's nose; blunder, bungle, boggle, fumble, muff, botch, bitch, flounder, loppet, stumble, trip; hobble &c. 275; put one's foot in it; make a -mess, - hash, - sad work- of; overshoot the mark.

play -tricks with, - Puck; mismanage, -conduct, -direct, -apply, -send.

stultify -, make a fool of -, commit-oneself; act foolishly; play the fool; put oneself out of court; lose one's -head, - cunning.

begin at the wrong end; do things by halves &c. (*not complete*) 730; make two

bites of a cherry; play at cross purposes; strain at a gnat and swallow a camel &c. (*caprice*) 608; put the cart before the horse; lock the stable door when the horse is stolen &c. (*too late*) 135.

not know -what one is about, - one's own interest, - on which side one's bread is buttered; stand in one's own light, quarrel with one's bread and butter, throw a stone in one's own garden, kill the goose which lays the golden eggs, pay dear for one's whistle, cut one's own throat, burn one's fingers; knock -, run- one's head against a stone wall; fall into a trap, catch a Tartar, bring the house about one's ears; have too many -eggs in one basket (*imprudent*) 863, - irons in the fire.

mistake &c. 495; take the shadow for the substance &c. (*credulity*) 486; be in the wrong box, aim at a pigeon and kill a crow; take -, get- the wrong sow by the ear, - the dirty end of the stick; put -the saddle on the wrong horse, - a square peg into a round hole, - new wine into old bottles.

cut a whetstone with a razor; hold a farthing candle to the sun &c. (*useless*) 645; fight with -, graps at- a shadow; catch at straws, lean on a broken reed, reckon without one's host, pursue a wildgoose chase; go on a fool's -, sleeveless- errand; go further and fare worse; lose -, miss- one's way; fail &c. 732.

Adj. un-skilful &c. 698; unskilled, inexpert; bungling &c. *v.*; awkward, clumsy, unhandy, lubberly, *gauche, maladroit*; left-, heavy-handed; slovenly, slatternly; gawky.

adrift, at fault.

in-, un-apt; inhabile; un-tractable, -teachable; giddy &c. (*inattentive*) 458; inconsiderate &c. (*neglectful*) 460; stupid &c. 499; inactive &c. 683; incompetent; un-, dis-, ill-qualified; unfit; quackish; raw, green, inexperienced, rusty, out of practice.

un-accustomed, -used, -trained &c. 537, -initiated, -conversant &c.

(*ignorant*) 491; shiftless; unbusinesslike, unpractical; unstatesmanlike.

un-, ill-, mis-advised; ill-devised, -imagined, -judged, -contrived, -conducted; un-, mis-guided; misconducted, foolish, wild; infelicitous; penny wise and pound foolish &c. (*inconsistent*) 608.

Phr. one's fingers being all thumbs; the right hand forgets its cunning.

il se noyerait dans une goutte d'eau.

incidit in Scyllam qui vult vitare Charybdim; out of the frying pan into the fire.

700. Proficient.—N. proficient, expert, adept, dab; *connoisseur* &c. (*scholar*) 492; master, -hand; topsawyer, *prima donna*, first fiddle, *chef de cuisine*; protagonist; past master; profess-or, -ional, specialist.

picked man; medallist, prizeman.

veteran; old -stager, - campaigner, - soldier, - file, - hand; man of -business, - the world.

nice -, good -, clean- hand; practised -, experienced- -eye, - hand; marksman; good -, dead -, crack- shot; ropedancer, funambulist, acrobat, contortionist; cunning man; conjuror &c. (*deceiver*) 548; wizard &c. 994.

genius; master-mind, - head, - spirit.

cunning -, sharp -blade, - fellow; jobber; cracksman &c. (*thief*) 792; politician, tactician, diplomat, -ist, strategist.

pantologist, admirable Crichton, Jack of all trades; prodigy of learning; walking encyclopædia; mine of information.

701. Bungler.—N. bungler; blunderer, -head; marplot, fumbler, lubber, lout, oaf, duffer, stick, clown; bad -, poor- -hand, - shot; butter-fingers.

no conjuror, flat, muff, slow coach, looby, lubber, swab; clod, yokel, hick, awkward squad, novice, greenhorn, jaywalker, *blanc-bec*.

land lubber; fresh water -, fair weather- sailor; horse-marine; fish out of water, ass in lion's skin, jackdaw in peacock's feathers; quack &c. (*deceiver*) 548; Lord of Misrule.

sloven, slattern, trapes.

Phr. *il n'a pas inventé la poudre*; he will never set the Thames on fire.

702. Cunning.—N. cunning, craft; cunningness, craftiness &c. *adj.*; subtlety, artificiality; manœuvring &c. *v.*; temporization; circumvention.

chicane, -ry; sharp practice, knavery, jugglery; concealment &c. 528; guile, duplicity &c. (*falsehood*) 544; foul play.

diplomacy, politics; Machiavellism; jobbery, back-stairs influence, gerrymandering.

art, -ifice; device, machination; plot &c. (*plan*) 626; manœuvre, stratagem, dodge, artful dodge, wile; trick, -ery &c. (*deception*) 545; *ruse, - de guerre; finesse*, side-blow, thin end of the wedge, shift, go by, subterfuge, evasion; white lie &c. (*untruth*) 546; juggle, *tour de force*; tricks -of the trade, - upon travellers; imposture, deception; *espièglerie*; net, trap &c. 545.

Ulysses, Machiavel, sly boots, fox, reynard; Scotch-, Yorkshire-man; Yankee; intriguer, *intrigant*, schemer, trickster.

V. be -cunning &c. *adj.*; have cut one's eye-teeth; contrive &c. (*plan*) 626; live by one's wits; manœuvre; intrigue, gerrymander, *finesse*, double, temporize, stoop to conquer, *reculer pour mieux sauter*, circumvent, steal a march upon; overreach &c. 545; throw off one's guard; surprise &c. 508; outdo, get the better of, snatch from under one's nose; snatch a verdict; waylay, undermine, introduce the thin end of the wedge; play -a deep game, - tricks with; have an axe to grind; *ambiguas in vulgum spargere voces*; flatter, make things pleasant.

Adj. cunning, crafty, artful; skilful &c. 698; subtle, feline, vulpine; cunning as a -fox, - serpent; deep, - laid; profound; designing, contriving; intriguing &c. *v.*; strategic, diplomatic, politic, Machiavellian, time-serving; artificial; trick-y, -sy; wily, sly, slim, insidious, stealthy, foxy; underhand &c. (*hidden*) 528; subdolous; deceitful &c.

545; double-tongued, -faced; shifty; crooked; arch, pawky, shrewd, acute; sharp, – as a needle; canny, astute, leery, knowing, up to snuff, too clever by half, not to be caught with chaff.

Adv. cunningly &c. *adj.*; slily, on the sly, by a side wind.

Phr. diamond cut diamond.

703. Artlessness.—N. artlessness &c. *adj.*; nature, simplicity; innocence &c. 946; *bonhomie, naïveté, abandon,* candour, sincerity; singleness of -purpose, – heart; honesty &c. 939; plain speaking; *épanchement.*

rough diamond, matter of fact man; *le palais de vérité; enfant terrible.*

V. be -artless &c. *adj.*; look one in the face; wear one's heart upon his sleeves for daws to peck at; think aloud; speak -out, – one's mind; be free with one, call a spade a spade.

Adj. artless, natural, pure, native, simple, plain, inartificial, untutored, unsophisticated, *ingénu,* unaffected, *naïve;* sincere, frank; open, – as day; candid, ingenuous, guileless, unsuspicious, childlike; honest &c. 939; innocent &c. 946; Arcadian; undesigning, straightforward, unreserved, unvarnished, aboveboard; simple-, single-minded; frank-, open-, single-, simple-hearted; open and above-board.

free-, plain-, out-spoken; blunt, downright, direct, matter of fact, unpoetical; unflattering.

Adv. in plain -words, – English; without mincing the matter; not to mince the matter &c. (*affirmation*) 535.

Phr. *Davus sum non Œdipus; liberavi animam meam.*

Section IV. Antagonism

1°. *Conditional Antagonism*

704. Difficulty.—N. difficulty; hardness &c. *adj.*; impracticability &c. (*impossibility*) 471; tough -, hard -, uphill-work; hard -, Herculean -, Augean-task; task of Sisyphus, Sisyphean labour, tough job, teaser, rasper, dead lift.

dilemma, embarrassment; perplexity &c. (*uncertainty*) 475; involvement; intricacy; entanglement &c. 59; cross fire; awkwardness, delicacy, ticklish card to play, deadlock, knot, Gordian knot, *dignus vindice nodus,* net, meshes, maze; coil &c. (*convolution*) 248; crooked path.

nice -, delicate -, subtle -, knotty-point; vexed question, *vexata quæstio,* poser; puzzle &c. (*riddle*) 533; paradox; hard -, nut to crack; bone to pick, *crux, pons asinorum,* where the shoe pinches.

nonplus, quandary, strait, pass, pinch, pretty pass, stress, brunt; critical situation, crisis; trial, rub, emergency, exigency, scramble.

scrape, hobble, slough, quagmire, hot water, hornet's nest; sea -, peck- of troubles; pretty kettle of fish; pickle, stew, *imbroglio,* mess, muddle, botch, fuss, bustle, ado; false position; set fast, stand; dead -lock, – set; fix, horns of a dilemma, *cul de sac;* hitch; stumbling block &c. (*hindrance*) 706.

V. be -difficult &c. *adj.*; run one hard, go against the grain, try one's patience, put one out; put to one's -shifts, – wit's end; go hard with -, try- one; pose, perplex &c. (*uncertain*) 475; bother, nonplus, gravel, bring to a dead lock; be -impossible &c. 471; be in the way of &c. (*hinder*) 706.

meet with -, labour under -, get into -, plunge into -, struggle with -, contend with -, grapple with- difficulties; labour under a disadvantage; be -in difficulty &c. *adj.*

fish in troubled waters, buffet the waves, swim against the stream, scud under bare poles.

have -much ado with, – a hard time of it; come to the -push, – pinch; bear the brunt.

grope in the dark, lose one's way, weave a tangled web, walk among eggs.

get into a -scrape &c. *n.*; bring a hornet's nest about one's ears; be put to one's shifts; flounder, boggle, struggle;

not know which way to turn &c. (*uncertain*) 475; get -tangled up, – wound up; *perdre son latin*; stick - at, – in the mud, – fast; come to a -stand, – dead lock; hold the wolf by the ears.

render -difficult &c. *adj.*; encumber, embarrass, ravel, entangle; put a spoke in the wheel &c. (*hinder*) 706; lead a pretty dance.

Adj. difficult, not easy, hard, tough; trouble-, toil-, irk-some; operose, laborious, onerous, arduous, Herculean, formidable; sooner –, more easily- said than done; difficult –, hard- to deal with; ill-conditioned, crabbed; not -to be handled with kid gloves, – made with rosewater.

awkward, unwieldy, unmanageable; intractable, stubborn &c. (*obstinate*) 606; perverse, refractory, plaguy, trying, thorny, rugged; knot-ted; -ty; invious; path-, track-less; labyrinthine &c. (*convoluted*) 248; intricate, complicated &c. (*tangled*) 59; impracticable &c. (*impossible*) 471; not -feasible &c. 470; desperate &c. (*hopeless*) 859.

embarrassing, perplexing &c. (*uncertain*) 475; delicate, ticklish, critical; beset with –, full of –, surrounded by –, entangled by –, encompassed with- difficulties.

under a difficulty; in -difficulty, – hot water, – the suds, – a cleft stick, – a fix, – the wrong box, – a scrape &c. *n.*, – deep water, – a fine pickle; *in extremis*; between -two stools, – Scylla and Charybdis; surrounded by -shoals, – breakers, – quicksands; at cross purposes; not out of the wood.

reduced to straits; hard -, sorely-pressed; run hard; pinched, put to it, straitened; hard -up, – put to it, – set; put to one's shifts; puzzled, at a loss &c. (*uncertain*) 475; at -the end of one's tether, – one's wit's end, – a nonplus, – a standstill; gravelled, nonplussed, stranded, aground; stuck -, set- fast; up a tree, at bay, *aux abois*, driven -into a corner, – from post to pillar, – to extremity, – to one's wit's end, – to the wall; *au bout de son latin*; out of one's -depth, – reckoning; put –, thrown -out.

accomplished with difficulty; hard-fought, -earned.

Adv. with -difficulty, – much ado; hardly &c. *adj.*; uphill; against the -stream, – grain; *à rebours*; *invitâ Minervâ*; in the teeth of; at –, upon- a pinch; at long odds.

Phr. ay there's the rub; *hic labor hoc opus*; things are come to a pretty pass.

705. Facility.—N. facility, ease; easiness &c. *adj.*; capability; feasibility &c. (*practicability*) 470; flexibility, pliancy &c. 324; smoothness &c. 255; convenience.

plain –, smooth –, straight- sailing; mere child's play, holiday task.

smooth water, fair wind; smooth -royal- road; clear -coast, – stage; *tabula rasa*; *full play* &c. (*freedom*) 748.

disen-cumbrance, -tanglement; deoppilation; permission &c. 760.

V. be -easy &c. *adj.*; go on –, run -smoothly; have -full play &c. *n.*; go –, run- on all fours; obey the helm, work well.

flow –, swim –, drift –, go- with the--stream, – tide; see one's way; have -it all one's own way, – the game in one's own hands; walk over the course, win -at a canter, – hands down; make -light of, – nothing of; be at home in &c. (*skilful*) 698.

render -easy &c. *adj.*; facilitate, smooth, ease; popularize; lighten, – the labour; free, clear; dis-encumber, -embarrass, -entangle, -engage; deobstruct, unclog, extricate, unravel; untie –, cut- the knot; disburden, unload, exonerate, emancipate, free from, deoppilate; humour &c. (*aid*) 707; lubricate &c. 332; relieve &c. 834.

leave -a hole to creep out of, – a loophole, – the matter open; give -the reins to, – full play, – full swing; make way for; open the -door to, – way; prepare –, smooth –, clear- the -ground, – way, – path, – road; pave the way, bridge over; permit &c. 760.

Adj. easy, facile; feasible &c. (*practicable*) 470; easily -managed, - accomplished; within reach, accessible, easy of access, for the million, open to.

manageable, wieldy; towardly, tractable; submissive; yielding, ductile; pliant &c. (*soft*) 324; glib, slippery; smooth &c. 255; on -friction wheels, - velvet; convenient.

un-, dis-burdened, -encumbered, -embarrassed; exonerated; un-loaded, -obstructed, -trammelled, -impeded, -restrained &c. (*free*) 748; at ease, light.

at -, quite at- home; in -one's element, - smooth water.

Adv. easily &c. *adj.*; readily, smoothly, swimmingly, *ad lib.*, on easy terms, single-handed.

Phr. touch and go.

Int. all clear!

2°. Active Antagonism

706. Hindrance.—N. prevention, preclusion, obstruction, stoppage; prohibition; inter-ruption, -ception, -clusion; hindrance, impedition; retardment, -ation; constriction; embarrassment, oppilation; coarctation, stricture, restriction; anchor &c. 666; restraint &c. 751 & 752; inhibition &c. 761; blockade &c. (*closure*) 261; picketing.

inter-ference, -position; obtrusion; dis-couragement, -countenance, -approval, -approbation; opposition &c. 708.

impediment, let, obstacle, obstruction, knot, knag; check, hitch, *contretemps, impasse*, screw loose, grit in the oil.

bar, stile, barrier; turn-stile, -pike; gate, portcullis; bulwark, parapet, barricade &c. (*defence*) 717; wall, dead wall, breakwater, groyne; bulkhead, block, buffer; stopper &c. 263; boom, dam, weir, burrock.

drawback, objection; stumbling-block, -stone; lion in the path; snag; snags and sawyers.

en-, in-cumbrance; clog, skid, shoe, spoke; brake, drag, - chain, - weight;

stay, stop; preventive, prophylactic; contraception; load, burden, fardel, *onus*, millstone round one's neck, *impedimenta*; dead weight; lumber, pack; nightmare, Ephialtes, incubus, old man of the sea; remora.

difficulty &c. 704; insuperable &c. 471- obstacle; estoppel; ill wind; head wind &c. (*opposition*) 708; trammel, tether &c. (*means of restraint*) 752; hold back, counterpoise; damper, wet blanket, hinderer, marplot, kill-joy, dog in the manger, interloper; trail of a red herring; opponent &c. 710.

V. hinder, impede, impedite, embarrass.

keep -, stave -, ward- off; picket; obviate; a-, ante-vert; turn aside, draw off, prevent, forefend, nip in the bud; retard, slacken, check, let; counter-act, -check; preclude, debar, foreclose, estop; inhibit &c. 761; shackle &c. (*restrain*) 751; restrict, restrain, cohibit.

obstruct, filibuster, stop, stay, bar, bolt, lock; block, - up; belay, barricade; block -, stop- the way; dam up &c. (*close*) 261; put on the -brake &c. *n.*; scotch -, lock -, put a spoke in- the wheel; put a stop to &c. 142; traverse, contravene; inter-rupt, -cept; oppose &c. 708; hedge -in, - round; cut off; interclude.

inter-pose, -fere, -meddle &c. 682.

cramp, hamper; clog, - the wheels; cumber; en-, in-cumber; handicap; choke; saddle -, load- with; overload, lay; lumber, trammel, tie one's hands, put to inconvenience; in-, dis-commode; discompose; hustle, drive into a corner; choke off.

run -, fall- foul of; cross the path of, break in upon.

thwart, frustrate, disconcert, balk, foil, baffle, snub, override, circumvent; defeat &c. 731; spike guns &c. (*render useless*) 645; spoil, mar, clip the wings of; cripple &c. (*injure*) 659; put an extinguisher on; damp; dishearten &c. (*dissuade*) 616; discountenance, throw cold water on, spoil sport; lay -, throw- a wet blanket on; cut the ground from under one, take the wind out of one's sails, undermine; be –, stand- in the way of; act as a drag; hang like a millstone round one's neck.

Adj. hindering &c. *v.*; obstr-uctive, -uent; impedi-tive, -ent; intercipient; prophylactic &c. (*remedial*) 662.

in the way of, unfavourable; onerous, burdensome; cumb-rous, -ersome; obtrusive.

hindered &c. *v.*; wind-bound, water-logged, heavy laden; hard pressed.

unassisted &c. (*see* assist &c. 707); single-handed, alone; deserted &c. 624.

707. Aid.—N. aid, -ance; assistance, help, opitulation, succour; support, lift, advance, furtherance, promotion; coadjuvancy &c. (*co-operation*) 709.

patronage, championship, countenance, favour, interest, advocacy, auspices.

sustentation, subvention, subsidy, bounty, alimentation, nutrition, nourishment, maintenance; manna in the wilderness; food &c. 298; means &c. 632.

ministr-y, -ation; subministration; accommodation.

relief, rescue; help at a dead lift; supernatural aid; *deus ex machinâ*.

supplies, reinforcements, succours, contingents, recruits; support &c. (*physical*) 215; adjunct, ally &c. (*helper*) 711.

V. aid, assist, help, succour, lend one's aid; come to the aid &c. *n.*- of; contribute, subscribe to; bring –, give –, furnish –, afford –, supply- aid &c. *n.*; render assistance; give –, stretch –, lend –, bear –, hold out- a -hand, – helping hand; give one a -lift, – cast, – turn; take -by the hand, – in tow; help a lame dog over a stile, lend wings to.

relieve, rescue; set -up, – agoing, – on one's legs; bear –, pull- through; give new life to, be the making of; reinforce, recruit; set –, put –, push- forward; give -a lift, – a shove, – an impulse- to; promote, further, forward, advance; speed, expedite, quicken, hasten.

support, sustain, uphold, prop, hold up, bolster.

cradle, nourish; nurture, nurse, dry nurse, suckle, put out to nurse; manure, cultivate, force; foster, cherish, foment; feed –, fan- the flame.

serve; do service to, tender to, pander to; ad-, sub-, minister to; tend, attend, wait on; take care of &c. 459; entertain; smooth the bed of death.

oblige, accommodate, consult the wishes of; humour, cheer, encourage.

second, stand by; back, – up; pay the piper, abet; work –, make interest –, stick up –, take up the cudgels- for; take up –, espouse –, adopt- the cause of; advocate, beat up for recruits, press into the service; squire, give moral support to, keep in countenance, countenance, patronize; lend -oneself, – one's countenance- to; smile –, shineupon; favour, befriend, take up, take in hand, enlist under the banners of; side with &c. (*co-operate*) 709.

be of use to; subserve &c. (*instrument*) 631; benefit &c. 648; render a service &c. (*utility*) 644; conduce &c. (*tend*) 176.

Adj. aiding &c. *v.*; auxiliary, adjuvant, helpful; coadjuvant &c. 709; subservient, ministrant, ancillary, accessory, subsidiary.

at one's beck; friendly, amicable, favourable, propitious, well-disposed; neighbourly; obliging &c. (*benevolent*) 906.

Adv. with –, by- -the aid &c. *n.*- of; on –, in- behalf of; in -aid, – the service, – the name, – favour, – furtherance- of; on account of; for the sake of, on the part of; *non obstante*.

Int. help! save us! to the rescue! S.O.S.!

708. Opposition.—N. opposition, antagonism; oppug-nancy, -nation; impugnation; contravention; counteraction &c. 179; counterplot.

cross-fire, under-current, head-wind.

clashing, collision, conflict, lack of harmony, contest.

competition, two of a trade, rivalry, emulation, race; war to the knife.

absence of -aid &c. 707; resistance &c. 719; restraint &c. 751; hindrance &c. 706.

V. oppose, counteract, run counter to; withstand &c. (*resist*) 719; control &c. (*restrain*) 751; hinder &c. 706; antagonize, oppugn, fly in the face of, go dead against, kick against, fall foul of; set -, pit- against; face, confront, cope with; make a -stand, - dead set- against; set -oneself, one's face- against; protest -, vote -, raise one's voice- against; disfavour, turn one's back upon; set at naught, slap in the face, slam the door in one's face.

be -, play- at cross purposes; counterwork, -mine; thwart, overthwart.

stem, breast, encounter; stem -, breast- the -tide, - current, - flood; buffet the waves; beat up -, make head-against; grapple with; kick against the pricks &c. (*resist*) 719; contend &c. 720 -, do battle &c. (*warfare*) 722- -with, - against.

contra-dict, -vene; belie; go -, run -, beat -, militate- against; come in conflict with.

emulate &c. (*compete*) 720; rival, spoil one's trade.

Adj. oppos-ing, -ed &c. *v.*; adverse, antagonistic; ambivalent; contrary &c. 14; at variance &c. 24; at issue, at war with; in opposition; 'agin the Government.'

un-favourable, -friendly; hostile, inimical, cross, unpropitious.

in hostile array, front to front, with crossed bayonets, at daggers drawn; up in arms; resistant &c. 719.

competitive, emulous.

Adv. against, *versus*, counter to, in conflict with, at cross purposes.

against the -grain, - current, - stream, - wind, - tide; with a headwind; with the wind -ahead, - in one's teeth.

in spite, in despite, in defiance; in the -way, - teeth, - face- of; across; a-, overthwart; where the shoe pinches.

though &c. 30; even; *quand même*; *per contra*.

Phr. *nitor in adversum.*

709.   Co-operation.—N. co-operation; coadju-vancy, -tancy; coagency, coefficiency; concert, concurrence, complicity, participation; union &c. 43; amalgamation, combination &c. 48; collusion.

association, alliance, colleagueship, jointstock, copartnership, trust, cartel, pool, ring, combine, interlocking directorate; confederation &c. (*party*) 712; federation, coalition, fusion; a long pull, a strong pull and a pull all together; logrolling, freemasonry.

unanimity &c. (*assent*) 488; *esprit de corps*, party spirit; clan-, partisan-ship; reciprocity, concord &c. 714.

V. co-operate, co-adjute, concur; conduce &c. 178; combine, cartelize, unite one's efforts; keep -, draw -, pull -, club -, hang -, hold -, league -, band -, be banded- together; stand -, put-shoulder to shoulder; act in concert, join forces, fraternize, cling to one another, conspire, concert, lay one's heads together; confederate, be in league with; collude, understand one another, play into the hands of, hunt in couples.

side -, take side -, go along -, go hand in hand -, join hands -, make common cause -, strike in -, unite -, join -, mix oneself up -, take -, play along -, cast in one's lot- with; join -, enter into- partnership with; rally round, follow the lead of; come to, pass over to, come into the views of; be -, row -, sail- in the same boat; sail on the same tack.

be a party to, lend oneself to; participate; have a -hand in, - finger in the pie; take -, bear- part in; second &c. (*aid*) 707; take the part of, play the game of; espouse a -cause, - quarrel.

Adj. co-operating &c. *v.*; in -co-operation &c. *n.*, - league &c. (*party*) 712; coadju-vant, -tant; hand and glove with.

favourable &c. 707- to; un-opposed &c. 708.

Adv. as one man &c. (*unanimously*) 488; shoulder to shoulder; in co-operation with.

710. Opponent.—N. opponent, antagonist, adversary; adverse party, opposition; enemy &c. 891; assailant.

oppositionist, obstructive; obscurantist; brawler, wrangler, disputant, extremist, irreconcilable, diehard, bitter-ender.

malcontent; Jacobin, Fenian &c. 742; demagogue, reactionist.

passive resister, conscientious objector.

rival, competitor, contestant.

711. Auxiliary.—N. auxiliary; recruit; assistant; adju-vant, -tant; adjunct; help, -er, -mate, -ing hand; midwife; colleague, partner, mate, *confrère*, co-operator; coadju-tor, -trix; collaborator.

ally; friend &c. 890, confidant, *fidus Achates*, pal, chum, buddy, *alter ego.*

confederate; ac-, complice; accessory, - after the fact; *particeps criminis.*

aide-de-camp, secretary, clerk, associate, marshal; right-hand; candle-, bottle-holder; hand-maid; servant &c. 746; puppet, cat's-paw, stooge, dependent, creature, jackal; tool, *âme damnée*, satellite, adherent, parasite.

votary, disciple; secta-rian, -ry; seconder, backer, upholder, supporter, abettor, advocate, partisan, champion, patron, friend at court, mediator.

friend in need, Jack at a pinch, *deus ex machinâ*, guardian angel, fairy godmother; special providence, tutelary genius.

712. Party.—N. party, faction, side, denomination, class, communion, set, crowd, crew, band, horde, posse, phalanx, regiment &c. 726; family, clan &c. 166.

Tories, Conservatives, Unionists, Whigs, Liberals, Radicals, Labour party, Socialists, Communists &c.; Republi-

cans, Democrats, Farmer-Labor; *Fascisti*, Revolutionaries &c. 742.

community, body, fellowship, sodality, solidarity; con-, fraternity; sorority; brother-, sister-hood.

Freemasons, Knights Templars, Odd Fellows, Ku Klux Klan &c.

knot, gang, *clique*, ring, circle; *coterie*, club, *casino.*

corporation, corporate body, guild; establishment, company; co-partnership; firm, house; joint concern, joint-stock company, trust, investment trust, combine &c. 709.

society, association; instit-ute, -ution; union; trade-union; league, syndicate, alliance, *Verein, Bund, Zollverein*, combination; league -, alliance- offensive and defensive; coalition; federation; confedera -tion, -cy; junto, cabal, *camarilla, camorra, brigue;* freemasonry; party spirit &c. (*co-operation*) 709.

staff; cast, *dramatis personæ.*

V. unite, join; club together &c. (*co-operate*) 709; cement -, form- a party &c. *n.*; associate &c. (*assemble*) 72.

Adj. in -league, - partnership, - alliance &c. *n.*

bonded -, banded -, linked &c. (*joined*) 43- together; embattled; confederated, federative, joint, corporate, leagued, fraternal, masonic, cliquish.

Adv. hand in hand, side by side, shoulder to shoulder, *en masse*, in the same boat.

713. Discord.—N. disagreement &c. 24; dis-cord, -accord, -sidence, -sonance; jar, clash, shock; jarring, jostling &c. *v.*; screw loose.

variance, difference, dissension, misunderstanding, cross purposes, odds, *brouillerie*; division, split, rupture, disruption, division in the camp, house divided against itself, rift within the lute; disunion, breach; schism &c. (*dissent*) 489; feud, faction.

quarrel, dispute, rippet, spat, tiff, *tracasserie*, squabble, altercation, words, high words; wrangling &c. *v.*; jangle, brabble, cross questions and crooked answers, snip-snap; family jars.

polemics; litigation; strife &c. (*contention*) 720; warfare &c. 722; outbreak, open rupture; breaking off of negotiations, recall of ambassadors; declaration of war.

broil, brawl, row, racket, hubbub, rixation; embroilment, embranglement, *imbroglio*, *fracas*, breach of the peace, piece of work, scrimmage, rumpus; breeze, squall; riot, disturbance &c. (*disorder*) 59; commotion &c. (*agitation*) 315; bear garden, Donnybrook Fair.

subject of dispute, ground of quarrel, battle ground, disputed point; bone -of contention, - to pick; apple of discord, *casus belli*; question at issue &c. (*subject of inquiry*) 461; vexed question, *vexata quæstio*, brand of discord.

troublous times; cat-and-dog life; contentiousness &c. *adj.*; enmity &c. 889; hate &c. 898; Kilkenny cats; disputant &c. 710; strange bedfellows.

V. be -discordant &c. *adj.*; disagree, come amiss &c. 24; clash, jar, jostle, pull different ways, conflict, have no measures with, misunderstand one another; live like cat and dog; differ; dissent &c. 489; have a -bone to pick, - crow to pluck- with.

fall out, quarrel, dispute; litigate; controvert &c. (*deny*) 536; squabble, wrangle, jangle, brangle, bicker, nag; spar &c. (*contend*) 720; have -words &c. *n.* with; fall foul of.

split; break -, break squares -, part company- with; declare war, try conclusions; join -, put in- issue; pick a quarrel, fasten a quarrel on; sow -, stir up- -dissension &c. *n.*; embroil, estrange, entangle, disunite, widen the breach; set -at odds, - together by the ears; set -, pit- against; rub up the wrong way.

get into hot water, fish in troubled waters, brawl; kick up a -row, - dust; turn the house out of window.

Adj. discordant; disagreeing &c. *v.*; out of tune, dissonant, inharmonious, harsh, grating, jangling, ajar, on bad terms; dissentient &c. 489; inconsistent, contradictory, incongruous, discrepant; un- -reconciled, -pacified.

quarrelsome, unpacific; gladiatorial, controversial, polemic, disputatious; factious; liti-gious, -gant; pettifogging.

at odds, at loggerheads, at daggers drawn, at variance, at issue, at cross purposes, at sixes and sevens, at feud, at high words; up in arms, together by the ears, in hot water, embroiled.

torn, disunited.

Phr. *quot homines tot sententiæ*; no love lost between them, *non nostrum tantas componere lites*.

714. Concord.—N. concord, accord, harmony, symphony, homology; agreement &c. 23; sympathy &c. (*love*) 897; response; union, unison, unity; bonds of harmony; peace &c. 721; unanimity &c. (*assent*) 488; league &c. 712; happy family.

rapprochement; *réunion*; amity &c. (*friendship*) 888; reciprocity; alliance, *entente cordiale*, good understanding, conciliation, arbitration, peacemaker &c. 724.

V. agree &c. 23; accord, harmonize with; fraternize; be -concordant &c. *adj.*; go hand in hand; blend -, tone in- with; run parallel &c. (*concur*) 178; understand one another; pull together &c. (*co-operate*) 709; put up one's horses together, sing in chorus.

side -, sympathize -, go -, chime in -, fall in- with; come round; be pacified &c. 723; assent &c. 488; enter into the -ideas, - feelings- of; reciprocate.

hurler avec les loups; go -, swim- with the stream.

pour oil on troubled waters, keep in good humour, render accordant, put in tune; come to an understanding, meet half-way; keep the -, remain at- peace.

Adj. concordant, congenial; agreeing &c. *v.*; in- accord &c. *n.*; harmonious, united, cemented; banded together &c. 712; allied; friendly &c. 888; fraternal; conciliatory; at one with; of one mind &c. (*assent*) 488.

at peace, in still water; tranquil &c. (*pacific*) 721.

Adv. with one voice &c. (*assent*) 488; in concert with, hand in hand; on one's side, unanimously.

715. Defiance.—N. defiance; daring &c. *v.*; dare, challenge, *cartel*; threat &c. 909; war-cry, -whoop.

V. defy, dare, beard; brave &c. (*courage*) 861; bid defiance to; set at -defiance, – naught; hurl defiance at; dance the war dance; snap the fingers at, laugh to scorn; disobey &c. 742.

show -fight, – one's teeth, – a bold front; bluster, look big, stand akimbo; double –, shake- the fist; threaten &c. 909.

challenge, call out; throw –, fling-down the -gauntlet, – gage, – glove.

Adj. defiant; defying &c. *v.*; with arms akimbo; rebellious, insolent; reckless, greatly daring.

Adv. in -defiance, – the teeth- of; under one's very nose.

Int. do your worst! come if you dare! come on! marry come up! hoity toity!

Phr. *noli me tangere; nemo me impune lacessit.*

716. Attack.—N. attack; assault, – and battery; onset, onslaught, charge.

aggression, drive, offence; incursion, inroad, invasion; irruption; outbreak; *estrapade, ruade; coup de main*, sally, *sortie, camisade*, raid, foray; run -at, – against; dead set at.

storm, -ing; boarding, *escalade*; siege, investment, obsession, bombardment, cannonade; air raid.

fire, volley; platoon –, file –, rapid-fire; *fusillade*; sharp-shooting, sniping; broadside; raking –, cross –, machine gun- fire; volley of grapeshot, *feu d'enfer*; salvo.

cut, thrust, lunge, pass, *passado*, *carte* and *tierce*, home thrust; *coup de pied*; kick, punch &c. (*impulse*) 276.

battue, razzia, Jacquerie, dragonnade; devastation &c. 162.

assailant, aggressor, invader.

base of operations, point of attack.

V. attack, assault, assail; set –, fall-upon; charge, impugn, break a lance with, enter the lists.

assume –, take- the offensive; be –, become- the aggressor; strike the first blow, fire the first shot, throw the first stone at; lift a hand –, draw the sword-against; take up the cudgels; advance –, march- against; march upon, invade, harry; come on, show fight.

strike at, poke at, thrust at; aim –, deal- a blow at; give –, fetch- one a -blow, – kick; have a -cut, – shot, – fling, – shy- at; be down –, pounce- upon; fall foul of, pitch into, launch out against; bait, slap on the face; make a -thrust, – pass, – set, – dead set- at; dunt; bear down upon.

close with, come to close quarters, bring to bay.

ride full tilt against; let fly at, dash at, run a tilt at, rush at, tilt at, run at, fly at, hawk at, have at, let out at; make a -dash, – rush at; attack tooth and nail; strike home; drive –, press-one hard; be hard upon, run down, strike at the root of.

lay about one, run amuck.

fire -upon, – at, – a shot at; shoot at, pop at, level at, let off a gun at; open fire, pepper, bombard, shell, pour a broadside into; fire -a volley, – red-hot shot; spring a mine.

throw -a stone, – stones- at; stone, lapidate, pelt; hurl -at, – against, – at the head of.

beset, besiege, beleaguer; lay siege to, invest, open the trenches, plant a battery, sap, mine; storm, board, scale the walls.

cut and thrust; bayonet, butt; kick, strike &c. (*impulse*) 276; whip &c. (*punish*) 972.

Adj. attacking &c. *v.*; aggressive, offensive, obsidional.

up in arms; on the warpath; over the top.

Adv. on the offensive.

Int. 'up and at them!'

717. Defence.—N. defence, protection, guard, ward; shielding &c. *v.*;

propugnation; preservation &c. 670; guardianship.

self-defence, -preservation; resistance &c. 719.

safeguard &c. (*safety*) 664; screen &c. (*shelter*) 666, (*concealment*) 530; barrage; fortification; muni-tion, -ment; bulwark, fosse, moat, ditch, intrenchment, trench, dugout, gas mask; dike, dyke; parapet, parados, sunk fence, embankment, mound, mole, bank; earthfield-work, gabions; fence, wall, dead wall, contravallation; paling &c. (*inclosure*) 232; palisade, haha, stockade, *stoccado*, *laager*, *sangar*; barri-er, -cade; boom; portcullis, *chevaux de frise*; aba-, abat-, abba-tis; *vallum*, circumvallation, battlement, rampart, scarp; e-, counter-scarp; glacis, casemate.

mine, countermine.

buttress, abutment; shore &c. (*support*) 215.

breastwork, *banquette*, curtain, mantlet, bastion, demilune, redan, ravelin; advanced -, horn -, out- work, lunette; barb-acan, -ican; redoubt; fort-elage, -alice; lines; coast defence.

loop-hole, machicolation; sally-port, postern gate.

hold, stronghold, fastness; asylum &c. (*refuge*) 666; keep, donjon, fortress, citadel; capitol, castle; tower, - of strength; fort, barracoon, pah, sconce, martello tower, peel-house, block-house, rath; wooden walls; turret, barbette.

buffer, corner-stone, fender, apron, mask, gauntlet, thimble, carapace, armour, shield, buckler; target, targe, ægis, breastplate, cuirass, plastron, habergeon, mail, coat of mail, brigandine, hauberk, lorication, helmet, helm, basinet, sallet, salade, heaume, morion, murrion, armet, cabaset, vizor, casquetel, siege-cap, head-piece, casque, steel helmet, tin hat; *pickelhaube*, csako; shako &c. (*dress*) 225; bearskin; panoply; truncheon &c. (*weapon*) 727.

garrison, picket, piquet; defender, protector; guardian &c. (*safety*) 664; trabant, body guard, champion; knight-errant, Paladin; propugner.

V. defend, forfend, fend; shield, screen, shroud; fence round &c. (*circumscribe*) 229; fence, intrench; guard &c (*keep safe*) 664; guard against; take care of &c. (*vigilance*) 459; bear harmless; keep -, ward -, beat- off; hinder &c. 706.

parry, repel, propugn, put to flight; give a warm reception to [*ironical*]; hold -, keep- at -bay, - arm's length.

stand -, act- on the defensive; show fight; maintain -, stand- one's ground; stand by; hold one's own; bear -, stand- the brunt; fall back upon, hold, stand in the gap.

Adj. defending &c. *v.*; defensive; mural; armed, - at all points, - *cap-à-pie*, - to the teeth; panoplied, accoutred, harnessed; iron-plated, -clad; loopholed, castellated, machicolated, casemated; defended &c. *v.*; proof against, bomb-, bullet-proof; protective.

Adv. defensively; on the -defence, - defensive; in defence; at bay, *pro aris et focis*.

Int. no surrender! *il ne passeront pas!*
Phr. defence not defiance.

718. Retaliation.—N. retaliation, reprisal, retort; counter-stroke, -blast, -plot, -project; retribution, *lex talionis*; reciprocation &c. (*reciprocity*) 12.

requital, desert, tit for tat, give and take, blow for blow, *quid pro quo*, a Roland for an Oliver, measure for measure, an eye for an eye, diamond cut diamond, the biter bit, a game at which two can play; boomerang.

recrimination &c. (*accusation*) 938; revenge &c. 919; compensation &c. 30; reaction &c. (*recoil*) 277.

V. retaliate, retort, turn upon; pay -off, - back; pay in -one's own, - the same- coin; cap; reciprocate &c. 148; turn the tables upon, return the compliment; give -a *quid pro quo* &c. *n.*, - as much as one takes; give and take, exchange -blows, - fisticuffs; be -quits, - even- with; pay off old scores.

serve one right, be hoist on one's own

petard, throw a stone in one's own garden, catch a Tartar.

Adj. retaliating &c. *v.*; retalia-tory, -tive; retributive, recriminatory, reciprocal.

Adv. in retaliation; *en revanche.*

Phr. *mutato nomine de te fabula narratur*; *par pari refero*; *tu quoque*; you're another; *suo sibi gladio hunc jugulo.*

719. Resistance.—N. resistance, stand, front, oppugnation; opposition &c. 708; renitence, reluctation, recalcitration, recalcitrance; repugnance; kicking &c. *v.*

repulse, rebuff.

insurrection &c. (*disobedience*) 742; strike; turn -, lock -, barring- out; *levée en masse*, *Jacquerie*; riot &c. (*disorder*) 59.

V. resist; not -submit &c. 725; repugn, reluctate, withstand; stand up -, strive -, bear up -, be proof -, make head- against; stand, - firm, - one's ground, - the brunt of, - out; hold -one's ground, - one's own, - out.

breast the -wave, - current; stem the -tide, - torrent; face, confront, grapple with; show a bold front &c. (*courage*) 861; present a front; make a -, take one's- stand.

kick, - against; recalcitrate, kick against the pricks; oppose &c. 708; fly in the face of; lift the hand against &c. (*attack*) 716; rise up in arms &c. (*war*) 722; strike, turn out; draw up a round robin &c. (*remonstrate*) 932; revolt &c. (*disobey*) 742; make a riot.

prendre le mors aux dents; take the bit between the teeth; sell one's life dearly, die hard, keep at bay; repel, repulse.

Adj. resisting &c. *v.*; resist-ive, -ant; refractory &c. (*disobedient*) 742; recalcitrant, re-nitent, -pulsive, -pellant; up in arms.

proof against; unconquerable &c. (*strong*) 159; stubborn, unconquered; indomitable &c. (*persevering*) 604a; unyielding &c. (*obstinate*) 606.

Int. hands off! keep off!

720. Contention.—N. contention, strife; contest, -ation; struggle; belligerency; opposition &c. 708.

controversy, polemics; debate &c. (*discussion*) 476; war of words, logomachy, litigation; paper war, ink slinging; high words &c. (*quarrel*) 713; sparring &c. *v.*

competition, rivalry; corrival-ry, -ship; agonism, *concours*, match, race, horse-racing, heat, steeple chase, point-to-point race, handicap; boat race, regatta; field-day; sham fight, Derby day; turf, sporting, bull-fight, tauromachy, *gymkhana*, rodeo, Olympiad.

wrestling, *ju-jitsu*, pugilism, boxing, fisticuffs, spar, mill, set-to, scrap, round, bout, event; prize-fighting; quarter-staff, single stick; gladiatorship; gymnastics; athletic-s, - sports; games of skill &c. 840.

shindy; *fracas* &c. (*discord*) 713; clash of arms; tussle, scuffle, broil, fray; affray, -ment; velitation; col-, luctation; brabble, *brigue*, scramble, *mêlée*, scrimmage, stramash, bush-fighting.

free -, stand up -, hand to hand -, running- fight.

conflict, skirmish; ren-, en-counter, *rencontre*, collision, affair, brush, fight; battle, - royal; combat, action, engagement, joust, tournament; tilt, -ing; tourney, list; pitched battle, guerilla warfare.

death-struggle, struggle for life or death, Armageddon; hard knocks, sharp contest, tug of war.

naval -engagement, - battle; *naumachia*, sea-fight.

duel, -lo; single combat, monomachy, satisfaction, *passage d'armes*, passage of arms, affair of honour; triangular duel; hostile meeting, digladiation; appeal to arms &c. (*warfare*) 722.

deeds -, feats- of arms; pugnacity; combativeness &c. *adj.*; bone of contention &c. 713.

V. contend; contest, strive, struggle, scramble, wrestle; spar, square; exchange -blows, - fisticuffs; scrap, mix with, fib, justle, tussle, tilt, box, stave, fence; skirmish; fight &c. (*war*) 722; wrangle &c. (*quarrel*) 713.

contend &c. –, grapple –, engage –, close –, buckle –, bandy –, try conclusions –, have a brush &c. *n.* –, tilt- with; encounter, fall foul of, pitch into, clapperclaw, run a tilt at; oppose &c. 708; reluct.

join issue, come to blows, be at loggerheads, set-to, come to the scratch, exchange shots, measure swords, meet hand to hand; take up the -cudgels, – glove, – gauntlet; enter the lists; couch one's lance; give satisfaction; appeal to arms &c. (*warfare*) 722.

lay about one; break the peace.

compete –, cope –, vie –, race- with; outvie, emulate, rival; run a race; contend &c. –, stipulate –, stickle- for; insist upon, make a point of.

Adj. contending &c. *v.*; together by the ears, at loggerheads, at war, at issue.

competitive, rival; belligerent; contentious, combative, bellicose, unpeaceful; warlike &c. 722; quarrelsome &c. 901; pugnacious; pugilistic, gladiatorial; palestric, -al.

Phr. *a verbis ad verbera*; a word and a blow.

721. Peace.—N. peace; amity &c. (*friendship*) 888; harmony &c. (*concord*) 714; tranquillity &c. (*quiescence*) 265; truce &c. (*pacification*) 723; pacificism; pipe –, calumet- of peace.

piping time of peace, quiet life, neutrality.

V. be at peace; keep the peace &c. (*concord*) 714; make peace &c. 723.

Adj. pacific; peace-able, -ful; calm, tranquil, untroubled, halcyon; bloodless; neutral.

Phr. the storm blown over; the lion lies down with the lamb.

722. Warfare.—N. warfare; fighting &c. *v.*; hostilities; war, arms, the sword; Mars, Bellona, grim visaged war, *horrida bella*, Armageddon.

appeal to -arms, – the sword; ordeal –, wager- of battle; *ultima ratio regum*, arbitrament of the sword.

battle array, campaign, crusade, expedition; mobilization; state of siege; battle-field &c. (*arena*) 728; warpath.

art of war, tactics, strategy, castrametation; general-, soldier-ship; aerial –, submarine –, naval –, chemical- warfare; military evolutions, ballistics, gunnery; chivalry; poison gas; gunpowder, shot, – and shell.

battle, tug of war &c. (*contention*) 720; service, campaigning, active service, tented field; fiery cross, trumpet, clarion, bugle, pibroch, slogan; war-cry, -whoop; battle cry, beat of drum, rappel, tom-tom; word of command; pass-, watch-word.

war to the -death, – knife; *guerre à -mort, – outrance*; open –, internecine –, civil- war.

V. arm; raise –, mobilize- troops; raise up in arms; take up the cudgels &c. 720; take up –, fly to –, appeal to- -arms, – the sword; draw –, unsheathe-the sword; dig up the hatchet; go to –, declare –, wage –, let slip the dogs of-war; cry havoc; kindle –, light- the torch of war; raise one's banner, send round the fiery cross; hoist the black flag; throw –, fling- away the scabbard; enrol, enlist, join up; take the field; take the law into one's own hands; do –, give –, join –, engage in –, go to- battle; flesh one's sword; set to, fall to, engage, measure swords, draw the trigger, cross swords; come to -blows, – close quarters; fight; combat; contend &c. 720; battle –, break a lance- with.

serve; see –, be on- -service, – active service; campaign; wield the sword, shoulder a musket, smell powder, be under the fire; spill –, imbrue the hands in- blood; be on the warpath.

carry on -war, – hostilities; keep the field; fight the good fight; go over the top; cut one's way through; fight -it out, – like devils, – one's way, – hand to hand; sell one's life dearly.

Adj. conten-ding, -tious &c. 720; armed, – to the teeth, – cap-à-pie; sword in hand; in –, under –, up in- arms; at war with; bristling with arms; in -battle array, – open arms, – the field; embattled.

unpacific, unpeaceful; belligerent, combative, armigerous, bellicose, martial, warlike, mili-tary, -tant; soldierlike, -ly; chivalrous; strategical, internecine.

Adv. *flagrante bello*, in the -thick of the fray, – cannon's mouth; at the -sword's point, – point of the bayonet.

Int. *væ victis!* to arms! to your tents O Israel!

Phr. the battle rages.

723. Pacification.—N. pacification, conciliation; reconcil-iation, -ement; shaking of hands, accommodation, arrangement, adjustment; terms, compromise; amnesty, deed of release.

peace-offering; olive-branch; overtures; pipe –, calumet –, preliminaries-of peace.

truce, armistice; suspension of -arms, – hostilities; breathing-time; convention; *modus vivendi*; flag of truce, white flag, *parlementaire, cartel.*

hollow truce, *pax in bello;* drawn battle.

V. pacify, tranquillize, compose; allay &c. (*moderate*) 174; reconcile, propitiate, placate, conciliate, meet halfway, hold out the olive-branch, heal the breach, make peace, restore harmony, bring to terms.

settle –, arrange –, accommodate--matters, – differences; set straight; make up a quarrel, *tantas componere lites;* come to -an understanding, – terms; bridge over, hush up; make -it, – matters- up; shake hands.

raise a siege; put up –, sheathe- the sword; bury the hatchet, lay down one's arms, turn swords into ploughshares; smoke the calumet of peace, close the temple of Janus; keep the peace &c. (*concord*) 714; be -pacified &c.; come round.

Adj. conciliatory, pacificatory; composing &c. *v.;* pacified &c. *v.*

Phr. *requiescat in pace.*

724. Mediation.—N. media-tion, -torship, -tization; inter-vention, -position, -ference, -meddling, -cession; parley, negotiation, arbitration; flag of truce &c. 723; good offices, peace-offering; diploma-tics, -cy; compromise &c. 774.

mediator, intercessor, peacemaker, make-peace, negotiator, go-between; diplomatist &c. (*consignee*) 758; moderator, propitiator, umpire, arbitrator.

V. media-te, -tize; inter-cede, -pose, -fere, -vene; step in, negotiate; meet half-way; arbitrate; *magnas componere lites.*

Adj. mediatory, propitiatory, diplomatic.

725. Submission.—N. submission, yielding, acquiescence, compliance; non-resistance; obedience &c. 743; submissiveness, deference.

surrender, cession, capitulation, resignation.

obeisance, homage, kneeling, genuflexion, courtesy, curtsy, *salaam, kowtow,* prostration.

V. succumb, submit, yield, bend, resign, defer to, accede.

lay down –, deliver up- one's arms; hand over one's sword; lower –, haul down –, strike- one's flag, – colours; deliver the keys of the city.

surrender, – at discretion; cede, capitulate, come to terms, retreat, beat a retreat; draw in one's horns &c. (*humility*) 879; give -way, – ground, – in, – up; cave in; suffer judgment by default; bend, – to one's yoke; bend, – before the storm; reel back; bend &c., knuckle--down, – to, – under; knock under.

humble oneself; eat -dirt, – the leek, – humble pie; bite –, lick- the dust; be –, fall- at one's feet; craven; crouch before, throw oneself at the feet of; swallow the -leek, – pill; kiss the rod; turn the other cheek; *avaler des couleuvres,* gulp down.

obey &c. 743; kneel to, bow to, pay homage to, cringe to, truckle to; bend the -neck, – knee; kneel, fall on one's

knees, bow submission, courtesy, curtsy, *kowtow*; make obeisance.

pocket the affront; make -the best of,
– a virtue of necessity; grin and abide,
shrug the shoulders, resign oneself; submit with a good grace &c. (*bear with*)
826.

Adj. surrendering &c. *v.*; submissive,
resigned, crouching; downtrodden;
down on one's marrow bones; on one's
bended knee; weakkneed, un-, non-
resisting; pliant &c. (*soft*) 324; undefended.

untenable, indefensible; humble &c.
879.

Phr. have it your own way; it can't be
helped; amen &c. (*assent*) 488.

726. Combatant.—N. combatant;
disputant, controversialist, polemic, litigant, belligerent; competitor, rival,
corrival; fighter, assailant, aggressor;
champion, Paladin; moss-trooper,
swashbuckler, fire-eater, duellist, bully,
bludgeon-man, rough, fighter, fighting-
man, prizefighter, pugilist, pug, boxer,
bruiser, the fancy, gladiator, athlete,
wrestler; fighting-, game-cock, swordsman, *sabreur*.

warrior, soldier, Amazon, man-at-
arms, armigerent; campaigner, veteran;
red-coat, military man, *rajpoot*, brave.

armed force, troops, soldiery, military, forces, sabaoth, the army, standing
army, regulars, the line, troops of the
line, militia, territorials, yeomanry, vol-
unteers, trainband, fencible; auxiliary –,
reserve- forces; reserves, *posse comitatus*, national guard, *gendarme*, beef-
eater; guards, -man; yeoman of the
guard, life guards, household troops.

janissary; myrmidon; Mama-, Mameluke, spahee, *spahi*, Cossack, Croat,
Pandour; irregular, free lance, *franc-
tireur, bashi-bazouk, guerilla, condottiere*; mercenary.

levy, draught, commando; *Landwehr, -sturm*; conscript, recruit, rookie,
cadet, raw levies.

private, – soldier; Tommy Atkins,
rank and file, peon, trooper, doughboy,

sepoy, *askari, légionnaire*, legionary,
food for powder, cannon fodder; officer
&c. (*commander*) 745; subaltern, ensign, shave-tail, standard bearer, non-
com; spear-, pike-man; halberdier, lancer; musketeer, carabineer, rifleman,
sharpshooter, yager, skirmisher; grenadier, fusileer; archer, bowman.

horse and foot; horse –, foot- soldier;
cavalry, horse, artillery, horse –, field
–, heavy –, mountain- artillery, infantry,
light horse, *voltigeur, Uhlan*, mounted
rifles, dragoon, hussar, trooper; light –,
heavy- dragoon; heavy; *cuirassier*; gunner, cannoneer, bombardier, artilleryman, matross; sapper, – and miner; engineer; light infantry, rifles, *chasseur,
zouave*; military train, supply and transport, coolie.

army, – corps, *corps d'armée*, host,
division, column, wing, detachment, *escadrille*, garrison, flying column, brigade, regiment, *corps*, battalion, squadron, company, platoon, battery,
subdivision, section, squad; piquet,
picket, guard, rank, file; legion, phalanx, cohort; cloud of skirmishers; impi.

war-horse, charger, *destrier*.

armoured -train, – car; tank.

marine, man of war's man &c. (*sail-
or*) 269; navy, first line of defence,
wooden walls; naval forces, fleet, flotilla, armada, squadron.

man-of-war, warship; H.M.S.,
U.S.S., capital ship; line-of-battle ship,
battle ship; super-, dreadnought, battle
–, armoured –, protected – light-cruiser;
scout, flotilla leader; destroyer, torpedo
boat; submarine, submersible, U-boat;
submarine chaser, eagle boat, mystery
ship, Q-boat; mine-layer, -sweeper; ship
of the line, iron-clad, turretship, ram,
Monitor, floating battery; first-rate, frigate, sloop of war, corvette, gunboat,
bomb-vessel, fire-boat; flag ship, guard
ship, cruiser; airplane carrier; privateer;
tender; depôt –, parent- ship; store –,
troop- ship; transport, catamaran.

aircraft &c. 273, air force, scout,
fighter, bomber, troop carrier, aerial patrol, seaplane, flying boat, torpedo

plane; airship, Zeppelin; rigid –, semi-rigid –, non-rigid- airship; dirigible –, free –, captive –, kite –, observation-balloon.

anti-aircraft guns, searchlights, sound locators; catapult.

727. Arms.—N. arm, -s; weapon, deadly weapon; arma-ment, -ture; panoply, stand of arms; armour &c. (*defence*) 717; armoury &c. (*store*) 636.

ammunition; powder, – and shot; explosive; propellant; gun-powder, -cotton; dynam-, melin-, cord-, lydd-ite; trinitrotoluene, T.N.T., ammonal; cartridge; ball cartridge, *cartouche*, fireball; dud, black Maria; 'villainous saltpetre'; poison –, mustard –, lachrymatory –, tear- gas.

sword, sabre, broadsword, cutlass, falchion, scimitar, cimeter, brand, whinyard, bilbo, glaive, glave, rapier, skean, Toledo, Ferrara, tuck, claymore, creese, kris, *kukri*, dagger, dirk, hanger, poniard, stiletto, stylet, dudgeon, bayonet; sword-bayonet, -stick; side arms, foil, blade, steel; axe, bill; pole-, battle-axe; gisarm, halberd, partisan, tomahawk, bowie-knife; at-, att-, yat-aghan; yatachan; good –, trusty –, naked-sword; cold –, naked- steel.

club, mace, truncheon, staff, bludgeon, cudgel, life-preserver, shillelagh, sprig; hand-, quarter-staff; bat, cane, stick, knuckle-duster, sand bag.

gun, piece; fire-arms; artillery, ordnance; siege –, battering-train; park, battery; cannon, gun of position, heavy –, siege –, field –, mountain –, anti-aircraft –, breech loading –, quick firing- gun; field piece, mortar, trench mortar, mine thrower, howitzer, carronade, culverin, basilisk; falconet, jingal, swivel, *pederero, bouche à feu*; smooth bore, rifled cannon; Armstrong –, Lancaster –, Paixhan –, Whitworth –, Parrott –, Krupp –, Gatling –, Maxim –, Vickers –, Hotchkiss –, Lewis –, machine- gun; tommy gun, Thompson's submachine gun; *mitrailleu-r, -se*; pompom; blow pipe.

small arms; musket, -ry, firelock, flintlock, fowling-piece, shot gun, rifle, *fusil*, caliver, carbine, blunderbuss, musketoon, Brown Bess, matchlock, harquebuss, *arquebuse*, haguebut; petronel; smallbore; breech-, muzzle-loader; Miniè –, Enfield –, Westley Richards –, Snider –, Springfield –, Martini-Henry –, Lee-Metford –, Lee-Enfield –, Mauser –, Männlicher –, magazine –, repeating- rifle; needle-gun, *chassepot*; pistol, -et; revolver, automatic pistol, automatic; wind-, air-gun; flame –, gas-projector.

bow, cross-bow, arbalest, balister, catapult, sling; battering-ram &c. (*impulse*) 276; gunnery; ballistics &c. (*propulsion*) 284.

missile, bolt, projectile, shot, pellet, ball; grape; grape –, canister –, bar –, cannon –, langrel –, langrage –, round –, chain- shot; explosive; incendiary –, expanding –, soft-nosed –, dum-dum-bullet; slug, stone, brickbat; hand –, rifle- grenade; high explosive –, incendiary –, star –, gas-shell; depth –, gas –, incendiary –, stink- bomb; petard, torpedo, carcass, rocket; congreve, – rocket; shrapnel, *mitraille*; thunderbolt; mine, land mine, infernal machine.

pike, lance, spear, spontoon, javelin, assagai, throwing stick, dart, djerrid, arrow, reed, shaft, bolt, boomerang, harpoon, gaff.

728. Arena.—N. arena, field, platform; scene of action, theatre; walk, course; hustings; stage, boards &c. (*playhouse*) 599; amphitheatre; Coli-, Colos-seum; Flavian amphitheatre, hippodrome, circus, race-course, track, *stadium, corso*, turf, cockpit, bear-garden, playground, playing fields, *gymnasium, palæstra*, ring, lists; tilt-yard, -ing ground; *Campus Martius, Champ de Mars*; aerodrome, airport, air base, flying field.

theatre –, seat- of war; battle-field, -ground; field of -battle, – slaughter; no man's land; Aceldama, camp; the enemy's camp; trysting-place &c. (*place of meeting*) 74.

Section V. RESULTS OF VOLUNTARY ACTION

729. Completion.—N. completion; accomplish-, achieve-, fulfil-ment; performance, execution; des-, dis-patch; consummation, culmination, climax; finish, conclusion, effectuation; close &c. (*end*) 67; terminus &c. (*arrival*) 292; winding up; *finale, dénouement*, catastrophe, issue, upshot, result; final -, last -, crowning -, finishing- -touch, - stroke; last finish, *coup de grâce*; crowning of the edifice; coping-, keystone; missing link &c. 53; superstructure, *ne plus ultra*, work done, *fait accompli*.

elaboration; finality; completeness &c. 52.

V. effect, -uate; accomplish, achieve, compass, consummate, hammer out; bring to -maturity, - perfection; perfect, complete; elaborate.

do, execute, make; go -, get- through; work out, enact; bring -about, - to bear, - to pass, - through, - to a head.

des-, dis-patch; knock -, finish -, polish- off; make short work of; dispose of, set at rest; perform, discharge, fulfil, realize; put in -practice, - force; carry -out, - into effect, - into execution; make good; be as good as one's word.

do thoroughly, not do by halves, go the whole hog; drive home; be in at the death &c. (*persevere*) 604a; carry through, play out, exhaust, deliver the goods, fill the bill.

finish, bring to a close &c. (*end*) 67; wind up, stamp, clinch, seal, set the seal on, put the seal to; give the -final touch &c. *n.* to; put the -last, - finishing- hand to; crown, - all; cap.

ripen, culminate; come to a -head, - crisis; come to its end; die -a natural death, - of old age; run -its course, - one's race; touch -, reach -, attain- the

goal; reach &c. (*arrive*) 292; get in the harvest.

Adj. completing, final; conclu-ding, -sive; crowning &c. *v.*; exhaustive, complete, mature, perfect, consummate.

done, completed &c. *v.*; done for, sped, wrought out; highly wrought &c. (*preparation*) 673; thorough &c. 52; ripe &c. (*ready*) 673.

Adv. completely &c. (*thoroughly*) 52; to crown all, out of hand.

Phr. the race is run; *actum est; finis coronat opus; consummatum est; c'en est fait*; it is all over, the game is played out, the bubble has burst.

730. Non-Completion.—N. non-completion, -fulfilment; shortcoming &c. 304; incompleteness &c. 53; drawn -battle, - game; work of Penelope, task of Sisyphus.

non-performance, inexecution; neglect &c. 460.

V. not -complete &c. 729; leave -unfinished &c. *adj.*, - undone; neglect &c. 460; let -alone, - slip; lose sight of.

fall short of &c. 304; do things by halves; scotch the snake, not kill it; hang fire; be slow to; collapse &c. 304.

Adj. not completed &c. *v.*; incomplete &c. 53; uncompleted, unfinished, unaccomplished, unperformed, unexecuted; sketchy, addle.

in progress, in hand; going on, proceeding; on one's hands; on the fire; on the stocks; in preparation; lacking the finishing touch.

Adv. *re infectâ*.

731. Success.—N. success, -fulness; speed; advance &c. (*progress*) 282.

trump card; hit, stroke; lucky -, fortunate -, good- -hit, - stroke; bold -, master- stroke; *coup de maître*, checkmate; half the battle, prize; profit &c. (*acquisition*) 775; best seller.

continued success; good fortune &c. (*prosperity*) 734; time well spent.

advantage over; edge; upper-, whip-hand; ascendancy, mastery; expugnation, conquest, victory, subdual; subjugation &c. (*subjection*) 749.

triumph &c. (*exultation*) 884; proficiency &c. (*skill*) 698; conqueror, victor, winner, champion; master of the -situation, - position.

V. succeed; be -successful &c. *adj.*; gain one's -end, - ends; crown with success.

gain -, attain -, carry -, secure -, win- -a point, - an object; put over; make a go of; manage to, contrive to; accomplish &c. (*effect, complete*) 729; do -, work- wonders.

come off -well, - successfully, - with flying colours; make short work of; take -, carry- by storm; bear away the bell; win -one's spurs, - the battle; win -, carry -, gain- the -day, - prize, - palm; climb on the bandwagon; have -the best of it, - it all one's own way, - the game in one's own hands, - the ball at one's feet, - one on the hip; walk over the course; carry all before one, remain in possession of the field; score a success, win hands down.

speed; make progress &c. (*advance*) 282; win -, make -, work -, find- one's way; strive to some purpose; prosper &c. 734; drive a roaring trade; make profit &c. (*acquire*) 775; reap -, gather- the -fruits, - benefit of, - harvest; make one's fortune, get in the harvest, turn to good account; turn to account &c. (*use*) 677.

triumph, be triumphant; gain -, obtain- -a victory, - an advantage; chain victory to one's car.

surmount -, overcome -, get over- -a difficulty, - an obstacle &c. 706; *se tirer d'affaire*; make head against; stem the -torrent, - tide, - current; weather -the storm, - a point; turn a corner, keep one's head above water, tide over; master; get -, have -, gain- the -better of, - best of, - upper hand, - ascendancy, - whip hand, - start of; distance; surpass &c. (*superiority*) 33.

defeat, conquer, vanquish, discomfit; over-come, -throw, -power, -master, -match, -set, -ride, -reach; out-wit, -do,

-flank, -manœuvre, -general, -vote; take the wind out of one's adversary's sails; beat, - hollow; rout, lick, drub, floor, worst; put -down, - to flight, - to the rout, - *hors de combat*, - out of court.

silence, quell, nonsuit, checkmate, upset, confound, nonplus, trump; baffle &c. (*hinder*) 706; circumvent, elude; trip up, - the heels of; drive -into a corner, - to the wall; run hard, put one's nose out of joint.

settle, do for; break the -neck of, - back of; capsize, sink, shipwreck, drown, swamp; subdue; subjugate &c. (*subject*) 749; reduce; make the enemy bite the dust; victimize, roll in the dust, trample under foot, put an extinguisher upon.

answer, - the purpose; avail, prevail, take effect, do, turn out well, work well, take, tell, bear fruit; hit -it, - the mark, - the right nail on the head; nick it; turn up trumps, make a hit, find one's account in.

Adj. succeeding &c. *v.*; successful; prosperous &c. 734; triumphant; flushed -, crowned- with success; victorious; set up; in the ascendant; unbeaten &c. (*see* beat &c. *v.*); well-spent; felicitous, effective, in full swing.

Adv. successfully &c. *adj.*; with flying colours, in triumph, swimmingly; *à merveille*, beyond all hope; to some -, good- purpose; to one's heart's content.

Phr. *veni vidi vici*, the day being one's own, one's star in the ascendant; *omne tulit punctum*.

732. Failure.—N. failure; non-success, -fulfilment; dead failure, successlessness; abortion, miscarriage; *brutum fulmen* &c. 158; labour in vain &c. (*inutility*) 645; no go; inefficacy; inefficaciousness &c. *adj.*; vain -, ineffectual -, abortive- -attempt, - efforts; flash in the pan, 'lame and impotent conclusion'; frustration; slip 'twixt cup and lip &c. (*disappointment*) 509.

blunder &c. (*mistake*) 495; fault, omission, miss, oversight, slip, trip, stumble, claudication, footfall; false -, wrong- step; *faux pas*, titubation, *bévue, faute*, lurch; botchery &c. (*want of skill*) 699; scrape, jam, mess, muddle, foozle, *fiasco*, breakdown.

mishap &c. (*misfortune*) 735; split, collapse, smash, blow, explosion.

repulse, rebuff, defeat, rout, overthrow, discomfiture; beating, drubbing; *quietus*, nonsuit, subjugation; check-, fool's-mate.

fall, downfall, ruin, perdition; wreck &c. (*destruction*) 162; death-blow; bankruptcy &c. (*non-payment*) 808.

losing game, *affaire flambée*.

victim, prey; bankrupt.

V. fail; be -unsuccessful &c. *adj.*; not -succeed &c. 731; make -vain efforts &c. *n.*; do -, labour -, toil- in vain; lose one's labour, take nothing by one's motion; bring to naught, make nothing of; wash a blackamoor white &c. (*impossible*) 471; roll the stone of Sisyphus &c. (*useless*) 645; do by halves &c. (*not complete*) 730; lose ground &c. (*recede*) 283; flunk; fall short of &c. 304.

miss, - one's aim, - the mark, - one's footing, - stays; slip, trip, stumble; make a -slip &c. *n.*, - blunder &c. 495, - mess of, - botch of; bitch it, miscarry, abort, go up like a rocket and come down like the stick, reckon without one's host; get the wrong sow by the ear &c. (*blunder, mismanage*) 699.

limp, halt, hobble, titubate; fall, tumble; lose one's balance; fall -to the ground, - between two stools; flounder, falter, stick in the mud, run aground, split upon a rock; run -, knock -, dash- one's head against a stone wall; break one's back; break down, sink, drown, founder, have the ground cut from under one; get into -trouble, - a mess, - a scrape; come to grief &c. (*adversity*) 735; go to -the wall, - the dogs, - pot; lick -, bite- the dust; be -defeated &c. 731; have the worst of it, lose the day, come off second best, lose; fall a prey to; succumb &c. (*submit*) 725; not have a leg to stand on.

come to nothing, end in smoke; fall-to the ground, - through, - dead, - still-born, - flat; slip through one's fingers; hang -, mis- fire; flash in the pan, collapse; topple down &c. (*descent*) 305; go to wrack and ruin &c. (*destruction*) 162.

go amiss, go wrong, go cross, go hard with, go on a wrong tack; go on -, come off -, turn out -, work- ill; take- a wrong, - an ugly- turn; gang agley.

be all -over with, - up with; explode; dash one's hopes &c. (*disappoint*) 509; defeat the purpose; upset the apple cart; sow the wind and reap the whirlwind, jump out of the frying pan into the fire.

Adj. unsuccessful, successless; failing, tripping &c. *v.*; at fault; unfortunate &c. 735.

abortive, addle, still-born; fruitless, sterile, bootless; ineffect-ual, -ive; inefficient &c. (*impotent*) 158; inefficacious; lame, hobbling, *décousu*; insufficient &c. 640; unavailing &c. (*useless*) 645; of no effect.

aground, grounded, swamped, stranded, cast away, wrecked, foundered, capsized, shipwrecked, nonsuited; foiled; defeated &c. 731; struck -, borne -, broken- down; down-trodden; over-borne, -whelmed; all up with; beaten to a frazzle.

lost, undone, ruined, broken; bankrupt &c. (*not paying*) 808; played out; done -up, - for; dead beat, ruined root and branch, *flambé*, knocked on the head; destroyed &c. 162.

frustrated, thwarted, crossed, unhinged, disconcerted, dashed; thrown -off one's balance, - on one's back, - on one's beam ends; unhorsed, in a sorry plight; hard hit.

stultified, befooled, dished, hoist on one's own petard; victimized, sacrificed.

wide of the mark &c. (*error*) 495; out of one's reckoning &c. (*inexpectation*) 508; left in the lurch; thrown away &c. (*wasted*) 638; unattained; uncompleted &c. 730.

Adv. unsuccessfully &c. *adj.*; to little or no purpose, in vain, *re infectâ*.

Phr. the bubble has burst, the game is up, all is lost; the devil to pay;

parturiunt montes &c. (*disappointment*) 509.

733. Trophy.—N. trophy; medal, prize, palm; ribbon, blue ribbon, *cordon bleu*; citation; cup; laurel, -s; bays, crown, chaplet, wreath, civic crown; Victoria Cross, V.C., *Croix de Guerre*, Iron Cross; Distinguished Service Cross, Medal of Honor, Congressional Medal; insignia &c. 550; feather in one's cap &c. (*honour*) 873; decoration &c. 877; garland, triumphal arch.

triumph &c. (*celebration*) 883; flying colours &c. (*show*) 882.

monumentum ære perennius.

734. Prosperity.—N. prosperity, welfare, well-being; affluence &c. (*wealth*) 803; success &c. 731; thrift, roaring trade; chicken in every pot, the full dinner pail; good -, smiles of- fortune; blessings, godsend.

luck; good -, run of- luck; sunshine; fair -weather, - wind; palmy -, bright -, halcyon- days; piping times, tide, flood, high tide.

Saturnia regna, Saturnian age; golden-time, - age; bed of roses; fat of the land, milk and honey, loaves and fishes, fleshpots of Egypt.

made man, lucky dog, *enfant gâté*, spoiled child of fortune.

upstart, *parvenu, nouveau riche*, profiteer, skipjack, mushroom.

V. prosper, thrive, flourish; be -prosperous &c. *adj.*; drive a roaring trade; go on -well, - smoothly, - swimmingly; sail before the wind, swim with the tide; run -smooth, - smoothly, - on all fours.

rise -, get on- in the world; work -, make- one's way; look up; lift -, raise- one's head, make one's -fortune, - pile, feather one's nest.

flower, blow, blossom, bloom, fructify, bear fruit, fatten, batten.

keep oneself afloat; keep -, hold- one's head above water; light -, fall- on one's -legs, - feet; drop into a good thing; bear a charmed life; bask in the sunshine; have a -good, - fine- time of

it; have a run, - of luck; have the -good fortune &c. *n.* to; take a favourable turn; live -on the fat of the land, - in clover.

Adj. prosperous; thriving &c. *v.*; in a fair way, buoyant; well -off, - to do, - to do in the world; set up, at one's ease; rich &c. 803; in good case; in -full, - high- feather; fortunate, lucky, in luck; born -with a silver spoon in one's mouth, - under a lucky star; on the sunny side of the hedge.

auspicious, propitious, providential.

palmy, halcyon; agreeable &c. 829; *couleur de rose*.

Adv. prosperously &c. *adj.*; swimmingly; as good luck would have it; beyond all -expectation, - hope, - one's wildest dreams.

Phr. one's star in the ascendant, all for the best, one's course runs smooth.

735. Adversity.—N. adversity, evil &c. 619; failure &c. 732; bad -, ill -, evil -, adverse -, hard- -fortune, - hap, - luck, - lot; frowns of fortune; evil -dispensation, - star, - genius; ups and downs of life, broken fortunes; hard -case, - lines, - life; sea -, peck- of troubles; hell upon earth; slough of despond; jinx.

trouble, humiliation, hardship, curse, blight, blast, load, pressure.

pressure of the times, iron age, evil day, time out of joint; hard -, bad -, sad- times; rainy day, cloud, dark cloud, gathering clouds, ill wind; visitation, infliction; affliction &c. (*painfulness*) 830; bitter -pill, - cup; care, trial; the sport of fortune.

mis-hap, -chance, -adventure, -fortune; disaster, calamity, catastrophe; accident, casualty, cross, reverse, check, *contretemps*, rub, pinch, setback.

losing game; falling &c. *v.*; fall, down-fall, come-down; ruin-ation, -ousness; undoing; extremity; ruin &c. (*destruction*) 162.

V. be -ill off &c. *adj.*; go hard with; fall on evil, - days; go on ill; not -prosper &c. 734.

go -downhill, - to rack and ruin &c.

(*destruction*) 162, – to the dogs; fall, – from one's high estate; decay, sink, decline, go down in the world; have seen better days; bring down one's grey hairs with sorrow to the grave; come to grief; be all -over, – up- with; bring a -wasp's, – hornet's- nest about one's ears.

Adj. unfortunate, unblest, unhappy, unlucky; im-, un-prosperous; luck-, hapless; out of luck; in trouble, in a bad way, in an evil plight; under a cloud; clouded; ill –, badly- off; in adverse circumstances; poor &c. 804; behindhand, down in the world, decayed, undone; on the road to ruin, on its last legs, on the wane; in one's utmost need.

planet-struck, devoted; born -under an evil star, – with a wooden ladle in one's mouth; ill-fated, -starred, -omened; inconspicuous, ominous, doomed, unpropitious.

adverse, untoward; disastrous, calamitous, ruinous, dire, deplorable.

Adv. if the worst come to the worst, as ill luck would have it, from bad to worse, out of the frying pan into the fire.

Phr. one's star is on the wane; one's luck -turns, – fails; the game is up, one's doom is sealed, the ground crumbles under one's feet, *sic transit gloria mundi, tant va la cruche à l'eau qu'à la fin elle se casse.*

736. Mediocrity.—N. moderate –, average- circumstances; respectability; middle classes, *bourgeoisie*; mediocrity; golden mean &c. (*midcourse*) 628, (*moderation*) 174.

V. jog on; go –, get on- -fairly, – quietly, – peaceably, – tolerably, – respectably; steer a middle course &c. 628.

Adj. middling, so-so, fair, medium, moderate, mediocre, second-, third- &c. -rate.

Division (II).
INTERSOCIAL VOLITION*

Section I. General
Intersocial Volition

737. Authority.—N. authority; influence, patronage, power, preponderance, credit, *prestige*, prerogative, jurisdiction, right &c. (*title*) 924.

divine right, dynastic rights, authoritativeness; absolut-eness, -ism; despotism, tyranny; *jus nocendi.*

command, empire, sway, rule; domin-ion, -ation; sovereignty, supremacy, suzerainty; lord-, head-ship; chiefdom, seignior-y, -ity, hegemony, patriarchate, patriarchy; master-y, -ship, -dom; government &c. (*direction*) 693; dictation, control.

* Implying the action of the will of one mind over the will of another.

hold, grasp; grip, -e; reach; iron sway &c. (*severity*) 739; fangs, clutches, talons; rod of empire &c. (*sceptre*) 747.

reign, regnancy, *régime*, dynasty; director-, dictator-ship; protector-ate, -ship; caliphate, pashalic, electorate; presiden-cy, -tship; administration; pro-, consulship; prefecture; seneschalship; magistra-ture, -cy; raj.

empire; monarchy; king-hood, -ship; royalty, regality, autocracy, monocracy, arist-archy, -ocracy; oligarchy, democracy, demogogy; republic, -anism, federalism; socialism, collectivism; communism, bolshevism, syndicalism; mob law, mobocracy, ochlocracy, ergatocracy;

vox populi, imperium in imperio; bureaucracy; beadle-, bumble-dom; stratocracy; martial law, military -power, -government; feodality, feudal system, feudalism.

Thearchy, diarchy; du-, tri-, heterarchy; du-, tri-umvirate; auto-cracy, -nomy; limited monarchy; constitutional -government, - monarchy; home rule, autonomy; self-government, -determination; representative government; Soviet government.

gyn-archy, -ocracy, -æocracy; petticoat government, matriarchate, matriarchy.

[Vicarious authority] commission &c. 755; deputy &c. 759; permission &c. 760.

country, state, realm, commonwealth, canton, constituency, toparchy, municipality, polity, body politic, *posse comitatus*.

person in authority &c. (*master*) 745; judicature &c. 965; cabinet &c. (*council*) 696; usurper; seat of -government, - authority; head-quarters.

[Acquisition of authority] accession; installation &c. 755; usurpation.

V. authorize &c. (*permit*) 760; warrant &c. (*right*) 924; dictate &c. (*order*) 741; have -, hold -, possess -, exercise -, exert -, wield- authority &c. *n.*

be -at the head of &c. *adj.*; hold -, be in -, fill an- office; hold -, occupy- a post; be -master &c. 745.

rule, sway, command, control, administer; govern &c. (*direct*) 693; lead, preside over, reign; possess -, be seated on -, occupy- the throne; sway -, wield- the sceptre; wear the crown.

have -, get- the -upper, - whip- hand; gain a hold upon, preponderate, dominate, boss, rule the roost; over-ride, - rule, -awe; lord it over, hold in hand, keep under, make a puppet of, lead by the nose, hold in the hollow of one's hand, turn round one's little finger, bend to one's will, hold one's own, wear the breeches; have- the ball at one's feet, - it all one's own way, - the game in one's own hand, - on the hip, - under one's

thumb; be master of the situation; take the lead, play first fiddle, set the fashion; give the law to; carry with a high hand; lay down the law; 'ride in the whirlwind and direct the storm'; rule with a rod of iron &c. (*severity*) 739.

ascend -, mount- the throne, take the reins, - into one's hand; assume -authority &c. *n.*, - the reins of government; take -, assume the- command.

be -governed by, - in the power of; be under -the rule of, - the domination of.

Adj. ruling &c. *v.*; regnant, at the head, dominant, paramount, supreme, predominant, preponderant, in the ascendant, influential; gubernatorial; imperious; authoritative, executive, administrative, clothed with authority, official, *ex officio*, ministerial, bureaucratic, departmental, imperative, peremptory, overruling, absolute; hegemonic, -al; arbitrary; compulsory &c. 744; stringent.

regal, sovereign; royal, -ist; monarchical, kingly; imperial, -istic; princely; feudal; aristo-, auto-cratic; oligarchic &c. *n.*; democratic, republican, dynastic.

at one's command; in one's -power, - grasp; under control; authorized &c. (*due*) 924.

Adv. in the name of, by the authority of, *de par le Roi*, in virtue of; under the auspices of, in the hands of.

at one's pleasure; by a -dash, - stroke- of the pen; *ex mero motu; ex cathedrâ*.

Phr. the grey mare the better horse; 'every inch a king.'

738. [Absence of authority.] **Laxity.—N.** laxity; lax-, loose-, slack-ness; toleration &c. (*lenity*) 740; freedom &c. 748.

anarchy, interregnum; relaxation; loosening &c. *v.*; remission; dead letter, *brutum fulmen*, misrule; licence, licentiousness; insubordination &c. (*disobedience*) 742; lynch law &c. (*illegality*) 964; nihilism.

[Deprivation of power] dethronement, deposition, usurpation, abdication.

V. be -lax &c. *adj.*; *laisser -faire, -
aller*; hold a loose rein; give -the reins
to, – rope enough, – a loose to; tolerate;
relax; misrule.

go beyond the length of one's tether;
have one's -swing, – fling; act without
-instructions, – authority; act on one's
own responsibility, usurp authority.

dethrone, depose; abdicate.

Adj. lax, loose; slack; remiss &c.
(*careless*) 460; weak.

relaxed; licensed; reinless, unbridled;
anarchical;   unauthorized   &c.
(*unwarranted*) 925.

739. Severity.—N. severity; strictness, formalism, harshness &c. *adj.*;
rigour, stringency, austerity; inclemency &c. (*pitilessness*) 914a; arrogance
&c. 885.

arbitrary power; absolut-, despotism;
dictatorship, autocracy, tyranny, domineering, oppression; assumption, usurpation; inquisition, reign of terror, martial law; iron -heel, – rule, – hand, –
sway; tight grasp; brute -force, –
strength; coercion &c. 744; strong –,
tight- hand.

hard -lines, – measure; tender mercies [ironical]; sharp practice; bureaucracy, red tape; pipe-clay, officialism.

tyrant, disciplinarian, martinet, stickler, formalist, bashaw, despot, hard
master, Draco, oppressor, inquisitor,
extortioner, harpy, vulture, bird of prey.

V. be -severe &c. *adj.*

assume, usurp, arrogate, take liber-
ties; domineer, bully &c. 885; tyrannize, inflict, wreak, stretch a point, put
on the screw; be hard upon; bear –, lay-
a heavy hand on; be –, come- down
upon; ill-treat; deal -hardly with, – hard
measure to; rule with a rod of iron,
chastise with scorpions; dye with blood;
oppress, override; trample –, tread-
-down, – upon, – under foot; crush under an iron heel, ride roughshod over;
rivet the yoke; hold –, keep- a tight
hand; force down the throat; coerce &c.
744; give no quarter &c. (*pitiless*) 914a.

Adj. severe; strict, hard, harsh, dour,

rigid, stiff, stern, rigorous, uncompromising, exacting, exigent, *exigeant*, inexorable, inflexible, obdurate, austere,
relentless, Spartan, Draconian, stringent, straitlaced, puritanical, prudish,
searching, unsparing, ironhanded, hard-
headed, peremptory, absolute, positive,
arbitrary, imperative; coercive &c. 744;
tyrannical, despotic, masterful, extortionate, grinding, withering, oppressive,
inquisitorial; inclement &c. (*ruthless*)
914a; cruel &c. (*malevolent*) 907;
haughty, arrogant &c. 885.

Adv. severely &c. *adj.*; with a -high,
– strong, – tight, – heavy- hand.

at the point of the -sword, – bayonet.

Phr. *Delirant reges plectuntur Achivi.*

740. Lenity.—N. leni-ty, -ence,
-ency; moderation &c. 174; toler-ance,
-ation; mildness, gentleness; favour; in-
dulgen-ce, -cy; clemency, mercy, forbearance, quarter; compassion &c. 914.

V. be -lenient &c. *adj.*; tolerate, bear
with; *parcere subjectis*, give quarter.

indulge, allow one to have his own
way, spoil.

Adj. lenient; mild, – as milk; gentle;
soft; tolerant, indulgent, easy-going;
clement &c. (*compassionate*) 914; forbearing; complaisant, long-suffering.

741. Command.—N. command, order, ordinance, act, *fiat*, bidding, *dictum*, hest, behest, call, beck, nod.

des-, dis-patch; message, direction;
injunction, charge, instructions; appointment, fixture.

demand, exaction, imposition, requisition, claim, reclamation, revendication; *ultimatum* &c. (*terms*) 770; request
&c. 765; requirement.

dictation; dict-, mand-ate; *caveat*, decree, decree -nisi, – absolute, *senatus
consultum*; precept; pre-, re-script; writ,
ordination, bull, edict, decretal, dispensation, prescription, brevet, placet,
ukase, *firman*, hattisheriff, warrant,
passport, *mittimus, mandamus*, summons, subpœna, *nisi prius*, interpellation, citation; word, – of command; *mot
d'ordre*; bugle -, trumpet- call; beat of

drum, tattoo; order of the day; enactment &c. (*law*) 963; *plébiscite* &c. (*choice*) 609.

V. command, order, decree, enact, ordain, dictate, direct, give orders.

prescribe, set, appoint, mark out; set –, prescribe –, impose- a task; set to work, put in requisition &c. 926.

bid, enjoin, charge, call upon, instruct; require, – at the hands of; exact, impose, tax, task; demand; insist on &c. (*compel*) 744.

claim, lay claim to, revendicate, reclaim.

cite, summon; call –, send- for; subpœna; beckon.

issue a command; make –, issue –, promulgate- -a requisition, – a decree, – an order &c. *n.*; give the -word of command, – word, – signal; call to order; give –, lay down- the law; assume the command &c. (*authority*) 737; remand.

be -ordered &c.; receive an order &c. *n.*

Adj. commanding &c. *v.*; authoritative &c. 737; decret-ory, -ive, -al; imperative, jussive, decisive, final.

Adv. in a commanding tone; by a -stroke, – dash- of the pen; by order, at beat of drum, on the first summons; at the word of command.

Phr. the decree is gone forth; *sic volo sic jubeo; le Roi le veut.*

742. Disobedience.—N. disobedience, insubordination, contumacy; infraction, -fringement; violation, noncompliance; non-observance &c. 773.

revolt, rebellion, mutiny, outbreak, rising, uprising, putsch, insurrection, *émeute*; riot, tumult &c. (*disorder*) 59; strike &c. (*resistance*) 719; barring out; defiance &c. 715.

mutinousness &c. *adj.*; mutineering; sedition, treason; high –, petty –, misprision of- treason; *premunire; lèse majesté*; violation of law &c. 964; defection, secession, revolution, *sabotage*, bolshevism, *Sinn Fein.*

insurgent, mutineer, rebel, revolter, rioter, traitor, *carbonaro, sansculottes,*

red republican, communist, Fenian, chartist, *frondeur*; seceder, runagate, brawler, anarchist, demagogue; suffragette; Spartacus, Masaniello, Wat Tyler, Jack Cade; bolshevist, bolshevik, maximalist, ringleader.

V. disobey, violate, infringe; shirk; set at defiance &c. (*defy*) 715; set authority at naught, run riot, fly in the face of, bolt, take the law into one's own hands; kick over the traces.

turn –, run- restive; champ the bit; strike &c. (*resist*) 719; rise, – in arms; secede; mutiny, rebel.

Adj. disobedient; uncompl-ying, -iant; unsubmissive, unruly, ungovernable; insubordinate, impatient of control; rest-iff, -ive; refractory, contumacious; recusant &c. (*refuse*) 764; recalcitrant; resisting &c. 719; lawless, mutinous, seditious, insurgent, riotous, revolutionary.

disobeyed, unobeyed; unbidden.

743. Obedience.—N. obedience; observance &c. 772; compliance; submission &c. 725; subjection &c. 749; nonresistance; passiveness, passivity, resignation.

allegiance, loyalty, fealty, homage, deference, devotion, fidelity, constancy.

submiss-ness, -iveness; ductility &c. (*softness*) 324; obsequiousness &c. (*servility*) 886.

V. be -obedient &c. *adj.*; obey, bear obedience to; submit &c. 725; comply, answer the helm, come at one's call; do -one's bidding, – what one is told, – suit and service; attend to orders, serve devotedly, – loyally, – faithfully.

follow, – the lead of, – to the world's end; serve &c. 746; play second fiddle.

Adj. obedient; compl-ying, -iant; law-abiding, loyal, faithful, leal, devoted; at one's -call, – command, – orders, – beck and call; under -beck and call, – control.

restrainable; resigned, passive; submissive &c. 725; henpecked; pliant &c. (*soft*) 324.

unresist-ed, -ing.

Adv. obediently &c. *adj.*; in compliance with, in obedience to.

Phr. to hear is to obey; as –, if- you please; at your service.

744. Compulsion.—N. compulsion, coercion, coaction, constraint, eminent domain, duress, enforcement, press, conscription.

force; brute –, main –, physical-force; the sword, *ultima ratio*; club –, mob –, lynch- law; *argumentum baculinum, le droit du plus fort*, martial law.

restraint &c. 751; necessity &c. 601; *force majeure*; Hobson's choice; the spur of necessity.

V. compel, force, make, drive, coerce, constrain, enforce, necessitate, oblige.

force upon, press; cram –, thrust –, force- down the throat; say it must be done, make a point of, insist upon, take no denial; put down, dragoon.

extort, wring from; put –, turn- on the screw; drag into; bind, – over; pin –, tie- down; require, tax, put in force; commandeer; restrain &c. 751.

Adj. compelling &c. *v.*; coercive, coactive; inexorable &c. 739; compuls-ory, -atory; obligatory, stringent, peremptory, binding.

forcible, not to be trifled with; irresistible &c. 601; compelled &c. *v.*; fain to.

Adv. by -force &c. *n.*, – force of arms; on compulsion, perforce; *vi et armis*, under the lash; at the point of the -sword, – bayonet; forcibly; by a strong arm.

under protest, in spite of one's teeth; against one's will &c. 603; *nolens volens* &c. (*of necessity*) 601; by stress of -circumstances, – weather; under press of; *de rigueur*.

745. Master.—N. master, *padrone*; lord, – paramount; command-er, -ant; captain; chief, -tain; *sahib*, sirdar, sachem, sheik, head, senior, governor, *duce*, ruler, dictator; leader &c. (*director*) 694.

lord of the ascendant; cock of the -walk, – roost; grey mare; mistress.

potentate; liege, – lord; suzerain, sovereign, monarch, autocrat, despot, tyrant, oligarch, overlord.

crowned head, emperor, king, anointed king, majesty, *imperator*, protector, president, stadtholder, judge.

cæsar, kaiser, czar, sultan, grand Turk, caliph, imaum, shah, padishah, sophi, mogul, great mogul, khan, cham; lama, tycoon, mikado, inca, cazique; domn; vaivode; wai-, way-wode; landamman; seyyid, cacique.

prince, duke &c. (*nobility*) 875; archduke, doge, elector; seignior; mar-, land-grave; rajah, emir, nizam, nawab, negus.

empress, queen, sultana, czarina, princess, infanta, duchess, margravine, begum, maharani.

regent, viceroy, exarch, palatine, khedive, hospodar, beglerbeg, three-tailed bashaw, pasha, pashaw, bashaw, bey, beg, dey, scherif, tetrarch, satrap, mandarin, subhadar, nabob, maharajah; burgrave; laird &c. (*proprietor*) 779; High Commissioner.

the -authorities, – powers that be, – government; staff, *état major*, aga, official, man in office, person in authority.

[Naval authorities] admiral, -ty, – of the fleet; rear-, vice-, port-admiral; senior-, naval officer, S.N.O., commodore, captain, commander, lieutenant-commander, lieutenant, sub-lieutenant, midshipman, warrant –, petty- officer, leading seaman; skipper, mate, master.

[Military authorities] marshal, field-marshal, *maréchal*; general, -issimo; commander-in-chief, *seraskier, hetman*; lieutenant-, major-general; commandant; colonel, lieutenant-colonel, major, captain, centurion, skipper, lieutenant, second-lieutenant, officer, staff-officer, *aide de camp*, brigadier, brigade-major, adjutant, *jemidar*, ensign, cornet, cadet, subaltern, warrant officer, quartermaster, noncommissioned officer, N.C.O.; sergeant, -major; top-sergeant, colour

sergeant; corporal, -major; lance-, act-
ing-corporal; drum major; shavetail.

[Air authorities] air -marshal, – commodore; group captain, squadron leader, wing commander, flight lieutenant,
flying –, pilot-officer.

[Civil authorities] judge &c. 967;
mayor, -alty; prefect, chancellor, archon, provost, magistrate, syndic; alcalde, alcaid; burgomaster, *corregidor*,
seneschal, alderman, warden, constable,
portreeve; lord mayor, sheriff; officer
&c. (*executive*) 965.

746. Servant.—N. subject, liegeman;
servant, retainer, follower, henchman,
servitor, domestic, menial, help, lady
help, *employé, attaché*; official.

retinue, suite, *cortège*, staff, court.

attendant, squire, usher, page, buttons,
donzel, footboy; dog robber; train-,
cup-bearer; waiter, busboy, tapster,
butler, livery servant, lackey, footman,
flunkey, valet, *valet de chambre*; boots;
scout, gyp; equerry, groom; jockey,
hostler, ostler, tiger, orderly, messenger, cad, gillie, caddie; *wallah*; journeyman, herdsman, swineherd.

bailiff, castellan, seneschal, chamberlain, *major-domo*, groom of the chambers.

secretary; under –, assistant- secretary; clerk; clerical staff, stenographer,
subsidiary; agent &c. 758; subaltern;
under-ling, -strapper; man.

maid, -servant, waitress; handmaid;
confidente, lady's maid, abigail, *soubrette*; nurse, *bonne, ayah*; nurse-,
nursery-, house-, parlour-, waiting-,
chamber-, kitchen-, scullery-, between
–, laundry –, dairy-maid; *femme –, fille
de chambre; camarista; chef de cuisine,
cordon bleu*, cook, scullion, Cinderella;
maid –, servant- of all work, tweeny,
general servant, girl, slavey; laundress,
bed-maker, goodie, char-woman &c.
(*worker*) 690.

serf, vassal, slave, negro, helot;
bondsman, -woman; bondslave; *âme
damnée, odalisque*, ryot, *adscriptus
glebæ*; vill-ain, -ein; bead-, bede-sman;

sizar; pension-er, -ary; client; dependant, -ent; hanger on, stooge, satellite;
parasite &c. (*servility*) 886; led captain;
protégé, ward, hireling, mercenary,
puppet, creature.

badge of slavery; bonds &c. 752.

V. serve; minister to, wait –, attend
–, dance attendance –, pin oneself-
upon; squire, tend, hang on the sleeve
of, char, do for; fag; valet.

Adj. in the train of; in one's -pay, –
employ; at one's call &c. (*obedient*) 743;
in bonds.

**747. [Insignia of authority.] Scep-
tre.—N.** sceptre, regalia, rod of empire,
sword of state, mace, *fasces*, wand; staff,
– of office; *bâton*, truncheon; flag &c.
(*insignia*) 550; ensign -, emblem –;
badge -, insignia- of authority, rank
marks, brassard, badge, sash; cocked
–, brass- hat.

epaulette, aiguilette, crown, star, eagle, bar, double bar, pip, stripe, chevron, curl, ring, anchor, shoulder-strap,
tab.

throne, chair, musnud, divan, dais,
woolsack.

toga, pall, mantle, robes of state, ermine, purple.

crown, coronet, diadem, tiara, triple
crown, mitre, crozier, cardinal's hat &c.;
cap of maintenance; decoration; title &c.
877; portfolio.

key, signet, seals, talisman; helm;
reins &c. (*means of restraint*) 752.

748. Freedom.—N. freedom, liberty,
independence; licence &c. (*permission*)
760; facility &c. 705.

scope, range, latitude, play; free -,
full- -play, – scope; free stage and no
favour; swing, full swing, elbow-room,
margin, rope, wide berth; Liberty Hall.

franchise, denization; free -, freed-,
livery- man; denizen.

autonomy, self-government, home
rule, self-determination, liberalism, free
trade; non-interference &c. 706.

immunity, exemption; emancipation
&c. (*liberation*) 750; en-, af-
franchisement; rights, privileges.

free land, freehold; allodium; fran-kalmoigne, mortmain.

independent, free-lance, -thinker, -trader.

V. be -free &c. *adj.*; have -scope &c. *n.*, – the run of, – one's own way, – a will of one's own, – one's fling; do what one -likes, – wishes, – pleases, – chooses; go at large, feel at home, paddle one's own canoe; stand on one's -legs, – rights; shift for oneself.

take a liberty; make -free with, – oneself quite at home; use a freedom; take -leave, – French leave.

set free &c. (*liberate*) 750; give the reins to &c. (*permit*) 760; allow –, give-scope &c. *n.* to; give a horse his head.

make free of; give the -freedom of, – franchise; en-, af-franchise.

laisser -faire, – aller; live and let live; leave to oneself; leave –, let- alone; mind one's own business.

Adj. free, – as air; out of harness, independent, at large, loose, scot free; left -alone, – to oneself.

in full swing; uncaught, uncon-strained, unbuttoned, unconfined, unre-strained, unchecked, unprevented, un-hindered, unobstructed, unbound, uncontrolled, untrammelled.

unsubject, ungoverned, unenslaved, unenthralled, unchained, unshackled, unfettered, unreined, unbridled, un-curbed, unmuzzled, unimpeded.

unrestricted, unlimited, uncondition-al; absolute; discretionary &c. (*option-al*) 600.

unassailed, unforced, uncompelled.

unbiassed, unprejudiced, uninflu-enced, spontaneous.

free and easy; at –, at one's- ease; *dé-gagé*, quite at home; wanton, rampant, irrepressible, unvanquished.

exempt; freed &c. 750; freeborn; au-tonomous, freehold, allodial; *gratis* &c. 815.

unclaimed, going a begging.

Adv. freely &c. *adj.; ad libitum* &c. (*at will*) 600.

749. Subjection.—N. subjection; de-pend-ence, -ance, -ency; subordination; thrall, thraldom, enthralment, subjuga-tion, bondage, serfdom; feudal- -ism, -ity; vassalage, villenage; slavery, en-slavement, involuntary servitude.

service; servi-tude, -torship; tend-ence, employ, tutelage, clientship; lia-bility &c. 177; constraint &c. 751; op-pression &c. (*severity*) 739; yoke &c. (*means of restraint*) 752; submission &c. 725; obedience &c. 743.

V. be -subject &c. *adj.*; be –, lie- at the mercy of; depend –, lean –, hang-upon; fall -a prey to, – under; play sec-ond fiddle.

be a -mere machine, – puppet, – foot-ball; not dare to say one's soul is his own; drag a chain.

serve &c. 746; obey &c. 743; submit &c. 725.

break in, tame; subject, subjugate; master &c. 731; tread -down, – under foot; weigh down; drag at one's chariot wheels; reduce to -subjection, – slavery; en-, in-, be-thral; enslave, lead captive; take into custody &c. (*restrain*) 751; rule &c. 737; drive into a corner, hold at the sword's point; keep under; hold in -bondage, – leading strings, – swaddling clothes.

Adj. subject, dependent, subordinate; feud-al, -atory; in subjection to, under control; in -leading strings, – harness; subjected, enslaved &c. *v.*; constrained &c. 751; subservient, servile, fawning, slavish, obsequious, cringing; down-trodden; over-borne, -whelmed; under the lash, on the hip, led by the nose, henpecked; the -puppet, – sport, – play-thing- of; under one's -orders, – com-mand, – thumb; like dirt under one's feet; a slave to; at the mercy of; in the -power, – hands, – clutches- of; at the feet of; at one's beck and call &c. (*obe-dient*) 743; liable &c. 177; parasitical; stipendiary.

Adv. under.

750. Liberation.—N. liberation, disengagement, release, disenthrall-ment, enlargement, emancipation; af-, enfranchisement; manumission; discharge, dismissal.

deliverance &c. 672; redemption, extrication, acquittance, absolution; acquittal &c. 970; escape &c. 671.

V. liberate, free; set -free, – clear, – at liberty; render free, emancipate, release; en-, af-franchise; manumit; enlarge; dis-band, -charge, -miss, -enthral; let -go, – loose, – out, – slip; cast -, turn- adrift; deliver &c. 672; absolve &c. (*acquit*) 970; reprieve.

unfetter &c. 751; untie &c. 44; loose &c. (*disjoin*) 44; loosen, relax; un-bolt, -bar, -close, -cork, -clog, -hand, -bind, -latch, -chain, -harness; dis-engage, -entangle; clear, extricate, unloose.

gain -, obtain -, acquire- one's -liberty &c. 748; get -rid, – clear- of; deliver oneself from; shake off the yoke, slip the collar; break -loose, – prison; tear asunder one's bonds, cast off trammels; escape &c. 671.

Adj. at -liberty, – large, free, liberated &c. *v.*; out of harness &c. 748; adrift.

Int. unhand me! let me go!

751. Restraint.—N. restraint; hindrance &c. 706; coercion &c. (*compulsion*) 744; cohibition, constraint, repression; discipline, control, self-restraint &c. 604.

confinement; durance, duress; im-, prisonment; incarceration, coarctation, entombment, mancipation, durance vile, thrall, -dom, limbo, captivity; blockade; quarantine; detention.

arrest, -ation; custody, keep, care, charge, ward, restringency.

curb &c. (*means of restraint*) 752; *lettres de cachet.*

limitation, restriction, protection, monopoly; prohibition &c. 761; economic pressure.

prisoner &c. 754.

V. restrain, check; put -, lay- under restraint; en-, in-, be-thral; restrict; debar &c. (*hinder*) 706; constrain; coerce &c. (*compel*) 744; curb, control; hold -, keep- -back, – from, – in, – in check,

– within bounds; hold in -leash, – leading strings; withhold.

keep under; repress, suppress; smother; pull in, rein in; hold, – fast; keep a tight hand on; prohibit &c. 761; in-, cohibit.

enchain; fasten &c. (*join*) 43; fetter, shackle, en-, trammel; bridle, muzzle, gag, pinion, manacle, handcuff, tie one's hands, hobble, bind hand and foot; swathe, swaddle; pin -, peg- down; tether, picket; tie, – up, – down; secure; forge fetters.

confine; shut -, clap -, lock -, box -, mew -, bottle -, cork -, seal -, button-up; shut -, hem -, bolt -, wall -, rail-in; impound, pen, coop; enclose &c. (*circumscribe*) 229; cage; in-, en-cage; close the door upon, cloister; imprison, immure; incarcerate, entomb; clap -, lay- under hatches; put in -irons, – a strait waistcoat; throw -, cast- into prison; put into bilboes.

arrest; take -up, – charge of, – into custody; take -, make- -prisoner, – captive; captivate; lead -captive, – into captivity; send -, commit- to prison; commit; give in -charge, – custody; subjugate &c. 749.

Adj. re-, con-strained; imprisoned &c. *v.*; pent up; jammed in, wedged in; under -restraint, – lock and key, – hatches; serving -, doing- time; in swaddling clothes; on *parole*; in custody &c. (*prisoner*) 754; cohibitive; coactive &c. (*compulsory*) 744.

stiff, restringent, straitlaced, hidebound.

ice-, wind-, weather-bound; 'cabined, cribbed, confined'; in Lob's pound, laid by the heels.

Adv. in captivity, under arrest, behind the bars, in -prison, – jail, – durance vile.

752. [Means of restraint.] **Prison.—N.** prison, -house; jail, gaol, cage, coop, den, death house, condemned -, cell; stronghold, fortress, keep, donjon, dungeon, *Bastille, oubliette,* bridewell, house of correction, hulks, toll-booth, panopticon, penitentiary, guard-room, clink, can, stir, tronk, jug, lock-up, hold; round –, watch –, station –, sponging-house; station; house of detention, black hole, pen, fold, pound; enclosure &c. 232; penal settlement; chain gang; debtors' prison; reformatory; federal penitentiary, state prison; criminal lunatic asylum; bilboes, stocks, limbo, quod.

Dartmoor, Newgate, Fleet, Marshalsea; King's (or Queen's) Bench; Sing Sing, Dannemora.

bond; strap, bandage, splint, tourniquet; irons, pinion, gyve, fetter, shackle, trammel, manacle, handcuff, bracelets, darbies, strait waistcoat, straitjacket.

yoke, collar, halter, harness; muzzle, gag, bit, brake, curb, snaffle, bridle; rein, -s; ribbons, lines, bearing-rein; martingale, leading string; tether, picket, band, guy, chain, cord &c. (*fastening*) 45.

bolt, bar, lock, padlock, rail, wall; paling, palisade; fence; barrier, barricade.

brake, drag &c. (*hindrance*) 706.

753. Keeper.—N. keeper, custodian, *custos*, ranger, warder, jailer, gaoler, turnkey, castellan, guard; watch, -dog, -man; Charley; sen-try, -tinel; watch and ward; *concierge*, coast-guard, *guarda costa*, gamekeeper.

escort, body guard, convoy.

protector, governor, duenna; guardian; governess &c. (*teacher*) 540; nurse, *bonne, ayah, amah.*

754. Prisoner.—N. prisoner, captive, *détenu*, close prisoner.

jail-bird, ticket-of-leave man.

V. stand committed; be -imprisoned &c. 751.

Adj. imprisoned &c. 751; in -prison, – quod, – durance vile, – limbo, – custody, – charge, – chains; under -lock and key, – hatches; on *parole*; detained at his Majesty's pleasure.

755. [Vicarious authority.] **Commis-**sion.**—N.** commission, delegation; con-, as-signment; procuration; deputation, legation, mission, embassy; agency, agentship; power of attorney, proxy; clerkship.

errand, charge, *brevet*, diploma, *exequatur*, permit &c. (*permission*) 760.

appointment, nomination, return; charter; ordination, installation, inauguration, investiture; accession, coronation, enthronement.

vicegerency; regency, regentship.

viceroy &c. 745; consignee &c. 758; deputy &c. 759.

V. commission, delegate, depute; consign, assign; charge; in-, en-trust; turn over to; commit, – to the hands of; authorize &c. (*permit*) 760.

put in commission, accredit, engage, hire, bespeak, appoint, name, nominate, return, ordain; install, induct, inaugurate, invest, crown; en-roll, -list.

employ, empower; give power of attorney to; set –, place- over; send out.

be commissioned, be accredited; represent, stand for; stand in the -stead, – place, – shoes- of.

Adj. commissioned &c. *v.*

Adv. *per procuratione.*

756. Abrogation.—N. abrogation, annulment, nullification; cancelling &c. *v.*; cancel; revo-cation, -kement; repeal, rescission, defeasance.

dismissal, *congé*, demission; deposal, -ition; sack, dethronement; disestablish-, disendow-ment; deconsecration.

aboli-tion, -shment; dissolution.

counter-order, -mand; repudiation, retractation; recantation &c. (*tergiversation*) 607.

V. abrogate, annul, cancel; destroy &c. 162; abolish; revoke, repeal, rescind, reverse, retract, recall; over-rule, -ride; set aside; disannul, dissolve, quash, nullify, declare null and void; disestablish, -endow; deconsecrate.

disclaim &c. (*deny*) 536; ignore, repudiate; recant &c. 607; divest oneself, break off.

counter-mand, -order; do away with;

sweep –, brush- away; throw -overboard, – to the dogs; scatter to the winds, cast behind.

dismiss, discard; cast –, turn- -off, – out, – adrift, – out of doors, – aside, – away; send -off, – away, – about one's business; discharge, get rid of, fire out, fire &c. (*eject*) 297; jilt.

cashier; break; oust; set down, unseat, -saddle; un-, de-, disen-throne; depose, uncrown; unfrock, strike off the roll; dis-bar, -bench.

be -abrogated &c.; receive its quietus.

Adj. abrogated &c. *v.; functus officio.*

Int. get along with you! begone! go about your business! away with!

757. Resignation.—N. resignation, retirement, abdication, renunciation, abjuration, disclaimer, abandonment, relinquishment.

V. resign; give –, throw- up; lay down, throw up the cards, wash one's hands of, abjure, renounce, forego, disclaim, abandon, relinquish, retract, demit; deny &c. 536.

abrogate &c. 756; desert &c. (*relinquish*) 624; get rid of &c. 782.

abdicate; vacate, – one's seat; accept the stewardship of the Chiltern Hundreds; retire; tender –, send in –, hand in- one's resignation.

Adj. abdicant, renunciatory &c. *v.*

Phr. 'Othello's occupation's gone.'

758. Consignee.—N. consignee, trustee, nominee, committee.

delegate; commiss-ary, -ioner; emissary, envoy, commissionaire; messenger &c. 534.

diplomatist, diplomat, *corps diplomatique*, embassy; am-, em-bassador; representative, resident, consul, legate, nuncio, internuncio, *chargé d'affaires, attaché.*

vicegerent &c. (*deputy*) 759; plenipotentiary.

functionary, placeman, curator; treasurer &c. 801; agent, factor, bailiff, steward, clerk, secretary, attorney, solicitor, proctor, broker, underwriter, commission agent, auctioneer, one's

man of business; factotum &c. (*director*) 694; caretaker.

negotiator, go between; middleman; under agent, *employé*; servant &c. 746.

salesman; commercial, – traveller; bagman, *commis-voyageur*, touter.

newspaper –, own –, war –, special-correspondent; reporter.

759. Deputy.—N. deputy, substitute, vice, proxy, *locum tenens*, delegate, representative, next friend, surrogate, secondary.

regent, vicegerent, vizier, minister, vicar; premier &c. (*director*) 694; chancellor, prefect, provost, warden, lieutenant, archon, consul, proconsul; viceroy &c. (*governor*) 745; commissioner &c. 758; plenipotentiary, *alter ego.*

team, eight, eleven; champion.

V. be -deputy &c. *n.*; stand –, appear –, hold a brief –, answer- for; represent; stand –, walk- in the shoes of; stand in the stead of.

substitute, ablegate, accredit; commission, empower, delegate &c. 755.

Adj. acting; vice, -regal; accredited to.

Adv. in behalf of, by proxy.

Section II. SPECIAL INTERSOCIAL VOLITION

760. Permission.—N. permission, leave; allow-, suffer-ance; toler-ance, -ation; liberty, law, licence, concession, grace; indulgence &c. (*lenity*) 740; favour, dispensation, exemption, release; connivance; vouchsafement.

authorization, warranty, accordance, admission.

permit, warrant, *brevet*, precept, sanction, authority, *firman*; pass, -port; furlough, licence, *carte blanche*, ticket of leave; grant, charter, patent.

V. permit; give -permission &c. *n.*, – power; let, allow, admit; suffer, bear with, tolerate, recognize; concede &c. 762; accord, vouchsafe, favour, humour, gratify, indulge, stretch a point; wink at, connive at; shut one's eyes to.

grant, empower, charter, enfranchise, privilege, confer a privilege, license, authorize, warrant; sanction; entrust &c. (*commission*) 755.

give *-carte blanche*, - the reins to, - scope to &c. (*freedom*) 748; leave -alone, - it to one, - the door open; open the -door to, - floodgates; give a loose to.

let off; absolve &c. (*acquit*) 970; release, exonerate, dispense with.

ask -, beg -, request- -leave, - permission.

Adj. permitting &c. *v.*; permissive, indulgent, permitted &c. *v.*; patent, chartered, permissible, allowable, lawful, legitimate, legal; legalized &c. (*law*) 963; licit; unforbid, -den; unconditional.

Adv. permissibly; by -, with -, on- -leave &c. *n.; speciali gratiâ*; under favour of; *pace; ad libitum* &c. (*freely*) 748, (*at will*) 600; by all means &c. (*willingly*) 602; yes &c. (*assent*) 488.

761. Prohibition.—N. pro-, inhibition; *veto*, disallowance; interdict, -ion; injunction; embargo, ban, *verboten*, taboo, proscription; *index expurgatorius*; restriction &c. (*restraint*) 751; hindrance &c. 706; forbidden fruit.

V. pro-, in-hibit; forbid, put one's *veto* upon, disallow; bar, debar &c. (*hinder*) 706, forefend.

keep -in, - within bounds; restrain &c. 751; cohibit, withhold, limit, circumscribe, clip the wings of, restrict, narrow; interdict, taboo; put -, place- under -an interdiction, - the ban; proscribe, censor; exclude, shut out; shut -, bolt -, show- the door; warn off; dash the cup from one's lips; forbid the banns.

Adj. prohibit-ive, -ory; interdictive; proscriptive; restrictive, exclusive; forbidding &c. *v.*

prohibited &c. *v.*; not -permitted &c. 760; unlicensed, contraband, under the ban of; illegal &c. 964; unauthorized, not to be thought of.

Adv. on no account &c. (*no*) 536.

Int. forbid it heaven! &c. (*deprecation*) 766.

hands -, keep- off! hold! stop! avast!

Phr. that will never do.

762. Consent.—N. consent; assent &c. 488; acquiescence; approval &c. 931; compliance, agreement, concession; yield-ance, -ingness; accession, acknowledgment, acceptance, agnition.

settlement, ratification, confirmation, adjustment.

permit &c. (*permission*) 760; promise &c. 768.

V. consent; assent &c. 488; yield assent, admit, allow, concede, grant, yield; come -over, - round; give in to, acknowledge, agnize, give consent, comply with, acquiesce, agree to, fall in with, accede, accept, embrace an offer, close with, take at one's word, have no objection.

satisfy, meet one's wishes, settle, come to terms &c. 488; not -refuse &c. 764; turn a willing ear &c. (*willingness*) 602; jump at; deign, vouchsafe; promise &c. 768.

Adj. consenting &c. *v.*; agreeable, compliant; agreed &c. (*assent*) 488; unconditional.

Adv. yes &c. (*assent*) 488; by all means &c. (*willingly*) 602; if -, as- you please; be it so, so be it, well and good, of course.

763. Offer.—N. offer, proffer, presentation, tender, bid, overture; propos-al, -ition; motion, invitation; candidature; offering &c. (*gift*) 784.

V. offer, proffer, present, tender; bid; propose, move; make -a motion, - advances; start; invite, hold out, place- at one's disposal, - in one's way, put forward.

hawk about; offer for sale &c. 796; press &c. (*request*) 765; lay at one's feet.

offer -, present- oneself; volunteer, come forward, be a candidate; stand -, bid- for; seek; be at one's service; go a begging; bribe &c. (*give*) 784.

Adj. offer-ing, -ed &c. *v.*; in the market, for sale, to let, disengaged, on hire.

764. Refusal.—N. refusal, rejection; non-, in-compliance; denial; declining &c. *v.*; declension; peremptory -, flat -, point blank- refusal; repulse, rebuff; discountenance.

recusancy, renunciation, abnegation, negation, protest, disclaimer; dissent &c. 489; revocation &c. 756.

V. refuse, reject, deny, decline; nill, negative; refuse -, withhold- one's assent; shake the head; close the -hand, - purse; grudge, begrudge, be slow to, hang fire.

be deaf to; turn -a deaf ear to, - one's back upon; set one's face against, discountenance, not hear of, have nothing to do with, wash one's hands of, stand aloof, forswear, set aside, cast behind one; not yield an inch &c. (*obstinacy*) 606.

resist, cross; not -grant &c. 762; repel, repulse; shut -, slam- the door in one's face; rebuff; send -back, - to the right about, - away with a flea in the ear; deny oneself, not be at home to; discard &c. (*repudiate*) 610; rescind &c. (*revoke*) 756; disclaim, protest; dissent &c. 489.

Adj. refusing &c. *v.*; rest-ive, -iff; recusant; uncomplying, noncompliant, unconsenting, uncomplaisant, protestant; not willing to hear of, deaf to.

refused &c. *v.*; ungranted, out of the question, not to be thought of, impossible.

Adv. no &c. 536; on no account, not for the world; no thank you.

Phr. *non possumus*; [ironically] your humble servant; *bien obligé.*

765. Request.—N. requ-est, -isition; claim &c. (*demand*) 741; petition, suit, prayer; begging letter, round-robin.

motion, overture, application, canvass, address, appeal, apostrophe; imprecation; rogation; proposal, proposition.

orison &c. (*worship*) 990; incantation &c. (*spell*) 993.

mendicancy; asking, panhandling, begging &c. *v.*; postulation, solicitation, invitation, entreaty, importunity, supplication, instance, impetration, imploration, obsecration, obtestation, invocation, interpellation.

V. request, ask; beg, crave, sue, pray, petition, solicit, invite, pop the question, make bold to ask; beg -leave, - a boon; apply to, call to, put to; call -upon, - for; make -, address -, prefer -, put up- a -request, - prayer, - petition; make -application, - a requisition; ask -, trouble- one for; claim &c. (*demand*) 741; offer up prayers &c. (*worship*) 990; whistle for.

beg hard, entreat, beseech, plead, supplicate, implore, apostrophize; conjure, adjure; obtest; cry to, kneel to, appeal to; invoke, evoke; impetrate, imprecate, ply, press, urge, beset, importune, dun, tax, clamour for; cry -aloud, - for help; fall on one's knees; throw oneself at the feet of; come down on one's marrow-bones.

beg from door to door; send the hat round, go a begging; mendicate, mump, cadge, panhandle, beg one's bread.

dance attendance on, besiege, knock at the door.

bespeak, canvass, tout, make interest, court; seek, bid for &c. (*offer*) 763; publish the banns.

Adj. requesting &c. *v.*; precatory; suppli-ant, -cant, -catory; invoc-, imprec-, rog-atory; postulant, mendicant.

importunate, clamorous, urgent; solicitous; cap in hand; on one's -knees, - bended knees, - marrow-bones.

Adv. prithee, do, please, pray; be so good as, be good enough; have the goodness, vouchsafe, will you, I pray thee, if you please.

Int. for -God's, - heaven's, - goodness', - mercy's- sake.

766. [Negative request.] **Deprecation.—N.** deprecation, expostulation; remonstrance; intercession, mediation.

V. deprecate, protest, expostulate, enter a protest, intercede for.

Adj. deprecatory, expostulatory, intercessory, mediatorial.

deprecated, protested.

un-, unbe-sought; unasked &c. (*see* ask &c. 765).

Int. cry you mercy! God forbid! forbid it Heaven! Heaven -forefend, – forbid! far be it from! hands off! &c. (*prohibition*) 761.

767. Petitioner.—N. petitioner, solicitor, applicant; suppli-ant, -cant; suitor, candidate, claimant, postulant, aspirant, competitor, bidder; place –, pot- hunter; prizer.

beggar, mendicant, mumper, sturdy beggar, cadger, panhandler.

canvasser, barker, touter &c. 768.

sycophant, parasite &c. 886.

Section III. CONDITIONAL INTERSOCIAL VOLITION

768. Promise.—N. promise, undertaking, word, troth, plight, pledge, *parole*, word of honour, vow; oath &c. (*affirmation*) 535; profession, assurance, warranty, guarantee, insurance, obligation; contract &c. 769.

engagement, pre-engagement: affiance; betroth, -al, -ment; marriage -compact, – vow.

V. promise; give a -promise &c. *n.*; undertake, engage; make –, form- an engagement; enter -into, – on- an engagement; bind –, tie –, pledge –, commit –, take upon- oneself; vow; swear &c. (*affirm*) 535, give –, pass –, pledge –, plight- one's word, – honour, – credit, – troth; betroth, plight faith; take the vows.

assure, warrant, guarantee, vouch for, avouch, covenant &c. 769; attest &c. (*bear witness*) 467.

hold out an expectation; contract an obligation; become -bound to, – sponsor for; answer –, be answerable- for; secure; give security &c. 771; underwrite.

adjure, administer an oath, put to one's oath, swear a witness.

Adj. promising &c. *v.*; promissory; votive; under hand and seal; upon -oath, – affirmation.

promised &c. *v.*; affianced, pledged, bound; committed, compromised; in for it.

Adv. as one's head shall answer for; upon my honour.

Phr. in for a penny, in for a pound.

768a. Release from engagement.— N. release &c. (*liberation*) 750.

Adj. absolute; unconditional &c. (*free*) 748.

769. Compact.—N. compact, contract, agreement, bargain, deal, transaction; affidation; pact, -ion; bond, covenant, indenture.

stipulation, settlement, convention; compromise, *cartel*.

protocol, treaty, *concordat, Zollverein, Sonderbund*, charter, *Magna Charta*, Pragmatic Sanction.

negotiation &c. (*bargaining*) 794; diplomacy &c. (*mediation*) 724; negotiator &c. (*agent*) 758.

ratification, completion, signature, seal, sigil, signet.

V. contract, covenant, agree for, engage &c. (*promise*) 768.

treat, negotiate, stipulate, make terms; bargain &c. (*barter*) 794.

make –, strike- a bargain; come to -terms, – an understanding; compromise &c. 774; set at rest; close, – with; conclude, complete, settle; confirm, ratify, clench, subscribe, underwrite; en-, indorse; put the seal to; sign, seal &c. (*attest*) 467; indent.

take one at one's word, bargain by inch of candle.

Adj. contractual, agreed &c. *v.*; conventional; under hand and seal; signed, sealed and delivered.

Phr. *caveat emptor.*

770. Conditions.—N. conditions, terms; articles, – of agreement.

clauses, provisions; proviso &c.

(*qualification*) 469; covenant, stipulation, obligation, *ultimatum, sine quâ non*; *casus fœderis*.

V. make –, come to- -terms &c. (*contract*) 769; make it a condition, stipulate, insist upon, make a point of; bind, tie up.

Adj. conditional, provisional, guarded, fenced, hedged in.

Adv. conditionally &c. (*with qualification*) 469; provisionally, *pro re natâ*; on condition; with a reservation.

771. Security.—N. security; guaranty, -tee; gage, warranty, bond, tie, pledge, plight, mortgage, debenture, hypothecation, bill of sale, lien, pignus, pawn, pignoration; real security; bottomry; collateral, vadium.

stake, deposit, earnest, handsel, caution.

promissory note; bill, – of exchange; I.O.U.; personal security, covenant, specialty; *parole* &c. (*promise*) 768.

acceptance, indorsement, signature, execution, stamp, seal.

spon-sor, -sion, -sorship; surety, bail; mainpernor, hostage.

recognizance; deed –, covenant- of indemnity.

authentication, verification, warrant, certificate, voucher, docket, doquet; record &c. 551; probate, attested copy.

receipt; ac-, quittance; discharge, release.

muniment, title-deed, instrument; deed, – poll; assurance, insurance, indenture; charter &c. (*compact*) 769; charter-poll; paper, parchment, settlement, will, testament, last will and testament, codicil.

V. give -security, – bail, – substantial bail; go bail; pawn, impawn, hock, spout, mortgage, hypothecate, impignorate.

guarantee, warrant, assure; accept, indorse, underwrite, insure.

execute, stamp; sign, seal &c. (*evidence*) 467.

let, sett; grant –, take –, hold- a lease; hold in pledge; lend on security &c. 787.

Adj. secure, -d; pledged &c. *v.*; in pawn, on deposit.

772. Observance.—N. observance, performance, compliance; obedience &c. 743; fulfilment, satisfaction, discharge; acquit-tance, -tal.

adhesion, acknowledgment; fidelity &c. (*probity*) 939; exact &c. 494- observance.

V. observe, comply with, respect, acknowledge, abide by; cling to, adhere to, be faithful to, act up to; meet, fulfil; carry -out, – into execution; execute, perform, keep, satisfy, discharge; do one's office.

perform –, fulfill –, discharge –, acquit oneself of- an obligation; make good; make good –, keep- one's -word, – promise; redeem one's pledge; keep faith with, stand to one's engagement.

Adj. observant, faithful, true, loyal, honourable &c. 939; true as the -dial to the sun, – needle to the pole; punct-ual, -ilious; meticulous; literal &c. (*exact*) 494; as good as one's word.

Adv. faithfully &c. *adj.*

773. Non-observance.—N. non-observance &c. 772; evasion, inobservance, failure, omission, neglect, laches, laxity, informality.

infringement, infraction; violation, transgression.

retractation, repudiation, nullification; protest; forfeiture.

lawlessness; disobedience &c. 742; bad faith &c. 940.

V. fail, neglect, omit, elude, evade, give the go by to, cut, set aside, ignore; shut –, close- one's eyes to, avoid.

infringe, transgress, pirate, violate, break, trample under foot, do violence to, drive a coach and six through.

discard, protest, repudiate, fling to the winds, set at naught, nullify, declare null and void; cancel &c. (*wipe off*) 552.

retract, go back from, be off, forfeit, go from one's word, palter; stretch –, strain- a point.

Adj. violating &c. *v.*; lawless,

transgressive; elusive, evasive; law, casual; non-observant.

unfulfilled &c. (*see* fulfill &c. 772).

774. Compromise.—N. compromise, -mutation, -position; middle term, *mezzo termine*; compensation &c. 30; adjustment, mutual concession.

V. com-promise, -mute, -pound; take the mean; split the difference, meet one half way, give and take; come to terms &c. (*contract*) 769; submit to -, abide by- arbitration; patch up, bridge over, fix up, arrange; adjust, - differences; agree; make -the best of, - a virtue of necessity; take the will for the deed.

Section IV. POSSESSIVE RELATIONS*

1°. *Property in general*

775. Acquisition.—N. acquisition; gaining &c. *v.*; obtainment; procuration, -ement; purchase, descent, inheritance; gift &c. 784.

recovery, retrieval, revendication, replevin; redemption, salvage, trover; find, *trouvaille*, foundling.

gain, thrift; money-making, -grubbing; lucre, filthy lucre, loaves and fishes, the main chance, pelf; emolument &c. 973; wealth &c. 803.

profit, earnings, winnings, innings, clean-up, pickings, perquisite, net profit; income &c. (*receipt*) 810; proceeds, -duce, -duct; out-come, -put; return, fruit, crop, harvest, tilth; second crop, aftermath; benefit &c. (*good*) 618.

sweepstakes, trick, prize, pool.

[Fraudulent acquisition] subreption, theft, stealing &c. 791.

V. acquire, get, gain, win, earn, obtain, procure, gather, annex; collect &c. 72; pick, - up; glean, take &c. 789.

find; come -, pitch -, light- upon; scrape -up, - together; get in, reap and carry, net, bag, sack, bring home, se-

*That is, relations which concern property.

cure, come across, derive, draw, get in the harvest.

profit; make -, draw- profit; turn to -profit, - to account; make -capital out of, - money by; obtain a return, reap the fruits of; reap -, gain- an advantage; turn -a penny, - an honest penny; make the pot boil, bring grist to the mill; make -, coin -, raise -money; raise -funds, - the wind; fill one's pocket &c. (*wealth*) 803.

treasure up &c. (*store*) 636; realize, clear; produce &c. 161; take &c. 789.

get back, recover, regain, retrieve, revendicate, replevy, redeem, come by one's own.

come -by, - in for; receive &c. 785; inherit; step into, - a fortune, - the shoes of; succeed to.

get -hold of, - between one's finger and thumb, - into one's hand, - at; take -, come into -, enter into- possession.

be -profitable &c. *adj.*; pay, answer.

accrue &c. (*be received*) 785.

Adj. acquir-ing, -ed &c. *v.*; acquisitive; productive, profitable, advantageous, gainful, remunerative, paying, lucrative.

776. Loss.—N. loss; de-, perdition; forfeiture, lapse.

privation, bereavement; deprivation &c. (*dispossession*) 789; riddance.

V. lose; incur -, experience -, meet with- a loss; miss; mislay, let slip, allow to slip through the fingers, squander; be without &c. (*exempt*) 777a; forfeit.

get rid of &c. 782; waste &c. 638.

be lost, lapse.

Adj. losing &c. *v.*; not having &c. 777a.

shorn of, deprived of; denuded, bereaved, bereft, *minus*, cut off; dispossessed &c. 789; rid of, quit of; out of pocket.

lost &c. *v.*; long lost; irretrievable &c. (*hopeless*) 859; irredentist; off one's hands.

Int. farewell to! adieu to! good riddance!

777. Possession.—N. possession,

seisin; ownership &c. 780; occupancy; hold, -ing; tenure, tenancy, feodality, dependency; villenage; socage, chivalry, knight service.

exclusive possession, impropriation, monopoly, corner; retention &c. 781; pre-possession, -occupancy; nine points of the law.

future possession, heritage, inheritance, heirship, reversion, fee, seigniority, feud, fief.

bird in hand, *uti possidetis, chose* in possession.

V. possess, have, hold, occupy, enjoy; be -possessed of &c. *adj.*; have -in hand &c. *adj.*; own &c. 780; command.

inherit; come -to, - in for.

engross, monopolize, forestall, regrate, impropriate, have all to oneself, corner; have a firm hold of &c. (*retain*) 781; get into one's hand &c. (*acquire*) 775.

belong to, appertain to, pertain to; be -in one's possession &c. *adj.*; vest in.

Adj. possessing &c. *v.*; worth; possessed of, seized of, master of, in possession of; endowed -, blest -, instinct -, fraught -, laden -, charged -, instilled -, with.

possessed &c. *v.*; on hand, by one; in hand, in store, in stock; in one's -hands, - grasp, - possession; at one's - command, - disposal; one's own &c. (*property*) 780.

unsold; unshared.

777a. Exemption.—N. exemption; exception, immunity, privilege, release &c. 927a; absence &c. 187.

V. not -have &c. 777; be -without &c. *adj.*

Adj. exempt from, devoid of, without, unpossessed of, unblest with, immune from.

not -having &c. 777; unpossessed; untenanted &c. (*vacant*) 187; without an owner.

unobtained, unacquired.

778. [Joint possession.] Participation.—N. participation; co-, joint- tenancy; possession -, tenancy- in com-

mon; joint -, common- stock; co-, partnership; communion; community of -possessions, - goods; communalism, communism, socialism, collectivism; co-operation &c. 709; profit sharing.

snacks, co-portion, picnic, hotchpotch; co-heirship, -parceny, -parcenary; gavelkind.

participator, sharer; co-, partner; shareholder; co-, joint-tenant; tenants in common; co-heir, -parcener.

communist, socialist.

V. par-ticipate, -take; share, - in; come in for a share; go -shares, - snacks, - halves; share and share alike.

have -, possess -, be seized- -in common, - as joint tenants &c. *n.*

join in; have a hand in &c. (*co-operate*) 709.

Adj. partaking &c. *v.*; communistic, socialistic, co-operative, profit sharing.

Adv. share and share alike.

779. Possessor.—N. possessor, holder; occup-ant, -ier; tenant; person -, man- -in possession &c. 777; renter, lodger, lessee, under-lessee; zemindar, ryot; tenant -on sufferance, - at will, - from year to year, - for years, - for life.

owner; propriet-or, -ress, -ary; impropriator, master, mistress, lord.

land-holder, owner, -lord, -lady; lord -of the manor, - paramount; heritor, laird, vavasour, landed gentry, mesne lord.

cestui-que-trust, beneficiary, mortgagor.

grantee, feoffee, relessee, devisee; legat-ee, -ary.

trustee; holder &c.- of the legal estate; mortgagee.

right -, rightful- owner.

[Future possessor] heir, - apparent; - presumptive; heiress; inherit-or, -ress, -rix; reversioner, remainder-man.

780. Property.—N. property, possession, *suum cuique, meum et tuum.*

owner-, proprietor-, lord-ship; seignority; empire &c. (*dominion*) 737.

interest, stake, estate, right, title, claim, demand, holding; tenure &c.

(*possession*) 777; vested -, contingent -, beneficial -, equitable- interest; use, trust, benefit; legal -, equitable- estate; seisin.

absolute interest, paramount estate, freehold; fee, - simple, - tail; estate -in fee, - in tail, - tail; estate in tail -male, - female, - general.

limitation, term, lease, settlement, strict settlement, particular estate; estate -for life, - for years, - *pur autre vie*; remainder, reversion, expectancy, possibility.

dower, dowry, *dot*, jointure, marriage portion, appanage, inheritance, heritage, patrimony, alimony; legacy &c. (*gift*) 784.

assets, belongings, means, resources, circumstances; wealth &c. 803; money &c. 800; what one -is worth, - will cut up for; estate and effects.

landed -, real- -estate, - property; realty; land, -s; subdivision; plot, site; tenements; hereditaments; corporeal -, incorporeal- hereditaments; acres; ground &c. (*earth*) 342; acquest; messuage.

territory, state, kingdom, principality, realm, empire, protectorate, margravate, dependancy, colony, sphere of influence, mandate.

manor, honour, domain, demesne; farm, ranch, plantation, *hacienda*; allodium &c. (*free*) 748; fieff, feoff, feud, zemindary, dependency.

free-, copy-, lease-holds; chattels real; fixtures, plant, heirloom easement; folkland; right of -common, - user.

personal -property, - estate, - effects; personalty, chattels, goods, effects, movables; stock, - in trade; things, traps, rattle-traps, paraphernalia; equipage &c. 633.

parcels, appurtenances.

impedimenta; lug-, bag-gage; bag and baggage; pelf; cargo, lading.

rent-roll; income &c. (*receipts*) 810.

patent, copyright; *chose* in action; credit &c. 805; debt &c. 806.

V. possess &c. 777; be the -possessor &c. 779- of own; have for one's own, - very own; come in for, inherit; enfeoff. savour of the realty.

be one's -property &c. *n.*; belong to; ap-, pertain to.

Adj. one's own; landed, predial, manorial, allodial, seigniorial; free-, copy-, lease-hold; feu-, feo-dal; hereditary, entailed, personal.

Adv. to one's -credit, - account; to the good.

to one and -his heirs for ever, - the heirs of his body, - his heirs and assigns, - his executors, administrators and assigns.

781. Retention.—N. retention; retaining &c. *v.*; keep, detention, custody; tenacity, firm hold, grasp, gripe, grip, iron grip.

fangs, teeth, claws, talons, nail, hook, tentacle, *tenaculum*; bond &c. (*vinculum*) 45.

clutches, tongs, forceps, pincers, nippers, pliers, tweezers, vise.

paw, hand, finger, wrist, fist, neaf, neif.

bird in hand; captive &c. 754.

V. retain, keep; hold, - fast, - tight, - one's own, - one's ground; clinch, clench, clutch, grasp, gripe, hug, have a firm hold of.

secure, withold, detain; hold -, keep-back; keep close; husband &c. (*store*) 636; reserve; have -, keep- in stock &c. (*possess*) 777; entail, tie up, settle.

Adj. retaining &c. *v.*; retentive, tenacious.

unforfeited, undeprived, undisposed, uncommunicated.

incommunicable, inalienable; in mortmain; in strict settlement.

Phr. *uti possidetis*.

782. Relinquishment.—N. relinquishment, abandonment &c. (*of a course*) 624; renunciation, expropriation, dereliction; cession, surrender, dispensation; resignation &c. 757; riddance.

derelict &c. *adj.*; jetsam; waif, foundling, orphan.

V. relinquish, give up, surrender, yield, cede; let -go, - slip; spare, drop, resign, forego, renounce, abjure, abandon, expropriate, give away, dispose of, part with; lay -aside, - apart, - down, - on the shelf &c. (*disuse*) 678; set -, put- aside; make away with, cast behind; discard, cast off, dismiss; maroon.

give -notice to quit, - warning; supersede; be -, get- -rid of, - quit of; eject &c. 297.

rid -, disburden -, divest -, dispossess- oneself of; wash one's hands of; divorce, desert; disinherit, cut off.

cast -, throw -, pitch -, fling- -away, - aside, - overboard, - to the dogs; cast -, throw -, sweep- to the winds; put -, turn -, sweep- away; jettison.

quit one's hold.

Adj. relinquished &c. *v.*; cast off, derelict; unowned, unappropriated, unculled; left &c. (*residuary*) 40; divorced; disinherited.

Int. away with!

2°. *Transfer of Property*

783. Transfer.—N. transfer, conveyance, assignment, alienation, abalienation; demise, limitation; conveyancing; transmission &c. (*transference*) 270; enfeoffment, bargain and sale, lease and release; exchange &c. (*interchange*) 148; barter &c. 794; substitution &c. 147.

succession, reversion; shifting -use, - trust; devolution.

V. transfer, convey; alien, -ate; assign; grant &c. (*confer*) 784; consign; make -, hand- over; pass, hand, transmit, negotiate; hand down; exchange &c. (*interchange*) 148.

change -hands, - from one to another; devolve, succeed; come into possession &c. (*acquire*) 775; take over.

abalienate; disinherit; dispossess &c. 789; substitute &c. 147.

Adj. alienable, negotiable, transferable, reversional.

Phr. estate coming into possession.

784. Giving.—N. giving &c. *v.*; be-

stowal, donation; present-ation, -ment; accordance; con-, cession; delivery, consignment, dispensation, communication, endowment; invest-ment, -iture; award.

almsgiving, charity, liberality, generosity; philanthropy &c. 910.

[Thing given] gift, donation, present, *cadeau*; fairing; free gift, boon, favour, benefaction, grant, offering, oblation, sacrifice, immolation.

grace, act of grace, *bonus, bonanza*.

allowance, contribution, subscription, subsidy, tribute, subvention.

bequest, legacy, devise, will, dotation, appanage; dowry; voluntary - settlement, - conveyance &c. 783; amortization.

alms, largess, bounty, dole, sportule, donative, help, oblation, offertory, Peter's pence, *honorarium*, gratuity, Maundy money, Christmas box, Easter offering, vail, tip, *douceur*, drink money, *pourboire, trinkgeld, backsheesh*; fee &c. (*recompense*) 973; consideration.

bribe, bait, ground-bait; peace-offering, handsel.

giver, grantor &c. *v.*; donor, feoffer, settlor; almoner; testator; investor, subscriber, contributor; fairy godmother; Santa Claus, benefactor &c. 816.

V. deliver, hand, pass, put into the hands of; hand -, make -, deliver -, pass -, turn- over.

present, give away, dispense, dispose of; give -, deal -, dole -, mete -, fork -, shell -, squeezeout.

pay &c. 807; render, impart, communicate.

concede, cede, yield, part with, shed cast; spend &c. 809.

give, bestow, confer, grant, accord, award, assign.

entrust, consign, vest in.

make a present; allow, contribute, subscribe, donate, furnish its quota.

invest, endow, settle upon; bequeath, leave, devise.

furnish, supply, help; ad-, minister to; afford, spare; accommodate -, indulge -, favour- with; shower down upon;

lavish, pour on, thrust upon; tip, bribe; tickle –, grease- the palm; offer &c. 763; sacrifice, immolate.

Adj. giving &c. *v.*; given &c. *v.*; allow-ed, -able; concessional; communicable; charitable, eleemosynary, sportulary, tributary; *gratis* &c. 815.

785. Receiving.—N. receiving &c. *v.*; acquisition &c. 775; reception &c. (*introduction*) 296; suscipiency, acceptance, admission.

re-, ac-cipient; assignee, devisee; lega-tee, -tary; grantee, feoffee, donee, relessee, lessee.

sportulary, stipendiary; beneficiary; pension-er, -ary; almsman.

income &c. (*receipt*) 810.

V. receive; take &c. 789; acquire &c. 775; admit.

take in, catch, touch; pocket; put into one's -pocket, – purse; accept; take off one's hands.

be received; come -in, – to hand; pass –, fall- into one's hand; go into one's pocket; fall to one's -lot, – share; come –, fall- to one; accrue; have -given &c. 784 to one.

Adj. receiving &c. *v.*; re-, suscipient.

received &c. *v.*; given &c. 784; second-hand.

not given, unbestowed &c. (*see* give, bestow &c. 784).

786. Apportionment.—N. apportion-, allot-, consign-, assign-, appointment; appropriation; dispensation, -tribution; allocation, division, deal; repartition; administration.

dividend, portion, contingent, share, allotment, lot, cut, split, measure, dose; dole, meed, pittance; *quantum*, ration; ratio, proportion, quota, *modicum*, mess, allowance.

V. apportion, divide; cut, split, divvy; distribute, administer, dispense; billet, allot, detail, cast, share, mete; portion -, parcel -, dole- out; deal, carve.

partition, assign, appropriate, appoint.

come in for one's share &c. (*participate*) 778.

Adj. apportioning &c. *v.*; respective.

Adv. respectively, each to each.

787. Lending.—N. lending &c. *v.*; loan, advance, accommodation, feneration; mortgage &c. (*security*) 771; investment.

mont de piété, pawnshop, hock shop, spout, my uncle's.

lender, pawnbroker, money lender, usurer.

V. lend, advance, loan, accommodate with; lend on security; pawn &c. (*security*) 771.

intrust, invest; place -, put- out to interest; sink, risk.

let, demise, lease, sett, under-, sub-let.

Adj. lending &c. *v.*; lent &c. *v.*; unborrowed &c. (*see* borrowed &c. 788).

Adv. in advance; on -loan, - security.

788. Borrowing.—N. borrowing, pledging, pawning.

borrowed plumes; plagiarism &c. (*thieving*) 791.

replevin.

V. borrow, desume; pawn.

hire, rent, farm; take a -lease, – demise; take -, hire- by the -hour, – mile, – year &c.

raise -, take up- money; float bonds; raise the wind; fly a kite, borrow of Peter to pay Paul; run into debt &c. (*debt*) 806.

make use of, plagiarize, pirate.

replevy.

789. Taking.—N. taking &c. *v.*; reception &c. (*taking in*) 296; deglutition &c. (*taking food*) 298; appropriation, prehension, prensation; capture, caption; ap-, de-prehension; abreption, seizure; ab-duction, -lation; subtraction &c. (*subduction*) 38; abstraction, ademption.

dispossession; depriv-ation, -ement; bereavement; divestment; disherison; distraint, distress; sequestration, confiscation, attachment, execution; eviction &c. 297.

rapacity, extortion, vampirism, predacity, blood-sucking; theft &c. 791.

resumption; repris-e, -al; recovery &c. 775.

clutch, swoop, wrench; grip &c. (retention) 781; haul, take, catch; scramble.

taker, captor, capturer; vampire; extortioner.

V. take, catch, hook, nab, bag, sack, pocket, put into one's pocket, scrounge; receive; accept.

reap, crop, cull, pluck; gather &c. (get) 775; draw.

ap-, im-propriate; assume, possess oneself of; take possession of; commandeer; lay –, clap- one's hands on; help oneself to; make free with, dip one's hands into, lay under contribution; intercept; scramble for; deprive of.

take –, carry –, bear- -away, – off; abstract; hurry off –, run away- with; abduct; steal &c. 791; ravish; seize; pounce –, spring- upon; swoop -to, – down upon; take by -storm, – assault; snatch, reave.

snap up, nip up, whip up, catch up; kidnap, crimp, capture, lay violent hands on.

get –, lay –, take –, catch –, lay fast –, take firm- hold of; lay by the heels, take prisoner; fasten upon, grip, grapple, embrace, gripe, clasp, grab, clutch, collar, throttle, take by the throat, claw, clinch, clench, make sure of.

catch at, jump at, make a grab at, snap at, snatch at; reach, make a long arm, stretch forth one's hand.

take -from, – away from; deduct &c. 38; retrench &c. (curtail) 201; dispossess, ease one of, snatch from one's grasp; tear –, tear away –, wrench –, wrest –, wring- from; extort; deprive of, bereave; disinherit, cut off with a shilling.

oust &c. (eject) 297; divest; levy, distrain, confiscate; sequest-er, -rate, accroach; usurp; despoil, strip, fleece, shear, displume, impoverish, eat out of house and home; drain, – to the dregs; gut, dry, exhaust, swallow up; absorb &c. (suck in) 296; draw off; suck, – like a leech, – the blood of.

retake, resume; recover &c. 775.

Adj. taking &c. v.; privative, prehensile; pred-aceous, -al, -atory, -atorial; rap-acious, -torial; ravenous; parasitic; all-devouring, -engulfing.

bereft &c. 776.

Adv. at one fell swoop.

Phr. give an inch and take an ell.

790. Restitution.—N. restitution, return; ren-, red-dition; reinstatement, restoration; reinvestment, recuperation; repatriation; rehabilitation &c. (reconstruction) 660; reparation, atonement, indemnity, compensation, recompense.

release, replevin, redemption, recovery &c. (getting back) 775; remitter, reversion.

V. return, restore; recondition; give –, carry –, bring- back; render, – up; give up; let go, unclutch; dis-, re-gorge; regurgitate; recoup, reimburse, repay, indemnify, reinvest, remit, rehabilitate; repair &c. (make good) 660.

redeem, recover &c. (get back) 775; take back again; revest, revert.

Adj. restoring &c. v.; recuperative &c. 660; in full restitution, to compensate for.

Phr. suum cuique.

791. Stealing.—N. stealing &c. v.; theft, thievery, robbery, latrociny, direption; abstraction, appropriation; plagiary, -ism; rape, kidnapping, depredation; raid, hold up.

spoliation, plunder, pillage; sack, -age; rapine, brigandage, highway robbery, foray, razzia; black-mail; piracy, privateering, buccaneering; filibustering, -ism; burglary; house-breaking, cattle-stealing, -rustling, -lifting.

peculation, embezzlement; fraud &c. 545; larceny, petty larceny, pilfering, shop-lifting.

thievishness, rapacity, kleptomania, Alsatia; den of -Cacus, – thieves.

licence to plunder, letters of marque.

V. steal, thieve, rob, purloin, pilfer, filch, lift, prig, bag, nim, crib, cabbage, palm; abstract; appropriate, plagiarize.

convey away, carry off, abduct,

kidnap, shanghai, impress, crimp; make –, walk –, run- off with; run away with; spirit away; seize &c. (*lay violent hands on*) 789.

plunder, pillage, rifle, sack, loot, ransack, spoil, spoliate, despoil, strip, sweep, gut, forage, levy, black-mail, pirate, pickeer, maraud, lift cattle, rustle, poach, smuggle, run.

stick –, hold- up.

swindle, peculate, embezzle; sponge, mulct, rook, bilk, pluck, pigeon, skin, fleece, diddle; defraud &c. 545; obtain under false pretences; live by one's wits.

rob –, borrow of- Peter to pay Paul; set a thief to catch a thief.

disregard the distinction between *meum* and *tuum*.

Adj. thieving &c. *v.*; thievish, light-fingered; fur-acious, -tive; piratical; pred-aceous, -al, -atory, -atorial; raptorial &c. (*rapacious*) 789.

stolen &c. *v.*

Phr. *sic vos non vobis.*

792. Thief.—N. thief, robber, *homo trium literarum*, pilferer, rifler, filcher, plagiarist.

spoiler, depredator, pillager, marauder; harpy, shark, land-shark, falcon, moss-trooper, bushranger, Bedouin, brigand, freebooter, bandit, thug, dacoit, pirate, corsair, viking, Paul Jones; buccan-eer, -ier; piqu-, pick-eerer; rover, ranger, privateer, filibuster; rapparee, wrecker, picaroon; smuggler, poacher, plunderer; racketeer.

highwayman, Dick Turpin, Claude Duval, Macheath, knight of the road, footpad, sturdy beggar; abductor, kidnapper.

cut-, pick-purse; pick-pocket, light-fingered gentry; sharper; card-, skittle-sharper; crook; thimble-rigger; rook, Greek, blackleg, leg, welsher, defaulter; Autolycus, Cacus, Barabbas, Jeremy Diddler, Robert Macaire, artful dodger, trickster; swell mob, *chevalier d'industrie*; shop-lifter.

swindler, peculator; forger, coiner,

counterfeiter, shoful; fence, receiver of stolen goods, duffer; smasher.

burglar, housebreaker; cracks-, magsman; Bill Sikes, Jack Sheppard, Jonathan Wild, Raffles, cat burglar.

793. Booty.—N. booty, spoil, plunder, prize, loot, graft, swag, pickings, boodle; *spolia opima*, prey; blackmail; stolen goods.

Adj. looting &c. *n.*; manubial, spoliative.

3°. Interchange of Property

794. Barter.—N. barter, exchange, scorse, truck system; interchange &c. 148.

a Roland for an Oliver; *quid pro quo*; com-mutation, -position.

trade, commerce, mercature, buying and selling, bargain and sale; traffic, business, nundination, custom, shopping; commercial enterprise, speculation, jobbing, stock-jobbing, *agiotage*, brokery, arbitrage.

dealing, transaction, negotiation, bargain.

free trade.

V. barter, exchange, truck, scorse, swop; interchange &c. 148; commutate &c. (*substitute*) 147; compound for.

trade, traffic, buy and sell, give and take, nundinate; carry on –, ply –, drive- a trade; be in -business, - the city; keep a shop, deal in, employ one's capital in.

trade –, deal –, have dealings- with; transact –, do- business with; open –, keep- an account with.

bargain; drive –, make- a bargain; negotiate, bid for; dicker, haggle, higgle; chaffer, huckster, cheapen, beat down; stickle, - for; out-, under-bid; ask, charge; strike a bargain &c. (*contract*) 769.

speculate, give a sprat to catch a herring; buy in the cheapest and sell in the dearest market; rig the market.

Adj. commercial, mercantile, trading; interchangeable, marketable, staple, in the market, for sale.

wholesale, retail.
Adv. across the counter; on 'change.

795. Purchase.—N. purchase, emption; buying, purchasing, shopping; preemption, refusal.

coemption, bribery; slave trade.

buyer, purchaser, *emptor*, vendee; patron, employer, client, customer, *clientèle*.

V. buy, purchase, invest in, procure; rent &c. (*hire*) 788; repurchase, buy in.

keep in one's pay, bribe, suborn; pay &c. 807; spend &c. 809.

make –, complete– a purchase; buy over the counter; pay cash for.

shop, market, go a shopping.
Adj. purchased &c. *v.*
Phr. *caveat emptor.*

796. Sale.—N. sale, vent, disposal; auction, roup, Dutch auction; custom &c. (*traffic*) 794.

vendi-bility, -bleness.

seller, salesman; peddler, smous; vender, vendor, consignor; merchant &c. 797; auctioneer.

V. sell, vend, dispose of, effect a sale; sell -over the counter, – by auction &c. *n.*; dispense, retail; deal in &c. 794; sell -off, – out; turn into money; realize; bring -to, – under- the hammer; put up to auction; auction, offer –, put up- for sale; hawk, peddle, bring to market; offer &c. 763; undersell; dump, unload.

let; mortgage &c. (*security*) 771.

Adj. under the hammer, in the market, for sale.

saleable, marketable, vendible, in demand, having a ready sale; unsaleable &c., unpurchased, unbought; on one's hands.

797. Merchant.—N. merchant, trader, dealer, monger, chandler, salesman; changer; regrater; shop-keeper, -man; trades-man, -people, -folk.

retailer; chapman, hawker, huckster, higgler; peddler, smous, pedlar, *colporteur*, cadger, Autolycus; sutler, *vivandière*; coster-man, -monger; market

woman; cheap jack; caterer &c. 637; tallyman.

money-broker, -changer, -lender; stock-broker, -jobber; cambist, usurer, moneyer, banker.

jobber; broker &c. (*agent*) 758; buyer &c. 795; seller &c. 796.

concern; firm &c. (*partnership*) 712.

798. Merchandise.—N. merchandise, ware, commodity, effects, goods, article, stock, produce, staple commodity; stock in trade &c. (*store*) 636; cargo &c. (*contents*) 190.

799. Mart.—N. mart; market, -place, *forum*; fair, bazaar, staple; stock –, exchange; 'change, *bourse*, Wall Street, Rialto, hall, guildhall; toll-booth, custom-house; Tattersalls.

shop, stall, booth; wharf; office, chambers, counting-house, *bureau*; coun-, comp-ter.

ware-house, -room; *dépôt*, interposit, *entrepôt*, emporium, establishment; store &c. 636.

open market, market-overt.

4°. *Monetary Relations*

800. Money.—N. money -matters, – market; finance; accounts &c. 811; funds, treasure; capital, stock; assets &c. (*property*) 780; wealth &c. 803; supplies, ways and means, wherewithal, sinews of war, almighty dollar, needful, cash.

sum, amount; balance, -sheet; sum total; proceeds &c. (*receipts*) 810.

currency, circulating medium, specie; coin, – of the realm; piece, hard cash, dollar, sterling coin; pounds shillings and pence; £ s. d., guineas; pocket, breeches pocket, purse; money in hand; the best, ready, – money; filthy lucre, shekels, roll, jack, rhino, blunt, dust, bawbees, brass, dibs, dough, mopus, tin, salt, chink, oof, spondulics, pile, wads.

precious metals, gold, silver, copper, nickel; bullion, bar, ingot, nugget.

petty cash; pocket-, pin-money; small –, change; small coin, loose cash; doit, stiver, rap, mite, farthing, *sou*, penny, shilling, bob, tanner, tester, groat, guinea, ducat; *rouleau*; *wampum*; good -, round -, lump-sum; power -, mint -, tons- of money; plum, lac of rupees, millions, money-bags, miser's hoard, stocking, mine of wealth &c. 803.

[Science of coins] numismatics, chrysology.

paper-money; money -, postal -, Post Office- order; note, - of hand; bank -, treasury- note; Bradbury; promissory note; I O U., bond; bill, - of exchange; draft, check, order, warrant, *coupon*, debenture, exchequer bill, *assignat*, greenback, gold -, silver- certificate.

cooper, nickel, dime, quarter, two bits, half a dollar, dollar, buck, simoleon, fiver, tenner, a twenty, a sawbuck, a century, a grand; eagle, double eagle.

gold standard, bimetallism, fiat money; rate of -, exchange; in-, de-flation.

remittance &c. (*payment*) 807; credit &c. 805; liability &c. 806; solvency &c. 803.

draw-er, -ee; oblig-or, -ee; moneyer, coiner, counterfeiter, forger.

false -, bad- money; base -, counterfeit- coin, flash note, slip, kite; Bank of Elegance.

argumentum ad crumenam.

V. amount to, come to, mount up to; touch the pocket; draw, - upon; endorse &c. (*security*) 771; issue, utter, circulate; discount &c. 813.

forge, counterfeit, coin, circulate -, pass- bad money.

Adj. monetary, pecuniary, crumenal, fiscal, financial, sumptuary, numismatical; sterling; solvent &c. 803.

801. Treasurer.—N. treasurer; bursar, -y; purser, purse-bearer; cashkeeper, banker; depositary; questor, receiver, steward, trustee, chartered -, accountant; Accountant-General, almoner, liquidator, paymaster, cashier, teller; cambist; money-changer &c. (*merchant*) 797.

financier, Chancellor of the Exchequer, minister of finance; Secretary of the Treasury, Director of the Budget, Controller of Currency.

802. Treasury.—N. treasury, bank, exchequer, almonry, fisc, hanaper, bursary; safe; strong-box, -hold, -room; coffer; chest &c. (*receptacle*) 191; depository &c. 636; till, -er; cash-box, -register, purse, pocketbook, wallet, money-bag, -belt, -box; *porte-monnaie*.

purse-strings; pocket, breeches pocket.

sinking fund; stocks; government -, public -, parliamentary- -stocks, - funds, - securities; bonds; gilt-edged securities; Consols, Liberty bonds, government bonds, *crédit mobilier*.

803. Wealth.—N. wealth, riches, fortune, handsome fortune, opulence, affluence; good -, easy- circumstances; independence; competence &c. (*sufficiency*) 639; solvency, soundness, solidity.

provision, livelihood, maintenance; alimony, dowry; means, resources, substance; property &c. 780; command of money.

income &c. 810; capital, money; round sum &c. (*treasure*) 800; mint of money, mine of wealth, *El Dorado*, Pactolus, Golconda, Potosi, *bonanza*; philosopher's stone.

long -, full -, well lined -, heavy-purse; purse of Fortunatus.

pelf, Mammon, lucre, filthy lucre; loaves and fishes; fleshpots of Egypt.

rich -, moneyed -, warm- man; man of substance; capitalist, millionaire, Nabob, Crœsus, Midas, Plutus, Dives, Timon of Athens; Timo-, Pluto-cracy; Danaë.

V. be -rich &c. *adj.*; roll -, wallow-in -wealth, - riches; have money to burn.

afford, well afford; command -money, - a sum; make both ends meet, hold one's head above water.

become -rich &c. *adj.*; fill one's - pocket &c. (*treasury*) 802; feather one's nest, clean up -, make- a fortune; make money &c. (*acquire*) 775.

enrich, imburse.

worship -Mammon, – the golden calf.

Adj. wealthy, rich, affluent, opulent, moneyed, monied, worth -a great deal, – much; well -to do, – off; warm; well –, provided for.

made of money; rich as Crœsus; rolling in -riches, – wealth.

flush, – of -cash, – money, – tin; in -funds, – cash, – full feather; solvent, solid, sound, pecunious, out of debt, all straight; able to pay 20s in the £.

Phr. one's ship coming in.

804. Poverty.—N. poverty, indigence, penury, pauperism, destitution, want; need, -iness; lack, necessity, privation, distress, difficulties, wolf at the door.

bad –, poor –, needy –, embarrassed –, reduced –, straitened- circumstances; slender –, narrow- means; straits; hand to mouth existence, *res angusta domi*, low water, impecuniosity.

beggary; mendi-cancy, -city; broken –, loss of- fortune; insolvency &c. (*non-payment*) 808.

empty -purse, – pocket; light purse; beggarly account of empty boxes.

poor man, pauper, mendicant, mumper, beggar, starveling; *pauvre diable*.

V. be -poor &c. *adj.*; want, lack, starve, live from hand to mouth, have seen better days, go down in the world, be on one's uppers, come upon the parish; go to -the dogs, -wrack and ruin; not have a -penny &c. (*money*) 800, – shot in one's locker; beg one's bread; *tirer le diable par la queue*; run into debt &c. (*debt*) 806.

render -poor &c. *adj.*; impoverish; reduce, – to poverty; pauperize, fleece, ruin, bring to the parish.

Adj. poor, indigent; poverty-stricken; badly –, poorly –, ill- off; poor as -a rat, – a church mouse, – Job's turkey, – Job; fortune-, dower-, money-, penniless; unportioned, unmoneyed; impecunious; broke, flat; out –, short- of -money, – cash; without –, not worth- a rap &c. (*money*) 800; *qui n'a pas le sou*, out of pocket, hard up; out at -elbows,

– heels; seedy, bare-footed; beggar-ly, -ed; destitute; fleeced, strapped, stripped; bereft, bereaved; reduced.

in -want &c. *n.*; needy, necessitous, distressed, pinched, straitened; put to one's -shifts, – last shifts; unable to -keep the wolf from the door, – make both ends meet; embarrassed, under hatches; involved &c. (*in debt*) 806; insolvent &c. (*not paying*) 808.

Adv. in formâ pauperis.

Phr. zonam perdidit.

805. Credit.—N. credit, trust, tick, score, tally, account.

letter of credit, circular note; duplicate; mortgage, lien, debenture, paper credit, floating capital; draft; securities.

creditor, lender, lessor, mortgagee; dun; usurer.

V. keep –, run up- an account with; entrust, credit, accredit.

place to one's -credit, – account; give –, take- credit; fly a kite.

Adj. credit-ing, -ed; accredited.

Adv. on -credit &c. *n.*; to the -account, – credit- of.

806. Debt.—N. debt, obligation, liability, indebtment, debit, score.

arrears, deferred payment, deficit, default; insolvency &c. (*non-payment*) 808; bad debt.

interest; usance, usury; premium; floating -debt, – capital.

debtor, debitor; mortgagor; defaulter &c. 808; borrower.

V. be -in debt &c. *adj.*; owe; incur –, contract- a debt &c. *n.*; run up -a bill, – a score, – an account; go on tick, put on the cuff; borrow &c. 788; run –, get- into debt; outrun the constable.

answer –, go bail- for; back one's note.

Adj. indebted; liable, chargeable, answerable for.

in -debt, – embarrassed circumstances, – difficulties; incumbered, involved; involved –, plunged –, deep –, over head and ears- in debt; deeply involved; fast tied up; insolvent &c. (*not paying*) 808; *minus*, out of pocket.

unpaid; unrequieted, unrewarded; owing, due, in arrear, outstanding.

807. Payment.—N. pay-, defrayment; discharge; ac-, quittance; settlement, clearance, liquidation, satisfaction, reckoning, arrangement.

acknowledgment, release; receipt, - in full, - in full of all demands; voucher.

repayment, reimbursement, retribution; pay &c. (*reward*) 973; money paid &c. (*expenditure*) 809.

ready money &c. (*cash*) 800; stake, remittance, instalment.

payer, liquidator &c. 801.

V. pay, defray, make payment; pay -down, - on the nail, - ready money, - at sight, - in advance; cash, honour a bill, acknowledge; redeem; pay in kind.

pay one's -way, - shot, - footing; pay -the piper, - sauce for all, - costs; do the needful; come across; shell -, forkout; come down with, - the dust; tickle -, grease- the palm; expend &c. 809; put -, lay- down.

discharge, settle, quit, acquit oneself of; account -, reckon -, settle -, be even -, be quits- with; strike a balance; settle -, balance -, square- accounts with; quit scores; foot the bill; wipe -, clear- off old scores; satisfy; pay in full; satisfy -, pay in full of- all demands; clear, liquidate; pay -up, - old debts.

disgorge, make repayment; repay, refund, reimburse, retribute; make compensation &c. 30.

Adj. paying &c., paid &c. *v.*; owing nothing, out of debt, all straight, clear of -debt, - encumbrance; unowed, never indebted.

Adv. to the tune of; on the nail; money -, cash- down; cash on delivery.

808. Non-payment.—N. nonpayment; default, defalcation; protest, repudiation; application of the sponge; whitewashing.

insolvency, bankruptcy, failure; overdraft, overdrawn account; insufficiency &c. 640; run upon a bank.

waste paper bonds; dishonoured -, protested- bills; bogus cheque.

bankrupt, insolvent debtor, lame duck, man of straw, welsher, stag, defaulter, absconder, levanter.

V. not -pay &c. 807; fail, break, stop payment; become -insolvent, - bankrupt; be gazetted.

protest, dishonour, repudiate, nullify.

pay under protest; button up one's pockets, draw the purse strings; apply the sponge; pay over the left shoulder, get whitewashed; swindle &c. 791; run up bills, fly kites.

Adj. not paying; in debt &c. 806; behindhand, in arrear; beggared &c. (*poor*) 804; unable to make both ends meet; *minus*; worse than nothing.

insolvent, bankrupt, in the gazette, gazetted, ruined.

unpaid &c. (*outstanding*) 806; *gratis* &c. 815; unremunerated.

809. Expenditure.—N. expenditure, money going out; out-goings, -lay; expenses, disbursement; prime cost &c. (*price*) 812; circulation; run upon a bank.

[Money paid] payment &c. 807; pay &c. (*remuneration*) 973; bribe &c. 973; fee, footing, garnish; subsidy; tribute, Peter's pence; contingent, quota; donation &c. 784.

pay in advance, earnest, handsel, deposit, instalment.

investment; purchase &c. 795.

V. expend, spend; run -, getthrough; pay, disburse; open -, loose -, untie- the purse strings; lay -, shell -, fork- out; bleed; make up a sum, invest, sink money.

fee &c. (*reward*) 973; pay one's way &c. (*pay*) 807; subscribe &c. (*give*) 784; subsidize, bribe.

Adj. expend-ing, -ed &c. *v.*; sumptuary, liberal &c. 816; openhanded, lavish &c. 818; extensive &c. 814.

810. Receipt.—N. receipt, accountable -, conditional -, binding -, returnreceipt; value received, money coming in; income, incomings, innings, revenue, return, proceeds; gross receipts; net profit; earnings &c. (*gain*) 775.

rent, - roll; rent-al, -age; rack-rent.

premium, *bonus*; sweepstakes, tontine, prize, drawing.

pension, annuity; jointure &c. (*property*) 780; alimony, pittance; emolument &c. (*remuneration*) 973.

V. receive &c. 785; take money; draw –, derive- from; get, be in receipt of, acquire &c. 775; take &c. 789.

bring in, yield, afford, pay, return; accrue &c. (*be received from*) 785.

Adj. receiv-ing, -ed &c. *v.*; profitable &c. (*gainful*) 775.

811. Accounts.—N. accounts, accompts; commercial –, monetary- arithmetic; statistics &c. (*numeration*) 85; money matters, finance, budget, bill, score, reckoning, account.

books, account book, ledger; day –, cash –, pass- book; journal; debtor and creditor –, cash –, petty cash –, running- account; account- current; balance, – sheet; *compte rendu*, account settled.

book-keeping, audit; double –, single- entry; reckoning &c. 85.

chartered –, certified public –, accountant; auditor, actuary, bookkeeper, financier &c. 801; accounting party.

V. keep accounts, enter, post, book, credit, debit, carry over; take stock; balance –, make up –, square –, settle –, wind up –, cast up –, add up –, tot up- accounts; make accounts square.

bring to book, audit, tax, surcharge and falsify.

falsify –, garble –, cook –, doctor- an account.

Adj. monetary &c. 800; account-able, -ing; statistical.

812. Price.—N. price, amount, cost, expense, prime cost, charge, figure, demand, damage, fare, hire; wages &c. (*remuneration*) 973.

dues, duty, toll, tax, impost, cess, sess, tallage, levy, capitation-, poll-, income-, sur-, sales-, super-tax; gabel, *gabelle*; gavel, *octroi*, custom, tariff, excise, assessment, taxation, benevolence, tithe, tenths, exactment, ransom, sal-

vage; broker-, wharf-, lighter-, ton-, freight-age.

worth, rate, value, valuation, appraisement, money's worth, par value; penny &c. -worth; price current, market price, quotation; what it will -fetch &c. *v.*

bill &c. (*account*) 811; shot.

V. bear –, set –, fix- a price; appraise, assess, price, charge, demand, ask, require, exact, run up; distrain; run up a bill &c. (*debt*) 806; have one's price; liquidate.

amount to, come to, mount up to; stand one in.

fetch, sell for, cost, bring in, yield, afford.

Adj. priced &c. *v.*; to the tune of, *ad valorem*; mercenary, venal.

Phr. no penny, no paternoster; *point d'argent*, *point de Suisse*, no longer pipe, no longer dance, no song, no supper.

one may have it for.

813. Discount.—N. discount, abatement, concession, reduction, depreciation, allowance, qualification, set off, drawback, poundage, *agio*, percentage; rebate, -ment; backwardation, contango; salvage; tare and tret.

V. discount, bate; a-, re-bate; deduct, reduce, mark down, take off, allow, give, make allowance; tax, depreciate.

Adj. discounting &c. *v.*

Adv. at a discount, below par.

814. Dearness.—N. dearness &c. *adj.*; high –, famine –, fancy- price; overcharge; extravagance; exorbitance; extortion; heavy pull upon the purse; Pyrrhic victory.

V. be -dear &c. *adj.*; cost -much, – a pretty penny; rise in price, look up.

overcharge, bleed, fleece, skin, extort.

pay -too much, – through the nose, – too dear for one's whistle.

Adj. dear; high, -priced; of great price, expensive, costly, precious, dear bought; unreasonable, extravagant, exorbitant, extortionate.

at a premium; not to be had, – for

love or money; beyond -, above- price; priceless, of priceless value.

Adv. dear, -ly; at great -, heavy- cost; *à grands frais*.

Phr. prices looking up; *le jeu ne vaut pas la chandelle*.

815. Cheapness.—N. cheapness, low price; depreciation; bargain; good penny &c.- worth, *bon marché*.

[Absence of charge] gratuity; free - quarters, - seats, - admission, - warren; pass, Annie Oakley; run of one's teeth; nominal price, peppercorn rent; labour of love.

drug in the market.

V. be -cheap &c. *adj.*; cost little; come down -, fall- in price.

buy for -a mere nothing, - an old song; have one's money's worth; cheapen, beat down.

Adj. cheap; low, - priced; moderate, reasonable; in-, un-expensive, well -, worth the money; *magnifique et pas cher*; good -, cheap- at the price; dirt -, dog- cheap; cheap, -as dirt, - and nasty; catchpenny.

reduced, marked down, half-price, depreciated, unsaleable.

gratuitous, *gratis*, free, for love, - nothing; cost-, expense-less; without charge, not charged, untaxed; scot -, shot -, rent- free; free of -cost, - expense; honorary, unbought, unpaid, complimentary.

Adv. for a mere song; at -cost price, - prime cost, - a reduction - a bargain; on the cheap.

816. Liberality.—N. liberality, generosity, munificence; bount-y, -eousness, -ifulness; hospitality; charity &c. (*beneficence*) 906.

benefactor, free giver, Lady Bountiful.

V. be -liberal &c. *adj.*; spend -, bleed- freely; shower down upon; open one's purse strings &c. (*disburse*) 809; spare no expense, give -with both hands, - *carte blanche*.

Adj. liberal, free, generous; charitable &c. (*beneficent*) 906; hospitable; bount-iful, -eous; handsome; unsparing,

ungrudging; open-, free-, full- handed; open-, large-, free-hearted; munificent, princely, unstinting.

overpaid.

Adv. liberally, ungrudgingly, with open hand.

817. Economy.—N. economy, frugality; thrift, -iness; prudence, care, husbandry, good housewifery, savingness, retrenchment.

savings; prevention of waste, save-all; cheese parings and candle ends; parsimony &c. 819.

V. be -economical &c. *adj.*; economize, save; retrench; cut- down expenses, - one's coat according to one's cloth, make both ends meet, keep within compass, meet one's expenses, pay one's way; keep one's head above water; husband &c. (*lay by*) 636; save -, invest-money; put out to interest; provide -, save- -for, - against- a rainy day; feather one's nest; look after the main chance.

Adj. economical, frugal, careful, thrifty, saving, chary, spare, sparing; parsimonious &c. 819.

underpaid.

Adv. sparingly &c. *adj.*; *ne quid nimis*.

818. Prodigality.—N. prodi-gality, -gence; unthriftiness, waste, -fulness; profus-ion, -eness; extravagance; squandering &c. *v.*; lavishness; malversation.

prodigal; spend-, waste-thrift; losel, play-boy, spender, squanderer, locust.

V. be -prodigal &c. *adj.*; squander, lavish, sow broadcast; pour forth like water; pay through the nose &c. (*dear*) 814; spill, waste, dissipate, exhaust, drain, eat out of house and home, overdraw, outrun the constable; run -out, - through; misspend; throw -good money after bad, - the helve after the hatchet; burn the candle at both ends; make ducks and drakes of one's money; squander one's substance, spend money like water; fool -, potter -, muddle -, fritter -, throw- away one's money; pour water into a sieve, kill the goose that lays the golden eggs; *manger son blé en herbe.*

Adj. prodigal, profuse, thriftless, unthrifty, improvident, wasteful, losel, extravagant, lavish, dissipated, over liberal; full handed &c. (*liberal*) 816.

penny wise and pound foolish.

Adv. with an unsparing hand; money burning one's pocket; recklessly profuse.

Int. hang the expense!

819. Parsimony.—N. parsimony, parcity; parsimoniousness, stinginess &c. *adj.*; stint; illiberality, avarice, tenacity, avidity, rapacity, extortion, venality, cupidity; selfishness &c. 943; *auri sacra fames.*

miser, niggard, churl, screw, tightwad, skinflint, crib, codger, muckworm, money-grubber, pinchfist, scrimp, lick-penny, hunks, curmudgeon, *Harpagon*, Silas Marner, harpy, extortioner, usurer.

V. be -parsimonious &c. *adj.*; grudge, begrudge, stint, skimp, pinch, gripe, screw, dole out, hold back, withhold, starve, famish, live upon nothing, skin a flint.

drive a -bargain, - hard bargain; cheapen, beat down; stop one hole in a sieve; have an itching palm, grasp, grab.

Adj. parsimonious, penurious, stingy, miserly, mean, shabby, peddling, scrubby, pennywise, near, niggardly, frugal to excess; close; fast-, close-, strait-handed; close-, hard-, tight-fisted; tight, sparing; chary; grudging, griping &c. *v.*; illiberal, ungenerous, churlish, hidebound, sordid, mercenary, venal, covetous, usurious, avaricious, greedy, extortionate, rapacious.

Adv. with a sparing hand.

CLASS VI

Words Relating to the
SENTIENT and MORAL POWERS.

Section I.
AFFECTIONS IN GENERAL

820. Affections.—N. affections, character, qualities, disposition, nature, spirit, tone; temper, -ament; *diathesis*, idiosyncrasy; cast -, habit -, frame- of-mind, - soul; predilection, turn; natural -, turn of mind; bent, bias, predisposition, proneness, proclivity; propen-sity, -sedness, -sion, -dency; vein, humour, mood, grain, mettle; sympathy &c. (*love*) 897.

soul, heart, breast, bosom, inner man; heart's -core, - strings, - blood; heart of hearts, *penetralia mentis*; secret and inmost recesses of the -, cockles of one's-heart; inmost -heart, - soul; back-bone.

passion, pervading spirit; ruling -, master- passion; *furore*; fulness of the heart, heyday of the blood, flesh and blood, flow of soul, force of character.

V. have -, possess- -affections &c. *n.*; be of a -character &c. *n.*; be -affected &c. *adj.*; breathe.

Adj. affected, characterized, formed, moulded, cast; at-, tempered; framed; pre-, disposed; prone, inclined; having a -bias &c. *n.*; tinctured -, imbued -, penetrated -, eaten up- with.

inborn, inbred, ingrained, in the grain, congenital, inherent, bred in the bone; deep-rooted, ineffaceable, inveterate; pathoscopic.

Adv. in one's -heart &c. *n.*; at heart; heart and soul &c. 821; in the -vein, - mood.

821. Feeling.—N. feeling; suffering &c. *v.*; endurance, tolerance, sufferance, supportance, experience, response; sympathy &c. (*love*) 897; impression, inspiration, affection, sensation, emotion, pathos, deep sense.

fire, warmth, glow, unction, *gusto*, vehemence; ferv-our, -ency; heartiness, cordiality; earnestness, eagerness; *empressement*, ardour, zeal, passion, enthusiasm, *verve, furore,* fanaticism; excitation of feeling &c. 824; fulness of the heart &c. (*disposition*) 820; passion &c. (*state of excitability*) 825; ecstasy &c. (*pleasure*) 827.

blush, suffusion, flush; hectic; tingling, thrill, kick, turn, shock; agitation &c. (*irregular motion*) 315; quiver, heaving, flutter, flurry, fluster, twitter, tremor; throb, -bing; pulsation, palpitation, panting; trepid-, perturb-ation; ruffle, hurry of spirits, pother, stew, ferment.

V. feel; receive an -impression &c. *n.*; be -impressed with &c. *adj.*; entertain -, harbour -, cherish- -feeling &c. *n.*

respond; catch the -flame, - infection; enter the spirit of.

bear, suffer, support, sustain, endure, brook, thole, aby; abide &c. (*be composed*) 826; experience &c. (*meet with*) 151; taste, prove; labour -, smart-under; bear the brunt of, brave, stand.

swell, glow, warm, flush, blush, change colour, mantle; turn -colour, - pale, - red, - black in the face; blench, crimson, whiten, pale, tingle, thrill, heave, pant, throb, palpitate, go pit-a-pat, tremble, quiver, flutter, twitter; stagger, reel; shake &c. 315; be -agitated, – excited &c. 824; look -blue, – black; wince, draw a deep breath.

impress &c. (*excite the feelings*) 824.

Adj. feeling &c. *v.*; sentient; sensuous; sensor-ial, -y; emo-tive, -tional; of –, with- feeling &c. *n.*

warm, quick, lively, smart, strong, sharp, acute, cutting, piercing, incisive; keen, – as a razor; trenchant, pungent, racy, *piquant*, poignant, caustic.

impressive, deep, profound, indelible; deep-, home-, heart-felt; swelling, soul-stirring, deep-mouthed, heart-expanding, electric, thrilling, rapturous, ecstatic.

earnest, wistful, eager, breathless; fervent, -vid; gushing, passionate, warm-hearted, hearty, cordial, sincere, zealous, enthusiastic, glowing, ardent, burning, red-hot, fiery, flaming; boiling, – over.

pervading, penetrating, absorbing; rabid, raving, feverish, fanatical, hysterical; impetuous &c. (*excitable*) 825; overmastering.

impressed –, moved –, touched –, affected –, penetrated –, seized –, imbued &c. 820- with; devoured by; wrought up &c. (*excited*) 824; struck all of a heap; rapt; in a -quiver &c. *n.*; enraptured &c. 829.

Adv. heart and soul, from the bottom of one's heart, *ab imo pectore, de profundis*, at heart, *con amore*, heartily, devoutly, over head and ears.

Phr. the heart -big, – full, – swelling, – beating, – pulsating, – throbbing, – thumping, – beating high, – melting, – overflowing, – bursting, – breaking.

822. Sensibility.—N. sensi-bility, -bleness, -tiveness; moral sensibility; impress-, affect-ibility; suscepti-bleness, -bility, -vity; mobility; viva-city, -ciousness; tender-, soft-ness; sentimentality, -ism.

excitability &c. 825; fastidiousness &c. 868; physical sensibility &c. 375.

sore -point, – place; where the shoe pinches.

V. be -sensible &c. *adj.*; have a -tender, – warm, – sensitive- heart.

take to –, treasure up in the- heart; shrink.

'die of a rose in aromatic pain'; touch to the quick.

Adj. sensi-ble, -tive; impressi-ble, -onable; suscepti-ve, -ble; alive to, impassion-able, -ed; gushing; warm-, tender-, soft-hearted; tender –, as a chicken; soft, sentimental, romantic; enthusiastic, highflying, spirited, mettlesome, vivacious, lively, expressive, mobile, tremblingly alive; excitable &c. 825; over-sensitive, without skin, thin-skinned; fastidious &c. 868.

Adv. sensibly &c. *adj.*; to the -quick, – inmost core.

823. Insensibility.—N. insensi-bility, -bleness; moral insensibility; inertness, *inertia, vis inertiæ*; impassi-bility, -bleness; inappetency, apathy, phlegm, dulness, hebetude, supineness, luke-warmness, insusceptibility, unimpressibility.

cold -fit, – blood, – heart; cold-, cool-ness; frigidity, *sang-froid*; stoicism, imperturbation &c. (*inexcitability*) 826; *nonchalance*, unconcern, dry eyes; *insouciance* &c. (*indifference*) 866; recklessness &c. 863; callousness; heart of stone, stock and stone, marble, deadness.

torp-or, -idity; obstupefaction, lethargy, coma, trance; sleep &c. 683; suspended animation; stu-por, -pefaction; paralysis, palsy; numbness &c. (*physical insensibility*) 376.

neutrality; quietism, vegetation.

V. be -insensible &c. *adj.*; have a rhinoceros hide; show -insensibility &c. *n.*; not -mind, – care, – be affected by; have no desire for &c. 866; have –, feel –, take- no interest in; *nil admirari*; not care a -straw &c. (*unimportance*) 643 for; disregard &c. (*neglect*) 460; set at naught &c. (*make light of*) 483; turn a deaf ear to &c. (*inattention*) 458; vegetate.

render -insensible, – callous; blunt, obtund, numb, benumb, paralyze, chloroform, deaden, hebetate, stun, stupefy; brut-ify, -alize.

inure; harden, – the heart; steel, caseharden, sear.

Adj. insensible, unconscious; impassive, -ble; blind to, deaf to, dead to; un-, in-susceptible; unimpress-ionable, -ible; passion-, spirit-, heart-, soul-less; unfeeling, unmoral.

apathetic; leuco-, phlegmatic; dull, frigid; cold, -blooded, -hearted; unemotional; cold as charity; flat, obtuse, inert, supine, sluggish, torpid; sleepy &c. (*inactive*) 683; languid, half-hearted, tame; numb, -ed; comatose; anæsthetic &c. 376; stupefied, chloroformed, palsy-stricken.

indifferent, lukewarm; Laodicean; careless, mindless, regardless; inattentive &c. 458; neglectful &c. 460; disregarding.

unconcerned, *nonchalant, pococurante, insouciant, sans souci*; unambitious &c. 866.

un-affected, -ruffled, -impressed, -inspired, -excited, -moved, -stirred, -touched, -shocked, -struck; unblushing &c. (*shameless*) 885; unanimated; vegetative.

callous, thick-skinned, pachydermatous, impervious; hard, -ened; inured, case-hardened; steeled –, proof- against; imperturbable &c. (*inexcitable*) 826; unfelt.

Adv. insensibly &c. *adj.*; *æquo animo*; without being -moved, – touched, – impressed; in cold blood; with -dry eyes, – withers unwrung.

Phr. never mind; it is of no consequence &c. (*unimportant*) 643; it cannot be helped; nothing coming amiss; it is all -the same, – one- to.

824. Excitation.—N. excitation of feeling; mental –, excitement; suscitation, galvanism, stimulation, piquancy, provocation, inspiration, calling forth,

infection; interest, animation, agitation, perturbation; subjugation, fascination, intoxication; en-, ravishment; entrancement, high pressure.

unction, impressiveness &c. *adj.*; emotional appeal; melodrama; psychological moment, crisis; sensationalism.

trial of temper, *casus belli*; irritation &c. (*anger*) 900; passion &c. (*state of excitability*) 825; thrill &c. (*feeling*) 821; repression of feeling &c. 826.

V. excite, affect, touch, move, impress, strike, interest, intrigue, animate, inspire, impassion, smite, infect; stir –, fire –, warm- the blood; set astir; a-, wake; a-, waken; call forth; e-, provoke; raise up, summon up, call up, wake up, blow up, get up, light up; raise; get up steam, rouse, arouse, stir, fire, kindle, enkindle, apply the torch, set on fire, inflame, illuminate.

stimulate; ex-, suscitate; inspirit; spirit up, stir up, work up; infuse life into, give new life to; bring –, introduce- new blood; quicken; sharpen, whet; work upon &c. (*incite*) 615; hurry on, give a fillip, put on one's mettle.

fan the -fire, – flame; blow the coals, stir the embers; fan, – into a flame; foster, heat, warm, foment, raise to a fever heat; keep -up, – the pot boiling; revive, rekindle; rake up, rip up.

stir –, play on –, come home to- the feelings; touch -a string, – a chord, – the soul, – the heart; go to one's heart, penetrate, pierce, go through one, touch to the quick, open the wound; possess –, pervade –, penetrate –, imbrue –, absorb –, affect –, disturb- the soul.

absorb, rivet the attention; sink into the -mind, – heart; prey on the mind; intoxicate; over-whelm, -power; *bouleverser*, upset, turn one's head.

fascinate; enrapture &c. (*give pleasure*) 829.

agitate, perturb, ruffle, fluster, flutter, shake, disturb, faze, startle, shock, stagger; give one a -shock, – turn; strike -dumb, – all of a heap; stun, astound, electrify, galvanize, petrify.

irritate, sting; cut, - to the -heart, - quick; try one's temper; fool to the top of one's bent, pique; infuriate, madden, make one's blood boil; lash into fury &c. (*wrath*) 900.

be -excited &c. *adj.*; flash up, flare up; catch the infection; thrill &c. (*feel*) 821; mantle; work oneself up; seethe, boil, simmer, foam, fume, flame, rage, rave; run mad &c. (*passion*) 825.

Adj. excited &c. *v.*; wrought up, on the *qui vive*, astir, sparkling; in a -quiver &c. 821, - fever, - ferment, - blaze, - state of excitement; in hysterics; black in the face, over-wrought; hot, red-hot, flushed, feverish; all -of a twitter, - of a flutter, - of a dither, - in a pucker; with -quivering lips, - tears in one's eyes.

flaming; boiling, - over; ebullient, seething; foaming, - at the mouth; fuming, raging, carried away by passion, wild, raving, frantic, mad, distracted, distraught, beside oneself, out of one's wits, amuck, ready to burst, *bouleversé*, demoniacal.

lost, *éperdu*, tempest-tossed; haggard; ready to sink.

stung to the quick, up, on one's high ropes.

exciting &c. *v.*; impressive, warm, glowing, fervid, swelling, imposing, spirit-stirring, thrilling; high-wrought; soul-stirring, -subduing; heart-swelling, -thrilling; agonizing &c. (*painful*) 830; telling, sensational, melodramatic, hysterical; over-powering, -whelming; more than flesh and blood can bear.

piquant &c. (*pungent*) 392; spicy, appetizing, provocative, *provoquant*, tantalizing.

Adv. till one is black in the face.

Phr. the heart -beating high, - going pit-a-pat, - leaping into one's mouth; the blood -being up, - boiling in one's veins; the eye -glistening, - 'in a fine frenzy rolling'; the head turned.

825. [Excess of sensitiveness.] **Excitability.—N.** excitability, impetuosity, vehemence; boisterousness &c. *adj.*;

turbulence; impatience, intolerance, non-endurance; irritability &c. (*irascibility*) 901; itching &c. (*desire*) 865; wincing; disquiet, -ude; restlessness; fidge-ts, -tiness; agitation &c. (*irregular motion*) 315.

trepidation, perturbation, ruffle, hurry, -skurry, fuss, flurry; fluster, flutter; pother, stew, ferment; whirl; thrill &c. (*feeling*) 821; state -, fever- of excitement; transport.

passion, excitement, flush, heat; fever, -heat; fire, flame, fume, blood boiling; tumult; effervescence, ebullition; boiling, - over; whiff, gust, storm, tempest; scene, breaking out, burst, fit, paroxysm, explosion; out-break, -burst; agony.

violence &c. 173; fierceness &c. *adj.*; rage, fury, *furor, furore*, desperation, madness, distraction, raving, delirium, brain storm; frenzy, hysterics; intoxication; tearing -, raging- passion, towering rage; anger &c. 900.

fascination, infatuation, fanaticism; Quixot-ism, -ry; *tête montée*.

V. be -impatient &c. *adj.*; not be able to -bear &c. 826; bear ill, wince, chafe, champ the bit; be in a -stew &c. *n.*; be out of all patience, fidget, fuss, not have a wink of sleep; toss, - on one's pillow.

lose one's temper &c. 900; break -, burst -, fly- out; go -, fly- -off, - off the handle, - off at a tangent; explode; flare up, flame up, fire up, burst into a flame, take fire, fire, burn; boil, - over; foam, fume, rage, rave, rant, tear; go -, run-wild, - mad; go into hysterics; run -riot, - amuck; *battre la campagne, faire le diable à quatre*, play the deuce; raise -Cain, - the devil.

Adj. excitable, easily excited, in an excitable state; highly strung; irritable &c. (*irascible*) 901; impatient, intolerant.

feverish, febrile, hysterical; delirious, mad, moody, maggoty-headed.

unquiet, mercurial, electric, galvanic, hasty, hurried, restless, fidgety, fussy; chafing &c. *v.*

startlish, mettlesome, high mettled, skittish.

vehement, demonstrative, violent, wild, furious, fierce, fiery, hot-headed, mad-cap.

over-zealous, enthusiastic, impassioned, fanatical; rabid &c. (*eager*) 865.

rampant, clamorous, uproarious, turbulent, tempestuous, tumultuary, boisterous.

impulsive, impetuous, passionate; uncontroll-ed, -able; ungovernable, irrepressible, stanchless, inextinguishable, burning, simmering, volcanic, ready to burst forth.

excit-ed, -ing &c. 824.

Int. pish! pshaw!

Phr. *noli me tangere.*

826. [Absence of excitability, or of excitement.] **Inexcitability.—N.** inexcit-, imperturb-, inirrit-ability; even temper, tranquil mind, dispassion; tolerance, toleration, patience.

passiveness &c. (*physical inertness*) 172; hebet-ude, -ation; impassibility &c. (*insensibility*) 823; stupefaction.

coolness, calmness &c. *adj.*; composure, placidity, indisturbance, imperturbation, *sang-froid*, tranquillity, serenity; quiet, -ude; peace of mind, mental calmness.

staidness &c. *adj.*; gravity, sobriety, Quakerism; philosophy, equanimity, stoicism, command of temper; self-possession, -control, -command, -restraint; presence of mind.

submission &c. 725; resignation; suffer-, support-, endur-, long-suffer-, forbear-ance; longanimity; fortitude; patience -of Job, - 'on a monument,' - 'sovereign o'er transmuted ill'; moderation; repression -, subjugation- of feeling; restraint &c. 751.

tranquillization &c. (*moderation*) 174.

V. be -composed &c. *adj.*

laisser -faire, - aller; take things -easily, - as they come; take it easy, run on, live and let live; take -easily, - coolly, - in good part; *æquam serva e mentem.*

bear, - well, - the brunt; go through, support, endure, brave, disregard.

tolerate, suffer, stand, bide; abide, aby; bear -, put up -, abide- with; acquiesce; submit &c. (*yield*) 725; submit with a good grace; resign -, reconcile-oneself to; brook, digest, eat, swallow, pocket, stomach; make -light of, - the best of, - a virtue of necessity; put a good face on, keep one's countenance; carry -on, - through; check &c. 751-oneself.

compose, appease &c. (*moderate*) 174; propitiate; repress &c. (*restrain*) 751; render insensible 823; overcome -, allay -, repress- one's -excitability &c. 825; master one's feelings.

make -oneself, - one's mind- easy; set one's mind at -ease, - rest.

calm -, cool- down; thaw, grow cool.

be -borne, - endured; go down.

Adj. in-, un-excitable; imperturbable; unsusceptible &c. (*insensible*) 823; un-, dis-passionate; cold-blooded, inirritable; enduring &c. *v.*; stoical, Platonic, philosophic, staid, stayed; sober, - minded; grave; sober -, grave- as a judge; sedate, demure, cool-, level-headed; steady.

easy-going, peaceful, placid, calm; quiet, - as a mouse; tranquil, serene; cool, - as -a cucumber, - custard; undemonstrative.

temperate &c. (*moderate*) 174; composed, collected; un-excited, -stirred, -ruffled, -disturbed, -perturbed, -impassioned; unoffended; unresisting.

meek, tolerant; patient, - as Job; submissive &c. 725; tame; content, resigned, chastened, subdued, lamblike; gentle, - as a lamb; *suaviter in modo*; mild, - as mother's milk; soft as peppermint; armed with patience, bearing with, clement, forbearant, long-suffering.

Adv. 'like patience on a monument smiling at grief'; *æquo animo*, in cold blood &c. 823; more in sorrow than in anger.

Int. patience! and shuffle the cards.

Section II. PERSONAL AFFECTIONS*

1°. Passive Affections

827. Pleasure.—**N.** pleasure, gratification, enjoyment, fruition; ob-, delectation; relish, zest; *gusto* &c. (*physical pleasure*) 377; satisfaction &c. (*content*) 831; complacency.

well-being; good &c. 618; snugness, comfort, ease; cushion &c. 215; *sans souci*, mind at ease.

joy, gladness, delight, glee, cheer, sunshine; cheerfulness &c. 836.

treat, refreshment; frolic, fun, lark, gambol, merry-making; amusement &c. 840; luxury &c. 377; hedonism.

mens sana in corpore sano.

happiness, felicity, bliss; beati-tude, -fication; enchantment, transport, rapture, ravishment, ecstasy; *summum bonum*; paradise, elysium &c. (*heaven*) 981; third -, seventh- heaven; unalloyed -happiness &c.

honeymoon; palmy -, halcyon- days; golden -age, - time; *Saturnia regna*, Eden, Arcadia, happy valley, Agape-mone; Cockaigne.

V. be pleased &c. 829; feel -, experience- pleasure &c. *n.*; joy; enjoy -, hug- oneself; be in -clover &c. 377, - elysium &c. 981; tread on enchanted ground; fall -, go- into raptures.

feel at home, breathe freely, bask in the sunshine.

be -pleased &c. 829- with; receive -, derive- pleasure &c. *n.*- from; take - pleasure &c. *n.*- in; delight in, rejoice in, indulge in, luxuriate in; gloat over &c. (*physical pleasure*) 377; enjoy, relish, like; love &c. 897; take -to, - a fancy to; have a liking for; enter into the spirit of.

take in good part.

treat oneself to, solace oneself with.

Adj. pleased &c. 829; not sorry; glad, -some; pleased as Punch.

happy, blest, blessed, blissful, beatified; happy as -a king, - the day is long; thrice happy, *ter quaterque beatus*; enjoying &c. *v.*; joyful &c. (*in spirits*) 836; hedonic.

in -a blissful state, - paradise &c. 981, - raptures, - ecstasies, - a transport of delight.

comfortable &c. (*physical pleasure*) 377; at ease; content &c. 831; *sans souci*, in clover.

overjoyed, entranced, enchanted; enraptured; en-, ravished; transported; fascinated, captivated.

with -a joyful face, - sparkling eyes.

pleasing &c. 829; ecstatic, beat-ic, -ific; painless, unalloyed, without alloy, cloudless.

Adv. happily &c. *adj.*; with pleasure &c. (*willingly*) 60; with -glee &c. *n.*

Phr. one's heart leaping with joy.

828. Pain.—**N.** mental suffering, pain, dolour; suffer-ing, -ance; ache, smart &c. (*physical pain*) 378; passion.

displeasure, dissatisfaction, discomfort, discomposure, disquiet; *malaise*; inquietude, uneasiness, vexation of spirit; taking; discontent &c. 832.

dejection &c. 837; weariness &c. 841.

annoyance, irritation, worry, infliction, visitation; plague, bore; bother, -ation; stew, vexation, mortification, chagrin, *esclandre; mauvais quart d'heure.*

care, anxiety, solicitude, trouble,

---

* Or those which concern one's own state of feeling.

trial, ordeal, fiery ordeal, shock, blow, cark, dole, fret, burden, load.

concern, grief, sorrow, distress, affliction, woe, bitterness, gloom, heartache; heavy –, aching –, bleeding –, broken-heart; heavy affliction, gnawing grief, unhappiness, infelicity, misery, tribulation, wretchedness, desolation; despair &c. 859; extremity, prostration, depth of misery.

nightmare, *ephialtes*, incubus.

anguish, agony; throe, tor-ture, -ment; crucifixion, martyrdom; pang, twinge, stab; the rack, the stake; purgatory &c. (*hell*) 982.

hell upon earth; iron age, reign of terror; slough of despond &c. (*adversity*) 735; peck –, sea- of troubles; ills that flesh is heir to &c. (*evil*) 619; miseries of human life; unkindest cut of all.

sufferer, victim, prey, martyr, object of compassion, wretch, shorn lamb.

V. feel –, suffer –, experience –, undergo –, bear –, endure- pain &c. *n.*; smart, ache &c. (*physical pain*) 378; suffer, bleed, ail; be the victim of; bear –, take up- the cross.

labour under afflictions; quaff the bitter cup, have a bad time of it; fall on evil days &c. (*adversity*) 735; go hard with, come to grief, fall a sacrifice to, drain the cup of misery to the dregs, sup full of horrors.

sit on thorns, be on pins and needles, wince, fret, chafe, worry oneself, be in a taking, fret and fume, take -on, - to heart.

grieve; mourn &c. (*lament*) 839; yearn, repine, pine, droop, languish, sink; give way; despair &c. 859; break one's heart; weigh upon the heart &c. (*inflict pain*) 830.

Adj. in –, in a state of –, full of- pain &c. *n.*; suffering &c. *v.*; pained, afflicted, worried, displeased &c. 830; aching, griped, sore &c. (*physical pain*) 378; on the rack, in limbo; between hawk and buzzard.

un-comfortable, -easy; ill at ease; in a -taking, - way; disturbed; discontent-

ed &c. 832; out of humour &c. 901*a*; weary &c. 841.

heavy laden, stricken, crushed, a prey to, victimized, ill-used.

unfortunate &c. (*hapless*) 735; to be pitied, doomed, devoted, accursed, undone, lost, stranded.

unhappy, infelicitous, poor, wretched, miserable, woe-begone; cheerless &c. (*dejected*) 837; careworn.

concerned, sorry; sorrow-ing, -ful; cut up, chagrined, horrified, horror-stricken; in –, plunged in –, a prey to- grief &c. *n.*; in tears &c. (*lamenting*) 839; steeped to the lips in misery; heart-stricken, -broken, -scalded; broken-hearted; in despair &c. 859.

Phr. 'the iron entered into our soul'; '*hæret lateri lethalis arundo*'; one's heart bleeding.

829. [Capability of giving pleasure; cause or source of pleasure.] **Pleasurableness.—N.** pleasurable-, pleasant-, agreeable-ness &c. *adj.*; pleasure giving, jocundity, delectability; amusement &c. 840.

attraction &c. (*motive*) 615; attractiveness, -ability; invitingness &c. *adj.*; charm, fascination, captivation, enchantment, witchery, seduction, winsomeness, winning ways, amenity, amiability, sweetness.

loveliness &c. (*beauty*) 845; sunny –, bright- side; sweets &c. (*sugar*) 396; goodness &c. 648; manna in the wilderness, land flowing with milk and honey.

treat; regale &c. (*physical pleasure*) 377; dainty; tit-, tid-bit; nuts, *sauce piquante*.

V. cause –, produce –, create –, give –, afford –, procure –, offer –, present –, yield- pleasure &c. 827.

please, charm, delight; gladden &c. (*make cheerful*) 836; take, captivate, fascinate; enchant, entrance, enrapture, transport, bewitch; en-, ravish.

bless, beatify; satisfy; gratify, – desire &c. 865; slake, satiate, quench; indulge, humour, flatter, tickle; tickle the palate &c. (*savoury*) 394; regale,

refresh; enliven; treat; amuse &c. 840;
take -, tickle -, hit- one's fancy; meet
one's wishes; win -, gladden -, rejoice
-, warm the cockles of- the heart; do
one's heart good.

attract, allure &c. (*move*) 615; stimulate &c. (*excite*) 824; interest, intrigue.

make things pleasant, popularize, gild
the pill, sweeten.

Adj. causing pleasure &c. *v.*; pleasure-giving; pleas-ing, -ant, -urable;
agreeable, cushy; grat-eful, -ifying; leef,
lief, acceptable; welcome, - as the roses
in May; welcomed; favourite; to one's
-taste, - mind, - liking, - heart's content; satisfactory &c. (*good*) 648.

refreshing; comfortable; cordial; genial; glad, -some; sweet, delectable, nice,
dainty; delic-ate, -ious; dulcet; luscious
&c. 396; palatable &c. 394; luxurious,
voluptuous; sensual &c. 377.

attractive &c. 615; inviting, prepossessing, engaging; win-ning, -some;
taking, fascinating, captivating, killing;
seduc-ing, -tive; alluring, enticing; appetizing &c. (*exciting*) 824; cheering
&c. 836; bewitching; interesting, absorbing, enchanting, entrancing, enrav-
ishing.

charming; delightful, felicitous, exquisite; lovely &c. (*beautiful*) 845; rav-
ishing, rapturous; heartfelt, thrilling,
ecstatic; beat-ic, -ific; seraphic; empyrean; elysian &c. (*heavenly*) 981.

palmy, halcyon, Saturnian.

Phr. *decies repetita placebit.*

830. [Capability of giving pain; cause
or source of pain.] **Painfulness.—N.**
painfulness &c. *adj.*; trouble, care &c.
(*pain*) 828; trial; af-, in-fliction; cross,
blow, stroke, burden, load, curse; bitter
-pill, - draught, - cup; waters of bitterness.

annoyance, grievance, nuisance, vexation, mortification, sickener; bore,
bother, pother, hot water, sea of troubles, hornet's nest, plague, pest.

cancer, ulcer, sting, thorn; canker &c.
(*bane*) 663; scorpion &c. (*evil-doer*)
913; dagger &c. (*arms*) 727; scourge &c.

(*instrument of punishment*) 975; carking
-, canker worm of- care.

mishap, misfortune &c. (*adversity*)
735; désagrément, esclandre, rub.

source of -irritation, - annoyance;
wound, sore subject, skeleton in the
closet; thorn in -the flesh, - one's side;
where the shoe pinches, gall and worm-
wood.

sorry sight, heavy news, provocation;
affront &c. 929; head and front of one's
offending.

infestation, molestation; malignity
&c. (*malevolence*) 907.

V. cause -, occasion -, give -, bring
-, induce -, produce -, create -, inflict-
pain &c. 828; pain, hurt, wound.

pinch, prick, gripe &c. (*physical
pain*) 378; pierce, lancinate, cut.

hurt -, wound -, grate upon -, jar
upon- the feelings; wring -, pierce -,
lacerate -, break -, rend- the heart;
make the heart bleed; tear -, rend-the
heart-strings; draw tears from the eyes.

sadden; make -unhappy &c. 828;
plunge into sorrow, grieve, fash, afflict,
distress; cut -up, - to the heart.

displease, annoy, incommode, dis-
commode, discompose, trouble, disquiet, disturb, thwart, cross, perplex, molest, tease, rag, tire, irk, vex, mortify,
wherret, worry, plague, bother, pester,
bore, pother, harass, harry, badger,
heckle, bait, beset, infest, persecute,
importune, be troublesome.

wring, harrow, torment, torture; put
to the -rack, - question; break on the
wheel, rack, scarify; cruci-ate, -fy; convulse, agonize; barb the dart; plant a
-dagger in the breast, - thorn in one's
side.

irritate, provoke, sting, nettle, try the
patience, pique, fret, rile, tweak the
nose, chafe, gall; sting -, wound -, cut-
to the quick; aggrieve, affront, enchafe,
enrage, ruffle, sour the temper; give offence &c. (*resentment*) 900.

maltreat, bite, snap at, assail, bully;
smite &c. (*punish*) 972.

sicken, disgust, revolt, nauseate, disenchant, repel, offend, shock, stink in

the nostrils; go against -, turn- the stomach; make one sick, set the teeth on edge, go against the grain, grate on the ear; stick in one's -throat, - gizzard; rankle, gnaw, corrode, horrify, appall, freeze the blood; chill the spine; make the -flesh creep, - hair stand on end; make the blood -curdle, - run cold; make one shudder.

haunt, - the memory; weigh -, prey-on the -heart, - mind, - spirits; bring one's grey hairs with sorrow to the grave; add a nail to one's coffin.

Adj. causing pain, hurting &c. *v.*; hurtful &c. (*bad*) 649; painful; dolorific, -ous; unpleasant; un-, dis-pleasing; disagreeable, unpalatable, bitter, distasteful; uninviting; unwelcome; undesir-able, -ed; obnoxious; unacceptable, unpopular, thankless.

unsatisfactory, untoward, unlucky, uncomfortable.

distressing; afflict-ing, -ive; joy-, cheer-, comfort-less; dismal, disheartening; depress-ing, -ive; dreary, melancholy, grievous, piteous; woeful, rueful, mournful, deplorable, pitiable, lamentable; sad, affecting, touching, pathetic.

irritating, provoking, stinging, annoying, aggravating, mortifying, galling; unaccommodating, invidious, vexatious; trouble-, tire-, irk-, weari-some; plaguing, -y; awkward.

importunate; teas-, pester-, bother-, harass-, worry-, torment-, cark-ing.

in-toler-, -suffer-, -support-able; un-bear-, -endur-able; past bearing; not to be -borne, - endured; more than flesh and blood can bear; enough to -drive one mad, - provoke a saint, - make a parson swear, - try the patience of Job.

shocking, terrific, grim, appalling, crushing; dreadful, fearful, frightful; thrilling, tremendous, dire; heart-breaking, -rending, -wounding, -corroding, -sickening; harrowing, rending.

odious, hateful, execrable, repulsive, repellent, abhorrent; horri-d, -ble, -fic, -fying; offensive; nause-ous, -ating; disgust-, sicken-, revolt-ing; nasty; loath-some, -ful; fulsome; vile &c. (*bad*) 649; hideous &c. 846.

sharp, acute, sore, severe, grave, hard, harsh, cruel, biting, acrimonious, caustic; cutting, corroding, consuming, racking, excruciating, searching, searing, grinding, grating, agonizing; envenomed.

ruinous, disastrous, calamitous, tragical; desolating, withering; burdensome, onerous, oppressive; cumb-rous, -ersome.

Adv. painfully &c. *adj.*; with -pain &c. 828; deuced.

Int. *hinc illæ lachrymæ!* woe is me!

Phr. *surgit amari aliquid*; the place being too hot to hold one; the iron entering into the soul.

831. Content.—N. content, -ment, -edness; complacency, satisfaction, entire satisfaction, ease, heart's ease, peace of mind; serenity &c. 826; cheerfulness &c. 836; ray of comfort; comfort &c. (*well-being*) 827.

re-, conciliation; resignation &c. (*patience*) 826.

waiter on Providence.

V. be -content &c. *adj.*; rest -satisfied, - and be thankful; take the good the gods provide, let well alone, feel oneself at home, hug oneself, lay the flattering unction to one's soul.

take -up with, - in good part; assent &c. 488; be reconciled to, make one's peace with; get over it; take -heart, - comfort; put up with &c. (*bear*) 826.

render -content &c. *adj.*; set at ease, comfort; set one's -heart, - mind- at -ease, - rest; speak peace; conciliate, reconcile, win over, propitiate, disarm, beguile; content, satisfy; gratify &c. 829.

be -tolerated &c. 826; go down, - with; do.

Adj. content, -ed; satisfied &c. *v.*; at -ease, - one's ease, - home; with the mind at ease, *sans souci, sine curâ,* easy-going, not particular; conciliatory; unrepining, of good comfort; resigned &c. (*patient*) 826; cheerful &c. 836.

un-afflicted, -vexed, -molested, -plagued; serene &c. 826; at rest; snug, comfortable; in one's element.

satisfactory, satisfying, ample, sufficient, adequate, tolerable.

Adv. to one's heart's content; *à la bonne heure*; all for the best.

Int. amen &c. (*assent*) 488; very well, so much the better, well and good; it -, that- will do; it cannot be helped.

Phr. nothing comes amiss.

832. Discontent.—N. discontent, -ment; dissatisfaction; dissent &c. 489; labour unrest.

disappointment, mortification; cold comfort; regret &c. 833; repining, taking on &c. *v.*; inquietude, vexation of spirit, soreness; heart-burning, -grief; querulousness &c. (*lamentation*) 839; hypercriticism.

malcontent, grumbler, growler, croaker, *laudator temporis acti*; censurer, complainer, faultfinder, murmurer, Adullamite, Diehard, Bitterender.

the Opposition, cave of Adullam, indignation, meeting, 'winter of our discontent.'

V. be -discontented &c. *adj.*; quarrel with one's bread and butter; repine; regret &c. 833; wish one at the bottom of the Red Sea; take -on, - to heart; shrug the shoulders; make a wry -, pull a long-face; knit one's brows; look -blue, - black, - black as thunder, - blank, - glum.

take -in bad part, - ill; fret, chafe, make a piece of work; grumble, croak, grouse; lament &c. 839.

cause -discontent &c. *n.*; dissatisfy, disappoint, mortify, put out, disconcert; cut up; dishearten.

Adj. discontented; dissatisfied &c. *v.*; unsatisfied, ungratified; dissident; dissentient &c. 489; malcontent, exigent, exacting, hypercritical.

repining &c. *v.*; regretful &c. 833; down in the mouth &c. (*dejected*) 837.

in -high dudgeon, - a fume, - the sulks, - the dumps, - bad humour; glum,

sulky; sour, - as a crab; soured, sore; out of -humour, - temper.

disappointing &c. *v.*; unsatisfactory.

Int. so much the worse!

Phr. that -, it- will never do.

833. Regret.—N. regret, repining; homesickness, nostalgia; *mal -, maladie- du pays*; lamentation &c. 839, contrition, compunction, penitence &c. 950.

bitterness, heart-burning.

laudator temporis acti &c. (*discontent*) 832.

V. regret, deplore; bewail &c. (*lament*) 839; repine, cast a longing lingering look behind; rue, - the day; repent &c. 950; *infandum renovare dolorem*.

prey -, weigh -, have a weight- on the mind; leave an aching void.

Adj. regretting &c. *v.*; regretful; home-sick.

regretted &c. *v.*; much to be regretted, regrettable; lamentable &c. (*bad*) 649.

Int. what a pity! hang it!

Phr. 'tis -pity, - too true.

834. Relief.—N. relief; deliverance; refreshment &c. 689; easement, softening, alleviation, mitigation, palliation &c. 174; soothing, lullaby; cradle song, *berceuse.*

solace, consolation, comfort, encouragement.

lenitive, restorative &c. (*remedy*) 662; poultice &c. *v.*; cushion &c. 215; crumb of comfort, balm in Gilead; aspirin.

V. relieve, ease, alleviate, mitigate, palliate, soothe, adduce; salve; soften, - down; foment, stupe, poultice; assuage, allay.

cheer, comfort, console; encourage, bear up, pat on the back, give comfort, set at ease; enliven, gladden -, cheer-the heart.

remedy; cure &c. (*restore*) 660; refresh; pour -balm into, - oil on.

smooth the ruffled brow of care, temper the wind to the shorn lamb, lay the flattering unction to one's soul.

disburden &c. (*free*) 705; take off a load of care.

be relieved; breathe more freely, draw a long breath; take comfort; dry -, wipe- the -tears, - eyes.

Adj. relieving &c. *v.*; consolatory, soothing; assua-ging, -sive; bal-my, -samic; lenitive, palliative; anodyne &c. (*remedial*) 662; curative &c. 660.

835. Aggravation.—N. aggravation, heightening; exacerbation; exasperation; overestimation &c. 482; exaggeration &c. 549.

V. aggravate, render worse, heighten, embitter, sour; ex-, acerbate; exasperate, envenom; tease, provoke, enrage.

add fuel to the -fire, - flame; fan the flame &c. (*excite*) 824; go from bad to worse &c. (*deteriorate*) 659.

Adj. aggravated &c. *v.*; worse, unrelieved; aggravable; aggravating &c. *v.*

Adv. out of the frying pan into the fire, from bad to worse, worse and worse.

Int. so much the worse!

836. Cheerfulness.—N. cheerfulness &c. *adj.*; geniality, gaiety, *l'allegro*, cheer, good humour, spirits; high -, animal -, flow of- spirits; glee, high glee, light heart; sunshine of the -mind, - breast; *gaieté de cœur, bon naturel*.

liveliness &c. *adj.*; life, alacrity, vivacity, animation, *allégresse*; jocundity, joviality, jollity; levity; jocularity &c. (*wit*) 842.

mirth, merriment, hilarity, exhilaration; laughter &c. 838; merry-making &c. (*amusement*) 840; heyday, rejoicing &c. 838; marriage bells.

nepenthe, Euphrosyne.

optimism &c. (*hopefulness*) 858; self-complacency.

V. be -cheerful &c. *adj.*; have the mind at ease, smile, put a good face upon, keep up one's spirits; view -the bright side of the picture, - things *en couleur de rose; ridentem dicere verum*, cheer up, brighten up, light up, bear up; chirp, take heart, cast away care, drive dull care away, perk up.

rejoice &c. 838; carol, chirrup, lilt; frisk, rollick, give a loose to mirth.

cheer, enliven, elate, exhilarate, gladden, inspirit, animate, raise the spirits, inspire; put in good humour; cheer -, rejoice- the heart; delight &c. (*give pleasure*) 829.

Adj. cheerful; happy &c. 827; cheer-y, -ly; of good cheer, smiling; blithe; in -, in good- spirits; in high -spirits, - feather; happy as -the day is long, - a king; gay, - as a lark; *allegro*; light, -some, -hearted; buoyant, *débonnaire*, bright, free and easy, airy; janty, jaunty, canty; spright-ly, -ful; spry; spirit-ed, -ful; lively; animated, breezy, vivacious; brisk, - as a bee; sparkling; sportive; full of -play, - spirit; all alive.

sunny, palmy; hopeful &c. 858.

merry, - as a -cricket, - grig, - marriage bell; joyful, joyous, jocund, jovial; jolly, - as a thrush, - as a sandboy; blithesome; glee-ful, -some; hilarious, rattling.

winsome, bonny, hearty, buxom.

play-ful, -some; *folâtre*, playful as a kitten, tricksy, frisky, frolicsome; gamesome; jocose, jocular, waggish; mirth-, laughter-loving; mirthful, rollicking.

elate, -d; exulting, jubilant, flushed; rejoicing &c. 838; cock-a-hoop.

cheering, inspiriting, exhilarating; cardiac, -al; pleasing &c. 829; flourishing, halcyon.

Adv. cheerfully &c. *adj.*

Int. never say die! come! cheer up! hurrah! &c. 838; 'hence loathed melancholy!' begone dull care! away with melancholy!

837. Dejection.—N. dejection; dejectedness &c. *adj.*; depression, prosternation; lowness -, depression- of spirits; weight -, oppression -, damp-on the spirits; low -, bad -, drooping -, depressed- spirits; heart sinking; heaviness -, failure- of heart.

heaviness &c. *adj.*; infestivity, gloom; weariness &c. 841; *tædium vitæ*, disgust of life; *mal du pays* &c. (*regret*) 833.

melancholy; sadness &c. *adj.; il penseroso, melancholia*, dismals, mumps, mopes, lachrymals, dumps, blues, blue devils, doldrums, vapours, megrims, spleen, horrors, hypochondriasis, pessimism; despondency, slough of Despond; disconsolateness &c. *adj.*; hope deferred, blank despondency.

prostration, – of soul; broken heart; despair &c. 859; cave of -despair, – Trophonius.

demureness &c. *adj.*; gravity, solemnity; long –, grave- face.

hypochondriac, seek-sorrow, self-tormentor, *heautontimorumenos, malade imaginaire, médecin tant pis*; croaker, pessimist; mope, mopus.

[Cause of dejection] affliction &c. 830; sorry sight; *memento mori*; damper, wet blanket, Job's comforter; death's head, skeleton at the feast.

V. be -dejected &c. *adj.*; grieve; mourn &c. (*lament*) 839; take on, give way, lose heart, despond, droop, sink.

lower, look downcast, frown, pout; hang down the head; pull –, make- a long face; laugh on the wrong side of the mouth; grin a ghastly smile; look -blue, – like a drowned man; lay –, take- to heart.

mope, brood over; fret; sulk; pine, – away; yearn; repine &c. (*regret*) 833; despair &c. 859.

refrain from laughter, keep one's countenance; be –, look- grave &c. *adj.*; repress a smile, keep a straight face.

depress; dis-courage, -hearten; dispirit; damp, dull, deject, lower, sink, dash, knock down, unman, prostrate, break one's heart; frown upon; cast a -gloom, – shade- on; sadden; damp –, dash –, wither- one's hopes; weigh –, lie heavy –, prey- on the mind, – spirits; damp –, depress- the spirits.

Adj. cheer-, joy-, spirit-less; uncheerful, -y; unlively; unhappy &c. 828; melancholy, dismal, sombre, dark, gloomy, adust, *triste*, clouded, murky, lowering, frowning, lugubrious, Acherontic, funereal, mournful, lamentable, dreadful.

dreary, flat; dull, – as -a beetle, – ditchwater; depressing &c. *v.*

'melancholy as a gib cat'; oppressed with –, a prey to- melancholy; downcast, -hearted; down -in the mouth, – on one's luck; heavy-hearted; in the -dumps, – suds, – sulks, – doldrums; in doleful dumps, in bad humour; sullen; mumpish, dumpish; mopish, moping; moody, glum; sulky &c. (*discontented*) 832; out of -sorts, – humour, – heart, – spirits; ill at ease, low-spirited, in low spirits, a cup too low; weary &c. 841; dis-couraged, -heartened; desponding; chop-, jaw-, crest-fallen.

sad, pensive, *penseroso*, tristful; dolesome, -ful; woebegone, lachrymose, in tears, melancholic, hypped, hypochondriacal, bilious, jaundiced, atrabilious, saturnine, splenetic; lackadaisical.

serious, sedate, staid, stayed; grave, – as -a judge, – an undertaker, – a mustard pot; sober, solemn, demure; grim; grim-faced, -visaged; rueful, wan, long-faced.

disconsolate; un-, in-consolable; forlorn, comfortless, desolate, *désolé*, sick at heart; soul-, heart-sick; *au désespoir*; in despair &c. 859; lost.

overcome; broken-, borne-, bowed-down; heart-stricken &c. (*mental suffering*) 828; cut up, dashed, sunk; unnerved, unmanned; down-fallen, -trodden; broken-hearted; care-worn.

Adv. with -a long face, – tears in one's eyes; sadly &c. *adj.*

Phr. the countenance falling; the heart -failing, -sinking within-one.

838. [Expression of pleasure.] **Rejoicing.—N.** rejoicing, exultation, triumph, jubilation, heyday, flush, revelling; merry-making &c. (*amusement*) 840; jubilee &c. (*celebration*) 883; pæan, *Te Deum* &c. (*thanksgiving*) 990; congratulation &c. 896; applause &c. 971.

smile, simper, smirk, grin; broad –, sardonic- grin.

laughter, giggle, titter, crow, cheer, chuckle, snicker, snigger, shout; Homeric laughter, horse –, hearty- laugh; guffaw; burst –, fit –, shout –, roar –, peal- of laughter; cachinnation.

risibility; derision &c. 856.

Momus; Democritus the Abderite; rollicker; Laughter holding both his sides.

V. rejoice; thank -, bless- one's stars; congratulate -, hug- oneself; rub -, clap- one's hands; smack the lips, fling up one's cap; dance, skip, caleer; sing, car- ol, chirrup, chirp; hurrah; cry for -, leap with- joy; exult &c. (*boast*) 884; tri- umph; hold jubilee &c. (*celebrate*) 883; make merry &c. (*sport*) 840; sing a pæan of joy.

smile, simper, smirk; grin, - like a Cheshire cat; mock, laugh in one's sleeve; laugh, - outright; giggle, titter, snigger, crow, smicker, chuckle, snick- er, cackle; burst -out, - into a fit of laughter; shout, split, roar.

shake -, split -, hold both- one's sides; roar -, die- with laughter.

raise laughter &c. (*amuse*) 840.

Adj. rejoicing &c. *v.*; jubilant, exul- tant, triumphant; flushed, elated; laugh- ing &c. *v.*; risible; ready to -burst, - split, - die with laughter; convulsed with laughter.

laughable &c. (*ludicrous*) 853.

Int. hip, hip, -hurrah! huzza! aha! hail! tolderolloll! tra-la la! Heaven be praised! *io triumphe! tant mieux!* so much the better.

Phr. the heart leaping with joy.

839. [Expression of pain.] **Lamenta- tion.—N.** lament, -ation; wail, com- plaint, plaint, murmur, mutter, grum- ble, groan, moan, whine, whimper, sob, sigh, suspiration, heaving, deep sigh.

cry &c. (*vociferation*) 411; scream, howl; outcry, wail of woe, frown, scowl.

tear; weeping &c. *v.*; flood of tears, fit of crying, lachrymation, melting mood, weeping and gnashing of teeth.

plaintiveness &c. *adj.*; languishment; condolence &c. 915.

mourning, weeds, willow, cypress, crêpe, crape, deep mourning; sackcloth and ashes; knell &c. 363; dump, death- song, dirge, coronach, keen, *nenia*, re- quiem, elegy, *epicedium*; threne; mon-, thren-ody; jeremiad; ululation.

mourner, professional mourner, keen- er; grumbler &c. (*discontent*) 832; Ni- obe; Heraclitus.

V. lament, mourn, deplore, grieve, weep over; be-wail, -moan; keen; con- dole with &c. 915; fret &c. (*suffer*) 828; wear -, go into -, put on- mourning; wear -the willow, - sackcloth and ashes; *infandum renovare dolorem* &c. (*regret*) 833; give sorrow words.

sigh; give -, heave -, fetch- a sigh; 'waft a sigh from Indus to the pole'; sigh 'like furnace'; wail.

cry, weep, sob, greet, blubber, pipe, snivel, bibber, whimper, pule; pipe one's eye; drop -, shed- -tears, - a tear; melt -, burst- into tears; *fondre en larmes*; cry -oneself blind, - one's eyes out.

scream &c. (*cry out*) 411; mew &c. (*animal sounds*) 412; groan, moan, whine, yammer; roar; roar -, bellow- like a bull; cry out lustily, rend the air, yell.

frown, scowl, make a wry face, gri- mace, gnash one's teeth, wring one's hands, tear one's hair, beat one's breast, roll on the ground, burst with grief.

complain, murmur, mutter, grumble, growl, clamour, make a fuss about, croak, grunt, maunder; deprecate &c. (*disapprove*) 932.

cry out before one is hurt, complain without cause.

Adj. lamenting &c. *v.*; in mourning, in sackcloth and ashes; crying, sorrow- ing, -ful &c. (*unhappy*) 828; mourn-, tear-ful; lachrymose; plaint-ive, -ful, quer-ulous, -imonious; in the melting mood.

in tears, with tears in one's eyes; with -moistened, - watery-eyes; bathed -, dissolved- in tears; 'like Niobe all tears.' elagiac, epicedial, threnetic.

Adv. *de profundis; les larmes aux yeux.*

Int. heigh-ho! alas! alack! O dear! ah -, woe is- me! lackadaisy! well -, lack -, alack- a day! well-a-way! alas the day! *O tempora! O mores!* what a pity! *mis- erabile dictu!* O lud lud! too true!

Phr. tears -standing in, - starting

from- the eyes; eyes -suffused, - swimming, - brimming -, overflowing- with
tears.

840. Amusement.—N. amuse-, entertain-ment; diver-sion, -tissement; reaction, relaxation, solace; pastime, *pas-
setemps*, sport; labour of love; pleasure
&c. 827.

fun, frolic, merriment, whoopee, jollity; jovial-ity, -ness; heyday; laughter
&c. 838; jocos-ity, -eness; droll-, buf-
foon-, tomfool-ery; mummery, masqu-
ing, pleasantry; wit &c. 842; quip,
quirk.

play; game, - at romps; gambol,
romp, prank, antic, rig, lark, spree,
skylarking, vagary, trick, monkey trick,
*gambade, fredaine, escapade, échap-
pée*, bout, *espièglerie*; practical joke &c.
(*ridicule*) 856.

dance; round -, square -, solo -, step
-, tap -, clog -, skirt -, sand -, folk -,
morris- dance, *pas seul*, step, turn,
chassé, cut, shuffle, double shuffle; hop,
reel, rigadoon, saraband, hornpipe, bolero, fandango, pavan, tarantella, minuet, waltz, polka; galop, -ade; Schottische, *pas de quatre*, Boston, one-, two-
step, rumba, tango, maxixe, fox-, turkey-trot, shimmy, ragtime, cakewalk,
jazz, blues, Charleston; jig, breakdown,
fling, strathspey; *allemande*; gavot, -te;
mazurka, morisco; quadrille, lancers,
country dance, *cotillon*, polonaise, Sir
Roger de Coverley, Swedish dance; *ballet* &c. (*drama*) 599; ball; *bal, - masqué, - costumé*; masquerade, fancy dress
ball; *thé dansant*; Terpsichore, choreography, Russian ballet, classical dancing; eurythmics; nautch dance, *danse du
ventre*, cancan.

festivity, merry-making; party &c.
(*social gathering*) 892; *fête*, festival,
gala, *ridotto*; revel-s, -ry, -ling; carnival, brawl, saturnalia, high jinks; feast,
banquet &c. (*food*) 298; regale, *symposium*, wassail; carous-e, -al; jollification, junket, wake, pic-nic, *fête champêtre*, garden party, gymkhana, regatta,
track meet, field-day, jamboree, treat.

round of pleasures, dissipation, a short
life and a merry one, racketing, holiday
making, high jinks.

rejoicing &c. 838; jubilee &c. (*celebration*) 883.

bonfire, fireworks, *feu-de-joie*, rocket, catherine wheel, roman candle &c.

holiday; gala -, red letter -, play- day;
high days and holidays; high -, Bank-
holiday; May -, Derby- day; Saint -,
Easter -, Whit- Monday; King's birthday, Empire Day; *mi-carême; Bairam*;
wayzgoose, bean feast, beano.

place of amusement, theatre &c. 599;
concert-, ball-, assembly-room; music-
hall, cinema, movies, talkies, vaudeville; hippodrome, circus, rodeo; *casino, kursaal*; winter garden; park, pleasance, arbour; garden &c. 371; pleasure-,
play-, cricket-, football-, polo-, cro-
quet-, archery-, hunting-ground; golf
links, race course, stadium, gridiron,
bowl, speedway, racing track, ring;
gymnasium, swimming pool; shooting
gallery; tennis-, racket-court; bowling-
green, -alley; croquet-lawn, rink, skating rink; roller-coaster, roundabout, carousel, merry-go-round; swing; *montagne russe*; switchback, scenic railway
&c.

game, - of -chance, - skill; athletic
sports, gymnastics; fencing; archery, ri-
fle-shooting; tournament, pugilism &c.
(*contention*) 720; sporting &c. 622;
horse-racing, the turf; aquatics &c. 267;
skating, roller skating; ski-running,
-joring, -jumping, bobsleighing, luging,
tobogganing, winter sports; sliding;
cricket, tennis, lawn -, table -, deck-
tennis, rackets, fives, squash, ping pong,
trap bat and ball, battledore and shuttlecock, badminton, *la grâce*; pall mall,
tip-cat, croquet, golf, curling, hockey,
basketball, soccer, football, Rugby, Association, *pallone*, polo; tent-pegging,
tilting at the ring, quintain, greasy pole;
quoits, *discus*; throwing the hammer,
putting the -weight, - shot, tossing the
caber; knurr and spell; leap-frog, hop,
skip and jump; French and English,
tug of war; blind man's buff, hunt the

slipper, hide-and-seek, kiss in the ring; snapdragon; cross questions and crooked answers; jig-saw puzzle; rounders, base-ball, *la crosse* &c.; angling; swimming, diving, water-polo.

billiards, pool, pyramids, snooker, bagatelle; bowls, skittles, ninepins, kail, American bowls.

cards; bridge, auction, contract, whist, rubber; round game, coon-can, loo, cribbage, *bésique*, pinocle, euchre, drole, *écarté*, skat, picquet, all-fours, quadrille, ombre, reverse, Pope Joan, commit; bo-, boa-ston; *vingt-et-un; quinze*, thirty-one, put-and-take, speculation, connections, brag, cassino, lottery, commerce, snip-snap-snorem, lift smoke, blind hookey, Polish bank, poker, banker; faro; Earl of Coventry, Napoleon, nap, patience, pairs; old maid, fright, beggar-my-neighbour; *baccarat, chemin de fer, monté, roulette*.

chess, draughts, backgammon, dominoes, checkers, mah jong, merelles, nine men's morris, go-bang, solitaire; game of -, fox and-goose; loto; &c.*

morra; gambling &c. (*chance*) 621.

toy, plaything, bauble; doll &c. (*puppet*) 554; teetotum; knick-knack &c. (*trifle*) 643; magic lantern &c. (*show*) 448; peep-, puppet-, raree-, gallantyshow; marionettes, Punch and Judy; toyshop; 'quips and cranks and wanton wiles, nods and becks and wreathed smiles.'

sportsman, gamester, gambler &c. 621; reveller, master of the -ceremonies, - revels; *arbiter elegantiarum*.

V. amuse, entertain, divert, enliven; tickle, - the fancy; titillate, raise a smile, put in good humour; cause -, create -, occasion -, raise -, excite -, produce -, convulse with- laughter; set the table in a roar, be the death of one.

recreate, solace, cheer, rejoice; please &c. 829; interest; treat, regale.

* A curious list of games is given in Sir Thomas Urquhart's translation of Rabelais' *Life of Gargantua*, book i. chapter 22.

amuse oneself; game; play, - a game, - pranks, - tricks; sport, disport, toy, wanton, revel, junket, feast, carouse, banquet, make merry; drown care; drive dull care away; frolic, gambol, frisk, romp; caper; dance &c. (*leap*) 309; keep up the ball; run a rig, sow one's wild oats, have one's fling, paint the town red, take one's pleasure; see life; *desipere in loco*, play the fool.

make -, keep- holiday; go a Maying.

while away -, beguile- the time; kill time, dally.

Adj. amusing, entertaining, diverting &c. *v.*; recreative, lusory; pleasant &c. (*pleasing*) 829; laughable &c. (*ludicrous*) 853; witty &c. 842; fest-ive, -al; jovial, jolly, jocund, roguish, rompish; sporting; playful, - as a kitten; sportive, ludibrious.

amused &c. *v.*; 'pleased with a feather, tickled with a straw.'

Adv. 'on the light fantastic toe,' at play, in sport.

Int. *vive la bagatelle! vogue la galère!*

Phr. *Deus nobis hæc otia fecit; dum vivimus vivamus.*

841. Weariness.—N. weariness, defatigation, boredom, *ennui*; lassitude &c. (*fatigue*) 688; drowsiness &c. 683.

disgust, nausea, loathing, sickness; satiety &c. 869; *tædium vitæ* &c. (*dejection*) 837.

wearisome-, tedious-ness &c. *adj.*; dull work, tedium, monotony, twice told tale.

bore, button-hole, proser, wet blanket; heavy hours, 'the enemy' [time].

V. weary; tire &c. (*fatigue*) 688; bore; bore -, weary -, tire- -to death, - out of one's life, -, out of all patience; set -, send- to sleep.

pall, sicken, nauseate, disgust.

harp on the same string; drag its -slow, - weary- length along.

never hear the last of; be -tired &c. *adj.* -of, - with; yawn; die with *ennui*.

Adj. wearying &c. *v.*; wearing; weari-, tire-, irk-some; uninteresting, stupid, bald, devoid of interest, dry, monotonous, dull, arid, tedious, humdrum, mortal, flat; pros-y, -ing; slow; soporific, somniferous, dormitive.

disgusting &c. *v.*; unenjoyed.

weary; tired &c. *v.*; drowsy &c. (*sleepy*) 683; uninterested, flagging, used up, worn out, *blasé*, life-weary, weary of life; sick of.

Adv. wearily &c. *adj.; usque ad nauseam.*

Phr. time hanging heavily on one's hands; *toujours perdrix; crambe repetita.*

842. Wit.—N. wit, -tiness; attic -wit, - salt; atticism; salt, *esprit*, point, fancy, whim, humour, drollery, pleasantry.

farce, buffoonery, fooling, tomfoolery; harlequinade &c. 599; broad -farce, - humour; fun, *espièglerie; vis comica.*

jocularity; jocos-ity, -eness; facetiousness; wagg-ery, -ishness; whimsicality; comicality &c. 853.

smartness, ready wit, banter, *badinage, persiflage,* retort, repartee, *quid pro quo*; ridicule &c. 856.

facetiæ, quips and cranks; jest, joke, capital joke; standing -jest, - joke; conceit, quip, quirk, crank, quiddity, *concetto, plaisanterie,* brilliant idea; merry -, bright -, happy- thought; sally; flash, - of wit, - of merriment; scintillation; *mot, - pour rire*; witticism, smart saying, *bon mot, jeu d'esprit,* epigram; jest book; dry joke, *quodlibet,* cream of the jest.

word-play, *jeu de mots*; play -of, - upon- words; pun, -ning; *double entendre* &c. (*ambiguity*) 520; quibble, verbal quibble; conundrum &c. (*riddle*) 533; anagram, acrostic, double acrostic, *nugæ canoræ,* trifling, idle conceit, *turlupinade.*

old joke, Joe Miller, chestnut, hoaryheaded jest.

V. joke, jest, cut jokes; crack a joke; perpetrate a -joke, - pun; make -fun of, - merry with; set the table in a roar &c. (*amuse*) 840; scintillate.

retort, flash back; banter &c. (*ridi-*

cule) 856; *ridentem dicere verum*; joke at one's expense.

Adj. witty, attic, salty; quick-, nimble-witted; keen, clever, smart, brilliant, pungent, jocular, jocose, funny, waggish, facetious, whimsical, humorous, gilbertian; playful &c. 840; merry and wise; pleasant, sprightly, *spirituel,* sparkling, epigrammatic, full of point, *ben trovato*; comic &c. 853.

Adv. in joke, in jest, in sport, in play.

843. Dulness.—N. dulness, heaviness, flatness; infestivity &c. 837; stupidity &c. 499; want of originality, dearth of ideas.

prose, matter of fact; heavy book, *conte à dormir debout*; platitude.

V. be -dull &c. *adj.*; prose, platitudinize, take *au sérieux,* be caught napping.

render -dull &c. *adj.*; damp, depress, throw cold water on, lay a wet blanket on; fall flat upon the ear; hang fire.

Adj. dull, - as ditch water; dry, insipid, jejune; unentertaining, uninteresting, unlively, unimaginative; heavisome, heavy-gaited; insulse; dry as dust; pros-y, -ing, -aic; matter of fact, commonplace, banal, pointless; 'weary, flat, stale and unprofitable.'

stupid, slow, flat, sluggish, ponderous, humdrum, monotonous; melancholic &c. 837; stolid &c. 499; plodding.

Phr. *Davus sum non Œdipus.*

844. Humorist.—N. humorist, wag, wit, reparteeist, epigrammatist, gag man, punster; *bel esprit,* life of the party; wit-snapper, -cracker, -worm; joker, jester, jokesmith, Joe Miller, *drôle de corps, gaillard,* spark, *persiffleur,* banterer.

buffoon, *farceur,* merry-andrew, mime, tumbler, acrobat, mountebank, charlatan, posturemaster, harlequin, punch, *pulcinella,* scaramouch, clown; wearer of the -cap and bells, - motley; motley fool; pantaloon, gipsy; jack -pudding, - in the green, - a dandy;

zany; mad-cap, pickle-herring, witling, caricaturist, *grimacier*.

2°. DISCRIMINATE AFFECTIONS

845. Beauty.—N. beauty, the beautiful, *le beau ideal*, loveliness.

[Science of the perception of beauty] Callæsthetics.*

form, elegance, grace, beauty unadorned; symmetry &c. 242; comeliness, fairness &c. *adj.*; pulchritude, polish, gloss; good -effect, - looks; *belle tournure*; bloom, brilliancy, radiance, splendour, gorgeousness, magnificence; sublimi-ty, -fication.

concinnity, delicacy, refinement; charm, *je ne sais quoi*, style, *chic*, swank.

Venus, - of Milo; Aphrodite, Hebe, the Graces, Peri, Houri, Cupid, Apollo, Hyperion, Adonis, Antinous, Narcissus; Helen of Troy.

peacock, butterfly; flower, flow'ret gay, rose, lily, asphodel; garden; flower of, pink of; *bijou*; jewel &c. (*ornament*) 847; work of art.

pleasurableness &c. 829.

beautifying; landscape gardening; decoration &c. 847; calisthenics.

V. be -beautiful &c. *adj.*; shine, beam, bloom; become one &c. (*accord*) 23; set off, grace, flatter one.

render -beautiful &c. *adj.*; beautify; polish, burnish; gild &c. (*decorate*) 847; set out.

'snatch a grace beyond the reach of art.'

Adj. beaut-iful, -eous; handsome; pretty; lovely, graceful, elegant; delicate, dainty, refined, exquisite; fair, personable, comely, seemly; bonny; good-looking; well-favoured, -made, -formed, -proportioned; proper, shapely; symmetrical &c. (*regular*) 242; harmonious &c. (*colour*) 428; sightly.

fit to be seen, passable, not amiss.

* Whewell, 'Philosophy of the Inductive Sciences.'

goodly, dapper, tight, jimp; gimp; janty, jaunty; natty, quaint, trim, tidy, neat, spruce, smart, tricksy.

bright, -eyed; rosy-, cherry-cheeked; rosy, ruddy; blooming, in full bloom.

brilliant, shining; beam-y, -ing; sparkling, swanky, splendid, resplendent, dazzling, glowing; glossy, sleek.

showy, specious; rich, gorgeous, superb, magnificent, grand, fine, sublime, imposing; majestic 873.

artistic, -al; æsthetic; pict-uresque, -orial; *fait à peindre*, paintable; well-composed, -grouped, -varied; curious.

enchanting &c. (*pleasure-giving*) 829; attractive &c. (*inviting*) 615; becoming &c. (*accordant*) 23; ornamental &c. 847.

undeformed, undefaced, unspotted; spotless &c. (*perfect*) 650.

846. Ugliness.—N. ugliness &c. *adj.*; deformity, inelegance; disfigurement &c. (*blemish*) 848; want of symmetry, inconcinnity; distortion &c. 243; squalor &c. (*uncleanness*) 653.

forbidding countenance, vinegar aspect, hanging look, wry face, '*spretæ injuria formæ.*'

eyesore, object, figure, sight, fright, spectre, scarecrow, hag, harridan, satyr, witch, toad, baboon, monster, Caliban, Æsop, '*monstrum horrendum informe ingens cui lumen ademptum.*'

V. be -ugly &c. *adj.*; look ill, grin horribly a ghastly smile, make faces.

render -ugly &c. *adj.*; deface; dis-, de-figure; deform, spoil, distort &c. 243; blemish &c. (*injure*) 659; soil &c. (*render unclean*) 653.

Adj. ugly, - as -sin, - a toad, - a scarecrow, - a dead monkey; plain, bald &c. 226; homely &c. (*unadorned*) 849; ordinary, unornamental, inartistic; unsightly, unseemly, uncomely, unshapely, unlovely; sightless, seemless; not fit to be seen; unbeaut-eous, -iful; beautiless; shapeless &c. (*amorphous*) 241; course; garish, over-decorated &c. 882.

mis-shapen, -proportioned; monstrous; gaunt &c. (*thin*) 203; dumpy &c.

(*short*) 201; curtailed of its fair proportions; ill-made, -shaped, -proportioned; crooked &c. (*distorted*) 243; hard-featured, -visaged; ill-, hard-, evil-favoured; ill-looking; unprepossessing.

graceless, inelegant; ungraceful, ungainly, uncouth; stiff; rugged, rough, gross, rude, awkward, clumsy, slouching, rickety; gawky; lump-ing, -ish; lumbering; hulk-y, -ing; unwieldy.

squalid, haggard; grim, -faced, -visaged; grisly, ghastly; ghost-, death-like; cadaverous, gruesome.

frightful, hideous, odious, uncanny, forbidding, repellant, repulsive; horri-d, -ble; shocking &c. (*painful*) 830.

foul &c. (*dirty*) 653; dingy &c. (*colourless*) 429; gaudy &c. (*colour*) 428; disfigured &c. *v.*; discoloured (*blemished*) &c. 848.

847. Ornament.—N. ornament, -ation, -al art; ornat-ure, -eness; adorn-ment, decoration, embellishment; architecture.

garnish, polish, varnish, French polish, gilding, japanning, lacquer, ormolu, enamel.

cosmetics, rouge, powder, lipstick, lip salve, mascara; manicure, nail polish; permanent –, Marcel –, fingerwave.

pattern, diaper, powdering, panelling, graining, pargeting, inlay, detail; texture &c. 329; richness; tracery, moulding, beading, reeding, fillet, listel, strapwork, *coquillage*, flourish, *fleur-de-lis*, arabesque, fret, *anthemion*; egg and -tongue, – dart; *astragal*, zigzag, *acanthus, cartouche*; pilaster &c. (*projection*) 250; cyma, ogee.

em-, broidery, needlework; knitting, crochet, tatting, brocade, *brocatelle*, beads, bugles; galloon, lace, gimp, *guipure*, fringe, trapping, border, edging, insertion, *motif*, trimming; *passementerie*; drapery, hanging, tapestry, arras; millinery, ermine.

wreath, festoon, garland, lei, chaplet, flower, nosegay, *bouquet*, posy, 'daisies pied and violets blue.'

tassel, knot; shoulder-knot, *épaulette*, epaulet, aigulet, *aiguillette*, frog; star,

rosette, bow; feather, plume, *panache, aigrette*.

jewel, -ry, -lery; bijoutry; *bijou, -terie*; diadem, tiara; pendant, trinket, locket, necklace, armilla, bracelet, bangle, armlet, anklet, ear-, nose- ring, carcanet, chain, *châtelaine,* albert, brooch, torque.

gem, precious stone; diamond, brilliant, beryl, aquamarine, alexandrite, cat's eye, emerald, calcedony, chrysoprase, cornelian, jasper, bloodstone, agate, heliotrope; girasol, -e; onyx, plasma; sard, -onyx; garnet, lapis-lazuli, opal, peridot, chrysolite, sapphire, ruby; spinel, -le; balais; oriental –, topaz; turquois, -e; zircon, jacinth, hyacinth, carbuncle, amethyst; moonstone; pearl, coral.

finery, frippery, gewgaw, gimcrack, knick-knack, tinsel, spangle, sequin, *clinquant*, pinch-beck, paste; excess of ornament &c. (*vulgarity*) 851; gaud, pride, ostentation; frills and furbelows.

illustration, illumination, *vignette; fleuron*; head-, tail-piece; *cul-de-lampe*; flowers of rhetoric &c. 577; work of art, article of vertu, *bric-à-brac*, curio, *bibelot*.

V. ornament, embellish, enrich, decorate, adorn, beautify, adonize.

smarten, furbish, polish, gild, varnish, whitewash, enamel, japan, lacquer, paint, grain.

garnish, trim, dizen, bedizen, prink, prank; trick –, fig- out; deck, bedeck, dight, bedight, array; dress, – up, preen, spruce up, titivate; spangle, bespangle, powder; embroider, work; chase, tool, emboss, fret; emblazon, blazon, illuminate; illustrate.

become &c. (*accord with*) 23.

Adj. ornamented, beautified &c. *v.*; ornate, rich, gilt, begilt, tessellated, enamelled, inlaid; festooned; topiary.

smart, gay, tricksy, flowery, glittering; new-gilt, -spangled; fine, – as -a Mayday queen, – fivepence, – a carrot fresh scraped; pranked out, bedight, well-groomed.

in full dress &c. (*fashion*) 852; *en
grande -tenue,* – *toilette*; in best bib and
tucker, in Sunday best, *endimanché*;
dressed to advantage.

showy, flashy; gaudy &c. (*vulgar*)
851; garish; gorgeous.

ornamental, decorative; becoming
&c. (*accordant*) 23.

848. Blemish.—N. blemish, disfigurement, deformity; defect &c. (*imperfection*) 651; flaw; injury &c. (*deterioration*) 659; spots on the sun; eyesore.

stain, blot, slur; spot, -tiness; speck,
-le; blur, freckle, mole, *macula*, patch,
blotch, birthmark, blain, maculation,
tarnish, smudge, smear; dirt &c. 653;
bruise, black eye, scar, wem; pustule;
excrescence, pimple &c. (*protuberance*)
250.

V. disfigure &c. (*injure*) 659; speckle; render ugly &c. 846.

Adj. pitted, freckled, discoloured,
bloodshot, bruised, disfigured; stained
&c. *n.*; imperfect &c. 651; injured &c.
(*deteriorated*) 659.

849. Simplicity.—N. simplicity;
plain-, homeliness; undress, nudity, na-
kedness, beauty unadorned, chastity,
chasteness.

V. be -simple &c. *adj.*

render -simple &c. *adj.*; simplify,
chasten, strip of ornament.

Adj. simple, plain; home-ly, -spun;
ordinary, household.

natural, unaffected; free from
-affectation, – ornament; *simplex
munditiis; sans façon, en déshabillé*,
nude, naked.

chaste, inornate, severe.

un-adorned, -ornamented, -decked, -gar-
nished, -arranged, -trimmed, -varnished.

bald, flat, dull, blank.

850. [Good taste.] Taste.—N. taste;
good -, refined -, cultivated- taste; delicacy, refinement, fine feeling, gust,
gusto, tact, *finesse*; nicety &c. (*discrimination*) 465; polish, elegance, grace.

virtu; dilettanteism, virtuosity; fine
art; cul-ture, -tivation.

[Science of taste] æsthetics.

man of -taste &c.; *connoisseur*, judge,
critic, *conoscente, virtuoso, amateur,
dilettante,* Aristarchus, Corinthian, *arbiter elegantiarum,* stagirite, euphemist.
'caviare to the general.'

V. appreciate, judge, criticize, discriminate &c. 465.

Adj. in good taste; tasteful, tasty; unaffected, pure, chaste, classical, attic;
cultivated, refined; dainty; æsthetic, artistic; elegant &c. 578; euphemistic.

to one's -taste, – mind; after one's
fancy; *comme il faut; tiré à quatre épingles.*

Adv. elegantly &c. *adj.*

Phr. *nihil tetigit quod non ornavit.*

851. [Bad taste.] Vulgarity.—N. vul-
gar-ity, -ism; barbar-, Vandal-, Gothic-
ism; *mauvais goût,* bad taste; Babbittry;
gaucherie, awkwardness, want of tact;
ill-breeding &c. (*discourtesy*) 895; un-
gentlemanly behaviour.

coarseness &c. *adj*; indecorum, misbehaviour.

low-, homeli-ness; low life, *mauvais
ton,* rusticity; boorishness &c. *adj.*;
brutality; rowdy-, ruffian-, blackguardism; ribaldry; slang &c. (*neology*) 563.

bad joke, *mauvaise plaisanterie.*

[Excess of ornament] gaudi-, tawdri-
ness; false ornament; finery, frippery,
trickery, tinsel, gewgaw, *clinquant.*

rough diamond, tomboy, hoyden, cub,
unlicked cub; clown &c. (*commonalty*)
876; Hun, Goth, Vandal, Bœotian; vul-
garian; snob, cad, bounder, gent; *parvenu* &c. 876; frump, dowdy; slattern
&c. 653.

V. be -vulgar &c. *adj.*; misbehave;
talk -, smell of the- shop.

Adj. in bad taste, vulgar, unrefined,
gutter.

coarse, indecorous, ribald, gross; unseemly, unbeseeming, unpresentable;
contra bonos mores; ungraceful &c.
(*ugly*) 846.

dowdy; slovenly &c. (*dirty*) 653;

ungenteel, shabby genteel; low &c. (*plebeian*) 876; uncourtly; uncivil &c. (*discourteous*) 895; ill-bred, -mannered; underbred; ungentleman-ly, -like; unladylike, unfeminine; wild, – as an unbacked colt.

unkempt, uncombed, untamed, unlicked, unpolished, uncouth, plebeian; incondite; heavy, rude, awkward; homely, -spun, -bred; provincial, hick, countrified, rustic, uncultivated, freshwater; boorish, clownish; savage, brutish, blackguard, rowdy, snobbish; barbarous, -ic; Gothic, unclassical doggerel, heathenish, tramontane, outlandish; Bohemian.

obsolete &c. (*antiquated*) 124; unfashionable, old-fashioned, out of date; new-fangled &c. (*unfamiliar*) 83; fantastic, odd &c. (*ridiculous*) 853.

particular; affected &c. 855; meretricious; extravagant, monstrous, horrid; shocking &c. (*painful*) 830.

gaudy, tawdry, bedizened, tricked out, gingerbread; obtrusive, flaunting, loud, flashy, garish, showy.

852. Fashion.—N. fashion, style, *ton, bon ton,* society; good –, polite-society; drawing room, civilized life, civilization, town, *beau monde,* high life, court; world; fashionable –, gay-world; Vanity Fair; show &c. (*ostentation*) 822.

manners, breeding &c. (*politeness*) 894; air, demeanour &c. (*appearance*) 448; *savoir faire;* gentlemanliness, gentility, decorum, propriety, *bienséance;* conventions –, dictates- of society; Mrs. Grundy; convention, -ality, punctilio; form, -ality; etiquette, point of etiquette; custom &c. 613; mode, vogue, style, go; rage &c. (*desire*) 865; prevailing taste, *dernier cri,* dress &c. 225.

man –, woman- of -fashion, – the world; height –, pink –, star –, glass –, leader- of fashion; *arbiter elegantiarum* &c. (*taste*) 850; upper ten thousand &c. (*nobility*) 875; *élite* &c. (*distinction*) 873.

V. be -fashionable &c. *adj.,* – the rage &c. *n.;* have a run, pass current.

follow –, conform to –, fall in with- the fashion &c. *n.;* go with the stream &c. (*conform*) 82; *savoir -vivre, – faire;* keep up appearances, behave oneself.

set the –, bring into- fashion; give a tone to –, cut a figure in- society, rub shoulders with nobility, keep one's carriage.

Adj. fashionable; in -fashion &c. *n.; à la mode, comme il faut;* admitted –, admissible- in -society &c. *n.;* presentable, decorous, punctilious, conventional &c. (*customary*) 613; genteel; well-bred, -mannered, -behaved, -spoken; gentleman-like, -ly; ladylike; civil, polite &c. (*courteous*) 894.

polished, refined, thoroughbred, courtly; *distingué,* aristocratic, unembarrassed, poised, *dégagé;* ja-, jau-nty; dashing, fast, showy, high toned, toney.

modish, stylish, in the latest style, *recherché;* new-fangled &c. (*unfamiliar*) 83.

in -court, – full, – evening- dress; *en grande tenue* &c. (*ornament*) 847.

Adv. fashionably &c. *adj.;* for fashion's sake.

853. Ridiculousness.—N. ridiculousness &c. *adj.;* comical-, odd-ity &c. *adj.;* extravagance, drollery.

farce, comedy; burlesque &c. (*ridicule*) 856; buffoonery &c. (*fun*) 840; frippery; doggerel verses; Irish bull, Hibernianism, Hibernicism; Spoonerism; absurdity &c. 497; bombast &c. (*unmeaning*) 517; anticlimax, bathos; monstrosity &c. (*unconformity*) 83; laughing stock &c. 857.

V. be -ridiculous &c. *adj.;* pass from the sublime to the ridiculous; make one laugh; play the fool, make a fool of oneself, commit an absurdity.

play a joke on, make a -fool of, – sucker of, – monkey of.

Adj. ridiculous, ludicrous; comic, -al; droll, funny, laughable, *pour rire,* grotesque, farcical, odd; whimsical, – as a dancing bear; fanciful, fantastic, queer, rum, quizzical, waggish, quaint, *bizarre;* eccentric &c. (*unconformable*)

83; strange, outlandish, out of the way, *baroque, rocaille,* rococo; awkward &c. (*ugly*) 846.

absurd, extravagant, *outré,* monstrous, preposterous, bombastic, inflated, stilted, burlesque, mock heroic.

drollish; serio-, tragic-comic; gimcrack, contemptible &c. (*unimportant*) 643; doggerel; ironical &c. (*derisive*) 856; risible.

Phr. '*risum teneatis amici?*' *rideret Heraclitus.*

854. Fop.—N. fop, fine gentleman; swell; dan-dy, -iprat; exquisite, coxcomb, toff, beau, macaroni, blade, blood, buck, man about town, fast man; fribble, jemmy, spark, popinjay, puppy, prig, *petit maître*; jacka-napes, -dandy; man milliner; Jemmy Jessamy, carpet-knight, masher, Dundreary, Johnnie, dude.

belle, fine lady, *coquette,* flirt.

855. Affectation.—N. affectation; affectedness &c. *adj.*; acting a part &c. *v.*; pretence &c. (*falsehood*) 544, (*ostentation*) 882; boasting &c. 884.

charlatanism, quakery, shallow profundity, humbug, pretension, airs, pedantry, purism, precisianism, euphuism, prunes and prisms; teratology &c. (*altiloquence*) 577.

mannerism, *simagrée,* grimace.

conceit, foppery, dandyism, man millinery, coxcombry, puppyism.

stiffness, formality, buckram; prudery, demureness, coquetry, mock modesty, *minauderie,* sentimentalism; *mauvaise honte,* false shame.

affector, performer, actor; pedant, pedagogue, *doctrinaire,* purist, euphuist, mannerist; shoneen; *grimacier*; lump of affectation, *précieuse ridicule, bas bleu,* blue stocking, poetaster; prig, hypocrite; charlatan &c. (*deceiver*) 548; *petit maître* &c. (*fop*) 854; flatterer &c. 935; *coquette,* prude, puritan; precisian, formalist.

V. affect, act a part, put on; give oneself airs &c. (*arrogance*) 885; boast &c. 884; coquet; simper, mince, attitudi-

nize, strike a pose, pose; flirt a fan; over-act, -play, -do.

Adj. affected, full of affectation, pretentious, pedantic, stilted, stagey, theatrical, big-sounding, *ad captandum,* canting, insincere.

not natural, unnatural; self-conscious; *maniéré*; artificial; overwrought, -done, -acted; euphuistic &c. 577.

stiff, starch, formal, prim, smug, demure, *tiré à quatre épingles,* quakerish, puritanical, prudish, pragmatical, priggish, conceited, coxcomical, foppish, dandified; fini-cal, -kin, -cky, mincing, simpering, namby-pamby, sentimental, languishing.

856. Ridicule.—N. ridicule, derision; sardonic -smile, - grin; irrision; snigger; scoffing &c. (*disrespect*) 929; mockery, quiz, banter, irony, *persiflage,* raillery, chaff, badinage; quizzing &c. *v.*

squib, satire, skit, quip, quib, grin.

parody, burlesque, travesty; farce &c. (*drama*) 599; caricature, take-off.

buffoonery &c. (*fun*) 840; practical joke, horseplay.

V. ridicule, deride; laugh at, grin at, smile at; snigger; laugh in one's sleeve; banter, rally, chaff, joke, twit, quiz, poke fun at, jolly, roast, rag; fleer; play -, play tricks- upon; fool, - to the top of one's bent; show up.

satirize, parody, caricature, burlesque, travesty.

turn into ridicule; make merry with; make -fun, - game, - a fool, - an April fool- of; rally; scoff &c. (*disrespect*) 929.

raise a laugh &c. (*amuse*) 840; play the fool, make a fool of oneself.

be ridiculous &c. 853.

Adj. deris-ory, -ive; mock; sarcastic, ironical, quizzical, burlesque, Hudibrastic; scurrilous &c. (*disrespectful*) 929.

Adv. in -ridicule &c. *n.*

857. [Object and cause of ridicule.] **Laughing-stock.—N.** laughing-, jesting-, gazing-stock; butt, game, fair game; April fool &c. (*dupe*) 547.

original, oddity; queer –, odd- fish; quiz, square toes; old –, fogey *or* fogy.

monkey; buffoon &c. (*jester*) 844; pantomimist &c. (*actor*) 599.

jest &c. (*wit*) 842.

3°. PROSPECTIVE AFFECTIONS

858. Hope.—N. hope, -s; desire &c. 865; fervent hope, sanguine expectation, trust, confidence, reliance; faith &c. (*belief*) 484; affiance, assurance; secur-eness, -ity; reassurance.

good -omen, – auspices; promise, well-grounded hopes; good –, bright- prospect; clear sky.

as-, pre-sumption; anticipation &c. (*expectation*) 507.

hopefulness, buoyancy, optimism, enthusiasm, heart of grace, aspiration; optimist, utop-ian, -ist; Pollyanna.

castles in the air, *châteaux en Espagne*, hope chest, *le pot au lait*, Utopia, millennium; day –, golden-dream; dream of Alnaschar; airy hopes, fool's paradise; *mirage* &c. (*fallacies of vision*) 443; fond hope.

beam –, ray –, gleam –, glimmer –, dawn –, flash –, star- of hope; cheer; bit of blue sky, silver lining of the cloud, bottom of Pandora's box, balm in Gilead.

anchor, sheet-anchor, main-stay; staff &c. (*support*) 215; heaven &c. 981.

V. hope, trust, confide, rely on, put one's trust in, lean upon; pin one's -hope, – faith- upon &c. (*believe*) 484.

feel –, entertain –, harbour –, indulge –, cherish –, feed –, foster –, nourish –, encourage –, cling to –, live in- hope &c. *n.*; see land; feel –, rest- -assured, – confident &c. *adj.*

presume; promise oneself; expect &c. (*look forward to*) 507.

hope for &c. (*desire*) 865; anticipate.

be -hopeful &c. *adj.*; look on the bright side of, view on the sunny side, make the best of it, hope for the best; put -a good, – a bold, – the best- face

upon; keep one's spirits up; take heart, – of grace; be of good –heart, – cheer; flatter oneself, lay the flattering unction to one's soul.

catch at a straw, hope against hope, count one's chickens before they are hatched.

give –, inspire –, raise –, hold out- hope &c. *n.*; raise expectations; encourage, hearten, cheer, assure, reassure, buoy up, embolden; promise, bid fair, augur well, be in a fair way, look up, flatter, tell a flattering tale.

Adj. hoping &c. *v.*; in -hopes &c. *n.*; hopeful, confident; secure &c. (*certain*) 484; sanguine, in good heart, buoyed up, buoyant, elated, flushed, exultant, enthusiastic; utopian.

unsus-pecting, -picious; fearless, free –, exempt from- -fear, – suspicion, – distrust, – despair; undespairing, self-reliant.

probable, on the high road to; within sight of -shore, – land; promising, propitious; of –, full of- promise; of good omen; auspicious, *de bon augure*; reassuring; encouraging, cheering, inspiriting, looking up, bright, roseate, *couleur de rose*, rose-coloured.

Adv. hopefully &c. *adj.*

Int. God speed! good luck!

Phr. *nil desperandum*; never say die, *dum spiro spero, latet scintillula forsan*, all is for the best, *spero meliora*; the wish being father to the thought; 'hope told a flattering tale'; *rusticus expectat dum defluat amnis*.

859. [Absence, want, or loss of hope.] **Hopelessness.—N.** hopelessness &c. *adj.*; despair, desperation; despondency &c. (*dejection*) 837; pessimism.

hope deferred, dashed hopes; vain expectation &c. (*disappointment*) 509.

airy hopes &c. 858; forlorn hope; bad -job, – business; *enfant perdu*; gloomy –, black spots in the- horizon; slough of Despond, cave of Despair.

Job's comforter; bird of -bad, – ill- omen.

V. despair; lose –, give up –, abandon

–, relinquish- -all hope, – the hope of; give -up, – over; yield to despair; falter; despond &c. (*be dejected*) 837; *jeter le manche après la cognée.*

inspire –, drive to- despair &c. *n.*; disconcert; dash –, crush –, shatter –, destroy- one's hopes; hope against hope.

Adj. hopeless, desperate, despairing, in despair, *au désespoir*, forlorn; inconsolable &c. (*dejected*) 837; brokenhearted.

out of the question, not to be thought of; impracticable &c. 471; past -hope, – cure, – mending, – recall; at one's last gasp &c. (*death*) 360; given -up, – over.

incurable, cureless, immedicable, remediless, beyond remedy; incorrigible; irreparable, -mediable, -coverable, -versible, -trievable, -claimable, -deemable, -vocable; ruined, undone; immitigable.

unpromising, unpropitious; inauspicious, ill-omened, threatening, clouded over, lowering, ominous.

Phr. '*lasciate ogni speranza voi ch'entrate*'; its days are numbered; the worst come to the worst.

860. Fear.—N. fear, timidity, diffidence, want of confidence; apprehensive-, fearful-ness &c. *adj.*; solicitude, anxiety, care, apprehension, misgiving; mistrust &c. (*doubt*) 485; suspicion, qualm; hesitation &c. (*irresolution*) 605.

nervous-, restless-ness &c. *adj.*; in-, dis-quietude; flutter, trepidation, fear and trembling, perturbation, tremor, quivering, shaking, trembling, throbbing heart, palpitation, ague fit, cold sweat; abject fear &c. (*cowardice*) 862; mortal funk, heart-sinking, despondency; despair &c. 859.

fright; affright, -ment; alarm, pavor, dread, awe, terror, horror, dismay, consternation, panic, scare, stampede [of horses].

intimidation, terrorism, reign of terror.

[Object of fear] bug-bear, -aboo; scarecrow; hobgoblin &c. (*demon*) 980; daymare, nightmare, Gorgon, Medusa, mormo, ogre, Hurlothrumbo, raw head and bloody bones, fee faw fum, *bête noire, enfant terrible.*

alarmist &c. (*coward*) 862.

V. fear, stand in awe of; be -afraid &c. *adj.*; have -qualms &c. *n.*; apprehend, sit upon thorns, eye askance; distrust &c. (*disbelieve*) 485.

hesitate &c. (be *irresolute*) 605; falter, funk, cower, crouch; skulk &c. (*cowardice*) 862; let 'I dare not' wait upon 'I would'; take -fright, – alarm; start, wince, flinch, shy, shrink; fly &c. (*avoid*) 623.

tremble, shake; shiver, – in one's shoes; shudder, flutter; shake –, tremble- -like an aspen leaf, – all over; quake, quaver, quiver, quail; get the wind up.

grow –, turn- pale; blench, stand aghast; not dare to say one's soul is one's own.

inspire –, excite- -fear, – awe; raise apprehensions; give –, raise –, sound- an alarm; alarm, startle, scare, cry 'wolf,' disquiet, dismay; fright, -en; affright, terrify; astound; frighten from one's propriety; frighten out of one's -wits, – senses, – seven senses; awe; strike -all of a heap, – an awe into, – terror; harrow up the soul, appall, unman, petrify, horrify.

make one's -flesh creep, – hair stand on end; – blood run cold, – teeth chatter; chill one's spine; take away –, stop- one's breath; make one -tremble &c.

haunt, obsess, beset; prey –, weigh- on the mind.

put in -fear, – bodily fear; terrorize, intimidate, cow, daunt, overawe, abash, deter, discourage; browbeat, bully; threaten &c. 909.

Adj. fearing &c. *v.*; frightened &c. *v.*; in -fear, – a fright &c. *n.*; haunted with the -fear &c. *n.*of.

afraid, fearful; tim-id, -orous; nervous, diffident, coy, fainthearted, tremulous, shaky, afraid of one's shadow, apprehensive, restless, fidgety; more frightened than hurt.

aghast; awe-, horror-, terror-,

panic- -struck, -stricken; frightened to death, white as a sheet; pale, – as -death, – ashes, – a ghost; breathless, in hysterics.

inspiring fear &c. *v.*; alarming; formidable, redoubtable; perilous &c. (*danger*) 665; portentous; fear-ful, -some; dread, -ful; fell; dire, -ful; shocking; terri-ble, -fic; tremendous; horri-d, -ble, -fic; ghastly; awful, awe-inspiring, eerie, weird; revolting &c. (*painful*) 830.

Adv. in terrorem.

Int. 'angels and ministers of grace defend us!'

Phr. ante tubam trepidat; horresco referens, one's heart failing one, *obstupui steteruntque comæ et vox faucibus hæsit.*

861. [Absence of fear.] **Courage.—**
N. courage, bravery, valour; resolute-, bold-ness &c. *adj.*; spirit, daring, gallantry, intrepidity; contempt –, defiance- of danger; derring-do; audacity; rashness &c. 863; dash; defiance &c. 715; confidence, self-reliance.

man-liness, -hood; nerve, pluck, mettle, game; heart, – of grace; spunk, gameness, grit, face, virtue, hardihood, fortitude; firmness &c. (*stability*) 150; heart of oak; bottom, backbone &c. (*perseverance*) 604a.

resolution &c. (*determination*) 604; tenacity, bull-dog courage.

prowess, heroism, chivalry.

exploit, feat, achievement; heroic -deed, – act; bold stroke.

man, – of mettle; hero, demigod, paladin, heroine, Amazon, Hector, Joan of Arc; lion, tiger, panther, bulldog; game-, fighting-cock; bully, fire-eater &c. 863; dare-devil.

V. be -courageous &c. *adj.*; dare, venture, make bold; face –, front –, affront –, confront –, brave, defy –, despise –, mock- danger; look in the face; look -full, – boldly, – danger- in the face; face; meet, – in front; brave, beard; defy &c. 715.

take –, muster –, summon up –, pluck up- courage; nerve oneself, take heart;

take –, pluck up- heart of grace; hold up one's head, screw one's courage to the sticking place; come -to, – up to- the scratch; stand, – to one's guns, – fire, – against; bear up, – against; hold out &c. (*persevere*) 604a.

put a bold face upon; show –, present- a bold front, face the music; envisage; show fight.

bell the cat, take the bull by the horns, beard the lion in his den, march up to the cannon's mouth, go through fire and water, run the gauntlet, go over the top.

give –, infuse –, inspire- courage; reassure, encourage, embolden, inspirit, cheer, hearten, nerve, put upon one's mettle, rally, raise a rallying cry; pat on the back, make a man of, keep in countenance.

Adj. courageous, brave; val-iant, -orous; gallant, intrepid; spirit-ed, -ful; high-spirited, -mettled; mettlesome, game, plucky; man-ly, -ful; resolute; stout, -hearted; iron-, lion-hearted; heart of oak; Penthesilean.

bold, – spirited; daring, audacious; fear-, daunt-, dread-, awe-less; undaunted, -appalled, -dismayed, -awed, -blenched, -abashed, -alarmed, -flinching, -shrinking, -blenching; apprehensive; confident, self-reliant; bold as -a lion, – brass.

enterprising, adventurous; ventur-ous, -esome; dashing, chivalrous; soldierly &c. (*warlike*) 722; heroic.

fierce, savage; pugnacious &c. (*bellicose*) 720.

strong-minded, hardy, doughty; firm &c. (*stable*) 150; determined &c. (*resolved*) 604; dogged, indomitable &c. (*persevering*) 604a.

up to, – the scratch; upon one's mettle; reassured &c. *v.*; unfeared, undreaded.

Phr. one's blood being up.

862. [Excess of fear.] **Cowardice.—**
N. cowardice, pusillanimity; cowardliness &c. *adj.*; timidity, effeminacy.

poltroonery, baseness; dastard-ness,

-y; abject fear, funk; Dutch courage; fear &c. 860; white feather, faint heart.

coward, poltroon, dastard, sneak, recreant; shy -, dunghill- cock; coistril, milksop, white-liver, nidget, cur, craven, one that cannot say 'Boo' to a goose; Bob Acres, Jerry Sneak.

alarm-, terror-, pessim-ist; runagate &c. (*fugitive*) 623; shirker.

V. quail &c. (*fear*) 860; be -cowardly &c. *adj.* , - a coward &c. *n.* ; funk; cower, skulk, sneak; flinch, shy, fight shy, slink, turn tail; run away &c. (*avoid*) 623; show the white feather, have cold feet, show a yellow streak.

Adj. coward, -ly; fearful, shy; tim-id, -orous; skittish; poor-spirited, spiritless, soft, effeminate.

weak-minded; infirm of purpose &c. 605; weak-, faint-, chicken-, lily-, pigeon-hearted; yellow; white-, lily-, milk-livered; milksop, smock-faced; unable to say 'Boo' to a goose.

dastard, -ly; base, craven, sneaking, dunghill, recreant; unwar-, unsoldier-like.

'in face a lion but in heart a deer.'

unmanned; frightened &c. 860.

Int. *sauve qui peut!* devil take the hindmost!

Adv. in fear and trembling, in fear of one's life, in a blue funk.

Phr. *ante tubam trepidat*, one's courage oozing out.

863. Rashness.—N. rashness &c. *adj.* ; temerity, want of caution, imprudence, indiscretion; over-confidence, presumption, audacity.

precipit-ancy, -ation; impetuosity; levity; foolhardi-hood, -ness; heed-, thought-lessness &c. (*inattention*) 458; carelessness &c. (*neglect*) 460; desperation; Quixotism, knight-errantry; fire-eating.

gam-ing, -bling; blind bargain, leap in the dark, fool's paradise; too many eggs in one basket.

desperado, rashling, mad-cap, daredevil, Hotspur, fire-eater, bully, *bravo*, Hector, scapegrace, *enfant perdu*; Don Quixote, knight-errant, Icarus; adventurer; gam-bler, -ester; dynamitard.

V. be -rash &c. *adj.* ; stick at nothing, play a desperate game; run into danger &c. 665; play with -fire, - edge tools.

carry too much sail, sail too near the wind, ride at single anchor, go out of one's depth.

take a leap in the dark, buy a pig in a poke.

donner tête baissée; knock one's head against a wall &c. (*be unskilful*) 699; rush on destruction; kick against the pricks, tempt Providence, go on a forlorn hope.

count one's chickens before they are hatched; reckon without one's host; catch at straws; trust to -, lean on- a broken reed.

Adj. rash, incautious, indiscreet, injudicious; imprudent, improvident, temerarious; uncalculating; heedless; careless &c. (*neglectful*) 460; without ballast, heels over head; giddy &c. (*inattentive*) 458; wanton, reckless, wild, madcap; desperate, devil-may-care.

hot-blooded, -headed, -brained; headlong, -strong; break-neck; foolhardy; harebrained; precipitate, impulsive.

over-confident, -weening; venturesome, -ous; adventurous, Quixotic; fire-eating, cavalier; free-and-easy.

off one's guard &c. (*inexpectant*) 508.

Adv. post haste, *à corps perdu*, hand over head, *tête baissée*, headforemost; happen what may.

Phr. neck or nothing, the devil being in one.

864. Caution.—N. caution; cautiousness &c. *adj.* ; discretion, prudence, cautel, heed, circumspection, calculation, deliberation; safety first.

foresight &c. 510; vigilance &c. 459; warning &c. 668.

coolness &c. *adj.* ; self-possession, -command; presence of mind, *sangfroid*; well-regulated mind; worldly wisdom, Fabian policy.

V. be -cautious &c. *adj.* ; take -care, - heed, - good care; have a care; mind,

– what one is about; be on one's guard &c. (*keep watch*) 459; make assurance double sure; ca' canny.

bespeak &c. (*be early*) 132.

think twice, look before one leaps, keep one's weather eye open, count the cost, look to the main chance, cut one's coat according to one's cloth; feel one's -ground, – way; see how the land lies &c. (*foresight*) 510; wait to see how the cat jumps; bridle one's tongue; *reculer pour mieux sauter* &c. (*prepare*) 673; let well alone, let sleeping dogs lie, *ne pas réveiller le chat qui dort.*

keep out of -harm's way, – troubled waters; keep at a respectful distance, stand aloof; keep –, be- on the safe side.

husband one's resources &c. 636.

caution &c. (*warn*) 668.

Adj. cautious, wary, guarded; on one's guard &c. (*watchful*) 459; *cavendo tutus*; *in medio tutissimus.*

care-, heed-ful; cautelous, stealthy, chary, shy of, circumspect, prudent, canny, safe, non-committal, discreet, politic; sure-footed &c. (*skilful*) 698.

unenterprising, unadventurous, cool, steady, self-possessed; over-cautious.

suspicious, leery, vigilant.

Adv. cautiously, gingerly &c. *adj.*

Int. have a care! look out! *cave canem!*

Phr. *timeo Danaos; festina lente.*

865. Desire.—N. desire, wish, fancy, fantasy; want, need, exigency.

mind, inclination, leaning, bent, *animus*, partiality, *penchant*, predilection; propensity &c. 820; willingness &c. 602; liking, love, fondness, relish.

longing, hankering; solicitude, anxiety; yearning, coveting; aspiration, ambition, vaulting ambition; eagerness, zeal, ardour, *empressement*, breathless impatience, over-anxiety; solicitude, impetuosity &c. 825.

appet-ite, -ition, -ence, -ency; sharp appetite, keenness, hunger, stomach, twist; thirst, -iness; drouth, mouthwatering; itch, -ing; prurience, *cacoëthes*, cupidity, lust, concupiscence.

edge of -appetite, – hunger; torment of Tantalus; sweet –, lickerish- tooth; itching palm; longing –, wistful –, sheep's eye.

avidity; greed, -iness; covetous-, ravenous-ness &c. *adj.*; grasping, craving, canine appetite, rapacity; voracity &c. (*gluttony*) 957.

passion, rage, *furore*, mania, *manie*; inextinguishable desire; dips-, klept-, mon-omania.

[Person desiring] desirer, lover, *amateur*, votary, devotee, aspirant, solicitant, candidate; cormorant &c. 957; sycophant.

[Object of desire] *desideratum*; want &c. (*requirement*) 630; 'consummation devoutly to be wished'; attraction, magnet, allurement, fancy, temptation, seduction, lure, fascination, *prestige*, height of one's ambition, idol; whim, -sey; maggot; hobby, -horse.

Fortunatus's cap, wishing cap, love potion.

V. desire; wish, – for; be -desirous &c. *adj.*; have a -longing &c. *n.*; hope &c. 858.

care for, affect, like, list; take to, cling to, take a fancy to; fancy; prefer &c. (*choose*) 609.

have -an eye, – a mind- to; find it in one's heart &c. (*be willing*) 602; have a fancy for, set one's eyes upon; cast a sheep's eye –, look sweet- upon; take into one's head, have at heart, be bent upon; set one's -cap at, – heart upon, – mind upon; covet.

want, miss, need, lack, desiderate, feel the want of; would fain -have, – do; would be glad of.

be -hungry &c. *adj.*; have a good appetite, play a good knife and fork; hunger –, thirst –, crave –, lust –, itch –, hanker –, run mad- after; raven –, die- for; burn to.

desiderate; sigh –, cry –, gape –, gasp –, cry –, pant –, languish –, yearn –, long –, be on thorns –, hope- for; aspire after; catch at, grasp at, jump at.

woo, court, solicit; fish –, spell –, whistle –, put up- for; ogle.

cause –, create –, raise –, excite –,
provoke- desire; whet the appetite; ap-
petize, titillate, allure, attract, take one's
fancy, tempt; hold out -temptation, – allurement; tantalize, make one's mouth
water, *faire venir l'eau à la bouche.*
gratify desire &c. (*give pleasure*) 829.
Adj. desirous; desiring &c. *v.*; orectic, appetitive; inclined &c. (*willing*)
602; partial to; fain, wishful, optative;
anxious, wistful, curious; at a loss for,
sedulous, solicitous.

craving, hungry, sharp-set, peckish,
ravening, with an empty stomach, esurient, lickerish, thirsty, athirst, parched
with thirst, pinched with hunger, famished, dry, drouthy; hungry as a -hunter,
– hawk, – horse, – church mouse.

greedy, – as a hog; over-eager, voracious; ravenous, – as a wolf; open-
mouthed, covetous, rapacious, grasping,
extortionate, exacting, sordid, *alieni appetens*; insati-able, -ate; unquenchable,
quenchless; omnivorous.

unsatisfied, unsated, unslaked.

eager, avid, keen; burning, fervent,
ardent; agog; all agog; breathless; impatient &c. (*impetuous*) 825; bent –, intent –, set- -on, – upon; mad after, *enragé*, rabid, dying for, devoured by
desire.

aspiring, ambitious, vaulting, sky-
aspiring.

desirable; popular; desired &c. *v.*; in
demand; pleasing &c. (*giving pleasure*)
829; appeti-zing, -ble; tantalizing.

Adv. wistfully &c. *adj.*; fain.

Int. would -that, – it were! O for! *esto
perpetua!* if only!

Phr. the wish being father to the
thought; *sua cuique voluptas; hoc erat
in votis,* the mouth watering, the fingers
itching; *aut Cæsar aut nullus.*

866. Indifference.—N. indifference,
neutrality; coldness &c. *adj.*; unconcern, *insouciance, nonchalance*; want of
-interest, – earnestness; anorexy, inappetency; apathy &c. (*insensibility*) 823;
supineness &c. (*inactivity*) 683; disdain

&c. 930; recklessness &c. 863; inattention &c. 458.

V. be -indifferent &c. *adj.*; stand
neuter; take no interest in &c. (*insensibility*) 823; have no -desire &c. 865, –
taste, – relish- for; not care for; care
nothing -for, – about; not care a -straw
&c. (*unimportance*) 643 -about, – for;
not mind.

set at naught &c. (*make light of*) 483;
spurn &c. (*disdain*) 930.

Adj. indifferent, cold, frigid, lukewarm; cool, – as a cucumber; unconcerned, *insouciant*, phlegmatic, *pococurante*, easy-going, devil-may-care,
careless, listless, lackadaisical, feckless;
half-hearted; un-ambitious, -aspiring,
-desirous, -solicitous, -attracted.

un-attractive, -alluring, -desired,
-desirable, -cared for, -wished, -valued,
all one to.

insipid &c. 391; vain.

Adv. for aught one cares.

Int. never mind.

867. Dislike.—N. dis-like, -taste,
-relish, -inclination, -placency.

reluctance; backwardness &c. (*unwillingness*) 603.

repugnance, disgust, queasiness, turn,
nausea, loathing; avers-eness, -ation,
-ion; abomination, antipathy, abhor-
rence, horror; mortal –, rooted-
-antipathy, – horror; hatred, detestation;
hate &c. 898; animosity &c. 900; hydrophobia.

sickener; gall and wormwood &c.
(*unsavoury*) 395; shuddering, cold
sweat.

V. dis-, mis-like, -relish; mind, object to; have rather not, not care for;
have –, conceive –, entertain –, take- -a
dislike, – an aversion- to; have no -taste,
– stomach- for.

shun, avoid &c. 623; eschew; withdraw –, shrink –, recoil- from; not be
able to -bear, – abide, – endure; shrug
the shoulders at, shudder at, turn up the
nose at, look askance at; make a -mouth,
– wry face, – grimace; make faces.

loathe, nauseate, abominate, detest,

abhor; hate &c. 898; take amiss &c. 900; have enough of &c. (*be satiated*) 869.

cause -, excite- dislike; disincline, repel, sicken; make -, render- sick; turn one's stomach, nauseate, wamble, disgust, shock, stink in the nostrils; go against the -grain, - stomach; stick in the throat; make one's blood run cold &c. (*give pain*) 830; pall.

Adj. disliking &c. *v.*; averse to, loth, adverse; shy of, sick of, out of conceit with; disinclined; heart-, dog-sick; queasy.

disliked &c. *v.*; uncared for, unpopular; out of favour; repulsive, repugnant, repellent; abhorrent, insufferable, fulsome, nauseous; loath-some, -ful; offensive; disgusting &c. *v.*; disagreeable &c. (*painful*) 830; unsavoury &c. 395.

Adv. *usque ad nauseam.*

Int. faugh! foh! ugh!

868. Fastidiousness.—N. fastidiousness &c. *adj.*; nicety, meticulosity, hypercriticism, difficulty in being pleased, *friandise*, epicurism, *omnia suspendens naso.*

discrimination, discernment, good taste, perspicacity.

epicure, gourmet.

[Excess of delicacy] prudery, prudishness, primness.

V. be -fastidious &c. *adj.*; split hairs, discriminate, have a sweet tooth.

mince the matter; turn up one's nose at &c. (*disdain*) 930; look a gift horse in the mouth, see spots on the sun.

Adj. fastidious, meticulous, exacting, nice, delicate, *délicat*, finical, finicky, difficult, dainty, lickerish, squeamish, thin-skinned; s-, queasy; hard -, difficult- to please; querulous, particular, over-particular, straitlaced, prudish, prim, scrupulous; censorious &c. 932; hypercritical, discriminating, discerning, perspicacious.

Phr. *noli me tangere.*

869. Satiety.—N. satiety, satisfaction, saturation, repletion, glut, surfeit; weariness &c. 841.

spoiled child; *enfant gâté*; too much of a good thing, *toujours perdrix; crambe repetita.*

V. sate, satiate, satisfy, saturate; cloy, quench, slake, pall, glut, gorge, surfeit; bore &c. (*weary*) 841; tire &c. (*fatigue*) 688; spoil.

have -enough of, - quite enough of, - one's fill, - too much of; be -satiated &c. *adj.*

Adj. satiated &c. *v.*; overgorged; *blasé*, used up, sick of, heart-sick.

Int. enough! hold! *eheu jam satis!*

4°. CONTEMPLATIVE AFFECTIONS

870. Wonder.—N. wonder, marvel; astonish-, amaze-, wonder-, bewilderment; amazedness &c. *adj.*; admiration, awe; stu-por, -pefaction; astound, fascination; sensation; surprise &c. (*inexpectation*) 508; cynosure.

note of admiration; thaumaturgy &c. (*sorcery*) 992.

V. wonder, marvel, admire; be -surprised &c. *adj.*; start; stare; open -, rub -, turn up- one's eyes; gloar; gape, open one's mouth, hold one's breath; look -, stand- -aghast, - agog; look blank &c. (*disappointment*) 509; *tomber des nues*; not believe one's -eyes, - ears, - senses.

not be able to account for &c. (*unintelligible*) 519; not know whether one stands on one's head or one's heels.

surprise, astonish, amaze, astound; dumbfound, -er; startle, dazzle; strike, - with -wonder, - awe; electrify; stun, stupefy, petrify, confound, bewilder, flabbergast; stagger, throw on one's beam ends, fascinate, turn the head, take away one's breath, strike dumb; make one's -hair stand on end, - tongue cleave to the roof of one's mouth; make one stare.

take by surprise &c. (*be unexpected*) 508.

be -wonderful &c. *adj.*; beggar -, baffle- description; stagger belief.

Adj. surprised &c. *v.*; aghast, all agog, breathless, agape; openmouthed; awe-, thunder-, moon-, planet-struck; spell-bound; lost in -amazement, - wonder, - astonishment; struck all of a heap, unable to believe one's senses, like a duck in thunder.

wonderful, wondrous; surprising &c. *v.*; unexpected &c. 508; unheard of; mysterious &c. (*inexplicable*) 519; miraculous; *foudroyant.*

in-describable, -expressible, -effable; un-utterable, -speakable.

monstrous, prodigious, stupendous, marvellous; in-conceivable, -credible; in-, un-imaginable; strange &c. (*uncommon*) 83; passing strange.

striking &c. *v.*; over-whelming; wonder-working.

Adv. wonderfully &c. *adj.*; fearfully; for a -, in the name of- wonder; strange to say; *mirabile -dictu, - visu;* to one's great surprise.

with -wonder &c. *n.*, - gaping mouth, - open eyes, - upturned eyes; eyes starting out of one's head.

Int. lo, - and behold! O! hey-day! halloo! what! indeed! really! surely! humph! hem! good -lack, - heavens, - gracious! - lord! by jove! gad so! well a day! dear me! only think! lack-a-daisy! my -stars, - goodness! gracious goodness! goodness gracious! mercy on us! heavens and earth! God bless me! bless -us, - my heart! odzookens! *O gemini!* adzooks! hoity-toity! strong! Heaven save -, bless- the mark! can such things be! zounds! 'sdeath! what -on earth, - in the world! who would have thought it! &c. (*inexpectation*) 508; fancy! did you ever? you don't say so! what do you say to that! how now! where am I? well I'm blowed! &c.

Phr. *vox faucibus hæsit;* one's hair standing on end.

871. [Absence of wonder.] **Expectance.—N.** expectan-ce, -cy &c. (*expectation*) 507; calmness, composure, tran-quillity, serenity, coolness, imperturbability &c. 826.

nine days' wonder.

V. expect &c. 507; not -be surprised, - wonder &c. 870; *nil admirari,* make nothing of.

Adj. expecting &c. *v.*; unamazed, astonished at nothing; *blasé* &c. (*weary*) 841; unimaginative, calm, serene, imperturbable &c. 826; expected &c. *v.*; foreseen.

common, ordinary &c. (*habitual*) 613.

Int. no wonder; of course; why not?

872. Prodigy.—N. prodigy, phenomenon; wonder, -ment; genius, marvel, miracle; freak, monster &c. (*unconformity*) 83; curiosity, lion, infant prodigy, sight, spectacle; *jeu -, coup- de théâtre;* gazing-stock; sign; portent &c. 512.

bursting of a -shell, - bomb; volcanic eruption, peal of thunder; thunder-clap, -bolt.

what no words can paint; wonders of the world; *annus mirabilis; dignus vindice nodus.*

5°. INTRINSIC AFFECTIONS*

873. Repute.—N. distinction, mark, name, figure; repute, reputation, character; good -, high-repute; note, notability, notoriety, *éclat,* 'the bubble reputation,' vogue, celebrity; fame, famousness; renown; popularity, *aura popularis*; esteem, approval, approbation &c. 931; credit, *succès d'estime, prestige,* talk of the town; name to conjure with.

glory, honour; lustre &c. (*light*) 420; illustriousness &c. *adj.*

account, regard, respect; reputableness &c. *adj.*; respectability &c. (*probity*) 939; good -name, - report; fair name.

dignity; stateliness &c. *adj.*;

---

* Or personal affections derived from the opinions or feelings of others.

solemnity, grandeur, splendour, nobility, majesty, sublimity.

rank, standing, brevet rank, precedence, *pas*, station, place, *status*; position, – in society; order, degree, *locus standi*, caste, condition.

greatness &c. *adj.*; eminence; height &c. 206; importance &c. 642; pre-, super-eminence; high mightiness, primacy; top of the -ladder, – tree.

elevation; ascent &c. 305; super-, exaltation; dignification, aggrandizement.

dedication, consecration, enthronement, canonization, apotheosis, deification, celebration, enshrinement, glorification.

hero, man of mark, great card, celebrity, worthy, lion, *rara avis*, notability, somebody; man of rank &c. (*nobleman*) 875; pillar of the -state, – society, – church.

chief &c. (*master*) 745; first fiddle &c. (*proficient*) 700; scholar &c. 492; cynosure, mirror; flower, pink, pearl; paragon &c. (*perfection*) 650; choice and master spirits of the age; *élite*; star, sun, constellation, galaxy.

ornament, honour, feather in one's cap, halo, aureole, nimbus; halo –, blaze- of glory; blushing honours; laurels &c. (*trophy*) 733.

memory, posthumous fame, niche in the temple of fame; immor-tality, -tal name; *magni nominis umbra*.

V. be conscious of glory; be proud of &c. (*pride*) 878; exult &c. (*boast*) 884; be vain of &c. (*vanity*) 880.

be -distinguished &c. *adj.*; shine &c. (*light*) 420; shine forth, figure; make –, cut- a -figure, – dash, – splash.

rival, surpass; out-shine, -rival, -vie, -jump; emulate, vie with, eclipse; throw –, cast- into the shade; overshadow.

live, flourish, glitter, scintillate, flaunt; gain –, acquire- honour &c. *n.*; play first fiddle &c. (*be of importance*) 642; bear the -palm, – bell; lead the way; take -precedence, – the wall of; gain –, win- -laurels, – spurs, – golden opinions &c. (*approbation*) 931; graduate, take

one's degree, pass one's examination, win a -scholarship, – fellowship.

make -a, – some- -noise, – noise in the world; leave one's mark, exalt one's horn, star, have a run, be run after; enjoy popularity, come -into vogue, – to the front; raise one's head.

enthrone, signalize, immortalize, deify, exalt to the skies; hand one's name down to posterity.

consecrate; dedicate to, devote to; enshrine, inscribe, blazon, lionize, blow the trumpet, crown with laurel.

confer –, reflect- honour &c. *n.* on; shed a lustre on; redound to one's honour, ennoble.

give –, do –, pay –, render- honour to; honour, accredit, pay regard to, dignify, glorify; sing praises to &c. (*approve*) 931; look up to; exalt, aggrandize, elevate, nobilitate.

Adj. distinguished, *distingué*, noted; of -note &c. *n.*; honoured &c. *v.*; popular; fashionable &c. 852.

in good odour; in –, in high- favour; reput-, respect-, credit-able.

remarkable &c. (*important*) 642; notable, notorious; celebrated, renowned, in every one's mouth, talked of; fam-ous, -ed; far-famed; conspicuous, to the front; foremost; in the -front rank, – ascendant.

imperishable, deathless, immortal, never fading, *ære perennius*; time-honoured.

illustrious, glorious, splendid, brilliant, radiant; bright &c. 420; full-blown; honorific.

eminent, prominent; high &c. 206; in the zenith; at the -head of, – top of the tree; peerless, of the first water; superior &c. 33; super-, pre-eminent.

great, dignified, proud, noble, honourable, worshipful, lordly, grand, stately, august, princely, imposing, solemn, transcendent, majestic, sacred, sublime, heaven-born, heroic, *sans peur et sans reproche*; sacrosanct.

Int. hail! all hail! *ave! viva! vive!* long life to! glory –, honour- be to!

Phr. one's name -being in every

mouth, – living for ever; *sic itur ad astra, fama volat, aut Cæsar aut nullus;* not to know him argues oneself unknown; none but himself could be his parallel, *palmam qui meruit ferat.*

874. Disrepute.—N. disrepute, discredit; ill-, bad- -repute, -name, -odour, -favour; disapprobation &c. 932; ingloriousness, derogation; a-, de-basement; abjectness &c. *adj.*; degradation, dedecoration; 'a long farewell to all one's greatness'; odium, obloquy, opprobrium, ignominy.

dishonour, disgrace; shame, humiliation; scandal, baseness, vileness; perfidy, turpitude &c. (*improbity*) 940; infamy.

tarnish, taint, defilement, pollution.

stain, blot, spot, blur, stigma, brand, reproach, imputation, slur.

crying –, burning- shame; *scandalum magnatum*, badge of infamy, blot in one's escutcheon; bend –, bar- sinister; champain, point champain; by-word of reproach; Ichabod.

argumentum ad verecundiam; sense of shame &c. 879.

V. be -inglorious &c. *adj.*; incur -disgrace &c. *n.*; have –, earn- a bad name; put –, wear- a halter round one's neck; disgrace –, expose- oneself.

play second fiddle; lose caste; pale one's ineffectual fire; recede into the shade; fall from one's high estate; keep in the background &c. (*modesty*) 881; be conscious of disgrace &c. (*humility*) 879; look -blue, – foolish, – like a fool; cut a -poor, – sorry- figure; laugh on the wrong side of the mouth; make a sorry face, go away with a flea in one's ear, slink away.

cause -shame &c. *n.*; shame, disgrace, put to shame, dishonour; throw –, cast -, fling –, reflect- dishonour &c. *n.* upon; be a -reproach &c. *n.* to; derogate from.

tarnish, stain, blot, sully, taint; discredit; degrade, debase, defile; beggar; expel &c. (*punish*) 972.

impute shame to, brand, post, stig-

matize, vilify, defame, slur, cast a slur upon, hold up to shame, send to Coventry; tread -, trample- under foot; show up, drag through the mire, heap dirt upon; reprehend &c. 932.

bring low, put down, snub; take down a peg, – lower, – or two.

obscure, eclipse, outshine, take the shine out of; throw –, cast- into the shade; overshadow; leave –, put- in the background; push into a corner, put one's nose out of joint; put out, – of countenance.

upset, throw off one's centre; discompose, disconcert; put to the blush &c. (*humble*) 879.

Adj. disgraced &c. *v.*; blown upon; shorn of -its beams, – one's glory; overcome, down-trodden; loaded with -shame &c. *n.*; in -bad repute &c. *n.*; out of -repute, – favour, – fashion, – countenance; at a discount; under -a cloud, – an eclipse; unable to show one's face; in the -shade, – background; out at elbows, down in the world, down and out.

inglorious; nameless, renownless, obscure, unknown to fame; un-noticed, -noted, -honoured, -glorified.

shameful; dis-graceful, -creditable, -reputable; despicable; questionable; unbecoming, unworthy; derogatory; degrading, humiliating, *infra dignitatem*, dedecorous; scandalous, infamous, too bad, unmentionable; ribald, opprobrious; arrant, shocking, outrageous, notorious, shady.

ignominious, scrubby, dirty, abject, vile, beggarly, pitiful, low, mean, shabby; base &c. (*dishonourable*) 940.

Adv. to one's shame be it spoken.

Int. fie! shame! for shame! *proh pudor! O tempora! O mores!* ough! *sic transit gloria mundi!*

875. Nobility.—N. nobility, rank, condition, distinction, optimacy, blood, *pur sang*, birth, high descent, order; quality, gentility; blue blood of Castile; *ancien régime.*

high life, *haut monde*; upper -classes, – ten thousand; *élite*, aristocracy, great folks; fashionable world &c. (*fashion*) 852; salariat.

peer, -age; house of -lords, – peers; lords, – temporal and spiritual; *noblesse*; baronage, knightage; noble, -man; lord, -ling; grandee, *magnifico, hidalgo*; don, -ship; aristocrat, swell, three-tailed bashaw; gentleman, squire, squireen, patrician, laureate.

gentry, gentlefolk; squirarchy, better sort, *magnates, primates, optimates*.

king &c. (*master*) 745; prince, crown prince, *Dauphin*; duke; marquis, -ate; earl, viscount, baron, thane, banneret; baronet, -cy; knight, -hood; count, armiger, laird; sig-, seig-nior; esquire, boyar, margrave, vavasour, sheik, emir, ameer, scherif, *pasha*, effendi, sahib.

queen &c. 745; princess, begum, duchess, marchioness; countess &c.; lady, dame.

personage –, man- of -distinction, – mark, – rank; nota-bles, -bilities; celebrity, big-wig, magnate, great man, star; *magni nominis umbra*; 'every inch a king'; grand Panjandrum.

V. be -noble &c. *adj.*

Adj. noble, exalted; of -rank &c. *n.*; princely, titled, patrician, aristocratic; high-, well-born; of gentle blood; genteel, *comme il faut*, gentlemanlike, courtly &c. (*fashionable*) 852; highly respectable.

Adv. in high quarters.

876. Commonalty.—N. commonalty, democracy; obscurity; low -condition, – life, – society, – company; *bourgeoisie*; mass of -the people, – society; Brown, Jones, and Robinson; Tom, Dick, and Harry; lower –, humbler- -classes, – orders; vulgar –, common- herd; rank and file, *hoc genus omne*; the -many, – general, – crowd, – people, – populace, – multitude, – million, – masses, – mobility, – peasantry; king Mob; proletariat, *fruges consumere nati*, great unwashed; man in the street.

mob; rabble, – rout; chaff, rout, horde, *canaille*; scum –, *residuum* –, dregs- of -the people, – society; swinish multitude, *fæx populi*; *profanum* –, *ignobile- vulgus*; vermin, riff-raff, tagrag and bobtail; small fry.

commoner, one of the people, democrat, plebeian, republican, proletary, *prolétaire, roturier*, Mr. Snooks, *bourgeois, épicier*, Philistine, cockney; *grisette, demi-monde*.

peasant, countryman, boor, carle, churl; vill-ain, -ein; serf, kern, tyke, tike, chuff, ryot, fellah; long-shoreman; swain, clown, hind; clod, -hopper; hobnail, yokel, hick, rube, cider squeezer, bog-trotter, bumpkin; ploughman, -boy; rustic, chawbacon, tiller of the soil; hewers of wood and drawers of water, groundling; gaffer, loon, put, cub, Tony Lumpkin, looby, lout, under-ling; *gamin*, guttersnipe, street arab, mudlark; rough, rowdy, ruffian, roughneck; potwallopper, slubberdegullion; vulgar –, low- fellow; cad, curmudgeon.

upstart, *parvenu, nouveau-riche*, skipjack; nobody, – one knows; *hesterni quirites, pessoribus orti*; *bourgeois gentilhomme, novus homo*, snob, gent, mushroom, no one knows who, adventurer; man of straw.

beggar, panhandler, gaberlunzie, muckworm, mudlark, *sans-culotte*, raff, tatterdemalion, caitiff, ragamuffin, Pariah, outcast of society, tramp, weary Willie, bum, vagabond, *chiffonnier*, ragpicker, Cinderella, cinderwench, scrub, jade; boots, gossoon.

Goth, Vandal, Hottentot, savage, barbarian, Yahoo; unlicked cub, rough diamond.

barbar-ousness, -ism; Bœotia.

V. be -ignoble &c. *adj.*, – nobody &c. *n.*

Adj. ignoble, common, mean, low, base, vile, sorry, scrubby, beggarly, below par; no great shakes &c. (*unimportant*) 643; home-ly, -spun; vulgar, low-minded; snobbish, *parvenu*.

plebeian, proletarian; of -low, – mean- -parentage, – origin, extraction; low-, base-, earth-born, low bred; mushroom, dunghill, risen from the ranks; unknown to fame, obscure, untitled.

rustic, uncivilized; lout-, boor-, clown-, churl-, brut-, raff-ish; rude, unlicked, unpolished.

barbar-ous, -ian, -ic, -esque; cockney, born within sound of Bow bells.

underling, menial, servile, subaltern.

Adv. below the salt.

877. Title.—N. title, honour; knighthood &c. (*nobility*) 875.

royal -, serene- highness, excellency, grace; lordship, worship. Rt. Hon., rever-ence, -end; esquire, sir; madam, *madame*; master, mistress, Mr., Mrs., *signor, señor, Mein Herr, mynheer*; your -, his- honour; handle to one's name.

decoration, laurel, palm, wreath, garland, bays, medal, ribbon, riband, blue ribbon, *cordon*, cross, crown, coronet, star, garter; feather, - in one's cap; chevron, epaulet, *épaulette*, colours, cockade; livery; order, arms, armorial bearings, shield, scutcheon, crest, reward &c. 973.

878. Pride.—N. dignity, self-respect, *mens sibi conscia recti*.

pride; haughtiness &c. *adj.*; high notions, *hauteur*; vainglory, crest; arrogance &c. (*assumption*) 885; pomposity &c. 882.

proud man, highflier; fine -gentleman, - lady; *grande dame*.

V. be -proud &c. *adj.*; put a good face on; look one in the face; stalk abroad, perk oneself up; presume, swagger, strut; rear -, lift up -, hold up- one's head; hold one's head high, look big, take the wall, 'bear like the Turk no rival near the throne,' carry with a high hand; ride the -, mount on one's- high horse; set one's back up, bridle, toss the head; give oneself airs &c. (*assume*) 885; boast &c. 884.

pride oneself on; glory in, take a pride in; pique -, plume -, hug- oneself; stand upon, be proud of; put a good face on; not -hide one's light under a bushel, - put one's talent in a napkin; not think small beer of oneself &c. (*vanity*) 880.

Adj. dignified; stately; proud, -crested; lordly, baronial; lofty-minded; high-

souled, -minded, -mettled, -handed, -plumed, -flown, -toned.

haughty, paughty, insolent, lofty, high, mighty, swollen, puffed up, flushed, blown; vain-glorious; purse-proud, fine; proud as -a peacock, Lucifer; bloated with pride.

supercilious, disdainful, bumptious, magisterial, imperious; high -handed, -and mighty; overweening, consequential; arrogant &c. 885; unblushing &c. 880.

stiff, -necked; starch; perked -, stuck-up; in buckram, straitlaced; prim &c. (*affected*) 855.

on one's -high horses, - tight ropes, - high ropes; on stilts; *en grand seigneur*.

Adv. with head erect, with one's nose in the air.

Phr. *odi profanum vulgus et arceo.*

879. Humility.—N. hum-ility, -bleness; meek-, low-ness; lowli-ness, -hood; abasement, self-abasement, -effacement; submission &c. 725; resignation.

condescension; affability &c. (*courtesy*) 894.

modesty &c. 881; verecundity, blush, suffusion, confusion; sense of -shame, - disgrace; humiliation, mortification; let -, set- down.

V. be -humble &c. *adj.*; deign, vouchsafe, condescend; humble -, demean- oneself; stoop, - to conquer; carry coals; submit &c. 725; submit with a good grace &c. (*brook*) 826; yield the palm.

lower one's -tone, - note; sing small, draw in one's horns, sober down; hide one's -face, - diminished head; not dare to show one's face, take shame to oneself, not have a word to say for oneself; feel -, be conscious of- -shame, - disgrace; drink the cup of humiliation to the dregs; eat -humble pie, - one's words, - dirt; be humiliated, receive a snub.

blush -for, - up to the eyes; redden, change colour; colour up; hang one's head, look foolish, feel small.

render humble; humble, humiliate; let
-, set -, take -, tread -, frown- down;
snub, abash, abase, make one sing
small, strike dumb; teach one -his distance, - his place; take down a peg, -
lower; throw -, cast- into the shade &c.
874; stare -, put- out of countenance;
put to the blush; confuse, ashame, mortify, disgrace, crush; send away with a
flea in one's ear.

get a set down.

Adj. humble, lowly, meek; modest
&c. 881; humble-, sober-minded; unoffended; submissive &c. 725; servile &c.
886.

condescending; affable &c. (*courteous*) 894.

humbled &c. *v.*; bowed down, resigned; abashed, ashamed, dashed; out
of countenance; down in the mouth;
down on one's -knees, - marrow-bones;
humbled in the dust, brow-beaten; chap-,
crest-fallen; dumbfoundered, flabber-
gasted, struck all of a heap.

shorn of one's glory &c. (*disrepute*)
874.

Adv. with -downcast eyes, - bated
breath, - bended knee; on all fours, on
one's feet.

under correction, with due deference.

Phr. I am your -obedient, - very
humble- servant; my service to you.

880. Vanity.—N. vanity; conceit,
-edness; self-conceit, -complacency,
-confidence, -sufficiency, -esteem, -love,
-approbation, -praise, -glorification,
-laudation, -gratulation, -applause, -ad-
miration; *amour-propre*; selfishness &c.
943.

airs, pretensions, mannerism; egotism; prig-gism, -gishness; coxcombery,
gaudery, vainglory, elation; pride &c.
878; ostentation &c. 882; assurance &c.
885.

*vox et præterea nihil; cheval de ba-
taille.*

ego-ist, -tist; peacock, coxcomb &c.
854; Sir Oracle &c. 887.

V. be -vain &c. *adj.*, - vain of; pique

oneself &c. (*pride*) 878; lay the flattering unction to one's soul.

have -too high, - an overweening-
opinion of -oneself, - one's talents; blind
oneself as to one's own merit; not think
-small beer, - *vin ordinaire*- of oneself;
put oneself forward; fish for compliments; give oneself airs &c. (*assume*)
885; boast &c. 884.

render -vain &c. *adj.*; inspire with
-vanity &c. *n.*; inflate, puff up, turn up,
turn one's head.

Adj. vain, - as a peacock; conceited,
assured, overweening, pert, forward,
perky; vain-glorious, high-flown; ostentatious &c. 882; puffed up, inflated,
flushed.

self-satisfied, -confident, -sufficient,
-flattering, -admiring, -applauding,
-glorious, -opinionated; *entêté* &c.
(*wrong-headed*) 481; wise in one's own
conceit, pragmatical, overwise, pretentious, priggish; egotistic, -al; *soi-disant*
&c. (*boastful*) 884; arrogant &c. 885.

un-abashed, -blushing; unconstrained, -ceremonious; free and
easy.

Adv. vainly &c. *adj.*

Phr. how we apples swim!

881. Modesty.—N. modesty; humility &c. 879; diffidence, timidity; retiring
disposition, unobtrusiveness, bashful-
ness &c. *adj.*; *mauvaise honte*; blush,
-ing; verecundity; self-knowledge.

reserve, constraint; demureness &c.
adj.; blushing honours.

V. be -modest &c. *adj.*; retire, reserve oneself; give way to; draw in one's
horns &c. 879; hide one's face.

keep -private, - in the background, -
one's distance; pursue the noiseless ten-
or of one's way, 'do good by stealth and
blush to find it fame,' hide one's light
under a bushel, cast a sheep's eye.

Adj. modest, diffident; humble &c.
879; timid, timorous, bashful; shy, nervous, skittish, coy, sheepish, shamefaced, blushing, over-modest.

unpreten-ding, -tious; un-obtrusive,

-assuming, -ostentatious, -boastful, -aspiring; poor in spirit.

out of countenance &c. (*humbled*) 879.

reserved, constrained, demure.

Adv. humbly &c. *adj.*; quietly, privately; without -ceremony, - beat of drum; *sans façon*.

882. Ostentation.—N. ostentation, display, show, flourish, parade, *étalage*, pomp, array, state, solemnity; dash, splash, glitter, strut, swank, side, swagger, pomposity; preten-se, -sions; showing off; fuss.

magnificence, splendour; *coup d'œil*; grand doings.

coup de théâtre; stage -effect, - trick; clap-trap; *mise en scène*; *tour de force*; *chic*.

demonstration, flying colours; tomfoolery; flourish of trumpets &c. (*celebration*) 883; pageant, -ry; spectacle, exhibition, procession; turn -, set- out; grand function; *fête*, gala, field-day, review, march past, promenade, insubstantial pageant.

dress; court -, full -, evening -, ball -, fancy- dress; tailoring, millinery, man-millinery, frippery; foppery, equipage.

ceremon-y, -ial; ritual; form, -ality; etiquette; punct-o, -ilio, -iliousness; starched-, stateli-ness.

mummery, solemn mockery, mouth honour.

attitudinarian; fop &c. 854.

V. be -ostentatious &c. *adj.*; come -, put oneself- forward; attract attention, star it.

make -, cut- a -figure, - dash, - splash; strut, blow one's own trumpet; figure, - away; make a show, - display; glitter.

show -off, - one's paces; parade, march past; display, exhibit, put forward, hold up; trot -, hang- out; sport, brandish, blazon forth; dangle, - before the eyes.

cry up &c. (*praise*) 931; *prôner*,

flaunt, emblazon, prink, set off, mount, have framed and glazed.

put a good, - smiling- face upon; clean the outside of the platter &c. (*disguise*) 544.

Adj. ostentatious, showy, dashing, pretentious; ja-, jau-nty; grand, pompous, palatial; high-sounding; turgid &c. (*big-sounding*) 577; garish, gorgeous; gaudy, - as a -peacock, - butterfly, - tulip; flaunting, flashing, flaming, glittering; gay &c. (*ornate*) 847; colourful.

splendid, magnificent, sumptuous.

theatrical, dramatic, spectacular, scenic, ceremonial, ritual, -istic.

solemn, stately, majestic, formal, stiff, ceremonious, punctilious, starch-ed, -y.

en grande tenue, in best bib and tucker, in Sunday best, *endimanché*.

Adv. with -flourish of trumpet, - beat of drum, - flying colours, - a brass band.

ad captandum vulgus.

883. Celebration.—N. celebration, solemnization, jubilee, diamond jubilee, commemoration, ovation, pæan, triumph, jubilation.

triumphal arch, bonfire, salute; salvo, - of artillery; *feu de joie*, flourish of trumpets, *fanfare*, colours flying, illuminations, fireworks.

inauguration, installation, presentation; *début*, coming out, birthday anniversary, bi-, ter-, centenary; silver -, golden -, diamond- wedding, -day; coronation; Lord Mayor's show; harvest home, red letter day, festival; trophy &c. 733; *Te Deum* &c. (*thanksgiving*) 990; *fête* &c. 882; holiday &c. 840.

V. celebrate, keep, signalize, do honour to, commemorate, solemnize, hallow, mark with a red letter, hold high festival, maffick.

pledge, drink to, toast, hob and nob.

inaugurate, install, instate, induct, chair.

rejoice &c. 838; kill the fatted calf, hold jubilee, roast an ox, fire a salute.

Adj. celebrating &c. *v.*; commemorative, celebrated, immortal.

Adv. in -honour, – commemoration, – celebration of.

Int. hail! all hail! *io -paean, – triumphe!* 'see the conquering hero comes!'

884. Boasting.—N. boasting &c. *v.*; boast, vaunt, crake; preten-ce, -sions; puff, -ery; flourish, *fanfaronnade*; gasconade; bluff, swank, brag, -gardism; bravado, bunkum, Buncombe; highfalutin; jact-itation, -ancy; bounce, rant, bluster; venditation, vapouring, rodomontade, bombast, fine talking, tall talk, magniloquence, teratology, heroics; jingoism, Chauvinism; exaggeration &c. 549; gas, hot air.

vanity &c. 880; *vox et praeterea nihil*; much cry and little wool, *brutum fulmen*.

exultation; glorification; flourish of trumpets; triumph &c. 883.

boaster; bragg-art, -adocio; hot air merchant; Gascon, *fanfaron*, pretender, fourflusher, *soi-disant*; windbag, blowhard, bluffer; chauvinist; blusterer &c. 887; charlatan, jack-pudding, trumpeter; puppy &c. (*fop*) 854.

V. boast, make a boast of, brag, vaunt, puff, show off, flourish, crake, crack, trumpet, strut, swagger, vapour, bluff; draw the long bow.

exult, crow over, neigh, chuckle, triumph; glory, gloat, jubilate; throw up one's cap; talk big, *se faire valoir, faire claquer son fouet*, take merit to oneself, make a merit of, sing *Io triumphe*, holloa before one is out of the wood.

Adj. boasting &c. *v.*; magniloquent, flaming, Thrasonic, stilted, gasconading, braggart, boastful, pretentious, *soi-disant*; vain-glorious &c. (*conceited*) 880.

elate, -d; jubilant, triumphant, exultant; in high feather; flushed, – with victory; cock-a-hoop; on stilts.

vaunted &c. *v.*

Adv. vauntingly &c. *adj.*; with a brass band.

Phr. 'let the galled jade wince.'

885. [Undue assumption of superiority.] **Insolence.—N.** insolence; haughtiness &c. *adj.*; arrogance, airs; overbearance, brashness, bumptiousness, contumely, disdain; domineering &c. *v.*; tyranny &c. 739.

impertinence; cheek, nerve, sauce; sauciness &c. *adj.*; flippancy, dicacity, petulance, procacity, bluster; swagger, -ing &c. *v.*; bounce; terrorism; jingoism, chauvinism.

as-, pre-sumption; beggar on horseback; usurpation.

impudence, assurance, audacity, selfassertion, hardihood, front, face, brass; shamelessness &c. *adj.*; effrontery, hardened front, face of brass.

assumption of infallibility.

malapert, saucebox &c. (*blusterer*) 887.

V. be -insolent &c. *adj.*; bluster, vapour, swagger, swell, give oneself airs, snap one's fingers, kick up a dust; swear &c.(*affirm*) 535; rap out oaths; roister.

arrogate; as-, pre-sume; make -bold, – free; take a liberty, give an inch and take an ell.

domineer, bully, dictate, hector; lord it over, bulldoze; *traiter de haut, regarder de haut en bas*; exact; snub, huff, beard, fly in the face of; put to the blush; bear –, beat- down; browbeat, intimidate; trample –, tread- -down, – under foot; dragoon, ride roughshod over, terrorize.

out-face, -look, -stare, -brazen, -brave; stare out of countenance; brazen out; lay down the law; teach one's grandmother to suck eggs; assume a lofty bearing; talk –, look- big; put on big looks, act the *grand seigneur*; mount –, ride- the high horse; toss the head, carry with a high hand.

tempt Providence, want snuffing.

Adj. insolent, haughty, arrogant, imperious, magisterial, dictatorial, arbitrary; high-handed, high and mighty; contumelious, supercilious, overbearing, intolerant, domineering; overweening, high-flown.

flippant, pert, cavalier, saucy, forward, impertinent, fresh, malapert.

precocious, assuming, would-be, bumptious.

bluff; brazen-, browed-faced, shameless, aweless, unblushing, unabashed; bold-, bare-faced; dead -, lost- to shame.

impudent, audacious, presumptuous, free and easy, devil-may-care, rollicking; janty, jaunty; roistering, blustering, hectoring, swaggering, vapouring; thrasonic, fire-eating, 'full of sound and fury.'

Adv. insolently, with a high hand; *ex cathedrâ.*

Phr. one's bark being worse than his bite.

886. Servility.—N. servility; slavery &c. (*subjection*) 749; obsequiousness &c. *adj.*; subserviency; abasement; pros-tration, -ternation; genuflexion &c. (*worship*) 990; fawning &c. *v.*; tuft-hunting, time-serving, flunkeyism; sycophancy &c. (*flattery*) 933; humility &c. 879.

sycophant, parasite, yes-man; toad, -y, -eater; tuft-hunter; snob, flunkey, lapdog, spaniel, lick-spittle, smell-feast, *Græculus esuriens*, hanger on, stooge, *cavaliere servente*, led captain, carpet knight; time-server, fortune-hunter, Vicar of Bray, Sir Pertinax Mac Sycophant, pick-thank; flatterer &c. 935; doer of dirty work; *âme damnée*, tool; reptile; slave &c. (*servant*) 746; courtier; sponge, jackal; truckler.

V. cringe, bow, stoop, kneel, bend the knee; fall on one's knees, prostrate oneself; worship &c. 990.

sneak, crawl, crouch, cower, truckle to, grovel, fawn, toady, lick the feet of, kiss the hem of one's garment.

pay court to; feed -, fatten -, batten-on; dance attendance on, pin oneself upon, hang on the sleeve of, *avaler des couleuvres*, keep time to, fetch and carry, do the dirty work of.

go with the stream, follow the crowd, worship the rising sun, hold with the hare and run with the hounds.

Adj. servile, obsequious; supple, - as a glove; soapy, oily, pliant, cringing, fawning, slavish, grovelling, snivelling, mealy-mouthed; beggarly, sycophantic, parasitical; abject, prostrate, down on one's marrow-bones; base, mean, sneaking; crouching &c. *v.*

Adv. hat -, cap- in hand.

887. Blusterer.—N. bluster-, swagger-, vapour-, roister-, brawl-er; brazenface; *fanfaron*; braggart &c. (*boaster*) 884; bully, terrorist, rough, rough-neck; hooligan, hoodlum, larrikin, ruffian; Mo-hock, -hawk; drawcansir, swashbuckler, Captain Boabdil, Sir Lucius O'Trigger, Thraso, Pistol, Parolles, Bombastes Furioso, Hector, Chrononhotonthologos; jingo; desperado, daredevil, fire-eater; fury &c. (*violent person*) 173; rowdy.

puppy &c. (*fop*) 854; prig; Sir Oracle, dogmatist, *doctrinaire*, stump orator, jack-in-office; saucebox, malapert, jackanapes, minx; bantamcock.

SECTION III.
SYMPATHETIC AFFECTIONS

1°. SOCIAL AFFECTIONS

888. Friendship.—N. friendship, amity; friendliness &c. *adj.*; brotherhood, fraternity, sodality, confraternity, sorosis, sisterhood; harmony &c. (*concord*) 714; peace &c. 721.

firm -, staunch -, intimate -, familiar -, bosom -, cordial -, tried -, devoted -, lasting -, fast -, sincere -, warm -, ardent- friendship.

cordiality, fraternization, *entente cordiale*, good understanding, *rapprochement*, sympathy, fellow-feeling, response, welcomeness; *camaraderie*.

affection &c. (*love*) 897; favouritism; goodwill &c. (*benevolence*) 906; partiality.

acquaintance, familiarity, intimacy, intercourse, fellowship, knowledge of; introduction.

V. be -friendly &c. *adj.*, - friends &c. 890, - acquainted with &c. *adj.*; know; have the ear of; keep company with &c. (*sociality*) 892; hold communication -, have dealings -, sympathize- with; have a leaning to; bear good will &c. (*benevolence*) 906; love &c. 897; make much of; befriend &c. (*aid*) 707; introduce to.

set one's horses together; hold out -, extend- the right hand of -friendship, - fellowship; become -friendly &c. *adj.*; make -friends &c. 890 with; break the ice, be introduced to; make -, pick -, scrape- acquaintance with; get into favour, gain the friendship of.

shake hands with, fraternize, embrace; receive with open arms, throw oneself into the arms of; meet half way, take in good part.

Adj. friendly; amic-able, -al; well affected, unhostile, neighbourly, brotherly, fraternal, sisterly, sympathetic, harmonious, hearty, cordial, warm-hearted, devoted.

friends -, well - at home -, hand in hand- with; on -good, - friendly, - amicable, - cordial, - familiar, - intimate--terms, - footing; on -speaking, - visiting- terms; in one's good -graces, - books.

acquainted, familiar, intimate, thick, hand and glove, hail fellow well met, free and easy; welcome.

Adv. amicably &c. *adj.*; with open arms; *sans cérémonie*; arm in arm.

889. Enmity.—N. enmity, hostility; unfriendliness &c. *adj.*; discord &c. 713.

alienation, estrangement; dislike &c. 867; hate &c. 898; antagonism.

heartburning; animosity &c. 900; malevolence &c. 907.

V. be -inimical &c. *adj.*; keep -, hold- at arm's length; be at loggerheads; bear malice &c. 907; fall out; take umbrage &c. 900; harden the heart, alienate, estrange.

Adj. inimical, unfriendly, hostile; at -enmity, - variance, - swords points, - daggers drawn, - open war with; up in arms against; in bad odour with.

on bad -, not on speaking- terms; cool; cold, -hearted; estranged, alienated, disaffected, irreconcilable.

890. Friend.—N. friend, - of one's bosom, intimate acquaintance, neighbour, well-wisher; *alter ego*; best -, bosom -, fast- friend; *amicus usque ad aras*; *fidus Achates*; *persona grata*.

favourer, *fautor*, patron, backer, Mæcenas; tutelary saint, good genius, advocate, partisan, sympathiser; ally; friend in need &c. (*auxiliary*) 711.

associate, compeer, comrade, mate, companion, *confrère, camarade, confidante*, colleague; old –, crony; side-kick; chum, buddy, bunkie, roommate, pal; play-fellow, -mate; classmate, schoolfellow; bed-fellow, -mate; maid of honour.

compatriot; fellow –, countryman, – townsman.

shop-, ship-, mess-mate; fellow –, boon –, pot- companion; co-partner.

Arcades ambo, Pylades and Orestes, Castor and Pollux, Nisus and Euryalus, Damon and Pythias, *par nobile fratrum*.

host, Amphitryon, Boniface; guest, visitor, frequenter, *habitué; protégé*.

891. Enemy.—N. enemy; antagonist, foeman; open –, bitter- enemy; opponent &c. 710; back friend.

public enemy, enemy to society, traitor, anarchist &c. 743.

Phr. every hand being against one.

892. Sociality.—N. soci-ality, -ability, -ableness &c. *adj.*; social intercourse; consociation; inter-course, -community; consort-, companion-, fellow-, comrade-ship; clubbism; *esprit de corps*.

conviviality; good -fellowship, – company, *camaraderie*; joviality, jollity, *savoir-vivre*, festivity, festive board, merry-making; loving cup; hospitality, heartiness; cheer.

welcome, -ness; greeting; hearty –, warm –, welcome- reception; urbanity &c. (*courtesy*) 894; intimacy, familiarity.

good –, jolly- fellow, good mixer, Rotarian; *bon enfant*.

social –, family- circle; circle of acquaintance, *coterie*, society, company.

social -gathering, – *réunion*; assembly &c. (*assemblage*) 72; party, entertainment, reception, *levée*, at home, *conversazione, soirée, matinée*, evening –, morning –, afternoon –, garden –, dinner –, tea –, cocktail- party; symposium, sing-song; kettle-, drum; *partie carrée*, dish of tea, *ridotto*, rout, house-

warming; ball, prom, hop, dance, *thé dansant*; festival &c. (*amusement*) 840; wedding breakfast; 'the feast of reason and the flow of soul.'

visit, -ing; round of visits; call, morning call; interview &c. (*interlocution*) 588; assignation; tryst, -ing place; appointment.

club &c. (*association*) 712.

V. be -sociable &c. *adj.*; know; be -acquainted &c. *adj.*; associate –, sort –, keep company –, walk hand in hand -with; eat off the same trencher, club together, consort, bear one company, join; make acquaintance with &c. (*friendship*) 888; make advances, fraternize, embrace; intercommunicate.

be –, feel –, make oneself- at home with; make free with; crack a bottle with; take pot luck with, receive hospitality, live at free quarters.

visit, pay a visit; interchange -visits, – cards; call -at, – upon; leave a card; drop in, look in; look one up, beat up one's quarters.

entertain; give a -party &c. *n.*; be at home, see one's friends, hang out, keep open house, do the honours; receive, – with open arms; welcome; give a warm reception &c. *n.* to; kill the fatted calf.

Adj. sociable, companionable, clubbable, clubby, conversable, cosy, cosey, chatty, conversational; homiletical.

convivial; fest-ive, -al; jovial, jolly, hospitable.

welcome, – as the roses in May; *fêté*, entertained.

free and easy, hail fellow well met, familiar, on visiting terms, acquainted.

social, neighbourly; international, cosmopolitan, gregarious.

Adv. *en famille*, in the family circle; *sans -façon, – cérémonie*, arm in arm.

893. Seclusion. Exclusion.—N. seclusion, privacy; retirement; concealment; reclusion, recess; snugness &c. *adj.*; delitescence; rustication, *rus in urbe*; solitude; solitariness &c. (*singleness*) 87; isolation; loneliness &c. *adj.*;

estrangement from the world, anchoritism, voluntary exile; aloofness.

cell, hermitage; convent &c. 1000; *sanctum sanctorum*; study, library, den; hide-out.

depopulation, desertion, desolation; wilderness &c. (*unproductive*) 169; howling wilderness; rotten borough, Old Sarum.

exclusion, excommunication, banishment, exile, ostracism, proscription; cut, – direct; dead cut.

inhospit-ality, -ableness &c. *adj.*; un-, dis-sociability; domesticity, Darby and Joan.

recluse, hermit, eremite, cenobite; anchor-et; -ite; Simon Stylites; Troglodyte, Timon of Athens, Santon, *solitaire*, ruralist, disciple of Zimmermann, closet cynic, Diogenes; outcast, Pariah, castaway, outsider, pilgarlic; wastrel, foundling, orphan.

V. be –, live- secluded &c. *adj.*; keep –, stand –, hold oneself- -aloof, – in the background; keep snug; shut oneself up; deny –, seclude- oneself; creep into a corner, rusticate, *aller planter ses choux*; retire, – from the world; hermetize, take the veil; abandon &c. 624.

cut, – dead; refuse to -associate with, – acknowledge; look cool –, turn one's back –, shut the door- upon; repel, blackball, excommunicate, exclude, exile, expatriate; banish, outlaw, maroon, ostracize, proscribe, cut off from, send to Coventry, keep at arm's length, draw a cordon round; boycott, blockade, lay an embargo on, isolate.

depopulate; dis-, un-people.

Adj. secluded, sequestered, retired, delitescent, private, bye; out of the -world, -way; in a backwater; 'the world forgetting by the world forgot.'

snug, domestic, stay-at-home.

unsociable; un-, dis-social; inhospitable, cynical, inconversable, unclubbable, *sauvage*, eremetic.

solitary; lone-ly, -some; isolated, single.

excluded, estranged; unfrequented; uninhabit-able, -ed; tenantless; un-tenanted, -occupied; abandoned; deserted, – in one's utmost need; unfriended; kith-, friend-, home-less; lorn, forlorn, desolate.

un-visited, -introduced, -invited, -welcome; under a cloud, left to shift for oneself, derelict, outcast, outside the gates.

banished &c. *v.*; under an embargo.

Phr. *noli me tangere.*

894. Courtesy.—N. courtesy; respect &c. 928; good -manners, – behaviour, – breeding; manners; politeness &c. *adj.*; *bienséance*, urbanity, comity, gentility; gentle –, breeding; polish, presence, cultivation, culture; civili-ty, -zation; amenity, suavity; good -temper, – humour; amiability, easy temper, complacency, soft tongue, mansuetude; condescension &c. (*humility*) 879; affability, complaisance, *prévenance*, amiability, gallantry, chivalry; pink of -politeness, – courtesy.

compliment; fair –, soft –, sweet-words; honeyed phrases, flattering remarks, ceremonial; salutation, reception, presentation, introduction, *accueil*, greeting, recognition; welcome, *abord*, respects, *devoir*, regards, remembrances; kind -regards, – remembrances; love, best love, duty; deference.

obeisance &c. (*reverence*) 928; bow, courtesy, curtsy, scrape, *salaam*, *kowtow*, bowing and scraping; kneeling; genuflexion &c. (*worship*) 990; obsequiousness &c. 886; capping, shaking hands &c. *v.*; grip of the hand, embrace, hug, squeeze, *accolade*, loving cup, *vin d'honneur*, pledge; love token &c. (*endearment*) 902; kiss, buss, salute.

mark of recognition, nod; 'nods and becks and wreathed smiles'; valediction &c. 293; condolence &c. 915.

V. be -courteous &c. *adj.*; show -courtesy &c. *n.*

mind one's P's and Q's, behave oneself, be all things to all men, conciliate, speak one fair, take in good part; make –, do- the amiable; look as if butter would not melt in one's mouth; mend one's manners.

receive, do the honours, usher, greet, hail, bid welcome; welcome, – with open arms; shake hands; hold out –, press –, squeeze- the hand; bid God speed; speed the parting guest; cheer, serenade.

salute; embrace &c. (*endearment*) 902; kiss, – hands; drink to, pledge, hob and nob; move to, nod to; smile upon.

uncover, cap; touch –, take off- the hat; doff the cap; pull the forelock; present arms; make way for; bow; make one's bow; scrape, curtsy, courtesy; bob a -curtsy, – courtesy; kneel; bow –, bend- the knee; salaam, *kowtow*.

visit, wait upon, present oneself, pay one's respects, pay a visit &c. (*sociability*) 892; dance attendance on &c. (*servility*) 886; pay attentions to; do homage to &c. (*respect*) 928.

prostrate oneself &c. (*worship*) 990.

give –, send- one's duty &c. *n.* to.

render -polite &c. *adj.*; polish, civilize, humanize.

Adj. courteous, polite, civil, mannerly, urbane; well-behaved, -mannered, -bred, -brought up, gently bred, of gentle -breeding, – manners, good-mannered, polished, civilized, cultivated; refined &c. (*taste*) 850; gentlemanlike &c. (*fashion*) 852; gallant, chivalrous, on one's good behaviour.

fine –, fair –, soft- spoken; honey-mouthed, -tongued; oily, unctuous, bland, suave; obliging, conciliatory, complaisant, complacent; obsequious &c. 886.

ingratiating, winning; gentle, mild; good-humoured, cordial, gracious, amiable, tactful, addressful, affiable, genial, friendly, familiar; neighbourly.

Adv. courteously &c. *adj.*; with a good grace; with -open, – outstretched-arms; *à bras ouverts*; *suaviter in modo*, in good humour.

Int. hail! welcome! well met! *ave!* all hail! good -day, – morning &c., – morrow! God speed! *pax vobiscum!* may your shadow never be less! *chin-chin!*

895. Discourtesy.—N. discourtesy; ill-breeding; ill -, bad -, ungainly- manners; insuavity; grouchiness; uncourteousness &c. *adj.*; tactlessness; rusticity, inurbanity; illiberality, incivility, displacency.

disrespect &c. 929; procacity, impudence; barbar-ism, -ity; misbehaviour, brutality, blackguardism, conduct unbecoming a gentleman, *grossièreté, brusquerie*; vulgarity &c. 851.

churlishness &c. *adj.*; spinosity, perversity; moroseness &c. (*sullenness*) 901a.

bad-, ill-temper; sternness &c. *adj.*; austerity; moodishness, captiousness &c. 901; cynicism; tartness &c. *adj.*; acrimony, acerbity, virulence, asperity.

scowl, black looks, frown; short answer, rebuff; hard words, contumely; unparliamentary language, personality.

bear, bruin, brute, grouch, blackguard, beast; unlicked cub; frump, cross-patch; saucebox &c. 887.

V. be -rude &c. *adj.*; insult &c. 929; treat with discourtesy; take a name in vain; make -bold, – free- with; take a liberty; stare out of countenance, ogle, point at, put to the blush.

cut; turn -one's back upon, – on one's heel; give the cold shoulder; keep at a -distance, – arm's length; look -cool, – coldly, – black- upon; show the door to, send away with a flea in the ear.

lose one's temper &c. (*resentment*) 900; sulk &c. 901a; frown, scowl, glower, pout; snap, snarl, growl.

render -rude &c. *adj.*; brut-alize, -ify.

Adj. dis-, un-courteous; uncourtly; ill-bred, -mannered, -behaved, -conditioned; unbred; unmanner-ly, -ed; im-, un-polite; un-polished, -civilized, -genteel; ungentleman-like, -ly; un-ladylike; blackguard; vulgar &c. 851; dedecorous; foul-mouthed, -spoken; abusive.

un-civil, -gracious, -ceremonious; cool; pert, forward, obtrusive, impudent, rude, saucy, precocious; insolent &c. 885.

repulsive; un-complaisant, -accom-
modating, -neighbourly, -gallant; inaffable; un-gentle, -gainly; rough, rugged,
bluff, blunt, gruff; churl- boor-, bear-
ish; brutal, *brusque*; stern, harsh, austere; cavalier.

tart, sour, crabbed, sharp, short,
trenchant, sarcastic, crusty, biting,
caustic, virulent, bitter, acrimonious,
venomous, contumelious; snarling &c,
v.; surly, – as a bear; perverse; grim.

sullen &c. 901*a*; peevish &c. (*irascible*) 901.

Adv. discourteously &c. *adj*.; with
-discourtesy &c. *n*., – a bad grace.

896. Congratulations.—N. con-,
gratulation; felicitation; salute &c. 894;
condolence &c. 915; compliments of the
season; good –, best- wishes.

V. con-, gratulate; felicitate, compliment; give –, wish one- joy; tender –,
offer- one's congratulations; wish -many
happy returns of the day, – a merry
Christmas and a happy new year.

congratulate oneself &c. (*rejoice*) 838.

Adj. con-, gratulatory.

897. Love.—N. love; fondness &c.
adj.; liking; inclination &c. (*desire*) 865;
regard, dilection, admiration, fancy.

affection, sympathy, fellow-feeling;
tenderness &c. *adj*.; heart, brotherly
love; benevolence &c. 906; attachment.

yearning, tender passion, *affaire de
coeur*, *amour*, gallantry, passion, flame,
devotion, fervour, enthusiasm, transport
of love, rapture, enchantment, infatuation, adoration, idolatry.

narcissim, Œdipus complex, Electra
complex.

Cupid, Venus, Eros; myrtle; true lover's knot; love -token, – suit, – affair, –
tale, – story; the old story, plighted love;
courtship &c. 902; *amourette*.

maternal love.

attractiveness, charm; popularity; favourite &c. 899.

lover, suitor, follower, admirer, adorer, wooer, amoret, beau, sweetheart, in-
amorato, swain, young man, flame, love,
truelove; leman, Lothario, gallant, par-

amour, *amoroso*, *cavaliere servente*,
captive, *cicisbeo*; *caro sposo*, Don Juan,
sheik, ladies' man, squire of dames,
Knave of Hearts.

inamorata, lady-love, idol, darling,
duck, Dulcinea, angel, goddess, *cara
sposa*; mistress.

betrothed, affianced, *fiancée*.

flirt, *coquette*; amorette; pair of turtle
doves; abode of love, *agapemone*.

V. love, like, affect, fancy, care for,
take an interest in, be partial to, sympathize with; be -in love &c. *adj.*- with;
have –, entertain –, harbour –, cherish-
a -love &c. *n*. for; regard, revere; take
to, bear love to, be wedded to; set one's
affections on; make much of, feast one's
eyes on; hold dear, prize, treasure; hug,
cling to, cherish, pet, caress &c. 902.

burn; adore, idolize, love to distraction, *aimer eperdument*; dote -on, –
upon.

take a fancy to, fall for, be stuck on,
look sweet upon; become -enamoured
&c. *adj*.; fall in love with, lose one's
heart; desire &c. 865.

excite love; win –, gain–, secure –,
engage- the -love, – affections, – heart;
take the fancy of; have a place in –, wind
round- the heart; attract, attach, endear,
charm, fascinate, captivate, bewitch, seduce, enamour, enrapture, turn the head.

get into favour; ingratiate –, insinuate
–, worm- oneself; propitiate, curry favour with, pay one's court to, make a
date with, *faire l'aimable*, set one's cap
at, flirt, coquet.

Adv. loving &c. *v*.; fond of; taken –,
struck- with; smitten, bitten; attached to,
wedded to; enamoured; charmed &c. *v*.;
in love; love-sick; over head and ears in
love.

affectionate, tender, sweet upon,
sympathetic, loving, fond, amorous,
amatory; erotic, uxurious, ardent, passionate, rapturous, devoted, motherly.

loved &c. *v*.; beloved; well -, dearly-
beloved; dear, precious, darling, pet,
little; favourite, popular.

congenial; to –, after- one's -mind, –
taste, – fancy, –own heart.

in one's good -graces &c. (*friendly*)
888; dear as the apple of one's eye, nearest to one's heart.

lovable, adorable; lovely, sweet; attractive, seductive, winning; charming, engaging, interesting, enchanting, captivating, fascinating, intriguing, bewitching; amiable, like an angel, angelic, seraphic.

898. Hate.—N. hate, hatred, vials of hate; Hymn of Hate.

dis-affection, -favour; alienation, estrangement, coolness; enmity &c. 889; animosity &c. 900.

umbrage, pique, grudge; dudgeon, spleen; bitterness, - of feeling; ill -, bad- blood; acrimony; malice &c. 907; implacability &c.(*revenge*) 919.

repugnance &c. (*dislike*) 867; odium, unpopularity; loathing, detestation, antipathy; object of -hatred, - execration; abomination, aversion, *bête noire*; enemy &c. 891; bitter pill; source of annoyance &c. 830.

V. hate, detest, abominate, abhor, loathe; recoil -, shudder- at; shrink from, view with horror, hold in abomination, revolt against, execrate; scowl &c. 895; disrelish &c. (*dislike*) 867.

owe a grudge; bear -spleen, - a grudge, - malice &c. (*malevolence*) 907; conceive an aversion to.

excite -, provoke- hatred &c. *n.*; be -hateful &c. *adj.*; stink in the nostrils; estrange, alienate, repel, set against, sow dissension, set by the ears, envenom, incense, irritate, rile, ruffle, vex; horrify &c. 830.

Adj. hating &c. *v.*; abhorrent; averse from &c. (*disliking*) 867; set against.

bitter &c. (*acrimonious*) 895; implacable &c. (*revengeful*) 919.

un-loved, -beloved, -lamented, -deplored, -mourned, -cared for, -endured, -valued; disliked &c. 867.

crossed in love, forsaken, rejected, love-lorn, jilted.

obnoxious, hateful, odious, abominable, repulsive, offensive, shocking; disgusting &c. (*disagreeable*) 830.

invidious, spiteful; malicious &c. 907. insulting, irritating, provoking.

[Mutual hate] at -daggers drawn, - swords points; not on speaking terms &c. (*enmity*) 889.

Phr. no love lost between.

899. Favourite.—N. favourite, pet, cosset, minion, idol, jewel, spoiled child, *enfant gâté*; led captain; crony; fondling; apple of one's eye, man after one's own heart; *persona grata*.

love, dear, darling, duck, honey, jewel; mopsey, moppet; sweetheart &c. (*love*) 897.

general -, universal- favourite; idol of the people; matinée idol, movie -, radio- star.

900. Resentment.—N. resentment, displeasure, animosity, anger, wrath, indignation; vexation, exasperation, bitter resentment, wrathful indignation.

pique, umbrage, huff, miff, soreness, dudgeon, acerbity, virulence, bitterness, acrimony, asperity, spleen, gall; heartburning, -swelling; rankling.

ill -, bad- -humour, - temper; irascibility &c. 901; ill blood &c. (*hate*) 898; revenge &c. 919.

excitement, irritation; warmth, bile, choler, ire, fume, pucker, dander, ferment, ebullition; towering -passion, - rage, *acharnement*, angry mood, taking, pet, tiff, passion, fit, tantrums.

burst, explosion, paroxysm, storm, rage, fury, desperation; violence &c. 173; fire and fury; vials of wrath; gnashing of teeth, hot blood, high words.

scowl &c. 895; sulks &c. 901*a*.

[Cause of umbrage] affront, provocation, offence; indignity &c. (*insult*) 929; grudge, crow to pluck, sore subject; red rag to a bull; *casus belli*.

Furies, Erinys, Eumenides, Alecto, Megæra, Tisiphone.

buffet, slap in the face, box on the ear, rap on the knuckles.

V. resent; take -amiss, - ill, - to heart, - offence, - umbrage, - huff, - exception; take in -ill part, - bad part,

– dudgeon; *ne pas entendre raillerie*; breathe revenge, cut up rough.

fly –, fall – get- into a -rage, – passion; bridle –, bristle – froth –, fire –, flare- up; open –, pour out- the vials of one's wrath.

pout, knit the brow, frown, scowl, lower, snarl, growl, gnarl, gnash, snap; redden, colour; look -black, – black as thunder, – daggers; bite one's thumb; show –, grind- one's teeth; champ the bit.

chafe, mantle, fume, kindle, fly out, take fire; boil, – over; boil with -indignation, – rage; rage, storm, foam; vent one's -rage, – spleen; lose one's temper, stand on one's hind legs, stamp the foot, kick up a row, fly off the handle, cut up rough; stamp –, quiver –, swell –, foam- with rage; burst with anger; raise Cain, breathe fire and fury.

have a fling at; bear malice &c. (*revenge*) 919.

cause –, raise- anger; affront, offend; give -offence, – umbrage; anger; hurt the feelings; insult, discompose, fret, ruffle, nettle, heckle, huff, pique; excite &c. 824; irritate, stir the blood, stir up bile; sting, – to the quick; rile, provoke, chafe, wound, incense, inflame, enrge, aggravate, add fuel to the flame, fan into a flame, widen the breach, envenom, embitter, exasperate, infuriate, kindle wrath; stick in one's gizzard; rankle &c. 919.

put out of humour; put one's -monkey, – back- up; set –, get- one's back up; raise one's -gorge, – dander, – choler; work up into a passion; make -one's blood boil, – the ears tingle; throw into a ferment, madden, drive one mad; lash into -fury, – madness; fool to the top of one's bent; set by the ears.

bring a hornet's nest about one's ears.

Adj. angry, wrath, irate; ire-, wrathful; cross &c. (*irascible*) 901; sulky &c. 901*a*; bitter, virulent; acrimonious &c. (*discourteous*) &c. 895; violent &c. 173.

warm, burning; boiling, – over; fuming, raging; foaming, – at the mouth; convulsed with rage.

offended &c. *v.*; waxy, *acharné*; wrought, worked up; indignant, hurt, sore, peeved; set against.

fierce, wild, rageful, furious, mad with rage, fiery, infuriate, rabid, savage; relentless &c. 919.

flushed with -anger, – rage; in a -huff, – stew, – fume, – pucker, – passion, – rage, – fury; on one's high ropes, up in arms; in high dudgeon.

Adv. angrily &c. *adj.*; in the height of passion; in the heat of -passion, – the moment.

Int. *tantœne animis cœlestibus irœ!* marry come up! zounds! 'sdeath!

Phr. one's -blood, – back, – monkey-being up; *fervens difficili bile jecur*; the gorge rising, eyes flashing fire; the blood -rising, – boiling; *hœret lateri lethalis arundo*.

901. Irascibility.—N. irascibility, temper; crossness &c. *adj.*; susceptibility, procacity, petulance, irritability, tartness, acerbity, protervity; pugnacity &c. (*contentiousness*) 720.

excitability &c. 825; bad -, fiery -, crooked -, irritable &c. *adj.*- temper; *genus irritabile*, hot blood.

ill humour &c. (*sullenness*) 901*a*; asperity &c., churlishness &c. (*discourtesy*) 895.

huff &c. (resentment) 900; a word and a blow.

Sir Fretful Plagiary; brabbler, Tartar; shrew, vixen, virago, termagant, dragon, scold, Xanthippe; porcupine; spitfire; fire-eater &c. (*blusterer*) 887; fury &c. (*violent person*) 173.

V. be -irascible &c. *adj.*; have a -temper &c. *n.*, – devil in one; fire up &c. (*be angry*) 900.

Adj. irascible; bad-, ill-tempered; irritable, susceptible; excitable &c. 825; thin-skinned &c. (*sensitive*) 822; fretful, fidgety; on the fret.

hasty, over-hasty, quick, warm, hot, testy, touchy, techy, tetchy; like -touchwood, – tinder; huffy; pet-tish, -ulant; waspish, snapp-y, -ish, peppery, fiery, passionate, choleric, shrewish, 'sudden and quick in quarrel.'

querulous, captious, mood-y, -ish; quarrelsome, contentious, disputatious; pugnacious &c. (*bellicose*) 720; cantankerous, exceptious; restive &c. (*perverse*) 901a; churlish &c. (*discourteous*) 895.

cross, – as -crabs, – two sticks, – a cat, – a dog, – the tongs; like a bear with a sore head; fractious, peevish, *acariâtre*.

in a bad temper; sulky &c. 901a; angry &c. 900.

resent-ful, -ive; vindictive &c. 919.

Int. pish!

901a. Sullenness.—N. sullenness &c. *adj.*; morosity, spleen; churlishness &c. (*discourtesy*) 895; irascibility &c. 901.

moodiness &c. *adj.*; perversity; obstinacy &c. 606; torvity, spinosity; crabbedness &c. *adj.*

ill -, bad- -temper, – humour; sulks, dudgeon, mumps, doleful dumps, doldrums, fit of the sulks, *bouderie*, black looks, scowl; huff &c. (*resentment*) 900.

V. be -sullen &c. *adj.*; sulk; frown, scowl, lower, glower, grouse, grouch, crab, gloam, pout, have a hang-dog look, glout.

Adj. sullen, sulky; ill-tempered, -humoured, -affected, -disposed; in -an ill, – a bad, – a shocking- -temper, – humour; out of -temper, – humour; knaggy, torvous, crusty, crabbed; sore as a boil; surly &c. (*discourteous*) 895.

moody; spleen-ish, -ly; splenetic, cankered.

cross, -grained; perverse, wayward, humoursome; restive; cantankerous, refractory, intractable, exceptious, sinistrous, deaf to reason, unaccommodating, rusty, crust, forward.

dogged &c. (*stubborn*) 606.

grumpy, glum, grim, grum, morose, frumpish; in the -sulks &c. *n.*; out of sorts; scowl-, glower-, growl-ing.

peevish &c. (*irascible*) 901.

902. [Expression of affection or love.] **Endearment.—N.** endearment, caress;

blandish-, blandi-ment; *épanchement*, fondling, billing and cooing, dalliance.

embrace, salute, kiss, buss, smack, osculation, deosculation; amorous glances; ogle, side glance, sheep's eyes.

courtship, wooing, suit, addresses, the soft impeachment; love-making; an affair; serenading; caterwauling.

flirting &c. *v.*; flirtation, gallantry; coquetry, spooning.

true lover's knot, plighted love, engagement, betrothal; love -tale, – token, – letter; *billet-doux*, valentine.

honeymoon; Strephon and Chloe, 'Arry and 'Arriet.

V. caress, fondle, pet, dandle, nurse; pat, – on the -head, – cheek; chuck under the chin, smile upon, coax, wheedle, cosset, coddle, cocker; make -of, – much of, pamper; cherish, foster, kill with kindness.

clasp, hug, cuddle; fold -, strain- in one's arms; nestle, nuzzle, neck, embrace, kiss, buss, smack, blow a kiss; salute &c. (*courtesy*) 894.

bill and coo, spoon, toy, dally, flirt, coquet; galli-, gala-vant; philander; make love; pay one's -court, – addresses, – attentions- to; serenade; court, woo; set one's cap at; be -, look- sweet upon; ogle, cast sheep's eyes upon; *faire les yeux doux*.

fall in love with, win the affections &c. (*love*) 897; die for.

propose; make -, have- an offer; pop the question; plight one's -troth, – faith; become -engaged, – betrothed.

Adj. caressing &c. *v.*; 'sighing like furnace'; love-sick, spoony.

caressed &c. *v.*

903. Marriage.—N. marriage, matrimony, wedlock, union, intermarriage, *vinculum matrimonii*, nuptial tie, knot.

married state, coverture, bed, cohabitation.

match; betrothment &c. (*promise*) 768; wedding, nuptials, Hymen, bridal; e-, spousals; leading to the altar &c. *v.*; nuptial benediction, *epithalamium*.

torch -, temple- of Hymen; hymeneal altar; honeymoon.

bride, bridegroom; brides-maid, -man.

best -, grooms-man, page, usher.

married -man, - woman, - couple; neogamist, Benedick, partner, spouse, mate, yokemate; husband, man, consort, baron; old -, good- man; wife of one's bosom; help-meet, -mate, rib, better half, grey mare, old woman, good wife; feme, - coverte; squaw, lady; matron, -age, -hood; man and wife; wedded pair, Darby and Joan.

affinity, soul-mate.

mono-, bi-, di-, deutero-, tri-, polygamy; mormonism; poly-andry; Turk, Bluebeard.

unlawful -, left-handed -, companionate -, morganatic -, ill-assorted-marriage; *mésalliance*; *mariage de convenance*; an affair.

match-maker, marriage broker, matrimonial agent.

V. marry, wive, take to oneself a wife; be -married, - spliced; go -, pair- off; wed, espouse, lead to the hymeneal altar, take 'for better, for worse,' give one's hand to, bestow one's hand upon; remarry; intermarry.

marry, join, handfast; couple &c. (*unite*) 43; tie the nuptial knot; give -away, - in marriage; affy, affiance; betroth &c. (*promise*) 768; publish -, bid-the banns; be asked in church.

Adj. married &c. *v.*; one, - bone and one flesh.

marriageable, nubile.

engaged, betrothed, affianced.

matrimonial, marital, conjugal, connubial, wedded; nuptial, hymeneal, spousal, bridal.

Phr. the grey mare the better horse.

904. Celibacy.—N. celibacy, singleness, single blessedness; bachelor-hood, -ship; miso-gamy, -gyny.

virginity, *pucelage*; maiden-hood, -head.

unmarried man, bachelor, Cœlebs,

agamist, old bachelor; miso-gamist, -gynist; celibate.

unmarried woman, spinster; maid, -en; virgin, *feme sole*, old maid; bachelor girl; nun &c.

V. live single; keep bachelor hall.

Adj. un-married, -wedded; wife-, spouse-less; single, virgin, celibate.

905. Divorce.—N. divorce, -ment; separation; judicial separation, separate maintenance; *separatio a -mensâ et thoro, - vinculo matrimonii*.

widowhood, viduage, viduity, weeds.

widow, -er; relict; dowager; *divorcée*; cuckold.

V. live -separately, - apart; separate, divorce, disespouse, put away; wear the horns.

2° DIFFUSIVE SYMPATHETIC AFFECTIONS

906. Benevolence. —N. benevolence, Christian charity; God's -love, - grace; good-will; philanthropy &c. 910; unselfishness &c. 942.

good -nature, - feeling, - wishes; kind-, kindli-ness &c. *adj.*; lovingkindness, benignity, brotherly love, charity, humanity, fellow-feeling, sympathy; goodness -, warmth- of heart; *bonhomie*; kind-heartedness; amiability, milk of human kindness, tenderness; love &c. 897; friendship &c. 888.

toleration, consideration, generosity; mercy &c. (*pity*) 914.

charitableness &c. *adj.*; bounty, alms-giving; good works, beneficence, the luxury of doing good.

acts of kindness, a good turn; good -, kind-offices, - treatment.

good Samaritan, sympathizer, well-wisher, philanthropist, *bon enfant*; altruist.

V. be -benevolent &c. *adj.*; have one's heart in the right place, bear good will; wish -well, - God speed; view -, regard- with an eye of favour; take in good part; take –, feel- an interest in; be –, feel- interested- in; sympathize with, feel for; fraternize &c. (*be friendly*) 888.

enter into the feelings of others, do as you would be done by, meet half-way.

treat well; give comfort, smooth the bed of death; do -good, – a good turn; benefit &c. (*goodness*) 648; render a service, be of use; aid &c. 707.

Adj. benevolent; kind, -ly; well-meaning; amiable; obliging, accommodating, indulgent, considerate, gracious, complacent, good-humoured.

warm-, soft-, kind-, tender-, large-, broad-hearted; merciful &c. 914; philanthropic &c. 910; charitable, beneficent, humane, benign, benignant; bounteous, -iful &c. 816.

good-, well-natured; spleenless; sympath-izing, -etic; complaisant &c. (*courteous*) 894; kindly, well-meant, -intentioned.

fatherly, motherly, brotherly, sisterly; pat-, mat-, frat-ernal; friendly &c. 888.

Adv. with -a good intention, – the best intentions.

Int. God speed! much good may it do!

907. Malevolence.—N. malevolence; bad intent, -ion; un-, dis-kindness; ill -nature, – will, – blood; bad blood; enmity &c. 889; hate &c. 898; malignity; malice, – aforethought, – prepense; maliciousness &c. *adj.*; spite, despite, resentment &c. 900.

uncharitableness &c. *adj.*; incompassionateness &c. 914a; gall, venom, rancour, rankling, virulence, mordacity, acerbity; churlishness &c. (*discourtesy*) 895.

hardness of heart, heart of stone, obduracy; cruelty; cruelness &c. *adj.*; brutality, savagery; fer-ity, -ocity; barbarity, inhumanity, immanity, truculence, ruffianism; evil eye, cloven -foot, – hoof; Inquisition; torture.

ill –, bad- turn; affront &c. (*disrespect*) 929; outrage, atrocity; ill usage; intolerance, bigotry, persecution; tender mercies [ironical]; 'unkindest cut of all.'

V. be -malevolent &c. *adj.*; bear –,

harbour-spleen, – a grudge, – malice; betray –, show- the cloven foot.

hurt &c. (*physical pain*) 378; annoy &c. 830; injure, harm, wrong; do -harm, – an ill office- to; outrage; disoblige, malign, plant a thorn in the breast.

molest, worry, harass, haunt, harry, bait, tease, throw stones at; play the devil with; hunt down, dragoon, hound; persecute, oppress, grind; maltreat; ill-treat, -use.

wreak one's malice on, do one's worst, break a butterfly on the wheel; dip –, imbrue- one's hands in blood; have no mercy &c. 914a.

Adj. male-, unbene-volent; unbenign; ill-disposed, -intentioned, -natured, -conditioned, -contrived; evil-minded, -disposed.

malicious; malign, -ant; rancorous; de-, spiteful; mordacious, caustic, bitter, envenomed, acrimonious, virulent; un-amiable, -charitable; maleficent, venomous, grinding, galling.

harsh, disobliging; un-kind, -friendly, -gracious; treacherous; inofficious; invidious; uncandid; churlish &c. (*uncourteous*) 895; surly, sullen &c. 901a.

cold, -blooded, -hearted; hard-, flint-, marble-, stony-hearted; hard of heart, unnatural; ruthless &c. (*unmerciful*) 914a; relentless &c. (*revengeful*) 919.

cruel; brut-al, -ish; savage, – as a -bear, – tiger; ferine, feral, ferocious; inhuman; barbarous, fell, untamed, tameless, truculent, incendiary; bloodthirsty &c. (*murderous*) 361; atrocious.

fiend-ish, -like; demoniacal; diabolic, -al; devilish, infernal, hellish, Satanic.

Adv. malevolently &c. *adj.*; with -bad intent &c. *n.*

908. Malediction.—N. malediction, malison, curse, imprecation, denunciation, execration, anathema, ban, proscription, excommunication, commination, thunders of the Vatican, fulmination, *maranatha*, aspersion, vilification, vituperation, scurrility.

abuse; foul –, bad –, strong –,

unparliamentary- language, Limehouse;
Billingsgate, sauce, evil speaking; cursing
&c. *v.*; profane swearing, oath.

threat &c. 909; more bark than bite;
invective &c. (*disapprobation*) 932.

V. curse, accurse, imprecate, damn,
swear at; slang; curse with bell, book
and candle; invoke -, call down- curses
on the head of; devote to destruction.

execrate, beshrew, scold; anathematize &c. (*censure*) 932; hold up to execration, denounce, proscribe, excommunicate, fulminate, thunder against;
threaten &c. 909; curse up hill and down
dale.

curse and swear; swear, - like a
trooper; fall a cursing, rap out an oath,
damn, cuss.

Adj. curs-ing, -ed &c. *v.*; maledicto-
ry.

Int. woe to! beshrew! *ruat cœlum!* ill
-, woe- betide! confusion seize! damn!
confound! blast! curse! devil take! hang!
out with! a plague -, out- upon! aroynt!
honi soit!

Phr. *delenda est Carthago.*

909. Threat.—N. threat, menace; defiance &c. 715; abuse, minacity, intimidation; fulmination; commination &c.
(*curse*) 908; gathering clouds &c.
(*warning*) 668.

V. threat, -en; menace; snarl, growl,
gnarl, mutter, bark, bully.

defy &c.715; intimidate &c. 860;
keep -, hold up -, hold out- *in terrorem*;
shake -, double -, clinch- the fist at;
thunder, talk big, fulminate, use big
words, bluster, look daggers.

Adj. threatening, menacing; minatory, -cious; comminatory, abusive; *in
terrorem*; ominous &c. (*predicting*) 511;
defiant &c. 715; under the ban.

Int. *væ victis!* at your peril! do your
worst!

910. Philanthropy.—N. philanthropy; altruism, humanit-y, -arianism; universal benevolence; *deliciæ humani generis*; cosmopolitanism, utilitarianism,
the greatest happiness of the greatest
number, social science, sociology.

common weal, public welfare, socialism, communism.

patriotism, civism, nationality, love of
country, *amor patriæ*, public spirit.

chivalry, knight errantry; generosity
&c. 942.

philanthropist, altruist &c. 906; uti-
itarian, Benthamite, socialist, communist, cosmopolite, citizen of the world,
amicus humani generis; knight errant;
patriot.

Adj. philanthropic, altruistic, humanitarian, utilitarian, cosmopolitan; pub-
lic-spirited, patriotic; humane, large-
hearted &c. (*benevolent*) 906; chival-ric,
-rous, generous &c. 942.

Adv. pro -bono publico, - aris et focis.

Phr. *'humani nihil a me alienum
puto.'*

911. Misanthropy.—N. misanthropy,
incivism; egotism &c.(*selfishness*) 943;
moroseness &c. 901*a*; cynicism; defeatism.

misanthrope, misanthropist, egotist,
cynic, man-hater, Timon, Diogenes.

woman-hater, misogynist.

Adj. misanthropic, antisocial, unpatriotic; egotistical &c. (*selfish*) 943; morose &c. 901*a*.

912. Benefactor.—N. benefactor,
saviour, good genius, tutelary saint, patron, guardian angel, fairy godmother,
good Samaritan; *pater patriæ*; salt of the
earth &c. (*good man*) 948; auxiliary &c.
711.

**913. [Maleficent being.] Evil-doer.—
N.** evil-doer, - worker; wrong doer &c.
949; mischief maker, marplot; oppressor, tyrant, firebrand, incendiary, pyromaniac, anarchist, destroyer, Hun,
Boche, Vandal, iconoclast; communist;
terrorist, *apache*, gunman, gangster,
racketeer.

savage, brute, ruffian, barbarian,
semi-barbarian, caitiff, desperado; Mo-
hock, -hawk; bludgeon man, bully,
rough, hooligan, larrikin, dangerous
classes, ugly customer; thief &c. 792.

cockatrice, scorpion, hornet; viper, adder; snake, – in the grass; serpent, cobra, asp, rattlesnake, anaconda; canker-, wire-worm; locust, Colorado beetle; torpedo; bane &c. 663.

cannibal; Anthropophag-us, -ist; bloodsucker, vampire, ogre, ghoul, gorilla; vulture; gyr-, ger-falcon.

wild beast, tiger, hyæna, butcher, hangman; cut-throat &c. (*killer*) 361; blood-, sleuth-, hell-hound.

hag, hellhag, beldam, Jezebel.

monster; fiend &c. (*demon*) 980; homicidal maniac, devil incarnate, demon in human shape; Frankenstein's monster.

harpy, siren, vampire; Furies, Eumenides &c. 900.

Attila, scourge of the human race.

Phr. *fœnum habet in cornu.*

3°. SPECIAL SYMPATHETIC AFFECTIONS

914. Pity.—N. pity, compassion, commiseration; bowels, – of compassion; condolence &c. 915; sympathy, fellow-feeling, tenderness, yearning, forbearance, humanity, mercy, clemency, exorability; leniency &c. (*lenity*) 740; charity, ruth, long-suffering.

melting mood; *argumentum ad misericordiam*; quarter, grace, *locus pœnitentiæ.*

sympathizer, champion, partisan.

V. pity; have –, show –, take- pity &c. *n.*; commiserate, compassionate; condole &c. 915; sympathize; feel –, be sorry –, yearn- for; weep, melt, thaw, enter into the feelings of.

forbear, relent, relax, give quarter, wipe the tears, *parcere subjectis*, give a *coup de grâce*, put out of one's misery; be cruel to be kind.

raise –, excite- pity &c. *n.*; touch, soften; melt, – the heart; appeal to one's better feelings; propitiate, disarm.

ask for -mercy &c. *n.*; supplicate &c.

(*request*) 765; cry for quarter, beg one's life, kneel; deprecate.

Adj. pitying &c. *v.*; pitiful, compassionate, sympathetic, touched.

merciful, clement, ruthful; humane; humanitarian &c. (*philanthropic*) 910; tender, – hearted, – as a chicken; soft, – hearted; unhardened; lenient &c. 740; exorable, forbearing; melting &c. *v.*; weak.

Int. for pity's sake! mercy! have –, cry you- mercy! God help you! poor -thing, – dear, – fellow! woe betide! *quis talia fando temperet a lachrymis!*

Phr. one's heart bleeding for; *haud ignara mali miseris succurrere disco.*

914a. Pitilessness.—N. pitilessness &c. *adj.*; inclemency; inexorability, hardness of heart; inflexibility; severity &c. 739; malevolence &c. 907.

V. have no –, shut the gates of- mercy &c. 914; give no quarter.

Adj. piti-, merci-, ruth-, bowel-less; unpitying, unmerciful, inclement; in-, un-compassionate; inexorable, inflexible; harsh &c. 739; cruel &c. 907; unrelenting &c. 919.

915. Condolence.—N. condolence; lamentation &c. 839; sympathy, consolation.

V. condole with, console, sympathize &c. 914, share one's misery; feel for; express –, testify- pity; afford –, supply-consolation; lament &c. 839- with; send one's condolences.

4°. RETROSPECTIVE SYMPATHETIC AFFECTIONS

916. Gratitude.—N. gratitude, thankfulness, gratefulness, feeling of obligation.

acknowledgment, recognition thanksgiving, giving thanks.

thanks, praise, benediction; pæan; *Te Deum* &c. (*worship*) 990; grace, – before, – after- meat; thank-offering. requital.

V. be -grateful &c. *adj.*; thank; give
-, render -, return -, offer -, tender-
thanks &c. *n.*; acknowledge, requite.

feel -, be -, lie- under an obligation;
savoir gré; not look a gift horse in the
mouth; never forget, overflow with gratitude; thank -, bless- one's stars; fall on
one's knees.

Adj. grateful, thankful, obliged, beholden, indebted to, under obligation.

Int. thanks! many thanks! gramercy!
much obliged! thank you! thank Heaven!
Heaven be praised!

917. Ingratitude.—N. ingratitude,
thanklessness, oblivion of benefits; un-
thankfulness.

'benefits forgot'; thankless -task, -
office.

V. be -ungrateful &c. *adj.*; forget
benefits; look a gift horse in the mouth.

Adj. un-grateful, -mindful, -thankful;
thankless, ingrate, wanting in gratitude,
insensible of benefits.

forgotten; un-acknowledged, -thanked,
-requited, -rewarded; ill-requited.

Int. thank you for nothing! *'et tu
Brute!'*

918. Forgiveness.—N. forgiveness,
pardon, condonation, grace, remission,
absolution, amnesty, oblivion; indulgence; reprieve.

conciliation; reconciliation &c. (*pacification*) 723; propitiation.

excuse, exoneration, quittance, release, indemnity; bill -, act -, covenant
-, deed- of indemnity; exculpation &c.
(*acquittal*) 970.

longanimity, placability, forbearance;
amantium iræ; *locus pœnitentiæ*.

V. forgive, - and forget; pardon, condone, think no more of, let bygones be
bygones, shake hands; forget an injury,
bury the hatchet; clean the slate.

excuse, pass over, overlook; wink at
&c. (*neglect*) 460; bear with; allow -,
make allowances- for; let one down
easily, not be too hard upon, pocket
the affront; blot out one's transgression.

let off, remit, absolve, give absolution, reprieve; acquit &c. 970.

beg -, ask -, implore: pardon &c. *n.*;
conciliate, propitiate, placate; make up
a quarrel &c. (*pacify*) 723; let the wound
heal.

Adj. forgiving, placable, conciliatory.

forgiven &c. *v.*; un-resented, -avenged,
-revenged.

Adv. cry you mercy.

Phr. *veniam petimusque damusque vicissim*; more in sorrow than in anger.

919. Revenge.—N. revenge, -ment;
vengeance; avenge-ment, -ance; sweet
revenge, *vendetta*, death-feud, eye for an
eye, blood for blood, a Roland for an
Oliver; retaliation &c. 718; day of reckoning.

rancour, vindictiveness, implacability; malevolence &c. 907; ruthlessness
&c. 914*a*.

avenger, vindicator, Nemesis, Eumenides.

V. re-, a-venge; take -, have one's-
revenge; breathe-revenge, - vengeance;
wreak one's -vengeance, - anger; give
no quarter.

have -accounts to settle, - a crow to
pluck, - a rod in pickle; pay off old
scores.

keep the wound green; harbour
-revenge, - vindictive feeling; bear malice; rankle, - in the breast; have at one's
mercy.

Adj. revenge-, venge-ful; vindictive,
rancorous; pitiless &c. 914*a*; ruthless,
rigorous, avenging, retaliative.

unforgiving, unrelenting; inexorable,
stony-hearted, implacable; relent-, re-
morse-less.

æternum servans sub pectore vulnus;
rankling, immitigable.

Phr. *manet -cicatrix, - altâ mente repostum.*

revenge is sweet.

920. Jealousy.—N. jealous-y, -ness;
jaundiced eye, heartburning; green-eyed
monster; yellows; Juno.

V. be -jealous &c. *adj.*; view with
-jealousy, - a jealous eye.

Adj. jealous, - as a Barbary pigeon; jaundiced, yellow-eyed, horn-mad.

921. Envy.—N. envy; enviousness &c. *adj*; rivalry; *jalousie de métier*.

V. envy, covet, lust after, crave, burst with envy, regard with envious eyes.

Adj. envious, invidious, covetous; *alieni appentens*.

Section IV. MORAL AFFECTIONS

1°. Moral Obligations

922. Right.—N. right; what -ought to, - should- be; fitness &c. *adj*.; *summum jus*.

justice, equity; equitableness &c. *adj*.; propriety; fair play, impartiality, measure for measure, give and take, *lex talionis*, square deal.

Astræa, Nemesis, Themis.

scales of justice, even-handed justice, retributive justice, *suum cuique*; clear stage -, fair field- and no favour; Queensberry rules.

morals &c. (*duty*) 926; law &c. 963; honour &c. (*probity*) 939; virtue &c. 944.

V. be -right &c. *adj*.; stand to reason.

see -justice done, –one righted, –fair play; do justice to; recompense &c. (*reward*) 973; hold the scales even, give and take; serve one right, put the saddle on the right horse; give -every one, – the devil- his due; *audire alteram partem*.

deserve &c. (*be entitled to*) 924.

Adj. right, good; just, reasonable; fit &c. 924; equ-al, -able, -itable; even-handed, fair, – and square.

legitimate, justifiable, rightful; as it -should, – ought to- be; lawful &c. (*permitted*) 760, (*legal*) 963.

deserved &c. 924.

Adv. rightly &c. *adj*.; in -justice, – equity, – reason.

without -distinction of, – regard to, – respect to- persons; upon even terms.

Int. all right!

923. Wrong.—N. wrong; what -ought

not to, – should not- be; *malum in se*; unreasonableness, grievance; shame.

injustice; unfairness &c. *adj*.; iniquity, foul play, partiality, leaning; favour, -itism; nepotism, party spirit, partisanship; undueness &c. 925; un-lawfulness &c. 964.

robbing Peter to pay Paul &c. *v.*; the wolf and the lamb; vice &c. 945.

a custom more honoured in the breach than the observance.

V. be -wrong &c. *adj*.; cry to heaven for vengeance.

do -wrong &c. *n*.; be -inequitable &c. *adj*.; favour, lean towards; en-croach; impose upon; reap where one has not sown; give an inch and take an ell; rob Peter to pay Paul.

Adj. wrong, -ful; bad, too bad; un-just, -fair; in-, un-equitable; unequal, partial, one-sided.

objectionable; un-reasonable, -allowable, -warrantable, -justifiable; not cricket, not playing the game; improper, unfit; unjustified &c. 925; illegal &c. 964; in-iquitous, criminal; immoral &c. 945; injurious &c. 649.

in the wrong, – box.

Adv. wrongly &c. *adj*.

Phr. it will not do; this is too bad.

924. Dueness.—N. due, -ness; right, privilege, prerogative, prescription, ti-tle, claim, pretension, demand, birthright.

immunity, licence, liberty, franchise; vested -interest, –right; licitness.

sanction, authority, warranty, charter;

warrant &c. (*permission*) 760; constitution &c. (*law*) 963; tenure; bond &c. (*security*) 771.

deserts, merits, dues.

claimant, appellant; plaintiff &c. 938.

V. be -due &c. *adj.* to, - the due &c. *n.* of; have -right, - title, - claim- to; be entitled to; have a claim upon; belong to &c. (*property*) 780.

deserve, merit, be worthy of, richly deserve.

demand, claim; call upon -, come upon -, appeal to- for; re-vendicate, -claim; exact; insist -on, - upon; challenge; take one's stand, make a point of, require, lay claim to, assert, assume, arrogate, make good; substantiate; vindicate a -claim, - right; make out a case.

give -, confer- a right; sanction, entitle; authorize &c. 760; sanctify, legalize, ordain, prescribe, allot.

give every one his due &c. 922; pay one's dues; have one's -due, - rights; stand upon one's rights.

use a right, assert, enforce, put in force, lay under contribution.

Adj. having a right to &c. *v.*; entitled to; claiming; deserving, meriting, worthy of.

privileged, allowed, sanctioned, warranted, authorized; ordained, prescribed, constitutional, chartered, enfranchised.

prescriptive, presumptive; absolute, indefeasible; un-, in-alienable; imprescriptible, inviolable, unimpeachable, unchallenged; sacrosanct.

due to, merited, deserved, condign, richly deserved, *emeritus*.

allowable &c. (*permitted*) 760; lawful, licit, legitimate, legal; legalized &c. (*law*) 963.

square, unexceptionable, right; equitable &c. 922; due, *en règle*; fit, -ting; correct, proper, meet, befitting, becoming, seemly; decorous; creditable, up to the mark, right as a trivet; just -, quite- the thing; *selon les règles*.

Adv. duly, *ex officio*, *de jure*; by -right, - divine right; as is -fitting, -

proper, - fitting and proper; *jure divino*, *Dei gratiâ*, in the name of.

Phr. *civis Romanus sum.*

925. [Absence of right.] **Undueness—N.** undueness &c. *adj.*; *malum prohibitum*; impropriety; illegality &c. 964.

falseness &c. *adj.*; emptiness -, invalidity- of title; illegitimacy.

loss of right, disfranchisement, forfeiture.

usurpation, assumption, tort, violation, breach, encroachment, presumption, seizure, stretch, exaction, imposition, lion's share.

usurper, pretender, Carlist; impostor.

V. be -undue &c. *adj.*; not be -due &c. 924.

infringe, encroach, trench on, exact; arrogate, - to oneself; give an inch and take an ell; stretch -, strain- a point; usurp, violate, do violence to; sail under false colours.

dis-franchise, -entitle, -qualify; invalidate.

relax &c. (*be lax*) 738; misbehave &c. (*vice*) 945; misbecome.

Adj. undue; unlawful &c. (*illegal*) 964; unconstitutional, *ultra vires*; illicit; un-authorized, -warranted, -allowed, -sanctioned, -justified; un-, dis-entitled, -qualified; un-privileged, -chartered.

illegitimate, bastard, spurious, false; usurped, tortious.

un-deserved, -merited, -earned; unfulfilled.

forfeited, disfranchised.

improper; un-meet, -fit, -befitting, -seemly; un-, mis-becoming; seemless; *contra bonos mores*; not the thing, out of the question, not to be thought of; preposterous, pretentious, would-be.

926. Duty.—N. duty, what ought to be done, moral obligation, accountableness, liability, *onus*, responsibility; bounden -, imperative- duty; call, - of duty.

allegiance, fealty, tie; engagement &c. (*promise*) 768; part; function, calling &c. (*business*) 625.

morality, morals, decalogue; case of conscience; conscientiousness &c. (*probity*) 939; conscience, inward monitor, still small voice within, sense of duty, tender conscience.

dueness &c. 924; propriety, fitness, seemliness, amenableness, decorum; the -thing, – proper thing; the -right, – proper- thing to do.

[Science of morals] eth-ics, -ology; deon-, are-tology; moral –, ethical-philosophy; casuistry, polity.

observance, fulfilment, discharge, performance, acquittal, satisfaction, redemption; good behaviour.

V. be -the duty of, – incumbent &c. *adj.* on, – responsible &c. *adj.*; behoove, become, befit, beseem; belong –, pertain- to; fall to one's lot; devolve on; lie -upon, – on one's head, – at one's door; rest -with, – on the shoulders of.

take upon oneself &c. (*promise*) 768; be –, become- -bound to, – sponsor for; be responsible for; incur a -responsibility &c. *n.*; be –, stand –, lie- under an obligation; have to answer for, owe it to oneself.

impose a -duty &c. *n.*; enjoin, require, exact; bind, – over; saddle with, prescribe, assign, call upon, look to, oblige.

enter upon –, perform –, observe –, fulfil –, discharge –, adhere to –, acquit oneself of –, satisfy- -a duty, – an obligation; act one's part, redeem one's pledge, do justice to, be at one's post; do duty; do one's duty &c. (*be virtuous*) 944.

be on one's good behaviour, mind one's P's and Q's.

Adj. obligatory, binding; imperative, peremptory; stringent &c. (*severe*) 739; behooving &c. *v.*; incumbent –, chargeable- on; under obligation; obliged –, bound –, tied- by; saddled with.

due –, beholden –, bound –, indebt-ed- to; tied down; compromised &c. (*promised*) 768; in duty bound.

amenable, liable, accountable, responsible, answerable.

right, meet &c. (*due*) 924; moral, ethical, casuistical, conscientious, ethological.

Adv. with a safe conscience, as in duty bound, on one's own responsibility, at one's own risk, *suo periculo*; *in foro conscientiæ*; *quamdiu se bene gesserit*; at one's post, on duty.

Phr. *dura lex sed lex.*

927. Dereliction of Duty.—N. dereliction of duty; fault &c. (*guilt*) 947- sin &c. (*vice*) 945; non-observance, -performance, -co-operation; neglect, carelessness, laziness, incompetence, eye-service, relaxation, infraction, violation, transgression, failure, evasion, indolence; dead letter.

slacker, loafer, striker; non-co-operator.

V. violate; break, – through; infringe; set -aside, – at naught; trample -on, – under foot; slight, neglect, evade, renounce, forswear, repudiate; wash one's hands of; escape, transgress, fail.

call to account &c. (*disapprobation*) 932.

927a. Exemption.—N. exemption, freedom, irresponsibility, immunity, liberty, licence, release, exoneration, excuse, dispensation, absolution, franchise, renunciation, discharge; exculpation &c. 970; *ægrotat.*

V. be -exempt &c. *adj.*

exempt, release, acquit, discharge, quit-claim, remise, remit; free, set at liberty, let off, pass over, spare, excuse, dispense with, give dispensation, license; stretch a point; absolve &c. (*forgive*) 918; exonerate &c. (*exculpate*) 970; save the necessity.

Adj. exempt, free, immune, at liberty, scot free; released &c. *v.*; unbound, unencumbered; irresponsible,

unaccountable, not answerable; excusable.

2°. MORAL SENTIMENTS

928. Respect.—N. respect, regard,
consideration; courtesy &c. 894; attention, deference, reverence, honour, esteem, estimation, veneration, admiration; approbation &c. 931.

homage, fealty, obeisance, genuflexion, kneeling, prostration; obsequiousness &c. 886; salaam, *kowtow*, bow,
presenting arms, salute.

respects, regards, duty, *devoirs*,
égards.

devotion &c. (*piety*) 987.

V. respect, regard; revere, -nce; hold
in reverence, honour, venerate, hallow;
esteem &c. (*approve of*) 931; think
much of; entertain -, bear- respect for;
have a high opinion of; look up to, defer
to; pay -attention, - respect &c. *n.*- to;
do -, render- honour to; do the honours,
hail; show courtesy &c. 894; salute,
present arms; do -, pay- homage to; pay
tribute to, kneel to, bow to, bend the
knee to; fall down before, prostrate oneself, kiss the hem of one's garment; worship &c. 990.

keep one's distance, make room, observe due decorum, stand upon ceremony.

command -, inspire- respect; awe,
impose, overawe, dazzle.

Adj. respecting &c. *v.*; respectful,
deferential, decorous, reverential, obsequious, ceremonious, bare-headed, cap
in hand, on one's knees; prostrate &c.
(*servile*) 886.

respected &c. *v.*; in high -esteem, -
estimation; time-honoured, venerable,
emeritus.

Adv. in deference to; with -all, - due,
- the highest- respect; with submission.

saving your -grace, - presence; *salva
sit reverentia*; *pace tanti nominis*.

Int. hail! all hail! *esto perpetua!* may
your shadow never be less!

929. Disrespect.—N. dis-respect,
-esteem, -estimation, -favour, -repute;
low estimation; disparagement
&c.(*dispraise*) 932, (*detraction*) 934.

irreverence; slight, neglect; *spretae
injuria formæ*; superciliousness &c.
(*contempt*) 930.

vilipendency, contumely, affront,
dishonour, insult, indignity, outrage,
discourtesy &c. 895; practical joking;
scurrility, scoffing, sibilation; ir-, derision; mockery; irony &c. (*ridicule*) 856;
sarcasm.

hiss, hoot, gibe, flout, jeer, scoff,
gleek, taunt, sneer, quip, fling, wipe,
slap in the face.

V. hold in disrespect &c. (*despise*)
930; misprize, disregard, slight, undervalue, depreciate, trifle with, set at
naught, pass by, push aside, overlook,
turn one's back upon, laugh in one's sleeve;
be -disrespectful &c. *adj.*. - discourteous
&c. 895; treat with -disrespect &c. *n.*; set
down, browbeat.

dishonour, desecrate; insult, affront,
outrage.

speak slightingly of; disparage &c.
(*dispraise*) 932; vilipend, call names;
throw -, fling- dirt; drag through the
mud, point at, indulge in personalities;
make -mouths, - faces; bite the thumb;
take -, pluck- by the beard; toss in a
blanket, tar and feather.

have -, hold- in derision; deride,
scoff, sneer, laugh at, snigger, ridicule,
gibe, mock, jeer, taunt, twit, niggle,
gleek, gird, flout, fleer; roast, turn into
ridicule; guy, burlesque &c. 856; laugh
to scorn &c. (*contempt*) 930; smoke;
fool; make -game, - a fool, - an April
fool- of; play a practical joke; rag; lead
one a dance, run the rig upon, have a
fling at, scout, hiss, hoot, mob.

Adj. disrespectful; aweless, irreverent; disparaging &c. 934; insulting &c.
v.; supercilious &c. (*scornful*) 930;
rude, derisive, contemptuous, sarcastic;
scurri-le, -lous; contumelious.

un-respected, -worshipped, -envied,
-saluted; un-, dis-regarded.

Adv. disrespectfully &c. *adj.*

930. Contempt.—N. contempt, disdain, scorn, sovereign contempt; despisal, -ciency; vilipendency, contumely; slight, sneer, spurn, by-word.

contemptuousness &c. *adj.*; scornful eye; smile of contempt; derision &c. (*disrespect*) 929.

[State of being despised] despisedness.

V. despise, contemn, scorn, disdain, feel contempt for, view with a scornful eye, disregard, slight, not mind; pass by &c. (*neglect*) 460.

look down upon; hold -cheap, - in contempt, - in disrespect; think -nothing, - small beer- of; make light of; underestimate &c. 483; esteem -slightly, - of small or no account; take no account of, care nothing for; set no store by; not care a -straw &c. (*unimportance*) 643; set at naught, laugh in one's sleeve, snap one's fingers at, shrug one's shoulders, turn up one's nose at, poohpooh, damn with faint praise; sneeze -, whistle -, sneer- at; curl up one's lip, toss the head, *traiter de haut*; laugh at &c. (*be disrespectful*) 929.

point the finger of -, hold up to -, laugh to- scorn; scout, hoot, flout, hiss, scoff at.

turn -one's back, - a cold shoulder-upon; tread -, trample- -upon, - under foot; spurn, kick; fling to the winds &c. (*repudiate*) 610; send away with a flea in the ear.

Adj. contemptuous; disdain-, scornful; withering, contumelious, supercilious, cynical, haughty, bumptious, cavalier; derisive.

contemptible, despicable; pitiable; pitiful &c. (*unimportant*) 643; despised &c. *v.*; down-trodden; unenvied.

Adv. contemptuously &c. *adj.*

Int. a fig for &c. (*unimportant*) 643; bah! never mind! away with! hang it! fiddle-de-dee!

931. Approbation.—N. approbation; approv-al, -ement; sanction, advocacy; nod of approbation; esteem, estimation, good opinion, golden opinions, admiration; love &c. 897; appreciation, regard, account, popularity, *kudos*, credit; repute &c. 873.

commendation, praise; laud, -ation; good word; meed -, tribute- of praise; encomium; eulog-y, -ium; *éloge*, panegyric; homage, hero worship; benediction, blessing, benison.

applause, plaudit, clap; clapping, - of hands; accl-aim, -amation; cheer; pæan, hosannah; shout -, peal -, chorus -, thunders- of -applause &c.; Kentish fire; Prytaneum; blurb.

V. approve; think -good, - much of, well of, - highly of; esteem, value, prize; set great store -by, - on.

do justice to, appreciate; honour, hold in esteem, look up to, admire; like &c. 897; be in favour of, wish God speed; hail, - with satisfaction.

stand -, stick- up for; uphold, hold up, countenance, sanction; clap -, pat-on the back; keep in countenance, endorse, give credit, recommend; mark with a white -mark, - stone.

commend, praise; be-, laud; compliment, pay a tribute, bepraise; clap, - the hands; applaud, cheer, acclaim, acclamate, encore; panegyrize, eulogize, cry up, *prôner*, puff; extol, - to the skies; magnify, glorify, exalt, boost, swell, make much of; flatter &c. 933; bless, give a blessing to; have -, say- a good word for; speak -well, - highly, - in high terms- of; sing -, sound -, chaunt -, resound- the praises of; sing praises to; cheer -, applaud- to the -echo, - very echo.

redound to the -honour, - praise, - credit- of; do credit to; deserve -praise &c. *n.*; recommend itself; pass muster.

be -praised &c.; receive honourable mention; be in -favour, - high favour-with; ring with the praises of, win golden opinions, gain credit, find favour with, stand well in the opinion of; *laudari a laudato viro*.

Adj. approving &c. *v.*; in favour of; lost in admiration.

commendatory, complimentary, benedictory, laudatory, panegyrical, eulogistic, encomiastic, acclamatory, lavish of praise, uncritical.

approved, praised &c. *v.*; un-censured, -impeached; popular, in good odour; in high esteem &c. (*respected*) 928; in -, in high- favour.

deserving -, worthy of- praise &c. *n.*; praiseworthy, commendable, of estima-tion; good &c. 648; meritorious, esti-mable, creditable, plausible, unim-peachable; beyond all praise.

Adv. commendably, with credit, to admiration; well &c. 681; with three times three.

Int. hear, hear! well done! *brav-o! -a! -i! bravissimo! euge! macte virtute!* so far so good, that's right, quite right; *op-time!* one cheer more; may your shadow never be less! *esto perpetua!* long life to! *viva! evviva!* God speed! *valete et plaudite! encore! bis!*

Phr. *probatum est.*

932. Disapprobation.—N. disappro-bation, -val; improbation; dis-esteem, -valuation, -placency; odium; dislike &c. 867; dissent &c. 489.

dis-praise, -commendation; blame, censure, obloquy; detraction &c. 934; disparagement, depreciation; denuncia-tion; condemnation &c. 971; ostracism; boycott; black-list, -ball; *index -expurgatorius, - librorum prohibitorum.*

animadversion, reflection, stricture, objection, exception, criticism; sardonic -grin, - laugh; sarcasm, insinuation, in-nuendo; bad -, poor -, lefthanded- com-pliment.

satire; sneer &c. (*contempt*) 930; taunt &c. (*disrespect*) 929; cavil, carping, censoriousness; hypercriticism &c. (*fastid-iousness*) 868.

reprehension, remonstrance, expostu-lation, reproof, reprobation, admoni-tion, increpation, reproach; rebuke, rep-rimand, castigation, jobation, lecture, curtain lecture, blow up, wigging, dressing, - down; rating, scolding, trim-ming; correction, set down, rap on the knuckles, *coup de bec*, rebuff; slap, - on

the face; home thrust, hit; frown, scowl, black look.

diatribe; jeremiad; *tirade*, philippic.

clamour, outcry, hue and cry; hiss, -ing; sibilation, cat-call; execration &c. 908.

chiding, upbraiding &c. *v.*; exprobra-tion, abuse, vituperation, invective, ob-jurgation, contumely, personal remarks; hard -, cutting -, bitter- words.

evil-speaking; bad language &c. 908; personality.

V. disapprove; dislike &c. 867; la-ment &c. 839; object to, take exception to; be scandalized at, think ill of; view with -disfavour, - dark eyes, - jaundiced eyes; *nil admirari*, disvalue, improbate.

frown upon, look grave; bend -, knit-the brows; shake the head at, shrug the shoulders; turn up the nose &c. (*con-tempt*) 930; look -askance, - black upon; look with an evil eye; make a wry -face, - mouth- at; set one's face against.

dis-praise, -commend, -parage; dep-recate, speak ill of, not speak well of, slate, condemn &c. (*find guilty*) 971.

blame; lay -, cast- blame upon; cen-sure, *fronder*, reproach, pass censure on, reprobate, impugn.

remonstrate, expostulate, recrimi-nate.

reprehend, chide, admonish; bring -, call- -to account, - over the coals, - to order; take to task, reprove, lecture, bring to book; read a -lesson, - lecture-to; rebuke, correct.

reprimand, chastise, castigate, lash, blow up, trounce, trim, *laver la tête*, overhaul; give it one, - finely; gibbet.

accuse &c. 938; impeach, denounce; hold up to -reprobation, - execration; expose, brand, gibbet, stigmatize; show -, pull -, take- up; cry 'shame' upon; be outspoken; raise a hue and cry against.

execrate &c. 908; exprobrate, speak daggers, vituperate; abuse, - like a pick-pocket; scold, rate, objurate, upbraid, fall foul of; jaw; rail, - at, - in good set terms; bark at; anathematize, call names; call by -hard, - ugly- names;

a-, re-vile; vili-fy, -pend; bespatter; back-bite; clapperclaw; rave -, thunder -, ful-minate- against; load with reproaches; lash with the tongue.

exclaim -, protest -, inveigh -, de-claim -, cry out -, raise one's voice-against.

decry; cry -, run -, frown- down; clamour, hiss, hoot, mob, ostracize; draw up -, sign- a round robin; black-ball, -list.

animadvert -, reflect- upon; glance at; cast -reflection, - reproach, - a slur-upon; insinuate, damn with faint praise; 'hint a fault and hesitate dislike'; not to be able to say much for.

scoff at, point at; twit, taunt &c. (*disrespect*) 929; sneer at &c. (*despise*) 230; satirize, lampoon; defame &c. (*detract*) 934; depreciate, find fault with, criticize, cut up; pull -, pick- to pieces; take exception; cavil; peck -, nibble -, carp-at; be -censorious &c. *adj.*; pick -holes, - a hole, - a hole in one's coat; make a fuss about.

take -, set- down; snub, snap one up; give a rap on the knuckles; throw a stone -at, - in one's garden; have a -fling, - snap- at; have words with, pluck a crow with; give one a -wipe, - lick with the rough side of the tongue.

incur blame, excite disapprobation, scandalize, shock, revolt; get a bad name, forfeit one's good opinion, be un-der a cloud, come under the ferule, bring a hornet's nest about one's ears.

take blame, stand corrected; have to answer for.

Adj. disapproving &c. *v.*; scandal-ized.

disparaging, condemnatory, damna-tory, denunciatory, reproachful, abu-sive, objurgatory, clamorous, vitupera-tive; defamatory &c. 934.

satirical, sarcastic, sardonic, cynical, dry, sharp, cutting, biting, severe, vir-ulent, withering, trenchant, hard upon; censorious, critical, captious, carping, hypercritical; fastidious &c. 868; spar-ing of -, grudging- praise.

disapproved, chid &c. *v.*; in bad

odour, blown upon, unapproved; un-blest; at a discount, exploded; weighed in the balance and found wanting.

blameworthy, reprehensible &c. (*guilt*) 947; to -, worthy of- blame, an-swerable, uncommendable, exceptiona-ble, not to be thought of, bad &c. 649; vicious &c. 945.

un-lamented, -bewailed, -pitied.

Adv. with a wry face; reproachfully &c. *adj.*

Int. it is too bad! it -won't, - will nev-er- do! marry come up! Oh! come! 'sdeath!

forbid it Heaven! God -, Heaven- for-bid! out -, fie- upon it! away with! tut! *O tempora! O mores!* shame! fie, - for shame! out on you!

tell it not in Gath!

933. Flattery.—N. flattery, adulation, gloze; bland-ishment, -iloquence; cajol-ery; fawning, wheedling &c. *v.*; capta-tion, coquetry, sycophancy, obsequious-ness, flunkeyism, toad-eating, tuft-hunting; snobbishness.

incense, honeyed words, flummery; bun-kum, -combe; blarney, *placebo*, butter; soft -soap, - sawder; rose water.

voice of the charmer, mouth honour, lip-homage; euphemism; unctuousness &c. *adj.*

V. flatter, praise to the skies, puff; wheedle, cajole, glaver, coax; fawn, - upon; humour, gloze, soothe, pet, co-quet, slaver, butter; be-spatter, -slubber, -plaster, -slaver; lay it on thick, over-praise; earwig, cog, collogue; truckle -, pander *or* pandar -, pay court- to; court; creep into the good graces of; curry favour with, hang on the sleeve of; fool to the top of one's bent; lick the dust.

lay the flattering unction to one's soul, gild the pill, make things pleasant.

overestimate &c. 482; exaggerate &c. 549.

Adj. flattering &c. *v.*; adulatory; mealy-, honey-mouthed; honeyed; smooth, - tongued; soapy, oily, unctu-ous, blandiloquent, specious; fine-, fair-spoken; plausible, servile, syco-phantic, fulsome; courtier-ly, -like.

Adv. *ad captandum.*

934. Detraction.—N. detraction, dis-paragement, depreciation, vilification, obloquy, scurrility, scandal, defamation, aspersion, traducement, slander, cal-umny, obtrectation, evil-speaking, back-biting, *scandalum magnatum.*

personality, libel, squib, lampoon, skit, pasquinade; *chronique scanda-leuse.*

sarcasm, cynicism; criticism (*disap-probation*) 932; invective &c. 932; en-venomed tongue; *spretæ injuria formæ.* detractor &c. 936.

V. detract, derogate, decry, depreci-ate, disparage; run -, cry- down; mini-mize, make light of; belittle, sneer at &c. (*contemn*) 930; criticize, pull to pieces, pick a hole in one's coat, as-perse, cast aspersions, blow upon, be-spatter, blacken; vili-fy, -pend; avile; give a dog a bad name, brand, malign, backbite, libel, lampoon, traduce, slan-der, defame, calumniate, bear false wit-ness against; speak ill of behind one's back.

'damn with faint praise, assent with civil leer; and without sneering, others teach to sneer.'

fling dirt &c. (*disrespect*) 929; anath-ematize &c. 932; dip the pen in gall, view in a bad light.

Adj. detracting &c. *v.*; defamatory, detractory, derogatory; disparaging, li-bellous; scurril-e, -ous; abusive; foul-spoken, -tongued, -mouthed; slander-ous; calumni-ous, -atory; sar-castic, -donic; satirical, cynical.

935. Flatterer.—N. flatterer, adula-tor; eu-logist, -phemist; optimist, enco-miast, *laudator,* whitewasher, booster.

toad-y, -eater; sycophant, courtier, pickthank, Sir Pertinax MacSycophant; *flâneur, prôneur;* puffer, touter, *cla-queur;* claw-back, ear-wig, doer of dirty work; parasite, hanger on &c. (*servility*) 886.

936. Detractor.—N. detractor, re-prover; cens-or, -urer; cynic, critic, cav-iller, carper, wordcatcher.

defamer, backbiter, slanderer, knock-er, Sir Benjamin Backbite, lampooner, satirist, traducer, libeller, calumniator, dearest foe, dawplucker, Thersites; Zo-ilus; good-natured -, candid- friend [sa-tirically]; reviler, vituperator, castiga-tor; shrew &c. 901.

disapprover, *laudator temporis acti.*

937. Vindication.—N. vindication, justification, warrant; exoneration, ex-culpation; acquittal &c. 970; white-washing.

extenuation; pallia-tion, -tive; soften-ing, mitigation.

reply, defence; recrimination &c. 938.

apology, gloss, varnish; plea &c. 617; salvo; excuse, extenuating circum-stances; allowance, - to be made; *locus pœnitentiæ.*

apologist, vindicator, justifier; defen-dant &c. 938.

justifiable charge, true bill.

V. justify, warrant; be an -excuse &c. *n.*- for; lend a colour, furnish a handle; vindicate; ex-, dis-culpate; acquit &c. 970; clear, set right, exonerate, white-wash.

extenuate, palliate, excuse, soften, apologize, varnish, slur, gloze; put a -gloss, - good face- upon; mince; gloss over, bolster up, help a lame dog over a stile.

advocate, defend, plead one's cause; stand -, stick -, speak- up for; contend -, speak- for; bear out, keep in counte-nance, support; plead &c. 617; say in defence; plead ignorance; confess and avoid, propugn, put in a good word for.

take the will for the deed, make al-lowance for, do justice to; give -one, - the Devil- his due.

make good; prove -the truth of, - one's case; be justified by the event.

Adj. vindicat-ed, -ing &c. *v.*; vindi-cat-ive, -ory; palliative; exculpatory; apologetic.

excusable, defensible, pardonable;

veni-al, -able; specious, plausible, justifiable.

Phr. *'honi soit qui mal y pense.'*

938. Accusation.—N. accusation,
charge, imputation, slur, inculpation,
exprobration, delation; crimination; in-,
ac-, re-crimination; *tu quoque* argument; invective &c. 932.

de-nunciation, -nouncement; libel,
challenge, citation, arraignment; im-,
ap-peachment; indictment, bill of indictment, true bill; lawsuit &c. 969;
condemnation &c. 971.

gravamen of a charge, head and front
of one's offending, *argumentum ad hominem*; scandal &c. (*detraction*) 934;
scandalum magnatum.

accuser, prosecutor, plaintiff, complainant, petitioner; relator, informer;
appellant.

accused, defendant, prisoner, panel,
co-, respondent; litigant.

V. accuse, charge, tax, impute, twit,
taunt with, reproach.

brand with reproach; stigmatize, slur;
cast a -stone at, - slur on; incriminate;
inculpate, implicate; call to account &c.
(*censure*) 932; take to -blame, - task;
put in the black book.

inform against, indict, denounce, arraign; im-, ap-peach; have up, show up,
pull up; challenge, cite, lodge a complaint; prosecute, bring an action against
&c. 969.

charge -, saddle- with; lay to one's
-door, - charge; lay the blame on, bring
home to; cast -, throw- in one's teeth;
cast the first stone at.

have -, keep- a rod in pickle for; have
a crow to pluck with.

trump up a charge.

Adj. accusing &c. *v.*; accusat-ory,
-ive; imputative, denunciatory; re-, crim-
inatory.

accused &c. *v.*; suspected; under
-suspicion, - a cloud, - *surveillance*; in
-custody, - detention; in the -lock up, -
watch house, - house of detention.

accusable, imputable; in-defensible,

-excusable; un-pardonable, -justifiable;
vicious &c. 945.

Int. look at home; *tu quoque* &c. (*retaliation*) 718.

3° MORAL CONDITIONS

939. Probity.—N. probity, integrity,
rectitude; uprightness &c. *adj.*; honesty, faith; honour; good faith, *bona fides*;
purity, clean hands.

fairness &c. *adj.*; fair play, justice,
equity, impartiality, principle; grace.

constancy; faithfulness &c. *adj.*; fidelity, loyalty; incorrupt-ion, -ibility.

trustworthiness &c. *adj.*; truth, candour, singleness of heart; veracity &c.
543; tender conscience &c. (*sense of
duty*) 926.

punctil-iousness, -io; delicacy, nicety; scrupul-osity, -ousness &c. *adj.*;
scruple; point, - of honour; punctuality.

dignity &c. (*repute*) 873; respectability, -bleness &c. *adj.*; gentleman;
man of -honour, - his word; *fidus Achates, preux chevalier, galantuomo*; true-
penny, trump, brick; true Briton, white
man, sportsman.

court of honour, a fair field and no
favour; *argumentum ad verecundiam*.

V. be -honourable &c. *adj.*; deal
-honourably, - squarely, - impartially, -
fairly; speak the truth &c. (*veracity*)
543; tell the truth and shame the devil,
vitam impendere vero; show a proper
spirit, make a point of; do one's duty
&c. 944; play the game.

redeem one's pledge &c. 926; keep -,
be as good as- one's -promise, - word;
keep faith with, not fail.

give and take, *audire alteram partem*,
give the devil his due, put the saddle on
the right horse.

redound to one's honour.

Adj. upright; honest, - as daylight;
veracious &c. 543; virtuous &c. 944;
honourable; fair, right, just, equitable,
impartial, even-handed, square; fair -,
open- and aboveboard.

constant, – as the northern star; faithful, loyal, staunch; true, – blue, – to
one's colours, – to the core, – as the
needle to the pole; true-hearted, trust-y,
-worthy; as good as one's word, to be
depended on, incorruptible.

manly, straightforward &c. (*ingenuous*) 703; frank, candid, open-hearted.

conscientious, tender-conscienced,
right-minded; high-principled, -minded;
scrupulous, religious, strict; nice, punctilious, correct, punctual; respect-, re-
put-able; gentlemanlike.

inviol-able, -ate; un-violated, -broken,
-betrayed; un-bought, -bribed.

innocent &c. 946; pure; stainless; un-
stained, -tarnished, -sullied, -tainted,
-perjured; uncorrupt, -ed; unde-filed,
-praved, -bauched; *integer vitæ scelerisque purus; justus et tenax propositi.*

chivalrous, jealous of honour, *sans
peur et sans reproche*; high-spirited.

supra-mundane, unworldly, overscru-
pulous.

Adv. honourably &c. *adj.; bona fide*;
on the square, in good faith, honour
bright, *foro conscientiæ*, with clean
hands; by fair means.

940. Improbity.—N. improbity;
dishon-esty, -our; deviation from rectitude; disgrace &c. (*disrepute*) 874; fraud
&c. (*deception*) 545; lying &c. 544; bad
–, Punic- faith; *mala –, Punica- fides*;
infidelity; faithlessness &c. *adj.*; Judas
kiss, betrayal; scrap of paper.

breach of -promise, – trust, – faith;
prodition, disloyalty, divided allegiance,
treason, high treason; apostacy &c. (*tergiversation*) 607; non-observance &c.
773.

shabbiness &c. *adj.*; villainy; baseness &c. *adj.*; abjection, debasement,
turpitude, moral turpitude, laxity, trimming, shuffling.

perfidy; perfidiousness &c. *adj.*;
treachery, double-dealing; unfairness
&c. *adj.*; knavery, roguery, rascality,
foul-play; jobb-ing, -ery; Tammany,
graft; venality, nepotism; corruption,
job, shuffle, fishy transaction, barratry;

sharp practice, heads I win, tails you
lose; mouth-honour &c. (*flattery*) 933.

V. be -dishonest &c. *adj.*; play false;
break one's -word, – faith, – promise;
jilt, betray, forswear; shuffle &c. (*lie*)
544; live by one's wits, sail near the
wind; play with marked cards.

disgrace –, dishonour –, demean –,
degrade- oneself; derogate, stoop, grovel, sneak, lose caste; sell oneself, go
over to the enemy; seal one's infamy.

Adj. dishon-est, -ourable; unconscientious, -scrupulous; fraudulent
&c. 545; knavish; disgraceful &c. (*disreputable*) 874; wicked &c. 945.

false-hearted, disingenuous; unfair,
one-sided; double, -tongued, -faced;
time-serving, crooked, tortuous, insidious, Machiavellian, dark, slippery;
questionable; fishy; perfidious, treacherous, perjured.

infamous, arrant, foul, base, vile, low,
ignominious, blackguard.

contemptible, abject, mean, shabby,
little, paltry, dirty, scurvy, scabby,
sneaking, grovelling, scrubby, rascally,
pettifogging; beneath one; not cricket.

low-minded, -thoughted, base-
minded.

undignified, indign; unbe-coming,
-seeming, -fitting; de-rogatory, -grading;
infra dignitatem; ungentleman-ly, -like;
un-knightly, -chivalric, -manly, -handsome;
recreant, inglorious.

corrupt, venal; debased, mongrel.

faithless, of bad faith, false, unfaithful, disloyal; untrustworthy; trust-, troth-
less; lost to shame, dead to honour.

Adv. dishonestly &c. *adj.; malâ fide*,
like a thief in the night, by crooked
paths; by foul means.

Int. *O tempora! O mores!*

941. Knave.—N. knave, rogue, villain; Scapin, rascal; Lazarillo de
Tormes; bad man &c. 949; blackguard
&c. 949.

traitor, betrayer, arch-traitor, conspirator, stool pigeon, Judas, Catiline; reptile, serpent, snake in the grass, wolf in
sheep's clothing, sneak, Jerry Sneak,

tell-tale, squealer, mischief-maker, trimmer; renegade &c. (*tergiversation*) 607; truant, recreant; sycophant &c. (*servility*) 886.

942. Disinterestedness.—N. disinterestedness &c. *adj.*; generosity; liberality, -ism; altruism; benevolence &c. 906; elevation, loftiness of purpose, exaltation, magnanimity; chival-ry, -rous spirit; heroism, sublimity.

self-denial, -abnegation, -effacement, -sacrifice, -immolation, -control &c. (*resolution*) 604; stoicism, devotion, martyrdom, *suttee*.

labour of love.

V. be -disinterested &c. *adj.*; make a sacrifice, lay one's head on the block; put oneself in the place of others, do as one would be done by, do unto others as we would men should do unto us.

Adj. disinterested; unselfish; self-denying, -sacrificing, -devoted; generous.

handsome, liberal, noble; noble-, high-minded; princely, great, high, elevated, lofty, exalted, spirited, stoical, magnanimous; great-, large-hearted, chivalrous, heroic, sublime.

un-bought, -bribed; uncorrupted &c. (*upright*) 939.

943. Selfishness.—N. selfishness &c. *adj.*; self-love, -indulgence, -worship, -interest; ego-tism, -ism; egocentrism, narcissism; *amour propre* &c. (*vanity*) 880; nepotism.

worldliness &c. *adj.*; world wisdom.

illiberality; meanness &c. *adj.*

time-server; tuft-, fortune-hunter; self-seeker; jobber, worldling; egotist, egoist, monopolist, nepotist, profiteer; temporizer, trimmer; dog in the manger, charity that begins at home.

V. be -selfish &c. *adj.*; please -, indulge -, coddle- oneself; consult one's own -wishes, - pleasure; look after one's own interest; feather one's nest; take care of number one, have an eye to the main chance, know on which side one's bread is buttered; give an inch and take an ell; wangle.

Adj. selfish; self-seeking, -indulgent, -interested; wrapt up -, centred- in self; egotistic, -al; egocentric.

illiberal, mean, ungenerous, narrow-minded; mercenary, venal; covetous &c. 819.

unspiritual; earthly, -minded; mundane; worldly, -minded, -wise; time-serving.

interested; *alieni appetens sui profusus.*

Adv. ungenerously &c. *adj.*; to gain some private ends; from selfish -, interested- motives.

Phr. *après nous le déluge.*

944. Virtue.—N. virtue; virtuousness &c. *adj.*; morality; moral rectitude; integrity &c. (*probity*) 939; nobleness &c. 873.

morals; ethics &c. (*duty*) 926; cardinal virtues.

merit, worth, desert, excellence, credit; self-control &c. (*resolution*) 604; self-denial &c. (*temperance*) 953.

well-doing; good -actions, –behaviour; discharge -, fulfilment -, performance- of duty; well-spent life; innocence &c. 946.

V. be -virtuous &c. *adj.*; practice virtue &c. *n.*; do -, fulfil -, perform -, discharge- one's duty; redeem one's pledge &c. 926; act well, - one's part; fight the good fight; acquit oneself well; command -, master- one's passions; keep -straight, - in the right path.

set -an, - a good- example; be on one's -good, - best- behaviour.

Adj. virtuous, good; innocent &c. 946; meritorious, deserving, worthy, desertful, correct; dut-iful, -eous; moral; right, -eous, -minded; well-intentioned, creditable, laudable, commendable, praiseworthy; above -, beyond- all praise; excellent, admirable; sterling, pure, noble.

exemplary; match-, peer-less; saintly, -like; heaven-born, angelic, seraphic, godlike.

Adv. virtuously &c. *adj.; e merito.*

945. Vice.—N. vice; evil -doing,

– courses; wrong doing; wickedness, viciousness &c. *adj.*; iniquity, peccability, demerit; sin, Adam; old –, offending-Adam.

immorality, impropriety, indecorum, scandal, laxity, looseness of morals; want of -principle, – ballast; obliquity, backsliding, infamy, demoralization, pravity, depravity, pollution; hardness of heart; brutality &c. (*malevolence*) 907; corruption &c. (*debasement*) 659; knavery &c. (*improbity*) 940; profligacy; lust &c. 961; flagrancy, atrocity; cannibalism.

infirmity; weakness &c. *adj.*; weakness of the flesh, frailty, imperfection; error; weak side; foible; fail-ing, -ure; crying –, besetting- sin; defect, deficiency, shortcoming; cloven foot.

lowest dregs of vice, sink of iniquity, Alsatian den; *gusto picaresco.*

fault, crime; criminality &c. (*guilt*) 947.

sinner &c. 949.

V. be -vicious &c. *adj.*; sin, commit sin, do amiss, err, transgress; misdemean –, forget –, misconduct- oneself; mis-do, -behave; fall, lapse, slip, trip, offend, trespass; deviate from the -line of duty, – path of virtue &c. 944; take a wrong course, go astray; hug a -sin, – fault; sow one's wild oats.

render -vicious &c. *adj.*; demoralize, brutalize; corrupt &c. (*degrade*) 659.

Adj.* vicious; sinful; sinning &c. *v.*; wicked, iniquitous, bad, immoral, unrighteous, wrong, criminal; naughty, incorrect; undut-eous, -iful.

unprincipled, lawless, disorderly, *contra bonos mores*, indecorous, unseemly, improper; dissolute, profligate, scampish; unworthy; worth-, desert-less; disgraceful, recreant; reprehensible, blameworthy, uncommendable; discreditable, -reputable.

base, sinister, scurvy, foul, gross, vile, black, grave, facinorous, felonious, nefarious, shameful, scandalous,

infamous, villainous, of a deep dye, heinous; flag-rant, -itious; atrocious, incarnate, accursed.

Mephistophelian, satanic, diabolic, hellish, infernal, stygian, fiend-ish, -like, hell-born, demoniacal, devilish.

mis-created, -begotten; demoralized, corrupt, depraved.

evil-minded, -disposed; ill-conditioned; malevolent &c. 907; heart-, grace-, shame-, virtue-less; abandoned, lost to virtue; unconscionable; sunk –, lost –, deep –, steeped- in iniquity.

incorrigible, irreclaimable, obdurate, reprobate, past praying for; culpable, reprehensible &c. (*guilty*) 947.

unjustifiable; in-defensible, -excusable; inexpiable, unpardonable, irremissible.

weak, frail, lax, infirm, imperfect, indiscreet; demoralizing, degrading.

Adv. wrong; sinfully &c. *adj.*; without excuse.

Int. *O tempora! O mores!*

946. Innocence.—N. innocence; guiltlessness &c. *adj.*; incorruption, impeccability.

clean hands, clear conscience, *mens sibi conscia recti.*

innocent, new born babe, lamb, dove.

V. be -innocent &c. *adj.; nil conscire sibi nullâ pallescere culpâ.*

acquit &c. 970; exculpate &c. (*vindicate*) 937.

Adj. innocent, not guilty; unguilty; guilt-, fault-, sin-, stain-, blood-, spotless; clear, immaculate; *rectus in curiâ;* un-spotted, -blemished, -erring; undefiled &c. 939; unhardened, Saturnian; Arcadian &c. (*artless*) 703.

in-, un-culpable; unblam-ed, -able; blameless, inerrable, above suspicion; irrepr-oachable, -ovable, -ehensible; un-exceptionable, -objectionable, -impeachable; salvable; venial &c. 937.

harmless; in-offensive, -noxious, -nocuous; dove-, lamb-like; pure, harmless as doves; innocent as -a lamb, – the

---

* Most of these adjectives are applicable both to the act and to the agent.

babe unborn; more sinned against than sinning.

virtuous &c. 944; un-reproved, -impeached, -reproached.

Adv. innocently &c. *adj.*; with clean hands; with a -clear, – safe- conscience.

947. Guilt.—N. guilt, -iness; culpability; crimin-ality, -ousness; deviation from rectitude &c. (*improbity*) 940; sinfulness &c. (*vice*) 945; peccability.

mis-conduct, -behaviour, -doing, -deed; malpractice, fault, sin, error, transgression; dereliction, delinquency; indiscretion, lapse, slip, trip, *faux pas, peccadillo*; flaw, blot, omission; fail-ing, -ure.

offence, trespass; mis-demeanour, -feasance, -prision; tort; mal-efaction, -feasance, -versation; crime, felony.

enormity, atrocity, outrage; deadly –, mortal –, unpardonable- sin; died without a name.

corpus delicti.

Adj. guilty, to blame, culpable, peccable, in fault, censurable, reprehensible, blameworthy, uncommendable, illaudable; weighed in the balance and found wanting; exceptionable, objectionable.

Adv. *in flagrante delicto*; red-handed, in the very act.

948. Good Man.—N. good man, worthy.

good woman, goddess, *madonna*, virgin.

model, paragon &c. (*perfection*) 650; good example; hero, demigod, seraph, angel; innocent &c. 946; saint &c. (*piety*) 987; benefactor &c. 912; philanthropist &c. 910; Aristides.

brick, trump, rough diamond, ugly duckling.

salt of the earth; one in ten thousand; one of the best.

Phr. *si sic omnes!*

949. Bad Man.—N. bad man, wrongdoer, worker of iniquity; evil-doer &c. 913; sinner; the -wicked &c. 945; bad example.

rascal, scoundrel, villain, miscreant, caitiff; wretch, reptile, viper, serpent, cockatrice, basilisk, urchin; tiger, monster; devil &c. (*demon*) 980; devil incarnate; demon in human shape, Nana Sahib; hell-hound, -cat; rake-hell.

bad woman, jade, Jezebel, adultress, &c. 962.

scamp, scapegrace, rip, runagate, ne'er-do-well, reprobate, *roué*, rake; limb; one who has sold himself to the devil, fallen angel, *âme damnée, vaurien, mauvais sujet*, loose fish, sad dog; lost -, black- sheep; castaway, recreant, defaulter; prodigal &c. 818; libertine &c. 962.

rough, rowdy, ugly customer, ruffian, hoodlum, bully; Jonathan Wild; hangman; incendiary; thief &c. 792; murderer &c. 361.

culprit, delinquent, criminal, malefactor, misdemeanant; felon; convict, jail-bird, ticket-of-leave man; outlaw.

blackguard, *polisson*, loafer, sneak; raps-, ras-callion; cullion, mean wretch, varlet, kern, *âme-de-boue, drôle*; cur, dog, hound, whelp, mongrel; lown, loon, runnion, outcast, vagabond; rogue &c. (*knave*) 941; scum of the earth, riffraff; *Arcades ambo.*

Int. sirrah!

950. Penitence.—N. penitence, contrition, compunction, repentance, remorse; regret &c. 833.

self-reproach, -reproof, -accusation, -condemnation, -humiliation; stings -, pangs -, qualms -, prickings -, twinge -, twitch -, touch -, voice- of conscience; compunctious visitings of nature.

acknowledgment, confession &c. (*disclosure*) 529; apology &c. 952; recantation &c. 607; penance &c. 952; resipiscence.

awakened conscience, deathbed repentance, *locus pœnitentiæ*, stool of repentance, cutty stool.

penitent, Magdalen, prodigal son, returned prodigal, a sadder and a wiser man.

V. repent, be sorry for; be -penitent &c. *adj.*; rue; regret &c. 833; think better of; recant &c. 607; knock under &c. (*submit*) 725; plead guilty; sing -miserere, – de profundis; cry *peccavi*; own oneself in the wrong; acknowledge, confess &c. (*disclose*) 529; humble oneself; beg pardon &c. (*apologize*) 952; turn over a new leaf, put on the new man, turn from sin; reclaim; repent in sackcloth and ashes &c. (*do penance*) 952; learn by experience.

Adj. penitent; repenting &c. *v.*; repentant, contrite; conscience-smitten, -stricken; self-accusing, -convicted.

penitenti-al, -ary; chastened, reclaimed; not hardened; unhardened.

Adv. meâ culpâ.

Phr. peccavi; erubuit; salva res est; vous l'avez voulu, Georges Dandin.

951. Impenitence.—N. impenitence, irrepentance, recusance.

hardness of heart, seared conscience, induration, obduracy.

V. be -impenitent &c. *adj.*; steel -, harden- the heart; die -game, – and make no sign.

Adj. impenitent, uncontrite, obdurate; hard, -ened; seared, recusant; unrepentant; relent-, remorse-, grace-, shrift-less.

lost, incorrigible, irreclaimable.

unre-claimed, -formed; unrepented, unatoned.

952. Atonement.—N. atonement, reparation; compromise, composition; compensation &c. 30; quittance, quits; indemni-ty, -fication; expiation, redemption, reclamation, conciliation, propitiation.

amends, apology, amende honorable, satisfaction; peace -, sin -, burnt- offering; scapegoat, sacrifice.

penance, fasting, maceration, sackcloth and ashes, white sheet, shrift, flagellation, lustration; purga-tion, -tory.

V. atone, – for; expiate; propitiate; make -amends, – good; reclaim, redeem, repair, ransom, absolve, purge,

shrive, do penance, stand in a white sheet, repent in sackcloth and ashes.

set one's house in order, wipe off old scores, make matters up; pay the -forfeit, – penalty.

apologize, beg pardon, express regret, faire amende honorable, give satisfaction; come -, fall- down on one's -knees, – marrow bones.

Adj. propitiatory, expiatory; sacrific, -ial, -atory; piacul-ar, -ous.

4°. MORAL PRACTICE

953. Temperance.—N. temperance, moderation, sobriety, soberness.

forbearance, abnegation; self-denial, -restraint, -control &c. (*resolution*) 604.

frugality; vegetarianism, teetotalism, total abstinence, prohibition; abstinence, -emiousness, asceticism &c. 955; system of -Pythagoras, – Cornaro; Pythagorism, Stoicism.

vegetarian; Pythagorean, gymnosophist; teetotaler &c. 958; abstainer.

V. be -temperate &c. *adj.*; abstain, forbear, refrain, deny oneself, spare; know when one has had enough; take the pledge; look not upon the wine when it is red.

Adj. temperate, moderate, sober, frugal, sparing; abst-emious, -inent; within compass; measured &c. (*sufficient*) 639.

Pythagorean; vegetarian; teetotal, pussy-foot.

954. Intemperance.—N. intemperance; sensuality, animalism, carnality; pleasure; effeminacy, silkiness; luxur-y, -iousness; lap of -pleasure, – luxury.

indulgence; high-, free- living, inabstinence, self-indulgence; voluptuousness &c. *adj.*; epicur-ism, -eanism; sybaritism.

dissipation; licentiousness &c. *adj.*; debauchery; crapulence.

revel-s, -ry; debauch, carousal, jollification, drinking bout, wassail, Saturnalia, orgies; excess, too much; intoxication &c. 959.

Circean cup; drug habit &c. 663.
V. be -intemperate &c. *adj.*; indulge,
exceed; live -well, – high, – on the fat
of the land; give a loose to -indulgence
&c. *n.*; dine not wisely but too well;
wallow in -voluptuousness &c. *n.*;
plunge into dissipation.

revel, rake, live hard, run riot, sow
one's wild oats; slake one's -appetite, –
thirst; swill; pamper.

Adj. intemperate, inabstinent, intoxicated &c. 958; sensual, self-indulgent;
voluptuous, luxurious, licentious, wild,
dissolute, rakish, fast, debauched.

brutish, crapulous, swinish, piggish,
hoggish, bestial.

Paphian, Epicurean, Sybaritical; bred
–, nursed- in the lap of luxury; in-
dulged, pampered, full-fed.

954a. Sensualist.—N. Sybarite, voluptuary, Sardanapalus, man of pleasure, carpet knight; epicure, -an; *gourmet, -and*; gormandizer, gutling, glutton,
pig, hog; votary –, swine- of Epicurus;
sensualist; Heliogabalus; free –, hard-
liver; libertine &c. 962; hedonist.

955. Asceticism.—N. asceticism,
puritanism, sabbatarianism; cynicism,
austerity; total abstinence.

mortification, maceration, sackcloth
and ashes, flagellation; penance &c.
952; fasting &c. 956; martyrdom.

ascetic; anchor-et, -ite; martyr; *Heautontimorumenos*; hermit &c. (*recluse*)
893; puritan, sabbatarian, cynic.

Adj. ascetic, austere, puritanical;
cynical; over-religious.

956. Fasting.—N. fasting; exropha-
gy; famishment, starvation; banting.

fast, *jour maigre*; fast –, banyan-day;
Lent, quadragesima; Rama-dan, -zan;
spare –, meagre- diet; lenten -diet, –
entertainment; *soupe maigre*, short
-rations, – commons; Barmecide feast;
hunger strike.

V. fast, starve, clem, famish, perish
with hunger; dine with Duke Humphrey;
make two bites of a cherry.

Adj. lenten, quadragesimal; unfed;

starved &c. *v.*; half-starved; fasting &c.
v.; hungry &c. 865.

957. Gluttony.—N. gluttony; greed;
greediness &c. *adj.*; voracity.

epicurism; good –, high- living; edacity, gulosity, crapulence; gutt-, guzz-
ling; over-indulgence.

good cheer, blow out; feast &c. (*food*)
298; gastronomy.

epicure, *bon vivant, gourmand*; glutton, cormorant, hog, belly-god, Apicius, gastronome, gormandizer.

V. gormandize, gorge; over-gorge,
-eat- oneself; engorge, eat one's fill,
cram, stuff, stodge, glut, satiate; guttle,
guzzle; bolt, devour, gobble up; gulp
&c. (*swallow food*) 298; raven, eat out
of house and home.

have the stomach of an ostrich; play a
good knife and fork &c. (*appetite*) 865.

pamper, indulge.

Adj. gluttonous, greedy; gormandiz-
ing &c. *v.*; edacious, omnivorous, crap-
ulent, swinish, voracious, devouring.

pampered; over-fed, -gorged.

958. Sobriety.—N. sobriety; teetotalism, temperance &c. 953.

water-drinker; teetotal-er, -ist; abstainer, Good Templar, Rechabite, band
of hope; prohibitionist, pussyfoot.

V. take the pledge.

Adj. sober, – as a judge; dry, on the
water wagon.

959. Drunkenness.—N. drunkenness
&c. *adj.*; intemperance; drinking &c. *v.*;
inebri-ety; -ation; ebri-ety, -osity; befuddlement; insobriety; intoxication; temulency, bibacity, wine-bibbing; com-,
potation; deep potations, bacchanals,
bacchanalia, libations.

oino-, dipso-mania; *delirium tremens*,
d.t.; alcohol, -ism.

drink; alcoholic drinks, alcohol,
booze; gin, blue ruin, grog, brandy, port
wine; punch, -bowl; cup, rosy wine,
flowing bowl; drop, – too much; dram;
beer, wine, spirits &c. (*beverage*) 298;
cocktail, nip, peg; stirrup cup.

drunkard, sot, toper, tippler, bibber,

wine-bibber; hard -, gin -, dram- drinker; soak, soaker, sponge, tun; love-, toss-pot; thirsty soul, reveller, carouser; Bacchanal, -ian; Bacch-al, -ante; devotee to Bacchus, dipsomaniac.

V. get -, be- drunk &c. *adj.*; see double; take a -drop, - glass- too much; drink, tipple, tope, booze, bouse, guzzle, swill, soak, sot, lush, bib, swig, carouse; sacrifice at the shrine of Bacchus; take to drinking; drink -hard, - deep, - like a fish; have one's swill, drain the cup, splice the main brace, take a hair of the dog that bit you.

liquor, - up; wet one's whistle, take a whet; lift one's elbow; crack a -, pass the- bottle; toss off &c. *(drink up)* 298; go to the -ale, - public-house.

make one -drunk &c. *adj.*; inebriate, fuddle, fuzzle, get into one's head.

Adj. drunk, tipsy; intoxicated; inebrious, -ate, -ated; in one's cups; in a state of -intoxication &c. *n.*; temulent, -ive; fuddled, mellow, cut, boosy, fou, fresh, merry, elevated, squiffy; plastered, befuddled, sozzled; flush, -ed; flustered, disguised, groggy, beery; topheavy; potvaliant, glorious; potulent; overcome, -taken; whittled, screwed, tight, primed, oiled, corned, raddled, sewed up, lushy, nappy, muddled, muzzy; bosky, obfuscated, maudlin; crapulous, dead -, blind- drunk.

inter pocula; in -, the worse for- liquor, having had a drop too much, half seas over, three sheets in the wind; under the table, blind to the world, one over the eight.

drunk as -a piper, - a fiddler, - a lord, - Chloe, - an owl, - David's sow, - a wheelbarrow.

drunken, bibacious, bibulous, sottish; given -, addicted- to -drink, - the bottle; toping &c. *v.*; wet.

Phr. *nunc est bibendum.*

960. Purity.—N. purity; decency, decorum, delicacy; continence, chastity, honesty, virtue, modesty, shame; pudicity, *pucelage*, virginity.

vestal, virgin, Joseph, Hippolytus; Lucretia, Diana; prude.

Adj. pure, undefiled, modest, delicate, decent, decorous; *virginibus puerisque*; chaste, continent, virtuous, honest, Platonic.

961. Impurity.—N. impurity; uncleanness &c. *(filth)* 653; immodesty; grossness &c. *adj.*; indelicacy, indecency; impudicity; obscenity, ribaldry, smut, bawdry, *double entendre, équivoque*; Aretinism; pornography.

concupiscence, lust, carnality, flesh, salacity; pruriency, lechery, lasciviency, lubricity, lewdness.

incontinence, intrigue, *faux pas; amour, -ette*; gallantry; debauchery, libertinism, *libertinage*, fornication; *liaison*; wenching, venery, dissipation.

seduction; defloration, defilement, abuse, violation, rape; incest.

social evil, harlotry, stupration, whoredom, concubinage, cuckoldom, adultery, advoutry, *crim. con.*; free love.

seraglio, harem, zenana; brothel, bagnio, stew, bawdy-house, *lupanar*, house of ill fame, *bordel*, kip.

V. be -impure &c. *adj.*; intrigue; debauch, defile, assault, attack, seduce; prostitute; abuse, violate, deflower; commit -adultery &c. *n.*

Adj. impure; unclean &c. *(dirty)* 653; not to be mentioned to ears polite; immodest, shameless; in-decorous, -delicate, -decent; loose, suggestive, *risqué*, coarse, gross, broad, free, equivocal, smutty, fulsome, ribald, obscene, bawdy, pornographic.

concupiscent, prurient, lickerish, rampant, lustful; carnal, -minded; lewd, lascivious, lecherous, libidinous, erotic, ruttish, salacious; Paphian; voluptuous; incestuous.

unchaste, light, wanton, licentious, adulterous, debauched, dissolute; of -loose character, - easy virtue; frail, gay, riggish, incontinent, meretricious, rakish, gallant, dissipated; no better than she should be; on the -town, - streets, - *pavé*, - loose.

adulterous, incestuous, bestial.

962. Libertine.—N. libertine; voluptuary &c. 954a; rake, debauchee, loose fish, rip, rake-hell, fast man; *intrigant*, gallant, seducer, fornicator, lecher, satyr, goat, whoremonger, *paillard*, adulterer, gay deceiver, Lothario, Don Juan, Blue-beard.

adulteress, advoutress, courtesan, prostitute, strumpet, tart, hustler, chippy, broad, harlot, whore, punk, *fille de joie*; woman, – of the town; streetwalker, Cyprian, miss, piece; frail sisterhood, fallen woman; demirep, wench, trollop, trull, baggage, hussy, drab, bitch, jade, skit, rig, quean, mopsy, slut, minx, harridan; woman -of easy virtue &c. (*unchaste*) 961; wanton, fornicatress; Jezebel, Messalina, Delilah, Thaïs, Phryne, Aspasia, Lais, *lorette, cocotte, petite dame, grisette; demimonde*; white slave.

concubine, mistress, fancy woman, kept woman, doxy, *chère amie, bona roba*.

pimp; pand-er, -ar; bawd, *conciliatrix*, procuress, mackerel; wittol.

5°. INSTITUTIONS

963. Legality.—N. legality; legitimacy, -teness, legitimization.

legislature; law, code, *corpus juris*, constitution, pandect, charter, act, enactment, statute, rule; canon &c. (*precept*) 697; ordinance, institution, regulation; by-, bye-law, rescript; decree &c. (*order*) 741; *ordonnance*; standing order; *plébiscite* &c. (*choice*) 609.

legal process; form, -ula, -ality; rite; arm of the law; *habeas corpus*.

[Science of law] jurisprudence, nomology; legislation, codification.

equity, common law; *lex -, lex nonscripta*, unwritten law; law of nations, international law, *jus gentium; jus civile*; civil -, criminal -, canon -, statute -, ecclesiastical- law; *lex mercatoria*.

constitutional-ism, -ity; justice &c. 922.

V. legalize, legitimize; enact, ordain; decree &c. (*order*) 741; pass a law; legislate; codify, formulate; authorize.

Adj. legal, legitimate; according to law; vested, constitutional, chartered, legalized; lawful &c. (*permitted*) 760; statut-able, -ory; legislat-orial, -ive.

Adv. legally &c. *adj.*; in the eye of the law; *de jure*.

964. [Absence or violation of law.] Illegality.—N. lawlessness; breach -, violation- of law; disobedience &c. 742; unconformity &c. 83.

arbitrariness &c. *adj.*; antinomy, violence, brute force, despotism, outlawry.

mob -, lynch -, club -, Lydford -, martial -, drumhead- law; *coup d'état; le droit du plus fort; argumentum baculinum*.

illegality, informality, unlawfulness, illegitimacy, bar sinister.

trover and conversion; smuggling, boot-legging, rum-running, poaching; simony.

speakeasy, speakie, blind pig.

V. offend against -, violate- the law; set the law at defiance, ride rough-shod over, drive a coach and six through a statute; make the law a dead letter, take the law into one's own hands.

smuggle, run, poach.

Adj. illegal; prohibited &c. 761; not allowed, unlawful, illegitimate, illicit, contraband, actionable.

unchartered, unconstitutional; unwarrant-ed, -able; unauthorized; informal, unofficial; in-, extra-judicial.

lawless, arbitrary; despotic, -al; summary, irresponsible; un-answerable, -accountable.

null and void; a dead letter.

Adv. illegally &c. *adj.*; with a high hand, in violation of law.

965. Jurisdiction. [Executive.]—N. jurisdiction, judicature, administration of justice, soc; executive, commission of

the peace; magistracy &c. (*authority*)
737.

judge &c. 967; tribunal &c. 966; municipality, corporation, bailiwick, shrievalty; lord lieutenant; lord -, mayor, city manager, alderman &c. 745; sheriff, bailie, shrieve, chief -, constable; police, - force; constabulary, bumbledom.

officer; proctor, high -, commissioner; bailiff, tipstaff, bum-bailiff, catchpoll, beadle; police-man, -constable, -sergeant; *sbirro, alguazil, gendarme,* kavass, *lictor,* macebearer, *huissier,* bedel.

press-gang; exciseman, gauger, custom-house officer, *douanier*.

coroner, edile, ædile, portreeve, paritor; *posse comitatus*.

V. judge, sit in judgment.

Adj. executive, administrative, municipal; inquisitorial, causidical; judicatory, -iary, -ial; juridical.

Adv. *coram judice*.

966. Tribunal.—N. tribunal, court, board, bench, judicatory, curia; court of -justice, - law, - arbitration; inquisition; guild.

justice -, judgment -, mercy- seat; woolsack; bar, - of justice; dock; forum, hustings, *bureau,* drum-head; jury-, witness-box.

senate-house, town-hall, theatre; House of -Lords, - Commons.

assize, eyre; ward-, burgh-mote; superior courts of Westminster; court of -record, - oyer and terminer, - assize, - appeal, - error; High court of -Judicature, - Appeal; Judicial Committee of the Privy Council; Star-Chamber; Court of -Chancery, - King's *or* Queen's Bench, - Exchequer, - Common Pleas, - Probate, - Arches, - Admiralty, - Criminal Appeal; Lords Justices' -, Rolls -, Vice Chancellor's -, Stannary -, Divorce -, Palatine -, ecclesiastical -, county -, police- court; sessions; quarter -, petty- sessions; court -leet, - baron, - of pie poudre, - of common council; board of green cloth.

court-martial; drum-head court-martial; *durbar,* divan; Areopagus; *rota*.

Adj. judicial &c. 965; appellate; curial.

967. Judge.—N. judge; justi-ce, -ciar, -ciary; chancellor; justice -, judge- of assize; recorder, common serjeant; puisne -, assistant -, county court-judge; conservator -, justice- of the peace, J.P.; court &c. (*tribunal*) 966; grand -, petty -, coroner's- jury; panel, juror, juryman; twelve men in a box; magistrate, police magistrate, stipendiary, the great unpaid, beak; his -worship, - honour, - lordship; deemster, moderator.

Lord -Chancellor, - Justice; Master of the Rolls, Vice-Chancellor; Lord Chief -Justice, - Baron; Mr. Justice; Baron, - of the Exchequer.

jurat, assessor; arbi-ter, -trator; umpire; refer-ee, -endary; revising barrister; domesman; censor &c. (*critic*) 480, official -, receiver.

archon, tribune, prætor, *ephor,* syndic, *podestà,* mullah, ulema, mufti, cadi, kadi; Rhadamanthus.

litigant &c. (*accusation*) 938.

V. adjudge &c. (*determine*) 480; try a -case, - prisoner.

Adj. judicial &c. 965.

Phr. 'a Daniel come to judgment.'

968. Lawyer.—N. lawyer, jurist, legist, civilian, pundit, publicist, jurisconsult, legal adviser, advocate; barrister, - at law; counsel, -lor; King's *or* Queen's counsel; K.C.; Q.C.; silk gown, leader; junior, - counsel; stuff gown, serjeant-at-law, bencher; tubman; judge &c. 967.

bar, legal profession, gentleman of the long robe; junior -, outer -, inner- bar; Inns of Court; equity draftsman, conveyancer, pleader, special pleader.

solicitor, attorney, proctor; notary, - public; scrivener, cursitor; writer, - to the signet; S.S.C.; limb of the law; pettifogger.

V. practise -at, - within- the bar; plead; call -, be called- -to, - within- the bar; take silk.

Adj. learned in the law; at the bar; forensic.

969. Lawsuit.—N. lawsuit, suit, action, cause, petition; litigation; dispute &c. 713.

citation, arraignment, prosecution, impeachment; accusation &c. 938; presentment, true bill, indictment.

apprehension, arrest; committal; imprisonment &c. (*restraint*) 751.

writ, summons, subpœna, *latitat, nisi prius; habeas corpus.*

pleadings; declaration, bill, claim; *procès-verbal*, bill of right, information, *corpus delicti*; affidavit, state of facts; answer, replication, plea, demurrer, rebutter, rejoinder; surre-butter, -joinder.

suitor, party to a suit; litigant &c. 938; libellant.

hearing, trial; verdict &c. (*judgment*) 480; appeal, – motion; writ of error; *certiorari.*

case, decision, precedent, ruling; decided case, reports.

V. go to –, appeal to the- law; bring to -justice, – trial, – the bar; put on trial, pull up; accuse &c. 938; prefer –, file a claim &c. *n.*; take the law of, inform against.

serve with a writ, cite, apprehend, arraign, sue, prosecute, bring an action against, indict, impeach, attach, distrain, commit; arrest; summon, -s; give in charge &c. (*restrain*) 751.

empanel a jury, implead, join issue; close the pleadings; set down for hearing.

try, hear a cause; sit in judgment; adjudicate &c. 480.

Adj. litigious &c. (*quarrelsome*) 713; *qui tam; coram –, sub- judice.*

Adv. *pendente lite.*

Phr. *adhuc sub judice lis est.*

970. Acquittal.—N. acquit-tal, -ment; clearance, exculpation, exoneration; discharge &c. (*release*) 750; *quietus*, absolution, compurgation, reprieve, respite; pardon &c. (*forgiveness*) 918.

[Exemption from punishment] impunity, immunity.

V. acquit, exculpate, exonerate, clear; absolve, whitewash, assoil, discharge, release; liberate &c. 750.

reprieve, respite; pardon &c. (*forgive*) 918; let off, – scot free.

Adj. acquitted &c. *v.*; un-condemned, -punished, -chastised; recommended to mercy.

971. Condemnation.—N. condemnation, conviction, proscription, damnation; death warrant; penalty &c. 974.

attain-der, -ture, -tment.

V. condemn, convict, cast, bring home to, find guilty, damn, doom, sign the death warrant, sentence, pass sentence on, attaint, confiscate, proscribe, sequestrate; non-suit.

disapprove &c. 932; accuse &c. 938.

stand condemned.

Adj. condem-, dam-natory; condemned &c. *v.*; non-suited &c. (*failure*) 732; self-convicted.

Phr. *mutato nomine de te fabula narratur.*

972. Punishment.—N. punishment, punition; chast-isement, -ening; correction, castigation.

discipline, infliction, trial; judgment; penalty &c. 974; retribution; thunderbolt, Nemesis; requital &c. (*reward*) 973; penology; retributive justice.

lash, scaffold &c. (*instrument of punishment*) 975; imprisonment &c. (*restraint*) 751; chain gang; transportation, banishment, expulsion, deportation, exile, involuntary exile, ostracism; penal servitude, hard labour; galleys &c. 975; beating &c. *v.*; flagellation, fustigation, gantlet, *strappado, estrapade, bastinado, argumentum baculinum*, stick law, rap on the knuckles, box on the ear; blow &c. (*impulse*) 276; stripe, cuff, kick, buffet, pummel; slap, – in the face; wipe, douse; *coup de grâce*; torture, rack; picket, -ing; *dragonnade*; capital punishment, extreme penalty; execution; hanging &c. *v.*; de-capitation, -collation; *garrot-te, -to*; electrocution, lethal chamber; crucifixion, impalement; martyrdom, *auto-da-fé; noyade; hara-kiri,* happy despatch.

V. punish; chast-ise, -en; castigate, correct, inflict punishment, administer correction, deal retributive justice.

visit upon, pay; pay -, serve- out; settle with, get even with, get one's own back; do for; make short work of, give a lesson to, strafe, serve one right, make an example of; have a rod in pickle for; give it one.

strike &c. 276; deal a blow to, administer the lash, smite; slap, - the face; smack, cuff, box the ears, spank, thwack, thump, beat, lay on, swinge, buffet; thresh, thrash, pummel, drub, leather, trounce, baste, belabour; lace, - one's jacket; dress, give a -dressing, - down; trim, warm, wipe, tund, cob, bang, strap, comb, lash, lick, larrup, whallop, whop, flog, scourge, whip, birch, cane, give the stick, switch, flagellate, horsewhip, *bastinado*, towel, rub down with an oaken towel, rib roast, dust one's jacket, fustigate, pitch into, lay about one, beat black and blue; beat to a -mummy, - jelly; give a black eye; hit on the head; sandbag.

tar and feather; pelt, stone, lapidate; mast-head, keelhaul.

execute; bring to the -block, - gallows; behead; de-capitate, -collate; guillotine; hang, turn off, gibbet, bowstring, hang, draw and quarter; shoot; decimate; burn; electrocute; break on the wheel, crucify; em-, im-pale; flay; lynch; put to death.

torture; put -on, - to- the rack; picket.

banish, exile; trans-, de-port; expel, ostracize; rusticate; drum out; dismiss, -bar, -bench; strike off the roll, unfrock; post.

suffer, - for, - punishment; be -flogged, - hanged &c.; come to the gallows, dance upon nothing, die in one's shoes; be rightly served.

Adj. punishing &c. *v.*; penal; punitory, -tive; inflictive, castigatory; punished &c. *v.*

Int. *à la lanterne!*

973. Reward.—N. reward, recompense, remuneration, prize, meed, guerdon, reguerdon; indemni-ty, -fication, price; quittance; compensation; reparation, *ersatz*, assythment, redress; retribution, reckoning, acknowledgment, requital, amends, sop; atonement; consideration, return, *quid pro quo*; salvage, perquisite; vail &c. (*donation*) 784; *douceur*, bribe, bait, baksheesh, tip; hush-, smart-money; blackmail; carcelage; *solatium*.

allowance, salary, stipend, wages; pay, -ment; emolument; tribute; batta, shot, scot; premium, fee, *honorarium*; hire.

crown &c. (*decoration of honour*) 877.

V. re-ward, -compense, -pay, -quite; re-, munerate; compensate; fee, tip, bribe; pay one's footing &c. (*pay*) 807; make amends, indemnify, atone; satisfy, acknowledge.

get for one's pains, reap the fruits of.

Adj. remunerat-ive, -ory; munerary, compensatory, retributive, reparatory.

974. Penalty.—N. penalty; retribution &c. (*punishment*) 972; pain, pains and penalties; *peine forte et dure*; penance &c. (*atonement*) 952; the devil to pay.

fine, mulct, amercement; forfeit, -ure; escheat, damages, deodand, sequestration, confiscation, *premunire*.

V. penalize, fine, mulct, amerce, sconce, confiscate; sequest-rate, -er; escheat; estreat, forfeit.

975. [Instrument of punishment.] Scourge.—N. scourge, rod, cane, stick; ra-, rat-tan; birch, - rod; rod in pickle; switch, ferule, cudgel, truncheon; rubber hose.

whip, lash, strap, thong, cowhide, knout; cat, - o'-nine-tails, *sjambok*, quirt; rope's end.

pillory, stocks, whipping-post; cuck-, duck-ing stool; brank; triangle, wooden horse, maiden, thumbscrew, boot, rack, wheel, iron heel; treadmill, crank, galleys.

scaffold; block, axe, *guillotine*; stake; cross; gallows, gibbet, Tyburn tree; drop, noose, rope, halter, bowstring; electric chair, lethal chamber.

house of correction &c. (*prison*) 752. gaol-, jail-er; executioner; hang-, heads-man; Jack Ketch; lyncher.

Section V. RELIGIOUS AFFECTIONS

1°. Superhuman Beings and Regions

976. Deity.—N. Deity, Divinity; God-head, -ship; Omnipotence, Providence.

[Quality of being divine] divin-eness, -ity.

God, Lord, Jehovah, *Deus*; The -Almighty, – Supreme Being, – First Cause; *Ens Entium*; Author –, Creator-of all things; Author of our being; The -Infinite, – Eternal; The All-powerful, -wise, -merciful, -holy; The Omni-potent, -scient.

[Attributes and perfections] infinite -power, – wisdom, – goodness, – justice, – truth, – love, – mercy; omni-potence, -science, -presence; unity, immutability, holiness, glory, majesty, sovereignty, infinity, eternity.

The -Trinity, – Holy Trinity, – Trinity in Unity, – Triune God; Three in One and One in Three.

God the Father; The -Maker, – Creator, – Preserver.

[Functions] creation, preservation, divine government; The-ocracy, -archy; providence; ways –, dealings –, dispensations –, visitations- of Providence.

God the Son, Jesus, Christ; The -Messiah, – Anointed, – Saviour, – Redeemer, – Mediator, – Intercessor, – Advocate, – Judge; The Son of -God, – Man, – David; The Only Begotten; The Lamb of God, The Word; Em-, Immanuel; The -King of Kings and Lord of Lords, – King of Glory, – Prince of Peace, – Good Shepherd, – Way, – Truth, – Life, – Bread of Life, – Light

of the World; The -Lord our, – Sun of -Righteousness.

The -Incarnation, – Hypostatic Union, – Word made Flesh.

[Functions] salvation, redemption, atonement, propitiation, mediation, intercession, judgment.

God the Holy Ghost, The Holy Spirit, Paraclete; The -Comforter, – Consoler, – Spirit of Truth, – Dove.

[Functions] inspiration, unction, regeneration, sanctification, consolation.

eon, æon, special providence, *Deus ex machinâ; Avatar.*

V. create, uphold, preserve, govern &c.

atone, redeem, save, propitiate, mediate &c.

predestinate, elect, call, ordain, bless, justify, sanctify, glorify &c.

Adj. almighty, holy, hallowed, sacred, divine, heavenly, celestial; messianic; sacrosanct; all-powerful, -wise, -seeing, -knowing; omnipotent, omniscient; supreme.

super-human, -natural; ghostly, spiritual, hyperphysical, unearthly; the-istic, -ocratic, deistic; anointed.

Adv. *jure divino*, by divine right; *Deo volente*, D.V.

977. [Beneficent spirits.] **Angel.—N.** angel, archangel; heavenly host, choir invisible, host of heaven, sons of God; Michael, Gabriel &c.; seraph, -im; cherub, -im; ministering spirit, morning star; saint, *Madonna*; Our Lady, the Blessed Virgin, the Virgin Mary.

Adj. angelic, seraphic, cherubic.

978. [Maleficent spirits.] Satan.—N. Satan, the Devil, Lucifer, Ahrimanes, Belial; Sammael, Zamiel, Beelzebub, the Prince of the Devils; Mephistopheles, his satanic majesty.*

the tempter; the evil -one, - spirit; the -author of evil, - wicked one, - old Serpent; the Prince of -darkness, - this world, - the power of the air; the -foul, - arch- fiend; the devil incarnate; the -common enemy, - angel of the bottomless pit; Abaddon, Apollyon, Mammon.

fallen angels, unclean spirits, devils; the -rulers, - powers- of darkness; inhabitants of Pandemonium; demon &c. 980.

diabolism; devil-ism, -ship, -dom, -ry, -worship; *diablerie*; satanism, manicheism; the cloven foot; black magic &c. 992.

Adj. satanic, diabolic, devilish, infernal, hell-born.

Heathen, Mythological and other fabulous Deities and Powers†

979. Jupiter.—N. god, -dess; heathen gods and goddesses; Pantheon; Jupiter, Jove, Zeus, Apollo, Mars, Mercury, Neptune, Vulcan, Bacchus, Pluto, Saturn, Cupid, Eros, Pan; Juno, Ceres, Proserpina, Dina, Minerva, Pallas, Athenae, Venus, Aphrodite, Vesta; The Fates &c. 601.

Allah, Brahma, Vishnu, Siva, Shiva, Krishna, Juggernaut, Buddha; Ra, Isis, Osiris; Belus, Bel, Baal, Asteroth &c.; Thor, Odin; Mumbo Jumbo; good -, tutelary- genius; demiurge, familiar, - spirit; Sibyl; fairy, fay; sylph, -id; Ariel, peri, nymph, nereid, dryad, oread, sea-maid, Banshee, Benshie, Ormuzd;

* The slang expressions 'the -deuce, - dickens, - old Gentleman; old -Nick, - Scratch, - Horny, - Harry, - Gooseberry,' have not been inserted in the text.

† Only a selection of those best known to literature is included.

Oberon, Titania, Mab, hamadryad, naiad, mermaid, kelpie, Ondine, nix, nixie, sprite; denizens of the air; pixy &c. (*bad spirit*) 980.

mythology; heathen -, fairy- mythology; Lemprière, folklore.

Adj. fairy-, sylph-like; sylphic.

980. Demon.—N. demon, -ry, -ism, -ology; evil genius, fiend, familiar, - spirit, devil; bad -, unclean- spirit; cacodemon, incubus, Frankenstein's monster, succubus and succuba, Titan, Shedim, Mephistopheles, Asmodeus, Moloch, Belial, Ahriman, fury, The Furies &c. 900; harpy; Friar Rush.

vampire, ghoul; af-, ef-freet; afrite; ogre, -ss; gnome, gin, djinn, imp, deev, *lamia*; bo-gie, -gle; nis, kobold, flibbertigibbet, fairy, brownie, pixy, elf, dwarf, urchin, Puck, Robin Goodfellow; lepre-, cluri-chaune; troll, dwerger, sprite, oaf, changeling, bad fairy, nixe, pigwidgeon, Will-o'-the-wisp; Erl King.

[Supernatural appearance] ghost, spectre, apparition, genie, spirit, shade, shadow, vision, phantom &c. 443; materialization (*spiritualism*) 992; hob-, goblin; wraith, spook, werwolf, boggart, banshee, *loup-garou, lemures*; evil eye.

nisse, necks; mer-man, -maid, -folk; siren, Lorelei; satyr, faun.

Adj. supernatural, weird, uncanny, unearthly, spectral; ghost-ly, -like; elf-in, -like; fiend-ish, -like; impish, demoniacal; haunted.

981. Heaven.—N. heaven; kingdom of -heaven, - God; heavenly kingdom; throne -, presence- of God; inheritance of the saints in light.

Paradise, Eden, abode of the blessed; Holy City, New Jerusalem; celestial bliss, glory.

[Mythological -heaven] Olympus; [- paradise] Elysium, Elysian fields, Arcadia, bowers of bliss, garden of the Hesperides, Islands of the Blessed; happy hunting-ground; third -, seventh- heaven; Valhalla (Scandinavian); Nirvana (Buddhist).

future state, eternity, eternal life, life after death, eternal home, resurrection, translation; resuscitation &c. 660; apotheosis, deification.

Adj. heavenly, celestial, supernal, unearthly, from on high, paradisiacal, beatific, elysian, Olympian, Arcadian.

982. Hell.—N. hell, bottomless pit, place of torment; habitation of fallen angels; Pandemonium, Abaddon, Domdaniel.

hell fire; everlasting -fire, - torment; lake of fire and brimstone; fire that is never quenched, worm that never dies.

purgatory, limbo, gehenna, abyss.

[Mythological hell] Tartarus, Hades, Avernus, Styx, Stygian creek, pit of Acheron, Cocytus, Phlegethon, Lethe; infernal regions, *inferno*, shades below, realms of Pluto.

Pluto, Rhadamanthus, Erebus, Charon, Cerberus; Tophet.

Adj. hellish, infernal, stygian.

2°. RELIGIOUS DOCTRINES

983. [Religious Knowledge.] Theology.—N. Theology (natural and revealed); Theo-gony, -sophy; Divinity; Hagio-logy, -graphy; Caucasian mystery; monotheism; religion; religious -persuasion, - sect, - denomination; cult; creed &c. (*belief*) 484; articles -, declaration -, profession -, confession- of faith.

theolog-ue, -ian; divine, schoolman, canonist, monotheist.

Adj. theological, religious; canonical; denominational; sectarian &c. 984.

983a. Orthodoxy.—N. orthodoxy; strictness, soundness, religious truth, true faith; truth &c. 494.

Christian-ity, -ism; Catholic-ism, -ity; 'the faith once delivered to the saints'; hyperorthodoxy &c. 984; iconoclasm.

the Holy -, the Orthodox- Church; Catholic -, Universal -, Apostolic -, Established- Church; temple of the Holy

Ghost; Church -, body -, members -, disciples -, followers- of Christ; Christian, - community; true believer; canonist &c. (*theologian*) 983; Christendom, collective body of Christians, the Church Militant.

canons &c. (*belief*) 484; thirty-nine articles; Apostles' -, Nicene -, Athanasian- Creed; Church Catechism; textuary.

Adj. orthodox, sound, literal, strict, faithful, catholic, schismless, Christian, evangelical, scriptural, divine, monotheistic; true &c. 494.

984. Heterodoxy. [Sectarianism.]— N. heterodoxy; error &c. 495; false doctrine, heresy, schism; schismantic-ism, -alness; recusancy, backsliding, apostasy; atheism &c. (*irreligion*) 989.

bigotry &c. (*obstinacy*) 606; fanaticism, iconoclasm; hyperorthodoxy, precisianism, bibliolatry, hagiolatry, sabbatarianism, puritanism; idolatry &c. 991; superstition &c. (*credulity*) 486; dissent &c. 489.

sectar-ism, -ianism; nonconformity; secularism; syncretism, religious sects; the clash of creeds.

protestant-, advent-, Arian-, Erastian-, Calvin-, quaker-, method-, anabapt-, Pusey-, tractarian-, ritual-, Origen-, Sabellian-, Socinian-, De-, The-, mon-, material-, positiv-, latitudinarian-ism &c.

High -, Low -, Broad -, Free-Church; ultramontanism; monasticism; pap-ism, -istry; papacy; Anglican-, Catholic-, Roman-ism; popery, Scarlet Lady, Church of Rome, Greek Church; Christian Science, The Church of Christ Scientist.

pagan-, heathen-, ethic-ism; mythology; animism; poly-, di-, tri-, pan-theism; dualism; heathendom.

Juda-, Gentil-, Mahometan-, Islam-, Turc-, Brahmin-, Hindoo-, Buddh-, Lama-, Confucian-, Shinto-, Sabian-, Gnostic-, Soofee-, Hylothe-, Mormonism.

Theosophy; Spiritualism, Occultism.

heretic, antichrist; pagan, heathen; pai-, pay-nim; *giaour*; gentile; pan-, poly-theist; idolator; misbeliever, apostate, backslider.

bigot &c. (*obstinacy*) 606; fanatic, dervish, abdal, iconoclast.

latitudinarian, limitarian, Deist, Theist, Unitarian; positivist, materialist; agnostic, sceptic &c. 989.

schismatic; sectar-y, -ian, -ist; seceder, separatist, recusant, dissenter; nonconformist, -juror; Huguenot, Protestant; orthodox dissenter, Congregationalist, Independent; Episcopalian, Presbyterian; Lutheran, Calvinist, Quaker, Methodist, Wesleyan; Ana-, Baptist; Dunker; Mormon, Latter-day Saint, Irvingite, Sandemanian, Glassite, Erastian; Sub-, Supra-lapsarian; Gentoo, Antinomian, Swedenborgian, Adventist, Plymouth Brother; Theosophist &c.

Catholic, Roman Catholic, Romanist, papist, ultramontane; Old Catholic, tractarian, Anglican, Puseyite, ritualist; Puritan.

Jew, Hebrew, Rabbist; Mahometan, Mohammedan, Mussulman, Moslem, Islamite, Osmanli; Brahm-in, -an; Parsee, Sofi, Soofee; Buddhist; Zoroastrian, Magi, Gymnosophist, fireworshipper, Sabian, Gnostic, Sadducee, Rosicrucian &c.

Adj. heterodox, heretical; unorthodox, -scriptural, -canonical; antiscriptural, apocryphal; un-, antichristian; schismatic, recusant, iconoclastic; sectarian; dis-senting, -sident; secular &c. (*lay*) 997.

pagan; heathen, -ish; ethnic, -al; gentile, painim; pan-, poly-theistic; agnostic, sceptic.

Judaical, Mohammedan, Moslem, Brahminical, Buddhist &c. *n.* Romish, Protestant &c. *n.*

bigoted &c. (*prejudiced*) 481, (*obstinate*) 606; superstitious &c. (*credulous*) 486; fanatical; idolatrous &c. 991; visionary &c. (*imaginative*) 515.

985. Revelation.—N. revelation, inspiration, *afflatus*.

Word, – of God; Scripture; the -Scriptures, – Bible, – Book of Books; Holy -Writ, – Scriptures; inspired writings, Gospel.

Old Testament, Septuagint, Vulgate, Pentateuch; Octateuch; the -Law, – Jewish Law, – Prophets; major –, minor-Prophets; Hagio-grapha, -logy; Hierographa; Apocrypha.

New Testament; Gospels, Evangelists, Acts, Epistles, Apocalypse, Revelation.

Talmud; Mishna, Masorah.

prophet &c. (*seer*) 513; evangelist, apostle, disciple, saint; the –, the Apostolical- fathers; Holy Men of old, inspired -writers, – penmen.

Adj. scriptural, biblical, sacred, prophetic; evangel-ical, -istic; apostolic, -al; inspired, theopneustic, apocalyptic, ecclesiastical, canonical, textuary.

986. Pseudo-Revelation.—N. the -Koran, – Alcoran; Ly-king, Shaster, Vedas, Zendavesta, Vedidad, Purana, Edda; Go-, Gau-tama; Book of Mormon.

[False prophets and religious founders] Buddha, Zoroaster, Zerdhusht, Confucius, Mahomet.

[Idols] golden calf &c. 991; Baal, Moloch, Dagon.

3°. RELIGIOUS SENTIMENTS

987. Piety.—N. piety, religion, theism, faith; religiousness, holiness &c. *adj.*; saintship; religionism; sanctimony &c. (*assumed piety*) 988; reverence &c. (*respect*) 928; humility, veneration, devotion; prostration &c. (*worship*) 990; grace, unction, edification; sancti-ty, -tude; consecration.

spiritual existence, odour of sanctity, beauty of holiness.

theopathy, beatification, adoption, regeneration, conversion, justification, sanctification, salvation, inspiration, bread of life; Body and Blood of Christ.

believer, convert, theist, Christian,

devotee, pietist; the -good, – righteous, – just, – believing, – elect; Saint, *Madonna*.

the children of -God, – the kingdom, – light.

V. be -pious &c. *adj.*; have -faith &c. *n.*; believe, receive Christ; revere &c. 928; worship &c. 950; be -converted &c.

convert, edify, sanctify, hallow, keep holy, beatify, regenerate, inspire, consecrate, enshrine.

Adj. pious, religious, devout, devoted, reverent, godly, heavenly minded, humble; pure, – in heart; holy, spiritual, pietistic; saint-ly, -like; seraphic, sacred, solemn.

believing, faithful, Christian, Catholic.

elected, adopted, justified, sanctified, regenerated, inspired, consecrated, converted, unearthly, not of the earth.

988. Impiety.—N. impiety; sin &c. 945; irreverence; profan-eness &c. *adj.*, -ity, -ation; blasphemy, desecration, sacrilege; scoffing &c. *v.*

[Assumed piety] hypocrisy &c. (*falsehood*) 544; pietism, cant, pious fraud; lip-devotion, -service, -reverence; misdevotion, formalism, austerity; sanctimon-y, -iousness &c. *adj.*; pharisaism, precisianism; sabbat-ism, -arianism; *odium theologicum*, sacerdotalism; bigotry &c. (*obstinacy*) 606, (*prejudice*) 481.

hardening, backsliding, declension, perversion, reprobation, apostacy, recusancy.

sinner &c. 949; scoffer, blasphemer; sacrilegist; worldling; hypocrite &c. (*dissembler*) 548; Scribes and Pharisees; Tartufe, Maw-worm.

bigot; saint [ironically]; Pharisee, sabbatarian, formalist, methodist, puritan, pietist, precisian, religionist, devotee, ranter, fanatic, wowser.

the -wicked, – evil, – unjust, – reprobate; son of -men, – Belial, – the wicked one; children of darkness.

V. be -impious &c. *adj.*; profane,

desecrate, blaspheme, revile, scoff; swear &c. (*malediction*) 908; commit sacrilege.

snuffle; turn up the whites of the eyes; idolize.

Adj. impious; irreligious &c. 989; desecrating &c. *v.*; profane, irreverent, sacrilegious, blasphemous.

un-hallowed, -sanctified, -regenerate; hardened, perverted, reprobate.

hypocritical &c. (*false*) 544; canting, pietistical, sanctimonious, unctuous, pharisaical, over-righteous, righteous over much.

bigoted, fanatical &c. 481 & 606; priest-ridden.

Adv. under the -mask, cloak, – pretence, – form, – guise- of religion.

989. Irreligion.—N. irreligion, indevotion; ungodliness &c. *adj.*; laxity, quietism, apathy, indifference, passivity.

scepticism, doubt; un-, dis-belief; incredul-ity, -ousness &c. *adj.*; want of -faith, – belief; pyrrhonism; doubt &c. 485; agnosticism.

atheism, deism; hylotheism; materialism; positivism; nihilism.

infidelity, freethinking, antichristianity, rationalism.

atheist, anti-christian, sceptic, unbeliever, deist, infidel, pyrrhonist; *giaour*, heathen, alien, gentile, Nazarene; *esprit fort*, freethinker, latitudinarian, rationalist; materialist, positivist, nihilist, agnostic.

V. be -irreligious &c. *adj.*; disbelieve, lack faith; doubt, question &c. 485.

dechristianize; serve Mammon, love darkness better than light.

Adj. irreligious; in-, un-devout; devout-, god-, grace-less; un-godly, -holy, -sanctified, -hallowed; atheistic, without God.

sceptical, free-thinking; un-believing, -converted; incredulous, faithless, lacking faith; deistical; un-, anti-christian.

worldly, mundane, earthly, carnal, unspiritual; worldly &c.-minded.

Adv. irreligiously &c. *adj.*

4°. ACTS OF RELIGION

990. Worship.—N. worship, adoration, devotion, aspiration, latria, homage, service, humiliation; kneeling, genuflexion, prostration.

prayer, invocation, supplication, rogation, intercession, orison, holy breathing; petition &c. (*request*) 765; collect, litany, Lord's prayer, paternoster, *Ave Maria*, rosary; bead-roll; latria, dulia, hyperdulia, vigils; revival; cult.

thanksgiving; giving -, returning-thanks; grace, praise, glorification, benediction, doxology, hosanna; h-, allelujah; *Te Deum, non nobis Domine, nunc dimittis*; pæan.

psalm, -ody; hymn, plainsong, chant, chaunt, response, anthem, motet; antiphon, -y.

oblation, sacrifice, incense, libation; burnt -, votive -, thank-offering; offertory, collection.

discipline; self-discipline, -examination, -denial; fasting.

divine service, office, duty; morning prayer; mass, matins, evensong, vespers, compline; holy day &c. (*rites*) 998.

worshipper, congregation, communicant, celebrant.

V. worship, lift up the heart, aspire; revere &c. 928; adore, do service, pay homage; humble oneself, kneel; bow -, bend- the knee; fall -down, - on one's knees; prostrate oneself, bow down and worship, recite the rosary.

pray, invoke, supplicate; put -, offer-up -prayers, - petitions; beseech &c. (*ask*) 765; say one's prayers, tell one's beads.

return -, give- thanks; say grace, bless, praise, laud, glorify, magnify, sing praises; give benediction, lead the choir, intone, chant, sing.

propitiate, offer sacrifice, fast, deny oneself; vow, offer vows, give alms.

work out one's salvation; go to church;

attend -service, - mass; communicate &c. (*rite*) 998.

Adj. worshipping &c. *v.*; devout, devotional, reverent, pure, solemn; fervid &c. (*heartfelt*) 821.

Int. h-, allelujah! hosanna! glory be to God! O Lord! pray God that! God - grant, - bless, - save, - forbid! *sursum corda.*

991. Idolatry.—N. idol-atry, -ism; demon-ism, -olatry; idol -, demon -, devil -, fire- worship; zoolatry, fetishism, Mari-, Bibli-, ecclesi-, heli-olatry.

deification, apotheosis, canonization; hero worship.

sacrifices, hecatomb, holocaust; human sacrifices, immolation, mactation, infanticide, self-immolation, *suttee*.

idol, golden calf, graven image, fetish, *avatar*, Juggernaut, joss, *lares et penates*; Baal &c. 986.

idolater &c. *n.*

V. worship -idols, - pictures, - relics; put on a pedestal, bow down to, prostrate oneself before, make sacrifice to; deify, canonize, idolize.

Adj. idolatrous.

992. Sorcery.—N. sorcery; superstition; occult -art, - sciences; black -, magic; the black art, necromancy, theurgy, thaumaturgy; demon-ology, -omy, -ship; *diablerie*, bedevilment; witchcraft, -ery; glamour; fetis-hism, -ism; ghost dance; hoodoo, voodoo; Shamanism [Esquimaux], vampirism; conjuration; bewitchery, exorcism, enchantment, incantation, obsession, possession, mysticism, second sight, mesmerism, animal magnetism; od -, odylic- force; electro-biology, *clairvoyance*; spiritualism, spirit-rapping, table-turning; thought reading, telepathy, thought transference, automatic writing, *planchette*, ouija board; crystal gazing; spirit manifestation, materialization, astral body, ectoplasm &c.

divination &c. (*prediction*) 511; sortilege, ordeal, *sortes Virgilianæ*; hocus-pocus &c. (*deception*) 545; oracle &c. 513.

V. practice -sorcery &c. *n.*; cast a -horoscope, – nativity; conjure, exorcise, charm, enchant; be-witch, -devil; over-look, look on with the evil eye; entrance, mesmerize, magnetize; fascinate &c. (*influence*) 615; taboo; wave a wand; rub the -ring, –lamp; cast a spell; call up spirits, – from the vasty deep; raise spirits from the dead; raise –, lay-ghosts; command genii.

Adj. magic, -al; mystic, weird, cabalistic, talismanic, phylacteric, incantatory; charmed &c. *v.*

993. Spell.—N. spell, charm, incantation, exorcism, weird, cabala, exsufflation, cantrap, runes, abracadabra, hocus-pocus, open *sesame*, counter-charm, Ephesian letters, bell, book and candle, Mumbo-jumbo, evil-eye, fee-faw-fum.

talisman, amulet, periapt, telesm, phylactery, philtre, wish-bone, merry-thought, mascot, scarab, swastika; fetish; *agnus Dei*.

wand, caduceus, rod, divining rod, lamp of Aladdin, magic carpet, seven-league boots; magic ring; wishing –, Fortunatus's- cap.

994. Sorcerer.—N. sorcerer, magician; thaumat-, the-urgist; conjuror, necromancer, seer, wizard, witch; fairy &c. 980; *lamia*, hag, warlock, charmer, exorcist, voodoo, mage, diviner, dowser; cunning –, medicine- man, witch doctor; Shaman, figure-flinger, ecstatica, medium, *clairvoyant*, mesmerist, hypnotist; *deus ex machinâ*; astrologer; soothsayer &c. 513.

Katerfelto, Cagliostro, Merlin, Comus, Mesmer, Rosicrucian; Hecate, Circe, Lilith, siren, weird sisters; witch of Endor.

5°. RELIGIOUS INSTITUTIONS

995. Churchdom.—N. church, -dom; ministry, apostleship, priesthood, prelacy, hierarchy, church government, christendom, pale of the church.

clerical-, sacerdotal-, episcopalian-, ultramontan-ism; Theocracy; ecclesiolog-y, -ist; priestcraft, *odium theologicum*.

monach-ism, -y; monasticism, monk-hood.

[Ecclesiastical offices and dignities] pontificate, primacy, archbishopric, archiepiscopacy; prelacy; bishop-ric, -dom; episcop-ate, -acy; see, diocese; deanery, stall; canon-ry, -icate; prebend, -aryship; benefice, incumbency, glebe, advowson, living, cure, – of souls; rectorship; vicar-iate, -ship; pastor-ate, -ship; deacon-ry, -ship; -curacy; chaplain, -cy, -ship; cardinal-ate, -ship; abbacy, presbytery.

holy orders, ordination, institution, consecration, induction, reading in, preferment, translation, presentation.

popedom, papacy; the -Vatican, – apostolic see, – see of Rome; religious sects &c. 984.

council &c. 696; conclave, college of cardinals, convocation, synod, consistory, chapter, vestry, presbytery; sanhedrim, *congé d'élire*; ecclesiastical courts, consistorial court, court of Arches.

V. call, ordain, induct, prefer, translate, consecrate, present, elect, bestow.

take -orders, – the veil, – vows.

Adj. ecclesi-astical, -ological; clerical, sacerdotal, priestly, prelatical, pastoral, ministerial, capitular, theocratic; hierarchical, archiepiscopal; episcopal, -ian; canonical; mon-astic, -achal; monkish; abbati-al, -cal; pontifical, papal, apostolic; ultramontane, priest-ridden.

996. Clergy.—N. clergy, clericals, ministry, priesthood, presbytery, the cloth, the pulpit.

clergyman, divine, ecclesiastic, churchman, priest, presbyter, hierophant, pastor, shepherd, minister, clerk in holy orders; father, – in Christ; *padre, abbé, curé*; patriarch; reverend; black coat; confessor; sky pilot.

dignitaries of the church; ecclesi-,

hier-arch; eminence, reverence, elder, primate, metropolitan, archimandrite, archbishop, bishop, prelate, diocesan, suffragan, dean, subdean, archdeacon, prebendary, canon, rural dean, rector, parson, vicar, perpetual curate, residentiary, beneficiary, incumbent, chaplain, curate, – in charge; deacon, -ess; preacher; lay reader, lecturer; capitular; missionary, propagandist, Jesuit, revivalist, field preacher.

churchwarden, sidesman; clerk, precentor, choir; almoner, *suisse*, verger, beadle, sexton, sacristan; acol-yth, -othyst, -yte; thurifer; chorister, choir boy.

[Roman Catholic priesthood] Pope, *Papa*, Holy Father, pontiff, high priest, cardinal; ancient –, flamen; confessor, penitentiary; spiritual director.

cenobite, conventual, abbot, prior, monk, friar, lay brother, beadsman, mendicant, pilgrim, palmer; canon-regular, -secular; Jesuit, Franciscan, Friars minor, Minorites; Observant, Capuchin, Dominican, Carmelite; Augustinian; Gilbertine; Austin-, Black-, White-, Grey-, Crossed-, Crutched-Friars; Bonhomme, Carthusian, Benedictine, Cistercian, Trappist, Cluniac, Premonstratensian, Maturine; Templar, Hospitaller.

abb-, prior-, canon-ess; mother superior; *religieuse*, nun, sister, *beguine*, novice, postulant.

[Under the Jewish dispensation] prophet, priest, high priest, Levite; Rabbi, -n; scribe.

[Mohammedan &c.] mullah, ulema, imauam, sheik; so-fi, -phi; mufti, hadji, muezzin, dervish; fa-kir, -quir; brahmin, gooroo, druid, bonze, santon, abdal, Lama, talapoin, caloyer &c.

V. take orders &c. 995.

Adj. the –, the very –, the Right-Reverend; ordained, in orders, called to the ministry.

997. Laity.—N. laity, flock, fold, congregation, assembly, brethren, people.

temporality, secularization.

layman, civilian; parishioner, catechumen; secularist.

V. secularize.

Adj. secular, lay, laical, civil, temporal, profane.

998. Rite.—N. rite; ceremon-y, -ial; ordinance, observance, function, duty; form, -ulary; solemnity, sacrament; incantation &c. (*spell*) 993; service, psalmody &c. (*worship*) 990; liturgies.

ministration; preach-ing, -ment; predication, sermon, homily, exhortation, lecture, discourse, pastoral.

baptism, christening, chrism, immersion; baptismal regeneration; font; circumcision.

confirmation; imposition –, laying on- of hands; churching, purification, ordination &c. (*churchdom*) 995; excommunication.

Eucharist, Lord's supper, communion; the –, the holy- sacrament; celebration, high celebration; *missa cantata*; offertory; introit; consecration; con-, transubstantiation; real presence; elements, bread and wine; mass; high –, low –, dry- mass.

matrimony &c. 903; burial &c. 363; visitation of the sick.

seven sacraments, impanation, extreme unction, last rites, *viaticum*, invocation of saints, canonization, transfiguration, auricular confession; fasting; maceration, flagellation, sackcloth and ashes; penance &c. (*atonement*) 952; absolution; telling of beads, reciting the rosary, processional; thurification, incense, holy water, aspersion.

relics, rosary, beads, reliquary, host, cross, rood, crucifix, pax, pix, pyx, *agnus Dei*, censer, thurible, patera, urceole; chalice, patten, Holy Grail, sangrail; seven-branch candle stick; monstrance, sacring bell.

ritual, rubric, canon, ordinal; liturgy, prayer-book, book of common prayer, pietas, euchology, litany, lectionary; missal, breviary, mass-book, bead-roll.

psalter; psalm -, hymn- book; hymnal, -ology; psalmody.

ritual-, ceremonial-ism; sabbat-ism, -arianism; ritualist, sabbatarian.

holyday, feast, fast; Sabbath, Passover, Pentecost; Advent, Christmas, Noel, Epiphany, Lent, Shrove Tuesday, Ash Wednesday, Maundy Thursday; Passion -, Holy- week; Good Friday, Easter, Ascension Day, Whitsuntide; Trinity Sunday, Corpus Christi; All-Saints' -, - Souls'-Day; Candle-, Lam-, Martin-, Michael-mas; hogmanay; Rama-dan, -zan; Bairam &c. &c.

V. perform service, do duty, minister, officiate, baptize, dip, sprinkle; confirm, lay hands on; give -, administer -, take -, receive -, attend-, partake of- the -sacrament, - communion; communicate; celebrate mass; administer -, receive- extreme unction; anele, shrive, absolve, confess; do penance; genuflect; cross oneself, make the sign of the cross.

excommunicate, ban with bell, book and candle.

preach, sermonize, predicate, lecture.

Adj. ritual, -istic; ceremonial, liturgic; baptismal, eucharistical; paschal.

999. Canonicals.—N. canonicals, vestments; robe, gown, Geneva gown, frock, pallium, surplice, cassock, dalmatic, scapulary, cope, scarf, tunicle, chasuble, alb, *alba*, stole; fan-on, -nel; tonsure, cowl, hood; calo-te, -tte; bands; capouch, amice, orarium, ephod; apron,

lawn sleeves, pontificals, pall; mitre, tiara, triple crown; shovel -, cardinal's-hat; biretta; crosier; pastoral staff; costume &c. 225.

1000. Temple.—N. place of worship; house of -God, - prayer.

temple, cathedral, minister, church, kirk, chapel, meeting-house, bethel, tabernacle, conventicle, *basilica*, fane, holy place, chantry, oratory.

synagogue; mosque; marabout; pantheon; pagoda; joss-house; dagobah, tope; kiosk.

parsonage, rectory, vicarage, manse, deanery, glebe, church house; Vatican; bishop's palace; Lambeth.

altar, shrine, sanctuary, Holy of Holies, *sanctum sanctorum*, sacrarium, -isty; communion -, holy -, Lord's- table; table of the Lord; pyx; baptistery, font; piscina, stoup; aumbry; sedile; reredos; rood-loft, - screen; jube.

chancel, quire, choir, nave, aisle, transept, lady chapel, vestry, crypt, cloisters, porch; triforum, clerestory, churchyard, *golgotha*, calvary, Easter sepulchre; stall, pew, sitting; pulpit, ambo, lectern, reading-desk, confessional, prothesis, credence, baldachin, *baldacchino*; jesse, apse, belfry; chapter-house; presbytery.

monastery, priory, abbey, friary, convent, nunnery, cloister.

Adj. claustral, cloistered; monast-ic, -erial; conventual.

INDEX

N.B.: The numbers refer to the headings under which the words or phrases occur. When the same word or phrase may be used in various senses, the several headings under which it, or its synonyms, will be found, according to those meanings, are indicated by the words printed in Italics. These words in Italics are not intended to explain the meaning of the word or phrase to which they are annexed, but only to assist in the required reference.

When the word given in the Index is itself the title or heading of a category, the number of reference is printed in blacker type, thus: **abode 189.**

371

abridge 596
take 789
steal 791
in the - *apart* 44
alone 87
- idea 453
- oneself inattention 458
- thought 451
attention 457
abstracted
inattentive 458
abstruse 519
absurdity
impossible 471
nonsense **497**
ridiculous 853
abundant *great* 31, 63
enough 639
abundanti cautelâ,
ex - 664
abuse *deceive* 545
ill-treat 649
misuse 679
malediction 908
threat 909
upbraid 932
violate 961
- of language 563
- of terms 523
abusive 895, 934
abut *near* 197 *touch* 199,
215
abutment 717
aby *remain* 141
endure 821, 826
abysmal *deep* 208
abyss *space* 180
depth 208
interval 198
danger 667
hell 982
A.C. 106
academic
teaching 537, 542
theory 514
academical
style 578
academicals
robes 225
academician 492
Royal - 559
academy 542
acanthus 847
a capite ad calcem 52
acariâtre 901
acarpous 169
acatalectic 597

acaudal 38
accede 488, 725, 762
accelerate
early 132
stimulate 173
velocity 274
hasten 684
accension 384
accent *sound* 402
tone of voice 580
rhythm 597
accentuate 642
accentuated 580
accept *assent* 488
consent 762
receive 785
take 789
acceptable 646, 829
acceptance 771
acceptation 522
acception 522
access 286
easy of - 705
means of - 627
accessible 470, 705
accession
increase 35
addition 37
adjunct 39
- to office 737, 755
consent 762
accessory
extrinsic 6
additive 37
adjunct 39
accompanying 88
aid 707
auxiliary 711
acciaccatura 413
accidence 567
accident *event* 151
chance 156
disaster 619
misfortune 735
fatal - 361
accidental
extrinsic 6
fortuitous 156
undesigned 621
accidents
trust to the chapter of -
621
accipient 785
acclamation
assent 488
approbation 931
acclimatize 370, 613

acclivity 217
accloy 641
accolade 894
accommodate
suit 23
adjust 27
aid 707
reconcile 723
give 784
lend 787
- oneself to 82
accommodation
space 180
accommodating
kind 906
accompaniment
adjunct 39
coexistence **88**
musical 415
accompany
add 37
coexist 88
concur 120
music 416
accompli, fait - 729
accomplice 711
accomplish
execute 161
complete 729
succeed 731
accomplishment 490, 698
accompts 811
accord
uniform 16
agree 23
music 413
assent 488
concord 714
grant 760
give 784
of one's own - 602
according
- as qualification 469
- to evidence 467
- to circumstances 8
- to law 963
- to rule
conformably 82
- rumour 527
accordingly
logically 476
accordion 417
accost 586
accoucheur 631, 662
accouchment 161
account *list* 86
adjudge 480

description 594
credit 805
money - 811
fame 873
approbation 931
call to – 932
find one's – in
useful 644
success 731
make no – of 483, 930
not – for 519
on – of *motive* 615
behalf 707
on no – 536
send to one's – 361
take into – 457, 469
small – 643
to one's – 780
turn to –
improve 658
use 677
success 731
gain 775
– as *deem* 484
– book 551
– for 155, 522
– with 794, 807
accountable
liable 177
debit 811
duty 926
accountant 301, 811
certified public – 811
accounts 811
accouple 43
accoutred
armed 717
accoutrement
dress 225
appliance 633
equipment 673
accoy 174
accredit
commission 755, 759
money 805
honour 873
accredited 484, 613
– to 755, 759
accretion 35, 46
accrimination 938
accroach 789
accrue *add* 37
result 154
acquire 775
be received 785, 810
accubation 213
accueil 894

accultural 35
accumbent 213
accumulate
collect 72
store 636
redundance 641
accurate 494
– knowledge 490
accurse 908
accursed
disastrous 649
undone 828
vicious 945
accusation 938
accuse
disapprove 932
charge 938
lawsuit 969
accustom 613
ace *small* 32
unit 87
within an – 197
aceldama *kill* 361
arena 728
acephalous 59
acerbate 659, 835
acerbity
acrimony 395
sourness 397
rudeness 895
spleen 900, 901
malevolence 907
acervate 72
acetous 397
acetylene 388
acharné 900
Achates, fidus – 890, 939
ache *physical* 378
mental 828
Acheron
pit of – 982
Acherontic
moribund 360
gloomy 837
achievable 470
achieve *end* 67
produce 161
do 680
accomplish 729
achievement 551, 861
Achilles, heel of –
vulnerable 665
achromatism 429
acicular 253
acid 397
acid test 463
acknowledge

answer 462
assent 488
disclose 529
avow 535
consent 762
observe 772
pay 807
thank 916
repent 950
reward 973
acknowledged
custom 613
acme 210
– of perfection 650
acology 662
acolyte 996
acomous 226
aconite 663
acoustic 418
– organs 418
acoustics 402
acquaint
– oneself with 539
– with 527
acquaintance
knowledge 490
information 527
friend 890
make – with 888
acquiesce
assent 488
willing 488
consent 762
tolerate 826
acquire
develop 161
get 775
receive 785
– a habit 613
– learning 539
acquirement
knowledge 490
learning 539
talent 698
receipt 810
acquisition
knowledge 490
gain 775
acquit
liberate 750
exempt 927a
vindicate 937
innocent 946
absolve 970
acquit oneself
behave 692
– of a debt 807

- of a duty 926
- of an obligation 772
acquittal 506, 970
acquittance 771
acres *space* 180
  land 342
  property 780
Acres, Bob 862
acrid 392, 395
acridity 171
acrimony
  physical 171
  caustic 830
  discourtesy 895
  hatred 898
  anger 900
  malevolence 907
acroamatism 490
acrobat
  strength 159
  actor 599
  proficient 700
  mountebank 844
Acropolis 210
across 219, 708
acrostic 533, 561, 842
act *imitate* 19
  physical 170
  - *of a play* 599
  personate 599
  voluntary 680
  statute 697
  in the - 680, 947
  - a part *feign* 544
  - one's part 625, 926
  - upon
  physical 170
  mental 615
  take steps 680
  - up to 772
  - well one's part 944
  - without authority 738
acting *deputy* 759
actinic 420
actinometer 445
action *physical* 170
  voluntary **680**
  battle 720
  law 969
  line of - 692
  put in - 677
  suit the - to the word 550
  thick of the - 682
actionable 964
activate 171
active *physical* 171
  voluntary 682

- service 722
- thought 457
activity 682
actor
  impostor 548
  player 599
  agent 690
  affectation 855
Acts *record* 551
  Apostolic 985
actual *existing* 1
  present 118
  real 494
actuary 85, 811
actuate 176, 615
actum est 729
acuity 253
aculeated 253
acumen 498
acuminated 253
acupuncture 260
acustics 402
acute *energetic* 171
  physically violent 173
  pointed 253
  physically sensible 375
  musical tone 410
  perspicacious 498
  cunning 702
  strong feeling 821
  morally painful 830
  - angle 244
  - ear 418
  - note 410
acutely 31
acuteness 465
acu tetigisti, rem 465, 494
ad
  - eundem 27
  - hominem 79
  - infinitum 105
  - instar 82
  - interim 106
  - lib 705
  - rem 23
A.D. 106
adage 496
adagio *slow* 275
  music 415
Adam *sin* 945
  -'s apple 250
adamant 159, 323
adapt 23, 27
  - oneself to 82
adaptable
  conformable 82
  useful 644

add *increase* 35
  join 37
  numerically 85
  - up 811
addendum 39
adder 913
addict *habit* 613
adding machine 85
additament 39
addition
  extrinsical 6
  increase 35
  adjunction **37**
  thing added 39
  arithmetical 85
addle *barren* 169
  incomplete 730
  abortive 732
  - the wits, 475, 503
addlehead 501
addleheaded 499
address
  residence 189
  direction 550
  speech 582
  speak to 586
  skill 698
  request 765
  - oneself to 673
addresses
  courtship 902
addressful 894
adduce
  bring to 288
  evidence 467
addulce 834
ademption 789
adenoid 250
adenology 329
adept 700
adequate *power* 157
  sufficient 639
  for a purpose 644
adhere *stick* 46
  - to 604a, 613
  - to an obligation 772
  - to a duty 926
adherent
  follower 711
adhesive, 46, 327, 352
adhibit 677
adhortation 695
adieu *departure* 293
  loss 776
adipocere 356
adipose 355
adit *orifice* 260

gain an - 775
set off to - 658
take - of 677, 698
- over *success* 731
advantageous
beneficial 648
profitable 775
advene 37
advent
futurity 121
event 151
approach 286
arrival 292
Advent 998
adventism 984
adventitious 6, 156
adventive 156
adventure *event* 151
chance 156
pursuit 622
danger 665
trial 675
the great - 360
adventurer
traveller 268
experimenter 463
deceiver 548
gambler 621
rash 863
ignoble 876
adventures 594
adventurous
undertaking 676
bold 861
rash 863
adversaria 551
adversary 710
adverse
contrary 14
opposed 708
unprosperious 735
disliking 867
- *party* 710
adversity 735
advert 457
advertise 531
advice *notice* 527
news 532
counsel 695
advisable 646
advise *predict* 511
inform 527
counsel 695
- with one's pillow 451
advised
predetermined 611
intended 620

better - 658
adviser 540, 695
advocacy 931
advocate
prompt 615
recommend 695
aid 707
auxiliary 711
friend 890
vindicate 937
counsellor 968
Advocate, the - 976
advocation 617
advoutress 962
advoutry 961
advowson 995
adynamic 160
adytum *room* 191
prediction 511
secret place 530
adze 253
adzooks 870
ædile 965
ægis 717
ægrescit medendo 659
ægrotat 927*a*
æolian 349
- *harp* 417
æon 976
æquam servare mentem
826
æquo animo 823, 826
ærate 334, 353
ære perennius 873
aerial 273
elevated 206
flying 267
gas 334
air 338
- navigation 267
- navigator 269
- mail 534
- patrol 726
- perspective 428
- warfare 722
aerie 189
aerify 334
aerodonetics 267
aerodrome 728
aerodynamics 267, 334,
349
aerolite 318
aerology 338
aeromancy 511
aeromechanics 267
aerometer 338
aeronaut 269

aeronautical 273
aeronautics 267, 338
aeroplane 273
aerostat *balloon* 273
aerostatics 267, 334
aerostation 338
aery 317
Æsculapius 662
Æsop 846
æsthetic
sensibility 375
beauty 845
taste 850
æstival 125
æternum servans sub
pectore vulnus 919
ætiology [*see* etiology]
afar 196
affable 879, 894
affair *event* 151
topic 454
business 625
battle 720
love 902, 903
- of honour 720
affaire de coeur 897
affaires, charge 'd - 758
affect *relate to* 9
tend to 176
qualify 469
feign 544
touch 824
desire 865
love 897
affectation 855
affected with
disease 655
feeling 821
affectibility 822
affecting 830
affection 821, 897
affections 820
affettuoso 415
affiance 768, 858
affianced 897, 903
affiche 531
affidation 769
affidavit
affirmation 535
record 551
lawsuit 969
affiliation
relation 9
kindred 11
attribution 155
affine 11
affinitive 9

affinity 9, 17
  mate 905
affirmation 535, 488
affix *add* 37
  sequel 39
  fasten 43
  letter 561
afflation 349
afflatus 349, 597, 985
afflict 830
  – *with illness* 655
affliction *adversity* 735
  pain 828
  infliction 830
affluence
  sufficiency 639
  prosperity 734
  wealth 803
affluent *river* 348
afflux 286
afford *supply* 784
  wealth 803
  yield 810
  sell for 812
  – *aid &c.* 707
afforestation 371
affranchise
  make free of 748
  liberate 750
affray 720
affreet 980
affriction 331
affright 860
affront *molest* 830
  provocation 900
  insult 929
  – *danger* 861
affuse 337
afield 186
afire 382
afloat *extant* 1
  unstable 149
  going on 151
  ship 273
  navigation 267
  ocean 341
  news 532
  preparing 673
  keep oneself – 734
  set – *publish* 531
afoot *on hand* 625
  preparing 673
  astir 682
afore 116
aforementioned 116
aforesaid
  preceding 62

  repeated 104
  prior 116
aforethought 611
aforetime 116
afraid 860
  be – *irresolute* 605
  – *to say uncertain* 475
afresh 104, 123
Afric heat 382
Afrikander 57
afrite 980
aft 235
after *in order* 63
  in time 117
  too late 135
  rear 235
  pursuit 622
  be – *intention* 620
  pursuit 622
  go – *follow* 281
  – *all for all that* 30
  qualification 469
  on the whole 476
  – *time* 133
after acceptation 516
after-age 124
after-clap 509
after-crop 65, 168
after-dinner 117
after-glow 40, 65, 420
after-growth 65
after-life 152
aftermath
  sequel 65
  fertile 168
  profit 775
aftermost 235
afternoon 126
  – *farmer* 683
after-part 65, 235
after-piece 599
after-taste 65, 390
after-thought
  thought 451
  memory 505
  change of mind 607
after-time 121
afterwards 117
age 745
agacerie 615
again 90, 104
  – *and again* 136
  come – *periodic* 138
  fall off – 661
  live – 660
against
  counteraction 179

  anteposition 237
  provision 673
  voluntary opposition 708
  chances – 473
  declaim – 932
  false witness – 934
  go – 708
  set – *actively* 898
  set one's face – 764, 932
  stand up – *resist* 719
  raise &c. one's voice –
    489
  – one's will 744
  – one's expectation 508
  – the grain *difficult* 704
  painful 830
  dislike 867
  – the stream 704
  – the time when 510
  – one's will 744
  – one's wishes 603
agamist 904
agape *open* 260
  curious 455
  expectant 507
  wonder 870
Agapemone 827, 897
agate 847
age *time* 106
  period 108
  long time 110
  era 114
  present time 118
  oldness 124
  advanced life **128**
  of – 131
  from age to – 112
agency
  physical **170**
  instrumentality 631
  means 632
  employment 677
  voluntary action 680
  direction 693
  commission 755
agenda 625, 626
agent *physical* 153
  intermediary 228
  voluntary **690**
  consignee 759
  – *provocateur* 615
agentship 755
age quod agis! 682
ages: for – 110
  – *ago* 122
agglomerate 46, 72
agglutinate 46

aggrandize
in degree 35
in bulk 194
honour 873
aggravate
increase 35
vehemence 173
exaggerate 549
render worse 659
distress 835
exasperate 900
aggravating 830
aggravation 835
aggregate 50, 72, 84
aggregation 46
aggression 716
aggressor 726
aggrieve 649, 830
aggroup 72
aghast
disappointed 509
fear 860
wonder 870
agile 274, 682
agio 813
agiotage 794
agitate *move* 315
inquire 461
activity 682
excite the feelings 824
– *a question* 476
agitation [*see* agitate]
changeableness 149
energy 171
motion **315**
in – *preparing* 673
agitator *leader* 694
aglet 554
agley, gang – 732
aglow 382, 420
agnate 11
agnition 762
agnomen 564
agnostic 487
agnosticism 984, 989
agnus Dei 993, 998
ago 122
not long – 123
agog *expectant* 507
desire 865
wonder 870
agoing 682
set – 707
agonism 720
agonizing 824, 830
agony 378, 828
– *of death* 360

– *of excitement* 825
agrarian 371
agree *accord* 23
concur 178
assent 488
concord 714
consent 762
compact 769
compromise 774
– *in opinion* 488
– *with salubrity* 656
agreeable
comfortable 82
physically 377
mentally 829
agreeably to 82
agreement **23** [*see* agree]
compact 769
agrestic 371
agriculture **371**
agronomy 371
aground *fixed* 150
in difficulty 704
failure 732
ague-fit 860
aguets, aux –
expectation 507
ambush 530
aguish *cold* 383
aha! *rejoicing* 838
ahead 234, 280
go – *progression* 282
shoot –
transcursion 303
activity 682
rock – 665, 667
ah me! 839
Ahrimanes 987, 980
aid 707, 906
by the – *of* 631, 632
aide-de-camp 711, 745
aidless 160
aigrette 847
aiguille 253
aiguillette 747, 847
aigulet 847
ail 655, 828
aileron 267, 273
ailment 655
aim 278, 620, 675
– *a blow at* 716
aimable 894
faire l' – 897
aimer éperdument 897
aimless *without*
motive 615a
chance 621

air *unsubstantial* 4
broach 66
lightness 320
gas 334
atmospheric **338**
wind 349
tune 415
appearance 448
refresh 689
demeanour 692
fashionable 852
beat the – 645
fill the – 404
fine – *salubrity* 656
fish in the – 645
fowls of the – 366
in the – 527
rend the – 404
take – 531
air-balloon 273
air base 728
air-commodore 745
aircraft 273, 726
air-drawn 515
airdrome 273
air-force 726
air-gun 727
airing 266
air-mail 273
airman 269
airmanship 698
air-marshal 745
air-passage 351
air-pipe 351
airport 273, 292, 728
air-pump 349
air-raid 716
airs *affectation* 855
pride 878
vanity 880
arrogance 885
air-shaft 351
air service 267
airship 273, 726
air-tight 261
airways 267
airworthy 273, 664
airy [*see* air]
windy 349
unimportant 643
gay 836
– *hopes* 858, 859
give to – nothing a local
habitation &c. 515
aisle *passage* 260
way 627
in a church 1000

ait 346
ajar *open* 260
  discordant 713
ajee 217
ajutage 260, 350
akimbo *angular* 244
  stand – 715
akin *related* 9
  consanguineous 11
  similar 17
alabaster *white* 430
alack! 839
alacrity *willing* 602
  active 682
  cheerful 836
Aladdin's lamp 993
alar 267
alarm *warning* 668
  notice of danger **669**
  fear 860
  cause for – 665
  give an – *indicate* 550
alarmist 862
alarum 114, 550, 669
alas! 839
alate 267
alb 999
albeit 30
albert
  chain 847
albification 430
albinescence 430
albinism 430
albino 443
album 593, 596
albumen
  semi-liquid 352
  protein 357
Alcaic 597
alcaid 745
alcalde 745
alcazar 189
alchemy 144
alcohol 995
Alcoran 986
alcove 191, 252
Aldebaran 423
alderman 745
ale 298
alea, jacta est – 601
aleatory 665
Alecto 173
alectromancy 511
alehouse 189
  go to the – 959
alembic
  conversion 144

vessel 191
  furnace 386
  laboratory 691
alentours 197
alert *watchful* 457, 459
  active 682
alerte 669
aleuromancy 511
Alexandrine
  ornate style 577
  verse 597
alexandrite 848
alexipharmic 662
alexiteric 662
al fresco 220
algebra 85
algid 383
algology 369
algorithm 85
alguazil 965
alias
  otherwise 18
  pseudonym 565
abili 187
alien *irrelevant* 10
  foreign 57
  transfer 783
  gentile 989
alienable 783
alienate
  estrange 44, 889
  transfer 783
  set against 898
alienation
  mental – 503
alieni appetens
  grasping 865
  envious 921
  selfish 943
alienism 54
alight *stop* 265
  arrive 292
  descend 306
  on fire 382
align 278
alike 17
  share and share – 778
aliment *food* 298
alimentary 662
  – canal 350
alimentation
  aid 707
alimony
  property 780
  provision 803
  income 810
aliquot 51, 84

aliter visum, diis – 601
alive
  living 359
  intelligent 498
  active 682
  cheerful 836
  be – with 102
  keep – *continue* 143
  keep the memory – 505
  look – 684
  – to *attention* 457
  cognizant 490
  informed 527
  able 698
  sensible 822
alkahest 335
all *whole* 50
  complete 52
  generality 78
  – absorbing 642
  in – ages 112
  – aboard 495
  – agog 865
  – in all 50
  – along 106
  – along of 154
  – but 32
  – colours 440
  – considered 451, 480
  – day long 110
  – devouring 190
  in – directions 278
  – engrossing 190
  at – events
  compensation 30
  qualification 469
  true 494
  resolve 604
  – fours *easy* 705
  cards 840
  – in good time 152
  – hail! *welcome* 292
  honour to 873
  celebration 883
  courtesy 894
  – hands *everybody* 78
  on – hands 488
  – of a dither 824
  – of a heap 72
  – knowing 976
  – manner of
  difference 15
  multiform 81
  with – one's might 686
  – at once 113
  – one 27, 866
  – out 52

- over *end* 67
universal 78
destruction 162
space 180
at - *points* 52
- in one's *power* 686
- *powerful*
mighty 159
God 976
in - *quarters* 180
with - *respect* 928
in - *respects* 52, 494
- *right!* 922
- *Saint's day* 998
- *searching* 461
- *seeing* 976
on - *sides* 227
- *sorts diverse* 16a
mixed 41
multiform 81
- *talk* 4
- *things to all men* 894
- *the time* 106
at - *times* 136
- *together* 50
- *ways* 243, 279
- *wise* 976
- *the world and his wife*
78
of - *work*
useful 644
maid - 746
Allah 979
allay
moderate 174
pacify 723
relieve 834
- *excitability* 826
allective 615
allege *evidence* 467
assert 535
plea 617
allegiance 743, 926
allegory 464, 521, 594
allegro *music* 415
cheerful 836
allelujah 990
allemande 840
all-embracing 76
alleviate 174, 834
alley *court* 189
passage 260
way 627
alliance *relation* 9
kindred 11
physical co-operation 178

voluntary co-operation
709
party 712
union 714
allied to *like* 17
alligation 43
allign 278
alliteration
similarity 17
style in writing 577
poetry 597
allocation 60, 786
allocution 586
allodium *free* 748
property 780
allopathy 662
alloquy 586
allot *arrange* 60
distribute 786
due 924
allow *assent* 488
admit 529
permit 760
consent 762
give 784
- *to have one's own way*
740
allowable 760, 924
allowance
qualification 469
gift 784
allotment 786
discount 813
salary 973
with *grains of* - 485
make - *for forgive* 918
vindicate 937
alloy *mixture* 41
combination 48
debase 659
allude *hint* 514
mean 516
refer to 521
latent 526
inform 527
allure *move* 615
create desire 865
alluring 829
allusive
relative 9
alluvial *level* 213
land 342
plain 344
alluvium
deposit 40
land 342
soil 653

ally *combine* 48
auxiliary 711
friend 891
alma mater 542
almanac
list 86
chronometry 114
record 551
almighty 157
Almighty, the - 976
almoner
treasurer 801
giver 784
church officer 996
almonry 802
almost *nearly* 32
not quite 651
- *all* 50
- *immediately* 132
alms *gift* 784
benevolence 906
worship 990
almshouse 189, 666
almsman 785
Alnaschar's dream 515,
858
aloes 395
aloft 206
alogy 497
alone *single* 87
unaided 706
let - *not use* 678
not restrain 748
along 200
get - *progress* 282
go - *depart* 293
go - *with concur* 178
assent 488
co-operate 709
- *of caused by* 154
- *with added* 37
together 88
by means of 631
alongside *near* 197
parallel 216
laterally 236
aloof *distant* 196
high 206
secluded 893
stand - *inaction* 681
refuse 764
cautious 864
alopecia 226
aloud 404
think - 589
naïveté 703
Alp 206

alpenstock 215
Alpha 66
 – and Omega 50
alphabet
 beginning 66
 letters 561
alphabetarian 541
alphabeticize 60
alphitomancy 511
alpine *high* 206
Alpine Club 268, 305
already
 antecedently 116
 even now 118
 past time 122
Alsatia 791, 945
also 37
altar 903, 1000
alter 140
 – *the case* 468
 – *one's course* 279
alterable 149
alteram partem, audire –
 468, 922
alterative
 substitute 634
 remedy 662
altercation 713
altered *worn* 668
 – *for the worse* 659
alter ego *similar* 17
 auxiliary 711
 deputy 759
 friend 890
alternate
 reciprocal 12
 sequence 63
 discontinuous 70
 periodic 138
 changeable 149
 oscillate 314
alternative
 substitute 147
 choice 609
 plan 626
although
 compensation 30
 counteraction 179
 unless 469
altiloquence 577
altimetry
 height 206
 angle 244
 measurement 466
altitude *height* 206
 – *and azimuth* 466
alto 410, 416

 – *part* 415
altogether 50, 51
 nude 226
alto-rilievo 250, 557
altruism 910, 942
altruist 906
alum 397
alumnus 541
alveolus 252
always
 uniformly 16
 generally 78
 during 106
 perpetually 112
 habitually 613
a.m. 114, 125
amability 829, 894
amah 753
amain 173, 684
amalgam, -ate 41, 48
amalgamation 709
Amalthæa's horn 639
amantium iræ 918
amanuensis 553, 590
amaranthine 112
amari aliquid
 bad 649
 imperfect 651
 painful 830
amaritude 395
amass *whole* 50
 collect 72
 store 636
amateur *volunteer* 602
 layman 699
 taste 850
 votary 865
amatory 897
amaurosis 442
amaze 870
amazingly 31
Amazon
 woman 374
 warrior 726
 courage 861
ambages
 convolutions 248
 circumlocution 573
 circuit 629
ambagious 573
ambassador
 messenger 534
 representative 758
 recall of –s 713
amber 356a
 – *colour* 436
ambidexter

 right and left 238
 fickle 607
 clever 698
ambient 227
ambigu 41
ambiguas spargere voces
 uncertain 475
 misteach 538
 false 544
 cunning 702
ambiguous
 uncertain 475
 unintelligible 519
 equivocal 520
 obscure 571
ambiloquy 520
ambit 230
ambition 620, 865
ambivalence 605, 708
amble 266
ambo *school* 542
 pulpit 1000
ambo, Arcades –
 alike 17
 friends 890
 bad men 949
ambrosia 298
ambrosial 394, 490
ambulance
 vehicle 272
 hospital 662
ambulation 266
ambuscade 530
ambush 530, 667
 lie in – 528
âme-de-boue 949
 – *damnée*
 catspaw 711
 servant 746
 servile 886
 bad man 949
 – *qui vive* 101, 187
ameer 875
ameliorate 658
amen *assent* 488
 submission 725
 content 831
amenable 177, 602, 926
 not – *to reason* 608
amend 658
amendatory 20
amende honorable 952
amends
 compensation 50
 atonement 952
 reward 973
amenity 829, 894

amentia 503
amerce 974
Americanism 563
American organ 417
amethyst
  purple 437
  jewel 847
amiable
  courteous 894
  loving 897
  kind 906
amicable 707, 888
amice 999
amicus – curiæ 527
  – humani generis 910
  – usque ad aras 890
amidships 68
amidst 41, 228
amiss 619
  come – *disagree* 24
  mistime 135
  inexpedient 647
  do – 945
  nothing comes – 823
  take – 867, 900
amity *concord* 714
  peace 721
  friendship 888
ammunition 635, 727
amnesia 506
amnesty 506, 723, 918
amnis, rusticus expectat
  dum defluat – *hope* 858
amœbæan 63
amok 503
among 41, 228
amor patriæ 910
amore, con – 602, 821
amoroso 599
amorous 897
  – glances 902
amorphism 241
amorphous 83, 241
amortization 784
amotion 270
amount
  quantity 25
  degree 26
  sum of money 800
  price 812
  gross – 50
  – to 27, 85
amour 897, 961
  – propre 880
ampere 466
amphibian 366
amphibious 83

amphibology 520
Amphictyonic council 696
amphigouri 497
amphitheatre
  prospect 441
  school 542
  theatre 599
  arena 728
Amphitryon 890
amphora 191
ample *much* 31
  spacious 180
  large 192
  broad 202
  copious 639
amplify
  expand 194
  exaggerate 549
  diffuse style 573
amplitude
  quantity 25
  degree 26
  size 192
  breadth 202
  enough 639
ampoulé 191
ampulla 191
amputate 38
amuck 824
  run – 503
amulet 247, 993
amusare la bocca, per –
  394
amuse 829, 840
amusement 840
  place of – 840
amussim, ad – 494
amylaceous 352
an *if* 514
ana 594
Anabaptist 984
anabasis 35
anachronism
  false time 115
  inopportune 135
  error 495
anacoluthon 70
anaconda 913
anacreontic 597
anæmia 160
anæsthesia 376, 381, 683
anaglyph 554, 557
anagoge 521, 526
anagram
  double sense 520
  secret 533
  letter 561

  wit 842
analecta 596
analeptic 662
analgesia 376
analogous 12
analogy 9, 17
analysis
  decomposition 49
  arrangement 60
  algebra 85
  inquiry 461
  experiment 463
  reasoning 476
  grammar 567
  compendium 596
analyst 461, 463
anamorphosis
  distortion 243
  optical 443
  misrepresentation 555
anapæst 597
anaphylaxis 375
anarchist
  destroyer 165
  disobedient 742
  evil-doer 913
anarchy 59, 738
anastatic printing 558
anastomosis 43, 219
anastrophe 218
anathema 908
anathematize 908
  censure 932
  detract 934
anatomize *dissect* 44
  investigate 461
anatomy
  dissection 44
  leanness 203
  texture 329
  science 357
  comparative – 368
anatriptic 331
ancestral
  bygone 122
  old 124
  aged 128
ancestry 166
anchor
  connection 45
  stop 265
  safeguard 666
  badge 747
  hope 858
  at – *fixed* 150
  stationed 184
  safe 664

cast – *settle* 184
 arrive 292
have an – to windward
 664
sheet – *means* 632
anchorage
 location 184
 roadstead 189
 refuge 866
anchored 150
anchorite 893, 955
ancien régime 875
ancient *old* 124
 flag 550
 – times 122
ancientness 122
ancillary 707
and 37, 88
andante 415
andiron 386
androgynous 83
anecdote 594
anele 998
anemography 349
ανεμωλια βαζειν 497
anemometer
 wind 349
 measure 466
anent 9
aneroid 338
anew *again* 104
 newly 123
anfractuosity 248
angel
 object of love 897
 good person 948
 supernatural being **977**
 fallen –
 bad man 949
 devil 978
 guardian –
 safety 664
 auxiliary 711
 benefactor 912
 – of Death 362
 – 's visits 137
angelic 944
angels and ministers of
 grace defend us! 860
angelus 550
anger 900
 more in sorrow than in –
 826, 918
angiology 329
angle 244
 try 463
 at an – 217

Anglicanism 984
angling 622, 840
**anguille au genou, rompre
 l'** – 158, 471
anguilliform 205, 248
anguish
 physical 378
 moral 828
anguis in herbâ 667
angular 244
 – *velocity* 264
angularity **244**
angusta domi, res – 804
angustation 203
anhelation 688
anhydrate 340
anhydrous 340
aniline dyes 437
anility 128, 499
animadvert
 consider 451
 attend to 457
 reprehend 932
animal **366**
 female – 374
 – *cries* 412
 – *economy* 359
 – *gratification* 377
 – *life* 364
 – *physiology* 368
 – *spirits* 836
 – and vegetable kingdom
 357
animalcule 193, 366
animalism
 sensuality 954
animality **364**
animate
 induce 615
 excite 824
 enliven 836
animation
 life 359
 animality 364
 activity 682
 vivacity 836
 suspended – 823
animism 984
animo, ex – 602
 quo – 620
animosity
 dislike 867
 enmity 889
 hatred 898
 anger 900
animus
 willingness 602

 intention 620
 desire 865
ankle 244
 – deep 208, 209
anklet 847
ankylosis 150
annalist 114, 553
annals
 chronology 114
 record 551
 account 594
anneal 673
annex
 addition 37
 adjunct 39
 junction 43
 acquire 775
Annie Oakley 815
annihilate 2, 162
anniversary 138
anno 106
Anno Domini
 era 106
 old age 124
annotation 522, 550
annotator 524
 scholar 492
 interpreter 524
 editor 595
annotto 434
announce
 predict 511
 inform 527
 publish 531
 assert 535
announcer 527
annoy
 molest 649, 907
 disquiet 830
annoyance 828
 source of – 830
annual *periodic* 138
 plant 367
 book 593
annuity 810
annul 162, 750
annular 247
annunciate 527
annus magnus 108
anodyne
 lenitive 174
 remedial 662
 relief 834
anoint *coat* 223
 lubricate 332
 oil 355
anointed

deity 976
king 745
anomaly 59, 83
disorder 59
irregularity 83
anon 132
anonymous 565
anopsia 442
anorexy 866
another
different 15
repetition 104
– *story* 468, 526
go upon – tack 607
– *time* 119
answer
to an inquiry **462**
confute 479
solution 522
succeed 731
pecuniary profit 775
pleadings 969
require an – 461
– for *deputy* 759
promise 768
go bail 806
I'll – for it 535
– the helm 745
– the purpose 731
– to *correspond* 9
– one's turn 644
answerable
agreement 23
liable 177
bail 806
duty 926
censurable 932
ant 690
Antæus 159, 192
antagonism
difference 14
physical 179
voluntary 708
enmity 889
antagonist 710, 891
antagonistic 24
antarctic 237
antecedence 62, 116
antecedent 64
antechamber 191
ante Christum 106
antedate 115
antediluvian 124
antelope 274
antemundane 124
antenna 379
anteposition 62

anterior
in order 62
in time 116
in place 234
– *to reason* 477
anteroom 191
antevert 706
anthem 990
anthemion 847
anthology
book 533
collection 596
poem 597
anthracite 388
anthropoid 372
anthropology
zoology 368
mankind 372
anthropomancy 511
anthropophagi 913
anthroposcopy 511
anthroposophy 372
anti-aircraft gun 564, 727
antic 840
antichambre, faire – 133
antichristian 984, 989
antichronism 115
anticipate
anachronism 115
priority 116
future 121
early 132
expect 507
foresee 510
prepare 673
hope 858
in – 116
anticlimax
decrease 36
bathos 497, 853
anticlinal 217
anticyclone 265
antidote 662
antigropelos 225
antilogarithm 84
antilogy 477
antimony 663
Antinomian 984
antinomy 964
Antinous 845
antiparallel 217
antipathy 867, 898
antiphon *music* 415
answer 462
worship 990
antiphrasis 563
antipodes

difference 14
distance 196
contraposition 237
antipoison 660
antiquary
past times 122
scholar 492
historian 553
antiquas vias, stare super
– 613, 670
antiquated 128
antique 124
antiquity 122
antiscriptural 984
antiseptic 652, 662
antisocial 911
antistrophe 597
antithesis
contrast 14
difference 15
opposite 237
style 574, 577
antitoxin 662
antitype 22
antler 253
antonomasia
metaphor 521
nomenclature 564
antonym 14
antrum 252
anvil *support* 215
on the –
intended 620
in hand 625
preparing 673
anxiety *pain* 828
fear 860
desire 865
anxious expectation 507
any *some* 25
part 51
no choice 609a
at – price 604a
at – rate
certain 474
true 494
at all hazards 604
anybody 78
anyhow 460, 627
anything one knows, for –
491
aorist 109, 119
aorta 350
apace *early* 132
swift 274
apache 913
apart 44, 87

set – 636
wide – 196
apartment 191
 –s 189
 –s to let
 imbecile 499
apathetic 275
apathy
 indifference 465
 insensibility 823
 irreligion 989
ape *imitate* 19
Apelles 559
aperçu 596
aperture 260
apex 210
aphasia 583
aphelion 196
aphonic 403
aphony 581
aphorism 496
aphrodite 845, 979
apiary 370
apiculture 370
Apicius 957
apiece 79
apish 19, 499
aplanatic 429
aplomb
 stability 150
 self-possession 498
 resolution 604
Apocalypse 985
Apocrypha 985
apocryphal
 uncertain 475
 erroneous 495
 heterodox 984
apodictic 478
apodosis 67
apogee 210
apograph 21
Apollo *sun* 318
 music 416
 luminary 423
 beauty 845
 god 979
 magnus – 500, 695
Apollyon 978
apologue
 metaphor 521
 teaching 537
 description 594
apology *excuse* 617
 vindication 937
 penitence 950
 atonement 952

apophthegm 496
apophysis 250
apoplexy 158, 655
aporetic 487
aposiopesis 585
apostasy
 recantation 607
 dishonour 940
 heterodoxy 984
apostate
 convert 144
 turncoat 607
 impiety 988
apostle *teacher* 540
 disciple 541
 inspired 985
 –'s creed 983*a*
apostolic 985
 – church 983*a*
 – see 995
apostrophe
 address 586
 soliloquy 589
 appeal 765
apothecary 662
 –'s weight 319
apothegm 496
apotheosis
 resuscitation 163
 canonization 873
 heaven 981
 hero worship 991
apozem 335, 384
appal 830, 860
appanage
 property 780
 gift 784
apparatus 633
apparel 225
apparent
 visible 446
 appearing 448
 probable 472
 manifest 525
 heir – 779
apparition
 fallacy of vision 443
 spirit 980
apparitor 534
appeach 938
appeal 586, 765
 court of – 966
 – to arms 722
 – motion 969
 – from Philip drunk to
 Philip sober 658
 – to *call to witness* 467

– to for (*claim*) 924
appear 446, 525
 – for 759
 – in print 591
appearance 448
 make one's – 292
 to all – 448
 probable 472
appearances
 keep up – 852
appease 174
appellant 924, 938
appellate 966
appellation 564
append *add* 37
 sequence 63
 hang 214
appendage 39
appendectomy 662
appendix
 adjunct 39
 sequel 65
 end 67
 book 593
appertain
 related to 9
 component 56
 belong 777
 property 780
appetite 865
 tickle the –
 savoury 394
appetizing 865
 exciting 824
applaud 931
apple – of discord 713
 golden –
 allurement 615
 – of one's eye *good* 648
 love 897
 favorite 899
 – off another tree 15
 how we –s swim! 880
apple-green 435
apple-pie order 58
appliance *use* 677
 –s *means* 632
 machinery 633
applicable *relevant* 23
 useful 644
 expedient 646
applicability 9
applicant 767
application *study* 457
 metaphor 521
 use 667
 request 765

apply *use* 677
- a match 384
- the match to a train 66
- the mind 457
- a remedy 662
appoggiatura 413
appointment
employment 625
order 741
charge 755
assignment 786
interview 892
appointments
gear 633
apportion *arrange* 60
disperse 73
allot 786
apportionment 786
appositeness 9
apposition
relation 9
relevancy 23
closeness 199
paraphrase 522
appraise 466, 812
appreciate
realize 450, 451
measure 466
judge 480
know 490
taste 850
approve 931
apprehend
believe 484
know 490
seize 789
fear 860
apprehension
idea 453
taking 789
apprentice 541
- oneself 676
apprenticeship 539, 673
apprise 527
apprised of 490
approach
of time 121
impend 152
nearness 197
move **286**
path 627
approaching 9
approbation 931
appropinquation 286
appropriate *fit* 23
peculiar 79
expedient 646

assign 786
take 789
steal 791
approval 488, 931
on - 609
approximate
related to 9
resemble 17
in mathematics 85
nearness 197
approach 286
appulse *meeting* 199
collision 276
approach 286
convergence 290
appurtenance
part 51
component 56
accompaniment 88
belongings 780
appurtenant 9
après nous le déluge 943
apricot *colour* 439
April
- fool 547, 857
make an - fool of 545
- showers 149
apron *extension* 39
clothing 225
defence 717
canonicals 999
àpropos [*see* à]
aprotype 591
apse 1000
apt *consonant* 23
tendency 176, 177
docile 539
willing 602
clever 698
aqua-fortis 335
aquamarine 435
aquarium 370
Aquarius 348, 636
aquatic *water* 337
aquatics 267
aqatinta 558
aqueduct 350
aqueous 337
aquiline 244
A.R. 106
Arab *wanderer* 268
horse 271
street - 876
araba 272
arabesque 847
Arabian
- perfumes 400

- nights 515
arable 371
arbalest 727
arbiter *critic* 480
director 694
adviser 695
judge 967
- elegantiarum
revels 840
taste 850
fashion 852
arbitrage 794
arbitrament 480
judgment 480
- of the sword 722
arbitary
without relation 10
irregular 83
wilful 606
capricious 608
authoritative 737
severe 739
insolent 885
lawless 964
- power 739
arbitrate
adjudicate 480
mediate 724
arbitration
court of - 966
submit to - 774
arbitrium, ad - 600
arbor 215, 312
arborescent
ramifiying 242
rough 256
trees 367
arboriculture 371
arbour *abode* 189
summer-house 191
plaisance 840
arc 245
heat 382
arcade *street* 189
curve 245
gateway 260
Arcades ambo
alike 17
friends 890
bad men 949
Arcadia 827, 981
Arcadian 703, 946
arcanum 533
arch *great* 31
support 215
curve 245
convex 250

pacification 723
armless 158
armlet *ring* 247
  gulf 343
  ornament 847
armorial bearings 550,
  877
armour *cover* 223
  defence 717
  arms 727
  buckle on one's - 673
  - plated 223
armoured
  - car 726
  - cruiser 726
  - train 726
armoury *store* 636
  workshop 691
arms 727 [*see* arm]
  heraldry 550
  war 722
  honours 877
  clash of - 720
  deeds of - 720
  with folded - 681
  in - *infant* 129
  throw oneself into the - of
    666, 880
  under - 722
  up in - *active* 682
  discord 713
  resistance 719
  enmity 889
  resentment 900
arm's length
  at - 196
  keep at -
  repel 289
  defence 717
  enmity 889
  seclusion 893
  discourtesy 895
Armstrong gun 727
army *collection* 72
  multitude 102
  troops 726
aroma 400
around 227
  lie - 220
arouse *move* 615
  excite 824
  - oneself 682
aroynt *begone* 297
  malediction 908
arquebusade 662
arquebuse 727
arraign 938, 969

arrange
  set in order 60
  plan 626
  compromise 774
  - with creditors 807
  - itself 58
  - matters
  pacify 723
  - music 413, 416
  - in a series 69
  - under 76
arrangement 23, **60** [*see*
  arrange]
  order 58
  temporary - 111
arrant *identical* 31
  manifest 525
  notorious 531
  bad 649
  disreputable 874
  base 940
arras 847
array *order* 58, 60
  series 69
  assemblage 72
  multitude 102
  dress 225
  prepare 673
  adorn 847
  ostentation 882
  battle - 722
arrear, in - 53, 808
arrears *debt* 806
arrectis auribus
  hear 418
  expect 507
arrest *stop* 142
  restrain 751
  in law 969
  - the attention 457
arrière-pensée
  after-thought 65
  mental reservation 528
  motive 615
  set purpose 620
arrival 292
arrive *happen* 151
  reach 292
  complete 729
  - at a conclusion 480
  - at the truth 480*a*
arrogant *severe* 739
  proud 878
  insolent 885
arrogate 885, 924
  - to oneself
  undue 925

arrondissement 181
arrosion 331
arrow *swift* 274
  missile 284
  arms 727
  broad - 550
arrow-head
  form 253
  writing 590
'Arry and 'Arriet 902
ars celare artem 698
arsenal *store* 636
  workshop 661
arsenic 663
arson 384
art *representation* 554
  business 625
  skill 698
  cunning 702
  fine - 850
  work of - 845, 847
  - gallery 556
artery 350, 627
artes, hæ tibi erunt - 627
artesian well 343
artful 544, 702
  - dodge 545, 702
article *thing* 3
  part 51
  matter 316
  chapter 593
  review 595
  goods 798
articled clerk 541
articles
  thirty-nine - 983*a*
  - of agreement 770
  - of faith 484, 983
articulate 366
articulation
  junction 43
  speech 580
articulo, in -
  transient 111
  dying 360
artifice 626, 702
artificer 690
artificial
  fictitious 545
  cunning 702
  affected 855
  - language 579
artillery
  explosion 404
  arms 727
artilleryman 726
artisan 690

artist *painter* &c. **559**
　contriver 626
　agent 690
artiste *music* 416
　drama 599
artistic *skilful* 698
　beautiful 845
　taste 850
　– *language* 578
artlessness 703
aruspex 513
aruspicy 511
arundo, hæret lateri
　lethalis – 828
as *motive* 615
　– broad as long 27
　– can be 52
　– good as 27
　– if *similar* 17
　suppose 514
　– little as may be 32
　– it may be
　circumstance 8
　event 151
　chance 156
　– much again 90
　– soon as 120
　– they say 496, 532
　– things are 7
　– things go 151, 613
　– to 9
　– usual 82
　– it were 17, 521
　– you were 141, 283
　– well as 37
　– the world wags 151
ascend *be great* 31
　increase 35
　rise 305
　improve 658
ascendancy
　power 157
　influence 175
　success 731
ascendant
　lord of the – 745
　in the –
　influence 175
　important 642
　success 731
　authority 737
　repute 873
　one's star in the –
　prosperity 734
ascension [*see* ascend]
　calefaction 384
　– Day 998

ascent [*see* ascend]
　gradient 217
　rise **305**
　glory 873
ascertain *fix* 150
　determine 480
ascertained 474, 490
ascertainment 480*a*
asceticism 955
ascititious
　intrinsic 6
　additional 37
　supplementary 52
ascribe 155
aseptic 652
ash 384
　– coloured 432
　– blond 430
ashamed 879
ashen 429
　Ash Wednesday 998
ashes *corpse* 362
　dirt 653
　lay in – 162
　pale as – 429, 860
　rise from one's – 660
ashore 342
　go – *arrive* 292
ashy 429
Asian mystery 533
aside *laterally* 236
　whisper 405
　private 528
　say – 589
　set &c. – *displace* 185
　neglect 460
　negative 536
　reject 610
　disuse 678
　abrogate 756
　discard 782
　step – 279
asinine *ass* 271
　fool 499
ask *inquire* 461
　request 765
　for sale 794
　price 812
　– leave 760
askance 217
　eye – *fear* 860
　look – *vision* 441, 443
　dissent 489
　dislike 867
　disapproval 932
askari 726
asked in church 903

askew 217, 243
aslant 217
asleep 683
aslope 217
Asmodeus 980
asomatous 317
asp *animal* 366
　evil-doer 913
Aspasia 962
aspect *feature* 5
　state 7
　situation 183
　appearance 448
aspen leaf
　shake like an – 315, 860
asperity
　roughness 256
　discourtesy 895
　anger 900
　irascibility 901
asperse 934
aspersion
　malediction 908
　rite 998
asphalte
　smooth 255
　resin 356*a*
　material 635
asphodel 845
asphyxia 360
asphyxiate 361
aspic 352
aspirant 767, 865
aspirate 580
aspirator 349
aspire *rise* 305
　hope 858
　desire 865
　worship 990
aspirin 834
asportation 270
asquint 217
ass *beast of burden* 271
　fool 501
　make an – of
　delude 545
　– between two bundles of
　hay 605
　–'s bridge 519
　– in lion's skin
　cheat 548
　bungler 701
assafœtida 401
assagai 727
assail 716, 830
assailant 710, 726
assassin, -ate 361

assault 716, 961
  take by – 789
assay 463
asseguay 727
assemblage 72
assembly
  council 696
  society 892
  religious 997
assembly hall 588
assembly room 189
assent *belief* 484
  agree **488**
  willing 602
  consent 762
  content 831
assert 535, 924
assess *measure* 466
  determine 480
  tax 812
assessor
  judge 967
assets 780, 800
asseverate 535
assiduity 110
assiduous 682
assign
  transfer 270, 783
  commission 755
  give 784
  allot 786
  – as cause 155
  – a duty 926
  – places 60
assignat 800
assignation 892
  place of – 74
assignee *donee* 785
assimilate
  uniform 16
  resemble 17
  imitate 19
  agree 23
  transmute 144
assist 707
  – at 186
assistant 711
assister *be present* 186
assize *measure* 466
  tribunal 966
  justice of – 967
associate *mix* 41
  unite 43
  collect 72
  accompany 88
  colleague 690
  auxiliary 711

friend 890
– with 892
association [*see* associate]
  relation 9
  combination 48
  co-operation 709
  partnership 712
  – of ideas
  intellect 450
  thought 451
  intuition 477
  hint 514
  – football 840
assoil *acquit* 970
assonance
  music 413
  poetry 597
assort *arrange* 60
assortment 72, 75
assuage 174, 834
assuetude 613
assume *believe* 484
  suppose 514
  falsehood 544
  take 789
  insolent 885
  right 924
  – authority 737
  – a character 554
  – command 741
  – a form 144
  – the offensive 716
assumed name 565
assumption [*see* assume]
  severity 739
  hope 858
  usurpation 925
assurance
  speculation 156
  certainty 474
  belief 484
  assertion 535
  promise 768
  security 771
  hope 858
  vanity 880
  insolence 885
  make – double sure
  safe 664
  caution 864
assuredly
  assent 488
assythment 973
astatic 320
asterisk 550
astern 235
  put the engines – 275

fall – 283
asteroid 318
Asteroth 979
asthenia 160
astigmatism 443
astir 682
  set – 824
astonish 870
astonished
  – at nothing 871
astonishing
  great 31
astound *excite* 824
  fear 860
  surprise 870
astra, sic itur ad – 360,
  873
Astræa 922
astraddle 215
astragal 847
astral 318
  – body 717, 992
  – influence 601
  – plane 317
astray 475, 495
  go – *deviate* 279
  sin 945
astriction 43
astride 215
astringent 195
astrolabe 466
astrologer 994
astrology 511
astromancy 511
astronomy 318
astute 498, 702
asunder 44, 196
  as poles – 237
asylum *hospital* 663
  retreat 666
  defence 717
asymptote 290
at, be – 620
  up and – them! 716
ataghan 727
atavism 144, 163
ataxia 158
atelier 556, 691
athanasia 112
Athanasian creed 983*a*
athanor 386
atheism 989
atheist 487
Athenae 979
Athens, owls to – 641
athirst 865
athlete *strong* 159

gladiator 726
athletic *strong* 159
  strenuous 686
  – sports
  contest 720
  games 840
athwart
  oblique 217
  crossing 219
  opposing 708
Atkins, Tommy 726
Atlantis 515
Atlas *arrangement* 60
  list 86
  strength 159
  support 215
  maps 554
atmosphere
  circumambience 227
  air 338
  painting 556
atmospheric blue 438
atoll 346
atom *small* 32, 193
atomic energy 157
atomizer 336
atoms
  crush to – 162
atomy 193
atonement
  restitution 790
  expiation **952**
  amends 973
  religious 976
atony 160
atrabilious 837
atramentous 431
atrium 191
atrocity
  malevolence 907
  vice 945
  guilt 947
atrophy
  shrinking 195
  disease 655
  decay 659
atropos 601
attach *join* 43
  love 897
  legal 969
  – importance to 642
attaché
  employé 746
  diplomatic 758
  – case 191
attack *singing* 580
  disease 655

assault **716**
  debauch 961
attaghan 727
attain *arrive* 292
  succeed 731
  – 'majority 131
attainable 470
attainder
  taint 651
  at law 971
attainment
  knowledge 490
  learning 539
  skill 698
attar 400
attempered 820
attempt 675
  vain – 732
  – impossibilities 471
attempter 41, 174
attend
  accompany 88
  be present 186
  follow 281
  apply the mind 457
  medically 662
  aid 707
  serve 746
  – to business 625
  – to orders 743
attendance on
  dance – 886
attendant [*see* attend]
attention 457
  care 459
  respect 928
  attract – 882
  call to – 457
  call – to 550
  give – 418
  pay –s to 894
  pay one's –s to 902
attenuate
  decrease 36
  weaken 158
  reduce 195
  rarefy 322
attenuated 203
attest
  bear testimony 467
  affirm 535
  adjure 768
attested copy 771
attic *simple* 42
  garret 191
  summit 210
  style 578

wit 842
  taste 850
Attila 913
attire 225
attitude
  circumstance 8
  situation 183
  posture 240
attitudinarian 882
attitudinize 855
attollent 307
attorney
  consignee 758
  at law 968
  power of – 755
attract
  bring towards 288
  induce 615
  allure 865
  excite love 897
  – the attention 457
  visible 446
attraction [*see* attract]
  natural power 157
  bring towards **288**
attractive [*see* attract]
  pleasing 829
  beautiful 845
attrahent 288
attribute
  speciality 79
  accompaniment 88
  power 157
  –s of the Deity 976
  – to 155
attribution **155**
attrite 330
attrition 330, 331
attroupement 72
attune *music* 415
  prepare 673
attuned to
  habit 613
attunement 23
auburn 433
A.U.C. 106
auction 796, 840
auctioneer 758, 796
auctorial 599
audacity
  courage 861
  rashness 863
  insolence 885
audible 402
  become – 418
  scarcely – 405
audience

hearing 418
conversation 588
before an – 599
audire alteram partem
counter-evidence 468
right 922
justice 939
audit
numeration 85
examination 461
accounts 811
auditive 418
auditor
hearer 418
accountant 811
auditorium 189, 588
auditory
sound 402
hearing 418
theatre 599
– *apparatus* 418
au fait 698
au fond 5
auf wiedersehen 293
Augean
– stable 653
– task 704
auger 262
aught 51
for – one cares
unimportant 643
indifferent 866
for – one knows
ignorance 491
conjecture 514
augment
increase 35
thing added 39
expand 194
augur 513
– well 858
augurate 511
augury 512
august 873
Augustinian 996
auk 366
auld lang syne 122
aulic council 696
aumbry 1000
aunt 11
aura *wind* 349
sensation 380
aurea mediocritas 628
aureate 436
aureola 420
aureole 420, 873
aureolin 436

auribus, arrectis – 418
auricular *hearing* 418
clandestine 528
– confession 998
auri sacra fames 819
aurist 662
aurora
dawn 125
light 420, 423
twilight 422
– australes 423
– borealis 423
auroral 236
ausculation 418
auspice *omen* 512
auspices
influence 175
prediction 511
protection 664
direction 693
aid 707
under the – of 693, 737
auspicious
opportune 134
prosperous 734
hopeful 858
austerity
harsh taste 395
severe 739
discourteous 895
ascetic 955
pietism 988
austral 237
austromancy 511
authentic 467
certain 474
true 494
authentication
evidence 467
security 771
author 164, 593
projector 626
dramatic – 599
– of our being 976
– of evil 978
– 's proof 591
authoritative 474, 741
authority
testimony 467
sage 500
informant 527
power **737**
permission 760
right 924
ensign of – 747
person in – 745
do upon one's own – 600

authorized *due* 924
legalized 963
authorship
production 161
style 569
writing 590
autobiography 594
autocar 272
autochthonous 188
autocracy 737, 739
autocrat 745
autocratic 600, 737
auto-da-fe 384, 972
autograph 550, 590
Autolycus *thief* 792
pedlar 797
automaniac 504
automatic 601, 663
– pistol 727
– writing 992
automaton 554, 601
automobile 272
automobilist 268
automotive 266
autonomasia 521
autonomy 737, 748
autopsy
post-mortem 363
vision 441
autoptical 446, 535
autotype 558
autumn 126
auxiliary 711
additional 34
helpful 707
– forces 726
avail *benefit* 618
useful 644
succeed 731
of no – 645
– oneself of 677
avalanche *fall* 306
snow 383
redundance 641
avaler les couleuvres 725,
886
avant-courier 64, 673
avant-propos 64
avarice 819
avast! *stop* 142, 265
desist 624
forbid 761
avatar *change* 140
deity 976
idol 991
avaunt! 297, 449
ave! *honour* 873

go – from *retract* 773
have at one's – 215
hold – *avoid* 623
keep – *reserve* 636
look – 505
on one's – *impotent* 158
 horizontal 213
 failure 732
pat on the –
 incite 615
 encourage 861
 approve 931
pay – *retaliate* **718**
put – *deteriorate* 659
 restore 660
send – 764
take – again 790
carry one's thoughts – 505
some time – 122
spring – 277
trace – 505
turn – 283
turn one's – 283
turn one's – upon
 repel 289
 inattention 458
 avoid 623
 oppose 708
 seclusion 893
 discourtesy 895
 disrespect 929
 contempt 930
set one's – against the wall
 604
– to back 235
– down 283
– one's note 806
– out *retire* 283
 change sides 607
 relinquish 624
– pedal 273
– up *support* 216
 influence 615
 aid 707
put one's – up
 anger 900
set one's – up
 pride 878
backbite 932, 934
backbiter 936
backbone
 intrinsic 5
 energy 171
 frame 215
 centre 222
 resolution 604
 persevere 604a

soul 820
game to the – 604
back door 627
back down 607
backer 711
back-fire 406
back friend 891
backgammon 840
background
 distance 196
 rear 235
in the –
 latent 526
 ignoble 874
keep in the –
 hide 528
 modest 881
 seclusion 893
put one in the – 874
throw into the – 460
backsheesh 784, 973
backside 235
backslider 607
backsliding
 regression 283
 tergiversation 607
 relapse 661
 vice 945
 heterodox 984
 impiety 988
backstairs
 ambush 530
 way 627
– *influence* 702
backward
 tardy 133
 regression 283
 unwilling 603
 deteriorate 659
backwardation 813
backwards 283
 bend – 325
– and forwards
 interchange 148
 oscillation 314
backwater 275, 283
 in a – 893
backwoodsman
 inhabitant 188
 agriculture 371
bacon
 butter upon – 641
 save one's – 664, 671
Baconian method 461
bacteria 193
bactericide 600
baculinum, argumentum –

compel 744
lawless 964
punish 972
bad 649
 unclean 653
 wrong 923
– blood 898, 907
go – 653, 659
– business 859
– case 477
– chance 473
put a – construction on
 523
– debt 806
– fairy 980
– faith 940
– grace 895
– habit 613
– hand 701
– humour
 discontent 832
 dejection 837
 anger 900
 sullen 901a
not a – idea 498
– intent 907
– job *evil* 619
 botch 699
 hopeless 859
– joke 851
– language 908
view in a – light 934
– luck &c. 735
– man **949**
– money 800
– name 932, 934
in – odour 889
take in – part 832, 900
– repute 874
– smell 401
– spirit 980
– spirits 837
– taste 579, 851
– temper 900, 901, 901a
on – terms 713, 889
– time of it 828
– turn 619, 907
in a – way
 disease 655
 worse 659
 danger 665
 adversity 735
– woman 949
from – to worse
 aggravation 835
badaud 501
badge 550

- of authority 747
- of infamy 874
- of slavery 746
badger 830
- dog 366
badinage 842, 856
badly off
adversity 735
poor 804
badminton 840
badness 649
Baedeker 266
baffle hinder 706
defeat 731
- description
unconformable 83
wonder 870
baffling
puzzling 519
bag put up 184
receptacle 191
protrude 250
acquire 755
take 789
steal 791
- and baggage 780
bagatelle
trivial 643
pastime 840
baggage 270
minx 129
materials 635
property 780
hussy 962
baggy 47
bagman 758
bagnio 961
bagpipes 417
bah! 930
bail 771
go - 806
leg - 623
bailie 965
bailiff
director 694
servant 746
factor 758
officer 965
bailiwick
region 181
jurisdiction 965
Bairam
holiday 840
rite 998
bairn 129
bait attraction 288
food 298

trap 545
lure 615
refresh 689
attack 716
bribe 784
harass 830
swallow the - 547
bake 384
bakehouse 386
baker 637
baker's dozen 98
baking heat 382
bal 840
balais 847
balaclava helmet 225
balance equal 27
mean 29
compensate 30
remainder 40
numeration 85
weigh 319
compare 464
style 578
hesitate 605
money 800
accounts 811
in the - 475
the mind losing its - 503
off one's -
irresolute 605
fail 732
want of - 579
- accounts with
pay 807
balanced 150, 242
balbucinate 583
balbutiate 583
balcony 250
theatre 599
bald bare 226
style 575
uninteresting 841
ugly 846
plain 849
baldachin 223, 1000
balderdash 517, 577
baldric 230, 247
bale bundle 72
load 190
ladle 270
evil 619
- out 297
baleful 649
balister 727
balize 550
balk disappoint 509
deceive 545

hinder 706
Balkanize 713
ball globe 249
missile 284
shot 727
dance 840
party 892
- at one's feet 731, 737
keep up the - 143, 682
ballad 415, 597
- monger 597
ballast
compensation 30
weight 319
wisdom 498
safety 666
without - rash 863
vicious 945
ballerina 599
ballet 599, 840
ballet-dancer 599
ballistics
projectiles 284
war 722
arms 727
ballon d'essai 463
balloon 273, 726
balloonist 269
balloonry 267
ballot 535, 609
ball-room 840
balm moderate 174
fragrance 400
remedy 662
relief 834
Balmoral boot 225
balmy
sleep 683
balneal 337
balourdise 699
balsam 662
balsamic
salubrious 834
balustrade
support 215
inclosure 232
bam 544
bambino 129
bamboozle 545
ban exclude 55
prohibit 761
denounce 908
under the - 909
- with bell, book, and
candle 998
banal 613, 843
band ligature 45

bandage
assemblage 72
filament 205
belt 230
ring 247
music 415, 416, 417
party 712
shackle 752
- of hope 958
- together 709
- with 720
bandage 43, 45
support 215
cover 223
remedy 662
restraint 752
the eyes –d 442
bandana 225
bandbox 191
banded together 178, 712
bandit 792
bandog 664, 668
bandolier 636
bandore 417
bandrol 550
bands 999
bandurria 417
bandy
exchange 148
agitate 315
- about 531
- legged 243
- words 476, 588
bane 619, **663**
baneful 649
bang *impel* 276
sound 406
beat 972
bangle 847
banish *eject* 297
seclude 893
punish 972
banister 215
banjo 417
bank *acclivity* 217
side of lake 342
store 636
sand 667
fence 717
money 802
sea - 342
- of elegance 800
- holiday 840
- up 670
banker 797, 801
game 840
bank-note 800
bankruptcy 732, 808

banlieue 197, 227
banner 550
enlist under the -s of 707
raise one's - 722
banneret 875
banns
forbid the - 761
publish the -
ask 765
marriage 903
banquet 298, 840
banquette 717
banshee 979, 980
bantam cock 887
banter 842, 856
banterer 844
banting 956
bantling 129, 167
banyan *stint* 640
fast 956
baptism *name* 564
rite 998
Baptist 984
baptistery 1000
bar *except* 38
exclude 55
hotel 189
line 200
support 215
inclosure 232
close 261
music 413
hindrance 706
insignia 747
prison 752
prohibit 761
ingot 800
tribunal 966
legal profession 968
- sinister *flaw* 651
disrepute 874
illegal 964
crossing the - 360
Barabbas 792
baragouin 517
barb *spike* 253
nag 271
- the dart *pain* 830
barbacan 717
barbarian
uncivilized 876
evil-doer 913
barbaric 851, 876
barbarism
neology 563
bad style 579
vulgarity 851

discourtesy 895
barbarous
unformed 241
plebeian 876
maleficent 907
barbette 717
barbican 717
barbouillage 590
barcarolle 415
bard 416, 597
bare *mere* 32
nude 226
manifest 525
disclose 529
scanty 640
- back 226
- bone 203
- faced
deceitful 544
insolent 885
- foot 226, 804
- headed 928
scud under - poles 704
- possibility 473
- supposition 514
bargain
compact 769
barter 794
cheap 815
into the - 37
- for 507
- and sale *transfer of
property* 783
barge 273
bargee 269
baritone 408
bark *rind* 223
strip 226
ship 273
yelp 412
- at *threaten* 909
censure 932
more - than bite 908
worse than bite 885
barker 767
barleycorn
little 193
Barleycorn, Sir John -
298
barm *leaves* 320
bubbles 353
Barmecide feast 956
barmy 320, 503
barn 189
barnacles 445
barndoor fowl 366
barograph 206, 338

barometer *air* 338
  measure 466
  consult the – 463
baron *peer* 875
  husband 903
  court – 966
  – of the Exchequer 967
baronet 875
baronial 878
baroque 853
baroscope 338
barouche 272
barque 273
barrack 189
barracoon 717
barrage 407, 717
barratry 940
barred 219, 440
barrel 191, 249
  – organ 417
barren 169, 645
barricade *fence* 232
  obstacle 706
  defence 717
  prison 752
barrier [*see* barricade]
barring *save* 38
  excluding 55
  except 83
  – out *resist* 719
  disobey 742
barrister 968
  revising – 967
barrow
  mound 206
  vehicle 272
  grave 363
barter
  reciprocate 12
  interchange 148
  commerce **794**
barytone 408
basal 215
bas-bleu
  scholar 492
  affectation 855
base
  site 183
  lowest part **211**
  support 215
  bad 649
  cowardly 862
  shameful 874
  servile 886
  dishonourable 940
  vicious 945
  – ball 840

– born 876
– coin 800
– note 408
– of operations
  plan 626
  attack 716
  – viol 417
baseball diamond 213
baseboard 211
based on *ground of belief*
  467
baseless 2, 4
basement *cellar* 191
  lowest part 207, 211
bash 276
bashaw 739, 745
bashful 881
bashi bazouk 726
basilica 1000
basilisk *sight* 441
  cannon 737
  serpent 949
basin *dock* 189
  vessel 191
  hollow 252
  plain 344
basinet 717
basis
  lowest part 211
  support 215
  preparation 673
bask *physical enjoyment*
  377
  warmth 382
  prosperity 734
  moral enjoyment 827
basket 191
  – of 190
bas-relief 250, 557
bass *music* 415
  – note 408
  – viol 417
basset horn 417
bassinet 191, 215
bassoon 417
basso-profondo 408
basso-rilievo 250, 557
bastard 545, 925
baste *beat* 276
  , *punish* 972
Bastille 752
bastinado 972
bastion 717
bat 276, 727
batch 25, 72
bate *diminish* 36
  subtract 38

  reduce price 813
bated breath
  with – *faint sound* 405
  expecting 507
  hiding 528
  whisper 581
  humble 879
bath 337, 652
  public –s 652
  warm – 386
  – room 191, 652
Bath chair 272
bathe *immerse* 300
  plunge 310
  water 337
bathos 497
bathysphere 208
batik 440
batman 637
bâton *support* 215
  sceptre 747
batrachian 366
batta 973
battalion 726
batten
  feed 298
  stage lighting 599
  – down the hatches 261
  – on 886
batter *destroy* 162
  beat 276
battered 659, 688
battering-ram 276
battering-train 727
battery *electric* 153
  artillery 726
  guns 727
  floating 726
  plant a – 716
battle 720, 722
  half the – 642
  win the – 731
  – array *order* 60
  prepare 673
  war 722
  – axe 727
  – cruiser 726
  – cry 550, 722
  – field *arena* 728
  – ground *discord* 713
  – ship 726
  – with *oppose* 708
battledore and shuttlecock
  interchange 148
  game 840
battlement 257, 717
battre

- la campagne
nonsense 497
diffuse style 573
excitable 825
- l'eau avec un bâton 645
- le fer sur l'enclume 134
- la générale 669
se - contre des moulins
  645
ne - que d'une aile 683
battology
repeat 104
diffuse style 373
battue *pursuit* 622
attack 716
kill 361
bauble 643, 840
bavardage 517, 584
bawd 962
bawdy, - house 961
bawl 411
bawn 189
bay *concave* 252
gulf 343
cry 412
brown 433
at - *danger* 665
difficulty 704
defence 717, 719
bring to - 716
- the moon 645
- window 260
bayadère 599
bayard 271
bayonet *kill* 361
attack 716
weapon 727
crossed -s 708
at the point of the
  - *war* 722
severity 739
coercion 744
bays *trophy* 733
crown 877
bazaar 799
B.C. 106
be 1
- all and end all
whole 50
intention 620
importance 642
- off *depart* 293
eject 297
retract 773
- it so 488
- that as it may 30
beach 231, 342

beach comber 268
beacon 550, 663
bead 249
beadle *janitor* 263
law officer 965
church 996
beadledom 737
beadroll *list* 86
prayers 990
ritual 998
beads
ornament 847
tell one's - 990, 998
beadsman
servant 746
clergy 996
beagle 366
beak *face* 234
nose 250
magistrate 967
beaker 161
beam *support* 215
plank 236
weigh 319
light 420
on - ends
powerless 158
horizontal 213
side 236
fail 732
wonder 870
beaming
beautiful 845
bean 276
beanfeast 840
bear *produce* 161
sustain 215
carry 270
admit of 470
suffer 821
endure 826
bring to - 677
more than flesh and blood
  can - 824
unable to -
excited 825
dislike 867
- away 789
- away the bell 648, 731
- the brunt 704, 717
- the burden 625
- the cross 828
- company 88
- down 173, 885
- down upon 716
- false witness 544
- fruit *produce* 161

useful 644
success 731
prosper 734
- a hand 680
- hard upon 649
- harmless 717
- ill 825
- off *deviate* 279
- on 215
- oneself 692
- out *evidence* 467
vindicate 937
- pain 828
- the palm 33
- a sense 516
- through 707
- up *approach* 286
persevere 604a
relieve 834
cheerful 836
- up against 719, 861
- upon
relevant 9, 23
influence 175
- with
tolerate 740
permit 760
take coolly 826
forgive 918
bear
savage 907
surly 895
had it been a - it would
  have bitten you 458
- garden
disorder 59
discord 713
arena 728
- leader 540
- pit 370
- skin *cap* 225
helmet 717
- with a sore back 901
bearable 651
beard *hair* 205
prickles 253
rough 256
defy 715
brave 861
insolence 885
pluck by the -
disrespect 929
- the lion 604
beardless 127, 226
bearer 271, 363
bearing *relation* 9
support 215

direction 278
meaning 516
demeanour 692
- *rein* 706, 752
bearings
  circumstances 8
  situation 183
  armorial - 550
beast *animal* 366
  unclean 653
  discourteous 895
  - of burden 271, 690
beat *be superior* 33
  periodic 138
  region 181
  impulse 276
  surpass 303
  oscillate 314
  agitation 315
  crush 330
  sound 407
  line of pursuit 625
  path 627
  overcome 731
  strike 972
  - about
  circuit 629
  - the air 645
  - against 708
  - one's breast 839
  - about the bush
  try for 463
  evade the point 477
  prevaricate 544
  diffuse style 573
  - down *destroy* 162
  cheapen 794, 819
  insolent 885
  - of drum
  music 416
  publish 531
  alarm 669
  wear 722
  command 741
  pomp 882
  without - of drum 528
  - into *teach* 537
  - off 717
  - a retreat
  retire 283
  avoid 623
  submit 725
  - time *clock* 114
  music 416
  - up *churn* 352
  - up against
  oppose 708

- up for *cater* 637
- up one's quarters
  seek 461
  visit 892
- up for recruits
  prepare 673
  aid 707
beaten track
  habit 613
  way 627
  leave the - 83
  tread the - 82
beatic 827
beatific 829, 981
beatification 827, 987
beating high
  the heart - 824
beatitude 827
beau *man* 373
  fop 854
  admirer 897
  - idéal 650, 845
  - monde 852
beautify 845, 847
beautiless 846
beauty 845
beaver *hat* 225
becalm 265
because *cause* 153
  attribution 155
  answer 462
  reasoning 476
  motive 615
bechance 151
beck *rill* 348
  sign 550
  mandate 741
  at one's - *aid* 707
  obey 743
beckon *sign* 550
  motive 615
  call 741
becloud *dark* 421
  hide 528
become
  accord with 23
  change to 144
  behoove 926
  - of 151
becoming
  accordant 23
  proper 646
  beautiful 845, 847
  due 924
becripple 158
bed *lodgment* 191
  layer 204

support 215
  garden 371
  marriage 903
  brought to - 161
  death - 360
  smooth the - of death 707
  go to - 265, 683
  keep one's - 655
  - of down 687
  - gown 255
  - maker 746
  - out 371
  - ridden 655
  - room 191
  - of roses 377, 734
  put to - with a shovel 363
  - time 126
bedarken 421
bedaub 223, 653
bedazzle 420
bedding 215
bedeck 847
bedel 965
bedesman [*see* beadsman]
bedevil *derange* 61
  sorcery 992
bedew 339
bedight 847
bedim 421, 422
bedizen *clothe* 225
  ornament 847
  vulgar 851
Bedlam
  - broke loose 59
  candidate for - 504
be-dog 281
Bedouin 792
bedraggled 59
bedwarf 195
bee 690
  busy - 682
  swarm like -s 102
  - in one's bonnet 503
  - in a bottle 407
  - line 246, 278
  -'s wax 352
beef-eater 726
beef-headed 499
beehive 250
Beelzebub 978
beer 298
beery 959
beetle *overhang* 206, 214
  project 250
  blind as a - 442
  Colorado - 913
  - head 501

befall 151
befit *agree* 23
  expedient 646
  due 924, 926
befog 353, 528
befool *mad* 503
  deceive 545
befooled
  victimized 732
before *in order* 62
  in time 116
  presence 186
  in space 234
  precession 280
  preference 609
  set – one 525
  – Christ 106
  – long 132
  – mentioned 62, 116
  – now 122
  – one's eyes 446, 525
  – one's time 132
  – you could –turn round, –
    say Jack Robinson 113
beforehand
  prior 116
  early 132
  foresight 510
  resolve – 611
befoul 653
befriend 707, 888
befuddlement 959
beg *Turk* 745
  ask 765
  – one's bread 765
  poor 804
  – leave 760
  – one's life 914
  – pardon 952
  – the question 477
beget 161
begetter 164, 166
beggar *idler* 683
  petitioner 767
  poor 804
  degrade 874
  low person 876
  sturdy – 792
  – description 83, 870
  – my neighbour 840
  – on horseback 885
beggared
  bankrupt 808
beggarly *mean* 643
  vile 874
  vulgar 876
  servile 886

– account of empty boxes
  640, 804
begging
  go a –
  too much 641
  useless 645
  offered 763
  free 748
  – letter 765
begilt 847
begin 66
  – again 104
beginner 541
beginning 66
begird 227, 229
beglerbeg 745
begone
  depart 293
  ejection 297
  abrogate 756
  – dull care 836
Begotten, the only – 976
begrime 653
begrudge
  unwilling 603
  refuse 764
  stingy 819
beguile *mislead* 495
  deceive 545
  reconcile 831
  – the time
  inaction 681
  amusement 840
beguine 996
begum 745, 875
behalf 618, 707
  in – of 759
behave oneself
  conduct 692
  fashion 852
  courtesy 894
behaviour 692
  on one's good – 894, 944
behead 361, 972
behemoth 192
behest 741
behind
  in order 63
  in space 235
  sequence 281
  – the age 124, 491
  – one's back 187
  speak ill of – one's back
   934
  – the bars 751
  – the scenes
  cause 153

  unseen 447
  cognizant 490
  latent 526
  hidden 528
  playhouse 599
  – time 133
behindhand
  late 133
  shortcoming 304
  adversity 735
  insolvent 808
behold 441, 457
beholden 916, 926
beholder 444
behoof 618
behoove 926
being 1, 3
  created – 366
  human – 372
  time – 106
Bel 979
belabour 276, 972
belated *late* 133
  ignorant 491
belaud 931
belay *join* 43
  restrain 706
belch 297
beldam 130, 913
beldame 173
beleaguer 716
bel esprit 844
belfry 206, 1000
Belial 978, 980
  sons of – 988
belie *deny* 536
  falsify 544
  contradict 708
belief **484,** 983
  easy of – 472
  hug a – 606
believe [*see* belief]
  suppose 514
  reason to – 472
  – who may 485
  not – one's senses 870
believer
  religious 987
  true – 983*a*
belike 472
belittle
  decrease 36
  underestimate 482
  disparage 934
bell 417, 550
  alarm – 669
  bear away the –

goodness 648
success 731
repute 873
church – 350
cracked – 408*a*
passing – 363
– book and candle
swear 535
curse 908
spell 993
rite 998
– the cat 861
– shape 249, 252
belladonna 663
belle 374, 854
a la – étoile 220, 845
belles-lettres 560
belli, casus – 824
bellicose 720, 722
bellied 250
belligerent
contentious 720
warlike 722
combatant 726
belling 412
bellman 354
bello, flagrante – 722
Bellona 722
bellow *loud* 404
cry 411
animal cry 412
wail 839
bellows 349, 580
bells, peal of – 407
bellwether 64, 694
belly *receptacle* 191
inside 221
convex 250
–ful 52, 639
– god 957
– timber 298
belomancy 511
belong to *related* 9
component 56
included 76
attribute 157
property 777, 780
duty 926
beloved 897
below 207
here – 318
– the mark 32
– par, 34, 207
bad 649
indifferent 651
discount 813
ignoble 876

– its full strength 651
– stairs 207
belt *outline* 230
ring 247
strait 343
swimming – 666
belting 633
Belus 979
belvedere 441
bemask 528
bemingle 41
bemire 653
bemoan 839
bemused 458
bench *support* 215
council 696
tribunal 966
Bench, King's – 752
bencher 968
bend *oblique* 217
angle 244
curve 245
incline 278
deviate 279
depression 308
circuit 311
give 324
submit 725
– backwards 235
– the bow 686
– the brows 932
– one's course 27
– the knee
bow down 308
submit 725
humble 879
servile 886
courtesy 894
respect 928
worship 990
– one's looks upon 441
– the mind 457
– over 250
– to rules &c. 82
– sinister 874
– one's steps 622
– to tend 176
– towards 278
– to one's will 737
beneath 207
– one 940
– notice 643
Benedick 903
Benedictine 996
benediction
gratitude 916
approval 931

worship 990
nuptial – 903
benefaction 784
benefactor 816, **912**
benefice 995
beneficent 906
beneficial 648
– interest 780
beneficiary
possessor 779
receive 785
clergy 996
benefit *good* 618
use 644
do good 648
aid 707
acquisition 775
property 780
benevolence 906
reap the – of 131
benefits forgot 917
bene gesserit, quamdiu se
– 926
benet 545
benevolence
tax 812
love 897
kindness **906**
universal – 910
Bengal heat 382
benighted
dark 421
ignorant 491
benign 656, 906
benignant 906
benison 618, 931
Benjamin's mess 33, 50
Benshie 979
bent *tendency* 176
angle 244
turn of mind 820
desire 865
fool to the top of one's –
856
– on *willing* 602
resolved 604
intention 620
desirous 865
Benthamite 910
ben trovato
likely 472
imagination 515
untruth 546
wit 842
benumb
insensible 376
cold 385

deaden affections 823
beplaster 933
bepraise 931
bequest 270
  gift 784
bereavement
  death 360
  loss 776
  take away 789
bereft *poor* 804
  – of life 360
  – of reason 503
béret 225
berg, ice – 383
bergamot 400
berlin 272
berth *lodging* 189
  bed 215
  office 625
beryl *green* 435
  jewel 847
beseech 765, 990
beseem 926
beserk 173, 503
beset *surround* 227
  follow 281
  attack 716
  entreat 765
  annoy 830
  haunt 860
  – with difficulties 704
besetting 78, 613
  – sin 945
beshrew 908
beside *except* 83
  near 197
  alongside 236
  – the mark 10, 495
  – oneself 503, 824
besides 37
besiege
  surround 227
  attack 716
  solicit 765
bésique 840
beslaver 933
beslime 653
beslubber 933
besmear 233, 653
besom 652
besotted 481
bespangle 847
bespatter *dirt* 653
  disapprove 932
  flatter 933
  detract 934
bespeak *early* 132

evidence 467
indicate 516
engage 755
ask for 765
bespeckle 440
bespot 440
besprinkle 41, 440
best 648, 650
  all for the –
  good 618
  prosper 734
  content 831
  hope 858
  bad is the – 649
  do one's –
  care 459
  try 675
  activity 682
  exertion 686
  have the – of it 731
  make the – of it
  over-estimate 482
  use 677
  submit 725
  compromise 774
  take easily 826
  hope 858
  the – 800
  to the – of one's belief 484
  – bib and tucker
  prepared 673
  ornament 847
  ostentation 882
  – friends 890
  – intentions 906
  – man 903
  – part 31, 50
  – seller 731
  make the – of one's time
    684
bestead 644
bestial 954, 961
bestir oneself
  activity 682
  haste 684
  exertion 686
bestow 784
  – one's hand 903
  – thought 451
bestraddle 215
bestrew 73
bestride 206, 215
bet 621
betake oneself to
  journey 266
  business 625
  use 677

bête, pas si – 498
bête noire *bane* 663
  fear 860
  hate 898
bethel 1000
bethink 451, 505
bethral 749, 751
betide 151
betimes 132
betoken
  evidence 467
  predict 511
  indicate 550
betray *disclose* 529
  deceive 545
  dishonour 940
  – itself *visible* 446
betrayer 941
betrim 673
betroth 768, 903
betrothed 897
better *good* 648
  improve 658
  appeal to one's – feelings
    914
  get – *health* 654
  improve 658
  restoration 660
  refreshment 689
  get the – of, 479, 702, 731
  think – of 658, 950
  seen – days
  deteriorate 659
  adversity 735
  poor 804
  – half 903
  only – than nothing 651
  – sort 875
  for – for worse
  choice 609
  marriage 903
between 228
  – cup and lip 111
  far – 198
  lie – 228
  – the lines 526
  vibrate – two extremes 149
  – ourselves 528
  – two fires 665
  – maid 746
betwixt 228
bevel 217
  – gearing 653
bever 298
beverage 298
bévue 732
bevy 72, 102

bewail *regret* 833
 lament 839
beware 665, 668
bewilder
 put out 458
 uncertainty 475
 astonish 870
bewitch
 fascinate 615
 please 829
 excite love 897
 exorcise 992
bey 745
beyond *superior* 33
 distance 196
 go – 303
 – compare 31, 33
 – control 471
 – one's depth 208, 519
 – expression 31
 – one's grasp 471
 – hope 731, 534
 – the mark 303, 641
 – measure 641
 – possibility 471
 – praise
 perfect 650
 approbation 931
 virtue 944
 – price 814
 – question 474, 494
 – reason 471
 – remedy 859
 – seas 57
bezel 217
bhang 663
bias *influence* 175
 tendency 176
 slope 217
 prepossession 481
 disposition 820
bib *pinafore* 225
 drink 959
bibber *weep* 839
 tope 959
bibble-babble 584
bibelot 847
bibendum, nunc est – 959
Bible 895
 – oath 535
biblioclasm 162
bibliography 593
bibliolatry
 learning 490
 heterodoxy 984
 idolatry 991
bibliomancy 511

bibliomania 490
bibliomaniac 492
bibliophile 492
bibliopole 593
bibliotheca 593
bibulous 298, 959
bicameral 90
bicapital 90
bice 435, 438
bicentenary 98, 138, 883
bicker *flutter* 315
 quarrel 713
bicolour 440
biconjugate 91
bicuspid 91
bicycle 272
bid *order* 741
 offer 763
 – the banns 903
 – defiance 715
 – fair *tend* 176
 probable 472
 promise 511
 hope 858
 – a long farewell 624
 – for *intend* 620
 offer 763
 request 765
 bargain 794
bidder 767
bide *wait* 133
 remain 141
 take coolly 806
 – one's time 133
 watch 507
 inactive 681
bidet 271
biennial
 periodic 138
 plant 367
bienséance 852, 894
bier 363
bifacial 90
bifarious 90
bifid 91
bifold 90
biform 90
bifurcate 91, 244
big *in degree* 31
 in size 192
 wide 194
 look – *defy* 715
 proud 878
 insolent 885
 talk – 885, 909
 – sounding
 loud 404

 words 577
 affected 855
 – swollen 194
 – with 161
 – with the fate of 511
bigamy 903
biggin 191
bight 343
bigot *positive* 474
 prejudice 481
 obstinate 606
 heterodox 984
 impious 988
bigotry 907
bigwig *scholar* 492
 sage 500
 nobility 875
bijou *goodness* 648
 beauty 845
 ornament 847
bilander 273
bilateral 90, 236
bilbao 727
bilboes 752
 put into – 751
bile 900
bilge *base* 211
 convex 250
 yawn 260
 – water 653
bilingual 560
bilious 837
bilk
 disappoint 509
 cheat 545
 steal 791
bill *list* 86
 hatchet 253
 placard 531
 ticket 550
 paper 593
 plan 626
 weapon 727
 money order 800
 money account 811
 charge 812
 in law 969
 true – 969
 – and coo 902
 – of exchange 771
 – of fare *food* 298
 plan 626
 – of indictment 938
 –s of mortality 360
 – of sale 771
billet *locate* 184
 ticket 550

apporrtion 786
billet *epistle* 592
– doux 902
billfold 191
billhook 253
billiard – ball 249
– room 191
– table *flat* 213
billiards 840
Billingsgate 563, 908
billion 98
billow *sea* 348
river 341
billy-cock 225
billy-goat 373
bimetallism 800
bin 191
binary 89
bind *connect* 43
cover 223
compel 744
condition 770
obligation 926
– hand and foot 751
– oneself 768
– over 744
– up wounds 660
binding 681, 744
bine 367
binnacle 693
binocular 445
binomial 89
biogenesis 161
biograph 448
biography 594
biology 357, 359
bioscope 448
biota 357
biparous 89
bipartite 44, 91
biplane 273
biplicity 89
biquadrate 96
birch *flog* 972
– rod 975
bird 366
kill two –s with one stone
682
–'s eye view 441, 448
–s of a feather 17
the – has flown 187, 671
– in hand 777, 781
– of ill omen
omen 512
warning 668
hopeless 859
– of passage 268

– of prey 739
a little – told me 527
birdcage 370
birdlime *glue* 45
trap 545
biretta 999
birth *beginning* 66
production 161
paternity 166
nobility 875
– place 153
– right 924
birthday 138, 883
– suit 226
birthmark 848
bis *repeat* 104
approval 931
biscuits, s'embarquer sans
– 674
bise 349
bisection 68, 91
bishop *punch* 298
clergy 996
–'s palace 1000
–'s purple 437
bishopric 995
bisque 33
bissextile 138
bistoury 253
bistre 433
bisulcate 259
bit
small quantity 32
part 51
interval 106
curb 752
just a – 26
– by bit
by degrees 26
by instalments 51
in detail 79
slowly 275
– between the teeth 600,
719
bitch animal 366
female 374
clumsy 699
fail 732
impure 962
bite *eat* 298
physical pain 378
cold 385
cheat 545
dupe 547
etch 558
mental pain 830
– the dust 725

– in 259
– the thumb 900, 929
– the tongue 392
biter bit 718
biting *pain* 378
cold 383
pungent 392
painful 830
discourteous 895
censorious 932
bitten 897
bitter *beer* 298
cold 383
taste 392, 395
painful 830
acrimonious 895
hate 898
angry 900
malevolent 907
– end 67
– ender 606, 710, 832
– pill 735
– words 932
bitterly *greatly* 31
bitterness [*see* bitter]
pain 828
regret 833
bitumen 356*a*
bituminous coal 388
bivouac
encamp 184
camp 189
repose 265
watch 668
bi-weekly 138
bizarre 83, 853
blab 529
blabber 584
black *colour* 431
crime 945
look – *feeling* 821
discontent 832
angry 900
– art 992
– and blue
beat 972
– board 590
– book 938
– eye 848, 972
– in the face
swear 535
excitement 821, 824
– flag 722
– hole *crowd* 72
prison 752
– lead 556
– letter *old* 124

barbarism 563
print 591
– list 932
– looks
  discourteous 895
  sullen 901*a*
  disapprove 932
  magic 998
– mail *theft* 791
  booty 793
  bribe 973
– sheep 949
– spots in the horizon 859
– swan 83
– and white
  chiaroscuro 420
  colourless 429
  record 551
  writing 590
prove that – is white 477
blackball 55, 893, 932
blackcoat 996
blacken [*see* black]
  defame 934
blackguard
  vulgar 851
  rude 895
  base 940
  vagabond 949
blackleg 792
black Maria 727
blackness **431**
blacksmith 690
bladder 191
blade *edge tool* 253
  man 373
  instrument 633
  sharp fellow 682
  proficient 700
  sword 727
  fop 854
blague 545
blain 250, 848
blame 155, 932
lay – on 938
take – 932
blameless 946
blameworthy
  disapprove 932
  vice 945
  guilt 947
blanc-bec 701
blanch 429, 430
blancmange 298
bland 174, 894
blandiloquence 933
blandishment

inducement 615
endearment 902
flattery 933
blank 2, 4
  empty 187
  simple 849
  look –
  disappointed 509
  discontent 832
  wonder 870
point – 576
– cartridge 158
– verse 597
blanket 223, 384
wet – 174
toss in a – 929
blare 404, 412
blarney 933
blasé 841, 869
blasphemy 988
blast
  destroy 162
  explosion 173
  wind 349
  sound 404
  adversity 735
  curse 908
– furnace 386
blatant *loud* 404
  cry 412
  silly 499
blather 584
blatter 412
blaze *heat* 382
  light 420
  mark 550
  excitement 824
– abroad 531
blazer 225
blazing
  luminary 423
blazon *publish* 531
  ornament 847
  repute 873
  ostentation 882
blé: manger son – on herbe
  818
bleach 429, 430
bleak 383
blear-eyed 443
bleary 422
bloat 412
blob 250
bleed
  physical pain 378
  remedy 662
  spend money 809

extort money 814
moral pain 828
make the heart – 830
– freely *liberal* 816
bleeding
  hemorrhage 299
  remedy 662
– heart 828
blemish
  imperfection 651
  injure 659
  ugly 846
  defect **848**
blench *avoid* 623
  whiten 821
  fear 860
blend 41, 48
– with 714
bless
  give pleasure 829
  approve 931
  divine function 976
  worship 990
– my heart 870
– one's stars 838, 916
blessed 827
abode of the – 981
blessedness
single – 904
blessing *good* 618
  approval 931
blessings 734
blest 827
– with 177
bletonism 511
blight
  deteriorate 659
  adversity 735
– hope 509
blighty 189
blimp 273
blind 223
  shade 424
  cecity 442
  inattentive 458
  ignorant 491
  conceal 528
  screen 530
  deception 545
  instinctive 601
  pretext 617
  insensible 823
  drunk 959
– alley 261
– bargain
  uncertain 475
  purposeless 621

rash 863
- the eyes *hide* 528
deceive 545
- hookey 840
- lead the blind 538
- man's buff 840
- man's holiday
evening 126
dark 421, 422
- to one's own merit 880
- to the world 959
- of one eye 443
- reasoning 486
- side *prejudice* 481
credulity 486
obstinacy 606
blinders 424, 443
blindness 442
blind pig 964
blink *wink* 443
neglect 460
falter 605
avoid 623
- at *blind to* 442, 458
blinkard 443
blinker 424, 530
bliss 827
celestial 981
blister 250
blithe 836
blizzard 349
bloated
expanded 194
misshapen 243
convex 250
- with pride 878
blob 250
block *mass* 192
support 215
dense 321
hard 323
fool 501
engraving 558
writing 590
hinder 706
execution 975
bring to the - 972
wood - 558
- of buildings 189
- out 230, 240, 973
- printing 591
- up, 261, 706
blockade
surround 227
close 261
restrain 751
exclude 893

blockhead 501
blockhouse 717
blockish 499
blond 429, 430
blood
consanguinity 11
fluid 333
kill 361
fop 854
nobility 875
dye with -
severe 739
hands in - *cruel* 907
in the - 5
life - 359
new - 658, 824
spill - *war* 722
- for blood 919
- boil *excite* 824, 825
anger 900
- run cold 830, 860
- heat 382
- horse 271
- hound 913
- letting 297, 662
- poisoning 655
- red 434
- stained 361
- sucker 789, 913
- thirsty
murderous 361
cruel 907
- up *excited* 824
angry 900
bloodless 160
peace 721
virtue 946
bloody [*see* blood]
red 434
unclean 653
cruel 907
bloom *youth* 127
flower 367
blue 438
health 654
prosperity 734
bloomer 495
bloomers 225
blooming 654, 845
blossom
flower 154, 161, 367
prosperity 734
blot *blacken* 431
error 495
obliterate 552
dirty 653
blemish 848

disgrace 874
guilt 947
- out *destroy* 162
forgive 918
blotch 848
blouse 225
blow *expand* 194
knock 276
wind 349
unexpected 508
disappointment 509
evil 619
action 680
get *wind* 688
failure 732
prosper 734
pain 828, 830
come to -s 720, 722
deal a - at 716
deal a - to 972
death - 360, 361
- for blow 718
- one's brains out 361
- the coals 824
- down 162
- the fire 384
- the gaff 529
- hole 351
- the horn 416
- hot and cold
lie 544
irresolute 605
tergiversation 607
caprice 608
- a kiss 902
- off *disperse* 73
- out *food* 298
darken 421
gorge 957
- over *past* 122
- pipe 349, 727
- the trumpet 873
- one's own trumpet 882
- up *destroy* 162
eruption 173
inflate 194
wind 349
excite 824
objurgate 932, 934
blower 349
blowhard 884
blown [*see* blow]
fatigued 688
proud 878
storm - over 664, 721
- upon 874, 932
blow-out 406

- clothes 225
- colour 556
- of doctrine 490
- forth 554
- guard 717, 753
- of knowledge 490
- politic
  mankind 372
  authority 737
  keep - and soul together
  654
- of water 438
Bœotian *rustic* 371
  stupid 499
  fool 501
  vulgar 851
  ignoble 876
Boer 371
bog 345, 653
- trotter 876
boggart 980
boggle *hesitate* 605
  awkward 699
  difficulty 704
bogie 980
  truck 272
bogle 980
bogus 545
Bohemian
  unconventional 83
  nomad 268
  ungenteel 851
boil *violence* 173
  effervesce 315
  bubble 353
  heat 382, 384
  ulceration 655
  excitement 824, 825
  anger 900
- down 195
boiler 386
boisterous
  violent 173
  hasty 684
  excitable 825
bold *prominent* 250
  unreserved 525
  vigorous 574
  brave 861
  make - with 895
  show a - front 715, 861
- faced 885
- push *essay* 675
- relief *visible* 446
- stroke *plan* 626
  success 731
bole 50

bolero 840
bollard 45
bolshevik 144, 146
bolshevist 737, 742
bolster *support* 215
  repair 658
  aid 707
- up *vindicate* 937
bolt *sift* 42
  fasten 43
  fastening 45
  close 261
  move rapidly 274
  propel 284
  run away 623
  escape 671
  hindrance 706
  shaft 727
  disobey 742
  shackle 752
  thunder - 872
- the door 761
- food 298, 957
- in 751
- upright 212
bolthead 191
bolus *mouthful* 298
  remedy 662
bomb 404, 727
- proof 664, 717
- vessel 726
bombard 716
bombardier 726
bombardon 417
bombast
  unmeaning 517
  exaggeration 549
  magniloquence 577
  ridiculous 853
  boasting 884
Bombastes Furioso 887
bomber
  aeroplane 726
bombilation 404
bon, de - augure 858
- enfant *social* 892
  kindly 906
- gré mal gré 601
- marché 815
- mot 842
- naturel 836
- ton 852
- vivant 957
- voyage 293
bona - fides
  veracity 543
  probity 939

- roba 962
bonanza 641, 784
  wealth 803
bonbon 396
bond *relation* 9
  tie 45
  compact 769
  security 771
  money 800
  right 924
- of union 9, 45
  government - 802
  Liberty - 802
bondage 749
bonded together 712
bonds [*see* bond]
  fetters 752
  funds 802
  in - *service* 746
  tear asunder one's - 750
- of harmony 714
bondsman 746
bone *strength* 159
  dense 321
  hard 323
  bred in the - 5
  feel it in one's - 510
- of contention 713, 720
  one - and one flesh 903
- to pick *difficulty* 704
  discord 713
- setter 662
bonehouse 363
boner 495
bones [*see* bone]
  corpse 362
  music 417
  break no - 648
  make no - 602, 705
boneyard 363
bonfire 382
  festivity 840
  celebration 883
  make a - of 384
bonhomie 703, 906
bonhomme 996
Boniface 890
bonne 746, 753
- bouche *end* 67
  pleasant 377
  savoury 394
  saving 636
  á la - heure 602, 831
  de - volonté 602
bonnet 225
bonny 836, 845
bono: cui -

409

intention 620
utility 644
inutility 645
pro – publico 644, 910
bonus *extra* 641
gift 784
money 810
bony 323
bonze 996
bonzer 648
booby 501
– trap 545
boodle 793
book *register* 86
publication 531
record 551
volume **593**
script 599
enter accounts 811
at one's –s 539
bring to –
evidence 467
account 811
reprove 932
mind one's – 539
school – 542
without –
by heart 505
– of Books 985
– club 593
– of fate 601
– learning 490
– shop 593
book-case 191
booked *dying* 360
bookish 490
bookkeeper 553
bookkeeping 811
bookless
unlearned 493
bookmaking 156
bookseller 593
bookworm 492, 593
boom
support 215
sail 267
rush 274
impulse 276
sound 404
obstacle 706
defence 717
boomerang
recoil 277
retribution 718
weapon 727
boon 784
beg a – 765

– companion 890
boor *clown* 876
boorish 851, 895
boost 276, 482, 931
booster 935
boot *box* 191
dress 225
advantage 618
punishment 975
to – added 37
– legging 964
booted and spurred 673
booth 189, 799
boothless 645, 732
boots *dress* 225
servant 746
low person 876
what – it? 643
booty 793
booze 959
bo-peep 441, 528
bordel 961
border *edge* 231
limit 233
flower bed 371
ornament 847
– upon 197, 199
bore *diameter* 202
hole 260
tide 348, 667
fatigue 688
trouble 828
plague 830
weary 841
bored 456
boreal
Northern 237
cold 383
Boreas 349
boredom 841
borer 262
born 359
– so 5
– under an evil star 735
– under a lucky star 734
borne 826
– down *failure* 732
defection 837
borné 499
borough 181, 189
rotten – 893
– council 696
borrow 19, 788
– of Peter &c. 147
borrowed plumes
deception 545
borrower 806

borrowing 788
bosh *absurdity* 497
unmeaning 517
untrue 546
trifling 643
bosky 959
bosom *breast* 221
mind 450
affections 820
in the – of 229
– of one's family 221
– friend 890
boss 250, 694, 737
straw – 694
boston 840
botanic garden 369, 371
Botanomancy 511
botany 367, **369**
botch *bungle* 59
mend 660
unskilful 699
difficulty 704
fail 732
both 89
listen with – ears 418
burn the candle at – ends 641
butter one's bread on – sides 641
bother
uncertainty 475
bustle 682
difficulty 704
trouble 828
harass 830
bothy 189
bottle
receptacle 191
preserve 670
bee in a – 407
crack a – 298
pass the – 959
smelling – 400
– green 435
– holder
auxiliary 177
mediator 724
– up *remember* 505
hide 528
restrain 751
bottom
lowest part 211
support 215
posterior 235
combe 252
ship 273
pluck 604a

strengthen 159
support 214
music 413
refresh 689
bracelet *circle* 247
 handcuff 752
 ornament 847
bracer 392
braces 45
brachial 633
Brachygraphy 590
bracing 656
bracken 367
bracket *tie* 43, 45
 couple 89
 support 215
brackish 392
brad 45
bradawl 262
Bradbury 800
Bradshaw 266
brae 206
brag *cards* 840
 boast 884
braggadocio 884
braggart 884
Brahma 979
Brahmin 984, 996
braid *tie* 43
 ligature 45
 net 219
 variegate 440
brain *kill* 361
 intellect 450
 skill 498
 blow one's –s out 361
 coinage of the – 515
 rack one's –s 451, 515
 suck one's –s 461
brainless 499
brainpan 450
brainsick 458
brain-storm 503, 825
brainwork 451
brainy 498
brake *carriage* 272
 copse 367
 hindrance 706
 curb 752
 apply the – 275
brakeman 268
bramble *thorn* 253
 bane 663
bran 330
brancard 272
branch *member* 51
 class 75

posterity 167
fork 244
tree 367
– off 91, 291
– out *ramify* 91
diffuse style 573
branching
 symmetry 242
brand *burn* 384
 fuel 388
 torch 423
 mark 550
 sword 727
 disrepute 874
 censure 932
 stigmatize 934
 – of discord 713
 – new 123
 – with reproach 938
brandish
 oscillate 314
 flourish 315
 display 882
brandy 959
brangle 713
brangler 710
brank 975
bras
 les – croisés 681
 à – ouverts 894
brashness 885
brasier 386
brass *alloy* 41
 money 800
 insolence 885
 bold as – 861
 – band 417, 882
 with a – 884
 – coloured 439
 – hat 745
 – farthing 643
brassard 550, 747
brat 129
brattice 224, 228
bravado 884
brave *confront* 234
 healthy 654
 defy 715
 warrior 726
 bear 821, 826
 courage 861
 – a thousand years 110
bravo
 assassin 361
 desperado 863
 applause 931
bravura 415

brawl *cry* 411
 discord 713
 revel 840
brawler
 disputant 710
 rioter 742
 blusterer 887
brawny 159, 192
bray *grind* 330
 cry 412
Bray, Vicar of – 607, 886
braze 43
brazen 525, 885
 – browned 885
 – faced 885
brazier [*see* brasier]
breach *crack* 44
 gap 198
 quarrel 713
 violation 925
 custom honoured in the –
 614
 – of faith 940
 – of law 83, 964
 – of the peace 713
bread 298
 beg – 765
 selfish 943
 quarrel with – and butter
 699
 – of idleness 683
 – of life *Christ* 976
 piety 987
 – upon the waters 638
 – and wine 998
breadbasket 191
breadth 202
 chiaroscuro 420
break
 fracture 44
 discontinuity 70
 change 140
 gap 198
 carriage 272
 crumble 328
 disclose 529
 cashier 756
 violate 773, 927
 bankrupt 808
 – away 623
 – bread 298
 – bulk 297
 – camp 293
 – of day *morning* 125
 twilight 422
 – down *destroy* 162
 fall short 304

decay 659
fail 732
dance 840
– one's fetters 614
– forth 295
– ground 66
– a habit 614
– the heart _pain_ 828, 830
dejection 837
– the ice 888
– in _ingress_ 294
domesticate 370
teach 537
tame 749
– in upon _derange_ 61
inopportune 135
hinder 706
– a lance 716, 722
– a law 83
– loose 671, 750
– one's neck _powerless_
158
die 360
task 676
success 731
– the news 529
– no bones 648
– of 660
– off _cease_ 142
relinquish 624
abrogate 756
– out _begin_ 66
violent 173
disease 655
excited 825
– the peace 173, 720
– Priscian's head 568
– prison 750
– the ranks 61
– short 328
– silence 582
– the teeth 579
– the thread 70
– through the clouds
visible 446
disclose 529
– through a custom 614
– up _disjoin_ 44
decompose 49
end 67
revolution 146
destroy 162
– up of the system, 360,
665
– on the wheel
physical pain 378
mental pain 830

punishment 972
– with 713
– with the past 146
– word _deceive_ 525
improbity 940
breaker
of horses 268
reef 346
wave 348
breakers 348, 667
surrounded by – 704
– ahead 665
breakfast 298
breakneck
precipice 217
rash 863
breakwater
refuge 666
obstruction 706
breast _interior_ 221
confront 234
convex 250
mind 450
oppose 708
soul 820
at the – 129
in the – of 620
– the current 719
– high 206
breastplate 717
breastwork 717
breath _instant_ 113
breeze 349
life 359
animality 364
faint sound 405
with bated – 581
hold – _quiet_ 265
expect 507
wonder 870
not a – of air 265, 382
out of – 688
in the same – 120
shortness of – 688
take – 265, 689
take away one's –
unexpected 508
fear 860
wonder 870
breathe _exist_ 1
blow 349
live 359
faint sound 405
evince 467
mean 516
inform 527
disclose 529

utter 580
speak 582
refresh 689
– freely 827, 834
– one's last 360
not – a word 528
breathing time 687, 723
breathless
voiceless 581
out of breath 688
feeling 821
fear 860
eager 865
wonder 870
– attention 457
– expectation 507
– impatience 865
– speed 684
bred in the bone 820
breech 235
– loader 727
breeches 225
wear the – 737
– buoy 666
– maker 225
– pocket
money 800, 802
breed _kind_ 75
multiply 161
progeny 167
animals 370
rear 537
breeding 161, 852, 894
breeze _wind_ 349
discord 713
breezy 836
brethren 997
breve 413
brevet
warrant 741
commission 755
permit 760
– rank 873
breviary 998
brevier 591
brevity 201, 572
brew 41, 673
brewing
impending 152
storm – 665
bribe _equivalent_ 30
tempt 615
offer 763
gift 784
buy 795
expenditure 809
reward 973

bric-à-brac 847
brick *hard* 323
　pottery 384
　material 635
　trump 939, 948
　make -s without straw 471
　- colour 434
brickbat 727
bricklayer 690
bride 903
bridewell 752
bridge 45, 627
　- over *join* 43
　facilitate 705
　make peace 723
　compromise 774
　cards 840
bridle *restrain* 751
　rein 752
　- road 627
　- one's tongue 585, 864
　- up 900
brief *time* 111
　space 201
　concise 572
　compendium 596
　hold a - for 759
　- case 191
briefly *anon* 132
brier
　sharp 253
　pipe 390
　bane 663
brig 273
brigade 726
brigadier 745
brigand 792
brigandage 791
brigandine 717
brigantine 273
bright *shine* 420
　colour 428
　intelligent 498
　cheery 836
　beauty 845
　glory 873
　- days 734
　- eyed 845
　- prospect 858
　- side 829
　look at the - side 836, 858
　- thought
　sharp 498
　good stroke 626
　wit 842
brighten up
　furbish 658

brigue 712, 720
brilliant
　shining 420
　good 648
　wit 842
　beautiful 845
　gem 847
　glorious 873
　- idea 842
brilliantine 356
brim 231
　- over 641
brimful 52
brimstone 388
brindled 440
brine 341, 392
bring 270
　- about 153, 729
　- back 790
　- back to the memory 505
　- to bear upon
　relation 9
　action 170
　- into being 161
　- to a crisis 604
　- forth 161
　- forward
　evidence 467
　manifest 525
　teach 537
　improve 658
　- grey hairs to the grave
　　735, 830
　- grist to the mill 644
　- home 775
　- home to 155
　- in *receive* 296
　income 810
　price 812
　- to life 359
　- to light 480*a*
　- low 874
　- to maturity 673, 729
　- to mind 505
　- under one's notice 457
　- off 672
　- out
　discover 480*a*
　manifest 525
　publish 591
　- over
　persuade 484
　- to perfection 677
　- into play 677
　- to a point 74
　- in question 461
　- up the rear 235

　- round
　persuade 615
　restore 660
　- to terms 723
　- to *convert* 144
　halt 265
　- together 72
　- in its train 88
　- to trial 969
　- up *develop* 161
　vomit 297
　educate 537
　- in a verdict 480
　- word 527
brink 231
　on the -
　almost 32
　coming 121
　near 197
　- on the grave 360
briny 392
　- ocean 341
brio *music* 415
　active 682
brisk *prompt* 111
　energetic 171
　active 682
　cheery 836
bristle 253
　- up *stick up* 250
　angry 900
　- with 639, 641
　- with arms 722
bristly 256
Britannia metal 545
Briticism 563
British 188
　- lion 604
Briton, true - 939
　work like a - 686
brittleness 328
britzska 272
broach *begin* 66
　found 153
　reamer 262
　tap 297
　publish 531
　assert 535
broad *general* 78
　space 202
　lake 343
　emphatic 535
　indelicate 961, 962
　- accent 580
　- awake 459, 682
　- daylight 420, 525
　- farce 842

- grin 838
- highway 627
- hint 527
- meaning 516
- minded 498
broadcast
disperse 73
spread 78
publish 531
sow - 818
broadcloth 219
broadhearted 906
broadsheet 593
broad-shouldered 159
broadside 236
publication 531
cannonade 716
broadsword 727
Brobdingnagian 192
brocade 847
brochure 593
Brocken, spectre of the
443
broder 549
brogue *boot* 225
dialect 563
broidery 847
broil *heat* 382
fry 384
fray 713, 720
broke *poor* 804
broken
discontinuous 70
weak 160
- colour 428
- down
decrepit 659
failing 732
dejected 837
- English 563
- fortune 735, 804
- heart 828, 837
hopeless 859
- reed 160, 665
- meat 645
- voice 581, 583
- winded
disease 655
fatigue 688
broker 758, 797
brokerage *pay* 812
brokery 794
bromidic 613
bronchia 351
bronze *alloy* 41
brown 433
sculpture 557

brooch 847
brood 102, 167
- over 451, 847
brooding
preparing 673
brook *stream* 348
bear 821, 826
broom 652
broth 298
brothel 961
brother *kin* 11
similar 17
equal 27
brotherhood 712
brotherly
friendship 888
love 897
benevolence 906
brougham 272
brought to bed 161
brouillerie 713
brouillon 626
brow *top* 210
edge 231
front 234
browbeat
intimidate 860
swagger 885
disrespect 929
-en *humbled* 879
brown 433
- Bess 727
- study 451, 458
Brown, Jones and
Robinson 876
brownie 980
browse 298
bruin 895
bruise *powder* 330
hurt 619
injure 649
blemish 848
bruiser 726
bruit
report 531, 532
brumal 126, 383
brumous 353
Brummagem 545
brunette 433
brunt *beginning* 66
impulse 276
bear the -
difficulty 704
defence 717
endure 821, 826
brush *rough* 256
rapid motion 274

graze 379
clean 652
fight 720
paint - 556
- away *reject* 297
abrogate 756
- up *clean* 562
furbish 658
prepare 673
brushwood 367
brusque *violent* 173
haste 684
discourtesy 895
brutal *vulgar* 851
rude 895
savage 907
brutalize [*see* brutal]
corrupt 659
deaden 823
vice 945
brute *animal* 366
rude 895
maleficent 913
- force
strength 159
violence 173
animal 450a
severe 739
compulsion 744
lawless 964
- matter 316, 358
Brute, et tu 917
brutish [*see* brute]
vulgar 851
ignoble 876
intemperate 954
brutum fulmen
impotent 158
failure 732
lax 738
boast 884
bubble
unsubstantial 4
transient 111
little 193
convexity 250
light 320
water 348
air 353
error 495
deceit 545
trifle 643
- burst
fall short 304
disappoint 509
fail 732
- reputation 873

bunting 550
buoy *raise* 307
  float 320
  hope 858
buoyant
  floating 305
  light 320
  elastic 325
  prosperous 734
  cheerful 836
  hopeful 858
bur *clinging* 46
  sharp 253
  rough 256
  in engraving 558
burden *lading* 190
  weight 319
  melody 413
  poetry 597
  too much 641
  clog 706
  oppress 828
  care 830
  - the memory 505
  - of a song
  repetition 104
burdensome [*see* burden]
  hurtful 649
  labouring 686
bureau *chest* 191
  office 691
  shop 799
  tribunal 960
bureaucracy 737
bureaucrat 694
burgee 550
burgeon [*see* bourgeon]
burgess 188
burgh 189
burgher 188
burghmote 966
burglar 792
  - alarm 669
burglary 791
burgomaster 745
burgrave 745
burial 363
buried *deep* 208
  imbedded 229
  hidden 528
  - in a napkin 460
  - in oblivion 506
burin 558
burke 361
burlesque
  imitation 19
  travesty 21

  absurdity 497
  misrepresent 555
  drama 599
  comic 853
  ridicule 856
burletta 599
burly 192
burn *near* 197
  rivulet 348
  hot 382
  consume 384
  near the truth 480a
  excited 825
  love 897
  punish 972
  - the candle at both ends
  waste 638
  exertion 686
  prodigal 818
  - daylight 683
  - one's bridges 604
  - one's fingers 699
  - in 384
  - out 385
  - to 865
burner 423
burning [*see* burn]
  passion 821
  angry 900
  - glass 445
  - with curiosity 455
  - pain 378
  - shame 874
burnish *polish* 255
  shine 420
  beautify 845
burnous 225
burnt [*see* burn]
  red 434
  - offering 952, 990
burr 410
burrock 706
burrow *lodge* 184
  excavate 252
bursar 801
bursary 802
burst *disjoin* 44
  instantaneous 113
  explosion 173
  brittle 328
  sound 406
  paroxysm 825
  bubble -
  disclosure 529
  all over 729
  ready to -
  replete 641

  excited 824
  - of anger 900
  - away 623
  - of eloquence 582
  - of envy 921
  - into a flame 825
  - forth *begin* 66
  expand 194
  be seen 446
  -ing with health 654
  - with grief 839
  - in 294
  - of laughter 838
  - out 295
  - upon *arrive* 292
  unexpected 508
  - into tears 839
burthen [*see* burden]
bury *enclose* 229
  inter 363
  conceal 528
  - the hatchet 918
  - one's talent 528
busboy 746
busby 225
bush *branch* 51
  jungle 344
  shrub 367
  beat about the - 629
bushel *much* 31
  multitude 102
  receptacle 191
  size 192
  hid under a - 460
  not hide light under a -
  878
bush-fighting 720
bushing 224
bushranger 792
bushy 256
business *event* 151
  topic 454
  occupation **625**
  commerce 794
  full of - 682
  man of -
  proficient 700
  consignee 758
  mind one's -
  incurious 456
  attentive 457
  careful 459
  let alone 748
  send about one's - 297
  stage - 599
business-like
  orderly 58

business 625
active 682
practical 692
skilful 698
buskin *dress* 225
drama 599
buss *boat* 273
courtesy 894
endearment 902
bust 554
bustle *energy* 171
dress 225
agitation 315
activity 682
haste 684
difficulty 704
bustling [*see* bustle]
eventful 151
busy 682
busybody 532, 682
but
on the other hand 30
except 83
limit 233
qualifying 469
– *now* 118
butcher *kill* 361
provisions 637
evil-doer 913
butler 746
butt *cask* 191
push 276
aim 620
attack 716
laughing-stock 857
– *in* 294, 682
– *end* 67
butte 206
butter 357
flattery 933
– *bread on both sides* 641
– *not melt in mouth* 894
buttered side
know – *skill* 698
selfish 943
not know – 699
butter-fingers 701
butterfly
variegated 440
fickle 605
beauty 845
gaudy 882
break – *on wheel*
waste 638
spite 907
butter-scotch 396
buttery 636

buttock 235
button *fasten* 43
fastening 45
little 193
hanging 214
knob 250
trifle 643
take by the – 586
– *hole* 586
– *up close* 261
restrain 751
– *up one's pockets* 808
buttoned-up
reserved 528
buttonholder 841
buttons *page* 746
button-top
useless 645
buttress
strengthen 159
support 215
defence 717
butyraceous 355
buxom 836
buy 795
– *a pig in a poke* 621
– *and sell* 794
buzz *hiss* 409
insect cry 412
publish 531
news 532
buzzard *fool* 501
blind as a – 442
between hawk
and –
agitation 315
worry 315
by *alongside* 236
instrumental 631
go – *pass* 303
– *air mail* 684
– *and by* 121, 132
– *the card* 82
– *the hour &c.*
hire 788
– *itself* 87
– *means of* 632
– *no means* 32
have – *one* 637, 777
– *my troth &c.* 535
– *the way*
à propos 9
beside the purpose 10
parenthetical 134
– *wire* 684
– *wireless* 684
bye *departure* 293

sequestered 893
bygone 122, 506
let –*s be bygones* 918
by-law 963
by-name 565
by-path 279
by-play 527, 550
byre 189
byssus 256
bystander 197, 444
byway 627
by-word
maxim 496
cant term 563, 564
reproach 574
contempt 930

C

C 3 160
cab 272
cabal *plan* 626
confederacy 712
cabala 526, 993
cabalistic 528, 992
cabaret 599
cabasset 717
cabbage 791
caber, *tossing the* – 840
cabin 189, 191
cabined, cribbed, confined
751
cabinet
receptacle 191
photograph 554
workshop 691
council 696
– *picture* 556
cabin plane 273
cable 45, 205
news 531, 532
slip – 623
telegraphic – 534
cabman 268, 694
caboose 386
cabriolet 272
cacation 299
cache 636
cachet 530
lettre de – 751
cachexy 160, 655
cachinnation 838
cacique 745
cackle *of geese* 412
chatter 584
talk 588

laugh 838
cacodemon 980
cacoëthes 613, 865
  – loquendi 584
  – scribendi 590
cacography 590
caconym 563
cacophony
  stridor 410
  discord 414
  style 579
Cacus 792
  den of – 791
cad *servant* 746
  vulgar 851
  plebeian 876
cadastre 86, 466
cadaverous
  corpse 362
  pale 429
  hideous 846
caddie 746
caddy 191
cadeau 784
cadence *pace* 264
  fall 306
  sound 402
  music 415
cadenza 415
cadet *junior* 129
  soldier 726
  officer 745
cadge 765
cadger *idler* 683
  beggar 767
  huckster 797
cadi 967
cadit quæstio 479
cadmium 439
cadre 726
caduceus 993
caducity
  fugacity 111
  age 128
  impotence 158
  decay 659
cæcal 261
Cæsar 745
  aut – aut nullus
  ambition 865
  fame 873
cæsura
  disjunction 44
  discontinuity 70
  cessation 142
  interval 198
cætera desunt 53

cæteris paribus 27
café 189
cafeteria 189
caftan 225
cage *receptacle* 191
  restrain 751
  prison 752
Cagliostro 548, 994
cahotage 59, 315
Cain 361
  mark of – 550
  raise – 825
caique 273
cairn 363, 550
caisse
  grand – 417
caisson 191
caitiff *churl* 876
  ruffian 913
  villain 949
cajolery
  imposition 544, 545
  persuasion 615
  flattery 933
cake *stick* 46
  food 298
  consolidate 321
  sweet 396
  – walk 840
calabash 191
calamity *evil* 619
  adversity 735
  suffering 830
calamo, currente – 590
calash *cap* 225
  vehicle 272
calcedony 847
calcine 384
calcitrate 276
calculate
  reckon 85
  investigate 461
  expect 507
  intend 620
  – upon 484
calculated
  tending 176
  premeditated 611
calculation [*see* calculate]
  caution 864
calculating [*see* calculate]
  prudent 498
  – machine 85
calculus 85
caldron
  convert 144
  vessel 191

heat 386
laboratory 691
calèche 272
caleer 838
calefaction 384
calembour 520
calendar *list* 86
  chronicle 114
  record 551
calender 255
calenture 503, 655
calf *young* 129
  give birth 161
  leather 223
  animals 366
  fool 501
  golden – 986, 991
Caliban 846
calibrate 26
calibre *degree* 26
  size 192
  breadth 202
  opening 260
  intellectual capacity 498
calidarium 356
calidity 382
caliginous 421
caliph 745
caliphate 737
calisthenics
  training 537
  beauty 845
caliver 727
calk 660
call *cry* 412
  signal 550
  name 564
  motive 615
  visit 892
  sanctify 976
  ordain 995
  at one's – 682, 743
  within – 197
  – to account 932
  – attention to 457
  – to the bar 968
  – into being 161
  – of duty 926
  – for *require* 630
  order 741
  ask 765
  – forth
  resort to 677
  excite 824
  – in *advice* 695
  – to mind 505
  – to the ministry 996

- names 929, 932
- into notice 525
- off the attention 458
- to order 741
- out *cry* 411
  challenge 715
- over *number* 85
- into play 677
- in question 485
- the roll 85
- up 527
- up spirits 992
- to 586
- up *recollect* 505
  motive 615
  excite 824
- upon
  demand 741
  request 765
  visit 892
  duty 924, 926
- to witness 467
callæsthetics 845
callant 129
call-boy
  theatre 599
called, so - 545
callidity 698
calligraphy 590
calling
  business 625
Calliope 417, 597
callipers 466
callosity 323
callous 376, 823
callow *young* 127
  infant 129
  bare 226
  unprepared 674
calm *physical* 174
  quiet 265
  dissuade 616
  leisure 685
  peace 721
  moral 826
  unamazed 871
- belief &c. 484
- before a storm 145
calmative 174
caloric 382
calorimeter 389
calote 999
calotype 556
caloyer 996
calumet *token* 550
- of peace 721, 723
calumniator 936

calumny 934
calvary 1000
Calvinism 984
calyx 191
cam 633
camarade 890
camaraderie 888, 892
camarilla 712
camarista 746
camber 250
cambist 797, 801
camboose 386
camel 271
  swallow a - 608, 694
cameo *convex* 250
  sculpture 557
camera 445, 553
  in - 528
- lucida 445
- obscura 445
camerated 191
camilla 274
camisade 716
camisole 225
camorra 712
camouflage 530
camp *locate* 184
  abode 189
  military 728
- bed 215
- stool 215
campagna 180, 344
campaign 692, 722
campaigner 726
campaigning 266
campaniform 249, 252
campanile 206
campestrian 344
Campus Martius 728
can *power* 157
  mug 191
  preserve 670
  jail 752
  best one - 686
- it be! 870
canaille 876
canal *opening* 260
  conduit 350
  way 627
- boat 273
canard 532, 546
canary 366
cancan
  dance 840
cancel
  compensate 30
  neutralize 179

  obliterate 552
  abrogate 756
  repudiate 773
cancellated 219
cancelli 191
cancer *disease* 655
  bane 663
  painful 830
candelabrum 423
candent 382
candid *white* 430
  sincere 543
  ingenuous 703
  honourable 939
candidate 767, 865
candidature 763
candle 423
  bargain by inch of - 769
  burn - at both ends 686
  not fit to hold a - to 34
- ends 40, 817
- holder 711
- light 126, 422
- power 466
- stick 423, 998
  hold - to sun 645
Candlemas 998
candour
  veracity 543
  artlessness 705
  honour 939
candy *dense* 321
  sweet 396
cane *weapon* 727
  punish 972
  scourge 975
canescent 430
Canicula 423
canicular 382
caniculated 259
canine 366
- appetite 865
canister 191
canker *disease* 655
  deterioration 659
  bane 663
  pain 830
canned goods 670
cannel coal 388
cankered
  sullen 901*a*
cankerworm 663
  evil-doer 913
- of care 830
cannibal 913
cannibalism 945
cannon

420

collision 276
loud 404
arms 727
– fodder 726
–'s mouth *war* 722
courage 861
cannonade 716
cannonball 249, 274
cannoneer 726
cannot 271
cannular 260
canny 498, 702
ca' – 864
canoe 273
paddle one's own – 748
canon *rule* 80
ravine 198
music 415
belief 484
precept 697
priest 996
rite 998
– law 697
canonical
regular 82
inspired 985
ecclesiastical 995
canonicals 999
canonist 983
canonization
repute 873
deification 991
rite 998
canonry 995
canopy 223
– of heaven 318
canorous 413
cant *oblique* 217
jerk 276
hypocrisy 544
neology 563
impiety 988
cantabile 415
cantankerous 901, 901*a*
cantata 415
missa – 998
cantatrice 416
canteen 189, 191
canter 266, 274
win at a – 705
canterbury
receptacle 191
Canterbury tale 546
cantharides 171
canticle 415
cantilever 215
canting 855

cantle 51
cantlet 32, 51
canto 597
canton 181, 737
cantonment 184, 189
cantrap 993
canty 836
canvas *sail* 267
picture 556
under press of – 274
canvass
investigate 461
discuss 476
dissert 595
solicit 765
canvasser 767
canyon 350
canzonet 415, 597
caoutchouc 325
cap *be superior* 33
height 206
summit 210
cover 223
hat 225
retaliate 718
complete 729
salute 894
fling up one's – 838
Fortunatus's – 993
set one's – at 897, 902
– and bells 844
– fits 23
– in hand
request 765
servile 886
respect 928
– of maintenance 747
capability
endowment 5
power 157
skill 698
facility 705
capacious *space* 180
– memory 505
capacity
endowment 5
power 157
space 180
size 192
intellect 450
wisdom 498
office 625
talent 698
cap-à-pie
complete 52
armed –
prepared 673

defence 717
war 722
caparison 225
cape *height* 206
cloak 225
projection 250
capella, alla – 415
caper *leap* 309
dance 840
capful *quantity* 25
small 32
– of wind 349
capillament 205
capillary
hairlike 205
thin 203
capital *city* 189
top 201
letter 561
important 642
excellent 648
money 800
wealth 803
make – out of
pretext 617
acquire 775
print in –s 642
– messuage 189
– punishment 972
ship 726
capitalist 803
capitation 85
– tax 812
capitol 189, 717
capitular 995, 996
capitulate 725
capnomancy 511
capon 373
caponize 38, 158
capote 225
capouch 999
capper 548
capriccio *music* 415
whim 608
caprice 608
out of – 615*a*
capricious
irregular 139
changeable 149
irresolute 605
whimsical 608
capriole 309
capsize 218, 731
capsized 732
capstan 307, 633
capstone 210
capsular 252

capsule *vessel* 190
 tunicle 223
 medicine 662
captain 269, 745
captandum, ad –
 sophistry 477
 deception 545
 affectation 855
 ostentation 882
 flattery 933
captation 933
caption
 beginning 66
 heading 564
 taking 789
captious
 capricious 608
 irascible 901
 censorious 932
captivate
 induce 615
 restrain 751
 please 829
captivated 827
captivating 829, 897
captive
 prisoner 754
 adorer 897
 lead – 749
 make – 751
 – balloon 273
captivity 751
capture 789
Capuchin 996
caput 696
 – mortuum 645, 653
caquet 584
car 272
carabineer 726
carack 273
caracole 309
caracoler 266
caraffe 191
carambole 276
caramel 396
carapace 717
cara sposa 897
carat 309
caravan 266, 272
caravansary 189
caravel 273
carbine 727
carbohydrates 298
carbon 388
 – dioxide 663
 – monoxide 663
carbonaro 742

carbonization 384
carboy 191
carbuncle red 434
 abscess 655
 jewel 847
carcanet 847
carcass
 structure 329
 corpse 362
 bomb 727
carcelage 973
carcinoma 655
card unravel 60
 ticket 550
 plan 626
 address – 550
 by the – 82
 great – 873
 house of –s 328
 leave a – 892
 on the –s 152, 177, 470
 play one's – 692
 play one's best – 686
 play one's –s well 698
 playing –s 840
 shuffle the –s
  begin again 66
  change 140
  chance 621
  prepare 673
 speak by the –
  care 459
  veracity 543
  phrase 566
 throw up the –s 757
 ticklish – 704
 trump – 626
 – index 60, 86, 551
 –s to play 632
cardcase 191
cardiac 836
cardigan 225
cardinal intrinsic 5
 dress 225
 red 434
 important 642
 excellent 648
 priest 995, 996
 –'s hat 747
 – points 278
 – virtues 944
cardioid 245
card-sharper 792
card-sharping 545
care attention **459**
 business 625
 adversity 735

 custody 751
 economy 817
 pain 828
 fear 860
 for aught one –s 643, 866
 begone dull – 836
 drive – away 840
 have the – of 693
 take – 665, 864
 take – of 459
 – for important 642
 desire 865
 love 897
careen slope 217
 repair 660
career 625, 692
careless
 inattentive 458
 neglectful 460, 927
 feeble 575
 insensible 823
 indifferent 866
caress 897, 902
caret incomplete 53
 want 640
careworn 828, 837
cargo 270
 large quantity 31
 contents 190
 property 780
 goods 798
 – boat 273
caricature
 likeness 19
 copy 21
 exaggerate 549
 misrepresent 555
 ridicule 856
caricaturist 844
caries 49, 653, 655
carillon 417
cariole 272
carious 563
carking 828
 – care 830
carle 876
Carlist 925
car-load 31
carman 694
Carmelite 996
carminative 662
carmine 434
carnage 361
carnal 364
 intemperate 954
 inpure 961
 irreligious 989

carnation 434
carnival 840
carnivorous 298
carol
  music 415, 416
  cheerful 836
  rejoice 838
caro sposo 897
carouse *feast* 298
  festivity 840
  intemperance 954
  drinking 959
carousel 840
carp at 932
carpe diem 134
carpenter 690
carper 936
carpet 211
  on the –
  topic 454
  project 626
  – bag 191
  – knight *fop* 854
  servile 886
  sybarite 954*a*
  – sweeper 652
carrefour 627
carriage *gait* 264
  transference 270
  vehicle 272
  aspect 448
  conduct 692
  keep one's – 852
carried
  – by acclamation &c. 488
  – away by passion 824
carrier 271
  – pigeon 534
carrion 362, 653
carronade 727
carroty 434
carry
  conduce to 176
  support 215
  transfer 270
  induce 615
  reap and – 775
  – all before one 731
  – coals 879
  – conviction 484
  – into execution 729, 772
  – with a high hand
  authority 737
  pride 878
  insolence 885
  – in the mind 505
  – off *take* 789

  steal 791
  – on [*see below*]
  – oneself 692
  – out *conduct* 692
  complete 729
  – over
  transfer 270
  accounts 811
  – a point 731
  – by storm 731
  – through 692, 729
  – weight
  influence 175
  evidence 467
  importance 642
carry on
  continue 143
  pursue 622
  undertake 676
  do 680
  conduct 692
  – an argument 476
  – business 625
  – an enquiry 461
  – a trade 794
  – war 722
cart 272
  – away 185
  – before the horse
  disorder 59
  inversion 218
  bungling 699
  – horse 271
  work like a – horse 686
  – load 31, 190
cartage 270
carte *list* 86
  à la – 298
  – blanche 760, 816
  – du pays 626
  – and tierce 716
  – de visite 550
  photograph 554
cartel
  combination 709
  defiance 715
  truce 723
  compact 769
cartelize 709
carter 268
cartes sur table 525, 543
Carthago, delenda est –
  908
Carthusian 996
cartilage
  dense 321
  hard 323

  tough 327
cartography 466, 554
cartoon 21, 556
cartoonist 559
cartouche
  ammunition 727
  ornament 847
cartridge 727
cartulary 86, 551
caruncle 250
carve *cut* 44
  make 161
  form 240
  sculpture 557
  apportion 786
  – one's way 282
carvel 273
carver 559
Caryatides 215
Cary's chickens, Mother –
  668
cascade 348
case *state* 7
  box 191
  sheath 223
  topic 454
  argument 476
  specification 527
  grammar 567
  affair 625
  patient 655
  law-suit 969
  be the – 1, 494
  in good – 654, 734
  in –
  circumstance 8
  event 151
  supposition 514
  make out a – 467, 924
  – in point 23, 82
caseation 321
caseharden
  strengthen 159
  habituate 613
case-hardened
  callous 376, 823
  obstinate 606
casemate 189, 717
casement 260
casern 189
cash *money* 800
  pay 807
  in – 803
  pay – for 795
  – account 811
  – book 551
  – box 802

- down 807
- register 85, 553, 802
cashier *dismiss* 756
 treasurer 801
casing 223
casino 712, 840
cask 191
casket 191
casque 717
Cassandra 513, 668
cassation 552
casserole 191
Cassiopeia's chair 318
cassock 999
cast *mould* 21
 small quantity 32
 spread 73
 tendency 176
 form 240
 throw 284
 tinge 428
 aspect 448
 drama 599
 reject 610
 plan 626
 company 712
 give 784
 allot 786
 condemn 971
 give one a – 707
 set on a – 621
 – about for 463
 – accounts 811
 – adrift *disperse* 73
 eject 297
 liberate 750
 dismiss 756
 – anchor 265, 292
 – aside 460
 – aspersions 934
 – away 610, 638
 lost 732
 – behind one
 forget 506
 refuse 764
 relinquish 782
 – away care 836
 – off clothes 645
 – of countenance 448
 – of the dice 156
 – in a different mould 18
 – dishonour &c. upon 874
 – to the dogs 162
 – down 308, 837
 – in the eye 443
 – the eyes back 122
 – eyes on 441

– the eyes over 457
 – a gloom 837
 – off a habit 614
 – iron 323
 resolute 604
 – in one's lot with 609
 – lots 621
 – lustre upon 420
 – of mind 820
 – a nativity 511, 992
 – one's net 463
 – off *divest* 226
 disused 678
 dismiss 756
 relinquish 782
 – over-board 678
 – the parts 60
 – reflection upon 932
 – in the same mould 17
 – a shade 421
 – the skin 226
 – a slur 874
 accuse 938
 – a spell 992
 – off trammels 750
 – up *add* 85
 happen 151
 eject 297
castanet 417
castaway *exile* 893
 reprobate 949
caste 75, 873
 lose – 940
castellan 746, 753
castellated 717
caster *cruet* 191
 wheel 312
castigate 932, 972
castigator 936
casting 21
 – vote 480
 – weight 28, 30
castle *at chess* 148
 abode 189
 defence 717
 – in the air
 impossible 471
 imagination 515
 hope 858
Castle of Indolence 683
castor *hat* 225
Castor and Pollux 89, 890
castrametation 189, 722
castrate *subduct* 38
 impotent 158
casual *extrinsic* 6
 chance 156

 uncertain 475
 lax 773
casualty *event* 151
 killed 361
 evil 619
 misfortune 735
casuist 476
casuistry
 sophistry 477
 falsehood 544
 duty 926
casus belli
 quarrel 713
 irritation 824, 900
casus fœderis 770
cat *nine lives* 359
 animal 366
 keen sight 441
 fall on one's feet 734
 cross 901
 gib –, tom – *male* 373
 rain –s and dogs 348
 let – out of bag 529
 – boat 273
 – burglar 792
 – call *whistle* 417
 disapproval 932
 –'s cradle 219
 – and dog life 713
 as the – jumps
 event 151
 see how the – jumps 510
 fickleness 607
 caution 864
 – o' nine tails 975
 – in pattens 652
 –'s paw *dupe* 547
 instrumental 631
 use 677
 auxiliary 711
catabasis 36
catachresis 521, 523
cataclysm
 convulsion 146
 destruction 162
 deluge 348
catacomb 363
catacoustics 402
catadupe 348
catafalque 363
catalectic 597
catalepsy 265, 376, 683
catalogue 60, 86
catalysis 49, 140
catamaran 273, 726
catamenial 138, 299
cataphonics 402

cataplasm 662
catapult 284, 726, 727
cataract
  waterfall 348
  blindness 442, 443
catarrh 299
catastrophe
  end 67
  disaster 619
  finish 729
  misfortune 735
catch *imitate* 19
  fastening 45
  song 415
  detect 480a
  joke 497
  gather the meaning 518
  cheat 545
  receive 785
  take 789
  by –es 70
  no great – 651
  – at *willing* 602
  desire 865
  – the attention 457
  – one's death 360
  – a disease 655
  – the ear 418
  – the eye 446
  – fire 384
  – a glimpse of 441
  – an idea 498
  – the infection
  excitation 824
  – a likeness 554
  – a sound 418
  – at straws
  overrate 482
  credulous 486
  unskilful 699
  rash 863
  – by surprise 508
  – a Tartar *dupe* 547
  retaliate 718
  – in a trap 545
  – tripping 480a
  – up 789
catching
  infectious 657
catchpenny
  deceiving 545
  trumpery 643
  cheap 815
catchpoll 965
catchword 550
catechism 461, 484
  church – 983a

catechize 461
catechumen 541, 997
categorical
  positive 474
  demonstrative 478
  affirmative 535
categorically true 494
category 7, 75
  in the same – 9
catena 69
catenary 245
catenation 69
cater 298, 637
caterpillar tractor 271
caterwaul
  cat-cry 412
  discord 414
  courting 902
cates 298
catgut 417
  – scraper 416
cathartic 652
cathedrâ, ex –
  affirm 535
  school 542
  authority 737
  audacity 885
cathedral 1000
Catherine wheel 840
catholic
  universal 78
  religious 987
  – church 983a
  Roman – 984
catholicon 662
Catiline 941
catopsis 441
catoptrics 420
catoptromancy 511
cattle 271, 366
  – truck 272
catwalk 273, 627
Caucasian mystery 983
caucus 696
caudal 67, 235
caudate 214
caudex 215
Caudine forks 162
cauf 370
caught tripping 491
caulk 660
cause *source* 153
  law-suit 969
  final – 620
  take up the – of 707
  tell the – of 522
  –d by 154

causeless
  casual 156
  aimless 621
causerie 588
causeway 627
causidical 965
caustic
  energetic 171
  feeling 821
  painful 830
  gruff 895
  malevolent 907
  – curve 245
cautel 864
cautelâ, ex abundanti –
  664
cautery 384
caution *warn* 668
  prudence 864
  security 771
  want of – 863
cavalcade 69, 266
cavalier
  horseman 268
  rash 863
  insolent 885
  discourteous 895
  contemptuous 930
cavaliere servente
  servile 886
  lover 897
cavalry 726
cavatina 415
cave *dwelling* 189
  cell 191
  cavity 252
  – canem 864
  – of Adullam 624, 832
  – in *hollow* 252
  submit 725
caveat
  warning 668
  command 741
  – emptor 769
cavendo tutus 664, 864
cavern [*see* cave]
cavernous 252
caviare 392, 393
  – to the general 850
cavil *sophistry* 477
  dissent 489
  censure 932
caviller 936
cavity 252
caw 412
cayak 273
cayenne 392, 393

cazique 745
cease 142
  – to breathe 360
  – to exist 2
ceaseless 112
cecity 442
cede *submit* 725
  relinquish 782
  give 784
ceiling 206, 210, 223
celare artem, ars – 698
cela va sans dire
  conformity 82
  consequence 154
celebrant 990
celebration **883**, 998
celebrity 873, 875
celerity 274
celeste 417
celestial
  physical 318
  religious 976
  heaven 981
celibacy **904**
cell *abode* 189
  receptacle 191
  cavity 221, 252
  prison 752
  hermitage 893
cellar 191
cellaret 191
cello 417
cellophane 223
cellular 191, 252
cement
  unite 43, 46, 48
  medium 45
  covering 223
  hard 323
  material 635
  – a party 712
cemented
  concord 714
cemetery 363
cenobite 893, 996
cenotaph 363
censer 998
censor
  moderate 174
  critic 480
  ban 761
  detractor 936
censorious 480, 932
censurable 947
censure 932
censurer 936
census 85, 86

  record 551
centaur 83, 366
centenarian 130
centenary
  hundred 98
  period 138
  celebration 883
centesimal 99
cento 597
centrality 222
centralize
  combine 48
centre 68, 222
  – round 72, 290
centrifugal 291
centripetal 290
centroidal 222
centuple 98
centurion 745
century
  hundred 98
  period 108
  long time 110
  money 800
ceramic
  bake 384
  – ware 557
cerate 662
Cerberus
  janitor 263
  custodian 664
  hades 932
  sop for – 615
cereal 298
cerebration 451
cerebrum 450
cere-cloth 363
cerement
  covering 223
  wax 356
  burial 363
ceremonious 928
ceremony
  parade 882
  courtesy 894
  rite 998
Ceres 979
cerise 434
cerography 558, 590
Ceromancy 511
ceroplastic 557
certain *special* 79
  indefinite number 100
  sure 474
  belief 484
  true 494
  make – of 480*a*

  of a – age 128
  to a – degree 32
certainly *yes* 488
certainness 474
certainty **474**
certes 474, 488
certificate
  evidence 467
  record 551
  security 771
certify 467, 535
certiorari 969
certitude 474
cerulean 438
cess *sewer* 653
  tax 812
cessation **142**
cession
  surrender 725
  of property 782
  gift 784
cesspool 653
cestui-que trust 779
cestus 45, 247
chafe
  physical pain 378
  warm 384
  irritate 825
  mental pain 828, 830
  discontent 832
  incense 900
chaff *trash* 643
  ridicule 856
  vulgar 876
  not to be caught with –
    698, 702
  winnow – from wheat 609
chaffer 794
chafing-dish 386
chagrin 828
chain *fasten* 43
  vinculum 45
  series 69
  measure 200
  interlinking 219
  measure 466
  gearing 633
  imprison 752
  ornament 847
  drag a – 749
  drag a lengthened – 686
  in –s 754
chain gang 752, 972
chain-shot 727
chair *support* 215
  vehicle 272
  professorship 542

president 694
throne 747
celebration 883
in the - 693
chairman 694
chaise 272
chalcography 558
chalet 189
chalice 191, 998
chalk *earth* 342
white 430
mark 550
drawing 556
- from cheese 14, 491
- out *plan* 626
challenge
question 461
doubt 485
defy 715
claim 924
accuse 938
- comparison 648
cham 745
chamber *room* 191
council 696
mart 799
sick - 655
chamberlain 746
chambermaid 746
chameleon 149, 440
chamfer 259
chamois 309
champ 298
- the bit *disobedient* 742
chafe 825
angry 900
champagne 298
champaign 344
champain 874
Champ de Mars 728
champêtre, fête - 840
champion
best 648
auxiliary 711
defence 717
combatant 726
representative 759
sympathizer 914
championship 707
chance 156, 621
be one's - 151
game of - 840
great - 472
small - 473
stand a - 177, 470
take one's - 675
-s against one 665

whirligig of - 156
as - would have it 152
chancel 1000
chancellor
president 745
deputy 759
judge 967
- of the exchequer 801
chancery
court of - 966
- suit *delay* 133
chandelier 214, 423
**chandelle, le jeu n'en vaut
pas la** - 638, 643
dear 814
chandler 797
change
alteration **140**
mart 799
small coin 800
inter- 148
radical - 146
sudden - 146
- about 149
- colour 821
- for 147
- hands 783
- of mind 607
- of opinion 485
- of place 264
changeableness 149, 605
changeful
fickle 607
changeling
substitute 147
fool 501
changeless 16
changer 797
channel
furrow 259
opening 260
conduit 350
way 627
chant *song* 415
sing 416
worship 990
chant du cygne 360
chanter 416
chanticleer 366
chantry 1000
chaomancy 511
chaos 59
chap *crack* 198
jaw 231
fellow 373
- book 593
chapel 1000

chaperon
accompany 88
watch 459
protect 664
chapfallen 878
chaplain 995, 996
chaplet *circle* 247
garland 550
trophy 733
ornament 847
chapman 797
chapter *part* 51
topic 454
book 593
council 696
church 995
- of accidents 156, 621
- house 1000
- and verse 467, 494
char *burn* 384
serve 746
char-à-banc 272
character
nature 5
state 7
class 75
oddity 83
letter 561
drama 599
disposition 820
reputation 873
characteristic
intrinsic 5
special 79
tendency 176
mark 550
characterize 564, 594
characterized 820
charade 533, 599
charcoal *fuel* 384, 388
black 431
drawing 556
charge *fill* 52
contents 190
business 625
requisition 630
direction 693
advice 695
precept 697
attack 716
order 741
custody 751
commission 755
bargain for 794
price 812
accusation 938
in - prisoner 754

justifiable –937
take – of 664
take in – 751
– on *attribute* 155
– with 155, 777
chargeable *debt* 806
– on *duty* 926
chargé d'affaires 758
charger
  carrier 271
  fighter 726
Charing Cross, proclaim
  at – 531
chariot 272
  drag at one's – wheels 749
charioteer 268, 694
charity *give* 784
  liberal 816
  beneficent 906
  pity 914
  Christian – 906
  cold as – 823
  – that begins at home 943
charivari 404, 407
charlatan
  ignoramus 493
  imposter 548
  mountebank 844
  boaster 884
charlatanism
  ignorance 491
  falsehood 544
  affectation 855
Charles's wain 318
Charleston 840
Charley 753
charm *motive* 615
  please 829
  beauty 845
  love 897
  conjure 992
  spell 993
  bear a –ed life 644, 734
charmer 994
  voice of the – 933
  not listen to voice of –
  604
charnel-house 363
Charon 982
chart 527, 554
charter
  commission 755
  permit 760
  compact 769
  security 771
  privilege 924
chartered

legal 963
– *accountant* 801, 811
– *libertine* 962
Chartist 742
charwoman 690, 746
chary
  economical 817
  stingy 819
  cautious 864
Charybdis 312, 665
chase *emboss* 250
  furrow 259
  drive away 289
  killing 361
  forest 367
  pursue 622
  ornament 847
  wild goose – 645
chaser 559
chasm *interval* 198
  opening 260
chassé 840
chassemarée 273
chassepot 727
chasser 297
  – *balancer* 605
chasseur 726
chassis 215
chaste
  shapely 242
  language 576, 578
  simple 849
  good taste 850
  pure 960
chasten
  moderate 174
  punish 972
chastened
  subdued spirit 826
  penitent 950
chastise 932, 972
  – with scorpions 739
chasuble 999
chat 588
château 189
  – en Espagne 858
chatelaine 847
chatoyant 440
chat qui dort 667, 668
chattels 633, 789
chatter 314, 584
chatterbox 584
chattering of teeth
  cold 383
chatty 584, 892
chauffeur 268
chaunt

song 415
sing 416
worship 990
chaussé 225
Chauvinism 884, 885
chawbacon 876
cheap 643, 815
  hold – 930
  – jack 797
cheapen *haggle* 794
  begrudge 819
cheapness 815
cheat 545, 548
check
  numerical 85
  stop 142
  moderate 174
  counteract 179
  slacken 275
  plaid 440
  experiment 463
  measure 466
  evidence 468
  ticket 550
  dissuade 616
  hinder 706
  misfortune 735
  restrain 751
  money order 800
  – the growth 201
  – oneself 826
checkered 149
checkers 440, 840
checkmate
  stop 142
  success 731
  failure 732
check-roll 86
check-string
  pull the – 142
cheek *side* 236
  impertinence 885
  – by jowl *with* 88
  near 197
cheeks *dual* 89
cheep 412
cheer *repast* 298
  cry 411
  aid 707
  pleasure 827
  relief 834
  mirth 836
  rejoicing 838
  amusement 840
  courage 861
  sociality 892
  welcome 894

applaud 931
good – *hope* 858
high living 957
cheerfulness 836
cheerless 830, 837
cheeseparings
remains 40
dirt 653
economy 817
chef de cuisine
proficient 700
servant 746
chef-d'œuvre 648, 698
cheka 696
chemin
– **de fer**
game 840
– *faisant* 270
chemise 225
chemist 662
Chemistry 144
organic – 357
cheque 800
chequer 440
– *roll* 86
cherchez la femme 155
chère amie 962
cherish *aid* 707
love 897
endearment 902
– a *belief* 484
– *feelings &c.* 821
– an *idea &c.* 451
cherry
– *red* 434
two bites of a –
overrate 482
roundabout 629
clumsy 699
cherry-cheeked 845
cherry-coloured 434
cheroot 392
cherub 977
Cheshire cat 838
chess 840
chessboard 440
chest 191, 802
chestnut-colour 433
cheval-de-bataille
plea 617
plan 626
vanity 880
cheval-glass 445
chevalier 875
– d'*industrie* 792
chevaux de frise 253, 717
chevron

angle 217
indication 550
badge 747
decoration 877
chew 298
– the *cud* 451
– *tobacco* 392
chiaroscuro
light 420
grey 432
painting 556
chiasma 43
chic 845, 882
chicane
sophistry 477
deceit 545
cunning 702
chicken 129, 366
– in every *pot* 733
count –s before hatched
858, 863
tender as a – *soft* 324
sensitive 822
compassionate 914
chickenhearted 862
chide 932
chief *principal* 642
master 745
evidence in – 467
– *constable* 765
– *part* 31
chiefdom 737
Chief Justice 967
chieftain 745
chiffonnier 876
chiffonnière 191
chignon 225
chilblain 383
child
infant 129
offspring 167
fool 501
– of *God* 987
–'s *play* 643, 705
with – 161
childbirth 161
childhood 127
childish
credulous 486
foolish 499
feeble 575
– *treble* 581
childlike 703
chiliad 98
chill *cold* 383
render cold 385
indispose 616

– the *spine* 830, 860
chillies 393
Chiltern Hundreds 757
chime
repetition 104
roll 407
resonance 408
melody 413
– in with *agree* 23
conform 82
assent 488
concord 714
chimera 83, 515
chimney 260, 351
– *corner* 189
– *pot* 249
china 384, 557
China to Peru 180
chine 235
chinese white 430
chink *gap* 198
sound 408
money 800
chip *small* 32
detach 44
bit 51
reduce 195
– of the old *block*
similar 17
copy 21
offspring 167
chippy 962
Chirography 590
Chirology 550
Chiromancy 511
chirp
bird-note 412
sing 416
cheerful 836
rejoice 838
chirrup [*see* chirp]
chirurgery 662
chisel
fabricate 161
form 240
sharp 253
sculpture 557
chit 129, 193
chit-chat 588
chitterlings 221
chivalry *war* 722
tenure 777
courage 861
courtesy 894
philanthropy 910
honour 939
generosity 942

429

chlamys 225
chloroform 376, 823
chlorophyl 435
chlorotic 655
chock full 52
chocolate
  food 298
  colour 433
choice *will* 600
  election 609
  excellent 648
  absence of - **609a**
  by - 600
  - spirits 873
  - of words 569
choir *sing* 416
  church music 996
  - boy 996
  - invisible 360, 977
choke *close* 261
  stifle 361
  redundant 641
  hinder 706
  - full *complete* 52
  replete 639
  - off 706
choler 900
choleric 901
choose 609
  do what one -s 748
chop *disjoin* 44
  change 140
  - logic 476
  - up 201
chopfallen 837
chopper 330
chopping
  large 192
  - sea 348
chops *mouth* 66
  jaws 231
  food 298
choral 415
chord 413
chore 625
choreography 840
chorister 416, 996
chorography 183
chorus
  shout 411
  song 415
  singers 416
  unanimity 488
  poetry 597
  opera 599
  concord 714
  - girl 599

chose
  - in action 780
  - in possession 777
chouse 545
choux gras, faire ses - 377
chrestomathy 560
chrism 998
Christ 976
  Church of - 893*a*
  receive - 987
Christ-cross-row 561
christen 564, 998
Christendom 983*a*, 995
Christian 983*a*, 987
  - charity 906
  - science 662, 984
Christmas 138, 998
Christmas-box 784
chromatic
  colour 428
  - scale *music* 413
chromato-pseudo-blepsis 443
chromatrope 445
chrome 436
chromolithograph 558
chromosphere 318
chronic 110
chronicle
  measure time 114
  annals 551
chronicler 553
chronography
  measure time 114
  description 594
chronology 114
chronometry 114
Chrononhotonthologos 887
chrysalis 129
chrysolite 847
  perfection 650
chrysology 800
chrysoprase 847
chubby 192
chuck *throw* 284
  animal cry 412
  - it 142
  - under chin 902
chuck-farthing 621
chuckle
  animal cry 412
  laugh 838
  exult 884
chuff 876
chum 711, 890
chunk 51
Church

infallible 474
  orthodox 983*a*
  Christendom 995
  temple 1000
  dignitaries of - 996
  go to - 990
  High -, Low - &c. 984
  - of Christ 983*a*
  - bell 550
  - house 1000
churchdom 995
churching 998
churchman 996
churchwarden 996
  pipe 392
churchyard 363, 1000
  - cough 655
churl *boor* 876
churlish
  niggard 819
  rude 895
  sulky 901*a*
  malevolent 907
churn 315, 352
chut! *silent* 403
  taciturn 585
chute 348
chutney 393
chypre 400
cibarious 298
cicatrix 551
  manet - 919
cicatrize 660
Cicero 582
cicerone 524, 527
ciceronian 578
cicisbeo 897
cicuration **370**
cider 298
cider squeezer 876
ci-devant 122
cigar 392
ci-git 363
cilia 205, 256
cimeter 727
Cimmerian 421
cinch 45
cincture 247
cinder
  combustion 384
  dirt 653
Cinderella
  servant 746
  commonalty 876
cinema 448, 599, 840
cinematograph 448
cinematographer 553

cinerary 363
cineration 384
cinereous 432
cingle 230
cinnabar 434
cinnamon 393, 433
cinque 98
cipher
  unsubstantial 4
  number 84
  compute 85
  zero 101
  concealment 528
  mark 550
  letter 561
  unimportant 643
  writing in – 590
Circe 615, 994
  –an cup 377, 954
circination 312
circle *region* 181
  embrace 227
  form 247
  party 712
  describe a – 311
  great – sailing 628
  – of acquaintance 892
  – of the sciences 490
circlet 247
circling 248
circuit *region* 181
  outline 230
  winding 248
  tour 266
  indirect path 311
  indirect course **629**
circuition **311**
circuitous 279, 311
  – method 629
circular *round* 247
  publication 531
  letter 592
  pamphlet 593
  – note 805
circularity **247**
circularize 592
circulate
  curcuit 311
  rotate 312
  publish 531
circulating medium 800
circulation [*see* circulate]
  in – *news* 532
  – of money 809
circumambient 227, 229,
  311, 629
circumambulate

travel 266
go round 311, 629
circumaviate 311
circumbendibus 248, 629
circumcision 44, 998
circumduction 552
circumference 230
circumferential 227
circumflex 311
circumfluent
  lie round 227
  move round 311
circumforaneous
  travelling 266
  circuition 311
circumfuse 73
circumgyration 312
circumjacence **227**
circumlocution 573
circumnavigate
  navigation 267
  circuition 311
circumrotation 312
circumscribe
  surround 229
  limit 233, 761
circumscription **229**
circumspection
  attention 457
  care 459
  caution 459
circumstance
  phase 8
  event 151
circumstances
  property 780
  bad – 804
  depend on – 475
  good – 803
  under the – 8
circumstantial 8
  – account 594
  – evidence 467
  probability 472
circumstantiality 459
circumstantiate 467
circumvallation
  enclosure 229, 232
  defence 717
  line of – 233
circumvent
  environ 227
  move round 311
  cheat 545
  cunning 702
  hinder 706
  defeat 731

circumvest 225
circumvolution
  winding 248
  rotation 312
circus
  buildings 189
  drama 599
  arena 728
  amusement 840
cirrus 353
Cistercian 996
cistern
  receptacle 191
  store 636
cit 188
citadel 717
citation 467, 733
cite
  quote as example 82
  as evidence 467
  summon 741
  accuse 938
  arraign 969
cithern 417
citizen 188
  – of the world 910
citriculture 371
citrine 436
city 189
  in the – 794
city manager 965
civet 400
civic 372
civil *courteous* 894
  laity 997
  – authorities 745
  – crown 733
  – law 963
  – war 722
civilian *lawyer* 968
  layman 997
civilization
  improvement 658
  fashion 852
  courtesy 894
civilized life 852
civism 910
clack *clatter* 407
  animal cry 412
  talkative 584
clad 225
claim requisition 630
  demand 741
  property 780
  right 924
  lawsuit 969
  – the attention 457

claimant
petitioner 767
right 924
clair-obscur 420
clairvoyance 992
clairvoyant 513, 994
clamant 411
clamber 305
clammy 352
clamorous [*see* clamour]
loud 404
excitable 825
clamour *cry* 411
wail 839
– against 932
– for 765
clamp *fasten* 43
fastening 45
clan *race* 11
class 75
family 166
party 712
clandestine 528
clangor 404
clank 410
clannishness 481
clanship 709
clap *explosion* 406
applaud 931
thunder –
prodigy 872
– the hands
rejoice 838
– on 31
– on the shoulder 615
– together 43
– up *imprison* 751
clapperclaw
contention 720
censure 932
claptrap
pretence 546
display 882
claquer 935
faire – son fouet 884
clarence 272
claret colour 434
clarify 652
clarinet 417
clarion *music* 417
war 722
clarity 518
clash *disagree* 24
cross 179
concussion 276
sound 406
oppose 708

discord 713
– of arms 720
clasp *fasten* 43
fastening 45
stick 46
come close 197
belt 230
embrace 902
class *arrange* 60
category **75**
learners 541
party 712
– prejudice 481
– room 542
classic *old* 124
symmetry 242
classical
elegant writing 578
taste 850
– art 556
– dancing 840
– education 537
– music 415
classicist 492
classics 560
classify 60
classmate 890
clatter 404, 407
claudication
slowness 275
failure 732
clause *part* 51
passage 593
condition 770
clausis, januis – 528
claustral 110
clavate 250
clavichord 417
clavier 417
claw *hook* 781
grasp 789
– back 935
clay *soft* 324
earth 342
corpse 362
material 635
– pipe 392
clay-cold 383
claymore 727
clean
entirely 52
perfect 650
unstained 652
– bill of health 654
– breast
disclose 529
– forgotten 506

– hand
proficient 700
with – hands
honesty 939
innocence 946
– out *empty* 297
– shaven 226
– sweep
revolution 146
destruction 162
clean-up 755
clear *simple* 42
sound 413
light 420
transparent 425
visible 446
certain 474
intelligible 518
manifest 525
easy 705
liberate 750
profit 775
vindicate 937
innocent 946
acquit 975
all – 664, 705
coast – 664
get – off 671
keep – of 623
make – 529
– for action
prepare 673
– articulation 580
– conscience 946
– the course 302
– cut 518
– the ground
facilitate 705
– of *distant* 196
– off *pay* 807
– out *empty* 297
clean 652
– sighted
vision 441
shrewd 498
– sky *hope* 858
– stage
occasion 134
easy 705
right 922
– thinking 498
– the throat 297
– up *light* 420
intelligible 518
interpret 522
clearheaded 498
clear-obscure 420

cleat 45
cleavage
  cutting 44
  structure 329
cleave *sunder* 44
  adhere 46
  bisect 91
cleaver 253
cledge 342
clef 413
cleft *divided* 44
  bisected 91
  chink 198
  in a – stick
  difficulty 704
clem 956
clement
  lenient 740
  long-suffering 826
  compassionate 914
clench *compact* 769
  retain 781
  take 789
clepe 564
clepsydra 114
clerestory 191, 1000
clergy 996
clerical 995, 996
  – *error* 495
  – *staff* 746
clerk *scholar* 492
  recorder 553
  writer 590
  helper 711
  servant 746
  agent 758
  clergy 996
  articled – 541
  – *in holy orders* 995
  – *of works* 694
clerkship
  commission 755
cleromancy 511
clever
  intelligent 498
  skilful 698
  smart 842
  too – by half 702
clew *ball* 249
  interpretation 522
  indication 550
  seek a – 461
click 406
client
  dependant 746
  customer 795
clientship

subjection 749
cliff *height* 206
  vertical 212
  steep 217
  land 342
climacteric 128
climate *region* 181
  weather 338
  fine – 656
climatology 338
climax
  supremacy 33
  summit 210
  culmination 729
climb 305
  – on the
  bandwagon 731
clime 181
clinal 217
clinch *fasten* 43
  close 261
  certify 474
  pun 563
  complete 729
  clutch 781
  snatch 789
  – an argument 47
  – the fist at 909
clincher 479
cling *adhere* 46
  – to *near* 197
  willing 602
  persevere 604a
  habit 613
  observe 772
  desire 865
  love 897
  – to hope 858
  – to one another 709
clinic 662
clink
  resonance 408
  stridor 410
  prison 752
clinker *brick* 384
  dirt 653
clinometer
  oblique 217
  angle 244
clinquant
  ornament 847
  vulgar 851
Clio 594
clip *shorten* 201
  – the wings
  powerless 158
  speed 264

slow 275
  useless 645
  hinder 706
  prohibit 761
  – one's words 583
clipper 273
clipping
  small piece 51
clique *conclave* 696
  party 712
cloaca *conduit* 350
  foul 653
Cloacina 653
cloak *dress* 225
  conceal 528
  disguise 530
cloaked 223
cloche 371
clock 114
clockwork 633
  by – *uniform* 16
  order 58
  regular 80
clod *lump* 192
  earth 342
  fool 501
  bungler 701
clodhopper 876
clodpated
  stupid 499
clog *shoe* 225
  hinder 706
  – *dance* 840
cloison 228
cloisonné 557
cloister *arcade* 189
  way 627
  restraint 751
  convent 1000
close *similar* 17
  tight 43
  end 67
  field 181
  court 189
  near 197
  narrow 203
  shut 261
  dense 321
  warm 382
  hidden 528
  concise 572
  taciturn 585
  complete 729
  stingy 819
  examine –ly 457
  keep – *hide* 528
  retain 781

tread – upon 281
 – the door upon
  restrain 751
 – the ears 419
 – the eyes
  die 360
  not see 442
 – one's eyes to
  not attend 458
  set at naught **773**
 – at hand
  to-morrow 121
  imminent 152
  near 197
 – the hand
  refuse 764
 – in upon 290
 – inquiry 461
 –ly packed 72
 – prisoner 754
 – quarters 197
  approach 286
  attack 716
  battle 722
 – one's ranks 673
 – study
  thought 451
  attention 457
 – up 197, 290
 – with *cohere* 46
  assent 488
  attack 716
  contend 720
  consent 762
  compact 769
close-mouthed 585
closet
 receptacle 191
 ambush 530
closeted with
 conference 588
 advice 695
close-up 197
closure 142, **261**
clot *solidify* 321
 earth 342
cloth *vocation* 625
 napkin 652
 clergy 996
clothes 225
 grave – 363
 – basket 191
clothier 225
Clotho 601
clotpoll 501
clotted 352
cloud

assemblage 72
multitude 102
mist 353
shade 424
screen 520
break through the –s
 446
drop from the –s 508
in a – 475, 528
in the –s
 lofty 206
 inattentive 458
 dreaming 515
under a –
 insane 503
 adversity 735
 disrepute 874
 secluded 893
 censured 932
 accused 938
 – burst 348
 – capt 206
 – of dust 330, 353
 –s gathering
 dark 421
 danger 665
 warning 668
 – no bigger than a man's
  hand 668
 – of skirmishers 726
 – of smoke 353
 – of words 573
clouded
 variegated 440
 dejected 837
 hopeless 859
 – perception 499
cloudiness 571
cloudland 515
cloudless
 light 420
 happy 827
cloudy *dim* 422, 426
clough 206
clout 276
cloven 91
cloven foot
 mark 550
 malevolence 907
 vise 945
 Satan 978
 see the – 480a
 show the – 907
clover
 luxury 377
 prosperity 734
 comfort 827

clown
 pantomime 599
 bungler 702
 buffoon 844
 vulgar 851
 rustic 876
cloy 641, 869
club
 place of meeting 74
 house 189
 association 712
 weapon 727
 sociality 892
 – law
 compulsion 744
 lawless 964
 – together
 co-operate 709
clubby 892
club car 272
clubfooted 243
cluck 412
clue 550
 seek a – 461
clump
 assemblage 72
 projecting mass 250
 – of trees 367
clumsy
 unfit 647
 awkward 699
 ugly 846
Cluniac 996
clurichaune 980
cluster 72
clutch *retain* 781
 seize 789
clutches 737
 in the – of 749
clutter 407
coacervation 72
coach
 carriage 272
 teach 537
 tutor 540, 673
 – painter 540
 – road 627
 drive a – and six through
  964
 – up 539
coachhouse 191
coachman 268, 694
coaction 744
coadjutant 709
coadjutor 711
coadjuvancy 709
coagency 178, 709

coagmentation 72
coagulate
cohere 46
density 321
semi-liquid 352
coal 388
call over the –s 932
carry –s 879
– black 431
carry –s to
Newcastle 641
coalesce
identity 13
combine 48
coalheaver
work like a – 686
coalition 43, 709, 712
coaming 232
coaptation 23
coarctation
decrease 36
contraction 195
narrow 203
impede 706
restraint 751
coarse *harsh* 410
dirty 653
unpolished 674
garish 846
vulgar 851
impure 961
– *grain* 329
coast *border* 231
slide 266
navigate 267
land 342
– *defence* 717
– *line* 230
coaster 273
coastguard 753
coat *layer* 204
paint 223
habit 225
cut – according to cloth
698
– of arms 550
– of mail 717
coating, inner – 224
coax *persuade* 615
endearment 902
flatter 933
cob *horse* 271
punish 972
cobalt 438
cobble *mend* 660
cobbler 225
cobbles 635

coble 273
cobra 913
cobweb *light* 320
fiction 545
flimsy 643
dirt 653
–s of antiquity 124
–s of sophistry 477
cocaine 376, 381, 663
cochineal 434
cock *bird* 366
male 373
game – 861
– boat 273
– and bull story 546
– the eye 441
– of the roost
best 648
master 745
– up *vertical* 212
convex 250
cockade *badge* 550
title 877
cock-a-hoop
gay 836
exulting 884
Cockaigne 827
cockatrice
monster 83
piercing eye 548
evil-doer 913
miscreant 949
cockcrow 125
cocked hat 225, 745
cocker *fold* 258
caress 902
Cocker
school book 542
according to – 82
cockle *fold* 258
– of one's heart 820
cockleshell 273
cockloft 191
cockney
Londoner 188
plebeian 876
cockpit *hold* 191
council 696
arena 728
cockshut
morning 125
evening 126
dusk 422
cock-sparrow 193
cocksure 484
cockswain 269
cocktail 298, 959

– *party* 892
cocoa 298
cocotte 962
coction 384
Cocytus 982
cod *shell* 223
coddle 902
– oneself 943
code *conceal* 528
precept 697
law 963
codex 593
codger 819
codicil *sequel* 65
testament 771
codify 60, 963
codlin 129
coecum 261
coefficient
factor 84
accompany 88
co-operate 709
Coelebs 904
coemption 795
coequal 27
coerce *compel* 744
restrain 751
coetaneous 120
coeternal
perpetual 112
synchronous 120
cœur, à contre – 603
coeval 120
– with birth 5
coexist *exist* 1
accompany 88
synchronism 120
contiguity 199
coextension
equality 27
parallelism 216
symmetry 242
coffee 298
coffee-house 189
coffee-pot 191
coffer *chest* 191
store 636
money chest 802
cofferdam 55
coffin 363
add a nail to one's – 830
cog *tooth* 253
boat 273
deceive 545
flatter 933
cogent
powerful 157

- reasoning 476
cogitate 451
cogitative faculties 450
cognate
  related 9
  consanguineous 11
  similar 16
cognition 490
cognitive faculties 450
cognizance 490
  take - of
  attention 457
  intellect 490
cognomen 564
cognoscence 490
cog-wheel 312
cohabitation
  location 184
  marriage 903
coheir 778
coherence *unite* **46**
  dense 321
cohesive 46
cohibit
  restrict 706
  restrain 751
  prohibit 761
cohobation 336
cohort 726
cohue 72
coif 225
coiffure 225
coign of vantage 33
coil *disorder* 59
  curve 245
  convolution 248
  circuition 311
  shuffle off this mortal -
  360
coin *fabricate* 161
  imagine 515
  money 800
  - *money* 775
  - *words* 563
coincidence
  identity 13
  in time 120
  chance 156
  concurrence 178
  in place 199
  in opinion 488
coiner *thief* 792
coistril 862
coition 42
coke 388
colander 260
colature 652

cold *frigid* **383**
  colour 429, 438
  style 575
  insensible 823
  indifferent 866
  in - blood
  premeditated 611
  purposely 620
  unfeeling 823
  dispassionate 826
  - comfort 832
  - shoulder
  discourtesy 895
  contempt 930
  - steel 727
  - storage 387
  - sweat *fear* 860
  dislike 867
  - water cure 662
  throw - water on
  dissuade 616
  hinder 706
  dull 843
cold feet 862
coldhearted
  unfeeling 823
  hostile 889
  malevolent 907
cold pack 670
Coliseum 189, 588, 728
collaboration 178
collaborator 690, 711
collapse
  prostration 158
  contract 195
  shortcoming 304
  deteriorate 659
  fatigue 688
  failure 732
collar *dress* 225
  circlet 247
  shackle 752
  seize 789
  slip the - 750
collate 464
collateral
  relation 9, 11
  parallel 216
  lateral 236
  security 771
  - evidence 467
collation
  repast 298
  comparison 464
colleague
  accompany 88
  co-worker 696

co-operation 709
  auxiliary 711
  friend 890
collect
  assemble 72
  opine 480
  understand 518
  acquire 775
  prayer 990
  - evidence 467
  - knowledge 539
  - one's thoughts 451
collectanea
  assemblage 72
  compendium 596
collected *calm* 826
collection
  assemblage 72
  offertory 998
collectively
  whole 50
  generality 78
  together 88
collectivism 737, 778
colleen 129
college 542
  go to - 539
  - of cardinals 996
  - education 537
colley 366
collide 276
collier 273
colligate 72
collimation 216, 278
colliquate 335
collision *disagreement* 24
  clash 179
  percussion 276
  opposition 708
  encounter 720
collocate
  arrange 60
  assemble 72
  place 184
collocution 588
collogue 933
colloid 352
collop 51, 298
colloquial
  figure of speech 521
  neology 563
  conversation 588
  - meaning 516
colluctation 720
collusion *deceit* 545
  conspiring 709
collusive 544

colluvies 653
collyrium 662
Cologne
eau de - 398
colon 142
colonel 745
colonist 188
colonize 184, 294, 295
colonnade
series 69
houses 189
colony 184, 188, 780
colophon 65
colophony 356a
Colorado beetle 913
coloration 428
coloratura 415, 416
Colosseum 728
colossus 192, 206
colour hue **428**
tone 431
appearance 448
probability 472
disguise 544
paint 556
plea 617
be angry 900
all -s 440
change -
shame 879
give a - to
change 140
qualify 469
probable 472
falsehood 472
lend a - to
plea 617
vindicate 937
man of - 431
show in true -s 543
- blindness 443
- printing 558
- sergeant 745
-ed spectacles 424
- too highly 549
- up redden 434
blush 879
colourable
ostensible 472
deceptive 545
colourful 882
colouring [see colour]
meaning 516
false - 523
- matter 428
colourless
weak 160

pale 429
colours
ensign 550
decoration 877
with - flying
resolution 604
false - 544, 545
flying -
display 882
celebration 883
lower one's - 735
nail one's - to the mast
604
show one's -
manifest 525
disclose 529
true to one's - 939
colporteur 797
colstaff 215
colt young 129
horse 271
fool 501
columbine 599
columella 215
column series 69
height 206
support 215
cylinder 249
caravan 266
monument 551
printing 591
troop 726
columnist 527, 553
colures 318
coma inactive 683
insensible 376, 823
comb teeth 253
clean 652
punish 972
combat 720, 722
combat, hors de -
useless 645
tired 688
combatant 726
combe 252
comber 348
combination 48
arithmetical 84
party 712
combine unite 48
co-operate 709
combustible 388
combustion 384
come happen 151
approach 286
arrive 292
cheer up! 836

out upon! 932
to - future 121
destiny 152
- about 658
- across
discover 480a
acquire 775
pay up 807
- after
sequence 63
posterior 117
- between 631
cut and - again 639
- of age 131
- amiss
disagreeable 24
ill-timed 135
- back 283
- before 116
- by 775
- at one's call 743
- to a determination 604
- down with 807
- into existence
be 1
begin 66
- first superior 33
precede 62
- forth
egress 295
appear 446
- forward 763
- from 154
- to the front 303
- and go 314
- to hand 785
- to a head
climax 33
complete 52
- in ingress 294
receipt 785
- in for
property 778, 780
- to one's knowledge 527
- to life 359
- what may 474
- near 286
- to nothing
unproductive 169
fail 732
- of 154
- off disjoin 44
event 151
loop-hole 617
escape 671
- on future 121
destiny 152

consignee 758
commission
  task 625
  delegate **755,** 759
  Royal – 696
  – of the peace 965
commissionaire
  doorkeeper 263
  messenger 534
  consignee 758
commissioner 758
commissure 43
commis-voyageur 758
commit *do* 680
  delegate 755
  cards 840
  arrest 969
  – an absurdity 853
  – oneself to a course 609
  – to the flames 384
  – to memory 505
  – oneself
  clumsy 699
  promise 768
  – to prison 751
  – sin 945
  – to writing 551
committee
  council 696
  consignee 758
  (director 694)
commix 41
commode 191
commodious 644
commodity 798
commodore 745
common
  general 78
  ordinary 82
  plain 344
  habitual 613
  trifling 643
  base 876
  in – *related* 9
  participate 778
  right of – 780
  short –s 640
  tenant in – 778
  make – *cause* 709
  – consent 488
  – council 966
  – course 613
  – herd 876
  – law *old* 124
  law 697, 963
  – measure 84
  – origin 153

– parlance 576
– place 82
– place book
  record 551
  compendium 596
  – saying 496
  – sense 498
  – sewer 653
  – stock 778
  – weal
  mankind 372
  good 618
  utility 644
  philanthropy 910
Common Pleas Court of –
  966
commonalty 876
commoner 876
commonplace
  usual 82
  known 490
  plain 576
  habit 613
  unimportant 643
  dull 843
commons 298
commonwealth
  territory 181
  community 372
  authority 737
commorant 188
commotion 315
communalism 778
commune
  township 181
commune with 588
  – oneself 451
communibus annis 29
communicant 990
communicate
  join 43
  tell 527
  correspond 592
  give 784
  sacrament 998
communication
  news 532
  of disease 657
  oral – 582, 588
communion
  discourse 588
  society 712
  participation 778
  sacrament 998
  hold – with 888
  – table 1000
communiqué 527

communism 737
communist
  party 712
  rebel 742
  participation 778
  philanthropy 910
  evil doer 913
community
  party 712
  – at large 372
  – of goods 778
commutation
  compensation 30
  substitution 147
  interchange 148
  compromise 774
  barter 794
commutual 12
compact
  joined 43
  united 87
  receptacle 191
  small 193
  compressed 195
  compendious 201
  dense 321
  bargain **769**
compages
  whole 50
  structure 329
compagination 43
companion *match* 17
  accompaniment 88
  ladder 305
  friend 890
companionable 892
companionship 892
companionway 305
company
  assembly 72
  actors 599
  party, partnership 712
  troop 726
  sociality 892
  bear – 88
  in – with 88
comparable 9
comparative 464
  degree 26
  – anatomy 368
comparatively 32
compare 464
  – notes 695
comparison 464
compartition 44
compartment
  part 51

region 181
place 182
cell 191
carriage 272
compass
degree 26
space 180
surround 227
measure 466
intend 620
guidance 693
achieve 729
box the –
azimuth 278
rotation 312
keep within –
moderation 174
fall short 304
economy 817
points of the – 236
in a small – 193
– about 229
– of thought 498
compassion 914
object of – 828
compatible
consentaneous 23
possible 470
compatriot
inhabitant 188
friend 890
compeer *equal* 27
friend 890
compel 744
compellation 564
compendency 43
compendious 201
compendium 596
book 593
compensate
make up for 30
requite 973
compensation 30
compère 599
competence
power 157
sufficiency 639
skill 698
wealth 803
competition
opposition 708
contention 720
competitor
opponent 710
combatant 726
candidate 767
compilation

collect 72
book 593
compendium 596
compile 54
complacent
pleased 827
content 831
courteous 894
kind 906
complain 839
complainant 938
complaint
illness 655
murmur 839
lodge a – 938
– without cause 839
complaisant
lenient 740
courteous 894
kind 906
complement
adjunct 39
remainder 40
part 52
arithmetic 84
complementary
correlation 12
colour 428
complete
entire 52
accomplish 729
compact 769
– answer 479
– circle 311
in a – degree 31
completeness 52
completion 729
complex 59
complexion
state 7
colour 428
appearance 448
compliance
conformity 82
obedience 743
consent 762
observance 772
complicate
derange 61
complicated
disorder 59
convolution 248
complice 711
complicity 709
compliment
courtesy 894, 896
praise 931

poor – 932
–s of season 896
complimentary
free 815
complot 626
comply [*see* compliance]
compo *coating* 223
material 635
component 56
componere lites 723, 724
comport
– oneself 692
– with 23
compos mentis 502
compose
make up 54, 56
produce 161
moderate 174
music 416
write 590
printing 591
pacify 723
assuage 826
composed
self-possessed 826
composer
music 413
composite 41
composition 54 [*see*
compose]
combination 48
piece of music 415
picture 556
style 569
writing 590
building material 635
compromise 774
barter 794
atonement 952
compositor
printer 591
compost 653
composure 826, 871
compotation 959
compote 298
compound
mix 41
combination 48
limited space 182
enclosure 232
compromise 774
– arithmetic 466
– for *substitute* 147
barter 794
comprador 637
comprehend
compose 54

include 76
know 490
understand 518
comprehension [*see*
comprehend]
intelligence 498
comprehensive 76
complete 50
general 78
wide 192
– argument 476
compress
contract 195
curtail 201
condense 321
remedy 662
compressible 322
comprise 76
comprobation
evidence 467
demonstration 478
compromise
dally with 605
mid-course 628
taint 659
danger 665
pacify 723
compact 769
compound **774**
atone 952
compromised
promised 768
compter 799
compte rendu
record 551
accounts 811
comptroller 694
compulsion 744
compunction 833, 950
compurgation
evidence 467
acquittal 970
compute 85
comrade 890
comradeship 892
con *think* 451
get by heart 505
learn 539
conation 600
**conatu magnas nugas,
magno** –
waste 638
unimportance 643
conatus 176
concamerate 245
concatenation
junction 43

continuity 69
concavity 252
conceal
invisible 447
hide 528
cunning 702
concealment 528, 893
concede
assent 488
admit 529
permit 760
consent 762
give 784
conceit *idea* 453
folly 499
supposition 514
imagination 515
wit 842
affectation 855
vanity 880
conceited
dogmatic 481
conceivable 470
conceive *begin* 66
beget 161
teem 168
believe 484
understand 490
imagine 515
plan 626
concent 413
concentrate
assemble 72
centrality 222
converge 290
concentric 216, 222
conception [*see* conceive]
intellect 450
idea 453
concern
relation 9
event 151
business 625
importance 642
firm 797
grief 828
– oneself with 625
concert
agreement 23
synchronism 120
music 415
act in – 709
in – *musical* 413
concord 714
– measures 626
concertina 417
concerto 415

concert-room 840
concession
permission 760
consent 762
compromise 774
giving 784
discount 813
concesso, ex –
reasoning 476
assent 488
concetto 842
conchoid 245
conchology 223
concierge 163, 753
conciliate
talk over 615
pacify 723
satisfy 831
courtesy 894
atonement 952
conciliatory [*see* conciliate]
concord 714
forgiving 918
conciliatrix 962
concinnity
agreement 23
style 578
beauty 845
conciseness 572
concision 201
conclave
assembly 72
council 696
church 995
conclude
end 67
infer 480
resolve 604
complete 729
compact 769
conclusion [*see* conclude]
sequel 65
germination 161
judgment 480
try –s 476
forgone – 611
hasty – 481
conclusive [*see* conclude]
answer 462
evidence 467
certain 474
proof 478
– reasoning 476
concoct *lie* 544
write 590
plan 626
prepare 673

concomitant
  accompany 88
  same time 120
  concurrent 178
concord *agree* 23
  music **413**
  assent 488
  harmony **714**
concordance 562
  book 593
concordant 173
concordat 769
concordia discors 24, 59
concours 720
concourse
  assemblage 72
  convergence 290
concremation 384
concrete *existent* 3
  mass 46
  definite 79
  density 321
  hardness 323
  materials 635
concubinage 961
concubine 926
concupiscence 865, 961
concur
  co-exist 120
  causation 178
  converge 290
  assent 488
  concert 709
concurrence **178,** 216
concussion 276
condemnation 932, **971**
condemned cell 752
condense
  compress 195
  dense 321
condensed
  concise 572
condescend 879
condign 824
condiment **393**
condisciple 541
condition *state* **7**
  modification 469
  supposition 514
  term 770
  repute 873
  rank 875
  in - *plump* 192
  in good - 648
  on - 770
  in perfect - 650
  physical - 316

conditional 8
conditions **770**
condolence 914, **915**
condone 918
condottiere
  traveller 268
  fighter 726
conduce
  contribute 153
  tend 176
  concur 178
  avail 644
conducive 631
conduct
  transfer 270
  music 416
  procedure **692**
  lead 693
  safe -
  passport 631
  safety 664
  - a funeral 363
  - an inquiry 461
  - to 278
conduction 264
conductor 269
  conveyer 271
  director 694
  lightning - 666
conduit **350**
conduplicate 89
condyle 250
cone *round* 249
  pointed 253
confabulation 588
confection 396
  confectionary 396
confectioner 637
confederacy
  co-operation 709
  party 712
confederate 711
confer *advise* 695
  give 784
  - *benefit* 648
  - *power* 157
  - *privilege* 760
  - *right* 924
  - *with* 588
conference [*see* confer]
  council 696
confess *assent* 488
  avow 529
  penitence 950, 998
  - and avoid 937
confession [*see* confess]
  auricular - 998

  - of faith 983
confessional 1000
confessions
  biography 594
confessor 996
confidant 711
confidante
  servant 746
  friend 890
confidence
  trust 484
  hope 858
  courage 861
  in - 528
  - *trick* 545
confident 535
configuration 240
confine
  region 182
  circumscribe 229
  limit 231, 233
  imprison 751
confined
  narrow judgment 481
  ill 655
confinement
  childbed 161
confines of
  on the - 197
confirm
  corroborate 467
  assent 488
  consent 762
  compact 769
  rite 998
confirmed 150
  - *habit* 613
confiscate *take* 789
  condemn 971
  penalty 974
confiture 396
conflagration 382, 384
conflexure 245
conflict
  opposition 708
  discord 713
  contention 720
conflicting
  contrary 14
  counteracting 179
  - *evidence* 468
confluence
  junction 43
  convergence 290
  river 248
conflux
  assemblage 72

convergence 290
conform *assent* 488
– to rule 494
conformable 23, 178
conformation 54, 240
conformity 82, 178
confound
  disorder 61
  destroy 162
  not discriminate 465a
  perplex 475
  defeat 731
  astonish 870
  curse 908
confounded
  great 31
  bad 649
confraternity
  party 712
  friendship 888
confrère
  colleague 711
  friend 890
confrication 331
confront *face* 234
  compare 464
  oppose 708
  resist 719
  – *danger* 861
  – *witnesses* 467
confucianism 984
Confucius 986
confuse *derange* 61
  perplex 458
  obscure 519
  not discriminate 465a
  abash 879
confused *disorder* 59
  invisible 447
  uncertain 475
  style 571
confusion [*see* confuse]
  – seize 908
  – of tongues 560, 563
  – of vision 443
  – worse-confounded 59
confutation 479
congé 293, 756
  – d'élire 995
congeal *dense* 321
  cold 385
congeneric
  similar 17
  included 76
congenial
  related 9
  agreeing 23

concord 714
love 897
congenital 5, 820
congeries 72
congestion 641
conglaciation 385
conglobation 72
conglomerate
  cohere 46
  assemblage 72
  dense 321
  council 696
conglutinate 46
congratulate 896
  – oneself 838
congratulation 896
congregation
  assemblage 72
  worshippers 990
  laity 997
Congregationalist 984
congress
  assembly 72
  convergence 290
  conference 588
  council 698
Congressional Medal 733
Congressional Record 551
congreve *fuel* 388
  – rocket 727
congruous
  agreeing 23
  (*expedient* 646)
conical *round* 249
  pointed 253
conjecture 475, 514
conjoin 43
conjoint 48
conjointly 37
conjugal 903
conjugate
  words 562
  grammar 567
  – in all its tenses &c. 104
conjugation
  junction 43
  pair 89
  phase 144
  grammar 567
conjunction 43
  in – with 37
conjuncture
  contingency **8**
  occasion 134
conjure *deceive* 545
  entreat 765
  sorcery 992

name to – with 873
  – up *recall* 505
  up a vision 505
conjuror
  deceiver 548
  sorcerer 994
connaître les dessous des
  cartes 490
connate
  intrinsic 5
  kindred 11
  cause 153
connatural
  uniform 16
  similar 17
connect *relate* 9
  link 43
connection [*see* connect]
  kin 11
  in – with 9
connections
  cards 840
connective 45
conned, well – 490
connive
  overlook 460
  co-operate 709
  allow 760
connoisseur
  critic 480
  scholar 492
  taste 850
connotate 550
connote 516, 550
  imply 526
connubial 903
connuted 9
conoscente 850
conquer 731
conquered
  (*failure* 732)
conquering hero comes
  883
conqueror 731
consanguinity 11
consciarecti, mens –
  pride 878
  innocence 946
conscience
  knowledge 490
  moral sense 926
  in all – *great* 31
  affirmation 535
  awakened – 950
  qualms of – 603
  clear – 946
  stricken – 950

tender – 926
honour 939
conscientious 926
scrupulous 939
– *objector* 489
conscious
intuitive 450
knowledge 490
– *of disgrace* 874
– *of glory* 873
conscript 726
conscription 744
consecrate *use* 677
dedicate 873
sanctify 987
holy orders 995
consecration
rite 998
consectory 478
– *reasoning* 476
consecution 63
consecutive
following 63
continuous 69
– *filth* 414
consecutively
slowly 275
consensus 488
– *of opinion* 23
consent *assent* 488
compliance **762**
with one – 178
consentaneous
agreeing 23
(expedient 646)
consequence
event 151
effect 154
importance 642
in – 478
of no – 643
take the –s 154
consequent 63
consequential
deducible 478
arrogant 878
consequently
effect 154
reasoning 476
conservation
permanence 141
storage 636
preservation 670
conservatism 141, 670
conservative 141, 712
– *policy* 681
conservatoire 542

conservator
of the peace 967
conservatory
receptacle 191
floriculture 371
furnace 386
store 636
conserve 396, 636
consider *think* 451
attend to 457
examine 461
adjudge 480
believe 484
considerable
in degree 31
in size 192
important 642
considerate
careful 459
judicious 498
benevolent 906
consideration
purchase money 147
thought 451
idea 453
attention 457
qualification 469
inducement 615
importance 642
gift 784
benevolence 906
respect 928
requital 973
deserve – 642
in – *of*
compensation 30
reasoning 476
on – 658
take into –
thought 451
attention 457
under –
topic 454
inquiry 461
plan 626
considered, all things –
collectively 50
judgment 480
premeditation 611
imperfection 651
consign
transfer 270
commission 755
property 783
give 784
– *to the flames* 384
– *to oblivion* 506

– *to the tomb* 363
consignee **758**
consignment
commission 755
gift 784
apportionment 786
consignor 796
consilience 178
consist
– *in* 1
– *of* 54
consistence
density 321
consistency
uniformity 16
agreement 23
consistently with 82
consistory
council 696
church 995
consolation
relief 834
condole 915
religious 976
console
table 215
Consoler
the – 976
consolidate
unite 46, 48
condense 321
consols 802
consommé 298
consonant
agreeing 23
musical 413
letter 561
consort
accompany 88
associate 892
spouse 903
– *with* 23
consortium 23
consortship 892
conspection 441
conspectus 596
conspicuous
visible 446
famous 873
conspiracy 626
conspirator 626
traitor 941
conspire
concur 178
co-operate 709
constable
policeman 664

governor 745
officer 965
constant
fixed 5
uniform 16
continuous 69
regular 80
continual 112
frequent 136
regular 138
immutable 150
exact 494
persevering 604a
obey 743
faithful 939
- *flow* 69
constellation
stars 318
luminary 423
glory 873
consternation 860
constipation
closure 261
density 321
constituency 181, 737
constituent 51, 56
constitute
compose 54, 56
produce 161
constitution
nature 5
state 7
composition 54
structure 329
charter 924
law 963
constitutional
walk 226
- *government* 737
constrain
compel 744
restrain 751
abash 881
constraint 195
constrict 195, 706
constringe 195
construct 161
construction 161
form 240
structure 329
meaning 522
put a false - upon 523
constructive
latent 526
- *evidence* 467
constructor 164
construe 522

consubstantiation 998
consuetude 618
consul 758, 759
consulship 737
consult 695
- one's pillow 133
- one's own wishes 943
- the wishes of 707
consultant 662
consultation 695, 696
consume
destroy 162
waste 638
use 677
- away 36
- time
time 106
inactivity 683
consumere natus, fruges -
683
consuming 830
consummate
great 31
complete 52
completed 729
- skill 698
consummation
end 67
completion 729
- devoutly to be wished
good 618
desire 865
consumption [*see* consume]
decrease 36
shrinking 195
disease 655
contact 199
come in -
arrive 292
contagion
transfer 270
disease 655
unhealthy 657
contain
be composed of 54
include 76
container 191
contaminate
soil 653
spoil 659
contaminated
diseased 655
contango 133, 813
contemn 930
contemper 174
contemplate
view 411

think 451
expect 507
purpose 620
contemporary 120
contemporation 174
contempt 930
- of danger 861
contemptible
unimportant 643
dishonourable 940
contend
reason 476
assert 535
fight 720
- with difficulties 704
- for
vindicate 937
content
assenting 488
willing 602
calm 826
satisfied **831**
- to one's heart's -
sufficient 639
success 731
contention **720**
contentious 901
contents
ingredients 56
list 86
components **190**
synopsis 596
conterminate
end 67
limit 233
conterminous 199
contesseration 72
contest 709, 720
contestant 710
context 591
from the - 516
contexture 329
contiguity **199**
continence 960
continent
land 342
continental 643
contingency
event 151
uncertainty 475
expectation 507
contingent
conditional 8
casual 156
liable 177
possible 470
uncertain 475

unforeseen 508
supply 635
aid 707
allotted 786
donation 809
- duration **108a**
- interest 780
continual
perpetual 112
frequent 136
continuance 143
continuation
adjunct 39
sequence 63
sequel 65
- school 542
continue
endure 106, 110
persist 143
continued 69
- success 731
continuity 69
uniformity 16
contortion
distortion 243
convolution 248
contortionist 599, 700
contour
outline 230
appearance 448
contra 14
per - 708
- bonos mores
vulgar 851
improper 925
vice 945
contraband
deceitful 545
prohibited 761
illicit 964
contrabasso 417
contraception 706
contract
shrink 195
narrow 203
promise 768
bargain 769
bridge 840
- a debt 806
- a habit 613
- an obligation 768
contractility 195
contraction 195
short-hand 590
compendium 596
contractor 690
contradict

contrary 14
answer 462
dissent 489
deny 536
oppose 708
contradictory
disagreement 24
evidence 468
discord 713
contradistinction 15
contraindicate
dissuade 616
warning 668
contraire, tout au - 536
contralto 408, 416
contraposition
inversion 218
reversion **237**
contrapuntist 413
contrariety 14
contrary
opposite 14
antagonistic 179
captious 608
opposing 708
quite the - 536
- to expectation
improbable 473
unexpected 508
- to reason 471
contrast
contrariety 14
difference 15
comparison 464
contravallation 717
contravene
contrary 14
counterevidence 468
deny 536
hinder 706
oppose 708
contre cœur, à - 603
contre-coup 277
contretemps
ill-timed 135
hindrance 706
misfortune 735
contribute
cause 153
tend 176
concus 178
aid 707
give 784
contribution 784
lay under - 789, 924
contrition
abrasion 331

regret 833
penitence 950
contrivance 633
contrive
produce 161
plan 626
- to succeed in 731
contriving
conning 702
control
power 157
influence 175
regulate 693
authority 737
restrain 751
board of - 696
under -
obedience 743
subjection 749
controller of currency 801
controls 273, 693
controversial
discussion 476
discordant 713
controversialist 476, 726
controversy
disagreement 24
discussion 476
debate 588
contention 720
controvert
deny 536
controvertible
uncertain 475
debatable 476
untrue 495
contumacy
obstinacy 606
disobedience 742
contumely
arrogance 885
rudeness 895
disrespect 929
scorn 930
reproach 932
contund 331
contuse 330
conundrum *pun* 520
riddle 533
wit 842
convalescence 654, 660
convection 270
convenance
mariage de - 903
convene 72
conveniences 632
convenient 646, 705

convent 1000
conventicle
  assembly 72
  council 696
  chapel 1000
convention
  agreement 23
  assembly 72
  rule 80
  council 696
  precept 697
  treaty of peace 723
  compact 769
  –s *of society* 852
conventional 82, 613
conventual 996, 1000
convergence 290
convergent 286
conversable
  talk 588
  sociable 892
conversant
  know 470
  skilful 698
conversation 588
conversational
  loquacious 584
  interlocution 588
  sociable 892
conversazione 588, 892
converse
  reverse 14
  talk 588
conversely 468
conversion 144
  trover and – 964
convert
  change to 140, 144
  opinion 484
  tergiversation 607
  religion 987
  – *to use* 677
convertible 13, 27
  – terms, 522
convexity 250
convey
  transfer 270
  mean 516
  assign 783
  – *away* 791
  – *the knowledge of* 527
conveyance [*see* convey]
  vehicle 272
conveyancer 968
conveyancing 783
convict
  convince 484

  condemned 949
  condemn 971
convicted, self – 950
conviction
  confutation 479
  belief 484
  prove guilty 971
convince
  confute 479
  belief 484
  teach 537
convivial 892
convocate 72
convocation
  council 696
  church 995
convoke 72
convolution
  coil **248**
  rotation 312
convoy
  accompany 88
  transfer 270
  guard 664
  escort 753
convulse
  derange 61
  violent 173
  agitate 315
  bodily pain 378
  mental pain 830
convulsed with
  – *laughter* 838
  – *rage* 900
convulsion [*see* convulse]
  disorder 59
  revolution 146
  in –s 325
coo 412
cook *heat* 384
  falsify 544
  improve 658
  prepare 673
  servant 746
  too many –s 699
  – accounts 811
cool *moderate* 174
  cold 383
  refrigerate 385
  grey 432
  dissuade 616
  cautious 864
  indifferent 866
  unamazed 871
  unfriendly 889
  discourteous 895
  look – upon

  unsocial 893
  take –ly 826
  – down 826
  – one's heels
  kept waiting 133
  inaction 681
cooler 387
coolheaded
  judicious 498
  unexcitable 826
coolie
  bearer 271
  military 726
coolness
  insensibility 823
  estrangement 898
coon-can 840
coop *abode* 189
  restrain 751
  prison 752
co-operation
  physical 178
  voluntary **709**
  participation 778
co-operator 690, 711
co-optation 609
co-ordinate
  equal 27
  arrange 60
  measure 466
cootie 653
cop 664
copal 356*a*
coparcener 778
copartner
  accompanying 88
  participator 778
  associate 890
copartnership
  co-operation 709
  party 712
cope *equal* 27
  oppose 708
  contend 720
  canonicals 999
copia verborum
  diffuse 573
  loquacious 584
coping stone
  top 210
  completion 729
copious
  diffuse style 573
  abundant 639
coportion 778
copper *policeman* 664
  money 800

copper-coloured 433, 439
copper-plate
  engraving 558
  writing 590
coppice 367
coprolite 653
copse 367
copula 45
copulation 43
copy
  imitate 19
  facsimile **21**
  prototype 22
  news 532
  record 551
  represent 554
  write 590
  for the press 591
  plan 626
  - book 22
copyhold 780
copyist
  imitator 19
  artist 559
  writer 590
copyright 780
coquet *lie* 544
  change the mind 607
  affected 855
  endearment 902
  flattery 933
  - with
  irresolute 605
coquette
  affected 854, 855
  flirt 897
coquillage 847
coracle 273
coral 847
  - reef 667
coram judice
  jurisdiction 965
  lawsuit 969
cor Anglais 417
corbeille 191
corbel 215
cord *tie* 45
  filament 205
cordage 45
cordated 245
cordial
  pleasure 377
  dram 392
  willing 602
  remedy 662
  feeling 821
  grateful 829

  friendly 888
  courteous 894
cordiform 245
cordite 727
cordon
  inclosure 232
  circularity 247
  decoration 877
  - blue 733, 746
  - sanitaire
  safety 664
  preservation 670
corduroy 259
cordwainer
  shoemaker 225
  artificer 690
core *gist* 5
  source 153
  centre 222
  gist 642
  true to the - 939
coriaceous 327
Corinthian 850
co-rival [*see* corrival]
cork *plug* 263
  lightness 320
  - jacket 666
  - up *close* 261
  restrain 751
corking pin 45
corkscrew
  spiral 248
  perforator 262
  circuition 311
cormorant
  desire 865
  gluttony 957
corn
  projection 250
Cornaro 953
cornea 441
corned 959
cornelian 847
corneous 323
corner *place* 182
  receptacle 191
  angle 244
  monopoly 777
  - creep into a - 893
  in a dark - 528
  drive into a - 706
  push into a - 874
  rub off -s 82
  - turn a - 311
  turn the - 658
  - stone
  support 215

  importance 642
  defence 717
cornet *music* 417
  officer 745
cornice 210
corniculate 253
cornification 323
Cornish hug 545
corno 417
cornopean 417
cornucopia 639
cornute
  projecting 250
  sharp 253
corollary
  adjunct 39
  deduction 480
corona 247
coronach 839
coronation
  enthronement 755
  celebration 883
coroner 363, 965
  -'s jury 967
coronet *hoop* 247
  insignia 747
  title 877
corporal
  corporeal 316
  officer 745
corporate 43
  - body 712
corporation
  bulk 192
  convex 250
  association 712
  jurisdiction 965
corporeal 3, 316, 364
  - hereditaments 780
corporeity 316
corps *assemblage* 72
  troops 726
  à - perdu
  haste 684
  rash 863
  - de reserve 636
corps 362
corpulence 192
corpus 316
  - Christi 998
  - delicti
  guilt 947
  lawsuit 969
  - juris
  precept 697
  law 963
corpuscle

small 32
little 193
corradiation
focus 74
convergence 290
corral 232, 370
correct
orderly 58
true 494
inform 527
disclose 529
improve 658
repair 660
due 924
censure 932
honourable 939
virtuous 944
punish 972
– ear 416, 418
– memory 505
– reasoning 476
– style
grammatical 567
elegant 578
correction [*see* correct]
house of – 752
under – 879
corrective 662
corregidor 745
correlation
relation 9
reciprocity **12**
correspondence
correlation 12
similarity 17
agreement 23
writing **592**
– course 537
correspondent
messenger 534
journalist 593
consignee 758
corresponding
similar 17
agreeing 23
corridor *region* 181
place 191
passage 627
– train 272
corrigendum 495
corrigible 658
corrival 726
corrivalry 720
corrivation 348
corroborant 662
corroboration
evidence 467

assent 488
corrode *burn* 384
erode 659
afflict 830
corrosive [*see* corrode]
acrid 171
destructive 649
– sublimate 663
corrugate
derange 61
constrict 195
roughen 256
rumple 258
furrow 259
corruption
decomposition 49
neology 563
foulness 653
disease 655
deterioration 659
improbity 940
vice 945
corrupting
noxious 649
corsage 225
corsair 273, 792
corse 362
corselet 225
corset 225
corso 728
cortège
adjunct 39
continuity 69
accompaniment 88
journey 266
suite 746
cortes 696
cortex
cortical 223
coruscate 420
corvette 273, 726
corybantic 503
coryphée 599
Corypheus
teacher 540
director 694
coscinomancy 511
cosey 892
cosignificative 522
cosine 217
cosmetic
remedy 662
ornament 847
cosmic 318
cosmogony &c. 318
cosmopolitan
abode 189

mankind 372
philanthropic 910
sociality 892
cosmorama 448
cosmos 60, 318
Cossack 726
cosset
darling 899
caress 902
cost 812
pay –s 807
to one's –
evil 619
badness 649
– what it may 604
– price 815
costermonger 797
costive
taciturn 585
costless 815
costly 814
costume 225
theatrical – 599
costumé 225
bal – 840
costumier 225
theatrical 599
cosy *snug* 377
sociable 892
cot *abode* 189
bed 215
cote 189
cotenancy 778
coterie *class* 75
junto 712
society 892
coterminous 120
cothurnus 599
cotillon 840
cottage 189
– piano 417
cottager 188
cotter 188
cotton 205
– seed oil 356
couch *lie* 213
bed 215
stoop 308
lurk 528
– one's lance 720
– in terms 566
couchant 213
couci-couci 651
cough 349
churchyard – 655
couleur de rose
good 648

449

prosperity 734
view en – 836
coulisses 599
coulter 253
council
senate **696**
church 995
hold a – 695
– of education 542
– school 542
councillor 696
counsel
advice 695
lawyer 968
keep one's own – 528
take – *think* 451
inquire 461
be advised 695
count *clause* 51
item 79
compute 85
estimate 480
lord 875
– one's chickens before
they are hatched 858,
863
– the cost 864
– upon
believe 484
expect 507
to be –ed on one's fingers
103
countenance
face 234
appearance 448
favour 707
approve 931
keep in –
conform 82
induce 615
encourage 861
vindicate 937
keep one's –
brook 826
not laugh 837
out of –
abashed 879
put out of – 874
stare out of – 885
– falling
disappointment 509
dejection 837
counter *contrary* 14
number 84
table 215
stern 235
token 550

shop-board 799
over the –
barter 794
buy 795
sell 796
run – 179
– to 708
counteract
compensate 30
physically 179
hinder 706
voluntarily 708
counteraction 14, **179**
counterbalance 30
counterblast
counteract 179
retaliate 718
counterchange
correlation 12
interchange 148
countercharge 462
countercharm 993
countercheck
mark 550
hindrance 706
counterclaim 30
counter-evidence **468**
counterfeit
imitate 19
copy 21
simulate 544
sham 545
coinage 792
counterfoil 550
countermand 756
countermarch 266, 283
countermark 550
countermine
plan 626
oppose 708
countermotion 283
counterorder 756
counterpane 223
counterpart
match 17
copy 21
reverse 237
counterplot
plan 626
oppose 708
retaliate 718
counterpoint 415
counterpoise
compensate 30
weight 319
hinder 706
counter-poison 662

counterpole 14
counter-project 718
counter-protest 468
counter-revolution 146
counterscarp 717
countersign
evidence 467
assent 488
mark 550
counterstroke 718
countervail
outweigh 28
compensate 30
evidence 468
counterwork 708
countess 875
counting-house 799
countless 105
countrified 189
vulgar 851
country
region 181
abode 189
rural 371
authority 737
love of – 910
country-dance 840
countryman
commonalty 876
friend 890
county 181
– seat 189
– town 189
– school 542
– council 696
– court 966
coup
instantaneous 113
action 680
– de bec
attack 716
censure 932
– d'épée dans
l'eau 645
– d'essai 675
– d'état
revolution 146
plan 626
action 680
lawless 964
– de grâce
end 67
death-blow 361
completion 729
punishment 972
– de main
violence 173

action 680
attack 716
– de maître
excellent 648
skilful 698
success 731
– d'œil
sight 441
appearance 448
display 882
– de plume 590
– de soleil
hot 384
mad 503
à – sûr 474
– de théâtre
appearance 448
display 882
coupé 272
couple
unite 43
two 89
–d with
added 37
accompanied 88
coupler 45
couplet 89, 597
coupling 45
coupon 800
courage 861
moral – 604
– oozing out 862
courant, au – 490
coureur, avant – 673
courier
traveller 268
guide 524
messenger 534
course *order* 58
continuity 69
time 106, **109**
layer 204
motion 264
locomotion 226, 267
direction 278
dinner 298
river 348
pursuit 622
way 627
conduct 692
arena 728
bend one's – 266
in due – 134
hold a – 278
in the – of
during 106
keep one's –

progress 282
persevere 604*a*
let things take
their –
continue 143
inaction 681
follow as of – 478
mark out a – 626
of –
conformity 82
effect 154
certain 474
assent 488
necessity 601
willingly 602
custom 613
consent 762
expect 871
race – 840
run its –
end 67
complete 729
take a – 622
take its – 151
– of action 692
– of business 625
– of events 151
– of inquiry 461
– of preparation 673
– runs smooth 734
– of study 537
– of things 151
– of time 121
courser
horse 271
swift 274
coursing
kill 361
pursue 622
court *close* 181, 182
house 189
hall 191
flatness 213
invite 615
pursue 622
council 696
retinue 746
solicit 765
gentility 852
wish 865
woo 902
flatter 933
tribunal 966
bring into – 467
friend at – 526, 711
pay – to
servile 886

love 897, 902
flatter 933
put out of – 731
– card 626
– of honour 939
courteous 894
courtesan 962
courtesy
stoop 308, 314
submit 725
politeness **894**
show –
respect 928
courtier
servile 886
flatterer 935
– like 933
courtly 852
courtship 902
courtyard 182
cousin 11
coûte-que-coûte
certainly 474
necessary 601
resolution 604
cove *cell* 191
hollow 252
bay 343
covenant
compact 769
condition 770
security 771
covenanter 488
Coventry
Earl of –
cards 840
send to –
eject 297
disrepute 874
seclusion 893
cover
compensate 30
include 76
superpose, lid 223
dress 225
stopper 263
meal 298
conceal 528
retreat 530
report 531
keep clean 652
keep safe 664
preserve 670
under –
hidden 528
pretence 545
safe 664

- with dust 653
covercle 223
covering 223
coverlet 223
Coverley, Sir Roger de -
840
covert *abode* 189
invisible 447
latent 526
refuge 666
feme -e 903
- *way* 627
coverture 903
covet *desire* 865
envy 921
covetous
miserly 819
covey
assemblage 72
multitude 102
cow
animal 366
female 374
intimidate 860
coward 862
cowardice 862
cowboy 370
cower *stoop* 308
fear 860
cowardice 862
servile 886
cowherd 370
cowhide 223, 975
cowhouse 189
cowkeeper 370
cowl *dress* 225
sacerdotal 999
cowled 223
cowl-staff 215
co-worker 690
coxcomb 854
coxcombry
affectation 855
vanity 880
coxswain 269
coy *timid* 860
modest 881
cozen 545
crab *sourness* 397
- like motion
deviation 279
regression 283
grouch 901a
crabbed *sour* 397
unintelligible 519
obscure style 571
difficult 704

uncivil 895
sulky 901a
crack *split* 44
discontinuity 70
instantaneous 113
fissure 198
furrow 259
brittle 328
sound 406
excellent 648
injure 659
skilful 698
boast 884
- a bottle
food 298
social 892
drunken 959
- of doom
end 67
future 121
destruction 162
- one's invention 515
- a joke 842
- shot 700
crackbrained 503
cracked
unmusical 410
fanatical 481
mad 503
faulty 651
- *bell* 408a
- *voice* 581
cracker 406
crackle 406
cracksman 792
crack-up 162
cradle
beginning 66
infancy 127
origin 153
placing 184
bed 215
training 673
aid 707
in the - 129
- *song* 415
craft *shipping* 273
business 625
skill 698
cunning 702
craftiness 498
craftsman 690
craftsmanship 680
crag *pointed* 253
hard 323
land 342
craggy

rough 256
craig *height* 206
crake 884
cram *crowd* 72
stuff 194
choke 261
teach 537
learn 539
gorge 957
- down the throat
induce belief 484
compel 744
crambe repetita
weariness 841
satiety 869
crambo 597
crammed 52
- to overflowing 641
crammer *teacher* 537
lie 546
cramp
fastening 45
paralyze 158
weaken 160
little 193
compress 195
spasm 378
hinder 706
cramped *style* 579
cran 191
cranch [see craunch]
crane *angle* 244
elevate 307
instrument 633
- *neck* 245
craniology &c. 450
cranium 450
crank
fanatic 504
instrument 633
wit 842
treadmill 975
crankle *fold* 258
crankling
rough 256
cranky *weak* 160
ill health 655
cranny 198
crape
crinkle 248
mourning 839
crapulence
intemperance 954
gluttony 957
drunken 959
crash
destruction 162

452

cribriform 260
Crichton, Admirable –
 scholar 492
 perfect 650
 proficient 700
crick *pain* 378
cricket *game* 840
 not – 940
 – ground 213
crier 534
 send round the – 531
crim. con. 961
crime 945, 947
criminal 923, 945
 culprit 949
 – law 963
 court of – appeal 966
criminality 947
criminate 938
crimp *crinkle* 248
 notch 257
 brittle 328
 deceiver 548
 take 789
 steal 791
crimple 258
crimson 434, 821
cringe *submit* 725
 subject 749
 servility 886
crinite 256
crinkle *angle* 244
 convolution 248
 roughen 256
 fold 258
crinoline 225
cripple *disable* 158
 weaken 160
 injure 649
crippled
 disease 655
crisis
 conjuncture 8
 present time 118
 opportunity 134
 event 151
 strait 704
 excitement 824
 bring to a – 604
 come to a – 729
crisp *rumpled* 248
 rough 256
 brittle 328
 style 572
Crispin 225
criss-cross 219
cristallomantia 511

criterion *test* 463
 evidence 467
 indication 550
crithomancy 511
critic *judge* 480
 taste 850
 detractor 936
critical
 contingent 8
 opportune 134
 discriminating 465
 important 642
 dangerous 665
 difficult 704
 censorious 932
criticism
 judgment 480
 dissertation 595
 disapprobation 932
 detraction 934
critique
 [*see* criticism]
croak *cry* 412
 hoarseness 581
 stammer 583
 warning 668
 discontent 832
 lament 839
croaker 832, 837
Croat 726
crochet 847
crock 191
crockery 384
crocodile tears 544
crocus *yellow* 436
Crœsus 803
croft 189, 232
Croix de Guerre 733
cromlech 363, 551
crone *veteran* 130
 fool 501
crony *friend* 890
 – *favourite* 899
crook *curve* 245
 deviation 279
 thief 792
crooked
 sloping 217
 distorted 243
 angular 244
 latent 526
 crafty 702
 ugly 846
 dishonourable 940
 – path 704
 – temper 901
 – ways 279

croon 580
crop
 harvest 154
 stomach 191
 shorten 201
 eat 298
 vegetable 367
 store 636
 gather 775
 take 789
 second – 167, 775
 – out *visible* 446
 disclose 529
 – up *begin* 66
 take place 151
 reproduction 163
cropper *fall* 306
croquet *game* 840
 – ground *level* 213
croquette 298
crosier 747, 999
cross *mix* 41
 across 219
 pass 302
 grave 363
 oppose 708
 failure 732
 disaster 735
 refuse 764
 pain 830
 decoration 877
 fretful 901
 punishment 975
 rites 998
 fiery – 722
 proclaim at the – roads 531
 red – 662
 –ed bayonets 708
 – breed 63
 – cut 628
 – fire *interchange* 148
 difficulty 704
 opposition 708
 attack 716
 –ed in love 898
 – the mind 451
 – the path of 706
 – and pile 621
 – purposes 14
 disorder 59
 error 495
 misinterpret 523
 unskilful 699
 difficulty 704
 opposition 708
 discord 713

- oneself 998
- questions
inquiry 461
discord 713
game 840
- road 627
- the Rubicon 609
- sea 348
- swords 722
crossbow 727
cross-examine 461
cross-grained 256
obstinate 606
sulky 901a
crossing 219
- sweeper 652
crosspatch 895
crossroads 8
cross-word puzzle 533
crotch 244
crotchet
eccentric 83
music 413
misjudgment 481
obstinacy 606
caprice 608
crouch *lower* 207
stoop 308
fear 860
servile 866
- before 725
croup 235
croupier 694
crow *cry* 412
black 431
rejoice 838
boast 884
pluck a - with 932
as the - flies 278
-'s foot (*age*) 128
-'s nest 210
- to pluck
discord 713
anger 900
accuse 938
crowbar 633
crowd 72
multitude 102
close 197
redundance 641
party 712
vulgar 876
in the - *mixed* 41
maddening - 682
crown *top* 210
circle 247
complete 729

trophy 733
sceptre 747
install 755
decoration 877
reward 973
to - all 33, 642
-ed head 745
- with laurel 873
- with success 731
crowning
[*see* crown]
superior 33
end 67
- point 210
cruche à l'eau &c.
tant va la - 735
crucial
crossing 219
proof 478
- test 463
cruciate
physical pain 378
mental pain 830
crucible
dish 191
conversion 144
furnace 386
experiment 463
laboratory 691
put into the - 163
crucifix 219, 998
crucifixion 828
cruciform 219
crucify
physical torture 378
mental agony 830
execution 972
crucis, experimen-
tum - 463
crude *colour* 428
-*style* 579
unprepared 674
cruel
painful 830
inhuman 907
- to be kind 914
cruelly *much* 31
cruet 191
cruise
vessel 191
navigation 267
cruiser 726
cruising 267
crumb *small* 32
powder 330
- of comfort 834
crumble

decrease 36
weak 160
destruction 162
brittle 328
pulverize 330
spoil 659
- into dust
decompose 49
- under one's feet 735
crumbling
[*see* crumble]
dangerous 665
crumenal 800
crump
distorted 243
curved 245
crumple
ruffle 256
fold 258
- up *destroy* 162
crush 195
crunch
shatter 44
chew 298
pulverize 330
crupper 235
crusade 722
crush *crowd* 72
destroy 162
compress 195
pulverize 330
humble 879
- under an iron heel 739
- one's hopes
disappoint 509
hopeless 859
crushed 828
crushing 830
crust 223
crustacean 366
crusty 895, 901a
crutch
support 215
angle 244
-ed Friars 996
crux 219, 704
- criticorum 533
cry *human* **411**
animal 412
publish 531, 532
call 550
voice 580
vogue 613
weep 839
far - to 196
full - *loud* 404
raise a - 550

455

- aloud
implore 765
- out against
dissuade 616
censure 932
- down 932, 934
- for 865
- before hurt 839
- for joy 838
- you mercy
deprecate 766
pity 914
forgive 918
- shame 932
- to *beseech* 765
- up 931
- for vengeance 923
- wolf *false* 544
alarm 669
- and little wool
overrate 482
disappoint 509
boast 884
crying [*see* cry]
urgent 630
weary 841
- evil 619
- shame 874
- sin 945
crypt *cell* 191
grave 363
ambush 530
altar 1000
cryptic 475, 528
cryptography
hidden 528
writing 590
crystal *hard* 323
transparent 425
snow - 383
- gazer 513
- gazing 511, 992
- oil 356
clear as - 519
crystalline
dense 321
hard 323
transparent 425
crystallization 321, 323
csako 225, 717
cub *young* 129
vulgar 851
clown 876
unlicked - 241
cubby-hole 191
cube
three dimensions 92, 93

form 244
cubicle 191
cubist 556
cubit 200
cucking stool 975
cuckold 905
cuckoldom 961
cuckoo
imitation 19
repetition 104
sound 407
cry 412
cuddle 196, 902
cudgel *beat* 276
weapon 727
punish 975
take up the -s
aid 707
attack 716
contention 720
- one's brains
think 451
imagine 515
cue *hint* 527
watchword 550
plea 617
rôle 625
take one's - from 695
in proper - 698
cuff *sleeve* 225
blow 276
punishment 972
cui bono 644, 645
cuique voluptas sui - 865
cuirass 717
cuirassier 726
cuisine 298
batterie de - 957
culbute
inversion 218
fall 306
cul-de-lampe
engraving 558
ornament 847
cul-de-sac
concave 252
closed 261
difficulty 704
culinary 298
- art 673
cull *dupe* 547
choose 609
take 789
cullender 260
cullibility 486
cullion 949
cully *deceive* 545, 547

culm 388
culminate
maximum 33
height 206
top 210
complete 729
culpability *vice* 945
guilt 947
culprit 949
cult 983
cultivate *till* 365, 371
sharpen 375
improve 658
prepare 673
aid 707
cultivated
courteous 894
- taste 850
cultivator 371
culture
knowledge 490
improvement 658
taste 850
politeness 894
culverin 727
culvert 350
cum multis aliis 37, 102
cumber *load* 319
obstruct 706
cumbersome
incommodious 647
disagreeable 830
cummerbund 225
cumulative 72
increasing 35
assembled 72
- evidence 467
- vote 609
cumulus 353
cunctando restituit rem
681
cunctation 133
cuneiform 244
- character 590
cunning
prepense 611
sagacious 698
artful **702**
- fellow 700
- man 994
cup *vessel* 191
hollow 252
beverage 298
remedy 662
trophy 733
tipple 959
between - and lip 111

in one's –s 959
– that cheers &c. 298
– of humiliation 879
dash the – from one's lips
  509
– too low 837
cupbearer 746
cupboard 191
cupellation 384
Cupid *beauty* 845
  love 897
  gods 979
cupidity
  avarice 819
  desire 865
cupola *height* 206
  roof 223
  dome 250
cup-tossing 621
cur *dog* 366
  coward 862
  sneak 949
curable 658, 660, 662
curacy 995
curare 663
curate 996
curative 660
curator 694, 758
curb *moderate* 174
  slacken 275
  dissuade 616
  restrain 751
  shackle 752
curb exchange 621
curbstone 233
curd *density* 321
  pulp 354
  (*cohere* 46)
curdle *condense* 321
  (*cohere* 46)
  make the blood – 830
curdled 352
cure *reinstate* 660
  remedy 662
  preserve 670
  benefice 995
curé 996
cureless 859
curfew 126
curia 966
curio 847
curiosa felicitas 698
curiosity
  unconformity 83
  inquiring **455**
  phenomenon 872
curious

exceptional 83
inquisitive 455
true 494
beautiful 845
desirous 865
curiously *very* 31
curl *bend* 245
  convolution 248
  hair 256
  cockle up 258
  badge 747
  – up one's lip 930
curling *game* 840
curmudgeon
  miser 819
  plebeian 876
currency
  publicity 531
  money 800
current *existing* 1
  usual 78
  present 118
  happening 151
  flow 264
  of water 348
  of air 349
  rife 531, 532
  language 560
  habit 613
  danger 667
  account – 811
  against the – 708
  go with the – 82
  pass –
  believed 484
  fashion 852
  stem the – 708
  – belief 488
  – of events 151
  – of ideas 451
  – of time 109
currente calamo 590
curricle 272
curriculum 537
curry *food* 298
  rub 331
  condiment 392, 393
  – favour with
  love 897
  flatter 933
curry-comb 370
curse *bane* 663
  adversity 735
  painful 830
  malediction 908
cursed *bad* 649
cursitor 968

cursive 590
cursory
  transient 111
  inattentive 458
  hasty 684
  take a – view of 457
  neglect 460
curst 901*a*
curt *short* 201
  concise 572
  taciturn 585
curtail *retrench* 38
  shorten 201
  –ed of its fair proportions
  distorted 243
  ugly 846
curtain 223
  shade 424
  hide 528, 530
  theatre 599
  fortification 717
  behind the –
  invisible 447
  inquiry 461
  knowledge 490
  close the – 528
  raise the – 529
  rising of the – 448
  – lecture 932
  – raiser 66, 599
curtsy
  stoop 308, 314
  submit 725
  polite 894
curule 696
curvature **245**
curvet *leap* 309
  turn 311
  oscillate 314
  agitate 315
curvilinear 245
  – motion 311
cushion *pillow* 215
  soft 324
  relief 834
cushy 829
cusp *angle* 244
  sharp 253
cuspidor 191
cuss 908
custard 298
custodes? quis custodiet –
  459
custodian 753
custody *safe* 664
  captive 751
  retention 781

457

in - *prisoner* 754
accused 938
take into - 751
custom *old* 124
habit 613
barter 794
sale 796
tax 812
fashion 852
- honoured in breach 614
customary [*see* custom]
regular 80
customer 795
custom-house 799
- officer 965
custos 753
- rotulorum 553
cut *divide* 44
bit 51
discontinuity 70
interval 198
curtail 201
layer 204
form 240
notch 257
blow 276
eject 297
reap 371
physical pain 378
cold 385
neglect 460
carve 557
engraving 558
road 627
attack 716
portion 786
affect 824
mental pain 830
dance step 840
decline acquaintance 893
discourtesy 895
tipsy 959
- short 628
unkindest - of all
pain 828
malevolence 907
- across 302
- adrift 44
- along 274
have a - at 716
- away 274
- a whetstone with a razor
sophistry 477
waste 638
misuse 679
- both ways 468
- capers 309

- according to cloth
economy 817
caution 864
- and come again
repeat 104
enough 639
- dead 893
- direct 893
- down *destroy* 162
shorten 201
fell 308
kill 361
- down expenses 817
- and dried
arranged 60
prepared 673
- a figure
appearance 448
fashion 852
repute 873
display 882
- the first turf 66
- the ground from under
one
confute 479
hinder 706
- to the heart 824, 830
- ice with
influence 175
- of one's jib 448
- jokes 842
- the knot 705
- off *subduct* 38
disjoin 44
kill 361
impede 706
bereft 776
secluded 893
- off with a shilling 789
- open 260
- out *surpass* 33
stop 142
substitute 147
plan 626
- out for 698
- out work
prepare 673
direct 693
- to pieces
destroy 162
kill 361
- a poor figure 874
- to the quick 830
- up root and branch 162
- up rough 900
- and run 274
depart 293

escape 623
- short *stop* 142
destroy 162
shorten 201
silence 581
- one's stick
depart 283
avoid 623
- one's own throat 699
- and thrust 716
- in two 91
- up *divide* 44
destroy 162
pained 828
give pain 830
discontented 832
dejected 837
censure 932
what one will - up for 780
- one's way through 302
cutaneous 223
cute 698
cuticle 223
cutlass 727
cutlery 253
cut-purse 792
cutter 273
cut-throat
killer 361
evil-doer 913
cutting *sharp* 253
cold 383
path 627
affecting 821
painful 830
reproachful 932
cuttings
excerpta 596
selections 609
cutty stool 950
cwt. 98, 319
cyanide of potassium
poison 663
cyanogen 438
cycle *time* 106
period 138
circle 247
ride 266
vehicle 272
- car 272
cyclist 268
cycloid 247
cyclometer 200
cyclone
rotation 312
wind 349
cyclopædia

knowledge 490
book 593
Cyclopean
  strong 159
  huge 192
Cyclops
  monster 83
  mighty 159
  huge 192
  dupe 547
cygne
  chant du – 360
  – noir 650
cylindric 249
cyma 847
cymbal 417
cymbalo 417
cymophanous 440
cynic
  misanthrope 911
  detractor 936
  ascetic 955
  closet – 893
cynical
  contemptuous 930
  censorious 932
  detracting 934
cynicism
  discourtesy 895
  contempt 930
cynosure *sign* 550
  direction 693
  wonder 870
  repute 873
Cynthia of the minute 149
cypher [*see* cipher]
cypress
  interment 363
  mourning 839
Cyprian 962
cyst 191
czar 745

D

dab *small* 32
  paint 223
  slap 276
  clever 700
dabble *water* 337
  dirty 653
  meddle 682
  fribble 683
dabbled *wet* 339
dabbler 493
da capo 104

dachshund 366
dacoit 792
dactyl 597
dactyliomancy 511
dactylogram 467
dactylonomy
  numeration 85
  symbol 550
dad 166
daddy 166
dado 211
dædal
  variegated 440
dædalion
  convoluted 248
  artistic 698
daft 503
dagger 727
  look –s *anger* 900
  threat 909
  air drawn – 515
  plant – in breast
    give pain 830
  speak –s 932
  at –s drawn
    opposed 708
    discord 713
    enmity 889
    hate 898
daggle *hang* 214
  dirty 653
dagobah 1000
Dagon 986
daguerreotype
  represent 554
  paint 556
dahabeah 273
Dail Eireann 696
daily
  frequent 136
  periodic 138
  – occurrence
    normal 82
    habitual 613
  – paper 531
dainty *food* 298
  savoury 394
  pleasing 829
  delicate 845
  tasty 850
  fastidious 868
dairy 191, 370
  – maid 946
dais *support* 215
  throne 747
daisy
  fresh as a – 654

– pied 847
dale 252
dally *delay* 133
  irresolute 605
  inactive 683
  amuse 840
  fondle 902
dalmatic 999
Daltonism 443
dam *parent* 166
  close 261
  pond 343
  obstruct 706
damage *evil* 619
  injure, spoil 659
  price 812
damages 974
damascene 440
damask 434
dame
  woman 374
  teacher 540
  lady 875
damn
  malediction 908
  condemn 971
  – with faint praise 932,
    934
damnable 649
damnatory
  disapprove 932
  condemn 971
damnify
  damage 649
  spoil 659
damnosa hereditas 663
Damocles
  sword of – 667
Damon and Pythias 890
damozel 129
damp
  moderate 174
  moist 339
  cold 385
  sound 405
  dissuade 616
  hinder 706
  depress 837
  dull 843
  – the sound 408*a*
damper 387
damsel
  youth 129
  female 374
Dan to Beersheba 52, 180
Danaë 803
Danaos, timeo –

doubt 485
caution 864
dance
  jump 309
  oscillate 314
  agitate 315
  rejoice 838
  sport 840
  sociality 892
  lead the – 175
  lead one a –
  run away 623
  circuit 629
  difficult 704
  practical joke 929
  St. Vitus' – 315
  – attendance
  waiting 133
  follow 281
  servant 746
  petition 765
  servility 886
  – the back step 283
  – upon nothing 972
  – the war dance 715
dance-band 417
dance-music 415
dander 900
Dandie Dinmont 366
dandiprat 193
dandle 902
dandruff 653
dandy
  ship 273
  fop 854
dandyism 855
danger 665
  in – *liable* 177
  source of – 667
  – past 664
  – signal 669
dangerous [*see* danger]
  – classes 913
  – illness 655
  – person 667
dangle *hang* 214
  swing 314
  display 882
dangler 281
Daniel *sage* 500
  judge 967
dank 339
Dannemora 752
danseuse 599
dapper
  little 193
  elegant 845

dapple 433
dappled 440
darbies
  handcuffs 752
Darby and Joan
  secluded 893
  married 903
dare *defy* 715
  face danger 861
  – not 860
  – say *probable* 472
  believe 484
  suppose 514
dare-devil
  courage 861
  rash 863
  bluster 887
daring 861
  unreserved 525
  – imagination 515
dark
  obscure 421
  dim 422
  black 431
  blind 442
  invisible 447
  unintelligible 519
  latent 526
  joyless 837
  insidious 940
  in the –
  ignorant 491
  leap in the –
  experiment 463
  chance 621
  rash 863
  keep – *hide* 528
  – ages 491
  – cloud 735
  view with – eyes 932
  – lantern 423
darkly
  see through a glass – 443
darkness [*see* dark] **421**
  children of – 988
  love – better than light
    989
  powers of – 978
darling *beloved* 897
  favourite 899
darn 660
dart *swift* 274
  propel 284
  missile 727
  – to and fro 684
Dartmoor 752
Darwinism 357

dash
  small quantity 32
  mix 41
  swift 276
  fling 284
  mark 550
  courage 861
  cut a – *repute* 873
  display 882
  – at *resolution* 604
  attack 716
  – board 666
  – cup from lips 761
  – down 308
  – hopes
  disappoint 509
  fail 732
  dejected 837
  despair 859
  – on 274
  – off *paint* 556
  write 590
  active 682
  haste 684
  – of the pen 590
dashed [*see* dash]
  humbled 879
dashing
  fashionable 852
  brave 861
  ostentatious 882
dastard 862
data *evidence* 467
  reasoning 476
  supposition 514
date *time* 106
  chronology 114
datum 673
daub *cover* 223
  paint 428
  misrepresent 555
  dirt 653
daughter 167
daunt 860
dauntless 861
Dauphin 875
davenport 191, 215
davit 214
Davus sum non
  Œdipus
  unintelligent 499
  artless 703
  dull 843
Davy Jones' locker 310
dawdle *tardy* 133
  slow 275
  inactive 683

dawk 534
dawn
  precursor 64
  begin 66
  priority 116
  morning 125
  light 420
  dim 422
  glimpse 490
dawplucker 936
day
  period 108
  present time 118
  light 410
  all - 110
  clear as -
    certain 474
    intelligible 518
    manifest 525
  close of - 126
  decline of - 126
  denizens of the - 366
  good old -'s 122
  have had its - 124
  one fine - 119
  open as - 703
  order of the - 613
  red letter - 642
  see the light of - 446
  - after day
    diuturnal 110
    frequent 136
  - by day
    repeatedly 104
    time 106
    periodic 138
  - after the fair 135
  -s gone by 122
  - of judgment 121
  happy as the - is long
    827, 836
  - and night
    frequent 136
  labour - and night 686
  -s numbered
    transient 111
    death 360
  - one's own 731
  - of rest 686
  - star 423
  - after to-morrow 121
  - before yesterday 122
  -s of week 138
  all in -'s work 625
daybed 215
daybook *record* 551
  accounts 811

daybreak
  morning 125
  dim 422
day-dream
  fancy 515
  hope 858
day-labourer 690
daylight 125, 420
  see - *intelligible* 518
  - saving 114
daymare 859
daze 420
dazed 376
dazzle
  light 420
  blind 422, 443
  put out 458
  astonish 870
  awe 928
dazzling [*see* dazzle]
  beautiful 845
de: - die in diem
  time 106
  periodic 138
  - facto 1
  - fond en comble 52
  - novo 104
  - omnibus rebus 81
  - profundis 821
deacon 996
deaconry 995
dead *complete* 52
  inert 172
  lifeless 360
  insensible 376
  colourless 429
  - against
    contrary 14
    oppose 708
  more - than alive 688
  - asleep 683
  - beat
    powerless 158
    certainty 474
  - colour 556
  - cut 893
  - drunk 959
  - failure 732
  - flat 213
  - heat 27
  - languages 560
  - letter
    impotent 158
    unmeaning 517
    useless 645
    laxity 738
    exempt 927

  illegal 964
  - level 16
  - lift *exertion* 686
  difficulty 704, 706
  - lock *cease* 142
  stoppage 265
  - march 363, 415
  - of night
    midnight 126
    dark 421
  - reckoning
    numeration 85
    measurement 466
  - secret 533
  - set against 708
  - set at
    attack 716
  - shot 700
  - silence 403
  - sound 408a
  - stop 142
  - to 823
  - wall
    hindrance 706
    defence 717
  - weight 706
  - water 343
deaden
  weaken 158
  moderate 174
  sound 405
  mute 408a
  benumb 823
dead-house 363
deadlock 142, 704
deadly *killing* 361
  pernicious 649
  unhealthy 657
  - sin 947
  - weapon 727
deads 645
deaf 419
  inattentive 458
  - to advice 606
  - and dumb 581
  turn - ear to
    neglect 460
    unbelief 487
    refuse 764
  - to reason 901a
  - to *insensible* 823
deafen *loud* 404
deafness 419
deal *much* 31
  arrange 60
  bargain 768
  allot 786

– a blow
injure 659
attack 716
punish 972
– board 323
– in 794
– out *scatter* 73
give 784
– with
treat of 595
handle 692
barter 794
dealer 797
dealings *action* 680
have – with
trade 794
friendly 888
dean 128, 694, 996
deanery *office* 995
house 1000
dear
high-priced 814
loved 897
favourite 899
O – ! *lament* 839
– at any price 646
– me *wonder* 870
pay – for whistle 647
dearest foe 936
dearness 814
dearth 640
– of ideas 843
death 360
house of – 363
in at the –
arrive 292
kill 361
persevere 604*a*
pale as –
colourless 429
fear 860
put to – 361, 972
still as – 265
violent – 361
be the – of one
amuse 480
–'s head 837
– in the pot
unhealthy 657
hidden danger 667
deathbed repentance 950
death-blow
end 67
killing 361
failure 732
death-house 752
deathless

perpetual 112
fame 873
deathlike
silent 403
hideous 846
death-song 839
death-struggle 720
death-warrant 971
death-watch 668
débâcle 145
destruction 162
downfall 306
torrent 348
debar *hinder* 706
restrain 751
prohibit 761
debark 292
debase *depress* 308
foul 653
deteriorate 659
degrade 874
debased
lowered 207
dishonoured 940
debate *reason* 476
talk 588
hesitate 605
dispute 720
debatable 475
debauch
spoil 659
intemperance 954
impurity 961
debauchee 962
debenture
security 771
money 800
credit 805
debility 160
debit *debt* 806
accounts 811
debitor 806
débonnaire 836
debouch 293, 295
débris
fragments 51
crumbled 330
useless 645
debt 806
out of – 803
get out of – 807
– of nature 360
debtor 806
– and creditor 811
debunk 529
début *beginning* 66
essay 675

celebration 883
débutant
learner 541
drama 599
decade *ten* 98
period 108
decadence 659
decagon 244
decalescence 382
decalogue 926
decamp
go away 293
run away 623
decant 270
decanter 191
decapitate *kill* 361
punish 972
decay *decrease* 36
decompose 49
shrivel 195
unclean 653
disease 655
spoil 659
adversity 735
natural – 360
– of memory 506
decayed [*see* decay]
old 124
rotten 160
decease 360
deceit
falsehood 544
deception 545
cunning 702
deceived
in error 495
duped 547
deceiver 548
gay – 962
decelerate 275
decennium 108
decent
mediocre 651
pure 960
decentralize 49
deception 545
deceptio visûs 443
deceptive reasoning 477
decession 293
dechristianize 989
decide
turn the scale 153
judge 480
choose 609
decided *great* 31
ended 67
certain 474

resolved 604
take a – step 609
deciduous
transitory 111
falling 306
spoiled 659
decies repetita placebit
829
decimal 84, 98, 99
decimate
subtract 38
tenth 99
few 103
weaken 160
kill 361
play havoc 659
punish 972
decipher 522
decision
judgment 480
resolution 604
intention 620
law case 969
decisive
certain 474
proof 478
commanding 741
take a – step 609
deck *floor* 211
beautify 847
declaim 531, 582
– against 932
declamatory
style 577
speech 582
declaration
affirmation 535
law pleadings 969
– of faith
belief 484
theology 983
– of war 713
declaratory
meaning 516
inform 527
declare
publish 531
declension [*see* decline]
grammar 567
backsliding 988
declensions 5
declination [*see* decline]
deviation 279
measurement 466
rejection 610
decline *decrease* 36
old 124

weaken 160
descent 306
grammar 567
be unwilling 603
reject 610
disease 655
become worse 659
adversity 735
refuse 764
– of day 126
– of life 128
declivity *slope* 217
descent 306
decoction 335, 384
decode 522
decollate 972
décolleté 226
decoloration 429
decomposition 49
deconsecrate 756
decontrol 158
décor 448, 599
decoration
insignia 747
ornament 847
title 877
decorative 556
decorous [*see* decorum]
fashionable 862
proper 924
respectful 928
decorticate 226
decorum
fashion 852
duty 926
purity 960
décousu
discontinuous 70
failure 732
decoy *attract* 288
deceive 545
deceiver 548
entice 615
decrease 36, 195
decree
judgment 480
order 741
law 963, 969
decrement
decrease 36
thing deducted **40a**
contraction 195
decrepit *old* 128
weak 158, 160
disease 655
decayed 659
decrepitate 406

decrescendo 36
decretal 741
decry *underrate* 483
censure 932
detract 934
decumbent 213
decuple 98
decursive 306
decurtation 201
decussation 219
dedecorous
disreputable 874
discourteous 895
dedicate *use* 677
inscribe 873
deduce *deduct* 38
infer 480
deducible
evidence 467
proof 478
deduct *retrench* 38
deprive 789
subtract 813
deduction [*see* deduce]
decrement 40a
reasoning 476
deed *evidence* 467
record 551
act 680
security 771
–s of arms 720
– without a name 947
deem 484
deemster 967
deep *great* 31
profound 208
sea 341
sonorous 404
cunning 702
plough the – 267
– colour 428
– in debt 806
– game 702
– knowledge 490
– mourning 839
– note 408
– potations 959
– reflection 451
– sense 821
– sigh 839
– study 457
in – water 704
deep-dyed
intense 171
black 431
vicious 945
deepen 35

deep-felt 821
deep-laid *plan* 626
deep-mouthed
  resonant 408
  bark 412
  thrilling 821
deep-musing 458
deep-read 490
deep-rooted
  stable 150
  strong 159
  belief 484
  habit 613
  affections 820
deep-sea 208
deep-seated 208, 221
deer 336
  in heart a – 862
deev 980
deface
  destroy form 241
  obliterate 552
  injure 659
  render ugly 846
defalcation
  incomplete 53
  contraction 195
  shortcoming 304
  non-payment 808
defame *shame* 874
  censure 932
  detract 934
defamer 936
defatigation 841
default
  incomplete 53
  shortcoming 304
  neglect 460
  insufficiency 640
  debt 806
  non-payment 808
  in – of 187
  judgment by – 725
defaulter *thief* 792
  non-payer 808
  rogue 949
defeasance 756
defeat
  confute 479
  succeed 731
  failure 732
  – one's hope 509
defeatism 911
defecate 652
defecation 299
defect
  decrement 40a

incomplete 53
imperfect 651
failing 945
defection
  relinquishment 624
  disobedience 742
defective
  incomplete 53
  insufficient 640
  imperfect 651
defence
  plea 462
  resist **717**
  vindication 937
  first line of – 726
defenceless
  impotent 158
  weak 160
  exposed 665
defendant 938
defensible *safe* 664
  excusable 937
defensive alliance 712
defer 133
  – to *assent* 488
  submit 725
  respect 928
deference
  obedience 743
  humility 879
  courtesy 894
  respect 928
defiance **715**, 909
  threat 909
  in – *opposition* 708
  set at – *disobey* 742
  – of danger 861
deficiency [*see* deficient]
  vice 945
deficient
  inferior 34
  incomplete 53
  shortcoming 304
  insufficient 640
  imperfect 651
deficit
  incompleteness 53
  debt 806
defigure 846
defile
  interval 198
  march 266
  dirt 653
  spoil 659
  shame 874
  impure 961
define

specify 79
limit 233
explain 522
name 564
definite [*see* define]
  visible 446
  certain 474
  exact 494
  intelligible 518
  manifest 525
  perspicuous 570
definition
  interpretation 521
definitive *final* 67
  affirmative 535
  decided 604
deflagration 384
deflate 195
deflation
  currency 800
deflect
  curve 245
  deviate 279
deflower
  spoil 659
  violate 961
defluxion
  egress 295
  flowing 348
defœdation 653, 659
deform 241
deformity
  distortion 243
  ugliness 846
  blemish 848
defraud *cheat* 545
  swindle 791
defray 807
deft *suitable* 23
  clever 698
defunct 360, 362
defy 715
  disobey 742
  threaten 909
  – danger 861
dégagé *free* 748
  fashion 852
degenerate 659
deglutition 298
degradation
  deterioration 659
  shame 874
  dishonour 940
degree 26
  term 71
  honour 873
  by –s 26

by slow –s 275
degustation 390
dehiscence 260
dehort
  dissuade 616
  advise 695
dehydrate 340
deification 873, 981
deify
  honour 873
  idolatry 991
deign
  condescend 762
  consent 879
Dei gratiâ 924
Deism
  heterodoxy 984
  irreligion 989
Deity 976
  tutelary – 664
dejection
  excretion 299
  melancholy **837**
déjeúner 298
délabrement 162
delaceration 659
delation 938
delator 527
delay 133
dele 552
delectable
  savoury 394
  agreeable 829
delectation 827
delectus 562
delegate
  transfer 270
  commission 755
  consignee 758
  deputy 759
delenda est Carthago
  destroy 162
  curse 908
delete 162
deleterious
  pernicious 649
  unwholesome 657
deletion 552
deletory
  destructive 162
deliberate
  slow 275
  think 451
  attentive 457
  leisure 685
  advise 695
  cautious 864

deliberately [*see* deliberate]
  late 133
  with premeditation 611
delicacy *weak* 160
  slender 203
  dainty 298
  brittleness 328
  texture 329
  savoury 394
  colour 428
  exact 494
  scruple 603
  ill health 655
  difficult 704
  pleasing 829
  beauty 845
  taste 850
  fastidious 868
  honour 939
  pure 960
  delicate ear 418
délice 377
delicious *taste* 394
  pleasing 829
delicti, corpus –
  guilt 947
  lawsuit 969
delicto, in flagrante – 947
delight
  pleasure 827
  pleasing 829
Delilah 962
delimit 233
delineate
  outline 230
  represent 554
  describe 594
delineator 559
delineavit 556
delinquency 304, 947
delinquent 949
deliquation 335
deliquesce 36
deliquescence 335
deliquium
  paralysis 158
  fatigue 688
delirant reges plectuntur
  Achivi 739
delirium
  raving 503
  passion 825
  – *tremens* 503, 959
delitescence
  invisible 447
  latency 526
  seclusion 893

deliver
  transfer 270
  utter 580, 582
  birth 662
  rescue 672
  liberate 750
  give 784
  relieve 834
  – *as one's act and deed*
   467
  – *the goods* 729
  – *judgment* 480
  – *a speech* 582
deliverance 672
delivery [*see* deliver]
  bring forth 161
  cash on – 807
dell 252
Delphic oracle
  prophetic 513
  equivocal 520
  latent 526
delta 342
delude *error* 495
  deceive 545
deluge *crowd* 72
  water 337
  flood 348
  redundance 641
delusion [*see* delude]
  insane 503
  self – *credulous* 486
delve *dig* 252
  till 371
  – *into inquire* 461
demagogue
  director 694
  malcontent 710
  rebel 742
demagogy 737
demand
  inquire 461
  order 741
  ask 765
  price 812
  claim 924
  in – *require* 630
  saleable 796
  desire 865
demarcation 233
dematerialize 317
demean oneself
  conduct 692
  humble 879
  dishonour 940
demeanour
  aid 448

conduct 692
fashion 852
demency 503
dementia 503
demerit 945
demesne
  abode 189
  property 780
demi- 91
demigod *hero* 861
  angel 948
demigration 266
demijohn 191
demi-jour 422
demi-lune 717
demi-monde
  plebeian 876
  licentious 962
démenti 536
demirep 962
demise *death* 360
  transfer 783
  lease 787
demisemiquaver 413
demission 756
demit 757
demiurge
  deity 979
demivolt 309
demobilize 73
democracy *rule* 737
  commonalty 876
Democrats
  party 712
Democritus 838
demoiselle 129
demolish 479
demon *violent* 173
  bane 663
  devil **980**
  – in human shape 913, 949
  – worship 991
demoniacal
  malevolent 907
  furious 824
  wicked 945
demonology
  demons 980
  sorcery 992
demonstration
  number 85
  proof **478**
  manifest 525
  ostentation 882
  ocular – 441, 446
demonstrative
  manifest 525

indicative 550
vehement 825
demonstrator 524
demoralize
  unnerve 158
  spoil 659
  vicious 945
Demosthenes 582
demotic 590
demulcent
  mild 174
  soothing 662
demur
  disbelieve 485
  dissent 489
  unwilling 603
  hesitate 605
  without – 602
demure
  grave 826
  sad 837
  affected 855
  modest 881
demurrage 132
demurrer 969
den *abode* 189
  study 191, 893
  sty 653
  prison 752
  – of thieves 791
denary 98
denaturalize
  corrupt 659
denaturalized
  abnormal 83
dendriform 242, 367
dendrology 369
denial
  negation 536
  refusal 764
  self – 953
denigrate 431
denization 748
denizen
  inhabitant 188
  freeman 748
  –s of the air 979
  –s of the day 366
Denmark, rotten in the
  state of – 526
denomination
  class 75
  name 564
  sect 712
  religious – 983
denominational
  dissent 489

theological 983
  – education 537
denominator 84
denote
  specify 79
  mean 516
  indicate 550
dénouement
  end 67
  result 154
  disclosure 529
  completion 729
denounce
  curse 908
  disapprove 932
  accuse 938
dense
  crowded 72
  ignorant 493
density **321**
dent 252, 257
dental 561
denticulated 253, 257
dentifrice 652
dentistry 662
denude 226
denuded *loss* 776
  – of
  insufficient 640
denunciation [*see*
  denounce]
deny *dissent* 489
  negative 556
  refuse 764
  – oneself
  avoid 623
  seclude 893
  temperate 953
  ascetic 990
deobstruct 705
deodand 974
deodorize 399
  clean 652
deontology 926
deoppilation 705
deorganization 61
deosculation 902
Deo volente 470, 976
depart 293
  – from
  deviate 15, 279
  relinquish 624
  – this life 360
departed
  non-existent 2
department
  class 75

disuse 678
desultory
disordered 59
fitful 70
multiform 81
irregular in time 139
changeable 149
deviating 279
agitated 315
desume 788
detach 44
detached
irrelated 10
loose 47
detachment
part 51
army 726
detail *special portions* 79
describe 594
allot 786
ornament 847
attention to - 457, 459
in - 51
details
minutiæ 32
unimportant 643
detain 781
detect 480a
detective 527, 664
detention 133, 751, 781
house of - 752
in house of - 938
détenu 754
deter *dissuade* 616
alarm 860
deterge *clean* 652
detergent
remedy 662
deterioration 659
determinate
special 79
exact 474
conclusive 480
intended 620
determine *end* 67
define 79
cause 153
direction 278
satisfy 462
make sure 474
judge 480
discover 480a
resolve 604
determined
resolute 604
determinism 601
deterration 529

detersion 652
detersive 662
detest *dislike* 867
hate 898
detestable 649
dethronement
anarchy 738
abrogation 756
detonate
explode 173
sound 406
detortion *form* 243
meaning 523
détour *curve* 245
circuit 629
detract *subduct* 38
underrate 483
defame 934
slander 938
detraction 934
detractor 936
detrain 292
detriment
evil 619
deterioration 659
detrimental 649
detrition 330
detritus
fragments 51
deposit 270
powder 330
detrude
cast out 297
cut down 308
detruncate 38
deuce *two* 89
devil 978
play the - 825
- is in him 608
deuced *great* 31
painful 830
deus 976
- ex machinâ
aid 707
auxiliary 711
deity 976
sorcerer 994
deuterogamy 903
devastate
destroy 162
havoc 659
develop
increase 35
produce 161
expand 194
evolve 313
development 144, 154

devexity
bending 217
curvature 245
deviate *wary* 20a
change 140
turn 279
diverge 291
circuit 629
- from 15
- from rectitude 940
- from virtue 945
deviation 279
device *motto* 550
expedient 626
artifice 702
devil
seasoned food 392
evil-doer 913
bad man 949
Satan 978
demon 980
fight like -s 722
have a - 503
machinations of the - 619
play the - with
injure 659
malevolent 907
printer's - 591
raise the - 828
- may care
rash 863
indifferent 866
insolent 885
give the - his due
right 922
vindicate 937
fair 939
- in one
headstrong 863
temper 901
- to pay
disorder 59
violence 173
evil 619
failure 732
penalty 974
- take 908
- take the hindmost
run away 623
haste 684
cowardice 862
-'s tattoo 407
devilish *great* 31
bad 649
malevolent 907
devious *curved* 245
deviating 279

circuitous 311
devisable 270
devise *imagine* 515
  plan 626
  bequeath 784
devised by the enemy 546
devisee *possess* 779
  receive 785
deviser 164
devitalize 158
devoid *absent* 187
  empty 640
  not having 777a
devoir *courtesy* 894
  respect 928
devolve 783
  - *on* 926
devote *destine* 601
  employ 677
  consecrate 873
  - *to destruction* 908
  - *the mind to* 457
  - *oneself to* 604
devoted
  habit 613
  ill-fated 735
  obedient 743
  undone 828
  friendship 888
  love 897
devotee
  zealot 682
  aspirant 865
  pious 987
  fanatic 988
devotion [*see* devotee,
  devoted]
  love 897
  piety 987
  worship 990
  self - 942
devour
  destroy 162
  eat 298
  gluttony 957
devoured by
  feeling 821
devouring element 382
devout 987, 990
devoutless 989
devoutly 821
dew 339
  shake as - drops from
  lion's mane 483
dewy eve 126
dexterous 238, 698
dextrality 238

dey 745
dhow 273
diable:
  avoir le - au corps 503
  - à quatre
    disorder 59
    violence 173
    loud 404
    excitement 825
  tirer le - par la queue 804
diablerie 978, 992
diabolic
  bad 649
  malevolent 907
  wicked 945
  Satanic 978
Diacoustics 402
diacritical 550
diadem 747, 847
diaeresis 49
diagnosis 465, 655
diagnostic
  special 79
  experiment 463
  indication 550
  (*intrinsic* 5)
diagonal 217
diagram 554
dial 114
  as the - to the sun
    veracious 543
    faithful 772
dialect 563
dialectic
  argument 476
  language 560
dialogism 586
dialogue 588
diameter 202
diametrically opposite
  contrariety 14
  contraposition 237
diamond
  lozenge 244
  type 591
  goodness 648
  ornament 847
  rough - 703
  - cut diamond
    cunning 702
    retaliation 718
  - jubilee 883
  - wedding 883
Diana *moon* 318
  chaste 960
  goddess 979
diapason 413

diaper 847
diaphanous 425
diaphonics 402
diaphoresis 299
diaphragm 68, 228
diaporesis 475
diarchy 737
diarrhœa 299
diary 114, 551
diastole 194
diatessaron 413
diathermancy 384
diathesis
  nature 5
  state 7
  temperament 820
diatonic 413
diatribe 932
dibble
  perforator 262
  till 371
dibs *money* 800
dicacity 885
dice 156, 621
  on the - 470
dicer 621
  false as -'s oaths 546
dichotomy
  bisect 91
  angle 244
dichroism 440
dichromatic 443
dickens 978
dicker 794
dicky 215, 225
dictaphone 553
dictate
  write 590
  enjoin 615
  advise 695
  authority 737
  command 741
dictator 694, 745
  -'s of society 852
dictatorial
  dogmatic 481
  wilful 600
  insolent 885
dictatorship 737, 739
diction 569
dictionary
  list 86
  words 562
  book 593
dictum
  judgment 480
  maxim 496

dimidiate 91
diminish
  lessen 36
  contract 195
  – the number 103
diminutive 32, 193
diminuendo
  decreasingly 36
  music 415
dimness 422
dimple 252, 257
dimsightedness 443
  unwise 499
din 404
  – in the ear
  repeat 104
  drum 407
  loquacity 584
dine 298
  – with Duke Humphrey 87
ding 408
ding-dong
  repeat 104
  chime 407
dingle 252
dingy *boat* 273
  dark 421, 422
  colourless 429
  black 431
  gray 432
dining-car 272
dining-room 191
dinner 298
  – jacket 225
  – party 892
dint *power* 157
  concavity 252
  blow 276
  by – of
  instrumentality 631
dio, sub – 220, 338
diocesan 996
diocese 181, 995
Diogenes
  recluse 893
  cynic 911
  lantern of –
  inquiry 461
dioptrics 420
diorama *view* 448
  painting 556
diorism 465
dip *slope* 217
  concavity 252
  ladle 270
  direction 278
  insert 300

descent 306
plunge 310
water 337
candle 423
baptize 998
– one's hands into
take 789
– into
glance at 457
inquire 461
learn 539
diphthong 561
diploma
  evidence 467
  commission 755
diplomacy
  artfulness 702
  mediation 724
  negotiation 769
diplomatist
  messenger 534
  expert 700
  consignee 758
dipper 191
dipsomania
  insanity 503
  desire 865
  drunkenness 959
dipsomaniac 504
diptych 86, 551
dire *hateful* 649
  disastrous 735
  grievous 830
  fearful 860
direct
  straight 246
  teach 537
  artless 703
  command 741
  – attention to **457**
  – one's course
  motion 278
  pursuit 622
  – the eyes to 441
direction [*see* direct
  tendency **278**
  indication 550
  management **693**
  precept 697
directly *soon* 132
director
  teacher 540
  theatre 599
  manager **694**
  master 745
  – of the budget 801
directorship 737

directory *list* 86
  council 696
diremption 44
direption 791
dirge
  funeral 363
  song 415
  lament 839
dirigible balloon 273, 726
dirk 727
dirt 653
  throw –
  defame 874
  disrespect 929
  – cheap 815
  like – under one's feet 749
dirty *dim* 222
  opaque 426
  unclean 653
  disreputable 874
  dishonourable 940
  – end of stick 699
  – sky 353
  – weather 359
  do – work
  servile 886
  flatterer 935
diruption 162
disability
  impotence 158
disable 158
  weaken 160
disabuse 527, 529
disaccord 713
disadvantage
  evil 619
  inexpedience 647
  at a – 34
  lie under a – 651
disadvantageous 647, 649
disaffection
  dissent 489
  enmity 889
  hate 898
disaffirm 536
disagreeable 830, 867
disagreement
  difference 15
  incongruity **24**
  dissent 489
  discord 713
disallow 761
disannul 756
disappearance 449
disappointment
  balk **509**
  fail 732

discontent 832
disapprobation 706, **932**
disapprover 936
disarm *disable* 158
  weaken 160
  reconcile 831
  propitiate 914
disarrange 61
disarray
  disorder 59
  undress 226
disaster *evil* 619
  failure 732
  adversity 735
  calamity 830
disastrous *bad* 649
disavow 536
disband
  separate 44
  disperse 73
  liberate 750
disbar
  abrogate 756
  punish 972
disbarment 55
disbelief 485, 487
  religious 989
disbench 756, 972
disbowel 297
disbranch 44
disburden
  facilitate 705
  – one's mine 529
  – oneself of 782
disburse 809
disc 220, 234
discard *eject* 297
  relinquish 624
  disuse 678
  abrogate 756
  refuse 764
  repudiate 773
  surrender 782
  – from one's thoughts 458
discarded 495
disceptation 476
discern *see* 441
  know 490
discernible 446
discernment 498, 868
discerption 44
discharge
  violence 173
  propel 284
  emit 297
  excrete 299
  sound 406

acquit oneself 692
  complete 729
  liberate 750
  abrogate 756
  pay 807
  exempt 927a
  acquit 970
  – a duty 926, 944
  – a function
  business 625
  utility 644
  – itself *egress* 295
  river 348
  – from the memory 506
  – from the mind 458
  – an obligation 772
discind 44
disciple *pupil* 541
  votary 711
  Christian 985
disciplinarian
  master 540
  martinet 739
discipline
  order 58
  teaching 537
  training 673
  restraint 751
  punishment 972
  religious 990
disclaim *deny* 536
  repudiate 756
  abjure 757
  refuse 764
disclosure 480a, **529**
discoid *layer* 204
  frontal 220
  flat 251
discoloration 429
discoloured
  shabby 659
  ugly 846
  blemish 848
discomfit 731
discomfiture 732
discomfort
  physical 378
  mental 828
discommend 932
discommode
  hinder 706
  annoy 830
discommodious 645, 647
discompose
  derange 61
  put out 458
  hinder 706

pain 830
  disconcert 874
  anger 900
discomposure 828
disconcert
  derange 61
  distract 458
  disappoint 509
  hinder 706
  discontent 832
  confuse 879
disconcerted
  hopeless 859
disconformity 83
discongruity 24
disconnected
  style 575
disconnection
  irrelation 19
  disjunction 44
  discontinuity 70
disconsolate 837
discontent **832**
discontinuance
  cessation 142
  relinquishment 624
discontinuity **70**
discord
  difference 15
  disagreement 24
  of sound **414**
  of colour 428
  dissension **713**
discount
  decrease 36
  decrement 40a
  money **813**
  at a –
  disrepute 874
  disapproved 932
discountenance
  disfavour 706
  refuse 764
discourage
  dissuade 616
  sadden 837
  frighten 860
discourse
  teach 537
  speech 582
  talk 588
  dissert 595
  sermon 998
discourtesy **895**
discous 202
discover
  perceive 441

solve 462
find 480*a*
disclose 529
– itself
be seen 446
discovery 480*a*
discredit
disbelief 485
dishonour 874
discreditable
vicious 945
discreet *careful* 459
cautious 864
discrepancy 15
discrepant 24, 713
discrete
separate 44, 70
single 87
discretion *will* 600
choice 609
skill 698
caution 864
surrender at – 725
use – 609
years of – 131
discrétion, à – 600
discrimination
difference 15
nice perception **465**
wisdom 498
taste 850
fastidiousness 868
disculpate 937
discumbency 213
discursion 266
discursive
moving 264
migratory 266
wandering 279
argumentative 476
diffuse style 573
conversable 588
disserting 595
discus 840
discuss *eat* 298
reflect 451
inquire 461
reason 476
dissert 595
discussion [*see* discuss]
open to – 475
under – 461
disdain
indifference 866
fastidious 868
pride 878
arrogance 885

contempt 930
disease 655
occupational – 655
–d *mind* 503
disembark 292
disembarrass 705
disembody
decompose 49
disperse 73
spiritualize 317
disembogue
emit 295
eject 297
flow out 348
disembowel 297, 301
disembroil 60
disenable 158
disenchant
discover 480*a*
dissuade 616
displease 830
disencumber 705
disendow 756
disengage
detach 44
facilitate 705
liberate 750
disengaged
to let 763
disentangle
separate 44
arrange 60
unroll 313
decipher 522
facilitate 705
liberate 750
disenthral 750
disenthrone 756
disentitle 925
disespouse 905
disestablish
displace 185
abrogate 756
disesteem 929, 932
disfavour
oppose 708
hate 898
disrespect 929
view with – 932
disfigure
deface 241
injure 659
deform 846
blemish 848
disfranchise 925
disgorge *emit* 297
flow out 348

restore 790
pay 807
disgrace
shame 874
dishonour 940
sense of – 879
disgraceful
vice 945
disgruntle 509
disguise
unlikeness 18
conceal 528
mask 530
falsify 544
untruth 546
disguised in drink 959
disgust *taste* 395
offensive 830
weary 841
dislike 867
hatred 898
– of life 837
dish *destroy* 162
plate 191
food 298
– of tea 892
dishabille
undress 225
unprepared 674
dishearten
dissuade 616
pain 830
discontent 832
deject 837
dished 252, 732
disherison 789
dishevel
loose 47
untidy 59
disorder 61
disperse 73
intermix 219
dishonest *false* 544
base 940
dishonour
disrepute 874
disrespect 929
baseness 940
– bills 808
dish-water 653
disillusion 509
disincline
dissuade 616
dislike 867
disinclined 603
disinfect
purify 652

disinfectant

restore 660
disinfectant 662
disingenuous
  false 544
  dishonourable 940
disinherit
  relinguish 782
  transfer 783
  deprive 789
disintegrate
  separate 44
  decompose 49
  pulverize 330
disinter *exhume* 363
  discover 480a
disinterested 942
disjecta membra
  separate 44
  disorder 59
  dispersed 73
  – poetæ 597
disjoin 44
disjointed
  disorder 59
  powerless 158
  style 575
disjunction 44
disjunctive 70
diskindness 907
dislike 867
  reluctance 603
  hate 898
dislocate
  separate 44
  put out of joint 61
dislocated
  disorder 59
dislodge
  displace 185
  eject 297
disloyal 940
dismal
  depressing 830
  dejected 837
dismantle
  destroy 162
  divest 226
  render useless 645
  injure 659
  disuse 678
dismask 529
dismast
  render useless 645
  injure 659
  disuse 678
dismay 860
dismember

separate 44
disperse 73
dismiss
  send away 289
  discharge 297
  discard 678
  liberate 750
  abrogate 756
  relinquish 782
  punish 972
  – from the mind 452, 458
dismount
  arrive 292
  descend 306
  render useless 645
disnest 185
disobedience 742
  non-observance 773
disoblige 907
disorder
  confusion 59
  derange 61
  turbulent 173
  disease 655
  –ed intellect 503
disorderly
  unprincipled 945
disorganize
  derange 61
  destroy 162
  spoil 659
disorganized 59
disown 536
dispair 44
disparage
  underrate 483
  disrespect 929
  dispraise 932
  detract 934
disparity
  different 15
  dissimilar 18
  disagreeing 24
  unequal 28
  isolated 44
dispart 44
dispassionate 826
  – opinion 484
dispatch [*see* despatch]
dispel *scatter* 73
  destroy 162
  displace 185
  repel 289
dispensable
  useless 645
dispensary 662
dispensation [*see* dispense]

command 741
licence 760
relinquishment 782
exemption 927a
–s of Providence 976
dispense
  disperse 73
  give 784
  apportion 786
  retail 796
  – with
  disuse 678
  permit 760
  exempt 927a
  cannot be –d with 630
dispeople
  eject 297
  expatriate 893
disperse
  separate 44
  scatter 73
  diverge 291
  waste 638
dispersion 73
  – of light 420
  chromatic – 428
dispirit
  discourage 616
  sadden 837
displacement
  derange 61
  remove 185
  transfer 270
displacency
  dislike 867
  incivility 895
  disapprobation 932
displant 185
display *appear* 448
  show 525
  parade 882
displease 830
displeasure 828
  anger 900
displosion 173
displume 789
disport 840
disposal [*see* dispose]
  at one's – 763, 777
dispose
  arrange 60
  tend 176
  induce 615
  – of *use* 677
  complete 729
  relinquish 782
  give 784

sell 796
disposed 620
disposition
  nature 5
  order 58
  arrangement 60
  inclination 602
  mind 820
dispossess
  transfer 783
  take away 789
  - *oneself of* 782
dispraise 932
dispread 73
disprize 483
disproof
  counter-evidence 468
  confutation 479
disproportion
  irrelation 10
  disagreement 24
disprove 479
disputable 475, 485
disputant 710, 726
disputatious 901
dispute
  discuss 476
  doubt 485
  deny 536
  discord 713
  in - 461
disqualification
  incapacitate 158
  useless 645
  unprepared 674
  unskilful 699
  disentitle 925
disquiet
  changeable 149
  agitation 315
  excitement 825
  uneasiness 828
  give pain 830
disquietude
  apprehension 860
disquisition 539, 595
disregard
  overlook 458
  neglect 460
  make light of 483
  insensible to 823, 826
  disrespect **929**
  contempt 930
  - *of time* 115
disrelish 867, 898
disreputable 874
  vicious 945

disrepute **874, 929**
disrespect **929**
  despise 930
disrobe 226
disruption
  disjunction 44
  destruction 162
  discord 713
dissatisfaction
  disappointment 509
  sorrow 828
  discontent 832
dissect
  anatomize 44, 49
  investigate 461
dissemblance 18
dissemble 544
dissembler 548
disseminate
  scatter 73
  pervade 186
  publish 531
  teach 537
dissension 713
  sow - 898
dissent
  disagree **489**
  refuse 764
  heterodoxy 984
dissentient 15
dissentious 24
dissertation **595**
disservice
  disadvantage 619
  useless 645
disserviceable 649
dissever 44
dissidence
  disagreement 24
  dissent 489
  discord 713
  discontent 832
  heterodoxy 984
dissilience 173
dissimilarity **18**
dissimulate 544
dissipate *scatter* 73
  destroy 162
  pleasure 377
  prodigality 818
  amusement 840
  intemperance 954
  dissolute 961
dissocial 893
dissociate 44
dissociation
  irrelation 10

separation 44
dissolute 961
  profligate 945
  intemperate 954
dissolution [*see* dissolve]
  decomposition 49
  destruction 162
  death 360
dissolve *vanish* 2, 4
  liquefy 335
  disappear 449
  abrogate 756
dissolving views 448, 449
dissonance
  disagreement 24
  unmusical 414
  discord 713
dissuasion **616**
dissyllable 561
distaff
  - *side* 374
distain *dirty* 653
  ugly 846
distal 196
distance **196**
  overtake 282
  go beyond 303
  defeat 731
  angular - 244
  keep at a -
    discourtesy 895
  keep one's -
    avoid 623
    modest 881
    respect 928
  teach one his - 879
  - *of time*
    long time 110
    past 122
distaste 867
distasteful 830
distemper 299, 428
  colour 428
  painting 556
  disease 655
distend 194
distended 192
distich 89, 597
distil *come out* 295
  extract 301
  evaporate 336
  drop 348
distinct
  disjoined 44
  audible 402
  visible 446
  intelligible 518

manifest 525
express 535
articulate 580
distinction
difference 15
discrimination 465
style 578
fame 873
rank 875
– without a difference 27
distinctive 15
– feature 79
distinctness 15
distingué 852, 873
distinguish
perceive 441
discriminate 465
– by the name of 564
distinguishable 15
distinguished
superior 33
repute 873
**Distinguished Service
Cross** 733
distortion
obliquity 217
twist **243**
of vision 443
misinterpret 523
falsehood 544
ugly 846
distract 458
distracted
confused 475
insane 503
excited 824
distraction
passion 825
love to – 897
distrain *take* 789
appraise 812
attach 969
distrait 458
distraught 824
distress
distraint 789
poverty 804
affliction 828
cause pain 830
signal of – 669
distressingly
excessively 31
distribute
arrange 60
disperse 44, 73
allot 786
district 181

– council 696
distrust
disbelief 485
fear 860
distrustful 487
disturb
derange 61
change 140
agitate 315
excite 824
distress 828, 830
disturbance 59
disunion
discord 24
separation 44
disorder 59
discord 713
disuse
desuetude 614
relinquish 624
unemploy **678**
disused
old 124
disvalue 932
ditch
inclosure 232
trench 259
water 343
conduit 350
defence 717
to the last – 606
ditch-water 653
ditheism 984
dither 315
dithyramb
music 415
poetry 597
dithyrambic 503
ditto 13, 104
say – to 488
ditty 415
– box 191
diurnal 138
diuturnity 110
diva 416
divagate 279, 629
divan *sofa* 215
council 696
throne 747
tribunal 966
divaricate *differ* 15
bifurcate 91
diverge 291
dive *swim* 267
fly 267
plunge 306, 310
– *into inquire* 461

divellicate 44
diver 208
divergence
difference 15
variation 20a
disagreement 24
deviation 279
separation **291**
divers *different* 15
multiform 81
many 102
– coloured 440
diverse 15
diversify
very 20a
change 140
diversion
change 140
deviation 279
pleasure 377
amusement 840
diversity
difference 15
irregular 16a
dissimilar 18
multiform 81
– of opinion 489
divert *turn* 279
deceive 545
amuse 840
– the mind 452, 458
divertissement
diversion 377
drama 599
amusement 840
Dives 803
divest *denude* 226
take 789
– oneself of
abrogate 756
relinquish 782
divestment 226
divide *differ* 15
separate 44
part 51
arrange 60
arithmetic 85
bisect 91
vote 609
apportion 786
dividend *part* 51
number 84
portion 786
divina particula auræ 450
divination
prediction 511
sorcery 992

divine *predict* 511
  guess 514
  perfect 650
  of God 976, 983, 983a
  clergyman 996
divine afflatus 515
  - right
  authority 737
  due 924
  - service 990
diving 840
diving-bell 208
divining-rod 550, 993
Divinity *God* 976
  theology 983
divisible
  number 84
division [*see* divide]
  part 51
  class 75
  arithmetic 85
  discord 713
  military 726
divisor 84
divorce
  separation 44
  relinquish 782
  matrimonial **905**
Divorce Court 966
divulge 529
divulsion 44
divvy 786
dixi 535
dizen 847
dizzard 501
dizzy
  dimsighted 443
  confused 458
  vertigo 503
  - height 206
  - round 312
djerrid 727
djinn 980
do *fare* 7
  suit 23
  produce 161
  cheat 545
  act 680
  complete 729
  succeed 731
  I beg 765
  all one can - 686
  plenty to - 682
  thing to - 625
  - away with
  destroy 162
  eject 297

abrogate 756
- battle 722
- one's bidding 743
- business 625
- to death 361
- as done by 906, 942
- for *destroy* 162
kill 361
conquer 731
serve 746
punish 972
- good 906
- harm 907
- honour 873
- into
translate 522
- justice to 595
- like 19
- little 683
- no harm 648
- nothing 681
- nothing but 136
- one's office 772
- as others do 82
- over 223
- as one pleases 748
- a service
useful 644
aid 707
- up 660
have to - with 680, 692
- without 678
- the work 686
- wrong 923
docere, pisces natare –
  641
docile *domesticated* 370
  learning 539
  willing 602
docimastic 463
dock *diminish* 36
  cut off 38
  port 189
  shorten 201
  edge 231
  store 636
  tribunal 966
docked
  incomplete 53
docker 690
docket
  list 86
  evidence 467
  note 550
  record 551
  security 771
dockyard 691

doctor
  learned man 492
  restore 660
  remedy 662
  after death the - 135
  - accounts 811
  when -s disagree 475
doctrinaire
  positive 474
  pedant 492
  affectation 855
  blusterer 887
doctrinal 537
doctrinarian 514
doctrine *tenet* 484
  knowledge 490
document 551
documentary evidence 467
dodder 315
doddering 128
dodecahedron 244
dodge *change* 140
  shift 264
  deviate 279
  oscillate 314
  pursue 461
  avoid 623
  stratagem 702
dodger, artful - 792
dodo 366
  extinct as the - 122
doe *swift* 274
  deer 366
  female 374
doer
  originator 164
  agent 690
doff 226
  - the cap 894
dog *follow* 281
  animal 366
  male 373
  pursue 622
  wretch 949
  cast to the -s
  destroy 162
  reject 610
  disuse 678
  abrogate 756
  relinquish 782
  fire - 386
  go to the -s
  destruction 162
  fail 732
  adversity 735
  poverty 804
  sea - 269

watch –
  safety 664
  warning 668
  keeper 753
  hair of – that bit you 959
  let sleeping –s lie 141
  – in manger 706, 943
  –tired 686
  –s of war 722
dog-cart 272
dog-cheap 815
dog-days 382
doge 745
dogged
  obstinate 606
  valour 861
  sullen 901a
dogger 273
doggerel
  verse 597
  ridiculous 851, 853
dog-hole 189
dog-Latin 563
dogma *tenet* 484
  theology 983
dogmatic
  certain 474
  positive 481
  assertion 535
  obstinate 606
dogmatist 887
dog robber 746
dog's ear 258
dog-sick 867
dog-star 423
dog-trot 275
dog-weary 688
doily 852
doing
 up and – 682
 what one is – 625
doings
  events 151
  actions 680
  conduct 692
doit *trifle* 643
  coin 800
dolce far niente 681
doldrums
  dejection 837
  sulks 901a
dole
  small quantity 32
  scant 640
  give 784
  allot 786
  parsimony 819

  grief 828
doleful 837
  – *dumps* 901a
doll *small* 193
  image 554
dollar 800
dolman 225
dolmen 363, 551
**dolorem, infandum
  renovare** – 833
dolorous 830
dolour
  physical 378
  moral 828
dolphin 341
dolt 501
doltish 499
domain
  class 75
  region 181
  property 780
Domdaniel 982
dome *high* 206
  roof 223
  curvature 245
  convex 250
Domesday book
  list 86
  record 551
domesman 967
domestic
  inhabitant 188
  home 189
  interior 221
  servant 746
  secluded 893
  – *animals* 366
domesticate
  locate 184
  acclimatize 613
  – *animals* 370
domicile 189
domiciled 186
domiciliary 188
  – *visit* 461
dominant 175
  note in music 413
domination 737
dominical 998
domineer
  tyrannize 739
  insolence 885
Domini, anno – 106
Dominican 996
Dominie 540
dominion 181, 737
domino *dress* 225

  mask 530
  game 840
domn 745
don *put on* 225
  scholar 492
  teacher 540
  noble 875
donation 784
done *finished* 729
 work – 729
 – for *spoilt* 659
  failure 732
 – up
  impotent 158
  tired 688
 have – with
  cease 142
  relinquish 624
  disuse 678
donee 785
donjon 717, 752
Don Juan 897
donkey *ass* 271
  fool 501
 talk a –'s hind leg off 584
donna 374
Donnybrook Fair
  disorder 59
  discord 713
donor 784
donzel 746
doodle 501
doom *end* 67
  fate 152
  destruction 162
  death 360
  judgment 480
  necessity 601
  sentence 971
 – sealed
  death 360
  adversity 735
doomed 735, 828
doomsday
  end 67
  future 121
 till – 112
door *entrance* 66
  cover 223
  brink 231
  barrier 232
  opening 260
  passage 627
 at one's – 197
 beg from door to – 765
 bolt the – 666
 close the – upon 751

death's – 360
keep within –s 265
lie at one's – 926
lock the – 666
open a – to
  liable 177
open the – to
  receive 296
  facilitate 705
  permit 760
show the – to
  eject 297
  discourtesy 895
  – mat 652
doorkeeper 263
doorway 260
dope 376, 545, 663
doquet
  security 771
Dorado, El – 803
Doric mode 413
dormant
  inert 172
  latent 526
  asleep 683
dormer 260
dormeuse 272
dormir debout, conte à –
  843
dormitive 841
dormitory 191
dormouse 683
dorp 189
dorsal 235
dorser 191
dorsum 235, 250
dory 273
dose *quantity* 25
  part 51
  medicine 662
  apportion 786
dosser 191
dossier *bundle* 72
  record 551
dossil 223, 263
dot *small* 32
  place 182
  little 193
  variegate 440
  mark 550
  dowry 780
  on the – 113
dotage 128, 499
dotard 130, 501
dotation 784
dote *drivel* 499, 503
  – upon 897

dottle 40, 645
douanier 965
double
  similar 17
  increase 35
  duplex 90
  substitute 147
  fold 258
  turn 283
  finesse 702
  march at the – 274
  see –
  dim sight 443
  drunk 959
  – acrostic
  letters 561
  wit 842
  – dutch 518
  – entry 811
  – the fist 909
  – march 684
  – meaning 520
  – a point 311
  in – quick time 274
  – reef topsails 664
  – sure 474
  work – tides 686
  – up
  render powerless 158
double bar 747
double-bass 417
doublecross 545
double-dealing
  lie 544
  cunning 940
double-distilled 171
double-dyed 428
double-eagle 800
double-edged 90, 171
double entendre
  ambiguity 520
  impure 961
double-faced
  lie 544
  cunning 702, 940
double-headed 90
double-minded 605
double-shotted 171
doublet 225
double-tongued
  lie 544
  cunning 702, 940
doubt
  uncertain 475
  disbelieve **485**
  sceptic 989
doubtful 475

more than – 473
  – meaning
  unintelligible 519
doubtless
  certain 474
  belief 484
  assent 488
douceur 784, 973
douche 337
dough 324, 354, 800
doughty 861
dour 739
douse
  immerse 310
  splash 337
  blow 972
Dove
  Holy Ghost 976
dove
  innocent 946
  roar like sucking – 174
dovecote 189
dovetail
  agree 23
  join 43
  intersect 219
  intervene 228
  angle 244
  insert 300
dowager 374, 905
dowdy 653, 851
dower 780, 803, 810
dowerless 804
down
  below 207
  light 320
  bear – upon 716
  bed of –
  pleasure 377
  repose 687
  come – 306
  get – 306
  go –
  sink 306
  calm 826
  keep – 36
  money – 807
  take –
  lower 308
  rebuff 874
  humble 879
  – on one's marrow-bones
  886
  – in the mouth 837
  – and out 874
  – in price 815
  go – like a stone 310

be – upon
  attack 716
  severe 739
downcast 306, 837
– eyes 879
downfall
  destruction 162
  fall 306
  failure 732
  misfortune 735
downhill 217, 306
go –
  adversity 735
downpour 348
downright
  absolute 31
  manifest 525
  sincere 703
downs 206, 344
down-trodden
  submission 725
  vanquished 732
  subject 749
  dejected 837
  disrepute 874
  contempt 930
downwards 306
downy
  smooth 255
  plumose 256
  soft 324
dowry 780, 784
dowse 276
dowser 994
doxology 990
doxy 897
doyer 128
doyley 652
doze 683
dozen 98
drab *colour* 432
  slut 653
  hussy 962
drabble 653
drachm 319
Draco 694, 739
draff 653
draft [*see also* draught]
  multitude 102
  drawing 554, 556
  write 590
  abstract 596
  plan 626
  cheque 800
  credit 805
– off *displace* 185
  transfer 270

draft-horse 271
drag *carriage* 272
  crawl 275
  traction 285
  impediment 706
put on the – 275
– a chain
  tedious 109, 110
  exertion 686
  subjection 749
– into
  implicate 54
  compel 744
– through mire
  disrepute 874
  disrespect 929
– on *tedious* 110
– into open day 531
– towards
  attract 288
– slow length
  long 200
  weary 841
draggle 285, 653
– tail 59
drag-net
  all sorts 78
dragoman 524
dragon *monster* 83
  violent 173
  animal 366
  irascible 901
dragonnade
  attack 716
  punish 972
dragoon
  soldier 726
  compel 744
  insolent 885
  worry 907
drain
  flow out 295
  empty 297
  dry 340
  conduit 350
  waste 638
  clean 652
  unclean 653
  exhaust 789
  dissipate 818
– the cup
  drink 298
  drunken 959
– the cup of misery 828
– into 348
– pipe 249
– of resources 640

drake *male* 373
fire – 423
dram *drink* 298
  pungent 392
  stimulus 615
– drinking 959
drama 599
dramatic 599
  ostentation 882
– author 599
– critic 599
– poetry 597
dramatis personæ
  mankind 372
  play 599
  agents 690
  party 712
drapery 225, 847
drast 645
drastic 171
draught [*see also* draft]
  depth 208
  traction 285
  drink 298
  stream of air 349
  delineation 554, 556
  plan 626
  physic 662
  troops 726
– off 73
draughts
  game 840
draughtsman
  artist 559
draw *equality* 27
  compose 54
  pull 285
  delineate 554, 556
– aside 279
– off the attention 458
– back
  deduction 40a
  regret 283
  avoid 623
– breath
  refresh 689
  feeling 821
  relief 834
– a cheque 800
– a curtain 424
– down 153
– forth 677
– from 810
– on futurity 132
– in one's horns
  tergiversation 607
  humility 879

- in 195
- an inference 480
- the line 465
- lots 621
- near *time* 121
  approach 286
- off *eject* 297
  hinder 706
  take 789
- on *time* 121
  event 151
  induce 615
- out
  protract 110
  late 133
  prolong 200
  extract 301
  discover 480a
  exhibit 525
  diffuse style 573
- over *induce* 615
- a parallel 9
- the pen through 552
- a picture 594
- profit 775
- and quarter 972
- the sword
  attack 716
  war 722
- the teeth of 158
- together
  assemble 72
  co-operate 709
- towards 288
- up *order* 58
  stop 265
  write 590
- up a statement 594
- upon *money* 800
- the veil 528

drawback *evil* 619
  imperfection 651
  hindrance 706
  discount 813
drawbar 45
drawbridge
  way 627
  escape 671
  raise the - 666
drawcansir 887
drawee 800
drawer
  receptacle 191
  artist 559
- of water 690
drawers
  dress 225

drawhead 45
drawing
  delineation 554, 556
  prize 810
drawing-room
  assembly 72
  room 191
  fashion 852
drawl *prolong* 200
  creep 275
  in speech 583
  sluggish 683
drawn *equated* 27
- battle
- irresistibly 601
  pacification 723
  incomplete 730
dray 272
- horse 271
drayman 268
dread 860
dreadful *great* 31
  bad 649
  dire 830
  depressing 837
  fearful 860
dreadless 861
dreadnought
  warship 726
dream
  unsubstantial 4
  error 495
  fancy 515
  sleep 683
  golden - 858
- of *think* 451
  intend 620
- on other things 458
dreamer
  madman 504
  imaginative 515
dreamy
  unsubstantial 4
  inattentive 458
  sleepy 683
dreary
  monotonous 16
  solitary 87
  melancholy 830, 837
dredge *collect* 72
  extract 301
  raise 307
dregs
  remainder 40
  refuse 645
  dirt 653
- of the people 876

- of vice 945
drench *drink* 298
  water 337
  redundance 641
- with physic 662
drencher 248
drenching rain 348
dress
  uniformity 16
  agree 23
  equalize 27
  clothes 225
  prepare 673
  ornament 847
  ostentation 882
  full - 852
- circle 599
- the ground 371
- up *falsehood* 544
  represent 554
- wounds 662
- to advantage 847
dress-coat 225
dresser
  sideboard 215
  surgeon 662
dressing 932, 972
- room 191, 599
dressing-gown 225
dressmaker 225
dribble 295, 348
driblet 25, 32
drift
  accumulate 72
  distance 196
  motion 264
  flying 267
  float 267
  transfer 270
  direction 278
  deviation 279
  approach 286
  wind 349
  meaning 516
  intention 620
  snow - 383
drifter 273
drifting 605
driftless 621
drill *fabric* 219
  bore 260
  auger 262
  teach 537
  prepare 673
- hall 191
drink
  swallow 296

liquor 298
tipple 959
– one's fill
enough 639
– in *imbibe* 296, 298
– in learning 539
– to *celebrate* 883
courtesy 894
drinking-bout 954
drink-money 784
drip 295, 348
dripping *wet* 330
fat 356
drive *airing* 266
impel 276
propel 284
break in 370
urge 615
haste 684
direct 693
attack 716
compel 744
– at *mean* 516
intend 620
– a bargain
barter 794
parsimony 819
– care away 836
– a coach and six through 83
– into a corner
difficult 704
hinder 706
defeat 731
subjection 749
– to despair 859
– matters to an extremity 604
– from *repel* 289
– one hard 716
– home 729
– in 300
– to the last 133
– out 297
– trade
business 625
barter 794
drivel *slobber* 297
imbecile 499
mad 503
rubbish 517
driveller 501, 584
driver 268
director 694
driving rain 348
drizzle 348
droil 683

droit du plus fort 744
drôle *cards* 840
drole 949
– de corps 844
drollery
amusement 840
wit 842
ridiculous 853
dromedary 271
drone *slow* 275
sound 407, 412, 413
inactive 683
drool 297
droop
weak 160
hang 214
sink 306
disease 655
decline 659
flag 688
sorrow 828
dejection 837
drop *small quantity* 32
discontinue 142
powerless 158
bring forth 161
spherule 249
emerge 295
fall 306
trickle 348
relinquish 624
discard 782
gallows 975
let – 308
ready to –
fatigue 688
– asleep 683
– astern 283
– from the couds 508
– dead 360
– by drop
by degrees 26
in parts 51
– in the bucket 32
– in upon 674
– into a good thing 734
– into the grave 360
– a hint 527
– all idea of 624
– in *arrive* 292
immerse 300
sociality 892
– the mask 529
– off *decrease* 36
die 360
sleep 683
–in the ocean

trifling 643
– the subject 458
– too much 959
dropping fire 70
drop-scene 599
dropsical 194, 641
droshki 272
dross
remainder 40
slag 384
trash 643, 645
dirt 653
drought
dryness 340
insufficiency 640
drouth *desire* 865
drove
assemblage 72
multitude 102
drover 370
drown
affusion 337
kill 361
ruin 731, 732
– care 840
– the voice 581
drowsy *slow* 275
sleepy 683
weary 841
drub
defeat 731, 732
punish 972
drudge *labour* 686
worker 682, 690
drug
render insensible 376
superfluity 641
trash 643
remedy 662
bane 663
– in the market 815
drugget
cover 223
clean 652
preserve 670
druggist 662
druid 996
drum
repeat 104
cylinder 249
sound 407
music 417
party 892
beat of –
signal 550
alarm 669
war 722

dynamitard 863
dynamite 727
dynamo 153
dynasty 737
dysentery 299
dyspepsia 655
dysphony 581

E

each 79
 – to each 786
 – other 12
 – in his turn 148
eager
 willing 602
 active 682
 ardent 821
 desirous 865
 – expectation 507
eagle
 standard 550
 money 800
 – boat 726
 – eye *sight* 441
 intelligence 498
 – winged *swift* 274
 insignia 747
eagre 348
ean 161
ear 418
 corn 154
 come to one's –s 527
 din in the –
 loud 404
 drum 407
 all – 418
 have the – of
 belief 484
 friendship 888
 lend an –
 hear 418
 attend 457
 meet the – 418
 nice – 418
 no – 419
 offend the – 410
 pick up the –s
 attention 457
 expectation 507
 put about one's –s 308
 quick – 418
 reach one's –s 527
 ring in the – 408
 set by the –s
 discord 713

 hate 898
 resentment 900
 split the –s 404
 together by the –s
 discord 713
 contention 720
 up to one's –s
 redundance 641
 active 680, 682
 willing – 602
 word in the – 586
 – for music 416, 418
 in at one – out at the other
 inattention 458
 forget 506
 not for –s polite 961
 make the –s tingle
 anger 900
 – ache 378
ear-drum 418
earl 875
earless 419
earliness 132
early 132
 get up – 682
earmark 550
earn 775
earnest *willing* 602
 determined 604
 emphatic 642
 pledge 771
 pay in advance 809
 eager 821
 in –
 affirmation 535
 veracious 543
 strenuous 682
ear-piercing 410
ear-ring 847
ear-shot 197
 out of – 405
ear-splitting 404
earth *ground* 211
 world 318
 land 342
 corpse 362
 what on –
 inquiry 461
 wonder 870
 – closet 653
earthenware
 baked 384
 sculpture 557
earthling 372
earthly 318
 end of one's – career 360
 of no – use 645

earthly-minded 943, 989
earthquake 146, 173
earthwork 717
earwig *flatter* 933, 935
ear-witness 467
ease *bodily* 377
 style 578
 leisure 685
 facility 705
 mental 827
 content 831
 at one's –
 prosperous 734
 mind at –
 cheerful 836
 set at – *relief* 834
 take one's – 687
 – off *deviate* 297
 – one of *take* 789
easel *support* 215
 painting 556
 – *picture* 556
easement
 porperty 780
 relief 834
easily [*see* easy]
 let one down – 918
 – accomplished 705
 – deceived 486
 – persuaded 602
East 236, 278
Easter *period* 138
 rite 998
 – Monday
 holiday 840
 – offering
 gift 784
 – sepulchre 1000
easy *gentle* 275
 style 578
 facile 705
 make oneself – about 484
 take it –
 inactive 683
 inexcitable 826
 – ascent 217
 – of belief 472
 – chair
 support 215
 repose 687
 – circumstances 803
 – going
 willing 602
 irresolute 605
 lenient 740
 inexcitable 826
 contented 831

indifferent 866
– sail
moderate 174
slow 275
– temper 894
– terms 705
– to understand 518
– virtue 961
eat *food* 298
tolerate 826
– dirt 725, 879
– one's fill
enough 639
gorge 957
– heartily 298
– one's words 879
– out of house and home
take 789
prodigal 818
gluttony 957
– of the same trencher 892
– one's words 607
eatables 298
eaten up with 820
eau, battre l' – 645
faire venir l' – à la bouche
865
mettre de l' – dans son vin
174
eaves 250
eavesdropper 455, 527
eavesdropping 418, 532
ébauche 626
ebb *decrease* 36
contract 195
regress 283
recede 287
waste 638
spoil 659
low – 36
low 207
depression 308
insufficient 640
– and flow 314
– of life 360
ebb-tide *low* 207
dry 340
ebony 431
ebriety 959
ebullient
violent 173
hot 382
excited 824
ebullition
energy 171
violence 173
agitation 315

heating 384
excitation 825
anger 900
écarté 840
ecce
– iterum Crispinus 104
– signum 550
eccentric 220
irregular 83
foolish 499
crazed 503, 504
capricious 608
ecchymosis 299
ecclesiastic
church 995
clergy 996
ecclesiastical
canonical 985
– court 966
– law 963
ecclesiolatry 991
écervelé 458
échafaudage 673
échappée 840
échapper belle 671
échelon 279
echo *imitate* 19
copy 21
repeat 104
reflection 277
resonance 408
answer 462
assent 488
applaud to the – 931
awake -es 404
éclaircissement 522
éclat 873
eclectic 609
eclipse *surpass* 33
disappearance 449
hide 528
outshine 873, 874
partial – *dim* 422
total – *dark* 421
under an –
invisible 447
out of repute 874
ecliptic 318
eclogue 597
economic pressure 751
economy
order 58
conduct 692
frugality **817**
animal – 359
écorcher les oreilles 410
ecphorize 615

écru 433
ecstasis 683
ecstasy
frenzy 515
transport 821
rapture 827
ecstatic 829
ecstatica 994
ectoplasm 992
ectype 21
ecumenical 78
edacity 957
Edda 986
eddy
whirlpool 348
current 312
danger 667
Eden 827
edge *energy* 171
height 206
brink **231**
sidle 279
advantage 731
cutting – 253
on – 256, 507
take the – off 174
– of hunger 865
– in 228
– one's way 282
edge-tools 253
play with – 863
edgewise 217
edging
obliquity 217
border 231
ornament 847
edible 298
edict 741
edification
building 161
teaching 537
learning 539
piety 987
edifice 161
edifying *good* 648
edile 965
edit
publication 531
condense 596
revise 658
edition, new – 658
editor 593
educate 537
educated 490
self – 490
education
knowledge 490

teaching 537
man of – 492
higher – 490
educational 537, 542
educe *extract* 301
  discover 480a
educt 40
eduction 40a
edulcorate 396, 652
eel 248
  wriggle like an – 315
eerie 860
efface
  delete 162
  disappear 449
  obliterate 552
  – from the memory 506
effect
  consequence **154**
  product 161
  impression 375
  complete 729
  carry into – 692
  with crushing – 162
  in – 5
  take – 731
  to that – 516
effective
  capable 157
  useful 644
effectuation 729
expedient 646
effects 780, 798
effectual 731
effectually 52
effectuate 729
effeminate
  weak 160
  womenlike 374
  timorous 862
  sensual 954
effeminize 158
effendi 875
effervesce
  energy 171
  violence 173
  agitate 315
  bubble 353
  excited 825
effervescent 338
effete *old* 128
  weak 160
  useless 645
  spoiled 659
efficacious [*see* efficient]
efficient
  power 157

agency 170
utility 644
skill 698
effigy 21, 554
effleurer *skim* 267, 460
efflorescence 330
effluence *egress* 295
  flow 348
effluvium 334, 398
efflux 295
effluxion of time 109
efformation 240
effort 686
effreet 980
effrontery 885
effulgence 420
effuse
  pour out 295, 297
  excrete 299
  speech 582
  loquacity 584
effusion of blood 361
effusive 573
eft 366
eftsoons 117
egad 535
égards 928
egesta 299
egestion 297
egg *beginning* 66
  cause 153
  food 298
  walk among –s 704
  too many –s in one basket
  unskilful 699
  (*imprudent* 863)
  – and dart
  ornament 847
  – on 615
egg-shaped 247, 249
ego *intrinsic* 5
  speciality 79
  immaterial 317
  non – 6
egocentrism 943
egotism
  vanity 880
  cynicism 911
  selfishness 943
egregious
  exceptional 83
  absurd 497
  exaggerated 549
  important 642
egregiously 31, 33
egress 295
Egyptian darkness 421

eheu! fugaces labuntur
  anni 111
eiderdown 223
eidouranion 318
Eiffel tower 206
eight *number* 98
  boat 273
  representative 759
eisteddfod 72, 416
eighty 98
either *choice* 609
  happy with – 605
ejaculate
  propel 284
  utter 580
ejecta 299
ejection 185, **297**
ejector 349
eke *also* 37
  – out *complete* 52
  spin out 110
ekka 272
elaborate
  improve 658
  prepare 673
  laborious 686
  work out 729
elaine 356
élan 276
elapse 109, 122
elastic fluid 334
elasticity
  power 157
  strength 159
  energy 171
  spring **325**
elate *cheer* 836
  rejoice 838
  hope 858
  vain 880
  boast 884
elbow *angle* 244
  projection 250
  push 276
  at one's –
  near 197
  advice 695
  lift one's –
  drink 959
  out at –s
  undress 226
  poor 804
  disrepute 874
  one's way
  progress 282
  pursuit 622
  active 682

elbow-chair 215
elbow-grease 331
elbow-room 180, 748
elder *older* 124
  aged 128
  veteran 130
  clergy 996
El Dorado 803
elect *choose* 609
  good 648
  predestinate 976
  pious 987
  clergy 996
election
  numerical 84
  nuecssity 601
electioneering 609
elector 745
electorate 737
Electra complex 897
electric
  car 272
  swift 274
  sensation 821
  excitable 825
  – blue 438
  – chair 974
  – light 423
  – piano 417
electrician 599, 690
electricity 157, 388
electrify
  unexpected 508
  excite 824
  astonish 870
electro-biology 992
electrocution 972
electrolier 214, 423
electrolyze 49
electro-magnetism 157
electromobile 272
electron 32
electroplate 223
electrotype 21, 591
electuary 662
eleemosynary 784
elegance
  in style 578
  beauty 845
  taste 859
  Bank of – 800
elegy *interment* 363
  poetry 597
  lament 839
element
  component 56
  beginning 66

cause 153
matter 316
in one's –
  facility 705
  content 831
devouring – 382
out of its – 195
elementary 42
  – education 537
  – school 542
elements
  Eucharist 998
elench 477
elephant
  large 192
  carrier 271
  white – *bane* 663
elevated
  tipsy 959
elevation
  height 206
  vertical 212
  raising **307**
  plan 554
  – of style 574
  improvement 658
  glory 873
  – of mind 942
  angular – 244
élève 541
eleven 98
  representative 759
eleventh hour
  evening 126
  late 133
  opportune 134
elf *infant* 129
  little 193
  imp 980
elicit *cause* 153
  draw out 301
  discover 480a
  manifest 525
eligible 646
Elijah's mantle 63
eliminant 299
eliminate
  subduct 38
  simplify 42
  exclude 55
  weed 103
  extract 301
  reject 610
elision 44, 201
élite *best* 648
  distinguished 873
  aristocratic 875

elixation 384
elixir 662
  – of life 471
elk 223
ell 200
  take an –
  take 789
  insolence 885
  wrong 923
  undue 925
  selfish 943
ellipse 247
ellipsis *shorten* 201
  style 572
ellipsoid 247, 249
elocation 185, 270
elocution 582
éloge 931
elongation 196, 200
elopement 623, 671
eloquence 572, 582
else 37
elsewhere 187
elucidate 522
elude
  sophistry 477
  avoid 623
  escape 671
  succeed 731
  palter 773
elusive 545
elusory 546
elutriate 652
elysian 829, 981
Elysium 827, 981
elytron 223
Elzevir edition 193
emaciation 195, 203, 640
emanate 151
  go out of 295
  excrete 299
  – from 544
emanation 398
emancipate
  facilitate 705
  free 748, 750
emasculate
  impotent 158
embalm
  interment 363
  perfume 400
  preserve 670
  – in the memory 505
embankment
  esplanade 189
  refuge 666
  fence 717

489

embar 229
embargo
  stoppage 265
  prohibition 761
  exclusion 893
embark
  transfer 270
  depart 293
  – in *begin* 66
  engage in 676
embarquer sans biscuits,
  s' – 674
embarras de
  – choix 609
embarrass 641, 704, 706
embarrassed 804, 806
embarrassing 475
embase 659
embassy
  errand 532
  commission 755
  consignee 758
embattled
  arranged 60
  leagued 712
  war array 722
embed
  locate 184
  base 215
  enclose 221
  insert 300
embellish 847
embers 384
embezzle 791
embitter
  deteriorate 659
  aggravate 835
  acerbate 900
emblazon
  colour 428
  ornament 847
  display 882
emblem 550, 747
embody
  join 43
  combine 48
  form a whole 50
  compose 54
embolden
  hope 858
  encourage 861
embolism 228, 261, 300
embonpoint 192
embosomed
  lodged 184
  interjacent 228
  circumscribed 229

emboss *convex* 250
  ornament 847
embouchure 260
embowel 297
embrace
  cohere 46
  compose 54
  include 76
  enclose 227
  choose 609
  take 789
  friendship 888
  sociality 892
  courtesy 894
  endearment 902
  – an offer 760
embrangle 61
embranglement 713
embrasure 257, 260
embrocation 662
embroider
  variegate 440
  lie 544
  ornament 847
embroidery
  adjunct 39
  exaggeration 549
embroil *derange* 61
  discord 713
embroilment 59
embrown 433
embryo
  beginning 66
  cause 153
  in – *destined* 152
  preparing 673
embryology 357
embryonic 193, 674
embus 293
embusqué 603
emendation 658
emerald *green* 435
  jewel 847
emerge 295, 446
emergency
  circumstance 8
  event 151
  difficulty 704
emeritus 500, 928
emersion 295, 446
emery
  sharpener 253
  – paper
  smooth 255
emetic *remedy* 662
émeute 742
emication 420

emigrant 57, 268
emigrate 266, 295
emigré 268, 295
eminence
  height 206
  fame 873
  church dignitary 996
eminent domain 744
eminently 33
emir 745, 875
emissary
  messenger 534
  consignee 758
emission 297
emit *eject* 297
  publish 531
  voice 580
  – vapour 336
Emmanuel 976
emmet 193
emollient 662
emolument
  acquisition 775
  receipt 810
  remuneration 973
emotion 821
  – al appeal 824
  – al drama 599
empale 260, 972
empanel 86, 969
empathy 515
emperor 745
emphasis 580
emphatic 535, 642
emphatically 31
empierce
  perforate 260
  insert 300
empire 737, 789
  – day 840
empiric 548
empirical 463, 675
empiricism 463
emplane 293
employ
  business 625
  use 677
  servitude 749
  commission 755
  in one's – 746
  – one's capital in 794
  – oneself 680
  – one's time in 625
employé
  servant 746
  agent 758
employer 795

endless
  multitudinous 102
  infinite 105
  perpetual 112
endlessly 16
endlong 200
endocrine 221
endogenous 367
endorse
  evidence 467
  assent 488
  compact 769
  - a bill 800
  approve 931
endorsement 550
endosmose 302
endow
  confer power 157
endowed with
  possessed of 777
endowment
  intrinsic 5
  power 157
  talent 698
  gift 784
endrogynous 83
endue 157
endure *time* 106
  last 110
  persist 143
  continue 141
  undergo 151
  feel 821
  submit to 826
  unable to - 867
  - for ever 112
  - pain 828
enduring
  indelible 505
endwise 212
enemy *time* 841
  foe 891
  the common - 978
  thing devised by the - 546
  - to society 891
energumen 504
energy *power* 157
  strength 159
  physical **171**
  resolution 604
  activity 682
enervate 158, 160
enfant, bon - 906
  - gâté
  prosperity 734
  satiety 869
  favorite 899

- perdu
  hopeless 859
  reckless 863
- terrible
  curiosity 455
  artless 703
  object of fear 860
enfeeble 160
enfeoff 780, 783
Enfield rifle 727
enfilade
  lengthwise 200
  pierce 260
  pass through 302
enfold 229
enforce *urge* 615
  advise 695
  compel 744
  require 924
enfranchise
  free 748
  liberate 750
  permit 760
enfranchised 924
engage
  bespeak 132
  induce 615
  undertake 676
  do battle 722
  commission 755
  promise 768
  compact 769
I'll -
  affirmation 535
  - the attention 457
  - with 720
engaged
  marriage 903
  be - 135
  - in *attention* 457
engagement
  business 625
  battle 720
  betrothal 902
engaging
  pleasing 829
  amiable 897
engender 161
engine 153, 633
engine-driver 268
engineer 690, 694, 726
engineering 633
engird 227
English 188
  broken - 563
  king's - 560
  murder the king's - 568

plain -
  intelligible 518
  interpreted 522
  style 576
  - horn 417
engorge
  swallow 296
  gluttony 957
engorgement
  too much 641
engrail 256
engrave
  furrow 259
  mark 550
  - in the memory 505
engraver 559
engraving 21, 22 **558**
engross *write* 590
  possess 777
  - the thoughts
  thought 451
  attention 457
engrossed in thought 451
engulf
  destroy 162
  swallow up 296
  plunge 310
enhance
  increase 35
  improve 658
enharmonic 413
enigma
  question 461
  secret 533
enigmatic
  uncertain 475
  unintelligible 517
  obscure 519
enigme, mot d' - 522
enjoin *advise* 695
  command 741
  prescribe 926
enjoy
  physically 377
  possess 777
  morally 827
  - health 654
  - popularity 873
  - a state 7
enkindle *heat* 384
  excite 824
enlarge
  increase 35
  swell 194
  in writing 573
  liberate 750
  - the mind 537

enlarged views 498
enlighten
  illumine 420
  inform 527
  teach 537
enlightened
  knowledge 490
enlist *engage* 615
  war 722
  commission 755
  under the banners of 707
  –into the service 677
enliven
  delight 829
  cheer 836
  amuse 840
enmity 889
ennoble 873
ennui 841
enormity
  crime 947
enormous *great* 31
  big 192
  – number 102
enough *much* 31
  no more! 142
  sufficient 639
  moderately 651
  satiety 869
  know when one has had –
    953
  – in all conscience 641
  – to drive one mad 830
  – and to spare 639
enounce 535, 580
enrage 830, 900
enragé 865
enrapture
  excite 824
  beatify 829
  love 897
enraptured 827
enravish 829
enravished 827
enravishment 824
enrich
  improve 658
  wealth 803
  ornament 847
enrobe 225
enroll *list* 86
  record 551
  – troops 722
  commission 755
ens *essence* 1
ensample 22
ensanguined 361

ensconce
  conceal 528
  safety 664
ensconced
  located 184
ensemble 50
Ens Entium 976
enshrine
  circumscribe 229
  repute 873
  sanctify 987
  – in the memory 505
ensiform 253
ensign
  standard 550
  officer 726
  master 745
  –of authority 747
ensilage 637
enslave 749
ensnare 545
ensue *follow* 63, 117
  happen 151
ensure 474
entablature 210
entail *cause* 153
  tie up property 781
entangle
  interlink 43
  derange 61
  ravel 219
  entrap 545
  embroil 713
entangled
  disorder 59
  – by difficulties 704
entend, cela s' – 613
entente
  agreement 23
  alliance 714
  friendship 888
enter *go in* 294
  appear 446
  note 551
  accounts 811
  – into the composition of
    56
  – into details
  special 79
  describe 594
  – into an engagement 768
  – into the feelings of 914
  – into the ideas of
  understand 518
  concord 714
  – in *converge* 290
  – the lists

  attack 716
  contention 720
  – the mind 451
  – a profession 625
  – into the spirit of
  feel 821
  delight 827
  – upon 66
  – into one's views 488
enterprise
  pursuit 622
  undertaking 676
  commercial – 794
enterprising
  active 171, 682
  courageous 861
entertain
  bear in mind 457
  support 707
  amuse 840
  sociality 892
  – doubts 485
  – feeling 821
  – an idea 451
  – an opinion 484
entertainment 840
  pleasure 377
  repast 298
entêté 481, 606
enthral
  subjection 749
  restraint 751
enthrone 873
enthronement 755
enthusiasm
  language 574
  willingness 602
  feeling 821
  hope 858
  love 897
enthusiast
  madman 504
  obstinate 606
  active 682
enthusiastic
  imaginative 515
  sensitive 822
  excitable 825
  sanguine 858
enthymeme 476
entice 615
enticing 829
entire *whole* 50
  complete 52
  continuous 69
  – horse 373
entirely *much* 31

entitle *name* 564
 ' *give a right* 924
entity 1
entoil 545
entomb *inter* 363
 imprison 751
Entomology 368
entourage 88, 183, 227
entozoon 193
entrails 221
entrammel 751
entrance
 beginning 66
 ingress 294
 way 627
 enrapture 827, 829
 magic 992
 give – to 296
entranced 515
entrancement 824
entrap 545
entrain 293
entreat 765
entrée
 reception 296
 dish 298
 give the – 296
 have the – 294
 – dish 191
entremet 298
entre nous 528
entrepôt 636, 799
entrepreneur 599
entre-sol 191
entrust
 commission 755
 give 784
 credit 805
entry *beginning* 66
 ingress 294
 record 551
entwine *join* 43
 intersect 219
 convolve 248
enucleate 522
enumerate 85
 – among 76
enumeration 86
enunciate
 inform 527
 affirm 535
 voice 580
envelop 225
envelope 223, 232
envenom
 deprave 659
 exasperate 835

hate 898
 anger 900
envenomed
 bad 649
 insalubrious 657
 painful 830
 malevolent 907
 – *tongue* 934
environ 227
environment 183
environs 197
 in such and such – 183
envisage 515, 861
envoy
 messenger 534
 consignee 758
envy 921
enwrap 225
enzyme 320
Eolian harp 417
Eolus 349
eon 976
epact 641
épanchement
 manifest 525
 artless 703
 endearment 902
épaulette
 badge 550,747
 ornament 847
 decoration 877
éperdu 824
épergne 191
ephemeral 111
ephemeris
 calendar 114
 record 551
 book 593
Ephesian letters 993
ephialtes
 physical pain 378
 hindrance 706
 mental pain 828
ephod 999
ephor 967
epic 594, 597
epicedium 839
epicene 81, 83
épicier 876
epicure
 fastidious 868
 sybarite 954a
 glutton 957
epicurean 954
Epicurus, system of – 954
epicy-cle, -cloid 247
epidemic

general 78
 disease 655
 insalubrity 657
epidermis 223
epigenesis 161
epigram 496, 842
epigrammatic 572
epigrammatist 844
epigraph 550
epilepsy 315, 655
epilogue
 sequel 65
 end 67
 drama 599
épingles, tiré à quatre –
 855
Epiphany 998
episcopal 995
Episcopalian 984
episcopate 995
episode
 adjunct 39
 discontinuity 70
 interjacence 228
episodic
 irrelative 10
 style 573
epistle 592
Epistles 985
epistrophe 104
epistyle 210
epitaph 363
epithalamium 903
epithem 662
epithet 564
epitome
 miniature 193
 short 201
 concise 572
epizoötic 657
epoch *time* 106
 instant 113
 date 114
 present time 118
epode 597
eponym 564
epopœa 597
epos 594
epulation 298
epulotic 662
epuration 652
equable 16, 922
equal *even* 27
 equitable 922
 – *chance* 156
 – *times* 120
 – *to power* 157

equality 13, **27**
equalize 213
equanimity 826
equate 27, 30
equations 85
equator 68, 318
equatorial 68, 236
equerry 746
equestrian 268
equibalanced 27
equidistant 68
equilibration 27
equilibrist 599
equilibrium 27
equine *carrier* 271
  horse 366
equinox 125, 126
equip 225, 673
equipage
  vehicle 272
  instruments 633
  display 882
equiparent 27
equipment 633
equipoise &c. 27, 30
equiponderate 30
equitable *wise* 498
  just 922
  due 924
  honourable 939
  – interest 780
equitation 266
equity *right* 922
  honour 939
  law 963
  in – 922
  – draftsman 968
equivalent
  identical 13
  equal 27
  compensation 30
  substitute 147
  translation 522
equivocalness
  dubious 475
  double meaning **520**
  impure 961
equivocate
  sophistry 477
  palter 520
  lie 544
equivocation [*see*
  equivocate]
  without – 543
équivoque
  double meaning 520
  impure 961

era *time* 106, 108
  date 114
eradicate
  destroy 162
  extract 301
erase *destroy* 162
  obliterate 331, 552
Erastian 984
erasure 552
Erato 416
ere 116
  – long 132
  – now 116
  past 122
Erebus *dark* 421
  hell 982
erect *build* 161
  vertical 212
  raise 307
  with head – 878
  – the scaffolding 673
erewhile 116, 122
ergatocracy 737
ergo 476
ergotism 480
ergotize 485
Erinys 900
eriometer 445
Erl King 980
ermine
  badge of authority 747
  ornament 847
erode 36, 659
Eros 897, 979
erosion 36
erotic 897, 961
err – *in opinion* 495
  – *morally* 945
errand
  message 532
  business 625
  commission 755
errand-boy 534
errant 279
erratic
  irregular 139
  changeable 149
  wandering 279
  capricious 608
erratum 495
erroneous 495
error *fallacy* **495**
  vice 945
  guilt 947
  court of – 966
  writ of – 969
ersatz 973

erst 122
erubescence 434
erubuit salva res est 95
eruct 297
eructate 297
erudition 490, 539
eruption
  upheaval 146
  violence 173
  egress 295, 297
  disease 655
  volcanic – 872
escadrille 726
escalade
  mounting 305
  attack 716
escalator 307
escalop 248
escapade
  absurdity 497
  freak 608
  prank 840
escape
  flight **671**
  liberate 750
  evade 927
  means of – 664, 666
  – the lips
    disclosure 529
    speech 582
  – the memory 506
  – notice &c.
    invisible 447
    inattention 458
    latent 526
escarp 717
escarpment
  stratum 204
  height 206
  oblique 217
escharotic
  caustic 171
  pungent 392
eschatology 67
escheat 144, 974
eschew
  avoid 623
  dislike 867
esclandre 828, 830
escort
  accompany 88
  safeguard 664
  keeper 753
escritoire 191
esculent 298
escutcheon 550
esoteric

private 79
concealed 528
Espagne, château en –
  fancy 515
  hope 858
espalier 232
especial 79
especially 33
espial 441
espiéglerie
  cunning 702
  fun 840
  wit 842
espionnage 441, 461
esplanade
  houses 189
  flat 213
espouse
  choose 609
  marriage 903
  – a cause *aid* 707
  co-operate 709
esprit
  shrewdness 498
  wit 842
  bel – 844
  – de corps
  bias 481
  co-operation 709
  sociality 892
  (*party* 712)
  – fort
  thinker 500
  irreligious 989
espy 441
esquire 875, 877
essay
  experiment 463
  dissertation 595
  endeavour **675**
essayist 593, 595
esse 1
essence
  nature 5
  scent 398
essential
  intrinsic 5
  great 31
  required 630
  important 642
essentially
  substantially 3
  intrinsically 5
essential stuff 5
establish
  settle 150
  create 161

place 184
evidence 467
demonstrate 478
– equilibrium 27
established
  permanent 141
  habit 613
  – church 983*a*
establishment
  party 712
  shop 799
estafette 534
estaminet 189
estate *condition* 7
  property 780
  come to man's – 131
esteem
  believe 484
  repute 873
  approve 931
  in high – 928
estimable 648
estimate
  measure 466
  adjudge 480
  information 527
  – too highly 482
estimation [*see* esteem,
  estimate]
estime
  succès d' – 873
estival 382
esto perpetua!
  perpetuity 112
  permanence 141
  desire 865
estop 706
estrade 213
estrange
  alienate 44, 889
  discord 713
  hate 898
estranged
  secluded 893
estrapade
  attack 716
  punishment 972
estreat 974
estuary 343
estuation 384
esurient 865
et – cætera
  add 37
  include 76
  plural 100
  – hoc genus omne
  similar 17

include 76
multiform 81
étalage 882
état major 745
etch *furrow* 259
  engraving 558
eternal 112
  – home 981
Eternal, the – 976
eterne 112
eternify 112
eternity 112
  an – 110
  launch into – 360, 361
ether
  lightness 320
  rarity 322
  vapour 334
  anæsthetic 376
ethereal 4
ethicism 984
ethics 926
Ethiopian 431
  –'s skin 150
Ethiopian's skin
  unchangeable 150
ethnic 984
ethnology 372
ethology 926
ethos 5
etiolate 429, 430
etiology *causes* 155, 359
  knowledge 490
  disease 655
etiquette
  custom 613
  fashion 832
  ceremony 882
étoile, à la belle –
  out of doors 220
  in the air 338
Eton jacket 225
étourderie
  inattention 458
  unskilfulness 699
etymological 560
etymology 562
etymon *origin* 153
  verbal 562
Eucharist 998
euchology 998
euchre 840
eudiometer
  air 338
  salubrity 656
euge! 931
eugenics 658

evident
concrete 3
visible 446
certain 474
manifest 525
evidently 516
evil *harm* 619
badness 649
impious 988
– day
prepare for – 673
adversity 735
– eye *vision* 441
malevolence 907
disapprobation 932
demon 980
sorcery 992
spell 993
– favoured 846
– fortune 735
– genius 980
– hour 135
– one 978
– plight 735
through – report &c. 604a
– star 649
evil-doer 913
evil-doing 945
evil-minded 907, 945
evil-speaking
malediction 908
censure 932
detraction 934
evince *show* 467
prove 478
disclose 529
eviscerate 297, 301
eviscerated 4
evoke *cause* 153
call upon 765
excite 824
evolution
numerical 85
production 161
motion 264
extraction 301
circuition 311
turning out **313**
organization 357
training 673
action 680
military –s 722
evolve
discover 480a
evolved from 154 [*and see*
evolution]
evulgate 531

evulsion 301
evivva! 931
ewe 366, 374
– lamb, 366
ewer 191
ex
– animo 602
– cathedra 542
– officio 494, 924
– parte 467
– pede Herculem 82
– post facto 122, 133
– tempore
instant 113
occasion 134
exacerbate
increase 35
exasperate 173
aggravate 659, 835
exact *similar* 17
special 79
true 494
style 572
require 741
tax 812
insolence 885
claim 924, 926
– meaning 516
– memory 505
– observance 772
– truth 494
exacting
severe 739
discontented 832
grasping 865
fastidious 868
exaction [*see* exact]
undue 925
exactly
just so 488
exaggeration
increase 35
expand 194
overestimate 482
magnify **549**
misrepresent 555
exalt
increase 35
elevate 307
extol 931
– one's horn 873
exalté 504
tête –e 503
exalted *high* 206
repute 873
noble 875
magnanimous 942

examination [*see* examine]
evidence 467
undergo – 461
examine 457, 461
example
pattern 22
instance 82
bad – 949
good – 948
make an – of 974
set a good – 944
exanimate
dead 360
supine 360
exarch 745
exasperate
exacerbate 173
aggravate 835
enrage 900
excavate 252
excecation 442
exceed *surpass* 33
remain 40
transgress 303
intemperance 954
excel *surpass* 33
– in *skilful* 698
excellence 648, 944
excellence, par – 642
excellency 877
excelsior 305
except *subduct* 38
exclude 55
reject 610
exception
unconformity 83
qualification 469
exemption 777a
disapproval 932
take –
qualify 469
resent 900
exceptionable
bad 649
guilty 947
exceptional
original 20
extraneous 57
unconformable 83
in an – degree 31
exceptious 901, 901a
exceptis excipiendis 469
excern 297
excerpt 609
excerpta *parts* 51
compendium 596
selections 609

excerption 609
excess
 remainder 40
 redundance 641
 intemperance 954
excessive 31
exchange
 reciprocity 12
 interchange 148
 transfer 783
 barter 794
 mart 799
 bill of – 771
 rate of – 800
 – blows &c.
 retaliation 718
 battle 720
Exchequer 802
 Baron of – 967
 Court of – 966
 – bill 800
excise 812
exciseman 965
excision 38
excitability 825, 901
excitation 824
excite *energy* 171
 violence 173
 – *morally* 824
 – attention 457
 – desire 865
 – hope 811
 – an impression 375
 – love 897
excited fancy 515
excitement 824, 825
 anger 900
exclaim 411
 – against 932
exclamation 580
 mark of – 550
exclude
 leave out 42, 55
 reject 610
 prohibit 761
 banish 893
exclusion 55, 57
exclusive
 simple 42
 omitting 55
 special 79
 irregular 83
 forbidding 761
 – of 38
 – possession 777
 – thought 457
excogitate 451, 515

excommunicate
 banish 893
 curse 908
 rite 998
excoriate 226
excrement
 excretion 299
 dirt 653
excrescence
 projection 250
 blemish 848
excreta
 excretion 299
 dirt 653
excretion 297, 299
excruciating 378, 830
exculpate
 forgive 918
 vindicate 937
 acquit 970
excursion 266, 311
excursionist 268
excursive
 deviating 279
 - *style* 573
excursus 595
excuse *plea* 617
 forgive 918
 exempt 927a
 vindicate 793
execrable 649, 830
execrate 898, 908
execution
 music 416
 action 680
 conduct 692
 signing 771
 observance 772
 punishment 972
 carry into –
 complete 729
 put in –
 undertaking 676
executioner 975
executive
 conduct 692
 direction 693
 authority 737
 judicature 965
executor 690
 to one and his –s &c.,
 property 780
exegetical 522
exemplar 22
exemplary 944
exemplify
 quote 82

 illustrate 522
exempt *free* 748
 dispensation 927a
 – from *absent* 187
 unpossessed 777a
exemption
 exception 83
 qualification 469
 deliverance 692
 permission 760
 non-possession 777a
 non-liability 927a
exenterate 297
exequatur 755
exequies 363
exercise
 operation 170
 teach 537
 task 625
 use 677
 act 680
 exert 686
 – authority 737
 – discretion 600
 – the intellect 451
 – power 157
exergue 231
exert *use* 677
 – authority 737
 – oneself 686
exertion 171, 686
exfoliate 226
exhalation
 ejection 297
 excretion 299
 vapour 336
 breath 349
 odour 398
exhaust
 paralyze 158
 empty 195
 waste 638
 fatigue 688
 complete 729
 drain 789
 squander 818
exhausted
 inexistent 2
exhauster 349
exhaustive
 complete 52
 – inquiry 461
exhaustless
 infinite 105
 enough 639
exhibit *evidence* 467
 show 525

extraneousness 57
extraordinary
　great 31
　exceptional 83
extraregarding 220
extravagant
　inordinate 31
　violent 173
　absurd 497
　foolish 499
　fanciful 515
　exaggerated 549
　excessive 641
　high-priced 814
　prodigal 818
　vulgar 851
　ridiculous 853
extravaganza
　fanciful 515
　drama 599
extravagation 303
extravasate 295, 297
extreme
　inordinate 31
　end 67
　– unction 998
extremis, in –
　dying 360
　difficulty 704
extremist 710
extremity *end* 67
　adversity 735
　tribulation 828
　drive matters to an – 604
　at the last – 665
extricate
　take out 301
　deliver 672
　facilitate 705
　liberate 750
extrinsicality 6
extrinsic *evidence* 467
extrusion 297, 299
exuberant
　– *style* 573
　redundant 639
exudation 295, 299
exulcerate 659
exult 838, 884
exultant 858
exulting 836
exunge 356
exuviæ 653
eye *circle* 247
　opening 260
　organ of sight 441

all my – and Betty Martin 546
appear to one's – 446
before one's –s
　front 234
　visible 446
　manifest 525
cast the –s on
　see 441
cast the –s over
　attend to 457
catch the – 457
close the –s
　death 360
　blind 442
　sleep 683
dry –s 823
fix the –s on 457
have an – to
　attention 457
　intention 620
　desire 865
in one's –
　visible 446
　expectant 507
in the –s of
　appearance 448
　belief 484
keep an – upon 459
look with one's own –s 459
make –'s at 441
mind's – 515
with moistened –s 839
open the –s to 480*a*
with open –s 870
set one's –s upon 865
shut one's –s to
　inattention 458
　permit 760
to the –s 448
under the –s of 186
up to one's –s 641
have one's –s about one 459
– askance 860
–s draw straws 683
an – for an – 718, 919
– glistening 824
in the – of the law 963
– of the master 693
– of a needle 260
–s open
　attention 457
　care 459
　intention 620
–s opened

disclosure 529
–s out 442
eye-ball 441
eyebrows 256
eyeglass 445
eyelashes 256
eyeless 442
eyelet 260
eyelid 223
eye-shade 443
eye-sight 441
eyesore 846, 848
eye-teeth
　have cut one's –
　adolescence 131
　skill 698
　cunning 702
eye-wash 544
eye-witness
　spectator 444
　evidence 467
eyot 346
eyre 966
eyry 189

F

Fabian policy
　delay 133
　inaction 681
　caution 864
fable *error* 495
　metaphor 521
　fiction 546
　description 590
fabric *state* 7
　effect 154
　texture 329
fabricate
　composition 54
　make 161
　invent 515
　falsify 544
fabrication *lie* 546
fabula narratur, de te –
　retaliate 718
　condemn 971
fabulist 594
fabulous
　enormous 31
　imaginary 515
　untrue 546
　exaggerated 549
faburden 413
façade 234
face *exterior* 220

covering 223
front 234
aspect 448
oppose 708
resist 719
brave 861
impudence 885
change the – of 146
fly in the – of
disobey 742
put a good – upon
sham 545
calm 826
cheerful 836
hope 858
pride 878
display 882
vindicate 93
in the – of
presence 186
opposite 708
look in the –
see 441
proud 878
make –s
distort 243
ugly 846
disrespect 929
on the – of the
manifest 525
show –
present 186
visible 446
not show –
disreputable 874
bashful 879
to one's – 525
wry – 378
– about 279
set one's – against 708
– of the country 344
on the – of the earth
space 180
world 318
– to face *front* 234
contraposition 237
manifest 525
– of the thing
appearance 448
facet 220
facetiæ 842
facetious 842
facia 234
facile *willing* 602
irresolute 605
easy 705
facile princeps 33

facilis descensus Averni
sloping 217
danger 665
facilitate 705
facility *skill* 698
easy **705**
facing *covering* 223
facinorous 945
façon de parler 521, 549
fac-simile 21, 554
fact *existence* 1
event 151
certainty **474**
truth 494
in – 535
faction 712, 713
factious 24
factitious 545, 546
factor
numerical 84
director 694
consignee 758
factory 691
factotum
agent 690
manager 694
employé 758
facts *evidence* 467
summary of – 594
at variance with – 471
facula 420
faculties 450
in possession of one's –
502
faculty
power 157
profession 625
skill 698
facundity 582
fad 481, 608
faddle 683
fade *vanish* 4
transient 111
become old 124
droop 160
grow dim 422
lose colour 429
disappear 449
spoil 659
– from the memory 506
fade 391
fadge 23
fæces 299, 653
fæx populi 876
fag *cigarette* 392
labour 686
fatigue 688

drudge 690, 746
– end
remainder 40
end 67
faggot 72, 388
fagots et fagots **15**, 465
faïence 557
fail *droop* 160
shortcoming 304
be confuted 479
illness 655
not succeed 732
not observe 773
not pay 808
dereliction 927
failing [*see* fail]
incomplete 53
insufficient 640
vice 945
guilt 947
– heart 837
– luck 735
– memory 506
– sight 443
– strength 160
failure **732**
heart – 360
fain *willing* 602
compulsive 744
wish 865
fainéant 683
faint
small in degree 32
impotent 158
weak 160
sound 405
dim 422
colour 429
swoon 688
– heart *fear* 860
cowardice 862
damn with – praise 930,
932, 934
faintness **405**
fair *in degree* 31
pale 429
white 430
wise 498
important 643
good 648
moderate 651
mart 799
beautiful 845
just 922
honourable 939
– chance 472
– copy *copy* 21

writing 590
– field
  occasion 134
– game 857
by – means 631, 940
– name 873
– play 922, 923
– question 461
– sex 374
in a – way
  tending 176
  probable 472
  convalescent 658
  prosperous 734
  hopeful 858
– weather 734
– weather sailor 701
– wind 705
– words 894
fairing 784
fairly *intrinsically* 5
get on – 736
– well 643
fair-spoken
  courtesy 894
  flattery 933
fairy *fanciful* 515
  fay 979
  imp 980
– godmother 711, 784, 912
– tale 545, 594
fairy-land 515
fait: au –
  knowledge 490
  skilful 698
– accompli
  certain 474
  complete 729
faith *belief* 484
  hope 858
  honour 939
  piety 987
declaration of – 983
bad – 544
i' – 535
keep – with
  observe 772
plight –
  promise 768
  love 902
true –
  orthodox 983a
want of –
  incredulity 487
  irreligious 989
– healing 662
faithful [*see* faith]

like 17
copy 21
exact 494
obedient 743
– memory 505
– to 772
faithless *false* 544
  dishonourable 940
  sceptical 989
fake 544, 545
fakir 996
falcate 244, 245
falchion 727
falciform [*see* falcate]
falcon 792
falconet 727
faldstool 215
fall *autumn* 126
  happen 151
  perish 162
  slope 217
  regression 283
  descend 306
  die 360
  fail 732
  adversity 73
  vice 945
let – *lower* 308
  inform 527
water– 348
– asleep 683
– astern 235, 283
– away 105
– back *return* 283
  recede 287
  relapse 661
– back upon 677, 717
have to – back upon 637
– a cursing 908
– of the curtain 67
– into a custom 82
– of day 125
– dead 360
– into decay 659
– down 990
– down before 928
– upon the ear 418
– flat on the ear 843
– at one's feet 725
– foul of *blow* 276
  hinder 706
  oppose 708
  discord 713
  attack 716
  contention 720
  censure 932
– for 897

– to the ground
  be confuted 479
  fail 732
– into a habit 613
– from one's high estate
  adversity 735
  disrepute 874
– in *order* 58
  continuity 69
  event 151
– into
  conversion 144
  river 348
– in with *agree* 23
  conform 82
  converge 2
  discover 480a
  concord 714
  consent 762
– on one's knees
  submit 725
  servile 886
  gratitude 916
  worship 990
– of the leaf 126
– from the lips 582
– in love with 897
– to one's lot
  event 151
  chance 156
  receive 785
  duty 926
– under one's notice 457
– into oblivion 506
– off *decrease* 36
  deteriorate 659
– off again 661
– out *happen* 151
  quarrel 713
  enmity 889
– into a passion 900
– to pieces
  disjunction 44
  destruction 162
  brittle 328
– a prey to 732, 749
– in price 815
– into raptures 827
– short *inferior* 32
  contract 195
  shortcoming 304
– of snow 383
– through *fail* 734
– to *eat* 298
  take in hand 676
  do battle 722
– into a trap 547

– under
inclusion 76
subjection 749
– upon
discover 480a
unexpected 508
devise 626
attack 716
– in the way of 186
– to work 686
fallacy *sophistry* 477
error 495
show the – of 497
fallen angel 949, 978
fallible 475, 477
falling-out 24
falling star 318, 423
fallow
unproductive 169
yellow 436
unready 674
inactive 681
false *imitation* 10
sophistry 477
error 495
untrue 544, 546
spurious 925
dishonourable 940
– alarm 669
– colouring
misinterpretation 523
falsehood 544
– construction 523, 544
– doctrine 984
– expectation 509
– hearted 940
– impression 495
– light *vision* 443
– money 800
– ornament 851
– plea *untruth* 546
plea 617
– position 704
– pretences 791
– prophet
disappoint 509
pseudo-revelation 986
– reasoning 477
– scent 495, 538
– shame 855
– statement 546
– step 732
– teaching 538
– witness
deceiver 548
detraction 934
falsehood 544, 546

falsetto *squeak* 410
want of voice 581
falsify *error* 495
falsehood 544, 546
– accounts 811
– one's hope 509
falter *slow* 275
stammer 583
hesitate 605
slip 732
hopeless 859
fear 860
faltering accents 605
fame *greatness* 31
news 532
renown 873
familiar
known 490
habitual 613
sociable 892
affable 894
– *spirit* 979, 980
on – terms 888
familiarize
teach 537
habit 613
famille, en – 892
family
kin 11
class 75
ancestors 166
posterity 167
party 712
in the bosom of one's –
221
happy – 714
– circle 892
– jars 713
– likeness 17
– tie 11
in the – way 161
famine 640
– price 814
famine-stricken 640
famish
stingy 819
fasting 956
famished
insufficient 640
hungry 865
famous 873
famously 31
fan *blow* 349
cool 385
refresh 689
stimulate 824
flirt a – 855

– the embers 505
– the flame
violence 173
heat 384
aid 707
excite 824
– into a flame
anger 900
–shaped 194
fanatic
madman 504
imaginative 515
zealot 682
religious – 988
fanatical
misjudging 481
insane 503
emotional 821
excitable 825
heterodox 984
over-righteous 988
fanaticism 606
fanciful
imaginative 515
capricious 608
ridiculous 853
fancy *think* 451
idea 453
believe 484
suppose 514
imagine 515
caprice 608
choice 609
pugilism 726
wit 842
desire 865
wonder 870
love 897
after one's – 850
indulge one's – 609
take a – to
delight in 827
desire 865
take one's –
please 829
– dog 366
– dress 840
– price 814
– woman 962
fandango 840
fandi, mollia tempora –
588
fane 1000
fanfare *loudness* 404
celebration 883
fanfaron 887
fanfaronnade 884

fangs *venom* 663
  rule 737
  retention 781
fan-light 260
fan-like 202
fannel 999
fanon 999
fantasia 415
fantastic *odd* 83
  absurd 497
  imaginative 515
  capricious 608
  unfashionable 851
  ridiculous 853
fantasy
  imagination 515
  desire 865
fantoccini 554, 599
faquir 996
far – *away* 196
  – be it from
  unwilling 603
  deprecation 766
  – between
  disjunction 44
  few 103
  interval 198
  – from it
  unlike 18
  shortcoming 304
  no 536
  – from the truth 546
  – and near 180
  – off 196
  – and wide 31, 180, 196
farce
  absurdity 497
  untruth 546
  drama 599
  wit 842
  ridiculous 853
  mere –
  unimportant 643
  useless 645
farceur
  actor 599
  humorist 844
fardel
  bundle 72
  hindrance 706
fare *state* 7
  food 298
  price 812
  bill of –
  list 86
farewell
  departure 293

  relinquishment 624
  loss 776
  – to greatness 874
far-famed 873
far-fetched 10
far-flung 73
far-gone
  much 31
  insane 503
  spoiled 654
farinaceous 330
farm *till* 371
  property 780
  rent 788
farmer 188, 342, 371
  afternoon – 683
Farmer-Labor 712
farm-house 189
faro 840
farrago 59
farrier 370
farrow
  multitude 102
  produce 161
  litter 167
far-sighted 442, 510
farther 196 [*and see*
  further]
farthing
  quarter 97
  worthless 643
  coin 800
  – candle 422
farthingale 225
fasces 747
fascia 205, 247
fasciculated 72
fascicule 51
fascinate
  influence 615
  excite 824
  please 829
  astonish 870
  love 897
  conjure 992
fascinated
  pleased 827
fascination [*see* fascinate]
  infatuation 825
  desire 870
fascine 72
Fascisti 712
fas et nefas, per – 604*a*,
  631
fash 830
fashion
  state 7

  form 240
  custom 613
  method 627
  ton **852**
  after a –
  middling 32
  after this – 617
  follow the – 82
  be in the – 488
  man of – 852
  set the –
  influence 175
  authority 737
  for –'s sake 852
fast *joined* 43
  steadfast 150
  rapid 274
  fashionable 852
  intemperate 954
  not eat 956
  worship 990
  rite 998
  stick – 704
  – asleep 683
  – by 197
  – day 956
  – friend 890
  – and loose
  sophistry 477
  falsehood 544
  irresolute 605
  tergiversation 607
  caprice 608
  – man *fop* 854
  libertine 962
fasten *join* 43
  hang 214
  restrain 751
  – on the mind 451
  – a quarrel upon 713
  – upon 789
fastening 45
fast-handed 819
fastidious
  censorious 932
fastidiousness **868**
fasting
  insufficiency 640
  penance 952
  abstinence **956**
  worship 990
fastness
  asylum 666
  defence 717
fat *corpulent* 192
  expansion 194
  unctuous 355

oleaginous 356
kill the -ted calf
celebration 883
sociality 892
- in the fire
disorder 59
violence 173
- of the land
pleasure 377
enough 639
prosperity 734
intemperance 95
fata - Morgana
occasion 134
ignis fatuus 423
- obstant 601
fatal 361
- disease 655
fatalism 601
fatality 601
fate *end* 67
necessity 601
chance 621
be one's - 156
sure as - 474
Fates 601, 979
fat-head 501
father *eldest* 128
paternity 166
priest 996
Apostolical -s 985
gathered to one's -s 360
heavy - 599
- upon 155
Father, God the - 976
fatherland 189
fatherless 158
fatherly 906
fathom
length 200
investigate 461
solve 462
measure 466
discover 480a
knowledge 490
fathomless 208
fatidical 511
fatigation 688
fatigue 688
fatras 643
fatten
expand 194
improve 658
prosperous 734
- on *parasite* 886
- upon
feed 298

fatuity 4, 499
fatuous 517
fat-witted 499
faubourg 227
fauces 231
faucet 252
faugh! 867
fault
break 70
error 495
imperfection 651
failure 732
vice 945
guilt 947
at -
uncertain 475
ignorant 491
unskilful 699
find - with 932
faultless 650, 946
faulty 495, 651
faun 980
fauna 366
faut: comme il -
taste 850
fashion 852
il s'en - bien 489
tant s'en - 536
faute 732
- de mieux
substitution 147
necessity 601
fauteuil 215
fautor 890
faux pas
error 568
failure 732
misconduct 947
intrigue 961
favour
resemble 16
badge 550
letter 592
aid 707
indulgence 740
permit 760
gift 784
partiality 923
appearances in - of 472
get into -
friendship 888
love 897
in - *repute* 873
approbation 931
in - of
approve 931
under - of 760

view with - 906
- with 784
favourable
occasion 134
willing 602
good 648
aid 707
- prospect 472
- to 709
take a - turn
improve 658
prosperity 734
favourably
well 618
favourer 890
favourite
pleasing 829
beloved 897, **899**
favouritism
friendship 888
wrong 923
fawn *colour* 433
cringe 749, 886
flatter 993
fay 979
fealty
obedience 743
duty 926
respect 928
fear 860
fearful
painful 830
timid 862
fearfully 31, 870
fearless *hope* 858
courage 861
fearsome 860
feasible 470, 705
feast *period* 138
repast 298
pleasure 377
revel 840
rite 998
- one's eyes 897
feast of reason
conversation 588
- and flow of soul
sociality 892
feat *action* 680
courage 861
- of arms 720
- of strength 159
feather
class 75
tuft 256
light 320
trifle 643

ornament 847
decoration 877
in full –
prepared 673
prosperous 734
rich 803
hear a – drop 403
in high –
health 654
cheerful 884
pleased with a – 840
– in one's cap
honour 873
decoration 877
– one's nest
prepare 673
prosperity 734
wealth 803
economy 817
selfish 943
– the oar 698
– in the scale 643
feather-bed 324
feathered tribes 366
feathery 256
featly 682
feature
character 5
component 56
form 240
appearance 448
press 531
lineament 550
– in 56
features
face 234
febrifuge 662
febrile 382, 825
fecal 653
fecit 556
feckless 866
feculence 653
fecund 168
fecundate 161
federal council 696
– penitentiary 752
federalism 737
federation 48, 709, 712
fee *possession* 777
property 780
pay 809
reward 973
feeble *weak* 160
illogical 477
feeble-minded 497, 605
feebleness
style **575**

feed *eat* 298
supply 637
– the flame 707
fee-faw-fum
bugbear 860
spell 993
feel *sense* 375
touch 379
emotion 821
– for *try* 463
benevolence 906
pity 914
condole with 915
– the pulse 461
– the want of 865
– one's way
essay 675
caution 864
feeler 379
inquiry 461
experiment 463
feeling 698, **821**
feet *low* 207
walkers 266
at one's –
near 197
subjection 749
humility 879
fall at one's –
submit 725
fall on one's –
prosper 734
lick the – of
servile 886
light upon one's –
safe 664
spring to one's – 307
throw oneself at the – of
entreat 765
feign 544, 546
feigned 545
feint 545
felicitas, curiosa – 698
felicitate 896
felicitous
agreeing 23
- *style* 578
skilful 698
successful 731
pleasant 829
felicity 827
feline *cat* 366
stealthy 528
cunning 702
fell *destroy* 162
mountain 206
lay flat 21

skin 223
lay low 308
moor 344
dire 860
malevolent 907
fellah 876
felloe 231
fellow *similar* 17
equal 27
companion 88
dual 89
man 373
scholar 492, 541
fellow-commoner 541
fellow-companion 890
fellow-countryman 890
fellow-creature 372
fellow-feeling
friendship 888
love 897
benevolence 906
pity 914
fellowship
partnership 712
distinction 873
friendship 888
companionship 890
good – 892
fellow-student 541
fellow-worker 690
felly 231
felo-de-se 361
felon 949
felonious 945
felony 947
felt *texture* 219
heart– 821
felucca 273
female 374
feme coverte 903
feme sole 904
femininality
weakness 160
woman 374
feminine 374
feminism 374
femme de chambre 746
fen 345
fence *enclose* 232
evade 544
defence 717
fight 720
prison 752
thief 792
– round 229
– with a question 528
fenced 770

the - of blood 361
- of inquiry
topic 454
inquiry 461
- of view
vista 441
idea 453
field-day
contention 720
amusement 840
display 882
field-glass 445
field-marshal 745
field-piece 727
field-preacher 996
field-work 717
fiend 913, 980
fiend-like
malevolent 907
wicked 945
fiend 980
fierce *violent* 173
passion 825
daring 861
angry 900
fiery *violent* 173
hot 382
strong feeling 821
excitable 825
angry 900
irascible 901
- *cross* 550, 722
- *furnace* 386
- *imagination* 515
- *ordeal* 828
fife 417
fifer 416
fifth 98, 99
fifty 98
fig
unimportance 643
in the name of the prophet
-s! 497
- out 847
fight
contention 720
warfare 722
show -
defence 717
courage 861
- one's battles again 594
- against destiny 606
- the good fight 944
- it out 722
- shy *avoid* 603, 623
coward 862
- one's way

pursue 622
active 682
exertion 686
fighter 726
fighting-cock 726, 861
fighting-man 726
figment 515
figurante 599
figurate number 84
figuration 240
figurative
metaphorical 521
representing 554
- *style* 577
figure
number 84
form 240
appearance 448
metaphor 521
indicate 550
represent 554
price 812
ugly 846
cut a -
repute 873
display 882
poor - 874
- to oneself 515
- of speech 521
- out 522
exaggeration 549
figure-flinger 994
figure-head 4, 550, 554, 643
figurine 554
figuriste 559
filaceous 205
filament 205
filamentous 256
filch 791
filcher 762
file *subduct* 38
arrange 60
row 69
assemblage 72
list 86
reduce 195
smooth 255
pulverize 330
record 551
store 636
soldiers 726
- a claim &c. 969
- off *march* 266
diverge 291
file-fire 716
filial 167

filiation
consanguinity 11
attribution 155
posterity 167
filibuster 133, 706, 792
filibustering 791
filiform 205
filigree 219
filings 330
fill *complete* 52
occupy 186
contents 190
stuff 224
provision 637
eat one's - 957
have one's -
enough 639
satiety 869
- the bill 229
- an office
business 625
government 737
- out
expand 194
-ed to overflowing 641
- one's pocket 803
- time 106
- up *compensate* 30
compose 54
close 261
restore 660
- up the time
inaction 681
fille
- de chambre 746
- de joie 962
filled
- to overflowing 641
filler 532
fillet *band* 45
filament 205
circle 247
insignia 550
ornament 847
fillibeg 225
filling 224
fillip
impulse 276
propulsion 284
stimulus 615
excite 824
filly 271
film *layer* 204
opaque 426
semitransparent 427
- over the eyes
dim sight 443

cinema 448
ignorant 491
filmy *texture* 329
filter *percolate* 295
  clean 652
filth 653
  –y *lucre* 800
filtrate 652
fimbriated 256
fin 267
final *ending* 67
  conclusive 474
  completing 729
  court of – *appeal* 474
  – *cause* 620
  – *stroke* 729
  – *touch* 729
finale *end* 67
  completion 729
finality 67, 729
finally
  for good 141
  on the whole 476
finance 800, 811
  minister of – 801
financier 801
finch 366
find
  eventuality 151
  adjudge 480
  discover 480a
  acquire 775
  – one's account in 644
  – the cause of 522
  – a clue to 480a
  – to one's cost 509
  – credence 484
  – it in one's heart 602
  – in *provide* 637
  – the key of 522
  – the meaning 522
  – means 632
  – oneself *be* 1
  present 186
  – out 480a
  – vent 671
  – one's way 731
  – one's way into 294
finding
  judgment 480
fine *small* 32
  large 192
  thin 203
  rare 322
  not raining 340
  exact 494
  good 648

beautiful 845
adorned 847
proud 878
mulct 974
in – *end* 67
  after all 476
  – air 656
  – arts 554
  – feather 159, 654
  – feeling 850
  – frenzy 515
  – gentleman
  fop 854
  proud 878
  – grain 329
  – lady 854, 878
  one – morning 106
  some – morning 119
  – powder 330
  – talking
  overrate 482
  boast 884
  – writing 577
  – time of it 734
  – voice 580
fine-draw 660
fine-fingered 698
finem, respicere – 510
finery 847, 851
fine-spoken 894, 933
fine-spun *thin* 203
  sophistry 477
finesse *tact* 698
  artifice 702
  taste 850
fine-toned 413
finger *touch* 379
  hold 781
  lay the – on
  point out 457
  discover 480a
  lift a – 680
  not lift a – 681
  point the – at 457
  turn round one's little – 737
  –'s breadth 203
  at one's –s' end
  near 197
  know 490
  remember 505
  – on the lips
  aphony 581
  taciturnity 585
  – in the pie
  cause 153
  interfere 228

act 680
active 682
co-operate 709
fingerling 193
finger-post 550
finger-print 467
finger-stall 223
fingle-fangle 643
finical
  trifling 643
  affected 855
  fastidious 868
finicky 855, 868
finikin 643
finis 67
  – coronat opus 729
finish *lend* 67
  symmetry 242
  skill 698
  complete 729
finished
  absolute 31
  perfect 650
  skilled 698
finishing
  – stroke 361
  – touch 729
finite 32
fiord 343
fire *energy* 171
  heat 382
  make hot 384
  stoke 388
  vigour 574
  discharge 756
  enthusiasm 821
  excite 824, 825
  catch – 384
  hell – 982
  on – 382
  open – *begin* 66
  play with – 863
  signal – 550
  take –
  excitable 825
  angry 900
  between two –s 665
  under – 665, 722
  – at 716
  – the blood 824
  – and fury 900
  – the first shot 716
  – of genius 498
  – off 284
  – a salute 883
  – and sword 162
  – up *excite* 825

anger 900
- a volley 716
go through - and water
   resolution 604
   perseverance 604*a*
   courage 861
fire-alarm 669
fire-annihilator 385
fire-arms 727
fire-ball *fuel* 388
   arms 727
fire-balloon 273
fire-barrel 388
fire-bell 669
fire-boat 726
fire-brand
   fuel 388
   instigator 615
   dangerous man 667
   incendiary 913
fire-brigade 385
fire-curtain 599
fire-drake 423
fire-eater
   fighter 726
   blusterer 887
fire-eating
   rashness 863
   insolence 885
fire-engine 348
fire-escape 671
fire-extinguisher 385
fire-fly 423
fireless cooker 386
fire-light 422
firelock 727
fireman *stoker* 268
   extinguisher 385
fire-place 386
fire-proof 385, 644
fireside 189
firewood 388
firework
   fire 382
   luminary 423
   amusement 840
   celebration 883
fire-worship 991
fire-worshipper 984
firing *fuel* 388
   explosion 406
firkin 191
firm
   junction 43
   stable 150
   hard 323
   resolute 604

partnership 712
merchant 797
brave 861
stand - 719
- as a rock 604
- belief 484
- hold 781
firmament 318
firman 741, 760
first 66
- blush
   morning 125
   leading 280
   vision 441
   appearance 448
   manifest 525
- blow 716
- cause 976
- that comes 609*a*
- fiddle
   importance 642
   proficient 700
   authority 737
- come first served 609*a*
- and foremost 66
- impression 66
- and last 87
- line 234
come back to - love 607
- move 66
- opportunity 132
at - sight 448
- stage 66
- stone
   preparation 673
   attack 716
on the - summons 741
of the - water
   best 648
   repute 873
first-born 124, 128
first-fruits 154
first-hand 20, 467
firstlings 128, 154
first-rate
   important 642
   excellent 648
   man-of-war 726
firth 343
fisc 802
fiscal 800
fish *food* 298
   sport 361, 622
   animal 366
food for -es 362
other - to fry
   ill-timed 135

busy 682
queer - 857
- in the air 645
- for compliments 880
-for *seek* 4
   experiment 463
   desire 865
-hatchery 370
-out *inquire* 461
   discover 480*a*
- in troubled waters
   difficult 704
   discord 713
-up *raise* 307
   find 480*a*
-out of water
   disagree 24
   unconformable 83
   displaced 185
   bungler 701
fisherman 361
fishery 370
fishing *kill* 361
   pursue 622
fishing-boat 273
fishpond 343, 370
fish-tail 267
fishy transaction 940
fisk 266, 274
fissile 328
fission 44
fissure 44
   chink 198
fist
   handwriting 590
   grip 781
shake the -
   defy 515
   threat 909
fisticuffs 720
fistula 260
fit *state* 7
   agreeing 23
   equal 27
   paroxysm 173
   agitation 315
   caprice 608
   expedient 646
   healthy 654
   disease 655
   excitement 825
   anger 900
   right 922
   due 924
   duty 926
in -s 315
think- 600

- of abstraction 458
- of crying 839
- for 698
-out *dress* 225
  prepare 673
- to be seen 845
by –s and starts
  irregular 59
  discontinuous 70
  agitated 315
  capricious 608
  haste 684
fitful
  irregular 139
  changeable 149
  capricious 608
fittings 633
five 98
  division by – 99
  – act play 599
  – and twenty 98
fiver 800
Five Year Plan 626
fives *game* 840
fix *join* 43
  arrange 60
  establish 150
  place 184
  immovable 265
  solidify 321
  resolve 604
  difficulty 704
  – the eyes upon 441
  – the foundations 673
  – the memory 505
  – the time 114
  – the thoughts 457
  – up 774
  – upon *discover* 480a
  choose 609
fixed *intrinsic* 5
  permanent 141
  stable 150
  quiescent 265
  habitual 613
  – idea 481
  – opinion 484
  – periods 138
fixity 141
fixity of purpose 141
fixture
  appointment 741
  property 780
fizgig 423
fizz 409
fizzle 353
  – out 304

flabbergast 870, 879
flabbiness 324
flabby 324
flabelliform 194
flaccid *weak* 160
  soft 324
  empty 640
flag *weak* 160
  flat stone 204
  floor 211
  smoothness 255
  slow 275
  leaf 367
  sign 550
  path 627
  infirm 655
  inactive 683
  tired 688
  weary 841
  lower one's - 725
  red – *alarm* 669
  yellow–
    warning 668
    alarm 669
  – man 668
  – ship 726
  – of truce 723
flag-bearer 534
flagellation
  penance 952
  asceticism 955
  flogging 972
  rite 998
flagelliform 205
flageolet 417
flagitious 945
flagon 191
flagrant
  great 31
  manifest 525
  notorious 531
  atrocious 945
flagrante
  – bello 722
  – delicto
  sure enough 474
  act 680
  guilt 947
flagration 384
flagstaff *tall* 206
  signal 550
flail 276
flair 450, 698
flake 204
  snow– 383
  – white 430
flam 544

flambé 732
flambeau 423
flamboyant 577
flame *fire* 382
  light 420
  luminary 423
  passion 824, 825
  love 897
  catch the - *emotion* 821
  consign to the –s 384
  add fuel to the - 173
  in –s 382
  – up 825
  –coloured
    red 434
    orange 439
flamen 996
flame-projector 527
flaming *violent* 173
  feeling 821
  excited 824
  ostentatious 882
  boasting 884
flâneur 935
flange *support* 215
  rim 231
  projection 250
flank *side* 236
  protect 664
flannel 384
flap *adjunct* 39
  hanging 214
  move to and fro 315
  – the memory 505
flapdoodle 517
flapper *girl* 129
flapping *loose* 47
flare *violent* 173
  glare 420
  light 423
  – up
    excited 824, 825
    angry 900
flaring *colour* 428
flash *instant* 113
  violent 173
  fire 382
  light 420
  eyes – *fire* 900
  – lamp 550
  – light 423
  – across the memory 505
  – on the mind
    thought 451
  disclose 529
  impulse 612
  – note 800

- in the pan
unsubstantial 4
transientness 111
impotent 158
unproductive 169
failure 732
- tongue 563
- up *excited* 824
- upon
unexpected 508
- of wit 842
flashing
ostentatious 882
flashy
gaudy colour 428
style 577
ornament 847
vulgar 851
flask 191
flat *inert* 172
abode 189
story 191
low 207
horizontal 213
vapid 391
low tone 408
musical note 413
positive 535
dupe 547
back-scene 599
shoal 667
bungler 701
poor 804
insensible 823
dejected 837
weary 841
dull 843
simple 849
fall - 732
- contradiction 536
- iron 255
- refusal 764
flatfoot 664
flatness 251
flatter *deceive* 545
cunning 702
please 829
grace 845
encourage 858
approbation 931
adulation 933
- oneself
probable 472
hope 858
- the palate 394
flatterer 935
flattering

- remarks 894
- tale
hope 858
- unction to one's soul
content 831
vain 880
flattery 933
flattery 544, **933**
flatulent
gaseous 334
air 338
wind 349
- style 573, 575
flatus 334, 349
flaunt 873, 882
flaunting *vulgar* 85
gaudy 428
unreserved 525
flautist 416
Flavian amphitheatre 728
flavour 390
flavouring 393
flavous 436
flaw *break* 70
crack 198
error 495
imperfection 651
blemish 848
fault 947
- in an argument 477
flaxen 436
flay *divest* 226
punish 972
flea *jumper* 309
dirt 653
- in one's ear
repel 289
eject 297
refuse 764
disrepute 874
abashed 879
discourteous 895
contempt 930
flea-bite 643
flea-bitten 440
fleck 32
flecked 440
flection 279
fled *escaped* 671
fledge 673
fledgling 123
flee *avoid* 623
fleece *tegument* 223
strip 789
rob 791
impoverish 804
surcharge 814

fleer *ridicule* 856
insult 929
fleet *ships* 273
swift 274
navy 726
Fleet *prison* 752
fleeting 4, 111
flesh *bulk* 192
animal 364
mankind 372
carnal 961
gain - 194
ills that - is heir to *evil*
619
disease 655
in the - 359
one - 903
way of all - 360
weakness of the - 945
- and blood
substance 3
materiality 316
animality 364
affections 820
make the - creep
pain 830
fear 860
flesh-colour 434
fleshly 316
flesh-pots 298
- of Egypt 734, 803
fleur-de-lis 847
fleuron 847
flexible 324, 705
flexion
curvature 245
fold 258
deviation 279
flexuous 248
flexure 245, 258
flibbertigibbet 980
flicker
changing 149
waver 314
flutter 315
light 420
dim 422
flickering 139
flier 621
flies *theatre* 599
flight *flock* 102
volitation 267
swiftness 274
departure 293
avoidance 623
escape 671
- lieutenant 745

put to –
propel 284
repel 717
vanquish 731
– of fancy 515
– of stairs 305, 627
– of time 109
flighty *inattentive* 458
mad 503
fanciful 515
flim-flam 544, 608
flimsy *unsubstantial* 4
weak 160
rarity 322
soft 324
sophistical 477
trifling 643
flinch *swerve* 607
avoid 623
fear 860
cowardice 862
fling *propel* 284
jig 840
jeer 929
have one's–
active 682
laxity 738
freedom 748
amusement 840
– aside 782
have a – at
attack 716
resent 900
disrespect 929
censure 932
– away *reject* 610
waste 638
relinquish 782
– down 308
– to the winds
destroy 162
not observe 773
flint *hard* 323
flint-hearted 907
flintlock 727
flip *beverage* 298
flippant *fluent* 584
pert 885
flipper *paddle* 267
flirt *propel* 284
coquet 607, 854
love 897
endearment 902
– a fan 855
flit *elapse* 109
changeable 149
move 264

travel 266
swift 274
depart 293
run away 623
flitter
small part 32
changeable 149
flutter 315
flitting 111
float *establish* 150
navigate 267
boat 273
buoy up 305
lightness 320
before the –s
on the stage 599
– on the air 405
– before the eyes 446
– bonds 788
– in the mind
thought 451
imagination 515
floater 683
floating [*see* float]
rumoured 532
– battery 726
– capital 805
– debt 806
– dock 189
flocculent
woolly 256
soft 324
pulverulent 330
flock
assemblage 72
multitude 102
laity 997
–s and herds 366
– together 72
floe *ice* 383
flog 972
hasten 684
flood *much* 31
crowd 72
river 348
abundance 639
redundance 641
prosperity 734
stem the – 708
– of the light 420
– of tears 839
flood-gate
limit 233
egress 295
conduit 350
open the –s
eject 297

permit 760
flood-light 423, 599
flood-mark 466
flood-tide
increase 35
complete 52
height 206
advance 282
water 337
floor *level* 204
base 211
horizontal 213
support 215
overthrow 731
ground – 191
flop 315
Flora 369
floral 367
florescence 154
floriculture 371
florid *colour* 428
red 434
style 577
health 654
florist 371
floss 256
flotilla 273, 726
flotsam and jetsam 73
flounce
trimming 231
jump 309
agitation 315
flounder
change 149
toss 315
uncertain 475
bungle 699
difficulty 704
fail 732
flour 330
flourish
brandish 314, 315
exaggerate 549
language 577
speech 582
prosper 618
healthy 654
prosperous 734
ornament 847
repute 873
display 882
boast 884
– of trumpets
loud 404
publish 531
cheerfulness 836
ostentation 882

celebrate 883
boast 884
flout 929, 936
flow *course* 109
  hang 214
  motion 264
  stream 348
  murmur 405
  abundance 639
  – from
  result 154
  – of ideas 451
  – in 294
  – into *river* 348
  – out 295
  – over 641
  – of soul
  conversation 588
  affections 820
  cheerful 836
  social 892
  – with the tide 705
  – of time 109
  – of words 582, 584
flower *essence* 5
  produce 161
  vegetable 367
  prosper 734
  beauty 845
  ornament 847
  repute 873
  – of age 131
  – of flock 648
  – of life 127
  – painting 556, 559
flowering plant 367
flowers
  anthology 596
  – of rhetoric 577
flowing [*see* flow]
  – periods 578
fluctuate
  change 149
  oscillate 314
  irresolute 605
flue *opening* 260
  down 320
  air-pipe 351
  dust 653
fluent
  differential 84
  fluid 333
  stream 348
  - *language* 578
  speech 584
fluff 256
  little bit of – 374

fluid 333
  – in motion 347
fluidity 333
fluke *hook* 244
  chance 621
flummery
  unmeaning 517
  flattery 933
flunk 732
flunkey
  servant 746
  servile 886
flunkeyism 933
flurry *hurry* 684
  agitation 821
  excitability 825
flush *flat* 251
  flood 348
  heat 382
  light 420
  colour 428
  red 434
  abundant 639
  wash 652
  health 654
  feeling 821
  passion 825
  rejoicing 838
  in liquor 959
  – of cash 803
flushed [*see* flush]
  excited 824
  cheerful 836
  hopeful 858
  proud 878
  vain 880
  – with rage 900
  – with success 731
  – with victory 884
fluster
  distract 458
  move 821
  excite 824, 825
flustered *tipsy* 959
flute
  furrow 259
  music 417
flutter
  variable 149
  agitation 315
  gamble 621
  hurry 684
  emotion 821
  excite 824, 825
  fear 860
fluvial 348
flux

conversion 144
  motion 264
  liquefaction 335
  flow 348
  – and reflux 314
  – of time 109
flux de paroles 584
fluxion 84
fluxions 85
fly *vanish* 4
  time 109
  transient 111
  burst 173
  minute 193
  wings 267
  vehicle 272
  swift 274
  depart 293
  break 328
  lose colour 429
  shun 623
  – to arms 722
  – at 716
  – back 277
  – in the face of
  oppose 708
  resist 719
  disobey 742
  insolence 885
  – in the face of facts 481,
    606
  – from 623
  – kites
  borrow 788
  credit 805
  not pay 808
  – off 291
  – in the ointment 651
  – open 260
  – out *violent* 173
  excitable 825
  angry 900
fly-blown 653
fly-boat 273
flyer 269
flying [*see* fly]
  – colours
  success 731
  display 882
  celebrate 883
  – boat 273, 726
  – column 726
  – field 728
  – fish 83
  – machine 273
  – officer 745
  – rumour 532

fly-leaf
  interjacent 228
  book 593
fly-wheel 312
foal 129, 271
foam *violent* 173
  boil 315
  spray 353
  excitement 824, 825
  - with rage 900
fob 191
  - off 545
focal 222
focis, pro aris et - 717
focus 74
  centre 222
  furnace 386
  bring into a -
  collect 72
  convergence 290
  in - *visible* 446
  out of - *dim* 447
  - the thoughts 457
fodder 298
foe 891
fœderis, casus - 770
foehn 349
fœnum habet in cornu
  668, 913
fœtor 401
fœtus 129, 153
fog 353, 475
  in a - 528
  London - 436
fogey 500, 857
foggy
  opaque 426
fog-signal 668, 669
foh! 867
foible 945
foil *contrast* 14
  lamina 204
  baffle 706
  weapon 727
  defeat 731
foiled 732
foin 276
foist *ship* 273
  - in 228
  - upon 545
folâtre 836
fold *fold* 39
  bisect 91
  inclosure 232
  plait **258**
  prison 752
  congregation 997

- one's arms 681
- in one's arms 902
- up 225
foliaceous 204
foliage 367
foliate 85
foliated 204
folio 593
folk 372
folk-dance 840
folk-lore 124, 979
folk-song 597
follicle *cyst* 191
  hollow 252
follicular 260
follow
  - *in order* 63
  conform to 82
  -in time 117
  - *in motion* 281
  understand 518
  pursue 622
  obey 743
  - advice 695
  - the dictates of 615
  - the example of 19
  - from
  result from 154
  be proved by 478
  - implicitly 486, 695
  - the lead of
  co-operate 709
  - suit *imitate* 19
  - the trail 461
  - up
  continue 143
  persevere 604a
follower [*see* follow]
  successor 65
  learn 541
  servant 746
  lower 897
folly
  building 189
  irrationality **499**
  act of -
  mismanagement 699
foment
  stimulate 173
  warm 384
  promote 707
  excite 824
  relieve 834
fond 897
  - hope 858
fondle 902
fondling 899, 902

fondness
  desire 865
fondre en larmes 839
fons et origo 153
font *origin* 153
  type 591
  rite 998
  altar 1000
food 298
  preparation of - 673
  - for the mind 454
  - for powder 726
fool 501
  pudding 354
  deceive 545
  ridicule 856
  disrespect 929
  make a - of oneself
  bungle 699
  motley - 844
  play the -
  folly 499
  amusement 840
  -'s errand
  deceived 545
  unskilful 699
  -'s mate 732
  -'s paradise
  unsubstantial 4
  misjudgment 481
  disappoint 509
  hope 858
  rash 863
  - to the top of one's bent
  excite 824
  anger 900
  flatter 933
  - away money 818
  - away time 683
foolhardy 863
fooling 842
foolish 499
  act -ly 699
  look -
  disrepute 874
  shame 879
foolscap 550, 559
foot
  length 200
  stand 211
  metre 597
  at the - of 207
  keep on -
  continue 143
  support 251
  provide 637
  prepare 673

not stir a – 681
on – *existing* 1
during 106
journey 266
topic 454
business 625
preparing 673
active 682
put one's – down
resolved 604
put one's – in
undertake 676
bungle 699
set – on land 342
trample under – 930
– the bill 807
– by foot 51
one – in the grave
age 128
death 360
it *journey* 266
dance 309
at – 's pace 275
foot-ball
subjection 749
game 840
footboy 746
footfall
motion 264
indication 550
stumble 732
footing
circumstances 8
rank 71
influence 175
situation 183
foundation 211
support 215
payment 809
friendly – 888
get a –
location 184
be on a–
state 7
pay one's – 807
footlights 599
footman 746
footmark 551
footpad 792
foot-passenger 268
footpath 627
foot pound 466
footprint 551
foot-soldier 726
footsore 688
footstep 551
footstool 215

foot-warmer 386
foozle 732
fop 854
foppery 882
foppish 855
for *cause* 155
tendency 176
reason 476
motive 615
intention 620
preparation 673
have –
price **812**
– all that
notwithstanding 30
qualification 469
– all the world like 17
– aught one knows 156
– better for worse 78
– ever 112
– example 82
– form's sake 82
– good
complete 52
diuturnity 110
permanence 141
– the most part
great 31
general 78
special 79
– the nonce 118
– nothing 815
– a season 106
– a time 111
– the time being 106
forage
food 298
provision 637
steal 791
forage-cap 225
foramen 260
foraminous 260
forasmuch as
relating to 9
cause 155
reason 476
motive 615
foray *attack* 716
robbery 791
forbear
avoid 623
spare 678
lenity 740
sufferance 826
pity 914
forbearance 918
abstain 953

forbid 761
God –
dissent 489
deprecation 766
censure 932
prayer 990
forbidden fruit
seduction 615
prohibition 761
forbidding
ugly 846
force *corps* 72
power 157
strength 159
agency 170
energy 171
violence 173
cultivate 371, 707
cascade 348
– *of style* 574
urge 615
exertion 686
compulsion 744
armed – 726
brute – 964
put in – 924
– of argument 476
– of arms 744
– of character 820
– down the throat
severe 739
compel 744
– majeure 744
– open 173
– one's way
progression 282
passage 302
forced *irrelative* 10
– *style* 579
be – to 601
– labor 603
– march 744
forcefully 601
forceps
extraction 301
grip 781
forces 726
forcible [*see* force]
ford 302, 627
fore 234
fore and aft
complete 52
lengthwise 200
– schooner 273
forearm 673
forebears 166
forebode 511

forecast
foresight 510
prediction 511
plan 626
foreclose 706
foredoom 152, 601
forefathers 166
forefend
prohibit 761
forefinger 379
forego
relinquish 624
renounce 757
surrender 782
foregoing 62, 116
foregone
past 122
– conclusion
prejudged 481
predetermined 611
foreground 234
in the –
manifest 525
forehead 234
foreign
alien 10
extraneous 57
– accent 580
– parts 196
foreigner 57
forejudge
prejudge 481
foresight 510
foreknow 510
foreland 206, 254
forelay 545
forelock
pull the – 894
take time by the –
early 132
occasion 134
foreman 694
foremost
superior 33
beginning 66
front 234
in advance 280
important 642
reputed 873
forenoon 125
forensic 968
foreordain 152
foreordination 601, 611
fore part 234
forerun 62, 116, 280
forerunner 64, 512
foresee 507, 510

foreseen 871
foreshadow 152, 511
foreshorten 201
foreshow 511
foresight 116, **510**
caution 864
forest 367
forestage 599
forestall
prior 116
early 132
possession **777**
forestry 371
foretaste 510
foretell 511
forethought 459, 510
foretoken 511
forewarn 511, 668
foreword 64
forfeit *fail* 773
lose 776
penalty 974
– one's good opinion 932
forfeiture
disfranchisement 925
forfend 706, 717
forgather 72
forge *imitate* 19
produce 161
furnace 386
trump up 544
workshop 691
– fetters 751
forged
false 546
forger
maker 690
thief 792
forgery
deception 545
forget 506
hand – cunning 699
– benefits 917
– injury 918
– oneself 945
forgive 918
forgo
relinquish 624
renounce 757
surrender 782
forgotten
past 122
ingratitude 917
not to be – 505
– by the world 893
fork *bifid* 91
pointed 244

– lightning 423
– out
give 784
pay 807
expenditure 809
forlorn
dejected 837
hopeless 859
deserted 893
– hope
danger 665
rashness 863
form *state* 7
likeness 21
make up 54
order 58
arrange 60
convert 144
produce 161
bench 215
shape **240**
educate 537
pupils 541
manner 627
beauty 845
fashion 852
etiquette 882
law 963
rite 998
– letter 592
– part of 56
– a party 712
– a resolution 604
formal [*see* form]
regular 82
definitive 535
– style 579
affected 855
stately 882
– speech 582
formalism 739, 988
formalist 82
formality [*see* formal]
ceremony 852
affection 855
law 963
formation
composition 54
production 161
shape 240
formative 153
formed [*see* form]
attempered 820
former
in order 62
prior in time 116
past 122

formication 380
formidable 704, 860
formless 241
formula *rule* 80
  arithmetic 84
  maxim 496
  precept 697
  law 963
formulary 998
formulate 590
fornication 961
fornicator 962
foro conscientiæ
  veracity 543
  duty 926
  probity 939
forsake 624
forsaken 898
forsooth 535
forspent 688
forswear *lie* 544
  tergiversation 607
  refuse 764
  transgress 927
  improbity 940
fort 666, 717
fort
  le droit du plus–
  compulsion 744
  illegality 964
  un peu – 641
fortalice 717
forte 415, 698
fortelage 717
forth 282
  come –
  egress 295
  visible 446
  go – *depart* 293
  the decree has gone – 741
forthcoming 152, 673
forthwith 132
fortification 717
fortify 159
fortiori, a – 467, 476
fortissimo 404
fortiter in re 171
fortitude 826, 861
fortnightly 138
fortress 717, 752
fortuitous
  extrinsic 6
  chance 156
  undersigned 621
  – concourse of atoms 59
fortunate
  opportune 134

  successful 731
  prosperous 734
Fortunatus's – cap
  wish 865
  spell 993
  – purse 803
fortune *chance* 156
  fate 601
  wealth 803
  be one's – 151
  clean up a – 803
  evil – 621, 735
  good – 734
  make one's –
  succeed 731
  wealth 803
  tempt –
  hazard 621
  essay 675
  trick of – 509
  try one's – 675
  wheel of – 601, 621
fortune-hunter 886, 943
fortuneless 804
fortunes of
  narrative 594
fortune-teller 513
fortune-telling 511
forty 98
  – winks 683
forum 799
  school 542
  tribunal 966
forward *early* 132
  transmit 270
  advance 282
  willing 602
  improve 658
  active 682
  help 707
  vain 880
  insolent 885
  uncourteous 895
  bend – 234
  come –
  in sight 446
  offer 763
  display 882
  look – to 507
  move – 282
  press – *haste* 684
  put – *aid* 507
  offer 763
  put oneself – 880
  set – 676
  – in *knowledge* 490
foss 348

fosse
  inclosure 232
  ditch 259
  defence 717
fossil
  ancient 124
  hard 323
  organic 357
  dry bones 362
foster *aid* 707
  excite 824
  caress 902
  – a belief 484
fou 959
foudroyant 870
foul
  collide 276
  bad 649
  dirty 653
  unhealthy 657
  ugly 846
  base 940
  vicious 945
  fall – of
  oppose 708
  quarrel 713
  attack 716
  fight 720
  censure 932
  run – of
  impede 706
  – fiend 978
  – means 940
  – language
  malediction 908
  – odour 401
  – play *evil* 619
  cunning 702
  wrong 923
  improbity 940
foul-mouthed 895
foul-spoken 934
found 153, 215
foundation
  beginning 66
  stability 150
  base 211
  support 215
  lay the –s 673
  sandy – 667
  shake to its –s 315
founded
  well – 472
  – on *base* 211
  evidence 467
founder
  originator 164

sink 310
fail 732
religious – 986
foundery 691
founding 22
foundling
trover 775
derelict 782
outcast 893
fount *type* 591
fountain
source 153
river 348
store 636
– head 210
– pen 590
four 95
on all –s 13, 23
horizontal 213
easy 705
prosperous 734
humble 879
– in hand 272
– score &c. 98
– square 244
– times 96
from the – winds 278
fourflusher 884
fourfold 96
four-oar 273
four-poster 215
fourth 96, 97
musical 413
– estate 531
four-wheeler 272
fowl 366
fowling-piece 727
fox *animal* 366
cunning 702
– chase 622
fox-trot 840
foxy *colour* 433, 434
cunning 720
foyer 191, 599
fracas
disorder 59
noise 404
discord 713
contention 720
fraction *part* 51
numerical 84
less than one **100a**
fractious 901
fracture
disjunction 44
discontinuity 70
fissure 198

fragile 160, 328
fragment
small 32, 193
part 51, 100*a*
fragrance 400
fragrant weed 392
frail *weak* 160
brittle 328
feeble 575
irresolute 605
imperfect 651
failing 945
impure 961
– sisterhood 962
frais, à grands – 481
frame
condition 7
make 161
support 215
border 231
form 240
substance 316
structure 329
contrive 626
cucumber – 371
have –d and glazed 822
– of mind
inclination 602
disposition 820
frame-up 626
framework
support 215
structure 329
franchise
voting 609
freedom 748
right 924
exemption 927*a*
Franciscan 996
franc-tireur 726
frangible 160, 328
frank *open* 525
sincere 543
artless 703
honourable 939
frankalmoigne 748
Frankenstein 913, 980
frankincense 400
frantic
violent 173
delirious 503
excited 824
fraternal
brother 11
concord 714
friendly 888
fraternity [*see* fraternal]

party 712
fraternize
co-operate 48, 709
agree 714
sympathize 888
associate 892
fratricide 361
Frau 374
fraud
falsehood 544
deception 545
pretender 548
dishonour 940
pious – 988
fraught *full* 52
pregnant 161
possessing 777
– with danger 665
fray *rub* 331
battle 720
in the thick of the – 722
frayed 659
frazzle
beaten to a – 732
freak 608, 872
– of Nature 83
freckle 848
freckled 440
fredaine 840
free
detached 44, 47
unconditional 52
liberate 672
unobstructed 705
at liberty 748, 750
gratis 815
liberal 816
insolent 885
exempt 927*a*
impure 961
– balloon 273
– and easy
cheerful 836
adventurous 863
vain 880
insolent 885
friendly 888
sociable 892
– fight 720
– from
simple 42
never – from 613
– gift 784
– from imperfection 650
– lance 726
– land 748
– liver 954*a*

- love 961
make – of 748
- play 170, 748
- quarters
cheap 815
hospitality 892
- space 180
- stage 748
- trade
commerce 794
- translation 522
- will 600
make – with
frank 703
take 789
sociable 892
uncourteous 895
freebooter 792
freeborn 748
freedman 748
freedom 748
free-handed 816
freehold 780
freely
willingly 602
freeman 748
freemasonry
unintelligible 519
secret 528
sign 550
co-operation 709
party 712
free-spoken 703
freethinker 989
freeze
benumb 381
cold 385
- the blood 830
freezing 383
- mixture 387
freight *lade* 184
cargo 190
transfer 270
freightage 812
freighter 273
freight train 272
French
peddler's – 563
- and English 840
- horn 417
- leave *avoid* 623
freedom 748
- polish 847
frenetic 503
frenzy
madness 503
imagination 515

excitement 825
frequency 136
frequent
in number 104
in time 136
in space 186
habitual 613
visit 892
fresco *cold* 383
painting 556
al –
out of doors 220
in the air 338
fresh *additional* 37
new 123
flood 348
cold 383
colour 428
remembered 505
unaccustomed 614
good 648
healthy 654
impertinent 885
tipsy 959
- breeze 349
- colour 434
- news 532
freshen 658, 689
freshet 348
freshman 541
freshwater 851
freshwater sailor 701
fret *suffer* 378
grieve 828
gall 830
discontent 832
sad 837
ornament 847
irritate 900
- and fume 828
fretful 901
fret-work 219
friable 328, 330
friandise 868
friar 996
- 's lantern 423
- Rush 980
Black –s 996
friary 1000
fribble
slur over 460
trifle 643
dawdle 683
fop 854
fricassee 298
frication 331
friction *force* 157

obstacle 179
rubbing 331
on – wheels 705
friend 711, **890**
candid – 936
next – 759
friendless 893
friendly 714, 894
friends, be – 888
see one's – 892
friendship 9, **888**
frieze 210
frigate 726
fright
cards 840
alarm 860
frightful 31, 830, 846
frightfully 31
frightfulness 860
frigid
cold 383
- *style* 575
callous 823
indifferent 866
frigidarium 387
frigorific 385
frill 231, 248
frills and furbelows 847
fringe
border 231
lace 256
exaggeration 549
ornament 847
frippery
trifle 643
ornament 847
finery 851
ridiculous 853
ostentation 882
frisk *prance* 266
leap 309
search 461
gay 836
amusement 840
frisky 682, 836
frith *chasm* 198
strait 343
forest 367
fritinancy 412
fritter *small* 32
- away *lessen* 36
waste 638
- away time 683
fritters 298
frivolous
unreasonable 477
foolish 499

capricious 608
trivial 643
frizz *curve* 245, 248
fold 258
frock *dress* 225
canonicals 999
– coat 225
frog *fastening* 45
leaper 309
ornament 847
frolic 827, 840
frolicsome 836
from *motive* 615
– this cause 155
– day to day 106, 138
– end to end 52
– that time 117
– time immemorial 122
– time to time 136
frond 367
fronder
censure 932
frondeur
disobey 742
front *foremost* 66
wig 225
fore part **234**
resist 719
insolence 885
bring to the –
manifest 525
come to the –
surpass 303
important 642
repute 873
in – 280
present a – 719
– danger 861
– to front 708
– of the house 599
– rank 234
in the – rank
important 642
repute 873
frontage 234
frontal 220
frontier 199, 233
fronting 237
fronti nulla fides
doubt 485
deception 545
frontispiece 64
frosh 541
frost 283
frostbite 383
frosted 430
– glass 427

froth
bubble 353
trifle 643
dirt 653
– up *angry* 900
frothy 320, 353
- *style* 573, 577
irresolute 605
frounce 258
frouzy 401
froward 901*a*
frown *lower* 837
scowl 839
discourteous 895
angry 900
sulky 901*a*
disapprove 932
– down·
abash 879
–s of fortune 735
frozen 383, 385
fructify
produce 161
be productive 168
improve 658
prosper 734
frugal 817, 953
– to excess 819
fruges consumere natus
drone 683
peasant 876
frugivorous 298
fruit *result* 154
produce 161
food 298
profit 775
forbidden – 615
reap the –s
succeed 731
reward 973
–tree 367
fruitful 168
fruition 161, 827
fruitless
unproductive 169
useless 645
failure 732
frump 851, 895
frumpish 901*a*
frustrate 179, 706
frustrated 732
frustum 51
fry *shoal* 102
child 129
heat 384
small –
unimportant 643

commonalty 876
frying-pan 386
out of – into fire
worse 659
clumsy 699
failure 732
misfortune 735
aggravation 835
fuddled 959
fudge 517, 643
fuel **388**, 638
add – to the flame 835
– oil 388
increase 35
heat 384
aggravate 835
anger 900
fugaces labuntur anni 111
fugacious 111
fugitive
transient 111
emigrant 268
avoiding 623
– writings 596
fugleman
pattern 22
director 694
fugue 415
fulciment 215
fulcrum 215
fulfil
complete 729
– a duty 926
– an obligation 772
fulgent 420
fuliginous
dim 422
opaque 426
black 431
full *much* 31
complete 52
large 192
loud 404
abundant 639
cleanse 652
hands –
active 682
receipt in – 807
– blooded 641
– bloom 131
health 654
beauty 845
– blown 131
expanded 194
glorious 873
– of business 682
– coloured 428

523

- cry *loud* 404
bark 412
pursuit 622
- dinner pail 734
dress 225
ornament 847
fashion 852
show 882
- drive 274
- feather
prepared 673
- force 159
- gallop 274
- heart 820
- of incident 151
- many 102
- of meaning 516
- measure 639
- of people 186
- play
facility 705
freedom 748
- of point 842
- scope 748
- score 415
- size 912
- of sound and fury &c.
unmeaning 517
- speech 274
- stop
cease 142
rest 265
- swing
strong 159
active 682
successful 731
free 748
- as a tick 52
- tide 348
- tilt *active* 682
haste 684
- view 446
- of whims 608
full-fashioned 240
full-fed 954
full-flavoured 392
full-grown 131, 192
full-handed 816, 818
full-length 556
full-mouthed 412
full-toned 413
fully 31
fulminate
violent 173
propel 284
loud 404
malediction 908

threat 909
- against
accuse 932
fulness [*see* full]
in the - of time 109
fulsome
nauseous 395
fetid 401
bad 649
abhorrent 867
adulatory 933
impure 961
fulvid 436
fulvous 436
fumble
derange 61
handle 379
grope 463
awkward 699
fumbler 701
fume
violent 173
exhalation 334, 336
froth 353
heat 382
odour 398
excitement 824, 825
anger 900
in a -
discontented 832
-s of fancy 515
fumid 426
fumigate
vaporize 336
cleanse 652
fumigator 388
fumo, dare pondus - 481
fun 827, 840, 842
make - of 856
funambulist 700
function
algebra 84
office 170
business 625
utility 644
pomp 882
duty 926
rite 998
functionary
director 694
consignee 758
functus officio 756
fund *store* 636
sinking - 802
fundamental
intrinsic 5
base 211

support 215
- bass 413
- note 413
fundamentally 31
funds 800
in - 803
public - 802
funebrial 363
funeral 363
- pace 275
- march 415
funereal
interment 363
dismal 837
fungiform 249
fungology 369
fungosity 250
fungus
projection 250
vegetable 367
fœtor 401
bane 663
funicle 205
funicular 627
funk 860, 862
- hole 530
funnel *opening* 260
conduit 350
air-pipe 351
funnel-shaped 252
funny *odd* 83
boat 273
humorous 842
comic 853
fur *covering* 223
hair 256
warm 384
dirt 653
furacious 791
furbelow 231
furbish
improve 658
prepare 673
adorn 847
furcated 244
furcation 91
furcular 244
furfur 653
furfuraceous 330
Furies *anger* 900
evil-doers 913
demons 980
furious *violent* 173
haste 684
passion 825
anger 900
furiously 31

furl 312
furlong 200
furlough 760
furnace 386
  workshop 691
  like a – *hot* 382
  sighing like –
    lament 839
  in love 902
furnish
  provide 637
  prepare 673
  give 784
  – aid 707
  – a handle 617
  – its quota 784
furniture 633
  – van 272
furor
  insanity 503
  passion 825
furore
  emotion 820, 821
  passion 825
  desire 865
furrow 259
further
  added 37
  distant 196
  aid 707
  go – and fare worse
    worse 659
    bungle 699
  not let it go – 528
furthermore 37
furtive
  clandestine 528
  stealing 791
furuncle 250
fury *violence* 173
  excitation 825
  anger 900
  demon 980
furze 367
fuscous 433
fuse *join* 43
  combine 48
  heat 382, 384
  torch 388
fuselage 215
fusel oil 356
fusiform 244, 253
fusil 727
fusileer 726
fusillade 361, 716
fusion *union* 48
  heat 384

  co-operation 709
fuss *agitation* 315
  activity 682
  haste 684
  difficulty 704
  excitement 825
  ostentation 882
  kick up a – 173
  make a – about
    importance 642
    lament 839
    disapprove 932
fussy *crotchety* 481
  bustling 682
  excitable 825
fustian
  absurd 497
  unmeaning 517
  - *style* 577, 579
fustigate 972
fusty 124, 401, 653
futhorc 590
futile 497, 645
future 121
  eye to the – 510
  – possession 777
  – state
    destiny 152
    heaven 981
futurity 121
fuzzle 959
fuzzy 447

G

gab 284
  gift of the – 582
gabardine 225
gabble 517, 583
gabelle 812
gaberlunzie 876
gabion 717
gable *side* 236
  – end 67
Gabriel 977
Gaby 501
gad
  about 266, 268
gadget 626
gad-so 870
gaff 727
gaffer *old* 130
  man 373
  clown 876
gag
  closure 261

  render mute 403, 581
  dramatic 599
  muzzle 751
  imprison 752
gage *measure* 466
  security 771
  throw down the – 715
gaggle 412
gag-man 844
gaieté de cœur 836
gaiety [*see* gay] 836
gaillard 844
gain
  increase 35
  advantage 618
  skilful 698
  acquisition 775
  – the confidence of 484
  – credit 931
  – one's end 731
  – ground
    progress 282
    improve 658
  – head 175
  – laurels 873
  – learning 539
  – over 615
  – a point 731
  – private ends 943
  – the start
    priority 116
    early 132
  – strength 35
  – time
    protract 110
    early 132
    late 133
  – upon
    approach 286
    pass 303
    become a habit 613
  – a victory 731
gainful *useful* 644
gainless 646
gainsay 536
gait 264, 627
gaiter 225
gala 840, 882
galactic circle 318
galantuomo 939
galavant 902
galaxy
  assemblage 72
  multitude 102
  stars 318
  luminary 423
  glory 873

gale 349
Galen 662
galenicals 662
galimatias 497
galipot 191
galopade 840
galore 639
gall *hurt* 378
  bitter 395
  annoy 830
  anger 900
  malevolence 907
  dip the pen in – 934
gallant *brave* 861
  courteous 894
  love 897
  licentious 961, 962
gallantry
  dalliance 902
gallanty-show 448, 840
galled jade wince, let the
  – 884
galleon 273
gallery *room* 191
  passage 260
  auditory 599
  museum 636
  picture – 556
galley *ship* 273
  punishment 972, 975
  work like a – slave 686
  – proof 591
galliass 273
Gallicism 563
galligaskin 225
gallimaufry 41
galliot 273
gallipot 191
gallivant 902
galloon 847
gallop
  pass away 111
  ride 266
  scamper 274
galloping consumption 655
galloway 271
gallows 361, 975
  come to the – 972
galoche 225
galore 102
galvanic
  excitable 825
galvanism 157
galvanize 824
gamache 225
Gamaliel

  brought up at the feet of –
  492
gambade *leap* 309
  prank 840
gambado
  gaiter 225
  leap 309
gambit 66
gamble 156
gambling
  chance 621
  rashness 863
gambling-house 621
gamboge 436
gambol 309, 827, 840
game *lame* 160
  food 298
  animal 366
  savoury 394
  resolute 604
  persevering 604a
  aim 620
  gamble 612
  pursuit 622
  tactics 692
  amusement 840
  laughing-stock 857
  brave 861
  make – of
  deceive 545
  ridicule 856
  disrespect 929
  play the – 709, 939
  – in one's hands
  easy 705
  succeed 731
  command 737
  – to the last 604a
  – at which two can play
  718
  – up 732
game-cock 726, 861
game-keeper 370, 753
gameness 861
gamesome 836
gamester
  chance 621
  play 840
  rash 863
gamey 392
gamin 876
gaming-house 621
gammer *old* 130
  woman 374
gammon 544, 545
gamut 413
gander 373

gang
  assemblage 72
  go 264
  party 712
  – agley 732
ganger 690
gangrene 655
gangster 361, 913
gangway 260, 627
gantlet 972
  run the –
  resolution 604
  dare 861
gaol 752
  – delivery 672
gaoler 753, 975
gap 70, 198, 252
  stand in the – 717
gape *open* 260
  curiosity 455
  wonder 870
  – for *desire* 865
gaping [*see* gape]
  expectant 507
gar 161
garage 191
garb 225
  under the – of 545
garbage 653
garble
  take from 38
  exclude 55
  erroneous 495
  misinterpret 523
  falsify 544
  – accounts 811
garbled
  incomplete 53
garden *grounds* 189
  horticulture 371
  beautiful 845
  botanic – 371
  zoological – 370
  – party 840
gardener 371
gardens *street* 189
Gargantua 192
gargle 337
gargoyle 350
garish
  light 420
  colour 428
  ugly 846
  ornament 847
  vulgar 851
  display 882
garland

garlic
circle 247
sign 550
trophy 733
ornament 847
decoration 877
garlic
condiment 393
fetid 401
garment 225
garner 636
garnet 847
red 434
garnish
addition 39
prepare 673
fee 809
ornament 847
garniture 225
garran 271
garret 191, 210
garrison
occupant 188
safety 664
defence 717
soldiers 726
garrotte
render powerless 158
kill 361
punishment 972
garrulity 584
garter
fastening 45
decoration 877
- blue 438
garth 181
gas 334
fuel 388
talk 482
boasting 883
- balloon 273
- stove 386
- bomb 727
- fitter 690
- mask 717
- projector 727
gasconade 884
gaseity 334
gaselier 214
gash *cut* 44
interval 198
wound 619
gasification 334, 336
gaskins 225
gas-light 423
gasoline 388
gasometer 636
gasp *blow* 349

droop 655
fatigue 688
at the last - 360
- for *desire* 865
gasper 392
gastriloquism 580
Gastromancy 511
gastronomy 298, 957
gate *beginning* 66
inclosure 232
mouth 260
barrier 706
water - 350
- way *way* 627
- keeper 263
gâté, enfant - 734
Gath, tell it not in -
conceal 528
disapprove 932
gather *collect* 72
expand 194
fold 258
conclude 480
acquire 775
take 789
- breath 689
- flesh 194
- from one
information 527
- fruits 731
gathered
- to one's fathers 360
gathering
assemblage 72
abscess 655
-clouds *dark* 421
shade 424
omen 512
danger 665
warning 668
adversity 735
gathering-place 74
gauche *clumsy* 699
gaucherie 699, 851
gaud 847
gaudery 880
gaudy *colour* 428
vulgar 851
showy 882
gauge 466
rain- 348
wind- 349
gauger 965
gaunt *bulky* 192
lean 203
ugly 846
gauntlet *glove* 225

armour 717
fling down the - 715
take up the - 720
gauntry 627
Gautama 986
gauze *shade* 424
semitransparent 427
gavel 72, 812
gavelkind 778
gavelock 633
gavot 840
gawky
awkward 699
ugly 846
(ridiculous 853)
gay *colour* 428
cheerful 836
adorned 847
showy 882
dissipated 961
- deceiver 962
- world 852
gaze 441
gazebo 441
gazelle *swift* 274
gazette
publication 531
record 551
in the -
bankrupt 808
gazetteer
list 86
information 527
record 551
gazing-stock
ridiculous 857
wondrous 872
géant, à pas de - 274
gear *clothes* 225
harness 633
high - 274
in - 673
low - 275
out of -
disjoin 44
derange 61
useless 645
unprepared 674
- wheel 633
geese are swans, all his -
482
gehenna 982
geisha 599
Geist 498
gel 352
gelatin 352
gelatinify 352

geld 38, 158
gelding 271, 373
gelid 383
Geloscopy 511
gem 648, 847
geminate 90
Gemini *twins* 89
  O - ! 870
gemote 72
gendarme 726, 965
gender 75
genealogy 69, 166
general
  generic 78
  habitual 613
  officer 745
  the -
  commonalty 876
  things in - 151
  - breaking up 655
  - favourite 899
  - information 490
  - meaning 516
  - public 372
  - run 613
  - servant 690, 746
generalissimo 745
generality
  mean 29
  universal 78
generalize 476
generally speaking 613
generalship 692, 722
generate 161, 168
generation
  consanguinity 11
  period 108
  production 161
  mankind 372
  rising - 167
  spontaneous - 161
  wise in one's - 498
generator 164
generic 78
generosity
  giving 784
  liberality 816
  benevolence 906
  disinterestedness 942
genesis
  beginning 66
  production 161
genet 271
Genethliacs 511
genetics 161
Geneva gown 996
genial

productive 161
sensuous 377
warm 382
willing 602
delightful 829
affable 894
geniality 836
geniculated 244
genie 980
genital 161
genitor 166
geniture 161
genius
  intellect 450
  talent 498
  skill 698
  proficient 700
  prodigy 872
  evil - 980
  good -
  friend 898
  benefactor 912
  spirit 979
  tutelary - 711
  - for 698
  - of a language 560
  - loci 664
genre 556, 559
gent 851, 876
genteel 852, 875
  - comedy 599
gentile 984, 989
gentility
  fashion 852
  rank 875
  politeness 894
gentium, jus - 963
gentle *moderate* 174
  slow 275
  domesticated 370
  faint sound 405
  lenient 740
  meek 826
  courteous 894
  - blood 875
  - breeding 894
  - hint 527
  - as a lamb 174
  - slope 217
gentlefolk 875
gentleman
  male 373
  squire 875
  man of honour 939
  the old - 978
  walking - 599
gentlemanly 852

gently bred 894
Gentoo 984
gentry 875
  landed - 779
genuflexion
  bowing 308
  submission 725
  servility 886
  courtesy 894
  respect 928
  worship 990, 998
genuine 494, 648
genus 75
  - irritabile vatum 597
geodesist 85, 318
geodesy 318, 466
geography 183, 318
geoid 249
geology &c. 358
geomancer 513
geomancy 511
geometry 466
geoponics 371
georama 448
Georgics 371
geotic 318
gerfalcon 913
germ 153
german 11
  - band 417
  - silver 545
germane 23
germicide 662
germinal 153
germinate 161, 194, 365
  - from 154
gerontic 128
gerrymander 545
gesso 556
gest 680
gestation
  propagation 161
  carriage 270
  maturation 673
gesticulate 550
gesture *hint* 527
  indication 550
get *become* 144
  beget 161
  acquire 775
  receive 810
  - ahead 35
  - ahead of 33
  - along 282
  - along with you
  ejection 297
  dismissal 756

– at 480*a*
– away 287
– back
retire 283
regain 775
– the best of 731
– better 658
– down
swallow 298
descend 306
– you gone 297
– into harness 673
– by heart 505
– home 292
– in *collect* 72
gather 775
– loose 44
– near 286
– off *depart* 293
escape 671
– on *advance* 282
prosper 734
– out *eject* 297
extract 301
publish 531
– over
recover from 660
succeed 731
be content 831
– over the ground 274
– for one's pains 973
– ready 673
– rid of 672
– a sight of 441, 490
– through
end 67
transact 692
complete 729
expend 809
– to
extend to 196
arrive 292
– together 72
– into trouble 732
– the wind up 860
– up *produce* 161
ascend 305
raise 307
learn 539
fabricate 544
prepare 673
rise early 682
foment 824
– into the way of 613
get-away 671
gewgaw
trifle 643

ornament 847
vulgar 851
geyser 382, 386
ghastly
pale 429
hideous 846
frightful 860
ghaut 203
ghetto 189
ghost *shade* 362
fallacy of vision 443
soul 450
writer 593
apparition 980
give up the – 360
needs no – to tell us 525
pale as a –
colourless 429
fear 860
– dance 992
Ghost, Holy – 976
ghost-like
ugly 846
ghostly
intellectual 450
supernatural 976, 980
ghoul 913, 980
ghyll 348
giant
large 192
tall 206
– refreshed
strong 159
refreshed 689
–'s strides
distance 196
swift 294
giaour 984, 989
gibber 583
gibberish 517, 563
gibbet
brand 932
execute 972
gallows 975
gibble-gabble 584
gibbous 249, 250
gib-cat *male* 373
gibe 929
giblets 298
gibus 225
giddy
inattentive 458
vertiginous 503
irresolute 605
capricious 608
bungling 699
giddy-head 501

giddy-paced 315
gift *power* 157
talent 698
given 784
– of the gab 582
look a – horse in the
mouth
fastidious 868
ungrateful 917
gifted 698
gig 272, 273
gigantic
strong 159
large 192
tall 206
giggle 838
giglamps 445
Gilbertian 842
Gilbertine 996
gild *coat* 223
colour 439
ornament 847
– refined gold 641
– the pill
deceive 545
tempt 615
please 829
flatter 933
Gilead, balm in – 834, 858
Giles's Greek, St. – 563
gill 348
gillie 746
gilt 436, 847
– edged 648
gimbals 312
gimcrack
weak 160
brittle 328
trifling 643
ornament 847
ridiculous 853
gimlet 262
gimp
clean 652
pretty 845
decoration 847
gin *trap* 545
instrument 633
intoxicating 959
demon 980
gingerbread
weak 160
vulgar 851
gingerly 174, 459, 864
gingle 408
gin mill 189
gin palace 189

gipsy
wanderer 268
wag 844
– lingo 563
giraffe 206
girandole 423
girasol 847
gird *bind* 43
strengthen 159
surround 227
jeer 929
– up one's loins
brace 159
prepare 673
girder 45, 215
girdle *bond* 45
encircle 227
circumference 230
circle 247
put a – round the earth 311
girl 129, 374
girlhood 127
girt 45
girth
bond 45
circumference 230
gisarm 727
gist *essence* 5
meaning 516
important 642
gît, ci – 363
gittern 417
give *yield* 324
melt 382
bestow 784
discount 813
– away 782, 784
in marriage 903
– back 790
– birth to 161
– with both hands 816
– in charge
restrain 751
– chase 622
– consent 762
– one credit for 484
– in custody 751
– expression to 566
– forth 531
– the go by 623
– a horse his head 748
– in *submit* 725
– into *consent* 762
– light 420
– the mind to 457
– notice
inform 527

warn 668
– it one
censure 932
punish 972
– out *emit* 297
publish 531
bestow 784
– over *cease* 142
relinquish 624
lose hope 859
– place to
substitute 147
avoid 623
– play to the imagination
515
– points to 27
– quarter 740
– rise to 153
– one the slip 671
– security 771
– and take
reciprocate 12
compensation 30
interchange 148
retaliation 718
compromise 774
barter 794
equity 922
honour 939
– tongue 531
– a turn to 140
– one to understand 527
– up
not understand 519
unwilling 603
reject 610
relinquish 624
submit 725
resign 757
surrender 782
restore 790
hopeless 859
– up the ghost 360
– way *weak* 160
brittle 328
submit 725
pine 828
despond 837
modest 881
given [*see* give]
circumstances 8
supposition 514
received 785
– over *dying* 360
– time 134
– to 613
giving 784

gizzard 191
stick in one's – 900
glabrous 225
glacial 383
glaciate 385
glacier 383
glacis 217, 717
glad 827, 829
give the – eye 441
would be – of 865
– tidings 532
gladden 834, 836
glade *hollow* 252
opening 260
shade 424
gladiator 726
gladiatorial 361, 713, 720
gladsome 827, 829
Gladstone bag 191
glair 352
glaive 727
glamour 992
glance *look* 441
sign 550
see at a – 498
– at
take notice of 457
allude to 527
censure 932
– off *deviate* 279
diverge 291
gland 221
glare *light* 420
stare 441
imperfection vision 443
visible 446
glaring [*see* glare]
great 31
colour 428
visible 446
manifest 525
glass *vessel* 191
smooth 255
brittle 328
transparent 425
lens 445
musical –es 47
see through a – darkly 491
– of fashion 852
live in a – house
brittle 328
visible 446
danger 665
– too much 959
glass-coach 272
glasshouse 191, 371
Glassite 984

glassy [*see* glass]
  shining 420
  colourless 429
glaucous 435
glave 727
glaver 933
glaze 255
gleam *small* 32
  light 420
glean 609, 775
gleanings 636
glebe *land* 342
  ecclesiastical 995
  church 1000
glee *music* 415
  satisfaction 827
  merriment 836
gleek 929
glen 252
glengarry 225
glib *voluble* 584
  facile 705
glide *lapse* 109
  move 264
  travel 266
  fly 267
  – *into*
  conversion 144
glider 273
glimmer
  light 420
  dim 422
  visible 446
  slight knowledge 490, 491
glimpse 441, 490
glint 420
glissade 306
glisten 420
glitter
  shine 420
  appear 446
  illustrious 882
glittering
  ornament 847
  display 882
gloam 901*a*
gloaming 126, 422
gloar *look* 441
  wonder 970
gloat 884
  – *on look* 441
  – *over* 441
  pleasure 377
  delight 827
globated 249
globe
  sphere 249

  world 318
  on the face of the – 318
  – *trotter* 268
globule 32, 249
glomeration 72
gloom 421, 827, 837
gloomy horizon 859
glorification 884
glorify
  honour 873
  approve 931
  worship 990
glorious
  illustrious 873
  tipsy 959
glory
  light 420
  honour 873
  heaven 981
  King of – 976
  – in 878, 884
  – be to God 990
gloss *smooth* 255
  sheen 420
  interpretation 522
  falsehood 546
  plea 617
  beauty 845
  – of novelty 123
  – over
  neglect 460
  sophistry 477
  falsehood 544
  vindicate 937
glossary 86, 562
glossographer 492
glossologist 492
glossology 560, 562
glossy [*see* gloss]
glottology 560
glout 901*a*
glove 225
  take up the – 720
  throw down the – 715
glow *warm* 382
  shine 420
  appear 446
  colour 428
  style 574
  passion 821
glower
  glare 443
  discourteous 895
  sullen 901*a*
glowing [*see* glow]
  orange 439
  excited 824

  beautiful 845
  – *terms* 574
glow-worm 423
gloze 933, 937
glucose 396
glue *cement* 45
  cementing 46
  semiliquid 352
glum
  discontented 832
  dejected 837
  sulky 901*a*
glut
  redundance 641
  satiety 869
glutinous 352
glutton 954*a*, 957
gluttony 957
glycerine 332, 356
glyphography 558
glyptography 558
glyptotheca 557
gnarl *protuberance* 250
  anger 900
  threat 909
gnarled 256, 321
gnash one's teeth 839, 900
gnat *little* 193
  strain at a – &c.
  caprice 608
gnaw *eat* 298
  rub 331
  injure 659
gnawing
  – *grief* 828, 830
  – *pain* 378
gnome 496, 980
gnomic 496
gnomon 114
Gnostic 984
go
  cease to exist 2
  energy 171, 682
  move 264
  recede 287
  depart 293
  fade 429
  disappear 449
  fashion 852
  come and – 314
  as things – 613
  – about
  turn round 311
  published 531
  undertake 676
  – across 302
  – after

in time 117
in motion 281
- ahead
energetic 171
precede 280
advance 282
active 682
- against 708
- astray 495
- away 293
- back 283, 624
- bad 659
- bail 771
- before 280
- between
interjacent 228
instrumental 631
mediate 631, 724
- beyond 303
- by the board 158
- about your business
ejection 297
dismissal 756
- by
conform to 82
elapse 109
past 122
outrun 303
subterfuge 702
give the - by to
neglect 460
deceive 545
avoid 623
not observe 773
- by the name of 564
- deep into 461
- down *sink* 306
decline 659
- down with
believed 484
tolerated 826
content 831
- forth *depart* 293
- further and fare worse
659
publish 531
- halves 91
- hand in hand
accompany 88
same time 120
- hard 704
- on ill 735
- in 294
- in for
resolution 604
pursuit 622
- into

ingress 294
inquire 461
dissert 595
- all lengths
complete 52
resolve 604
exertion 686
- mad 503
- near 286
- no further
keep secret 528
- for nothing
sophistry 477
unimportant 643
- off *explode* 173
depart 293
die 360
wither 659
marry 903
- on *time* 106
continue 143
advance 282
- on for ever 112
- one better 303
- out
cease 142
egress 295
extinct 385
- out of one's head 506
- over
passage 302
explore 461
apostate 607
faithless 940
- to pieces 162
- on record 551
- round 311
- shares 778
- to sleep 683
- through
meet with 151
pass 302
explore 461
perform 599
conduct 692
complete 729
endure 826
- to *extend* 196
travel 266
direction 278
remonstrance 695
- up 305
- to war 722
- with
assent 488
concord 714
- with the stream

conform 82
servile 886
- from one's word 773
goad 615
hasten 684
goal *end* 67
reach 292
object 620
reach the -
complete 729
goat *substitute* 147
jumper 309
lecher 962
he - *male* 373
play the - 499
gob 269
gobang 840
gobbet
small piece 32
food 298
gobble *eat* 298
cry 412
gormandize 957
gobemouche 501, 547
go-between 758
goblet 191
goblin 980
go-cart 272
God 976
house of - 1000
kingdom of - 981
sons of - 977
-'s acre 363
- bless me! 870
- bless you
farewell 293
- forbid 766
-'s grace 906
- grant 990
- knows 491
-'s love 906
for -'s sake 765
-'s will 601
- willing 470
god 979
household -s 189
tutelary - 664
goddess *love* 897
good woman 948
heathen 979
Godhead 976
godlike 987
godly 944
godsend *good* 618
prosperity 734
Godspeed
farewell 293

hope 858
courtesy 894
benevolence 906
approbation 931
goer *horse* 271
goes [*see* go]
as one – 270
here – 676
Gog and Magog 192
goggle 441
– eyes 443
goggles 445
going [*see* go]
general 78
rumour 532
– to happen 152
– on
incomplete 53, 730
current 151
transacting 625
goitre 250
Golconda 803
gold *yellow* 436
orange 439
money 800
write in letters of – 642
worth its weight in – 648
gold certificate 800
golden [*see* gold]
– age
prosperity 734
pleasure 827
– apple 615
– calf
wealth 803
idol 985
idolatry 991
– dream
imagination 515
hope 858
– mean
moderation 174
mid-course 628
– opinions 931
– opportunity 134
– rule
precept 697
season of life 127
– *wedding* 883
golf 840
Golgotha 363, 1000
Goliath 159, 192
goloshes 225
gondola 273
gondolier 269
gone [*see* go]
past 122

absent 187
dead 360
– bad 653
– by
antiquated 124
– out of one's recollection 506
gonfalon 550
gong 417
goniometer 244, 466
good
complete 52
palatable 394
assent 488
benefit **618**
beneficial 648
right 922
virtuous 944
pious 987
as – as 197
be so – as 765
do – 906
for –
diuturnal 110
permanent 141
make –
evidence 467
provide 637
restore 660
complete 729
substantiate 924
vindicate 937
atone for 952
so far so – 931
think – 931
to the – 780
turn to – account 731
what's the – 645
– actions 944
– at 698
– auspices 858
– behaviour
contingent 108a
duty 926
virtue 944
in one's – books 888
– bye 293
in – case 192
– chance 472
– cheer *food* 298
cheerful 826
– circumstances 803
– condition 192
– day
arrival 292
departure 293
courtesy 894

– effect
goodness 648
beauty 845
– enough
not perfect 651
be – enough 765
put a – face upon
cheerful 836
proud 878
– fellow 892
– fight *war* 722
virtue 944
– for
useful 644
salubrious 656
– fortune 734
– Friday 998
– genius
friend 890
benefactor 912
god 979
in one's – graces 888
– hand 700
– humour
concord 714
cheerfulness 836
amuse 840
courtesy 894
kindly 906
– intention 906
– judgment 498
– lack! 870
– living
food 298
gluttony 957
– look-out 459
– looks 845
– luck 734
– man *man* 373
husband 903
worthy **948**
– manners 894
much – may it do 906
– morrow 292
– name 873
– nature 906
– night 293
– for nothing
impotence 158
useless 645
in – odour
repute 873
approbation 931
– offices
mediation 724
kind 906
– old time 122

– omen 858
– opinion 931
take in – part
pleased 827
courteous 894
kind 906
– pennyworth 815
– at the price 815
to – purpose 731
– repute 873
– sense 498
– society 852
– taste 578, 850
– temper 894
– thing 648
– time *early* 132
opportune 134
prosperous 734
– turn
kindness 906
– understanding 714
– wife
woman 374
spouse 903
– will
willingness 602
benevolence 906
– word
approval 931
vindication 937
– as one's word
veracity 543
observance 772
probity 939
– works 906
goodie 652, 746
goodly
great 31
large 192
handsome 845
good mixer 892
goodness [*see* good] **648**
virtue 944
have the –
request 765
– gracious! 870
– of heart 906
goods *effects* 270, 780
merchandise 798
good taste 868
Goodwin sands 667
goody 374
gooroo 996
goose *hiss* 409
game of – 840
giddy as a – 458
tailor's – 255

kill the – with golden eggs
699, 818
a wild – chase 545
gooseberry
old – 978
play – 459
– eyes 411, 443
goosecap 501
goose egg 101
gooseflesh 383
goosequill 590
goose-skin 383
Gordian knot 59, 704
gore *stab* 260
blood 361
gorge *ravine* 198
conduit 350
fill 641
satiety 869
gluttony 957
raise one's – 900
– the hook 602
gorge de pigeon 440
gorgeous
colour 428
beauty 845
ornament 847
ostentation 882
Gorgon 860
gorilla 913
gormandise 298, 954*a*, 957
gorse 367
gory *red* 434
murderous 361
unclean 653
gospel
certainty 474
truth 494
take for – 484
Gospels 985
gossamer
filament 205
light 320
texture 329
gossip *news* 532
babbler 584
conversation 588
gossoon 876
Gotama 986
Goth 851, 876
Gotham, wise men of –
501
gothic
amorphous 241
gouache 556
gouge *concave* 252
perforator 262

goulash 298
gourd 191
gourmand 954*a*, 957
gourmet 868, 954*a*
gout 378
goût, haut – 392
goutte d'eau, il se noyerait
dans une – 699
govern 693, 737
governess 540 [*see* govern]
ruling power 745
divine – 976
petticoat – 699
governor
tutor 540
director 694
ruler 745
keeper 753
gowk 501
gown *dress* 225
canonicals 999
gownsman 492
grab *take* 789
miser 819
grabble 379
grace *style* 578
permission 760
concession 784
elegance 845
polish 850
title 877
pity 914
forgiveness 918
honour 939
piety 987
worship 990
act of – 784
God's – 906
with a bad – 603
with a good –
willing 602
courteous 894
in one's good –s 888
heart of – 861
say – 990
submit with a good – 826
– before meat 916
grâce: coup de – 914
la – 840
graceless
inelegant 579
ugly 846
vicious 945
impenitent 951
irreligious 989
Graces 845
gracile 203

gracious
  willing 602
  courteous 894
  kind 906
  good – 870
grade *degree* 26
  arrange 60
  term 71
  ascent 217
  on the down – 658
  on the up – 659
gradatim
  gradually 26
  in order 58
  continuous 69
  slow 275
gradation
  degree 26
  order 58
  continuity 69
gradient 217
gradual *degree* 26
  continuous 69
  slow 275
graduate
  adjust 23
  calibrate 26
  arrange 60
  series 69
  measure 466
  scholar 492, 873
graduated scale 466
gradus 86, 562
Græculus esuriens 886
graft *join* 43
  locate 184
  insert 300
  trees 371
  teach 537
  booty 794
  corruption 940
Grail
  holy – 998
grain *essence* 5
  small 32
  tendency 176
  little 193
  rough 256
  weight 319
  texture 329
  powder 330
  paint 428
  temper 820
  ornament 847
  against the –
  rough 256
  unwilling 603

  opposing 708
  in the – 820
  –s of allowance
  qualification 469
  doubt 485
  like –s of sand
  incoherent 47
gramercy 916
graminivorous 298
grammar
  beginning 66
  teaching 537
  school 542
  language **567**
  bad – 568
  comparative – 560
grammarian 492
gramme 319
gramophone 417, 418, 553
granary 636
grand
  great 31
  style 574
  important 642
  money 800
  handsome 845
  glorious 873
  ostentatious 882
  – climacteric 128
  – doings 882
  – duchy 181
  – jury 967
  en – seigneur
  proud 878
  insolent 885
  en –e tenue
  ornament 847
  show 882
  – piano 417
  – style 556
  – tour 266
  – Turk 745
  – vizier 694
grandam 130
grandchildren 167
grande dame 878
grandee 875
grandeur 873
grandfather 130, 166
grandiloquent 577
grandiose 577
grandmother 166
  simple 501
  teach – 538
grandsire 130, 166
grange 189
granite 323

granivorous 298
grano salis, cum 469, 485
grant *admit* 529
  permit 760
  consent 762
  confer 784
  God – 990
  – a lease 771
granted 488
  take for –
  believe 484
  suppose 514
grantee
  possessor 779
  receiver 785
granular 330
granulate 330
granule 32
grapes, sour –
  unattainable 471
  falsehood 544
  excuse 617
grape-shot
  attack 716
  arms 727
graph 554
graphic
  intelligible 518
  painting 556
  descriptive 594
graphite 332
graphito 556
graphology 590
graphometer 244
graphotype 558
grapnel 666
grapple
  fasten 43
  clutch 789
  – with
  – a question 461
  – difficulties 704
  oppose 708
  resist 719
  contention 720
grappling-iron
  fastening 45
  safety 666
grasp
  comprehend 518
  power 737
  retain 781
  seize 789
  in one's – 737
  possess 777
  tight – *severe* 739
  – at 865

- of intellect 498
grasping
  miserly 819
  covetous 865
grass 344, 367
  let the – grow under one's
    feet
  neglect 460
  inactive 683
  not let the – &c.
  active 682
grasshopper 309
grass-plat 371
grate *rub* 330
  physical pain 378
  stove 386
  – on the ear
  harsh sound 410
  – on the feelings 830
grated
  barred 219
grateful
  physically pleasant 377
  agreeable 829
  thankful 916
grater 260, 330
gratification
  animal - 377
  moral - 827
gratify 829
  permit 760
  please 829
grating [*see* grate]
  lattice 219
  harsh 713
gratis 815
gratitude **916**
gratuitous
  inconsequent 477
  supposititious 514
  voluntary 602
  payless 815
gratuity
  gift 784
  gratis 815
gratulate 896
gravaman 642
  – of a charge 938
grave *great* 31
  engrave 259, 558
  tomb 363
  important 642
  composed 826
  distressing 830
  sad 837
  heinous 945
  beyond the – 360

look –
  disapprove 932
  rise from the – 660
  silent as the – 403
  sink into the – 360
  on this side of the – 359
  – in the memory 505
  – note 408
  – trap 599
gravel
  earth 342
  material 635
  puzzle 704
graven image 991
graveolent 398
graver 558
graving dock 189
gravitate
  descend 306
  weigh 319
  – towards 176
gravity *force* 157
  weight **319**
  vigour 574
  importance 642
  sedateness 826
  seriousness 827
  centre of – 222
  specific –
  weight 319
  density 321
gravy 333
  – boat 191
gray 432 [*and see* grey]
graze *touch* 199
  browse 298
  rub 331
  brush 379
grazier 370
gré, savoir – 916
grease
  lubricate 332
  oil 356
  – the palm
  tempt 615
  give 784
  pay 807
greasy 355
great *much* 31
  big 192
  glorious 873
  magnanimous 942
  (*important* 642)
  – bear 318
  – circle sailing 628
  – coat 225
  – doings

  importance 642
  bustle 682
  – folks 875
  – gun 626
  – hearted 942
  – Mogul 745
  – number 102
  – primer 591
  – quantity 31
greater 33
  – number 102
  – part 31
  nearly all 50
greatest 33
greatness **31**
greave 225
greed
  desire 865
  gluttony 957
greedy
  avaricious 819
green
  new 123
  young 127
  lawn 344
  grass 367
  unripe 397
  colour 435
  credulous 486
  novice 491
  unused 614
  healthy 654
  immature 674
  unskilled 699
  board of – cloth 966
  – memory 505
  – old age 128
greenback 800
green-eyed monster 920
greenhorn
  novice 493
  dupe 547
  bungler 701
greenhouse
  receptacle 191
  horticulture 371
greenness **435**
green-room 599
greensward 344
Greenwich time 114
greenwood 367
Greek
  unintelligible 519
  sharper 792
  St. Giles's – 563
  – Church 984
  – Kalends 107

greet *weep* 839
  hail 894
greeting
  sociality 892
  –s! 292
gregarious 892
grenade 727
grenadier
  tall 206
  soldier 726
grey 432
  – beard 130
  – friar 996
  – hairs 128
  bring – hairs to the grave
    adversity 735
    harass 830
  – mare
    rule 737
    master 745
    wife 903
  – matter
    brain 498
  – hound
    swift 274
    animal 366
  ocean –hound 273
gridelin 437
gridiron
  flatness 213
  crossing 219
  stove 386
  stage 599
  stadium 840
grief 828
  come to – 735
grievance
  evil 619
  painful 830
  wrong 923
grieve *mourn* 828
  pain 830
  dejected 837
  complain 839
grievous 649, 830
grievously 31
griffin 83, 366, 493
griffo 41
griffonage 590
grig *merry* 836
grill 382, 384, 461
  – room 189
grille 219
grim
  resolved 604
  painful 830
  doleful 837

  ugly 846
  discourteous 895
  sullen 901a
  –visaged war 722
grimace 243, 839, 855
grimacier
  actor 599
  humorist 844
  affected 855
grimalkin 366
grimy 652
grin *laugh* 838
  ridicule 856
  – and abide 725
  – a ghastly smile
    dejected 837
    ugly 846
grind
  reduce 195
  sharpen 253
  pulverize 330
  pain 378
  learn 539
  oppress 907
  – the organ 416
  – one's teeth 900
grinder
  teacher 330
  noise 404
grinding 739, 830
grindstone 253, 330
grip
  indication 550
  power 737
  retention 781
  clutch 789
  – of the hand 894
gripe [*see* grip]
  pain 378
  parsimony 819
grisaille
  grey 432
  painting 556
grisette
  woman 374
  commonalty 876
  libertine 962
grisly 846
grist
  materials 635
  provision 637
  – to the mill
    useful 644
    acquire 775
gristle 321, 327
grit
  strength 159

  powder 330
  stamina 604a
  courage 861
  – in the oil
    hindrance 706
gritty 323
grizzled
  grey 432
  variegated 440
groan 411, 839
groat 800
grocer 637
grocery 396
grog 298, 959
groin 244
groom 370, 746
  – of the chambers 746
  –'s man 903
groove
  furrow 259
  habit 613
  in a – 16
  move in a – 82
  put in a – for 673
grope
  feel 379
  experiment 463
  try 675
  in the dark 442, 704
gross
  great 31
  whole 50
  number 98
  ugly 846
  vulgar 851
  vicious 945
  impure 961
  – credulity 486
  – receipts 810
grosshead 501
grossheaded 499
grossièreté 895
grot [*see* grotto]
grotesque
  odd 83
  distorted 243
  - style 579
  ridiculous 853
grotto
  alcove 191
  hollow 252
grouch 895, 901a
ground
  cause 153
  region 181
  base 211
  lay down 213

support 215
coating 223
land 342
plain 344
evidence 467
teach 537
motive 615
plea 617
above – 359
down to the – 52
dress the – 371
fall to the – 732
get over the – 274
go over the – 302
level with the – 162
maintain one's –*persevere*
　604a
play– 840
prepare the – 673
stand one's –
　defend 717
　resist 719
– bait 784
– cut from under one 732
– floor
　chamber 191
　low 207
　base 211
– on
　attribute 155
– plan 554
– of quarrel 713
– sliding from under one
　665
– swell
　agitation 315
　waves 348
grounded
　stranded 732
well– 490
– on *basis* 211
　evidence 467
groundless
　unsubstantial 4
　illogical 477
　erroneous 495
groundling 876
grounds
　dregs 653
groundwork
　precursor 64
　cause 153
　basis 211
　support 215
　preparation 673
group
　marshal 60

cluster 72
– captain 745
grouping 60
grouse 852, 901a
grout 45
grove
　street 189
　glade 252
　wood 367
grovel
　below 207
　move slowly 275
　cringe 886
　base 940
grow
　increase 35
　become 144
　expand 194
– from
　effect 154
– into 144
– less 195
– taller 206
– together 46
– up 194
– upon one 613
grower 164
growl *cry* 412
　complain 839
　discourtesy 895
　anger 900
　threat 909
growler *cab* 272
　discontented 832
　sulky 901a
grown up 131
growth [*see* grow]
　development 161
– *in size* 194
　tumour 250
　vegetation 367
groyne 706
grub
　small animal 193
　food 298
– up
　eradicate 301
　discover 480a
Grub-street writer 593
grudge
　unwilling 603
　refuse 764
　stingy 819
　hate 898
　anger 900
bear a – 907
owe a – 898

grudging 603
– praise 932
gruel 298
gruesome 846
gruff
　harsh sound 410
　discourteous 895
grum
　harsh sound 410
　morose 901a
grumble
　cry 411
　complain 832, 839
grume 321, 354
grumous 321, 354
grumpy 901a
Grundy, Mrs. 852
grunt 412
　complain 839
guano 653
guarantee 768, 771
guard
　travelling 268
　safety 664
　defence 717
　soldier 726
　sentry 753
advanced – 668
mount –
　care 459
　safety 664
off one's –
　inexpectant 508
throw off one's –
　cunning 702
on one's –
　careful 459
　cautious 864
rear – 668
– against
　prepare 673
　defence 717
– ship 664, 726
guarda costa 753
guarded
　conditions 770
guardian
　safety 664
　defence 717
　keeper 753
– angel
　helper 711
　benefactor 912
guardless 665
guard-room 752
gubernation 693
gubernatorial 737

gudgeon 547
guerdon 973
guernsey 225
guerre:
  nom de – 565
  – à outrance &c. 722
guerrilla 726
  – warfare 720
guess 514
guesswork 514
guest 890
  paying – 188
guet:
  mot de – 550
  –à-pens 545
guffaw 838
guggle
  gush 348
  bubble 353
  resound 408
  cry 412
guide
  pattern 22
  courier 524
  teach 537
  teacher 540
  indicate 550
  direct 693
  director 694
  advise 695
guide-book 527
guided by, be – 82
guideless 665
guide-post 550
guiding star 693
guild 712, 966
guildhall 799
guile
  deceit 544, 545
  cunning 702
guileless 543, 703
guillotine 972, 975
guilt 947
guiltless 946
guilty:
  find – 971
  plead – 950
guindé 579
guinea 800
guipure 847
guisard 599
guise
  state 7
  dress 225
  appearance 448
  plea 617
  mode 627

  conduct 692
guiser 599
guitar 417
gulch 198
gules 434
gulf
  interval 198
  deep 208
  lake 343
gull 545, 547
gullet *throat* 260
  rivulet 348
gullible 486
gully *gorge* 198
  hollow 252
  opening 260
  conduit 350
gulosity 957
gulp *swallow* 296
  take food 298
  – down
  credulity 486
  submit 725
gum *fastening* 45
  fasten 46
  resin 356a
  – elastic 325
  – tree 367
gumbo 298
gummy 352
gumption 498
gun *report* 406
  weapon 727
  great – 626
  blow great –s 349
  sure as a – 474
gunboat 726
gunfire 404
gunman 361
gunner 776
gunnery
  warfare 722
  cannon 727
gunlayer 284
gunpowder
  warfare 722
  ammunition 727
  not invent – 665
  sit on barrel of – 501
gunroom 193
gun-shot 197
gunwale 232
gurge 312, 348
gurgle
  flow 348
  bubble 353
  faint sound 405

  resonance 408
gurgoyle 350
gush
  flow out 295
  flood 348
  exaggeration 482
  talk 584
gushing
  emotional 821
  impressible 822
gusset 43
gust *wind* 349
  physical taste 390
  passion 825
  moral taste 850
gustation 390
gustful 394
gustless 391
gusto [*see* gust]
  physical pleasure 377
  emotion 821
gut *destroy* 162
  opening 260
  strait 343
  eviscerate 297
  sack 789
  steal 791
gutling 954a
guts *inside* 221
guttapercha 325
gutter *groove* 259
  conduit 350
  vulgarity 851
guttersnipe 876
guttle 957
guttural
  letter 561
  inarticulate 583
guy
  fastening 45, 752
  fellow 373
  grotesque 853
  disrespect 929
guzzle
  gluttony 957
  drunkenness 959
gybe [*see* jibe]
gymkhana 720, 840
gymnasium 191
  school 542
  arena 728, 840
gymnast 159
gymnastics
  training 537
  exercise 686
  contention 720
  sport 840

gymnosophist
abstainer 953
sectarian 984
gynander 83
gynarchy 727
gynecæum 374
gynecology 662
gyniatrics 374
gynics 374
gyp 545, 746
gyrate 312
gyre 311
gyrfalcon 913
gyromancy 511
gyrostat 312
gysart 599
gyve 752

H

habeas corpus 963, 969
haberdasher 225
habergeon 717
habiliment 225
habilitation 698
habit
essence 5
coat 225
custom **613**
want of – 614
–s of business 682
– of mind 820
habitant 188
habitat 189
habitation 189
habit-maker 225
habitual
unvariable 16
orderly 58
ordinary 82
customary 613
habituate 537, 613
habitude
state 7
habit 613
habitué 613
hacienda 189, 780
hack *cut* 44
shorten 201
horse 271
writer 594
worker 690
literary – 593
hackle 44
hackney-coach 272
hackneyed

known 490
trite 496
habitual 613
Hades 982
Hadji
traveller 268
priest 996
hæret lateri lethalis
arundo
displeasure 828
anger 900
hæ tibi erunt artes 627
haft 633
hag *age* 128
ugly 846
wretch 913
witch 994
haggard
insane 503
tired 688
wild 824
ugly 846
haggis 298
haggle *cut* 44
chaffer 794
Hagiographa 985
Hagiolatry 984
Hagiology 983, 985
haguebut 727
ha-ha *trench* 198, 719
haik 225
hail *welcome* 292
ice 383
call 586
rejoicing 838
honour to 873
celebration 883
courtesy 894
salute 928
approve 931
–fellow well met
friendship 888
sociality 892
hailstone 383
hair *small* 32
filament 205
roughness 256
to a – 494
–'s breadth
near 197
narrow 203
–breadth escape
danger 665
escape 671
–s on the head
multitude 102
make one's – stand on end

distressing 830
fear 860
wonder 870
hairless 226
hairy *rough* 256
halberd 727
halberdier 726
halcyon *calm* 174
peace 721
prosperous 734
joyful 827, 829
hale 654
half 91
– the battle
important 642
success 731
– distance 68
– a dozen *six* 98
several 102
see with – an eye
intelligent 498
intelligible 518
manifest 525
– a gale 349
– and half
equal 27
mixed 41
incomplete 53
– a hundred 98
– light 422
– measures
incomplete 53
vacillating 605
mid-course 628
– moon 245
– price 815
– rations 640
– scholar 493
– seas over 959
– sight 443
– speed
moderate 174
slow 275
– truth 546
half-blind 443
half-blood
mixture 41
unconformity 83
imperfect 651
half-frozen 352
half-hearted
irresolute 605
insensible 823
indifferent 866
half-learned 491
half-melted 352
halfpenny

trifle 643
half-starved
insufficient 640
fasting 956
half-way
small 32
middle 68
between 228
go - *irresolute* 605
mid-course 628
meet -
willing 602
compromise 774
half-witted 499, 501
hall *chamber* 189
receptacle 191
mart 799
music - 599
- of audience 588
- mark 550
hallelujah 990
halliard 45
halloo *cry* 411
look here! 457
call 586
wonder 870
hallow
celebrate 883
respect 928
hallowed 976
hallucination
error 495
insanity 503
halo *light* 420
glory 873
Halomancy 511
halser 45
halt *cease* 142
weak 160
rest 265
go slowly 275
lame 655
fail 732
at the - 265
halter *rope* 45
restraint 752
punishment 975
wear a - 874
with a - round one's neck 665
halting
style 579
- place 292
halve [*see* half]
halves
do by -
neglect 460

not complete 730
not do by - 729
go - 778
ham *house* 189
hamadryad 979
hamlet 189
hammam 386, 652
hammer
repeat 104
knock 276
stammer 583
under the -
auction 796
between the - and the anvil 665
- at *think* 451
work 686
- out *form* 240
prepare 673
complete 729
hammock 215
hamper *basket* 191
obstruct 706
hamstring 158, 659
hanaper 802
hand
measure of length 200
side 236
transfer 270
man 372
organ of touch 379
indicator 550
writing 590
medium 631
agent 690
grasp 781
transfer 783
at - *future* 121
destined 152
near 197
useful 644
bad - 590
bird in - 781
come to - 292, 785
fold one's -s 681
give one's - to
marry 903
good -
writing 590
skill 698
proficiency 700
helping - 707, 711
hold in - 737
hold out the - 894
hold up the -
vote 609
in -

incomplete 53
business 625
preparing 673
not finished 730
possessed 777
money 800
in the -s of
authority 737
subjection 749
lay -s on
discover 480a
use 677
take 789
rite 998
much on one's -s 682
on one's -s
business 625
redundant 641
not finished 730
for sale 796
on the other - 468
no - in 623
poor - 701
put into one's -s 784
put one's - to 676
ready to one's - 673
shake -s 918
stretch forth one's - 680
take by the - 707
take in -
teach 537
undertake 676
time hanging on one's -s
inaction 681
leisure 685
weary 841
try one's - 675
turn one's - 675
turn one's - to 625
under one's -
in writing 590
promise 768
compact 769
- back 683
- cart 272
- of death 360
- down
record 551
transfer 783
have one's -s full 682
- gallop 274
- glass 445
- and glove 709, 888
- in hand
joined 43
accompanying 88
same time 120

concur 178
co-operate 709
party 712
concord 714
friend 888
social 892
– to hand
touching 199
transfer 270
fight 720, 722
– over head
inattention 458
neglect 460
reckless 863
have a – in
cause 153
act 680
co-operate 709
have one's – in
skill 698
keep one's – in 613
live from – to mouth
insufficient 640
unprepared 674
poor 804
–s off! *avoid* 623
leave alone 681
prohibition 761
– over
transfer 783
give 784
win –s down 731
with the –s in the pockets
　681
hand-bag 191
hand-barrow 272
handbook
travel 266
information 527
book 593
handcuff 751, 752
handfast 903
handful
quantity 25
small 32
few 103
handicap
equalize 27
inferiority 34
encumber 706
race 720
handicraft 625, 680
handicraftsman 690
effect 154
doing 680
handkerchief
clothes 225

cleaner 652
handle
feel, touch 379
name 565
dissert 595
plea 617
instrument 633
use 677
manage 693
furnish a – 937
make a – of 677
– a case 693
– to one's name
name 564
honour 877
handmaid
instrumentally 631
auxiliary 711
servant 746
handpost 550
handsel
begin 66
security 771
gift 784
pay 809
handsome
liberal 816
beautiful 845
disinterested 942
– fortune 803
handspike 633
handstaff 727
handwriting
signature 550
autograph 590
– on the wall
warning 668
handy
near 197
useful 644, 646
ready 673
dexterous 698
hang
pendency 214
kill 362
curse 908
execute 972
– about 133, 197
– back 133, 197
– in the balance 133
– in doubt 485
– fire *late* 133
cease 142
unproductive 169
inert 172
slow 275
reluctance 603

inactive 683
not finish 730
fail 732
refuse 764
dullness 843
– on hand 641
– down the head 837
– over the head 152
– it! *regret* 833
contempt 930
– out a light 420
– upon the lips of 418
– on
accompany 88
– out
display 882
entertain 892
– over
destiny 152
height 206
project 250
– out a signal 550
– on the sleeve of
servant 746
servility 886
flattery 933
– in suspense 605
– by a thread 665
– together
joined 43
cohere 46
concur 178
co-operate 709
– upon
effect 154
dependency 749
hangar 191, 273
hang-dog look 901*a*
hanged if, I'll be – 489
hanger
weapon 727
suspender 45, 214
pothooks and –s 590
– on
accompaniment 88
servant 746
servile 886
hanging [*see* hang]
elevated 307
ornament 847
– look 846
hangman
evil-doer 913
bad man 949
executioner 975
hank *tie* 45
hanker 865

542

hanky-panky 545
Hansard 551
hansom 272
hap 156
haphazard
  chance 156, 621
hapless
  unfortunate 735
  (*miserable* 828)
  (*hopeless* 859)
haply
  possibly 470
  (*by chance* 156)
happen 151
  – as it may
  chance 621
  – what may
  certain 474
  reckless 863
happening 151
happiness [*see* happy]
  the greatest – of the
    greatest number 910
happy *fit* 23
  opportune 134
  style 578
  glad 827
  cheerful 836
  – despatch 972
  – go lucky 674
  – hunting grounds 981
  – returns of the day 896
  – thought 842
  – valley
  imagination 515
  delight 827
hara-kiri 972
harangue 582
harass
  fatigue 688
  vex 830
  worry 907
harbinger
  precursor 64
  omen 512
  informant 527
harbour
  abode 189
  haven 292
  refuge 666
  cherish 821
  natural – 343
  – a design 620
  in – 664
  – an idea 451
  – revenge 919
harbourless 665

hard *strong* 159
  dense 323
  physically insensible 376
  sour 397
  difficult 704
  severe 739
  morally insensible 823
  grievous 830
  impenitent 951
  blow – 349
  go –
  difficult 704
  failure 732
  adversity 735
  pain 828
  hit – 276
  look – at 441
  not be too – upon 918
  strike –
  energy 171
  impulse 276
  try – 675
  work – 686
  – at it 682
  – bargain 819
  – of belief 487
  – to believe 485
  – by 197
  – case 735
  – cash 800
  – earned 704
  – and fast rule 80
  – fought 704
  – frost 383
  – of hearing 419
  – heart
  malevolent 907
  vicious 945
  impenitent 951
  – hit 732
  – knocks 720
  – life 735
  – lines
  adversity 735
  severity 739
  – liver 954*a*
  – lot 735
  – master 739
  – measure 739
  – names 932
  – necessity 601
  – nut to crack 704
  – to please 868
  – pressed
  haste 684
  difficulty 704
  hindrance 706

  – put to it 704
  – set 704
  – tack 298
  – task 703
  – time 704
  – up 704, 804
  – upon
  attack 715
  severe 739
  censure 932
  – winter 383
  – words
  obscure 571
  rude 895
  censure 932
  – work 686
  – at work 682
harden [*see* hard]
  strengthen 159
  accustom 613
  – the heart
  insensible 823
  enmity 889
  impenitence 951
hardened
  impious 988
  – front
  insolent 885
hardening
  habit 613
hard-featured 846
hard-fisted 819
hard-headed 498, 739
hardihood 861, 885
hardly
  scarcely 32
  deal – with 739
  – any *few* 103
  – anything
  small 32
  unimportant 643
  – ever 137
hard-mouthed 606
hardness 323
  – of heart 914*a*
hardship 735
hardy
  strong 159
  healthy 654
  brave 861
hare 274
  hold with the – and run
    with the hounds
  fickle 607
  servile 886
hare-brained 458, 863
harem 961

hariolation 511
hark 418, 457
- back 283
harl 205
harlequin
changeable 149
nimble 274
motley 440
pantomimic 599
humorist 844
harlequinade 599
harlot 962
harlotry 961
harm
evil 619
badness 649
malevolence 907
harmattan 349
harmless
impotent 158
good 648
perfect 650
salubrious 656
safe 664
innocent 946
bear - 717
harmonica 417
harmonics 413
harmonist 413
harmonium 417
harmonize 178, 416
harmony
agreement 23
order 58
music 413
colour 428
concord 714
peace 721
friendship 888
harness
fasten 43
fastening 45
accoutrement 225
yoke 370
instrument 633
restraint 752
in -
prepared 673
in action 680
active 682
subjection 749
- up 293
harp
repeat 104
musical instrument 417
weary 841
Harpagon 819

harper 416
harpist 416
harpoon 727
harpsichord 417
harpy
relentless 739
thief 792
miser 819
evil-doer 913
demon 980
harquebuss 727
harridan 846, 962
harrier 366
harrow
agriculture 371
- up the soul 860
harrowing 830
harry *pain* 830
attack 716
persecute 907
Harry, old - 978
harsh
acrid 171
sound 410
style 579
discordant 713
severe 739
disagreeable 830
morose 895
malevolent 907
- voice 581
hart 366, 373
hartal 142, 489
harum-scarum 59, 458
haruspice 513
Haruspicy 511
harvest
effect 154
profit 618
store 636
acquisition 775
get in the -
complete 729
succeed 731
- home
celebration 883
- time
autumn 126
exertion 686
has been 122
hash *mix* 41
cut 44
confusion 59
food 298
make a - 699
hashish 863
hasp 43, 45

hassock 215
hastate 253
haste
velocity 274
activity 682
hurry **684**
hasten
promote 707
hasty
transient 113
hurried 684
impatient 825
irritable 901
- pudding 298
hat 225
cardinal's - 999
send round the - 765
shovel - 999
- in hand 886
hatch
produce 161
gate 232
opening 260
chickens 370
fabricate 544
shading 556
plan 626
prepare 673
- a plot 626
hatches, under -
restraint 751
prisoner 754
poor 804
hatchet
cutting 253
bury the - 918
dig up the - 722
throw the helve after the - 818
hatchet-faced 203
hatchment
funeral 363
arms 550
record 551
hatchway 260
hate 867, **898**
hateful 649, 830
hath been, the time - 122
hatrack 215
hatter 225
mad as a - 503
hatti-sheriff 741
hatred [*see* hate]
object of - 898
hauberk 717
haud passibus
æquis 28, 275

haugh 344
haughty
  proud 878
  insolent 885
  contemptuous 930
haul *drag* 285
  catch of fish &c. 789
  – down one's flag 725
  – in 10
haunch 236
haunt *focus* 74
  presence 186
  abode 189
  alarm 860
  persecute 907
  – the memory
  remember 505
  trouble 830
haunted 980
haut
  traiter de –
  insolence 885
  contempt 930
hautboy 417
hauteur 878
haut-goût 392
haut-monde 875
have *confute* 479
  ken 490
  possess 777
  – the advantage 28, 33
  – at 716
  – no choice 609*a*
  – done! 142
  – to do with 9
  – no end 112
  – other fish to fry 135
  – it
  discover 480*a*
  believe 484
  – one to know 527
  – some knowledge of 490
  – nothing to do with 10
  – for one's own 780
  – rather 609
  – one's rights 924
  – the start 116
  – in store 152, 637
  – to 620
  – up 638
  – it your own way
  submission 725
haven 292, 666
haversack 191
havoc
  destruction 162
  cry – *war* 722

play – *spoil* 659
haw 583
hawk *spit* 297
  stammer 583
  eye of a – 498
  – about
  publish 531
  offer 763
  sell 796
  – at 716
  between – and buzzard
  315, 828
  know a – from a handsaw
  465, 698
hawker 796
hawk-eyed 441
hawking *chase* 622
hawser 45
hay while the sun shines,
  make – 134
haycock 72
hazard
  chance 156, 621
  danger 665
  at all –s 604
  – a conjecture 514
  – a proposition 477
haze *mist* 353
  uncertainty 475
  in a –
  hidden 528
hazel 433
hazy *opaque* 426
he 373
head *precedence* 62
  beginning 66
  class 75
  summit 210
  coiffure 225
  lead 280
  froth 353
  person 372
  intellect 450
  topic 454
  wisdom 498
  picture 556
  nomenclature 564
  chapter 593
  direct 693
  director 694
  master 745
  at the – of
  direction 693
  authority 737
  repute 873
  bow the – 308
  bring to a – 729

come into one's – 451
come to a – 729
drive into one's – 505
gain – 175
get into one's –
  thought 451
  belief 484
  learn 505
  intoxicate 959
give a horse his – 748
hang one's – 879
have in one's – 490
from – to heels 52, 200
hit on the – 912
knock on the – 361
knock one's – against
  impulse 276
  unskilful 699
  fail 732
lie on one's – 926
lift up one's – 878
make – against
  oppose 708
  resistance 719
  success 731
never entered into one's –
  458
have no – 506
on one's – 218
off one's – 503
can't get out of one's –
  505
over – and ears
  deep 641
  debt 806
  love 897
put into one's –
  supposition 514
  information 527
put out of one's – 458
run in the – 505
not know whether one
  stands on – or heels
  uncertain 475
  wonder 870
take into one's –
  thought 451
  caprice 608
  intention 620
turn the – 824
trouble one's – about 457
as one's – shall answer for
  768
with – erect 878
from – to foot 200
– and front
  important 642

- and front of one's
 offending
provocation 830
charge 938
- over heels
 inversion 218
 rotation 312
- light 423
- line 591
- and shoulders
 irrelevant 10
 complete 52
 haste 684
make neither - nor tail of
 519
hold one's - up 307
above water
 safe 664
 prosperous 743
 wealth 803
with a - on 353
headache 378
head-dress 225
header 310
head-foremost
 violent 173
 rash 863
head-gear 225
heading *prefix* 64
 beginning 66
 indication 550
 title 564
headland
 height 206
 projection 250
headlong
 hurry 684
 rush 863
rush -
 violence 173
headman 694
headmost
 front 234
 precession 280
head-piece
 summit 210
 intellect 450
 helmet 717
 ornament 847
head-quarters
 focus 74
 abode 189
 authority 737
head-race 350
heads
 compendium 596
- or tails 156, 621

lay - together
 advice 695
 co-operate 709
- I win tails you lose
 unfair 940
headship 737
headsman 975
head-stone 363
headstrong
 violent 173
 obstinate 606
 rash 863
headway *space* 180
 navigation 267
 progression 282
headwind 708
headwork 451
heady 606
heal *restore* 660
 remedy 662
let the wound -
 forgive 918
- the breach
 pacify 723
healing art 662
health 654
picture of - 654
healthiness 655
health resort 189
healthy 656
heap *quantity* 31
 collection 72
 store 636
 too many 641
heaps 102
rubbish - 645
hear
 audition 418
 be informed 527
not - of (refuse) 764
- a cause
 adjudge 480
 lawsuit 969
- hear! 931
- and obey 743
- out 457
hearer 418
hearing 418, 696 [*see* hear]
gain a - 175
give a - 418
hard of - 419
out of - 196
within - 197
hearken 457
hearsay 532
- evidence 467
hearse 363

heart
 intrinsicality 5
 interior 221
 centre 222
 mind 450
 willingness 602
 essential 642
 affections 820
 courage 861
 love 897
man after one's own - 899
with all one's - 438, 602
at - 820, 821
from bottom of - 543
beating - 821, 824
break the - 830
by -
 memory 505
go to one's - 824
in good - 858
with a heavy - 603
know by - 490
lay to - 837
learn by - 539
lift up the - 990
lose - 837
lose one's - 897
nearest to one's - 897
not find it in one's - 603
have a place in the - 897
put one's - into 604
set one's - upon 604
take -
 content 831
 hope 858
 courage 861
take to -
 sensibility 822
 discontent 832
 dejection 837
 anger 900
warm - 822
wind round the - 897
- bleeding for 914
to one's -'s content
 willing 602
 enough 639
 success 731
 pleasure 829
-'s core
 mind 450
 affections 820
- expanding 821
- failing one 837, 860
do one's - good 829
- of grace 858
- in hand 602

- leaping with joy 827, 838
- leaping into one's mouth 824
- of oak
  strong 159
  hard 323
- in right place 906
- sinking *fear* 860
- and soul
  completely 52
  willing 602
  resolute 604
  exertion 686
  feeling 821
- of stone 823, 907
- swelling 824
heartache 828
heart-breaking 821, 830
heart-broken 828
heartburning
  discontent 832
  regret 833
  enmity 889
  anger 900
  jealousy 920
hearten 858, 861
heartfelt 821, 829
hearth
  home 189
  fireplace 386
heartless 823, 945
heart-rending 830
heartsease 831
heart-shaped 245
heart-sick
  dejection 837
  dislike 867
  satiety 869
heart-stricken 828
heart-strings, tear the – 830
hearty
  willing 602
  healthy 654
  feeling 821
  cheerful 836
  friendly 888
  social 892
- laugh 838
- meal 298
- reception 892
heat *warmth* **382**
  make hot 384
  contest 720
  excitement 824, 825
  dead – 27

- of passion 900
- wave 382
heated imagination 515
heater 386
heath *moor* 344
  plant 367
heathen 984, 989
- mythology 979
heathenish 851
heather *moor* 344
  plant 367
heaume 717
heautontimorumenos 837, 955
heave *raise* 307
  emotion 821
- the lead 208, 466
- a sigh 839
- in sight 446
- to 265
heaven 827, **981**
  call – to witness 535
  in the face of – 525
  light of – 420
  move – and earth 686
  will of – 601
- forfend! 766
- knows 475, 491
- be praised 838, 916
  for –'s sake 765
heaven-born
  wise 498
  repute 873
  virtue 944
heaven-directed 498
heaven-kissing 206
heavenly
  celestial 318
  rapturous 829
  divine 976
  of heaven 981
- bodies 318
- host 977
- kingdom 981
heavenly-minded 987
heavens 318
- and earth! 870
Heaviside layer 338
heavisome 843
heavy *great* 31
  inert 172
  weighty 319
  stupid 499
  actor 599
  sleepy 683
  dull 843
  brutish 851

- affliction 828
- artillery 726
- cost 814
- dragoon 726
- father 599
- gaited 843
- gun 727
- hand
  clumsy 699
  severe 739
- on hand 641
- heart *loth* 603
  pain 828
  dejection 837
- hours 841
- on the mind 837
- news 830
- sea
  agitation 315
  waves 348
- sleep 683
- type 591
- wet 298
heavy-laden 706, 828
hebdomadal 138
Hebe 845
hebetate 823, 826
hebetude
  imbecile 499
  insensible 823
  inexcitable 826
Hebrew
  unintelligible 519
  Jew 894
Hecate 994
hecatomb
  number 98
  sacrifice 991
heckle 830, 900
hectic 382, 821
Hector *brave* 861
  rash 863
  bully 885, 887
hedge
  compensate 30
  inclosure 232
- in
  circumscribe 229
  hinder 706
  conditions 770
hedgehog 253
hedonism 377, 827
hedonist 954*a*
heed *attend* 457
  care 459
  beware 668
  caution 864

heedful 457
heedless
inattentive 458
neglectful 460
oblivious 506
rash 863
heel *support* 215
lean 217
deviate 279
go round 311
iron – 975
lay by the –s 162
turn on one's –
go back 283
go round 311
avoid 623
– of Achilles 665
heel-piece
sequel 65
back 235
repair 660
heel-tap
remainder 40
dress 653
heels *lowness* 207
at the – of
near 197
behind 235
cool one's – 681
follow on the – of 281
laid by the – 751
lay by the – 789
show a light pair of – 623
take to one's – 623
tread on the – of
near 197
follow 281
approach 286
– over head
inverted 218
hasty 684
rash 863
heft *handle* 633
exertion 686
hegemony
influence 175
direction 693
authority 737
heifer 366
heigho! 839
height *degree* 26
altitude **206**
summit 210
at its –
great 31
supreme 33

draw oneself up to his full
– 307
– finder 206
heighten
increase 35
elevate 307
exaggerate 549
aggravate 835
hegira [*see* hejira]
heinous 945
heir *futurity* 121
posterity 167
inheritor 779
heirloom 780
heirship 777
hejira 293
Helen of Troy 845
heliacal 318
helical 248
Helicon 597
helicon-horn 417
helicopter 273
Heliogabalus 954*a*
heliograph
signal 550
picture 556
heliography 550
light 420
painting 556
Helios 423
heliotrope 847
heliotype 558
helix 248
hell *abyss* 208
gaming-house 621
gehenna **982**
– upon earth
misfortune 735
pain 828
– broke loose 59
hell-born 945, 978
hellebore 663
hell-hound 913, 949
hellish
malevolent 907
vicious 945
hell 982
helluo librorum 492
helm *handle* 633
sceptre 747
(*authority* 737)
answer the – 743
at the – 693
obey the – 705
take the – 693
helmet 225, 717
helminthology 368

helmsman 269, 694
helot 746
help *benefit* 618
utility 644
remedy 662
aid 707
servant 746
give 784
it can't be –ed
submission 725
never mind 823
content 831
God – you 914
so – me God 535
– oneself to 789
helper 711
helpless 158, 665
helpmate
auxiliary 711
wife 903
helter-skelter 59, 684
helve
throw the – after the
hatchet 818
hem *edge* 231
fold 258
indeed! 870
kiss the – of one's garment
886
– in *enclose* 220
restrain 751
hemi- 91
hemisphere 181
hemispheric 250
hemlock 663
hemorrhage 299
hemp 205
hen 366, 374
female 374
– with one chicken
busy 682
henbane 663
hence
arising from 155
departure 293
deduction 476
– loathed melancholy 836
henceforth 121
henchman 746
hencoop 370
hendiadis 91
henna 433
henpecked 743, 749
heptagon 244
heptarchy 98
Heraclitus 839
rideret – 853

herald
  precursor 64
  precession 280
  predict 511
  forerunner 512
  proclaim 531
  messenger 534
heraldry 550
herb 367
herbage 365
herbal 369
herbivorous 298
herborize 369
herculean
  strong 159
  exertion 686
  difficult 704
Herculeum, ex pede – 550
Hercules 159, 215
  pillars of – 233, 550
herd 72, 102
herdsman 746
here
  situation 183
  presence 186
  arrival 292
  come –! 286
  – below 318
  – goes 676
  – and there
  dispersed 73
  few 103
  place 182, 183
  – there and everywhere
  diversity 16a
  space 180
  omnipresence 186
  – to-day and gone to-
  morrow 111
hereabouts 183, 197
hereafter 121, 152
hereby 631
hereditament 780
hereditary
  intrinsic 5
  derivative 154, 167
heredity 167
herein 221
heresy 495, 984
heretic 984
heretofore 122
hereupon 106
herewith 88, 632
heritage
  futurity 121
  possession 777
  property 780

heritor 779
hermaphrodite 83
  – brig 273
hermeneutics 522
Hermes 534, 582
hermetically 261
hermit 893, 955
hermitage
  house 189
  cell 191
  seclusion 893
hero *brave* 861
  glory 873
  good man 948
  – worship 931, 991
Herod, out-Herod – 549
heroic [*see* hero]
  magnanimous 942
  mock – 853
heroics 884
heroin 663
heroine 861
herpetology 368
Herr 373
herring
  pungent 392
  – pond 341
  draw a – across the trail
  545
  trail of a red – 615, 706
herring-gutted 203
hesitate
  uncertain 475
  sceptical 485
  stammer 583
  reluctant 603
  irresolute 605
  fearful 860
Hesperian 236
Hesperides, garden of the
  – 981
Hesperus 423
Hessian boot 225
hest 741
hesterni quirites 876
heterarchy 737
heteroclite 83
heterodoxy 489, **984**
heterogeneity 15, 16a
heterogeneous
  unrelated 10
  different 15
  mixed 41
  multiform 81
  exceptional 83
heteromorphism 16a
hetman 745

hew *cut* 44
  shorten 201
  fashion 240
  – down 308
hewers of wood
  workers 690
  commonalty 876
hexagon 98, 244
hexahedron 244
hexameter 98, 597
hey! 586
heyday
  exultation 838
  festivity 840
  wonder 870
  – of the blood 820
  – of youth 127
hiation 260
hiatus 198
hibernal 383
hibernate 683
Hibernicism 497, 563
hic:
  – jacet 363
  – labor hoc opus 704
hiccup 349
hick 701, 851, 876
hidalgo 875
hidden 528
  – meaning 526
hide *skin* 223
  conceal 528
  – diminished head
  inferior 34
  decrease 36
  humility 879
  – one's face
  modesty 881
  – and seek
  deception 545
  avoid 623
  game 840
hide-bound 751, 819
hideous 846
hide-out 893
hiding-place
  abode 189
  ambush 530
  refuge 666
hid under a bushel 460
hie 264, 274
  – to 266
hiemal 126
hierarch 996
hierarchy 995
hieratic 590
hieroglyphic

depend upon 154
rotate 312
hinny 271
hint *reminder* 505
suppose 514
inform 527
take a – 498
– a fault &c. 932
hinterland 235
hip 236
have on the –
confute 479
success 731
authority 737
subjection 749
– hip, hurrah! 838
hipped [*see* hypped]
hippocentaur 80
Hippocrates 662
hippocratic 360
hippodrome
drama 599
arena 728
amusement 840
hippogriff 83
Hippolytus 960
hippophagy 298
hippopotamus 192
hirdie-girdie 218
hire
commission 755
borrowing 788
price 812
reward 973
on – 763
hireling 746
hirsute 256
hispid 256
hiss *sound* 409
animal cry 412
disrespect 929
contempt 930
disapprobation 932
hist! 585, 586
histology 329
historian 553
historic 594
historical:
– painter 559
– painting 556
historiette 594
historiographer 553
historiography 594
history *past* 122
record 551
narrative 594
History, Natural – 357

histrionic 599
hit *chance* 156
strike 276
reach 292
succeed 731
censure 932
(*punish* 972)
good – 626
make a – 731
– one's fancy 829
– the mark 731
– off 545
– upon
discover 480a
plan 626
hitch
fasten 43
knot 45
stoppage 142
hang 214
jerk 315
harness 370
difficulty 704
hindrance 706
– up 293
hither 278, 292
come – 286
hitherto 122
hive
multitude 102
location 184
abode 189
bees 870
workshop 691
H.M.S. 726
hoar *aged* 128
white 430
– frost 383
hoard 636
hoarse
husky 405
harsh 410
voiceless 581
talk oneself – 584
hoary [*see* hoar]
hoax 545
hob *support* 215
stove 386
– and nob
celebration 883
courtesy 894
hobble
limp 275
awkward 699
difficulty 704
fail 732
shackle 751

– skirt 225
hobbledehoy 129
hobby
crotchet 481
pursuit 622
desire 865
hobby-horse 272
hobgoblin
fearful 860
demon 980
hobnail 876
hobo 268
Hobson's choice
necessity 601
no choice 609a
compulsion 744
hoc genus omne 876
hock 771
hockey 840
hockey rink 213
hock shop 787
hocus 545
hocus-pocus
interchange 148
unmeaning 517
cheat 545
conjuration 992
spell 993
hod
receptacle 191
support 215
vehicle 272
hoddy-doddy 501
hodge-podge 41, 59
hoe 272, 371
hog *animal* 366
sensualist 954a
glutton 957
greedy as a – 865
go the whole – 604
hogmanay 998
hog's back 206
hogshead 191
hog-wash 653
hoist 307
– the black flag 722
– a flag 550
– on one's own petard
retaliation 718
failure 732
hoity-toity! 815, 870
hold *cohere* 46
contain 54
remain 141
cease 142
go on 143
happen 151

receptacle 191
cellar 207
base 211
support 215
halt 265
believe 484
be passive 681
defend 717
power 737
restrain 751
prison 752
prohibit 761
possess 777
retain 781
enough! 869
have a firm – 781
have a – upon 175
gain a – upon 737
get – of 789
quit one's – 782
take – 175
– aloof
　stay away 187
　distrust 487
　avoid 623
– an argument 476
– authority 737
– back *avoid* 623
　store 636
　hinder 706
　restrain 751
　retain 781
　miserly 819
– one's breath
　wonder 870
– converse 588
– a council 695
– fast 751, 781
– forth *teach* 537
　speak 582
– good 478, 494
– one's ground 141
– in hand 737
– one's hand
　cease 142
　relinquish 624
– hard 265
– up one's head 861
– a lease 771
– a meeting 72
– off 623
– office 693
– on
　continue 141, 143
　persevere 604a
– out [*see below*]
– one's own

preserve 670
defend 717
resist 719
– oneself in readiness 673
– in remembrance 505
– both one's sides 838
– a situation 625
– in solution 335
– to 602
– together 43, 709
– one's tongue 403, 585
– up [*see below*]
– oneself up 307
holder 779
holdfast 45
holding
tenancy 777
property 780
hold out
endure 106
affirm 535
persevere 604a
resist 719
offer 763
brave 861
– expectation
predict 511
promise 768
– temptation 865
hold up
continue 143
support 215
not rain 340
aid 707
rob 791
display 882
extol 931
– one's hand
sign 550
threat 609
– to execration
curse 908
censure 932
– the mirror 525
– to scorn 930
– to shame 874
– to view 525
hole *place* 182
hovel 189
receptacle 191
opening 260
ambush 530
– in one's coat 651
– and corner
place 182
peer into – 461
hiding 528, 530

– to creep out of
plea 617
escape 671
facility 705
holiday *leisure* 685
repose 687
amusement 840
– task *easy* 705
holiness *God* 976
piety 987
holloa 411
– before one is out of the
　wood 884
hollow
unsubstantial 4
completely 52
incomplete 53
depth 208
concavity 252
channel 350
- *sound* 408
specious 477
false 544
voiceless 581
beat – 731
– truce 723
holm 346
holocaust
kill 361
sacrifice 991
(*destruction* 162)
holograph 590
holster 191
holt 367
holus bolus 684
Holy *of God* 976
pious 987
keep – 987
– breathing 990
– Church 983a
– City 981
– day 998
– Ghost 976
temple of the – Ghost
　983a
– men of old 985
– orders 995
– place 1000
– Scriptures 985
– Spirit 976
– water 998
– week 998
holystone 652
homage
submission 725
fealty 743
reverence 928

approbation 931
worship 990
home *focus* 74
habitation 189
near 197
interior 221
arrival 292
refuge 666
at – *party* 72
present 186
within 221
at ease 705
social gathering 892
be at –
– *to visitors* 892
feel at –
freedom 748
pleasure 827
content 831
look at –
accusation 938
make oneself at –
free 748
sociable 892
not be at – 764
stay at – 265
at – in
knowledge 490
skill 698
at – with
friendship 888
bring – to
evidence 467
belief 484
accuse 938
condemn 971
come – 292
eternal – 98
from – 187
get – 292
go – 283
go from – 293
long – 363
strike –
energy 171
attack 716
– stroke 170
– thrust
attack 716
censure 932
home-bred 851
home-felt 821, 824
homeless
unhoused 185
banished 893
homely
language 576

unadorned 849
common 851, 876
Homeric
– laughter 838
home-rule 737, 748
home-sick 833
home-spun
texture 329
home-stall 189
homestead 189
homeward bound 292
homicidal maniac 913
homicide 361
homiletical 892
homily
teaching 537
advice 595
sermon 998
hominem, argumentum ad
– 938
homœpathic
small 32
little 193
Homœpathy 662
homogeneity
relation 9
identity 13
uniformity 16
simplicity 42
homogenesis 161
homologous 23
homology
relation 9
uniformity 16
equality 27
concord 714
homonym
equivocal 520
vocal sound 580
homophony 413
homunculus 193
Hon. 817
hone 253
honest
veracious 543
honourable 939
pure 960
– meaning 516
turn an – penny 775
– truth 494
honey
sweet 396
favourite 899
mild and – 734
honeycomb
concave 252
opening 260

deterioration 659
honeyed
– phrases 894
– words
allurement 615
flattery 933
honeymoon
pleasure 827
endearment 902
marriage 903
honey-mouthed 894, 933
honeysuckle 396
honorarium 784, 973
honorary 815
honour
demesne 780
glory 873
title 877
respect 928
approbation 931
probity 939
affair of – 720
do – to 883
do the –s
sociality 892
courtesy 894
respect 928
his – *judge* 967
in – of 883
man of – 939
upon my – 535, 768
word of – 768
– be to 873
– a bill 807
– in the breach 923
– bright
veracity 543
probity 939
honte, mauvaise – 881
hood 225, 999
hooded 223
hoodlum 887
hoodoo 649
hoodwink
blind 442
ignore 491
hide 528
deceive 545
hoof 211
cloven – 907
hook *fasten* 43
fastening 45
hang 214
curve 245
deceive 545
retain 781
take 789

by – or by crook 631
hookah 392
hooker *ship* 273
hookey, blind – 840
hooks, go off the 360
hooligan 887, 913
hoop *circle* 247
cry 411
hoot *cry* 411, 412
deride 929
contempt 930
censure 932
hop *leap* 309
dance 840, 892
– off 293
– skip and jump
leap 309
agitation 315
haste 684
game 840
– the twig 360
hope **858**
band of – 958
beyond – 658, 734
dash one's –s 837
excite – 511
foster – 858
well-grounded – 472
– against hope 859
– for the best 858
– deferred
dejection 837
lamentation 859
– for *expect* 507
desire 865
hope chest 858
hopeful *infant* 129
probable 472
hope 858
hopelessness 471, **859**
Hop-o'-my-thumb 193
hopper 191
horary 108
horde
assemblage 72
party 712
commonalty 876
horizon
distance 196
view 441
expectation 507
appear on the – 525
gloomy – 859
horizontality **213**
horn
receptacle 191
sharp 253

music 417
draw in one's –s
recant 607
submit 725
humility 879
exalt one's – 873
wear the –s 905
–s of a dilemma
reasoning 476
difficulty 704
– in 294
– mad 920
– of plenty 639
hornbook 542
hornet
evil-doer 913
–'s nest
pitfall 667
difficulty 704
adversity 735
painful 830
resentment 900
censure 932
hornpipe 840
hornwork 717
horny 323
Horny, old – 978
horology 114
horoscope 511, 992
horresco referens 860
horrible *great* 31
noxious 649
dire 830
ugly 846
fearful 860
horrid [*see* horrible]
vulgar 851
horrida bella 722
horrific [*see* horrible]
horrified 828, 860
horrify 830, 860
horripilation 383
horrisonous 410
horror 860, 867
view with – 898
horrors 837
sup full of – 828
horror-stricken 828
hors de combat
impotent 158
useless 645
tired out 688
put – 731
hors-d'œuvre 298
horse *hang on* 214
stand 215
carrier 271

animal 366
male 373
cavalry 726
ride the high – 885
put the –s to 673
put up one's –s at 184
put up one's –s together
concord 714
friendship 888
take – 266
to – 293
war – 726
work like a – 686
– artillery 726
– of another colour 15
– doctor 370
– and foot 726
– laugh 838
– marine 701
like a – in a mill 613
– racing
pastime 840
contention 720
– soldier 726
– track 627
horseback 266
horse-cloth 225
horseman 268
horsemanship
riding 266
skill 698
horseplay 856
horse power 466
horse-shoe 245
horse-whip 972
hortation 615, 695
hortative 537
horticulture 371
hortus siccus 369
hosanna 931, 990
hose
stockings 225
pipe 348, 350
extinguisher 385
hosier 225
hospice 189, 662
hospitable 816, 892
hospital 189, 662
in – 655
hospitality [*see* hospitable]
hospodar 745
host *collection* 72
multitude 102
army 726
friend 890
rite 998
reckon without one's –

howl
wind 349
human cry 411
animal cry 412
lamentation 839
howler 495
howling wilderness 169,
893
hoy 273
hoyden *girl* 129
rude 851
hub 222
hubble-bubble 392
hubbub *stir* 315
noise 404
discord 713
huckster 794, 797
huddle
disorder 59
derange 61
collect 72
hug 197
– on 225
Hudibrastic 856
– verse 597
hue 428
– and cry cry 411
proclaim 531
pursuit 622
alarm 669
raise a – and cry 932
hueless 429
huff 885, 900
huffy 901
hug *cohere* 46
border on 197
retain 781
courtesy 894
love 897
endearment 902
– a belief 606
– oneself
pleasure 827
content 831
rejoicing 838
pride 878
– the shore
navigation 267
approach 286
– a sin 945
huge 31, 192
hugger-mugger 528
Huguenot 984
huis clos, à *–* 528
huissier 965
huke 225
hulk *body* 50

ship 273
hulks 752
hulky *big* 192
unwieldy 647
ugly 846
hull 50
hullabaloo 404, 411
hullo! 292
hum
faint sound 405
continued sound 407
animal sound 412
sing 416
deceive 545, 546
– and haw
stammer 583
irresolute 605
busy *– of men* 682
human 372
– race 372
– sacrifices 991
humane
benevolent 906
philanthropic 910
merciful 914
humanitarian 372, 910
humanities 560
humanize 894
humano capiti cervicem
jungere equinam 24
humation 363
humble *meek* 879
modest 881
pious 987
–r classes 876
– oneself
submit 725
meek 879
penitent 950
worship 990
eat *– pie* 725, 879
your – servant
dissent 489
refusal 764
humbug
falsehood 544
deception 545
deceiver 548
trifle 643
affectation 855
humdrum 841, 843
humectate 337, 339
humid 339
humiliate 308
humiliation
adversity 735
disrepute 874

sense of shame 879
worship 990
self *–* 950
humility **879**, 987
humming-top 417
hummock 206, 250
humorist **844**
humorous 842
humour *essence* 5
tendency 176
liquid 333
disposition 602
caprice 608
aid 707
indulge 760
affections 820
please 829
wit 842
flatter 933
(fun 840)
in the *–* 602
out of *–* 901*a*
peccant –
unclean 653
disease 655
humoursome
capricious 608
sulky 901*a*
hump 250
hump-backed 243
humph! 870
Humphrey, dine with
Duke *–* 956
Humpty-dumpty 193
Hun 165, 851, 913
hunch 250, 612
hunch-backed 243
hundred
number 98
many 102
region 181
the same a *– years hence*
460
hundredth 99
hundredweight 319
hunger 865
hunger-strike 956
hunks 819
hunt *inquiry* 461
pursuit 622
– after 622
– in couples 709
– down 907
– out inquiry 461
discover 480*a*
– slipper 840
hunter *horse* 271

killer 361
pursuer 622
place &c. – 767
hunting 361, 622
hunting-ground 840
happy – 981
hurdle 272
hurdy-gurdy 417
hurl 284
– against 716
– defiance 715
hurler avec les loups 82, 714
Hurlothrumbo 860
hurly-burly 315
hurrah 411, 836, 838
hurricane 349, 667
– deck 210
hurry *haste* 684
excite 825
– forward 684
– off with 789
– on 615
– of spirits 821
– up 684
hurst 367
hurt
physical pain 378
evil 619
maltreat 649
injure 659
more frightened than – 860
– the feelings
pain 830
anger 900
hurtful 649
hurtle 276
hurtless 648
husband
store 636
director 694
spouse 903
husbandman 371
husbandry
agriculture 371
conduct 692
economy 817
hush *moderate* 174
stop 265
silence 403
taciturn 585
– up
conceal 528
pacify 723
hush-money 30, 973
husk 223, 226

husky *strong* 159
dry 340
faint sound 405
hoarse 581
hussar 726
hussy 962
hustings
school 542
arena 728
tribunal 966
hustle
perturb 61
push 276
agitate 315
activity 682
hinder 706
hustler 682, 962
hut 189
hutch 189
huzza 838
hyacinth
jewel 847
hyæna 913
hyaline 425
hybrid
mixture 41
exception 83
hydra
monster 83, 366
productive 168
– headed 163
hydrant 348, 385
hydraulics 333, 348
hydro-aeroplane 273
hydrodynamics 333, 348
hydrography 341
hydrology 333
hydrolysis 49
hydromancy 511
hydromel 396
hydropathy 662
hydrophobia 867
hydroplane 273
hydrostatics 333
hyemal 383
hyetology 348
hygeian 656
hygiantics 670
hygienic 656, 670
hygre 348
hygrometry 339
hyle 316
hylism 316
hylotheism 984, 989
Hymen 903
hymeneal 903
hymn *song* 415

worship 990
– of hate 898
hymn-book 998
hyoscine 663
hypallage 218
hyperbation 218
hyperbola 245
hyperbole 549
hyperborean
far 196
cold 383
hypercriticism
misjudgment 481
discontent 832
fastidiousness 868
censure 932
hyperdulia 990
Hyperion 423, 845
– to a satyr 14
hyperorthodoxy 984
hyperphysical 976
hypertrophy 194
hyphen 45
hypnology 683
hypnotic
remedy 662
sleep 683
hypnotize 376
hypocaust 386
hypochondriac
madman 504
low spirits 837
hypochondriasis 837
hypocrisy
falsehood 544
religious – 988
hypocrite 548, 855
play the – 544
hypostasis 1, 3
Hypostatic union 976
hypothecate 771
hypothenuse 217
hypothesis 514
hypothesize 514
hypothetical 475, 514
hypped *insane* 503
dejected 837
hypsometer 206
Hyrcynian wood 533
hysteria
insanity 503
hysteric *violent* 173
hysterical
spasmodic 608
emotional 821
excitable 825
hysterics 173

in – *excited* 824
　frightened 860
hysteron proteron 218

I

I 79
iambic 597
ibidem 13
Icarus
　navigator 269
　rash 863
　fate of – 306
ice *cold* 383
　refrigerate 385
iceberg 383
ice-bound 383
　restraint 751
ice-chest 385
ice-house 387
ice-yacht 273
Ichabod 874
ichnography 554
ichor 333
ichthyology 368
ichthyomancy 511
ichthyophagous 298
icicle 383
icon 554
iconoclasm 983*a*, 984
iconoclast 165, 913
iconography 554
icosahedron 244
idea
　small quantity 32
　notion **453**
　give an – of 537
ideal *unreal* 2
　completeness 52
　erroneous 495
　imaginary 515
　perfect 650
ideality 450, 515
idée fixe 481
identification
　identity 13
　comparison 464
　discovery 480*a*
identity **13**
　– book 206
Ideology 450
Ides of March 601
id est 522
idiocrasy
　essence 5
　tendency 176

idiocy 499
idiom 560, 566
idiomatic 79
idiosyncrasy
　essence 5
　speciality 79
　unconformity 83
　tendency 176
　temperament 820
idiot 501
　tale told by an – 517
idiotic
　foolish 499
idiotism
　folly 499
　phrase 566
idle *foolish* 499
　trivial 643
　slothful 683
　lie – *inaction* 681
　– conceit 842
　– hours 681
　be an – man
　leisure 685
　– talk 588
　– time away 683
idler 683
Ido 560
idol *desire* 865
　favourite 899
　fetich 991
　– of the people 899
idolater 984
idolatry 897, **991**
idolize *love* 897
　impiety 988
idoneous 23
idyl 597
if *circumstance* 8
　qualification 469
　supposition 514
　– you please 765
　– possible 470
igloo 189
igneous 382
ignis fatuus
　ignite 384
　luminary 423
　phantom 443
ignoble 876
ignominy 874, 940
ignoramus **493**
ignorance **491**
　keep in – 528
　plead – 937
ignoratio elenchi 477
ignore

　neglect 460
　incredulity 487
　not known 491
　repudiate 756, 773
ignotum per ignotius 477
ilk 13
ill *evil* 619
　badness 649
　sick 655
　go on – *fail* 732
　adversity 735
　look – 846
　take –
　discontent 832
　anger 900
　– betide 908
　– blood *hate* 898
　malevolence 907
　– at ease *pain* 828
　dejection 837
　house of – fame 961
　–s that flesh is heir to *evil*
　619
　disease 655
　– humour
　anger 900
　sullenness 901*a*
　– luck 735
　as – luck would have it
　135
　– off
　insufficient 640
　adversity 735
　poor 804
　do an – office to 907
　bird of – omen 668
　– repute 874
　– turn *evil* 619
　spiteful 907
　– usage 907
　– will 907
　– wind *bad* 649
　hindrance 706
　adversity 735
ill-adapted 24
ill-advised
　foolish 499
　inexpedient 647
　unskilful 699
ill-affected 901*a*
illapse
　conversion 144
　ingress 294
illaqueate 545
ill-assorted 24
illation 480
illaudable 947

ill-balanced 28
ill-bred 851, 895
ill-conditioned
  bad 649
  difficult 704
  discourteous 895
  malevolent 907
  vicious 945
ill-conducted 699
ill-contrived
  inexpedient 647
  bad 649
  unskilful 699
  malevolent 907
ill-defined 447
ill-devised 499, 699
ill-digested 674
ill-disposed 901*a*, 907
illegality **964**
illegible 519
 render – 552
 – hand 590
illegitimate
  deceitful 545
  undue 925
  illegal 964
ill-fated 735
ill-flavoured 395
ill-furnished 640
illiberal
  narrow-minded 481
  stingy 819
  uncourteous 895
  selfish 943
illicit 925, 964
ill-imagined 499, 699
illimited 105
ill-intentioned 907
illiterate 491, 493
ill-judged 499, 699
ill-judging 481
ill-made 243, 846
ill-mannered 851, 895
ill-marked 447
ill-matched 24
ill-mated 24
ill-natured 907
illogical 477, 495
ill-omened 605, 859
ill-proportioned 243
ill-provided 640
ill-qualified 699
ill-requited 917
ill-spent 646
ill-tempered 901
ill-timed 135
ill-treat *bad* 649

  severe 739
  malevolent 907
illuminant 388
illuminate
  enlighten 420
  colour 428
  excite 824
  ornament 847
illuminati 492
illumination [*see*
  illuminate]
  book-illustration 558
  celebration 883
ill-use 907
ill-used 828
illusion
  fallacy of vision 443
  error 495
illusive, illusory
  sophistical 477
  erroneous 495
  deceitful 545, 546
illustrate
  exemplify 82
  interpret 522
  represent 554
  engravings 558
  ornament 847
illustrious 873
image
  likeness 17
  copy 21
  appearance 448
  idea 453
  metaphor 521
  representation 554
  graven – *idol* 991
imagery *fancy* 515
  metaphor 521
  representation 554
imaginable 470
imaginary
  non-existing 2
  fancied 515
  – *quantity* 84
imagination **515**
imaum 745, 996
imbecile 158, 499
imbécile 501
imbecility **499**
imbed [*see* embed]
imbedded 229
imbibe 296
 – *learning* 539
imbrangle 61
imbricated 223
imbroglio

  disorder 59
  difficulty 704
  discord 713
imbrue
  impregnate 300
  moisten 339
 – one's hands in blood
  killing 361
  war 722
 – the soul 824
imbue *mix* 41
  impregnate 300
  moisten 339
  tinge 428
  teach 537
imbued
  affections 820
 – with
  belief 484
  habit 613
  feeling 821
imburse 803
imitation
  copying **19**
  copy 21
  representation 554
immaculate
  perfect 650
  clean 652
  innocent 946
immanent 5, 132
immanity 907
Immanuel 976
immaterial
  unsubstantial 4
immateriality
  spiritual **317**
  trifling 643
immature 123, 674
immeasurable 31, 105
immediate
  continuous 69
immediately 113, 132
immedicabile vulnus 619
immedicable 859
immelodious 414
immemorial 124
 from time – 122
 – *usage* 613
immense *great* 31
  infinite 105
  - *size* 192
immerge, immerse
  introduce 300
  dip 337
immersed in 229
immethodical 59

immigrant
  alien 57
  entering 294
immigration 266, 294
imminent 152, 286
immiscible 47
immission 296
immitigable
  hopeless 859
  revenge 919
immix 41
immobility 150, 265
immoderately 31
immodest 961
immolation
  killing 361
  giving 784
  sacrifice 991
immoral 923, 945
immortal
  perpetual 112
  glorious 873
  celebrated 883
immotile 265
immovable
  stable 150
  quiescent 265
  obstinate 606
immundicity 653
immunity
  health 656
  freedom 748
  right 924
  exemption 777a, 927a
immure 751
immutable
  stable 150
  deity 976
imo pectore, ab - 821
imp 980
impact contact 43
  impulse 276
  insertion 300
impair 659
impale transfix 260
  execute 972
impalpable
  small 193
  powder 330
  intangible 381
impanation 998
imparity 28
impar sibi 608
impart inform 527
  give 784
impartial
  judicious 498

neutral 628
  just 922
  honourable 939
  - opinion 484
impassable
  closed 261
  impossible 471
impasse 706
impassible 823
impassion 824
impassionable 822
impassioned
  - language 574
  excited 825
impassive 823
impatient 825
  - of control 742
impawn 771
impeach
  censure 932
  accuse 938
  go to law 969
impeachment, soft - 902
impeccability 650, 946
impecunious 804
impede 706
impediment 706
  - in speech 583
impedimenta 633, 780
impel push 276
  induce 615
impend
  future 121
  imminent 132
  destiny 152
  overhang 206
impenetrable
  closed 261
  solid 321
  unintelligible 519
  latent 526
impenitence 951
imperative
  require 630
  command 737, 741
  severe 739
  duty 926
imperator 745
imperceptible
  small 32
  minute 193
  slow 275
  invisible 447
  latent 526
impercipient 376
imperdible 664
imperfect

incomplete 53
  failing 651
  vicious 945
imperfection 651
  inferiority 34
  vice 945
imperfectly 32
imperforate 261
imperial
  trunk 191
  beard 256
  authority 737
imperil 665
imperious
  command 737
  proud 878
  arrogant 885
  - necessity 601
imperishable 112
  stable 150
  glorious 873
imperium in imperio 737
impermanent 111
impermeable
  closed 261
  dense 321
impersonal
  general 78
  neuter 316
impersonate 19, 554
impersonator 19
imperspicuity 519
impersuasible 606
impertinent
  irrelevant 10
  insolent 885
imperturbable 823, 826
impervious
  closed 261
  impossible 471
  insensible 823
  - to light 426
  - to reason 606
impetiginous 653
impetrate 765
impetuous
  boisterous 173
  hasty 684
  excitable 825
  rash 863
  eager 865
impetus 276
impi 726
impiety 988
impignorate 787
impinge 276
implacable 848, 919

improviste, à l'- 508, 612
imprudent 460, 863
impudent 885, 895
impudicity 961
impugn *deny* 536
  attack 716
  blame 932
impugnation 708
impuissance 158
impulse *push* **276**
  sudden thought **612**
  motive 615
  blind - 601
  creature of - 612
  give an - to
  propel 284
  aid 707
impulsive [*see* impulse]
  intuitive 477
  excitable 825
  rash 863
impunity *escape* 671
  acquittal 970
  with - *safely* 664
impurity 653, **961**
imputation
  ascribe 155
  slur 874
  accuse 938
in 221
  go - 294
  - as much as
  relation 9
  degree 26
  - the circumstances 8
  - doors 221
  - durancevile 751
  - force 1
  undertake 676
  promise 768
  - re 9
  - and out 314
  -s and outs 182
in: - articulo 111
  - extenso *whole* 50
  diffuse 573
  - jail 751
  - limine 66
  - loco 23
  - medias res 68
  - prison 751
  - propriâ personâ 79
  - toto 52
  - transitu
  transient 111
  transfer 270
  - statu pupillari 127

  - statu quo 141
  - vogue 1
inability 158, 699
inabstinent 954
inaccessible 196, 471
inaccurate 495, 568
inaction 172, **683**
inactivity 172, **683**
inadequate
  powerless 158
  insufficient 640
  useless 645
  imperfect 651
inadmissible
  incongruous 24
  excluded 55
  extraneous 57
  inexpedient 647
inadvertence 458
inadvisable 647
inaffable 895
inalienable
  retention 781
  right 924
inamorata 897
inane *void* 4
  unmeaning 517
  unthinking 452
  insufficient 640
  trivial 643
  useless 645
inanimate 360
  - matter 358
inanition 158
inanity [*see* inane]
inappetency 823, 866
inapplicable 10, 24
inapposite 10, 24
inappreciable 33, 193
  unimportant 643
inapprehensible
  stolid 499
  unintelligible 519
inappropriate 24, 647
inapt
  incongruous 24
  impotent 158
  useless 645
  inexpedient 647
  unskilful 699
inarticulate 581, 583
inartificial 703
inartistic 846
inasmuch *whereas* 9
  however 26
  because 476
inattention 458

inaudible
  silence 403
  faint sound 405
  deaf 419
  voiceless 581
inaugural
  precursor 64
inaugurate
  begin 66
  cause 153
  install 755
  celebrate 883
inauspicious
  untimely 135
  untoward 649
  hopeless 859
inbeing 5
inborn, inbred
  intrinsic 5
  affections 820
  - proclivity 601
inca 745
incage 751
incalculable 31, 105
incalescence 382
incandescence 382
incandescent 423
incantation
  invocation 765
  sorcery 992
  spell 993
incantatory 992
incapable 158
incapacious 203
incapacitate 158
incapacity
  impotence 158
  ignorance 491
  stupidity 499
incarcerate 751
incarnadine 434
incarnate
  intrinsic 5
  bodily 316
  fleshly 364
  vicious 945
  devil -
  bad man 949
  Satan 978
Incarnation 976
incase 223, 229
incautious 863
incendiary
  destroy 162
  burn 384
  influence 615
  malevolent 907

evil-doer 913
bad man 949
incense *fuel* 388
fragrant 400
hate 898
anger 900
flatter 933
worship 990
rite 998
incension
burning 384
incentive 615
inception 66
inceptive 153
inceptor 541
incertitude 475
incessant
repeated 104
ceaseless 112
frequent 136
incest 961
inch *small* 32
length 200
by –es 275
to an – 494
not yield an – 606
give an – and take an ell
　789
– by inch
by degrees 26
in parts 51
slowly 275
not see an – beyond one's
　nose 699
inchoation 66, 673
incide 44
incidence 278
incident 151
incidental
extrinsic 6
circumstance 8
irrelative 10
occurring 151
casual 156
liable 177
chance 621
trivial 643
– music 415
incinerate 384
incipience 66
incircumspect 460
incision 44, 259
incisive *energy* 171
vigour 574
feeling 821
incisor 253
incite

exasperate 173
urge 615
incivility 895
incivism 911
inclasp 229
inclement
violent 173
cold 383
severe 739
pitiless 914a
inclination [*see* incline]
will 600
affection 820
desire 865
love 897
incline *tendency* 176
slope 217
direction 278
willing 602
induce 615
– an ear to 457
– the head 308
inclined
disposed 620
– *plane* 633
inclose
surround 227
inclosure 232
include
composition 54
- *in a class* 76
inclusion 76
inclusive
additive 37
component 56
class 76
incogitancy 452
incognita, terra – 491
incognito 528
incognizable 519
incoherence
physical **47**
mental 503
incombustible 385
income *means* 632
profit 775
property 780
wealth 803
receipt 810
– *tax* 812
incoming
ingress 294
receipt 810
incommensurable 10
– *quantity* 84, 85
incommode 706
hinder 706

incommunicable
unmeaning 517
unintelligible 519
retention 781
incommunicado 528
incommutable 150
incomparable 33
incompassionate 914a
incompatible 24
incompatibility 15
incompetence
inability 158
incapacity 499
unskilful 699
dereliction 927
incompleteness 53
non-completion 730
incompliance 764
incomprehensible
infinite 105
unintelligible 519
incomprehension 491
incompressible 321
inconcealable 525
inconceivable
unthinkable 452
impossible 471
improbable 473
incredible 485
unintelligible 519
wonder 870
inconceptible 519
inconcinnity
disagreement 24
ugliness 846
inconclusive 477
inconcoction 674
incondite 851
incongruous
differing 15
disagreeing 24
illogical 477
ungrammatical 568
discordant 713
inconnection 10, 44
inconsequence
irrelation 10
inconsequential 477
inconsiderable 32, 643
inconsiderate
thoughtless 452
inattentive 458
neglectful 460
foolish 699
inconsistent
contrary 14
disagreeing 24

illogical 477
absurd 497
foolish 499
capricious 608
discord 713
inconsolable 837
inconsonant
disagreeing 24
fitful 149
inconspicuous 447
inconstant 149
incontestable 159, 474, 525
incontiguous 196
incontinent 961
incontinently 132
incontrollable 173
incontrovertible 150, 474
inconvenience 647
put to – 706
inconversable 585, 893
inconvertible 143
inconvincible 487
incorporate 48
combine 48
include 76
materialize 316
incorporation 761
incorporeal 317
– hereditaments 780
incorrect
illogical 477
erroneous 495
solecism 568
vicious 945
incorrigible
obstinate 606
hopeless 859
vicious 945
impenitent 951
incorruption
probity 939
innocence 946
incrassate
increase 194
density 321
– *fluids* 352
increase
– *in degree* **35**
– *in number* 102
– *in size* 194
incredible
great 31
impossible 471
improbable 473
doubtful 485
wonderful 870
incredulity 487, 989

increment
increase 35
addition 37
adjunct 39
expansion 194
increpation 932
incriminate 938
incrust 223, 224
incubate 370
incubation 673
incubus
hindrance 706
pain 828
demon 980
inculcate 6, 537
inculpable 946
inculpate 938
inculture 674
incumbency
business 625
churchdom 995
incumbent
inhabitant 188
high 206
weight 319
duty 926
clergyman 996
incumber 706
incumbered 806
incunabula 66, 127
incur 177
– blame 932
– danger 665
– a debt 806
– disgrace 874
– a loss 776
– the risk 621
incurable
ingrained 5
disease 655
hopeless 859
incuriam, per – 458, 460
incuriosity 456
incursion 294, 716
incurvation 245
indagation 461
indebted
owing 806
gratitude 916
duty 926
indecent 961
indeciduous 150
indecipherable 519
indecision 475, 605
indecisive 475
indeclinable 150
indecorous

vulgar 851
vicious 945
impure 961
indeed *existing* 1
very 31
assent 488
truly 494
assertion 535
wonder 870
indefatigable
persevering 604a
active 682
indefeasible
stable 150, 474
due 924
indefectible 650
indefensible
powerless 158
submission 725
accusable 938
wrong 945
indeficient 650
indefinite
great 31
unspecified 78
infinite 105
misty 447
uncertain 475
inexact 495
vague 519
indeliberate 612
indelible *stable* 150
memory 505
mark 550
feeling 821
indelicate 961
indemnity
compensation 30
restitution 790
forgiveness 918
atonement 952
reward 973
deed of – 771
indenizen 184
indent *scollop* 248
list 86
indentation 252, 257
indenture 769, 771
independence
irrelation 10
freedom 748
wealth 803
independent 984
indescribable 31, 870
indesinent 112
indestructible 150
indeterminate

inelegance 579, 846
ineluctable 474
inept 24, 158, 645
inequality 28
inequitable 923
ineradicable
 intrinsic 5
 stable 150
inerrable 946
inertia 172
inertness
 physical **172**
 inactive 683
 moral 823
inestimable 648
inevitable 474, 601
inexact
 erroneous 495
 feeble 575
inexcitability 826
inexcusable
 accusable 938
 vicious 945
inexecution 730
inexhaustible 105, 639
inexistence 2
inexorable
 unavoidable 601
 resolved 604
 stern 739
 compelling 744
 pitiless 914a
 revengeful 919
inexpectation 508
inexpedience 647
inexpensive 815
inexperience 491, 699
inexpert 699
inexpiable 945
inexplicable 519
inexpressible
 great 31
 unmeaning 517
 unintelligible 519
 wonderful 870
inexpressibles 225
inexpression
 latency 526
inexpressive 517
inexpugnable 664
inextension 180a
 littleness 193
 immateriality 317
inextinguishable
 stable 150
 strong 159
 excitable 825

 – *desire* 865
inextricable
 coherent 46
 disorder 59
 impossible 471
infallibility 474
 assumption of – 885
infamy *shame* 874
 dishonour 940
 vice 945
infancy 66, 127
infandum renovare
 dolorem 505, 833
infant 129
 fool 501
 – *prodigy* 872
Infanta 745
infanticide 361, 991
infantine 129
 foolish 499
infantry 726
infarction 261
infatuation
 misjudgment 481
 credulity 486
 folly 499
 insanity 503
 obstinacy 606
 passion 825
 love 897
infeasible 471
infect *mix with* 41
 contaminate 659
 excite 824
infectâ, re –
 shortcoming 304
 non-completion 730
 failure 732
infection
 transference 270
 disease 655
infectious 270, 657
infecund 169
infelicitous 24
infelicity
 inexpertness 699
 misery 828
infer 472
inference 476, 480
 by – 467
inferential
 demonstrative 478
 latent 526
inferiority
 in degree **34**
 in size 195
 imperfection 651

 personal – 34
infernal *bad* 649
 malevolent 907
 wicked 945
 satanic 978
 – *machine* 727
 – *regions* 982
infertility 169
infest 830
infestivity 837, 843
infibulation 43
infidel 487, 989
infidelity
 dishonour 940
 irreligion 989
infiltrate *mix* 41
 intervene 228
 interpenetrate 294
 moisten 337, 339
 teach 537
infiltration
 passage 302
Infinite, the – 976
infinite 105
 – *goodness* 976
infinitely *great* 31
infinitesimal
 small 32
 little 193
 – *calculus* 85
infinity 105
infirm *weak* 160
 disease 655
 vicious 945
 – *of purpose* 605
infirmary 662
infirmity [*see* infirm]
infix 537
inflame
 render violent 173
 burn 384
 excite 824
 anger 900
inflamed 382
inflammable 384, 388
inflammation
 heating 384
 disease 655
inflate *increase* 35
 expand 194
 blow 349
inflated
 overestimation 482
 style 573, 577
 ridiculous 853
 vain 880
inflation [*see* inflate]

rarefaction 322
currency 800
inflect 245
inflexible *hard* 323
  resolved 604
  obstinate 606
  stern 739
  inexorable 914a
inflexion
  change 140
  curvature 245
  grammar 567
inflict *act upon* 680
  severity 739
  - *evil* 649
  - *pain*
  bodily pain 378
  mental pain 830
  - *punishment* 972
infliction
  adversity 735
  mental pain 828, 830
  punishment 972
influence 153
  change 140
  physical - **175**
  inducement 615
  instrumentality 631
  authority 737
  absence of - **175a**
  sphere of - 780
  make one's - felt 631
influx 294
infold 232
inform 527
  - against
  accuse 938
  go to law 969
informal 83, 964
informality 773
informant 527
information
  knowledge 490
  communication **527**
  learning 539
  lawsuit 969
  pick up - 539
informer 532
informity 241
infraction
  trespass 303
  disobedience 742
  non-observance 773
  exemption 927
  - of usage &c.
  unconformity 83
  desuetude 614

infra dignitatem 874, 940
infrangible
  combined 46
  dense 321
infra-red rays 420
infrequency 137
infrigidation 385
infringe
  transgress 303
  disobey 742
  not observe 773
  undueness 925
  dereliction 927
  - a law &c. 83
infundibular 252, 269
infuriate
  violent 173
  excite 824
  anger 900
infuscate 431
infuse *mix* 41
  insert 300
  teach 537
  - courage 861
  - life into 824
  - new blood 658
infusible 321
infusion [*see* infuse]
  liquefaction 335
infusoria 193
ingannation 545
ingathering 72
ingemination 90
ingenerate 5
ingenious 515, 698
ingenite 5
ingenium, perfervidum -
  682
ingénu *artless* 703
ingénue *actress* 599
ingenuity 698
ingenuous 703
ingesta 298
ingestion 296
ingle 388
inglorious 874, 940
ingluvies 191
ingot 800
ingraft *add* 37
  join 43
  insert 300
  teach 537
ingrafted
  extrinsic 6
  habit 613
ingrain
  insinuate 228

  colour 428
ingrained
  intrinsic 5
  combined 48
  habit 613
  character 820
ingrate 917
ingratiate 897
ingratiating 894
ingratitude **917**
ingredient 51, 56
ingress **294**
  forcible - 300
ingurgitate 296
ingustible 391
inhabile 699
inhabit 186
inhabitant **188**
inhale *receive* 296
  breathe 349
  smell 398
inharmonious
  discord 713
  - colour 428
  - sound 414
inhere 1
inherent 5, 820
inherit 775, 777
inheritance 780
  - of the saints 981
inherited
  intrinsic 5
inheritor 779
inhesion 5
inhibit *hinder* 706
  restrain 751
  prohibit 761
inhospitable 893
inhuman 907
inhume 363
inimaginable
  impossible 471
  improbable 473
  wonderful 870
inimical 708, 889
inimitable
  non-imitation 20
  supreme 33
  very good 648
  perfect 650
iniquity 923, 945.
  worker of - 949
inirritability 826
initial 66
  - letter 558
initiate *begin* 66
  admit 296

teach 537
initiated *skilful* 698
initiative 66
inject 300, 337
injection 662
injudicial 964
injudicious 499, 863
injunction
  acquirement 630
  advice 695
  command 741
  prohibition 761
injure *evil* 619
  damage 659
  spite 907
injuria formæ, spretæ –
  846, 930
injury *evil* 619
  badness 649
  damage 659
injustice 923
ink 431
  pen and – 590
  before the – is dry 132
  – slinging 720
inkle 45
inkling
  knowledge 490
  supposition 514
  information 527
inkstand 590
inland 221
inlay 440, 847
inlet *beginning* 66
  interval 198
  opening 260
  ingress 294
  - *of the sea* 343
inly 221
inmate 188
inmost 221
  to the – core 822
  – soul 820
  – thoughts 451
inn 189
  –s of Court 968
innate 5, 601
innavigable 471
inner 221
  – coating 224
  – man *intellect* 450
  affections 820
innermost recesses 221
innings *land* 342
  acquisition 775
  receipt 810
innkeeper 601

innocence 946
innocent *fool* 501
  good 648
  healthy 656
  artless 703
  guiltless 946
innocuous *good* 648
  healthy 656
  innocent 946
innominate 565
innovation
  variation 20a
  new 123
  change 140
innoxious
  salubrious 656
  innocent 946
innuendo *hint* 527
  censure 932
innumerable 105
innutritious 657
inobservance 773
inoccupation 681
inoculate
  insert 300
  teach 537
  influence 615
inodorous 399
inoffensive 648, 946
inofficious 907
inoperative
  powerless 158
  unproductive 169
  useless 645
inopportune
  untimely 135
  inexpedient 647
inordinate 31, 641
inorganization 358
inornate 849
inosculate *join* 43
  intersect 219
  convoluted 248
inquest 461
inquietude
  changeable 149
  uneasy 828
  discontent 832
  apprehension 860
inquinate 659
inquire 461
  – into 595
inquirer 461
inquiring mind 455
inquiry 461
inquisition
  inquiry 461

severity 739
  torture 907
  tribunal 966
inquisitive 455
inquisitorial
  prying 455
  inquiry 461
  severe 739
  jurisdiction 965
inroad *ingress* 294
  devastation 659
  invasion 716
inrolment 551
insalubrity 657
insanity 503
insatiable 865
inscribe 590, 873
inscription 551
inscroll 551
inscrutable 519
insculpture 557
insculptured 558
insecable 43, 87
insect *minute* 193
  animal 366
  – cry 412
insecure
  uncertain 475
  danger 665
insensate
  foolish 499
  insane 503
insensibility
  slow 275
  physical **376**
  moral **823**
  – of benefits 917
  – to the past 506
inseparable 43, 46
insert *locate* 184
  interpose 228
  enter 294
  put in 300
  record 551
  – itself 300
insertion 300
  adjunct 39
  ornament 847
inservient 645
inseverable 43, 87
inside 221
  – out 218
  turn – out 529
insidious
  deceitful 545
  cunning 702
  dishonourable 940

insight 465, 490
insignia 550
  – of authority 747
insignificant
  unmeaning 517
  unimportant 643
insincere 544, 855
insinuate
  intervene 228
  ingress 294
  insert 300
  latency 526
  hint 527
  ingratiate 897
  blame 932
insipid
  style 575
  dull 840
insipidity
  tasteless **391**
  indifferent 866
insist *argue* 476
  command 741
  – upon *affirm* 535
  dwell on 573
  be determined 604
  contend 720
  compel 744
  conditions 770
  due 924
insnare 545
insobriety 959
insolation 382, 384
insolence 878, 885
insoluble *dense* 321
  unintelligible 519
insolvable 519
insolvent
  poverty 804
  debt 806
  non-payment 808
insomnia 682
insouciance
  thoughtlessness 458
  supineness 823
  indifference 866
inspan 293
inspect 441, 457
inspector 444
  inquisitor 461
  judge 480
  director 694
inspiration
  wisdom 498
  imagination 515
  poetry 577
  impulse 612

  motive 615
  feeling 821
  Deity 976
  revelation 985
  religious - 987
inspire *improve* 658
  prompt 615
  animate 824
  cheer 836
  – *courage* 861
  – *hope* 858
  – *respect* 928
inspirit *incite* 615
  animate 824
  encourage 861
inspiriting
  hopeful 858
inspissate 321, 352
instability 149
install *locate* 184
  commission 755
  celebrate 883
instalment
  portion 51
  payment 807, 809
instance
  example 82
  motive 615
  solicitation 765
instant *moment* 113
  present 118
  destiny 152
  required 630
  importance 642
  active 682
  lose not an – 684
  on the – 132
instantaneity **113**
instanter 113, 132
instar omnium 17, 82
instate 883
instauration 660
instead 147
instep 245
instigate 615
instil *extrinsic* 6
  mix 41
  insert 300
  teach 537
instinct
  intellect 450
  intuition 477
  impulse 601
  – with *motive* 615
  possession 777
  brute – 450*a*
instinctive

  inborn 5
institute *begin* 66
  cause 153
  produce 161
  academy 542
  society 712
  – an inquiry 461
institution
  academy 542
  society 712
  political - 963
  church 995
institutor 540
instruct *teach* 537
  advise 695
  precept 697
  order 741
instructed 490
instructor 540
instrument
  implement **633**
  security 771
  musical – 417
  optical – 445
  recording – 553
instrumental 631
  – *music* 415
instrumentalist 416
instrumentality **631**
insuavity 895
insubordinate 742
insubstantial 4
  – pageant 882
insufferable
  painful 830
  dislike 867
insufficiency **640**
insufflation 349
insular *unrelated* 10
  detached 44
  single 87
  local 181
  island 346
  prejudice 481
insulate 44
insulse 499, 843
insult *rudeness* 895
  offence 900
  disrespect 929
insulting 898
insuperable 471
  – obstacle 706
insupportable 830
insuppressible 173
insurance 768, 771
insure
  make sure 474

obtain security 771
insurgent 742
insurmountable 471
insurrection 719, 742
insusceptible 823
– of change 150
inswept 195
intact
permanent 141
perfect 650
preserved 670
intaglio *mould* 22
concave 252
sculpture 557
engraving 558
intangible *little* 193
numb 381
integer 50, 84
**integer vitæ scelerisque
    purus** 939
integral 50
– *calculus* 85
– *part* 56
integrate 50
integrity *whole* 50
probity 939
virtue 944
integument 223
intellect 450
absence of – **450a**
exercise of the – 451
intellectual 450
intelligence
mind 450
capacity **498**
news 532
intelligencer 527
intelligentsia 492
intelligibility 518
intemperance 954
drunkenness 959
intempestivity 135
intend 620
intendant 694
intended *will* 600
predetermined 611
intense *great* 31
energetic 171
– *colour* 428
– *thought* 457
intensification 35
intensify
increase 35
stimulate 171
intensity *degree* 26
greatness 31
energy 171

intensive culture 371
intent *attention* 457
will 600
design 620
active 682
– upon *desire* 865
resolved 604
intention 620
bad – 607
good – 906
intently, look – 441
**intents and purposes, to
    all** – 27, 52
inter 363
inter: – **alia** 82
– **nos** 528
interact 12
interaction 170
interbreeding 41
intercalate 228
intercalation 300
intercede
mediate 724
deprecate 766
intercept
hinder 706
take 789
intercession [*see* intercede]
worship 990
Intercessor 976
interchange 148
barter 794
– *visits &c.* 892
interchangeable 12
intercipient 706
interclude 706
intercommunication 527
intercommunity 892
interconnection 9
intercourse
copulation 43
friendship 888
sociality 892
verbal – 582, 588
intercurrence
interchange 148
interjacence 228
passage 302
interdependence 12
interdict 761
interdictive 55
interdigitate 219, 228
interest *concern* 9
influence 175
curiosity 455
advantage 618
importance 642

property 780
debt 806
excite 824
please 829
amuse 840
devoid of – 841
feel an – in 906
not know one's own – 699
make – for 707
place out at –
lend 787
economy 817
take an – in
curiosity 455
love 897
take no – in
insensibility 823
indifference 866
want of – 866
interested
selfish 943
– in 457
interesting
lovable 897
interfere *disagree* 24
counteract 179
intervene 228
activity 682
thwart 706
mediate 724
interference
light 420
interfretted 219
interfusion 41
interim 106, 120
interior 221
painting 556
interjacence 68, **228**
interject 228, 300
interlace *join* 43
twine 219
interlacing 41
interlard 41, 228
interleave 228
interline
interpolate 288
write 590
interlineation 39
interlink 43, 219
interlocation 228
interlocking directorate
709
interlocution 588
interlocutor 582
interloper
extraneous 57
intervene 228

obstruct 706
interlude
  time 106
  dramatic 599
intermarriage 903
intermeddle 682, 706
intermeddling 724
intermediary 534
intermediate
  mean 29
  middle 68
  intervening 228
  ministerial 631
  – time 106
intermedium
  mean 29
  link 45
  intervention 228
  instrument 631
interment 363
  insertion 300
intermezzo 415
intermigration 266
interminable
  infinite 105
  eternal 112
  long 200
intermingle 41
intermission 106, 142
intermit
  interrupt 70
  recur 138
  discontinue 142
intermittence
  time 106
intermix 41, 48
intermural 278
intermutation 148
intern 221
internal 5, 221
  – evidence 467
international
  reciprocal 12
  sociality 892
  – law 963
internecine 361
  – war 722
internuncio 534, 758
interpel 142
interpellation
  inquiry 461
  address 586
  summons 741
  appeal 765
interpenetration
  interjacence 228
  ingress 294

passage 302
interplanetary 228
interpolation
  adjunct 39
  analytical 85
  interpose 228
  insertion 300
interpose
  intervene 228
  act 682
  hinder 706
  mediate 724
interposit 799
interpretation 522
interpreter 524
interregnum
  intermission 106
  transient 111
  discontinuance 142
  interval 198
  laxity 738
interrelation 9, 12
interrogate 461
interrupt
  discontinuity 70
  cessation 142
  hinder 706
interruption
  derangement 61
  interval 198
intersect 219
interspace 198, 221
intersperse 73, 228
interstellar 228
interstice 198
interstitial 221, 228
intertexture
  intersection 219
  tissue 329
inter-twine, -twist
  unite 43
  cross 219
interval
  – of time 106
  – of space **198**
  – in music 413
  at –s
  discontinuously 70
  at regular –s 138
intervene
  – in order 70
  – in time 106
  – in space 228
  be instrumental 631
  mediate 724
intervert 140, 279
interview 588, 892

intervolved 43
interweave *join* 43
  cross 219
  interjacence 228
interworking 170
intestate 552
intestine 221
inthral 749, 751
intimacy 9
intimate
  personal 79
  close 197
  inside 221
  tell 527
  friendly 888, 892
intimately
  joined 43
intimidate
  frighten 860
  insolence 885
  threat 909
intitule 564
into: go – 294
  put – 300
  run – 300
intolerable 830
intolerance
  prejudice 481
  dissent 489
  obstinacy 606
  impatience 825
  insolence 885
  malevolence 907
intomb 363
intonation
  sound 402
  musical 313
  voice 580
intone 416, 992·
intort 248
intoxicant 663
intoxication
  excitement 824, 825
  inebriation 959
intra, ab – 221
intractable
  obstinate 606
  difficult 704
  sullen 901*a*
intramural 221
intransient 110
intransigeance 604
intransitive 110
intransmutable 110, 150
intrap 545
intraregarding 221
intrench 717

– on 303
intrepid 861
intricate
  confused 59
  convoluted 248
  difficult 704
intrigant
  meddlesome 682
  cunning 702
  libertine 962
intrigue *fascinate* 615, 897
  plot 626
  activity 682
  cunning 702
  excite 824
  interest 829
  licentiousness 961
intrinsic 5
  – evidence 467
  – habit 613
  – truth 494
intrinsicality 5
introception 296
introduce *lead* 62
  interpose 228
  precede 280
  insert 300
  – new blood 140
  – new conditions 469
  – to 888
introduction [*see*
  introduce]
  preface 64
  reception 296
  drama 599
  friendship 888
  courtesy 894
introductory
  precursor 64
  beginning 66
  priority 116
introgression 294
introit 998
intromission 228
intromit
  discontinue 142
  receive 296
introspection 441, 457
introspective 451
introvert 218
intrude
  interfere 24
  inopportune 135
  intervene 228
  enter 294
  encroach 303
intruder 57

intrusiveness 682
intrust 755, 787
intuition *mind* 450
  unreasoning **477**
  knowledge 490
intumescence 194, 250
intwine 43, 243
inunction 223
inundate
  effusion 337
  flow 348
  redundance 641
inunderstanding 452
inurbanity 895
inure 613, 673
inured
  insensible 823
inusitation 614
inutility **645**
invade *ingress* 294
  encroach 303
  attack 716
invalid
  powerless 158
  illogical 477
  diseased 655
  undue 925
invalidate
  disable 158
  weaken 160
  confute 479
invaluable 648
invariable
  intrinsic 5
  uniform 16
  conformable 82
  stable 150
invasion
  ingress 294
  attack 716
invective 932
inveigh 932
inveigle 545, 615
invent
  discover 480a
  imagine 515
  lie 544
  devise 626
invented
  untrue 546
invention 480a
inventive
  skilful 698
inventor 164
inventory 86
inverse 14, 218
inversion

  derangement 61
  change 140
  reversion 145
  of position **218**
  contraposition 237
  language 577
invertebrate 158
invest
  empower 157
  clothe 225
  besiege 227, 716
  commission 755
  give 784
  lend 787
  expend 809
  – in *locate* 184
  purchase 795
  – money 817
  – with *ascribe* 155
investigate 461
investment **225**
  – trust 712
  make –s 673
inveterate *old* 124
  established 150
  inborn 820
  – belief 484
  – habit 613
invidious
  painful 830
  hatred 898
  spite 907
  envy 921
invigorate
  strengthen 159
invigorating
  healthy 656
invincible 159
inviolable
  secret 528
  right 924
  honour 939
inviolate
  permanent 141
  secret 528
  honourable 939
invious *closed* 261
  pathless 704
invisibility **447**
invisible *small* 193
  not to be seen 447
  concealed 526
  – ink 528
  become – 4
invitâ Minervâ 603, 704
invite *induce* 615
  offer 763

jammed in 751
jangle
 harsh sound 410
 quarrel 713
janissary 726
janitor 263
janty *gay* 836
 pretty 845
 stylish 852
 showy 882
 insolent 885
January 138
januis clausis 528
Janus *deceiver* 607
 tergiversation 607
 close the temple of – 723
Janus-faced 544
japan *coat* 223
 resin 356a
 ornament 847
jar *clash* 24
 vessel 191
 agitation 315
 stridor 410
 discord 713
 – *upon the feelings* 830
jardinière 191
jargon
 absurdity 497
 no meaning 517
 unintelligible 519
 neology 563
jarvey 694
jasper 847
jaundiced
 yellow 436
 prejudiced 481
 dejected 837
 jealous 920
 view with – eyes
  disapprove 932
jaunt 266
jaunting car 272
jaunty [*see* janty]
javelin 727
jaw *chatter* 584
 scold 932
jaw-fallen 837
jaws *mouth* 231
 eating 298
 – *of death* 360
jay 584
jaywalker 701
jazz 415, 840
 – *band* 417
jealous of honour 939
jealousy 920

suspicion 485
jecur, difficili bile – 900
jeer 929
Jehovah 976
Jehu 268, 694
jejune *insipid* 391
 style 575
 scanty 640
 dull 843
jell 352
jelly 298, 352
 beat to a – 972
jemidar 745
jemmy *lever* 633
 dandy 854
je ne sais quoi
 exceptional 83
 what d'ye call 'em 563
 beauty 845
jennet 271
jeopardy 665
jerboa 309
jeremiad
 lament 839
 invective 932
Jericho, send to – 297
jerk *start* 146
 throw 284
 pull 285
 agitate 315
jerkin 225
jerks, by – 70
Jerry Sneak 862, 941
jersey 225
Jerusalem
 the new – 981
Jessamy, Jemmy – 854
jesse 1000
jest *trifle* 643
 wit 842
jest-book 842
jester 844
jesting-stock 857
Jesuit *deceiver* 548
 priest 996
jesuitical 477, 544
Jesus 976
jet *stream* 348
 – *black* 431
jetsam 73, 782
jettison 782
jetty *protection* 250
 harbour 666
jeu
 le – n'en vaut pas la
  chandelle
 waste 638

unimportant 643
 dear 814
 – d'esprit 842
 – de mots 842
 – de théâtre 599
jeune
 – premier 599
 – veuve 599
jewel *gem* 648
 ornament 847
 favourite 899
jewellery, false – 545
Jew's harp 417
Jezebel *wicked* 913
 wretch 949
 courtesan 962
jib *front* 234
 regression 283
 cut of one's –
  form 240
  appearance 448
jibe 140
jiffy 113
jig 840
jig-saw puzzle 840
jilt *disappoint* 509
 deceive 545
 deceiver 548
 cast off 756
 dishonour 940
jilted 898
jimp 845
jingal 727
jingle 408
jingo 887
jingoism 884
jinks, high – 840
jinriksha 272
jinx 649, 735
Joan of Arc 861
job *business* 625
 action 680
 unfair 940
 tough – 704
Job:
 patience of – 826, 830
 poor as – 804
 –'s comforter
  dejection 837
  hopeless 859
jobation 932
jobber
 deceiver 548
 tactician 700
 merchant 797
 trickster 943
jobbernowl 501

jobbery 702, 940
jobbing *barter* 794
jockey *rider* 268
  deceive 545
  deceiver 548
  servant 746
jocose 836, 842
jocoseness *fun* 840
jocular 836, 842
jocund 836, 840
jocundity 829
Joe Miller 842, 844
jog *push* 276
  shake 315
  - the memory 505
  - on *continue* 143
  trudge 266
  slow 275
  advance 282
  mediocrity 736
joggle 315
jog-trot
  trudge 266
  slow 275
  habit 613
John Doe and Richard
  Roe 4
Johnny 894
John's 653
Johnsonian 577
joie, feu de - 883
join *connect* 43
  assemble 72
  contiguous 199
  arrive 292
  party 712
  sociality 892
  marry 903
  - battle 722
  - in the chorus 488
  - forces, hands, 709
  - in 778
  - issue *discuss* 476
  deny 536
  quarrel 713
  contend 720
  lawsuit 969
  - the majority 360
  - up
  enlist 723
  - with 709
joint *junction* 43
  part 51
  accompanying 88
  concurrent 178
  meat 298
  - concern 721

joint-stock 709, 778
joint-tenancy 778
jointure 780
joist 215
joke *absurdity* 497
  trifle 643
  wit 842
  ridicule 856
  in - 842
  mere - 643
  no - *existing* 1
  important 642
  practical -
  deception 545
  ridicule 856
  disrespect 929
  take a - 498
joker 844
jokesmith 844
joking apart 535, 604
jole 236
jollification
  amusement 840
  intemperance 954
jollity 840, 892
jolly *plump* 192
  marine 269
  gay 836
  ridicule 856
  - boat 273
  - fellow 892
jolt 276, 315
jolthead 501
Jonah 649
Jones
  Davy -' locker 360
  Paul - 792
jorum 191
Joseph 960
  -'s coat 440
joss 991
  - house 1000
jostle *rush* 276
  jog 315
  clash 713
jot 32, 643
jotting 550, 551
jounce 315
journal *annals* 114
  newspaper 531
  record 551
  magazine 593
  narrative 594
  accounts 811
journalist
  messenger 534
  recorder 553

  author 593
journey **266**
journeyman
  artisan 690
  servant 746
joust 720
Jove 979
  by - 870
  sub -
  out of doors 220
  air 338
jovial *gay* 836
  amusement 840
  social 892
jowl 236
joy 827
  give one - 896
joyful 836
joyless *painful* 830
  sad 837
joy stick 693
J.P. 967
Juan, Don - 962
jube 1000
jubeo, sic volo sic - 741
jubilant *gay* 836
  rejoicing 838
  boastful 884
jubilee 138, 883
jubilitate 884
Judæus Apella, credat -
  disbelief 485
  absurdity 497
Judaism 984
Judas *deceiver* 548
  knave 941
  - kiss
  hypocrisy 544
  base 940
judge *decide* 480
  master 745
  taste 850
  magistrate **967**
Judge *deity* 976
Judgment
  Day of - 67
judgment
  intellect 450
  discrimination 465
  decision **480**
  wisdom 498
  sentence 972
judgment-seat 966
judicata, res -
  certain 574
  judgment 480
judication 480

lament 839
witty 842
eager 865
– blast 349
keener 839
keen-eyed 441
keep *do often* 136
persist 141
continue 143
food 298
store 636
provision 637
refuge 666
preserve 670
citadel 717
custody 751
prison 752
observe 772
retain 781
celebrate 883
– alive 359, 670
– aloof 196, 623
– accounts 811
– an account with 805
– apart 44
– at it 143
– away 187
– back *late* 133
conceal 528
dissuade 616
not use 678
restrain 751
retain 781
– the ball rolling 143
– one's bed 655
– body and soul together
  life 359
health 654
– within bounds 304
– close 781
– company 88
– one in countenance
conformity 82
induce 615
aid 707
encourage 861
– one's countenance
unexcitable 826
sad 837
– one's course 282
– an eye upon 459
– the field 722
– firm 150
– on foot
continuance 143
support 215
preparation 673

– from *conceal* 528
refrain 623
not do 681
restrain 751
– going
continue 143
move 264
– one's ground 141
– one's hand in 613
– one's head above water
  731, 817
– hold 150
– holy 987
– house 184
– in ignorance 528
– in *restrain* 751
prohibit 761
– on one's legs 654
– a good look out for 507
– in mind 505
– moving 682
– off *avoid* 623
hinder 706
defend 717
resist 719
prohibition 761
– on *do often* 136
continue 143
persevere 604a
– to oneself 528
– in order 693
– out
 – *of the way* 187
 – *of harm's way* 864
– pace with 27, 120
– the peace 714
– posted 527
– the pot boiling 143
– one's promise 772
– quiet 265
– a secret 528
– a shop 625
– in sight 459
– silence 585
– straight 944
– in suspense
uncertainty 475
irresolution 605
– in the thoughts 505
– time
punctual 132
music 416
– to 604a
– together 709
– under
authority 737
subjection 749

restraint 751
– up [*see below*]
– in view
attend to 457
remember 505
expect 507
– waiting 133
– watch 459
– one's word 939
keeper 370, **753**
keeping
congruity 23
in – 82
safe – *safety* 664
preservation 670
keepsake 505
keep up
continue 143
preserve 670
stimulate 824
– appearances 852
– the ball 682, 840
– a correspondence 592
– the memory of 505
– one's spirits 836
– with 274
keg 191
kelpie 979
kelson 211
kempt 652
ken 441, 490
beyond mortal – 360
kennel
assemblage 72
hovel 189
ditch 259
conduit 350
Kentish fire 931
képi 225
kerb-stone 233
kerchief 225
wave a – 550
kern *quern* 330
low fellow 876
varlet 949
kernel *heart* 5
cause 153
central 222
important 642
kerosene 356
ketch
ship 273
Ketch, Jack – 975
kettle *vessel* 191
caldron 386
– drum *music* 417
tea-party 892

- of fish
 disorder 59
 difficulty 704
key *cause* 153
 opener 260
 music 413
 colour 428
 interpretation 522
 indication 550
 instrument 631, 633
 emblem of authority 747
 deliver the –s of the city
  725
key-hole 260
key-note *model* 22
 rule 80
 music 413
key-stone
 support 215
 motive 615
 importance 642
 completion 729
khaki 225, 433
khan *inn* 189
 governor 745
khedive 745
kibitka 272
kibitzer 682
kick *impulse* 276
 recoil 277
 assault 716
 thrill 821
 spurn 930
 punish 972
– against
 oppose 708
 resist 719
– against the pricks
 useless 645
 rash 863
 unequal 28
 superior 33
– up a dust
 active 682
 discord 713
 insolent 885
– a row 900
– one's heels
 kept waiting 133
 nothing to do 681
– off 62
– up a row
 violent 173
 discord 713
– over the traces 742
kicking, alive and - 359
kickshaw *food* 298

 trifle 643
kid *child* 129
 progeny 167
 leather 223
 not to be handled with –
  gloves
 dirty 653
 difficult 704
kidnap
 deceive 545
 take 789
 steal 791
kidney *class* 75
kilderkin 191
Kilkenny cats 713
kill 361
– or cure 662
– the fatted calf 883
– the goose with golden
  eggs 699
– with kindness 902
– the slain 641
– time 106
 inactivity 683
 amusement 840
– two birds with one stone
  682
killing 361
 delightful 829
kill-joy 706
kiln 386
kilowatt 466
kilt 225
kimbo 244
kimono 225
kin 75
kind *class* 75
 benevolent 906
– regards 894
kinder-garten 542
kindle *cause* 153
 produce 161
 quicken 171
 inflame 173
 set fire to 384
 excite 824
 incense 900
kindling wood 388
kindred 9, 11
kine 366
kinematics 264
kinetic energy 157
king 745
 every inch a–
 authority 737
 rank 875
 –maker 694

King –'s Bench 752, 966
 –'s birthday 268
 –'s counsel 968
– Death 360
 –'s English 560
 –'s evidence 529
 –'s highway 627
 –'s ransom 648
– of Kings 976
kingcraft 693
kingdom
 region 181
 property 780
– of heaven 981
kingly 737
king-post 215
kink 248, 378, 608
kiosk 189, 1000
kip 961
kirk 1000
kirtle 225
kismet 601
kiss *touch* 199
 courtesy 894
 endearment 902
– the book 535
– the hem of one's
  garment 928
– in the ring 840
– the rod 725
kit *class* 75
 equipment 191
 fiddle 417
– bag 191
kitcat 556
kitchen 191, 691
– maid 746
– range 386
kitchener 386
kitchenette 691
kite *fly* 273
 bill 800
 fly a – *credit* 805
 insolvency 808
– balloon 273, 726
kith 11
kithless 87
kitten *animal* 366
 young 129
 bring forth 161
 playful as a – 836, 840
kleptomania
 insanity 502
 stealing 791
 desire 865
kleptomaniac 504
knack 698

get into the – 613
knacker 361
knag 706
knaggy 901*a*
knap 206
knapsack 191
knave 548, **941**
– of hearts 897
knavery
deception 545
cunning 702
improbity 940
vice 945
knead *mix* 41
mould 240
soften 324
stroke 379
knee *angle* 244
bend the –
stoop 30
submission 725
down on one's –s
humble 879
on one's –s
beg 765
respect 928
atone 952
on the –s of the gods 121,
152
knee-deep 208, 209
kneel *stoop* 308
submit 725
beg 765
servility 886
courtesy 894
ask mercy 914
respect 928
worship 990
knell 363
strike the death – 361
knickerbockers 225
knicknack 643, 847
knife 253
play a good – and fork *eat*
298
appetite 865
war to the – 708
knight 875
– errant
madman 504
defender 717
rash 863
philanthropist 910
–'s move 279
– service 777
– of the road 792
– Templar 71

knit 43
well – 159
– the brow
discontent 832
anger 900
disapprobation 932
knitting 847
knob *pendency* 214
ball 249
protuberance 250
knock *blow* 276
sound 406
hard –s 720
– at the door
death 360
request 765
– down
destroy 162
lay flat 213
lower 308
injure 659
dishearten 837
– on the head
kill 361
– one's head against 699
– off *complete* 729
– out 162
– over 162
– under 725
– up 688
knock-down argument 479
knocked
– to atoms 162
– on the head
failure 732
knocker 936
knock-kneed 243, 244
knoll 206
knot *ligature* 45
entanglement 59
group 72
intersection 219
round 249
dense 321
difficulty 704
hindrance 706
junto 712
ornament 847
marriage 903
true lover's – *love* 897
endearment 902
tie the nuptial – 903
knotted *rough* 256
knout 975
know *believe* 484
knowledge 490
friendly 888

associate 892
I'd have you to – 457, 535
not that one –s 491
– what one is about 698
– all 474
I – better 536
– no bounds
great 31
infinite 105
redundance 641
– for certain 484
– by heart 505
– one's own mind 604
– one's stuff 465
– one's way about 465
– nothing of 491
– what's what 698
– which is which 465
knowing 702
knowingly 620
knowledge **490** [*and see*
know]
acquire – 539
come to one's – 527
practical – 698
– of the world 698
known:
become – 529
make – *inform* 527
publish 531
well – 490
habitual 613
– as 564
– by 550
knuckle 244
– down 725
knuckle-duster 727
knurl 256
knurr and spell 840
kobold 980
Koh-i-noor 650
kopje 206
Koran 986
kowtow *bow* 308
submission 725
courtesy 894
respect 928
kraal 189, 232
kraken 83
kris 727
Krishna 979
kudos 931
Ku Klux Klan 712
kursaal 840
kyanize 670
kyles 343

L

laager 717
labarum 550
labefy 659
label 39, 550
labent 306
labial *lip* 231
  letter 561
labitur et labetur 112, 143
laboratory 691
labor hoc opus, hic - 704
laborious
  active 682
  exertion 686
  difficult 704
labour
  parturition 161
  work 680
  exertion 686
  hard -
  punishment 972
  mountain in - 638
  - for 620
  - of love
  willing 602
  amusement 840
  disinterested 942
  - party 712
  - under *state* 7
  disease 655
  difficulty 704
  feeling 821
  affliction 828
  - in vain
  fall short 304
  useless 645
  - in one's vocation 625
  - unrest 832
laboured - *style* 579
  prepared 673
  - study 457
labourer 690
labouring
  - man 690
  - oar 686
labyrinth
  disorder 59
  convolution 248
  secret 533
lac *number* 98
  resin 356a
  - of rupees 800
lace *stitch* 43
  netting 219
  ornament 847
  - one's jacket 972

lacerable 328
lacerate 44
  - the heart 830
laches 460, 773
Lachesis 601
lachrymæ, hinc illæ - 830
lachrymatory gas 727
**lachrymis, quis temperet
  a** - 914
lachrymose 837
lack *require* 630
  insufficient 640
  destitute 804
  desire 865
  - faith 989
  - harmony 708
  - preparation 674
  - wit 501
lackadaisical
  inactive 683
  melancholy 837
  indifferent 866
lackadaisy! 839, 870
lack-brain 499, 501
lacker [*see* lacquer]
lackey 746
lack-lustre 422, 429
laconic 572
lacquer
  covering 223
  resin 356a
  adorn 847
lacrosse 840
lacteal 352
lacuna 198, 252
lacustrine 343
lad 129
ladder 305, 627
  kick down the - 604
lade *load* 184
  transfer 185
  contents 190
  dip 270
  - out 297
laden 52
  heavy - 828
  - with 777
ladies' man 897
lading 190, 780
  bill of - *list* 86
ladle *receptacle* 191
  transfer 270
  vehicle 272
lady *woman* 374
  rank 875
  wife 903
  our - 977

  - day 138
  - help 746
  -'s maid 746
lady chapel 1000
ladylike
  womanly 374
  fashionable 852
lady-love 897
lag *linger* 275
  follow 281
  dawdle 683
  - behind 133
lager *beer* 298
laggard 603, 683
lagoon 343
laical 997
laid: - on one's back 158
  - by the heels 751
  - low 160
  - up 655
lair 189, 653
laird *master* 745
  proprietor 779
  nobility 875
Lais 962
laisse manger, cela se -
  394
laisser: - aller, - faire
  permanence 141
  neglect 460
  inaction 681
  laxity 738
  freedom 748
  inexcitable 826
laity 997
lake *water* **343**
  pink 434
  - of fire and brimstone
  982
Lama 745, 996
Lamaism 984
Lamarkism 357
lamb *infant* 129
  animal 366
  gentle 826
  innocent 946
  go out like a - 174
  lion lies down with - 721
lambent
  touching 379
  - flame *heat* 382
  light 420
Lambeth 1000
Lamb of God 976
lame *incomplete* 53
  impotent 158
  weak 160

imperfect 651
disease 655
injury 659
failing 732
– conclusion
illogical 477
failure 732
help a – dog over a stile
aid 707
vindicate 937
– duck 808
– excuse 617
lamellar 204
lamentable *bad* 649
painful 830
sad 837
lamentably *very* 31
lamentation 839
lamia 980, 994
lamina 51, 204
lamination 204
Lammas 998
lamp 423
rub the – 992
safety – 666
smell of the –
style 577
prepared 673
lamplighter
quick 682
lampoon 932, 934
lampooner 936
lanâ caprinâ, de – 643
lanary 636
lanate 25, 256
lance *pierce* 260
throw 284
spear 727
break a – with
attack 716
warfare 722
couch one's – 720
– corporal 745
lancer 726
–'s *dance* 340
lancet 253, 262
lancinate 378, 830
land *arrive* 292
ground **342**
estate 780
gone to a better – 360
hug the – 286
make the – 286
on – 342
see – 858
– covered with water 343

– flowing with milk and
honey 168
how the – lies
circumstances 8
experiment 463
foresight 510
in the – of the living 359
landamman 745
landau 272
landed
– estate 780
– gentry 779
landgrave 745
landholder 779
landing field 273
landing-place 215, 292
landlady 779
land-locked 229, 343
landloper 268
landlord 779
land-lubber 343, 701
landmark
limit 233
indication 550
land-mine 727
landreeve 694
landscape
prospect 448
– gardening
agriculture 71
beauty 845
– painter 559
– painting 556
land-shark 792
land-slip 306
landsman 342
Landsturm 726
land-surveying 466
Landwehr 726
lane 189, 260, 627
langrel 727
lang-syne 122
language 560
command of – 582
strong –
vigour 574
malediction 908
languid *weak* 160
inert 172
slow 275
– *style* 575
inactive 683
torpid 823
languish
decrease 36
ill 655
inactive 683

repine 828
– for 865
languishing
weak 160
affected 855
languishment
lament 839
languor [*see* languid]
lank 200
lanky 203, 206
lantern
window 260
lamp 423
magic – 448
– of Diogenes 461
– jaws 203
lanterne, à la – 972
lanuginous 256
lanyard 45
Laodicean 822
lap *abode* 189
support 215
interior 221
wrap 225
encompass 227, 229
drink 298
– of luxury
pleasure 377
inactivity 683
voluptuousness 954
lap-dog *animal* 366
servile 886
lapel 39
lapidary 559
lapidate *kill* 361
attack 716
punish 972
lapidescence 323
lapis lazuli
blue 438
jewel 847
lappet 39, 214
lapse *course* 109
past 122
conversion 144
fall 306
degeneracy 659
relapse 661
loss 776
vice 945
guilt 947
– of memory 506
– of time 109
lapsus calami 495
lapsus linguæ
mistake 495
solecism 568

stammering 583
Laputa, college of – 538
larboard 239
larceny 791
lard 356
lardaceous 355
larder 636
  contents of the – 298
lares et penates
  home 189
  idols 991
large
  quantity 31
  size 192
  at – *diffuse* 573
  free 748
  become – 194
  – number 102
  – type 642
large-hearted
  liberal 816
  benevolent 906
  disinterested 942
larger 194
largest 784
largest portion 192
larghetto 275, 415
largiloquent 573
largo 275, 415
lariat 45, 247
lark *ascent* 305
  pleasure 827
  spree 840
  with the – 125
larmes:
  fondre en – 839
  – aux yeux 839
larmoyante, comédie – 599
larrikin 887, 913
larrup 972
larum 404, 669
larva 129
larynx 351
lascar 269
lasciate ogni speranza 859
lascivious 961
lash *tie together* 43
  violence 173
  incite 615
  censure 932
  punish 972
  scourge 975
  under the –
  compelled 744
  subject 749
  – into fury 909
  – with the tongue 931

– the waves 645
lass *girl* 129
lassitude 680, 841
lasso 45, 247
last *model* 22
  – *in order* 67
  endure 106
  durable 110
  – *in time* 122
  continue 141
  at – 133
  breathe one's – 360
  game to the – 604a
  never hear the – of 104
  – but one &c. 67
  die in the – ditch 604a
  – for ever 112
  at the – extremity 665
  – finish 729
  – gasp 360
  go to one's – home 360
  on – legs *weak* 160
  dying 360
  spoiled 659
  adversity 735
  – resort 666
  – rites 998
  – shift 601
  – sleep 360
  – stage 67
  – straw 153
  – stroke 729
  – touch 729
  – word
  affirmation 535
  obstinacy 606
  – year &c. 122
latch 43, 45
latchet 45
latch-key 631
late *past* 122
  new 123
  tardy 133
  dead 360
  too – 135
lately 122, 123
latency 526
lateness 133
latent 172, 526
  – organism 153
later 117
laterality 236
lateritious 434
latest 118
latet anguis in herbâ 66
lath 205
  thin as a – 203

lathe
  region 181
  machine 633
lather 332, 353
Latin
  au bout de son – 704
  perdre son – 704
  thieves' – 563
latitancy 528
latitat 969
latitude *extent* 180
  region 181
  breadth 202
  measurement 466
  freedom 748
  – and longitude
  situation 183
latitudinarian 984, 989
latration 412
latria 990
latrines 653
latrociny 791
latter *sequent* 63
  past 122
Latter-day Saint 984
latterly 123
lattice *crossing* 219
  opening 260
laud 931, 990
laudable 944
laudanum 174
laudari a laudato viro 931
laudator 935
  – *temporis acti*
  past 122
  habit 613
  discontent 832
  detractor 936
laudatory 931
laugh 838
  make one – 853
  raise a – 840
  – at *ridicule* 856
  sneer 929
  (*undervalue* 483)
  – to scorn *defy* **715**
  despise 930
  – in one's sleeve
  latent 526
  ridicule 856
  disrespect 929
  contempt 930
  – on the wrong side of
    one's mouth
  disappointed 509
  dejected 837
  in disrepute 874

laughable 853
laughing:
no – matter 642
– gas 376
laughing-stock 857
laughter-loving 836
launch *begin* 66
boat 273
propel 284
– forth 676
– into 676
– into eternity 360, 361
– out 573
– out against 716
laundress 652, 746
laundry *room* 191
heat 386
clean 652
– maid 746
– man 652
laureate 875
poet – 597
laurel *trophy* 733
glory 873
decoration 877
repose on one's –s 265
lava *excretion* 299
semiliquid 352
lavatory 652
lave *water* 337
clean 652
lavender *colour* 437
laver la tête 932
lavish *profuse* 641
give 784
squander 818
– of praise 931
law *regularity* 80
statute 697
permission 760
legality 963
court of – 966
give the – 737
go to – 969
Jewish – 985
lay down the –
certainty 474
affirm 535
command 741
learned in the – 968
set the – at defiance 964
take the – into one's own
hands 722, 742
– of the Medes and
Persians 80, 148
take the – of 969
law-abiding 743

lawful
permitted 760
due 924
legal 963
lawgiver 694
lawless 59
irregular 83
mutinous 742
non-observant 773
vicious 945
arbitrary 964
lawn *plain* 344
grass 367
agriculture 371
– sleeves 999
– tennis 840
lawsuit 969
lawyer 968
lax *incoherent* 47
soft 324
error 495
– *style* 575
remiss 738
non-observance 773
dishonourable 940
licentious 945
irreligious 989
laxity 738
lay *moderate* 174
place 184
ley 344
music 415
poetry 597
bet 621
secular 997
– about one
active 682
exertion 686
attack 716
contend 720
punish 972
– one's account for 484
– apart
exclude 55
relinquish 782
– aside
neglect 460
reject 610
disuse 678
give up 782
– on the table 133
– the axe at the root of
tree 162
– bare 529
– before 527
– brother 996
– by *store* 636

sickness 655
disuse 678
– to one's charge 938
– claim to 924
– in the dust 162
– eggs 161
– at the door of 155
– down [*see below*]
– at one's feet 763
– figure *nonentity* 4
model 22
representation 554
– one's finger upon 480*a*
– the first stone 66
– the flattering unction to
one's soul 831, 834
– the foundations 153, 673
– ghosts 992
– hands on
use 677
take 789
rite 998
– under hatches 751
– one's head on the block
942
– heads together 695, 709
– in *eat* 298
store 636
provide 637
– on 972
– open *divest* 226
opening 260
show 525
disclose 529
– oneself open to 177
– out
horizontal 213
corpse 363
plan 626
expend 809
– oneself out for 673
– over 133
– reader 996
– under restraint 751
– in ruins 162
– siege to 716
– stress on 642
– to *attribute* 155
rest 265
– it on thick
cover 223
too much 641
flatter 933
– together 43
– train 626
– up *store* 636
sickness 655

disuse 678
- *waste* 162
lay down *locate* 184
  horizontal 213
  assert 535
  renounce 757
  relinquish 782
  pay 807
- one's arms
  pacification 723
  submission 725
- the law
  certain 474
  assert 535
  command 741
  insolence 885
- one's life 360
- a plan 626
layer 204
layette 225
layman 699, 997
laystall 653
lazaret 662
lazar-house 662
lazy 683, 927
lazzarone 683
lb. 319
lea *land* 342
  plain 344
leach 335
lead *superiority* 33
  in order 62
  pioneer 64
  influence 175
  tend 176
  soundings 208
- *in motion* 280
  heavy 319
  rôle 599
  induce 615
  direct 693
  authority 737
heave the - 466
red - 434
take the -
  influence 175
  importance 642
  authority 737
white - 420
- to the altar 903
- astray 495
- captive
  subject 749
  restraint 751
- a merry chase 623
- the choir 990
- a dance

run away 623
  circuit 629
  difficulty 704
  disrespect 929
- the dance 280
- one to expect 511
- a life 692
- on 693
- to no end 645
- by the nose 737
- off 62
- the way
  precedence 62
  begin 66
  precession 280
  importance 642
  direction 693
  repute 873
leaden *dim* 422
  colourless 429
  grey 432
  inactive 683
leader
  precursor 64
  dissertation 595
  director 694
  counsel 968
- *writer* 593
leading
  beginning 66
  important 642
- article 595
- lady 599
- note *music* 413
- part 175
- question 461
- seaman 745
- strings
  childhood 127
  child 129
  pupil 541
  subject 749
  restraint 751, 752
leads 223
leaf *part* 51
  layer 204
  plant 367
- *of a book* 593
turn over a new - 658
- green 435
leafless 226
leaflet 531
leafy 256
league *length* 200
  co-operation 709
  party 712
- of Nations 696

leak *crack* 198
  dribble 295
  waste 638
spring a -
  injury 659
- out
  disclosure 529
leaky *imperfect* 651
leal 743
lean *thin* 203
  oblique 217
- on 215
- to *shed* 191
  willing 602
- towards 923
- upon *belief* 484
  subjection 749
  hope 858
leaning
  tendency 176
  willingness 602
  desire 865
  friendship 888
  favouritism 923
leap
  sudden change 146
  ascent 305
  jump **309**
-s and bounds 274
make a - at 622
- in the dark
  experiment 463
  uncertain 475
  chance 621
  rash 863
- with joy 838
- year 138
leap-frog 840
learn 490, 539
- by experience 950
- by heart 505
learned 490
learner 541
learning 490, **539**
lease *property* 780
  lending 787
grant a - 771
take a new - of life 654
- and release 783
leasehold 780
leash *lie* 43
  three 92
hold in - 751
least
- in quantity 34
- in size 193
at the - 32

leather *skin* 223
  tough 327
  beat 972
  nothing like – 481
  – bottle 191
  – or prunello 643
leave *remainder* 40
  part company 44
  relinquish 624
  permission 760
  bequeath 784
  French – 623
  take – *depart* 293
  freedom 748
  – alone
  inaction 681
  freedom 748
  permit 760
  – the beaten track 83
  – to chance 621
  – an inference 526
  – a loophole 705
  – in the lurch
  pass 303
  decisive 545
  – no trace
  be no more 2
  disappear 449
  obliterate 552
  – it to one 76
  – to oneself 748
  – off *cease* 142
  desuetude 614
  relinquish 624
  disuse 678
  – out 55
  – out of one's calculation
    460
  – a place 293
  – ad referendum 605
  give me – to say 535
  – undecided 609*a*
  – undone 730
  – a void *regret* 833
  – word 527
leaven
  component 56
  cause 153
  lighten 320
  qualify 469
  unclean 653
  deterioration 659
  bane 663
leavings
  remainder 40
  useless 645
lecher 962

lechery 961
lectern 1000
lection *special* 79
  interpretation 522
lectionary 998
lecture *teach* 537
  speak 582
  dissertation 595
  censure 932
  sermon 998
  – room 542
lecturer
  teacher 540
  preacher 996
lectureship 542
led – captain
  follower 746
  servile 886
  favourite 899
  – by the nose 749
ledge *height* 206
  horizontal 213
  shelf 215
  projection 250
ledger *list* 86
  record 551
  accounts 811
lee 236
leech 662, 695
leef 829
leek eat the –
  recant 607
  submit 725
Lee-Metford
  rifle 727
leer *stare* 441
  dumb-show 550
leery 702, 864
lees 653
lee-shore 665, 667
leet, court – 966
lee-wall 666
leeward 236
lee-way *tardy* 133
  space 180
  navigation 267
  deviation 279
  progression 282
  shortcoming 304
left *residuary* 40
  sinistral 239
  over the – 545
  – alone 748
  – in the lurch 732
  – to shift for oneself 893
  pay over the – shoulder
    808

left-handed
  clumsy 699
  – compliment 932
  – marriage 903
leg *support* 215
  walker 266
  thief 792
  best – foremost 686
  fast as –s will carry 274
  have a – to stand on 470
  keep on one's –s 654
  last –s *spoiled* 659
  fatigue 688
  light on one's –s 734
  make a – 894
  not a – to stand on
  illogical 477
  confuted 479
  failure 732
  off one's –s
  propulsion 284
  on one's –s
  upright 212
  elevation 307
  speaking 582
  in health 654
  active 682
  free 748
  set on one's –s 660
  – bail 623
legacy 270, 780, 784
legal *permitted* 760
  legitimate 924
  relating to law 963
  – adviser 968
  – estate 780
legality 963
legate 534
legatee 779, 785
legation 755
legato 415
legend 551, 594
legendary
  imaginary 515
legerdemain 146, 545
légèreté 605
leggings 225
leghorn hat 225
legible 518
  – hand 590
legion
  multitude 102
  army 726
legionary 726
legislation 693, 963
legislative assembly 696
legislator 694

legislature 693, 696
legist 968
legitimate *true* 494
  permitted 760
  right 922
  due 924
  legal 963
legume 367
lei 847
leisure 685
  at one's – *late* 133
leisurely 275
leman 897
lemma 476
lemon *colour* 436
Lemprière 979
lemures 980
lend 787
  – aid 707
  – countenance 707
  – a hand 680
  – oneself to
    assent 488
    co-operate 709
  – on security 789
  – wings to 707
lender *creditor* 805
lending 787
length 200
  go all –s
    resolution 604
    activity 682
    exertion 686
  at – *in time* 133
  full – *portrait* 556
  go great –s 549
  – and breadth of 50
  – and breadth of the land
    space 180
    publication 531
  – of time 110
lengthen 35, 200
  – out
    diuturnity 110
    late 133
lengthwise 200
lengthy *long* 200
  diffuse 573
lenient
  moderate 174
  mild 740
  compassioante 914
lenify 174
lenitive
  moderating 174
  remedy 662
  relieving 834

lenity 740
lens 445
Lent 956, 998
lenten 956
lenticular 245, 250
lentor *slowness* 275
  spissitude 352
  inactivity 683
lentous 352
leonem, ex ungue – 550
leonine verses 597
leopard
  variegated 440
  –'s spots
    unchanging 150
leprechaune 980
leprosy 655
lerret 273
lèse-majesté 742
less *inferior* 34
  subduction 38
  – than no time 113
lessee
  possessor 779
  receiver 785
lessen
  – in quantity or degree 36
  – in size 195
  – an evil 658
lesson *teaching* 537
  warning 668
  give a – to
    punish 972
  read a – to
    censure 932
  say one's –
    memory 505
lessor 805
lest 623
let *hindrance* 706
  permit 760
  lease 771
  lend 787
  sell 796
  apartments to –
    fool 499
  to – 763
  – alone *besides* 37
    permanence 141
    quiescence 265
    avoid 623
    disuse 678
    inaction 681
    not complete 730
    free 748
  – be
    permanence 141

  continuance 143
  inaction 681
  – blood 297
  – 'I dare not' wait upon 'I
    would' 605
  – down
    depress 308
    humble 879
  – down easily
    forgive 918
  –fall *drop* 308
    inform 527
    speak 582
  – fly *violence* 173
    propel 284
  – fly at 716
  – go *neglect* 460
    liberate 750
    relinquish 782
    restitution 790
  – in *interpose* 228
    admit 296
    trick 545
  – into *inform* 490
    disclose 529
  – one know 527
  – off *violent* 173
    propel 284
    permit 760
    forgive 918
    exempt 927a
    acquit 970
  – out *disperse* 73
    lengthen 200
    eject 297
    disclose 529
    liberate 750
  – out at 716
  – pass 460
  – slip
    miss an opportunity 135
    neglect 460
    not complete 730
    lose 776
    relinquish 782
  – the matter stand over
    133
  – things take their course
    143
  – well alone
    content 831
    caution 864
lethal 361
  – chamber 975
lethalis arundo,
  hæret lateri – 900
lethargy 683, 823

Lethe 982
  waters of – 506
lethiferous 361
letter *mark* 550
  character **561**
  epistle 592
  to the – 494
  – card 524
  – of credit 805
  – of the law 494
  – writer 592
letter-bag 534
letter-carrier 534
lettered 490
letterpress 591
letters
  knowledge 490
  language 560
  description 594
  in large – 642
  man of – 492
  – of marque 791
lettres de cachet 751
leucophlegmatic 823
leucorrhea 299
Levant *east* 236
levant *abscond* 623
levanter *wind* 349
  defaulter 808
levée *assemblage* 72
  sociality 892
  – en masse 719
level *uniform* 16
  equal 27
  destroy 162
  horizontal 213
  instrument 213, 217
  flat 251
  smooth 255
  lower 308
  – at *direct* 278
  intend 620
  attack 716
  – best 686
  – headed 826
  – off 27
  – with the ground 207
lever *cause* 153
  instrument 633
  – de rideau 599
leverage 175
leviathan 192
levigate 255, 330
levitate 320
Levite 996
levity *lightness* **320**
  irresolution 605

trifle 643
jocularity 836
rashness 863
levy *muster* 72
  military 726
  distrain 789
  demand 812
lewd 961
Lewis gun 727
lex – mercatoria 963
  – scripta 697
  – scripta et nonscripta 963
  – talionis
  retaliation 718
  right 922
lexicography 562
lexicology 562
lexicon 86, 562
ley 344
liability **177**
  debt 806
  duty 926
liaison 961
liar 548
libation
  potation 298
  drunkenness 959
  worship 990
libel 934, 938
libelant 989
libeller 936
liberal *ample* 639
  – party 712
  generous 816
  disinterested 942
  over – 818
  – education
  knowledge 490
  teaching 537
liberalism
  freedom 748
liberality
  giving 784
  generosity **816**
liberate 672
liberation **750**
liberavi animam meam 703
libertinage 961
libertine **962**
libertinism 961
liberty *freedom* 748
  permission 760
  right 924
  exemption 927a
  gain one's – 750
  set at – *free* 750

exempt 927a
take a –
  arrogate 739
  make free 748
  insolence 885
  discourtesy 895
libidinous 961
libitum, ad –
  at *will* 600
  enough 639
  freely 748
librarian 593, 694
library *room* 191, 593
  books 593
  storehouse 636
librate 314
libretto 593, 599
licence *laxity* 738
  permission 760
  right 924
  exemption 927a
  – to plunder 791
licentiate 492
licentious *lax* 738
  dissolute 954
  debauched 961
lichgate 363
lichen 367
licit 760, 924
lick *lap* 298
  conquer 731
  punish 972
  – the dust 933
  – into shape 240
lickerish
  savoury 394
  desirous 865
  fastidious 868
  licentious 961
lickpenny 819
lickspittle 886
lictor 965
lid 223
lie *situation* 183
  presence 186
  recline 213
  falsehood 544
  untruth 546
  give the – to 536
  white – 617
  – abed 683
  – in ambush 528
  – by 681
  – at one's door 926
  – down *flat* 213
  rest 687
  – fallow 674

– hid 528
– in *be* 1
  give birth 161
– low 528
– under a necessity 601
– in a nutshell 32
– on 215
– over *defer* 133
  destiny 152
– in one's power 157
– at the root of 153
– still 265
– to *quiescence* 265
  inaction 681
– under 177
– in wait for
  expect 507
  inaction 681
lief *pleasant* 829
  as – *willing* 602
  choice 609
liege 745
liegeman 746
lien 771, 805
lienteria 653
lieu 182
  in – of 147
lieutenant 745, 759
  lord – 965
life *essence* 5
  events 151
  vitality **359**
  biography 594
  activity 682
  conduct 692
  cheerful 836
  animal – 364
  battle of – 682
  come to – 660
  infuse into
  excite 824
  put – into 359
  recall to – 660
  see – 840
  support – 359
  take away – 361
  tenant for – 779
  – to come 152
  – after death 981
  – or death
  need 630
  important 642
  contention 720
  – and spirit 682
Life, the 976
life-blood 5, 359
life-boat 273, 666

life-giving 168
lifeguards 726
lifeless 172, 360
lifelike 17
lifelong 110
life-preserver 666, 727
life-size 192
lifetime 108
life-weary 841
lift *raise* 307
  aid 707
  steal 791
  – cattle 791
  – up the eyes 441
  – a finger 680
  – hand against 716
  – one's head 734
  – up the heart 990
  – the mask 529
  – the voice
  shout 411
  speak 582
lift-smoke 840
ligament 45
ligation 43
ligature 45
light *state* 7
  small 32
  window 260
  velocity 274
  arrive 292
  descend 306
  levity 320
  kindle 384
  watch 388
  luminosity **420**
  luminary 423
  - *in colour* 429
  white 430
  aspect 448
  knowledge 490
  interpretation 522
  unimportant 643
  easy 705
  gay 836
  loose 961
  blue – *signal* 550
  bring to –
  discover 480a
  manifest 525
  disclose 529
  children of – 987
  come to – 529
  false – 443
  foot –s 599
  half – 422
  make – of

  underrate 483
  easy 705
  inexcitable 826
  despise 930
  in one's own – 699
  obstruct the – 426
  side – 490
  see the – *life* 359
  publication 531
  transmit – 425
  throw – upon 522
  a – breaks in upon one
    529
  – under a bushel
  hide 528
  not hide 878
  modesty 881
  – comedy 599
  – cruiser 726
  – fantastic toe 309
  – upon one's feet 664
  – heart 836
  – of heel 274
  – horse 726
  – infantry 726
  – purse 804
  – and shade 420
  – of truth 543
  – up *illumine* 420
  excite 824
  cheer 836
  – upon *chance* 156
  arrive at 292
  discover 480a
  acquire 775
lighten
  make light 320
  illume 420
  facilitate 705
lighter *boat* 273
lighterage 812
lighterman 269
light-fingered 791, 792
light-footed 274, 682
light-headed 503
lighthouse 550
lightless 421
light-minded 605
lightning
  velocity 274
  flash 420
  spark 423
Light of the World 976
  like greased – 113
lightsome
  luminous 420
  irresolute 605

cheerful 836
ligneous 367
lignite 388
lignography 558
ligulate 205
like *similar* 17
 enjoy 377, 827
 relish 394
 wish 865
 love 897
 do what one –s 748
 look – 448
 we shall not look upon his
  – again 33
 – master like man 19
 – a pin in paper 58
likely 472
 think – 507
likeness 21, 554
 bad – 555
likewise 37
liking 865, 897
 have a – for 827
 to one's – 829
lilac *colour* 437
Liliputian 193
Lillith 994
lilt 416, 836
lily *white* 430
 beauty 845
 paint the – 641
lily-livered 862
limæ labor
 improve 658
 toil 686
limature 330, 331
limb *member* 51
 instrument 633
 scamp 949
 – of the law 968
limber 272, 324
limbo *prison* 751, 752
 pain 828
 purgatory 982
lime *entrap* 545
 – light 423, 531, 599
Limehouse 908
limine, in – 66
limit *complete* 52
 end 67
 circumscribe 229
 boundary 233
 qualify 469
 restrain 751
 prohibit 761
limitarian 984
limitation [*see* limit]

estate 780, 783
limited
 – *in quantity* 32
 – *in size* 393
 to a – extent
  imperfect 651
limitless 105
limitrophe 197
limn 556
limner 559
limousine 272
limp *weak* 160
 slow 275
 supple 324
 fail 723
limpid 425
lin 343, 348
lincture 662
line *fastening* 45
 continuous 69
 ancestors 166
 descendants 167
 length 200
 no breadth 203
 string 205
 lining 224
 outline 230
 straight 246
 of steamers 273
 direction 278
 music 413
 appearance 448
 measure 466
 mark 550
 writing 590
 verse 597
 vocation 625
 army and navy 726
 boundary – 233
 draw the – 465
 drop a – to 526
 in a –
  continuous 69
  straight 246
 in a – with 278
 read between the –s 522
 sounding – 208
 straight – 246
 troops of the – 726
 – of action 692
 – of battle 69
 – of battle ship 726
 – engraving 558
 – of march 278
 – of road 627
lineage *kindred* 11
 series 69

ancestry 166
 posterity 167
lineament
 outline 230
 feature 240
 appearance 448
 mark 550
linear
 continuity 69
 pedigree 166
 length 200
linen 225
liner 273
lines
 fortification 717
 hard –
  adversity 735
  severity 739
  reins 752
linger *protract* 110
 delay 133
 loiter 275
lingerie 225
lingo 560, 563
linguacious 584
lingua franca 563
lingual 560, 582
linguist 492
linguistics 560
liniment 356, 662
lining 224
link *relation* 9
 connect 43
 connecting – 45
 part 51
 term 71
 crossing 219
 torch 423
 golf –s 840
 missing – 53, 729
linked together
 party 712
linoleum 223
linotype 591
linseed oil 356
linsey-wolsey 41
linstock 388
lint 223
lintel 215
lion
 courage 861
 prodigy 872
 repute 873
 come in like a – 183
 as dewdrops from the –'s
  mane 483
 in the –'s den 665

– lies down with the lamb 721
put one's head in the –'s mouth 665
– in the path 706
–'s share *more* 33
  chief part 50
  too much 641
  undue 925
lioness 374
lion-hearted 861
lionize 455, 873
lip *beginning* 66
  edge 231
  side 236
  prominence 250
between cup and – 111
finger on the –s
  silent 581
  speechless 585
hang on the –s of 418
open one's –s
  speak 582
seal the –s 585
smack the –
  taste 390
  savoury 394
–homage
  flattery 933
– service
  falsehood 544
  hypocrisy 988
– wisdom 499
lip salve 847
lipstick 847
lipothymy 688
lippitude 443
liquefaction 335, 384
liquescence 335
liqueur 298, 396
liquid
  fluid 333
  sound 405
  letter 561
liquidate 807, 812
liquidator 801
liquor *potable* 298
  fluid 333
in – 959
– up 959
liquorice 396
liquorish [*see* lickerish]
lisp 583
lissom 324
list *catalogue* **86**
  strip 205
  leaning 217

fringe 231
hear 418
record 551
will 600
choose 609
arena 728
desire 865
enter the –s
  attack 716
  contend 720
listed 440
listel 847
listen 418
– in 455
– to 457
be –ed to 175
– to reason 498
listless
  inattentive 458
  inactive 683
  indifferent 866
litany 990, 998
lite, pendente – 969
literæ scriptæ 590
literal
  imitated 19
  exact 494
  manifest 525
  letter 561
  word 562
  orthodox 983a
– meaning 516
– translation 522
literarum
homo multarum – 492
homo trium – 792
literary 560
– hack 593
– man 492
– power 569
literati 492
literatim [*see* literal]
literature 490, 560
lithe 324
lithic 323
lithograph 558
lithology 358
lithomancy 511
lithotint 558
litigant
  litigious 713
  combatant 726
  accusation 938
litigation
  quarrel 713
  contention 730
  lawsuit 969

litigious 713
litter *disorder* 59
  derange 61
  multitude 102
  brood 167
  support 215
  vehicle 272
  useless 645
littéraire, la morgue – 569
littérateur 492, 593
little
– *in degree* 32
– *in size* 193
  darling 897
  mean 940
cost – 815
do – 683
make – of 483
signify – 643
think – of 458
– did one think 508
– by little
  degree 26
  slowly 275
– Mary 191
– one 129
to – purpose
  useless 645
  failure 732
littleness 193
littoral 342
liturgy 978
live *exist* 1
  continue 141
  energetic 171
  dwell 186
  life 359
  repute 873
– apart 905
– to fight again 110
– from hand to mouth 674
– hard 954
– in hope 858
– and let live
  inaction 681
  freedom 748
  inexcitability 826
– in the memory 505
– upon nothing 819
– on 298
– separately 905
– by one's wits 545
livelihood 803
livelong 110
lively *keen* 375
– *style* 574
  active 682

rascal 949
loop 245, 247, 629
– the loop 245
loop-hole
opening 260
vista 441
plea 617
device 626
escape 671
fortification 717
loose *detach* 44
incoherent 47
pendent 214
desultory 279
illogical 477
vague 519
– *style* 575
lax 738
free 748
liberate 750
debauched 961
give a – to
– *imagination* 515
laxiety 738
permit 760
indulgence 954
let – 750
on the – 961
screw – 713
– character 961
at a – end 685
– fish 949, 962
– morals 945
– rein 738
– suggestion 514
– thread 495
leave a - 460
take up a - 664
loosen 47, 750
loot 791, 793
lop 201
– and top 371
lop-eared 53
lopped
incomplete 53
loppet 699
lop-sided 28
loquacity 584
loquendi
cacoëthes – 584
jus et norma – 567
usus – 582
lorcha 273
Lord, lord
ruler 745
nobleman 875
God 976

O – *worship* 990
– Chancellor 967
– of the creation 372
–'s day 687
–s Justices 966, 967
the – knows 491
– lieutenant 965
– of Lords 976
– of the manor 779
– it over 737, 885
–'s prayer 990
–'s supper 998
–'s table 1000
lordling 875
lordly 873, 878
Lord Mayor 745, 965
–'s show 883
lordship
authority 737
property 780
title 877
judge 967
lore 490, 539
Lorelei 980
lorette 962
lorgnette 445
loricated
clothed 223
lorication
armour 717
lorn 893
lorry 272
lose *forget* 506
unintelligible 519
fail 732
loss 776
no time to – 684
– one's balance 732
– breath 688
– caste 874, 940
– the clew 475, 519
– colour 429
– one's cunning 699
– the day 732
– flesh 195
– ground
slow 275
regression 283
shortcoming 304
– one's head
bewildered 475
– heart 837
– one's heart 897
– hope 859
– interest in 624
– labour 732
– one's life 360

– no time 682, 684
– oneself 475
– an opportunity 135
– one's reason 503
– sight of
blind 442
disappear 449
neglect 460
oblivion 506
not complete 730
– one's temper 900
– time 683
– one's way
wander 279
uncertainty 475
unskilful 699
difficulty 704
losel 818
losing game 732, 735
loss *decrement* 40a
death 360
evil 619
deterioration 659
privation **776**
at a –
uncertain 475
at a – for
desiring 865
– of fortune 804
– of health 655
– of life 360
– of right 925
– of strength 160
lost *non-existing* 2
absent 187
invisible 449
abstracted 458
uncertain 475
failure 732
loss 776
over-excited 824
pain 828
dejection 837
impenitent 951
– in admiration 931
– in astonishment 870
– in iniquity 945
– labour 645
– to shame
insolent 885
improbity 940
bad man 949
– to sight 449
– in thought 458
– to virtue 945
lot *state* 7
quantity 25

group 72
multitude 102
necessity 601
chance 621
sufficient 639
allotment 786
be one's – 151
cast –s 621
cast in one's – with 609,
  709
fall to one's – 156
in –s 51
where one's – is cast 189
loth 603, 867
Lothario 897, 962
lotion *liquid* 337
  clean 652
  remedy 662
loto 840
lottery 156, 840
  put into a – 621
lotus-eater 683
loud 404, 525
  vulgar 851
lough 343
lounge 191, 683
  – suit 225
loup
  hurler avec les –s 714
  –garou 980
louse 653
lout 501, 701, 876
louvre 351
lovable 897
love *desire* 865
  courtesy 894
  affection **897**
  favourite 899
  abode of – 897
  labour of –
    willing 602
    inexpensive 815
    amusement 840
    disinterest 942
  God's – 906
  make – 902
  no – lost 713
  – affair 897
  – of country 910
  – lock 256
  not for – or money 640,
    814
love-knot *token* 550
love-lorn 898
lovely 845, 897
love-making 902
love-pot 959

love-potion 865
lover [*see* love]
love-sick 897, 902
love-story 897, 902
love-token 897, 902
loving-cup 892, 894
loving-kindness 906
low *small* 32
  not high 207
  - *sound* 405
  moo 412
  vulgar 851
  disreputable 874
  common 876
  base 940
  bring – 308
  – condition 876
  – comedy 599
  at a – ebb
  small 32
  inferior 34
  depressed 308
  waste 638
  deteriorated 659
  – fellow 876
  – life 851
  – note 408
  – origin 876
  – price 815
  – spirits 837
  – tide 207
  – tone *black* 431
  mutter 581
  – water *low* 207
  dry 340
  insufficient 640
  poor 804
low-born 876
low-brow 491
lower *inferior* 34
  decrease 36
  overhang 214
  depress 308
  dark 421
  dim 422
  predict 511
  sad 837
  irate 900
  sulky 901a
  – one's flag 725
  – one's note 879
  – orders 876
lowering 668, 859
low-lands 207
lowly 879
low-minded 876, 940
lown 501, 949

lowness [*see* low] **207**
  humility 879
loy 272
loyal *obedient* 743
  observant 772
  honourable 939
lozenge 244, 662
L. s. d. 800
lubbard [*see* lubber]
lubber 683, 701
lubberly 192, 699
lubricant 332
lubrication 255, **332**
lubricity
  slippery 255
  unctuous 355
  impure 961
lucent 420
lucid
  luminous 420
  transparent 425
  intelligible 518
  - *style* 570
  – interval 502
lucidus ordo 58
lucifer 388
Lucifer 423, 978
lucimeter 445
luck *chance* 156, 621
  prosperity 734
  good – 858
luckless 735
lucky 134, 731
lucrative 775
lucre 775, 803
Lucretia 960
luctation 720
lucubration 451
luculent 420
lucus a non lucendo 18,
  565
lud! O – 839
ludibrious 840
ludicrous 853
luff 267
lug *pull* 285
  ear 418
luge 272
luggage 270, 780
  – van 272
lugger 273
lugubrious 837
lukewarm
  temperate 382
  irresolute 605
  torpid 823
  indifferent 866

lull *cessation* 142
  mitigate 174
  silence 403
  – to sleep 265
lullaby
  moderate 174
  song 415
  verses 597
  inactivity 683
  relief 834
lumbago 378
lumbar 235
  disorder 59
  slow 275
  store 636
  useless 645
  hindrance 706
lumbering 647, 846
lumber-room 191
lumbriciform 249
luminary *star* 318
  light **423**
  sage 500
luminescence 420
luminous *light* 420
  intelligible 518
  – paint 423
lump *whole* 50
  chief part 51
  amass 72
  mass 192
  projection 250
  weight 319
  density 321
  in the – 50
  – of affectation 855
  – sum 800
  – together *join* 43
  combine 48
  assemble 72
lumpish [*see* lump]
  inactive 683
  ugly 846
Luna 318
lunacy 503
lunar 318
  – caustic 384
lunatic 503, 504
luncheon 298
lune avec les dents,
  prendre la – 158, 471
lunette 717
lunge 276, 716
lungs *wind* 349
  loudness 404
  shout 411
  voice 580

luniform &c. 245
lupanar 961
lurch *incline* 217
  sink 306
  oscillation 314
  failure 732
  leave in the –
  outstrip 303
  deceive 545
  relinquish 624
  left in the –
  defeated 732
lure *attraction* 288, 865
  deceive 545
  entice 615
lurid *dark* 421
  dim 422
  red 434
lurk *unseen* 447
  latent 526
  hidden 528
lurking-place 530
luscious 394, 829
lush *vegetation* 365
  drunkenness 959
lushy 959
lusk 683
lusory 840
lust 865, 961
  – after 921
lustily 404, 686
  cry out – 839
lustless 158
lustration 652, 952
lustre
  brightness 420
  chandelier 423
  glory 873
lustrum 108
lusty 159, 192
lusus naturæ 80
lute *cement* 45, 46
  guitar 417
luteous 436
Lutheran 984
luxation 44
luxuriant 168, 639
luxuriate in 377, 827
luxurious
  pleasant 377
  delightful 829
  intemperate 954
luxury
  physical - 377
  redundance 641
  enjoyment 827
  sensuality 954

lycanthropy 503
Lyceum 542
lyddite 727
Lydford law 964
Lydian measure 415
lying
  decumbent 213
  deceptive 544
  faithless 986
Ly-king 986
lymph *fluid* 333
  water 337
  transparent 425
lymphatic 337
lynch 972
  – law 964
lyncher 975
lynching 361
lynx-eyed 441, 498
lyre 417
lyric 415
  – poetry 597
lyrist 597

M

Mab 979
macadamize 255, 635
Macaire, Robert - 792
macaroni 854
macaronic
  absurdity 497
  neology 563
  verses 597
Macchiavel [*see*
  Machiavelism]
mace
  weapon 727
  sceptre 747
mace-bearer 965
maceration
  saturation 337
  atonement 952
  asceticism 955
  rite 998
Macheath 792
Machiavelism
  falsehood 544
  cunning 702
  dishonesty 940
machicolation 257, 717
machination
  trick 545
  plan 626
  cunning 702
  –s of the devil 619

machinator 626
machine 633
  like a – 698
  – gun 407, 727
  be a mere – 749
machinist
  theatrical – 599
  workman 690
macilent 203
mackerel
  mottled 440
  procuress 962
  – sky 349, 353
mackintosh 225
macrobiotic 110
macrocosm 318
macrography 441
macrology 577
mac Sycophant, Sir
  Pertinax – 886, 935
mactation 991
macte virtute 931
macula 848
maculate
  unclean 653
maculation 440, 848
mad *insane* 503
  excited 824
  drive one – 900
  go – 825
  – after 865
  – with rage 900
madam 374
mad-brained 503
madcap
  violent 173
  lunatic 504
  excitable 825
  buffoon 844
  rash 863
madder colour 434
made
  – to one's hand 673
  – man 734
  – to order 673
madefaction 339
madman 504
Madonna
  good 948
  angel 977
  pious 987
madrigal *music* 415
  verses 597
Mæcenas 492, 890
Maelstrom
  whirl 312
  water 348

  pitfall 667
maestro 415
maffick 883
magazine
  periodical 53
  record 551
  book 593
  store 636
  – rifle 727
Magdalen 950, 962
mage 994
magenta 434
maggot *little* 193
  fancy 515
  caprice 608
  desire 865
maggoty
  capricious 608
  unclean 653
  – headed
  silly 499
  excitable 825
Magi *sage* 500
  sect 984
magic 175, 992
  – lantern
  instrument 445
  show 448
magician 548, 994
magilp 356*a*
magisterial 878, 885
magistery 30
magistracy 737, 965
magistrate 745, 967
magistrature 737
magistri, jurare in verba
  – 481
  nullius – 487
magma 41
Magna Charta 769
magnanimity 942
magna pars fui, quorum –
  690
magnate 875
magnet *attract* 288
  desire 865
magnetism
  power 157
  influence 175
  attraction 288
  motive 615
  animal – 992
magnetize
  influence 175
  motive 615
  conjure 992
magnificent

  large 192
  fine 845
  grand 882
magnifico 875
magnifier 445
magnifique et pas cher 815
magnify
  increase 35
  enlarge 194
  over-rate 482
  exaggerate 549
  approve 931
  praise 990
magniloquent 577, 884
magni nominis umbra
  wreck 659
  repute 873
  rank 875
magnitude 25, 31, 192
magno conatu magnas
  nugas 638, 643
Magnus Apollo 500
magpie 584
magsman 792
maharajah 745
maharani 745
mah jong 840
mahl-stick [*see* maulstick]
mahogany
  colour 433
Mahomet 986
Mahometan 984
maid *girl* 129
  servant 631, 746
  spinster 374, 904
  – of all work 690
  – of honour 890
maiden *first* 66
  girl 129
  punishment 975
  – speech 66
maidenhood 904
maidenly 374
maigre 956
mail *post* 270, 534
  armour 717
  – coach 272, 534
  – steamer 273
  – van 272, 534
maim 158, 659
main *tunnel* 260
  ocean 341
  conduct 350
  principal 642
  coup de – 680
  in the –
  intrinsically 5

greatly 31
on the whole 50
principally 642
with might and – 686
plough the – 267
main-chance 156
good 618
important 642
profit 775
look to the –
foresight 510
skill 698
economy 817
caution 864
selfish 943
main-force
strength 159
violence 173
compulsion 744
mainland 342
main-part 31, 50
mainpernor 771
main-spring 153, 633
mainstay
support 215
refuge 666
hope 858
maintain
permanence 141
continue 143
sustain 170
support 215
assert 535
preserve 670
– one's course
persevere 604a
– the even tenor of one's
way 623
– one's ground 717
maintenance [*see* maintain]
assistance 707
wealth 803
maintien 692
maison de santé 662
maisonette 189
maître: coup de –
goodness 648
skill 698
l'œil e – 459
majesté, lèse– 742
majestic 873, 882
majesty *king* 745
rank 873
deity 976
major *greater* 33
officer 745
–domo

director 694
retainer 746
–general 745
– key 413
– part *great* 31
all 50
majority
superiority 33
multitude 102
age 131
join the – 360
majusculæ 561
make
constitute 54, 56
render 144
produce 161
form 240
arrive at 292
complete 729
compel 744
– acquainted with 527,
539
– after 622
– its appearance 446
– away with 162, 361
– believe 544, 545, 546
– the best of 725
– bold to differ 489
– a date with 897
– choice of 609
– fast 43
– a fool of 853
– for 278
– one's fortune 734
– fun of 842, 856
– a fuss 642, 682
– good
compensation 30
complete 52, 729
establish 150
evidence 467
demonstrate 478
provide 637
restore 660
– one's escape 671
– one's word 772
– a go of 731
– haste 684
– hay while the sun shines
134
– interest 765
– known 527
– the land 292
– light of 483, 705, 934
– oneself master of 539
– money 775
– a monkey of 853

– much of 549, 642
– no doubt 484
– no secret of 525
– no sign 526, 528
– nothing of
unintelligible 519
not wonder 871
– of 902
– off 623, 671
– off with 791
– out *see* 441
evidence 467
demonstrate 478
discover 480a
know 490
intelligible 518
interpret 522
due 924
– over 658, 783, 784
– peace 723, 724
– a piece of work 832
– things pleasant 702
– a present 784
– public 531
– a push 682
– ready 673
– a requisition 741, 765
– a speech 582
– a sucker of 853
– sure 150, 673
– terms 769
– time 110
– tracks 293
– towards 278
– up [*see below*]
– use of 677
– way 282
– one's way 302, 734
– way for 147, 623
– a wry face 867
maker *artificer* 690
Maker, the – 976
makeshift 147, 617
make up
complete 52
compose 54
– accounts 811
– for 30
– matters 952
– one's mind
judgment 480
belief 484
resolve 604
– a quarrel 723
– a sum 809
– to *approach* 286
address 586

make-weight
　inequality 28
　compensation 30
　completeness 52
making of, be the –
　utility 644
　goodness 648
　aid 707
malachite 435
malacology 368
malade imaginaire 837
maladie du pays 833
maladministration 699
maladroit 699
malady 655
mala fides 940
malaise 378, 828
malapert 885, 887
Malaprop, Mrs. – 565
malapropism 495
mal à propos 24, 135
malaria 657, 663
malconformation 243
malcontent 710, 832
mal du pays 833
male 159, 373
　– animal 373
malediction 908
malefaction 947
malefactor 949
malefic 649
maleficent 907
　– being 913
malevolence 907
malfeasance 647
malformed 241
malformation 243
malgré 179
　– soi 603
malice *hate* 898
　spite 907
　bear – *revenge* 919
　– aforethought 907
　– prepense 907
malign *bad* 649
　malevolent 907
　detract 934
malignant 649, 907
malignity
　violence 173
malinger 544, 655
malison 908
malkin 653
mall *walk* 189
　club 276
malleable 324
mallet 276

malnutrition 655
mal-odour 401
malpractice 947
malt liquor 298
maltreat
　injure 649
　aggrieve 830
　molest 907
malum
　– prohibitum 925
　– in se 923
malversation 818, 947
mamelon 250
Mameluke 726
mamma 166
mammal 366
mammiform 250
mammilla 250
Mammon 803, 978
　serve – 989
mammoth 192
man *adult* 131
　mankind 372
　male **373**
　prepare 673
　workman 690
　servant 746
　courage 861
　husband 903
　make a – of 648, 861
　Son of – 976
　straight – 599
　to a – 488
　–at-arms 726
　one's – of business 758
　–'s estate 131
　– in office 745
　– in the street 876
　–of-war 273, 726
　–of-war's man 269
　– at the wheel 694
　– and wife 903
manacle 751, 752
manage 693
　– to succeed 731
manageable 705
management
　conduct 692
　skill 698
manager
　stage – 599
　director 694
managery 693
**manche après la cognée,
　jeter le –** 859
mancible 637
mancipation 751

mandamus 741
mandarin 745
mandate 630, 741
mandible 298
mandolin 417
mandragora 174
mandrel 312
manducation 298
mane 256
man-eater 361
manége 266, 370
manes 362
manet: – altâmente
　repostum 505
　– cicatrix 919
manful *strong* 159
　resolute 604
　brave 861
manger 191
manger:
　cela se laisse – 394
　– son blé en herbe 818
mangle
　separate 44
　smooth 255
　injure 659
mangled 53
mangy 655
man-hater 911
manhood 131, 861
mania *insanity* 503
　desire 865
maniac 504
manibus pedibusque 686
manic 503
manic-depressive 503
manicheism 978
manichord 417
manicure 847
manie 865
maniéré 855
manifest
　list 86
　visible 446
　obvious 525
　disclose 529
manifestation 525
manifesto 531
manifold 81, 102
manikin *dwarf* 193
　image 554
maniple 103
manipulate
　handle 379
　use 677
　conduct 692
manipulator 621

mankind 372
manly
  adolescent 131
  strong 159
  male 373
  brave 861
  honest 939
manna *food* 396
  – in the wilderness
  aid 707
  pleasing 829
manner *kind* 75
  style 569
  way 627
  conduct 692
  in a – 32
  by all – of means 536
  by no – of means 602
  to the – born 5
mannered 579
mannerism
  special 79
  unconformity 83
  affectation 855
  vanity 880
mannerly 894
manners 852, 894
manœuvre 680, 702
manor 780
  lord of the – 779
  – house 189
manorial 780
Mansard roof 223
manse 1000
mansion 189
manslaughter 361
mansuetude 894
mantelpiece 215
mantilla 225
mantle *spread* 194
  dress 225
  foam 353
  shade 424
  redden 434
  robes 747
  flush 821, 824
  anger 900
mantlet *cloak* 225
  defence 717
Mantology 511
manual *guide* 527
  schoolbook 542
  book 593
  advice 695
  – labour 686
manubial 793
manufactory 691

manufacture 161, 680
manufacturer 690
manumission 750
manure
  agriculture 371
  dirt 653
  aid 707
manuscript 22, 590
many 102
  the – 876
  for – a day 110
  – irons in the fire 682
  – men many minds 489
  – times
  repeated 104
  frequent 136
many-coloured 440
many-sided 81, 236
many-tongued 532
map 234, 527, 554
  – out 626
mar 659, 706
marabou 83
marabout 1000
maranatha 908
marasmus
  shrinking 195
  atrophy 655
  deterioration 659
maraud 791
marauder 792
marble 440
  ball 249
  hard 323
  sculpture 557
  tablet 590
  insensible 823
marble-hearted 907
march *region* 181
  journey 266
  progression 282
  music 415
  dead – 363
  forced – 684
  on the – 264
  steal a –
  advance 280
  go beyond 303
  deceive 545
  active 682
  cunning 702
  – against 716
  – of events 151
  – of intellect
  knowledge 490
  improvement 658
  – off 293

  – on a point 278
  – past 882
  – of time 109
  – with 199
March, Ides of – 601
marches 233
marchioness 875
marcid 203
marconigram 523
marcor 203
mare *horse* 271
  female 374
  –'s nest 497, 546
  –'s tail *wind* 349
  cloud 353
marechal 745
margarine 356
margin *space* 180
  edge 231
  redundance 641
  latitude 748
margravate 780
margrave 745, 875
marimba 417
marine *sailor* 269
  fleet 273
  oceanic 341
  soldier 726
  tell it to the –s 489, 497
  – painter 559
  – painting 556
mariner 269
Mariolatry 991
marionnette
  representation 554
  drama 599
  amusement 840
marish 345
marital 903
maritime 267, 341
mark *degree* 26
  term 71
  take cognizance of 450
  attend to 457
  indication 550
  record 551
  writing 590
  object 620
  importance 642
  repute 873
  beyond the – 303
  leave one's – 873
  man of – 873, 875
  near the – 197
  overshoot the – 699
  put a – upon 457
  save the – 870

up to the –
  enough 639
  good 648
  skill 698
  due 924
wide of the – 196, 495
within the – 304
– down 813
– off 551
– out *choose* 609
  plan 626
  command 741
– of recognition 894
– with a red letter 883
– time
  chronometry 114
  halt 265
  wait 507
– with a white stone 931
marked [*see* mark]
  great 31
  affirmed 535
well– 446
in a – degree 31
play with – cards 545
– down 815
marker 550
market *buy* 795
  mart 799
bring to – 796
buy in the cheapest &c. –
    794
in the –
  offered 763
  barter 794
  sale 796
rig the – 794
– garden 371
– overt
  manifest 525
  mart 799
– place *street* 189
  mart 799
– price 812
– woman 797
marketable 794, 796
marksman 700
marksmanship 698
marl 342
marmalade 396
marmot 683
maroon
  colour 433, 434
  abandon 782, 893
marplot
  bungler 701
  obstacle 706

malicious 913
marque, letters of – 791
marquee 223
marquetry 440
marquis 875
marriage 903
  companionate – 903
  ill-assorted – 904
  – bells 836
  – portion 780
marriageable 131, 903
marrow *essence* 5
  interior 221
  central 222
chill to the – 385
marrow-bones, on one's –
  submit 725
  beg 765
  humble 879
  servile 886
  atonement 952
marrowless 158
marry *combine* 48
  assertion 535
  wed 903
– come up
  defiance 715
  anger 900
  censure 932
Mars 722, 979
– orange 439
marsh 345
marshal
  arrange 60
  messenger 534
  auxiliary 711
  officer 745
Marshalsea 752
marsupial 191, 366
mart 799
Marte, suo –
  exertion 686
  skill 698
martello tower 717
martial 722
  court– 966
  – law 737, 739
  compulsory 744
  illegal 964
  – music 415
martinet 739
martingale 752
Martinmas 998
martyr
  bodily pain 378
  mental pain 828
  ascetic 955

– to disease 655
martyrdom
  killing 361
  agony 378, 828
  unselfish 942
  punishment 972
marvel 870, 872
– whether 514
marvellous 31, 870
deal in the – 549
Masaniello 742
mascaro 847
mascot 993
masculine 159, 373
mash *mix* 41
  disorder 59
  soft 324
  semiliquid 253
  pulpify 354
masher 854
mask *dress* 225
  shade 424
  concealment 528
  ambush 530
  deceit 545
  shield 717
put on the – 544
mason 690
Masorah 985
masque 599
masqué, bal – 840
masquerade
  dress 225
  concealment 528
  disguise 530
  frolic 840
mass *quantity* 25
  much 31
  whole 50
  heap 72
  size 192
  gravity 319
  density 321
  worship 990
  rite 998
attend – 990
in the – 50
– book 998
– of society 876
massacre 361
massage 33, 379, 662
masse, en – 712
masses, the – 876
massive *large* 31
  huge 192
  heavy 319
  dense 321

mast 206
master
 boy 129
 influence 175
 man 373
 know 490
 understand 518
 learn 539
 teacher 540
 director 694
 proficient 698, 700
 succeed, conquer 731
 ruler **745**
 possession 777
 possessor 779
 title 877
 eye of the – 693
 hard – 739
 past – 700
 – of Arts 492
 – one's feelings 826
 – hand 700
 – key *open* 260
 instrument 631
 – mariner 269
 – mind *sage* 500
 proficient 700
 – passion 820
 – one's passions 944
 – of the position 731
 – of the revels 840
 – of the Rolls 553, 967
 – of self 604
 – of the situation 731, 737
 – spirit of the age 500, 873
 – of one's time 685
masterdom 737
masterpiece
 good 648
 perfect 650
 skill 698
master-stroke 626, 731
mastery 731, 737
 get the – over 175
masthead
 punish 972
mastic *viscid* 352
 resin 356a
masticate 298
mastiff 366
mat *support* 215
 woven 219
 misty 427
 cover 652
matador 361
match *coincide* 13

similar 17
copy 19
equal 27
fuel 388
contest 720
marriage 903
matchless
 supreme 33
 excellent 648
 virtuous 944
matchlock 727
mate *similar* 17
 equal 27
 duplicate 89
 mariner 269
 auxiliary 711
 master 745
 friend 890
 wife 903
 check– 732
maté 298
mater alma – 542
 –familias 166
material
 substance 316
 stuff 635
 important 642
 – for thought 454
 – point 32
materialism
 matter 316
 heterodoxy 984
 irreligion 989
materiality 316
materialize 446
materials 635
materia medica 662
matériel 633
maternal
 parental 166
 benevolent 906
 – love 897
maternity 166
mathematical
 precise 494
 – point 193
mathematics 25
mathesis 25
matin 125
matinée 892
matins 990
matrass 191
matriarch 11, 166
matriarchate 737
matriculate 86
matriculation 539
matrilinear 11, 166

matrimony
 mixture 41
 wedlock 903
matrix *mould* 22
 workshop 691
matron 374, 903
matronly 128, 131
matross 726
matter *substance* 3
 material world 316
 topic 454
 meaning 516
 type 591
 business 625
 importance 642
 pus 653
 no – 460
 what – 643
 what's the – 455, 461
 – of course
 conformity 82
 certain 474
 habitual 613
 – in dispute 461
 – of fact *event* 151
 certainty 474
 truth 494
 language 576
 artless 703
 dull 843
 – in hand 454, 625
 – of indifference 866
 – nothing 643
mattock 253
mattress 215
mature *old* 124
 adolescent 131
 conversion 144
 scheme 626
 perfect 650
 improve 658
 prepare 673
 complete 729
 – thought 451
maturely considered 611
maturine 996
maturity [*see* mature]
 bring to – 729
matutinal 125
matzoon 298
maudlin
 inactive 683
 drunk 959
maugre 30
maukin 562
maul *hammer* 276
 hurt 649

maulstick 215
maund *basket* 191
  mumble 583
maunder
  diffuse style 573
  mumble 583
  talk 584
  lament 839
maundy
  – money 784
  – Thursday 988
Mauser rifle 727
mausoleum 363
mauvais
  – goût 851
  – quart d'heure 828
  – sujet 949
  – ton 851
mauvaise:
  – honte
  affectation 855
  modesty 881
  – plaisanterie 851
mauve 437
maw 191
mawkish 391
Mawworm
  deceiver 548
  sham piety 988
maxim 80, **496**
maximal 33
maximalist 742
Maxim gun 727
maximum 33, 210
maxixe 840
may be 470
  as it – 156
May-day 138, 840
May-fly 111
mayhap 470
mayonnaise 298
mayor 745, 965
maypole 206
May-queen 847
mazard 298
maze
  disorder 59
  convolution 248
  enigma 533
  difficulty 704
  in a –
  uncertain 475
mazed 503
mazurka 840
me 317
meâ culpâ 950
mead *plain* 344

  sweet 396
meadow *plain* 344
  grass 367
  – land 371
meagre *small* 32
  incomplete 53
  thin 203
  – *style* 575
  scanty 640
  poor 643
  – diet 956
meal *repast* 298
  powder 330
mealy-mouthed
  falsehood 544
  servile 886
  flattering 933
mean *average* **29**
  small 32
  middle 68, 228
  signify 516
  intend 620
  contemptible 643
  stingy 819
  shabby 874
  ignoble 876
  sneaking 886
  base 940
  selfish 943
  golden – 174
  take the – 774
  – nothing 517
  – parentage 876
  – time 114
  – wretch 949
meander
  convolution 248
  deviate 279
  circuition 311
  river 348
  – around Robin Hood's
    barn 279
meandering
  diffuse 573
meanest capacity 499
  intelligible to the – 518
meaning 516
meaningless 517
means
  appliances **632**
  property 780
  wealth 803
  by all – 602
  by any – 632
  by no – 536
  – of access 627
meantime 106

meanwhile 106
measurable 466
  within – distance 470
measure *extent* 25
  degree 26
  moderation 174
  music 413
  compute 466
  verse 597
  proceeding 626
  action 680
  apportion 786
  angular – 244
  full – 629
  out of – 641
  without – 641
  – of inclination 217
measured
  moderate 174
  sufficient 639
  temperate 953
measureless 105
measurement 25, **466**
measures
  have no – with 713
  take – *plan* 626
  prepare 673
  conduct 692
  – of length 200
meat 298
  broken – 645
  one man's – is another
    man's poison 15
mechanic 690
mechanical 601, 633
  – powers 633
  – warfare 722
mechanician 690
mechanism 633
medal
  record 551
  sculpture 557
  palm 733
  decoration 877
  – of Honor 733
medallion 557
medallist 700
meddle 682
médecin tant pis 837
médecine expectante 133,
  662
Medes and Persians, law
  of the – 80, 141
mediæval 124
mediævalism 122
medial 29, 68
median 228

mediant 413
medias res, in - 68
  plunge - 300, 576
mediation *instrumen-*
  tality 631
  intercession **724**
  deprecation 766
  Christ 976
mediator 711
Mediator
  Saviour 976
medical 662
medicament 662
medicaster 548
medicate
  compound 41
  heal 660
medicine 662
  - man 994
medico 662
mediety 68
mediis rebus, in - 682
mediocritas, aurea - 628
mediocrity
  average 29
  smallness 32
  imperfect 651
  - of fortune **736**
medio tutissimus, in - 864
meditate *think* 451
  purpose 620
mediterranean 68, 228
medium *mean* 29
  middle 68
  atmosphere 227
  intermediary 228
  colour 428
  oracle 513
  impostor 548
  instrument 631
  seer 994
  transparent - 425
medley 41, 59
  music 415
  chance - 156
medullary 324
Medusa 860
meed
  apportion 786
  reward 973
  - of praise 931
meek 826, 879
meerschaum 392
meet *agreement* 23
  assemble 72
  touch 199
  converge 290

arrive 292
expedient 646
fulfil 772
proper 924
make both ends -
  wealth 803
  economy 817
unable to make both ends
  -
  poverty 804
  not pay 808
  - with attention 457
  - one's death 360
  - the ear 418
  - one at every turn
  present 186
  redundant 641
  - one's expenses 817
  - the eye 446
  - in front 861
  - half way
  willing 602
  concord 714
  pacification 723
  mediation 724
  compromise 774
  friendship 888
  benevolence 906
  - hand to hand 720
  - one's wishes
  consent 762
  pleasurable 829
  - with *event* 151
  find 480a
meeting [*see* meet]
  junction 43
  hostile - 720
  place of - 74
meeting-house
  hall 189
  chapel 1000
megacosm 318
Megæra 173, 900
megalomania 482, 504
megaphone 404, 418
megascope 445
megatherium 124
megrims *fits* 315
  melancholy 837
mehari 271
Mein Herr 877
meister-singer 597
me judice 484
melancholia
  insanity 503
  dejection 837
melancholy 830, 837

away with - 836
mélange 41
mêlée *disorder* 59
  contention 720
melinite 727
meliora, spero - 858
meliorate 658
meliorism 658
melius inquirendum, ad -
  658
melliferous
  sweet 396
mellifluous
  music 413
  - *language* 578
mellow
  old 128
  grow into 144
  soft 324
  sound 413
  colour 428
  improve 658
  prepare 673
  tipsy 959
melodeon 417
melodious 413
melodist 416
melodrama 599, 824
melody **413**
Melpomene 599
melt *convert* 144
  liquefy 335
  fuse 384
  pity 914
  - in the air 405
  - away
  cease to exist 2
  unsubstantial 4
  decrease 36
  disappear 111, 449
  waste 638
  - the heart 914
  - into one 48
  - into tears 839
melting-pot 691
member *part* 51
  component 56
  councillor 696
membrane 204
même, quand - 708
memento 505
  - mori 363, 837
meminisse juvabit 505
memoir 594, 595
memorabilia
  reminiscences 505
  important 642

memorable 642
memorandum
　memory 505
　record 551
　plan 626
　- book 505, 551
　compendium 596
memorial
　record 551
memorialist 553
memorialize 505
memorials 594
memoriam, in - 363, 505
memory **505**
　fame 873
　failing - 506
　short - 506
　in the - of man 122
　- runneth not to the
　　contrary 124
mem-sahib 374
menace 909
ménage 692
menagerie
　collection 72
　animals 370
　store 636
mend 658, 660
　- one's manners 894
mendacity 544
mendicancy 765, 804
mendicant
　beggar 767
　poor 804
　monk 996
menhir 363
menial 746, 876
meniscus 245, 445
mensâ et thoro, separatio
　a - 905
menses 299
mens sana 502
　- in corpore sano 827
mens sibi conscia recti 878
menstrual 138
menstruum 335
mensuration 466
mental 450
　- calm 826
　- excitement 824
　- pabulum 454
　- philosophy 450
　- reservation 528
　- suffering 828
menteur à triple étage 548
menticulture 658
mention 527

above -ed 104
not worth -ing 643
mentis gratissimus error
　481
mentor *sage* 500
　teacher 540
　adviser 695
menu 86, 298
Mephistopheles 980
Mephistophelian 945
mephitic 401, 657
mephitis 663
meracious 392
mercantile 794
mercatoria, lex - 963
mercature 794
mercenary
　soldier 726
　servant 746
　price 812
　parsimonious 819
　selfish 943
mercer 225
merchandise **798**
merchant **797**
merchantman 273
merciful 914
merciless 914*a*
mercurial
　changeable 149
　mobile 264
　quick 274
　excitable 825
Mercury 979
　traveller 268
　quick 274
　messenger 534
mercy *lenity* 740
　pity 914
　at the - of
　liable 177
　subject 749
　cry you - 766
　have at one's - 919
　have no - 914*a*
　- on us! 870
　for -'s sake 765
　- seat 966
mere *simple* 32
　lake 343
　trifling 643
　- nothing
　small 32
　trifle 643
　buy for a - nothing 815
　- pretext 617
　- words 477

- wreck 659
merelles 840
meretricious
　false 495
　vulgar 851
　licentious 961
merfolk 980
merge *combine* 48
　include 76
　insert 300
　plunge 337
　- in 56
　- into *become* 144
merged 228
meridian
　region 181
　room 125
　summit 210
　light 420
　- of life 131
merit
　goodness 648
　due 924
　virtue 944
　make a - of 884
　- notice 642
merito, e - 944
meritorious 931
Merlin 994
mermaid 341
　monster 83
　mythology 979, 980
merman 341
mero motu, ex - 600
merriment
　cheerful 836
　amusement 840
merry *cheerful* 836
　drunk 959
　make - *sport* 840
　make - with
　wit 842
　ridicule 856
　wish a - Christmas &c.
　896
　- and wise 842
merry-andrew 844
merry-go-round 312, 840
merry-making 827, 840,
　892
merry-thought 842
mersion 337
meruit ferat, palmam qui
　- 873
merveille, à - 731
mesa 344
mésalliance 24, 903

meseems 484
mesh 198, 219
meshes *trap* 545
  difficulty 704
  - *of sophistry* 477
meshwork 219
mesial
  middle 68
mesmerism 992
mesmerist 994
mesne *lord* 779
mess *mixture* 41
  disorder 59
  barracks 191
  meal 298
  difficulty 704
  portion 786
  make a –
  unskilful 699
  fail 732
message
  intelligence 532
  command 741
Messalina 962
messenger 271
  envoy **534**
  servant 746
  - *balloon* 463
Messiah 976
messianic 976
messmate 890
messuage 189
messy 59
metabolism 140
metacentre 222
metachronism 115
metage 466
metagenesis 140
metagrammatism 561
metal 635
  Brittania – 545
metalepsis 521
metallic *sound* 410
metallurgy 358
metamorphosis 140
metaphor
  comparison 464
  figure **521**
  (*analogy* 17)
metaphrase 522
metaphrast 524
metaphrastic 516
metaphysics 450
metastasis, metathesis
  change 140
  inversion 218
  displacement 270

mete *measure* 466
  distribute 786
  - out *give* 784
metempsychosis 140
meteor 318, 423
meteoric 173, 420
meteorology 338
meteoromancy 466
meter 466
metheglin 396
methinks 484
method *order* 58
  way **627**
  want of – 59
methodical 60
Methodist 984
methodist
  journalist 988
methodize 60
Methuselah 130
  old as – 12
  since the days of – 124
methylated spirit 388
meticulous 772
métier 625
métis 83
metonymy 521
metoposcopy
  front 234
  appearance 44
  interpret 522
metre
  length 200
  poetry 597
metrical
  measured 466
  verse 597
metrology 466
  moderation 174
  mid-course 628
metropolis 189
metropolitan
  archbishop 996
mettle *spirit* 820
  courage 861
  man of – 861
  on one's –
  resolved 604
  put on one's –
  excite 824
  encourage 861
mettlesome
  energetic 171
  sensitive 822
  excitable 825
  brave 861

mettre de l'eau dans son
  vin 160
meum et tuum 780
  disregard distinction
    between – 791
mew *moult* 226
  cry 412
  - up 751
mewed up 229
mewl 412
mews 189
mezzanine floor 191, 599
Mezzofanti 492
mezzo rilievo
  convex 250
  sculpture 557
mezzosoprano 416
mezzo termine
  middle 68
  mid-course 628
  compromise 774
mezzotint 420, 558
miasm 663
mica 425
micacious 204
mi-carême 840
Micawber 460
Michael 977
Michaelmas 998
Micomicon 515
microbe 163, 193
microcosm 193
micrography 193, 441
micrometer 193
micro-organism 193
microphone 418
microscope 193, 445
microscopic 32, 193
mid 68
Midas 803
mid-course 628
mid-day 125
midden 653
middle – *in degree* 29
  - *in order* **68**
  - *in space* 222, 228
  - classes 736
  - constriction 203
  - course 29, 628
  - man *director* 694
  agent 758
  - point 29
  - term 68
  compromise 774
middlemost 222
middling 29, 32, 68, 651
middy 225, 269

midge 193
midget 193
midland 342
midnight *night* 126
 dark 421
 – oil 539, 689
mid-progress 282
midriff 68, 228
midshipman 269, 745
midships 68
midst - *in order* 68
 central 222
 interjacent 228
 in the – of
 mixed with 41
 doing 680
midsummer 125
 – day 138
midway 68
midwife
 instrument 631
 remedy 662
 auxiliary 711
midwifery 161, 662
mien 448, 692
miff 900
might *power* 157
 violence 173
 energy 686
mightily 31
mighty *much* 31
 strong 159
 large 192
 haughty 878
migraine 378
migrate 266, 295
mikado 745
milch cow
 productive 168
 animal 366
 store 636
mild *moderate* 174
 warm 382
 insipid 391
 lenient 740
 calm 826
 courteous 894
mildew 653, 663
mildewed
 spoiled 659
mile 200
milestone 550
 whistle jigs to a – 645
milieu, juste – 174, 628
militant 722
 church – 983*a*
military

 warfare 722
 soldiers 726
 – authorities 745
 – band 417
 – power 737
 – time 132
 – train 726
militate against 708
militia 726
milk *moderate* 174
 semiliquid 352
 cows &c. 370
 white 430
 mild 740
 – a he-goat into a sieve
 471
 flow with – and honey
 plenty 639
 prosperity 734
 pleasant 829
 – of human kindness 906
 – the ram 645
 – and water
 weak 160
 insipid 391
 unimportant 643
 imperfect 651
milk-livered 862
milksop
 incapable 158
 fool 501
 coward 862
milky [*see* milk]
 semitransparent 427
 whiteness 430
 – way 318
mill 330
 notch 257
 machine 633
 workshop 691
 fight 720
 like a horse in a – 312
millennium
 number 98
 period 108
 futurity 121
 utopia 515
 hope 858
millesimal 99
millet seed 193
milliard 98
milliner 225
 man – 854
millinery *dress* 225
 ornament 847
 display 882
 man – 855

million 98
 multitude 102
 people 372
 populace 876
 for the –
 intelligible 518
 easy 705
 –s *money* 800
millionaire 803
mill-pond *level* 213
 pond 343
 store 636
mime 19, 599, 844
mimeograph 19
mimeotype 19
mimic 19
mimodrama 599
minacity 909
minaret 206
minatory 668
minauderie 855
mince *cut up* 44
 slow 275
 food 298
 stammer 583
 affected 855
 extenuate 937
 – the matter 868
 not – the matter
 affirm 525
 artless 703
 – the truth 544
mincemeat of
 make – 162
mincing 855
 – steps 275
mind *intellect* 450
 attend to 457
 take care 459
 believe 484
 remember 505
 will 600
 willing 602
 purpose 620
 warning 668
 desire 865
 dislike 867
 bear in – 451, 457
 bit of one's – 527
 food for the – 454
 give the – to 457
 have a – 602, 865
 in the –
 thought 451
 topic 454
 willing 602
 make up one's – 484, 604

never – *neglect* 460
 unimportant 643
not – 866
out of – 506
set one's – upon 604
speak one's – 582, 703
to one's – *taste* 850
 love 897
willing – 602
– one's book 539
– one's business 456, 457
– at ease 827
make one's – easy 826
–'s eye 515
– what one is about 864
minded 602, 620
mindful 457, 505
mindless
 inattentive 458
 imbecile 499
 forgetful 506
 insensible 823
mine
 sap 162
 hollow 252
 open 260
 snare 545
 store 636
 abundance 639
 damage 659
 attack 716
 defence 717
 explosive 727
 dig a – *plan* 626
 prepare 673
 spring a –
 unexpected 508
 attack 716
 – of information 700
 –layer 726
 –sweeper 726
 –thrower 727
 – of wealth 803
miner 252
 sapper and – 726
mineral 358
 – oil 356
mineralogy 358
Minerva 979
 – invita 603, 709
 – press 577, 594
mingle 41
miniature *small* 193
 portrait 556
 painter 559
Minié rifle 727
minikin 193

minim *small* 32
 music 413
minimize 36, 483, 934
minimum *small* 32
 inferior 34
minion 899
 type 591
minister *instrumentality*
 631
 remedy 662
 director 694
 aid 707
 deputy 759
 give 784
 clergy 996
 rites 998
 – to 746
ministerial
 clerical 995
ministering spirit 977
ministration
 direction 693
 aid 707
 rite 998
ministry
 direction 693
 aid 707
 church 995
 clergy 996
miniver 223
minnesinger 597
minnow 193
minor *inferior* 34
 infant 129
 – *key* 413
Minorites 996
minority *few* 103
 youth 127
Minos 694
minotaur 83
minster 1000
minstrel 416, 597
minstrelsy 415
mint *mould* 22
 workshop 691
 wealth 803
 – of money 800
minuend 38
minuet 415, 840
minus *less* 34
 subtracted 38
 absent 187
 deficient 304
 loss 776
 in debt 806
 non-payment 808
minusculæ 561

minute
 – *in degree* 32
 – *of time* 108
 instant 113
 – *in size* 193
 record 551
 compendium 596
 to the – 132
 – account 594
 – attention 457
minuteness
 care 459
minutiæ 32, 79, 643
minx 887, 962
mirabile
 – dictu &c. 870
mirabilis, annus – 872
miracle 83, 872
 – play 599
miraculous 870
mirage 443
mire 653
mirror *imitate* 19
 reflector 445
 perfection 650
 glory 873
 hold up the – 525
 hold the – up to nature
 554
 magic – 443
mirth 836
misacceptation 235
misadventure 735
misadvised 699
misanthropy 911
misapply
 misinterpret 523
 misuse 679
 mismanage 699
misapprehend 495, 523
misappropriate 679
misarrange 61
misbecome 925
misbegotten 243, 945
misbehave 851, 945
misbehaviour 895, 947
misbelief 485
misbeliever 487, 984
miscalculate
 misjudge 481
 err 495
 disappoint 509
miscall 565
miscarry 732
miscegenation 41
miscellany
 mixture 41

collection 72
generality 78
compendium 596
mischance 619, 735
mischief 619
do – 649
make – 649
mischief-maker 913, 941
miscible 41
miscite 544
miscompute 481, 495
misconceive 495, 523
misconduct 699, 947
– oneself 945
misconjecture 481
misconstrue 523
miscorrect 538
miscount 495
miscreance 485
miscreant 949
miscreated 945
misdate 115
misdeed 947
misdemean 945
misdemeanant 949
misdemeanour 947
misdevotion 988
misdirect 538, 699
misdo 945
misdoing 947
misdoubt 485, 523
misemploy 679
mise en scène
appearance 448
drama 599
display 882
miser 819
–'s hoard 800
miserabile dictu 839
miserable *small* 32
contemptible 643
unhappy 828
miserably *very* 31
miserere 215
sing – 950
misericordiam,
argumentum ad – 914
miseries of human life 828
miseris succurrere disco
914
miserly 819
misery 828
put out of one's – 914
misestimate
misjudge 481
misfeasance 699, 947
misfit 24

misfortune
adversity 735
unhappiness 830
misgiving 485, 860
misgovern 699
misguide 495, 538
misguided 699
mishap *evil* 619
failure 732
misfortune 735
painful 830
Mishna 985
misinform 538
misinformed 491
misinstruct 538
misintelligence 538
misinterpretation 523
misjoined 24
misjudgment
sophistry 477
misjudge **481**
misinterpretation 523
mislay *derange* 61
lose 776
mislead *error* 495
misteach 538
deceive 545
mislike 867
mismanage 699
mismatch 15, 24
misname 565
misnomer **565**
misogamist 904, 911
misogyny 904
mispersuasion 538
misplace
derange 61
misplaced
intrusive 24
unconformable 83
displaced 185
misprint 495
misprision
concealment 528
guilt 947
– of treason 742
misprize 483, 929
mispronounce 583
misproportioned 243, 846
misquote 544
misreckon 481, 495
misrelish 867
misreport 495, 544
misrepresent
misinterpret 523
misteach 538
lie 544

misrepresentation **555**
untruth 544, 546
misrule
misconduct 699
laxity 738
Lord of – 701
miss *girl* 19
neglect 460
error 495
unintelligible 519
fail 732
lose 776
want 865
courtesan 962
– one's aim 732
– fire 732
– stays 304
– one's way
uncertain 475
unskilful 699
missa cantata 998
missal 998
missay 563, 583
missend 699
misshapen 243, 846
missile 727
missing
non-existent 2
absent 187
disappear 449
– link 53, 83, 729
mission 625, 755
missionary 540, 996
missive 592
misspell 523
misspend 818
misstate 495, 544
misstatement 495, 546
mist 353, 424
in a – 528
seen through a – 519
–s of error 495
– before the eyes 443
mistake *error* 495
misconstrue 523
mismanage 699
failure 732
never was a greater – 536
misteaching **538**
mister 373
misterm 565
misthink 481
mistime 135
mistral 349
mistranslate 523
mistress *lady* 374
master 745

possessor 779
title 877
love 897
concubine 962
mistrust 485
misty [*see* mist]
semi-transparent 427
misunderstand
misinterpret 523
misunderstanding 495, 713
misuse 679
mite *bit* 32
small 193
insufficiency 649
money 800
little – 129
Mithridate 662
mitigate *abate* 174
improve 658
relieve 834
mitigation [*see* mitigate]
extenuation 937
mitraille 727
mitrailleur 727
mitre *junction* 43
angle 244
crown 747, 999
mitten 225
mittimus 741
mix 41
– oneself up with
meddle 682
co-operate 709
– with 720
mixen 653
mixture 41
mere – 59
mix-up 59
mizzen 235
mizzle 348
mnemonics 505
Mnemosyne 505
moa 366
moan 405
cry 411
lament 839
moat *enclosure* 232
ditch 259
canal 350
defence 717
mob *crowd* 72
multitude 102
vulgar 876
hustle 929
scold 932
king – 876
– cap 225

– law
authority 737
illegality 964
mobile
inconstant 149
movable 264
sensitive 822
mobility, the – 876
mobilize
assemblage 72
render movable 264
– troops 722
mobocracy 737
mobster 361
moccasin 225
mock *imitate* 17, 19
repeat 104
erroneous 495
deceptive 545
chuckle 838
ridicule 856
disrespect 929
– danger 861
– modesty 855
– sun 423
mockery [*see* mock]
unsubstantial 4
solemn – 882
– delusion and snare
sophistry 477
deception 545
mocking-bird 19
modal 6, 7, 8
mode *state* 7
music 413
habit 613
method 627
fashion 852
– of expression 569
mode, à la – 852
model *copy* 21
prototype 22
rule 80
form 240
representation 554
sculpture 557
perfection 650
good man 948
new – 658
– after 19
– condition 80
modeller 559
moderate
average 29
small 32
allay **174**
slow 275

sufficient 639
cheap 815
temperate 953
– circumstances
mediocrity 736
moderately
imperfect 651
moderation [*see* moderate]
174
mid-course 628
inexcitability 826
moderato *music* 415
moderator 174
lamp 423
director 694
mediator 724
judge 967
modern 123
music 415
art 556
modest *small* 32
modesty
humility **881**
purity 960
mock – 855
modicum *little* 32
allotment 786
modification
difference 15
variation 20a
change 140
qualification 469
modish 852
modulation
variation 20a
change 140
music 413
module 22
modulus 84
modus: – operandi
method 627
conduct 692
– in rebus 174
– vivendi 723
mogul 745
Mohammedan 984
Mohawk
swaggerer 887
evil-doer 913
moider 458, 475
moiety 51, 91
moil *active* 682, 686
exertion 686
moisture *wet* 337
humid **339**
mokes 219
molar 330

molasses 396
mole *mound* 206
  prominence 250
  colour 432
  refuge 666
  defence 717
  spot 848
molecular 32
molecule 193
molehill *little* 193
  low 207
  trifling 643
molest *trouble* 830
molestation
  damage 649
  malevolence 907
mollia tempora 134
  - *fandi* 588
mollify *allay* 174
  soften 324
mollusk 366
mollycoddle 158
Molly Maguire 548
Moloch
  slaughter 361
  demon 980
  heathen deity 986
molten 384
moment
  - *of time* 113
  importance 642
  for the – 111
  lose not a – 684
  not have a – 682
  on the spur of the – 612
momentous 152
momentum 276
Momus 838
monachism 995
monad 193
monarch 745
monarchy 737
monastery 1000
monastic 995
monasticism 984
monetary 800
  – *arithmetic* 11
money 800
  wealth 803
  bad – 800
  command of – 803
  for one's – 609
  made of – 803
  make – 775
  raise – 788
  save – 817
  throw away one's – 818

– to burn 641, 803
– burning one's pocket 818
– coming in 810
– down 807
– going out 809
– market 800
– matters 811
– paid 809
–'s worth
  useful 644
  price 812
  cheap 815
money-bag 800, 802
money-belt 800
money-broker 797
money-changer 797, 801
moneyed 803
moneyer 797
money-grubbing 775
moneyless 804
monger 797
mongrel
  mixture 41
  anomalous 83
  dog 366
  base 949
moniker 565
moniliform 249
monism 984
monition 527, 668
  information 527
  warning 668
monitor *hear* 418
  oracle 513
  pupil-teacher 540
  director 694
  adviser 695
  war-ship 726
  inward – 926
monitory
  prediction 511
  dissuasion 616
  warning 668
monk 996
monkey
  imitative 19
  support 215
  catapult 276
  ridiculous 857
  play the – 499
  – jacket 225
  – trick
  absurdity 497
  sport 840
  – up 900
monkhood 995
monkish Latin 563

monochord 417
monochrome 429, 556
monocracy 737
monoculous 443
monode 445
monodrame 599
monody 597, 839
monogamist 904
monogamy 903
monogram
  cipher 533
  sign 550
  diagram 554
  letter 561
monograph
  publication 531
  writing 590
  book 593
  description 594
monolith 551
monolithic 983*a*
monologue
  soliloquy 589
  drama 599
monomachy 720
monomania 503
  obstinacy 606
  fanaticism 825
monomaniac 504
monomark 550
monoplane 273
monopolist 943
monopoly
  restrain 751
  possession 777
monostich 572
monosyllable 561
monotheism 983
monotonous
  uniform 16
  equal 27
  repetition 104
  permanent 141
  - *style* 575
  weary 841
  dull 843
monotype 591
monsieur 370
monsoon 349
monster
  exception 83
  large 192
  ugly 846
  prodigy 872
  evil-doer 913
  ruffian 949
monstrance 998

monstrosity [*see* monster]
  distortion 243
monstrous
  excessive 31
  exceptional 83
  huge 192
  ugly 846
  vulgar 851
  ridiculous 853
  wonderful 870
montagne russe
  slope 217
  sport 840
mont-de-piété 787
monté *cards* 840
Montgolfier 273
month 108
monthly 138
  magazine 531
  - nurse 662
monticle 206
monument *tall* 206
  tomb 363
  record 551
monumentum ære
  perennius 733
moo 412
mood *nature* 5
  state 7
  change 140
  tendency 176
  willingness 602
  temper 820
moodish 895, 901
moods and tenses 15, 20*a*
moody *furious* 825
  sad 837
  sullen 901*a*
moon *changes* 149
  world 318
  luminary 423
  bay the - 645
  jump over the - 309
  man in the - 515
  - of green cheese
  credulity 486
moonbeam 420, 422
mooncalf 501
moon-eyed 443
moonshee 493, 540
moonshine
  unsubstantial 4
  dim 422
  absurdity 497
  unmeaning 517
  untrue 546
  excuse 617

moonstone 847
moonstruck 503, 870
moor *fasten* 43
  open space 180
  locate 184
  highland 206
  plain 344
Moore, Old - 513
moored *firm* 150
mooring mast 184
moorings 45, 184
moorish 345
moorland 180, 206
moot *inquire* 461
  argue 476
  - point *topic* 454
  question 461
  discuss 514
mooted 514
mop 243, 652
mope 837
mope-eyed 443
moppet 899
mopsy 962
mopus *dreamer* 515
  drone 683
  money 800
  sad 837
moral *judgment* 480
  maxim 496
  right 922
  duty 926
  virtuous 944
  point a - 537
  - certainty 474
  - courage 604
  - education 537
  - obligation 926
  - support 707
  - tuition 537
  - turpitude 940
morality play 599
moralize 476
moral philosophy
  mind 450
  duty 926
morals *duty* 926
  virtue 944
mora nec requies, nec -
  682
morass 345
moratorium 133
morbid 655
morbific 657
mordacity 907
mordant *keen* 171
  pungent 392

  colour 428
  language 574
more *superior* 33
  added 37
  - than enough 641
  - than flesh and blood can
    bear 830
  - last words 65
  - or less
  quantity 25
  small 32
  inexact 495
  - than a match for 33, 159
  - than meets the eye 526
  - more than one 100
more:
  - majorum 82
  - solito
  conformable 82
  habitual 613
  - suo 613
moreover 37
mores, O - 932
Morgana, Fata - 423
morganatic marriage 903
morgue 363
  - littéraire 569
mori, memento - 363
moribund 369, 655
  dying 360
  sick 655
morient 360
morion 717
morisco 840
mormo 860
Mormon 984
Mormonism 903, 984
morning 125
  - coat 225
  - dress 225
  - noon and night
  repetition 104
  diuturnal 110
  frequent 136
  - star 423, 977
morocco 223
moron 493, 501
moronic 499
morose 895, 901*a*
morosis 503
Morpheus 683
morphew 653
morphia 381, 663
morphology
  form 240
  zoology 368
morra 840

morris
nine men's – 840
morris-dance 840
morrow 121
**mors aux dents, prendre
le** – 719
morse 45
morsel *small* 32
portion 51
food 298
mort, guerre à – 722
mortal
transient 111
fatal 361
man 372
wearisome 841
– antipathy 867
– blow 619
– coil 362
– funk 860
– remains 362
– sin 947
mortality
evanescence 111
death 360
mankind 372
bills of – 360
mortar *cement* 45
pulverizer 330
cannon 727
mortem, post – 360, 363
mortgage
security 771
lend 787
sale 796
credit 805
mortgagee 779, 805
mortgagor 779, 806
mortician 363
mortiferous 361
mortification
disease 655
pain 828
vexation 830
discontent 832
humiliation 879
asceticism 955
mortise *unite* 43
intersect 219
interjacence 228
mortmain 748
in – 781
Morton's fork 475
mortuary 360, 363
mosaic *mixture* 41
multiform 81
variegation 440

painting 556
Moslem 984
mosque 1000
moss *tuft* 256
marsh 345
vegetation 367
moss-grown 659
moss-trooper 726, 792
most 31
at – 32
make the – of
over-estimate 482
exaggerate 549
improve 658
use 677
skill 698
the – 33
– often 136
for the – part 78, 613
make the – of one's time
682
mot 496
– de l'énigme 522
– du guet 550
– à mot 19
– d'ordre 741
– de passe 550
– pour rire 842
mote *small* 32
light 320
– in the eye
dim-sighted 443
misjudging 481
motet 990
moth *bane* 663
moth-eaten 124, 653, 659
mother *parent* 166
mould 653
– country 189
– of-pearl 440
– superior 996
– tongue 560
– wit 498
motherly *love* 897
kind 906
motif 415, 847
motile 264
motion
change of place **264**
topic 454
plan 626
proposal 763
request 765
make a – 763
put in – 284
put oneself in – 680
set in – 677

– downwards 306
– from
recession 287
repulsion 289
– into *ingress* 294
reception 296
– out of 295
– through 302
– towards
approach 286
attraction 288
– upwards 305
motionless 265
motive 615
absence of – **615a**
– power 264
motivity 264
motley 81, 440
wearer of the – 844
motor 153, 266
vehicle 271, 272
instrument 633
–boat 273
–car &c. 272
–driver 268
–man 694
motorist 268
motory 264
mottled 440
motto *maxim* 496
device 550
phrase 566
motu: ex mero – 737
suo – 600
mouchard 527
mould *condition* 7
matrix 22
convert 144
form 240
structure 329
earth 342
vegetation 367
model 554
carve 557
decay 653
turn to account 677
moulded 820
– on 19
moulder 653, 659
moulding 847
mouldy 653, 659
moulin:
se battre contre des –s 645
– à paroles 584
moult 226
mound *large* 192
hill 206

defence 717
mount *increase* 35
   hill 206
   horse 271
   ascend 305
   raise 307
   display 882
   - guard *care* 459
   safety 664
   - up to *money* 800
   price 812
mountain *large* 192
   hill 206
   weight 319
   - artillery 726
   - in labour
   waste 638
   make -s of molehills 482
   - brought forth mouse
   disappoint 509
mountaineer 268
mountainous 206
mountebank
   quack 548
   drama 599
   buffoon 844
mounted rifles 726
mourn 828, 839
mourner 363
mournful
   afflicting 830
   sad 837
   lamentable 839
mourning *dress* 225
   in - *black* 431
   lament 839
mouse *little* 193
   search 461
   mountain brought forth -
     509
   not a - stirring 265
mouse-coloured 432
mousehole 260
mouser 366
mousetrap 545
mousseux 353
moustache 256
mouth *entrance* 66
   receptacle 191
   brink 231
   opening 260
   eat 298
   estuary 343
   enunciate 580
   drawl 583
   deep -ed
   resonant 408

bark 412
down in the - 879
make -s 929
open one's - 582
stop one's - 581
word of - 582
- honour
   falsehood 544
   show 882
   flattery 933
pass from - to mouth 531
- wash 652
- watering 865
mouthful
   quantity 25
   small 32
   food 298
mouthpiece
   speaker 524
   information 527
   speech 582
mouthy *style* 577
moutonné 250
moutons, revenons à nos -
   660
movable 264, 270
movables 780
move *begin* 66
   motion 264
   propose 514
   induce 615
   undertake 676
   act 680
   offer 763
   excite 824
get a - on 684
good - 626
on the - 293
- forward 282
- from 287
- in a groove 82
- heaven and earth 686
- off 293
- on *progress* 282
   activity 682
- out of 295
- quickly 274
- slowly 275
- to 894
moveless 265
movement
   motion 264
   music 415
   action 680
   activity 682
moved with 821
mover 164

movies 448, 599, 840
movie star 899
moving
   keep - 682
   self - 266
   - pictures 448
mow *shorten* 201
   smooth 255
   agriculture 371
   store 636
   - down
   destroy 162
moxa 384
M.P. 696
Mr. 373, 877
Mrs. 374
MS. 22, 590
much 31
make - of
   importance 642
   friends 888
   love 897
   endearment 902
   approval 931
not say - for 932
think - of 928, 931
- ado *exertion* 686
   difficulty 704
- ado about nothing
   over-estimate 482
   exaggerate 549
   unimportant 643
   unskilful 699
- cry and little wool 884
- the same
   identity 13
   similarity 17
   equality 27
- speaking 584
mucid 352, 653
mucilage 352
muck 653
   run a - *kill* 361
   attack 716
   excitement 825
muckle 31
muckworm 819, 876
mucor 653
mucosity 352
mucronate 253
muculent 352
mud *marsh* 345
   semiliquid 352
   dirt 653
clear as - 519
stick in the - 704
- guard 666

muddle *disorder* 59
  derange 61
  inattention 458
  absurd 497
  difficulty 704
  failure 732
  – one's brains 475
muddled 959
muddle-headed 499
muddy *moist* 339
  dim 422
  opaque 426
  colour 429
  stupid 499
mudlark *dirty* 653
  commonalty 876
muezzin 550, 996
muff *incapable* 158
  dress 225
  bungle 699
  bungler 701
muffettee 225
muffle *wrap* 225
  silent 403
  deaden 408a
  conceal 528
  voiceless 581
  stammer 583
muffled *faint* 405
  latent 526
  – drums
  funeral 363
  non-resonance 408a
muffler 225, 384
mufti *undress* 225
  judge 967
  priest 996
mug *cup* 191
  face 234, 448
  pottery 384
  dupe 547
muggy *moist* 339
  dim 422
  opaque 426
mug-house 189
mugient 412
mugwump 607
mulatto
  mixture 41
  exception 83
mulct *steal* 791
  fine 974
mule *mongrel* 83
  beast of burden 271
  obstinate 606
muleteer 694
muliebrity 374

mull
  prominence 250
  sweeten 396
mullah 967, 996
muller 330
mullion 215
mullioned 219
multifarious
  irrelevant 10
  diverse 16a
  multiform 81
multiferous 102
multifid
  divided 51
multifold 81
multiformity 81
multigenerous 81
multilateral 236, 244
multilocular 191
multiloquence 582, 584
multinomial 102
multiparous 168
multipartite 44
multiple 84, 102
multiplex 81
multiplicand 84
multiplicate 81
multiplication
  increase 35
  arithmetic 85
  multitude 102
  reproduction 163
  productiveness 168
multiplicator 84
multiplicity 102
multiplier 84
multiply 35
multipotent 157
multisonous 404
multitude 72, **102**
  the – 876
multum in parvo 596
multure 330
mum 581, 585
  –'s the word 403
mumble *chew* 298
  mutter 583
Mumbo Jumbo 979, 993
mummer 599
mummery
  absurdity 497
  imposture 545
  masquerade 840
  parade 882
mummify 363
mummy *dry* 340
  corpse 362

  beat to a – 972
mump *mutter* 583
  beg 765
mumper 767, 804
mumpish *sad* 837
mumps 837, 901a
munch 298
Munchausen 549
mundane
  world 318
  selfish 943
  irreligious 989
mundation 652
mundivagant 266
munerary 973
munerate 973
municipal 965
municipality 737
munificent 816
muniment
  evidence 465
  record 551
  defence 717
  security 771
munition
  materials 635
  defence 717
mural 717
murder 361
  – the King's English
  solecism 568
  stammering 583
  the – is out 529
murderer 361
muricated 253
murky *dark* 421
  opaque 426
  black 431
  gloomy 837
murmur *purl* 348
  sound 405
  voice 580
  complain 839
murmurer 832
murrain 655
Murray *travel* 266
  Lindley – 542
murrey 434
murrion 717
mus, nascitur ridiculus –
  509, 643
muscadine 400
muscle 159
muscular 159
muse 451 [*and see* musing]
Muse *poetry* 597
  historic – 594

unlettered – 579
musette 417
Muses, the – 416
museum
 collection 72
 store 636
mush 354
mushroom
 new 123
 fungus 367
 upstart 734
 low-born 876
 spring up like –s 163
 – anchor 666
music 415
 face the – 861
 set to – 416
 – of the spheres
 order 58
 universe 318
musical 413, 415, 416
 – comedy 599
 – ear
 musician 416
 hearing 418
 – instruments **417**
 – note 413
 – voice 580
music-hall 599, 840
musician 416
musing 451
 – on other things 458
musk 400
musket 727
 shoulder a – 722
musketeer 726
musketry 727
muslin
 semi-transparent 427
musnud
 support 215
 council 696
 sceptre 747
muss 59
Mussulman 984
must *necessity* 601
 mucor 653
 compulsion 744
 it – follow 478
 I – say 535
mustachio 256
mustard 392, 393
 after meat – 135
 – gas 663, 727
mustard-seed 193
muster 72, 85
 pass – 639

not pass – 651
 – courage 861
muster-roll 86
musty 401, 653
mutable 149
mutation 140
mutatis mutandis
 correlation 12
 change 140
 interchange 148
mutato nomine de te &c.
 parable 521
 retaliation 718
mute *funeral* 363
 silent 403
 sordine 405, 408a, 417
 letter 561
 speechless 581
 taciturn 585
 dramatis persona 599
 deaf – 419
 render – 581
mutilate
 retrench 38
 deform 241
 injure 659
mutilated 53
mutilation 619
mutineer 742
mutiny 742
mutt 366
mutter
 faint sound 405
 mumble 583
 grumble 839
 threaten 909
mutton-chop
 whiskers 256
mutual 12, 148
mutualize 12
mutual understanding 23
muzzle
 powerless 158
 edge 231
 opening 260
 silence 403
 render speechless 581
 restrain 751
 gag 752
muzzle-loader 727
muzzy 458
 in liquor 959
my: all – eye 546
 – stars! 870
mycology 369
mynheer 877
myology 329

myomancy 511
myopia 443
myriad 98, 102
myrmidon 726
myrrh 400
myrtle 897
myself *I* 79
 immateriality 317
mysterious
 invisible 447
 uncertain 475
 obscure 519
 concealed 528
mystery [*see* mysterious]
 latency 526
 secret 533
 play 599
 craft 625
 – ship 726
mystic
 puzzle 475
 uncertain 475
 obscure 519
 latent 526
 concealed 528
 sorcery 992
mystify *falsify* 477
 hide 528
 misteach 538
 deceive 545
myth 515, 546
mythology 979, 984

N

nab *deceive* 545
 seize 789
Nabob 745, 803
nacelle 273
nacre 440
nadir 211
nag *horse* 271
 quarrel 713
nager entre deux eaux 607
Naiad 341, 979
nail *fasten* 43
 fastening 45
 measure of length 200
 peg 214
 sharp 253
 hard 323
 retain 781
 on the –
 present 118
 pay 807
 hit the right – on the head

discover 480*a*
skill 698
– polish 847
naïveté 703
naked *denuded* 226
  manifest 525
  simplicity 849
  – eye 441
  – fact 151
  – steel 727
  – sword 727
  – truth 494
namby-pamby 643, 855
name
  indication 550
  appellation 564
  appoint 755
  celebrity 873
  assume a – 565
  call –s
  disrespect 929
  disapprobation 932
  fair – 873
  good – 873
  in the – of
  aid 707
  authority 737
  due 924
  – to conjure with 873
nameless 565, 874
namely 79, 522
namesake 564
Nana Sahib 949
Nanny-goat 374
nap *down* 256
  texture 329
  sleep 683
  cards 840
nape *back* 235
napery 652
Napier's bones 85
napkin 652
  buried in a – 460
  lay up in a – 678
napless 226
Napoleon *food* 298
  cards 840
napping
  inattentive 458
  inexpectant 508
  dull 843
nappy *frothy* 353
  tipsy 959
narcissism 897, 943
Narcissus 845
narcosis 376
narcotic 657, 662

nard 356
narration 594
narrow
  contract 195
  thin 203
  intolerant 481
  restrict 761
  – down 42
  – end of the wedge 66
  – escape 671
  – house 363
  – means 804
  – search 461
narrow-minded 481, 943
narrowness 203
narrows 343
nasal accent 583
nascent 66
nascitur: – ridiculus mus
  509
  – a sociis 82
naso, omnia suspendens –
  868
nasty
  unsavoury 395
  foul 653
  offensive 830
  cheap and – 815
natâ, pro re – 770
natal *birth* 66
  indigenous 188
natation 267
natatorium 652
nathless 30
nation 372
national 188, 372
  – guard 726
nationality 372, 910
nations, law of 963
native
  inhabitant 188
  artless 703
  – accent 580
  – land 189
  – soil 189
  – tongue 560
nativity *birth* 66
  cast a –
  predict 511
  sorcery 992
natty 845
natura il fece e poi roppe
  la stampa 87
naturæ, vis medicatrix –
  662
natural *intrinsic* 5
  musical note 413

true 494
fool 501
– *style* 576, 578
spontaneous 621
not prepared 674
artless 703
simple 849
– course of things 613
– death *death* 360
completion 729
– impulse 601
– meaning 516
– order of things 82
– state 90
– turn 820
Natural – History 357
  – Philosophy 316
  – Theology 983
naturalist 357
naturalization
  conformity 82
  conversion 144
  location 184
naturalize
  habit 613
naturalized
  inhabitant 188
naturally 154
nature *essence* 5
  rule 80
  tendency 176
  world 318
  reality 494
  artlessness 703
  affections 820
  animated – 357
  organized – 357
  second – 613
  state of –
  naked 226
  raw 674
  in –'s garb 226
naught *nothing* 4
  zero 101
  bring to – 732
  set at –
  make light of 483
  opposition 708
  disobey 742
  not observe 773
  disrespect 929
  contempt 930
naughty 945
naumachia 720
nausea 841, 867
nauseate 395, 830
nauseous

unsavoury 395
unpleasant 830
disgusting 867
nautch dancer 840
nautical 267
naval 267
  – authorities 745
  – engagement 720
  – forces 726
nave *middle* 68
  centre 222
  church 1000
navel 68, 222
navigation 267
navigator 269
navvy 673, 690
navy 273, 726
  – blue 438
nay 536
  – rather 14
Nazarene 989
naze 250
N.C.O. 745
ne plus ultra
  supreme 33
  complete 52
  distance 196
  summit 210
  limit 233
  perfection 650
  completion 729
neaf 781
neap 195, 207
  – tide 36, 340
near *like* 17
  – *in space* 197
  – *in time* 121
  soon 132
  impending 152
  approach 286
  stingy 819
  bring – 17
  draw – 197
  come – 286
  – one's end 360
  – at hand 132
  – the mark 32
  – run 32
  – side 239
  – sight 443
  – the truth 480*a*
  – upon 3
  sail – the wind
  skilful 698
  rash 863
nearly 32
nearness 197

neat *simple* 42
  order 58
  in writing 572, 576, 578
  clean 652
  spruce 845
  –'s foot oil 356
  – as a pin 58
neat-handed 698
neatherd 370
neb 250
nebula *stars* 318
  mist 353
nebular *dim* 422
nebulous *misty* 353
  obscure 519
necessarian 601
necessaries 630
necessarily 154
necessitate 630
necessity *fate* **601**
  requirement 630
  compulsion 744
  indigence 804
  make a virtue of – 698
neck
  contraction 195
  narrow 203
  make love 902
  break one's – 360
  – and crop
  completely 52
  turn out - 297
  – of land 342
  – and neck 27
  – or nothing
  resolute 604
  rash 863
neckcloth 225
necklace 247, 847
necks 980
necrology 360, 594
necromancer 548, 994
necromancy 992
necropsy 363
necroscopic 363
necrosis 49
nectar 394, 396
need *necessity* 601
  requirement 637
  insufficiency 640
  indigence 804
  desire 865
  friend in – 711
  in one's utmost – 735
needful
  necessary 601
  requisite 630

money 800
  do the – *pay* 807
needle *sharp* 253
  perforator 262
  compass 693
  as the – to the pole
  veracity 543
  observance 772
  honour 939
  – in a bottle of hay 475
needle-gun 727
needle-shaped 253
needless 641
needle-witted 498
needlewoman 690
needlework 847
ne'er-do-well 949
nefarious 945
negation 536, 764
negative
  inexisting 2
  contrary 14
  prototype 22
  quantity 84
  confute 479
  deny 536
  photograph 558
  refuse 764
  prove a – 468
neglect 460
  disuse 678
  leave undone 730
  omit 773
  evade 927
  disrespect 929
  – of time 115
négligé 225, 674
negligence 460
negotiable 270
negotiate
  mediate 724
  bargain 769
  transfer 783
  traffic 794
negotiations
  breaking off – 713
negotiator 724, 758
negro 431, 746
negus
  drink 298
  king 745
neif 781
neigh *cry* 412
  boast 884
neighbour 197, 890
neighbourhood 183, 197,
  227

neighbourly
aid 707
friendly 888
social 892
courteous 894
neither 610
– here nor there
irrelevant 10
absent 187
– more nor less
equal 27
true 494
– one thing nor another 83
nem. con. 488
Nemesis
vengeance 919
justice 922
punishment 972
nemine contradicente 488
nemo me impune lacessit
715
nenia 839
neogamist 903
neologism 123
neology 563
neophyte 144, 541
neoteric 123
nepenthe 662, 836
nephelogy 353
nephew 11
nepotism
nephew 11
wrong 923
dishonest 940
selfish 943
Neptune 341
Nereid 341, 979
nerve 159, 861, 885
exposed – 378
nerveless 158
nervous *weak* 160
style 574
timid 860
modest 881
nescience 491
nest
multitude 102
cradle 153
lodging 189
– of boxes 204
nest-egg 636
nestle *lodge* 186
safety 664
endearment 902
nestling 129
Nestor *veteran* 130
sage 500

advice 695
net *remainder* 40
receptacle 191
intersection 219
inclosure 232
snare 545
difficulty 704
gain 775
– profit *gain* 775
receipt 810
nether 207
nethermost 211
netting 219
nettle *bane* 663
sting 830
incense 900
network
disorder 59
crossing 219
neuralgia 378
neurasthenia 655
neuritis 378
neurology 329
neurotic 662
neuter *matter* 316
no choice 609a
remain –
irresolute 605
stand –
indifferent 866
neutral *mean* 29
no choice 609a
avoidance 623
– tint
colourless 429
grey 432
peace 721
neutrality
mid-course 628
peace 721
insensibility 823
indifference 866
neutralize
compensate 30
counteract 179
névé 383
never 107
– say die
persevere 604a
cheerful 836
hope 858
it will – do
inexpedient 647
prohibit 761
discontent 832
disapprobation 932
–dying 112

–ending 112
–fading
perpetual 112
glory 873
– forget 916
– to be forgotten 642
– indebted 807
– hear the last of 841
– mind
neglect 460
unimportant 643
insensible 823
indifferent 866
– more 107
– a one 4
– otherwise 16
– to return 122
– was seen the like 83
– so 31
– tell me 489
– thought of 621
– tired *active* 682
– tiring
persevering 604a
neverness 107
nevertheless 30
new *different* 18
additional 37
novel 123
unaccustomed 614
– birth 660
– blood *change* 140
improve 658
excite 824
– brooms 614, 682
– comer 57
– conditions 469
– departure 66
– edition
repetition 104
reproduction 163
improvement 658
– ideas 537
turn over a – leaf
change 140
repeat 950
give – life to 707, 824
view in a – light 658
put on the – man 950
newaub 745
new-born 123, 129
Newcastle, carry coals to –
641
new-fangled
unfamiliar 83
change 140

neology 563
new-fashioned 123
new-fledged 129
Newfoundland dog 366
Newgate 752
new-gilt 847
new-model
　convert 144
　revolutionize 146
　improve 658
newness 123
news 532
－ sheet 531
newsmonger
　curious 455
　informant 527
　news 532
newspaper 531, 551
－ correspondent 758
newspaperman 534
newt 366
New Year's Day 138
next
　following 63
　later 117
　future 121
　near 197
　－ friend 759
　－ of kin 11
　－ to nothing 32
　－ world 152
nexus 45
Niagara 348
niais 501
niaiserie 517
nib *cut* 44
　end 67
　summit 210
　point 253
nibble *eat* 298
　－ at *censure* 932
　－ at the bait
　dupe 547
　willing 602
nice
　savoury 394
　discriminative 465
　exact 494
　good 648
　pleasing 829
　fastidious 868
　honourable 939
　－ ear 418
　－ hand 700
　－ perception 465
　－ point 704
nicely

completely 52
Nicene Creed 983*a*
nicety 466
niche *recess* 182
　receptacle 191
　angle 244
　－ in the temple of fame
　873
nicher, se － 184
nick *notch* 257
　deceive 545
　mark 550
　－ it 731
　－ of time 124
Nick, Old － 978
nickel
　money 800
nicknack 643
nickname 565
nicotine 392, 663
nictitate 443
nidget 862
nidification 189
nidor 398
nidorous 401
nidus 153, 189
niece 11
niggard 819
niggle *mock* 929
niggling 643
nigh 197
night 421
　labour day and － 686
　orb of － 318
　－ and day 136
　－ school 542
night-cap 225
nightfall 126
night-gown 225
nightingale 416
nightmare
　bodily pain 378
　dream 515
　incubus 706
　mental pain 828
　alarm 860
nightshade 663
nigrescent 431
nigrification 431
nihil － ad rem 10
　－ tetigit quod non ornavit
　850
nihilism 989
nihilist 165
nihility 2, 4
nil 2, 4
　－ admirari

insensible 823
　no wonder 871
　disapproval 932
　－ conscire sibi nullâ
　　pallescere culpâ 946
　－ desperandum 858
nill *unwilling* 604
　refuse 764
nim 791
nimble 274, 682
nimble-witted 498, 842
nimbus
　cloud 353
　halo 420
　glory 873
nimiety 641
nimis, ne quid － 817
nimium ne crede colori
　485
n'importe 643
Nimrod 361, 622
nincompoop 501
nine 98
　tuneful －
　　music 416
　　poetry 597
　－ days' wonder
　　transient 111
　　unimportant 643
　　no wonder 871
　－ lives 359
　－ men's morris 840
　－ points of the law 777
ninefold 98
ninepins 840
ninety 98
ninny 501
Niobe 839
nip *cut* 44
　destroy 162
　shorten 201
　dram 298
　freeze 385
　pungent 392
　drink 959
　－ in the bud
　check 201
　kill 361
　hinder 706
　－ up 789
nipperkin 191
nippers 781
nipple 250
Nirwana 981
nis 980
nisi prius 741, 969
Nisus and Euryalus 890

- deficit alter 100
- est in ventus 187
- hæc in fœdera 536, 610
- nobis Domine 990
- obstante 707
- placet 489
- possumus
  impossible 471
  obstinate 606
  refusal 764
- nostrum tantas
  componere lites 471,
  713
lex - scripta 963
- semper erit æstas 111
- sequitur 477
- sum qualis eram 140,
  160
non-addition 38
non-admission 55
nonage 127
nonagenarian 98
non-appearance 447
non-assemblage 73
non-attendance 187
nonce 188
for the - 118, 134
nonchalance
  neglect 460
  insensibility 823
  indifference 866
non-cohesive 47
non-coincidence 14
non-com. 726
non-commissioned officer
  745
non-committal 528, 864
non-completion 730
non-compliance 742, 764
nonconformity
  difference 15
  exception 83
  dissent 489
  sectarianism 984
non-content 489
non-cooperation 489, 927
nondescript 83
none 101
- else 87
- to spare 640
- such
  superior 33
  exceptional 83
  very good 648
- in the world 4
- the worse 660
non-endurance 825

nonentity
  inexistence 2
  unsubstantial 4
  unimportant 643
non esse 2
non-essential 6, 643
non-existence 2
non-expectance 508
non-extension 180*a*
non-fulfilment 730, 732
- of one's hopes 509
non-imitation 20
non-interference
  inaction 681
  freedom 748
nonius 466
non-juror 489, 984
non-naturals 657
nonny 501
non-observance
  inattention 458
  desuetude 614
  infraction **773**
  dereliction 927
nonpareil 648
  type 591
non-payment 808
non-performance
  non-completion 730
  dereliction 927
non-plus
  uncertain 475
  difficulty 704
  conquer 731
non-preparation 674
non-prevalence 614
non-residence 187
non-resistance 725, 743
non-resonance 408*a*
nonsense
  absurdity 497
  unmeaning 517
  trash 643
talk - *folly* 499
non-subsistence 2
non-success 732
nonsuch [*see* none]
nonsuit *defeat* 731
  fail 732
  condemn 971
**nonum prematur in
  annum** 133
non-uniformity 16*a*
noodle 501
nook *place* 182
  receptacle 191
  corner 244

noology 450
noon *mid-day* 125
noon-day *light* 420
clear as -
  intelligible 518
  manifest 525
nooscopic 450
noose *ligature* 45
  loop 247
  snare 545
  gallows 975
norma loquendi 567
normal
  intrinsic 5
  mean 29
  regular 82
  perpendicular 212
- condition
  rule 80
normality 80, 502
Normand, répondre en -
  544
Norns 601
North 278
- and South 237
Northern 237
- light 423
- star
  constant 939
North-west passage 311
nose *prominence* 250
  smell 398
with one's - in the air 878
lead by the - 615, 737
led by the - 749
not see beyond one's -
  misjudge 481
  folly 499
  unskilful 699
speak through the - 583
thrust one's - in
  interjacence 228
  busy 682
under one's -
  present 186
  near 197
  manifest 525
  defy 715
put one's - out of joint
  defeat 731
  disrepute 874
- ring 847
nose-dive 306
nosegay 400, 847
nosey 455
nosology 655
nostalgia 833

nostril 351
  breath of one's –s 359
  stink in the –s 401
nostrum 626, 662
not *negation* 536
  what is – 546
  what ought – 923
  – at all 32
  – allowed 964
  – amiss 618, 651, 845
  – any 101
  – bad 651
  – bargain for 508
  – a bit 536
  – to be borne 830
  – a Chinaman's chance
    471
  – come up to 34
  – cricket 923
  – to be despised 642
  it will – do 923
  – of the earth 987
  – expect 508
  – fail 939
  – far from 197
  – a few 102
  – fit to be seen 846
  – following 477
  – grant 764
  – guilty 946
  – to be had 471, 640
  – having 187, 777*a*
  – hardened 950
  – hear of 764
  – included 55
  – know what to make of
    519
  – a leg to stand on 158
  – likely 473
  – a little 31
  – matter 643
  – to mention 37
  – mind 823, 930
  – often 137
  – on your life 489
  – one 101
  – a particle 4
  – particular 831
  – pay 808
  – a pin to choose 27
  – playing the game 923
  – within previous
    experience 137
  – to be put down 604
  – quite 32
  – reach 304
  – right 503

  – sorry 827
  – a soul 101
  – on speaking terms 889
  – the thing 925
  – to be thought of
  incogitancy 452
  impossible 471
  refusal 764
  hopeless 859
  undue 925
  disapprobation 932
  – trouble oneself about
    460
  – understand 519
  – vote 609*a*
  – wonder 871
  – for the world 603, 764
  – worth
  trifling 643
  useless 645
nota bene 457
notabilia 642
notabilities 875
notable
  manifest 525
  important 642
  active 682
  distinguished 873
notables 875
notably 31
notary 553, 968
notation 85
notch 198, **257**, 550
note *cry* 412
  music 413
  take cognizance 450
  remark 457
  explanation 522
  sign 550
  record 551
  printing 591
  epistle 592
  minute 596
  money 800
  fame 873
  change one's – 607
  make a – of 551
  of – 873
  take – of 457
  – of admiration 870
  – of alarm 669
  – of preparation 673
note-book
  memorandum 505
  record 551
  compendium 569
  writing 590

noted 490, 873
noteworthy
  great 31
  exceptional 83
  important 642
nothing *nihility* 4
  zero 101
  trifle 643
  come to – 304, 732
  do – 681
  for – 815
  go for – 643
  good for – 646
  make – of
  under-estimate 483
  fail 732
  take – by 732
  think of – 930
  worse than – 808
  – comes amiss 831
  – to do 681
  – to do with 764
  – doing 681
  – to go upon 471
  – in it 4
  – of the kind 18, 536
  – loth 602
  – on 226
  – more to be said 478
  – to signify 643
nothingness 2
notice *intellect* 450
  observe 457
  review 480
  information 527
  warning 668
  bring into – 525
  deserve – 642
  give –
  manifest 525
  inform 527
  indicate 550
  short – 111
  take – of 450
  this is to give – 457
  worthy of – 642
  – is hereby given
  publication 531
  – to quit 782
noticeable 31
notification 527
notion *idea* 453
notional 515
notoriety 531, 873
notorious
  known 490
  public 531

compendium 596
nutation 314
nutriment 298
nutrition 707
nutritious *food* 298
　healthy 656
　remedy 662
nutty 499
nuzzle 902
nyctalopy 443
nymph *girl* 129
　woman 374
　mythology 979
　sea - 341
nystagmus 443

O

O! *wonder* 870
　discontent 932
　- for *desire* 865
oaf *fool* 501
　bungler 701
　changeling 980
oak *strong* 159
　heart of -
　hard 323
　brave 861
oakum 205
oar *paddle* 267
　oarsman 269
　instrument 633
　labouring - 686
　lie upon one's -s 681
　ply the -
　navigate 267
　exert 686
　pull an - 680
　put in an - 228, 682
　rest on one's -
　cease 142
　quiescence 265
　repose 687
　stroke - 693
oarsman 269
oasis *separate* 44
　exceptional 83
　land 342
oast-house 386
oath
　assertion 535
　bad language 908
　on - 543
　rap out -s 885
　upon - 768
oatmeal 298

obbligato 88, 415
obduction 223
obdurate
　obstinate 606
　severe 739
　malevolent 907
　graceless 945
　impenitent 951
obedience 743
obeisance *bow* 308
　submission 725
　courtesy 894
　reverence 928
obelisk 206, 551
Oberon 979
obese 194
obesity 192
obey 743
　be subject to 749
　- a call 615
　- the helm 705
　- rules 82
obfuscate 421, 426
obfuscated
　drunk 959
obit 360, 363
　post - 360, 363
obiter dictum
　irrelevant 10
　occasion 134
　interjacent 228
obituary 360, 594
object *thing* 3
　matter 316
　take exception 469
　intention 620
　ugly 846
　disapprove 932
　be an -
　important 642
　- to *dislike* 867
　- lesson 82
objection 706, 932
　no - 762
objectionable
　inexpedient 647
　wrong 923, 947
objective
　extrinsic 6
　material 316
objector
　conscientious - 710
objurgate 932
oblate 201
　- spheroid 249
oblation *gift* 784
　religious - 990

oblectation 827
obligation
　necessity 601
　promise 768
　conditions 770
　debt 806
　confer an - 648
　feeling of - 916
　under an - 916, 926
oblige *benefit* 707
　compel 744
　duty 926
oblige, bien -
　refusal 764
obliged
　necessity 601
　grateful 916
　duty 926
obligee 800
obliging
　helping 707
　courteous 894
　kind 906
obliquation 279
obliquity
　slope **217**
　vice 945
　- of judgment 481
　- of vision 443
obliteration 552
　- of the past 506
oblivion 506
　nothingness 2
　pardon 506
　forgiveness 918
　redeem from - 505
　- of benefits 917
　- of time 115
oblivious 506
oblong 200
　- spheroid 249
obloquy
　disrepute 874
　disapprobation 932
　detraction 934
obmutescence 581, 585
obnoxious
　pernicious 649
　unpleasing 830
　hateful 898
　- to *liable* 177
obnubilated 422
oboe 417
obreption 528
obscene 653, 961
obscurantist 421, 519, 710
obscure *dark* 421

dim 422
unseen 447
uncertain 475
unintelligible 519
eclipse 874
ignoble 876
obscurity *style* **571**
obscurum per obscurius
519
obsecration 765
obsequies 363
obsequious
subject 749
servile 886
courteous 894
respectful 928
flattery 932
observance *rule* 82
attention 457
habit 613
practice 692
fulfilment **772**
duty 926
rite 998
observant
friar 996
observation
intellect 450
idea 453
attention 457
assertion 535
– car 272
observatory 318
observe [*see* observance,
observation]
remark 535
– a duty 926
– rules 82
observer 444
obsess 860, 992
obsession 716
obsidional 716
obsolete *old* 124
words 563
effete 645
obstacle 179, 706
obstant, Fata – 601
obstetrician 631
obstetrics 161, 662
obstinacy **606**
prejudice 481
obstipation 261
obstreperous 173, 404
obstruct *close* 261
hinder 706
– the passage of light 426
– the view 424

obstructive
opponent 710
obstruent 706
obstupefaction 823
obstupui steterunt que
comæ 860
obtain *exist* 1
prevail 78
get 775
– under false
pretences 791
obtainable 470
obtenebration 421
obtestation 765
obtrectation 934
obtrude
interfere 228
insert 300
meddle 682
obtruncate 201
obtrusion 228, 706
obtrusive
interfering 228
vulgar 851
rude 895
obtund *mitigate* 174
blunt 254
deaden 376
paralyze 823
obturate 261
obturator 263
obtuse *blunt* 253
insensible 376
imbecile 499
dull 823
– angle 244
obtuseness 456*a*
obumbrate 421
obverse 234
obviate 706
obvious *visible* 446
evident 474
clear 518
manifest 525
ocarina 417
occasion
juncture 8
opportunity **134**
cause 153
befit the – 646
have – for 630
on the present – 118
on the spur of – 612
occasional 475
occasionally 136
occidental 236, 560
occiput 235

occision 361
occlusion 261
unintelligible 919
latent 526
hidden 528
– art 992
occultation 449, 528
occultism 984
occupancy 186, 777
occupant 188, 779
occupation
business 625
in the – of 188
– road 627
occupied 682
– by 188
– with 457, 625
occupier 188, 779
occupy 186, 777
– the chair 693
– oneself with 457, 625
– the mind 451, 457
– a post 737
– time 106
occur 1, 151
– to the mind 451
– in a place 186
occurrence 151
of daily – 613
occursion 276
ocean **341**
plough the – 267
oceanography 341
ochlocracy 737
ochre 433, 439
yellow – 436
o'clock 114
know what's – 698
octagon 244
octahedron 244
Octateuch 895
octave
eight 98
music 413
period 108
octavo 593
octet 98
octifid 99
octodecimo 593
octogenarian 98, 130
octoroon 41
octroi 812
octuple 98
ocular 441
– demonstration
see 441
visible 446

– inspection 441
oculis subjecta fidelibus
446
oculist 662
odalisque 746
odd *remaining* 40
  exception 83
  single 87
  insane 503
  vulgar 851
  ridiculous 853
– fellows 712
– fish 857
oddity 857
oddments 51
odds *inequality* 28
  superiority 33
  chance 156
  discord 713
  at – 24, 713
  long – 704
  what's the – 643
  – against one 665
  the – are 472
  – and ends
  remainder 40
  mixture 41
  part 51
  useless 645
ode 597
od force 992
Odin 979
odious
  disagreeable 830
  ugly 846
  hateful 898
odi profanum vulgus 878
odium *disgrace* 874
  hatred 898
  blame 932
odium theologicum 481,
  988
  church 995
odograph 200
odometer 200
odontoid 250, 253
odour 398
  in bad – 932
  – of sanctity 897
odylic force 992
odzookens 870
oecumenical 78
oedematous 194, 324
Œdipus 462, 524
  – complex 897
  Davus sum non – 703
œil de maître 459

o'er [*see* over]
œsophagus 260
œuvre 161
of: – all things 33
  – course 82, 154
  – late 123
  – one mind 23
  – no effect 169
  – old 122
  – a piece
  uniform 16
  similar 17
  agreeing 23
off 196
  be – 623
  keep – 623
  make – with 791
  move – 287
  sheer – 287
  stand – 287
  start – 293
  – one's balance 605
  throw – one's centre 874
  – one's guard 260, 508
  – one's hands 776
  take – one's hands 785
  – one's head 503
  – one's legs 284, 309
  – one's mind 452
  – and on
  periodical 138
  changeable 149
  irresolute 605
  throw – the scent
  uncertain 475
  avoid 623
  – side 238
  – with you 297
offal 653
offence *attack* 716
  anger 900
  guilt 947
offend 830, 945
  – against the law 964
offensive
  unsavoury 395
  fetid 401
  foul 653
  aggressive 716
  displeasing 830
  distasteful 867
  obnoxious 898
  – and defensive alliance
  712
  – to ears polite 579
offer *proposal* **763**
  – the alternative 609

– a choice 609
– of marriage 902
– oneself 763
– up prayers 990
– sacrifice 990
– for sale 796
offering *gift* 784
  burnt – 990
  sin – 952
offertory *gift* 784
  worship 990
  rite 998
off-hand *soon* 132
  inattentive 458
  careless 460
  spontaneous 612
office *doing* 170
  room 191
  business 625
  mart 799
  worship 900
  do one's – 772
  good –s 724, 906
  hold – 693
  kind –s 906
  do an ill – 907
  man in – 694
officer *director* 694
  commander 745
  constable 965
offices
  kitchen &c. 191
official *certain* 474
  true 494
  business 625
  man in office 694
  authoritative 737
  master 745
  servant 746
officialism 739
officiate
  business 625
  act 680
  conduct 692
  religious 998
officinal 613
officio, ex –
  officer 694
  authority 737
  duly 924
officious 682
offing 196, 341
offscourings 645, 653
offset
  compensation 30
  offspring 167
offshoot *adjunct* 39

part 51
effect 154
offspring 167
offspring *effect* 154
posterity 167
offuscate 121, 426
often *repeated* 104
frequent 136
most – 613
– to be met with 136
ogee 847
Ogham 590
ogive 215
ogle *look* 441
desire 865
rude 895
endearment 902
ogpu 696
ogre *bugbear* 860
evil-doer 913
demon 980
oil *lubricate* 332
grease 355, **356**
pour – on
relieve 834
– on the troubled waters
174, 714
– lamp 423
– stove 386
oilcloth 223
oiled *drunk* 959
oilskin 386
oil-painting 556
oily *smooth* 255
greasy 355
servile 886
courteous 894
flattery 933
oinomania 959
ointment
grease 356
remedy 662
O.K. 58
old 124
of – 122
– age 128
die of – age 729
– bachelor 904
– clothes 225
– fashioned 851
– fogey 501, 857
– joke 842
– maid *cards* 840
spinster 904
– man *veteran* 130
husband 903
– man of the sea 706

– Nick 978
– school 124
obstinate 606
habit 613
pay off – scores 718
– song
repetition 104
trifle 643
cheap 815
– stager
veteran 130
actor 599
proficient 700
– story
repetition 104
stale news 532
love 897
– times 122
one's – way 613
– woman *fool* 501
wife 903
Oldbuck 122
olden 124
older 128
oldest inhabitant
not in memory of – 137
old-fashioned 124, 851
oldness 124
oleagine 356
oleaginous 355
oleomargarine 356
oleum addere camino 35,
173
olfactory 398
olid 401
oligarch 745
oligarchy 737
olio 41
olive-branch
infant 129
offspring 167
pacification 723
olive-green 435
olla podrida 41
Olympiad 720
Olympus 981
ombre 840
ombres chinoises 448
omega *end* 67
omelet 298
omen **512**
ominate 511
ominous
predicting 511
indicating 550
danger 665
hopeless 859

omission
incomplete 53
exclusion 55
neglect 460
failure 732
non-observance 773
guilt 947
omitted 2, 187
omne tulit punctum 731
omnibus 272
omnifarious 81
omnific 168
omniform 81
omnigenous 81
omnipotence 157, 976
omnipresence 186, 976
omniscience 490, 976
omnium gatherum
mixture 41
confusion 59
assemblage 72
omnivorous
eating 298
desire 865
gluttony 957
omphalos 68
on *forwards* 282
– account of 155
– all accounts 52
– that account 155
– approval 463
– an average 29
– the brink of 32
– the cards 152
– foot *duration* 106
event 151
doing 170
– the fire 730
– all fours 13, 23
– the other hand 30
– one's head 218
– the increase 35
– a large scale 31
– these lines 627
– the move 264
– the nail 118
– no account 32
– no occasion 107
– a par 27
– the part of 9
– the point of 111
– the present occasion 118
– trial 463
– the whole 50
once *past* 119, 122
seldom 137
at – 113, 132

– the lock 480*a*
– market 799
– one's mind 529
– order 194
– one's pursestrings 809
– question 461, 475
– rupture 713
– sesame 631, 993
– the sluices 297
– space 180
– to suspicion 485
– to *liable* 177
facile 705
– the trenches 716
– up *begin* 66
disclose 529
– to the view 446
– war 722, 889
– warfare 722
– the wound 824
open-handed 809, 816
open-hearted
veracious 543
artless 703
liberal 816
honourable 939
opening
beginning 66
opportunity 134
space 180
gap 198
aperture **260**
open-mouthed
cry 411
expectation 507
speak 582
loquacious 584
desire 865
wonder 870
opera *music* 415
poetry 597
drama 599
– glass 445
– hat 225
– house 599
opéra bouffe 599
operæ pretium est 646
operandi, modus 627, 692
operate *cause* 153
produce 161
act 170
work 680
– upon *motive* 615
operation [*see* operate]
arithmetical – 85
in – 680
put in – 677

surgical – 662
operative
acting 170
workman 690
operator
surgeon 662
doer 690
operculated 261
operculum 223
operetta 415
operose 686, 704
ophicleide 417
ophiology 368
ophiomancy 511
ophthalmia 443
ophthalmic 441
opiate 174
opine 484
opiniative 481
opiniator 606
opiniâtre 481
opinion 484
give an – 480
have too high an – of
oneself 880
popular – 488
system of –s 484
wedded to an – 606
opinionate 481, 606
opinionated 474
self– 880
opinionist 474, 606
opitulation 707
opium *soothe* 174
deaden sense 376
bane 663
opium-eater 683
oppidan 188
oppilation 706
opponent **710**, 891
opportune
well-timed 134
expedient 646
opportunism 605, 646
opportunity 134
lose an – 135
oppose *contrary* 14
counteract 179
evidence 468
clash 708
opposite 14
– scale 30
– side 237
opposition [*see* oppose]
708
the – 710
oppositionist 710

oppress *molest* 649
severe 739
malevolence 907
oppressed with
melancholy 837
oppressive *hot* 382
painful 830
oppressor 739, 913
opprobrium 874
oppugnation 708, 719
optative 865
optical 441
– instruments **445**
– lantern 448
optician 445
optics *light* 420, 445
sight 441
optimacy 875
optimates 875
optime! 931
optimism 482, 858
optimist 858
flatterer 935
option 609
optional 600
optometer 443
optometry 445
opulence 803
opuscule 593
or *yellow* 436
self– 880
orange 439
alternative 609
oracle 500, **513**
Oracle, Sir –
positive 474
vanity 880
blusterer 887
oracular
answering 462
ambiguous 475
wise 498
prediction 511
oral *information* 527
voice 580
speech 582
– communication 588
– evidence 467
orange *round* 249
colour **439**
orangery 371
orarium 999
oration 582
funeral – 363
orator 582
oratoric 415
oratory
speaking 582

place of prayer 1000
orb *region* 181
  circle 247
  luminary 423
  eye 441
  sphere of action 625
  – of day *sun* 318
  luminary 423
  – of night 318
orbicular 247
orbit *circle* 247
  heavens 318
  path 627
orchard 371
orchestra
  music 415
  musicians 416
  instruments 417
  theatre 599
orchestral 415
orchestrate 60, 413, 416
orchestration 413
orchestrelle 417
ordain
  command 741
  commission 755
  due 924
  legal 963
  God 976
  church 995
ordained *due* 924
  clergy 996
ordeal
  experiment 463
  trouble 828
  sorcery 992
  – of battle 722
order
  regularity **58**
  arrangement 60
  class 75
  record 551
  requisition 630
  direct 693
  command 741
  money 800
  rank 873
  quality 875
  decoration 877
  law 963
  at one's – 743
  call to – 932
  in – 620
  keep in – 693
  money – 800
  out of – 651
  put in – 60

recur in regular – 138
  set in – 60
  set one's house in – 673
  standing – 613
  in working – 673
  – of the day
    conformity 82
    events 151
    habit 613
    plan 626
    command 741
  pass to the – of the day
    624
orderless 59
orderly
  regular 58, 80
  arrange 60
  conformable 82
  servant 746
  – of succession 63
  – of things 80
orders, holy – 995
  in – 996
ordinal 998
ordinance
  command 741
  law 963
  rite 998
ordinary *usual* 82
  meal 298
  habitual 613
  imperfect 651
  ugly 846
  simple 849
  in – *store* 636
  lie in – 681
  – condition
    rule 80
  – course of things 613
ordinate 466
ordination
  measurement 466
  command 741
  commission 755
  church 995
  rite 998
ordnance 727
ordonnance 963
ordure 653
ore 635
oread 979
orectic 865
ore rotundo 577
organ *music* 417
  voice 580
  instrument 633
  internal –s 221

– point 413
organic *state* 7
  structural 329
  protoplastic 357
  – change 146
  – chemistry 357
  – remains 357
  ' dead 329
organism 329
organist 416
organization 60
  production 161
  structure 329
  animated nature 357
organize
  arrange 60
  produce 161
  plan 626
organized hypocrisy 544
organology 329
orgasm 173
orgies 954
oriel *recess* 191
  corner 244
  window 260
  chapel 1000
Orient 236, 420
orifice
  beginning 66
  opening 260
oriflamme 550
Origenism 984
origin 66, 153
  derive its – 154
original
  dissimilar 18
  not imitated 20
  model 22
  initial 66
  individual 79
  exceptional 83
  cause 153
  invented 515
  unaccustomed 614
  laughing-stock 857
  return to – state 660
originality 600
  want of – 843
originate *begin* 66
  cause 153
  invent 515
  – in 154
originator 164
originative 168
Orion's belt 318
orismology 562, 564
orison *request* 765

worship 990
orlop deck 211
ormoln
sham 545
ornament 847
Ormuzd 979
ornament
in writing **577**
adornment **847**
glory 873
excess of – 851
ornamental art 847
painting 556
ornate
– *writing* 577
ornamental 847
ornavit, nihil tetigit quod non – 850
orniscopy 511
ornithology 368
ornithomancy 511
orotundity 577
orphan 893
Orpheus 416
orpiment 436
orrery 318
orthodox
conformable 82
– *religion* 983a
– *dissenter* 984
orthodoxy 983a
orthoepy 562, 580
orthogonal 212
orthography 561
orthology 494
orthometry 466, 597
orthopædy 662
orthopraxy 662
orts *remnants* 40
useless 645
(trifles 643)
oryctology
minerals 358
organic remains 368
oscillation
change 149
motion **314**
centre of – 222
oscitancy
opening 260
sleepy 683
osculation
contact 199
endearment 902
Osiris 979
Osmanli 984
osmose 302

Ossa on Pelion 72, 319
osseous 323
ossify 323
ossuary 363
ostensible
appearance 448
probable 472
manifest 525
plea 617
ostentation 882
osteology 329
ostiary
doorkeeper 263
mouth 260
estuary 343
ostler 370, 746
ostracize *exclude* 55
eject 297
banish 893
censure 932
punish 972
ostrich, stomach of an – 957
Othello's occupation's gone 757
other 15, 37
do unto –s as we would men should do unto us 942
enter into the feelings of – s 906
every – 138
put oneself in the place of –s 942
the – day 123
– extreme 14
– side of the shield 468
– than 18
– things to do 683
– time 119
just the – way 14
in – words 522
otherwise 18
otia fecit, Deus nobis hæc – 840
otiose 683
otium cum dignitate 685
ottar, otto 400
ottoman 215
oubliette
ambush 530
prison 752
ough! 874
ought:
– to be 922, 926
ouï-dire 532
oui-ja board 992

ounce *weight* 319
ourselves 372
oust *eject* 297
dismiss 756
deprive 789
out *exterior* 220
in error 495
come – 446
go – *egress* 295
cool 385
play – 729
send – 297
time – of joint 735
waters – 337
– at elbows 874
– at heels 804
– of [*see below*]
– and out 52
– in one's reckoning 495
– upon it
malediction 908
censure 932
– with it
disclose 529
obliterate 552
out of *motive* 615
insufficient 640
get well – 671
– breath 688
– cash 804
– character 24
– whole cloth 544
– the common 83
– conceit with 867
– countenance
disrepute 874
humbled 879
– danger 664
– date
anachronism 115
old 124
ill-timed 135
unfashionable 851
– one's depth
deep 208
shortcoming 340
difficult 704
rash 863
– doors 220, 338
turn – doors 297
– employ 681
– favour 867
– focus 447
– gear
disorder 59
powerless 158
unprepared 674

– hand *soon* 132
completed 729
– harness 748
– health 655
– hearing 196, 419
– humour
discontent 832
anger 900
– a job 681
– joint
disorder 59
impotent 158
evil 619
– luck 735
– one's mind 503
– order
disorder 59
unconformity 83
imperfect 651
– patience 825
– the perpendicular 217
– place
disorder 59
unconformable 83
displaced 185
inexpedient 647
– pocket *loss* 776
poverty 804
debt 806
– one's power 471
– print 552
– all proportion 31
– the question
impossible 471
dissent 489
rejection 610
refusal 764
hopeless 859
undue 925
– reach 196, 471
– one's reckoning
uncertain 475
error 495
inexpectation 508
disappointment 509
– repair 659
– repute 874
– season 135
– shape 243
put – sight
invisible 447
neglect 460
conceal 528
– sorts *disorder* 59
dejection 837
– the sphere of 196
– spirits 837

– one's teens 131
– time
unmusical 414
imperfect 651
spoiled 659
discord 713
– the way
irrelevant 10
exceptional 83
absent 187
distant 196
ridiculous 853
secluded 893
get – the way 623
go – one's way 629
– one's wits 824
– work 681
– the world
dead 360
secluded 893
outbalance 30, 33
outbid 794
outbrave 885
out-brazen 885
outbreak
beginning 66
violence 173
egress 295
discord 713
attack 716
revolt 742
passion 825
outburst
violence 173
egress 295
revolt 825
outcast
unconformable 83
pariah 876
secluded 893
bad man 949
outcome *effect* 154
egress 295
produce 775
outcry *noise* 411
complaint 839
censure 932
outdo *superior* 33
transcursion 303
activity 682
cunning 702
conquer 731
outdoor 220
outer 220
outermost 220
outface 885
outfit 225, 673

outflank *flank* 236
defeat 731
outgate 295
outgeneral 731
outgo 303
outgoing 295
outgoings 809
outgrow 194
outgrowth 154
out-Herod 33, 174
outhouse 191
outing 266
outjump
transcursion 303
repute 873
outlander 57
outlandish
foreign 10
extraneous 57
irregular 83
barbarous 851
ridiculous 853
outlast 110
outlaw *irregular* 83
secluded 893
reprobate 949
outlawry 964
outlay 809
outleap 303
outlet *opening* 260
egress 295
outline *contour* **230**
form 240
features 448   •
sketch 554
painting 556
plan 626
outlines
rudiments 66
principles 596
outlive 110, 141
outlook *view* 448
outstare 885
outlying
remaining 40
exterior 220
outmanœuvre
trick 545
defeat 731
outnumber 102
outpost
distant 196
circumjacent 227
front 234
outpouring
egress 295
information 527

level 308
confute 479
vanquish 731
overthrown
vanquished 732
overthwart 708
overtired 688
overtone 413
overtop 31, 33, 206
overture
precursor 64
music 415
peace 723
offer 763
request 765
overturn
destroy 162
invert 218
level 308
confute 479
overvalue 482
overweening
excess 641
rash 863
pride 878
conceit 880
insolence 885
overweigh
exceed 33
influence 175
overrate 482
overwhelm
ruin 162
redundant 641
affect 824
overwhelmed
defeated 732
subjection 749
overwhelming
strong 159
wonderful 870
over-wise 880
overwork 679, 688
overwrought
exaggerated 549
emotion 824
affectation 855
over-zealous 825
oviform 249
ovo, in - 153
ovoid 247, 249
ovule 247
owe 806
- it to oneself 926
owing *debt* 806
- to *effect* 154
attribution 155

owl *fool* 501
-'s light 422
-s to Athens 641
own *assent* 488
divulge 529
possess 777
property 780
come by one's - 775
condemned out of one's -
mouth 479
consult one's - pleasure
943
hold one's - 737
know one's - mind 604
not know one's - interest
699
not know one's - mind
605
will of one's - 604
of one's - accord 600, 602
pay in one's - coin 718
look with one's - eyes 459
- flesh and blood 11
throw a stone in one's -
garden
clumsy 699
retaliation 718
take the law into one's -
hands 722, 964
out of one's - head 600
after one's - heart 897
look after one's - interest
943
stand in one's - light 699
act on one's -
responsibility 738
at one's - risk 926
have one's - way
will 600
easy 705
succeed 731
authority 737
freedom 748
- oneself in the wrong 950
owner *possessor* 779
without an - 777a
ownership
property 780
ox 366, 373
hot enough to roast an -
382
oxidation 659
oxymoron 24
**oyer and terminer, court
of** - 966
O yes 531

Oyez! *hear* 418
publication 531

P

P:
mind one's -'s and Q's
care 459
polite 894
duty 926
pabulum 298, 316
mental - 454
pace *walk* 264
journey 266
measure 466
permission 760
keep - with
concur 178
velocity 274
put through one's -s 525
show one's -s
ostentation 882
- tanti nominis 928
- up and down 266
pachydermatous 376, 823
pacific 172, 721
pacification 723
pacificism 721
pacify 174
pack *arrange* 60
assemblage 72
locate 184
squeeze 195
prepare 673
burden 706
send -ing 297
- of nonsense 643
- off *depart* 293
eject 297
- up 229
package
assemblage 72
location 184
packer 673
packet
assemblage 72
ship 273
pack-horse 271
pack-saddle 215
pack-thread 205
pact 23, 769
Pactolus 803
pad *thicken* 194
line 224
horse 271
soft 324

expatiate 577
tablet 590
padding *lining* 224
  stopper 263
  soft 324
  words 573
paddle *walk* 260
  row 267
  oar 633
  – one's own canoe
  conduct 692
  free 748
  – steamer 273
paddock 232
padishah 745
padlock 45, 752
  put a – on one's lips 585
padre 996
padrone 745
pæan
  rejoicing 838
  celebration 883
  gratitude 916
  approbation 931
  worship 990
paganism 984
page
  numeration 85
  printing 591
  book 593
  attendant 746
  wedding 903
  – proof 591
pageant 448, 882
paginate 85
pagoda 206, 1000
pah 717
pail 191
paillard 962
paillasse 215
pain *physical* - **378**
  moral - **828**
  penalty 974
painfulness 830
painfully *very* 31
painim 984
painless 827
pains 686
  get for one's – 973
  take – 686
  – and penalties 974
painstaking
  active 682
  laborious 686
paint *coat* 223
  colour 428
  deceive 545

delineate 556
  ornament 847
  – the lily 641
paintable 845
painter *rope* 45
  artist 559
painting 556
pair *similar* 17
  combine 48
  couple 89
  – off *average* 29
  marry 903
pair-oar 273
pairs *cards* 840
pal 711, 890
palace 189
  bishop's – 1000
  floating – 273
Paladin 717, 726
  hero 861
palæocrystic 124
palæology [*see* paleology
    &c.]
palæstra
  school 542
  arena 728
palais de vérité 703
palanquin 272
palatable 394, 829
palatal *letter* 561
palate 390
  tickle the – 394
palatial *palace* 189
  ostentatious 882
palatinate 181
palatine 745
Palatine Court 966
palaver
  unmeaning 517
  speech 582
  loquacity 584
  colloquy 588
  council 696
pale *stake* 45
  region 181
  inclosure 232
  limit 233
  dim 422
  colourless 429
  emotion 821
  frightened 860
  turn –
  lose colour 429
  emotion 821
  fear 860
  – of the church 995
  – its ineffectual fire

dim 422
  out of repute 874
pale-faced 429
paleography
  past 122
  philology 560
paleology *past* 122
  language 160
paleontology 368
paleozoic 124
palestric 686, 720
paletot 225
palette 556
palfrey 271
palimpsest 147, 528
palindrone
  inversion 218
  neology 563
paling 232, 752
palingenesia 163
palingenesis 660
palinode 597
palinody 607
palisade
  wall 212
  defence 717
  prison 752
pall *covering* 223
  mantle 225
  funeral 363
  disgust 395
  insignia 747
  weary 841
  dislike 867
  satiety 869
  canonicals 999
palladium
  safety 664
Pallas 979
pall-bearer 363
pallet *support* 215
  painter's - 556
palliament 225
palliate
  moderate 174
  mind 658
  relieve 834
  extenuate 937
palliative 174
  remedy 662
pallid 429
pallium 999
pall-mall 840
pallone 840
pallor 429
palm
  measure of length 200

trophy 733
steal 791
laurel 877
bear the – 873
grease the –
induce 615
give 784
itching – 865
win the – 731
– off, – upon 545
– tree 367
palmated 257
palmer
traveller 268
clergy 996
palmist 513
palmistry 511
palmy
prosperous 734
pleasant 829
– days
prosperous 734
pleasure 827
palpable
material 316
tactile 379
obvious 446
manifest 525
– obscure 421
palpation 379
palpitate
tremble 315
colour 440
emotion 821
fear 860
palsy
impotence 158
physical insensibility 376
disease 655
mental insensibility 823
palter
falsehood 544
shift 605
elude 773
paltry *small* 32
unimportant 643
mean 940
paludal 345
pampas 344.
pamper 902, 954, 957
pamphlet 531, 593
pamphleteer 595
Pan 979
pan 191
panacea 662
panache 256, 847
panama *hat* 225

panary 636
pancake 298
pandar [*see* pander]
Pandean pipes 417
pandect
knowledge 490
dissertation 595
compendium 596
code 963
pandemic 657
pandemonium 59, 404, 982
inhabitants of – 978
pander *pimp* 962
– to *instrument* 631
help 707
flatter 933
pandiculation
expansion 194
opening 260
sleepy 683
Pandoor 726
Pandora's box 619
bottom of – 858
paned 440
panegyric 931
panegyrize 482
panel *list* 86
layer 204
partition 228
accused 938
jury 967
sliding – 545
panelling 847
pang 378, 828
Pangloss 492
panguid 355
panhandle 765, 767, 876
panic 860
panier 225
Panjandrum 875
pannel 213
pannier 191
pannikin 191
panoply 717, 727
panopticon 752
panorama 448, 556
panoramic 78, 446
– view 441
pansophy 490
pant *heat* 382
fatigue 688
emotion 821
– for 865
pantaloon
old man 130
pantomimist 599

buffoon 844
pantaloons 225
pantechnicon 272, 636
pantheism 984
Pantheon 979, 1000
panther 861
pantile 223, 350
pantologist 492, 700
pantology 490
pantomime 550, 599
pantry 191, 636
pants 225
panurgy 698
pap 250, 354
papa *father* 166
Papa *pope* 996
papacy 984, 995
papal 995
paper *cover* 223
white 430
writing 590
book 593
security 771
exist only on – 4
– credit 805
– money 800
– pellet 643
– war 476, 720
Paphian 954, 961
papilla 250
papistry 984
papoose 129
pappous 256
papula 250
papulose 250
papyrus 590
par 27
above – 648
below – *low* 207
imperfect 651
– excellence 33
– nobile fratrum
alike 17
friends 890
de – le roi 737
– parenthèse 134
– pari refero 718
– value 812
parable
metaphor 521
teaching 537
description 594
parabola *curve* 245
parabolic
metaphorical 521
paracentesis 297
parachronism 115

parachute
balloon 273
means of safety 666
- *light* 423
Paraclete 976
parade *procession* 69, 266
walk 189
ostentation 882
paradigm 22, 567
Paradise *bliss* 827
heaven 981
in - 827
parados 717
paradox
absurdity 497
obscurity 519
difficulty 704
paradoxical 475, 519
paraffine 356
paragon
perfect 650
glory 873
good man 948
paragram
ambiguous 520
neology 563
paragraph *part* 51
phrase 566
article 593
paraleipsis 460
parallax 196
parallel
similarity 17
imitate 19
harmonious 178
- *position* 216
symmetry 242
draw a - 464
none but himself can be
his - 873
run - 178
parallelism 216
agreement 23
parallelogram 244
parallelopiped 244
paralogism 477
paralogize 477
paralysis
impotence 158
physical insensibility 376
disease 655
moral insensibility 823
paralyze 158, 376, 823
paramount
supreme 33
important 642
authority 737

lord - *master* 745
possessor 779
- *estate* 780
paramour 897
paranoia 503, 504
parapet 717
papaph 550
paraphernalia
machinery 633
belonging 780
paraphrase
imitation 19
copy 21
synonym 522
phrase 566
paraphrast 524
paraphrastic 19, 522
parasite *auxiliary* 711
servile 886
flatterer 935
parasitic
subjection 749
grasping 789
servile 886
parasol *covering* 223
shade 424
paratus:
in utrumque -
resolved 604
ready 673
semper - 673
parboil 384
parbuckle 633
Parcæ 601
parcel *part* 51
group 72
part and - 56
- out *arrange* 60
allot 786
parcels
property 780
parcere subjectis 740, 914
parch *dry* 340
heat 382
bake 384
parched with thirst 865
parchment
writing 590
security 771
parcity 819
pardi 535
pardon 506, 918
beg - 952
- me 489
pardonable 937
pare *cut* 38
reduce 195

peel 204
divest 226
- down
shorten 201
paregoric 662
parenchyma 316, 329
parent 166
- *ship* 726
parentage 11, 166
parenthesis
discontinuity 70
inversion 218
interjacence 228
by the way of - 134
parenthetical
irrelative 10
pargeting 847
parhelion 423
Pariah
outlaw 83
commonalty 876
outcast 893
parian
sculpture 557
parietal 236
parietes 224
paring 32
pari passu 27, 120
parish 181
bring to the - 804
come upon the - 804
- *council* 696
parishioner 997
paritor 965
parity 17, 27
park *house* 189
plain 344
trees 367
artillery 727
pleasure ground 840
- *paling* 232
parkway 627
parlance 582
in common - 576
parlante 415
parlementaire 534, 723
parler:
façon de - 521
- a tort et à travers
illogical 477
nonsense 497
parley *talk* 588
conference 695
mediation 724
parliament 696
parliamentary securities
802

parlour 191
parlour-maid 746
parlous 665
Parnassus 597
parochial 181, 189
  prejudiced 48
parody
  imitation 19
  copy 21
  misinterpret 523
  misrepresent 555
  travesty 865
parole *speech* 582
  on – *restraint* 751
  prisoner 754
  promise 763
Parolles 887
paronomasia
  neology 563
  ornament 577
paronymous 562
paroxysm
  violence 173
  agitation 315
  emotion 825
  anger 900
parquetry 440
Parr, Old – 130
parricide 361
parrot
  imitation 19
  repetition 104
  loquacity 584
  repeat as a – 505
parry *confute* 479
  avert 623
  defend 717
parse 461, 567
Parsee 984
parsimony 819
pars magna fui, quorum –
  690
parson 996
parsonage 1000
part *divide* 44
  portion **51**
  diverge 291
  music 413
  book 593
  rôle 599
  function 625
  duty 926
  act a – *action* 680
  take an active – 682
  bear – in 709
  component – 56
  fractional – 100*a*

in – *a little* 32
for my – 79
on the – of 707
play a – in 175
principal – 642
take the – of 709
take – with 709
take a – in 680
take no – in 623
– company
  disjunction 44
  avoid 623
  quarrel 713
– and parcel 56
– by part 51
–song 415
– of speech 567
– with 782, 784
partake 778
  – of the sacrament 998
parte, ex – 481
parterre *level* 213
  cultivation 371
Parthis mendacior 544
partial *unequal* 28
  incomplete 51
  special 79
  misjudging 481
  unjust 923
  – *shadow* 422
partiality
  preponderance 33
  desire 865
  friendship 888
  love 897
partially 32, 51
partible 44
particeps criminis 690, 711
participate 709, 778
  – in *be a doer* 680
participation **778**
participator 690
particle 32, 330
parti-coloured 440
particular *item* 51
  event 151
  attentive 457
  careful 459
  exact 494
  capricious 608
  odd 851
  fastidious 868
  in – 79
  – account 594
  – estate 780
particularize
  special 79

  describe 594
particularly 31, 33
particulars 79, 594
partie carrée 892
parting 44
parti pris 611
partisan
  auxiliary 711
  weapon 727
  friend 890
  sympathizer 914
partisanship
  warped judgment 481
  co-operation 709
  partiality 923
partition *wall* 228
  allot 786
partlet 366
partly 51
partner
  companion 88
  auxiliary 711
  sharer 778
  friend 890
  spouse 903
  sleeping – 683
partnership
  party 712
  join – with 709
parts *intellect* 450
  skill 698
  wisdom 498
parturition 161
parturiunt montes 482,
  509
party *assemblage* 72
  special 79
  person 372
  association **712**
  sociality 892
  – spirit
  warped judgment 481
  cooperation 709
  wrong 923
  – to *action* 680
  agent 690
  co-operate 709
  – to a suit 969
  – wall 228
parva componere magnis
  464
parvenu
  new 123
  successful 734
  vulgar 851
  low-born 876
parvitude 193

pas *precedence* 62
  term 71
  precession 280
  rank 873
 – de quatre 840
 – seul 840
paschal 998
pasha 875
pashalic 737
pashaw 745
pasigraphie 560
pasigraphy 590
pasquinade 934
pass *conjuncture* 8
  be superior 33
  course 109
  lapse 122
  happen 151
  interval 198
  defile 203
  move 264
  transfer 270
  move through 302
  exceed 303
  vanish 449
  way 627
  difficulty 704
  thrust 716
  passport 760
  gratuity 815
 - *as property* 783, 784
 barely – 651
 let it – 460
 make a – at 716
 pretty – 704
 – away
  cease to exist 2
  end 67
  transient 111
  past 122
  cease 142
  die 360
 – by *course* 109
  inattention 458
  neglect 460
  disrespectful 929
 – comprehension 519
 – current 484
 – an examination 648, 873
 – the eyes over 457
 – the fingers over 379
 – into one's hand 785
 – through one's hands 625
 – into 144
 – judgment 480
 – a law 963
 – in the mind 451

 – muster
  conform to 82
  sufficient 639
  good 648
  approbation 931
 barely – muster 651
 – under the name of 564
 – off *be past* 122
  egress 295
 – off for 544
 – on 282
 – an opinion 480
 – to the order of the day 624
 – out of 295
 – over
  exclude 55
  cross 302
  give 784
  forgive 918
  exemption 927a
 – over to 709
 – and repass 302, 314
 – in review 457, 461
 – the Rubicon 609
 – sentence on 971
 – time *exist* 1
  time 106
  do nothing 681
 – one's time in 625
 – to 144
 – through
  event 151
  motion 302
 – one's word 768
passable *small* 32
  unimportant 643
  imperfect 651
  pretty 845
passado 716
passage [*see* pass]
  part 51
  conversion 144
  street 189
  corridor 191
  opening 260
  navigation 267
  moving through **302**
  music 413
 - *in a book* 593
  action 680
 cut a – 260
 force a – 302
 – of arms 720
passant, en -
  transit 270
  incidentally 621

pass-book 811
passe: mot de – 550
passé
  antiquated 124
  aged 128
  spoiled 659
passed away 122
passementerie 847
passenger 268
 – train 272
passe-partout
  key 260
  instrument 631
passer by 444
passer le temps, pour – 681
passeront pas, il ne – 717
passe-temps 840
pas si bête 498
passim
  dispersed 73
  place 182
  situation 183
passing *very* 31
  transient 111
 – bell 363
 – strange 870
 – word 527
passion
  emotion 820, 821
  excitability 825
  pain 828
  desire 865
  love 897
  anger 900
 ruling – 606
passionate
  warm 825
  irascible 901
passionless 823
Passion-week 998
passive *inert* 172
  inaction 681
  obedient 743
  inexcitable 826
 – resister 489
passivity 172, 989
pass-key 631
Passover 998
passport
  indication 550
  instrumentality 631
  order 741
  permission 760
pass-word
  answer 462
  sign 550

military 722
past 122
  danger – 664
  insensibility to the – 506
  obliteration of the – 506
  thing of the – 124
  – bearing 830
  – comprehension 519
  – cure 859
  – dispute 474
  – praying for 945
  – one's prime 128
  – recollection 506
  – work
    uselss 645
    impaired 659
paste *attach* 43
  cement 45
  to cement 46
  pulp 354
  sham 545
  tinsel 847
  scissors and – 609
pastel 556
pasteurize 652
pasticcio 21, 41
pastil 400
pastime 840
pastor 996
pastoral
  bucolic 370
  music 415
  poem 597
  religious 995
  sermon 998
pastorale 415
pasty *food* 298
  sweets 396
pasturage
  meadow 344
  herbage 367
pasture *food* 298
pastry *tart* 298
  like paste 352
pat *pertinent* 23
  strike 276
  (*expedient* 646)
  – on the back
  induce 615
  comfort 834
  encourage 861
  approve 931
  – on the cheek 902
  – on the head
  endearment 902
Patagonian 206
patch *small* 32

change 140
region 181
blemish 848
– up *restore* 660
compromise 774
patchwork
  mixture 41
  discontinuous 70
  variegation 440
pate *summit* 210
  brain 450
patefaction 260
patella 191
paten 191
patent *open* 260
  manifest 525
  licence 760
  property 780
  – medicine 662
pater 166
  – patriæ 912
patera *cup* 191
  sacramental 998
paterfamilias 166
paternal
  father 166
  benevolent 906
  – domicile 189
paternity 166
paternoster 990
path *direction* 278
  way 627
  cross the – 706
  secret – 530
pathetic 830
pathless
  spacious 180
  closed 261
  difficult 704
pathognomonic 550
pathology 655, 662
pathos 821
pathoscopic 820
pathway 627
patience
  perseverance 604a
  endurance 826
  cards 840
patient *sick* 655
patisserie 298
patois 563
patriæ: amor – 910
  pater – 912
patriarch
  family 11
  veteran 130
  ancestors 166

priest 996
patriarchal
  ancient 124
  ancestral 166
patriarchate 737
patrician 875
patrilineal 11, 166
patrimony 780
patriot 910
patrol *walk* 266
  safeguard 664
  (*warning* 668)
patrolman 664
patron
  auxiliary 711
  customer 795
  friend 890
  benefactor 912
patronage
  influence 175
  aid 707
  authority 737
patronize 693, 707
patronymic 564
patte de
  – mouche 590
  – velours 544, 545
patten 225, 998
patter *strike* 276
  sound 407
  meaningless 417
  talk 584
  stage 599
patterer 582
pattern *model* 22
  perfection 650
  ornament 847
  – after 20
patty 298
patulous 194
pauciloquy 585
paucity *small* 32
  few 103
  scanty 640
paughty 878
Paul Jones 792
paulo post futurum 121
Paul Pry
  curious 455
  prattle 588
paunch 191, 250
pauper 804
pause
  discontinue 70
  cease 142
  quiescence 265
  doubt 485

irresolution 605
repose 687
pauvre diable 804
pavanne 840
pave 223
– the way 705
pavé, on the – 961
pavement *base* 211
covering 223
path 627
pavilion 189
paving 211
paviour 673
pavor 859
paw *touch* 379
retention 781
– the ivories 416
pawky 702
pawl 45
pawn 771
pawnbroker 787
pax *hush!* 403
– in bellow 723
– vobiscum 894
pay *paint* 223
profitable 775
defray 807
expend 809
income 810
punish 972
remunerate 973
in one's –
servant 746
hired 795
– in advance 809
– attention to 457
– back 718
– down 807
– dues 924
– in full 807
– homage
submission 725
worship 990
– the debt of nature 360
– no attention &c. to 458,
460
– through the nose 814
– off 718
– off old scores 919
– old debts 807
– out 200, 972
– in one's own coin 718
– the penalty 952
– the piper 707
– regard to 484
– one's respects 894
– too much 814

– a visit 892, 894
– one's way
defray 807
economy 817
paymaster 801
payment 807
remuneration 973
paynim 984
pays, mal du –
regret 833
sociality 892
pea 249
peace
silence 403
concord 714
amity **721**
at – 714
commission of the – 965
justice of the – 967
keep the –
moderation 174
concord 714
make – 723
make – with 831
Prince of – 976
speak – 831
peaceable
moderate 174
peaceably, get on – 736
peaceful
inexcitable 826
peace-maker 714
mediator 724
contented 831
peace-offering
pacification 723
mediation 724
gift 784
atonement 952
peach 529
peach-coloured 434
peacock
variegation 440
beauty 845
proud 878
vain 880
guady 882
jackdaw in –'s feathers 701
pea-green 435
pea-jacket 225
peak *height* 206
summit 210
sharp 253
sicken 655
peaked 253
peaky 203
peal *loud* 404

roll 407
music 415
– of bells 407, 417
– of laughter 838
pearl *type* 591
goodness 648
ornament 847
glory 873
mother-of- 440
cast –s before swine 638
pearly
semitransparent 427
colour 428
white 430
grey 432
variegated 440
pear-shape 249
peasant 876
peat 388
pebble *little* 193
hard 323
– dash 223
peccability 945
peccable 947
peccadillo 947
peccant *bad* 649
unclean 653
diseased 655
– humour 653, 655
peccavi 950
peck *much* 31
multitude 102
eat 298
– at *censure* 932
– of troubles
difficulty 704
adversity 735
pain 828
peckish 865
Pecksniff 548
pectinated 253
peculate 791
peculator 792
peculiar 79, 83
peculiarly 31, 33
pecuniary 800
pecunious 803
pedagogic 537
pedagogue
scholar 492
teacher 540
pedantic 855
pedagogy 537
pedal 633
– note 408
– point 416
pedant *scholar* 492

pedantic
  half-learned 491
  - *style* 577
  affected 855
pedantry 481
peddle *meddle* 683
  hawk 796
peddler 796, 797
peddling
  trifling 643
  miserly 819
pederero 727
pedestal 215
  place on a - 307, 931
pedestrian 268
pedicel 215
pedicle 215
pedigree 69, 166
pediment 210, 215
pedlar 797
  -'s French 563
pedometer 200
peduncle 215
peek 441
peel *layer* 204
  skin 223
  uncover 226
  - off *separate* 44
peeler 664
peel-house 717
peep 441
  - behind the curtain 461
  - of day 125
  - into the future 510
  - out 446, 529
peep-hole 260
peep-show 448, 840
peer *equal* 27
  pry 441
  inquire 461
  lord 875
  - out 446
peerless *supreme* 33
  first rate 648
  glorious 873
  virtuous 944
peeved 900
peevish 895, 901
peg *grade* 71
  hang 214
  project 250
  drink 298, 959
  come down a - 306
  let down a - 308
  not stir a - 265, 681
  - away 682
  - to hang on 617

- on *journey* 266
-out *die* 360
Pegasus 271
pegomancy 511
pegs *legs* 266
peignoir 225
peindre, fait à - 845
peine forte et dure 974
pejorative 483
pelagic 341
pelerine 225
pelf *gain* 775
  property 780
  money 803
Pelion, Ossa on - 72, 319
pelisse 225
pellet 249, 727
  paper - 643
pellicle 204, 223
pell-mell 59
pellucid 425
pelote 249
pelt *skin* 223
  dress 225
  throw 276
  attack 716
  punish 972
peltry 223
pemmican 298
pen *inclosure* 232
  write 590
  writer 593
  restrain 751
  imprison 752
  ready - 569
  slip of - 495, 568
  stroke of the -
  write 590
  authority 737
  command 741
  - in hand 590
  - and ink 590
  - name 565
  draw the - through 552
penal 972
  - servitude 972
  - settlement 752
penalty 974
  extreme - 972
penance 952, 974
  do - 998
penates, lares et - 189,
  991
penchant
  willing 602
  desire 865
  love 897

pencil *bundle* 72
  - *of light* 420
  write 590
pencil-drawing 556
pencraft 590
pendant *match* 17
  flag 550
  ornament 847
pendency *time* 106
  hanging **214**
pendente lite 106
  uncertain 475
  lawsuit 969
pendule 114
pendulous 214, 314
pendulum 114, 214
  motion of a - 314
Penelope, work of - 645,
  730
penetralia 221
  - *mentis* 450, 820
penetrate
  ingress 294
  passage 302
  sagacity 498
  - the soul 824
penetrated with 484, 821
penetrating
  sagacious 498
  feeling 821
  - glance 441
penfold 232
peninsula 342
penitence 950
penitentiary 752, 996
pen-knife 253
penman 590
  inspired - 985
penmanship 590
pennant 550
pennate 267
penniless 804
pennon 550
penny 800
  not have a - 804
  cost a pretty - 814
  turn a - 775
  no - no paternoster 812
  in for a - in for a pound
  768
  - dreadful 594
  - trumpet 410
  - whistle 410
penny-a-liner 534, 593
penny-a-lining 573
pennyweight 319
penny-wise 819

- and pound foolish
  caprice 608
  waste 638
  prodigal 818
pennyworth 812
penology 972
penscript 590
pensée, arrière - 528
penseroso 837
pensile 214
pension *income* 810
pensioner
  student 541
  servant 746
  receiver 785
pensive 451, 837
penstock 350
pentagon 98, 244
pentahedron 244
pentameter 98, 597
Pentateuch 98, 985
Pentecost 998
Penthesilean 861
penthouse 189, 191
pentile 223
pent up 751
- in one's memory 505
penultimate 67
penumbra 421
penurious 819
penury 804
peon 726
people
  kinsfolk 11
  multitude 102
  inhabit 186
  mankind 372
  commonalty 876
  laity 997
pep 171
- up 171
pepastic 662
pepper *pungent* 392
  condiment 393
  attack 716
- and salt 432, 440
peppercorn 643
- rent 815
peppery
  irascible 901
peptic 662
per 631
- contra
  contrariety 14
  counter-evidence 468
  opposition 708
- procuratio 755

- saltum 70, 113
- se 87
peradventure 470
peragrate 266
perambulate 266
perambulator
  measure of length 200
  vehicle 272
perceivable 446
perceive
  be sensible of 375
  see 441
  know 490
percentage 84, 813
perceptible 446
perception 453, 490
perceptive 375
perch *location* 184
  abide 186
  habitation 189
  length 200
  height 206
  support 215
- up 307
perchance 156, 470
percipience 450
percolate 295, 348
percolator 191
percursory 458
percussion 276
  centre of - 222
percussive 277
perdition
  destruction 162
  ruin 732
  loss 776
perdre son Latin 704
perdrix, toujours - 841
perdu 528
  enfant - 859, 863
perdurable 110
perdy 535
peregrination 266
peregrinator 268
peremptory
  assertion 535
  firm 604
  authoritative 737
  rigorous 739
  compulsory 744
  duty 926
- denial 536
- refusal 764
perennial
  continuous 69
  diuturnal 110
- *plants* 367

perennius, ære - 873
pererration 266
perfect
  great 31
  entire 52
  excellent 650
  complete 729
perfection 650
  bring to - 729
perfervidum ingenium 682
perfidy 874, 940
perflate 349
perforate 260
perforator 262
perforce 601, 744
perform
  produce 161
  do 170
- *music* 416
  action 680
  achieve 729
  fulfil 772
- a circuit 629
- a duty 926
- the duties of 625
- a function 644
- an obligation 772
- a part 599, 680
- a service 998
performable 470
performance [*see* perform]
  effect 154
performer
  musician 416
  stage-player 599
  agent 690
  affectation 855
perfume 400
perfunctory 53, 460
pergola 191
perhaps 470, 514
peri 845, 979
periapt 993
pericranium 450
periculous 665
peridot 847
perihelion 197
peril 665
  at your - 909
  take heed at one's - 668
perilepsis 476
perimeter 230
period *end* 67
  point 71
- *of time* 106, **108**
  recurrence 138
  at fixed -s 138

well rounded –s 577, 578
periodical
 recurring 138
 book 593
periodicity 138
peripatetic 266, 268
periphery 230
periphrase 566, 573
periplus 267
periscope 441, 445
periscopic 446
 – lens 445
perish
 cease to exist 2
 be destroyed 162
 die 360
 decay 659
 – with cold 383
 – with hunger 956
perishable 111
perissology 573
peristaltic 248
peristyle 189
periwig 225
perjured 940
perjurer 548
perjury 544
perk *dress* 225
 – up *elevate* 307
 revive 689
perked up
 proud 878
perky 880
perlustration 441
permanence
 durability 110
 unchanging **141**
 unchangeable 150
permanent
 habitual 613
permeable 260
permeate
 insinuate 228
 pervade 186
 pass through 302
 –d with 613
permissible 760
permission 760
permissive 760
permit 760
permitting
 weather &c. – 469, 470
permutation
 numerical – 84
 change 140
 interchange 148
pernicious 649

pernicity 274
perorate
 diffuse style 573
peroration
 sequel 65
 end 67
 speech 582
perpend *think* 451
perpendicular 212
perpension
 attention 457
perpetrate 680
 – a pun &c. 842
perpetrator 690
perpetua, esto – 928, 931
perpetual 112
 frequent 136
 – curate 996
 – motion 467
perpetuate 112
 continue 143
 establish 150
perpetuity 69, **112**
perplex *derange* 61
 distract 458
 uncertainty 475
 bother 830
perplexed 59, 248
perplexity
 disorder 59
 uncertainty 475
 unintelligibility 519
 difficulty 704
perquisite 775, 973
perquisition 461
perron 627
perscrutation 461
persecute
 oppress 469
 annoy 830
 malevolence 907
perseverance 143, **604a**
Persides 215
persiflage 842, 856
persifleur 844
persist *duration* 106
 permanence 141
 continue 143
 persevere 604a
persistence
 diuturnity 110
person 3, 372
 without distinction of –s
 922
personable 845
personæ, dramatis – 599,
 690

personage 372
persona grata 890, 899
personal [*see* person]
 special 79
 subjective 317
 – narrative 594
 – property 780
 – remarks 932
 – security 771
personality [*see* personal]
 discourtesy 895
 disrespect 929
 censure 932
 detraction 934
personalty 780
personate 19, 554
personify 521, 554
personnel 56, 590
perspective
 view 448
 expectation 507
 painting 556
 aerial – 428
 in – 200
perspicacity
 sight 441
 intelligence 498
 fastidiousness 868
perspicuity
 intelligibility 518
 style **570**
perspiration 295, 299
 in a – 382
perstringe 457
persuadable 602
persuade *belief* 484
 induce 615
persuasibility
 willingness 602
persuasion
 class 75
 opinion 484
 teaching 537
 inducement 615
 religious – 983
persuasive
 reasoning 476
pert
 vain 880
 insolent 885
 discourteous 895
pertain to
 relate to 9
 included under 76
 power 157
 belong 777
 property 780

duty 926
perte de vue, à – 196, 447
pertinacity 604*a*
pertinent 9, 23
pertingent 199
perturbation
  derange 61
  ferment 171
  agitation 315
  emotion 821
  excitation 824, 825
  fear 860
pertusion 260
peruke 225
peruse 539
pervade
  influence 175
  extend 186
  affect 821
  – the soul 824
pervading spirit 820
perverse
  obstinate 606
  difficult 704
  churlish 895
  sulky 901*a*
perversion
  sophistry 477
  misinterpretation 523
  misteaching 538
  falsehood 544
  untruth 546
  injury 659
  impiety 988
pervert 144, 607 [*see*
  perversion]
perverted 495
pervestigation 461
pervicacious 606
pervigilium 682
pervious 260
pessimism
  overrate 482
  underrate 483
  dejection 837
  hopeless 859
pessimist [*see* pessimism]
  coward 862
pessomancy 511
pessoribus orti 876
pest 663, 830
pester 830
pest-house 662
pestiferous 657
pestilence 655
pestle 330
pet *love* 897

favourite 899
  anger 900
  fondle 902
  flatter 933
  – lamb 266
petal 367
petard 727
  hoist on one's own – 718,
  732
Peter to pay Paul:
  borrow of – 788
  rob – *steal* 791
    wrong 923
  –'s pence 784, 809
  peter out 142
petite dame 962
petition 765, 969, 990
petitioner 767
petitio principii 477
petit-maître 854
petrel *warning* 668
petrify *dense* 321
  hard 323
  freeze 385
  thrill 824
  affright 860
  astonish 870
petrol 388
petroleum 356
pétroleuse 384
petronel 727
petticoat *dress* 225
  woman 374
  – government
  authority 737
pettifogger 968
pettifogging
  sophistry 477
  deception 545
  litigious 713
  dishonourable 940
pettish 901
petto, in –
  mental 450
  thought of 454
  concealed 528
  intention 620
petty *little* 32, 193
  unimportant 643
  – cash 800, 811
  – jury 967
  – larceny 791
  – officer 745
  – sessions 966
  – treason 742
petulance 885, 901
petulant

– *language* 574
peu de chose 643
peu s'en faut 32
pew *cell* 191
  church 1000
pewter 41
Phaethon 423
phaeton 272
phalanx 712, 726
phantasm
  unsubstantiality 4
  illusion 443
  appearance 448
  imagination 515
phantasmagoria 448
phantasy 453, 515
phantom *unreal* 4
  fallacy of vision 443
  imaginary 515
pharisaical 544, 988
Pharisee 548, 988
pharmacy 662
pharos 550
phase *aspect* 8
  transition 144
  form 240
  appearance 448
  have many –s 149
  assume a new – 144
  view in all its –s 461
phasis 448
phasma 443
phenomenon
  event 151
  appearance 448
  prodigy 872
phial 191
Phidias 559
philander 902
philanthropy 784, 906, 910
Philip drunk to Philip
  sober, appeal from –
  658
philippic 932
Philistine 491, 876
philologist 492
philology 560
philomath 492
philomel 416
philosopher 492, 500
  –'s stone
  impossibility 471
  perfect 650
  remedy 662
  wealth 803
philosophical
  thoughtful 451

calm 826
philosophy
calmness 826
knowledge 490
Moral – 450
– of the Mind 450
philtre 993
phiz *face* 234
look 448
phlebotomy
ejection 297
remedy 662
Phlegethon 982
phlegm *viscid* 352
insensibility 823
phlegmatic *indifferent*
866
phlogiston 382
pho! 497
Phœbus *sun* 318
luminary 423
phœnix
exception 83
reproduction 163
paragon 650
restoration 660
phonate 402
phonetic
sound 402
voice 580
speech 582
– spelling 561
phonics 402
phonograph 417, 418
phonography
sound 402
letter 361
writing 590
phonology 562
Phosphor 423
phosphorescence 420, 423
phosphorus 423
photo-engraving 558
photograph *like* 17
photographer 559
photography 445
light 420
representation 554
photogravure 558
photolysis 49
photometer 445
photosphere 318
photostat 553
phrase *part* 51
music 413
language **566**
phrasemonger 577

phraseology 569
phrenetic 503
phrenitis 503
phrenology 450
phrenotypics 505
Phryne 962
phthisozoics 361
phylacteric
sorcery 992
phylactery
maxim 496
spell 993
physic
cure 660
remedy 662
physical 316
– education
material 316
teaching 537
– force
strength 159
compulsion 744
– nature 3
– pleasure **377**
– pain **378**
– science 316
physician
remedy 662
advice 695
physics 316
physiognomy
face 234
appearance 448
interpret 522
physiology
organization 357
life 359
vegetable – 369
physique
strength 159
animality 364
phytivorous 298
phytology 369
pi 591
piacere, al – 600
piacular 952
pianino 417
pianissimo 415
pianist 416
piano *gentle* 174
music 415
– organ 417
– player 417
pianoforte 417
pianola 417
piazza 189, 191
pibroch *music* 415

war 722
pica 591
picaresco, gusto – 945
picaroon 792
piccolo 410, 417
pick *axe* 253
eat 298
select 609
best 648
clean 652
gain 775
– a-back 215
– the brains of 461
– holes
censure 932, 934
– the lock 480*a*
– me up 662
– out *extract* 301
select 609
– to pieces
separate 44
destroy 162
find fault 932
– a quarrel 713
– one's steps 459
– up *learn* 539
get better 658
gain 775
– one's way 675
pickaxe 253
picked 648
– men 700
pickeer 791
pickeerer 792
pickelhaube
armour 717
picket *join* 43
locate 184
fence 229
guard 668
defence 717
soldiers 726
restrain 751
imprison 752
torture 972
– boat 273
pickings 775, 793
pickle *condition* 7
macerate 337
pungent 392
condiment 393
preserve 670
difficulty 704
have a rod in – 673
pickle-herring 844
pickpocket 792
abuse like a – 932

pickthank *busy* 682
  servile 886
  flatterer 937
picnic *food* 298
  participation 778
  amusement 840
picquet 840
pictorial
  painting 556
  beauty 845
picture
  appearance 448
  representation 554
  painting 556
  description 594
  - to oneself 515
picture-gallery 556
picturesque
  painting 556
  beauty 845
picture-theatre 599
piddle *dawdle* 683
piddling *trivial* 643
pidgin English 563
pie *food* 298
  sweet 396
  printing 591
piebald 440
piece *bit* 32
  adjunct 59
  painting 556
  drama 599
  cannon 727
  coin 800
  courtesan 962
  fall to -s 162
  go to -s 162
  in -s 330
  of a - 42
  pull to -s 162
  give a - of advice 695
  - of good fortune 618
  - of music 415
  - of news 532
  - out 52
  - together 43
  - of work 713
  make a - of work about
    642
pièce
  - justificative 467
  - de résistance 298
piecemeal 51
pied *variegated* 440
pied de la lettre, au - 494
pie-poudre, court of - 966
pier 189, 666

pierce
  perforate 260
  bodily pain 378
  chill 385
  hurt 649
  wound 659
  affect 824
  mental pain 830
  - the head 410
  - the heart 830
piercer 262
piercing *cold* 383
  loud 404
  shrill 410
  intelligent 498
  feeling 821
  - eye 441
  - pain 378
pier-glass 445
Pierian spring 597
pierre fendre, à - 383
Pierrot 599
pietas 998
pieté, mont de - 787
pietism 988
pietist 987, 988
piety 987
pig *animal* 366
  sensual 954a
  - in a poke
  uncertain 475
  chance 621
  rash 863
  - together 72
pigeon
  dupe 547
  steal 791
  gorge de - 440
pigeon-hearted 862
pigeon-hole 191, 260
piggin 191
piggish 954
pig-headed 499, 606
pigment 428
pigmy 193
pignoration 771
pignus 771
pig-sticking 361
pigsty 653
pigtail 214
pigwidgeon 193, 980
pike *hill* 206
  sharp 253
  highway 627
  weapon 727
pikeman 726
pikestaff *tall* 206

  plain 525
pilaster
  support 215
  projection 250
  ornament 847
pile *stake* 45
  heap 72
  edifice 161
  post 215
  velvet 256
  money 800
  funeral - 363
  - up 549, 641
pile-driver 276
pilfer *steal* 791
pilferer 792
pilgarlic
  outcast 893
pilgrim 268, 996
pilgrimage 266, 676
pill *sphere* 249
  medicine 662
  bitter - 735
pillage 659, 791
pillager 792
pillar *stable* 150
  lofty 206
  support 215
  monument 551
  tablet 590
  -s of Hercules 550
  - of the state &c. 873
  from - to post
  transfer 270
  agitation 315
  irresolute 505
  circuit 629
pillion 215
pillory 975
pillow
  support 215
  soft 324
  consult one's -
  temporize 133
  reflect 451
pilot *mariner* 269
  inform 527
  guide 693
  director 694
pilot-balloon 463
pilot-boat 273
pilot-jacket 225
pilot-officer 745
pilous 256
pimp 962
pimple 250, 848
pin *fasten* 43

fastening 45
locate 184
sharp 253
axis 312
trifle 643
might hear a – drop 403
point of a – 193
not a – to choose 27, 609a
– down 744, 751
– one's faith upon 484
– oneself upon 746, 886
pinafore 225
pince-nez 445
pincers 781
pinch *emergency* 8
contract 195
pain 378
chill 385
need 630
difficulty 704
adversity 735
grudge 819
hurt morally 830
at a – 630, 704
jack at a – 711
where the shoe –es 830
– of snuff 643
pinchbeck 545, 847
pinched [*see* pinch]
thin 203
poor 804
– with hunger 865
pinching 383, 819
Pindaric 597
pine *disease* 655
dejection 837
suffer in mind 828
– away 837
– for 865
pinery 371
ping-pong 840
pinguid 355
pin-hole 260
pinion *fasten* 43
wing 267
instrument 633
restrain 751
fetter 752
pink *notch* 257
pierce 260
thrust 276
colour 434
perfection 650
glory 873
pink of *beauty* 845
– fashion 852
– perfection 650

– politeness 894
pinnace 273
pinnacle 210
pinocle 840
pin-prick 180a
pins *legs* 266
– and needles
bodily pain 378
numb 381
mental pain 828
pinscher 366
Pinto, Fernam Mendez –
548
pioneer
precursor 64
leader 234
teacher 540
prepare 673
pious 987
– fraud 546, 988
pip 747
pipe *tube* 260
conduit 350
vent 351
tobacco 392
sound 410
cry 411
music 416, 417
weep 839
no – no dance 812
– one's eye 839
– of peace 721, 723
pipeclay *habit* 613
strictness 739
piper 416
pay the – 707, 807
piping – hot 382
– time 721, 734
pipkin 191
piquant
pungent 392
- *style* 574
impressive 821
piquante, sauce – 393, 829
pique *fly* 267
excite 824
pain 830
hate 898
anger 900
– oneself
pride 878
piqueerer 792
piquet 717, 726
pirate 773, 791, 792
piroque 273
pirouette 218, 312
turn a – 607

Pisa, tower of – 217
pis-aller 147
piscatorial 366
pisces natare docere 538,
641
pisciculture 370
piscina 350, 1000
pish! *absurd* 497
trifling 643
excitable 825
irascible 901
piste 551
Pistol 887
pistol 727
pistol-shot 197
piston 263
pit *deep* 208
hole 252
opening 260
extract 301
grave 363
theatre 599
danger 667
bottomless – 982
– of Acheron 982
– against 708, 713
– against one another 464
pit-a-pat
agitation 315
rattle 407
feeling 821
excitation 824
pitch *degree* 26
term 71
location 184
height 206
summit 210
erect 212
throw 284
descent 306
depression 308
reel 314
resin 356a
musical - 413
black 431
absolute – 416
– of one's breath 411
– dark 421
– into *attack* 716
contend 720
punish 972
– overboard 782
– one's tent 292
– and toss 621
– upon *reach* 292
discover 480a
choose 609

get 775
pitched battle 720
pitcher 191
pitchfork 273, 284
    rain –s 348
pitch-pipe 417
piteous 830
piteously *much* 31
pitfall 545, **667**
pith *gist* 5
    strength 159
    interior 221
    centre 222
    meaning 516
    important part 642
pithless 158
pithy *meaning* 516
    concise 572
    vigorous 574
pitiable *bad* 649
    painful 830
    contemptible 930
pitied, to be – 828
pitiful
    unimportant 643
    bad 649
    disrepute 874
    pity 914
pitiless **914a**
    revengeful 919
pittance
    quantity 25
    dole 640
    allotment 786
    income 810
pitted 848
pituitous 352
pity 914
    express – 915
    what a –
    regret 833
    lament 839
    for –'s sake 914
pivot *junction* 43
    cause 153
    support 215
    axis 222, 312
pix *box* 191, 998
    assay 463
pixy 980
pizzicato 415
placable 918
placard 531
placate 723, 918
place
    circumstances 8
    order 58

arrange 60
term 71
situation **182**, 183
locate 184
abode 189
office 625
rank 873
give – to 623
have – 1
in – 183
in – of 147
make a – for 184
out of – 185
take – 151
– to one's credit 805
– itself 58
– in order 60
– upon record 551
– under
    include 76
placebit, decies repetita –
    829
placebo 933
place-hunter 767
placeman 758
placet 488, 741
placid 826
placket 260
plagiarism
    imitation 19
    borrowing 788
    theft 791
plagiarist 792
Plagiary, Sir Fretful – 901
plagiedral 217
plague *disease* 655
    pain 828
    worry 830
plague-spot 657
plaguy 704, 830
plaid *shawl* 225
    variegation 440
plaidoyer 476
plain
    horizontal 213
    country **344**
    obvious 446
    meaning 518
    manifest 525
    style 576
    artless 703
    ugly 846
    simple 849
speak –ly 576
tell one –ly 527
– English 576
– dealing 543

– interpretation 522
– question 461
– sailing 705
– sense 498
– speaking 525, 703
– terms
    intelligible 518
    interpreted 522
    language 576
– truth 494
– words 703
plainness 576
plainsong 990
plain-spoken 525, 703
plaint 411, 839
plaintiff 938
plaintive 839
plaisance [*see* pleasance]
plaisanterie 842
plaister 223
plait 219, 258
plan *itinerary* 266
    information 527
    representation 554
    scheme **626**
according to – 82
planchette 992
plane *horizontal* 213
    flat 251
    smooth 255
    fly 267
    aeroplane 273
    soar 305
inclined – 633
planet *world* 318
    luminary 423
    fate 601
planet-struck
    adversity 735
    wonder 870
planimeter 466
planish 255
plank *board* 204
    programme 626
    path 627
    safety 666
plant *place* 184
    insert 300
    vegetable 367
    agriculture 371
    trick 545
    tools 633
    property 780
– a battery 716
– a dagger in the breast
    830
– oneself 184

– a thorn in the side 830
plantation
  location 184
  agriculture 371
  estate 780
planter 188
planter ses choux, aller –
  893
plaque 204
plash *lake* 343
  stream 348
  sound 405, 408
plashy 345
plasm 22
plasma 847
plasmic 240
plaster *cement* 45
  covering 223
  remedy 662
  – up *repair* 660
plastered 959
plastic *alterable* 149
  form 240
  soft 324
  – arts 557
plastron 717
plat *weave* 219
  ground 344
plate *dish* 191
  layer 204
  covering 223
  flat 251
  food 298
  engraving 558
  – layer 690
  – printing 558, 591
plateau 213, 344
plated 545
platform
  horizontal 213
  support 215
  stage 542
  scheme 626
  arena 728
  – orator 582
platinum-blond 430
platitude 517, 843
Platonic
  contemplative 451
  inexcitable 826
  chaste 960
  – bodies 244
Platonism 451
platoon 726
  – fire 716
platter 191
  layer 204

flat 251
clean the outside of the –
  544
plaudit 931
plausible
  probable 472
  sophistical 477
  false 544
  approbation 931
  flattery 933
  vindication 937
play *operation* 170
  influence 175
  scope 180
  oscillation 314
  music 416
  drama 599
  use 677
  action 680
  freedom 748
  amusement 840
  at – 840
  bring into – 677
  full – 175
  full of – 836
  in – 842
  – along with 709
  – one's best card 686, 698
  – of colours 440
  – at cross purposes 59,
    523
  – a deep game 702
  – the deuce 825
  – the devil 907
  – one false
    disappoint 509
    falsehood 544
    deception 545
  – fast and loose
    falsehood 544
    irresolute 605
    tergiversation 607
    caprice 608
  – on the feelings 824
  – first fiddle 642, 873
  – the fool
    folly 499
    clumsy 699
    amusement 840
    ridiculous 853
    ridicule 856
  – for *chance* 621
  – a game
    pursue 622
    conduct 692
    pastime 840
  – the game 939

– into the hands of 709
– havoc 659
– hide and seek 528, 623
– a joke 853
give – to the imagination
  515
– of light 420
– the monkey 499
– off 545
– a part
  false 544
  drama 599
  action 680
– one's part 625, 692
– second fiddle 34, 749
– one a trick 509, 545
– tricks with 699, 702
– truant 623
– upon 545, 856
– with 460
– upon words
  misinterpret 523
  neology 563
  wit 842
play-boy 818
play-day 840
played out
  end 67
  fatigue 688
  completion 729
  failure 732
player
  musician 416
  actor 599
  – piano 417
playfellow 890
playful 836
  – imagination 515
playground 728, 840
play-house 599
playmate 890
playsome 836
plaything
  trifle 643
  toy 840
  make a – of 749
playwright 599
plea
  defence 462
  argument 476
  excuse **617**
  vindication 937
  lawsuit 969
plead *argue* 467
  plea 617
  beg 765
  – one's cause 937

- guilty 950
pleader *lawyer* 968
pleading, special – 477
pleadings 969
pleasance 189, 840
pleasant
agreeable 829
amusing 840
witty 842
make things –
deceive 545
induce 615
please 829
flatter 933
pleasantry 840, 842
please 829
as you – 743
do what one –s 748
if you –
obedience 743
consent 762
request 765
– onself 943
pleasurableness 829
pleasure
physical - **377**
will 600
moral - **827**
dissipation 954
at – 600
at one's – 737
during – 108*a*
give – 829
man of – 954*a*
make a toil of – 682
take one's – 840
will and – 600
with –
willingly 602
pleasure-giving 829
pleasure-ground
demesne 189
amusement 840
pleat 258
plebeian 851, 876
plébiscite 480, 609
plectrum 417
plectuntur Achivi 739
pledge *affirmation* 535
promise 768
security 771
borrow 788
drink to 883, 894
hold in – 771
take the – 771, 958
– oneself 768
– one's word 768

pledget 263, 662
Pleiades 72, 318
plenary 31, 52
plenipotent 157
plenipotentiary
consignee 758
deputy 759
plenitude 639
in the – of power 159
plenty
multitude 102
sufficient 639
– to do 682
plenum *substance* 3
matter 316
pleonasm
repetition 104
diffuseness 573
redundance 641
plerophory 484
plethora 64
plexal 219
plexus 219
pliable 324
pliant *soft* 324
irresolute 605
facile 705
servile 886
plicature 258
pliers 301, 781
plight *state* 7
promise 768
security 771
evil – 735
– one's faith 902
– one's troth 768, 902
plighted love 897, 902
Plimsoll mark 466
plinth 211, 215
plod *journey* 266
slow 275
persevere 604*a*
work 682
– along 143
plodding 604*a*, 682
dull 843
plot - *of ground* 181
plain 344
story 594
plan 626
realty 780
the – thickens
assemblage 72
plough *furrow* 259
agriculture 371
– the ground 673
– in 228

– the waves 267
– one's way 266
ploughboy
commonalty 876
ploughman 371
ploughshare 253
pluck *cheat* 545
resolution 604
persevere 604*a*
reject 610
take 789
steal 791
courage 861
– up courage 861
– a crow with 932
– out 301
plug 261, 263
– along 143
plum *number* 98
sweet 396
money 800
plumage 256
plumb *vertical* 212
close 261
measure 466
plumber 690
plumb-line 212
plum-coloured 437
plume *feather* 256
ornament 847
borrowed –s 788
– oneself 878
plume
coup de – 590
nom de – 565
plumigerous 256
plummet 208, 212
plumose 256
plump
instantaneous 113
fat 192
plunge 310
unexpected 508
– down 306
– upon 292
plumper
expansion 194
vote 609
plunder 791, 793
plunderer 792
plunge
revolution 146
insert 300
dive 306, **310**
immerse 337
hurry 684
– into difficulties 704

– into dissipation 954
– headlong 684
– into 676
– in medias res 576, 604
– into sorrow 830
plunged
– in debt 806
– in grief 828
plunger 621
plurality 100
plus 37
plus fours 225
plush 256
Pluto 979, 982
  realms of – 982
Plutocracy 803
plutonic 382
Plutus 803
pluvial 348
ply *layer* 204
  fold 258
  use 677
  exert 686
  request 765
  – one's task 680
  – one's trade 625
  – a trade 794
Plymouth Brother 984
p.m. 114, 126
pneumatics 334, 338
pneumatology 450
pneumatoscopic 317
poach 791, 964
poacher 792
poachy 345
pock 250
pocket *place* 184
  pouch 191
  diminutive 193
  receive 785
  take 789
  money 800
  treasury 802
  brook 826
  button up one's – 808
  out of – 776, 806
  touch the – 800
  – the affront 725, 918
pocket-book 551
pocket-handkerchief 225
pocket-money 800
pocket-pistol
  bottle 191
pococurante 823, 866
pocula, inter – 959
pod 191, 223
podestà 967

podgy 201
poem 597
  book of –s 593
pœnitentiæ, locus –
  pity 914
  forgive 918
  vindicate 937
  repent 950
poesy 597
poet 597
poetaster 597, 855
poetic *style* 574
poetic frenzy 515
poetry 597
pogrom 361
poignancy
  physical energy 171
  pain 378
  pungency 392
  feeling 821
point *condition* 8
  degree 26
  small 32
  end 67
  term 71
  poignancy 171
  no magnitude 180a
  place 182
  speck 193
  sharp 253
  topic 454
  mark 550
  vigour 574
  intention 620
  wit 842
  punctilio 939
  at the – of 197
  come to the –
  special 79
  attention 457
  reasoning 476
  plain language 576
  culminating – 210
  disputed – 713
  from all –s 180
  full of – 574
  give –s to 27
  go straight to the – 278
  in – *relative* 9
  agreeing 23
  conformable 82
  knotty – 704
  make a – of
  resolution 604
  contention 720
  compulsion 744
  conditions 770

  due 924
  honour 939
  nice – 697
  on the – of 111, 121
  to the – 572, 642
  – an antithesis 578
  – at *direction* 278
  direct attention 457
  intend 620
  discourtesy 895
  disrespect 929
  censure 932
  – of attack 716
  at the – of the bayonet 173
  – of the compass 278
  – of convergence 74
  – of death 360
  – in dispute 461
  – of etiquette 852
  in – of fact 1
  – the finger of scorn 930
  – of honour 939
  – of land 250
  – a moral 537
  – out 155, 457, 527
  – to – race 720
  at the – of the sword
  violence 173
  severity 739
  compulsion 744
  – to *attribute* 155
  direction 278
  probable 472
  predict 511
  mean 516
  – of view 441, 448
point-blank
  direct 278
  plain language 576
  refusal 764
point-champain 874
point d'appui 215
pointed
  great 31
  sharp 253
  affirmation 535
  marked 550
  concise 572
  language 574
pointedly
  intention 620
pointer *dog* 366
  indicator 550
pointless 843
poise 27, 319, 852
  mental – 498
poison 659, 663

- gas 722, 727
poisoned 655
  commend the – chalice 544
poisonous 657, 665
poke
  pocket 191
  pig in a –
  uncertain 475
  chance 621
  dawdle 683
  rash 863
  – at 276, 716
  – the fire 384
  – fun at 856
  – one's nose in 682
  – out *project* 250
poker 386
  cards 840
polacca 273
polacre 273
polar 210
  cold 383
  – co-ordinates 466
polarization 420
polariscope 455
polarity
  duality 89
  counteraction 179
  contraposition 237
pole *measure of length* 200
  tall 206
  summit 210
  axis 222
  punt 267
  rotation 312
  greasy – 840
  opposite –s 237
  from – to pole 180
pole-axe 727
polecat 401
polemic
  discussion 476
  discord 713
  contention 720
  combatant 726
polemoscope 445
pole-star 550, 693
police 965
  – court 966
  – magistrate 967
policeman 664, 965
policy 626, 692
polish *smooth* 255
  rub 331
  furbish 658
  beauty 845

  ornament 847
  taste 850
  politeness 894
  – off *finish* 729
Polish bank 840
polished
  – *language* 578
  fashionable 852
  polite 894
polisson 949
polite 894
  offensive to ears – 579
  – literature 560
  – society 852
politic *wise* 498
  cunning 702
  cautious 864
  body –
  mankind 372
  government 737
political economy 692
politician
  director 694
  proficient 700
politics 702
polity *conduct* 692
  authority 737
  duty 926
polka 840
poll 85, 609
  parrot 584
  – tax 812
pollard 193, 201
  tree 367
pollute *soil* 653
  corrupt 659
  disgrace 874
pollution
  disease 655
  vice 945
Pollyanna 858
polo 840
polonaise 840
poltroon 862
polyandry 903
polychord 417
polychromatic 428, 440
polychrome 440, 556
polygamy 903
polygastric 191
polyglot 522, 560
polygon
  buildings 189
  figure 244
polygraphy 590
polylogy 573
polymorphic 81

polyphonism 580
polypus 250
polyscope 445
polysyllable 561
polytheism 984
pomade 356
pomatum 356
pommel
  support 215
  round 249
  beat 972
Pomona 369
pomp 882
pom-pom 727
pomposity 882
pompous
  language 577
poncho 225
pond 343, 636
  fish – 370
ponder 451
ponderable 316, 319
ponderation 319, 480
ponderous 319
  – *style* 574, 579
  dull 843
pondus fumo, dare – 481
poniard 727
pons asinorum 519, 704
pontifical 995
pontificals 999
pontificate 995
pontiff 996
pontoon
  vehicle 272
  boat 273
  way 627
pony 271
poodle 366
pooh, pooh!
  unimportance 643
  contempt 930
pool *lake* 343
  combination 709
  prize 775
  billiards 840
poop 235
poor *weak* 160
  – *reasoning* 477
  – *style* 575
  insufficient 640
  trifling 643
  indigent 804
  unhappy 828
  cut a – figure 874
  – hand 701
  – head 499

– house 189
– man 804
– in spirit 881
– stick 501
– thing 914
poorly 160, 655
– off 804
poor-spirited 862
pop *noise* 406
  unexpected 508
– at 716
– in *ingress* 294
  insertion 300
– off *die* 360
– a question 461
– the question
  request 765
  endearment 902
– upon *arrive* 292
  discover 480a
Pope
  infallibility 474
  priest 996
Popedom 995
Pope Joan 840
Popery 984
pop-gun *trifle* 643
popinjay 854
poplar *tall* 206
poppy *sedative* 174
populace 876
popular
  in demand 865
  celebrated 873
  favourite 897
  approved 931
– opinion 488
popularis, aura – 873
popularize
  render intelligible 518
  facilitate 705
  make pleasant 829
populate 184
population 188, **372**
populi, vox –
  publication 531
  election 609
  authority 737
populous
  crowded 72
  multitude 102
  presence 186
porcelain
  baked 384
  sculpture 557
porch *entrance* 66
  lobby 191

mouth 231
opening 260
church 1000
porcupine 253, 901
pore *opening* 260
  egress 295
  conduit 350
– over *look* 441
  apply the mind 457
  learn 539
porism 461, 480
pornographic 961
porous 260
porpoise 192
porridge 298
porringer 191
port *abode* 189
  sinistral 239
  gait 264
  arrival 292
  carriage 448
  harbour 666
in – 664
make – 666
– admiral 745
– fire 388
– wine 959
portable *small* 193
  transferable 270
  light 320
portage 270
portal *entrance* 66
  mouth 231
  opening 260
portative 193, 270
portcullis 706, 717
  let down the – 666
porte-monnaie 802
portend 511
portent 512
portentous
  prophetic 511
  fearful 860
porter *janitor* 263
  carrier 271, 690
porterage 270
portfolio *case* 191
  book 593
  magazine 636
  direction 693
  insignia 747
porthole 260
portico 66, 191
portion 51, 786
– out 786
portly 192
portmanteau 191

– word 116
portrait 554
portrait painter 559
portrait painting 556
portraiture 554, 556
portray 19, 554
portreeve 745, 965
posada 189
pose *situation* 183
  form 240
  puzzle 475
  difficulty 704
  affectation 855
– as 554
  strike a – 855
posited 184
position
  circumstances 8
  term 71
  situation 183
  proposition 514
  assertion 535
– in society 873
positive *real* 1
  great 31
  strict 32
  certain 474
  narrow-minded 481
  belief 484
  unequivocal 518
  assertion 535
  obstinate 606
  absolute 739
  Philosophie – 316
– colour 428
– degree 31
– fact 474
– quantity 84
positivism 984, 989
posnet 191
posology 662
posse 72, 712
  in – 470
– comitatûs
  collection 72
  army 726
  authority 737
  jurisdiction 965
possess 777
– knowledge 490
– the mind 484
– oneself of 789
– the soul 824
– a state 7
possessed with a devil 503
possession **777**, 780
  sorcery 992

come into – 775, 783
in one's – 777
person in – 779
put one in – of 527
remain in – of the field
731
possessor 779
posset 298
possibility
chance 156
liability 177
may be **470**
property 780
– upon a possibility 475
possidetis, uti –
possession 777
retention 781
post *fastening* 45
situation 183
location 184
support 215
transmit 270
swift 274
publish 531
mail 534
beacon 550
record 551
employment 625
accounts 811
stigmatize 874
punish 972
at one's –
persist 604a
prepared 673
on duty 926
sign – 550
stand like a – 265
– hoc ergo propter hoc 477
drive from – to pillar 704
postal order 800
postboy 268
post-card 592
postcenal 117
post-chaise 272
postcibal 117
post-date 115
post-diluvial 117
poster 531
posterior
in order 63
in time 117
in space 235
posteriority 117
posterity 121, **167**
hand down to – 551, 873
postern *portal* 66
back 235

opening 260
post-existence 152
postfix 37
post-graduate 492
– student 541
post-haste
swift 274
haste 684
rash 863
post-horse 271
posthumous 117, 133
– fame 873
postilion 268, 694
postliminious 117, 133
postman 534
post-meridiem 126
post-mortem 360, 363
postnate 117
post-obit 360, 363
post-office 534
– order 800
– red 434
postpone 133
postprandial 117
postscript 39, 65
postulant
asking 765
petitioner 767
nun 996
postulate 496
reasoning 476
supposition 514
postulation
supposition 514
request 765
posture
circumstance **8**
situation 183
form 240
posture-master 599, 844
post-war 116
posy *motto* 550
poem 597
flowers 847
pot *much* 31
mug 191
heat 384
saucepan 386
preserve 670
death in the – 657
go to – 162, 732
keep the – boiling 143,
682
make the – boil 775
le – au lait
imagination 515
hope 858

potable 298
potage 298
potager 191
potation 298, 959
pot-bellied 194
pot-companion 890
potency 157
potent 157, 159
potentate 745
potential
inexistent 2
potentiality 157, 470
pot-herbs 393
pother *disorder* 59
feeling 821
excitement 825
annoyance 830
pot-hooks 590
pot-house 189
pot-hunter 767
potion
beverage 298
medicine 662
cordial 992
pot-luck *eating* 298
chance 621
non-preparation 674
take – with 892
Potosi 803
pot-pourri
mixture 41
fragrance 400
music 415
pottage 298
pottering 682, 683
pottery *baked* 384
art 557
pottle 191
potulent 298, 959
pot-valiant 959
potwalloper 876
pouch 191
poudre:
qui n'a pas inventé la –
501, 701
jeter de la – aux yeux 442
poultice *pulp* 354
remedy 662
relief 834
poultry 298, 366
pounce upon
unexpected 508
attack 716
seize 789
pound *inclose* 232
weight 319
bruise 330

imprison 752
- together 41
poundage 813
pounds, shillings, and pence 800
pour *emerge* 295
   stream 348
   sufficient 639
it never rains but it -s 641
- out blood like water 361
- a broadside into 716
- forth *eject* 297
   speak 582
   loquacity 584
- forth like water 818
- in *converge* 290
   ingress 294
   sufficiency 639
- on *lavish* 784
- with rain 348
- water into a sieve 638, 818
- out 295, 297
pourboire 784
pourparler
   interlocution 588
   advice 695
   council 696
pout *project* 250
   sad 837
   discourteous 895
   irate 900
   sulky 901*a*
poverty
   insufficiency 640
   unimportance 643
   indigence **804**
- of intellect 499
powder 330
   cosmetics 847
food for - 726
gun- 727
smell - 722
keep one's - dry 673
- and shot 727
waste - 638
not worth - 645
powdered
   variegated 440
powdering
   ornament 847
power
   much 31, 102
   numerical 84
   efficacy **157**
   loud 404
- *of style* 574

authority 737
do all in one's - 686
give - 760
in the - of
   authority 737
   subjection 749
literary - 569
- of attorney 755
- behind the throne 694
- of money 800
powerful 159, 171
- voice 580
powerless 158, 160
powers that be 745
pow-wow 588, 696
pox 655
praam 273
practicable 470, 644
practical
   acting 170
   expedient 646
   executive 692
- joke
   absurdity 497
   deception 545
   ridicule 856
   disrespect 929
- knowledge 698
practically
   intrinsically 5
practice
   arithmetic 85
   training 537
   habit 613
   conduct 692
in - *prepared* 673
   skilled 698
put in - *use* 677
   action 680
   conduct 692
   complete 729
out of - 699
- of medicine 662
practise *train* 537
   use 677
   act 680
- at the bar 968
- on one's credulity 545
- upon
   experiment 463
   deceive 545
practised
   skilled 698
- eye 700
- hand 700
practitioner
   medical - 662

doer 690
præcognita 467
prænomen 564
prætor 967
pragmatical 855, 880
Pragmatic Sanction 769
pragmatism 677
prahu 273
prairie *space* 180
   plain 344
   vegetation 367
praise *thanks* 916
   commendation 931
   worship 990
praiseworthy 931, 944
prame 273
prance 266, 315
prandial 298
prank *caprice* 608
   amusement 840
   adorn 847
prate 584
prattle 582, 584
pravity 945
praxis
   grammar 567
   action 680
Praxiteles 559
pray 765, 990
prayer 765, 990
house of - 1000
prayer-book 998
preach *teach* 537
   speak 582
   predication 998
- to the winds 645
- to the wise 538
preacher
   teacher 540
   priest 996
preachment 998
preadamite 124, 130
preamble 64
preapprehension 481
prebend 995
prebendary 996
precarious
   transient 111
   uncertain 475
   dangerous 665
precatory 765
precaution
   care 459
   expedient 626
   safety 664
   preparation 673
precede

superior 33
- *in order* 62
- *in time* 116
- *in motion* 280
precedence 873
precedent [*see* precede]
  prototype 22
  precursor 64
  habit 613
  legal decision 969
follow -s 82
precentor 694, 996
precept *adage* 496
  maxim **697**
  order 741
  permit 760
preceptor 540
precession 62, **280**
précieuse ridicule 855
precinct *region* 181
  place 182
  environs 227
  boundary 233
precious *great* 31
  excellent 648
  valuable 814
  beloved 897
  - *metals* 800
  - *stone* 648, 847
preciosity 578
precipice
  vertical 212
  slope 217
  dangerous 667
on the verge of a - 665
precipitancy 684, 863
precipitate
  early 132
  sink 308
  consolidate 321
  refuse 653
  haste 684
  rash 863
  - *oneself* 306
precipitous 217
précis 596
precise *exact* 494
precisely
  literally 19
  assent 488
precisianism
  affectation 855
  heterodoxy 984
  over-religious 988
preclude 55, 706
precocious
  early 132

immature 674
pert 885
rude 895
precognition
  forethought 490
  knowledge 510
preconceived idea 481
preconception 481
preconcert 611, 626
preconcertation 673
precursor
  - *in order* 62, **64**
  - *in time* 116
  predict 511
predatory 789, 791
predecessor 64
predeliberation 510, 611
predella 215
predesigned 611
predestination
  fate 152
  necessity 601
  predetermination 611
  Deity 976
predetermination **611**
predial
  land 342
  agriculture 371
  manorial 780
predicament 8, 75
predicate
  affirm 535
  preach 998
prediction **511**
predilection
  bias 481
  affection 820
  desire 865
predispose 615, 673
predisposed
  willing 602
predisposition 176, 820
predominant 175, 737
predominate 33
pre-eminent 33, 873
pre-emption 795
preen 847
pre-engage 132
pre-engagement 768
pre-establish 626
pre-examine 461
pre-exist 1, 116
preface 62, 64
prefect 745, 759
prefecture 737
prefer *choose* 609
  - *a claim* 969

- *a petition* 765
preference 62
preferment
  improvement 658
  ecclesiastical - 995
prefigure 511
prefix 62, 64
  letter 561
pre-glacial 124
pregnable 158
pregnant
  producing 161
  productive 168
  predicting 511
  - *style* 572
  important 642
  - *with meaning* 516
prehensile 789
prehension 789
pre-historic 124
pre-instruct 537
prejudge 481
prejudicate 481
prejudice ▬▬
  misjudge 481
  evil 619
  detriment 659
prejudicial 481, 649
prelacy 995
prelate 996
prelation 609
prelection 537, 582
prelector 540
preliminaries:
  settle - 673
  - of peace 723
preliminary 62, 64
prelude 62, 64
  beginning 66
  music 415
premature 132, 674
premeditate 611, 620
prémices 154
premier 694, 759
  - *pas* 66
premiership 693
premise *prefix* 62
  precede 116
  announce 511
premises
  precursor 64
  prior 116
  ground 182
  evidence 467
  logic 476
premium
  debt 805

receipt 810
reward 973
at a – 814
premonish 668
premonitory 511, 668
Premonstratensian 996
premonstration
appearance 448
prediction 511
manifestation 525
premunire 742, 974
prendre la balle au bond
134
prenotion
misjudgment 481
foresight 510
prensation 789
prentice 541
prenticeship 539
preoccupancy
possession 777
preoccupation
inattention 458
preoption 609
preordain 152, 601
preparation 673
music 413
instruction 537
in – 730
in course of – 626
preparatory
preceding 62
prepared *expectant* 507
ready 698
prepare the way
facilitate 705
preparing
destined 152
prepense
spontaneous 600
predetermined 611
intended 620
malice – 907
prepollence 157
πρέπεον, τέο – 850, 926
preponderance
superiority 33
influence 175
dominance 737
prepossessed
obstinate 606
prepossessing 829
prepossession
prejudice 481
possession 777
preposterous
great 31

absurd 497
exaggerated 549
ridiculous 853
undue 925
prepotency 157
pre-Raphaelite 122, 124,
556
pre-require 630
pre-resolve 611
prerogative 737, 924
presage 511, 512
presbyopia 443
presbyter 996
Presbyterian 984
presbytery 995, 996, 1000
prescience 510
prescious 511
prescribe *direct* 693
advice 695
order 741
entitle 924
enjoin 926
prescript 697, 741
prescription
remedy 662
prescriptive *old* 124
unchanged 141
habitual 613
due 924
presence
in space **186**
appearance 448
breeding 894
in the – of
near 197
real – 998
saving one's – 928
– of God 981
– of mind 826, 864
presence-chamber 191
present
– *in time* 118
– *in space* 186
offer 763
give 784
church preferment 995
at – 118
these –s 590, 592
– arms 894, 928
– a bold front 861
– a front 719
– itself *event* 151
visible 446
thought 451
– oneself
presence 186
offer 763

courtesy 894
– to the mind 457, 505
– time **118**
instant 113
– to the view 448
presentable 852
presentation 883, 894
presentiment
instinct 477
prejudgment 481
foresight 510
presently 132
presentment
information 527
law proceeding 969
preservation
continuance 141
conservation **670**
Divine attributes 976
preserve *sweets* 396
preserver 664
preshow 511
preside 693, 737
presidency 737
president 694, 745
press *crowd* 72
closet 191
weight 319
public – 531
printing 591
book 593
move 615
compel 744
offer 763
solicit 765
go to – 591
under – of 744
writer for the – 593
– of business 682
– one hard 716
– in 300
– on *course* 109
progression 282
haste 684
– into the service 677, 707
– out 301
press-agent 599
pressed: hard – 704
– for time 684
press-gang 965
pressing *need* 630
urgent 642
pressure *power* 157
influence 175
weight 319
urgency 642
exertion 686

adversity 735
centre of – 222
high – 824
work under – 684
Prester John 515
prestidigitation 545
prestidigitator 548
prestige *bias* 481
  authority 737
  fascination 865
  fame 873
prestigiation 545
prestissimo 415
presto
  instantly 113
  music 415
prestriction 442
presumable 472
presume
  misjudge 481
  believe 484
  suppose 514
  hope 858
  pride 878
presumption [*see* presume]
  probability 472
  expectation 507
  rashness 863
  arrogance 885
  unlawfulness 925
presumptive
  probable 472
  supposed 514
  due 924
heir – 779
– evidence
  evidence 467
  probability 472
presumptuous 885
presuppose
  misjudge 481
  suppose 514
presurmise 510, 514
pretence
  imitation 19
  falsehood 544
  untruth 546
  excuse 617
  ostentation 882
  boast 884
pretend *assert* 535
  simulate 544, 546
pretended 545
pretender
  deceiver 548
  braggart 884
  unentitled 925

pretending 544
pretension
  ornament 577
  affectation 855
  due 924
pretentious
  affected 855
  vain 880
  ostentatious 882
  boasting 884
  undue 925
preterite 121
preterition 122
preterlapsed 122
pretermit 460
preternatural 83
preterperfect 122
pretext 546, 617
pretty
  much 31
  imperfectly 651
  beautiful 845
  – fellow 501
  – good 651
  – kettle of fish, pass &c.
    59, 704
  – well *much* 31
  little 32
  trifling 643
preux chevalier 939
prevail *exist* 1
  superior 33
  general 78
  influence 175
  habit 613
  succeed 731
  – upon 615
prevailing 78
  – taste 852
prevalence [*see* prevail]
prevaricate 544
prévenance 894
prevenient 62, 132
prevention
  prejudice 481
  hindrance 706
  – of waste 817
preventive 55
preventorium 656
previous 116
  move the – question 624
  not within – experience
    137
prevision 510
pre-war 116
prewarn 668
prey *food* 298

quarry 620
booty 793
victim 732, 828
fall a – to
  be defeated 732
  subjection 749
– to grief 828
– to melancholy 837
– on the mind
  excite 824
  regret 833
  fear 860
– on the spirits 837
price
  consideration 147
  value 648
  money **812**
  reward 973
at any – 604a
beyond – 814
cheap at the – 815
of great –
  good 648
  dear 814
have one's – 812
price-current 812
priceless
  valueless 645
  dear 814
prick *sharp* 253
  hole 260
  sting 378
  sensation of touch 380
  incite 615
  mental suffering 830
  kick against the –s
  useless 645
  resistance 719
– up one's ears
  hear 418
  curiosity 455
  attention 457
  expect 707
prickle 253, 380
pride
  ornament 847
  loftiness **878**
take a – in 878
prie-dieu 211
priest 996
priestcraft 995
priesthood 995, 996
priest-ridden 988, 995
prig *steal* 791
  puppy 854
  affected 855
  blusterer 887

priggish 855, 880
prim *affected* 855
  fastidious 868
  proud 878
prima: – donna
  actress 599
  important 642
  proficient 700
  – facie *sight* 441
  appearance 448
  probable 472
  - *meaning* 516
  manifest 525
primacy
  superiority 33
  celebrity 873
  church 995
primary
  original 20
  cause 153
  important 642
  - *colour* 428
  - *education* 537
primarily 66
primate 996
primates 875
prime
  primeval 124
  early 132
  teach 537
  important 642
  excellent 648
  prepare 673
  in one's – 131
  in the – of manhood 159
  - cost *price* 812
  cheap 815
  - of life *youth* 127
  adolescence 131
  - and load 673
  - minister 694
  - of the morning 125
  - mover 153
  - number 84
prime constituent 1
primed
  skilled 698
  tipsy 959
primer 542
primeval 124
  - forest 367
primigenous 124
primitive 124, 153
  - *colour* 428
primogenital 66
primogeniture
  old 124

  age 128
  posterity 167
primordial 20, 124, 153
primordinate 124
primrose-coloured 436
primum:
  - mobile 153, 615
primus inter pares 33
prince
  perfection 650
  master 745
  nobility 875
  - of darkness 978
princely
  authoritative 737
  liberal 816
  famous 873
  noble 875
  generous 942
princeps
  facile – 33
princess 745, 875
principal
  important 642
  director 694
  - part 31, 50
principality 181, 780
principally 33
principia 66, 496
principiis obstare 673
principle
  intrinsic 5
  rule 80
  cause 153
  element 316
  idea 453
  reasoning 476
  tenet 484
  maxim 496
  motive 615
  probity 939
  on – 615
  want of – 945
principled, high- 939
prink 847, 882
print *copy* 21
  mark 550
  engraving 558
  letter-press 591
  out of – 552
printer 591
printing 531, **591**
  - telegraph 553
prior
  - *in order* 62
  - *in time* 116
  clergy 996

priori reasoning, a – 476
priority 116, 234
priory 1000
Priscian's head, break –
  568
prism
  angularity 244
  optical 445
  see through a – 443
prismatic
  colour 428
  variegated 440
prison 752
  cast into – 751
  in – 754
prisoner 754, 938
  take – 751, 789
prison-house
  secrets of the – 529, 533
pristine 20, 122
prithee 765
prittle-prattle 588
private *special* 79
  hidden 528
  secluded 893
  to gain some – ends 943
  in – 528
  keep – 881
  talk to in – 586, 588
  - road 627
  - soldier 726
privateer 726, 792
privateering 791
privately 881
privation 776, 804
privative 789
privilege
  freedom 748
  permission 760
  exemption 777a
  due 924
privity 490
privy *hidden* 528
  latrines 653
  - to 490
Privy Council 966
prize *good* 618
  palm 733
  gain 775
  booty 793
  receipt 810
  love 897
  approve 931
  reward 973
  win the – 731
  - open 173
prizer 767

prize-fighter 726
prize-fighting 720
prizeman 700
pro: – and con 476, 615
– formâ 82
– hâc vice
special 79
present time 118
occasion 134
seldom 137
– rata 23
– re natâ
circumstances 8
relation 9
special 79
occasion 134
conditions 770
– tanto 26, 32
– tempore 111
proa 273
probability 156, **472**
probable 858
probate 771
Probate Court 966
probation
trial 463
demonstration 478
probationary 463, 675
probationer 541
probative 478
probatum est 478, 931
probe *depth* 208
perforator 262
investigate 461
measure 466
probity 939
problem *topic* 454
question 461
enigma 533
problematical 475
proboscis 250
procacity
insolence 885
rudeness 895
irascibility 901
procedure
method 627
action 680
conduct 692
proceed *time* 109
advance 282
– from 154
– with 692
proceeding
incomplete 53
event 151
action 680

not finished 730
course of – 692
proceedings 551
proceeds *gain* 775
money 800
receipts 810
procerity 206
process
projection 250
conduct 692
legal – 963
– *engraving* 558
– *of time* 109
in – *of time* 117
procession
continuity 69
march 266
ceremony 882
processional
rite 998
procès-verbal
record 551
law proceeding 969
prochronism 115
proclaim 531
proclivity 176, 820
proconsul 759
proconsulship 737
procrastination 133, 460, 683
procreant 168
procreate 161, 168
procreator 166
procrustean 82
– *law* 80
Procrustes:
stretch on the bed of – 27
proctor *teacher* 540
officer 694, 965
consignee 758
lawyer 968
proctorship 693
procumbent 213
procuration 170, 755
procurator 694
procure *cause* 153
induce 615
get 775
buy 795
procurement 170
procuress 962
prod 276
prodigal 641, 816
prodigality **818**
prodigious 31, 870
prodigy 83, **872**
– *of learning* 700

prodition 940
prodrome 64
produce
increase 35
cause 153
effect 154
create 161
prolong 200
show 525
stage 599
fruit 775
merchandise 798
– *itself* 446
producer **164**
product
multiple 85
effect 154
harvest 636
gain 775
finished – 154
production 54, **161** [*and see* produce]
productive
cause 153
power 157
inventive 515
profitable 775
productiveness **168**
proem 64
proemial
preceding in order 62
beginning 66
profane
desecrate 679
impious 988
laical 997
– *swearing* 908
profanum vulgus 876
profession
assertion 535
pretence 546
business 625
promise 768
enter a – 625
– *of faith* 484, 983
professional 700
– *mourner* 363, 839
professor 492, 540, 700
professorship 542
proffer 763
proficient
knowledge 490
skill 698
adept **700**
proficuous 644
profile
outline 230

side 236
appearance 448
portraiture 556
profit
  increase 35
  advantage 618
  utility 644
  acquisition 775
  - by *use* 677
  - *sharing* 778
profitable
  useful 644
  good 648
  gainful 775
profitless 646
profligacy 945
profluent
  progressive 282
  stream 348
profound
  great 31
  deep 208
  learned 490
  wise 498
  sagacious 702
  feeling 821
  - *attention* 457
  - *knowledge* 490
  - *secret* 533
profundis, de - 839, 950
profuse
  diffuse style 573
  redundant 641
  prodigal 818
profusion 102, 639
prog 298
progenerate 161
progenitive 163
progenitor 166
progeny 167
prognosis 510, 511, 522, 655
prognostic 511, 512
prognosticate 511
prognostication 507
programme
  catalogue 86
  publication 531
  plan 626
progress
  growth 144
  motion 264
  advance 282
in - *incomplete* 53, 730
make - 282
in mid - 270
- of science 490

- of time 109
progression
  gradation 58
  series 69
  numerical - 84
  motion **282**
progressive
  continuous 69
  course 109
  advancing 282
  improving 658
prohibition **761**
  exclusion 55
  stoppage 706
  teetotalism 953, 958
project *bulge* 250
  impel 284
  intend 620
  plan 626
projectile 727
projection *map* 554
projector
  lantern 423
  film 445
  designer 626
prolation 580, 582
prole, sine - 169
prolegomena 64
prolepsis 64, 115
proletarian 876
prolific 168
prolix 573
prolocutor
  interpreter 524
  teacher 540
  speaker 582
prologue
  precursor 64
  drama 599
prolong
  protract 110
  late 133
  continue 143
  lengthen 200
prolongation 63, 143
prolusion 64
prom 892
promenade 266
  on pier 189
  display 882
Promethean 359
prominent
  convex 250
  manifest 525
  important 642
  eminent 873
prominently 31, 33

promiscuous
  mixed 41
  irregular 59
  indiscriminate 465a
  casual 621
promise
  predict 511
  engage **768**
  hope 858
keep one's - 939
keep - to ear and break to
  hope 545
- oneself 507, 858
promissory 768
- *note* 771, 800
promontory
  height 206
  projection 250
  land 342
promote 153, 658, 707
promoter 626
promotion 658
prompt *early* 132
  remind 505
  tell 527
  induce 615
  active 682
  advise 695
  - *memory* 505
prompter
  drama 599
  motive 615
  adviser 695
promptuary 636
promulgate 531
- a *decree* 741
pronation and supination
218
prone
  horizontal 213
proneness
  tendency 176
  disposition 820
prôner 882, 931
prôneur 935
prong 91
pronounce
  judge 480
  assert 535
  voice 580
  speak 582
pronounced 525
pronouncement 531
pronunciamento 531
pronunciation 580
pronunciative 535
proof *hard* 323

insensible 376
test 463
demonstration 478
printing 591
draft 626
ocular - 446
- against
strong 159
resolute 604
safe 664
defence 717
resistance 719
insensible 823
prop 215, 707
propædeutics 537
propagable 168
propaganda 537, 542
propagandism 537
propagandist 540, 996
propagate
produce 161
be productive 168
publish 531
propel 284
propellant 727
propeller 267, 312
propend 602
propendency
predetermination 611
inclination 820
propense 602
propension 820
propensity 176, 820
proper *special* 79
expedient 646
handsome 845
due 924
- name 564
in its - place 58
show a - spirit 939
the - thing 926
- time 134
properties
theatrical - 225, 599
property *power* 157
possessions **780**
wealth 803
property-man 599
prophecy 511
prophet 513, 996
false -s 986
in the name of the - figs!
497
prophetic 511, 985
Prophets, the - 985
prophylactic
healthful 656

remedy 662
preservative 670
hindrance 706
prophylaxis 670
propinquity 197
propitiate
pacify 723, 724
calm 826
content 831
love 897
pity 914
forgive 918
atone 952
worship 990
propitious
timely 134
beneficial 648
helping 707
prosperous 734
auspicious 858
proplasm 22
proportion
relation 9
degree 26
mathematical 84
symmetry 242
style 578
allotment 786
proportionate
agreeing 23
proportions 180, 192
proposal *plan* 626
propose
suggest 514
broach 535
intend 620
offer 763
offer marriage 912
- a question 461
proposition
supposition 454
reasoning 476
project 626
suggestion 514
offer 763
propound 514, 535
- a question 461
propriâ personâ
in - *speciality* 79
presence 186
proprietary 779
proprietor 779
proprietorship 780
propriety
agreement 23
elegance 578
expedience 646

fashion 852
right 922
duty 926
proprio motu 600
props 599
propter hoc 155
propugn
resist 717
vindicate 937
propulsion 284
propylon 66
prore 234
prorogue 133
proruption 295
prosaic *usual* 82
- *style* 575, 576
dull 843
prosaism *prose* 598
proscenium
front 234
theatre 599
proscribe
interdict 761
banish 893
curse 908
condemn 971
prose
diffuse style 573
prate 584
not verse **598**
- run mad 517, 597
- writer 598
prosecute
pursue 622
act 680
accuse 938
arraign 969
- an inquiry 461
prosecutor 938
proselyte
convert 144, 607
learner 541
proselytism 537
proser 841
prosody 597
prosopopœia 521
prospect
futurity 121
view 448
probability 472
expectation 507
landscape painting 556
good - 858
in - *intended* 620
prospective 121
prospector 463
prospectus *list* 86

foresight 510
compendium 596
scheme 626
prosper 618
prosperity 734
prospicience 510
prosternation
dejection 837
servility 886
prostitute
corrupt 659
misuse 679
impure 961
courtesan 962
prostrate
powerless 158
destroyed 162
low 207
horizontal 213
depress 308
laid up 655
exhausted 688
dejected 837
servile 886
fall – 306
– oneself
servile 886
obeisance 928
worship 990, 991
prostration [*see* prostrate]
submission 725
pain 828
prosy 841, 843
prosyllogism 476
protagonist
actor 599
proficient 700
protasis
precursor 64
beginning 66
maxim 496
protean 149
protect *safe* 664
protective 717
protection
influence 175
defence 717
restrain 751
protected cruiser 726
protector 664, 717
master 745
keeper 753
protectorate 737, 780
protégé *servant* 746
friend 890
proteiform 149
protein 298

semiliquid 352
organic 357
protervity 901
protest *dissent* 489
assert 535
deny 536
refuse 764
deprecate 766
not observe 773
not pay 808
counter – 468
enter a – 766
under – 603, 744
– against 708, 932
protestant 489, 764
Protestant 984
protested bills 808
Proteus 149
prothesis 1000
prothonotary 553
protocol *scheme* 626
compact 769
protogram 572
protoplasm
prototype 22
material 316
organization 357
protoplast 22
prototypal 20
prototype 22
prediction 511
protozoon 366
protract *time* 110
late 133
lengthen 200
diffuse style 573
protreptical 615
protrude 250
protuberance 250
protypify 511
proud 873, 878
– flesh 250
prove
arithmetic 85
turn out 151
try 463
demonstrate 478
affect 821
– one's case
vindication 937
– true 494
provender 298, 637
proverb 496
proverbe *acting* 599
proverbial 490
provide
furnish 637

– against
prepare 673
– against a rainy day 817
provided
conditionally 8
qualification 469
supposition 514
well – 639
– for 803
providence
foresight 510
preparation 673
divine government 976
Providence 976
special – 711
waiter on – 683, 831
provident
careful 459
wise 498
prepared 673
providential
opportune 134
fortunate 734
province
department 75
region 181
abode 189
office 625
provincial [*see* province]
prejudiced 481
vulgar 851
provincialism
neology 563
provision *food* 298
supply **637**
preparation 673
wealth 803
– merchant 637
provisional
circumstances 8
uncertain 475
temporary 111
preparing 673
provisions
conditions 770
proviso 469, 770
provisory 111
provoke *cause* 153
incite 615
excite 824
vex 830
anger 900
– desire 865
– hatred 898
provoquant 824
provost *master* 745
deputy 759

prow 234
prowess 861
prowl *walk* 266
  lurk 528
  – after 622
proximate
  next 63
  near 197
  – cause 153
proximity *near* 197
  adjacent 199
proximo 121
proximus ardet
  danger 665, 667
proxy 634, 759
prude *affected* 855
  chaste 960
prudent
  careful 459
  wise 498
  economical 817
  cautious 864
prudery 855, 868
prudish 739
prune
  take away 38
  lop 201, 371
  repair 658
prunello, leather or – 643
prunes and prisms 855
prurience 865, 961
Prussian blue 438
Prussic acid 663
pry *look* 441
  curiosity 455
  inquire 461
  – into the future 510
Prytaneum 931
psalm 415, 990
psalm-book 998
psalmody 415, 998
psalter 998
psaltery 417
psephomancy 511
pseudo 17, 545
pseudoblepsis 443
pseudonym 565
pseudo-revelation 986
pseudoscope 445
pshaw
  trifling 643
  excitement 825
psychiatry 662
psychical 450
psycho-analysis 662
psychological moment 824
psychology 450

psycho-therapy 662
ptisan 662
ptomaine poisoning 663
ptyalism 229
puberty 127
pubescent 131
public, general – 372
  make – 531
  – enemy 891
  – good 644
  – opinion 488
  – press 531
  – school 542
  – spirit 910
  – welfare 910
publican 637
publication 531
  production 161
  book 593
public-house 189
  go to the – 959
publicist 593, 595, 968
publicity 531
publicly rumoured 532
publico, pro bono – 644,
  910
publish 531
  – the banns 765
publisher 593
puce 433, 437
pucelage *youth* 127
  celibacy 904
  purity 960
Puck 980
  play – 699
pucker *fold* 258
  anger 900
  in a – 824
pudder
  disorder 59
pudding *food* 298
  soft 324
  pulpy 354
  sweets 396
  in – time 132
Pudding, Jack – **599**
puddle 343
pudicity 960
pudor, proh – 874
puerile *boyish* 129
  foolish 499
  feeble 575
  trifling 643
puerperal 161
puff *inflate* 194
  wind 349
  tartlet 396

  exaggerate 482
  advertisement 531
  pant 688
  boast 884
  praise 931
  flatter 933
  – of smoke 330
  – out 194
  – up *vanity* 880
puffed up
  exaggerated 482
  pride 878
puffer 935
puffery 884
puffy 194
pug *short* 201
  dog 366
  pugilist 726
pugh! 643
pugilism 720
pugilist 726
pugilistic 720
pugnacity 720, 901
puisné
  posterior 117
  young 127
puissant 157, 159
puke 297
pukka 494
pulchritude 845
pulcinella 599, 844
pule *cry* 411, 412
  weep 839
pull *superiority* 33
  influence 175
  row 267
  draw 285
  printing 591
  a long and a strong – 709
  strong – 636
  – the check string 142
  – different ways 713
  – down 162, 308
  – about one's ears 308
  – in 751
  – an oar 680
  – out 301
  – to pieces
  separate 44
  destroy 162
  censure 932
  detract 934
  – upon the purse 814
  – by the sleeve 505
  – the strings 631
  – through 660, 707
  – together 709

- towards 288
- up *stop* 142
  rest 265
  root out 301
  reprimand 932
  accuse 969
- the wires 693
pulled down 160, 688
pullet 129
pulley 633
Pullman car 272
pullulate
  produce 161
  multiply 168
  grow 194
pulmonary 349
pulmotor 349
pulp 354
pulpiness 354
pulpit *rostrum* 542
  church 1000
  the – 996
pulsate
  periodic 138
  oscillate 314
  agitate 315
pulsation
  feeling 821
pulse [*see* pulsate]
  vegetable 367
  feel the –
  inquire 461
  test 463
pulsion 276
pultaceous 354
pulverize 330
  destroy 162
  dust 358
pulverulence 330
pulvil 400
pummel [*see* pommel]
pump *shoe* 225
  water supply 348
  inquire 461
  – up 349
pump-room
  house 189
  remedy 662
pun *similarity* 17
  absurdity 497
  ambiguity 520
  wit 842
punce 276
punch *mould* 22
  perforate 260
  perforator 262
  nag 271

strike 276
beverage 298
engrave 558
vigour 574
Punch *buffoon* 844
– and Judy 599, 840
punchbowl
  vessel 191
  hollow 252
  tippling 959
puncheon
  vessel 191
  perforator 262
punchinello 599
punctated 440
punctilio 852
punctilious
  exact 494
  observant 772
  ostentation 882
  scrupulous 939
puncto 882
punctual *early* 132
  periodical 138
  exact 494
  observance 772
  scrupulous 939
punctuation 567
puncture 260
pundit
  learned man 492, 500
  lawyer 968
pungency 392
  physical energy 171
  taste 392
pungent *taste* 392
  odour 398
  vigour 574
  feeling 821
  wit 842
Punica fides 940
punishment 972
punition 972
punk 962
punkah 349
punnet 191
punster 844
punt 267, 273
punter 621
puny 193
pup *infant* 129
  give birth 161
  dog 366
pupil 541
  – of the eye 441
pupilage *youth* 127
  learning 539

pupillari, in statu – 541
puppet *little* 193
  dupe 547
  effigy 554
  auxiliary 711
  tool 746
  make a – of 737
  be the – of 749
puppet-show 599, 840
puppy *dog* 366
  fop 854
  braggart 884
  blusterer 887
puppyism 855
pur: – sang 875
Purana 986
purblind 443, 481
purchase
  support 215
  acquisition 775
  buy **795**
purchase-money 147
purchaser 795
purdah 374, 531
pure *simple* 42
  true 494
  truthful 543
  – *style* 576, 578
  clean 652
  artless 703
  – *taste* 850
  honourable 939
  virtuous 944
  innocent 946
  chaste 960
  devout 987, 990
  – accent 580
  – colour 428
  – and simple 42
purée 298
purely 31, 32
purgation
  cleansing 652
  atonement 952
purgative 652
purgatory
  suffering 828
  atonement 952
  hell 982
purge *cast out* 297
  clean 652
  atone 952
purification 998
purify 652, 658
puris naturalibus, in – 226
purist *style* 578
  affected 855

– practice 692
– remembrance 505
– shape 60
– trim 60, 673
– the way of 470
– a word 582, 588
put out
　destroy 162
　outside 220
　extinguish 385
　darken 421
　distract the attention 458
　uncertain 475
　difficult 704
　discontent 832
– of countenance 874
oneself – of court
　sophistry 477
　bungling 699
– of gear 158
– of one's head 458
– of joint 61
– of one's misery 914
– to nurse 707
– of order 59
put to *attribute* 155
　request 765
– the blush 879
– death 361
– the door 261
– it 704
– one's oath 768
– press 591
– the proof 463
– the question 830
– the rack 830
– rights 60
– sea 293
– shame 874
– silence 581
– the sword 361
– task 677
– use 677
– the vote 609
put up *assemble* 72
　locate 184
　store 636
– to auction 796
– for 865
– a petition, – a prayer,
　765, 990
– for sale 796
– a shutter 424
– the sword 723
– to 615
– with 147, 826
putative

　attributed 155
　believed 484
　supposed 514
putid 643
putrefy 653
putrescence 49
putrid 653
putsch 742
puttee 225
putter 683
putting the weight 840
putty 45
puzzle *uncertain* 475
　conceal 528
　enigma 533
– out 522
puzzled 475, 533
puzzle-headed 499
puzzling 519
pyæmia 655
pyjamas 225
Pylades and Orestes 890
pylon 206
pyramid *heap* 72
　height 206
　point 253
pyramids
　billiards 840
pyre 363
pyriform 249
pyrology 282
pyromancy 511
pyromaniac 384, 504, 913
pryometer 389
pyrotechnics 423
protechny 382
Pyrrhic victory 814
pyrrhonism 487, 989
Pythagorean 953
Pythia *oracle* 513
Python, -ess 513
pyx *vessel* 191, 998
　temple 1000

Q

Q-boat 726
Q.C. 968
Q.E.D. 478
quack *cry* 412
　imposter 548
quackery
　falsehood 544
　want of skill 699
　affectation 855
quacksalver 548

quad 189
quadragesima 956
quadrangle
　four-sided 95
　precinct 182
　house 189
　angular 244
quadrant 244, 247
quadrate with 23
quadratic 95
quadrature
　four 95
　angle 244
quadrennial 95
quadrible 96
quadrifid 97
quadriga 95, 272
quadrilateral
　sides 236
　angles 244
quadrille 840
quadripartition 97
quadrisection 97
quadrivalent 95
quadroon 41
quadruped 366
quadruplet 96
quadruplex 96
quadruplication 96
quære 461
quaff 298
– the bitter cup 828
quaggy 345
quagmire
　marsh 345
　dirty 653
　difficult 704
quail 860, 862
quaint *odd* 83
　pretty 845
　ridiculous 853
quake *oscillate* 314
　shake 315
　cold 383
　fear 860
quakerish 826, 855
Quakerism 984
qualification [*see* qualify]
　power 157
　modification **469**
　skill 698
　discount 813
qualify *change* 140
　modify 469
　deny 536
　teach 537
qualis ab incepto 141

qualities
character 820
quality *nature* 5
power 157
tendency 176
nobility 875
qualm *disbelieve* 485
unwilling 603
fear 860
qualms of conscience 950
quamdiu se bene gesserit
108*a*
quand même
compensating 30
opposed 708
quandary 475, 704
quantity 25, 31, 102
quantum *amount* 25
allotment 786
– *mutatus* 140
– *sufficit* 639
quaquaversum 278
quarantine 664, 751
quarrel 24, 713
– with one's bread and
butter
bungling 699
discontent 832
quarrelsome 901
quarry *object* 620
mine 636
quart 97
quarter *cut up* 44
fourth 95
quadrisection 97
period 108
region 181
locate 184
abode 189
side 236
direction 278
forbearance 740
money 800
mercy 914
give – 914
give no –
kill 361
severe 739
pitiless 914*a*
revenge 919
– of a hundred 98
– upon 184
quarter-day 138
quarter-deck 210
quarterly
periodical 531
quartermaster 637

quartern 95
quarteron 41
quarters *abode* 189
take up one's – 184
quarter sessions 966
quarter-staff
contention 720
weapon 727
quartet *four* 95
music 415
quartic 95
quarto 593
quartz 323
quash 162, 756
quasi *similar* 17
supposed 514
quassia 395
quaternity 95
quatrain 597
quatrefoil 95
quaver *oscillate* 314
shake 315
sound 407
music 413, 416
fear 860
quay 189, 666
edge 231
quean 962
queasiness 867
queasy 868
queen 745
Queen's – Bench
prison 752
court 966
– counsel 968
– English 560
– evidence 529
– highway 627
Queensberry rules 922
queer 83, 853
– fish 857
quell *destroy* 162
moderate 174
quiescence 265
subdue 731
quench *destroy* 162
cool 385
dissuade 616
gratify 829
satiate 869
quenchless 865
querimonious 839
querist 461
quern 330
querulous
complaining 839
fastidious 868

irritable 901
query 461, 485
quest 461
question
inquiry 461
doubt 485
deny 536
in – *event* 151
topic 454
inquiry 461
danger 665
pop the – 902
put to the – 830
– at issue 461
questionable
uncertain 475
doubtful 485
disreputable 874
dishonest 939
questionary 461
questioner 455
questionist 541
questionless
certain 541
questionnaire 461
questor 801
queue 65, 214
quib 856
quibble
sophistry 477
unmeaning 517
equivocation 520
falsehood 544
wit 842
verbal –
absurdity 497
quick *transient* 111
rapid 274
alive 359
intelligent 498
active 682
skilful 698
feeling 821
irascible 901
cut to the – 824
probe to the – 461
sting to the – 830, 900
to the – 375, 822
touch to the – 822, 824
– ear 418
– eye 441
– as a flash 113
– succession 136
– time 274
– as thought 113
quicken *work* 170
violence 173

R

Ra 423, 979
R's, three – 537
rabbet 43
Rabbi 996
Rabbist 984
rabbit
  productive 168
rabble 72, 876
rabid *insane* 502
  emotion 821
  eager 865
  angry 900
rabies 503
raccroc 156
race *relation* 11
  sequence 69
  kind 75
  lineage 166
  run 274
  stream 348
  conduit 350
  pungency 392
  course 622
  business 625
  haste 684
  career 692
  opposition 708
  contention 720
  run a – 720
  run in a – 680
  run one's – 729
  one's – is run 360
  – prejudice 479
race-course 728
racehorse
  horse 271
  swift 274
racing car 272
rack *receptacle* 191
  frame 215
  cloud 353
  physical pain 378
  purify 652
  moral pain 828
  torture 830
  punish 972
  instrument of torture 975
  on the – 507
  – one's brains
  thought 451
  imagination 515
  –rent 810
  go to – and ruin 735
racket
  agitation 315

  loud 404
  roll 407
  scheme 626
  discord 713
racket-court 840
racketeer 913
racketeering 361, 792
racketing 682, 840
rackets 840
rackety *loud* 404
raconteur 594
racy *strong* 171
  pungent 392
  - *style* 574
  feeling 821
raddle *weave* 219
raddled *tipsy* 959
radiance *light* 420
  beauty 845
radiant
  diverging 291
  glorious 873
  – *heat* 420
radiate 73, 291
radiation 420
radiator 386
radical
  essential 5
  complete 52
  algebraic root 84
  cause 153
  important 642
  reformer 658
  party 712
  – *change* 146
  – *cure* 662
  – *reform* 658
radically 31
radication 613
radio 532
radio-active 171
radio-activity 420
radiogram
  wireless 532
  X-ray 554
radio-graph 421, 554
radiometer 420, 445
radiomicrometer 389
radiophone 418
radio star 899
radiotelegraph 534
radiotelephone 534
radium 423
radius 200, 202
radix 153
radoter 499
radoteur 501

raff 653, 876
raffle 156
Raffles
  thief 792
raft 273
rafter 215
rag 32
  tease 830, 856, 929
ragamuffin 876
rage *violence* 173
  influence 175
  excitement 824, 825
  fashion 852
  desire 865
  wrath 900
  the battle –s 722
ragged 226
ragoût 41, 298
rag-picker 876
rags *clothes* 225
  useless 645
  do to – 384
  tear to – 162
  worn to – 659
ragtime 415, 473
raid 716, 791
rail *inclosure* 232
  prison 752
  – at 932
  – in
  circumscribe 229
  restrain 751
railing 232
raillerie, ne pas entendre
  – 900
raillery 856
railway 627
  – *speed* 274
  – *station* 292
raiment 225
rain *stream* 348
  sufficient 639
  – or shine 474, 604
rainbow 440
raincoat 225
rainless 340
rains but it pours, never –
  641
rainy day 735
  provide against a – 673,
  817
rainy season 348
raise *increase* 35
  produce 161
  erect 212
  elevate 307
  excite 824

- alarm 860
- anger 900
- one's banner 722
- a cry 531
- a dust 682
- expectations 858
- the finger 550
- funds 775
- one's head
  improve 658
  refresh 689
  prosperity 734
  repute 873
- ghosts 992
- hope 511
- a hue and cry against
  932
- a laugh 840
- the mask 529
- money 788
- a question 461, 485
- a report 531
- a siege 723
- the spirits 836
- spirits from the dead
  992
- a storm 173
- troops 722
- up 212, 824
- the voice 441
- one's voice 535, 932
- the wind 775, 778

raised *convex* 250

raison:
- d'être 620
- de plus 467

raj 737
rajah 745
rajpoot 726
rake *drag* 285
  gardening 371
  clean 652
  profligate 949
  intemperance 954
  libertine 962
- out 301
- up *collect* 72
  extract 301
  recall 505
  excite 824
- up evidence 467
rake-hell 949, 962
raking-fire 716
rakish
  intemperate 954
  licentious 961
rallentando 415

rally *arrange* 60
  improve 658
  restore 660
  ridicule 856
  encourage 861
- round *order* 58
  co-operate 709
rallying: - cry 550, 861
- point 74
ram *impulse* 276
  sheep 366
  male 373
  man-of-war 726
  milk the - 645
- down 261, 321
- in 300
Ramadan 956, 993
ramage 367
ramble *stroll* 266
  wander 279
  folly 499
  delirium 503
  digress 573
rambler 269
rambling 139
ramification *part* 51
  bisection 91
  posterity 167
  filament 205
  symmetry 242
  divergence 291
rammer 263, 276
ramose 242
ramp *slope* 217
  climb 305
  leap 309
rampage 173
rampant
  violent 173
  prevalent 175
  vertical 212
  raised 307
  free 748
  vehement 825
  licentious 961
rampart 717
ramrod 263
ramshackle 665
ranch 780
rancid 401, 653
rancour 907, 919
randan 273
random *casual* 156
  carriage 272
  uncertain 475
  aimless 621
  talk at -

  sophistry 477
  exaggerate 549
  loquacity 584
- *experiment* 463
  chance 621
range *extent* 26
  collocate 60
  series 69
  term 71
  class 75
  space 180
  distance 196
  roam 266
  direction 278
  stove 386
  freedom 748
  out- 196
  long - 196
  within - 197
  -finder 200
- itself 58
- under, - with 76
ranger
  director 694
  keeper 753
  thief 792
rank *have place* 1
  degree 26
  thorough 31
  collocate 60
  row 69
  term 71
  vegetation 365
  fetid 401
  estimate 480
  bad 649
  soldiers 726
  glory 873
  nobility 875
  man of - 875
- and file
  continuity 69
  soldiers 726
  commonalty 876
- marks 745
rankle *unclean* 653
  corrupt 659
  painful 830
  animosity 900
  malevolence 907
  revenge 919
ranks
  fill up the - 660
  risen from the - 876
ransack *seek* 461
  deliver 672
  plunder 791

price 812
atonement 952
- one's brains 451, 515
ransom 672
rant
  unmeaning 517
  exaggeration 549
  diffuse style 573
  turgescence 577
  speech 582
  acting 599
  excitement 825
  boasting 884
ranter *talker* 584
  false piety 988
rantipole 458
rap *blow* 276
  sound 406
  trifle 643
  money 800
  not worth a - 804
  - on the knuckles
  angry 900
  censure 932
  punish 972
  - out *affirm* 535
  voice 580
  speak 582
  - out oaths 885, 908
rapacity
  taking 789
  stealing 791
  avarice 819
  greed 865
rape 791, 961
  - oil 356
rapid 274
  - slope 217
  - strides
  progress 282
  velocity 274
  - succession 136
rapids 348
rapier 727
rapine 791
rapparee 792
rappel 722
rapping, spirit - 992
rapport 9
rapports, sous tous les -
  494
rapprochement 714, 888
rapscallion 949
rapt *attention* 457
  inattention 458
  emotion 821
  - in thought 451

raptorial 789, 791
rapture 827, 897
rapturous 827
rara avis
  exceptional 83
  good 648
  famous 873
rare *exceptional* 83
  few 103
  infrequent 137
  light 322
  excellent 648
raree show 448, 840
rarefaction 194, 322
rari nantes 103
rarity 322
rasa, tabula - 552
rascal 941, 949
rascality 940
rase *obliterate* 552
rash
  skin disease 655
  reckless 863
rasher 204
rashness 863
rasp 330, 331
rasper *difficult* 704
rasure 552
rat *recant* 607
  smell a -
  discover 480a
  doubt 485
rataplan 407
rat-a-tat 407
ratchet 253
rate *degree* 26
  motion 264
  measure 466
  estimation 480
  price, tax 812
  abuse 932
  at a great - 274
rath *early* 132
  fort 717
rather 32, 643
  have - 609
  - good 651
  have - not 867
ratification
  confirm 467
  affirm 488
  consent 762
  compact 769
ratio *relation* 9
  degree 26
  proportion 84
  apportionment 786

ratiocination 476
ration *quantity* 25
  food 298
  provisions 637
  allotment 786
  short -s 956
rational
  - *quantity* 84
  intellectual 450
  judicious 498
  sane 502
rationale *cause* 153
  attribution 155
  answer 462
  interpretation 322
rationalism 476, 989
rationalization 60
rats in the upper story
  503
rattan 975
ratten 158
rattle *noise* 407
  music 417
  prattle 584
  death - 360
  watchman's - 669
  - on 584
rattle-snake 913
rattle-traps 780
rattling 836
  - pace 274
raucity 405, 410
raucous *hoarse* 581
ravage 162, 659
ravages of time 659
rave *madness* 503
  excitement 824, 825
  - against 932
ravel *untwist* 60
  derange 61
  entangle 219
  difficulty 704
ravelin 717
ravelled 59
raven *black* 431
  hoarse 581
  gorge 957
  - for 865
ravening 173, 865
ravenous 789, 865
raver 504
ravine *interval* 198
  narrow 203
  dike 259
  channel 350
raving *mad* 503
  feeling 821

excitement 824, 825
ravish *seize* 789
  please 829
ravished
  pleased 827
ravishment 824
raw *immature* 123
  sensitive 378
  cold 383
  colour 428
  unprepared 674
  unskilled 699
  – head and bloody bones
    860
  – levies 726
  – material 635
raw-boned 203
ray 420
  – of comfort 831
rayah 745
rayless 421
raze 162
  – to the ground 308
razor 253
  cut a whetstone with a –
    638
  misuse 679
  unskilful 699
  keen as a – 821
razzia
  destruction 162
  attack 716
  plunder 791
re, in – 9
reabsorb 296
reach *degree* 26
  equal 27
  distance 196
  fetch 270
  arrive at 292
  river 348
  deceive 545
  grasp 737
  take 789
  within – *near* 197
  possible 470
  – the ear
  hearing 418
  information 527
  – of thought 498
  – to *distance* 196
  length 200
reach-me-down 673
reaction
  compensation 30
  reversion 145
  counteraction 179

recoil 277
  restoration 660
reactionary 145, 607
reactionist 710
read 522, 539
  well – 490
  – a lecture 537
readable 578
reader *teacher* 540
  printer 591
  clergyman 996
readership 542
readily 705
reading
  speciality 79
  knowledge 490
  interpretation 522
  learning 539
  – glass 445
  – in 995
reading-desk 1000
readjust 23, 27
readmit 296
ready
  expecting 507
  willing 602
  useful 644
  prepare 673
  active 682
  skilful 698
  cash 800
  get – 673
  make – 673
  – to burst forth 825
  – made 673
  – memory 505
  – money 800
  – pen 569
  – to sink 824
  – wit 842
reaffirm 535
reagent 463
real *existing* 1
  substantial 3
  – *number* 84
  true 494
  – estate 780
  – property 780
  – security 771
realism 494
realistic 17
realize
  speciality 79
  intellect 450
  think 451
  discover 480a
  believe 484

conceive 490
  imagine 515
  accomplish 729
  acquire 775
  sell 796
really *wonder* 870
realm *region* 181
  people 372
  government 737
  property 780
realness 1
realty 780
ream 593
reamer 262
reanimate
  reproduce 163
  life 359
  resuscitate 660
reap *shorten* 201
  agriculture 371
  take 789
  – the benefit of
  be better for 658
  – and carry 775
  – the fruits
  succeed 731
  acquire 775
  reward 973
  – where one has not sown
    923
  – the whirlwind
  product 154
  failure 732
reappear
  repetition 104
  reproduce 163
  visible 446
  restore 660
rear *sequel* 65
  end 67
  bring up 161
  erect 212
  back **235**
  elevate 307
  teach 537
  in the – 281
  – its head
  manifest 525
  – one's head
  pride 878
rear-admiral 745
reason *cause* 153
  intellect 450
  thought 451
  argue 476
  wisdom 498
  motive 615

by – of 615
feast of – 588
in – *moderate* 174
   right 922
listen to – 498
stand to –
   certain 474
   proof 478
   manifest 525
what's the – ? 461
without rhyme or – 615a
– in a circle 477
– why 153, 615
reasonable
   moderate 174
   probable 472
   judicious 498
   sane 502
   cheap 815
   right 922
– prospect 472
reasoner 476
reasoning 476
reasonless 499
reasons 476
reassemble 72
reassert 535
reassure 858, 861
reasty 401, 653
reave 789
rebate
   subtract 38
   decrement 40a
   moderate 174
   discount 813
rebeck 417
rebel 742
rebellion 715
rebellow 412
rebirth 660
reboation 412
rebound 277, 283
rebours, à –
   reversion 145
   regression 283
   difficult 704
rebuff *recoil* 277
   resist 719
   repulse 732
   refuse 764
   discourtesy 895
   censure 932
rebuild 660
rebuke 932
rebus 533
rebut *answer* 462
   counter evidence 468

confute 479
deny 536
rebutter 462, 969
recalcitrant 719, 742
recalcitrate 277, 719
recalescence 382
recall
   recollect 505
   recant 607
   cancel 756
– to life 660
recant *deny* 536
   retract 607
   resign 756
recapitulate
   enumerate 85
   repeat 104
   describe 594
   summarize 596
recast
   revolution 146
   scheme 626
recede 283, 287
– into the shade 874
receipt
   scheme 626
   prescription 662
   precept 697
   security 771
   payment 807
   – *of money* **810**
   – in full 807
receive *include* 76
   admit 296
   belief 484
   assent 488
   acquire 775
   take in 785
   take 789
   – *money* 810
   welcome 892, 894
   – Christ 987
received *known* 490
   habitual 613
   – *maxim* 496
receiver
   vessel 191
   treasurer 801
   official – 967
   – of stolen goods 792
receiving 785
recension 85
recent 122, 123
receptacle 191
reception
   comprehension 54
   inclusion 76

arrival 292
ingestion **296**
interview 588
receiving 785
welcome 892, 894
warm – 892
reception-room 191
recess
   receptacle 191
   corner 244
   regression 283
   ambush 530
   vacation 687
   retirement 893
recesses
   interior 221
   secret – of one's heart 820
recession
   motion from **287**
Rechabite 958
réchauffé *copy* 21
   repetition 104
   food 298
   made hot 384
   restored 660
recherché 648, 852
recidivation
   regression 283
   relapse 607, 661
recipe *remedy* 662
   precept 697
recipient 191, 785
reciprocal 12, 84
reciprocate
   correlation 12
   interchange 148
   assent 488
   concord 714
   retaliate 718
reciprocity 709
recision 38
recital 415
recitativo 415
recite
   enumerate 85
   speak 582
   narrate 594
reck 459
reckless
   careless 460
   defiant 715
   rash 863
recklessly profuse 818
reckon *count* 85
– among 76
– upon 484, 507
– with 807

677

- without one's host
unskilful 699
fail 732
rash 863
reckoning
numeration 85
measure 466
expectation 507
payment 807
accounts 811
reward 973
day of - 919
out of one's - 704
reclaim *restore* 660
command 741
due 924
atonement 952
reclaimed
penitent 950
recline *lie flat* 213
depress 308
repose 687
- on 215
recluse 893
recognition [*see* recognize]
courtesy 894
thanks 916
means of - 550
recognizable 446, 518
- by 550
recognizance 771
recognize *see* 441
attention 457
discover 480a
assent 488
know 490
remember 505
understand 518
permit 760
recognized
influential 175
customary 613
- maxim 496
recoil *reaction* 179
repercussion **277**
reluctance 603
shun 623
from which reason –s 471
- at *hate* 898
- from *dislike* 867
recollect 505
recommence 66
recommend 695, 931
- itself
approbation 931
recompense [790, 973
reconcile *agree* 23

pacify 723
content 831
forgive 918
- oneself to 826
recondite 519, 528
recondition 660, 790
reconnaissance 441
reconnoitre 441, 461
reconsideration 451
on - 658
reconstitute 660
reconstruct 660
reconvert 660
record 551
break the - 33
court of - 966
gramophone - 551
recorder 553
judge 967
recount 594
recoup 30, 790
recourse 677
recovery
improvement 658
reinstatement 660
getting back 775
restitution 790
- of strength 689
recreant
coward 862
base 940
knave 941
vicious 945
bad man 949
recreation 840
recrement 653
recriminate 932
recrimination 938
recrudescence 661
recruit *strength* 159
learner 541
provision 637
health 654
repair 658
reinstate 660
refresh 689
aid 707
auxiliary 711
soldier 726
beat up for –s 673, 707
rectangle 244
rectangular 214, 244
rectify
straighten 246
improve 658
re-establish 660
rectilinear 346

rectitude 939, 944
rector 694, 996
rectorship 995
rectory 1000
rectus in curiâ 946
reculer pour mieux sauter
673, 702
reculons, à - 283
recumbent 213, 217
recuperation 790
recuperative 660
recur
repeat 104
frequent 136
periodic 138
- to the mind 505
- to 677
recure 660
recursion 292
recurvity 245
recusant
dissenting 489
denying 536
disobedient 742
refusing 764
impenitent 951
heterodox 984
red 434
paint the town - 840
turn - *feeling* 821
- book *list* 86
- coat 726
- cross 662
- flag 668
- hot *great* 31
violent 173
hot 382
emotion 821
excited 824
- letter 550, 883
-letter day
important 642
rest 687
amusement 840
celebration 883
- light 669
- rag to a bull 900
- republican 742
- tape 613
- tapist 694
- and yellow 439
redact 590, 658
redan 717
redargue 479
red cap 271
redden *colour* 434
humble 879

angry 900
reddition
  interpretation 522
  restitution 790
redeem
  compensate 30
  substitute 147
  reinstate 660
  deliver 672
  regain 775
  restore 790
  pay 807
  atone 952
  – from oblivion 505
  – one's pledge 772, 926
Redeemer 976
redemption [*see* redeem]
  liberation 750
  duty 926
  salvation 976
red-handed
  murder 361
  in the act 680
  guilty 947
redict 905
redingote 225
redintegrate 660
redintegratio amoris 607
redivivus 660
redness 434
redolence
  odour 398
  fragrance 400
redouble
  increase 35
  duplication 90
  repeat 104
  – one's efforts 686
redoubt 717
redoubtable 860
redound to
  conduce 176
  – one's honour
  glory 873
  approbation 931
  honour 939
redress *restore* 660
  remedy 662
  reward 973
red-tape 694, 739
reduce *lessen* 36
  – *in number* 103
  weaken 160
  contract 195
  shorten 201
  lower 308
  subdue 731

discount 813
– to ashes 384
– to demonstration 478
– to a mean 29
– to order 60
– to poverty 804
– to powder 330
– the speed 275
– in strength 160
– to subjection 749
– to *convert* 144
– to writing 551
reduced [*see* reduce]
  impoverished 804
  – to the last extremity 665
  – to a skeleton 659
  – to straits 704
reductio ad absurdum
  476, 479
reduction [*see* reduce]
  arithmetical 85
  conversion 144
  at a – 815
  – of temperature 385
redundance
  diffuseness 573
  too much **641**
redundancy 104
reduplication 19, 90
re-echo *imitate* 19
  repeat 104
  resonance 408
reechy 653
reed *weak* 160
  pan 590
  arrow 727
  trust to a broken – 699
  – instrument 417
reef *slacken* 275
  shoal 346
  danger 667
  take in a – 664
  double – topsails 664
reefer 269
reek *gas* 334
  vaporize 336
  liquid 337
  hot 382
  fester 653
reeking 339, 653
reel *rock* 314
  agitate 315, 851
  dance 840
  – back *yield* 725
re-embody
  junction 43
  combination 48

re-enter 245
re-entrant angle 244
re-establish 660
re-estate 660
refashion 163
refect
  strengthen 159
refection
  meal 298
  refreshment 689
  (*restoration* 660)
refectory 191
refer to *relate* 9
  include 76
  attribute 155
  cite 467
  allude 521
  take advice 695
referable 9, 155
referee
  judgment 480
  judge 967
reference [*see* refer]
referendary 967
referendum 480, 609
  ad – 461, 605
referrible 9, 155
refine *clean* 652
  – upon 658
refined *colour* 428
  fashionable 852
refinement
  discrimination 465
  wisdom 498
  elegance 578, 845
  improvement 658
  taste 850
  over– 477
refit 660
reflect *imitate* 19
  think 451
  – *dishonour* 874
  – *light* 420
  – upon *censure* 932
reflecting 498
reflection 408, 453
reflector *mirror* 445
reflex *copy* 21
  recoil 277
  regressive 283
reflexion 21, 277
  light 420
refluence *recoil* 277
  regress 283
reflux *decrease* 36
  recoil 277
  regress 283

current 348
refocillate
strengthen 159
refresh 689
reform *convert* 144
improve 658
reformatory 542, 752
reformer 658
refound 144
refraction
deviation 279
light 420
fallacy of vision 443
refractory
obstinate 606
difficult 704
mutinous 742
ill-tempered 901a
refrain *repetition* 104
poetry 597
avoid 623
do nothing 681
temperate 953
- *from laughter* 837
- *from voting* 609a
refresh
strengthen 159
cool 385
refit 658
restore 660
recruit 689
relieve 834
- *the memory* 505
refreshing 377, 829
refreshment
food 298
recruiting **689**
delight 827
refrigeration
anæsthetic 376
making cold **385**
refrigerator 387
reft 44
refuge **666**
refugee 268, 623
refulgence 420
refund 807
refurbish 673
refusal **764**
pre-emption 795
refuse *remains* 40
useless 645
not consent 764
- *assent* 489
- *to associate with* 893
- *to believe* 487
- *to hear* 460

refute 479
refuted 495
regain 775
- *breath* 689
regal 737
regale *feast* 298
physical pleasure 377
refresh 689
pleasing 829
amusement 840
regalia 747
regality 737
regard
relation 9
view 441
attention 457
judge 480
credit 873
love 897
respect 928
approbation 931
have - *to* 457
merit - 642
pay - *to*
believe 484
honour 873
- *as* 484
regardful 457, 459
regardless 458, 823
regards 894, 928
regatta 720, 840
regency 755
regenerate
reproduce 163
restore 660
piety 987
regeneration
divine function 976
baptismal - 998
regent 745, 759
regicide 361
régime
circumstances **8**
conduct 692
authority 737
ancien - 875
regimen *diet* 298
remedy 662
conduct 692
regiment 72, 726
regimentals 225
region 181
register
arrange 60
list 86
chronicle 114
record 551, 553

registrar 553
registration 551
registry 114
règle: en - 924
regnant 175, 737
regni, anno - 106
regorge 790
regrade 283
regrate 777
regrater 797
regression **283**
regret **833**, 950
express - 952
regretted, to be - 833
reguerdon 973
regular
uniform 16
complete 52
order 58
arrangement 60
rule 80
conformity 82
periodic 138
symmetric 242
habitual 613
by - *intervals* 58
- *return* 138
regulars 726
regulate
adjust 23
arrange 60
direct 693
regulated by
conformity 82
regulation 697, 963
regurgitate
return 283
flow 348
restore 790
rehabilitate 660, 790
rehearse
repeat 104
try 463
describe 594
drama 599
prepare 673
Reichsrath 696
reign 175, 737
- *of terror* 739, 860
reimburse 790, 807
rein 752
- *in* 275, 751
reincarnation 163
reindeer 271
re infectâ 304, 681
reinforce
strengthen 159

restore 660
aid 707
reinforced concrete 635
reinforcement
  addition 37
  adjunct 39
  materials 635
  provision 637
  aid 707
reinless 738
reins [*see* rein]
  direction 693
  give the − to
   facilitate 705
   lax 738
   permit 760
  hold the − 693
  take the − 737
  give − to the imagination
   515
reinstall 660
reinstate 660, 790
reinvest 790
reinvigorate 658, 689
Reis Effendi 694
reiterate 104
reject
  exclude 55
  eject 297
  refuse 764
rejected
  hateful 898
rejection 610
rejoice *exult* 838
  amuse 840
  − the heart
   gratify 829
   cheer 836
  − in 827
  − in the name of 564
rejoicing 838
rejoin *assemble* 72
  arrive 292
rejoinder
  answer 462
  law pleadings 969
rejuvenescence 660
rekindle
  ignite 384
  excite 824
relapse
  turn back 145, 283
  fall back **661**
relate *narrate* 594
  − to *refer* 9
related *kin* 11
relation 9

kin 11
narrative 594
relationship 9
relative 11, 464
relativity 9
relator
  accuser 938
relax *loose* 47
  weaken 160
  moderate 174
  slacken speed 275
  soften 324
  inactive 683
  repose 687
  misrule 738
  liberate 750
  relent 914
  − one's efforts 681
  − the mind 452
relaxation [*see* relax]
  amusement 840
  dereliction 927
relaxed *weak* 160
relay 635, 637
release *death* 360
  deliverance 672
  liberate 750
  exempt 760
  from engagement **768a**
  security 771
  restore 790
  repay 807
  forgive 918
  exempt 927a
  discharge 970
  deed of − 923
relegate *banish* 55
  transfer 270
  remove 297
relent *moderate* 174
  soften 324
  pity 914
relentless
  resolute 604
  severe 739
  wrathful 900
  malevolent 907
  revenge 919
  impenitent 951
relessee
  possessor 779
  receiver 785
relevancy 9, 23
relevé 298
reliable 474
reliance
  confidence 484

hope 858
relic *remainder* 40
  reminiscence 505
  token 551
relics *corpse* 362
  sacred 998
relict 40, 905
relief
  prominence 250
  aid 707
  comfort **834**
  bas − 250, 557
  in strong − 446, 525
relieve *improve* 658
  aid 707
  comfort 834
relievo 250, 557
religieuse 996
religion 983, 987
  under the mask of − 988
religionist 988
religious
  honourable 939
  theological 983
  pious 987
  over− 955
  − education 537
  − persuasion 983
  − sects 984
religiously exact 494
relinquish 757
  − hope 859
  − life 360
  − property 782
  − a purpose 624
  recant 607
relinquishment 624, 782
reliquary 191, 998
reliquiæ 362
relish *pleasure* 377
  savour 390
  condiment 393
  savoury 394
  delight 827
  desire 865
relive 660
relucent 420
reluct 720
reluctance
  dissuasion 616
  unwilling 603
  dislike 867
reluctation 719
relume 384, 420
rely 484, 858
rem acu tetigisti 23
remain *be left* 40

endure 106
long time 110
continue 141
be present 186
stand 265
– firm 150
– on one's hands 641
– in one's mind 505
– neuter 605
– in possession of the field 731
remainder 40
estate 780
in – *posterior* 117
remainder-man 779
remains
remainder 40
corpse 362
vestige 551
organic – 357
remand *defer* 133
order 741
remanet 40
remark *observe* 457
affirmation 535
worthy of – 642
remarkable
great 31
exceptional 83
important 642
remarry 903
Rembrandtesque 160
remediable, remedial 660, 662
remediless 859
remedy 660, **662**
remembrance 505
remembrances 894
rememoration 505
remigration
regression 283
arrival 292
egress 295
remind 505
that –s me 134
reminiscence 505
remise 927*a*
remiss
neglectful 460
reluctant 603
idle 683
lax 738
remission
cessation 142
moderation 174
laxity 738
forgiveness 918

exemption 927*a*
remit [*see* remission]
– one's efforts 681
remittance 807
remittent
periodic 138
remitter 790
remnant 40
remodel
convert 144
revolutionize 146
improve 658
remonstrance 615, 766, 932
remora *cohere* 46
hindrance 706
remorse 950
remorseless 919
remote 10, 196
– age 122
– cause 153
– future 121
remotest idea, not have – 491
remotion 270
remount 147
remove *subduct* 38
term 71
displace 185
transfer 270
recede 287
depart 293
dinner 298
extract 301
school 541
– the mask 529
removedness
distance 196
remugient 412
remunerate 973
remunerative 644, 775
renaissance 660
renascence 660
renascent 163
rencounter
contact 199
meeting 292
fight 720
rend 44
– the air 404, 411, 839
– the heart-strings 830
render *convert* 144
interpret 522
give 784
restore 790
– an account
inform 527

describe 594
– *hors de combat* 645
– a service 644
rendering
covering 223
rendezvous 72, 74
rendition
interpretation 522
restore 790
renegade
convert 144
turncoat 607
fugitive 623
apostate 941
renew *twice* 90
repeat 104
reproduce 163
recollect 505
improve 658
restore 660
– one's strength 689
reniform 245
renitence
counteraction 179
hardness 323
elasticity 325
unwillingness 603
resistance 719
renitency
light 420
renounce
recant 607
relinquish 624
resign 757
abnegate 764
– *property* 782
repudiate 927
renovare dolorem, infandum – 833
renovate 160, 660
renovated *new* 123
renown 873
renownless 874
rent *tear* 44
fissure 198
hire 788
purchase 795
rental 810
renter 188, 779
rent-free 815
rent-roll 780, 810
rents *houses* 189
renunciation [*see* renounce]
exemption 927*a*
reorganize
order 60

convert 144
improve 658
restore 660
repair
  mend 658
  make good 660
  refresh 689
  out of – 659
  – to 266
reparation [*see* repair]
  compensation 30
  restitution 790
  atonement 952
  reward 973
repartee 462, 842
reparteeist 844
repartition 786
repass, pass and – 314
repast 298
repatriation 790
repay 790, 807, 973
repeal 756
repeat *imitate* 19
  duplication 90
  iterate 104
  reproduce 163
  affirm 535
  – by rote 505
repeated 104, 136
repeater
  watch 114
  fire-arm 727
repel *repulse* 289
  deter 616
  defend 717
  resist 719
  refuse 764
  give pain 830
  disincline 867
  banish 893
  excite hate 898
repent 950
repercussion 277
répertoire 599
repertory 636
repetend
  arithmetical 84
  iteration 104
repetition 19, **104**
repine
  pain 828
  discontent 832
  regret 833
  sad 837
replace
  substitute 147
  locate 184

restore 660
replenish 52, 637
repletion
  filling 639
  redundance 641
  satiety 869
replevin
  recovery 775
  borrow 788
  restore 790
replica 21
replication
  answer 462
  law pleadings 969
reply 462, 937
répondre en Normand 544
report *noise* 406
  judgment 480
  inform 527
  publish 531
  news 532
  rumour 532
  record 551
  statement 594
  good – 873
  through evil report and
    good – 604*a*
  – progress 527
reporter
  informant 527
  messenger 534
  recorder 553
  journalist 593, 758
reports *law* 969
repose
  quiescence 265
  leisure 685
  rest **687**
  – confidence in 484
  – on *support* 215
  evidence 467
  – on one's laurels 142
reposit 184
repository 636
**repostum, manet alta
    mente** – 919
repoussé 250
reprehend 932
reprehensible 945, 947
represent *similar* 17
  imitate 19
  exhibit 525
  intimate 527
  declare 535
  denote 550
  delineate 554
  commission 755

deputy 759
  – to oneself 515
representation [*see*
    represent]
  copy 21
  portrait **554**
  drama 599
representative
  typical 79
  commissioner 758
  deputy 759
  – government 737
  – of the people 696
  – of the press
  messenger 534
  writer 593
repress 751
  – one's feelings 826
  – a smile 837
reprieve
  respite 133, 970
  deliverance 672
  release 750
  pardon 918
reprimand 932
reprint
  copy 21
  repetition 104
  reproduce 183
reprisal
  retaliation 718
  resumption 789
reprise 40*a*
reproach
  disgrace 874
  blame 932
  accusation 938
reprobate
  disapproved 932
  vicious 945
  bad man 949
  sinner 988
reprobation 932, 988
reproduce
  imitate 19
  repeat 104
  renovate 163
reproduction [*see*
    reproduce] 21, **163**
reproductive 163
reproof 932
reprover 936
reptile
  animal 366
  servile 886
  knave 941
  miscreant 949

discover 480a
interpret 522
determine 604
predetermine 611
intend 620
– into elements 49
– into *convert* 144
resonance 402, **408**
resorb 296
resort *assemble* 72
focus 74
dwelling 189
converge 290
last – 601
– to *be present* 186
travel 266
employ 677
resound *loud* 404
ring 408
– *praises* 931
resourceful 698
resources
means 632
property 780
wealth 803
respect *relation* 9
observe 772
fame 873
salutation 894
deference **928**
have – to 9
in no – 536
with – to 9
respectability
mediocrity 736
repute 873
probity 939
respectable
unimportant 643
respectful 928
– distance 623, 864
respective 79, 786
respectless 458
respects 894, 928
resperse 73
respicere finem 510
respire *breathe* 349
live 359
refresh 689
respite
intermission 106
defer 133
pause 142
deliver 672
repose 687
reprieve 970
resplendent

luminous 420
splendid 845
respond *accord* 23
answer 462
feel 821
respondent 462
accused 938
response
answer 462, **587**
concord 714
feeling 821
friendship 888
worship 990
responsible 177, 926
responsibility
upon one's own – 600
responsive 375
rest *remainder* 40
pause 141
cessation 142
support 215
quiescence 265
death 360
silence 403
music 413
inaction 681
repose 687
at – *repose* 687
content 831
home of – 189
set at –
answer 462
ascertain 474
complete 729
compact 769
set one's mind at –
calm 826
set the question at – 478,
480
– assured 484, 858
– on *support* 215
– on one's oars 142, 687
– satisfied 831
– and be thankful 681, 687
– upon
evidence 467
confide 484
– with *duty* 926
restaurant 189
– car 272
restaurateur 637
restful 265
resting place
support 215
quiet 265
arrival 292
restitution 660, **790**

restive *averse* 603
obstinate 606
disobedient 742
refusal 764
perverse 901a
restless
changeable 149
moving 264
agitated 315
active 682
excited 825
fearful 860
restoration 660
restorative
salubrious 656
remedial 662
relieving 834
restore *reinstate* 660
refresh 689
return 790
– equilibrium 27
– harmony 723
– to health 654
restrain 616, 706, 751
restrainable 743
restrained 751
restraint 578, **751**
self – 826, 953
restrict *hinder* 706
restrain 751
prohibit 761
restringency 751
result *remainder* 40
follow 117
effect 154
conclusion 480
completion 729
resultant 48, 154
resume *begin* 66
repeat 104
change 140
restore 660
take 789
résumé 596
resupination 213
resurgence 163, 660
resurrection
reproduction 163
restoration 660
heaven 981
resuscitate
reproduce 163
reinstate 660
retable 215
retail *distribute* 73
inform 527
barter 794

piety 987
clergy 996
reverenced 500
reverend 877, 996
reverent 987, 990
reverential 928
reverie
train of thought 451
inattention 458
imagination 515
reversal 218, 607
reverse *contrary* 14
inversion 218
- *of a medal* 235
anteposition 237
adversity 735
abrogate 756
cards 840
- *of the shield* 468
reverseless 150
reversible 605
reversion [*see* reverse]
posterity 117
return **145**
possession 777
property 780
succession 783
remitter 790
reversioner 779
revert *repeat* 104
return 145
turn back 283
revest 790
- *to* 457
revest 790
revet 223
reviction 660
review *consider* 457
inquiry 461
judge 480
recall 505
periodical 531
dissertation 595
compendium 596
entertainment 599
revise 658
parade 882
reviewer 480, 595
revile 932, 988
reviler 936
revise *copy* 21
consider 457
printing 591
plan 626
improve 658
revising barrister 967
revision, under - 673

revisit 186
revival
reproduction 163
restoration 660
worship 990
revivalist 996
revive
reproduce 163
improve 658
resuscitate 660
excite 824
revivify
reproduce 163
life 359
improve 658
resuscitate 660
revocable 605
revoir, au - 293
revoke 607, 756
revolt, *resist* 719
disobey 742
shock 830
disapproval 932
- *against hate* 898
- *at the idea*
dissent 489
revolting
painful 830
revolution
periodicity 138
change **146**
rotation 312
disobedience 742
revolutionize 140, 146
revolve [*see* revolution]
- *in the mind* 451
revolver 727
revue 599
intimate - 599
revulsion
reversion 145
revolution 146
inversion 218
recoil 277
reward **973**
reword 104
Reynard
animal 366
cunning 702
rez-de-chaussée 191, 207
rhabdology 85
rhabdomancy 511
Rhadamanthus 967, 982
rhapsodical
irregular 139
imaginary 515
rhapsodist

fanatic 504
rhapsody
discontinuity 70
music 415
nonsense 497
fancy 515
poetry 597
rhetoric *speech* 582
flowers of - 577
rheum
excretion 299
fluidity 333
water 337
rhino 800
rhinoceros hide 376, 823
rhomb 244
rhumb 278
rhyme
similarity 17
verse 597
without - or reason
absurd 497
caprice 608
motiveless 615a
rhymeless 598
rhymester 597
rhythm
periodicity 138
melody 413
elegance 578
verse 597
rhythmical
- *style* 578
rialto 799
rib *support* 215
ridge 250
wife 903
ribald *vulgar* 851
disreputable 874
impure 961
riband [*see* ribbon]
ribbed 259
ribbon *tie* 45
filament 205
record 550
decoration 877
-s *reins* 152
handle the - 693
ribroast 972
rich *savoury* 394
colour 428
language 577
abundant 639
wealthy 803
beautiful 845
ornament 847
- *man* 803

rill 348
rim 231
rime *chink* 198
  frost 283
rimer 262
rimple 258
rind 223
ring
  fastening 45
  pendency 214
  circle 247
  loud 404
  resonance 408
  test 463
  combination 709
  clique 712
  arena 728, 840
  badge 747
  rub the – 992
  have the true – 494
  – the changes
  repeat 104
  change 140
  changeable 149
  – in the ear 408
  in a – fence 229, 232
  – with the praises of 931
  – the tocsin 669
  – up 527
ringleader
  director 694
  mutineer 742
ringlet 247, 256
rink 840
rinse 652
rinsings 653
riot *confusion* 59
  derangement 61
  violence 173
  discord 713
  resist 719
  mutiny 742
  run – *activity* 682
  excitement 825
  intemperance 954
  – in *pleasure* 742
rioter 742
riotous 173
rip 949, 962
  – open 260
  – up *tear* 44
  recall the past 505
  excite 824
riparian 342
ripe 673
  – age *old* 128
ripen *perfect* 650

improve 658
prepare 673
complete 729
– into 144
rippet 713
riposte 462
ripple *ruffle* 256
  shake 315
  water 348
  murmur 405
ripuarian 342
Rip van Winkle 130
rire, pour – 853
rise *grow* 35
  begin 66
  slope 217
  progress 282
  ascend 305
  stir 682
  revolt 742
  – again 660
  – in arms 722
  – from 154
  – to the occasion 612
  – up in price 814
  – up *elevation* 307
  – in the world 734
risible 838, 853
rising [*see* rise]
  – of the curtain 66, 448
  – generation 127, 167
  – ground
  height 206
  slope 217
  worship the – sun 886
risk *chance* 621
  danger 665
  invest 787
  at any – 604
risqué 961
rissole 298
risum teneatis amici? 853
rite 963, **998**
  funeral – 363
ritornello 64, 104
ritual
  ostentation 882
  rite 998
ritualism 984
rival
  emulate 648
  oppose 708
  opponent 710
  compete 720
  combatant 726
  outshine 873
rivalry *envy* 921

rive 44
rivel 258
river **348**
rivet 43, 45
  – the attention 457, 824
  – the eyes upon 441
  – in the memory 505
  – the yoke 739
riveted *firm* 150
rivulet 348
rixation 713
Ro 560
road *street* 189
  direction 278
  way 627
  on the –
  transference 270
  progression 282
  approach 286
  on the high – to 278
  – to ruin
  destruction 162
  danger 665
  adversity 735
road-book 266
roads *lake* 343
roadstead 154
  abode 189
  refuge 666
roadster 271
roadway 627
roam 266
roan, *horse* 271
  colour 433
roar *violence* 173
  wind 349
  sound 404, 407
  bellow 411, 412
  laugh 838
  weep 839
roaring *great* 31
  – trade 731, 734
roast *heat* 384
  ridicule 856
  rib – 972
  – and boiled 298
  – an ox 883
rob 354, 791
robber 792
robbery 791
robe 225, 999
  robes – of state 747
Robin Goodfellow 980
Robinson
  say Jack – 132
Robot 554
robust *strong* 159, 654

roc 83
rocaille 853
rock *firm* 150
  oscillate 314
  hard 323
  land 342
  safety 664
  danger 667
  build on a - 150
  founded on a - 664
  split upon a - 732
  - ahead 665
  -bound coast 342
  - oil 356
rocket *rapid* 274
  rise 305
  light 423
  signal 550
  arms 727
  fireworks 840
  go up like a - and come
    down like the stick 732
rocking-chair 215
rococo 124, 853
rod *support* 215
  measure 466
  scourge 975
  divining 993
  kiss the - 725
  sounding - 208
  - of empire 747
  - in pickle
  prepared 673
  accusation 938
  punishment 972
  scourge 975
rodeo 720, 840
rodomontade
  exaggeration 482
  unmeaning 517
  boast 884
roe 366, 374
Roentgen rays 420
rogation
  request 765
  worship 990
rogue *cheat* 548
  knave 941
  scamp 949
  -'s march 297
roguery 940
roguish
  playful 840
Roi le veut, le - 741
roister 885
roisterer 887
Roland for an Oliver

retaliation 716
revenge 719
barter 794
rôle *drama* 599
  business 625
  plan 626
  conduct 692
roll *list* 86
  fillet 205
  convolution 248
  rotundity 249
  make smooth 255
  move 264
  fly 267
  rotate 312
  rock 314
  flow 384
  sound **407**
  record 551
  money 800
  strike off the - 756, 972
  - along 312
  - in the dust 731
  - on the ground 839
  - of honour 86
  - in 639, 461
  - on 109
  - into one 43
  - in riches 803
  - up 312
  - up in 225
  - in wealth 803
roll-call 85
roller *fillet* 45
  round 249
  clothing 255
  rotate 312
roller-coaster 840
rollers *billows* 348
rollick 836
rollicker 838
rollicking
  frolicsome 836
  blustering 885
rolling: - pin 249
  - stock 272
  - stone 312
Rolls: Master of
  the -
  recorder 553
  judge 967
  - Court 966
Roman candle 840
Roman Catholic 984
romance
  music 415
  absurdity 497

  imagination 515
  untruth 546
  fable 594
Romanism 984
romantic
  imaginative 515
  art 556
  sensitive 822
romanticism 515
Romanus sum, civis - 924
Romany 563
Rome: Church of 984
  do at - as the Romans do
    82
romp *violent* 173
  game 840
rondeau *music* 415
  poem 597
rondel 597
rondolette 597
rood *area* 180
  cross 998
  - loft 1000
roof 189, 223
roofless 226
rook 791, 792
rookie 726
rookery *nests* 189
  dirt 653
room *occasion* 134
  space 180
  lodge 186
  chamber 191
  plea 617
  assembly - 840
  in the - of 147
  make - for
  opening 260
  respect 928
roommate 890
rooms
  lodgings 189
roomy 180
roost 189
  rule the - 737
rooster 366
root *algebraic* - 84
  cause 153
  place 184
  abide 186
  base 211
  etymon 562
  lie at the - of 642
  pluck up by the -s 301
  strike at the - of 716
  take -
  influence 175

locate 184
habit 613
– and branch 52
cut up – and branch 162
– out *eject* 297
extract 301
discover 480a
rooted
old 124
firm 150
located 184
habit 613
deep – 820
– antipathy 867
– belief 484
rope *fastening* 45
cord 205
freedom 749
scourge 975
give – enough 738
–'s end 975
– of sand
incoherence 47
weakness 160
impossible 471
– way 627
rope-dancer 700
rope-dancing 698
ropy 352
roquelaure 225
roric 339
rosâ, sub – 528
rosary 990, 998
Roscius 599
rose *pipe* 350
fragrant 400
red 434
beauty 845
bed of –s 377, 734
couleur de –
red 434
good 648
prosperity 734
hope 858
under the – 528
welcome as the –s in May
829, 892
roseate *red* 434
hopeful 858
rose-coloured
hope 858
Rosetta stone 522
rosette 847
rose-water
moderation 174
flattery 933
not made with – 704

Rosicrucian
sect 984
sorcerer 994
rosin *rub* 331
resin 356a
Rosinante 271
roster 86
rostrum *beak* 234
pulpit 542
rosy 434
– wine 959
rosy-cheeked 845
rot *decompose* 49
absurdity 497
rubbish 517
putrefy 653
disease 655
decay 659
rota 86, 138
Rotarian 892
rotate 138
rotation 312
periodicity 138
rote, by – 505
know – 490
learn – 539
rôti 298
rôtisserie 189
rotogravure 531, 558
rotten *weak* 160
bad 649
foul 653
decayed 659
– at the core
deceptive 545
diseased 655
– borough 893
rotulorum, custos – 553
rotund 249
rotunda 189
rotundity 249
roturier 876
roué 949
rouge 434, 847
rouge-et-noir 621
rough *violent* 173
shapeless 241
uneven 256
pungent 392
unsavoury 395
sour 397
sound 410
unprepared 674
fighter 726
ugly 846
low fellow 876
bully 887

churlish 895
evil-doer 913
bad man 949
cut up – 900
– copy *writing* 590
unprepared 674
– diamond
uncouth 241
unprepared 674
artless 703
vulgar 851
commonalty 876
good man 948
– draft 626
– guess 514
– it 686
– sea 348
– side of the tongue 932
– and tumble 59
– weather 173, 349
rough-cast 256
covering 223
shape 240
scheme 626
unpolished 674
rough-hew 240, 673
roughly
nearly 197
rough-neck 876, 887
roughness 256
rough-rider 268
roughshod over, ride – 739
roulade 415
rouleau
assemblage 72
cylinder 249
money 800
roulette 621, 840
round *series* 69
revolution 138
– of a ladder 215
curve 245
circle 247
rotund 249
music 415
fight 720
all – 227
bring – 660
come –
periodic 138
recant 607
persuade 615
dizzy – 312
get – 660
go – 311
go one's –s 266
go the –

publication 531
make the – of 311
run the – of 682
go the same – 104
turn – *invert* 218
retreat 283
revolve 311
– assertion 535
– a corner 311
– dance 840
– game 840
– hand 590
– like a horse in a mill 613
– of the ladder 71
– number 84, 102
in – numbers 29, 197
– pace 274
– of pleasures 377, 840
– robin
information 527
petition 765
censure 932
– and round 138, 312
– sum 800
– terms 566
– trot 274
– up 370
– of visits 892
round about
circumjacent 227
deviation 279
circuit 311
amusement 840
– phrases 573
– way 729
rounded periods 577, 578
roundelay 597
rounders 840
round-house 752
roundlet 247
round-shouldered 243
roup 796
rouse 615, 824
– oneself 682
rousing 171
rout *crowd* 72
agitation 315
overcome 731
discomfit 732
rabble 876
assembly 892
put to the – 731
– out 652
route 627
en – 270
en – for 282
routine

uniform 16
order 58
rule 80
periodic 138
custom 613
business 625
rove *travel* 266
deviate 279
rover *traveller* 268
pirate 792
roving commission 475
row *disorder* 59
series 69
violence 173
street 189
navigate 267
discord 713
– in the same boat 88
rowdy *vulgar* 851, 876
blusterer 887
bad man 949
rowel 253, 615
rower 269
rowlock 215
royal 737
– blue 438
– highness 877
– road 627, 705
Royal Academician 559
royalist 737
royaliste que le roi, plus –
33
royalty 737
Rt. Hon. 877
ruade *impulse* 276
attack 716
ruat cœlum 908
rub *friction* 331
touch 379
difficulty 704
adversity 735
painful 830
– off corners 82
– down *lessen* 195
powder 330
– down with an oaken
towel 972
– one's eyes 870
– one's hands 838
– up the memory 505
– off 552
– on *slow* 275
progress 282
inexcitable 826
– out 552
– up 658
– up the wrong way 713

rubadub 407
rubber 325
whist 840
rubber boots 225
rubber hose 975
rubber-stamp 82
rubbish
absurdity 497
unmeaning 517
trifling 643
useless 645
rubble 645
rube 876
rubescence 434
Rubicon *limit* 233
pass the –
begin 66
cross 303
choose 609
rubicund 434
rubify 434
rubigo 653
rubric 550, 697, 998
rubricate
redden 434
ruby *red* 434
gem 648
ornament 847
ruck 29, 258
in the – 235
rucksack 191
ructation 297
rudder 273, 693
rudderless 158
ruddle 434
ruddy *red* 434
beautiful 845
rude *violent* 173
shapeless 241
ignorant 491
inelegant 579
ugly 846
vulgar 851
uncivilized 876
uncivil 895
disrespect 929
– health 654
rudera 645
rudiment 66, 153
rudimental 193, 674
rudimentary 66
rudiments 490, 542
rudis indigestaque moles
59, 241
rue *bitter* 395
regret 833
repent 950

rueful 830, 837
ruff 225
ruffian 876
  blusterer 876
  maleficent 913
  scoundrel 949
ruffianism 851, 907
ruffle *disorder* 59
  derange 61
  roughen 259
  fold 258
  feeling 821
  excite 824, 825
  pain 830
  anger 900
rufous 434
rug 215, 223
Rugby
  football 840
rugged
  shapeless 241
  rough 256
  difficult 704
  ugly 846
  churlish 895
rugose 256
ruin *destruction* 162
  evil 619
  failure 732
  adversity 735
  poverty 804
ruined
  bankrupt 808
  hopeless 859
ruinous
  painful 830
ruins *remains* 40
rule *mean* 29
  regularity **80**
  influence 175
  length 200
  measure 466
  decide 480
  custom 613
  precept 697
  government 737
  law 963
  absence of – 699
  as a – 613
  by – 82
  golden – 697
  obey –s 82
  – of three 85
  – of thumb
    experiment 463
    unreasoning 477
    essay 675

  unskilled 699
ruler 745
ruling 697, 969
  – *passion* 606, 820
rum *liquor* 298
  queer 853
  – *running* 964
rumba 840
rumble 407
ruminate
  chew 298
  think 451
rummage 461
rummer 191
rumour 531, 532
rump 235
rumple
  disorder 59
  derange 61
  roughen 256
  fold 258
rumpus
  confusion 59
  violence 173
  discord 713
run *generality* 78
  repetition 104
  continuance 106, 143
  course 109
  eventuality 151
  motion 264
  speed 274
  sequence 281
  liquefy 335
  flow 348
  habit 613
  smuggle 791
  contraband 964
  have a – 852, 873
  have – of 748
  near – 197
  ordinary – 29
  race is – 729
  time –s 106
  – abreast 27
  – after 622, 873
  – against 276, 708, 716
  – at 716
  – away 623
  – away with 789, 791
  – away with a notion
    misjudge 481
    credulous 486
  – back 283
  – a chance
    probable 472
    chance 621

  – counter to 468, 708
  – its course
    course 109
    past 122
    complete 729
  – into danger 665
  – into debt 806
  – down
    underestimate 483
    pursue 622
    bad 649
    finished 678
    attack 678
    attack 716
    depreciate 932
    detract 934
  – dry 638, 640
  – the eye over 441, 539
  – the fingers over 379
  – foul of 276
  – the gauntlet 861
  – on in a groove 613
  – hard *danger* 665
    difficult 704
    success 731
  – in the head 451, 505
  – high *great* 31
    violent 173
  – in *introduce* 228
  – into
    conversion 144
    insert 300
  – low 36
  – of luck 156, 734
  – mad 503, 825
  – mad after 865
  – like mad 274
  – of the mill 29
  – amuck
    violent 173
    kill 361
    mad 503
    attack 716
  – on 143
  – out *end* 67
    course 109
    past 122
    antiquated 124
    egress 295
    prodigal 818
  – out on 573
  – over *count* 85
    – *in the mind* 451
    examine 457
    describe 594
    synopsis 596
    overflow 641

sacerdotal 995
sacerdotalism 988
sachel 191
sachem 745
sachet 400
sack *bag* 191
  discharge 297, 756
  gain 775
  take 789
  plunder 791
  give the – to 297
sackbut 297
sackcloth and ashes
  lament 839
  atonement 952
  ascetic 955
  rite 998
sacrament 998
sacrarium 1000
sacred
  dignified 873
  holy 976
  revelation 985
  piety 987
sacrifice
  destroy 162
  gift 784
  atonement 952
  worship 990
  idolatry 991
  at any – 604
  fall a – 828
  make a – 942
  make the supreme – 361
  self – 942
sacrificed 732
sacrilege 988
sacring bell 550, 998
sacristan 996
sacristy 1000
sacrosanct
  honourable 873
  inviolable 924
  holy 976
sad *great* 31
  grey 432
  bad 649
  painful 830
  dejected 837
  – disappointment 509
  – dog 949
  – times 735
  – work 699
sadden 830, 837
sadder and wiser man 950
saddle 215
  in the – 673

– on 37, 43
– on the right horse
  discovery 480a
  skill 698
  right 922
  fair 939
– with *add* 37
  attribute 155
  quarter on 184
  clog 706
  impose a duty 926
  accuse 938
– on the wrong horse 495,
  699
– up 293
saddle-bags 191
Sadducee 984
sadness, in – 535
safe *cupboard* 191
  hiding place 530
  secure 664
  treasury 802
  cautious 864
– conduct 631
– conscience 926, 946
– deposit 636
– keeping 670
– and sound 654
on the – side 864
safety 664
– bicycle 272
– curtain 599
– first 665, 864
– match 388
– valve 666
saffron *colour* 436
sag 214, 217, 245
saga 594
sagacious 498, 510
sage 498, **500**
– maxim 496
saggar 386
sagittal 253
sagittary 83
sagum 225
Sahara 169
sahib 373, 745, 875
saick 273
said *preceding* 62
  repeated 104
  prior 116
  it is – 532
  thou hast – 488
  more easily – than done
  704
sail *navigate* 267
  ship 273

  set out 293
easy – 174
full – 274
press of – 274
shorten – 275
take in – 174
take the wind out of one's
  –s 706
too much – 863
under – 267
– before the wind 734
– near the wind 698
– too near the wind 863
sailing: plain – 705
– vessel 273
sailor 269
fair weather – 701
saint *angel* 977
  revelation 985
  piety 987
  false piety 988
  tutelary – 664
saintly 944, 987
Saint Monday 840
sais quoi, je ne – 563
sake:
for the – of 615, 707
for goodness – 765
salaam
  bow 308
  submit 725
  courtesy 894
  respect 928
salacity 961
salad 41
– oil 356
salade 717
salamander 386
salariat 875
salary 973
sale **796**
bill of – 771
for – *offer* 763
  barter 794
saleable 796
salebrosity 256
salesman 797
salient
  projecting 250
  sharp 253
  manifest 525
  important 642
– angle 244
– points 642
saline 392
saliva 299, 332
salivate 297

salle-à-manger 191
sallet 717
sallow
  colourless 429
  yellow 436
sally *issue* 293
  attack 716
  wit 842
sally-port 295, 717
salmagundi 41
salmi 298
salmon-coloured 434
saloon 189, 191
salt *sailor* 269
  pungent 392
  condiment 393
  importance 642
  preserve 670
  money 800
  wit 842
  below the – 876
  worth one's – 644
  – of the earth 648, 948
  – water 341
saltation 309
saltatory 315
saltinbanco 548
saltpetre 392, 727
saltum, per – 315
salubrity 656
salutary 656
salutatory 582
salute
  allocution 586
  celebration 883
  courtesy 894
  kiss 902
  respect 928
salutiferous [*see* salutary]
salva:
  – res est 664
  – sit reverentia 928
salvable 946
salvage
  acquisition 775
  tax 812
  discount 813
  reward 973
salvation
  preservation 670
  deliverance 672
  religious 976
  piety 987
  work out one's – 990
salve *unguent* 356
  remedy 662
  relieve 834

salver 191
salvo *exception* 83
  explosion 406
  qualification 469
  plea 617
  attack 716
  excuse 937
  – of artillery
  celebration 883
Samaritan, good – 906,
  912
same 13
  all the – to 823
  in the – boat 709
  in the – breath 113, 120
  go over the – ground 104
  of the – mind 488
  on the – tack 709
  adds up to the – thing 27
  at the – time 30, 120
sameness 16
samiel 349
samisen 417
Sammael 978
samovar 191
sampan 273
sample 82, 463
Samson 159
sana, mens – 502
  – in corpore sano 827
sanation 660
sanative 662
sanatorium 662
sanctification 976
sanctify 926, 987
sanctimony 988
sanction
  permission 760
  dueness 924
  approbation 931
sanctitude 987
sanctity 987
sanctuary 666, 1000
sanctum 191
  – sanctorum
  abode 189
  privacy 893
  temple 1000
sand *powder* 330
  –bag 727
  built upon – 665
  –dance 840
  sow the – 645
sandal 225
sand-blind 442
Sandemanian 984
sand-paper 255

sands *danger* 667
  – on the seashore
  multitude 102
sand-storm 330
sandwich-wise 228
sandy *yellow* 436
sane 502
sangar 717
sang-froid
  insensibility 823
  inexcitability 826
  presence of mind 864
sangrail 998
sanguinary 361
sanguine *red* 434
  hopeful 858
  – expectation 507, 858
  – imagination 515
sanhedrim 696, 995
sanies 333
sanitaire, cordon – 670
sanitarian 656
sanitarium 656, 662
sanitary 656
sanity *mental* **502**
  bodily - 654
sans 187
  – cérémonie 888, 892
  – façon
  simple 849
  modest 881
  social 892
  – pareil 33
  – peur et sans reproche
  perfect 650
  heroic 873
  honourable 939
  – souci
  insensible 823
  pleasure 827
  content 831
sans-culotte 742, 876
Santa Claus 874
santé, maison de - 662
santon 893, 996
sap *essence* 5
  destroy 162
  excavate 252
  juice 333
  damage 659
  attack 716
  – the foundations 162, 659
sapid 390
sapient 498
sapless 160, 340
sapling 129, 367
saponaceous 355

saporific 390
sapper 252, 726
sappers and miners
  preparers 673
Sapphic 597
sapphire *blue* 438
  gem 847
sappy
  young 127
  juicy 333
  foolish 499
saraband 840
sarà sarà, che – 601
sarcasm
  disrespect 929
  censure 932
  detraction 934
sarcastic 856, 895
sarcoma 250
sarcophagus 363
sarculation 103
sard 847
Sardanapalus 954*a*
sardonic 932, 934
 – *grin*
  laughter 838
  ridicule 856
  discontent 932
sardonyx 847
sark 225
sartorial 225
Sarum, old – 893
sash 247
Satan 978
satanic
  malevolent 907
  vicious 945
  diabolic 978
satchel 191
sate 869
satellite
  companion 88
  follower 281
  heavenly body 318
  auxiliary 711
  servant 746
satiate 957
satiety
  sufficient 639
  pleasant 829
  cloy **869**
satin 255
satire 521, 856, 932
satirical 546, 932
  detraction 934
satirist 936
satis: *jam* – 869

– *superque* 641
satisfaction [*see* satisfy]
  duel 720
  pleasure 827
  atonement 952
  hail with – 931
satisfactorily 618
satisfactory 648
satisfy *answer* 462
  convince 484
  sufficient 639
  consent 762
  observance 772
  pay 807
  gratify 829
  content 831
  satiate 869
  reward 973
 – *an obligation* 926
 – *oneself* 484
satrap 745
saturate *fill* 52
  moisten 339
  satiate 869
Saturn 979
saturnalia
  disorder 59
  games 840
  intemperance 954
Saturnian 829, 946
 – *age* 734
Saturnia regna 734, 827
saturnine 837
satyr *ugly* 846
  libertine 962
  demon 980
sauce *adjunct* 39
  mixture 41
  food 298
  condiment 393
  impertinence 885
  abuse 908
 – *boat* 191
 pay – *for all* 807
sauce-box 887
saucepan 191
sauce piquante 829
saucer 191
 – *eyes* 441
saucy 885, 895
saunter 133, 266, 275
sausage 298
saute aux yeux, cela – 525
sauvage 893
sauve qui peut
  run away 623
  alarm 669

  haste 684
  cowardice 862
savage *violent* 173
  vulgar 851
  brave 861
  boorish 876
  angry 900
  malevolent 907
  evil-doer 913
savanna 344
savant 490, 492
save *subduct* 38
  exclude 55
  except 83
  store 636
  preserve 670
  deliver 672
  economize 817
  God – 990
 – *one's bacon* 671
 – *and except* 83
 – *money* 817
 – *the necessity* 927*a*
 – *us* 707
save-all 817
saving 817
 – *clause* 469
 – *one's presence* 928
savings 636, 817
saviour 912
Saviour 976
savoir: – *faire* 698, 852
 – *gré* 916
 – *vivre skill* 698
  fashion 852
  sociality 892
savour 390
 – *of resemble* 17
 – *of the reality* 780
savouriness 394
savourless 391
savoury 394
saw *cut* 44
  jagged 257
  maxim 496
 – *the air*
  gesture 550
sawbuck 800
sawder, soft –
  flattery 933
sawdust 330
sawney 501
sax-horn 417
Saxon
  style 576, 578
saxophone 417
say *nearly* 32

assert 535
speak 560, 582
you don't – so 870
go without –ing 525
have one's – 535, 582
that is to – 522
what do you – to that 870
– by heart 505
– no 489
– nothing 585
– to oneself 589
– one's prayers 990
– what comes uppermost 612
saying 496, 535
sbirro 965
scabbard 191
throw away the –
resolution 604
war 722
scabby 940
scabrous 256
scaffold
support 215
preparation 673
execution 975
scagliola 545
scalawag 193
scald *burn* 384
poet 597
scale *transcend* 31
portion 51
series 69
term 71
slice 204
skin 223
mount 305
weigh 319
gamut 413
measure 466
hold the –s 480
turn the –
reversion 145
influence 175
counter evidence 468
motive 615
hold the –s even 922
–s of justice 922
– the heights 305
– the walls 716
–s falling from the eyes 441, 529
scalene 243
scallop 248, 257
scalp 226
scalpel 253
scamble 44

scamp *neglect* 460
shirk 603
rascal 949
scamped *sham* 545
scamper *speed* 274
– *off* 623
scampish 945
scan *see* 441
attend to 457
inquire 461
know 490
prosody 597
scandal *news* 532
obloquy 934
scandaleuse, chronique – 934
scandalize 932
scandal-monger 532
scandalous 874, 945
scandalum magnatum
infamy 874
detraction 934
accusation 938
scandent 305
scansion 597
scant *small* 32
few 103
little 193
narrow 203
insufficient 640
scantling *model* 22
scrap 32
dimensions 192
scanty [*see* scant]
scape 671
scapegoat 147, 952
scapegrace 863, 949
Scapin 548, 941
scapulary 999
scar *shore* 342
record 551
blemish 848
scarab 993
scaramouch 844
scarce
few 103, 137, 640
make oneself – 187, 623
scarcely 32
– any 103
– anything 643
– ever 137
scarcity 103
scare 860
scarecrow 846, 860
scarf 225, 999
scarfskin 223
scarify *notch* 257

torment 830
scarlet 434
– Lady 984
scarp *oblique* 217
defence 717
scathe 649, 659
scatheless 650
scatter *derange* 61
disperse 73
diverge 291
– to the winds
destroy 162
confute 479
scatterbrained 458, 503
scattering 268
scavenger 652
scenario 594, 626
scene
appearance 448
painting 556
drama 599
excitement 825
– of action 728
look behind the –s 461
scene-painter 559
scene-painting 556
scenery 448, 559
scenic 599, 882
– railway 840
scenography 556
scent *smell* 398
discovery 480a
disbelieve 485
knowledge 490
sign 550
trail 551
get – of 527
put on a new – 279
on the – 622
throw off the – 623
on the right – 462
– from afar 510
scent-bag 400
scent-bottle 400
scented 400
scentless 399
sceptre 747
sway the – 737
schedule 86
schematist 626
scheme *draft* 554
plan 626
schemer 626
scherif 745, 875
scherzo 415
schesis 7
schism *dissent* 489

discord 713
heterodoxy 984
schismless 983*a*
schistose 204
scholar 492, 541
scholarly 539
scholarship
  knowledge 490
  learning 539
  distinction 873
scholastic
  knowledge 490
  teaching 537
  learning 539
  school 542
scholiast 496, 522
scholium 496, 522
school
  herd 72
  multitude 102
  system of opinions 484
  knowledge 490
  teaching 537
  academy **542**
  painting 556
  go to – 539
  send to – 537
schoolboy 129, 541
  familiar to every – 490
schooldays 127
schoolfellow 541
schoolgirl 129, 541
schoolman 492, 983
schoolmaster 540
  – abroad 490, 537
schoolroom 191
schooner 273
schottische 840
sciatica 378
science 490, 698
scientific *exact* 494
scientist 476, 492
scimitar 727
scintilla *small* 32
  spark 420, 423
scintillate 446, 873
scintillation
  heat 382
  light 420
  wit 842
scintillula forsan, latet –
  858
sciolism 491
sciolist 493
sciomachy 497
Sciomancy 511
scion *part* 51

child 129
posterity 167
scire: – facias 461
  – quid valeant humeri 698
scission 44
scissors 253
  – and paste 609
scissure 198
sclerotics 195
scobs 330
scoff *ridicule* 856
  deride 929
  impiety 988
  – at *despise* 930
  censure 932
scold *shrew* 901
  malediction 908
  censure 932
scollop 248, 257
sconce *top* 210
  candlestick 423
  brain 450
  defence 717
  mulct 974
scone 298
scoop
  depression 252
  perforator 262
scooter 272
scope *degree* 26
  opportunity 134
  extent 180
  meaning 516
  freedom 748
scorch
  rush 274
  heat 382, 384
scorching
  violent 173
score
  music 60, 415
  count 85
  list 86
  twenty 98
  notch 257
  furrow 259
  mark 550
  success 731
  credit 805
  debt 806
  accounts 811
  on the – of
  relation 9
  motive 615
scores *many* 102
scoriæ *ash* 384
  dirt 653

scorify 384
scoring board 551
scorn 930
scorpion
  painful 830
  evil-doer 913
  (*bane* 663)
  chastise with –s 739
scorse 794
scot *reward* 973
scotch *notch* 257
  injure 659
  – the snake
  maim 158
  insufficient 640
  non-completion 730
  – the wheel 706
scot free *free* 748
  cheap 815
  exempt 927*a*
  escape –
  escape 671
  let off – 970
scotomy 443
Scotsman
  canny 702
Scotticism 563
scoundrel 913, 949
scour *run* 274
  rub 331
  clean 652
  – the country 266
  – the plain 274
scourge *bane* 663
  painful 830
  punish 972
  instrument of punishment
  975
  – of the human race 913
scourings 645
scout 234
  observer 444
  feeler 463
  messenger 534
  reject 610
  watch 664
  warning 668
  warship 726
  servant 746
  disrespect 929
  disdain 930
  (*looker* 444)
  (*underrate* 483)
  (*ridicule* 856)
scow 273
scowl
  complain 839

frown 895
anger 900
sullen 901*a*
disapprobation 932
scrabble
unmeaning 517
scribble 590
scrag 32, 203
scraggy *lean* 193, 203
rough 256
scramble
confusion 59
climb 305
pursue 622
haste 684
difficulty 704
contend 720
seize 789
scranch 330
scrannel 643
scrap 32, 720
– *of paper* 158, 940
scrap-book 596
scrape *subduct* 38
reduce 195
pulverize 330
abrade 331
mezzotint 558
difficulty 704
mischance 732
bow 894
– *together*
assemble 72
acquire 775
scraper 652
scratch *groove* 259
abrade 331
mark 550
daub 555
draw 556
write 590
hurt 619
wound 649
come to the – 720, 861
mere – 209
old – 978
up to the – 861
without a – 654, 670
– *the head* 461
– *out* 552
scrawl 590
scrawny 203
screak 411
scream *cry* 411, 839
screech 411, 412
screech owl 412
screed 582, 593

screen *sift* 60
sieve 260
shade 424
cinema 448
hide 528
hider 530
side-scene 599
clean 562
safety 664
shelter 666
defence 717
– *from sight* 442
screw *fasten* 43
fastening 45
distort 243
oar 267
rotation 312
instrument 633
miser 819
put on the – 739, 744
– *one's courage to the sticking place* 861
– *loose insane* 503
imperfect 651
unskilful 699
hindrance 706
attack 713
– *up fasten* 43
strengthen 159
prepare 673
– *up the eyes* 443
screw-driver 633
screwed
drunk 959
screw-steamer 273
scribble 517, 590
scribbler 593
scribe *recorder* 553
writer 590, 593
priest 996
–*s and Pharisees* 988
scribendi, cacoëthes – 580
scrimmage 713, 720
scrimp *short* 201
insufficient 640
stingy 819
scrimshanker 603
scrip 191
script 590, 599
scripta, lex – 963
scriptæ, literæ – 590
scriptural 983*a*
Scripture
certain 474
revelation 985
scrivener *writer* 590
lawyer 968

scroll 86, 551
scrub *rub* 331
bush 367
clean 652
dirty person 653
commonalty 876
scrubby *small* 193
trifling 643
stingy 819
disreputable 874
vulgar 876
shabby 940
scruff 235
scruple
small quantity 32
weight 319
doubt 485
reluctance 603
probity 939
scrupulous
careful 459
incredulous 487
exact 494
reluctant 603
fastidious 868
punctilious 939
scrutator 461
scrutiny 457, 461
scrutoire 191
scud *sail* 267
speed 274
shower 348
cloud 353
– *under bare poles* 704
scuffle 720
scull *row* 267
brain 450
scull-cap 225
scullery 191
scullion 746
sculpsit 558
sculptor 559
sculpture 240, **557**
scum *dirt* 653
– *of the earth* 949
– *of society* 876
scupper 350
scurf 653
scurrilous
ridicule 856
malediction 908
disrespect 929
detraction 934
scurry 274, 684
scurvy
insufficient 640
unimportant 643

base 940
wicked 945
scut 235
scutcheon
  standard 550
  honour 877
scutiform 251
scuttle *destroy* 162
  receptacle 191
  speed 274
  - along *haste* 684
Scylla and Charybdis,
  between -
  danger 665
  difficulty 704
Scyllam, incidit in - 699
scythe *pointed* 244
  sharp 253
'sdeath! *wonder* 870
  anger 900
  disapprobation 932
se non e vero e ben
  trovato 546
sea *multitude* 102
  ocean 341
  at - 341
  uncertain 475
  erroneous 495
  go to - 293
  on the high -s 41
  heavy - 315
  the seven -s 341
  - of doubt 475
  - of troubles
  difficulty 704
  adversity 735
seaboard 342
seafarer 269
seafaring 267, 273
sea-fight 720
sea-girt 346
sea-going 267, 341
sea-green 435
seal
  matrix 22
  close 261
  evidence 467
  mark 550
  resolve 604
  complete 729
  compact 769
  security 771
  break the - 529
  under - 769
  - the doom of 162
  - one's infamy 940
  - the lips 585

- of secrecy 528
- up *restrain* 751
sealed:
  one's fate is - 601
  hermetically - 261
  - book
  ignorance 491
  unintelligible 519
  secret 533
sealing-wax 747
seals *insignia* 747
sealskin 223
seam 43
sea-maid 979
sea-man 269
seamanship 692, 698
sea-mark 550
seamless 50
seamstress 225, 690
seamy side 651
séance 525, 696
sea-piece 556
seaplane 273, 736
sea-port 666
sear *dry* 340
  burn 384
  deaden 823
  - and yellow leaf 128, 659
search *inquire* 461
searching
  severe 739
  painful 830
searchless 519
searchlight 423, 726
seared conscience 951
searing 830
seascape 556
sea-serpent 83
seaside 342
season *mix* 41
  time 106
  pungent 392
  accustom 613
  preserve 670
  prepare 673
seasonable 23, 134
seasoning 393
seasons 138
seat *place* 183
  locate 184
  abode 189
  support 215
  posterior 235
  parliament 693
  country - 189
  judgment - 966
  - of government 737

- of war 728
seated, firmly - 150
seaway 180
seaweed 367
seaworthy 273, 664
sebaceous 355
secant 219
secede *dissent* 489
  relinquish 624
  disobey 742
seceder
  heterodox 984
secern 297
seclusion 893
second
  duplication 90
  - *of time* 108
  instant 113
  - *in music* 413, 415
  abet 707
  play or sing a - 416
  - best 651, 732
  - childhood 128, 499
  - crop 168, 775
  - edition 104
  play - fiddle
  obey 743
  subject 749
  disrepute 874
  - nature 613
  - to none 33
  one's - self 17
  - rate 659
  - sight
  foresight 510
  sorcery 992
  - thoughts
  sequel, 65
  thought 451
  improvement 658
  - youth 660
secondary
  inferior 34
  following 63
  imperfect 651
  deputy 759
  - education 537
  - evidence 467
  - school 542
seconder 711
second-hand
  imitation 19
  old 124
  deteriorated 659
  received 785
secondly 90
second-rate 651

secret *key* 522
 latent 526
 hidden 528
 riddle **533**
 in the – 490
 keep a – 585
 – motive 615
 – passage 627, 671
 – place 530
 – writing 590
secrétaire 191
secretary
 recorder 553
 writer 590
 director 694
 auxiliary 711
 servant 746
 consignee 758
 – of state 694
 – of the treasury 801
secrete *excrete* 297
 conceal 528
secretion 299
secretive 528
sect 75
 religious – 983, 984
sectarian
 dissent 489
 ally 711
 heterodox 984
sectary 489
section *division* 44
 part 51
 class 75
 chapter 593
 troops 726
sector *part* 51
 circle 247
secular
 centenary 98
 periodic 138
 laity 997
 – education 537
secularism 984
secula seculorum, in – 112
secundum artem 82, 698
secure *fasten* 43
 bespeak 132
 belief 484
 safe 664
 restrain 751
 engage 768
 gain 775
 confident 858
 – an object 731
securities 802–805
security *safety* 664

 pledge **771**
 hope 858
 lend on – 787
Sedan
 disaster 162
sedan chair 272
sedate
 thoughtful 451
 calm 826
 grave 837
sedative 174, 662
sedentary 265
sedge 367
sedile 1000
sediment *dregs* 653
sedimentary 40
sedition 742
seduce *entice* 615
 love 897
 debauch 961
seducer 962
seduction 829, 865
sedulous 682, 865
see *view* 441
 look 457
 believe 484
 know 490
 bishopric 995
 we shall – 507
 – after 459
 – daylight 480*a*
 – double 959
 – fit 600, 602
 – at a glance 498
 – justice done 922
 – life 840
 – the light
 born 359
 published 531
 – service 722
 – sights 455
 – through 480*a*, 498
 – to *attention* 457
 care 459
 direction 693
 – one's way
 foresight 510
 intelligible 518
 skill 698
 easy 705
seed *small* 32
 cause 153
 posterity 167
 grain 330
 run to – *age* 128
 lose health 659
 sow the – 673

seedling 129
seed-plot 168, 371
seed-time of life 127
seedy *weak* 160
 disease 655
 deteriorated 659
 exhausted 688
 needy 804
seeing that 8, 476
seek *inquire* 461
 pursue 622
 offer 763
 request 765
 – safety 664
seek-sorrow 837
seel 217
seem 448
 as it –s good to 600
seeming 488
seemingly 472
seemless 846, 925
seemliness 926
seemly
 expedient 646
 handsome 845
 due 924
seep 295
seer *veteran* 130
 madman 504
 oracle 513
 sorcerer 994
see-saw 12, 314
seethe *wet* 339
 hot 382
 make hot 384
 excitement 824
seething caldron 386
segar 392
segment 44, 51
segnitude 683
s'égosiller 411
segregate
 not related 10
 separate 44
 exclude 55
segregated
 incoherent 47
seigneur, grand –
 pride 878
 insolence 885
seignior 745, 875
seigniority
 authority 737
 possession 777
 property 780
seigniory 737
seine net 232

wonder 870
sensational 574, 824
sensation drama 599
sensations of touch 380
sense 498, 516
 deep – 821
 horse – 498
 in no – 565
 accept in a particular –
 522
 – of duty 926
senseless
 insensible 376
 absurd 497
 foolish 499
 unmeaning 517
senses
 external - 375
 intellect 450
 sanity 502
sensibility 375, 822
sensible
 material 316
 wise 498
sensitive 375, 822
sensorial 821
sensorium 450
sensual 377, 954
sensualist 954*a*
sensuous
 sensibility 375
 pleasure 377
 feeling 821
sentence
 decision 480
 maxim 496
 affirmation 535
 phrase 566
 condemnation 971
sententious 572, 574
sentient 375, 821
sentiment 453
sentimental
 sensitive 822
 affected 855
sentinel, sentry 263
 guardian 664
 watch 688
 keeper 753
separate *disjoin* 44
 exclude 55
 bisect 91
 diverge 291
 divorce 905
 – the chaff from the wheat
 discriminate 465
 select 609

– into elements 49
– maintenance 905
separation 49
separatist 489, 984
sepia 433
seposition 44, 55
sepoy 726
sept *kin* 11
 class 75
 clan 166
Septentrional 237
septet 415
septic 655, 657
septicæmia 655
septuagenarian 98
Septuagint 985
septum 228
sepulchral
 interment 363
 resonance 408
 stridor 410
 hoarse 581
sepulchre 363
 whited – 545
sepulture 363
sequacious 63
sequacity *soft* 324
 tenacity 327
sequel 65, 117
sequela 65, 154
sequence
 - *in order* **63**
 - *in time* 117
 motion **281**
 logical – 476
sequent 63
sequester 789, 974
sequestered 893
sequestrate
 seize 789
 condemn 971
 confiscate 974
sequin 847
serac 383
seraglio 961
seraph 948, 977
seraphic
 blissful 829
 virtuous 944
 pious 987
seraphina 417
seraskier 745
sere and yellow leaf 128
serein 339, 348
serenade *music* 415
 compliment 894
 endearment 902

serene
 pellucid 425
 calm 826
 content 831
 imperturbable 871
 – highness 877
serf *slave* 746
 clown 876
serfdom 749
sergeant 745
serial
 continuous 69
 periodic 183
 book 593
seriatim
 in order 58
 continuously 69
 each to each 79
 slowly 275
series 69, 84
sérieux, take au – 843
serio-comic 853
serious *great* 31
 resolved 604
 important 642
 dejected 837
seriously 535
serjeant:
 common – 967
 –at-law 968
sermon *lesson* 537
 speech 582
 dissertation 595
 pastoral 998
 funeral – 363
sermonizer 584
seroon 72
serosity 333, 337
serpent
 tortuous 248
 snake 366
 hiss 409
 wind instrument 417
 wise 498
 deceiver 548
 cunning 702
 evil-doer 913
 knave 941
 demon 949
 the old – 978
 great sea – 515
serpentine 248
serrated 244, 257
serried 72, 321
serum 333, 337
servant *instrumentality* 631
 help 711

retainer **746**
- of all work 690
serve *benefit* 618
  business 625
  utility 644
  aid 707
  warfare 722
  obey 743
  servant 746
- an apprenticeship 539
- faithfully 743
- loyally 743
- notice 527
- out 972
- one right
  retaliation 718
  right 922
  punish 972
- as a substitute 147
- one's turn 644
- with a writ 969
service *good* 618
  utility 644
  use 677
  warfare 722
  servitude 749
  worship 990
  rite 998
  hold - 363
  at one's - 763
  press into the - 677
  render a - 644, 906
serviceable 644, 648
serviette 652
servile 749, 876, **886**
servitor 746
servitorship 749
servitude 749
  penal - 972
sesame, open - 260
  watchword 550
  spell 993
sesqui- 87
sesquipedalia verba 577
sesquipedalian 200
sess 812
sessile 46
session *council* 696
sessions *law* 966
sestet 597
set
  condition 7
  join 43
  coherence 46
  group 72
  class 75
  firm 150

tendency 176
place 184
form 240
sharpen 253
direction 278
go down 306
dense 321
stage 599
habit 613
prepare 673
gang 712
impose 741
make a dead - at 716
- about 66, 676
- abroach 73
- one's affections on 897
- afloat 153, 531
- against
  oppose 708
  quarrel 713
  hate 898
  angry 900
- against one another 464
- agoing
  impulse 276
  propulsion 284
  aid 717
- apart
  separate 44
  exclude 55
  select 609
- aside
  displace 185
  disregard 458
  neglect 460
  negative 536
  reject 610
  disuse 678
  annul 756
  refuse 764
  not observe 773
  relinquish 782
  dereliction 927
- one's back up 878
- before
  inform 527
  choice 609
- before oneself 620
- by 636
- one's cap at 897, 902
- on a cast 621
- down [see below]
- by the ears 898
- at ease 831
- an example
  model 22
  motive 615

- the eyes on 441
- one's face against
  oppose 708
  refuse 764
  disapprove 932
- the fashion
  influence 175
  authority 737
  fashion 852
- fast 704
- on fire
  ignite 384
  excite 824
- on foot 66
- foot on 294
- forth *show* 525
  assert 535
  describe 594
- forward 293
- free 750
- going [see - agoing]
- one's hand to 467
- one's heart upon 604, 865
- at hazard 665
- in *begin* 66
  rain 348
- on its legs 150
- on one's legs 159, 669
- in motion 264, 677
- to music 416
- at naught
  make light of 483
  reject 610
  oppose 708
  defy 715
  disobey 742
  not observe 773
  dereliction 927
- no store by 483, 930
- off
  compensation 30
  depart 293
  improve 658
  discount 813
  adorn 845
  display 882
- on 615
- in order 60
- out *arrange* 60
  begin 66
  depart 293
  decorate 845
  display 882
- over 755
- phrase 566
- a price 85, 812

- purpose 620
- at rest *end* 67
answer 462
adjudge 480
complete 729
compact 769
- right
inform 527
disclose 529
teach 537
reinstate 660
vindicate 937
- to rights 60
- sail 293
- the seal on 729
- one's seal to 467
- store by 642
- straight 246, 723
- the table in a roar 840
- one's teeth 604
- terms
manifest 525
phrase 566
style 574
- a trap for 545
- to 720, 722
- in towards 286
- up
printing 54
originate 153
strengthen 159
produce 161
upright 212
raise 307
successful 731
prosperous 734
- up shop 676
- upon
resolved 604
attack 716
desirous 865
- too high a value upon 482
- watch 459
- one's wits to work *think* 451
imagine 515
plan 626
- to work
undertake 676
impose 741
setaceous 256
set-back 735
set down
record 551
unseat 756
humiliate 879

slight 929
censure 932
give one a –
confute 479
- as 484
- for 484
- a cause for hearing 969
- to 155
- in writing 551
seton 662
setose 256
sett *lease* 771, 787
settee 215
setter 366
settle *regulate* 60
establish 150
be located 184
bench 215
come to rest 265
subside 306
kill 361
decide 480
choose 609
vanquish 731
consent 762
compact 769
pay 807
- accounts 807, 811
- down 133
stability 150
moderate 174
locate oneself 184
- into 144
- matters 723
- preliminaries 673
- property 781
- the question 478
- to sleep 683
- upon *give* 784
- with 807, 992
settled [*see* settle]
characteristic 5
ended 67
account - 811
- opinion 484
- purpose 620
settlement [*see* settle]
location 184
colony 188
dregs 653
compact 769
deed 771
property 780
strict - 781
settler 188
settlor 784
seven 98

-league boots 274, 992
wake the - sleepers 404
seventy 98
sever 38, 44
several *special* 79
plural 100
many 102
- times 104
severalize 465
severally 44, 79
severalty 44
severance 38
severe
energetic 171
symmetry 242
exact 494
- *style* 576
harsh 739
painful 830
simple 849
critical 932
severely *very* 31
severity **739**
sew 43
sewage 299, 653
sewed up
drunk 959
sewer 350, 653
sewerage 652, 653
sewer-gas 663
sewing-silk 205
sex *kind* 75
women 374
fair - 374
sexagenarian 98, 130
sexagenary 99
sextant 217, 244, 247
sextet 98
sextodecimo 593
sexton 363, 996
sextuple 98
seyyid 745
sforzando 415
shabbiness 34
shabby *trifling* 643
deteriorated 659
stingy 819
mean 874
disgraceful 940
shabby-genteel 851
shack 189
shackle
fastening 45
hinder 706
restrain 751
fetter 752
shade *degree* 26

small quantity 32
manes 362
darkness 421
shadow **424**
colour 428
conceal 528
screen 530
paint 556
ghost 980
eye – 443
in the – 528, 874
shadow of a – 32, 422
throw into the –
surpass 303
conceal 528
glory 873
throw all else into the –
642
thrown into the – 34, 874
under the – of 664
without a – of doubt 474
shades:
– below 982
– of death 360
– of difference 15
– of evening 422
shading 421
– off 26
shadow
unsubstantial 4
copy 21
small 32
accompaniment 88
thin 203
be behind 235
sequence 281
dark 421
shade 424
pursue 461, 622
dream 515
demon 980
fight with a – 699
follow as a – 281
partial – 422
without a – of turning 141
worn to a –
thin 203
worse for wear 659
– of coming events 511
– forth dim 422
predict 511
metaphor 521
represent 554
may your – never be less
courtesy 894
respect 928
approbation 931

take the – for the
substance
credulous 486
mistake 495
unskilful 699
under the – of one's wing
664
shadowy 4, 447
shady 874
shaft deep 208
frame 215
pit 260
missile 284
axis 312
air-pipe 351
handle 633
weapon 727
shaggy 256
shagreen 223
shah 745
shake totter 149
weak 160
vibrate 314
agitation 315
shiver 383
trill 407
music 416
dissuade 616
injure 659
impress 821
excited 824
fear 860
– one's fatih 485
– hands
pacification 723
friendship 888
courtesy 894
forgive 918
– the head
dissent 489
deny 536
refuse 764
disapprove 932
– off 297
– off the yoke 759
– to pieces 162
– one's sides 838
– up 315
shakedown bed 215
shakes, no great – 643,
651
shako 225, 717
shaky weak 160
in danger 665
fearful 860
shallop 273
shallow

not deep 32, 209
ignorant 491
ignoramus 493
foolish 499
trifling 643
– pretext 617
– profundity 855
shallow-brain 501
shallowness 209
shallow-pated 499
shallows
danger 667
sham imitation 19
falsehood 544
deception 545, 546
– fight 720
shaman 994
shamanism 992
shamble 275, 315
shambles 361
shame
disrepute 874
wrong 923
censure 932
chastity 960
cry – upon 932
false – 855
for – 874
sense of – 879
– the devil 939
to one's – be it spoken 874
shamefaced 881
shameful
disgraceful 874
profligate 945
shameless
bold 525
impudent 885
profligate 945
indecent 961
shampoo 652
shandredhan 272
shanghai 791
shank support 215
instrument 633
Shanks's mare 266
shanty 189
shape 240, 448
– one's course
direction 278
pursuit 622
conduct 692
– out a course 626
shapeless 241, 846
shapely 242, 845
shard 51
share

part 51
participate 778
allotted portion 786
– *and share alike* 778
shareholder 778
shark 792
sharp
energetic 171
violent 173
acute 253
sensible 375
pungent 392
- *sound* 410
musical tone 413
intelligent 498
active 682
clever 698
cunning 702
feeling 821
painful 830
rude 895
censorious 932
look – 459, 682
- *appetite* 865
- *contest* 720
- *ear* 418
- *eye* 441
- *fellow* 682, 700
- *frost* 383
- *look-out* 459, 507
- *pain* 378
- *practice*
cunning 702
severity 739
improbity 940
- *set* 865
sharpen [*see* sharp]
excite 824
- *one's tools* 673
- *one's wits* 537
sharpener 253
sharper 792
sharpness 253
sharpshooter 726
sharpshooting 716
Shaster 986
shatter *disjoin* 44
disperse 73
render powerless 158
destroy 162
shatter-brained 503
shattered 160, 688
shave *reduce* 195
shorten 201
layer 204
smooth 255
grate 330

lie 546
close – 671
shaved 226
shaving *small* 32
layer 204
filament 205
shave-tail 726, 745
shawl 225
shawm 417
shay 272
she 374
sheaf 72
shear *reduce* 195
shorten 201
sheep 370
take 789
shears 253
sheath 191, 223
sheathe 225
moderate 174
- *the sword* 723
sheathing 223
sheave 633
shed *scatter* 73
building 189
divest 226
emit 297
give 784
- *blood* 361
- *light upon* 420
- *a lustre on* 873
- *tears* 839
Shedim 980
sheen 420
sheep 366
sheep-dog 366
sheep-fold 232
sheepish 881
sheep's eye, cast a –
desire 865
modest 881
endearment 902
sheer *simple* 42
complete 52
deviate 279
- *off avoid* 623
sheet *layer* 204
covering 223
paper 593
come down in –s
rain 348
white – 952
winding – 363
- *of fire* 382
- *of water* 343
sheet-anchor
safety 664, 666

hope 858
sheet-lightning 423
sheik *ruler* 745, 875
lover 897
priest 996
shelf 215, 667
on the –
powerless 158
disused 678
inaction 681
shell *cover* 223
coffin 363
bombard 716
bomb 727
–*burst* 404
–*shock* 655
- *out* 784, 807, 809
shellac 356*a*
shellback 269
shell-fish 366
shelter 664, 666
- *oneself under plea of* 617
sheltie 271
shelve *defer* 133
locate 184
slope 217
neglect 460
disuse 678
shelving beach 217
shend 659
shepherd *tender of sheep*
370
director 694
pastor 996
Shepherd, the Good – 976
shepherd's dog 366
Sheppard, Jack – 792
shere 32
sheriff 745, 965
Shetland pony 271
shew [*see* show]
shibboleth 550
shield
heraldry 550
safety 664
buckler 666
defend 717
scutcheon 877
look only at one side of
the – 481
reverse of the – 235, 468
under the – of 664
shift *change* 140
convert 144
substitute 147
changeable 149
chemise 225

move 264
transfer 270
deviate 279
prevaricate 546
plea 617
cunning 702
last – 601
make a – with 147, 677
put to one's –s 704, 840
– one's ground 607
– off *defer* 133
– for oneself 692, 748
left to – for oneself 893
– one's quarters 264
– the scene 140
– to and fro 149
shifting [*see* shift]
transient 111
– sands 149
– trust or use 783
shiftless 674, 699
shillelagh 727
shilling 800
cut off with a – 789
– shocker 594
shilly-shally 605
shimmer 420
shimmy
dance 840
shindy 720
shine *light* 420
beauty 845
glory 873
take the – out of 874
– in conversation 588
– forth 873
– upon
illumine 420
aid 707
shingle 330
shingled
hair 53
shingles 223
shining [*see* shine]
– light *sage* 500
Shintoism 984
shiny 420
ship *lade* 190
transfer 270
vessel **273**
take – 267, 293
one's – coming in 803
– of the line 726
shipboard, on – 273
ship-load 31, 190
shipman 269
shipmate 890

shipment
contents 190
transfer 270
shippen 189
shipping 273
shipshape *order* 58
conformity 82
skill 698
shipwreck
destruction 162
vanquish 731
failure 732
shire 181
shirk 603, 623, 742
shirker 862
shirt 225
Shiva 979
shive 22, 204
shiver
small piece 32
divide 44
destroy 162
filament 205
shake 315
brittle 328
cold 383
fear 860
go to –s 162
– in one's shoes 860
shivery *brittle* 328
powdery 330
shoal
assemblage 72
multitude 102
shallow 209
shoals *danger* 667
surrounded by –
difficulty 704
shoat 366
shock *sheaf* 72
violence 173
concussion 276
agitation 315
unexpected 508
disease 655
discord 713
affect 821
move 824
pain 828
give pain 830
dislike 867
scandalize 932
shocking *bad* 649
painful 830
ugly 846
vulgar 851
fearful 860

disreputable 874
hateful 898
in a – temper 901*a*
shockingly *much* 31
shod 225
shoddy 645
shoe *support* 215
dress 225
hindrance 706
stand in the –s of
commission 755
deputy 759
where the – pinches
badness 649
difficulty 704
opposition 708
sensibility 822
painful 830
shoemaker 225
shofle 272
shoful 792
shog 173
shoneen 855
shoot
offspring 167
expand 194
dart 274
propel 284
kill 361
sprout 365, 367
pain 378
execute 972
teach the young idea to –
537
– ahead 282
– ahead of 303
– at 716
– out beams 420
– up *increase* 35
prominent 250
shooting [*see* shoot]
chase 622
– pain 378
– star 318, 423
shooting-coat 225
shop 795, 799
keep a – 625, 794
shut up – *end* 67
cease 142
relinquish 624
rest 687
smell of the – 851
shopkeeper 797
shoplifter 792
shoplifting 791
shopman 797
shopmate 890

shopping 794, 795
shore
  support 215
  border 231
  land 342
  buttress 717
  hug the – 286
  on – 342
  – up 215, 670
shoreless 180
shorn *cut short* 21
  deprived 776
  – of its beams 422, 874
  – lamb 828
short
  not long 201
  brittle 328
  concise 572
  uncivil 895
  come – of, fall – of
  inferior 34
  shortcoming 304
  insufficient 640
  in – 572, 596
  – allowance 640
  – answer 895
  – breath 688
  – by 201
  – of cash 804
  – commons
  insufficiency 640
  fasting 956
  – circuit 279, 628
  – cut *straight* 246
  mid-course 628
  – distance 197
  – life and merry 840
  – measure 53
  at – notice 111, 132
  – of *small* 32
  inferior 34
  subtraction 38
  incomplete 53
  shortcoming 304
  insufficient 640
  – sea 348
  make – work of
  destroy 162
  active 682
  haste 684
  complete 729
  conquer 731
  punish 972
shortage 53
shortcoming
  inequality 28
  inferiority 34

  motion short of **304**
  non-completion 730
  deficiency 945
shorten 201
  – sail 275
shorthand 590
short-handed 651
shorthorn 366
short-lived 111
shortly *soon* 132
shortness 201
  for – sake 572
shorts 225
short-sighted
  myopic 443
  misjudging 481
  foolish 499
short-story 594
short-winded 160, 688
short-witted 499
shot *missile* 284
  report 406
  variegated 440
  guess 514
  war material 722, 727
  price 812
  reward 973
  bad – 701
  exchange –s 720
  good – 700
  have a – at 716
  like a – 113
  off like a – 623
  pistol – 406
  random – 463, 621
  round – 727
  – in the locker 632
  not have a – in one's
    locker 804
  – and shell 722
shot-free 815
shot-gun 727
should be:
  no better than she – 961
  what – 922
shoulder
  support 215
  projection 250
  shove 276
  broad –ed 159
  cold – 289
  have on one's –s 625
  on the –s of
  high 206
  elevated 307
  instrumentality 631
  shrug the –s [*see* shrug]

  rest on the –s of 926
  rub –s with nobility 852
  take upon one's –s 676
  – arms 673
  – a musket 722
  – to shoulder 709, 712
  – to the wheel 604, 676
shoulder-knot 847
shoulder-strap 747
shout
  loud 404
  cry 411
  rejoice 838
shove 276
  give a – to
  aid 707
shovel
  receptacle 191
  transfer 270
  vehicle 272
  fire-iron 386
  cleanness 652
  put to bed with a – 363
  – away 297
shovel-hat 999
show *visible* 446
  appear 448
  draw attention 457
  evidence 467
  demonstrate 478
  manifest 525
  entertainment 599
  parade 882
  dumb – 500
  make a – 544
  mere – 544
  peep– 840
  – off 525
  – one's cards 529
  – cause 527
  – one's colours, 550
  – one's face
  presence 186
  manifest 525
  disclose 529
  – fight *defy* 715
  attack 716
  defend 717
  brave 861
  – forth 525
  – in front 303
  – one's cards 529
  – one's hand 529
  – a light pair of heels 623
  – itself 446
  – of 17, 472
  – off 882, 884

– one's teeth 715
– up *visible* 446
manifest 525
ridicule 856
degrade 874
censure 932
accuse 938
shower
assemblage 72
rain 348
– bath 386
– down
abundance 639
– down upon 784, 816
showman 524
showy *colour* 428
beauty 845
ornament 847
vulgar 851
fashion 852
ostentatious 882
shrapnel 727
shred 32, 205
shredder 260
shrew 901
shrewd
knowing 490
wise 498
cunning 702
shriek 410, 411
shrievalty 965
shrieve 965
shrift
confession 529
absolution 952
shriftless 951
shrill 410, 411
shrimp 193
shrine 363, 1000
receptacle 191
shrink
decrease 36
shrivel 195
go back 283, 287
unwilling 603
avoid 623
sensitive 822
– from *fear* 860
dislike 867
hate 898
shrive 952, 998
shrivel 195
shrivelled *thin* 203
shroud *cover* 225
funeral 363
hide 528
safety 664

defend 717
–ed in mystery 519
shrouds 45
Shrove Tuesday 998
shrub *plant* 367
plantation 371
shrug *sign* 550
– the shoulders
dissent 489
submit 725
discontent 832
dislike 867
contempt 930
disapprobation 932
shrunk 193, 195
shudder *cold* 383
fear 860
make one –
painful 830
– at *aversion* 867
hate 898
shuffle *mix* 41
derange 61
change 140
interchange 148
changeable 149
move slowly 275
agitate 315
falsehood 544
untruth 546
irresolute 605
recant 607
dance 840
improbity 940
– the cards
begin again 66
change 140
chance 621
prepare 673
patience and – the cards
826
– off *run away* 623
– off this mortal coil 360
– on 266
shuffler 548
shun 623, 867
shunt 270, 279
shunted
shelved 460
shut 261
– the door 761
– the door in one's face
764
– the door upon 893
– one's ears 419, 487
– the eyes 442
– one's eyes to

not attend to 458
neglect 460
not believe 487
permit 760
not observe 773
– the gates of mercy 914*a*
– in 751
– oneself up 893
– out 55, 761
– up shop *end* 67
cease 142
silence 403
relinquish 624
repose 687
– up *close* 261
confute 479
imprison 751
shutter 424
shuttle 314
shuttlecock 605
shy *deviate* 279
draw back 283
propel 284
avoid 623
fearful 860
cowardly 862
modest 881
fight – of 623
have a – at 716
– of belief 487
– cock 862
– of *doubtful* 485
unwilling 603
cautious 864
dislike 867
Shylock 787
Siamese twins 89
sib 11
Siberia 383
sibi gladio hunc jugulo,
suo – 718
sibilation *hiss* **409**
disrespect 929
disapprobation 932
Sibyl *oracle* 513
ugly 846
Sibylline 511
– leaves 513
sic *imitation* 19
exact 494
si – omnes! 948
– transit gloria mundi 111
– volo sic jubeo 600
– vos non vobis 791
siccity 340
sick *ill* 655
make one – 830, 867

visitation of the – 998
 – at heart 837
 – of *weary* 841
  dislike 867
  satiated 869
 in –ness and in health 604
sick-chamber 655
sicken *nauseate* 395
 disease 655
 pain 830
 weary 841
 disgust 867
sickener
 too much 641
sickle 244, 253
sickly *weak* 160
sick-room 655
side
 consanguinity 11
 edge 231
 laterality 236
 party 712
 ostentation 882
 at one's – 197
 on every – 277
 one one – 243
 on one's – 714
 look only at one – of the
  shield 481
 pass from one – to another
  607
 take up a – 476
 wrong – up 218
 – by side
  accompaniment 88
  near 197
  laterality 236
  party 712
 from – to side 314
 – with *aid* 707
  co-operate 709
  concord 714
side-arms 727
side-blow 702
sideboard 191
side-car 272
side-dish 298
side-drum 417
side issue 643
side-kick 890
sideling 279
sidelong 236
sideration 158
sidereal 318
 – time 114
siderite 288
Sideromancy 511

side-saddle 215
side-scene 599
sideslip 267
sidesman 996
side-track 287
sidewalk 627
sideways 217, 236
side-wind
 oblique 217
 circuit 629
 cunning 702
sidle *oblique* 217
 lateral 236
 deviate 279
siege 716
 lay – to 716
 state of – 722
siege-train 727
siesta 683
sieve *sort* 60
 perforate 260
 clean 652
 memory like a – 506
 pour water into a – 638,
  818
 stop one hole in a – 819
sift *simplify* 42
 sort 60
 inquire 461
 discriminate 465
 clean 652
 – the chaff from the wheat
  609
sigh 405, 839
 – for 865
sighing like furnace 902
sight *much* 31
 multitude 102
 vision 441
 appearance 448
 ugly 846
 prodigy 872
 at – 132, 441
 dim – 443
 in – 446
 in – of 197, 441
 in plain – 525
 keep in – 457
 within – of shore 858
sightless
 blind 442
 invisible 447
 ugly 846
sightly 845
sights, see – 455
sightseeing 441
sightseer 444, 455

sigil *seal* 550
 evidence 769
sigmoidal 248
sign *attest* 467
 omen 512
 indication 550
 record 551
 write 590
 compact 769
 prodigy 872
 give – of 525
 make no – 585
 – of the cross 998
 –s of the times
  indication 550
  omen 512
  warning 668
 –s of the zodiac 318
signal *great* 31
 sign 550
 important 642
 give the – 741
 – of distress 669
signalize
 indicate 550
 glory 873
 celebrate 883
signally 31
signal oil 356
signal-post 668
signature
 mark, identification 550
 writing 590
 compact 769
 security 771
sign-board 550
signet
 mark, identification 550
 sign of authority 747
 compact 769
 writer to the – 968
significant 642 [*see* signify]
 evidence 467
 important 642
signifies, what – 643
signify
 forebode 511
 mean 516
 inform 527
signior 875
sign-manual 550, 590
signor 373, 877
signora 374
sign-painter 559
sign-painting 555
sign-post 550
signum, ecce – 550

sike 348
silence *disable* 158
  no sound **403**
  confute 479
  latency 526
  concealment 528
  aphony 581
  taciturn 585
  check 731
silencer 405, 408
silentio, sub –
  silent 403
  inattention 458
  latent 526
silhouette
  outline 230, 448
  shadow 421
  portrait 556
siliquose 191
silk 255, 324
  – gown
  barrister 968
  – hat 225
  make a – purse out of a
    sow's ear 471
silken repose 686
silkiness 954
sill 215
silly
  credulous 486
  imbecile 499
  insane 503
silo 636
silt *deposit* 321
  dirt 653
silvan 367
silver *bright* 420
  white 430
  grey 432
  money 800
  bait with a – hook 615
  German – 545
  – lining of the cloud 858
  – wedding 883
silver certificate 800
silver-toned 413
silviculture 371
simagrée 855
similarity 17
  – of form 240
simile
  similarity 17
  comparison 464
  metaphor 521
similitude 17, 21
simmer
  agitation 315

  boil 382, 384
  excitement 824
simmering 825
simoleon 800
Simon, Simple – 501, 547
Simon Pure
  the real – 494
Simon Stylites 893
simony 964
simoon 249, 382
simper *smile* 838
  affectation 855
simple *mere* 32
  unmixed 42
  credulous 486
  ignorant 493
  silly 499
  – *language* 576
  herb 662
  artless 703
  unadorned 849
  – *meaning* 516
simple-hearted 543
simpleness **42**
Simple Simon 501, 547
simpleton 501
simplex munditiis 849
simplicity [*see* simple] **849**
  ignorance 491
simplify [*see* simple]
  elucidate 518
simply 32, 87
  more – 522
simulacrum 19
simulate
  resemble 17
  imitate 19
  cheat 544
simultaneous 120
sin 945, 947
sinapism 662
since *under the*
  circumstances 8
  after 117
  cause 155
  reason 476
sincere
  veracious 543
  ingenuous 703
  feeling 821
sine 217
sine: – curâ 831
  – die 107, 133
  – ictu 158
  – quâ non
  required 630
  important 642

  condition 770
sinecure 681
  no – 682
sinew 159
sinewless 158
sinews of war 800
sinful 945
sing *resonance* 408
  bird 412
  music 416
  voice 580
  poetry 597
  rejoice 838
  – Io triumphe 884
  – out 411
  – praises
  approve 931
  worship 990
  – in the shrouds 349
  – small 879
singe 382, 384
singer 416
single *unmixed* 42
  unit 87
  secluded 893
  unmarried 904
  ride at – anchor 863
  – combat 720
  – file 69
  – out 609
single-handed
  one 87
  easy 705
  unassisted 706
single-minded 703
singleness [*see* single]
  – of heart 703, 939
  – of purpose 604a, 703
single-stick 720
singlet 225
Sing Sing 752
sing-song 414, 892
singular *special* 79
  exceptional 83
  one 87
singularly *very* 31
sinister *left* 239
  bad 649
  vicious 945
  bar –
  imperfect 651
  disrepute 874
sinistrality **239**
sinistromanual 239
sinistrous
  left-handed 239
  sullen 901a

sink *disappear* 4
  destroy 162
  descend 306
  lower 308
  submerge 310
  neglect 460
  conceal 528
  cloaca 653
  fatigue 688
  vanquish 731
  fail 732
  adversity 735
  invest 787
  pain 828
  depressed 837
  – back 661
  – of corruption 653
  – into the grave 360
  – of iniquity 945
  – in the mind
  thought 451
  memory 505
  excite 824
  – money 809
  – into oblivion 506
  – or swim
  certainty 474
  perseverance 604a
sinking
  heart – 837
  – fund 802
sinless 946
sinned against than
  sinning, more – 946
sinner 949
Sinn Fein 742
sin-offering 952
sinuous 243, 248
sinus 252
sip *small* 32
  drink 298
siphon 350
sippet 298
sir *man* 373
  title 877
  – Oracle 887
sirdar 745
sire 166
siren
  sea-nymph 341
  loud sound 404
  musician 416
  seducing 615
  warning 668
  alarm 669
  evil-doer 913
  demon 980

  sorcerer 994
  song of the –s 615
  – strains 415
sirene *musical instrument*
  417
siriasis 053
sirius 423
sirocco *wind* 349
  heat 382
sirrah! 949
sister *kin* 11
  likeness 17
  nurse 662
  nun 996
sisterhood
  party 712
  frail – 962
sisterly 906
sisters:
  weird – 994
  – three 601
sistrum 417
Sisyphus, task of –
  useless 645
  difficult 704
sit 308
  – down *settle* 184
  lie 213
  stoop 308
  – in judgment
  adjudge 480
  jurisdiction 965
  lawsuit 969
  – on 215
  – on thorns
  annoyance 828
  fear 860
site 183, 780
sith 476
sitting [*see* sit]
  incubation 673
  convocation 696
  – up *late* 133
  work 686
sitting-room 191
situ, in – 183, 265
situation
  circumstances 8
  place **183**
  location 184
  business 625
  out of a – 185
Siva 979
six 98
  – of one and half-a-dozen
    of the other 27

sixes and sevens, at – 59,
  713
sixty 98
sizar 746
size *degree* 26
  magnitude 31
  glue 45
  arrange 60
  dimensions **192**
  viscid 352
  – up 480
sizzle 409
sjambok 975
skat 840
skate
  locomotion 266
  vehicle 272
skating 840
skean 727
skedaddle 623
skeel 191
skein 219
  tangled – 59
skeleton
  remains 40
  essential part 30
  thin 203
  support 215
  corpse 362
  plan 626
  reduced to a – 659
  – in the closet 649, 830
  – at the feast 836
skelter 276
skepticism
  doubt 485
  incredulity 487
  irreligion 989
sketch
  form 240
  represent 554
  paint 556
  describe 594
  plan 626
sketcher 559
sketchy
  incomplete 53
  feeble 575
  unfinished 730
skew 217
  –bald 440
skewer 45
ski 266, 272
  –running 840
  –joring 840
  –jumping 840
skiagraphy 421, 554, 556

skid *support* 215
  hindrance 706
skies:
  exalt to the – 873
  praise to the – 933
skiff 273
skill 698
  acquisition of – 539
  game of – 840
skillet 191
skilly 293
skim *move* 266
  navigate 267
  rapid 274
  neglect 460
  summarize 596
skimp 460, 819
skimpy 640
skin *outside* 220
  tegument 223
  peel 226
  swindle 791
  fleece 814
  wet to the – 339
  with a whole – 670
  without – 822
  mere – and bone 203
  – a flint 471, 819
  – over 660
skin-deep
  shallow 32, 209
  external 220
skinned: thick– 376
  thin– 375
skinny 203, 223
skip *jump* 309
  neglect 460
  rejoice 838
skipjack
  prosperous 734
  low-born 876
skipper
  sea captain 269
  captain 745
skippingly 70
skips, by – 70
skirmish 720
skirmisher 726
skirt
  appendix 39
  pendent 214
  dress 225
  surrounding 227
  edge 231
  side 236
  – dance 840
skirting 231

skirts of:
  hang upon the –
  sequence 281
  on the –
  near 197
skit *ridicule* 856
  detraction 934
  prostitute 962
skittish
  capricious 608
  excitable 825
  timid 862
  bashful 881
skittles 840
skittle sharper 792
skiver 253
skulk 528, 862
skull 450
skull-cap 225
skunk 401
skurry 684
sky *summit* 210
  world 318
  air 338
  necessity 601
sky-aspiring 865
sky-blue 438
sky-lark 305
sky-larking 840
sky-light 260
sky-line 196
sky-pilot 996
sky-rocket 305
sky-scraper 206, 210
slab *layer* 204
  support 215
  flat 251
  viscous 352
  record 551
slabber *slaver* 297
  unclean 653
slack *loose* 47
  weak 160
  inert 172
  slow 275
  cool 385
  fuel 388
  neglectful 460
  unwilling 603
  insufficient 640
  inactive 683
  lax 738
slacken
  loosen 47
  moderate 174
  repose 687
  hinder 706

  – one's pace 275
slacker 460, 603, 623, 927
slag *embers* 384
  inutility 641
  dirt 653
slake *quench* 174
  gratify 829
  satiate 869
  – one's appetite
  intemperance 954
slam 276, 406
  – the door in one's face
  oppose 708
  refuse 764
slammerkin 653
slander 934
slanderer 936
slang 560, 563, 908
slant 217
slap *instantly* 113
  strike 276
  censure 932
  punish 972
  – in the face
  opposition 708
  attack 716
  anger 900
  disrespect 929
  disapprobation 932
  – the forehead 461
slap-dash 684
slash 44, 308
slashing *style* 574
slate
  writing tablet 590
  election 609
  disparage 932
  clean the – 918
  – loose *mad* 503
slate-coloured 432
slates *roof* 223
slattern
  disorder 59
  dirty 653
  bungler 701
  vulgar 851
slatternly 699
slaughter 361
slaughter-house 361
slave *instrumentality* 631
  toil 686
  servant 746
  a – to 749
  – trade 795
slaver *ship* 273
  slobber 297
  dirt 653

flatter 933
slavery 686, 749
slavish 749, 886
slay 361
sleave 59
sled 272
sledge 272
sledge-hammer 276
  with a – 162, 686
sleek 255, 845
sleep 683
  last – 360
  rock to – 174
  send to – 841
  not have a wink of – 825
  – with one eye open 459
  – at one's post 683
  – upon 133, 451
  – walker 268
  – walking 266
sleeper *support* 215
  wake the seven –s 404
sleeping partner 683
sleepless 682
sleepy 683
sleet 383
sleeve *skein* 219
  dress 225
  hang on the – of 746
  wear one's heart upon his
    – 525, 703
  in one's – 528
  laugh in one's – 838, 856
sleeveless 499, 608
  – errand 645, 699
sleigh 272
sleight *skill* 698
  – of hand 545
slender *small* 32
  thin 203
  trifling 643
  – means 804
sleuth 527
  – hound 913
slew round 312
slice *cut* 44
  piece 51
  layer 204
slick 682, 698
slicker 225
slide *elapse* 109
  smooth 255
  pass 264
  locomotion 266
  descend 306
  – back 661
  – in 228

– into 144
sliding 840
sliding-panel 545
sliding-rule 85
slight *small* 32
  slender 203
  rare 322
  neglect 460
  disparage 483
  feeble 575
  trifle 643
  dereliction 927
  disrespect 929
  contempt 930
slight-made 203
slily
  surreptitiously 544
  craftily 702
slim 203
  cunning 702
slime *viscous* 352
  dirt 653
sling *hang* 214
  project 284
  weapon 727
slink *hide* 528
  cowardice 862
  – away *avoid* 623
  disrepute 874
slip *small* 32
  elapse 109
  child 129
  strip 205
  petticoat 225
  descend 306
  error 495
  workshop 691
  fail 732
  false coin 800
  vice 945
  guilt 947
  give one the – 671
  let – *liberate* 750
  lose 776
  relinquish 782
  – away 187, 623
  – cable 623
  – the collar 671, 750
  – 'twixt cup and lip 509
  let – the dogs of war 722
  – in, – into 294
  – the memory 506
  – on 225
  – out 187
  – over *neglect* 460
  – of the pen 568
  – of the tongue

solecism 568
stammering 583
– through the fingers *miss*
  an opportunity 135
escape 671
fail 732
slipper 225
  hunt the – 840
slippery
  transient 111
  smooth 255
  greasy 355
  uncertain 475
  vacillating 607
  dangerous 665
  facile 705
  faithless 940
  – ground 667
slipshod 575
slipslop
  absurdity 497
  solecism 568
  weak language 575
slit *divide* 44
  chink 198
  furrow 259
slither 264
sliver 51
slobber *drivel* 297
  slop 337
  dirt 653
sloe *black* 431
slog 143
slogan 722
sloop 273
  –of-war 726
slop *spill* 297
  water 337
  dirt 653
slope *oblique* 217
  run away 623
sloppy *moist* 339
  marsh 345
  - *style* 575
slops *clothes* 225
slosh 337, 653
slot 44, 260
sloth 683
slouch *low* 207
  oblique 217
  move slowly 275
  inactive 683
slouching *ugly* 846
slough
  quagmire 345
  dirt 653
  difficulty 704

adversity 735
- of Despond 859
sloven untidy 59
  bungler 701
slovenly *untidy* 59
  careless 460
  - *style* 575
  dirty 653
  awkward 699
  vulgar 851
slow *tardy* 133
  inert 172
  moderate 174
  motion 275
  inactive 683
  wearisome 841
  dull 843
  by - degrees 26
  - movement
  music 415
  march in - time 275
  - as molasses in January
    275
  be - to
  unwilling 603
  not finish 730
  refuse 764
slow-coach 701
slowness 275
sloyd 537
slubber 653
slubberdegullion 876
sludge 653
slug *slow* 275
  inaction 681
  inactivity 683
  bullet 727
sluggard 275, 683
sluggish 172, 823, 843
sluice *limit* 233
  egress 295
  river 348
  conduit 350
  open the -s 297
slum 653
slumber 683
slump 304
slur *blemish* 847
  stigma 874
  gloss over 937
  reproach 938
  - over *neglect* 460
  slight 483
slush *marsh* 345
  semiliquid 352
  dirt 653
slut *untidy* 59

female 374
dirty 653
unchaste 962
sly *stealthy* 528
  cunning 702
smack
  small quantity 32
  mixture 41
  boat 273
  impulse 276
  taste 390
  thud 406
  kiss 902
  strike 972
  - the lips
  pleasure 377
  taste 390
  savoury 394
  rejoice 838
  - of *resemble* 17
small
  - *in degree* 32
  - *in size* 193
  become - 195
  feel - 879
  of - account 643
  esteem of - account 930
  - arms 727
  - beer 643, 880, 930
  - coin 800
  - chance 473
  - fry 193, 643, 876
  - matter 643
  - number 103
  - part 51
  - pica 591
  in the - hours 125
  on a - scale 32, 193
  - talk 588
small-bore 727
small-clothes 225
smaller 34, 195
smallness 32
smalls 225
smalt 438
smart *pain* 378
  active 682
  clever 698
  feel 821
  grief 828
  witty 842
  pretty 845
  ornamental 847
  - pace 274
  - saying 842
  - under 821
smarten 847

smart-money 973
smash 162, 732
smasher 792
smatch 390
smatterer 493
smattering 491
smear *cover* 223
  soil 653
  blemish 848
smell 398
  bad - 401
  - of the lamp
  ornate style 577
  prepared 673
  - powder 722
smell-feast 886
smelling-bottle 400
smelt *heat* 384
  prepare 673
smicker 838
smile 836, 838
  raise a - 840
  - at 856
  - of contempt 930
  - of fortune 734
  - upon *aid* 707
  courtesy 894
  endearment 902
smirch 431, 653
smirk 838
smite *maltreat* 649
  excite 824
  afflict 830
  punish 972
smith 690
smithereens 161
smitten *love* 897
  - with *moved* 615
smock 225, 258
smock-faced 862
smock-frock 225
smoke
  dust 330
  vapour 336
  heat 382
  tobacco 392
  discover 480a
  suspect 485
  unimportant 643
  dirt 653
  cure 670
  disrespect 929
  end in -
  shortcoming 304
  failure 732
  - the calumet of peace 723
  -ed glasses 424

– screen 424
– stack 260
smoking hot 382
smoking-jacket 225
smoking-room 191
smoky *opaque* 426
  dirty 653
smooth *uniform* 16
  calm 174
  flattery 213, 251
  not rough 255
  easy 705
– the bed of death 707,
  906
– down 174
– over 174
– the ruffled brow of care
  834
– sailing 705
– water *easy* 705
– the way 705
smooth-bore 727
smoothly, go on –
  prosperous 734
smoothness 255
smooth-tongued 544, 933
smother
  repress 174
  kill 361
  stifle sound 581
  restrain 751
smoulder *inert* 172
  burn 382
  latent 526
smous 796, 797
smudge 431, 653, 848
smug *affected* 855
smuggle
  introduce 288
  steal 791
  illegal 964
smuggler 792
smut
  dirt 653
  impurity 961
smutch 431
snack
  small quantity 32
  food 298
snacks, go – 778
snaffle 752
snag *projection* 250
  sharp 253
  danger 667
  hindrance 706
snail *slow* 275
snake *undulation* 248

serpent 366
hissing 406
miscreant 913
scotch the – 640
– in the grass
hidden 528
deceiver 548
bad 649
source of danger 667
evil-doer 913
knave 941
snake-like
  convoluted 248
snap *break* 44
  eat 298
  brittle 328
  noise **406**
  rude 895
– at *seize* 789
  bite 830
  censure 932
– of the fingers
  trifle 643
– one's fingers at
  defy 715
  insolence 885
  despise 930
– the thread 70
– up *seize* 789
– one up
  censure 932
–shot 554
snap-dragon 840
snappish 901
snare *deception* 545
snarl *growl* 412
  rude 895
  angry 900
  threaten 909
snatch
  small quantity 32
  seize 789
– at *pursue* 622
  seize 789
– a grace beyond the reach
  of art 845
– from one's grasp 789
– from the jaws of death
  662, 672
– from under one's nose
  702
– a verdict 545, 702
snatches, by – 70
sneak *hide* 528
  coward 862
  servile 886
  base 940

knave 941
bad man 949
– off, – out of 623
sneer *disparage* 929
  contempt 930
  blame 932
sneeze *blow* 349
  snuffle 409
– at *despise* 930
sneezed at, not to be – 642
snick 32, 51
snicker 838
sniff *blow* 349
  odour 398
  discovery 480a
sniffle 349
snigger *laugh* 838
  ridicule 856
  disrespect 929
sniggle 545
snip
  small quantity 32
  cut 44
  short 201
  tailor 225
sniping 716
snippet 32
snip-snap 713
snip-snap-snorem 840
snivel *weep* 839
snivelling
  servile 886
snob *vulgar* 851
  plebeian 876
  servile 886
snobbishness
  flattery 933
snood
  headdress 225
  circle 247
snooker 840
Snooks, Mr. – 876
snooze 683
snozzle 250
snore 411, 683
snort 411, 412
snout 250
snow *ship* 273
  ice 383
  white 430
snow-ball 72
snow-blindness 443
snow-drift 72
snow-shoe 272
snow-storm 383
snub *short* 201
  hinder 706

cast a slur 874
humiliate 879
bluster 885
censure 932
snub-nosed 243
snuff *blow* 349
  pungent 392
  odour 398
  up to – 698, 702
  go out like the – of a
    candle 360
  – out 162, 421
  – up 296, 398
snuff-colour 433
snuffing, want –
  pert 885
snuffle *blow* 349
  hiss 409
  stammer 583
  hypocrisy 988
snuffy 653
snug *closed* 261
  comfortable 377
  safe 664
  prepared 673
  content 831
  secluded 893
  keep – 528, 893
  make all – 673
snuggery 189
snugness 827
so *similar* 17
  very 31
  therefore 476
  method 627
  – be it 488, 762
  – far so good 618
  – let it be 681
  – much the better 831, 838
  – much the worse 832,
    835
  – to speak 17, 521
soak *immerse* 300
  water 337
  moist 339
  drunkenness 959
  – up 340
So-and-so, Mr. –
  neology 563
soap *lubricate* 332
  oil 356
  cleanser 652
soapy *unctuous* 355
  servile 886
  flattery 933
soar *great* 31
  height 206

fly 267
rise 305
sob 839
sober *moderate* 174
  wise 498
  sane 502
  style 576
  grave 837
  temperate 953
  abstinent 958
  – down 174, 502
  humility 879
  in – sadness
    affirmation 535
  – senses 502
  – truth *fact* 494
sober-minded 502
  calm 826
  humble 879
sobriety 958
sobriquet 565
sob sister 534
soc *jurisdiction* 965
socage 777
so-called 545, 565
soccer 840
sociable
  carriage 272
  sociality 892
social *mankind* 372
  sociable 892
  – circle 892
  – evil 961
  – gathering 892
  – science 910
socialism
  government 737
  participation 778
  philanthropy 910
socialist 712
sociality 892
society
  mankind 372
  party 712
  fashion 852
  sociality 892
  position in – 873
Socinianism 984
sociology 712
sock *hoisery* 225
  drama 599
socket 191, 252
socle 215
Socratic method 461
sod 344
  beneath the – 363
sodality 712, 888

sodden 339, 384
sofa 215
Sofi 984, 996
soft *stop!* 142
  weak 160
  moderate 174
  smooth 255
  not hard 324
  moist 339
  marsh 345
  silence! 403
  – sound 405
  dulcet 413
  credulous 486
  silly 499
  lenient 740
  tender 822
  timid 862
  own to the –
    impeachement 529
  – music 415
  – pedal 405
  – sawder 617, 933
  – soap 356, 933
  – tongue, – words 894
soften [*see* soft]
  moderate 174
  relieve 834
  pity 914
  palliate 937
softening of the brain 158
softer sex 374
soft-hearted 914
softling 160
softness 324
  persuasibility 615
soft-spoken 894
soggy 339
soho
  attention 457
  parley 586
  hunting 622
soi-disant
  asserting 535
  pretender 548
  misnomer 565
  vain 880
  boastful 884
soil *region* 18
  land 342
  dirt 653
  deface 846
  till the – 371, 673
soirée 892
sojourn 186, 189
sojourner 188
soke 181

solace *relief* 834
　recreation 840
　– oneself with *pleasure* 827
solar 318
　– system 318
　– time 114
solatium 973
sold to the devil 949
soldan [*see* sultan]
solder *join* 43
　cement 45
　cohere 46
soldier 726
soldier-like 722, 861
sole *alone* 87
　base 211
　support 215
　feme – 904
solecism 568
soleil, coup de –
　hot 384
　mad 503
solemn
　affirmation 535
　important 642
　grave 837
　glorious 873
　ostentatious 882
　religious 987
　worship 990
　– mockery 882
　– silence 403
solemnity *rite* 998
solemnization 883
sol-fa 416
solfeggio 415
solicit *induce* 615
　request 765
　desire 865
　– the attention 457
solicitor *agent* 758
　petitioner 767
　lawyer 968
solicitous 865
solicitude *care* 459
　pain 828
　anxiety 860
　desire 865
solid *complete* 52
　dense 321
　certain 474
　learned 490
　exact 494
　wise 498
　persevering 604a
　solvent 803

– angle 244
solidarity
　party 712
solidify 321
soliloquy 589
solitaire *game* 840
　hermit 893
solitary, solitude
　alone 87
　secluded 893
solmization 416
solo 87, 415
　– dance 840
Solomon, Solon
　wise 498
　sage 500
solstice 125, 126
soluble *fluid* 333
　liquefy 335
solus 87
solution
　liquefaction 335
　answer 462
　explanation 522
　– of continuity 70
solve *liquefy* 335
　discover 480a
　unriddle 522
solvent
　liquefier 335
　monied 803
somatics 316
sombre *dark* 421
　black 431
　grey 432
　sad 837
sombrero 225
some *indefinite quantity* 25
　small quantity 32
　more than one 100
　–body *person* 372
　important or distinguished 642
　in – degree
　degree 26
　small 32
　at – other time 119
　in – place 182
　– ten or a dozen 102
　– time ago 122
　– time or other 119
somehow or other
　cause 155
　instrument 631
somersault 218
something *thing* 3
　small degree 32

　matter 316
　– else 15
　– like 17
　– or other 475
sometimes 136
somewhat
　a little 32
　a trifle 643
somewhere 182
　– about 32
somnambulism
　walking 266
　trance 515
somnambulist
　walker 268
　dreamer 515
somniferous
　sleepy 683
　weary 841
somnolence 683
son 167
Son, God the – 976
sonant 402
　letter 561
sonata 415
Sonderbund 769
song *music* 415
　poem 597
　death – 360, 839
　love– 597
　for a mere – 815
　no – no supper 812
　old – 643
songster 416
soniferous 402
sonnet 597
sonneteer 597
sonorous *sound* 402
　loud 404
　language 577
sons of:
　– Belial 988
　– God 977
Soofeeism 984
soon *transient* 111
　future 121
　early 132
　too – for 135
sooner: – or later
　another time 119
　future 121
　– said than done 704
soot 431, 653
sooth 511
　in good – 543
soothe
　allay 174

relieve 834
flatter 933
soothing
faint sound 405
– syrup 174
soothsay 511
soothsayer 513, 994
soothsaying 511
sop
small quantity 32
food 298
fool 501
inducement 615
reward 973
– to Cerberus 458
– in the pan 615
soph 492, 541
Sophi 745, 996
sophism 477, 497
sophist *scholar* 492
dissembler 548
sophister 492
student 541
sophistical 477
sophisticate *mix* 41
debase 659
sophisticated
spurious 545
sophistry 477
sophomore 541
soporific 683, 841
soporous 683
soprano 410, 416
sorbet 298
sorcerer **994**
sorcery **992**
sordes 653
sordet 417
sordid *stingy* 819
covetous 865
sordine 417
sore
bodily pain 378
disease 655
mental suffering 828, 830
discontent 832
anger 900
– as a boil 901*a*
– place 822
– subject 830, 900
sorely *very* 31
s'orienter 278
sorites 476
sorority 712
sorrel 433, 434
sorrow 828
give – words 839

sorry *trifling* 643
grieved 828
mean 876
make a – face 874
cut a – figure 874
be – for 750, 914
in a – plight 732
– sight 830, 837
sort *degree* 26
arrange 60
kind 75
– with
sociality 892
sortable, sortance
agreement 23
sortes
chance 156, 621
– Virgilianæ
sorcery 992
sortie 716
sortilege
prediction 511
sorcery 992
sortilegy 621
sortition 621
sorts, out of –
ill-health 655
sulky 901*a*
S.O.S. 669, 707
so-so *small* 32
trifling 643
imperfect 651
sostenuto 415
sot *fool* 501
drunkard 959
sot à triple étage 501
sotto voce
faint sound 405
conceal 528
voiceless 581
sou *money* 800
qui n'a pas le – 804
soubrette 599, 746
sough *conduit* 350
noise 405
cloaca 653
soul *essence* 5
person 372
intellect 450
genius 498
affections 820
cure of –s 995
flow of – 588
not a – 187
not dare to say one's – is
his own *subjection* 749
fear 860

– of wit 572
have one's whole – in his
work 686
soulless 683, 823
soul-mate 905
soul-sick 837
soul-stirring 821, 824
sound *great* 31
comfortable 82
stable 150
strong 159
fathom 208
bay 343
noise **402**
investigate 461
measure 466
true 494
wise 498
sane 502
good 648
perfect 650
healthy 654
solvent 803
orthodox 983*a*
catch a – 418
safe and – 654, 670
– the alarm
indication 550
warning 668
alarm 669
fear 860
– asleep 683
full of – and fury
unmeaning 517
insolent 885
– the horn 416
– of limb 654
– locator 726
– mind 502
– the praises of 931
– the note of preparation
673
– reasoning 476
– a retreat 283
– sleep 683
– a trumpet
publish 531
alarm 669
– of wind 654
sounding: big – 577
– brass 517
sounding-board 417
soundings 208
soundless
unfathomable 208
silent 403
soup 298, 352

soupçon 32, 41
souplé 298
sour *acid* 397
  discontented 832
  embitter 835
  uncivil 895
  sulky 901
  – grapes
    impossible 471
    excuse 617
  – the temper 830
source *beginning* 66
  cause 153
sourdet 417
sourdine 417
  à la – *noiseless* 405
  concealed 528
sourdough 463
soured 832
sourness 397
sous tous les rapports 52
souse 310, 337
South *direction* 278
  North and –
  opposite 237
Southern
  antipodes 237
  – Cross 318
souvenir 505
sovereign
  superior 33
  all-powerful 159
  authorities 737
  ruler 745
  – *contempt* 930
  – *remedy* 662
Soviet 696, 737
sow *scatter* 73
  pig 366
  agriculture 371
  female 374
  get the wrong – by the ear
  misjudgment 481
  error 495
  mismanage 699
  fail 732
  – broadcast 818
  – dissension 713, 898
  – the sand 645
  – the seed
  prepare 673
  – the seeds of
  cause 153
  teach 537
  – one's wild oats
  improve 658
  amusement 840

vice 945
  intemperance 954
sozzled 959
spa *town* 189
  sanatorium 662
space *distribute* 60
  time 106
  extension **180**
  musical 413
  celestial –s 318
  wide open –s 180
spaddle 272
spade 272
  call a – a spade
  plain language 576
  straightforward 703
spade-husbandry 371
spahi 726
span *join* 43
  link 45
  duality 89
  time 106
  transient 111
  distance 196
  near 196
  length 200
  short 201
  measure 466
  – new 124
spangle *spark* 420
  ornament 847
spaniel *dog* 366
  servile 886
spanish fly 171
spank *swift* 274
  flog 972
spanking *large* 192
  – pace 274
spanner 633
spar *beam* 214
  quarrel 713
  contend 720
spare *extra* 37
  small 193
  meagre 203
  refrain 623
  store 636
  scanty 640
  redundant 641
  disuse 678
  inaction 681
  relinquish 782
  give 784
  economy 817
  exempt 927a
  temperate 953
  enough and to – 639

not a moment to – 682
  to – 641
  – diet 956
  – no expense 816
  – no pains 686
  – room 180
  – time 685
spared: be –
  live 359
  it cannot be – 630
sparge 337
spargefaction
  scatter 73
  wet 337
sparing [*see* spare]
  small 32
  economy 817
  parsimony 819
  temperate 953
  with a – hand 819
  with no – hand 639
  – of praise 932
  – of words 585
spark *small* 32
  heat 382
  light 420
  luminary 423
  wag 844
  fop 854
  as the –s fly upwards *habit* 613
sparkle
  bubble 353
  glisten 420
sparkling
  vigorous 574
  excitement 824
  cheerful 836
  wit 842
  beauty 845
  with – eyes 827
sparse 73
sparsity 103
Spartacus 742
spartan 739
spasm
  sudden change 146
  violence 173
  agitation 315
  pain 378
spasmodic
  discontinuous 70
  irregular 139
  changeable 149
  violent 173
spat 225, 713
spate 348

spathic 204
spatter *dirt* 653
spatterdash 225
spatula 191, 272
spavined 655
spawn *produce* 161
  offspring 167
  dirt 653
spay 38, 158
speak 560, 580, 582
  – one fair 894
  – for 937
  – ill of 932, 934
  – for itself 518, 528
  – low 581
  – of *meaning* 516
  publish 531
  speak 582
  – out *make manifest* 525
  artless 703
  – softly 581
  – to 586
  – up 411
  – up for 937
  – volumes 467
  – well of 931
speakeasy 189, 964
speaker
  interpreter 524
  chairman 694
speakie 964
speaking: much – 584
  way of – 521
  – likeness 554
  on – terms 888
speaking-trumpet 418
spear 260, 727
  – shaped 253
spearman 726
special 79
  – correspondent 593
special pleader 968
special pleading
  sophistry 477
speciali gratiâ 760
specialist 662, 700
speciality 79
specialty
  security 771
specie 800
species *kind* 75
  appearance 448
  human – 372
specific *special* 79
  remedy 662
  – gravity 321
specification 594

specify
  particularize 79
  tell 527
  name 564
specimen 82
specious
  probable 472
  sophistical 477
  beauty 845
  flattering 933
  pardonable 937
speck 32
speckle 440, 848
spectacle
  appearance 448
  drama 599
  prodigy 872
  show 882
spectacles 445
  look through rose
    coloured – 523
spectacular 882
spectator 444
spectral 4, 980
spectre
  fallacy of vision 443
  ugly 846
  ghost 980
spectroscope
  light 420
  colour 428
  optical instrument 445
spectrum
  colour 428
  variegation 440
  optical illusion 443
speculate
  view 441
  think 451
  suppose 514
  chance 621
  essay 675
  traffic 794
speculation
  experiment 463
  cards 840
speculative 463, 514
speculum 445
  veluti in – 446
sped *completed* 729
speech 582
  figure of – 521
  parts of – 567
speechify 582
speechless 403, 581
speechmaker 582
speed

  velocity 274
  activity 682
  haste 684
  help 707
  succeed 731
  with breathless – 684
  God – 731, 906
speedily *soon* 132
speedometer 200, 274, 553
speedway 840
speer 455, 461
spell *period* 106
  influence 175
  read 539
  letter 561
  necessity 601
  motive 615
  exertion 686
  charm **993**
  cast a – 992
  wonder 870
  knurr and – 840
  – for 865
  – out *interpret* 522
spell-bound 601, 615
spence 636
spencer 225
spend *effuse* 297
  waste 638
  give 784
  purchase 795
  expend 809
  – freely 816
  – time 106
  – time in 683
  – one's time in 625
spender 818
spendthrift 818
spent 160, 688
spermaceti 356
spermatic 168
spermatize 168
spero, dum spiro – 858
spes sibi quisque 604
spew 297
sphacelus 655
sphere *rank* 26
  domain 74
  space 180
  region 181
  ball 249
  world 318
  business 625
  – of influence 181, 780
spheroid 249
spherule 249
sphery 318

sphinx *monster* 83
  oracle 513
  ambiguous 520
  riddle 533
spial 668
spice
  small quantity 32
  mixture 41
  pungent 392
  condiment 393
spiced 390
spicilegium 72, 596
spick and span 123
spiculate 253
spiculum 253
spicy 400, 824
spigot 263
spike *sharp* 253
  pierce 260
  plug 263
  – *guns* 158, 645
spikebit 262
spikenard 356
spill *filament* 205
  stopper 263
  shed 297
  splash 348
  match 388
  waste 638
  lavish 818
  – *blood* 722
  – *and pelt* 59
spin *flying* 267
  rotate 312
  pluck 610
  – *out protract* 110
  late 133
  prolong 200
  diffuse style 573
  – *the wheel* 140
  – *a long yarn* 549
spindle 312
spindle-shanks 203
spindle-shaped 253
spindling 203
spindrift 353
spine 222, 253
spinel 847
spinet *copse* 367
  harpsichord 417
spinner of yarns 594
spinney 367
spinosity
  unintelligible 519
  discourtesy 895
  sullenness 901*a*
spinous *prickly* 253

spinster 374, 904
spiracle 351
spiral 248
spire *height* 206
  convolution 248
  peak 253
  soar 305
spirit *essence* 5
  immateriality 317
  fuel 388
  intellect 450
  meaning 516
  vigorous language 574
  activity 682
  affections 820
  courage 861
  ghost 980
  bad – 980
  keep one's – *up*
  hope 858
  with life and – 682
  unclean – 978
  – *away* 791
  – *up* 615, 824
Spirit, the Holy – 976
spirited
  language 574
  active 682
  sensitive 822
  cheerful 836
  brave 861
  generous 942
spiritless
  insensible 823
  sad 837
  cowardly 862
spirit-level 213
spiritoso *music* 415
spirit-rapping 992
spirits *drink* 298, 959
  cheer 836
spirit-stirring 824
spiritual
  immaterial 317
  psychical 450
  heterodoxy 984
  divine 976
  pious 987
  – *director* 996
  – *existence* 987
spiritualism
  immateriality 317
  intellect 450
  sorcery 992
spiritualize 317
  reasoning 476
spirituel 842

spirt *eject* 297
  stream 348
  haste 684
  exertion 686
spirtle *disperse* 73
  splash 348
spissitude 321, 352
spit *pointed* 253
  perforate 260
  eject 297
  rotate 312
  rain 348
  – *fire irascible* 901
spite 907
  in – *of*
  disagreement 24
  notwithstanding 30
  counteraction 179
  opposition 708
  in – *of one's teeth*
  unwilling 603
  compulsion 744
spiteful 898, 907
  hating 898
spittle 299
spittoon 191
splanchnology 329
splash *affuse* 337
  stream 348
  spatter 653
  parade 882
  make a –
  fame 873
  display 882
  –*board* 666
splay 291
  –*footed* 243
spleen
  melancholy 837
  hatred 898
  anger 900
  sullen 901*a*
  harbour – 907
spleenless 906
splendour
  bright 420
  beautiful 845
  glorious 873
  display 882
splenetic 837, 901*a*
splice *join* 43
  cross 219
  interjacent 228
  repair 660
  – *the main brace*
  tipsy 959
spliced, be –

marriage 903
splint 215
splinter
　small piece 32
　divide 44
　filament 205
　brittle 328
split *divide* 44
　discontinuity 70
　bisect 91
　brittle 328
　divulge 529
　quarrel 713
　fail 732
　portion 786
　laugh 838
　– the difference 29, 774
　– the ears, – the head 404,
　　410
　– hairs
　discriminate 465
　sophistry 477
　fastidiousness 868
　– upon a rock 732
　– one's sides 838
splutter *energy* 171
　spit 297
　stammer 583
　haste 684
spoil *vitiate* 659
　hinder 706
　lenity 740
　plunder 791
　booty 793
　deface 846
　satiate 869
　– sport 706
　– trade 708
spoiled child 869, 899
　– of fortune 734
spoiler 792
spoke *radius* 200
　tooth 253
　obstruct 706
　put a – in one's wheel
　　render powerless 158
　hinder 706
spokesman 524, 582
spolia opima 793
spoliate 791
spoliative 793
spondee 597
spondulics 800
sponge *moisten* 339
　dry 340
　pulp 354
　clean 652

despoil 791
hanger on 886
drunkard 959
apply the –
　obliterate 552
　non-payment 808
– out 552
sponging-house 752
spongy *porous* 252
　soft 324
　marshy 345
sponsion 771
sponsor
　witness 467
　security 771
　be – for
　promise 768
　obligation 926
sponsorship 771
spontaneous
　voluntary 600
　willing 602
　impulsive 612
spontoon 727
spoof 545
spook 980
spool 312
spoon
　receptacle 191
　ladle 272
　bill and coo 902
　born with a silver – in
　　one's mouth 734
Spoonerism 218, 853
spoonful 25, 32
spoon-like 252
spoon-meat 298
spoony *foolish* 499
　lovesick 902
spoor 551
sporadic 73, 137, 657
spore 330
sport *killing* 361
　chase 622
　amusement 840
　show off 882
　in – *pastime* 840
　humour 842
　the – of 749
　– of fortune 735
sporting *killing* 361
　contention 720
　amusement 840
　– dog 366
sportive 836, 840
sports 686
sportsman 361, 622, 840

sportulary 784, 785
sportule 784
sporule 330
spot *place* 182
　discover 480a
　mark 550
　dirt 653
　blemish 848
　blot 874
　on the –
　instantly 113
　present time 118
　soon 132
　in one's presence 186
spotless *perfect* 650
　clean 652
　innocent 946
spot light 423, 599
spots in the sun, see –
　fastidious 868
spotted
　variegated 440
　damaged 659
spousal 903
spouse 88, 903
spouseless 904
spout *egress* 295
　flow out 348
　conduit 350
　speak 582
　act 599
　pawn 771, 787, 788
sprag 215
sprain 158, 160
sprat to catch a:
　– herring 794
　– whale 699
sprawl *length* 200
　horizontal 213
　descend 306
spray *sprig* 51
　vaporizer 336
　foam 353
spread *enlarge* 35
　disperse 73
　broadcast 78
　expanse 180
　expand 194
　diverge 291
　feast 298
　publish 531
　– abroad 531
　– canvas 267
　– out 194
　– sail 267
　– a shade 421
　– to 196

- the toils 545
spree 840
spretæ injuria formæ
  ugly 846
  disrespect 929
  detraction 934
sprig *branch* 51
  child 129
  shillelagh 727
sprightly 836, 842
spring *early* 125
  source 153
  strength 159
  velocity 274
  recoil 277
  fly 293
  leap 309
  elasticity 325
  rivulet 348
  instrument 633
  store 636
  -s of *action* 615
  - back 277
  - to one's feet 307
  - from 154
  - a leak 651, 659
  - a mine
  destroy 162
  unexpected 508
  attack 716
  - a project 626
  - up *begin* 66
  event 151
  grow 194
  ascend 305
  visible 446
  hot - 382
  - upon 789
spring balance 319
springe 545
spring-gun 545
spring tide
  greatness 31
  increase 35
  completeness 52
  youth 127
  high 206
  low 207
  water 337
  wave 348
springy 325
sprinkle *add* 37
  mix 41
  scatter 73
  wet 337
  rain 348
  variegate 440

  baptize 998
sprinkler 348, 385
sprinkling
  small quantity 32
sprint 274
sprit *sprout* 167
  support 215
sprite 979, 980
sprout *grow* 35
  germinate 161
  offspring 167
  expand 194
  - from *result* 154
spruce 652, 845
  - up 847
sprue 653
sprung 651, 659
spry 682, 836
spud 272
spume 353
spunk 861
spun out 110, 573
spur
  pointed 250
  sharp 253
  incite 615
  hasten 684
  win -s *succeed* 731
  glory 873
  on the - of the moment
  instantly 113
  now 118
  soon 132
  opportune 134
  impulse 612
  - *gearing* 633
  the - of *necessity* 745
spurious
  erroneous 495
  false 544
  deceptive 545
  illegitimate 925
spurlos versenkt 2, 449
spurn *reject* 55
  disdain 930
spurred 253
spurt
  transient 111
  swift 274
  gush 348
  impulse 612
  haste 684
  exertion 686
sputa 299
sputter *emit* 297
  splash 348
  stammer 583

spy *see* 441
  spectator 444
  inquire 461
  informer 527
  emissary 534
  watcher 664
  warning 668
spy-glass 445
squab *large* 192
  short 201
  broad 202
  bench 215
squabble 713
squad 72, 726
squadron 726
  - *leader* 745
squalid 653, 846
squall *violent* 173
  wind 349
  cry 411
  quarrel 713
squalor 653
squamous 204, 223
squander *waste* 638
  misuse 679
  lose 776
  prodigal 818
square
  congruous 23
  compensate 30
  four 95
  limited space 182
  houses 189
  perpendicular 212
  form 244
  sparring 720
  justice 924
  honourable 939
  make all - 660
  on the - 939
  - accounts
  pay 807
  account 811
  - dance 840
  - deal 922
  - the circle 471
  - inches 180
  - peg into a round hole
    699
  - up 556
  - with 23
  - yards 180
square-toes 857
squash *destroy* 162
  flatten 251
  blow 276
  soft 324

marsh 345
semiliquid 352
hiss 409
game 840
squashy 345, 352
squat 308
  locate oneself 184
  little 193
  short 201
  thick 202
  low 207
squatter 188
squaw *woman* 374
  wife 903
squeak, squeal 411, 412
squeamish 655
  unwilling 603
  fastidious 868
squeasy 868
squeezable 762
squeeze
  contract 195
  condense 321
  embrace 894
squeeze out 301, 784
squelch 162
squib *sound* 406
  lampoon 856, 934
squiffy 959
squilgee 652
squint
  peephole 260
  look 441
  defective sight 443
squirarchy 875
squire *aid* 707
  attendant 746
  gentry 875
  – *of Dames* 897
squirm 315
squirrel 274, 682
squirt 297, 348
S.S.C. 968
stab *pierce* 260
  kill 361
  pain 378, 649, 828
  injure 659
stabilimeter 150
stabilisator 150
stability 16, **150**
stable *firm* 150
  house 189
  lock the – door when the
    steed is stolen
  too late 135
  useless 645
  bungling 699

– *equilibrium* 150
staccato 415
stack 72, 636
staddle 215
stade 252
stadium 728, 840
stadtholder 745
staff *support* 215
  music 413
  measure 466
  signal 550
  council 696
  party 712
  weapon 727
  chief 745
  retinue 746
  pastoral – 999
  – *of life* 298
  – *of office* 747
  – *officer* 745
stag *deer* 366
  male 373
  defaulter 808
stage *degree* 26
  term 71
  time 106
  position 183
  layer 205
  platform 215
  forum 542
  drama 599
  arena 728
  come upon the – 446
  on the – 525, 599
  go off the – 293
  revolving – 599
  – *business* 599
  – *coach* 272
  – *craft* 599
  – *direction* 697
  – *effect* 882
  – *hand* 599
  – *manager* 599
  – *name* 565
  – *play* 599
  – *player* 599
  – *struck* 599
  – *whisper* 580
stager *player* 599
  doer 690
  old – 130
stagger *slow* 275
  totter 314, 821
  agitate 315
  unexpected 508
  dissuade 616
  affect 824

  astonish 870
  – belief *doubt* 485
  – like a drunken man 605
staggers 315
stagirite 850
stagnant 265
stagnation 681
stagy 599, 855
staid *wise* 498
  calm 826
  grave 837
stain *paint* 223
  colour 428
  dirt 653
  spoil 659
  blemish 848
  disgrace 874
  – *paper writing* 590
stained, travel- 266
stainless *clean* 652
  honourable 939
  innocent 946
stair 305, 627
stake *fastening* 45
  wager 621
  danger 665
  security 771
  property 780
  lay down 807
  execution 975
  at – *intended* 620
  in danger 665
  the – *agony* 828
  burn at the – 384
stalactite 224
stalagmite 224
stale *old* 124
  insipid 391
  deteriorated 659
  – flat and unprofitable 645
  – *news* 532
stale-mate 27, 731
stalk *stem* 153
  support 215
  walk 266
  – *abroad*
  generality 78
  pursue 622
  proud 878
stalking-horse
  ambush 530
  plea 617
stall *cease* 142
  abode 189
  receptacle 191
  support 215
  play-house 599

mart 799
churchdom 995
cathedral 1000
finger– 223
stallion 271, 373
stalwart 159, 192
stamina 159, 604*a*
stammel 434
stammering 583
stamp
character 7
prototype 22
kind 75
form 240
mark 550
engraving 558
complete 729
security 771
– the foot
anger 900
– in the memory 505
– out 162, 385
stampede 860
stanch - *a flow* 348
persevering 604*a*
health 654
reinstate 660
stanchion 215
stanchless 825
stand *exist* 1
rank 71
long time 110
permanent 141
support 215
quiescence 265
difficulty 704
resistance 719
brook 821
patience 826
brave 861
at a – 681
come to a – 704
make a – 708, 719
take one's –
resolve 604
resist 719
due 924
take one's – upon
reasoning 476
affirm 535
plea 617
– aghast 870
– aloof 623, 681
– of arms 727
– at attention 507
– the brunt 717
– by *near* 197

aid 707
defend 717
– a chance 470, 472
– committed 754
– at ease 458
– to one's engagement 772
– fair for 472
– fire 861
– firm 150, 719
– first 66
– for *indicate* 550
deputy 759
candidate 763
– forth 446
– one's ground
preserved 670
resist 719
– the hazard of the die 621
– one in 812
– in need of 630
– no nonsense 604
– off 287, 623
– on 215
– out *project* 250
visible 446
obstinate 606
– over 133
– the proof 648
– to reason
proof 478
manifest 525
right 922
– on one's rights 748
– in the shoes of 147
– one in good stead 644
– still *remain* 141
stop 265
difficulty 704
– the test 494, 648
– up [*see below*]
– upon *pride* 878
– upon one's rights 924
– in the way of 706
– well in the opinion of 931
standard *model* 22
degree 26
mean 29
rule 80
measure 466
flag 550
good 648
perfect 650
gold – 800
standard-bearer 726
standardize 22, 60, 466
standing *footing* 8

degree 26
long time 110
permanence 141
situation 183
note 873
– army 726
– dish *rule* 80
permanent 141
– jest *wit* 842
– order 613, 963
– type 591
– water 343
stand-pipe 348, 385
stand-point 183, 441
stand up 212, 307
– against 719
– fight 720
– for 931, 937
– to 459
Stannary Court 966
stanza 597
staple
fastening 45
whole 50
peg 214
texture 329
material 635
trade 794
mart 799
– commodity 798
star *luminary* 423
actor 599
destiny 601
badge 747
ornament 847
glory 873
noble 875
decoration 877
– in the ascendant
success 731
prosperity 734
– of fashion 852
– it *drama* 599
fame 873
display 882
– shell 423
– trap 599
starboard 238
starch *stiff* 323
viscid 352
affected 855
proud 878
Star Chamber 966
starched
ostentatious 882
stare *look* 441
curiosity 455

wonder 870
make one – 870
– out of countenance
  humiliate 879
  insolent 885
  discourteous 895
– one in the face
  destiny 152
  manifest 525
Death –s one in the face
  360
stare super antiquas vias
  continue 143
  habit 613
  preservation 670
  inaction 681
star-gazing 318
staring 446
stark *very* 31
  sheer 32
  complete 52
  hard 323
– blind 442
– naked 226
stark staring 31
  manifest 525
– mad 503
starlight 422
starlike
  pointed 253
starry 318
stars [*see* star]
  'worlds' 318
  bless one's – 916
– in the firmament
  multitude 102
– and stripes 550
start *begin* 66
  sudden change 146
  arise 151
  impulse 276
  move 284
  depart 293
  leap 309
  unexpected 508
  suggest 514
  crack 659
  offer 763
  fear 860
  wonder 870
  get the –
  precede 280
  success 731
  give a – to 276
  have the –
  prior 116
  early 132

get before 280
– afresh 66
– a doubt 485
– game 622
– off 293
– a question 461
– up *project* 250
  arise 305
  appear 446
starting: – hole
  plea 617
– point
  departure 293
  reasoning 476
  eyes – out of one's head
  870
startle *doubt* 485
  unexpected 508
  excile 824
  fear 860
  wonder 870
startling 508
startlish 825
starts, by fits and – 608
starvation 640, 956
starve *cold* 383,385
  poverty 804
  parsimony 819
  fast 956
starveling *thin* 203
  insufficient 640
  poor 804
state *condition* 7
  speciality 79
  nation 372
  inform 527
  affirm 535
  government 737
  realm 780
  ostentation 882
  robes of – 747
  secretary of – 694
– of affairs 151
–'s evidence 529
– of facts
  description 594
  lawsuit 969
– paper 551
– room 191
– of siege 722
statecraft 693
stated periods, at – 138
stately *grand* 873
  proud 878
  pompous 882
statement 535, 594
statemonger 694

state prison 752
states-general 696
statesman 694
statesmanlike 698
statesmanship 692, 693
static 404
statics *strength* 159
  gravity 319
station *degree* 26
  term 71
  place 182
  situation 183
  locate 184
  rank 873
stationary
  permanent 141
  quiescent 265
stationery 590
station-house 752
statist 694
statistics 85, 86
statu:
  in – pupillari 127
  in – quo 141, 660
statuary 557, 559
statue 554
  still as a – 265
stature 206
status *position* 8
  terms 71
  situation 183
  repute 873
status quo
  past 122
  unchanged 145
  restoration 660
– ante bellum 145
statute 697, 963
staunch *health* 654
  reinstate 660
  honest 939
– belief 484
stave *music* 413, 415
  contention 720
– in *concave* 252
  hole 260
– off 133, 706
stay *remain* 106
  wait 133
  continue 141
  stop 142
  dwell 186
  support 215
  not move 265
  prevent 706
– away 187
– one's hand

729

cease 142
relinquish 624
rest 687
– at home 893
stayed [*see* staid]
stays *corset* 225
stead 644
in the – of
  substitution 147
  commission 755
  deputy 759
stand one in good – 644
steadfast *stable* 150
  persevering 604a
– belief 484
– thought 457
steady *uniform* 16
  regular 80
  periodic 138
  stable 150
  persevering 604a
  unexcitable 826
  cautious 864
steal 791
– along 275, 528
– away 623
– on the ear 405
– a march
  prior 116
  early 132
  precede 280
  deceive 545
  active 682
  cunning 702
– upon one 508
stealing 791
stealth 528
do good by – &c. 881
stealthy 528
  cunning 702
  caution 864
steam *navigate* 267
  gas 334
  vaporize 336
  bubbles 353
under – 267
under sail and – 274
– car 272
– up 171
get the – up 673
steamboat 273
steam-engine to crack a
  nut
  waste 638
  redundance 641
  misuse 679
steamer 273

– track 343
stearine 356
steed 271
steel *strong* 159
  sharp 253
  hard 323
  sword 727
  harden the sensibility 823
– gray 432
– the heart 951
– helmet 717
– oneself 604
steeled against 604, 823
steel-engraving 558
steelyard 319
steep *height* 206
  cliff 212
  slope 217
  soak 337
steeped in
– iniquity 945
– misery 828
steeple 206, 253
steeple-chase
  swift 274
  pursuit 622
  contest 720
steer *beast* 366
  mate 373
  direct 693
– clear 279, 623
– one's course 692
– for 278
steerage 279, 693
steersman 269, 694
steganographic 526
steganography
  unintelligible 519
  hidden 528
  writing 590
stellar 318
stellated 253
St. Elmo's fire 423
stelography 590
stem *origin* 153
  ancestor 166
  front 234
  oppose 708
– to stern 200
– the tide 142, 719
– the torrent 731
stench 401
stencil 556
stenographer 553, 746
steonography 590
stentor *cry* 411
stentorian *loud* 404

step *degree* 26
  term 71
  support 215
  motive 264, 266
  measure 466
  expedient 626
  act 680
dance the back – 283
but a – 197
take a decisive – 609
not stir a – 265
–dance 840
– forward 282
– in *mediate* 724
– into *acquire* 775
– on *be supported by* 215
– in the right direction 644
– into the shoes of
  sequence 63
  posteriority 117
  substitution 147
– short 275
– by step
  degree 26
  order 58
  seriatim 69
  slowly 275
– of time 109
steppe 180, 344
stepping-stone
  link 45
  way 627
  instrument 631
  resource 666
  preparation 673
steps *way* 627
bend one's –
  travel 266
  direction 278
flight of – 305
retract one's – 283
take – *plan* 626
  prepare 673
  conduct 692
tread in the – of 281
stercoraceous 653
stereography 591
stereometry 466
steropticon 445
stereoscope 445
stereoscopic 446
stereotype *copy* 21
  mark 550
  engraving 558
  printing 591
stereotyped
  uniform 16

stable 150
habit 613
sterile 169, 645, 732
sterilize 652
sterling *true* 494, 944
 – coin 800
stern *rear* 235
severe 739
discourteous 895
 – necessity 601, 603
 – truth 494
sternmost 235
sternutation
sneeze 349
sound 409
sternway 267
stertorous 402, 580
stet 150
 – pro ratione voluntas 600
stethoscope 418
stevedore 271, 613, 690
stew *food* 298
heat 382
cook 384
difficulty 704
emotion 821
excitement 825
annoyance 828
bagnio 961
in a – *angry* 900
steward 637
director 694
agent 758
treasurer 801
stewardship 692, 693
stewpan 386
stichomancy 511
stick *adhere* 46
cease 142
staff 215
stab 260
remain quiet 265
fool 501
bungler 701
weapon 727
scourge 975
dirty end of the – 699
give the – to 972
 – at *doubt* 485
averse 603
 – fast *firm* 150
difficulty 704
 – in one's gizzard 830, 900
 – in 300
 – law 972
 – in the mud 304, 732

 – at nothing
resolve 604
active 682
rash 863
 – out 250
 – to 143, 604a
 – in the throat
hoarse 581
not say 585
dislike 867
 – up 212, 307, 791
 – up for *aid* 707
applaud 931
vindicate 937
stickle 603, 616
 – for 720, 794
stickler 606
severity 739
sticky
cohering 46
viscid 352
stiff *rigid* 323
style 579
severe 739
coactive 751
ugly 846
affected 855
haughty 878
pompous 882
 – breeze 349
stiffen 323
stiff-necked 606
stiffness
stability 150
stifle *kill* 361
silence 403
conceal 528
stifled
faint sound 405
stifling *hot* 382
stigmatize 874
censure 932
accuse 938
stile *way* 627
hindrance 706
help a lame dog over a –
707
stiletto 262, 727
still
on the other hand 30
moderate 174
not moving 265
vaporization 336
furnace 386
silent 403
 – less 467
 – life *matter* 316

painting 556
 – more
superior 33
evidence 467
 – small voice 405
in – water 714
still-born 360, 732
stillicidium 348
stillroom 636
stilted
elevated 307
 - *style* 577
ridiculous 853
affected 855
boasting 884
stilts *support* 215
on – *high* 206
elevated 307
hyperbolical 549
proud 878
boasting 884
stimulant 662
stimulate
energy 171
violence 173
incite 615
excite 824
stimulating
suggestive 514
stimulus 615
sting *pain* 378
tingle 380
poison 663
excite 824
mental suffering 830
anger 900
stinging
pungent 392
stingo 298
stingy 819
stink 401
 – in the nostrils
unpleasant 830
dislike 867
hate 898
stink-bomb 727
stink-pot 401
stint *degree* 26
limit 233
scanty 640
begrudge 819
stintless 639
stipend *salary* 973
stipendiary
subject 749
receiving 785
magistrate 967

stipple
  variegate 440
  painting 556
  engraving 558
stipulate 769, 770
  – for 720
stipule 51
stir *energy* 171
  move 264
  agitation 315
  excite 375
  activity 682
  jail 752
  emotion 824
  make a – 642, 682
  – about 682
  – the blood 824, 900
  – up dissension 713
  – the embers 163, 824
  –the feelings 824
  – the fire 384
  – a question 461, 476
  – one's stumps 266, 682
  – up *mix* 41
  violent 173
  excite 824
stirps *kin* 11
  source 153
  paternity 166
stirring *events* 151
  important 642
  active 682
  – news 532
stirrup
  support 215
  with a foot in the – 293
stirrup-cup 293, 959
stitch *junction* 43
  pain 378
  work 680
  – in time 132
  – of work 686
stive 384
stiver 800
stoat 401
stoccado 717
stock *kinship* 11
  quantity 25
  origin 153
  paternity 166
  collar 225
  soup 298
  fool 501
  habitual 613
  materials 635
  store 636
  property 780

  merchandise 798
  money 800
  in – 777
  laughing – 857
  lay in a – 637
  take – *inspect* 457
   accounts 811
  – exchange 799
  – still 265
  – in trade
   means 632
   store 636
   property 780
   merchandise 798
  – with 637
stockade 717
stocked, well – 639
stock exchange 621
stock-farm 370
stocking 225
  hoard 800
stock-jobbing 794
stock operator 621
stocks *prison* 752
  funds 802
  punishment 975
  on the –
   business 625
   preparation 673
   incomplete 730
stocky 201
stodge 957
stoicism
  insensibility 823
  inexcitability 826
  disinterested 942
  temperance 953
stoke 388
stoker 268
stole 999
stolen: – away 671
  – goods 793
stolid 499, 843
stomach *pouch* 191
  taste 390
  brook 826
  desire 865
  not have the – to 603
  turn the – 830
  – of an ostrich 957
stomacher 225
stone *heavy* 319
  dense 321
  hard 323
  kill 361
  lithography 558
  material 635

  attack 716
  weapon 727
  punish 972
  corner – 642
  go down like a – 310
  cast the first – at 938
  heart of – 823, 907
  key- 642
  musical –s 417
  no – unturned 461, 686
  philosopher's – 662
  precious – 648
  stepping – 627
  throw a – at
   attack 716
   censure 932
   accuse 938
  throw –s at 907
  tomb- 363
  mark with a white – 642
  throw a – in one's own
   garden 699
  – dead 360
  – of Sisyphus 645
stone-blind 442
stone-coloured 432
stone-deaf 419
stone's throw 197
stoneware 384
stony 323
stony-hearted 907, 919
stooge 711, 746, 886
stook 72
stool 215
  between two –s 704
  – of repentance 950
  – pigeon 527, 548
stoop *slope* 217
  lower 308
  humble 879
  servile 886
  dishonourable 940
  – to conquer 702
stop *end* 67
  cease 142
  close 261
  rest 265
  silent 403
  danger 665
  inaction 681
  hinder 706
  prohibit 761
  put a – to 142
  – the breath 361
  – the ears 419
  – a flow 348
  – a gap 600

- the mouth 479, 581
- payment 808
- press news 532
- short 142, 265
- short of 304
- the sound 408a
- up 261
- the way 706
stopcock 263
stopgap
  substitute 147
  stopper 263
stoppage
  cessation 142
  hindrance 706
stopper 263
stopping place 292
store *store* 184
  stock **636**
  shop 799
  in - *destiny* 152
  preparing 673
  lay in a - 637
  set - by 642, 931
  set no - 483
  - of knowledge 490
  - in the memory 505
store-house 636
store-keeper 636
store-ship 273, 726
storied 594
storm *crowd* 72
  convulsion 146
  violence 173
  agitation 315
  wind 349
  danger 667
  attack 716
  passion 825
  anger 900
  ride the - 267
  take by -
  conquer 731
  seize 789
  - brewing 665
  - in a teacup
  overrate 482
  exaggerate 549
  unimportance 643
storthing 696
story *rooms* 191
  layer 204
  news 532
  lie 546
  history 594
  the old - 897
  as the - goes 532

story-teller 548, 594
stot 366
stound 870
stoup *cup* 191
  altar 1000
stour 59
stout *strong* 159
  large 192
  drink 298
stout-hearted 861
stove *fireplace* 386
  - in 252
stow *locate* 184
  pack close 195
  store 636
stowage 180, 184
stowaway 528, 673
strabism 443
straddle 266, 607
Stradivarius 417
strafe 972
straggle 266, 279
straggler 268
straggling 44, 59
straight
  vertical 212
  rectilinear 246
  direction 278
  all - *rich* 803
  solvent 807
  - course 628
  - descent 167
  - face 837
  - sailing 705
straighten 246
  - up 60
straightforward 278
  truthful 543
  artless 703
  honourable 939
straightness 246
straight shot 278
straightway 132
strain *race* 11
  weaken 160
  operation 170
  violence 173
  percolate 295
  transgress 303
  sound 402
  melody 415
  overrate 482
  exaggerate 549
  style 569
  poetry 597
  voice 580
  clean 652

  effort 686
  fatigue 668
  - in the arms 902
  - one's eyes 441, 507
  - at a gnat and swallow a
    camel 608
  - one's invention 515
  - the meaning 523
  - every nerve 686
  - a point
  go beyond 303
  exaggerate 549
  not observe 773
  undue 925
  - the throat 411
strait
  interval 198
  water 343
  difficulty 704
straitened
  poor 804
strait-handed 819
strait-jacket 752
strait-laced
  severe 739
  restraint 751
  fastidious 868
  haughty 878
strait-waistcoat 751, 752
strake 205
stramash 720
strand *thread* 205
  shore 231, 342
stranded
  stuck fast 150
  in difficulty 704
  failure 732
  pain 828
strange
  unrelated 10
  exceptional 83
  ridiculous 853
  wonderful 870
  - bedfellows 713
  - to say 870
strangely *much* 31
stranger 57
  a - to 491
strangle
  render powerless 158
  contract 195
  kill 361
strap *fasten* 43
  fastening 45
  restraint 752
  punish 972

instrument of punishment
975
strappado 972
strapping
mighty 31
strong 159
big 192
pace 274
strapwork 847
stratagem
deception 545
plan 626
artifice 702
strategic *plan* 626
artifice 702
strategist
planner 626
director 694
proficient 700
strategy 692, 722
strath 252
strathspey 840
stratification 204, 329
stratocracy 737
stratosphere 338
stratum 204
stratus 353
straw *scatter* 73
light 320
unimportant 643
care not a – 866, 930
catch at –s
overrate 482
credulous 486
misuse 679
unskilful 699
hope 858
rash 863
the eyes drawing –s 683
in the – 161
man of –
unsubstantial 4
cheat 525
insolvent 808
low person 876
not worth a – 643, 645
– to show the wind 463
straw-coloured 436
straw-hat 225
stray *dispersion* 73
exceptional 83
random 156
wanderer 268
deviate 279
streak *intrinsicality* 5
long 200
narrow 203

furrow 259
light 420
stripe 440
mark 559
streaked 219, 440
stream *assemble* 72
move 265
– *of fluid* **347**
– *of water* 348
– *of air* 349
– *of light* 420
abundance 639
against the – 708
with the –
conformity 82
progression 282
assent 488
facility 705
concord 714
fashion 852
servility 886
– *of events* 151
– *of time* 109
streamer *flag* 550
streaming 47, 73
streamlet 348
street 189, 627
man in the – 876
streets:
in the open – 525
on the – 961
street-walker 962
strength
quantity 25
degree 26
greatness 31
vigour **159**
energy 171
tenacity 327
animality 364
put all one's – into 686
lose – 655
tower of – 717
– *of mind* 604
strengthen 35
strengthless 160
strenuous
persevering 604a
active 682
exertion 686
Strephon and Chloe 902
stress *emphasis* 580
requirement 630
importance 642
strain 686
difficulty 704
by – of 601

lay – on 476
– of circumstances
compulsion 744
– of weather 349
stretch *expanse* 180
expand 194
extend 200
exaggerate 549
exertion 686
encroach 925
at a – 69
mind on the – 451
on the – 686
upon the – 457
– away to 196
– forth one's hand 680,
789
– of the imagination 515,
549
– the meaning 523
– a point 83, 303
exaggerate 549
severity 739
permit 760
not observe 773
undue 925
exempt 927a
– *to distance* 196
length 200
stretcher 215, 272
strew 73
striæ, striated 259, 440
stricken *pain* 828
terror– 860
be – by 655
– in years 128
strict
in conformity 82
exact 494
severe 739
conscientious 939
orthodox 983a
– inquiry 461
– interpretation 522
– search 461
– settlement 780
strictly speaking
literally 19
exact 494
interpreted 522
stricture
constriction 203
hindrance 706
censure 932
stride *distance* 196
motion 264
walk 266

parade 882
boast 884
– and fret one's hour upon
  a stage 359, 599
strychnine 663
stub 40, 550
stubbed 201
stubble *remains* 40
  useless 645
stubborn
  strong 159
  hard 323
  obstinate 606
  resistance 719
stubby 201
stucco 45, 223
stuck [*see* stick]
  – *fast* 150,704
  be – on 897
stuck-up 878
stud *hanging-peg* 214
  knob 250
  horses 271
studded *many* 102
  spiked 253
  variegated 440
student 541
stud-farm 370
studied
  predetermined 611
studio *room* 191
  painting 556
  workshop 691
studious
  thoughtful 451
  docile 539
  intending 620
study *copy* 21
  room 191
  thought 451
  attention 457
  research 461
  learning 539
  painting 556
  intention 620
  retreat 893
  brown – 515
stuff *substance* 3
  contents 190
  expand 194
  line 224
  matter 316
  texture 329
  absurdity 497
  unmeaning 517
  material 635
  trifle 643

overeat 957
such – as dreams are made
  of 515
– *gown* 968
– *in* 300
– the memory with 505
– and nonsense
  unsubstantial 4
  absurdity 497
  unmeaning 517
– up *close* 261
  hoax 545
stuffed
  redundancy 641
stuffing *contents* 190
  lining 224
  stopper 263
stuffy 321, 382
stultified 732
stultify oneself 699
stultiloquy 497
stumble *fall* 306
  flounder 315
  error 495
  unskilful 699
  failure 732
– on *chance* 156
  discover 480a
stumbling-block
  difficulty 704
  hindrance 706
stump
  remainder 40
  trunk 51
  walk 266
  drawing 556
  speak 582
  stir your –s
  active 682
  worn to the – 659
– along *slow* 275
stump orator 582, 887
stumpy *short* 201
stun *physically insen-*
  sible 376
  loud 404
  deafen 419
  unexpected 508
  morally insensible 823
  affect 824
  astonish 870
stung [*see* sting]
– to the quick 824
stunt *shorten* 201
  performance 680
stunted 193, 195
  insufficient 640

stupe 834
stupefaction 826
stupefy
  – *physically* 376
  – *morally* 823
  astonish 870
stupendous
  great 31
  large 192
  wonderful 870
stupid
  unsubstantial 4
  misjudging 481
  credulous 486
  unintelligent 499
  tiresome 841
  dull 843
stupor
  insensibility 823
  wonder 870
stupration 961
sturdy *strong* 159
  persevering 604a
– *beggar* 767, 792
stutter 583
sty *house* 189
  enclosure 232
  dirt 653
Stygian *dark* 421
  diabolic 945
  infernal 982
  cross the – ferry
  die 360
– shore
  death 360
style *state* 7
  time 114
  painting 556
  graver 558
  name 564
  diction **569**
  writing 590
  beauty 845
  fashion 852
stylet
  awl 262
  dagger 727
stylist 578
Stylites, Simon – 893
stylographic pen 590
stylography 590
stylus 590
styptic 397
Styx 982
suasible 602
suasion 615
suave mari magno 664

law – 969
love – 897
– the action to the word 550
– the occasion 646
do – and service 743
suitable 23, 646
– season 134
suit case 191
suite *sequel* 65
  series 69
  escort 88
  retinue 746
– of rooms 189, 191
suitor
  petitioner 767
  lover 897
  lawsuit 969
sulcated 259
sulky *carriage* 272
  obstinate 606
  discontented 832
  dejected 837
  sullen 901*a*
sullen
  obstinate 606
  gloomy 837
  discourteous 895
  sulky 901*a*
sullenness 901a
sully 653, 874
sulphur 388
– coloured 436
sultan 745
sultry 382
sum *number* 84
  money 800
– and substance
  meaning 516
  synopsis 596
  important part 642
– total 800
– up *reckon* 85
  description 594
  compendium 596
sumless 105
summation 37, 85
summary
  transient 111
  early 132
  short 201
  concise 572
  compendious 596
  illegal 964
– of facts 594
summer *season* 125
  support 215

heat 382
Indian – 125
St. Luke's – 125
St. Martin's – 125
– lightning 423
– time 114
summer-house 191
summerset 218
summit *top* **210**
summon 741, 969
– up 505, 824
– up courage 861
summum:
– bonum 618, 827
– jus 922
sump *base* 211
  pool 343
  slough 345
  store 636
  cess 653
sumpter-horse 271
sumptuary 800, 809
sumptuous 882
sum-total 50
sun 318
  luminary 423
  glory 873
  bask in the – 377
  going down of the – 126
  farthing candle to the – 645
  under the – 180, 318
  as the – at noonday
  bright 420
  certain 474
  plain 525
– oneself 384
Sun:
– of Righteousness 976
sunbeam 420
–s from cucumbers 471
sunburn *heat* 384
sunburnt *brown* 433
Sunday:
– Monday &c. 138
–'s best 847, 882
– school 542
sunder 44
sundial 114
sundown 126
sundry 102
sunk [*see* sink]
  deep 208
– fence 717
– in iniquity 945
– in oblivion 508
sunken rocks 667

sunless 421
sunlight 420
sunny *warm* 382
  luminous 420
  cheerful 836
sunny side 829
  view the – 858
– of the hedge 734
sun-painting 556
sunrise 125
sunset 126
  at – 133
sunshade 223, 424
sunshine *light* 420
  prosperity 734
  happy 827
  cheerful 836
sunstroke 384, 503
sun-up 125
suo: – periculo 926
– sibi gladio hunc jugulo
  absurdity 479
  retaliation 718
sup *small quantity* 32
  feed 298
– full of horrors 828
super *theatrical* 599
superable 470
superabound 641
superadd 37
superannuated 128
superb 845
supercargo 694
supercherie 545
supercilious
  proud 878
  insolent 885
  disrespectful 929
  scornful 930
superdreadnought 726
supereminence 648, 873
supererogation 641, 645
superexaltation 873
superexcellence 648
superfetation 37, 168
superficial
  shallow 209
  outside 220
  misjudging 481
  ignorant 491
– extent 180
superficies 220
superfine 648
superfluitant 305
superfluity 40, 641
superfluous 645
superhuman 650, 976

superimpose 233
superimposed 206
superincumbent 206, 319
superinduce
  change 140
  cause 153
  produce 161
superintend 693
superintendent 694
superior *greater* 33
  – *in size* 194
  important 642
  good 648
  director 694
superiority 33
superjunction 37
superlative 33
superlatively good 648
superman 33
supernal 206, 210, 981
supernatant 206, 305
supernatural 976, 980
  – *aid* 707
supernumerary
  adjunct 39
  theatrical 599
  reserve 636
  redundant 641
superpose 37, 223
supersaturate 641
superscription 550, 590
supersede
  substitute 147
  disuse 678
  relinquish 782
supersensible 317
superstition
  credulity 486
  error 495
  religion 984
superstratum 220
superstructure 729
supertax 812
supertonic 413
supervacaneous 641
supervene
  extrinsic 6
  be added 37
  succeed 117
  happen 151
supervise 693
supervisor 694
supination 213
supine
  horizontal 213
  inverted 218
  sluggish 683

  mentally torpid 823
suppediate 637
supper 298
supplant 147
supple *soft* 324
  servile 886
supplement
  addition 37
  adjunct 39
  completion 52
  publication 531
  book 593
suppletory 37
suppliant 765, 767
supplicate *beg* 765
  pity 914
  worship 990
supplies
  materials 635
  aid 707
  money 800
supply *store* 636
  provide 637
  give 784
  – *aid* 707
  – *deficiencies* 52
  – *the place of* 147
  – *and transport* 726
support *perform* 170
  sustain **215**
  evidence 467
  preserve 670
  aid 707
  feel 821
  endure 826
  vindicate 937
  – *life* 359
supporter 711
  –s *heraldic* 550
suppose 514
supposing 469
supposition **514**
supposititious 546
suppress
  destroy 162
  conceal 528
  silent 581
  restrain 751
suppression of truth 544
suppuration 653
suppute 85
supralapsarian 984
supramundane 939
supremacy 33, 737
supreme 33
  summit 210
  authority 737

  in a – *degree* 31
Supreme Being 976
surbate 659
surbated 688
surcease 142
surcharge 641
  – *and falsify* 811
surcingle 45
surcoat 225
surd *number* 84
  deaf 419
  silent letter 561
sure *certain* 474
  belief 484
  safe 664
  make – *against* 673
  make – *of*
  inquire 461
  take 789
  you may be – 535
  to be – *assent* 488
  on – *ground* 664
  security 771
sure-footed
  careful 459
  skilful 698
  cautious 864
surely 489, 602, 870
sureness 474
surety 474, 664
surf 348, 353
surface *outside* 220
  texture 329
  below the – 526
  lie on the – 518, 525
  skim the – 460
Surface, Joseph – 548
surfeit 641, 869
surge *swarm* 72
  swell 305
  rotation 312
  wave 348
surgeon 662
surgery 662
surgit amari aliquid 651
surly *gruff* 895
  sullen 901*a*
  unkind 907
surmise 514
surmount *be superior* 33
  tower 206
  transcursion 303
  ascent 305
  – *a difficulty*
  overcome 731
surmountable 470
surname 564

surpass
be superior 33
grow 194
go beyond 303
outshine 873
surplice 999
surplus 40, 641
surplusage 641
surprint 550
surprise
non-expectation 508
unprepared 674
wonder 870
surprisingly 31
surrebutter &c.
answer 462
pleadings 969
surrender 725, 782
– *one's life* 360
surreptitious
furtive 528
deceptive 545
untrue 546
surrogate 759
surround 227, 229
surroundings
amidst such and such –
183
sursum corda 990
surtax 812
surtout *coat* 225
surveillance
care 459
direction 693
under – 938
survene 151
survey 441, 466
surveyor 85, 694
survive *remain* 40
long time 110
permanent 141
susceptibility
power 157
tendency 176
liability 177
sensibility 375
motive 615
impressibility 822
irascibility 901
suscipient 785
suscitate *cause* 153
produce 161
stir up 173
excite 824
suspect *doubt* 485
suppose 514
suspected 938

suspectless 484
suspend *defer* 133
discontinue 142
hang 214
suspended animation 823
suspender 45, 214
suspense
cessation 142
uncertainty 475
expectation 507
irresolution 605
in – *inert* 172
suspension
cessation 142
hanging 214
music 413
– *of arms* 723
suspicion *doubt* 485
incredulity 487
knowledge 490
supposition 514
fear 860
under – 938
suspiration 839
sustain
continue 143
strength 159
perform 170
support 215
preserve 670
aid 707
endure 821
sustained note 413
sustenance 298
sustentation [*see* sustain]
food 298
susurration 405
sutler 637, 797
suttee *killing* 361
arson 384
unselfishness 942
idolatry 991
suture 43
suum cuique 780, 922
suzerain 945
suzerainty 737
swab *dry* 340
clean 652
lubber 701
swaddle *clothe* 225
restrain 751
swaddling clothes, in –
infant 129
subjection 749
swag *hang* 214
lean 217
curve 245

drop 306
oscillate 314
booty 793
ostentation 887
swag-bellied 194
swage 174
swagger
pride 878
boast 884
bluster 885
swaggerer 887
swain *man* 373
rustic 876
lover 897
swale 659
swallow *gulp* 296
eat 298
believe 484
credulous 486
brook 826
– *the bait* 547, 602
– *flight* 274
– *the leek* 607, 726
– *up destroy* 162
store 636
use 677
take 789
– *hook, line and sinker*
602
– *whole* 468a, 484
swallow-tail coat 225
swamp *destroy* 162
marsh 345
defeat 731
swamped
failure 732
swampy *moist* 339
swank 845, 882, 884
swan-pan 85
swan-song 360
swap *exchange* 148
blow 276
sward 344
swarm *crowd* 72
multitude 102
climb 305
sufficiency 639
redundance 641
swarthy 431
swash *affuse* 337
spurt 348
swashbuckler 726, 887
swashy 339
swastika 621, 993
swat 276
swath 72
swathe *fasten* 43

741

clothe 225
restrain 741
sway *power* 157
  influence 175
  lean 217
  oscillate 314
  agitation 315
  induce 615
  authority 737
  – to and fro 149
sweal 659
swear *affirm* 535
  promise 768
  curse 908
  just enough to – by 32
  – at 908
  – by *believe* 484
  – false 544
  – a witness 768
sweat *exude* 295
  excretion 299
  heat 382
  exertion 686
  fatigue 688
  cold – 860
  in a – 382
  – of one's brow 686
sweater 225
Swedenborgian 984
Swedish dance 840
sweep *space* 180
  curve 245
  oar 267
  rapid 274
  bend 279
  clean 652
  dirty fellow 653
  steal 791
  make a clean – of 297
  – along 264
  – away
  destroy 162
  eject 297
  abrogate 756
  relinquish 782
  – the chords 416
  – off 297
  – out 297, 652
  – of time 109
sweeper 652
  mine– 726
sweeping *whole* 50
  complete 52
  general 78
  – change 146
sweepings
  useless 645

dirt 653
sweepstakes 775, 810
sweet
  saccharine 396
  melodious 413
  colour 428
  clean 652
  agreeable 829
  lovely 897
  look – upon
  desire 865
  love 897
  endearment 902
  – smell 400
  – tooth 865, 868
  – wine 396
  – words 894
sweeten 396, 829
sweetheart 897
sweetmeat 396
sweetness 396
sweets 298, 396
sweet-scented 400
swell *increase* 35
  expand 194
  wave 348
  sound 404
  emotion 821
  fop 854
  nobility 875
  swagger 885
  extol 931
  ground – 315
  – over 250
  – with rage 900
  – the ranks of 37
  – out
  diffuse style 573
swelling
  expansion 194
  prominence 250
  - *style* 577
  excitement 824
swell-mob 792
swelter 382
swerve *change* 140
  deviate 279
  demur 603
  tergiversation 607
swift 274
swig 298, 959
swill *dirt* 653
  drink 298
  intemperance 954
  drunkenness 959
swim *navigate* 267
  float 305

light 320
– against the stream 704
– in *pleasure* 377
  abundance 639
– with the stream 82, 683
– with the tide 734
swimming 840
  - *eyes* 443
  - *head* 503
  - belt 666
  - pool 652, 840
swimmingly
  easily 705
  success 731
  prosperity 734
swindle 545, 791
swindler 548, 792
swine 366
  cast pearls before – 638
  – of Epicurus 954*a*
swineherd 746
swing
  operation 170
  space 180
  hang 214
  oscillate 314
  freedom 748
  amusement 840
  full – 682, 731
  give full – 705
  have one's – 738
  – the lead 544
swinge 972
swinging *great* 31
swinish 954, 957
  – multitude 876
swink 686
swipe 276
swirl 312
swish 409
switch *shunt* 279
  flog 972
  rod 975
switchback 840
Swithin, reign of St. – 348
swivel *hinge* 312
  cannon 727
swivel-eye 443
swollen 194, 878
swoon 158, 688
swoop 274
  descend 306
  seize 789
  at one fell – 173
swop 794
sword *weapon* 727

draw the –, flesh one's –
722
measure –s 720, 722
at the point of the – 722,
889, 898
severity 739
compulsion 744
subjection 749
put to the – 361
– of Damocles 667
– in hand
prepare 673
war 722
turn –s into ploughshares
723
– of state 747
swordsman 726
Sybarite 954*a*
sybaritism 954
sycophancy 933
sycophant 886, 935
syenite *blue* 438
syllable 561
breathe not a – 528
syllabus 86, 596
syllogism 476
sylph 979
sylvan 367
symbol
copy 21
mathematical – 84
sign 550
symbolize 526, 550
represent 554
symmetrical 80
symmetry
equality 27
order 58
conformity 82
centrality 222
regular form **242**
style 578
beauty 845
want of – 846
sympathizer
partisan 890
sympathy
concord 714
friendship 888
love 897
kindness 906
pity 914
condolence 915
symphonious 413
symphony
overture 64
music 415

concord 714
symphysis 43
symposium 72, 840, 892
symptom 550, 668
symptomatology 522
synagogue 1000
synchronism **120**
synchysis 218
syncopation 415
syncope
impotence 158
musical 413
rhetoric 572
fatigue 688
syncretic 61
syncretism 24, 984
syndic 745, 967
syndicate 696, 712
synecdoche 521
synod 696, 995
synonym
identity 13
meaning 516
interpretation 522
term 564
synonymous 13
synopsis
arrangement 60
list 86
compendium 596
synovia 332, 356
syntagma 60
syntax 567
synthesis
combination 48
composition 54
reasoning 476
synthesize 54
syntony 23, 120
syringe 337, 348
syrup 352, 396
system *order* 58
rule 79
plan 626
– of knowledge 490
– of opinions 484
systematize 60, 626
systole 195
syzygy 199

T

T, to a – 494
tab 39, 550, 747
tabard 225
tabby *mottled* 440

gossip 588
tabefaction 195
tabernacle 189, 1000
house 189
temple 1000
tabescent 195
tabid *shrunk* 195
thin 203
disease 655
deteriorated 659
table
arrangement 60
list 86
defer 133
layer 204
support 215
flat 251
repast 298
writing 590
on the – 626, 673
turn the –s 218, 468
under the –
hidden 528
drunk 959
– of the Lord 1000
– the motion 624
tableau *list* 86
appearance 448
painting 556
theatrical 599
table-cloth 652
table d'hôte 298
table-land 213, 344
tablet *layer* 204
flat 251
record 551
writing 590
remedy 662
table-talk 532, 588
tablets of the memory 505
table-turning 992
tabloid 531, 662
taboo 762, 992
tabor 417
tabouret 215
tabret 417
tabula rasa
inexistence 2
absence 187
ignorance 491
obliterated 552
facility 705
tabulate 60, 69
tabulation 551
tachometer 274
tachy case 191
tachygraphy 590

tacit 526
taciturnity 585
Tacitus
　concise style 572
tack *join* 43
　nails 45
　change course 140
　sharp 253
　direction 278
　turn 279
　food 289
　way 627
　go upon another – 607
　wrong – 732
　– to *add* 37
tackle
　fastening 45
　gear 633
　try 675
　undertake 676
　manage 693
tacky 352
tact *touch* 379
　discrimination 465
　wisdom 498
　skill 698
　taste 850
　want of – 851
tactful 894
tactician 700
tactics 692, 722
tactile &c. 379
tactless 895
tadpole 129
tædium vitæ 837, 841
tag *small* 32
　addition 37
　adjunct 39
　fastening 45
　sequel 65
　end 67
　point 253
　sheep 366
　– after 281
tagrag and bobtail 876
tail *sequel* 65
　end 67
　pendent 214
　back 235
　aircraft 273
　estate – 780
　turn – 623
　– off *decrease* 36
tail-coat 225
tailor 225, 690
tailoring 225, 882
tail-piece *sequel* 65

rear 235
engraving 558
ornament 847
tail-race 350
taint
　imperfection 651
　dirt 653
　decay 659
　disgrace 874
tainted 401, 655
taintless 652
taj 225
take *eat* 298
　believe 484
　know 490
　understand 518
　succeed 731
　receive 785
　appropriate 789
　captivate 829
　give and – 718
　– a back 508, 870
　– an account of 85
　– action 680
　– advice 695
　– after 17
　– aside 586
　– away
　annihilate 2
　subtract 38
　remove 185
　seize 789
　– back again 790
　– a back seat 34
　– by [*see below*]
　– the cake 33
　– care 668, 864
　– care of 459, 664
　– no care of 460
　– off 293
　– one's chance 621, 675
　– one's choice 609
　– things as they come 683,
　　826
　– comfort 831, 834
　– the consequences 154
　– coolly 826
　– a course 692
　– its course 143, 151
　– no denial 606, 744
　– a disease 655
　– down
　swallow 298
　depress 308
　record 551
　write 590
　dismantle 681

humiliate 874
censure 932
　– easily 826
　– effect 151, 170
　– an ell 885
　– exception 932
　– one's fancy 829, 865
　– fire 384
　– flight 623
　– from 38, 789
　– for [*see below*]
　– the good the gods
　　provide 831
　– heart 831, 836
　– to heart 828, 832
　– heed 864
　– a hint 498
　– hold of 46, 789
　– hold of the mind 484
　– ill 832
　– in [*see below*]
　– an infection 655
　– no interest in 823
　– into [*see below*]
　– it 484, 514
　– the lead 62
　– a leaf out of another's
　　book 19
　– a lease 788
　– leave of 624
　– a liberty 748
　– away life 361
　– a likeness 554
　– measures 626
　– money 810
　– no note of 460
　– no note of time 115
　– notice 457
　– one's oath 535
　– off [*see below*]
　– oneself off 293
　– on [*see below*]
　– one with another 29
　– out 301, 552
　– over 783
　– part with 709
　– pattern by 19
　– a peep 441
　– pen in hand 590
　– to pieces 44, 681
　– place 151
　– the place of 147
　– possession of 589
　– precedence 33, 62
　– its rise 66, 154
　– root 150, 184
　– the shine out of 33

744

- ship 267
- steps 673, 680
- stock 85
- time
  duration 106
  late 133
  leisure 685
- time by the forelock 132
- to *habit* 613
  pursuit 622
  use 677
  like 827
  desire 865
  love 897
- on trust 484
- a turn 140
- up [*see below*]
- upon oneself 676, 768
- warning 668
- wing 293
- one at one's word 769

take by
- the button 586
- the hand 707
- surprise 508, 675

take for 484
- better or for worse 609
- gospel 486
- granted 484

take in *include* 54
  shorten 201
  admit 296
  understand 518
  deceive 545
  receive money 785
- good part
  be calm 826
  be pleased 827
  content 831
- hand *teach* 537
  undertake 676
  aid 707
- an idea 498
- sail 275

take into
- account
  include 76
  discriminate 465
  qualify 469
- consideration 451
- custody 751
- one's head 514, 608

take off *mimic* 19
  destroy 162
  remove 185
  divest 226
  depart 293

discount 813
ridicule 856
- one's hands 785
- the hat 894

take on
  attempt 675
  discontent 832
  melancholy 837
- credit 484
- trust 484

take up
  elevate 307
  inquire 461
  dissent 595
  choose 609
  undertake 676
  befriend 707
  arrest 751
  borrow 788
  censure 932
- arms 722
- a case 476
- one's abode 184
- the cudgels 716, 720
- an inquiry 461
- money 788
- one's pen 590
- with
  attention 457
  use 677
  content 831

taken, be –
  die 360
- ill 655
- with 897

taker 789

taking 789
  infectious 657
  in a – *pained* 828
  angry 900

talapoin 996

talbotype 556

tale
  counting 85
  narrative 594
  thereby hangs a – 526
  twice-told –
    diffuse style 573
    weary 841

tale-bearer 532

talent 698
  bury one's – in a napkin 528
  not put one's – in a napkin 878

talionis, lex – 718, 922

taliped 243

talisman 747, 993

talismanic 992

talk
  unsubstantial 4
  rumour 532
  speak 582
  conversation 588
  small – 588
- big *boast* 884
  insolent 885
  threat 909
- glibly 584
- nonsense 497
- of *signify* 516
  publish 531
  intend 620
- to oneself 589
- oneself out of breath 584
- over
  confer 588
  persuade 615
- to in private 586
- at random
  illogical 477
  loquacity 584
- together 588
- against time
  time 106
  protract 110
  inaction 681
- of the town
  gossip 588
  fame 873

talkative 582, 584

talked of 873

talkies 599, 840

talking, fine –
  over-estimation 482

tall 206
- hat 225
- talk 884

tallage 812

tallies 85

tallow 356
- candle 423

tallow-faced 429

tally *agree* 23
  list 85, 86
  sign 550
  credit 805
- with *conform* 82

tally-ho 622

tally-man 797

talma 225

Talmud 985

talons
  authority 737

tattoo
  drumming 407
  mottled 440
  summons 741
taught [*see* teach]
  fastened 43
taunt 929, 938
tauromachy 720
taut 43
tautology 104, 573
tavern 189
tawdry 851
tawny 433, 436
tax *inquire* 461
  employ 677
  fatigue 688
  command 741
  compel 744
  request 765
  accounts 811
  impost 812
  discount 813
  accuse 938
  – one's energies 686
  – the memory 505
taxi 266
taxi-cab 272
taxi-driver 268
taxidermy 368
taxis 60
taxonomy 60
tazza 191
Te Deum 990
te fabula narratur, de –
  retaliate 718
  condemn 971
tea 298
teach 537
  – one's grandmother 641,
  885
  – one his place 879
teachable 539
teacher 540, 673
teaching 537
  false – 538
teacup, storm in a –
  overrate 482, 549
  exaggerate 549
teagown 225
team *assemblage* 69, 72
teamster 694
tea-party 892
tea-pot 191
tear *separate* 44
  violence 173
  move rapidly 274
  excite 825

  weeping 839
  – away from 789
  – oneself away 623
  – asunder one's bonds 750
  – one's hair 839
  – out 301
  – to pieces
  separate 44
  destroy 162
  – up *destroy* 162
tear-gas 663, 727
tearful 839
tearing passion 839
tears: draw – 830
  shed – 839
  – in one's eyes
  excited 824
  sad 837
tease *annoy* 830
  spite 907
teaser *difficult* 704
teasing 830
teat 250
tea-table talk 588
technic 698
technica, memoria – 505
technical
  comfortable 82
  workmanlike 698
  – college 542
  – education 537
  – knowledge 698
  – school 542
  – term 564
technicality
  special 79
  cant term 563
  formulary 697
technique 556, 698
technocracy 698
technology 698
techy 901
tedious 841
  while away the – hours
  681
tedium 841
tee 66
teem
  produce 161
  productive 168
  abound 639
  – with *multitude* 102
teemful 168
teeming *crowd* 72
teemless 169
'teens 98
  in one's – 127, 129

teeter 314
teeth 330, 781
  armed to the – 673, 717,
  722
  between the – 405
  cast in one's – 938
  chattering of – 383
  have cut one's eye – 698
  in the – of 704, 708
  grind one's – 900
  the run of one's – 815
  set one's – 604
  show one's – 900
  in spite of one's – 708,
  744
  make one's – chatter 385,
  860
  set the – on edge
  scrape 331
  saw 397
  stridor 410
  pain the feelings 830
teetotalism 953, 958
teetotum 312, 840
teg 366
tegument 223
teind 99
teinoscope 445
tekel upharsin 668
telautograph 553
telegram 532
telegraph
  velocity 274
  messenger 534
  signal 550
  – boy 534
  by – *haste* 684
telegraphone 553
telegraphy
  publication 531
telemeter 200
teleology 620
telepathy 992
telephone 418
  inform 527
  messenger 534
telescope 445
  – word 572
telescopic 196
telesis 658
telesm 993
tell *count* 85
  influence 175
  evidence 467
  inform 527
  speak 582
  describe 594

succeed 731
let me – you 535
who can – 475
– one's beads 990, 998
– the cause of 522
– fortunes 511
– how 155
– a lie 544
– a piece of one's mind
  529
– of 467
– off 85
– one plainly 527
– its own tale 518
– tales
  disclose 529
– the truth 543
teller *treasurer* 801
– of tales 594
telling 175
  graphic 518
  important 642
  exciting 824
with – effect 171, 175
telltale *news* 532
  indicator 550
  knave 941
telluric 318
telum imbelle 158
temerity 863
temper *nature* 5
  state 7
  moderate 174
  elasticity 323
  pliability 324
  modify 469
  prepare 673
  affections 820
  irascibility 901
  command of – 826
  lose one's – 900
  out of – 901*a*
  trial of – 824
  – the wind to the shorn
    lamb 834
tempera 556
temperament
  nature 5
  tendency 176
  musical 413
  affections 820
temperance 174, **953**
temperate [*see* temperance]
  mild 826
temperature 382
  increase of – 384
  reduction of – 385

tempest
  violence 173
  agitation 315
  wind 349
  excitement 825
tempestivity 134
tempest-tossed 824
tempestuous 59
Templar 996
  Good – 958
temple *house* 189
  side 236
  church **1000**
  – of the Holy Ghost 983*a*
templet 22
tempora:
  O –! O mores!
  lament 839
  disreputable 874
  disapprobation 932
  improbity 940
  vice 945
  – mutantur 140
temporal
  transient 111
  laical 997
  lords – and spiritual 875
temporality 997
temporary 111
temporize
  protract 110
  defer 133
  cunning 702
temporizer 943
tempt *entice* 615
  attempt 675
  desire 865
  – fortune 621, 675
  – Providence 863, 885
tempter 615
  Satan 978
  voice of the – 615
temulency 959
ten 98
  – to one 472
  – thousand 98
tenable 664
tenacity
  coherence 46
  toughness **327**
  memory 505
  resolution 604
  obstinacy 606
  retention 781
  avarice 819
  courage 861
  – of life 357

– of purpose 604*a*
tenaculum 781
tenancy 777
tenant
  present 186
  occupier 188
  possessor 779
tenantless
  absence 187
  seclusion 893
tenax propositi 204, 939
tend *conduce* 176
  – *animals* 370
  aid 707
  serve 631, 746
  – towards 278
tendence 749
tendency **176**
tender *slight* 32
  ship 273
  soft 324
  painful 378
  colour 428
  war vessel 726
  offer 763
  susceptible 822
  affectionate 897
  compassionate 914
  – age 127
  – conscience 926
  – heart
  susceptible 822
  kind 906
  compassionate 914
  – mercies [ironical]
  badness 649
  severity 739
  cruelty 907
  – passion 897
  – one's resignation 757
  – to 707
tenderfoot 57, 541
tendon 45
tendril *fastening* 45
  offshoot 51
  infant 129
  filament 205
  convoluted 248
  plant 367
tenebrious 421
tenebrosity 421
tenement 189, 780
  – of clay 362
tenet *belief* 484
tenner 800
tennis 840
  – ground 213

tenor *course* 7
 degree 26
 direction 278
 high note 410
 singer 416
 violin 417
 meaning 516
 pursue the noiseless – of
  one's way 881
tense *hard* 323
tensile 325
tension 159, 200
tensure 200
tent *abode* 189
 covering 223
 pitch one's –
  locate 184
  arrive 292
tentacle 781
tentative 463, 675
tente d'abri 223
tented field 722
tenter-hook 214
 on –s 507
tenth 99
tenths
 tithe 812
tent-pegging 840
tents, O Israel, to your –
 722
tenue, en grande – 847,
 882
tenuity
 smallness 32
 thinness 203
 rarity 322
tenuous
 shadowy 4
tenure
 possession 777
 property 780
 due 924
tepee 189
tepefaction 384
Tephramancy 511
tepid 382
tepidarium 386
teratology
 unconformity 83
 distortion 243
 altiloquence 577
 boasting 884
tercentenary 98, 138, 883
terceron 41
terebration 260
teres atque rotundus 249
 in seipso – 650

tergiversation 283, **607**
term *end* 67
 place in series **71**
 period of time 106
 limit 233
 word 562
 name 564
 lease 780
termagant 901
terminal 67, 253, 292
terminate 67, 292
 limit 233
termination 154
termine, mezzo – 628
terminology 562
terminus *end* 67
 limit 233
 arrival 292
termless 105
terms [*see* term]
 circumstances **8**
 reasoning 476
 pacification 723
 conditions 770
 bring to – 723
 come to –
  assent 488
  pacify 723
  submit 725
  consent 762
  compact 769
 couch in – 566
 on friendly – 888
 in no measured – 574
ternary 93
ternion 92
ter quaterque beatus 827
Terpsichore 416, 840
terra: – cotta
 baked 384
 sculpture 557
 – firma
  support 215
  land 342
  safety 664
 – incognita 419
terrace *houses* 189
 level 213
terrain 181
terraqueous 318
terrene 318, 342
terre verte 435
terrestrial 318
terrible 860
terribly *greatly* 31
terrier *list* 86
 auger 262

 dog 366
terrific 31, 830, 860
terrify 860
terrine 191
territorial *land* 342
 soldier 726
territory 181, 780
terror 860
 King of –s 360
 reign of – 739, 828
terrorem, in – 860, 909
terrorism 860
 insolence 885
terrorist
 coward 862
 blusterer 887
 evil-doer 913
terse 572
tertian *periodic* 138
tertiary *three* 92
tertium quid
 dissimilar 18
 mixture 41
 combination 48
 uncomfortable 83
tessellated 440, 847
tesseræ
 mosaic 440
 counters 550
test 463
testa, voce di – 410
testament 771
Testament 985
tester *bedstead* 215
 sixpence 800
testify 467, 550
testimonial 467
testy 901
tetanus 315
tetchy 901
tête: – baissée 863
 – exaltée 503
 – montée 503, 825
 –à-tête *two* 89
 near 197
 confer 588
tether *fasten* 43
 locate 184
 restrain 751
 means of restraint 752
 go beyond the length of
  one's – 738
tethered *firm* 150
tetrachord 413
tetractic 95
tetrad 95
tetrahedral 95

749

tetrahedron 244
tetrarch 745
text *prototype* 22
  topic 454
  meaning 516
  printing 591
  -book 542, 596
textile 219, 329
textuary 983*a*, 985
texture *mixture* 41
  roughness 256
  fabric **329**
Thais 962
Thalia 599
Thames on fire
  set the - 471
  never set the - 501, 701
thane *nobility* 875
thank 916
  no - you 764
  - one's stars 838
  - you for nothing 917
thankful 916
  rest and be - 265, 831
thankless
  painful 830
  ungrateful 917
thank-offering 916, 990
thanksgiving
  gratitude 916
  worship 990
thanks to 155
that 79
  - is 118
  - is to say 79
  - being so 8
  at - time 119
thatch *roof* 223
thaumatrope 445
thaumaturgist 994
thaumaturgy 992
thaw *melt* 335
  heart 382
  heating 384
  calm the mind 826
  pity 914
Thearchy
  authority 737
  Deity 976
theatre
  spectacle 441
  school 542
  drama 599
  arena 728
  amusement 840
  tribunal 966
théâtre: coup de -

appearance 448
  prodigy 872
  display 882
  jeu de - 448, 872
  nom de - 565
theatrical 599
  affected 855
  ostentatious 882
Theban, learned - 492
theca 223
thé dansant 840
theft 775, 791
theism 984, 987
theistic *of God* 976
theme *topic* 454
  dissertation 595
Themis 922
then *time* 106
  therefore 476
thence
  caused by 155
  departure 293
  therefore 476
thenceforward 121
theocracy 976, 995
theodolite 217, 244
theogony 983
theologicum, odium -
  misjudgment 481
  false piety 988
  churchdom 995
theology **983**
theomancy 511
theopathy 987
theopneustic 985
theorbo 417
theorem
  topic 454
  maxim 496
  supposition 514
theoretical 514
theorize 155, 514
theory
  attribution 155
  knowledge 490
  supposition 514
theosophy 983, 984
therapeutics 655, 662
therapy 662
there 183, 186
thereabouts
  almost 32
  place 183
  near 197
thereafter 117
thereby 631
  - hangs a tale 154

therefore
  attribution 155
  reasoning 476
  motive 615
therein 221
thereof 9
theretofore 116
thereupon 106, 117
therewith
  accompanying 88
  means 632
theriac 662
thermal 382
thermion 330
thermogenic 382
thermology 382
thermometer
  heat **389**
thermopile 389
thermoscope 389
Thersites 936
thesaurus
  list 86
  words 562
  book 593
  store 636
thesis *theme* 454
  proposition 514
  dissertation 595
Thespian 599
Thetis 341
theurgist 994
theurgy 992
thews and sinews 159
thick *crowded* 72
  numerous 102
  broad 202
  dense 321
  semiliquid 352
  turbid 426
  dirty 653
  friends 888
  come - 102
  in the - of
  middle 68
  imbedded 228
  action 680
  lay it on -
  cover 223
  redundance 641
  flattery 933
  - of the action 682
  - of the fray 722
  through - and thin 173,
    604*a*
thick-coming
  many 102

repeated 104
frequent 136
- fancies 515
thicken 35
thickens, the plot - 682
thicket 367
thick-head 501
thickness 202, 204
thick-ribbed 159
- ice 383
thickset *short* 201
broad 202
dense 321
thick-skinned 376, 823
thick-skull 499, 501
thief 792
set a - to catch a thief 791
like a - in the night
unexpected 508
concealment 528
dishonourable 940
thievery 791
thieves' Latin 563
thimble
receptacle 191
defence 617
thimbleful 25, 32
thimblerig 545
thimblerigger 792
thin *subduct* 38
few 103
small 193
narrow 203
rare 322
scanty 640
- end of the wedge 66
- out 371
thing *substance* 3
matter 316
just the - 924
the - 926
- to do 625
- of naught 4
know a - or two 698
things
events 151
clothes 225
chattels 780
as - go 613
thingumbob 563
think 451, 484
only - 873
reason to - 472
- aloud 589, 703
- better of 607, 658
- fit 600, 602
- highly 931

- ill 932
- likely 472
- no more of
inattention 458
forgive 918
- of *intend* 620
- out 457
as one -s proper 600
- twice 605, 864
- upon
remember 505
thinker 500
thinking principle 450
thinness 203
thin-skinned
physically sensible 375
morally sensitive 822
fastidious 868
irascible 901
third 93
trisection 94
music 413
- degree 461
- heaven 981
- part 94
- person 664
- power 92
thirdly 93
thirst 965
- for knowledge 455
thirsty soul 959
thirteen 98
thirty-nine articles 983*a*
thirty-one
cards 840
this 79
- that or the other 15
at - time of day 118
thistle *prickly* 253
thistle-down 320
thither 278
thole 821
- pin 215
**Thompson sub-machine
gun** 727
thong *fastening* 45
scourge 975
Thor 979
thorn *sharp* 253
bane 663
painful 830
plant a - 830
spiteful 907
- in the flesh 663, 830
- in the side
badness 649
bane 663

annoyance 830
thorns: sit on -
physical pain 378
moral pain 828
fear 860
on - for 868
thorny 253, 704
thorough 52
thorough-bass 413, 415
thorough-bred
intrinsic 5
horse 271
skill 698
fashionable 852
thoroughfare 260, 627
thorough-going 52
thoroughly, do - 729
thorough-paced 31
thorp 189
though
compensation 30
qualification 469
opposition 708
thought *little* 32
reflection **451**
idea 453
give a - to 457
not to be - of 610, 761
organ of - 450
quick as - 274
seat of - 450
subject of - 454
want of - 458
who could have - it? 508
- of 454
thoughtful 451, 498
thoughtless
incogitant 452
inattentive 458
careless 460
improvident 674
thoughts:
- that breathe 574
- elsewhere 458
thousand 98, 102
one in a - 648, 948
thraldom 749, 750
thrash 972
Thraso 887
Thrasonic 884, 885
thread
arrange 60
series 69
weak 160
filament 205
pass through 302
not have a dry - 339

hang by a – 665
life hangs by a – 360
worn to a – 659
– one's way 266, 302
threadbare 226, 659
threadpaper 203
threat 909
threaten
　future 121
　destiny 152
　danger 665
threatening
　warning 668
　unhopeful 859
three 93
– in one and one in – 976
sisters – 601
go through – hundred and
　sixty degrees 311
– sheets in the wind 959
– times three
　number 98
　approbation 931
threefold 93
three-score 98
– years and ten 128
three-tailed bashaw
　master 745
　nobility 875
threne 938
threnody 839
thresh 972
– out 461
threshold
　beginning 66
　edge 231
at the – *near* 197
– of an inquiry 461
thrice 93
– happy 827
–told tale 573
thrid 302
thrift
　prosperity 734
　gain 775
　economy 817
thriftless 818
thrill
　physical pain 378
　touch 380
　feeling 821
　excitation 824
thrilling
　pleasing 829
　painful 830
thrive 734
throat *opening* 260

　pipe 350, 351
cut the – 361
force down the – 739
stick in one's – 581, 585
take by the – 789
throb 315, 821
throbbing: – heart 860
– pain 378
throe
　revolution 146
　violence 173
　agitation 315
　physical pain 378
　agony 828
birth– 161
throne *abode* 189
　seat 215
　emblem of authority 747
ascend the – 737
occupy the – 737
power behind the – 526
– of God 981
throng 72
throttle
　render powerless 158
　close 261
　kill 361
　seize 789
– down 275
through
　owing to 154
　viâ 278
　by means of 631
get – 729
go – one 824
wet – 339
– thick and thin
　complete 52
　violence 173
　perseverance 604a
throughout 50, 52
– the world 180
throw *impel* 276
　propel 284
　exertion 686
– oneself into the arms of
　664
– away *reject* 610
　waste 638
　relinquish 782
– back 144
– cold water on 616
– of the dice 156
– doubt upon 485
– down 162, 308
– oneself at the feet of 725

– good money after bad
　818
– in 228
– off [*see below*]
– open 260, 296
– out [*see below*]
– over *destroy* 162
– overboard
　exclude 55
　destroy 162
　eject 297
　abrogate 756
– on paper 590
– away the scabbard 722
– into the shade
　superior 33
　lessen 36
　surpass 303
　important 642
– a tub to catch a whale
　545
– up [*see below*]
– a veil over 528
throw off 297
– all disguise 529
– one's guard 508
– the mask 529
– the scent
　misdirect 538
　avoid 623
throw out 284, 297
　eject 297
– a feeler 379
– of gear
　disjoin 44
　derange 61
– a hint 527
– a suggestion 514
throwing stick 727
thrown out 704
thrown up *eject* 297
　resign 757
– one's cap 884
– the game 624
thrum 416
thrush 416
thrust *push* 276
　attack 716
– in *insert* 300
　(*interpose* 228)
– one's nose in 682
– out 55
– down one's throat 744
– upon 784
thud 406, 408a
thug *murderer* 361
　thief 792

thumb *touch* 379
bite the – 929
one's fingers all –s 699
rule of –
  experiment 463
  unreasoning 477
  essay 675
twiddle one's –s 681
under one's –
  authority 737
  subjection 749
– over 539
– screw 975
Thumb, Tom – 539
thump
  beat 276
  thud 406
  non-resonance 408a
  punish 972
thumping *great* 31
  big 192
thunder
  violence 173
  noise 404
  prodigy 872
  threaten 909
look black as – 832, 900
– against 908, 932
– of applause 931
– forth 531
– at the top of one's voice
  411
–s of the Vatican 908
thunderbolt
  weapon 727
  prodigy 872
thunder-clap 508, 872
thundering *great* 31
  big 192
thunderstorm 173
thunderstruck 870
thurible 400, 998
thurifer 996
thuriferous 400
thurification
  fragrance 400
  rite 998
thus *circumstance* 8
  therefore 476
  – far *little* 32
  limit 233
thwack 276, 972
thwart
  across 219
  harm 649
  obstruct 706
  oppose 708

cross 830
thwarted 732
tiara *insignia* 747
  ornament 847
  canonicals 999
Tib's eve 107
tick *graze* 199, 379
  oscillation 314
  sound 407
  mark 550
  credit 805
  go on – 806
  – off *record* 551
ticker 553
ticket 86, 550, 609
  – man 754, 949
ticket of leave 760
tickle *touch* 380
  please 829
  amuse 840
  – the fancy 829, 840
  – the ivories 416
  – the palate 394
  – the palm 784, 807
ticklish
  uncertain 475
  dangerous 665
  difficult 704
tidal wave 348, 667
tid-bit 648, 829
tide *ocean* 341
  wave 348
  abundance 639
  prosperity 734
  against the – 708
  drift with the – 705
  go with the – 82
  high &c. – 348
  stem the – 708
  swim with the – 734
  turn of the – 210
  – of events 151
  – over *time* 106
  defer 133
  safe 664
  inaction 681
  succeed 731
  – of time 109
tidings 532
tidy *orderly* 58
  arrange 60
  good 648
  clean 652
  pretty 845
  – up 60
tie *relation* 9
  equality 27

fasten 43
fastening 45
neckcloth 225
security 771
obligation 926
nuptial – 903
ride and – 266
–s of blood 11
– down
  hinder 706
  compel 744
  restrain 751
– the hands 158, 751
– oneself 768
– up *restrain* 751
  condition 770
  entail 771
tie-beam 45
tied up
  busy 135
  in debt 806
tier *continuity* 69
  layer 204
tierce 92
  – and carte 716
tiff 713, 900
tiffin 298
tiger *violent* 173
  servant 746
  courage 861
  savage 907
  evil-doer 913
  bad man 949
tight *fast* 43
  closed 261
  smart 845
  drunk 959
  – grasp 739
  – hand 739
  – rope dancing 698
  keep a – hand on 751
  on one's – ropes 878
tighten 43, 195
tight-fisted 819
tights 225
tightwad 819
tigress 374
tike 876
tilbury 272
tile *roof* 223
  hat 225
  – loose *insane* 503
till *up to the time* 106
  coffer 191
  cultivate 371
  treasury 802
  – doomsday 112

tipsy 959
tip-top 210, 648
tirade 582, 932
tire *dress* 225
 fatigue 688
 worry 830
 weary 841
tiré à quatre épingles 850
tirer d'affaire 672
 se – 731
Tiresias 513
tiresome [*see* tire]
Tisiphone 173, 900
tissue *whole* 50
 assemblage 72
 matted 219
 texture 329
tit *small* 193
 pony 271
Titan 159, 980
Titania 979
titanic 192
titbit 291, 394, 829
tit for tat 718
tithe *tenth* 99
 tax 812
tithing 181
titillate 840, 865
titillation 377, 380
titivate 847
title
 indication 550
 name 564
 printing 590
 right to property 780
 distinction **877**
 right 924
titled 875
title-deed 771
title-page 66
titter 838
tittle 32
 to a – 494
tittle-tattle 532, 588
titubancy 583
titubate 306, 732
titular 562, 564
tmesis 218
T.N.T. 727
to *direction* 278
 lie – 681
 – all intents and purposes
  27, 52
 – a certain degree 32
 – come 121, 152
 – the credit of 805
 – crown all 33, 642

– do 59
– the end of the chapter 52
– the end of time 112
– and fro 12, 314
– the full 52
– a great extent 31
– the letter 19
– a man 78
– the point 23
– the purpose 23
– a small extent 32
– some extent 26
– be sure 488
– this day 118
– wit 79
toad 649, 846
– under a harrow 378
toad-eater 886, 935
toad-eating
 flattery 933
toadstool 367
toady 886
toast *roast* 384
 celebrate 883
tobacco 392
toboggan 272, 840
toby *jug* 191
toccata 415
tocsin 669
tod 319
to-day 118
toddle 266, 275
toddy 298
toe 211
 on the light fantastic 309,
  840
toes turn up the –
 die 360
toff 854
toffee 396
toga 225, 747
 assume the – virilis 131
together 88, 120
 come – 290
 get – 72
 hang – 709
 lay heads – 695
 – with 37, 88
toggery 225
toil
 activity 682
 exertion 686
 – of a pleasure 682
 –s *trap* 545
toilet 225
 – water 400
toilette 225

en grande – 847
toilsome 686, 704
toilworn 688
token 550
 give – 525
 – of remembrance 505
told, do what one is – 743
tolderolloll 838
Toledo 727
tolerable
 a little 32
 trifling 643
 pretty good 648
 not perfect 651
 satisfactory 831
tolerably, get on – 736
toleration
 laxity 738
 lenity 740
 permission 760
 feeling 821
 calmness 826
 benevolence 906
toll *sound* 407
 tax 812
 – the knell 363
tollbooth
 prison 752
 market 799
tomahawk 727
tomb 363
 lay in the – 363
 – of the Capulets 506
tombé des nues 83, 870
tombola 156
tomboy 129, 851
tombstone 363
tom-cat 373
tome 593
tomentous 256
tomfool 501
tomfoolery
 absurdity 497
 amusement 840
 wit 842
 ostentation 882
Tommy Atkins 726
tommy-gun 727
Tom Noddy 501
to-morrow 121
 – and to-morrow 104, 109
tompion 263
Tom Thumb 193
tomtit 193
tom-tom 417, 722
ton *weight* 319
 fashion 852

toque 225
tor 206
torch 388, 423
  apply the - 824
  light the - of war 722
  - of Hymen 903
Tories 712
torment
  physical 378
  moral 828, 830
  place of - 982
Tormes, Lazarillo de - 941
torn [*see* tear]
  discord 713
tornado 312, 349
torpedo *bane* 663
  sluggish 683
  weapon 727
  evil-doer 913
  - boat 726
  - boat destroyer 726
  - plane 276
torpid, torpor
  inert 172
  inactive 683
  insensible 823
torque 847
  torrefy 384
torrent
  violence 173
  rapid 274
  flow 348
  rain in -s 348
torrid 382
torsion 248
torso 50
tort 925, 947
tort et à travers, à -
  disagreement 24
  absurdity 497
  resolution 604
tortile 248
tortious 925
tortive 248
tortoise 275
tortoise-shell 440
tortuous
  twisted 248
  dishonourable 940
torture
  physical 378
  moral 828, 830
  cruelty 907
  punishment 972
  - a question 476
torvity 901*a*
toss *derange* 61

throw 284
  oscillate 314
  agitate 315
  - in a blanket 929
  - the caber 840
  - the head
  pride 878
  insolence 885
  contempt 930
  - off *drink* 298
  - overboard 610
  - on one's pillow 825
  - up 156, 621
tosspot 959
tot *child* 129
total 50, 84
  sum - 800
  - abstinence 953, 955
  - eclipse 421
totalisator 621
totality 52
totally 52
tot homines, tot sententiæ
  15
totidem verbis 19, 494
totient 84
toties quoties 136
totis viribus 686
totitive 84
toto: in - 52
  - cœlo 52
totter
  changeable 149
  weak 160
  limp 275
  oscillate 314
  agitate 315
  decay 659
  danger 665
  - to its fall 162
touch *relate to* 9
  small quantity 32
  mixture 41
  contact 199
  sensation **379, 380**
  music 416
  test 463
  indication 550
  act 680
  receive 785
  excite 824
  pity 914
  - and go
  instant 113
  soon 132
  changeable 149
  easy 705

  - the guitar 416
  - the hat 894
  - the heart 824
  - on 516
  - to the quick 822
  - up 658
  - upon 595
  in - with 9
touched *crazy* 503
  tainted 653
  compassion 914
  - in the wind 655
  - with *feeling* 821
touching 830
touchstone 463
touchwood
  fuel 388
  irascible 901
touchy 901
tough *coherent* 46
  tenacious 327
  difficult 704
toujours perdrix
  repetition 104
  weary 841
  satiety 869
toupee 256
tour 266
tour de force
  skill 698
  stratagem 702
  display 882
touring car 272
tourist 268
tournament 720
tourniquet 263
tournure 230, 448
  belle - 845
tous les rapports, sous -
  494
tousle 61
tout *solicit* 765
tout: - au contraire 14
  - court 265
  - ensemble 50
  - le monde 78
touter *agent* 758
  solicitor 767
  eulogist 935
tow 285
  take in - *aid* 707
towage 812
towardly 705
towards 278
  draw - 288
  move - 286
towel *clean* 652

fetter 752
cast –s off 750
tramontane
foreign 57
distant 196
wind 349
outlandish 851
tramp *stroll* 266
stroller 268
idler 683
vagabond 867
on the – 264
trample
– in the dust
destroy 162
prostrate 308
– out 162
– under foot
vanquish 731
not observe 773
disrepute 874
insolence 885
dereliction 927
contempt 930
– upon 649, 739
tramway 627
trance *insensibility* 376
dream 515
sleep 683
lethargy 823
tranquil *calm* 174
quiet 265
peaceful 721
calmness 871
– mind 826
tranquillize
moderate 174
pacify 723
soothe 826
transact *act* 680
conduct 692
– business 625
– business with 794
transaction 151, 625, 680, 769
transactions 551
transalpine 196
transanimation 140
transatlantic 196
transcalency 384
transcend *great* 31
superior 33
go beyond 303
transcendency 641
transcendent 33, 873
transcendental 78, 519
transcendentalism 450

transcolate 295
transcribe 19, 590
transcript 21, 590
transcursion 303
transept 1000
transfer
copy 21
displace 185
– *of things* 270
– *of property* **783**
transference **270**
transfiguration
change 140
divine – 998
transfix 260
transfixed *firm* 150
transform 140
transformation scene 599
transfuse 41, 270
– the sense of 522
transgress
go beyond 303
infringe 773
violate 927
sin 945
transgression 947
transi de froid 383
transient 111, 149
transientness 111
transilience 146, 303
transit
conversion 144
motion 264
transference 270
– *circle* 244
transit gloria mundi, sic – 735, 874
transition 144, 270
transitional 140
transitory 111
transitu, in –
transient 111
journey 266
transference 270
translate
interpret 522
promote 955
translation
transference 270
resurrection 981
translator 524
translocation 270
translucence 425
transmarine 196
transmigration 140, 144
transmission
moving 270

passage 302
– *of property* 783
transmit light 425
transmogrify 140
transmutation 140, 144
transom 215
transparency **425**
transparent
transmitting light 425
obvious 518
transpicuous
transmitting light 425
obvious 518
transpierce 260
transpire
evaporate 336
appear 525
be disclosed 529
transplace 270
transplant 270
transplendent 420
transpontine 196
transport
transfer 270
ship 273
war vessel 726
excitement 825
delight 827
please 829
punish 972
– of love 897
– plane 273
transpose
exchange 148
displace 185
invert 218
transfer 270
– *music* 413
transubstantiation
change 140
sacrament 998
transude 295, 302
transume 140
transumption 270
transverse 217, 219
tranter 271
trap *closure* 261
gig 272
snare 545
stage – 599
pitfall 667
fall into a – 547, 699
lay a – for 545
trapan 545
trap bat and ball 840
trap-door
opening 260

snare 545
pitfall 667
trapes 701
trappings
  adjunct 39
  clothes 225
  equipment 633
  ornament 847
Trappist 996
traps
  clothes 225
  baggage 780
trash
  unmeaning 517
  trifling 643
  useless 645
trashy – *style* 575
traulism 583
traumatic 662
travail 161, 686
trave 215
travel 266
  – *out of the record* 477
traveller 268
  bagman 758
  tricks upon –s 545, 702
  –'s *tale* 546, 549
travelling bag 191
traverse *move* 266
  pass 302
  negative 536
  obstruct 706
travesty
  imitate 19, 21
  misinterpret 523
  misrepresent 555
  ridicule 856
travis 215
trawl 285, 463
trawler 273
tray 191
treacherous 907, 940
  – *memory* 506
treachery 545, 940
treacle 352, 396
tread 264, 266
  – *the beaten track* 82, 613
  – *the boards* 599
  – *down* 739, 879
  – *on the heels of* 281
  – *a path* 266, 622
  – *the stage* 599
  – *in the steps of* 19
  – *under foot*
    destroy 162
    subjection 749
    disrepute 874

insolence 885
contempt 930
– *upon* 649
treadle 633
treadmill 975
treason 742, 940
treasure *cherish* 897
  store 636
  goodness 648
  money 800
  – *trove* 618
  – *up in the memory* 505
treasurer 801
treasury 802
  – *note* 800
treat *physical pleasure* 377
  manage 692
  bargain 769
  delight 827, 829
  amusement 840
  – *of* 595
  – *oneself to* 827
  – *well* 906
treatise 593, 595
treatment
  painting 556
  conduct 692
  ill – 649
  medical – 662
treaty 769
treble
  three 93
  shrill 410
  childish – 581
tree *pedigree* 166
  plant 367
  gallows 975
  top of the – 210
  up a – 704
  as the – *falls* 151
  – *of knowledge* 493
treenail 45
trefoil 92
trek 266
trellis 219
tremble
  fluctuate 149
  weakness 160
  shake 315
  cold 383
  emotion 821
  fear 860
  make one – 860
trembling:
  – *in the balance* 475, 665
  – *to its fall* 160
tremblingly alive 822

tremendous 830, 860
tremendously 31
tremolo 415
tremor
  agitation 315
  emotion 821
  fearful 860
tremulous
  agitated 315
  – *voice* 583
  irresolute 605
  fear 860
trench *moat* 232
  furrow 259
  concavity 252
  defence 717
  – *mortar* 727
  – *on near* 197
  trespass 303
  moral trespass 925
trenchant
  energetic 171
  assertive 535
  concise style 572
  vigorous language 574
  important 642
  emotion 821
  discourteous 895
  censure 932
trench-coat 225
trencher *plate* 191
  layer 204
trenches, open the – 716
trend *tendency* 176
  bend 278
  deviate 279
trennel 45
trepan 260
  borer 262
  snare 545
trephine 260, 267
trepidation
  agitation 315
  emotion 821
  excitement 825
  fear 860
tres juncta in uno 92
trespass
  go beyond 303
  vice 945
  guilt 947
tress 256
trestle 215
trevet 215 [*see* trivet]
trews 225
trey 92
triad 92

triagonal 244
trial *inquiry* 461
  experiment 463
  essay 675
  difficulty 704
  adversity 735
  suffering 828, 830
  lawsuit 969
  punishment 972
  - of temper 824
triality 92
trialogue 588
triangle 92, 244
  music 417
  punishment 975
triangular duel 720
triarchy 737
tribe *race* 11
  assemblage 72
  class 75
  clan 166
tribulation 828
tribunal 966
tribune
  rostrum 542
  judge 967
tributary *river* 348
  giving 784
tribute
  compensation 30
  donation 784
  money paid 809
  reward 973
  pay - to 928, 931
trice 113, 633
  - up 43
  in a - 113
trichotomy 94
trichroism 440
trick *deception* 545
  trait 550
  habit 613
  contrivance 626
  skill 698
  artifice 702
  - *at cards* 775
  play -s
  bungle 699
  cunning 702
  amusement 840
  ridicule 856
  - of fortune 509
  - out 847, 851
  -s of the trade 702
trickery *deceit* 545
  finery 851
trickle 295, 348

trickster
  deceiver 548
  cunning 702
  rogue 792
tricksy *cheery* 836
  pretty 845
  ornamented 847
tricolour
  variegated 440
  flag 550
tricycle 272
trident 92, 341
triennial
  periodical 138
  plant 367
triennium 92
trifid 94
trifle *small* 32
  neglect 460
  folly 499
  unimportant 643
  not to be -d with 744
  not stick at -s 604
  - time away 683
  - with *neglect* 460
  deceive 545
  disrespect 929
trifler 460, 501
trifling 499, 643
  wit 842
triforium 1000
triform 92
trifurcate 94
trigamy 903
trigger 633
  draw the - 722
Trigger, Sir Lucius O' -
  887
trigon 244
trigonometry 244
trihedral 93
trilateral 236, 244
trilogistic 93
trilogy 93
  drama 599
trill *stream* 348
  sound 407
  music 416
trillion 98
trim *state* 7
  adjust 27
  dress 225
  form 240
  lie 544
  waver 605
  change sides 607
  clean 652

  beautify 845
  adorn 847
  scold 932
  flog 972
  in - *order* 58
trimmer *fickle* 607
  apostate 941
  selfish 943
trimming
  border 231
  ornament 847
  dishonesty 940
trinal 92
trine 93
trinitrotoluene 727
trinity 92
  - Sunday 998
Trinity, Holy - 976
trinket 643, 847
trinkgeld 784
trinomial 92
trio *three* 92
  music 415
triolet 597
trip *jaunt* 266
  run 274
  fall 306
  mistake 495
  leap 509
  bungle 699
  fail 732
  vice 945
  guilt 947
  - up *deceive* 545
  overthrow 731
tripartition 94
triplane 273
triple 93
  - *crown* 747, 999
triplet *three* 92
  verse 597
triplex 93
triplication 93
triplicity 93
tripod 215
tripos 461
tripotage 588
tripping [*see* trip]
  style 578
  nimble 682
  caught - 491
trippingly on the tongue
  584
Triptolemus 371
trireme 273
trisection 94
triste 837

tristful 837
trisulcate
  trisected 94
  furrow 259
trite
  known 490
  conventional 613
  - *saying* 496
tritheism 984
Triton *sea* 341
  - among the minnows
  superior 33
  huge 192
  important 642
trituration 330
trium literarum, homo -
  792
triumph
  success 731
  trophy 733
  exult 838
  celebrate 883
  boast 884
triumvirate 92, 737
triune 93
Triune God 976
trivet 215, 386
  right as a - 650, 924
trivia 643
trivial
  unmeaning 517
  trifling 643
  useless 645
troat 412
trocar 262
trochaic 597
trochee 597
trochilic 312
trodden: down- 749
  well - 613, 677
Troglodyte 893
troika 92
troll
  roll 312
  fairy 980
trolley 272
  - omnibus 272
trollop 962
trombone 417
tronk 752
troop 72, 726
  raise -s 722
  - carrier
  aeroplane 726
trooper 726
  lie like a - 544
  swear like a - 908

troop-ship 726
trop, de - 641
trope 521
Trophonius, cave of - 837
trophy 551, **733**
tropical 382
troposphere 338
trot 266, 274
  - out 525, 882
troth *belief* 484
  veracity 543
  promise 768
  by my - 535
  plight one's - 902
trothless 544, 940
trotters 266
trottoir 627
troubadour 597
trouble *disorder* 59
  derange 61
  exertion 686
  difficulty 704
  adversity 735
  pain 828
  painful 830
  bring into - 649
  get into - 649, 732
  in - 619, 735
  take - 686
  - one's head about 682
  - one for 765
  - oneself 686
troubled waters, fish in -
  704
troublesome 686, 704, 830
troublous 59, 173
  - times 713
trough *hollow* 252
  trench 259
  conduit 350
trounce 932, 972
troupe 72
trousers 225
trousseau 225
trouvaille 775
trouvère 597
trover 775, 964
trow *think* 451
  believe 484
  know 490
trowel 191
troy-weight 219
truant *absent* 187
  runaway 623
  idle 682
  apostate 941
truce *cessation* 142

  deliverance 672
  peace 721
  pacification 723
  flag of - 724
trucidation 361
truck *summit* 210
  vehicle 272
  barter 794
truck driver 268
truck farm 371
truckle to
  submit 725
  servile 886
  flatter 933
truckle-bed 215
truck-load 31
truckman 268
truculent 907
trudge 266, 275
truditur dies die 109
true *real* 1
  straight 246
  assent 488
  accurate 494
  veracious 543
  faithful 772
  honourable 939
  orthodox 983a
  - bill
  vindicate 937
  accuse 938
  lawsuit 969
  see in its - colours 480a
  - meaning 516
  - to nature 17
  - to oneself 604a
  - saying 496
  - to scale 494
true-hearted 543, 939
true-love 897
true-lover's knot 897, 902
true-penny 939
truism *axiom* 496
  unmeaning 517
trull 962
truly *very* 31
  assent 488
  really 494
  indeed 535
trump *perfect* 650
  honourable 939
  good man 948
  turn up -s 731
  - card *device* 626
  success 731
  - up *falsehood* 544
  accuse 938

trumped up 468, 545, 546
trumpery 517, 643
trumpet *music* 417
  war cry 722
  boast 884
  flourish of –s
  ostentation 882
  celebration 883
  boasting 884
  ear– 418
  penny –
  skill 410
  sound of –
  alarm 669
  speaking – 418
  – blast 404
  – call 550, 741
  – forth 531
trumpeter
  musician 416
  messenger 534
  boaster 884
trumpet-toned 410
trumpet-tongued 404, 531
truncate 201, 241
truncated 53
truncheon
  weapon 727
  staff of office 747
  instrument of punishment
  975
trundle 284, 312
trunk *whole* 50
  origin 153
  paternity 166
  box 191
trunk-hose 225
trunnion
  support 215
  projection 250
truss *tie* 43
  pack, packet 72
  support 215
trust
  belief 484
  combination 709
  property 780
  credit 805
  hope 858
  – to a broken reed 699
  – to the chapter of
  accidents 621
trustee
  consignee 758
  possessor 779
  treasurer 801
trustful 484

trustless 940
trustworthy
  certain 474
  belief 848
  - *memory* 505
  veracious 543
  honourable 939
truth
  exactness **494**
  veracity 543
  probity 939
  arrive at the – 480*a*
  in – *certainly* 474
  love of – 543
  of a – 535, 543
  prove the – of 937
  religious – 983*a*
  speak the – 529, 543
  in very – 543
Truth, Spirit of – 976
truthless 544
trutination 319
try *experiment* 463
  adjudge 480
  endeavour 675
  use 677
  lawsuit 969
  – a case 967
  – a cause 480
  – conclusions
  discuss 476
  quarrel 713
  contend 720
  – one's hand 675
  – one's luck 621
  – one 704
  – out 463
  – the patience 830
  – a prisoner 967
  – one's temper 824
  – one's utmost 686
trying 688, 704
tryst 892
trysting-place 74
tsar [*see* czar]
tu quoque 718
  – argument
  counter-evidence 468
  confutation 479
  accuse 938
tub 191
  – thumper 582
  – to a whale 545, 617
tuba 417
tubam trepidat, ante –
  860, 862
tubby 202

tube 260
  test – 144
tubercle 250
tuberculous 655
tuberosity 250
tubman 968
tubular 260
tubulated 260
tubule 260
tuck *fold* 258
  dagger 727
  – in *locate* 184
  eat 298
  insert 300
tucker 225
tuft *collection* 72
  rough 256
tufted 256
tuft-hunter 836, 943
tuft-hunting 886, 933
tug *ship* 273
  pull 285
  effort 686
  – of war 720, 722
  athletic sport 840
tuition 537
tulip *variegated* 440
  gaudy 882
tumble *derange* 61
  destruction 162
  fall 306
  agitate 315
  fail 732
  rough and – 59
  – down 665
tumbler *athlete* 159
  glass 191
  actor 599
  buffoon 844
tumbrel 272
tumefaction 194
tumid
  expanded 194
  - *style* 577
tumour
  expansion 194
  prominence 250
tumult *disorder* 59
  agitation 315
  revolt 742
  emotion 825
tumultuous 59, 173
tumulus 363
tun *receptacle* 191
  large 192
  drunkard 959
tunable 413

tund 972
tundra 344
tune 402, 415
  in – 413
  out of –
    unmusical 414
    imperfect 651
    deteriorated 659
  put in –
    prepare 673
    concord 714
  to the – of
    quantity 25
    payment 807
    price 812
  – up 416
tuneful *music* 413
  poetry 597
  – nine 416, 597
tuneless 414
tunic 225
tunicle 999
tuning-fork 417
tunnage 192
tunnel *concave* 252
  opening 260
  passage 627
tup 366, 373
turban 225
turbary 267
turbid 426, 653
turbinated 248, 312
turbine 153
turbulence
  violence 173
  agitation 315
  excitation 825
turbulent 59
Turcism 984
tureen 191
turf *lawn* 344
  grass 367
  fuel 388
  gambling 621
  races 720
  race-course 728
  amusement 840
turgid
  expanded 194
  - *style* 577
  redundant 641
  ostentatious 882
Turk
  polygamist 903
  grand – 745
  'bear like the – no rival
    near the throne' 878

turkey-trot 840
Turkish bath 386, 652
turlupinade 842
turmoil
  confusion 59
  violence 173
  agitation 315
turn *state* 7
  crisis 134
  period of time 138
  change 140
  tendency 176
  form 240
  curve 245
  blunt 254
  stroll 266
  deviate 279
  circuition 311
  rotate 312
  aptitude 698
  affections 820
  emotion 821
  dance 840
  nausea 867
  by –s 138, 148
  come in its – 138
  each in its – 148
  meet one at every – 641
  take a favourable – 658
  give one a –
    aid 707
    excite 824
  do a good – 648, 906
  ill – 907
  in – 58, 138
  one's luck –s 735
  serve one's – 644
  to a – 494
  take a wrong – 732
  – about 148
  – to account 677, 775
  – adrift 73, 297
  – aside *change* 140
    deviate 279
    hinder 706
  – one's attention from 458
  – away *eject* 297
    not look 442
    avoid 623
    dismiss 756
    relinquish 782
  – back 145, 283
  – one's back upon
    oppose 708
    refuse 764
    disrespect 929
    contempt 930

  – the brain 503
  – of the cards 156
  – colour 821
  – a corner
    go round 311
    succeed 731
  – the corner 140, 658
  – a deaf ear to
    deaf 419
    refuse 764
  – down 258
  – of expression 566
  – the eyes upon 441
  – for 698
  – from *repent* 950
  – to good account 658
  – one's hand to 625
  – the head
    induce 615
    excite 824
    astonish 870
    vanity 880
    hate 898
  – on one's heel
    avoid 623
    discourtesy 895
  – the house out of window
    713
  – in *go to bed* 683
  – inside out 529
  – into
    conversion 144
    translate 522
  - *money* 796
  - *ridicule* 856
  – of mind 820
  – the mind to 457
  – off 972
  – on the tap 297
  – the other cheek 725
  – out *become* 144
    happen 151
    exterior 220
    clothes 225
    carriage 272
    eject 297
    strike 719
    - *well* 731
    - *ill* 732
    dismiss 756
    display 882
  – over [*see below*]
  – a penny 775
  – round
    inversion 218
    revolve 311
    rotate 312

recant 607
- *one's little finger* 737
- the scale
unequal 28
superior 33
change 140
reverse 145
cause 153
counter-evidence 468
induce 615
- the stomach 395, 867
- the tables 14, 718
- of the table 156
- tail *go back* 283
run away 623
cowardice 862
- the tide 145
- of the tide 145, 218
- topsy turvey 61, 218
- and turn about 148, 149
- turtle 218
- and twist 248
- under 258
- up [*see below*]
- upon
depend upon 154
retaliate 718
turn-coat 605, 607
turned of 128
turn over *give* 784
invert 218
entrust 755
- the leaves 457, 539
- in the mind 451
- a new leaf
change 140
improve 658
repent 950
- to 270
turnover 298
turning-point
crisis 8
end 67
occasion 134
reversion 145
cause 153
summit 210
limit 233
turnkey 753
turnpike 706
- road 627
turnscrew 633
turnspit 366
turnstile 553, 706
turn up *happen* 151
chance 156
visible 446

unexpected 508
- one's eyes
wonder 870
hypocrisy 988
- one's nose at
aversion 867
fastidious 868
contempt 930
turpentine and beeswax 255
Turpin, Dick - 792
turpitude 874, 940
turquoise *blue* 438
jewel 847
turret 206
turret-ship 726
turtle *savoury* 394
turtle-doves 897
tush *silence* 403
taciturn 585
trifling 643
tusk 253
tussle 720
tussock 256
tut [*see* tush]
censure 932
tutelage
teaching 537
learning 539
safety 664
subjection 749
tutelary *safety* 664
- genius
auxiliary 711
god 979
- god 664
- saint 890, 912
tutor *cultivate* 375
teach 537
teacher 540
tutus, cavendo - 664
tuyère 386
twaddle
absurd 497
unmeaning 517
diffuseness 573
talk 584
twain 89
in - 44
twang *taste* 390
pungency 392
sound 402
stridor 410
music 416
voice 583
twattle [*see* twaddle]
tweak 378

- the nose 830
tweed 219
tweedle *touch* 379
music 416
**tweedledum and
tweedledee** 415
tweeny 746
tweezers 781
twelfth 99
twelve 98
twentieth century 118
twenty &c. 98
- shillings in the pound 803
twice 90
twice-told tale 104, 841
twiddle 379
twig 51
hop the - 360
twilight
morning 125
evening 126
dusk 422
- sleep 376
twill *crossing* 219
convolution 248
fold 258
twin *similar* 17
accompanying 88
two 89
duplicate 90
twine *string* 205
intersect 219
convolution 248
- round 43, 227
twinge 378, 828
twinkle
instantaneous 113
light 420
dimness 422
twinkling of an eye,
in the - 113
twins 11
twire 315
twirl *convolute* 248
revolve 311
rotate 312
twist *join* 43
thread 205
oblique 217
crossing 219
distort 243
convolution 248
deviate 279
bend 311
prejudice 481
insanity 503

unintelligible 519
irresponsible 927a
arbitrary 964
unaccustomed
unusual 83
unused 614
unskilful 699
unachievable 471
unacknowledged 489, 917
unacquainted 491
unacquired 777a
unadmonished 665
unadorned 576, 849
beauty - 845
unadulterated 42, 494, 652
unadventurous 864
unadvisable 647
unadvised 665, 699
unaffected
genuine 494
sincere 543
- *style* 578
obstinate 606
artless 703
insensible 823
simple 849
taste 850
unafflicted 831
unaided *weak* 160
unalarmed 861
unalienable 924
unallayed 159
unallied 10
unallowable 923
unallowed 925
unalloyed 42
- happiness 827
- truth 494
unalluring 866
unalterable 150
unaltered 13, 150
unamazed 871
unambiguous 518
unambitious 866
unamiable 907
unanimated 823
unanimity 23, 488, 714
unannexed 44
unanswerable
demonstrative 478
irresponsible 927a
arbitrary 964
unanswered 478
unanticipated 508
unappalled 861
unappareled 226

unapparent 526
unappeasable 173
unappetizing 398
unapplied 678
unappreciated 482
unapprehended 491
unapprehensive 861
unapprized 491
unapproachable
great 31
infinite 105
distant 196
unapproached 33
unappropriated 782
unapproved 932
unapt
incongruous 24
important 158
unskilful 699
unarmed 158
unarranged 59, 674
unarrayed 849
unascertained 475, 491
unasked 602, 766
unaspiring 866, 881
unassailable 664
unassailed 748
unassembled 73
unassisted 160, 706
- eye 441
unassociated 44
unassuming 881
unatoned 951
unattached 44
unattackable 664
unattainable 471
unattained 732
unattempted 623
unattended 87
- to 460
unattested 468
unattracted
indifferent 866
unattractive 866
unauthenticated
unproved 468
uncertain 475
error 495
unauthoritative 475
unauthorized
prohibited 761
undue 925
lawless 964
unavailing 645, 918
unavenged 918
unâ voce 488
unavoidable 474, 601

unavowed 489
unawakened 683
unaware 491, 508
take -s 674
unawed 861
unbalanced 28
unbar 750
unbearable 830
unbeaten 123
unbeauteous 846
unbecoming
incongruous 24
disreputable 874
undue 925
dishonourable 940
- a gentleman 895
unbefitting 24, 925, 940
[*see* unbecoming]
unbegotten 2
unbeguile 527, 529
unbegun 67, 674
unbelief 485, 989
unbeloved 898
unbend
straighten 246
repose 687
- the mind 452
unbending 323
unbenevolent 907
unbenign 907
unbeseeming 851, 940
unbesought 766
unbetrayed 939
unbewailed 932
unbiassed 498, 748
unbidden 600, 742
unbigoted 498
unbind 44, 750
unblamable 946
unblamed 946
unblemished 650, 946
unblenching 861
unblended 42
unblest 735, 932
- with 777a
unblown 674
unblushing
proud 878
vain 880
imprudent 885
unboastful 881
unbodied 317
unboiled 674
unbolt 750
unbookish 491
unborn 2, 152
unborrowed 787, 788

unbosom oneself 529
unbought
  not bought 796
  honorary 815
  honourable 939
  unselfish 942
unbound 748, 927*a*
unbounded 105
unbrace 160, 655
unbreathed 526
unbred 895
unbribed 939, 942
unbridled
  violent 173
  lax 738
  free 748
unbroken
  entire 50
  continuous 69
  preserved 670
  unviolated 939
unbruised 50
unbuckle 44
unburden
  - one's mind 529
unburdened 705
unburied 362
unbusinesslike 699
unbuttoned 748
uncalculating 863
uncalled for
  redundant 641
  useless 645
  not used 678
uncandid 544, 907
uncanny 846, 980
uncanonical 984
uncared for
  neglected 460
  indifference 866
  disliked 867
  hated 898
uncase 226
uncaught 748
uncaused 156
unceasing 112
uncensured 931
unceremonious 880, 895
uncertain
  irregular 139
  not certain 475
  doubtful 485
  in an - degree 32
uncertainty 475
unchain 44, 750
unchained 748
unchallenged 488, 924

unchangeable 150, 604*a*
unchanged 16, 141
unchanging 5
uncharitable 907
unchartered 925, 964
unchaste 961
unchastised 970
unchecked 748
uncheckered 141
uncheerful 837
unchivalric 940
unchristian 984, 989
uncial 590
uncinated 244
uncircumscribed 180
uncircumspect 460
uncivil 851, 895
uncivilized 876, 895
unclaimed 748
unclassical 851
uncle *kin* 11
  my -'s
  pawnship 787
unclean 653
  - spirit 978, 980
uncleanness 653
unclipped 50
unclog 705, 750
unclose 260, 750
unclothe 226
unclouded 420, 446
unclubbable 893
unclutch 790
uncoif 226
uncoil 313
uncoloured
  achromatic 429
  true 494
uncombed 653, 851
uncombined
  simple 42
  incoherent 47
uncomeatable 471
uncomely 846
uncomfortable 828, 830
uncommenced 67
uncommendable
  blamable 932
  bad 945
  guilt 947
uncommensurable 24
uncommon 31, 83, 137
uncommonly 31
uncommunicated 781
uncommunicative 528
uncompact 322
uncompassionate 914*a*

uncompelled 748
uncomplaisant 764
uncompleted
  incomplete 53
  unfinished 730
  failure 732
uncomplying 742, 764
uncompounded 42
uncompressed 320, 322
uncompromising
  conformable 82
  severe 739
unconcealable 525
unconceived
  uncreated 12
  unintelligible 519
unconcern 823, 866
unconcocted 674
uncondemned 970
unconditional
  complete 52
  free 748
  permission 760
  consent 762
  release 768*a*
unconducive 175*a*
unconfined 748
unconfirmed 475
unconformity
  disagreement 24
  irregularity **83**
unconfused
  methodical 58
  clear 518
unconfuted 478, 494
uncongealed 333
uncongenial 24, 657
unconnected
  irrelative 10
  disjointed 44
  discontinuous 70
  illogical 477
unconquerable
  strong 159
  persevering 604*a*
  - will 604
unconquered 719
unconscientious 940
unconscionable
  excessive 31
  unprincipled 945
unconscious
  ignorant 491
  insensible 823
unconsenting 603, 764
unconsidered 452
unconsolable 837

unconsolidated 47
unconsonant 24
unconspicuous 447
unconstitutional 925, 964
unconstrained 748, 880
unconsumed 40
uncontested 474
uncontradicted 488
uncontrite 951
uncontrollable
  violent 173
  necessity 601
  emotion 825
uncontrolled
  free 748
  excitability 825
uncontroverted 488
unconventional 83, 614
unconversant 491, 699
unconverted
  dissenting 489
  irreligious 989
unconvinced 489
uncooked 674
uncopied 20
uncork 750
uncorrupted 939
uncounted 475
uncouple 44
uncourteous 895
uncourtly 851, 895
uncouth
  - *style* 579
  ugly 846
  vulgar 851
uncover
  denude 226
  open 260
  disclose 529
  bow 894
uncreated 2
uncritical 931
uncropped 50
uncrown 756
unction
  emotion 821, 824
  divine functions 976
  piety 987
  extreme - 998
  lay the flattering
  - to one's soul 834, 858
unctuous *oily* 355, 894
  flattering 933
  hypocritical 988
unctuousness **355**
unculled
  unused 678

relinquished 782
unculpable 946
uncultivated
  vulgar 85
  ignorant 491
  unprepared 674
uncurbed 748
uncurl 246
uncustomary 83
uncut 50
undamaged 648
undamped 340
undated
  without date 115
  waving 248
undaunted 861
undazzled 498
undebauched 939
undeceive 527, 529
undeceived 490
undecided
  inquiring 461
  uncertain 475
  irresolute 605
leave - 609*a*
undecipherable 519
undecked 849
undecomposed 42
undefaced 845
undefended 725
undefiled
  honest 939
  innocent 946
  chaste 960
undefinable
  uncertain 475
  unmeaning 517
  unintelligible 519
undefined
  invisible 447
  uncertain 475
undeformed 845
undemolished 50
undemonstrable 485
undemonstrated 475
undemonstrative 826
undeniable 474, 478
undeplored 898
undepraved 939
undeprived 781
under *less* 34
  below 207
  subject to 749
  range - 76
  - advisement 454
  - age 127
  - agent 758

- arrest 751
- breath 405
- the conditions 8
- one's control 743
- cover
  covered 223
  hidden 528
  safe 664
- the domination of 737
- one's eyes 446
- foot [*see below*]
- full strength 651
- the head of 9
- lock and key 664
- the mark 34
- press of 744
- protest 489, 744
- restraint 751
- the rule of 737
- seal 467
- subjection 749
- the sun 1
- way 282
underbid 794
underbreath 405
underbred 851
underclothing 225
undercurrent
  cause 153
  stream 348, 349
  latent 526
  opposing 708
underestimation **483**
underfed 640
underfoot 207
  tread - 739
undergo 151
  - a change 144
  - pain 828
undergraduate 541
underground
  low 207
  deep 208
  latent 526
  hidden 528
underhand 526, 528
- dealing 528
underhung 250
underived 20
underlessee 779
underlet 787
underlie 207, 526
underline
  mark 550
  emphatic 642
underling
  servant 746

clown 876
undermine
  weaken 158
  burrow 252
  damage 659
  stratagem 702
  hinder 706
undermost 211
underneath 207
undernourished 640
underpaid 817
underpin 215
underplot 626
underprop 215
underrate 483
underreckon 483
undersell 796
underset 215
undershot 250
undersign 467
undersized 193
understand
  know 490
  intelligible 518
  latent 526
  be informed 527
  give one to - 572
  - by 516, 522
  - one another 709, 714
understanding
  agreement 23
  intellect 450
  intelligence 498
  come to an - 488
  intelligible 518
  agree 714
  pacification 723
  compact 769
  good - 714, 888
  by a mutual - 526
  with the - 469
understate 489
understood
  meaning 516
  implied 526
  customary 613
understrapper 746
understudy 134
undertake
  endeavour 676
  promise 768
undertaker 363
undertaking 625, **676**
undertone 405
undertow 348
undervalue 483
underwood 367

underwrite
  promise 768
  compact 769
  insurance 771
underwriter 758
undescribed 83
undeserved 925
undeserving of belief 485
undesigned 621
undesigning 703
undesirable 647, 830
undesired 830, 866
undesirous 866
undespairing 858
undestroyed
  existing 1
  whole 50
  persisting 141
undetermined
  chance 156
  inquiry 461
  uncertain 475
  unintelligible 519
  irresolute 605
undeveloped 526
undeviating
  uniform 16
  unchanged 150
  straight 246
  direct 278
  persevering 604a
undevout 989
undigested 674
undignified 940
undiminished 31, 35, 50
undirected 279, 621
undiscernible 447, 519
undiscerning
  blind 442
  inattentive 458
undisciplined 608
undisclosed 526, 528
undiscoverable 519
undiscovered 526
undiscriminating 465a
undisguised
  true 494
  manifest 525
  sincere 543
undismayed 861
undisposed of 678, 781
undisputed 474
undissembling 543
undissolved
  entire 50
  dense 321
undistinguishable 465a

undistinguished 465a
undistorted 246, 494
undistracted 457
undisturbed
  quiescent 265
  repose 685
  unexcited 826
undivided 50, 52
undo *untie* 44
  reverse 145
  destroy 162
  neutralize 179
  not do 681
undoing *ruin* 735
undone *failure* 732
  adversity 735
  pained 828
  hopeless 859
undoubted 474
undraped 226
undreaded 861
undreamt of 452
undress *clothes* 225
  nude 226
  simple 849
undressed 226, 674
undried 339
undrilled 674
undrooping 604a
undubitably 488
undueness 925
undulate 248, 314
unduly 32
undutiful 945
undying 112, 150
une aile, ne battre que d'
  - 683
unearned 925
unearth *eject* 297
  disinter 363
  inquire 461
  discover 480a
unearthly
  immaterial 317
  Deity 976
  demon 980
  heavenly 981
  pious 987
uneasy 828
uneatable 395
unedifying 538
uneducated 491, 674
unembarrassed 705, 852
unembodied 317
unemotional 823
unemployed 678, 681
unencumbered 705, 927a

unendeared 898
unending 112
unendowed 158
 – with reason 450*a*
unendurable 830
unenjoyed 841
unenlightened 491, 499
unenslaved 748
unenterprising 864
unentertaining 843
unenthralled 748
unentitled 925
unenvied 929, 930
unequal 28, 139
 inequitable 923
 – to 640
unequalled 33
unequipped 674
unequitable 923
unequivocal
 great 31
 sure 474
 clear 518
unerring
 certain 474
 tone 494
 innocent 946
unessayed 678
unessential 643
unestablished 185
uneven *diverse* 16*a*
 unequal 28
 irregular 139
 rough 256
uneventful 643
unexact 495
unexaggerated 494
unexamined 460
unexampled 83
unexceptionable
 good 648
 legitimate 924
 innocent 946
unexcitable 826
unexcited 823, 826
unexciting 174
unexecuted 730
unexempt 177
unexercised 674, 678
unexerted 172
unexhausted 159, 639
unexpanded 195, 203
unexpected
 exceptional 83
 inexpectation 508
unexpensive 815
unexplained

 not known 491
 unintelligible 519
 latent 626
unexplored
 neglected 460
 ignorant 491
 unseen 526
unexposed 526
unexpressed 536
unexpressive 517
unextended 317
unextinguished 173, 382
unfaded 428
unfading 112
unfailing 141
unfair *false* 544
 unjust 923
 dishonourable 940
unfaithful 940
unfaltering 604*a*
unfamiliar 83
unfashionable 83, 851
unfashioned 241, 674
unfasten 44
unfathomable
 infinite 105
 deep 208
 mysterious 519
unfavourable
 out of season 135
 hindrance 706
 obstructive 708
 – chance 473
unfeared 861
unfeasible 471
unfed 640, 956
unfeeling 376, 823
unfeigned 543
unfelt 823
unfeminine
 manly 373
 vulgar 851
unfertile 169
unfetter 750
unfettered 748
unfinished 53, 730
unfit
 inappropriate 24
 impotence 158
 inexpedient 647
 unskilful 699
 wrong 923
 undue 925
unfitted
 not prepared 674
unfix 44
unfixed 149

unflagging 604*a*
unflammable 385
unflattering 494, 703
unfledged
 young 127, 129
 unprepared 674
unflinching
 firm 604
 persevering 604*a*
 brave 861
unfold
 straighten 246
 evolve 313
 interpet 522
 manifest 525
 disclose 529
 – a tale 594
unforbidden 760
unforced 602, 748
unforeseen 508
unforfeited 781
unforgettable 505
unforgiving 919
unforgotten 505
unformed 241, 674
unfortified
 pure 42
 powerless 158
unfortunate
 ill-timed 135
 failure 732
 adversity 735
 unhappy 828
 – woman 962
unfounded 546
unfrequent 137
unfrequented 893
unfriended
 powerless 158
 secluded 893
unfriendly
 opposed 708
 hostile 889
 malevolent 907
unfrock 756, 972
unfrozen 382
unfruitful 169
unfulfilled 713, 925
unfurl
 unfold 313
 – a flag 525, 550
unfurnished 640, 674
ungainly 846, 895
ungallant 895
ungarnished 849
ungathered 678
ungenerous 819, 943

continuing 143
persevering 604*a*
uninterrupted
continuous 69
perpetual 112
unremitting 893
unintroduced 893
uninured 614
uninvented 526
uninvestigated 491
uninvited 893
uninviting 830
union
agreement 23
junction 43
combination 48
concurrence 178
workhouse 189
party 712
concord 714
marriage 903
unionist 712
union-jack 550
union-pipes 417
unique
dissimilar 18
original 20
exceptional 83
alone 87
unirritating 174
unison
agreement 23
melody 413
concord 714
unit 51, 87
Unitarian 984
unite *join* 43
combine 48
assemble 72
concur 178
converge 290
party 712
- one's efforts 709
- in pairs 89
- with 709
united 46, 714
unity *identity* 14
uniformity 16
whole 50
complete 52
single **87**
concord 714
- of time 120
Unity, Trinity in - 976
universal 78
- Church 983*a*
- favourite 899

universality 52
universe 318
university 542
- education 537
- extension 537
go to the - 539
unjust *wrong* 923
impious 988
unjustifiable
wrong 923
inexcusable 938
wicked 945
unjustified 923
undue 925
unkempt
unclean 753
vulgar 851
unkennel *eject* 297
disclose 529
unkind 907
-est cut of all 828
unknightly 940
unknit 44
unknowable 519
unknowing 491
unknown
ignorant 491
latent 526
- to fame
inglorious 874
low-born 876
- quantities 491
unlaboured
- *style* 578
unprepared 674
unlace 44
unlade 297
unladylike
vulgar 851
rude 895
unlamented
hated 898
disapproved 932
unlatch 44, 750
unlawful
undue 925
illegal 964
unlearn 506
unlearned 491
unleavened 674
unless
circumstances 8
except 83
qualification 469
unlettered 491
- Muse 579
unlicensed 761

unlicked
unprepared 674
vulgar 851
clownish 876
- cub
youngster 129
shapeless 241
unmannerly 895
unlike 18
unlikely 473
unlikeness 15
unlimber 323
unlimited
great 31
infinite 105
free 748
- space 180
unliquefied 321
unlively 837, 843
unload
displaced 185
eject 297
disencumber 705
unlock *unfasten* 44
discover 480*a*
unlooked for 508
unloose
unfasten 44
liberate 750
unloved 898
unlovely 846
unlucky
inopportune 135
bad 649
unfortunate 735
in pain 830
unmade 2
unmaimed 654
unmake 145
unman
mutilate 38
render powerless 158
madden 837
frighten 860
unmanageable
unwieldy 647
perverse 704
unmanly
effeminate 374
dishonourable 940
unmanned
dejected 837
cowardly 862
unmannered 895
unmannerly 895
unmarked 460
unmarred 654, 670

unmarried 904
unmask 529
unmatched
different 15
dissimilar 18
unparalleled 20
unmeaningness **517**
unmeant 517
unmeasured
infinite 105
undistinguished 465a
abundant 639
unmeditated 612
unmeet 925
unmellowed 674
unmelodious 414
unmelted 321
unmentionable 874
-s 225
unmentioned 526
unmerciful 914a
unmerited 925
unmethodical 59
unmindful
inattentive 458
neglectful 460
ungrateful 917
unmingled 42
unmissed 460
unmistakable
certain 474
intelligible 518
manifest 525
unmitigable 173
unmitigated
great 31
complete 52
violent 173
unmixed 42
unmolested 664, 831
unmoneyed 804
unmoral 823
unmourned 898
unmoved
quiescent 265
obstinate 606
insensible 823
unmusical 424
- *voice* 581
unmuzzled 748
unnamed 565
unnatural
exceptional 83
affected 855
spiteful 907
unnecessary
redundant 641

useless 645
inexpedient 647
unneeded 645
unneighbourly 895
unnerved
powerless 158
weak 160
dejected 837
unnoted, unnoticed 460, 874
unnumbered 105
unnurtured 674
unobeyed 742
unobjectionable
good 648
pretty good 651
innocent 946
unobnoxious 648
unobscured 420
unobservant 458
unobserved 460
unobstructed 705, 749
unobtainable 471
unobtained 777a
unobtrusive 881
unoccupied
vacant 187
unthinking 452
doing nothing 681
inactive 683
untenanted 893
unoffended
enduring 826
humble 879
unofficial 964
unoften 137
unopened 261
unopposed 709
unorganized 674
- matter 358
unornamental 846
unornamented
- *style* 576
simple 849
unorthodox 984
uno saltu 113
unostentatious 881
unowed 807
unowned 782
unpacific 713, 722
unpacified 713
unpack
unfasten 44
take out 297
unpaid *debt* 806
honorary 815
the great -

magistracy 967
- worker 602
unpalatable 395, 830
unparagoned
supreme 33
best 648
perfect 650
unparalleled
unimitated 20
supreme 33
exceptional 83
unpardonable 938, 945
unparliamentary language 895, 908
unpassable 261
unpassionate 826
unpatriotic 911
unpeaceful 720, 722
unpeople
emigration 297
banishment 893
unperceived
neglected 460
unknown 491
unperformed 730
unperjured 543, 939
unperplexed 498
unpersuadable 606
unpersuaded 616
unperturbed 826
unphilosophical 499
unpierced 261
unpin 44
unpitied 932
unpitying 914a
unplaced 185
unplagued 831
unpleasant 830
unpleasing 830
unpoetical 598, 703
unpolished
rough 256
inelegant 579
unprepared 674
vulgar 851, 876
rude 895
unpolite 895
unpolluted
good 648
perfect 650
unpopular 830, 867
unpopularity 898
unportioned 804
unpossessed 777a
unpractical 699
unprecedented 83, 137
unprejudiced 498, 748

unpremeditated
impulsive 612
undesigned 621
unprepared 674
unprepared 508, 674
unprepossessed 498
unprepossessing 846
unpresentable 851
unpretending 881
unprevented 748
unprincipled 945
unprivileged 925
unprized 483
unproclaimed 526
unproduced 2
unproductive 645
unproductiveness 169
unproficiency 699
unprofitable
unproductive 169
useless 645
inexpedient 647
bad 649
unprolific 169
unpromising 859
unprompted 612
unpronounceable 519
unpronounced 526
unpropitious
ill-timed 135
opposed 708
hopeless 859
unproportioned 24
unprosperous 735
unprotected 665
unproved 477
unprovided
scanty 640
unprepared 674
unprovoked 616
unpublished 526
unpunctual
tardy 133
untimely 135
irregular 139
unpunished 970
unpurchased 796
unpurified 653
unpurposed 621
unpursued 624
unqualified
incomplete 52
impotent 158
certain 474
unprepared 674
inexpert 699
unentitled 925

– *truth* 494
unquelled 173
unquenchable
strong 159
desire 865
unquenched
violence 173
heat 382
unquestionable 474
unquestionably 488
unquestioned 474, 488
unquiet
motion 264
agitation 315
excitable 825
unravel *untie* 44
arrange 60
straighten 246
evolve 313
discover 480a
interpret 522
disembarrass 705
unreached 304
unread 491
unready 674
unreal
not existing 2
erroneous 495
imaginary 515
unreasonable
impossible 471
illogical 477
misjudging 481
foolish 499
exorbitant 814
unjust 923
unreclaimed 951
unrecognizable 146
unreconciled 713
unrecorded 552
unrecounted 55
unreduced 31
unrefined 851
unreflecting 458
unreformed 951
unrefreshed 688
unrefuted 478, 494
unregarded
neglected 460
unrespected 929
unregenerate 988
unregistered 552
unreined 748
unrelated 10
unrelenting 914a, 919
unreliable
uncertain 475

irresolute 605
dangerous 665
unrelieved 835
unremarked 460
unremembered 506
unremitting
continuous 69
continuing 110
unvarying 143
persevering 604a
unremoved 184
unremunerated 808
unrenewed 141
unrepealed 141
unrepeated 87, 103
unrepentant 951
unrepining 831
unreplenished 640
unrepressed 173
unreproached 946
unreproved 946
unrequited 806, 917
unresented 918
unresenting 826
unreserved
manifest 525
veracious 543
artless 703
unresisted 743
unresisting 725
unresolved 605
unrespected 929
unrest 149, 264
unrestored 688
unrestrained
capricious 608
unencumbered 705
free 748
unrestricted
undiminished 31
free 748
unretracted 535
unrevenged 918
unreversed 143
unrevoked 143
unrewarded 806, 917
unrhymed 598
unriddle 480a, 529
unrig 645
unrighteous 945
unrip 260
unripe
young 127
sour 397
immature 674
unrivalled 33
unroll *evolve* 313

display 525
unromantic 494
unroot 301
unruffled
calm 174
quiet 265
unaffected 823
placid 826
unruly *violent* 173
obstinate 606
disobedient 742
unsaddle 756
unsafe 665
unsaid 526
unsaleable
useless 645
selling 796
cheap 815
unsaluted 929
unsanctified 988, 989
unsanctioned 925
unsated 865
unsatisfactory
inexpedient 647
bad 649
displeasing 830
discontent 832
unsatisfied 832, 865
unsavouriness 395
unsay *recant* 607
unscanned 460
unscathed 654
unschooled 491
unscientific 477
unscoured 653
unscriptural 984
unscrupulous 940
unseal 529
unsearched 460
unseasonable 24, 135
unseasoned 614, 674
unseat 756
unseemly
inexpedient 647
ugly 846
vulgar 851
undue 925
vicious 945
unseen
invisible 447
neglected 460
latent 526
unseldom 136
unselfish 942
unseparated 46
unserviceable 645
unsettle *derange* 61

unsettled
mutable 149
displaced 185
uncertain 475
– in one's mind 503
unsevered 50
unsex 146
unshaded 525
unshaken 159
– belief 484
unshapely 846
unshapen 241
unshared 777
unsheathe
– the sword 722
unsheltered 665
unshielded 665
unshifting 143
unship 185, 297
unshocked 823
unshorn 50
unshortened 200
unshrinking 604, 861
unsifted 460
unsightly 846
unsinged 670
unskilfulness 699
unslaked 865
unsleeping 604*a*, 682
unsmooth 256
unsociable 893
unsocial 893
unsoiled 652
unsold 777
unsoldierlike 862
unsolicitous 866
unsolved 526
unsophisticated
simple 42
genuine 494
artless 703
unsorted 59
unsought
avoided 623
unrequested 766
unsound
illogical 477
erroneous 495
deceptive 545
imperfect 651
– mind 503
unsown 674
unsparing
abundant 639
severe 739
liberal 816
with an – hand 818

unspeakable 31, 870
unspecified 78
unspent 678
unspied 526
unspiritual 316, 989
unspoiled 648
unspotted
clean 652
beautiful 845
innocent 946
unstable 218
changeable 149
uncertain 475
irresolute 605
precarious 665
– equilibrium 149
unstaid 149
unstained
clean 652
honourable 939
unstatesmanlike 699
unsteadfast 605
unsteady
mutable 149
irresolute 605
in danger 665
unstinted 639
unstinting 816
unstirred 823, 826
unstopped
continuing 143
open 260
unstored 640
unstrained
turbid 653
relaxed 687
– meaning 516
unstrengthened 160
unstruck 823
unstrung 160
unstudied 460
unsubject 748
unsubmissive 742
unsubservient
usless 645
inexpedient 647
unsubstantial 4
weak 160
rare 322
erroneous 495
imaginary 515
unsubstantiality 4
unsuccessful 732
unsuccessive 70
unsuitable
incongruous 24
(*inexpedient* 647)

– time 135
unsullied *clean* 652
  honourable 939
  (*guiltless* 946)
unsung 526
unsupplied 640
unsupported
  weak 160
  (*unassisted* 706)
  – by evidence 468
unsuppressed 141
unsurmountable 471
unsurpassed 33
unsusceptible 823
unsuspected
  belief 484
  latent 526
unsuspecting
  hopeful 858
unsuspicious
  belief 484
  artless 703
  hope 858
unsustainable 495
unsweet 395
unswept 653
unswerving
  straight 246
  direct 278
  persevering 604*a*
unsymmetric 83
unsymmetrical 59, 243
unsystematic 59
untainted *pure* 652
  healthy 654
  honourable 939
untalked of 526
untamed 851, 907
untarnished 939
untasted 391
untaught 491, 674
untaxed 815
unteach 538
unteachable 499, 699
untenable
  powerless 158
  illogical 477
  undefended 725
untenanted 187, 893
unthanked 917
unthankful 917
unthawed 321, 383
unthinkable 471
unthinking
  unconsidered 452
  involuntary 601
unthought of 452, 460

unthreatened 664
unthrifty
  unprepared 674
  prodigal 818
unthrone 756
untidy 59, 653
untie 44, 750
  – the knot 705
until 106
  – now 118
untilled 674
untimely 135
  – end 360
untinged 42
untired 689
untiring 604*a*
untitled 876
untold
  countless 105
  uncertain 475
  latent 526
  secret 528
untouched
  disused 678
  insensible 823
untoward
  ill-timed 135
  bad 649
  unprosperous 735
  unpleasant 830
untraced 526
untracked 526
untractable 606, 699
untrained
  unaccustomed 614
  unprepared 674
  unskilled 699
untrammelled 705, 748
untranslatable 523
untranslated 523
untravelled 265
untreasured 640
untried *new* 123
  not decided 461
untrimmed 674, 849
untrodden *new* 123
  impervious 261
  not used 678
untroubled 174, 721
untrue 495, 546
untrustworthy
  uncertain 475
  erroneous 495
  danger 665
  dishonourable 940
untruth 544, **546**
untunable 414

unturned 246
untutored
  ignorant 491
  unprepared 674
  artless 703
untwine 313
untwist 313
unused
  new 123
  unaccustomed 614
  unskilful 699
unusual 83
unusually *very* 31
unutterable 31, 519, 870
unvalued
  underrated 483
  undesired 866
  disliked 898
unvanquished 748
unvaried
  continuing 143
  - *style* 575, 576
unvarnished
  true 494
  - *style* 576
  unreserved 703
  simple 849
  – tale 494, 543
unvarying 16, 143
unveil 525, 529
unventilated 261
unveracious 544
unversed 491
unvexed 831
unviolated 939
unvisited 893
unwakened 683
unwarlike 862
unwarmed 383
unwarned 508, 665
unwarped judgment 498
unwarrantable 923
unwarranted
  illogical 477
  undue 925
  illegal 964
unwary 460
unwashed 653
  great – 876
unwatchful 460
unwavering 604*a*
unweakened 159
unwearied
  persevering 604*a*
  indefatigable 682
  refreshed 689
unwedded 904

unweeded garden 674
unweeting 491
unweighed 460
unwelcome 830, 893
unwell 655
unwept 831
unwholesome 657
unwieldy
  large 192
  heavy 319
  cumbersome 647
  difficult 704
  ugly 846
unwilling 489
unwillingness 603
unwind *evolve* 313
unwiped 653
unwise 499
unwished 866
unwithered 159
unwitting
  ignorant 491
  involuntary 601
unwittingly 621
unwomanly 373
unwonted 83, 614
unworldly 939
unworn 159
unworshipped 929
unworthy
  shameful 874
  vicious 945
  – of belief 485
  – of notice 643
unwrap 246
unwrinkled 255
unwritten
  latent 526
  obliterated 552
  spoken 582
  – law 697, 963
unwrought 674
unyielding
  tough 323
  resolute 604
  obstinate 606
  resisting 719
up
  aloft 206
  vertical 212
  effervescing 353
  excited 824
  the game is – 735
  prices looking – 814
  time – 111
  – in arms
  prepared 673

active 682
opposition 708
attack 716
resistance 719
warfare 722
– and at them 716
– and doing 682
– and down 314
– on end 212
– in 698
– to [*see below*]
all – with
  destruction 162
  failure 732
  adversity 735
Upas tree 663
upbear 215, 307
upbraid 932
upcast 307
upgrow 206
upgrowth 194, 305
upheaval 146
upheave 307
uphill
  acclivity 217
  ascent 305
  laborious 686
  difficult 704
uphoist 307
uphold
  continue 143
  support 215
  evidence 467
  aid 707
  praise 931
upholder 488, 711
upholstery 633
uplands 180, 206, 344
uplift 307, 658
upon:
  – my honour 535
  – oath 535
  – which 117, 121
upper 206
  – boxes, – circle 599
  – classes 875
  – hand
  influence 175
  success 731
  sway 737
  – story
  summit 210
  intellect 450
  wisdom 498
  – ten thousand 875
  be on one's –s 804
uppermost 210

say what comes – 612
– in the mind
  thought 451
  topic 454
  attention 457
  – in one's thoughts
  memory 505
upraise 307
uprear 307
upright
  vertical 212
  honest 939
uprise 305
uprising 742
uproar
  disorder 59
  violence 173
  noise 404
uproarious 825
uproot 301
ups and downs of life 151,
  735
upset *destroy* 162
  invert 218
  throw down 308
  defeat 731
  excite 824
  disconcert 874
  – the apple cart 732
upshot *result* 154
  judgment 480
  completion 729
upside down 218
upstairs 206
upstart
  new 123
  prosperous 734
  plebeian 876
up to
  time 106
  power 157
  knowing 490
  skilful 698
  brave 861
  – the brim 52
  – date 123
  – one's ears 641
  – one's eyes 641
  – the mark
  equal 27
  sufficient 639
  good 648
  due 924
  – snuff 702
  – this time
  time 106
  past 122

– suggestion 514
vail *panel* 228
  donation 784
  reward 973
vain *unreal* 2
  unprofitable 645
  unvalued 866
  conceited 880
  in – *failure* 732
  labour in –
  come short 304
  useless 645
  fail 732
  take a name in – 895
  – attempt 732
  use – efforts 645
  – expectation 509
vainglorious
  haughty 878
  vain 880
  boasting 884
vaivode 745
valance 231
vale 252
  – of years 128
valeat quantum 467
valediction 293, 894
valedictory 293
valentine 902
valet 631, 746
  – de chambre 746
  – de place 524, 527
valetudinarian 655, 656
Valhalla 981
valiant 861
valid *confirmed* 150
  powerful 157
  strong 159
  true 494
  sufficient 639
  – reasoning 476
valise 191
valley 252
  – of the shadow of death
  360
vallum 717
valoir, se faire – 884
valorem, ad – 812
valour 861
valuable 644, 648
value *colour* 423
  measure 466
  estimate 480
  importance 642
  utility 644
  goodness 648
  price 812

  approbation 931
  of priceless – 814
  set a – upon 482
  – received 810
  –s *painting* 556
valueless 645
valve *stop* 263
  conduit 350
safety – *safety* 664
  refuge 666
  escape 671
vamp *change* 140
  music 463
  – up *improve* 658
  restore 660
  prepare 673
vampire 913, 980
vampirism 789, 992
van *beginning* 66
  front 234
  wagon 272
  in the – 234
  precession 280
van-courier 64
Vandal
  destroyer 165
  vulgar 851
  commonalty 876
  evil-doer 913
vandalism 851
vandyke 257
Vandyke brown 433
vane *wind* 349
  indication 550
vanguard 234
vanish
  unsubstantial 4
  transient 111
  disappear 449
vanishing 32, 193
vanity *useless* 645
  conceit **880**
  – bag 191
Vanity Fair 852
vanquish 731
vantage ground
  superiority 33
  power 157
  influence 175
  height 206
vapid *insipid* 391
  – *style* 575
vaporization **336**
vaporous
  opaque 426
  imaginary 515
vapour *gas* 334

  bubbles 353
  fancy 515
  boast 884
  insolence 885
  – bath 386, 652
vapourer 887
vapours
  dejection 837
variable 149, 605
variance
  difference 15
  disagreement 24
  discord 713
  at – *enmity* 889
  at – with 489
variant 15
variation
  difference 15
  diverseness **20a**
  number 84
  chance 140
  music 415
varied 15
variegated 16a, 440
variegation **440**
variety
  difference 15
  class 75
  multiformity 81
  exception 83
  entertainment 599
variform 81
various 15, 102
  – places 182
  – times 119
varlet 949
– **varnish**
  overlay 223
  resin 356a
  sophistry 477
  falsehood 544
  painting 556
  decorate 847
  excuse 937
vary *differ* 15
  dissimilar 18
  variation 20a
  change 140
  fluctuate 149
va sans dire, cela – 474,
  525
vascular *cells* 191
  holes 260
  pipes 350
vase 191
vassal 746
vassalage 749

vast *great* 31
  spacious 180
  large 192
  – learning 490
vasty deep 341
vat 191
Vatican 995, 1000
  thunders of the – 908
vaticination 511
vatum, genus irritabile –
  597
vaudeville 599, 840
vault
  cellar 191
  curve 245
  leap 309
  tomb 363
  store 636
  – of heaven 318
vaulted 245, 252
vaulting 33, 865
vaunt 884
vaurien 949
vavasour
  possessor 779
  nobleman 875
V.C. 733
vection 270
Vedas 986
vedette 668
Vedidad 986
veer
  change 140
  deviate 279
  go back 283
  change intention 607
vegetability 365
vegetable 367
  – kingdom 367
  – life 386
  – oil 356
  – physiology 369
vegetarian 298, 953
vegetate 365
  exist 1
  grow 194
  stagnate 265
  inactive 681, 683
  insensible 823
vegetation 365
vehemence
  violence 173
  feeling 821
  emotion 825
vehement
  – *language* 574
vehicle

  carriage **272**
  instrument 631
veil *covering* 225
  shade 424
  concealment 526, 527
  conceal 528
  ambush 530
  behind the – 360
  draw aside the – 529
  take the – 893, 995
veiled
  uncertain 475
  invisible 447
  concealed 528
vein *temper* 5
  tendency 176
  thin 203
  thread 205
  channel 350
  humour 602
  mine 636
  affections 820
  in the – 602
  not in the – 603
veined 440
veld 344
velis et remis 274
velitation 720
velleity 600
vellicate 315
vellicating 392
vellum 590
veloce *music* 415
velocipede 272
velocity 264, **274**
  angular – 244
veluti in speculum 17
velvet 255, 256
  pleasure 377
  on – *easy* 705
venal *price* 812
  stingy 819
  dishonest 940
  selfish 943
venation 622
vend 796
vendee 795
vender 796
vendetta 919
vendible 796
venditation 884
vendor 796
veneer 204, 223
venenation 659
venerable *old* 124
  aged 128
  sage 500

  respected 928
veneration
  respect 928
  piety 987
venereal disease 665
venery *killing* 361
  hunting 622
  impurity 961
venesection
  ejection 297
  remedy 662
Venetian blinds 351
vengeance 919
  cry to heaven for – 923
  with a – 31, 173
vengeful 919
venial 937
veniam petimusque
  damusque vicissim 918
venienti occurrere morbo
  673
venison 394
veni vidi vici 731
venom 663, 907
venomous *bad* 649
  poisonous 657
  rude 895
  maleficent 907
vent *opening* 260
  egress 295
  air-pipe 351
  disclose 529
  escape 671
  sale 796
  find – *egress* 295
  passage 302
  publish 531
  escape 671
  give – to 297, 529
  – one's rage 900
  – one's spleen 900
venter 191
ventiduct 351
ventilate
  begin 66
  air 338
  wind 349
  discuss 595
  – a question 461, 476
ventilator 349, 351
ventosity 349
vent-peg
  stopper 263
  safety 666
  escape 671
ventre
  – à terre 274

churchdom 995
church 1000
vesture 225
vesuvian
   match 388
veteran *old* **130**
   adept 700
   warrior 726
veterinary art 370
veteris vestigia flammæ
   505, 613
veto 761
vetturino 694
vex 830, 898
vexata quæstio 704, 713
vexation 828, 830
   – of spirit 828
   discontent 832
   resentment 900
vexatious 830
vexed question 704, 713
viâ 278, 627
viable 359
viaduct 627
vial 191
via lactea 318
vials:
   – of hate 898
   – of wrath 900
viands 298
viaticum
   provision 637
   rite 998
vibrate 314
   – between two extremes
   149
vibrato 415
vibratory 149
vibroscope 314
vicar *deputy* 759
   clergyman 996
   – of Bray 607, 886
vicarage 1000
vicariate 995
vicarious 147
vicarship 995
vice *deputy* 759
   holder 781
   wickedness **945**
vice-admiral 745
Vice-Chancellor 967
   –'s Court 966
vicegerency 755
vicegerent 758, 759
vice-president 694
vice-regal 759
viceroy

governor 745
deputy 759
vicesimal 98
vice versâ
   reciprocal 12
   contrary 14
   interchange 148
vicinage 197
vicinism 145
vicinity 197, 227
vicious 173, 945
   render – 659
   – reasoning 477
vicissitude 149
Vickers gun 727
victim *dupe* 547
   defeated 732
   sufferer 828
victimize *kill* 361
   deceive 545
   injure 649
   baffle 731
victis, væ – 722, 909
victor 731
victoria
   carriage 272
Victoria Cross 733
victory 731
victual *provide* 637
victuals 298
videlicet 79, 522
viduage 905
viduity 905
vie *good* 648
   – with 720
vielle 417
vi et armis
   violence 173
   exertion 686
   compulsion 744
view
   sight 441
   appearance 448
   attend to 457
   opinion 484
   landscape painting 556
   intention 620
   bring into – 525
   come into – 446
   commanding – 441
   in – *visible* 446
   intended 420
   expected 507
   keep in – 457
   on – 448
   present to the – 448
   with a – to 620

– as 484
– in a new light 658
viewer 444
viewless 447
view-point 441
vigesimal 98
vigil *care* 459
vigilance *care* 459
   wisdom 498
   activity 682
   caution 864
vigils *worship* 990
vignette 558, 594, 847
vigour *strength* 159
   energy 171
   style **574**
   resolution 604
   health 654
   activity 682
viking 792
vile *valueless* 643
   bad 649
   painful 830
   disgraceful 874
   plebeian 876
   dishonourable 940
   vicious 945
vilify *shame* 874
   malediction 908
   censure 932
   detract 934
vilipend
   disrespect 929
   censure 932
   detract 934
vilipendency 930
villa 189
village 189
   – talk 588
villager 188
villain
   servant 746
   serf 876
   knave 941
   rascal 949
villainous 649, 945
   – saltpetre 727
villainy 940
villein [*see* villain]
villenage 749, 777
villi 256
villous 256
vim 171
vin: – d'honneur 292, 894
   not think – ordinaire of
   oneself 880
vinaigrette 400

vincible 158
vincture 43
vincula matrimonii,
  separatio a – 905
vinculum 45
  – matrimonii 903
vindicate 467, 937
  – a right 924
vindication 937
vindicator 919
vindictive 901, 919
vine 367
  – grower 371
vinegar 397
  – aspect 846
vinery 191
vineyard 371, 691
vingt et un 840
vintage 371, 636
vintner 637
viol 417
violate
  disobey 742
  non-observance 773
  undue 925
  dereliction 927
  ravish 961
  – a law 83
  – the law 964
  – a usage 614
violence 173
  arbitrary 964
  do – to *bad* 649
  non-observance 773
  undue 925
violent 173
  excitable 825
  – death 360, 361
  in a – degree 31
  lay – hands on 789
violet 437
violin 417
violinist 416
violoncello 417
viper *snake* 366
  bane 663
  evil-doer 913
  bad man 949
  – in one's bosom 667
virago 901
virent 435
vires acquirit eundo
  increase 35
  energy 171
  velocity 274
virescence 435
Virgilianæ, sortes – 621

virgin *new* 123
  girl 129
  woman 374
  spinster 904
  good 948
  pure 960
  – forest 367
  – soil
  ignorance 491
  untilled 674
  the – Mary 976
virginals 417
virginibus puerisque 960
viribus, totis – 686
viridity 435
virile
  adolescent 131
  strong 159
  manly 373
virtu 850
  article of – 847
virtual 2, 5
  – image 443
virtue *power* 157
  courage 861
  goodness **944**
  purity 960
  by – of 157, 631
  in – of 737
  make a – of necessity *no*
    choice 609a
  skill 698
  submit 725
  compromise 774
  bear 826
virtueless 945
virtuoso 416, 850
virtuous 944, 960
virulence
  energy 171
  noxiousness 649
  insalubrity 657
  discourtesy 895
  anger 900
  malevolence 907
virulent 932
virum volitare per ora 531
virus 655, 663
vis:
  – comica 842
  – conservatrix 670
  – inertiæ
  power 157
  inertness 172
  insensibility 823
  – medicatrix 600, 662
  – mortua 157

  – a tergo 284
  – viva 157
visa 488
visage 234, 448
vis-à-vis *front* 234
  opposite 237
  carriage 272
viscera 221
viscid 352
viscount 875
viscous 352
vise 781
Vishnu 979
visibility 446
visible 446
  be – 448
  become – 448
  darkness – 421
  – radiation 420
vision *sight* **441**
  phantasm 443
  dream 515
  spectre 980
  organ of – 441
visionary
  inexistence 2
  unsubstantial 4
  impossible 471
  imaginary 515
  heterodox 984
visionless 442
visit *arrival* 292
  social 892
  courtesy 894
  – upon 972
  pay a surprise – 647
visitation
  disease 655
  adversity 735
  suffering 828
  –s of Providence 976
  – of the sick 998
visiting:
  – card 550
  on – terms 888, 892
visitor *incomer* 294
  director 694
  friend 890
visor 530
vista
  convergence 260
  sight 441
  appearance 448
  expectation 507
visual 441
  – organ 441
vitability 359

- over the course 705, 731
- in the shoes of 19
walker 268
walking gentleman 599
wall *vertical* 212
　parietes 224
　inclosure 232
　refuge 666
　obstacle 706
　defence 717
　prison 752
　driven to the - 704
　go to the -
　destruction 162
　die 360
　fail 732
　pushed to the - 601
　take the - 873, 878
　wooden -s 726
　-eyed 442
　- in 229, 751
wallah 746
wallet 191
wallop 315
wallow *low* 207
　plunge 310
　rotate 312
　- in 377, 641
　- in the mire 653
　- in riches 803
　- in voluptuousness 954
wallsend 388
Wall-street 799
　- slang 563
waltz 415, 840
wamble
　vacillate 149
　oscillate 314
　dislike 867
wampum 800
wan 429, 837
wand *sceptre* 747
　magic 993
　wave a - 992
wander *move* 264
　journey 266
　deviate 279
　delirium 503
　the attention -s 458
wanderer 268
wandering
　exceptional 83
　- Jew 268
wane
　decrease 36
　age 128
　contract 195

decay 659
one's star on the - 735
wax and - 140
wangle 943
want
　inferiority 34
　shortcoming 304
　requirement 630
　insufficiency 640
　poverty 804
　desire 865
wanted 187
wanting
　incomplete 53
　absent 187
　inbecile 499
　found -
　imperfect 651
　disapproval 932
　guilt 947
wantless 639
wanton
　unconformable 83
　capricious 608
　unrestrained 748
　amusement 840
　rash 863
　impure 961
wapentake 181
war 722
　at - 24, 720
　at - with 708, 722
　declare - 713
　man of - 727
　seat of - 728
　- correspondent 534, 593
　- of words 588, 720
warble 416
war-cry *alarm* 669
　defiance 715
　war 722
ward *part* 51
　parish 181
　safety 664
　asylum 666
　dependent 746
　restraint 751
　watch and - 459, 753
　- off 706, 717
war-dance 715
warden
　guardian 664
　master 745
　deputy 759
warder
　perforator 262
　porter 263

guardian 664
keeper 753
wardmote 966
wardrobe 191, 225
ward-room 191
war-drum 417
wardship 664
ware
　warning 668
　merchandise 798
warehouse 636, 799
warfare 722
　discord 713
war-horse 726
warlike 722
warlock 994
warm
　violent 173
　hot 382
　make hot 384
　red 434
　orange 439
　wealthy 803
　ardent 821
　excited 824
　angry 900
　irascible 901
　flog 972
　- bath 386
　- the blood 824
　- the cockles of the heart
　829
　- imagination 515
　- man 803
　- reception
　repel 717
　welcome 892
　- up 658, 660
　- work 686
warm-hearted
　feeling 821
　sensibility 822
　friendship 888
　benevolence 906
warming 384
warming-pan
　locum tenens 147
　heater 386
　preparation 673
warmth
　vigorous language 574
warn *dissuade* 616
　caution 668
　- off 761
warning *omen* 512
　dissuasion 616
　caution **668**

give – *dismiss* 678
 relinquish 782
 – voice *alarm* 666
warp *change* 140
 tend 176
 contract 195
 distort 243
 navigate 267
 deviate 279
 prejudice 481
 deteriorate 659
 – and weft 329
war-paint 673
war-path 72
 on the – 716
warped 651
warped notion 495
warrant
 evidence 467
 protest 535
 order 741
 permit 760
 promise 768
 security 771
 money order 800
 justify 937
 death – *die* 360
 kill 361
 condemn 971
 I'll – you 535
 – officer 745
warranted 924
warranty
 permission 760
 promise 768
 security 771
 sanction 924
warren 168
 free – 815
warrior 726
warship 726
wart 250
wary 864
wash *cover* 223
 water 337
 marsh 345
 colour 428
 paint 556
 cleanse 652
 – down 298
 – one's hands of
 relinquish 624
 depute 757
 refuse 764
 part with 782
 dereliction 927
 – out

discolour 429
 obliterate 552
 deteriorate 659
 – up 659
washer 247
washerwoman 652
washhouse 386, 652
washy *weak* 160
 unmeaning 517
 feeble style 575
wasp *narrow* 203
 bring a –'s nest about
 one's ears 735
waspish 173, 901
wassail
 beverage 298
 feast 840
 drunkenness 954
wastage 40a
waste *decrease* 36
 decrement 40a
 destroy 162
 unproductive 169
 space 180
 contract 195
 plain 344
 consumption **638**
 useless 645
 spoiled 659
 misuse 679
 loss 776
 prodigality 818
 run to – 641, 659
 watery – 341
 – away 655
 – time 683
wasted 160, 659
wasteful 818
waste-paper 158, 645
 – basket 191, 645
 – bonds 808
waste-pipe 350
waster 460
waste-thrift 818
wasting, wide – 649
wastrel 268, 893
watch *clock* 114
 observe 441
 attend to 457
 take care of 459
 expect 507
 guardian 664
 warning 668
 keeper 753
 death – *death* 360
 warning 668
 on the – 459, 507

– for 507
 – out for 668
 – over 664
 – and pray 673
 – and ward 459, 753
watch-dog 664, 753
watchet 438
watch-fire 550
watchful 459
watch-glass 191
watch-house 752
 in the – 938
watchman
 guardian 664
 sentinel 668
 keeper 753
watch-tower
 view 441
 signal 550
 warning 668
watchword
 sign 550
 military 722
water 337
 transparent 425
 keep one's head above –
 664
 back – 283
 cast one's bread upon the
 –s 638
 throw cold – on 174
 depth of – 208
 of the first – 648
 great –s 341
 hold – 478, 494
 land covered with – 343
 pour forth like – 818
 make one's mouth – 507
 running – 348
 walk the –s 267
 pour – into a sieve 638
 –bearer, carrier 348
water-colour 556
watercourse 350
water-cure 662
water-dog 361
water-drinker 958
watered
 variegated 440
waterfall 348
water-glass 556
water-gruel 160
watering
 – cart 348
 – place 189
 – pot 348
waterless 340

water-logged
powerless 158
danger 665
hindrance 706
waterman 269
water-pipe 350
water-polo 840
waterproof
dress 225
dry 340
protection 664
waters
– of bitterness 830
– of oblivion 506
watershed 210
water-spaniel 366
waterspout 348
water-tight 261, 340
waterworks 350
watery *wet* 337
moist 339
– eyes 839
– grave 360
wattle 219
Wat Tyler 742
wave *sinuous* 248
oscillate 314
hair 847
- *of water* 348
[*see* waive]
brain – 498
– a banner 550
– a wand 992
waver
changeable 149
doubt 485
irresolute 605
waverer 605
waves 341
buffet the –
navigate 267
difficult 704
oppose 708
lash the – 645
plough the – 267
wax *increase* 35
become 144
expand 194
soft 324
lubrication 332
viscid 352
substance 356
close as – 528
– and wane 140
– candle 423
waxwork 554
waxy *unctuous* 355

irate 900
way *degree* 26
space 180
habit 613
road 627
in a bad – 655
by – of 278, 627
by the –
in transitu 270
accidental 621
fall in the – of 186
fight one's – 622, 722
find its – 302
gather – 267
get into the – of 613
go one's – 293
go your – 297
let it have its – 681
it must have its – 601
have one's own – 748
in a – 828, 900
in the – *near* 197
in the – of 706, 708
make – 302
make one's –
journey 266
progression 282
passage 302
prosperity 734
make – for
substitution 147
opening 260
turn aside 279
avoid 623
facilitate 705
courtesy 894
on the – 282
place in one's – 763
put in the – of 470, 537
see one's – 490
show the – 693
under – *move* 264
sail 267
progression 282
depart 293
wing one's – 267
– in 294
long – off 196
have – on 267
– out 295
– of speaking 521
– of thinking 484
not know which – to turn
475
Way, the – 976
wayfarer 268
wayfaring 266

waylay 545, 702
wayless 261
ways 692
in all manner of – 278
– and means 632, 800
wayward
changeable 149
obstinate 606
capricious 608
sullen 901a
waywode 745
wayworn 266, 688
wayzgoose 840
weak *feeble* 160
water 337
insipid 391
illogical 477
foolish 499
- *style* 575
irresolute 605
trifling 643
lax 738
compassionate 914
vicious 945
– point 477, 651
expose one's – point 479
– side 499, 945
weaken
decrease 36, 37
enfeeble 160
refute 468
weaker vessel 374
weak-headed 499
weak-hearted 862
weak-kneed 725
weakness 160
– of the flesh 945
weal 618
common – 644
weald 367
wealth 780, **803**
wean 484, 614
– from 616
– one's thoughts from 506
weanling 129
weapon 727
weaponless 158
wear *decrease* 36
clothes 225
deflect 279
use 677
– away *cease* 142
deteriorate 659
– the breeches 737
– off 142, 614
– on 109
– out 659, 688

- and tear
decrease 36
waste 638
injury 659
exertion 686
weariness 841
wearing 841
- apparel 225
wearisome
laborious 686
fatiguing 688
painful 830
weary *fatigue* 688
painful 828
sad 837
ennuyant 841
- flat, stale, and
unprofitable 843
- waste 344
- Willie 876
weasand 260, 351
weasel asleep,
catch a - 471, 682
weather 338
keep one's - eye open 864
rough - 173, 349
- the storm
stability 150
recover 660
safe 664
succeed 731
weather-beaten
weak 160
damaged 659
fatigue 688
weather-bound 751
weathercock
changeable 149
wind 349
indication 550
fickle 607
weathered 659
weather-gauge 338
weather-glass 338
weather permitting 469,
470
weather-proof 654, 664
weatherwise 338
foresight 510
weave *produce* 161
interlace 219
- a tangled web 704
weazen 193
web
complexity 59
intersection 219
texture 329

wed 48, 903
wedded: - pair 903
- to *belief* 484
habit 613
loving 897
- to an opinion
misjudgment 481
obstinacy 606
wedding 903
- breakfast 892
- day 883
wedge *join* 43
angular 244
sharp 253
instrument 633
thin edge of the -
begin 66
insinuate 228
cunning 702
- in 228
wedged in 751
wedlock 903
wee 193
weed *exclude* 55
few 103
plant 367
agriculture 371
cigar 392
trifle 643
clean 652
- out 297, 301
weeds *dress* 225
useless 645
mourning 839
widowhood 905
weedy 203, 643
week 108
weekly 138
- paper 531
ween *judge* 480
believe 484
know 490
weeny 32
weep 839, 914
weet 480, 490
weetless 491
weft, warp and - 329
weigh *influence* 175
lift 307
heavy 319
ponder 451
under - [*see* way]
- anchor 293
- carefully 465
- down 649, 749
- on the heart 830
- heavy on 649

- on the mind
regret 833
dejection 837
fear 860
- with 615
weighed and found
wanting 34, 932
weighing machine 319
weight
influence 175
gravity 319
importance 642
short - 53
attach - to 484
carry - 175
drag - 706
have - 467
throw one's - into the
scale 175
weightless 320
weights and measures 466
weighty
style 574
weir *conduit* 350
hindrance 706
weird 860
demon 980
mystic 992
spell 993
- sisters 994
welcome
arrival 292
grateful 829
friendly 888
sociality 892
reception 894
weld 43, 46
welfare 734
welkin 318, 338
make the - ring 404
well *much* 31
origin 153
deep 208
welcome 292
exude 295
pool 343
flow 348
assent 488
good 618
store 636
healthy 654
spa 662
act - 944
all's - 664
drop a bucket into an
empty - 645
get - 660

go on – 734
let – alone, 265, 681
  inaction 681
think – of 931
treat – 906
turn out – 731
work – 731
– and good
  assent 488
  consent 762
  content 831
– done! 931
– enough 32, 651
– out 295
– over 641
– up in 698
– with 888
well-a-day 839, 870
well-advised 498
well-affected 888
well-behaved 852, 894
well-being 734, 827
well-beloved 897
well-born 875
well-bred 852
well-composed 845
well-defined
  visible 446
  exact 494
  predetermined 611
well-disposed 707
well-doing 944
well-favoured 845
well-fed 192
well-formed 845
well-founded
  existent 1
  probable 472
  certain 474
  - *belief* 484
  true 494
well-grounded
  existent 1
  informed 490
  - *hope* 858
well-informed 490
Wellington boots 225
well-intentioned 906, 944
well-knit 159
well-known 490, 613
well-made 845
well-mannered 894
well-marked 446
well-meaning 906
well-meant 906
well-met 894
well-natured 906

well-nigh 32, 197
well-off 734, 803
well-proportioned 845
well-provided 639
well-regulated
  order 58
  conformity 82
  circumspect 864
well-set 242
well-spent
  successful 731
  virtuous 944
well-tasted 394
well-timed 134
well-to-do 734, 803
well-turned periods 578
well-weighed 611
well-wisher 890, 906
welsher 792, 808
welt 321
welter 310, 312
  - in one's blood 361
wem 848
wen 250
wench *girl* 129
  woman 374
  impure 962
wenching 961
wend 266
were, as you – 660
werewolf 980
Wesleyan 984
West *lateral* 236
  direction 278
  go – *die* 360
Westminster
  superior courts of – 966
wet 337, 339
  - blanket
  dissuade 616
  hindrance 706
  sadden 837
  weary 841
  dull 843
  just enough to – one's feet
  209
  - one's whistle 298, 959
wether 366
whack 276
  out of – 59
whacking 32, 192
whale *large* 192
  sprat to catch a – 699
  tub to a – 545, 617
whalebone 325
whaler 273
whallop 972

whap 276
wharf *houses* 189
  workshop 691
  mart 799
wharfage 812
what 461, 870
  know –'s what
  discriminate 465
  intelligent 498
  skill 698
  - d'ye call 'em 563
  - on earth 83
  -'s his name 563
  - next 455
  and – not 81
  - is the reason? 461
  - signifies 643
  -'s up 461
  - in the world 83, 870
whatever 78
  - may happen 474
wheal 250
wheat
  winnow the chaff from
  the – 609
wheedle
  coax 615
  endearment 902
  flatter 933
wheel *circle* 247
  deviate 279
  turn back 283
  circuition 311
  rotation 312
  rack 975
  break on the – 378, 972
  get the – out of the rut
  672
  paddle – 267
  scotch the – 706
  stern – 267
  - about 279
  - and axle 633
  - of Fortune
  changeable 149
  chance 156, 621
  rotation 312
  necessity 601
  - round 218, 607
wheelbarrow 272
wheel-chair 272
wheelman 268
wheels within wheels 59,
  633
wheel-work 633
wheeze 349, 409
whelm 641

whelp *infant* 129
  produce 161
  dog 366
  rogue 949
when *inquiry* 461
  in the time – 106
whence
  attribution 155
  departure 293
  inquiry 461
  reasoning 476
where 186, 461
  – am I? 870
whereabouts 183, 197
whereas 9, 476
whereby 631
wherefore
  attribution 155
  inquiry 461
  reasoning 476
  motive 615
wherein 221
whereness 186
whereupon 106, 121
wherever 180, 182
wherewith 632, 800
wherret 830
wherry 273
whet *sharpen* 253
  meal 298
  incite 615
  excite 824
  take a –
  tipple 959
  – the appetite 865
  – the knife 673
whether or not 609
whetstone, cut a – with a
  razor 638
which:
  at – time 119
  know – is which 465
whiff 349, 825
whiffle 349
Whig 712
while *time* 106
  in a – 132
  worth – 646
  – away time
  inaction 681
  pastime 840
  – speaking of 9, 134
whilom 122
whilst 106
whim *fad* 481
  fancy 515
  caprice 608

  wit 842
  desire 865
whimper 839
whimsey 515, 865
whimsical [*see* whim] 853
whimwam 608, 643
whin 367
whine 411, 839
whinyard 727
whip *collect* 72
  coachman 268
  strike 276
  stir up 315
  urge 615
  hasten 684
  director 694
  flog 972
  scourge 975
  – and spur 274
  – away 293
  – hand 731, 737
  – in 300
  – on 684
  – off 293
  – up 789
whipcord 205
whipper-in 694
whippersnapper 129
whipping-post 975
whipster 129
whir *rotate* 312
  sound 407
whirl *rotate* 312
  flurry 825
whirligig 312
whirlpool *rotate* 312
  agitation 315
  water 348
  danger 667
whirlwind
  disorder 59
  agitation 315
  wind 349
  reap the –
  product 154
  fail 732
  ride the –
  resolution 604
  authority 737
whisk *rapid* 274
  circuition 311
  agitation 315
  – off 297
whisker 256
whisket 191
whisky
  vehicle 272

  drink 298
whisper
  faint sound 405
  tell 527
  conceal 528
  stammer 583
  stage – 580
  – about
  disclose 529
  publish 531
  – in the ear
  voice 580
whist *hush* 403
  cards 840
whistle *wind* 349
  hiss 409
  play music 416
  musical instrument 417
  clean as a –
  thorough 52
  perfect 650
  neatly 652
  pay too dear for one's –
  inexpedient 647
  unskilful 699
  dear 814
  police – 669
  wet one's –
  drink 298
  tipple 959
  – at 930
  – for *request* 765
  desire 865
  – jigs to a milestone 645
  – for want of thought
  inaction 681
whit *small* 32
white 430
  – of the eye 41
  – feather 862
  – flag 723
  – frost 383
  – heat 382
  – horses 348
  – lie *equivocal* 520
  concealment 528
  untruth 546
  plea 617
  – liver 862
  – as a sheet 860
  – slave 962
  stand in a – sheet 952
  mark with a – stone 642,
  931
whitechapel
  vehicle 272
Whitefriars 996

whiteness 430
whitewash
  cover 223
  whiten 430
  cleanse 652
  ornament 847
  justify 937
  acquit 970
whitewashed
  get – 808
whitewasher 935
white wings 652
whitey-brown 433
whither
  tendency 176
  direction 278
  inquiry 461
whit-leather 327
whitlow 655
Whit-Monday 840
Whitsuntide 998
whittle 44, 253
whittled
  drunk 959
whiz 409
who 461
  – goes there? 669
  – would have thought?
    508, 870
whoa! 265
whole *entire* **50**
  healthy 654
  make – 660
  as a – 50
  on the – 476, 480
  go the – hog 729
  the – time 106
  – truth
  truth 494
  disclosure 529
  veracity 543
wholesale
  large scale 31
  whole 50
  abundant 639
  trade 794
wholesome 656
wholly 50, 52
whoop 411
  war – 715, 722
whoopee 840
whop *flog* 972
whopper *lie* 546
whopping *huge* 192
whore 962
whoredom 961
whoremonger 962

whorl 248
why *cause* 153
  attribution 155
  inquiry 461
  indeed 535
  motive 615
  – not 868
wibble-wabble 314
wick 388, 423
wicked 945
  the – *bad men* 949
  impious 988
  the – one 978
wicker 219
wicket 66, 260
wide 202
  – apart 15
  – awake *hat* 225
  intelligent 498
  – away 196
  – berth 748
  – of the mark
  distance 196
  deviation 279
  error 495
  – of *distant* 196
  – open 194, 260
  – of the truth 495
  – world 180, 318
  in the – world 180
widen 194
  – the breach 713, 900
wide-spread
  great 31
  dispersed 73
  space 180
  expanded 194
widow 905
widowhood 905
width 202
wield
  brandish 315
  handle 379
  use 677
  – authority 737
  – the sword 722
wieldy 705
wife 903
wig 225
wigging 932
wiggle 315
wight 373
wigwam 189
wild 851
  unproductive 169
  violent 173
  plain 344

  inattentive 458
  mad 503
  shy 623
  unskilled 699
  excited 824, 825
  untamed 851
  rash 863
  angry 900
  licentious 954
  run – 825
  – animals 366
  – beast *fierce* 173
  evil-doer 913
  – goose chase
  caprice 608
  useless 645
  unskilful 699
  – imagination 515
  sow one's – oats
  grow up 131
  improve 658
  amusement 840
  vice 945
  intemperance 954
Wild, Jonathan –
  thief 792
  bad man 949
wilderness
  disorder 59
  unproductive 169
  space 180
  solitude 893
wild-fire 382
  spread like –
  violence 173
  influence 175
  expand 194
  publication 531
wile 545, 702
wilful
  voluntary 600
  obstinate 606
will
  volition **600**
  resolution 604
  testament 771
  gift 784
  at – 600
  at one's own sweet – 608
  have one's own – 600, 748
  make one's – 360
  tenant at – 779
  – be 152
  – for the deed 774, 937
  – of Heaven 601
  – he nil he 601
  – power 600

- and will not 605
- you 765
willingness 602
willing or unwilling 601
Will o' the wisp
  luminary 423
  imp 980
willow 839
willy-nilly 601, 744
wilted 659
wily 702
wimble 262
wimple 225
win 731, 775
- the affections 897
- golden opinions 931
- the heart 829
- laurels 873
- out 33
- over *belief* 484
  induce 615
  content 831
wince
  bodily pain 378
  emotion 821
  excitement 825
  mental pain 828
  flinch 860
winch 307, 633
wind *convolution* 248
  velocity 274
  deviate 279
  circuition 311
  blast **349**
  life 359
against the - 278, 708
before the - 278, 734
cast to the -s
  repudiate 610
  disuse 678
  not observe 773
  relinquish 782
close to the - 278
fair - 705
to the four -s 180
get - 531
get the - up 860
see how the - blows
  direction 278
  experiment 463
  foresight 510
  fickle 607
in the - 151, 152
lose - 688
sail near the -
  direction 278
  skill 698

  sharp practice 940
outstrip the - 274
preach to the -s 645
raise the - 775
scatter to the -s 756
see where the - lies 698
short -ed 688
sport of -s and waves 315
sound of - and limb 654
take the - out of one's
  sails
  render powerless 158
  hinder 706
  defeat 731
touched in the - 655
what's in the -? 461
- ahead 708
- bag 584
in the -'s eye 278
- the horn 416
hit between - and water
  659
- and weather permitting
  qualification 469
  possibility 470
- round the heart 897
- up *strengthen* 159
  prepare 673
  complete 729
- accounts 811
windbag 884
wind-bound 706
windfall 618
wind-gauge 349
wind-gun 727
winding 248, 311
winding-sheet 363
windings and turnings 248
wind instruments 417
wind-jammer 273
windlass 307, 633
windless 688
windmill 312
tilt at -s 638
window 260
make the -s shake
  loud noise 404
- dressing 544
wind-pipe 351
wind-up 67
windward, to - 236, 278
windy 349
wine 298, 959
put new - into old bottles
  699
look upon the - when it is
  red 953

wine-bibbing 959
wine-cooler 387
wineglass 191
wing *extension* 39
  part 51
  side 236
  fly 267
  side-scene 599
  instrument 633
  refuge 666
  army 726
clip the -s 275
lend -s to 707
on the -
  motion 264
  flying 267
  transference 270
  departure 293
take - *journey* 266
  fly 267
  depart 293
under the - of
  safe 664
with -s *active* 682
- one's flight 293
- one's way 267
on the -s of the wind 274
wing-commander 747
winged *swift* 274
wink 443, 550
tip the - 550, 527
- at
  be blind to 442
  disregard 458
  neglect 460
  permit 760
  forgive 918
- of sleep 683
winning [*see* win]
  pleasing 829
  courteous 894
  lovable 897
winnings 775
winnow *sift* 42
  exclude 55
  inquire 461
  pick 609
  clean 652
- the chaff from the wheat
  465
winsome 829, 836
winter 126, 383
- of our discontent 832
- garden 840
- sports 840
wintry 126
wipe *dry* 340

clean 652
disrespect 929
flog 972
give one a –
  rebuke 932
– away 552
– the eyes
  relieve 834
– off old scores 807, 952
– the tears 914
wire *ligature* 45
filament 205
telegraph 527, 534
pull the –s 693
wire-drawn
long 200
wireless 531
– telegram 532
– telegraph 534
– telephone 534
wire-puller 526, 694
wire-worm 913
wiry *strong* 159
wis 514
wisdom 498
have cut one's – teeth 698
worldly – 864
wise
intelligent 498
sage 500
manner 627
in such – 8
word to the – 695
– in one's own conceit 880
– after the event 135
– man 500
– maxim 496
dine out –ly but too well
  953
wiseacre 493, 500
wiser, nobody the– 528
wish *will* 600
intention 620
desire 865
do what one –es 748
– at the bottom of the Red
  Sea 832
– the father to the thought
misjudge 481
credulous 486
hope 858
desire 865
– joy 896
– well 906
wishing-cap 993
wish-wash
unmeaning 517

wishy-washy
languid 160
insipid 391
feeble style 575
unimportant 643
wisket 191
wisp 72
wistful
thought 451
care 459
feeling 821
desire 865
wit *intellect* 450
wisdom 498
humour **842**
humorist 844
mother – 498
soul of – 572
to – 522
at one's –'s end 475, 704
witch *oracle* 513
ugly 846
sorceress 994
– doctor 994
witchcraft 992
witchery
attraction 615
pleasing 829
sorcery 992
witching time 126, 421
witenagemote 696
with *added* 37
mixed 41
ligature 45
accompanying 88
means 632
go – 178
– all its parts 52
– regard to 9
– a vengeance 31, 52
– a witness 31
withal
in addition 37
accompanying 88
enough 639
withdraw
subduct 38
absent 187
turn back 283
recede 287
depart 293
– from
recant 607
relinquish 624
dislike 867
withe 45
wither 195, 659

– one's hopes 837
withered *weak* 160
disease 655
withering
harsh 739
painful 830
contempt 930
censure 932
withers 250
– unwrung 159, 323
withhold *hide* 528
restrain 751
prohibit 761
retain 781
stint 819
– one's assent 764
within 221
derived from – 5
place – 221
keep – 221
– an ace 32
– bounds
small 32
shortcoming 304
restraint 751
– call 197
– compass
shortcoming 304
temperate 953
– the mark 304
– one's memory 505
– reach 197, 705
without *unless* 8
subduction 38
exception 83
absence 187
exterior 220
circumjacent 227
exemption 777a
derived from – 6
not be able to do – 630
– alloy 827
– ballast 605, 945
– ceasing 136
– ceremony 881
– charge 815
– fear of contradiction 535
– a dissentient voice 488
– end 105, 112
– exception 16, 79
– excuse 945
– fail 474, 604a
– God 989
– a leg to stand on 158
– limit 105
– measure 105
– notice 508

– number 105
– parallel 33
– a rap 804
– reason 499
– regard to 10
– reluctance 602
– reserve 525
– rhyme or reason 615*a*
– a shadow of turning 141
– stint 639
– warning 508
withstand 708, 719
withy 45
witless 491
witling 501, 844
witness [*see* 441]
  spectator 444
  evidence 467
  voucher 550
  call to – 467
witness-box 966
wits 450
  live by one's –
  deceive 545
  skill 698
  cunning 702
  steal 791
  dishonourable 940
  set one's – to work
  think 451
  invent 515
  plan 626
  all one's – about one
  care 459
  intelligence 498
  skill 698
  one's – gone a
    woolgathering 458
witsnapper 844
witticism 842
wittingly 620
wittol 962
wive 903
wiveless 904
wizard *sage* 500
  proficient 700
  sorcerer 994
wizen *wither* 195
  throat 260
woad 438
wobble 605
woe 828
– betide 908, 914
– is me 839
– to 908
woebegone 828, 837
woeful 649, 830

woefully *very* 31
wold 344
wolf *ravenous* 865
  cry – *false* 544
  alarm 669
  fear 860
  hold the – by the ears 704
  keep the – from the door
    359
  unable to keep the – from
    the door 804
  – at the door 667, 804
  – and the lamb 923
  – in sheep's clothing 548,
    941
woman 131, **374**
– of the town 962
woman-hater 911
womanhood 131, 374
womanish 160
womanly
  adolescent 131
  feminine 374
womb *cause* 153
  interior 221
– of time 121, 152
wonder
  exception 83
  astonishment **870**
  prodigy 872
  do –s 682, 731
  for a – 870
  nine days' – 643
  not – 507
  – whether
  uncertain 475
  ignorant 491
  suppose 514
  –s of the world 872
wonderfully 31
wonder-working 870
wondrous 870
wont *habitual* 613
won't do, it – 932
woo 865, 902
wood *trees* 367
  material 635
  not out of the – 665, 704
  take to the –s 166
woodcut 558
woodcutter 371
wooded, well- 256
wooden 635
– horse 975
– spoon 493
– walls 717, 726
wood engraving 558

woodlands 367
wood-note 412
wood pavement 255
woody 367
wooer 897
woof
  warp and – 329
wool *flocculent* 256
  warm 238
  much cry and little – 482
woolgathering 458
woolly 255, 256
woolpack *cloud* 353
woolsack
  pillow 215
  authority 747
  tribunal 966
word *maxim* 496
  intelligence 532
  assertion 535
  vocable **562**
  phrase 566
  command 741
  promise 768
  give the – 741
  good as one's –
  veracious 543
  complete 729
  probity 939
  in a – 572
  keep one's – 939
  man of his – 939
  not a – to say 585, 879
  pass– 550
  put in a – 582
  take at one's – 484, 762
  upon my – 535
  watch– 722
  – and a blow
  hasty 684
  contentious 720
  irascible 901
  – of command
  indication 550
  military 722
  command 741
  – in the ear 527, 586
  – of honour 768
  – it 566
  – of mouth 582
  – to the wise
  intelligible 518
  advice 695
  – for word 19, 494
Word *Deity* 976
– of God 985
word-catcher 936

– the rising sun 886
worshipful 873
worst *defeat* 731
do one's – 659, 907
do your – 715, 909
have the – of it 732
make the – of 482
worst come to the –
 certain 474
 bad 649
 hopeless 859
worsted 205
worth *value* 644
 goodness 648
 possession 777
 price 812
 virtue 944
penny – 814
what one is – 780
– a great deal 803
– the money 815
– much 803
– one's salt 644
– while 646
worthless
 trifling 643
 useless 645
 profligate 945
worthy
 famous 873
 virtuous 944
 good 948
– of 924
– of belief 484
– of blame 932
– of notice 642
– of remark 642
wot 490
would: – fain 865
– that! 865
would-be *pert* 885
 usurping 925
wound *evil* 619
 injure 659
 pain 830
 anger 900
keep the – green 919
– the feelings 830
– up 704
woven fabrics 219
wowser 988
wrack 162
go to – and ruin
 perish 162
 fail 732
 bankrupt 804
wraith 980

wrangle
 disagreement 24
 reason 476
 quarrel 713
 contend 720
wrangler
 reasoner 476
 scholar 492
 opponent 710
wrap 223, 225
wrapped in
 attention 457
– clouds 528
– self 943
– thought 458
wrapper 223, 225
 inclosure 232
wraprascal 225
wrath 900
wreak *violent* 173
 harsh 739
– one's anger 919
– one's malice on 907
wreath *woven* 219
 circle 247
 trophy 733
 ornament 847
 honour 877
wreathe *weave* 219
wreathy 248
wreck
 remainder 40
 destruction 162
 damage 659
 defeat 732
wrecker 792
wrench *disjoin* 44
 draw 285
 extract 301
 twist 311
 tool 633
 seize 789
wrest *distort* 243
– from 789
– the sense 523
wrestle 720
wrestler 726
wretch *sufferer* 828
 sinner 949
wretched
 unimportant 643
 bad 649
 unhappy 828
wretchedly
 small 32
wriggle 314, 315
– into 294

– out of 671
wright 690
wring *twist* 248
 pain 378
 clean 652
 torment 830
– from
 extract 301
 compel 744
 take 789
– one's hands 839
– the heart 830
wringing wet 339
wrinkle *fold* 258
 hint 527
wrinkled 128
wrist 781
wristband 225
writ 741, 969
Writ, Holy – 985
write *compose* 54
 style 569
 writing 590
– down *record* 551
– music 416
– off 624
– out 590
– prose 598
– to 592
– upon 595
– word 527
writer 590, 593
dramatic – 599
pen of a ready – 569
– to the Signet 968
writhe *distort* 243
 agitate 315
 pain 378
writing 590, 593
put in – 551
– in cipher 590
written, it is – 601
wrong *error* 495
 evil 619
 injury 649
 spite 907
 improper **923**
 vice 945
go – 732
in the – *error* 495, 923
own oneself in the – 950
– box 699, 704
 wrong 923
– course 945
begin at the – end 699
– in one's head 503
in the – place 647

- side out 145, 218
- side up 218
- side of the wall 665
- sow by the car 699, 732
- step 732

wrong-doer 949
wrong-doing 945
wrongful 923
wrong-headed 481
wrought:
 highly –
  prepared 673
  complete 729
 – iron 323
 – out 729
 – up *excited* 824
  angry 900
wry 217, 243
 – face *pain* 378
  discontent 832
  lamentation 839
  ugly 846
  disapproval 932
wynd 189
wyvern 83

X

xanthic 436
Xanthippe 901
xebec 273
xenogenesis 161
xerophagy 956
X-rays 420, 554
xylography 558
xylophone 417
x, y, z 491

Y

yacht 273
yachting 267
yachtsman 269
yager 726
Yahoo 702
yammer 839
yap 412
yard *abode* 189
 length 200
 enclosure 232
 workshop 691
yardarm to yardarm 197
yare 682
yarn *filament* 205
 story 532

 untruth 546
 exaggeration 549
 mingled – 41
 spin a long – 549
 diffuse style 573
yarr 412
yashmak 225
yataghan 727
yaup 411
yaw 279
yawl *ship* 273
 cry 412
yawn *open* 260
 sleepy 683
 tired 688
 weary 841
yawning *gulf* 198
 deep 208
yclept 564
yea *more* 33
 assent 488
yean 161
year 106, 108
 – in and – out 104
 since the – one 124
 all the – round 110
 – after year 104
 tenant from – to year 779
yearling 129
yearly 138
yearn 828, 837
 – for *desire* 865
 pity 914
yearning *love* 897
years 128
 in – 128
 tenant for – 779
 – ago 122
 come to – of discretion
  131
 – old 128
yeast *leaven* 320
 bubbles 353
yell *cry* 411
 scream 839
yellow 436
 – flag 668
 – streak 862
 – and red 439
yellow-eyed 920
yellowness 436
yelp 412
yeoman 371, 373
 – of the guard 726
 –'s service 644
yeomanry 726
yerk *strike* 276

yes 488, 762
yes-man 886
yesterday *past* 122
 of – *new* 123
yet *in compensation* 30
 exception 83
 time 106
 prior 116
 past 122
 qualification 469
yeux doux, faire les – 902
yield *soft* 324
 harvest 636
 submit 725
 consent 762
 resign 782
 furnish 784
 gain 810
 price 812
 – assent 488, 762
 – one's breath 360
 – to despair 859
 – up the ghost 360
 – the palm 34, 879
 – to temptation 615
yielding *soft* 324
 facile 705
 submissive 725
yodel 580
yoicks 622
yoke *join* 43
 vinculum 45
 couple 89
 subject 749
 means of restraint 752
 rivet the – 739
yokel 701, 876
yokemate 903
yonder 79, 196
yore 122
Yorkshireman 702
you: – don't say so 870
 –'re another 718
young 127
 – man *lover* 897
younger generation 127
youngster 129
younker 129
youth 127, 129
yule log 388

Z

Zadkiel 513
zambo 41
Zamiel 978